D1271002

PRODUCTION AND INVENTORY CONTROL HANDBOOK

PRODUCTION AND INVENTORY CONTROL HANDBOOK

APICS®

**Prepared under the Supervision of the
Handbook Editorial Board of the
American Production and
Inventory Control Society (APICS)**

James H. Greene, Ph.D., CFPIM   Editor in Chief

Third Edition

Boston, Massachusetts   Burr Ridge, Illinois
Dubuque, Iowa   Madison, Wisconsin   New York, New York
San Francisco, California   St. Louis, Missouri

IUPUI
UNIVERSITY LIBRARIES
COLUMBUS CENTER
COLUMBUS, IN 47201

Library of Congress Cataloging-in-Publication Data

Production and inventory control handbook / James H. Greene, editor
in chief.—3rd ed.
    p.   cm.
    "Prepared under the supervision of the Handbook Editorial Board of
the American Production and Inventory Control Society (APICS)"
    Includes bibliographical references and index.
    ISBN 0-07-024428-6
    1. Production management—Handbooks, manuals, etc. 2. Inventory
control—Handbooks, manuals, etc. I. Greene, James H. (James
Harnsberger), date. II. American Production and Inventory Control
Society. Handbook Editorial Board.
  TS155.P74   1997
  658.5—dc20   96-39980
                                                    CIP

McGraw-Hill

A Division of The McGraw-Hill Companies

Copyright © 1997, 1987, 1970 by The McGraw-Hill Companies, Inc. All rights
reserved. Printed in the United States of America. Except as permitted under the
United States Copyright Act of 1976, no part of this publication may be reproduced or distributed in any form or by any means, or stored in a data base or
retrieval system, without the prior written permission of the publisher.

3 4 5 6 7 8 9 BKM BKM   9 0 9 8 7 6 5 4 3 2 1

ISBN 0-07-024428-6

*The assistant editor for this book was Allyson Arias, the editing supervisor
was David E. Fogarty, and the production supervisors were Donald Schmidt
and Pamela A. Pelton. It was set in Times Roman by Renee Lipton of
McGraw-Hill's Professional Book Group composition unit.*

Printed and bound by R. R. Donnelley & Sons Company.

McGraw-Hill books are available at special quantity discounts to use as premiums and sales promotions, or for use in corporate training programs. For more
information, please write to the Director of Special Sales, McGraw-Hill, 11 West
19th Street, New York, NY 10011. Or contact your local bookstore.

Information contained in this work has been obtained by The
McGraw-Hill Companies, Inc. ("McGraw-Hill") from sources
believed to be reliable. However, neither McGraw-Hill nor its
authors guarantee the accuracy or completeness of any information published herein, and neither McGraw-Hill nor its authors
shall be responsible for any errors, omissions, or damages arising
out of use of this information. This work is published with the
understanding that McGraw-Hill and its authors are supplying
information but are not attempting to render engineering or other
professional services. If such services are required, the assistance
of an appropriate professional should be sought.

EDITORIAL BOARD, James H. Greene, Editor in Chief

James H. Greene, Ph.D., CFPIM
Department of Industrial Engineering
Purdue University
West Lafayette, Indiana

Stephen A. DeLurgio, Ph.D.
Professor of Operations Management
Bloch School of Business
University of Missouri —Kansas City
Kansas City, Missouri

Hank Grant, Ph.D.
Director, School of Industrial
 Engineering
University of Oklahoma
Norman, Oklahoma

Timothy J. Greene, Ph.D.
Associate Dean for Research
College of Engineering
Oklahoma State University
Stillwater, Oklahoma

Trevor Kaye
Development Manager
Information Services
Universal Flavor Corporation
Indianapolis, Indiana

Marty Muscatello
Assistant Plant Manager
Litton Poly-Scientific Co.
Blacksburg, Virginia

June Sheaks, CPIM
Bendix Energy & Control Division
South Bend, Indiana

Ralph B. Tower, Ph.D.
Professor of Accounting
Wake Forest University
Winston-Salem, North Carolina

CONTENTS

Section 7 Managing the PIC Function

Section 8 Quantitative Methods for PIC

Section 9 Certification

CHAPTER EDITORS AND CONTRIBUTORS

Lloyd Andreas, CFPIM, *Application Manager, Marcam Corp., Atlanta, Ga.* (CHAPS. 8, 30)

Carl D. Bhame, CFPIM, *Vice President, American Software, Atlanta, Ga.* (CHAP. 23)

John H. Blackstone, Ph.D., CFPIM, *Professor of Management, University of Georgia, Athens* (CHAP. 9)

Ronald W. Bohl, CFPIM, *Vice President, Jack Gipps, Inc., Chagrin Falls, Ohio* (CHAP. 10)

Steven F. Bolander, Ph.D., *Professor and Chair of Departmant of Management, College of Business, Colorado State University, Fort Collins* (CHAP. 15)

J. Thomas Brown, CFPIM, *Principal Consultant, PowerCerv, Inc., Duluth, Ga.* (CHAP. 8)

Robert G. Brown, CFPIM, *President, Materials Management Systems, Inc., Thetford Center, Vt.* (CHAP. 19)

Lloyd M. Clive, Ph.D., CFPIM *Coordinator of Industrial Engineering Technology Programs, Center for Integrated Manufacturing, Sir Sandford Fleming College, Peterborough, Ontario, Canada* (CHAP. 13)

Janet L. Cohen, CPIM, *Consultant, IBM Corporation, Milwaukee, Wis.* (CHAP. 28)

David W. Cornell, Ph.D., CPA, CMA, *Bloch School of Business, University of Missouri—Kansas City* (CHAP. 27)

James F. Cox, Ph.D., CFPIM, *Robert O. Arnold Prof. of Business, Terry College of Business, University of Georgia, Athens, Ga.* (CHAP. 9)

Stephen A. De Lurgio, Ph.D., CFPIM, *Professor of Operations Management, Henry W. Bloch School of Business, University of Missouri—Kansas City* (CHAPS. 13, 23, 34)

Quentin Ford, *President, Manufacturing Control Associates, Palatine, Ill.* (CHAP. 20)

Walter E. Goddard, *President and Chairman of the Board, Oliver Wight International, Concord, N.H.* (CHAP. 3)

Hank Grant, Ph.D., *Director, School of Industrial Engineering, University of Oklahoma, Norman* (CHAPS. 13, 36)

William M. Grauf, *Client Manager, J. D. Edwards World Solution Company, Oak Brook, Ill.* (CHAP. 29)

Timothy J. Greene, Ph.D., *Associate Dean for Research, College of Engineering, Architecture, and Technology, Oklahoma State University, Stillwater* (CHAP. 13)

Frank Gue, *Partner, Industrial Education Services, Burlington, Ontario, Canada* (CHAP. 6)

Robert W. Hall, Ph.D., *Association for Manufacturing Excellence, Professor, School of Management, Indiana University, Indianapolis* (CHAP. 16)

Michael F. Hatch, CFPIM, *President, Hatch and Associates, Industry Consultants, Fond du Lac, Wis.* (CHAP. 11)

Thomas R. Hoffman, Ph.D., CFPIM *Carlson School of Management, University of Minnesota, Minneapolis* (CHAP. 37)

Norman Hopwood, *Chief Engineer, MACH System Consultants, Dearborn, Mich.* (CHAP. 7)

James Hunt, *Manager, Special Projects, Arrowhead Metals, Ltd., Toronto, Ontario, Canada* (CHAP. 13)

David Hunting, *Free Lance Technical Writer, Everett, Wash.* (CHAP. 31)

Henry H. Jordan, Jr., CMC, CFPIM, *Chairman, Center for Inventory Management, Sugar Hill, Ga.* (CHAP. 8)

Henry H. Jordan, III, CMC, CPIM, CIRM, *Professor, DeVry Institute, Atlanta, Ga.* (CHAP. 8)

C. Patrick Koelling, Ph.D., *Professor of Industrial Engineering, Virginia Polytechnic Institute and State University, Blacksburg* (CHAP. 32)

Henry W. Kraebber, P.E., CPIM, *Professor, School of Technology, Purdue University, West Lafayette, Ind.* (CHAP. 4)

Robert A. Leavey, CFPIM, CIRM, *Consultant, Atlanta, Ga.* (CHAP. 8)

Kimberly Lombard, *Public Relations Manager, Intermec Corp., Everett, Wash.* (CHAP. 31)

John E. Martin, CFPIM, CIRM, *Curriculum Manager, IBM Solutions Institute, A. J. Watson Education Center, Brussels, Belgium* (CHAP. 22)

John M. McKeller, D.B.A., CFPIM, *Director of Education, National Association of Purchasing Management, Tempe, Ariz.* (CHAP. 24)

Patricia Moody, *Patricia Moody Consulting, Marblehead, Mass.* (CHAP. 33)

James L. Morgan, *Business Science Specialist, Midland, Mich.* (CHAP. 23)

Charles J. Murgiano, CPIM, *Principal, Waterloo Manufacturing Software, Twinsburg, Ohio* (CHAP. 10)

Selim Noujaim, *Past President of APICS, Waterbury, Conn.* (CHAP. 1)

George W. Plossl, CFPIM, *President, G. W. Plossl and Co., Inc., Fort Myers, Fla.* (CHAP. 2)

James W. Rice, Ph.D., P.E., CFPIM, *Management Consultant, Eldorado, Wis., and Professor Emeritus, University of Wisconsin-Oshkosh* (CHAPS. 11, 20)

Stephen Roberts, Ph.D., *Head, Department of Industrial Engineering, North Carolina State University, Raleigh* (CHAP. 35)

Paul R. Rouse, CPIM, *Senior Consultant, IBM Corporation, Romulus, Mich.* (CHAP. 28)

Gerald A. Sanderson, CFPIM, CIRM, *President, Gerald A. Sanderson, Inc., Roeland Park, Kan.* (CHAP. 18)

F. John Sari, CFPIM, *President, John Sari & Company, Winston-Salem, N.C.* (CHAP. 12)

Rick Scott, *Managing Consultant, EDS, Troy, Mich.* (CHAP. 5)

Sam G. Taylor, Ph.D., *Professor, College of Business, University of Wyoming, Laramie, Wyoming* (CHAP. 15)

Ernest C. Theisen, CFPIM, *Consultant, Stone Mountain, Ga.* (CHAP. 8)

Ralph Tileston, *Vice President, Manufacturing Control Associates, Palatine, Ill.* (CHAP. 20)

James A. Tompkins, Ph.D., *President, Tompkins Associates, Inc., Raleigh, N.C.* (CHAP. 25)

Eileen Van Aken, Ph.D., *Professor of Industrial Engineering, Virginia Polytechnic Institute and State University, Blackburg* (CHAP. 32)

William T. Walker, CFPIM, CIRM, *Supply Chain Management, Hewlett-Packard Company, Rockaway, N.J.* (CHAP. 21)

William R. Wassweiler, CFPIM, CIRM, *Manufacturing Industry Consultant, Milwaukee, Wis.* (CHAP. 14)

Carl Watkins, *President, Manufacturing Information and Control Systems, Eugene, Oreg.* (CHAP. 17)

Nancy Weatherholt, Ph.D., CPA, *Associate Professor, Henry W. Bloch School of Business and Public Administration, University of Missouri—Kansas City* (CHAP. 27)

Bill Winchell, J.D., P.E., *Associate Professor of Manufacturing Technology, Ferris State University, Big Rapid, Mich.* (CHAP. 26)

FOREWORD

This third edition of the *Production and Inventory Control Handbook* reveals the extent to which the profession has matured. The previous edition saluted a new era of integrating the manufacturing function into a closed-loop manufacturing resource planning and control system that encompassed strategic planning, service parts management, and distribution resource management.

Manufacturers were just starting to realize the potential of computer-aided design (CAD), computer-aided manufacturing (CAM), and cellular manufacturing. Robots were just finding their way to the factory floor and the bar code standards were being developed. New organization structures were being implemented and improved. The protagonist relationships between vendor and manufacturer, and manufacturer and customer were being resolved. Management was learning a new improved approach to personnel problems. These new attitudes improved product quality and shipping schedules.

None of these changes could have come about without improved methods of communication. To comprehend the change consider the new language that has evolved—e-mail, LAN, PC, FAX, laptops, and many other terms were not in use just a few years ago.

The development of this Handbook started out with a detailed outline that included all pertinent subjects. This outline was screened and revised by the editorial committee and other interested professionals. Then began the search for chapter editors and contributors who were experts in the field and who were willing to give of their time and their knowledge. Thus the Handbook evolved.

As mentioned in the previous edition, the premise *keep it simple* is just as important to manufacturers today as it was to Eli Whitney, Thomas Edison, and Henry Ford. This edition of the Handbook is rededicated to this concept.

The American Production and Inventory Control Society members and I would like to thank the officers, in particular the presidents, for staying the course and steering the society toward a goal of education. In addition, I would like to thank each member of the editorial committee for his or her direction and cooperation. Without their willing assistance this third edition of the Handbook would not have come about.

I am very aware of the contributions made by chapter editor secretaries. I am very grateful to them for helping to make my task easier. I wish to express my sincere thanks for all of the assistance given by Cathy Ralston in preparing this and the previous edition.

James H. Greene

PREFACE

In 1957, some twenty dedicated business practitioners founded the American Production and Inventory Control Society. In the ensuing three decades, changes in the field have occurred at an explosive rate and provide us today with a fundamentally expanded management science of techniques, concepts, and applications.

The era of the 1960s was one of education, a sharing of knowledge by practitioners and academicians. Increased productivity was inevitable, and production and inventory control (PIC) gained respect and legitimacy in the business environment. By the end of the decade, the initial handful of practitioners had expanded to over seven thousand active APICS members. In 1970, the first edition of the *Production and Inventory Control Handbook* joined other APICS efforts in providing members with current state-of-the-art techniques.

During the 1970s and continuing into the early 1980s, the dominant theme of production operations management was material requirement planning. Today, MRP techniques have been adopted by the majority of large manufacturing firms and are being taught and researched in many major universities. What will be the theme of the future that will enable American firms to meet the challenges of tomorrow and maintain an edge over the competition?

Business managers today are faced with a highly volatile set of problems and opportunities. One of the most difficult and yet rewarding continues to be the challenge of learning from the previous experience of others. APICS remains dedicated to the sharing of information and it is with this objective in mind that the third edition of the *Production and Inventory Control Handbook* is published.

Section 1.   The American Production and Inventory Control Society is a professional society that extends its members' knowledge by publications, clinics, and conferences. The society members maintain their high standards by an extensive certification which is becoming a requirement to practice in the field.

Section 2.   This section is an introduction to the basics of production and inventory control. First comes an overview and then a discussion of the information required. Manufacturing brings labor, materials, and facilities together to produce a product of desired quality at the time desired. This section discusses how the information for manufacturing is derived and used.

Section 3.   After the product and process information has been assembled, the product is placed in a schedule depending on capacity available. This section is a comprehensive coverage of scheduling techniques.

Section 4.   In the profitable factory, inventory and production control go hand-in-hand. Inventory theory records and practices are included in this section. The scope of inventory control has been extended to include remote warehouses.

Section 5.   Production and inventory control can't operate in isolation. Supporting function including forecasting, sales, purchasing, warehousing, quality assurance, cost accounting are the subjects included in this section.

Section 6.   It is apparent that the flow of timely information is needed for an effective production and inventory control system. Can you ship a certain product? If not, when? What is its cost? Is a certain machine up and running? Computer systems discussed in this section can help answer these questions.

Section 7.   Managing the relationships between personnel in PIC and other functions may be the most difficult task of the PIC manager. This section covers not only the classical but also the most modern concepts of management.

Section 8.   Probably the biggest change in production and inventory control in the past half century has been the application of quantitative methods. The quantitative methods, statistics, and simulation chapters will give you a basic understanding of these subjects and will also present the state of the art.

Section 9.   Certification is important to the professional and this section discusses the structure of the certification program, the various levels, and how you can successfully prepare for the examinations.

James H. Greene

SECTION 1

PRODUCTION AND INVENTORY CONTROL PROFESSION

Chapter 1. Professionalism

CHAPTER 1
PROFESSIONALISM

Editor
Selim Noujaim
Past President, American Production and Inventory Control Society
Waterbury, Connecticut

THE APICS HANDBOOK AND THE PROFESSION*

A handbook on production and inventory control (PIC) serves professionals engaged in production and inventory management and control, students preparing for professional certification, students of management, and persons designing control systems. More importantly, it is a resource for general managers and chief operating officers, sales managers, and general production managers—all those whose policy-making decisions impact directly on the inventory investment.

The meaning of the word *control* in the title is much broader than the more common meaning of exercising restraint or direction. It is broader, also, than the definition of *controlling,* which refers to testing, or verifying by a standard. *Control,* as used in the title of this book, begins with a plan, which is used as a standard.

A *plan* is a scheme of action for a definite purpose. *Planning* means arranging for work, or for enterprise, or projecting a course of action. Synonyms of plan include model and system. A plan, as a system, broadens the scope of this book. A system is an assemblage or a combination of things or parts forming a complex or unitary whole. It is also an ordered, comprehensive assemblage of facts, principles, doctrines, or the like in a particular field of knowledge or thought. It is also a coordinated body of methods, a complex scheme, or a plan of procedures.

The existence of controls and plans and systems suggest that a method of managing is being used, or suggest management itself. To *manage* means to bring about, to succeed in accomplishments, to take charge of, to conduct business or commercial affairs. *Management* is accomplished through an organization. An *organization* is a body of persons organized for some end or work.

This book, then, is about planning, controlling, and managing production and inventories through systems and an organization; applying principles, methods, and models,

---

*Contributed to by Frederic E. Bulleit, CFPIM, Vice President, Armstrong Industries; Past President of APICS.

based on facts, knowledge, forecasts, and predictions to accomplish goals and objectives. This book covers production and inventory control in its broadest sense.

A handbook of PIC must be broad enough to include the large businesses as well as the small. It should cover the process industries as well as the assembly and fabrication industries. It should cover the businesses that produce to order as well as those that ship "off the shelf." It should concern itself with distribution inventories as well as with manufactured inventory, from the simple manufacturing processes to the very complex. This is such a book.

The act of writing a book of production and inventory control implies that a professional field of endeavor exists; and, in fact, it does. But the recognition of the profession is recent, and it has resulted from a combination of various actions and extensive work on the part of dedicated people over the past quarter-century.

DEVELOPMENT OF PROFESSIONALISM

Professionalism in PIC most likely developed in industry when the various functions relating to the field were assigned to a single manager. That manager, in that business, became a potential professional when the manager carried the responsibility for controlling production and inventories, in its broadest definition. Consolidation of these functions in a single department began in the 1920s in the automobile industry, a necessary outgrowth of the assembly line, and extended to some other industries in the 1930s. However, this trend was not common or universal. More commonly, the functions were scattered among many departments or staff areas.

Following World War II, three trends began to be noticed. First, many functions relating to scheduling, shop floor control, and inventory control were assigned to a single department, which reported to a general production manager, or plant manager. Second, PIC professionals began to talk with one another, across companies. As an example, the New Bedford Production and Inventory Control Association, located in New Bedford, Massachusetts, began functioning officially in 1946. Other PIC associations, independent of one another, began to be organized in Los Angeles; the Minneapolis/St. Paul area; Louisville, Kentucky; Cleveland, Ohio; and many other places.

Third, after World War II more sophisticated techniques became available to attack the problems of both inventory control and production flow through the manufacturing process. These included the *operations research techniques,* many developed in World War II by the British and Americans. These techniques have names that are quite common today, such as *Monte Carlo, queuing,* and *linear programming.* Industrial engineering schools and some business schools began teaching the use of these techniques as well as extending class studies in shop floor control and scheduling. *Economical-order-quantity (EOQ) models* were studied and used more intensively. *Gantt charts* and *machine loading systems* were examined for possible applications.

In 1956, some 26 production and inventory control professionals met in Cleveland, Ohio, many representing local professional associations already functioning. The purpose was to discuss the organization of a national PIC society. In a pioneering spirit, with a strong commitment to professionalism, the American Production and Inventory Control Society (APICS) was formed. And in 1957 the first national conference was held in Cleveland.

By 1960, the fourth national conference had been held, and 47 chapters of the APICS were scattered throughout the country. Approximately 1500 members were listed nationally. Growth during the 1960s was rather slow. Local and regional seminars were held, and national conferences were held annually. Speakers became more professional in knowledge, principles, and applications.

By 1970, 114 chapters existed with a combined membership of 8387. The first handbook of production and inventory control was published. Also in 1970 a milestone decision was reached by the APICS to establish the Curriculum and Certification Council. The first assignment was to develop the criteria for testing an individual's knowledge in PIC and to award a certification of professionalism in that field. Simultaneously, with the encouragement of the council, the APICS began extensive work with universities and colleges through the local chapters and regions to develop curricula and courses for training in PIC. The APICS itself began to expand its training, adding more seminars and course material. The production and inventory technical journal had existed since the early 1960s; in the 1970s it was recognized as the professional journal in the field of PIC.

In 1971 and 1972, professional examinations were being written and developed by the Curriculum and Certification Council with the assistance of the Educational Testing Service. In the fall of 1972, the first examinations were given for the granting of the designation of *Certified in Production and Inventory Management* (CPIM) and *Certified Fellow in Production and Inventory Management* program (CFPIM) in 1973. The CFPIM recognizes those who actively educate others in the industry. At that time there were four modules in the examination structure (there are now six): forecasting, shop floor control, materials requirements planning, and inventory planning.

By 1975, APICS membership had increased to 14,177. More significantly, 91 people had achieved the CPIM, and 50 had achieved the CFPIM. A half decade later, membership had grown to 41,045, while the number of CPIMs had risen to 3459, and CFPIMs to 916.

By 1991—with membership at more than 60,000—the society took certification to the next level by unveiling the *Certified in Integrated Resource Management* (CIRM) program. The CIRM was designed to help transform manufacturing professionals from functional specialists into organizational leaders by giving them knowledge of 13 business functions in a manufacturing organization and how they interact. CIRM—an important learning tool to help manufacturing professionals adapt to structural changes in the workforce—also helps companies use cost-effective education to create a better trained, knowledgeable, and flexible professional staff which promotes the company's overall competitiveness.

In 1993, APICS unveiled the *Business Outlook Index,* a monthly manufacturing-based survey report based on confidential production, sales, and inventory data from about 100 APICS-affiliated companies.

In 1995, the society took a major step to better serve its customers with the introduction of *computer-based testing* (CBT) for its CPIM and CIRM programs, becoming one of the first organizations of its kind to offer the benefits of computerized testing to its membership. CPIM exams are available on demand in most locations 6 days a week, from 8 to 10 hours per day.

At present, within 2 years of its fortieth birthday, the society serves nearly 70,000 members. More than 52,000 people have achieved the CPIM, and over 2000 have earned the CFPIM. In addition, in less than 4 years since its implementation, more than 1500 people have achieved the CIRM.

When APICS was first formed, there was no well-defined body of knowledge. Today, such knowledge exists, and much of the credit should go to the APICS for its efforts to encourage colleges and universities to pursue education in the field, for its efforts in developing technical manuals and educational programs, and finally, for its very fine certification program that continues to stress education and learning as its joint goal with professionalism. Certification has been the rallying point around which so many of these more important activities have been carried out.

SECTION 2

ESSENTIALS OF PRODUCTION AND INVENTORY CONTROL

CHAPTER 2

THE PRODUCTION AND INVENTORY CONTROL ENVIRONMENT

Editor

George W. Plossl, CFPIM

President, G.W. Plossl & Company, Fort Myers, Florida

Industry in North America and Europe has lost control of many markets to companies in the Far East including Japan, Korea, and Malaysia. The list of affected industries is long; it includes steel, machine tools, fasteners, castings, electronic equipment, optical devices, automobiles, motorcycles, and wristwatches, and the list is still growing. Computers, medical equipment, and aircraft are in jeopardy. Additional losses can be expected in other industries if corrective actions are not taken quickly.

Many vocal individuals in economics, government, academia, and the media speak glibly about the necessity for abandoning the "smokestack" industries and fostering the "sunrise" companies, those high-technology businesses where we are supposed to retain leadership. Little study is required to see that we have lost leadership already in many markets considered high tech—among them machine tools and semiconductors. Even if successful, the electronics companies, now supposed to be the hope of the future, are just not capable of generating the wealth, replacing the number of jobs already lost, or maintaining the supporting businesses so necessary to preserving our present standard of living.

The knowledge and resources necessary to reestablish and to maintain our manufacturing leadership in world markets are available in the professional activities of planning and control. This is evident in the performance of excellent companies in many industries. No new inventions or concepts are needed. A major investment is required, however, in the education of managers and workers on the compelling need to change their ways and get their houses in order. There is no better way or any so well proven.

What has been called "the Japanese industrial miracle" was not accomplished through sophisticated computer systems. They concentrated on the fundamentals of flawless execution of production tasks supporting a coherent strategy and sound planning, based on two beliefs: inventory is an evil, and perfection of the process is possible. These beliefs and the tactics based on them are applicable to all manufacturing businesses anywhere.

SCOPE OF PRODUCTION AND INVENTORY CONTROL

Definitions

The *APICS Dictionary* defines most terms used in PIC. Definitions of important terms used in this chapter are:

Capacity. The capability of a manufacturing entity (plant, work center, machine, worker, or supplier) to produce an amount of output in a specified time period; not to be confused with *load,* that is, the amount of work planned for a manufacturing entity at some point in time.

Control. Comparing execution to corresponding plans, detecting significant deviations, and alerting someone or something to take corrective actions.

Cycle time. The total time from recognition of a need to fulfilling that need in manufacturing processes.

Execution. Converting plans to reality.

Inventory. Any material required for the manufacturing process, whether or not it is used in the finished products.

Lead time. The time required to complete one operation on a component (work center lead time) or all operations on an order (order lead time) in manufacturing or purchasing. Includes preparation, setup, all processing operations, move time, and waiting (queue) elements.

Manufacturing. The business of converting lower value materials into products of higher value to customers.

Planning. Assigning numbers to future events.

Production. All activities supporting the processing of materials.

Resources. Everything necessary in manufacturing, including people, money, materials, plant and equipment, tooling, energy, utilities, and data.

Functions

Manufacturing planning and control has three primary functions:

1. Preproduction planning, including:
   a. Research and development of new products
   b. Application design and prototype making and testing
   c. Process selection, tool design, and standard setting
   d. Plant layout and utilities
   e. Plant and equipment procurement
2. Planning and control, including:
   a. Long-term strategic and business planning
   b. Midterm production planning
   c. Near-term master production scheduling
   d. Capacity planning and control
   e. Priority planning and control
3. Execution, including:
   a. Activities of suppliers of goods and services
   b. Production in plant work centers

    c. Maintenance of plant, equipment, tooling, and systems
    d. Solving problems and eliminating causes

Evolution

The twentieth century saw the evolution of production and inventory control from simple production support to an activity influencing every facet of manufacturing. About 1900, a clerk was added to the staff of a production supervisor, then called "foreman," to provide clerical assistance and to serve as "gofer" tracking down raw materials, jobs from other work centers, tooling, and other needed items. While this could hardly be called "control," the duties soon evolved into close communication with internal sales people plus monitoring schedules and expediting the movement of urgent work through production.

    By the 1940s, these production clerks were organized into "production control" groups. Concurrently, another clerical group, called "inventory control," was organized to issue and track purchase and work orders for production materials. The development of economic order quantity (1915) and statistical safety stock (1934) techniques and the introduction of computers (1960s) improved this group's ability to plan the timing and size of orders for purchased and manufactured materials. In the 1950s an increasing number of companies combined these two groups into one called "production and inventory control," which became the name of the field of activities and its technical society, American Production and Inventory Control Society (APICS).

    As its ability grew to handle a wide scope of activities, it became evident that "production and inventory control" was an inadequate name; it embraced only one segment, albeit a vital part, of planning and control activities. The communion of interests of this group with purchasing, receiving, stores, materials handling, and shipping personnel led to the concept of "materials management." Organizing them into one group was intended to improve control of production and inventories, but this concept was only marginally successful. New names have been applied to the field; the most popular are production and inventory management, manufacturing resources planning (MRPII), and manufacturing planning and control.

    By the mid-1970s, all important techniques for priority and capacity planning and control were developed and implemented using sophisticated computer software and powerful computers. The body of knowledge was codified, principles and techniques identified, and applications widely tested in that decade. The details of these make up this handbook.

    By the early 1970s, it was clear that PIC was a true profession; it had its unique body of knowledge, language, principles, and techniques and was making significant contributions to society. APICS recognized this professionalism with its program for certification in production and inventory management (CPIM). The number of individuals, both APICS members and nonmembers, certified at both the practitioner (CPIM) and fellow (CFPIM) levels rose rapidly in the United States and abroad, passing 43,000 in 1994, and continuing to grow steadily.

    In 1991, a new set of examinations leading to Certification in Integrated Resource Management (CIRM) was introduced to cover activities related to PIC in marketing and sales, engineering, quality control, finance, information systems, and other organizational groups. The CIRM has been very popular.

    Manufacturing is now seen as *a process integrating the activities of three participants: suppliers of materials and services, manufacturing plants, and customers.* Two flows are involved: materials and information. One integrated planning and control system is needed to handle data related to planned and actual events from which information is drawn for people to use in execution and control activities.

The term *inventory* has meaning far beyond the usually accepted raw materials, work-in-process, stocked components, and finished goods related to a company's products. For effective control, all materials required for manufacture must be considered in both planning and control. These materials obviously include tools, fixtures, gauges, cutters, test equipment, and other devices used in production processing operations. These cannot be managed properly independent of operating schedules and without utilizing applicable inventory management techniques. Supplies such as lubricants, grinding materials, cleaning and sterilizing compounds, and fuels also must be part of the formal inventory plan.

Equally important and more frequently neglected are items needed to keep processing equipment and machinery in operation. Unscheduled breakdowns cannot be tolerated. Preventive maintenance, scheduled in harmony with production, to increase the average time between failures can eliminate such problems.

Clearly, *production and inventories can be controlled in any industry using any processing operations to make any type of product.* New success stories appear daily; however, many common practices—based on long-held misconceptions—must be changed to achieve success:

- Production problems must and can be eliminated; they cannot be covered up successfully with cushions of inventory and time.
- Inventory is more of a liability than an asset, having real value only when it is flowing through operations or used to support them.
- Replanning is admitting failure; it is no substitute for sound execution.
- Greater precision in the plan, such as computing daily, rather than weekly, time periods, does not make it more accurate.

Effective planning, control, and execution of manufacturing operations in any company requires a complete system capable of integrating planning and control data for all activities related to demand, procurement, production, warehousing, shipment, and field service. Computer-based systems built around the proper techniques are necessary but not sufficient. Greater sophistication in the system provides only more opportunities for underqualified people to self-destruct at higher speeds. Skill in operating businesses with systems determines success.

TYPES OF PRODUCTION

Classification of a manufacturing facility depends on equipment configuration, materials movement, and production processes.

Facilities Classifications

Equipment Configuration.   Equipment may be configured three ways: functionally, linearly, or as a combination of these two. Early emphasis on the advantages of specialization resulted in grouping machinery, equipment, and people performing similar operations into functional work centers or departments, each performing one basic function such as milling, mixing, or assembling. More recent recognition of the benefits of faster, smoother flow of work led to lining up equipment needed to perform a series of operations to produce a single product or a family of similar products. A manufacturing facility with functional equipment configuration is commonly referred to as a *job shop*, a misnomer that is explained later. A plant composed only of production lines is commonly referred to as a *flow shop*. A facility combining functional and linear equipment configurations at different stages in the production process is called a *mixed shop*.

A concept called *group technology* was introduced in the 1970s to identify manufactured parts suitable for production in a line of different machines. Classification and coding systems were used to group parts requiring similar processing sequences although different in specific dimensions, shapes, and materials. Interest in this approach lagged until the late 1980s when the importance of improving materials flow was recognized.

Materials Movement.   Materials can be moved in discrete batches or in a continuous flow, or they can be moved in some combination of batch and continuous flow. The term *pure batch operation* implies that each unique batch is completed in one work center and the entire batch is moved to the next work center. This is commonly assumed in *materials requirements planning* (MRP). The term *pure continuous flow* implies that a single component or product is moved, in an uninterrupted flow, through a dedicated production line. The term *just in time* (JIT) refers to a continuous flow operation with the rates of production calculated in time periods. Pure batch or continuous flow plants are not common; most plants use a combination of both types of materials movement schemes, with a strong trend to continuous flow.

Most batch-oriented facilities allow for overlapping operations and/or splitting batches; thus a single batch can be spread over several work centers at one time. This practice introduces severe problems of control, first believed to require sophisticated data-handling equipment and systems. A better solution was recognized in the 1980s when it became apparent that reducing setup time, and making smaller batches and never splitting them was more practical and beneficial.

Most flow-oriented facilities produce a variety of similar products on each production line or in each process unit; the flow of specific items in this type of environment is, therefore, intermittent. Most flow facilities also incorporate discrete batch control at some point in the manufacturing process, commonly for blending, reacting, materials handling, production reporting, quality assurance, and/or packaging. The planning of these batches is an important factor in the design of planning and control systems. Using only the type of production as the sole factor in selecting the planning and control method is dangerous.

Production Processes.   These are grouped into two major categories: discrete and process. *Discrete operations* produce a single component or unit of product each time an operation is performed. Machining, fabrication, and assembly operations are typical. *Process operations* produce a large quantity of each component or product continuously. Petroleum-refining and chemical reaction operations are typical. Steel and aluminum extrusion or rolling operations may produce various lengths of a product at relatively slow rates and be classified as "discrete." Or they may produce long lengths of product at very high rates and be classified as "process." Mass production units, such as screw machines and injection molding machines that produce large volumes of discrete units in a very short time, can be controlled as continuous flow processes, although they are discrete by definition. Categorizing manufacturing processes is at best indefinite and can be misleading, particularly when selecting optimal planning and control strategies and techniques.

Production Classifications

Common classifications of production are *job shop, intermittent, repetitive,* and *continuous*; many real plants will fall into more than one of these categories. Clearer identification of all of their characteristics is necessary if systems and activities for planning and control are to be chosen well and be effective.

Job Shop. A more definitive term for this category is *single job lot.* In the true job shop, each unit of work processed is unique; products are engineered and/or made to order. Examples are tooling, special machinery, custom clothing, and pre-engineered, prefabricated steel buildings. Production work centers are functional, and most machines are general-purpose types. Materials move from work center to work center in small discrete batches, and there is very little overlapping or splitting. The routing of each component through the plant is unique. Inventory is carried only as raw material, work in process, and support materials. The term *job shop* is often confused with the term *intermittent production.* Many people consider a *job shop* to be an environment that is difficult to control.

Intermittent. A more definitive term for this category is *job lot.* Many jobs are repeated frequently. Products are typically stocked but may be assembled or finished to order, with a limited number of made-to-order products. Examples are home appliances, office equipment, power tools, and electric machinery. Most production equipment has been functionally configured, although trends now are toward more work cells and flow centers. Individual machines and equipment are less capable of general-purpose activities and are more functionally specific, particularly where automation has been introduced. There is consistency in the routings among jobs, and materials are moved between work centers in discrete batches. Job splitting and/or overlapping is common. Batch quantities can vary from a few to many thousands of units. Inventories are carried at all levels of the product's bills of material, and work-in-process is usually large.

Repetitive. A more definitive term for this category is *modified flow.* The same job runs steadily for a few hours or days. Products—typically cosmetics, hand tools, small household appliances, and fasteners—are made on production lines to stock, with a limited number assembled or finished to order. Machines and equipment are configured linearly, with the exception of a few feeder departments processing raw materials into components used on several lines. Machines and equipment are specialized and product specific. Materials are moved between operations in very small batches, approximating continuous flow. Jobs are typically grouped and scheduled by rates of product flow in time periods. Routings of all items are almost identical. Inventories are carried in finished goods, purchased raw materials, and components, and small quantities, if any, of manufactured components. Work-in-process is low.

Continuous. This category is often called "process flow." Products are typically bulk commodities, some of which may be packaged to order, and include petroleum products, chemicals, paint, pharmaceuticals, and foods. All equipment is linearly configured, with the exception of material preparation (blending, mixing, and weighing) and packaging. Material flows at a variable, specified rate through production lines from raw material to finished product. Routings are the same for each product processed in a specific plant or production unit. Production runs are expressed in units per time period, and run lengths vary from short periods to continuous operation. Cleanout of equipment to avoid contamination between runs of different materials requires a significant amount of time and work. Only raw materials and finished-product inventories are carried. Work-in-process is very small, usually just enough to fill the process units.

Degree of External Regulation

When production operations are run as they can and should be, the planning and control system can be essentially simple. In many companies, however, information requirements of customers, particularly local, state, and federal governments, introduce more complexity. These requirements fall into two categories: periodic reports and operation restrictions.

Periodic Reports.   Manufacturers must issue up-to-date reports often to people outside the firm, such as financial information to government taxing departments, and to people inside the firm, such as progress information to the marketing department. Usually the tracking of data for reporting purposes does not influence operations directly as such tracking simply records what has happened or is occurring. Often the reporting departments use the same data for planning and control that management gets and therefore require no added system elements. When systems must be modified, changes are usually minor.

Operation Restrictions.   These regulations do influence operations, causing changes in the ways companies would otherwise conduct business. Sometimes external requirements on industries cannot be met without very significant systems enhancements. Among these industries are producers of atomic power, radioactive materials, pharmaceuticals, foods, aircraft, weapons, and major structures (e.g., bridges and buildings) for public use. Well-run manufacturing operations are able to meet such external requirements with few and simple changes in their planning and control systems.

Influences on Production and Inventory Control

For many years during early development of the production and inventory control body of knowledge, so-called process industries were convinced that they were different from metal, wood, and plastics working and that APICS teachings could not be applied. While it is true that very few process industry facilities fall into the job shop and intermittent job lot categories, the distinction between repetitive and continuous production for specific plants is often arbitrary, based more on tradition than reality. Even in the process industries, few plants run continuously as the petroleum refineries do, making the same products; most plants are repetitive, modified flow facilities.

This smoke screen of semantics began to lift when the first APICS Special Interest Group (SIG) was formed in 1980 by process industry people. They undertook as their first task the definition of the PIC system framework for their businesses; the diagram they produced was obviously applicable to all types of production, showing the same core system elements as previous charts for other industries.

In reality, the similarities between process and other industries far outnumber their differences. Planning and control of production operations are based on data involving the use of facilities and the movement of materials. The system structure and use of data within one of the above production categories is influenced very little by differences in materials, processing, and markets served. The core planning and control system needed is common to all categories regardless of what is made, how it is made, and for whom it is made.

REQUIREMENTS FOR EFFECTIVE CONTROL

By the mid-1970s all the basic requirements for achieving control of production operations had been identified:

1. A complete, integrated planning and control system
2. A valid master production schedule
3. Accurate data
4. Qualified people
5. An organization to plan, execute, and control

The integrated system, including its design, installation, and operation, is the only one of the five that is primarily technical. The remaining four are people oriented and, as such, are much more difficult to achieve and utilize.

Planning and Control Systems

The role of the planning and control system is often misunderstood. The purpose of planning is to define the resources needed to produce planned output. The system is the means to make an integrated plan linking all production activities requiring resources. Since plans are future projections, what has been planned is rarely what customers really want when plans are executed. The purpose of execution, very different from that of planning, is to apply available resources to make what customers want now. The control elements of the system compare planned and immediate needs, sort significant from trivial differences, and produce signals to initiate corrective actions, which may include revising plans and/or refocusing execution.

Manufacturing, as a process, is subject to varying degrees of control depending on the complexity of the process, the power and sophistication of the system, and the characteristics of the environment, including its disciplines, variability, and predictability. Manual systems are now obsolete; computers are needed to achieve the processing speed required and to accumulate the masses of data involved. Computer hardware and software, however, are now available to any company at affordable prices (see Chapters 28 to 30).

Control systems may be *open-loop* or *closed-loop*. The former simply handles planning data, making them available to those responsible for preparing and revising plans and transmitting them to people running the manufacturing process; most early PIC systems were open-loop. Control theory defines *closed-loop* as capable of adjusting the process, which is rarely possible in manufacturing. Planning and control systems are often called "closed-loop," however, when they are capable of tracking execution activities and adjusting plans, although they may depend on human intervention for corrective actions to adjust the process.

Two fundamental questions must be answered affirmatively for sound planning:

1. Is output adequate to meet total demands?
2. Are the right items being worked on now?

The first question is more vital for control, but the second question usually receives far more attention. If a plant cannot make enough of everything, it will not be able to make all of the right things. Plans impossible to execute are worse than useless.

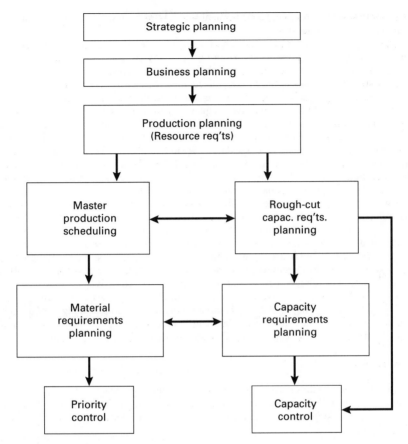

FIGURE 2.1 Core system.

Basic Elements. The elements of the core PIC system common to all types of production are shown in Fig. 2.1. The lower left side shows the priority elements, and the right shows the capacity ones. The core system is linked directly to the hierarchy of the long-range (1 to 5 years) plans—strategic, business, and production—covered in detail in other chapters. *Strategic plans* incorporate management's goals, policies, and methods for operating the total business. *Business plans* focus on product families sold in various markets. *Production plans* are expressed in dollar values or number of units of families of similar items and are used to identify needed resources. Time periods often vary over the planning horizon from monthly, in the near term, to quarterly, semiannually, and annually further out.

The master production schedule (MPS) and rough-cut capacity planning boxes in the figure represent the next level of planning. One important role of the MPS is linking long- and short-range plans. Driven by the MPS, the formal system develops detailed plans and schedules supporting the production plan, or the system indicates clearly through feedback that the plan cannot be executed. These details must be realistic and achievable so that individuals can be held responsible for execution. The MPS must be tested for realism via rough-cut capacity analyses, comparison with previous operations, or more detailed evaluations.

The third (and final) phase of planning includes detailed materials and capacity requirements determinations, as shown in Fig. 2.1. Modern formal systems ensure that all details are integrated, so that all people involved in execution are "singing to the same music." The arrows in the figure indicate how the elements relate to each other.

As mentioned, capacity control is more important than priority control. With rare exceptions, most companies try to get adequate capacity to execute the plan set by the MPS. Input-output capacity control techniques measure flow rates of work into and out of suppliers and plant work centers to detect significant deviations promptly, so that lead times can be controlled. Average data over moderately long horizons are quite adequate. This is the "acid test" of the validity of the MPS. The arrow bypassing the capacity requirements box in the figure conveys an important message: *Input-Output must operate even if it is based on only rough-cut capacity data.*

The priority control element utilizes work sequences established by materials requirements planning; based on order completion dates and (sometimes) work content, these requirements are communicated to suppliers and plant work centers via lists variously called *daily dispatches, orders of work,* or *work schedules.* Erratic loads that often result must be examined to ascertain whether near-term capacity permits holding schedules. Excessive overloads require revisions to the material plan and possibly to the MPS; the latter should be avoided unless costs of adherence are excessive.

Tailoring PIC systems to the wide variety of production processes is accomplished mainly by formatting the database and output reports and by emphasizing various techniques. For example, detailed forecasting is little used in aerospace and defense operations, and batch identification and tracking are mandatory in regulated businesses.

Foundations.   Sound PIC systems require:

1. An adequate database, up-to-date and having no significant errors in customer orders, active bills of material, on-hand inventory, open purchase and manufacturing orders, processing operations, work standards, tooling, equipment specifications, and costs.

2. Performance measures indicating the health of the system including file data accuracy, number of action messages by category, lists of data omissions, and aged transaction errors not yet corrected.

3. People whose qualifications match their system's capabilities. Businesses change, and there will never be an ultimate system; people and systems must evolve together.

Supporting Subsystems.   In addition to the core elements, PIC systems need many supporting subsystems, including:

Demand forecasting	Customer order processing
Master production schedules	Inventory transactions
Open orders, purchasing	Open orders, manufacturing
Bills of materials processing	Engineering change control
Process data	Methods change control
Production reporting	Quality control
Tooling	Maintenance
Costs	Budgets

Need for Variations.   As already mentioned, the PIC core system framework is identical for all types of production. The framework diagram developed by the APICS Process Industry Special Interest Group (discussed under "Influences on PIC," above) was almost identical to Fig. 2.1; the differences are only minor details and arrows. Another APICS Special Interest Group for repetitive industries has identified no essential differences required in their system elements.

While core-system elements are common to all, individual companies will have differences in emphases, techniques, databases, output reports, and subsystems. Underqualified people are often confused by myriad details of production, failing to understand the essential simplicity of the process. Combined with the chaos of poorly planned, executed, and controlled operations, they believe their companies need unique, expensive, and sophisticated systems. When manufacturing firms are run the way they can and should be, systems can be much simpler than most now in use.

Frequency and Causes of Replanning.   Modern computer-based systems create an illusion of precision. Neatly tabulated reports, arithmetically perfect, look highly credible; this illusion is enhanced greatly by short time periods. Weekly planning periods and weekly updating of the plan are satisfactory for practically all manufacturing companies; shorter planning periods should be utilized only with fast operations where significant benefits can be identified. However, many believe the ultimate is the 1-day, so-called bucketless, plan. Computer power and economics make instant, on-line, transaction-driven replanning possible; in most applications it is impractical.

There are two fallacies in thinking that planning can be accurate and that replanning improves accuracy and control and aids execution. Dealing as it does with uncertain future activities, planning will never be accurate; the perfect plan will never be made. Replanning is necessary, of course, when customer demands or internal resources change significantly. Replanning to cope with unsolved production problems is just an admission of failure to execute and should be used only as a last resort.

Myriad planning changes introduced too frequently result in nervous prostration, making the system incapable of helping people execute plans at the very time such help is needed most. Systems are very flexible and responsive; plant operations are not. Efforts to dampen nervousness by "fences" defining periods in which the MPS should not be changed are evidence of a lack of understanding of the different purposes of planning and execution and are doomed to failure. This is explained in detail in the section "Replanning Versus Execution" later in this chapter.

Uses in Planning, Control, and Execution.   Primarily PIC systems make integrated plans for all future important activities involved with production operations so that needed resources can be identified. Secondarily, they must accept data tracking actual performance, compare it to planned performance, and highlight significant deviations for control. In the near term, planning cannot be expected to coincide with reality, and it is counterproductive to attempt to make it do so. Actual data on customers' orders and resources must drive execution. PIC systems can help by producing shortage lists and work center overloads caused by decisions to build specific products needed now, whether planned or not, and revising plans to adjust for the changes resulting.

Planning data (called "soft" data) represent future expected or desired events like dates for receiving purchased materials or completing work orders, levels of inventory targeted, or value of weekly shipments. Execution data (called "hard" data) show realities like the amount of purchased material received, inventory on hand now, or quantity completed through an operation on a work order. Planning data should be updated periodically; execution data must be up to date when users need them for decision making. Real-time entry of transactions to adjust hard data is possible but not necessary for effective execution. Timely, accurate data updated within a few hours of execution is usually adequate.

A key activity in the execution process is solving problems; this involves analyzing any problem threatening proper execution of the plan. A late component, unusual scrap loss, unexpected tool breakdown, equipment failure, record error, or other upset must trigger analysis of formal systems data to decide on proper corrective actions. Snap decisions made with partial or invalid data or made by people unfamiliar with the system or with production processes create more problems than they solve. The future use of PIC systems in problem solving will occupy more time and be more important than their use in planning. This fact must be a prime consideration in the design of the system, particularly in the selection of enhancements, which often add sophistication without significantly improving utility. Education and training must develop people's skill in using systems to solve problems.

Master Production Schedules

Sound planning and control of manufacturing operations require valid, realistic master production schedules (MPSs). To be valid, an MPS must support long-term strategic, business, and production plans; to be realistic, resources must be adequate to produce all of the items planned. The MPS is the most important set of planning numbers, and, at the same time, it is the most difficult to develop.

What MPSs Are and Are Not.   MPSs are planning devices; they are not part of execution. They are statements of what items are planned to be produced, when, and in what quantities. They do not indicate what items are expected to be bought by customers; these are shown in demand forecasts. Each item in an MPS is described by a bill of materials (see other chapters for details). MPSs for simple products (hardware, hand tools, and fasteners) usually represent finished products, ready for sale. For more complex products (home appliances or lawn mowers) and those with product options offered to customers in myriad combinations (automobiles or machine tools), MPS items represent subassemblies or convenient artificial groupings called *planning modules.*

Assembly, finishing, packaging, and shipping schedules for finished products, called *shippables,* are part of execution. Where modular bills of materials describe MPS items and products are finished to customer orders, the MPS will be very different from assembly, finishing, packaging, and shipping schedules.

MPSs are not intended to be constraints setting rigid programs to be followed at all costs. They are planning devices to initiate and control the procurement of necessary materials and other resources. Master scheduling, the development of this set of numbers, should involve the top-level managers in marketing, manufacturing, engineering, finance, and general management. This activity provides the mechanism whereby conflicting policies and objectives of these people can be reconciled and a consensus developed for an operating plan for the whole company.

MPSs are not schedules in the usual sense of assigning times for the start and completion of activities. Quantities in the MPS are not "orders." MPSs and their supporting formal planning programs provide integrated sets of data from which to determine quantitatively and specifically what materials and work centers are affected when significant changes become necessary.

MPSs are short- to medium-range plans. Their minimum horizon is the longest sum of the lead times required to procure materials and process them through sequences of production operations for all levels of the bill of materials of each MPS item. In the past a year was commonly used, but attention to shortening lead times has made 3- and 6-

month horizons common. Most frequently, time periods (buckets) are 1 week; longer intervals make the plan too insensitive. One-day time intervals (bucketless) are possible but impractical; they give an illusion of precision to inherently approximate planning data.

Objectives. The objectives of the MPSs are to:

1. Provide top management with the means to authorize and control procurement of resources
2. Serve as a mechanism to coordinate all functions (finance, engineering, marketing, and production) of the business and to measure the performance of each
3. Aid in making valid customer delivery promises, reconciling customers' wants with plant capabilities
4. Make budgets for formal planned activities such as purchased-material commitments, direct and indirect labor, and inventories of raw materials, stocked components, and works-in-process
5. Provide means to coordinate related activities in organization groups supporting production

Sources of Data. The MPS receives input data from a variety of sources. Among the important ones are:

1. Demand forecasts, necessary when customers will not wait for manufacturing companies to procure materials and make them into products. Forecasts must cover, or be convertible into, the same items, time periods, and units of measure as the MPS and extend over the same horizon, over which the level of detail may broaden.
2. Unshipped customer orders, due within the planning horizon. These are not substitutes for the MPS; they must drive execution. They should be considered when developing the MPS, particularly if they represent heavy demands on resources. For make-to-order products, customer orders are viewed as "consuming the MPS" and unconsumed balances as "available to promise." When customer orders have been released to production, components have been issued or allocated and there are no longer demands for available materials, although capacity is still needed to complete work. Possible problems are handled in execution, not planning.
3. Planning to increase or decrease safety stocks subtracts from or adds to the production totals planned in the MPS.
4. Decreasing or increasing inventory totals has the same effect on the MPS as safety stock level changes.
5. Lot sizes planned for economies in machine changeover may require revising MPS quantities in specific time periods if they result in undesirable lumps of demand.
6. Lead times of operations required for production items must be considered when changes in rates are planned in the MPS; procurement and work cannot be done in the past.
7. Time-phased order points develop profiles of planned orders that may be used directly in the MPS for products stocked for future customer demand or warehouse supply.
8. Demand for components used or sold as spare, repair, service, or maintenance parts must be considered in the MPS if they are significant users of resources.

TABLE 2.1   Master Production Schedule

MPS for Product Family #4321									
Week	15	16	17	18		27	28	29	30
Product A	50	—	50	—		60	—	60	—
Product B	610	610	610	610		610	610	610	610
Product C	340	360	380	400		460	430	400	370
Product D	180	180	175	175		155	155	150	150
Product E	—	15	—	—		—	—	20	—
Product F	205	205	205	205		225	225	225	225
Spares sets	18	18	18	18		20	20	20	20
Monthly totals		5637					5830		

Typical Format.   MPS formats vary widely according to the type of business, sources of data, users' needs, and many other factors. A typical format is shown in Table 2.1 for a family of finished products and their spare parts sold for field replacement. This MPS has a 1-year horizon and weekly data. Product models are grouped into families meaningful to both marketing and production people. Product A has low demand, B's is level, and C's is seasonal. D is dwindling in its markets, E has one customer who orders intermittently, and F is expected to grow. Service parts are included as "sets" defined by kit-bills of materials. The weekly data *show when final assembly is to begin*; they are not demand forecasts or orders but planned production quantities. Monthly total units are shown for comparison to production plans, providing a check on aggregate loads on plant and suppliers.

Ensuring Realism.   The greatest difficulty in developing and maintaining a valid MPS lies in determining the facilities' ability to produce all of the products desired. Both overstated or understated MPSs produce invalid detailed plans; they are the most prevalent reasons for PIC system failures. People, particularly those in authority, refuse to accept constraints or agree on compromises. Front-end MPS overloads persist when viewed as "delivery commitments to customers" or, in defense and aerospace companies, as "contract requirements." The root cause is failure to understand the differences between planning and execution and the proper uses of the MPS.

Effective use of capacity requirements planning is vital for writing a valid MPS. This is made more difficult by rapid proliferation of products and technologies employed in their processing. The most successful plants, called *focused factories,* produce a limited product line utilizing relatively few production operations.

Lack of detailed data in work or machine standards is no excuse to avoid capacity requirements planning. Rough-cut methods are widely applicable, require only approximate data, are simple to employ, and provide very useful results. In Fig. 2.1, the arrow on the core system, originating in the rough-cut capacity requirements planning element and bypassing capacity requirements planning, indicates that capacity control is necessary and can be effective without myriad details.

Uses.   MPS data have a wide variety of uses in planning and control of resources needed for manufacturing:

1. Providing a mechanism for developing consensus and coordination among all functions of the business
2. Linking detailed planning to broader-based, longer-range strategic, business, and production plans
3. Measuring the ability of major business functions (finance, engineering, marketing, and production) to make and execute plans
4. Driving formal core systems that develop integrated detailed materials and capacity requirements plans and procurement and production schedules for all components at all levels of the bills of materials
5. Making possible valid revisions of plans and schedules
6. Providing means to make sound customer delivery promises and revise them when necessary
7. Scheduling marketing, design engineering, internal sales, and other activities related to production

Replanning Versus Execution.   As stated earlier, the perfect plan will never be made; if one were, it would never be executed perfectly. The obvious conclusions are that:

1. Companies must be prepared to make something different from what they planned to make.
2. Formal plans, however sound, will never eliminate shortages of resources.

Revising the plan (replanning) can be helpful but only if adequate time remains to react. Defining *adequate time* is difficult; it is a function of people's resolve to change and the flexibility of operations permitting quick changes.

"Fences" in the MPS are useful only to define the front end of the horizon within which revising the plan is useless. Suggestions that this part of the MPS be "firm" or "frozen" are worthless, based as they are implicitly on two fallacies:

1. Items not planned in this period cannot be made in it now.
2. What is planned must be made whether needed now or not.

Fences should indicate periods in which replanning ceases and execution activities begin. Tentative schedules of customer orders or other firm demands can be tested, using the formal PIC system to allocate the sets of components needed to build desired items. Negative available balances from such allocations indicate shortages of components. Each shortage can be analyzed to determine whether the item can be obtained in time at reasonable cost. Tentative schedules are revised until shortages can be overcome.

The locations of MPS fences are determined by the time periods covered by firm demands, but they should not exceed a few weeks to avoid committing resources too soon. Finished-product warehouse replenishment orders can be firmed up and included in the same periods. Customer orders on hand for delivery beyond the fence are often susceptible to design, option definition, quantity, and delivery date changes and should not be included.

The proper sequence of planning and execution is:

1. Develop a realistic MPS.
2. Work to improve its validity by cutting lead times, matching customer orders to avoid changing the plan, and weeding out dead or dying products from lines.

3. Revise the plan for significant customer-related or design changes.
4. Attempt to execute the plan to obtain components, but expect some shortages.
5. Within the fence period, use allocation routines to determine specific shortages that will prevent completion of desired products whether planned or not.
6. Concentrate on overcoming shortages to enable shipment of a maximum number of desired orders.
7. Identify problems preventing execution of plans, and eliminate them or minimize their effects.

The number of shortages uncovered in the allocation process will be manageable if:

1. Continual efforts are made to make a better plan.
2. Flexibility in operations is provided by shortening lead times, standardizing components, and avoiding early assignment of resources to specific items.
3. Problems interfering with execution are discovered immediately, attacked vigorously, and eliminated.

Accurate Data

Planning and control systems simply manipulate data on which all manufacturing plans are based. Plans cannot be more accurate than the data; the system cannot correct errors. Integrated manufacturing systems pass errors from level to level through the entire product structure and the total system, multiplying their effects. Errors in items common to many product structures have devastating results not limited to class A or B items. The quality of plan data limits the effectivity of execution and control.

The 1970s saw dramatic developments in effective elimination of record errors. Previously, most managers believed that getting and maintaining accurate records would be tremendously expensive, take an inordinate amount of time, and offer little in tangible benefits. All three of these are fallacies.

Vital Records.   Myriad files and records are found in even small manufacturing companies. All are useful to someone, but the following are essential for planning and control:

- Customers' orders
- Open purchase orders
- Processing routines:
    Work centers
    Standards
    Tooling and equipment
- Bills of material
- Open manufacturing orders
- On-hand inventory balances and transactions
- Costs

Causes of Errors.   Errors are caused primarily by humans: carelessness in writing or keying data, incorrect counting, wrong identification, loss of documents, or mistakes in simple calculations. Poor design of forms, lack of documentation, and inadequate training also lead to errors. Mechanical and electronic devices like bar-code readers and counting scales are being used increasingly in data transfer activities. These sometimes fail and add errors; more often, poorly trained users get erroneous results. Long, alphanumeric part numbers contribute to error problems. Few firms have more than 100,000 items to plan and control; only five digits are necessary to assign individual identifications to this many items. Naive attempts to have part numbers describe, not just identify, items are unnecessary; item master records can be coded in other fields for desired descriptive information.

Requirements for Accuracy. Fundamental to achieving accurate records is management's intolerance of sloppy data handling and processing. All people handling data must understand that errors will not be tolerated. High levels of record accuracy are possible. The goal should be *100 percent of data having no significant errors.* "Significant" refers to the effect of errors on operations; it is a function of an item's value, ease of procurement, method of counting, and type of control. Achieving the goal is not expensive; it can be accomplished in a remarkably short time by five essential activities, not limited to inventory records but applied to all records and files supporting planning and control. These five activities are:

Establish a Climate of High Expectations. People cannot be held responsible for performance that is poorly defined and measured. Management must make clear the importance of accuracy, set high goals, and be intolerant of errors. This can be done through meetings, posters, banners, letters, and gimmick programs stressing that errors are unacceptable. The costs involved in developing such a climate are minimal.

Assign Responsibility. Management must assign responsibility clearly for accuracy in all transactions updating record data. This should be shown in job descriptions, and performance should be measured periodically. It is best if an individual is assigned specific records. For example, one person should be accountable for individual receipts and issues and the accuracy of balances for specific inventory items in a section of a stockroom. If more than one person is responsible for a record segment, no one can be held really accountable.

Materials planners should be responsible for open purchase and manufacturing order data on a specified list of items. Design engineering should be responsible for the accuracy of bills of material, including phasing in engineering changes. Routings and standards should be the responsibility of manufacturing engineering. Plant engineering should be held accountable for machine data, spares inventories, and utilities information. The cost of assigning such responsibilities and monitoring performance is small. The primary benefit is making clear to each individual what is expected in accuracy of data handling.

Provide Adequate Tools. Simply understanding and stressing the need for record accuracy is not enough; people must be given adequate tools with which to do their jobs. Tools fall into two categories:

System tools	Physical tools
Bar coding	Locked stockrooms
Checking digits	Good housekeeping
Hash totals	Bar-code readers
Edit checks	Counting scales
Serial numbers	Marking hand counters
Form design	Standard containers
Documentation	Stamped part numbers
Short part numbers	On-line data access

The costs of providing these tools originally, plus training in their use, can be significant, but they will be a one-time expense. Some have other tangible benefits; for example, standard containers often reduce materials-handling costs and accidents along with improving accuracy.

Measure Record Accuracy.   The principle that "you cannot control what you do not measure" is particularly true of record accuracy. Job descriptions should contain specific references to data to be handled and accuracy levels desired. Individuals' performance should be compared periodically to desired standards. Help should be given to poor performers, and, if they are unable to improve, they should be transferred to other work. Posted charts showing groups' (e.g., storekeepers or receiving clerks) performance stimulate rapid improvement.

Find and Eliminate Causes of Error.   It is far easier to find errors than to find out what caused them, but eliminating causes of errors is required to achieve high levels of accuracy. The best technique to find errors, *cycle counting,* is well known and widely tested. Cycle counting involves a physical count of a sample of items, comparing record data, and identifying "significant" errors as defined above under the heading "Requirements for Accuracy." Cycle counts can be made to check all records, not just inventory balances. When properly made, they are a quick, easy, inexpensive means to find errors. Identifying the causes of errors requires experienced people with a thorough understanding of the company's operations and its planning and control system. Eliminating errors from records can be a speedy, highly rewarding process; the real tragedy of poor data is that it is unnecessary.

Sources of Tangible Benefits.   The tangible benefits that can be achieved by improving data accuracy are surprisingly large and far exceed the costs of the five activities. They include:

1. Elimination of annual physical inventories
2. Elimination of year-end write-offs to reconcile actual inventory investment with book values
3. Elimination of "staging" (physically isolating and counting) materials to be sure items needed for production are really on hand
4. Reduced time and effort of manually counting when items are needed urgently
5. Reduction in obsolete inventory
6. Reductions in operating expenses (overtime, extra setups, substitute materials, alternate operations, extra freight) incurred to recover from unexpected errors

Even if tangible benefits did not cover the costs of making and keeping records accurate, significant errors must be eliminated from planning and control data if sound decisions are to be made.

Qualified People

The art and science of production planning and control have been developed only in the last three decades. During this time schools, colleges, and universities have focused on intellectually challenging aspects of PIC and have derived solutions with only limited practical application. APICS activities have attracted many seminar leaders, speakers, and writers with little knowledge of laws, principles, and correct applications of techniques. Literature has proliferated but has been heavily weighted with misinformation.

As a result, few PIC professionals have understood fully how manufacturing should be controlled. This has changed slowly.

Recent rapid developments in production planning and control have resulted in job requirements rising beyond the level of competence of many people holding them. Newer, more sophisticated computer systems embodying new techniques and providing much more information more quickly in an environment of rapid changes dictate the need for people with faster and more intelligent responses who can operate under severe pressures. The need for adequate preparation of individuals for planning and control jobs was never greater.

Common Misconceptions. To become qualified, people must learn new ideas, facts, and skills, and they must also unlearn many misconceptions. The latter is by far the more difficult task. Misunderstandings have persisted through the years, held by people at all organization levels. The most insidious are:

Manufacturing problems cannot be eliminated. Inventory and time cushions must be provided to reduce their harmful effects. In spite of the evident failure of safety stock and time cushions to solve the problems, people persist in pursuing this approach. This wastes inventory, makes planning less valid, and actually aggravates the problems. Even worse, it diverts attention from the real solution—eliminating the problems. It is clear now that this is possible.

More frequent and precise replanning will improve execution. Computer systems can easily handle myriad revisions, but plants and people cannot. The real problem arising from this myth is neglect of efforts to make a more valid plan, requiring short horizons and quick execution.

Lead times cannot be controlled; they can only be monitored and adjusted. This fiction also leads to actions that aggravate the problem. Two truths about lead time must be recognized:

1. A difference between *planned* and *measured actual* lead times cannot be eliminated by changing the planned figure. If it is increased, the gap will widen. The vicious cycle thus generated is disastrous. Cutting planned lead times will be less damaging but will not wipe out the differences resulting from unplanned work-in-process levels caused by excess or inadequate capacity. These are eliminated only by adjusting capacity.
2. Actual lead times will follow planned figures, increasing or decreasing with them. The reasons for this become obvious immediately if the inevitable reactions of ordering techniques and people employing them are thought through.

Idle time must be prevented. The tangible costs of idle people or machines are easily calculated, but the true total cost of avoiding them are not. Among the latter are excess inventory, commitment of flexible resources to the wrong items, poor reaction to customers' needs, and less valid planning data. Successful companies tolerate some downtime while striving to eliminate the causes.

It is not worth the effort to reduce setup costs. These are usually included in factory overhead, calculated by dividing setup cost by standard lot size. Compared to per-piece material, labor, and overhead costs, setup costs appear negligible, but the insidious effect on all elements of lead time (setup, running, move, and queue times) must be recognized. Cutting setup time not only shortens the working elements but also makes possible dramatic reductions in the dominant element, queue time, by smoothing and speeding up materials flow through all operations.

Who Must Be Qualified?   The activities of planning and control are not limited to any single department; they involve all departments and all organization levels within them. These activities represent the sensory system, intelligence, communication media, and muscles of the organization. No company can realize its full potential if some part of its organization lacks understanding or is mishandling its proper role.

The major concerns of the principal departments in manufacturing firms have little in common. Engineering sees its role as technical, inventing and developing products, improving methods and tooling, and managing the physical plant and equipment. Marketing focuses on defining and meeting customers' needs through a variety of products, and it desires a flexible response to changes. Production is preoccupied with stability of operation, level loads, getting the necessary resources, and keeping costs low. Finance concentrates on acquisition of the needed capital, cash flow, budgets, and policing others' performance.

Top management and department heads try to direct operations to achieve desired goals. While it is easy to get agreement among functional departments on specific goals (for example, profits), each has its own ideas on methods of achieving these goals. Reconciling their differences and coordinating the groups is management's task. The planning and control system provides a common source of information that all need, ending perennial arguments about whose data are correct. It also provides the mechanism whereby each can contribute to the development of a consensus on how the business will be operated and then can be measured on the effectiveness with which the resulting plans are executed.

Getting Qualified.   Several avenues are open to those wishing to become qualified. A few business schools now recognize the need to include courses on manufacturing operations in their MBA curriculum. Many colleges, particularly in their extension services, offer courses leading to degrees in production management. The APICS, many consultants, and most computer hardware and software companies conduct courses on various topics. Videotapes, games, books, articles, training aids, and a wealth of other published materials are available.

No special skills in mathematics, statistics, computer technology, or other high-level science are required. Few individuals, when given the proper education, are unable to master the requirements for jobs in the field. There are three phases:

Understand the state of the art. This takes broad-based education led by someone with experience and understanding of the field's language, laws, principles, and techniques and their applications in various industries.

Understand the individual's role. This phase focuses on the support that systems need from users and the help systems provide to users. It details how individuals must change their ways of life and why.

Monitor actual performance. Daily, on-the-job use of the system and the data it provides must be reviewed regularly to ensure people's adherence to policies and standard practices, to prevent misguided shortcuts, to adapt to changing needs, and to handle employee turnover.

Professionalism.   The day of the amateur in PIC has passed. Manufacturing can be controlled, but it takes professionals to do it. Failure to control now means failure to survive; few companies are exceptions. PIC progressed from a collection of loosely related techniques to a recognized profession during the 1960s and 1970s. It has its unique body of knowledge, language, principles, and techniques as well as the requirement of skill in applying these to specific situations.

PIC affects the welfare of individuals, companies, industries, and countries as much as any other profession. People in law, medicine, dentistry, commercial airline flying, engineering, and accounting cannot perform activities affecting the public without society's sanction through licensing or registration. The APICS recognizes qualified individuals in certification programs.

Unfortunately, it is not yet possible to define rigorously what is required to be a professional manager in a manufacturing company. Clearly, it must include knowledge of the fundamentals of effective planning and control. All managers in positions of responsibility for engineering, marketing and sales, financial, or production activities will be required in the not too distant future to demonstrate their familiarity with these fundamentals in addition to their capabilities in their special fields.

Organization

Management of manufacturing operations can be effective only when sound plans are successfully executed; planning and control are necessary but not sufficient. Successful execution requires people to work together effectively toward common goals. Contrast professional sporting teams with the typical management team, a collection of all-stars. Managers must agree not only on company goals but also on the methods of achieving them.

Operating the total business, not just an individual portion of it, must be seen more clearly as a primary objective of each group. Sound planning and effective execution make it mandatory that these groups know their real jobs, know how to do them properly, and know when they are and are not performing well.

Internal Relationships.   The activities of manufacturing planning and control span all departments. Some believe it must be part of the chief executive's office if it is to be effective. This is nonsense. A clear understanding of its relationships with other functions rather than a particular form of organization is needed. In fact, formal organization structure is only a minor factor; it should be developed to utilize the strengths of individuals and to compensate for weaknesses, rather than to suit specific functional relationships.

The primary roles of each group in a manufacturing organization must be defined properly, usually requiring reevaluation. The basic objective is to break down the compartmentalization of specialty groups such as purchasing, production, engineering, and cost accounting and to create instead their roles as team members in an organized effort. When the primary role of each group is properly defined, its interrelationships with other groups become clear. Typical primary roles are:

Planning and control. Develop realistic plans for all important resources; measure promptly and accurately actual performance executing these plans, detect and identify significant deviations, and initiate corrective actions. This role does not include execution.

Production. Manage plant, equipment, and line personnel to execute plans, converting materials into products to satisfy market needs and meet internal goals.

Design engineering. Improve present products and develop new products to serve desired markets, utilizing present plant and equipment, and informing others of needed details via drawings, specifications, and properly structured bills of material.

Manufacturing engineering. Improve present methods and develop new methods of processing materials to improve function, quality, and durability of products, smooth out the materials flow through the plant, and reduce processing costs.

Plant engineering. Lay out and maintain buildings, machinery, and equipment, and provide energy sources to ensure continuity of production.

Marketing and sales. Identify markets, customers, and their product needs, define distribution methods, get orders, forecast expected customer demand, and reconcile customer and company interests.

Finance. Provide capital and operating funds, manage cash and investments, coordinate budgeting and highlight significant variations, assist in financial analyses, report financial information needed by managers, stockholders, and governments, and maintain cost accounting data.

Information services. Provide specialized assistance in applying computer-based systems, including database design, selecting hardware and software, programming, providing documentation, but not necessarily operating computers.

Purchasing. Locate sources for materials and services, negotiate prices, terms, and conditions, prepare legal purchase orders, and work with suppliers to ensure smooth flow of quality materials and services in adequate quantities and short lead times.

Top management. Direct and coordinate all activities to achieve goals while adhering to policies and strategies.

External Relationships.   Planning and control groups, because they work intimately and are familiar with their own systems, have taken on responsibilities for communications with organizations outside their own companies. These include:

Suppliers. Purchasing handles supplier selection and negotiation of prices, terms, and conditions but schedules and other details are handled by "planner-buyers" who have system data on which to base communications. In some cases, customer and supplier systems are linked directly, and people are needed only for exceptions.

Customers. Marketing and sales has responsibility for customer contacts to obtain orders. Once in-house, however, planning and control people approve requested (or develop revised) delivery promises, respond to status requests, and handle order quantity and delivery date changes.

Oversight agencies. Defense contractors and other regulated manufacturers funnel communications on inspection and test schedules, specification changes, delivery performance, and compliance problems through planning and control.

MAKING PIC WORK

Two phases and five stages for improving PIC performance are:

* Planning phase:
    Set production strategies.
    Lay out systems plan.
* Implementation phase:
    Develop specifications.
    Implement plan.
    Improve performance.

Setting production strategies will be discussed here; other chapters cover well the other stages. Before work is undertaken in any stage, basic principles must be understood and applied. Failures in the past of intelligent people to implement powerful techniques in sophisticated systems and gain potential benefits have been due directly to ignorance or misapplication of such principles.

Fundamental Principles

There are many principles of manufacturing that professional people need to know. These are well covered in PIC literature. Eight important ones are:

1. *Time is the most precious resource.* It cannot be stored, reused, or slowed. This principle demands intolerance of delays and time cushions, concentration on speeding up all needed activities, and eliminating unneeded ones. Lost time is the worst waste.

2. *There is one system framework common to all types of manufacturing.* This is illustrated in Fig. 2.1. This principle is true regardless of products made, materials used, processes employed, and customers served.

3. *Well-run operations do not require complex systems.* The bulk of complexity in PIC systems is involved in coping with unexpected upsets, correcting data errors, and recovering from surprises. This principle focuses attention on eliminating problems, not coping with their effects.

4. *Any manufacturing problem can be minimized; most can be eliminated.* Contrary to popular opinion, this principle emphasizes that chaos is not normal in manufacturing. One problem solved produces much better results than any system enhancement to handle its effects.

5. *Plans impossible to execute are worse than useless.* The final result will be poor customer service, excess, unbalanced inventories, and above-budget costs. This principle stresses the importance of realistic planning.

6. *Plan capacity over long horizons; schedule specifics in the near term.* Errors and changes increase with the length of planning horizons; only resources requiring long periods for actions should be planned far ahead, always in aggregate terms. Detailed plans should cover only very short horizons.

7. *Planning defines resources needed to make what is planned; execution applies available resources to make what customers want now.* This principle highlights the difference between planning and execution. Implicit is the fallacy of trying to do both with the same system programs.

8. *Educate all employees continuously.* Manufacturing is a living activity, constantly changing to meet market needs, utilize latest technologies, comply with government regulations, and respond to management goals and policies. This principle points out that all employees need constant improvement in understanding and skills. Next to time, people are a company's most important resource.

Setting Production Strategies

In 1969 in a *Harvard Business Review* article, "Manufacturing—Missing Link in Corporate Strategy," Wickham Skinner criticized managers of U.S. manufacturing companies for failing to integrate manufacturing and corporate strategies. He stated that top managers had the wrong perception of manufacturing, that plants were mismanaged, and that business school teachings were faulty. The indictments were both justified and prophetic. At that time, two powerful forces were emerging that together would change the course of U.S. industry as no other influences had since the industrial revolution:

1. Rapidly rising productivity and quality, coupled with better cost control, by foreign competitors, especially in Japan and West Germany, was eroding the supremacy of U.S. companies in manufacturing technology and management.

2. New concepts of manufacturing planning and control were emerging to join with an increase in capability and availability of computers to create the systems revolution of the 1970s.

Since then, the two imperatives of manufacturing management have been to respond to the challenge of foreign competition and to master the use of manufacturing systems as weapons in a worldwide competitive struggle. The first requires radical changes in most companies, the second extensive education of their people.

It has not been unusual to find marketing strategy well defined: "Offer a wide line of high-quality, low-cost products and options to all classes of customers with quick delivery." Production usually has no defined strategy and is measured on low-cost, high-labor efficiency, and high machine utilization; this implies a strategy of stable schedules, long production runs, and inflexibility, incompatible with marketing!

A production strategy coherent with those of research and development, marketing, and finance is a prerequisite for developing planning and control systems supporting competitive performance. This must include explicit policies consistent with the strategy to provide operating people with guidelines for using the systems. In the past, many newly implemented manufacturing systems—perhaps a majority—failed outright or did not yield benefits expected when the investment decision was made. There were many reasons, but a frequent one was poor strategic planning.

The first step is a corporate strategic plan. The principal objectives and strategies from this are translated to corresponding mandates for the principal functions. For production, this covers process technology, human resources, and control systems. Defining the manufacturing mission forces resolution of conflicting objectives, such as the tradeoff between flexibility and finished-product inventory investment. The resulting collection of objectives and action plans is the production strategy.

The corporate strategy usually views the business as a group of segments involving specific products and markets, with strategies for gaining advantages in each segment. Often, the several market strategies mandate different production strategies. A diversity of manufacturing missions imposed on the same production facility will result in confusion of purpose and suboptimal performance. Failure to achieve "factory focus" will be very troublesome to PIC and will force harmful compromises in the design of planning and control systems.

This does not necessarily imply that separate facilities are needed for each business segment. Focus can be achieved by a "plant within a plant," dividing existing facilities organizationally into separate units, each with its own manufacturing mission, organizational structure, control systems, and policies. With an explicit production strategy, the elements of the planning and control system can be analyzed for capabilities, focus, and staffing. Frequently, since practically every company has some system in place, this requires significant system revisions.

Requirements for Success

There are six keys to effective competitive performance of manufacturing companies:

1. Fully Qualified People at All Organizational Levels.   Characteristic of PIC's early days was a proliferation of techniques, each with strong, vocal advocates, and practitioners seeking panaceas in single, simple techniques. Failure to understand both a technique's capabilities and the manufacturing process in which it must work made frustration and disappointment epidemic. An understanding throughout the whole organization of the manufacturing process and how it should be run is essential.

Modern manufacturing firms are improving operations along well-defined paths. Fewer layers of supervisors are serving as coaches and facilitators, not bosses, to employees *empowered, educated, and trained* to make decisions on improving their work, emphasizing total quality, doing it right the first time. Production facilities divided into cells focus on families of similar items. Performance measures of specific activities rather than traditional charts of accounts provide earlier alerts to problem areas. The scope of planning and control systems is broadening to include the whole manufacturing business.

Overcoming popular misconceptions, who must be qualified, and how they get qualified is covered in the section "Qualified People" earlier in this chapter. The topic of professionalism is also covered in that section; APICS's role and aids in developing fully qualified people is the subject of other chapters.

2. Complete and Integrated Planning and Control Systems.   The core elements of planning and control systems, supporting systems, replanning, and uses in manufacturing operations are covered in the section "Planning and Control Systems" earlier in this chapter. Workable systems must include all core elements; incomplete systems are like vehicles short one or more wheels—they won't take you anywhere. In the early preoccupation with materials requirements planning, most companies that adopted this powerful technique neglected master scheduling, capacity management, or both. A major development in manufacturing planning and control was the concept of the integrated manufacturing system.

Many techniques, touted highly by proponents, have played only minor roles in PIC. These include linear programming, operation sequencing (formerly "finite loading"), simulation, and other rigorous optimizing techniques. Techniques used successfully abroad—for example, Swedish cyclical planning and Japanese Kanban—were adopted as panaceas by those who understood neither their strengths nor limitations. All techniques have a role in specific production environments, and any will be misapplied in the wrong environment. Fully qualified people will apply system tools most suited to the specific tasks.

System improvements can be implemented without causing serious disruption with a well-structured system plan and sound management of the implementation project. The key is user education in the broad aspects of new programs and training in the specifics of user applications.

The heart of user preparation is system documentation. This is not the technical documentation of programming details; it shows how the system can aid users in running their part of the business. It should contain details of:

1. Conceptual approaches in the application—for example, the rationale and structure of planning bills of material

2. Functional uses of each system module—for example, the conversion of sales forecasts to production plans

3. System elements used in specific functional tasks—for example, examination of transaction records for data error detection

4. Management policies to ensure consistent application of manufacturing strategy— for example, the use of an MPS in making delivery promises to customers

5. Procedures in performing functional tasks—for example, mechanics of introducing engineering changes

6. Criteria for measurement of progress in vital functions—for example, goals for customer delivery performance

User documentation, best when written by users with help from others, is the vehicle that converts manufacturing strategy to workable tactics. It produces three important results: user involvement in system implementation, user mastery of system tools, and highlighted conflicts and difficulties affecting the use of the system in improving operations.

3. Valid and Realistic Planning.   The temptation to avoid realistic planning appears inescapable in manufacturing. The impossibility of turning away customer orders, coupled with difficulties in adding resources quickly, make overloaded plans common in times of rising demand. When demand is slowing, lack of orders and reluctance to cut back on production cause underloaded plans. Both have the same ultimate effects: poor customer service, high costs, and excess inventories. More details are included under "Master Production Schedules" earlier in this chapter, and also in Chapter 12.

4. High Integrity of All Data.   Myriad data and transactions, together with human error tendencies, make this difficult to achieve. The common belief that it is an enormous, costly, and impractical task with few tangible benefits deter too many companies from attacking the problems of data errors although it is obvious to all that accurate data are fundamental to effective planning and control. Proof now abounds that the probability of making errors can be made inconsequential in any business serious about reducing them. It does not take long, it is not difficult, and it yields tangible benefits. The section "Accurate Records" in this chapter and many other chapters in this handbook, principally 8 and 18, present details on error reduction methods.

5. Tightly Managed Cycle Times.   Another set of common fallacies is found in management of cycle and lead times, believed by many to be a contradiction in terms. "They can't be managed, only tracked and adjusted." "Just allow more time, and more work will be completed on schedule." These are popular beliefs. The truth is that *cycle and lead times will be as long or as short as planned, and everything will be better if they are shortened.* Chapters 6 and 16 focus on this topic, and comments are found in many others.

6. Teamwork in Planning and Execution.   Improving the total manufacturing process is an every-day duty of everyone in the organization. To achieve flexibility of production increasingly demanded to support strategic manufacturing objectives, companies must:

1. Simplify all processes and adapt modern planning and control systems and procedures

2. Shorten setup and changeover times, aiming for lot sizes approaching one and the shortest possible cycle times

3. Work toward continuous material flow of various batches

Obviously, these activities involve people from several organization groups. In the past, militarylike line-and-staff organizations in business added excess layers of managers and supervisors, and specialization of work caused delays and conflict. Now reengineering teams are streamlining organizations and eliminating redundant and unnecessary tasks. In normal operations, teams are smoothing out and speeding up processes spanning several organization groups. Members come from organization groups with interest in the activities studied, plus others with skills to contribute to the solutions.

Instead of a single team focused on specific improvement in one activity (like design and implementation of a PIC system), many teams attack simultaneously multiple areas and move companies rapidly toward world-class performance. Management direction has shifted from telling specialized groups how to do things to defining what should be done, setting new goals, coordinating teams whose work overlaps, and aiding team members working on specific changes. Managers and the people they manage experience a new way of life.

Performance Measures

Past manufacturing controls were primarily financial, designed by those keeping score in money units rather than those playing the physical game. Measures were those easily counted rather than those that really counted. Decision makers were swamped with mostly irrelevant data, unrelated to formal plans and precise but inaccurate.

Performance measures should define desired important goals and objectives (e.g., customer service and cycle times), concentrate people's actions on achieving these, and be accurate and timely. Physical measures (pieces and hours) are better than financial; they are more accurate, timely, specific and relevant, simpler, cheaper, easier to get and show causes, easier to correct, and more accountable. Visible measures are more timely and meaningful than data from systems. Aggregates are cheaper and more accurate than details—data on families, not just individual items; flow rates of work, not just specific orders; and trends, not absolute values—and are of more value to decision makers.

The most effective performance reports show both planned and actual data and focus on a vital few activities; common budgets often contain myriad data on trivial items. The objective of measuring performance is to detect aberrant conditions promptly and start corrective actions immediately. Emphasis is now on individual worker self-improvement, not professional specialists analyzing long-after-the-fact signals and instructing them how to change future actions. Prevention of problems, not just later detection and correction, is the ideal.

Potential Benefits

The tangible and intangible benefits of improved control of manufacturing operations are literally enormous. A sound plan coupled with effective execution is the key to success. No other actions, including investment in automated equipment, aggressive marketing programs, or wage and salary incentives, can generate anything approaching these benefits. Failure to achieve tight control has put apparently impregnable firms in desperate straits and has been fatal for many companies.

All businesses have three basic objectives:

1. Customer service superior to competitors
2. Higher productivity and lower costs
3. Better utilization of capital assets, particularly inventories

Often, these are viewed as conflicting—progress in attaining one comes at the expense of the others. When run right, firms can improve all three simultaneously. Here are typical ranges of benefits that well-run companies have received quickly:

1. Quality and Customer Service

- Rejects measured in parts per million, not percent within acceptable quality levels
- On-time delivery, 85 to 95 percent and higher
- Quicker deliveries, 25 to 75 percent
- Excess freight costs, cut 75 to 95 percent
- Internal sales costs, cut 50 to 90 percent
- Sales productivity, up 20 to 40 percent

Product quality has become a given; customers expect appearance, reliability, and performance in excess of their needs. On-time delivery and some fraction of product delivered in much shorter than standard lead times can be major factors in improving a company's market share in a competitive industry. Makers of capital equipment command higher prices when delivery schedules are reliable. The ability to beat a competitor's delivery time or to react more quickly to customers' changes provides major competitive advantages and often commands premium prices. When products are late, penalty clauses in delivery contracts or the cost of premium freight to overcome delays can add tremendously to costs. A sales force on the defensive, making excuses for the failure of their plant to deliver past orders on time, will be severely handicapped in getting new orders.

2. Productivity and Costs.

2. Productivity and Costs.   Benefits in higher productivity and lower costs have been achieved in the following ranges:

- Direct labor productivity, up 10 to 50 percent
- Factory indirect productivity, up 25 to 60 percent
- Office productivity, up 20 to 40 percent
- Unplanned overtime, down 50 to 90 percent
- Alternate operations, down 50 to 85 percent
- Substitute materials, down 50 to 95 percent
- Obsolete materials, down 25 to 80 percent
- Material costs, down 5 to 25 percent
- Storage, interest, and insurance, down 20 to 40 percent

Increasing productivity and lowering costs can be even more important to a company's survival than reducing capital investment in inventories. Significant gains can be made for direct, indirect, and office workers, although the latter two classes are much more difficult to measure. In a well-planned operation with effective execution, many costs can be cut, but idle time of people and machines may actually be increased. Some idle time is an indication of tight control; it usually costs much less than the actions taken and the inventories carried to avoid it.

3. Inventory Reductions.   Zero Inventory was the title of an APICS crusade in 1984. Like JIT (just in time), the term describes a concept, not a technique, a journey, not an objective. Here are typical inventory reductions companies have made:

- Raw materials, 20 to 40 percent
- Purchased and manufactured components, 20 to 40 percent

- Safety stocks, 50 to 95 percent
- Work-in-process, 25 to 75 percent
- Finished products, 10 to 40 percent
- Repair parts (customers'), 25 to 50 percent
- Repair parts (internal), 40 to 60 percent
- Tooling, gauging, and so on, 20 to 40 percent
- Obsolete items, 50 to 90 percent

To achieve the higher figures, a company does not have to be poorly managed when it starts its attack. Very few companies are already doing such a good job that high potentials no longer exist. The low end of the range is easy to achieve; the higher numbers take more time and work.

Work-in-process (WIP) should be the first class of inventory attacked since it comprises half the total of inventories in most companies. Technically the easiest to reduce, WIP is in reality the most difficult to cut because the needed actions are counterintuitive. It involves the least planning effort but requires the greatest execution attention. It is the most visible of wasted inventories and yet the most vitally needed to support a sound plan and execution. Reducing work-in-process will ease the task of reducing all other classes of inventories, open up additional space for more production equipment, increase capacity, avoiding the necessity of expanding plants and buildings, and freeing up capital for automated equipment and other investments.

Raw materials, purchased and manufactured components, and finished-product inventories can be reduced significantly by:

- Procuring materials and producing components just in time to meet customer's delivery needs
- Eliminating redundant safety stocks at several levels in bills of material
- Constantly reducing order quantities (lot sizes)
- Better managing of finished products in central and branch warehouses

Inventories of internal repair parts, tooling, gauges, fixtures, and the like are very fertile areas for improved inventory management. Few companies include these items in the formal planning and control system, ignoring operating schedules, a very serious omission.

PIC CONCEPTS IN NONMANUFACTURING

The concepts, principles, techniques, and systems making improvements possible in manufacturing have applications in nonmanufacturing activities and businesses also.

Manufacturing Support Activities

Design, manufacturing, and plant engineering, marketing and sales, distribution, quality, field service, and cost accounting and finance are finding increasing uses for data found in the planning and control system. Now often called "the business system," its linking of support and production activities results in better coordination among all. This topic is part of many chapters in this handbook. It is the basis for the second APICS certification program, "Integrated Resource Management."

Service Industries

Well over half of the working people in the United States are now employed in service industries. Personnel in medical, legal, financial, insurance, retail sales, transportation, power generation, and repair and maintenance industries make up the private sector. These industries are like manufacturing in:

1. Needing strategic planning, defining what business they are really in, and stating supporting policies
2. Having customers whose future demand, current orders, and past relations need to be planned, tracked, and recorded
3. Dealing with limited resources requiring capital
4. Having masses of data to enter, massage, store, and retrieve with significant penalties for errors
5. Having some kinds of inventory to be managed and several activities to be scheduled
6. Benefiting from use of computer hardware and software programs for specific applications similar, sometimes identical, to those used in manufacturing

Education

Elementary schools, secondary schools, trade schools, and colleges and universities as well as their extension services—all could apply some PIC knowledge. They have extensive and varied inventories, complex scheduling problems, changing designs of teaching aids, and sophisticated equipment loading, in addition to masses of current and historical data to handle. The help of professionals in PIC could be useful to educators.

Health Care

Hospitals, nursing homes, clinics, physicians and surgeons, dentists, and other specialists are benefiting from the use of computer hardware and software very similar to PIC systems. They have extensive customer (patient) data records, complex invoicing, critical inventories, expensive and sophisticated equipment scheduling and maintenance, diagnostic reference and technical data files for physicians and surgeons, and many more requirements similar to manufacturers. They lead in understanding the need for fast reaction and flexibility.

Government

As in other nonmanufacturing areas, government has many activities that could be improved by use of PIC theory and practices. The principal reason privatization usually results in dramatic improvement in government-run entities is that knowledge and skills from commercial fields are applied and operations are treated more like a business. Obviously, some government activities (military, judicial, legislative, executive, emergency relief, and welfare are examples) cannot be run in businesslike fashion; they are political.

But many others like the post office, trash and garbage collection, road building and maintenance, public housing, licensing, and others should focus on serving customers rather than operating rigid bureaucracies. This is happening at revolutionary pace in former communist and socialist countries and is proceeding steadily, if too slowly, in the

United States. The body of knowledge, principles, techniques, and skills of PIC will assist in making these changes when applied inside or outside government.

BIBLIOGRAPHY

Brown, R. G.: *Statistical Forecasting for Inventory Control,* McGraw-Hill, New York, 1959.

Burbidge, J. L.: *Principles of Production Control,* MacDonald & Evans, London, 1971.

Dertouzos, M. L., R. K. Lester, and R. M. Solow: *Made in America,* MIT Press, Cambridge, Mass., 1991.

Dickie, H. F.: *ABC Inventory Analysis Shoots for Dollars,* Factory Management & Maintenance, New York, July 1951.

Drucker, P.: *Managing for the Future,* Truman Tally/Dutton, New York, 1992.

Ford, Henry: *Today and Tomorrow,* Reprint Productivity Press, Cambridge, Mass., 1988.

Gue, F.: *Increased Profits through Better Control of Work in Process,* Prentice-Hall, Englewood Cliffs, N.J., 1980.

Hall, R. W.: *Attaining Manufacturing Excellence,* Dow Jones-Irwin/APICS Series, Homewood, Ill., 1987.

————, *Zero Inventories,* Dow Jones-Irwin/APICS Series, Homewood, Ill., 1983.

Hammer, M., and J. Champy: *Reengineering the Corporation,* Harper Business, New York, 1993.

Harris, F. W.: *Operations and Cost,* Factory Management Series, A.W. Shaw, 1915.

Harty, J. D., G. W. Plossl, and O. W. Wight: *Management of Lot-size Inventories,* APICS Special Report, Falls Church, Va., 1963.

Lankford, R. L.: *Input/Output Control: Making It Work,* APICS 1980 Conference Proceedings, Falls Church, Va.

Magee, J. F.: *Production Planning and Inventory Control,* McGraw-Hill, New York, 1958.

Mather, H.: *Competitive Manufacturing,* Prentice-Hall, Englewood Cliffs, N.J., 1988.

Osborne, D., and T. Gaebler: *Reinventing Government,* Plume, New York, 1992.

Plossl, G. W.: *Managing in the New World of Manufacturing,* Prentice-Hall, Englewood Cliffs, N.J., 1991.

————, *Production and Inventory Control: Principles and Techniques,* 2d ed., Prentice-Hall, Englewood Cliffs, N.J., 1985.

————, *Production and Inventory Control: Applications,* George Plossl Educational Services, Atlanta, Ga., 1983.

————, *Orlicky's Material Requirements Planning,* 2d ed., McGraw-Hill, New York, 1994.

Plossl, K. R.: *Engineering for the Control of Manufacturing,* Prentice-Hall, Englewood Cliffs, N.J., 1987.

Sandras, W. A., Jr.: *Just-In-Time: Making It Happen,* Oliver Wight Publications, Essex Junction, Vt., 1989.

Schonberger, R. J.: *Japanese Manufacturing Techniques,* Macmillan Free Press, New York, 1982.

Shigeo Shingo: *Study of Toyota Production System,* Japan Management Association, Tokyo, 1981.

Taylor, S. G., S. M. Seward, S. F. Bolander, and R. C. Heard: "Process Industry Production and Inventory Planning Framework," *APICS Production and Inventory Management Journal,* first quarter, 1981.

Welch, W. E.: *Tested Scientific Inventory Control,* Management Publishing, Greenwich, Conn., 1956.

Wight, O. W.: *MRPII: Unlocking America's Productivity Potential,* CBI Publishing, Boston, 1974.

————, *Production and Inventory Management in the Computer Age,* Cahners Publishing, Boston, 1974.

Wilson, R. H.: "A Scientific Routine for Inventory Control," *Harvard Business Review,* 1934.

CHAPTER 3
PRODUCTION AND INVENTORY CONTROL INFORMATION REQUIREMENTS

Editor
Walter E. Goddard
President and Chairman of the Board
Oliver Wight International
Concord, New Hampshire

Production and inventory control (PIC) can be thought of as a manufacturing company within a manufacturing company. PIC acquires information from various sources, analyzes it, and delivers planning information to its customers. Many customers are other departments within the same company such as the factory, purchasing, engineering, distribution, sales and marketing, and the general manager. Other customers work for other divisions and outside companies such as suppliers, subcontractors, warehouses, and paying customers—those that buy products and services.

The value of the output from PIC is determined by these internal and external customers. As users of the planning information, they are constantly testing it: Does the information correctly reflect the needs of the company? Are the recommendations attainable? Are the plans believable? Yes answers mean that PIC is producing high-quality information.

The objective of this chapter is to provide an overview of the information that PIC requires, where it comes from, and how it's used. Subsequent chapters will expand upon the techniques for analyzing data, ensuring its accuracy, preparing plans, and communicating them in a timely manner. Before more advanced approaches can be effectively utilized, however, a correct understanding of the basics must occur.

FUNDAMENTAL MANUFACTURING EQUATION

The late Oliver Wight contributed greatly to the body of knowledge that encompasses PIC. Among his many insights is the "fundamental manufacturing equation." All manufacturing companies regardless of their size, types of processes, or complexity of products must answer these five questions:

- What are we going to sell?
- What do we need to make?
- What does it take to make it?
- What do we have?
- What do we need to get?

Answering these questions is inescapable. The only choices are who and how: Who will do them, and how will they be done? In addition to being robust, the fundamental manufacturing equation is eloquently simple. "It is common sense, organized," is how one executive described it.

The fundamental manufacturing equation offers a structured approach to describing what PIC is all about. PIC is immersed in all five questions, receiving answers for some and supplying answers to others. The following sections analyze what is required to successfully respond to each question.

What Are You Going to Sell?

The demands of the marketplace come in various flavors. They include:

- Customer orders booked but not yet shipped, called *backlog*
- Quotes entered but not yet approved
- Forecasts of anticipated business
- Anticipated replenishment of distribution centers
- Needs for spare or repair parts
- Interplant demands

Demand management is the term that covers the activities that deal with the marketplace. Forecasting, advertising, promotions, pricing, adding and deleting products, field sales reporting, handling of abnormal demands, answering inquiries, processing changes to existing orders, and entering new orders are all part of demand management. Sales and marketing are typically responsible for performing these activities. In their absence, other departments would be accountable, frequently PIC. Regardless of who is doing them, they all impact the answer to the question, "What do we expect to sell?"

Forecasting is guaranteed to be the most contentious activity. Attempting to predict future business warrants skilled people, good analytical tools, reliable history of past demands, and close communications among customers, sales, marketing, and PIC. Even then the results will be inaccurate. As a prime user of forecasts, PIC has a vested interest in improving forecasts. There are many productive things that can be done:

- *Determine the minimum planning horizon.* This means identifying the need for forecasts and then estimating the lead time required to service them. Forecasting any farther into the future generates unnecessary work and produces less accurate estimates.
- *Attack lead times.* Rather than accept lead times as "givens," aggressively reduce them. A major contributor to lead times are queues, that is, time spent waiting for the next activity to occur. Attacking queue times slashes lead times.

- *Convert independent demand to dependent.* Independent demands must be forecasted whereas dependent demands can be calculated. For example, customers prepared to share requirements need not be part of their suppliers' forecasting activity. Although the customers' needs may change, it is still better than suppliers' trying to out-guess them. An organized effort should be in place to receive demands from customers and to provide requirements to suppliers.

- *Separate forecasts into two categories, aggregate and detail.* Aggregate forecasts by broad groupings, such as product lines, become input for long-range financial planning, purchasing of capital equipment, and determining rates of production. Detail forecasts by specific configurations are needed for materials and capacity planning.

- *Routinely update forecasts.* With the help of exception reporting, a review process should be in place that produces updated projections. Typically this is done monthly.

- *Measure performance.* Although the projections will be inaccurate, there should be clear-cut accountability for who is responsible for making the forecast. Additionally, goals should be established for reducing the variability of forecast errors.

- *Improved flexibility.* PIC must be ever alert to significant changes to maintain high-quality plans. Quickly recognizing forecast errors and being able to swiftly respond to them minimizes the impact on cost and customer service. Speedy reactions by the factory, engineering, and suppliers also reduce the effect of forecast errors.

- *Evaluate protection against forecast errors.* Extra inventory or extra time is protection against uncertainties of demand. Caution is needed in this area as both approaches create extra investments and hurt credibility of dates. Instead of planning events when they are needed, using safety stock or safety time causes them to be scheduled sooner.

To be useful for PIC, demands must be described by specific configuration, quantity, and timing: What is being demanded, how many are needed, and when. For make-to-stock products, the configuration would be *end items,* that is, the saleable configurations being shipped from finished goods. When make-to-order products are received, they would be given a unique identification representing the saleable configuration. Prior to arriving, the forecasted demand often is expressed in configurations that represent options, features, or representative models.

Having quick access to pertinent data and displaying data in a convenient format are helpful aids for PIC. There are numerous ways to display demand. Some people prefer to consolidate all demands into one figure for each time period; others see value in separating the total quantity into "streams of demand." The example shown in Table 3.1 distinguishes forecasted demand from customer demands. Knowing what we need to sell leads to the next question in the fundamental equation.

TABLE 3.1 Displaying Demands

Part number: XYZ

	Weeks							
	1	2	3	4	5	6	7	8
Customer orders	16	5		1				
Forecasts	0	0	9	9	10	10	10	10
Total requirements	16	5	9	10	10	10	10	10

What Do We Need to Make?

There are two categories of answers for "What do we need to make?": aggregate and detail. The aggregate is expressed in rates of production for families of products; the detail answer becomes the build plan for specific configurations.

Establishing rates of production for families of products is the job of the general manager and his or her staff. As discussed in the previous section, aggregate demand is a major input to this process. Equally important are the capabilities of manufacturing, purchasing, and engineering to economically support various alternatives of production. The process of arriving at a decision is called *sales and operations planning*. The approved rates of production provide the framework for what resources will be required.

For make-to-stock products, the rate of output determines the size of finished-goods inventory. If management wants to increase finished-goods inventory, the rate of output for manufacturing must exceed the incoming order rate; to decrease finished-goods inventory, setting a rate of output less than demand will accomplish it. For make-to-order products, the rate of output determines the size of the backlog. When the rate of output exceeds the incoming order rate, backlog will shrink; if the output rate is less than the incoming order rate, backlog will grow.

At the detail level, answering "What do we need to make?" generates the *master production schedule* (MPS). This is the anticipated build plan expressed in specific configurations, quantity, and date. There is no more important scheduling task for PIC. The word *master* says it all: If this plan is not maintained properly, all of PIC's subsequent analysis will produce very little benefit for the company. The goals are to satisfy existing customer commitments and to cover the forecast of anticipated orders, both in an economical manner.

The MPS for make-to-stock products determines when finished-goods inventory will be replenished. By comparing the projected requirements against existing inventory plus the current master production schedule, a master scheduler evaluates the need to change. If he or she believes that more inventory than necessary is building up, the MPS should be reduced or rescheduled to a later time period. On the other hand, if finished goods is dropping faster than desired, the master scheduler must evaluate increasing the existing quantities or rescheduling quantities earlier.

The MPS for make-to-order products is aimed at satisfying customer orders. Many times this means that the MPS is directly aligned with the customer commitments. Other times, however, it may be practical to build products in advance. To gain the economies of a larger order quantity, the master schedule quantity may cover future commitments. Another common situation is the need to level the load on the factory, avoiding costs that come from working overtime one week and lacking work the next week. Where the backlog tails off and forecasts of anticipated business begins, the master scheduler's job is to address both types of demands.

Prior to initiating changes to the MPS, there are important considerations to take into account such as safety stock levels, order quantities, lead times, and the availability of components and capacity. Each can influence the size and timing of the change. The master scheduler is responsible for producing a "can-do" schedule, which is frequently different from what he or she would like to do. Common constraints are the lack of capacity and the lack of components. Ignoring these issues makes the MPS simply a wish list, one that is impossible to carry out.

Promising new customer orders is an important company activity. The master production schedule is the right source for promising incoming orders. Part of the current MPS is committed, spoken for by existing customer orders. The balance is uncommitted, available for new orders. The term *available for promise* is the calculation that reflects the uncommitted portion. By calculating the available to promise on an ongoing basis, quick and reliable promises can be made as new orders arrive (Table 3.2).

TABLE 3.2 Available to Promise (ATP)

Part number: XYZ; on hand (OH) = 4

		Weeks							
		1	2	3	4	5	6	7	8
Customer orders		16	5		1				
Forecasts		0	0	9	9	10	10	10	10
Projected balance	OH4	8	3	14	4	14	4	14	4
Master schedule		20		20		20		20	
ATP (noncumulative)		3		19		20		20	

The production plans and master production schedules are converted into great detail in the next step of the fundamental manufacturing equation.

What Does It Take to Make It?

To produce products, there are many resources required. Six critical ones are:

- *Materials.* These are the manufactured and purchased ingredients in the products. The bills of material identify these components, although some companies use the terms *formulas* or *recipes.*

- *Labor.* The personnel required to produce components as well as the saleable products is estimated in the routings. Often the routing contains estimated setup and changeover times as well. The routings represent what operations are required, the engineering standards to perform them, and the sequence in which the operations occur.

- *Equipment.* Typically the routing would also define the machinery needed and the work center that it belongs to.

- *Tooling.* Sometimes the routing includes tooling identification, but in many cases it does not. The responsibility for providing the tooling is generally the responsibility of the factory, not PIC. It is critical, however, that good planning occur to avoid tooling being a cause of poor service and extra costs.

- *Engineering specifications.* In addition to maintaining bills of material and routings, the engineering group is usually responsible for providing blueprints to the factory and purchasing. Without the specifications, components cannot be produced nor raw materials purchased.

- *Constraints.* Whenever space, weight, height, containers, and so on affect planning, they must become part of the process. For example, transportation issues could include limitations on the number of railcars or trucks that can arrive for delivery or for shipments.

- *Money.* Converting plans into financial terms is an important consideration. Decision making is always better when people know the financial consequences: shipping dollars, profit margins, cash flow, and monies tied up in inventory.

To be effective, PIC must know which of these resources must be incorporated into the planning process. It is safe to predict that it will always include material, labor, and equipment.

The next step is to predict the impact on the selected resources. This is an excellent application of dependent planning. There is no need to speculate what components, how many of them, or when they will be needed. All of this can be derived by exploding the master production schedule against a structured bill of material. In the same manner, capacity can be determined in terms of either employee hours or machine hours, by time period, or by multiplying the standards contained in the routings against what components must be manufactured. Likewise, the need for tooling, engineering specifications, space, and money can be tied directly to the master production schedule and material plans.

Attempting to manage these resources independently would be a nightmare. Without close coordination, only on rare occurrences would all be available at the right time. The lack of any one stops the others. A traffic jam of mismatched resources is the consequence: too much of some, too little of others. Whenever this occurs, costs soar and service plummets. Synchronizing the availability of resources is a critical part of PIC's job.

Accurately predicting resources does not mean that the company is in good shape. The answers to the next two steps of the fundamental manufacturing equation are needed as well.

What Do We Have?

PIC needs to have up-to-date information with regard to what's currently available for each of the selected key resources. This means the following:

- *Materials.* What's on hand, what's reserved and/or allocated, and what's scheduled to be received, both quantity and date, must be known for every saleable product plus all components, including raw materials.

- *Capacities.* The most recent, average output from a work center represents "demonstrated capacity" as opposed to theoretical capacity. Actual output reflects the expected and unexpected events that prevent operators and machinery from running at peak performance. Until corrective action is taken, demonstrated capacity should be used as the benchmark for determining what's available today. This can be expressed either in terms of employee hours or machine hours, or other units of measures such as tons, pieces, or feet.

- *Constraints.* Often called *bottlenecks* or *pinch points,* these are areas that define the limitation of what a company is able to do. They exist in various places in the factory as well as in engineering and at suppliers. Producing doable plans depends on knowing the capabilities of the constraining areas.

- *Tooling, engineering specifications, and space.* Whenever PIC is responsible for taking these into account, they need to know what's available today, what commitments exist, and when more or less will be available in the future. Companies that design and make their own tools and/or repair them have specific skills that are frequently in scarce supply.

Accuracy and timeliness are prerequisites for this information to be of value. *Trustworthy data* means information in which users have high confidence; if the records show it is there, they can count on it. Timeliness is also essential. Even if it is accurate, old information becomes a serious handicap to making good decisions. Ongoing audits for accuracy and timeliness are appropriate to verify the quality of the data, catch discrepancies early, and, importantly, to identify causes of problems so that they can be corrected quickly.

What Do We Need to Get?

Demand versus supply summarizes what PIC is constantly analyzing. The goal is to satisfy the needs of the marketplace in a timely, economical manner. If demand exceeds supply, PIC must figure out how to change existing plans or create new ones. When supply is greater than demand, the opposite actions must be considered. The ideal resolution is to find the balance between demand and supply that best achieves the goals of the company.

At the aggregate level, balancing demand and supply occurs in the process called *sales and operations planning*. This process cycles on a monthly basis in most companies. Forecasts are reviewed and revised in order to produce an updated sales plan. In a similar manner, manufacturing, engineering, finance, and purchasing must review their performance plus expected changes in order to update the supply plans. Inventory and backlog targets are seldom fixed because they need to reflect the latest conditions. The general manager and his or her staff make appropriate changes to the rates of production in response to these latest conditions. At the detail level, PIC does the same on a more frequent basis. They would be reviewing plans at least weekly or daily in many cases.

Job titles vary greatly from company to company. *Master schedulers, material planners, supplier schedulers,* and *capacity planners* are some of the most common ones. These are the people charged with the responsibility of answering the fifth question in the fundamental equation, "What do we need to get?" Analyzing information and initiating actions is how they do it.

There is, however, an essential prerequisite: Pertinent data must be collected and presented in a useful manner. To perform these functions, manual systems have proved to be inadequate unless a company has few transactions, limited variety of products and components, and straightforward manufacturing operations. Otherwise, volume and complexity overwhelm manual systems. Computers have elevated the planning function. With them, great amounts of data can be stored, tremendous volumes of transactions can be processed, and data can be projected in helpful formats.

PIC AND THE COMPUTER

It is no coincidence that the growth of APICS has followed the popularity of computers. PIC used to be widely regarded as performed simply by clerks and expediters. Many people were posting records and triggering orders with limited knowledge, while others were running around fighting fires. The combination of computers and software has given these same people an opportunity to be skilled as "problem preventers" and more effective when unavoidable problems do occur.

Here is what the computer's job consists of:

- *Store data.* All of the answers to the fundamental equation should be stored. Rather than having to re-create the answers, this feature permits the planners to focus on maintaining the answers.
- *Display data.* Not only should the information be displayed in easily digestible formats, ideally it should be capable of being retrieved in a timely, convenient manner.
- *Critique the data.* Through action messages, the computer can call attention to situations and recommend corrective action.

What the computer cannot do is to separate significant from insignificant action messages nor make decisions. Differentiating between trivial and important needs to be done by skilled planners; decisions must be made by people if someone is going to be held accountable.

FIVE ACTION MESSAGES

Five action messages greatly assist master schedulers and material planners. They are:

- *Reschedule out (Table 3.3)*. Whenever there is a scheduled receipt arriving earlier than needed to satisfy demands plus safety stock, the action message would recommend changing the due date later, to where it is needed. This avoids users working on the wrong priorities, building unnecessary inventory, and consuming scarce resources needed for more urgent items.

TABLE 3.3   Reschedule Later

Part number: MNO; on hand (OH) = 2; order quantity = 5; safety stock = 0; and lead time = 4.

					Weeks				
		1	2	3	4	5	6	7	8
Total requirements		1		3					
Scheduled receipts			5						
Projected available	OH2	1	6	3	3	3	3	3	3
Planned order release									

    Action: Reschedule from week 2 to week 3.

- *Reschedule in (Table 3.4)*. The opposite condition is where the need date precedes the current scheduled due date. The message would recommend rescheduling earlier to avoid the potential shortage.
- *Cancel (Table 3.5)*. If none of the scheduled receipt is required, the recommended action would be to cancel it. Even if this is not possible because it has been started, preventing any additional costs being added is the next best possibility.

TABLE 3.4   Reschedule Earlier

Part number: MNO; on hand (OH) = 2; order quantity = 5; safety stock = 0; and lead time = 4.

					Weeks				
		1	2	3	4	5	6	7	8
Total requirements		1		3					
Scheduled receipts					5				
Projected available	OH2	1	1	−2	3	3	3	3	3
Planned order release									

    Action: Reschedule from week 4 to week 3.

TABLE 3.5 Cancel

Part number: MNO; on hand (OH) = 2; order quantity = 5; safety stock = 0; and lead time = 4.

		Weeks							
		1	2	3	4	5	6	7	8
Total requirements		1							
Scheduled receipts					5				
Projected available	OH2	1	1	1	6	6	6	6	6
Planned order release									

Action: Cancel scheduled receipt in week 4.

- *Time to order (Table 3.6).* The supply side consists of inventory on hand plus scheduled receipts. The demand side includes projected requirements, existing allocations, and safety stock. If the sum of the supply side is less than the sum of the demand side, more material must be ordered. The next issue is when should this be authorized. Affecting the answer is lead time; the expected time to replenish each part number. Ordering material prematurely, that is, authorizing the factory or purchasing to make or buy more, is undesirable because conditions may change. On the other hand, authorizing new orders in less than average lead time puts undesired pressure on the factory and purchasing to compress lead times. Consequently, the right time to order new material is when the need date equals today plus the lead time.

TABLE 3.6 Time to Order

Part number: MNO; on hand (OH) = 2; order quantity = 5; safety stock = 0; and lead time = 4.

		Weeks							
		1	2	3	4	5	6	7	8
Total requirements		1		3		4			
Scheduled receipts				5					
Projected available	OH2	1	1	3	3	−1	−1	−1	−1
Planned order release		5							

Action: Convert planned order to scheduled receipt in week 4.

- *Past due (Table 3.7).* Whenever a scheduled receipt should have been received prior to today, a warning message should be given to the planner. In a similar manner, if the time to order is late, that is, it should have been ordered earlier than today to give the factory or purchasing average lead time, the planner needs to be aware of this potential problem. Schedule the planned order last week.

Effective scheduling is tied directly to *need dates*. This is the date when resources are required. In an ideal world, the scheduled due date would always equal the need date. Because of the uncertainties in demand and/or uncertainties of supply, the due date is often scheduled earlier than the need date. The gap represents safety stock or safety

TABLE 3.7   Past Due

Part number: MNO; on hand (OH) = 2; order quantity = 5; safety stock = 0; and lead time = 4.

		Weeks							
		1	2	3	4	5	6	7	8
Total requirements		1		3	4				
Scheduled receipts				5					
Projected available	OH2	1	1	3	-1	-1	-1	-1	-1
Planned order release		5							

Action: Past-due planned order; scheduled receipt needed in week 4.

time. Many planners feel that this is their friend when in fact it can be a Trojan horse. When opened up, there is an enemy inside. Safety stock pollutes credibility; users are being asked to complete something sooner than it is needed. At times this does not cause a problem. But whenever a number of jobs are competing for scarce resources, working on one ahead of when it is needed may prevent working on another that is needed. Furthermore, it is hard to justify a factory working overtime simply to make components or products early. In a similar manner, it is hard to explain paying suppliers a premium or paying for air-freight shipments only to have the materials arrive sooner than required.

Credibility is a fragile commodity. Once broken, it is hard to put back together. To have credibility in the plans, "drop-dead dates" should be the goal: containing no fat, no lies, and no padding. Where safety stock is judged to be necessary, two good rules are: Use as little as practical, and make it visible. When users can see the gap between due dates and need dates, they can make better decisions leading to better performance.

PLANNER'S JOB

Where the computer's job ends, the planner's job begins. There are four important aspects of it:

- *Review action messages.* The first question is whether the situation is significant or insignificant. If it is deemed to be insignificant, it should be ignored. No sense in wasting time and incurring unnecessary costs by addressing it. If the message is judged to be significant, the next issue is whether it can be implemented. At times this is straightforward. The planner knows enough about the situation to make a confident decision. In other cases, the planner needs to turn to other information and/or other people prior to arriving at the right response. For example, he or she may have to look up the availability of components or capacity or check with people in the factory or purchasing to see how quickly they can change plans.

- *Respond to changes.* Communications are constantly flowing among planners as well as other users, especially in manufacturing, purchasing, engineering, and sales and marketing. Examples would be a notice of an emergency order from a customer, significant scrap, or a serious problem with a supplier. Each would trigger a review and require a response.

- *Maintain data.* There are many pieces of data under the responsibility of PIC that must be maintained. These include lead times, order quantities, safety stocks, and scrap factors. Periodically they need to be analyzed and adjusted as required.

- *Maintain credibility.* "Silence is approval" is the bond that holds a team together. Discussions typically precede a decision. But once an action plan has been approved, silence means that everyone can do his or her job. Silence on the part of PIC is all the users need to hear to know that the plans are correct. The users do not have to ask for reassurance. Silence on the part of the users carrying out the plan is all that PIC needs to hear that they will be completed on time. Questioning the user's ability to accomplish this is inappropriate. Without this principle of silence in place, neither the planners nor the executors can trust the information they are working with. The performance of the company will be hurt: Customer service will suffer, and costs will increase.

In working with suppliers, many companies have found it productive to separate the task into two categories: several assigned to supplier schedulers and others to buyers. *Supplier schedulers* operate identically as materials planners, but work with the "outside shop" suppliers. As such, they order materials, reschedule existing commitments, provide routine communications, and resolve minor problems. *Buyers* are responsible for negotiating relationships with suppliers, arriving at the terms and conditions that include price, lead time, and order quantity. They monitor supplier performance and, if the supplier scheduler requests help, work with the suppliers to correct problems. Buyers would be key members of a team that developed close partnerships with suppliers addressing quality, value analysis, new technologies, process capabilities, and cost reductions. Additional important functions of buyers are determining how many sources are appropriate, working with existing sources to improve their performance, and developing new sources.

The skills necessary to do these activities are different. Rather than expecting one person to do all well, the separation of responsibilities, some being given to supplier schedulers while others assigned to buyers, has proved to be productive.

Capacity planners operate in a similar manner as materials planners. They are judging the comparison between demonstrated capacity and required capacity. Whenever the gap between the two is significant, they need to correct it. Normally their first choice to avoid problems is to change the demonstrated capacity. If the required capacity is greater than demonstrated capacity, commitments will not be met. If demonstrated capacity exceeds required capacity, idle operators and/or equipment will be the eventual consequence.

If a reasonable balance cannot be found, the capacity planners must speak up. Identifying choices, predicting consequences, and making recommendations are part of their job just as it is when materials planners are confronted with unavoidable problems.

When manufactured components are released to the factory, operational dates are often helpful. These represent benchmarks for when the job should pass through the conversion steps, culminating with the scheduled due date representing the completion of the last activity. Operational dates are calculated with the use of the routings and scheduling rules. The routings contain the operations with estimates of time to perform each. The scheduling rules take into account the order quantity, the engineering standards, the number of shifts, move time, and queue time. Queue times represent the average wait time for each work center, and the total of the queue times generally adds up to the bulk of the time spent in the factory.

DISPATCHING

Dispatching is a term that is used for describing the operational dates communicated to the factory. As jobs pass through the various work centers, dispatch reports reflect their progress plus the sequence of the jobs based on latest priorities. With this information, factory supervisors and operators are up to date on what jobs are available and when they are needed. Each department should be held accountable for completing work on time, as determined by the operational due dates. Doing so gives the downstream departments a fair chance of meeting their operational dates and the last operation being completed on the scheduled due date. Dispatch lists are generally issued daily, or maintained on-line, to keep up with the constant movement of jobs and the ever-changing priorities.

What happens, however, when the ideal balance between supply and demand cannot be found? Invariably, it will be impossible or economically impractical to service all demands due to the lack of required resources. How managers respond to these situations determines how PIC operates:

- *Least worse choice.* When all practical alternatives have been exhausted and still the demands cannot be met, PIC plays a very important role. Identifying choices, predicting the consequences of each, and recommending a course of action helps the company deal with the problem. Managers who realistically face the situation and make the best choice gain important benefits. First, the integrity of PIC's plans is enhanced, not destroyed. Once a "do-this-first" list comes ahead of the priorities established by the scheduling system, all schedules are suspect; the *hot list* becomes longer, and eventually schedules are ignored. Second, cutting losses quickly is less painful than waiting and hoping that the passage of time will somehow make the problem disappear. Damage control avoids compounding the predicament.

- *Denial.* Unfortunately, some managers are convinced that any crisis can be overcome. "Try harder" is their reaction. Miracles are their expectations. If this becomes the way of doing business, expediting replaces planning. Priorities will no longer come from the formal system. Rather, they will be generated by expediters using hot lists and red tags. As they solve one problem, they are inadvertently creating several others. Firefighting is highly visible and very satisfying. Far more productive, however, is fire prevention. Expediters start with a problem whereas effective planning predicts problems so that the users can prevent them. Furthermore, expediters can only make jobs "hotter" whereas planning can also unexpedite. Rescheduling jobs later makes expediting more efficient.

What happens when supply exceeds demands? This situation can create costly consequences. PIC must respond as urgently as when demand is greater than supply. The first action is to send early warning signals to management. Catching a downturn quickly minimizes its impact by avoiding such unnecessary activities as hiring people, working overtime, and releasing new orders to suppliers as well as to the factory. Other choices include shifting materials and capacities from products that are not selling to those that may be selling faster than predicted. Generally speaking, the strategy is to avoid completing products: stopping progress at the lowest level is the least costly place. It is often the most flexible place to store material waiting for the upturn to arrive.

If the decision is to stockpile products in the expectation of selling them at a later date, then selecting which products to build becomes critical. The ideal choice would be those products high in popularity, low in costs, high in profit margins, and low in risk of obsolescence. Before these steps are incurred, the pressure is on sales and marketing to gain more orders. Increasing their field sales efforts, employing telemarketing, running promotions, and changing pricing—all are ways to influence the marketplace.

An effective planning system does not operate as an "eraser" system, always alleviating the need for extra effort by changing the plans. Rather, it must be dedicated to achieving the company's goals and expecting that the users will do whatever is possible to make this happen.

Changing the master production schedule because of a problem is a last choice. Before reaching this stage, all other solutions should have been applied. There are many things that can be done: compressing lead times, utilizing safety stocks, cutting lot sizes, authorizing overtime, employing subcontractors, approving air-freight shipments, using alternative components, substituting other products, and checking with other customers. Although rare, there are times when the sales department can find a customer whose order can be delayed, solving the conflict.

Feedback

Feedback is the opposite of "silence is approval." Feedback communicates problems that the users have with the current plans. The flow of information is going in the opposite direction; instead of PIC sending it to the users, it is from the users back to PIC. *Bottom-up replanning* is the process that closes the planning loop. A partnership must be formed whereby PIC provides users with excellent plans and users execute the plan in an excellent manner. To keep everyone up to date with changes, both partners must implement a smooth, two-way flow of information.

Neither partner likes surprises, but everyone knows that they will occur. Quickly responding to them is essential. One executive described its importance as, "Bad news early is better than bad news late." Waiting rarely helps the situation; delays typically aggravate it. As bad as the problem may be, it will never be less than today. Now's the time to deal with such events as:

- Emergency customer orders and customer cancellations
- Major revisions to forecasts
- Engineering changes that must be implemented immediately
- Unexpected scrap and rework in the factory
- Equipment breaking down or tooling not available
- Suppliers who cannot meet their commitments

Anticipated delay reports (*Table 3.8*) are one way to provide feedback. When the users—be they in engineering, manufacturing, or purchasing—cannot carry out the plan, they must speak up. This report would contain what is affected, what is wrong,

TABLE 3.8 Anticipated Delay Report

Work Center: 40; Date: 2/17

Shop order	Part no.	Due date	Cause	New date	Action
138	4898	3/15	Fixture Broke	3/22	Split Order

what is being done to correct it, when it is expected to be corrected, and who is responsible for the correction.

Honest communications become mandatory for PIC to do its job effectively. It must provide honest information to help internal and external customers and insist that they do the same.

Measurements

PIC, like all other departments, has the responsibility for measuring its performance. Frequently it is also charged with measuring how well activities are being performed by other departments. In all cases, the main objective is to contribute to the success of the company. Knowing what is happening, comparing performance to predetermined goals, uncovering the cause of poor performance, and highlighting outstanding performance are positive contributions that come from measuring the right things in the right manner.

Data accuracy is a major concern when making measurements. Inaccurate data are worse than worthless—reviewing them costs money, and, if decisions are made on the basis of them, the wrong answers add additional costs. Aspects of this concern for accuracy include:

Inventory accuracy. A generally agreed-upon standard is that the on-hand plus the on-order (scheduled receipts) should be at least 95 percent accurate, not in aggregate but by part number. Tolerances defining when "good" ends and "bad" begins is a necessary part of this process in order to reflect different conditions. Much like upper and lower limits from the engineering department, these tolerances reflect the pain of being wrong. Some part numbers deserve zero tolerance as any error hurts. High-volume, low-cost, short lead time items do not warrant this precision.

Bills of material. They must be judged by three questions: Are the part numbers correct? Is the quantity per product for each correct? And, is it structured properly? If the wrong part numbers are on the bill of material or the right ones missing, problems of having too much of some and too little of the other will be the consequences. A wrong component quantity per product produces the same poor results. The structure must reflect how the factory builds the product. Otherwise, the timing of when components are needed will either be too early or too late. The general agreed-upon standard is that the bill of materials must be at least 98 percent accurate, level by level.

Routings. There are three questions to be asked in checking the routings: Are the right operations listed? Is the sequence of them accurate? and, Are the engineering standards reasonable? Leaving off operations or adding ones that are not needed hurts both capacity planning and dispatching. A wrong sequence hurts dispatching even though it may be insignificant to the prediction of capacity. Often engineering standards do not need to be precise. In a number of companies, operators out-produce the standards by a wide margin; the opposite occurs in other companies. If the gap is predictable, it is questionable whether a great investment in fine-tuning is appropriate. Although no one wants poor data, the cost may exceed the payback. Judging the need to fix it also involves the impact on cost accounting and pricing.

Other data. Factors such as lead times, safety stock, scrap, and costs all influence decisions that planners are making. All are subject to change as improvements are initiated in the factory, at suppliers, and engineering. There is no agreed-upon level of accuracy that can be used as standards in this area. Yet all deserve to be audited.

Within the PIC department, there are a number of ways for measuring how well jobs are being performed:

Education and training. Growing people is an ongoing process. In the heat of the battle this is often ignored. Only when it is treated as a high priority will companies gain the benefits of improved skills of its people.

Action messages. Tracking the types of action messages for each planner can be revealing: Is there a balance between rescheduling out and rescheduling in? Are the number of past dues increasing? Is there a change in the normal pattern? These indicators do not necessarily mean that a planner is not performing well; they are signals that further investigation is warranted.

Reconciliation. Reports should reflect a reconciliation between aggregate planning and detail planning. Specifically, the sum of the master schedule quantities, per time period, per family, should add back to the production plan as approved by the general manager. Whenever this total is judged to be too high or too low, PIC must do one of two things: present a recommendation to the general manager why the detail plan is the right one to follow and gain approval or adjust the detail plan so that it reconciles with the aggregate.

Reporting causes of problems. Identifying causes of poor performance becomes a major contributor to correcting them. There are three broad categories: the plan was wrong, or the execution was poor, or it was a problem beyond the control of either.

There are a number of company measurements that PIC often maintains. They include:

Customer service. Measuring how well customers are being served in terms of quantity and timing is a major indicator of success. There are a number of dates involved: date that the customer's order was entered, requested ship date, original promise date, and revised promise date, if one was necessary. Comparing actual shipping dates against each of these is important. Some companies also measure whether the shipment arrived at the customer's location when it was wanted.

Execution of schedules. The users responsible for carrying out the plan should be judged on how well they are doing their jobs. All schedules should be measured for on-time completions: from engineering, factory, and purchasing. A generally accepted level of performance is at least 95 percent.

Inventory turnovers. The number of turns for the company can be calculated by dividing the average inventory investment into the cost of shipments. All companies do this in hindsight, reviewing what has occurred. Additionally, many companies do it in foresight, projecting these figures forward. In addition to the aggregate answer, it is helpful to know how each of the major categories are doing: distribution, finished goods, work-in-process, component inventory, and raw materials.

Costs. Companies establish budgets for operating expenses and goals for improving costs. PIC should live within its budget and have action plans for achieving its goals. A lucrative area for helping to reduce costs occurs with suppliers. Effective planning provides buyers with excellent negotiating information. More efficient communications with suppliers, such as electronic data interchange, not only can improve timeliness but can also reduce clerical expenses. When problems occur either at the supplier's company or the customer's, a genuine effort to sort out the choices and arrive at a reasonable solution avoids unnecessary costs for both parties.

Productivity. Bad plans can hurt productivity; good plans can help. The sequence of schedules, practical order quantities, and matched sets of resources can make a significant difference between saving money and spending money.

Providing performance measurements is an important part of PIC's job. Successful companies establish standards to motivate their people, monitor progress against these benchmarks, and encourage departments to work together to solve problems.

SUMMARY

PIC's performance is directly connected to how well the fundamental manufacturing equation is being managed. Although the equation is straightforward and easily understood, answering the five questions is challenging. There are many factors involved, and many of them are interrelated. Fixing one situation can knock others off stride. Furthermore, the marketplace does not stand still for long, and the capabilities of the company are constantly shifting. The same swirl of activity is also happening at suppliers. The unexpected becomes the expected—change is constant.

The challenge for PIC is not planning but replanning. The need to maintain valid plans never ends. As the needs and the capabilities of the company change, plans must be reviewed. PIC must keep the plan so thorough and up to date that the users can follow it, confident that the execution of the plan will generate predictable, desired results for the company.

Integrity and credibility are the standards of excellence that PIC must be striving for. No doubt the toughest test occurs when users encounter problems. Will the users turn to the plans for help or turn away? Passing this test is not simply a compliment to PIC; it means that the company has a competitive advantage. Significant paybacks in terms of better customer service, improved productivity, reduced costs, and greater flexibility will be the results.

CHAPTER 4
PROCESS DESIGN

Editor

Professor Henry W. Kraebber, P.E., CPIM

Purdue University, School of Technology
West Lafayette, Indiana

A manufacturing process transforms raw materials and component parts into higher-level products and assemblies. The details of the process used to complete the transformation require careful attention, planning, and control and must not be left to chance.

Planning the manufacturing process involves the collection of a number of pieces of information from many sources. Inputs for process planning include the details of the product design and data related to the manufacturing processes used to produce the product. The process planning information flow is presented in Fig. 4.1.[1]

Usually no single individual is responsible for the accumulation of data that describes the product structure and routing requirements. In fact, these data come from many sources and people throughout the organization. Product routing and process information is developed best by cross-functional teams representing the areas of design, engineering, manufacturing, and materials. The people who should prepare the processing sheet, and/or have inputs to it, include: industrial engineers, manufacturing engineers, product designers, process designers, tool engineers, cost estimators, production managers, and supervisors.

The modern concepts of "designing for manufacturing" and "designing for assembly" drive a company to open the discussion of how the process should be designed for all personnel who can have an impact on it. Each functional area brings to the process a different perspective. Knowledgeable people from all areas should be invited to participate in the design of the manufacturing process. Sales and marketing representatives bring knowledge of the customer's requirements and their concerns about product reliability and quality. The product designers translate the customer's requirements into specific products with unique features. Industrial engineers address how the product can be manufactured using current or proposed new processes, equipment, methods, and layouts. Supervisors and production operators bring their experience and skills related to manufacturing and the effectiveness of proposed production operations. Purchasing and materials management representatives provide critical inputs on material availability and lead time as well as alternative material and parts. Accounting assures complete and accurate assignment of costs. Early and open communication among all departments during the planning and manufacturing processing leads to more effective production processes to meet the customer's and the company's needs.

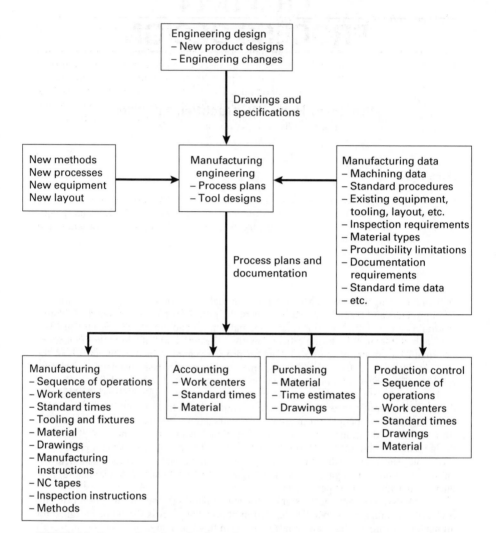

FIGURE 4.1 Process plan information flow. (*Courtesy D. D. Bedworth, M. R. Henderson, and P. M. Wolfe,* Computer-Integrated Design and Manufacturing, *McGraw-Hill, New York, 1991. Reproduced with permission of McGraw-Hill, Inc.*)

DEFINITIONS OF KEY TERMS

A description of the steps required to transform raw materials and components into a finished product or subassembly is essential for effective manufacturing. The information and instructions included in the description of the manufacturing process are needed by many of the functional departments. The descriptive information telling how a product is to be manufactured is known by many names in industry. The information that describes the manufacturing process is often documented using a form known as a *routing*.

Process Sheet

According to the *APICS Dictionary, "the process sheet is the detailed manufacturing instructions issued to the plant."* The instructions may include specifications on speeds, feeds, depths of cuts, temperatures, tools, fixtures, machines, and sketches of setups and semifinished dimensions.

Routing

The *APICS Dictionary* defines *routing* as *"a set of instructions detailing the method of manufacturing a particular item."* It includes the operations to be performed, their sequence, the specific machines or work centers to be involved, and the time standards for setup and run. In some companies, the routing also includes information on tooling, operator skill levels, inspection operations, testing requirements, and the location of materials to be used.

The routing sheet, as contrasted with a process sheet, is prepared for a particular work order. For example, a turned part could be produced on a lathe, turret lathe, or single- or multiple-spindle automatic screw machine. The routing would indicate which one of the processes to use and might even indicate which particular machine to use. This decision would depend on the quantity, cost, quality, tooling, availability of machine, capacity, and other considerations.

A route sheet is an essential key to effective management, yet few operations management books discuss it in any detail. The routing information may be known by other names depending on the industry, the software package used for manufacturing planning and control, and the company's preference. Some of the alternative names for the routing form include:

Operation sheet

Instruction sheet

Bill of operations

Manufacturing data sheet

Operation chart

Operation list

Formula or recipe

Though not true synonyms for *routing,* these terms are closely related.

DEFINING PRODUCTION FACILITIES

Where will the steps in the production process actually take place? Production work may be completed at a specific machine, a group of machines, or on an assembly line. Machines and departments will be designed by a code. The decision of where the work will be done should not be left to chance.

Before the detailed work can begin and the route sheets prepared, there is important preliminary information that must be completed. Representatives from all functional areas working together must answer the following questions related to the work centers and other production facilities:

Is each machine a work center, or does a work center define a group of machines? For example, to produce coils might require a wire stripper, a coil winder, and a press, which would form a work center.

What information is required to define each work center?

What are the capacity constraints of the work centers?

Will a work center operate on single or multiple shifts?

Will a work center normally operate 5 workdays per week?

Are the production machines and processes capable of producing the required quality?

These questions appear to be very simple, but developing answers that satisfy all the functional areas often leads to serious discussions. These questions address fundamental issues related to how the facilities will operate. The answers directly impact the development of the routing sheet so it is essential that the people in all manufacturing areas understand how the work centers are defined and how they will operate.

The facilities where work is done must be determined before the routing for a particular product can be defined and entered into a database system. This is similar to the process of creating a master-file record for each material type before using it in a product structure.

PRODUCTION FACILITY DOCUMENTATION

To describe production facilities and work centers requires considerable information. These data should be made available to people in many different functional areas. Consequently, many computer-based formal systems include a central database that contains the important information related to the production facilities.

Computer-based manufacturing systems typically provide work center information on a formatted screen to guide the user in making the proper entries on a route sheet. Some common fields include:

- Facility or work center identification number
- Responsible supervisor's code
- Work center location code
- Labor-hour rates for costing
- Overhead rates
- Machine-time cost

- Planned capacity of the work center
- Standard allowances for moving or waiting time

These data are fairly static. Once defined in a formal database system, they should require little attention or change.

DEFINING AND DOCUMENTING THE MANUFACTURING STEPS

Many texts have lists of critical information elements needed to define the transformation process. These key information elements for describing the process for a particular item could include:

- A brief description of the work to be performed
- Work center or machine where the work will be performed
- The staffing required to complete the work
- The sequence in which work is to be performed
- The labor and machine time(s) for each operation or production rate
- The time required for each material move
- The time required for each setup
- Specific tool information including tool number or requirements (List any special tools.)
- The customer's name
- The name of the person who prepared the sheet
- The name of the person who designed the process
- The effective date of process revisions

The specific type of manufacturing information required to produce a product will usually be defined by the software package being used. The previous list includes much more than the minimum information required for most systems. Each company must decide how much information to enter and maintain in the routing data file. A typical format for basic route sheet information is shown in Table 4.1. Table 4.2 shows a routing example as it would be presented in a popular software package. Note the use of the *time basis code* (TBC) to control the data in the time fields.

TABLE 4.1 Basic Routing Data for Finished Burner Assembly

Oper	Oprn description	Run labor min	Setup min	Crew	Work center
0010	Assemble end fitting	2.50	10.00	1	130
0020	Weld end fitting	3.50	10.00	1	130
0030	Weld brackets	3.00	0.00	1	130
0040	Leak test	2.00	5.00	1	200
0050	Inspect and pack	2.00	0.00	1	200

Source: Adapted from the 1992 CIM in Higher Education Faculty Training Institute, presented by Lansing Community College.

TABLE 4.2   Routing Information Formatted for a Formal System

Item	Oper	Description	TBC	Run mach	Run labor	Setup	Crew	FAC
4400	0010	Assemble end fitting	*m*	0.00	2.50	0.00	1	130
	0020	Weld end fitting	*m*	0.00	3.50	0.00	1	130
	0030	Weld brackets	*m*	0.00	3.00	0.00	1	130
	0040	Leak test	*m*	0.00	2.00	0.00	1	200
	0050	Inspect and pack	*m*	0.00	2.00	0.00	1	200

Note: TBC (time basis code) = *m* implies here that the labor and machine time values are to be read as minutes per piece. Other TBC codes are typically available such as hours per piece, or hours per 100 pieces.

Source: Adapted from the 1992 CIM in Higher Education Faculty Training Institute, presented by Lansing Community College.

ROUTING SINGLE ITEMS AND ASSEMBLIES

As you can imagine, there is a difference in appearance for an assembly route sheet and one for individual parts. A route sheet for a gearbox assembly looks quite different from a route sheet for an individual part used in the gearbox. If the parts are made in-house, there will be a route sheet for each part number and one for each subassembly and assembly. To keep track of each part number, some companies will have a route sheet for purchased parts as well and stamp the sheet PURCHASED PART. Companies producing clothing, furniture, paint, pharmaceuticals, and other products may also use route sheets for single parts and assemblies.

PREPARING A ROUTE SHEET FOR A SINGLE PART

These are the steps for producing a route sheet for a single part:

Step 1. Identify and list all suboperations as shown in Fig. 4.2.   A *suboperation* is the work done without interruption. Typical suboperations would be: Drill hole, saw to a particular dimension, tap, solder, sew button, and so on. If there are three holes to be drilled, there would be three suboperations listed. If each hole was to be tapped, there would be three "tap hole" suboperations.

It is essential that all suboperations are identified since they are the basis for the operation. If one suboperation is missed, it will mean that the product will take longer to produce and therefore be underpriced. Also, the schedule could be affected.

Step 2. Group the suboperations into operations.   An operation can be defined as:

- One or more suboperations
- All the work done at one location
- The work combined into one operator's instruction
- The work combined for 1 pay unit

Grouping the suboperations into operations requires extensive knowledge of the factory, personnel, and facilities. For example, there are a number of ways three holes can be drilled in a piece of metal depending on the size of the holes, whether they are all the same, and whether the drill presses are single spindle or gang drills. It may even be possible to drill the holes while other work is being performed on the piece. All the time one must consider which method is most efficient.

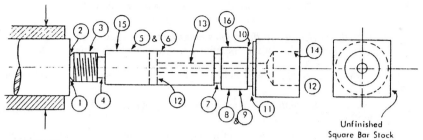

Unfinished
Square Bar Stock

FIRST STEP

List of Suboperations:

1. Face and cut-off
2. Chamfer
3. Thread
4. Neck
5. Rough turn
6. Finish turn
7. Neck
8. Rough turn

9. Finish turn
10. Neck
11. Washer face
12. Drill lateral hole
13. Drill concentric hole (small)
14. Drill concentric hole (large)
15. Grind small diameter
16. Grind large diameter

SECOND STEP

Operation Groupings:

Drill lateral hole

Grind small diameter

Grind large diameter

Face and cut-off, chamfer,
neck, rough turn,
finish turn, neck, rough turn,
neck, washer face,
drill concentric hole (small)
drill concentric hole (large)
Thread

THIRD STEP

Operation Sheet

PRODUCT NAME _Fuel Pin_____ PRODUCT NO. _12-562_

MATERIAL _1020 C.R.S._____ PRINT NO. _1-A-391_

PLANNER _T.I.M._____ DATE _6/5/--_ REVISIONS _R.C._

OPERATION NO.	OPERATION DESCRIPTION	OPERATION	TOOLS
10	Face and cut-off, chamfer, neck, rough turn, finish turn, neck, rough turn, neck, washer face, drill large concentric hold, drill small concentric hole.	--	T.L.
15	Thread		T.L.
20	Drill lateral hole	--	D.
30	Grind small diameter	--	Gr
40	Grind large diameter	--	Gr.

For special tools only

FIGURE 4.2   The logic of process planning.

4.7

Step 3. Place the operations in the proper manufacturing sequence.   Often there is a preferred or required order for the operations. Consider the following:

- *First things first. Example:* Drill holes before tapping. Inspect the product before packing it.

- *Cost of operation. Example:* If taps are breaking, do not tap holes last after other costs have been invested in the part.

- *Finish coats of paint.* Do not apply a finish coat of paint until the end of the process.

- *Materials handling and transportation.* Consider how materials handling and travel distance can be minimized.

Operations should be numbered in a series that identifies the correct sequence for production. The numbering scheme should allow room for additions and future revisions without renumbering all operations. A numbering pattern with planned "steps" such as 0010, 0020, 0030,..., has proven to work well. Later on if an operation is required between 0020 and 0030, it can be called 0025 without disturbing the sequence.

Coordinating the information on an engineering print with the route sheet can cause confusion. For example, an engineering print may call for a $\frac{1}{2}$-in hole and the route sheet also indicates a $\frac{1}{2}$-in hole is to be drilled. Later on, an engineering change may be made that calls for a $\frac{3}{8}$-in rather than a $\frac{1}{2}$-in hole. The engineering change may never get made on the route sheet, and the operator produces a $\frac{1}{2}$-in hole. In some way the engineering changes must also be made on the route sheet.

This problem becomes even more confusing if there are three $\frac{1}{2}$-in holes and only one is to be changed. Perhaps the dimensions should be avoided on a route sheet so the operator will always work with the engineering print.

Often several related or similar operations can be completed as a group. Drilling a series of holes of various sizes is a typical example. Grouping several suboperations into one larger operation leads to simplification of the processing and the related documentation, less materials handling, and simplified reporting of the actual work completed.

Step 4. Determine the work center or facility where the work is to be done.   The work center identified in the routing should be the primary choice for the operation. There may also be alternate work centers identified, but the alternates will not come into play unless there is a specific schedule and capacity issue that must be resolved. The identification number of the required work center is entered in the facility ID field (FAC).

Step 5. Determine the production time required for the operation.   Requirements may be stated for both labor and machine times. Many formal systems provide great flexibility in how time elements may be defined. The formal system may use a time basis code (TBC), as shown in the last table, to define the time units applied to specific time data fields. Typically, codes are provided for "hours per piece," "hours per 10 pieces," "hours per 100 pieces," "hours per 1000 pieces," "minutes per piece," and so on. Be sure to check out the codes available in the software package you are using. The TBC may apply to both the run machine and run labor time fields.

Step 6. Determine the estimated setup or changeover time.   The times obtained may be for one or more operators required to complete the changeover. Excessive changeover times should be analyzed and reduced whenever possible.

Setup time starts when production work stops and the new job begins. Setup time is the total labor-hours required by the crew to complete the setup. It may be included in the routing form if it is significant and if it makes sense to load and maintain the data. Controversy between manufacturing and engineering personnel on the amount of setup time required should be avoided. Setup time requirements may add a significant amount of time to the workload. Be sure to keep the amount of time loaded on a work center realistic. An impossible overload will lead to confusion, frustration, and an increase in work-in-process and throughput time.

ROUTE SHEETS FOR AN ASSEMBLY

Figure 4.3 shows how several material elements come together to produce an assembled finished product. The finished product described is a desktop accessory that holds a paperweight and a 2- by 2-inch square pad of notepaper. The production process begins with milling two pockets into the blank base plate. The next operation is the engraving of a customer-selected design inside the round milled pocket. A CAD drawing of the milled and engraved base is shown in Fig. 4.4. Assembly of this simple product involves placing the finished base plate into a box, a casting into the circular pocket, a pad of notepaper into the square pocket, and a felt product structure pad strip into the box.

The simple example shows the routing for the sequence of steps in the manufacturing process required to make and assemble the product. It must be in agreement with the product structure information and show the operations required to complete the product. The *product structure* and the *routing* work together to document the steps in a production process. Table 4.3 is a description of the first nine operations required to produce the desktop accessory discussed. This has been a simple product that permits fabrication and assembly to be combined in one route sheet.

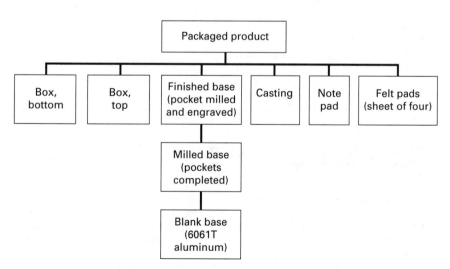

FIGURE 4.3.   Product structure tree diagram.

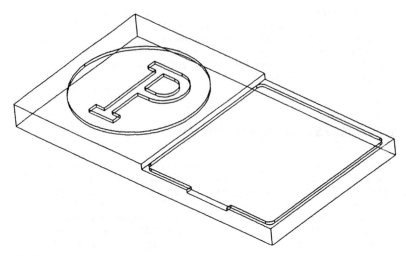

FIGURE 4.4   CAD drawing of a base plate. (*Courtesy Professor B. Harriger, CIM Technology, Purdue University.*)

TABLE 4.3   Partial List of Production Operations for Desk Accessory

Descriptions of the first nine operations required to complete the production of the product
0010   Part from feeder 1 (or 2 if 1 is empty) is loaded onto a fixture by robot 1.
0020   Pallet is moved to product stop at mill 1.
0030   Robot 2 loads part into machine tool (pallet is released to clear path).
0040   Mill 1 cuts pockets (signal as mill is nearing completion calling for a pallet).
0050   Robot 2 loads part onto pallet.
0060   Pallet is moved to product stop at mill 2.
0070   Robot 3 loads part into machine tool (pallet is released to clear path).
0080   Mill 2 engraves "logo" (signal as mill is nearing completion calling for a pallet).
0090   Robot 3 loads part onto pallet.
⋮

RELATIONSHIP OF ROUTING SHEET AND PRODUCT STRUCTURE

The information presented in the routing for an assembly is closely related to the *structured bill of material* for that assembly. The structured bill of material describes how the required material elements come together, level by level, to complete the product or assembly. The routing sheet describes the processing steps that the material follows during the manufacturing process.

The product structure describes how the materials and components come together to produce the finished product. It does not provide details of the manufacturing operations required to transform the raw materials into a finished product.

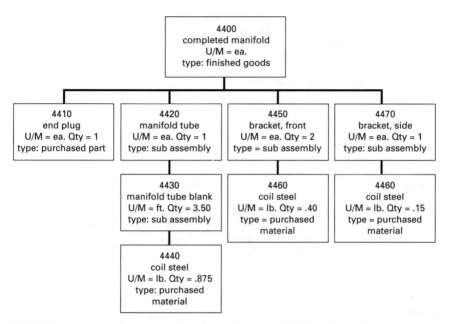

FIGURE 4.5   Product structure for manifold. (*Adapted from the 1992 CIM in Higher Education Faculty Training Institute, presented by Lansing Community College.*)

TREE DIAGRAM

An example of a product structure *tree diagram* is shown in Fig. 4.5. The product structure is for a manufactured item, number 4400. Table 4.4 identifies the work centers where item 4400 and its components will be produced and tested.

TABLE 4.4   Facility Identification Codes and Descriptions

Facility ID	Description
100	Stamping department
110	Heat treat (an off-site vendor)
120	Roll forming line
130	Assembly (home to several different types of operation)
200	Leak test and inspection

Source: Adapted from the 1992 CIM in Higher Education Faculty Training Institute, presented by Lansing Community College.

USES FOR ROUTING INFORMATION

Route sheets provide a detailed description of the manufacturing process. Routings primarily support the planning, control, and manufacturing functions, but the routing information is used in other areas as well. The route sheet information is the basis for production scheduling, costing, and the manufacturing order paperwork and instructions provided to the factory.

Production Control Applications

The route sheet instructions and shop floor paperwork generated for a specific production order are often inserted in a clear plastic envelope and placed with material prior to its being delivered to the first work center. This paperwork "traveler" goes through the shop with the material. It identifies the order, shows where material is to be moved next, and describes the operations that are to be performed on the material at each work station. Employees often are instructed to "sign off" on each operation as it is completed, making the shop floor paperwork serve as a production reporting tool.

The movement of jobs through the shop is often erratic. The typical "job shop" environment groups similar machines and processes into a shop area. For example, all lathes might be grouped together into one production area so jobs are routed from one production area to another. The traveling documents produced for each order, based on data in the routing file, are important control tools in the job shop environment.

Applications of Routing

- Some industries (garment and furniture) use several copies of the routing as "turnaround" documents for data entry to the production control system. Workers record their time and production activity on a copy of the route sheet and turn it in to a clerk for entry into the manufacturing system.
- The department numbers have been used to represent a particular operation. This can be very confusing if a product has to be processed in a department more than once, which results in two or more identical numbers on the routing.
- Some companies invert the sequence of operations so that the first operation is printed at the bottom of the routing page. The operator completes the assigned work, then cuts off the operation information from the bottom of the printout, has it signed by the supervisor, and sent to the operations office for entry into the system. The information reported is typically used for payroll and scheduling purposes.

Just in Time (JIT)

Just-in-time (JIT) manufacturing is growing in popularity with many manufacturing companies. JIT requires fundamental changes in the way products are produced. The layout of the production process is improved to minimize the distance that material must travel. Work cells are designed to bring the processes required to produce the product together into one area. JIT techniques have been shown to reduce work-in-process and simplify the production flow. Work that requires multiple operations in a job shop environment may be produced in one JIT work cell with a substantial reduction in throughput time and simplified tracking and reporting.

Cost Accounting and Performance Measurement

The time requirements as defined in the routing can become the basis for detailed cost analysis and performance measurements. Many formal manufacturing systems provide the ability to "roll up" material costs through the bill of material and the labor and overhead costs from the operations defined in the routings. The operations described in the routing file may become the basis for the development of "current" and "future" standard costs used by the accounting system.

The operation records developed for a specific manufacturing order can become the basis for work reporting and actual job costing. Production operators can be instructed to report how much time was spent on each operation and the amount of good product produced. From this, cost accounting variances can be determined and used as a tool to improve the manufacturing operation.

Order-Specific Routings

Sometimes the routing sheet is customized to describe a specific set of operations for an order. In this case, an *order-specific operation sheet* is created from the standard routing by additions or changes to the basic routing operations for a particular customer order or job. Usually these order-specific changes are made on a one-time-only basis. Ongoing changes should be processed through a formal *change-order* process that revises the original or primary routing information.

Routing Information and Capacity

Formal planning systems are known for their ability to plan material while ignoring the constraints of the operation's capacity (infinite loading). Most traditional manufacturing systems provide only visibility of workloads at specific work centers including the information in the product structure, routing, and work center data files. New systems, featuring finite scheduling capability, use sophisticated algorithms to fit work requirements into the available capacity.

Capacity can be defined in several ways. It is important to understand capacity at the *maximum, effective,* and *demonstrated levels:*

- The *maximum capacity level* considers the use of every possible minute of each working day, defining a true maximum level of possible output.

- *Effective capacity* makes allowances for the scheduled hours of operation and the estimated production efficiency. This is a more realistic view of what output can be expected.

- *Demonstrated capacity* is the level of output that has actually been achieved by production. Often the demonstrated output rate is substantially less than the effective rate.

FEATURES OF COMPUTER-BASED ROUTING SYSTEMS

The difficult and time-consuming preparation and control of process documentation can often be simplified with the use of a computer-based system. The systems generally provide structure and formats for the required routing data, as well as security and control of the data entry and editing processes. The brief process description found on the route sheet may be expanded by the computer to include longer and more detailed operation descriptions, additional text information, operation instructions, and quality-control information.

ROUTING SIMILAR PARTS

Many items are often produced using similar standard process routings, or routing steps. Modern software systems allow the users to copy information from an existing routing sheet and apply it to a new routing sheet. This technique permits the computer operator to reduce the number of keystrokes required for entering new routings. Significant time savings and a reduction of data entry errors can be expected from this feature. Many software systems provide a "same-as-except" feature to simplify the loading and maintenance of routing data for similar parts.

Consider the following example: A new part is to be produced that has a geometry similar to an existing part but has different critical dimensions. A copy of the routing sheet for the known similar part may be copied, then edited or modified as needed to represent the new item. Features such as "alternate operations" and "extended text" offered in many computer-based systems can help make the modification process easier to complete and produce better information for the shop floor. System features that support the copying and editing of existing routings to create new routings result in less work and fewer process planning errors.

Additional system features that simplify the management of routing data include database "where-used" and "search" capabilities. Often changes take place that impact a group of similar parts routed through a particular work center. The ability to search the database for all items that are routed through a given work center is very helpful. This feature helps people assess the effect of changes on downtime, maintenance, equipment replacements, and potential bottlenecks. The routing system features offered in a software package should be carefully considered during the evaluation of routing system software.

COMPUTER-ASSISTED PROCESS PLANNING (CAPP)

Many firms today, faced with extreme competition, must meet special customer delivery requirements and special product features at competitive prices. Competitive pressures are causing companies to consider automating as many planning and production processes as possible.

The manual preparation of process plans involves many subjective judgments. The personal preferences of planners for particular machines and work centers may influence the final process decision. Larger companies with a number of planners have found significant differences in the process plans produced for similar parts. The competitive manufacturing environment is requiring companies to move toward increased standardization and simplification, available from computer software.

Imagine a computer-based system that can plan the manufacturing process automatically. The system utilizes an extensive database that includes design and process information. Searches of the database for existing parts with similar characteristics are routine. Design and process standards are the basis for production plans so documentation is simplified. The creation of plans for new items and revisions to existing items can be handled quickly. This type of computer-assisted process planning system is no longer just a dream.

Computer-assisted process planning (CAPP) is becoming a reality as the computer power in manufacturing is increasing and the cost of computer systems and networks continues to fall. These systems use the computer to enter, store, retrieve, and edit the production process data. CAPP systems now range from fairly simple "variant" systems that use data inputs to describe the specific operations to the highly complex, but more automated "generative" systems that develop the process plan using less input data.

Most CAPP systems are based on the concept of group technology. *Group technology* involves the identification of families of parts based on their geometry and the manufacturing processes required to produce them. Group technology has been a recognized technique of manufacturing planning and control for many years, so it provides a solid base for the development and operation of CAPP systems!

Some companies can accomplish the same thing by combining an engineering print with the route sheet. For example, manufacturers of bolts have a drawing of a bolt on the route sheet. The dimensions are filled in for the particular size of bolt desired.

GIGO CAUTION

Any data-driven system is only as good as the data it uses as reflected by *GIGO* (garbage in equals garbage out). Knowing that change is an ongoing reality in the manufacturing environment, it is essential that the data in the system be kept accurate and up to date. Processing must be coordinated with engineering changes to assure that the routing information remains correct.

An engineering change system must be developed and implemented that directs the personnel what to do. This system usually goes beyond the controls provided through the software, but the ultimate responsibility for the system's data quality must be assigned to somebody. So developing standard change procedures and training the people to follow them correctly is an essential element of a well-developed system.

SUMMARY

Routing information provides the details of the process used to complete the transformation process. The routing documents the story of how and where the materials and production equipment will come together to produce the product. The preparation and documentation of the process and routing information requires careful attention, control, and planning and must not be left to chance.

Properly defining the steps of the manufacturing process and where these steps are to be performed involves the collection of a quantity of information from many sources. Processing information is essential and will be used by people in many functional areas of the company for decisions that will have an impact on the business by reducing manufacturing costs and improving customer service levels.

The contents and format of the routing sheet must be defined for each company. There are many ways to capture the data and display the required information. It is important when developing a system to have input from all the departments that will use the routing and processing data.

Many companies will plan to use some type of computer-based system for data entry, editing, control, and reporting. The available systems should be reviewed carefully by the company representatives that will be using them. The use of a computer is not a requirement for a routing system; however, computer systems can offer users advantages. Many routing-related activities are made easier by a computer system to assist with the data control, storage, and retrieval. Systems that are not well planned and supported by the users can cause major problems for the company.

The future offers even more opportunities as the power of the computer and information databases for manufacturing are expanded. Computer-assisted process planning is becoming a reality so companies are able to take advantage of process planning systems that require minimal manual inputs. Continuing advancements in computer hardware and software will make the routing and process information easier to create, manage, and integrate throughout the factory.

REFERENCE

1. D. D. Bedworth, M. R. Henderson, and P. M. Wolfe: *Computer-Integrated Design and Manufacturing,* McGraw-Hill, New York, 1991.

BIBLIOGRAPHY

Bedworth, D. D., M. R. Henderson, and P. M. Wolfe: *Computer-Integrated Design and Manufacturing,* McGraw-Hill, New York, 1991.

Chang, T. C., R. A. Wysk, and H. P. Wang: *Computer-Aided Manufacturing,* Prentice-Hall, Englewood Cliffs, N.J., 1991.

Foston, A. L., C. L. Smith, and T. Au: *Fundamentals of Computer-Integrated Manufacturing,* Prentice-Hall, Englewood Cliffs, N.J., 1991.

Koenig, D. T.: *Manufacturing Engineering: Principles for Optimization,* Taylor & Francis, Washington, D.C., 1994.

Turner, W. C., J. H. Mize, K. E. Case, and J. W. Nazemetz: *Introduction to Industrial and Systems Engineering,* 3rd ed., Prentice-Hall, Englewood Cliffs, N.J., 1993.

CHAPTER 5
BILLS OF MATERIALS AND ROUTINGS

Editor

Rick Scott, CPIM
Managing Consultant, EDS, Troy, Michigan

The importance of bills of materials and routings databases cannot be overemphasized. These two databases must be solidly in place for a manufacturing concern to achieve its operational objectives and to effectively compete in today's environment. Bills of materials and routings databases are used in conjunction with each other to provide basic part-related information, product-structure-related information, and information describing the sequence of events that take place to produce a finished product along with the supporting resources (labor). A hierarchical depiction of the basic components of product structure is shown in Fig. 5.1.

This chapter is organized into three major sections. In the first section basic concepts regarding a bill of materials database are discussed. In the second section, basic concepts regarding a routings database are discussed. Once these basic concepts are understood, we can look at some practical applications of bills of materials and routings databases. This will be done in the third section of this chapter.

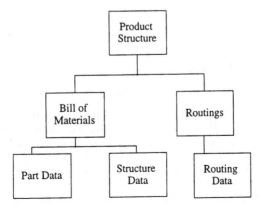

FIGURE 5.1 Hierarchical product structure.

5.1

BILL OF MATERIALS DATABASE CONCEPTS

Topics discussed in this section include the following:

- Definition of a bill of materials
- Types of bills of materials
- Information typically contained in a bill of materials database

Bill of Materials Defined

The *American Production and Inventory Control Society* (APICS) *Dictionary* tells us that a bill of materials database is "a listing of all of the subassemblies, intermediates, parts, and raw materials that go into a parent assembly showing the quantity of each required to make an assembly....It may also be called a *formula, recipe,* or *ingredients list* in certain industries." These subassemblies, intermediates, parts, and raw materials can generally be categorized as components or parents with the item being produced as the parent and the materials required to produce the parent as the components.

Bill of Materials Types

Bill of materials databases can be generally classified in one of two ways:

- Formal:

  All business systems are integrated with the bill of materials system.

  The use of the systems is documented in a consistent format.

- Informal:

  Multiple bill of materials systems exist either as separate databases or as extracts from the main database.

  Documentation is either nonexistent (committed to memory) or exists in multiple, inconsistent formats.

Generally, successful businesses and business systems demand that a formal bill of materials be in place.

Bills of materials can be generally grouped into various types by a specific format, and they can also be grouped by how they support the materials planning process.

Formatted Bills of Materials

These types of bills of materials include the following:

- *Multilevel bills of materials (Fig. 5.2).* This type displays the parent and all of its components used directly or indirectly, together with the quantity required of all components. If a component is, say, a subassembly or an intermediate, then all of its components will also be displayed, as will all subsequent components at all levels down to raw materials and purchased parts. Refer to Fig. 5.2 to understand the remainder of the formatted bill of materials.
- *Single-level bills of materials (Table 5.1).* This type displays only the components required for the parent along with a description, the quantity per, and the unit of mea-

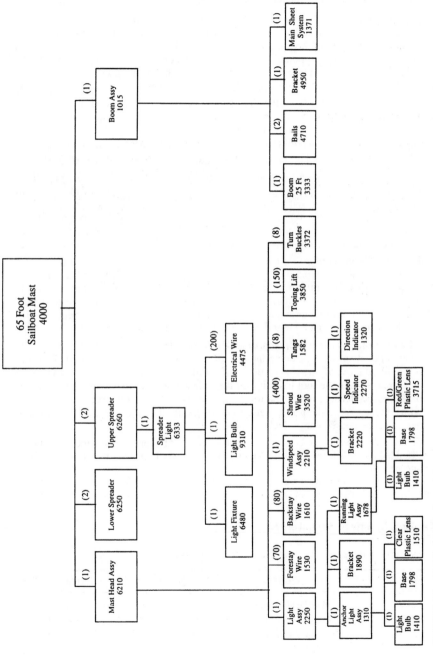

FIGURE 5.2 Multilevel bill of materials.

sure. Thus an explosion of the parent part, sailboat mast (4000), would produce the four components and associated information listed.

- *Indented bills of materials (Table 5.2).* The highest-level parents are listed farthest to the left of the margin, and all of the components going into these parents are shown indented to the right of the margin. All subsequent levels of components are indented farther to the right. Components used in more than one parent will appear more than once, under every assembly or subassembly in which they are used.

- *Summarized where-used bills of materials (Table 5.2).* This type is the same as Table 5.2 without the levels. Also, the light bulbs (1410) would only appear once with a quantity of 2. All like components used in the product are grouped, and the total quantity of each component used in the product is shown.

- *Matrix bills of materials (Table 5.3).* This type groups all the parts for a product family in a matrix, allowing all common part requirements to be readily totaled.

- *Single-level where-used bills of materials (Table 5.4).* This type is a listing of all the parents in which a component part is used. It could be considered an upside-down bill of materials. A where-used bill of materials is sometimes called a *goes-into* bill of materials since the components literally "go into" an assembly. This is a useful tool when verifying the accuracy of a bill of material because it provides an auditor with a simple means of verifying all of the parents with which a component is associated.

- *Multilevel where-used bill of materials (Table 5.5).* This type is a listing for a component showing all the parents in which that component is directly used and the next higher level parents into which each of those parents is used. This form is repeated until all top-level (level 0) parents are shown. This tool is useful when verifying the accuracy of a bill of materials because it provides a map of all the part relationships of a particular component.

- *Top-level where-used bills of materials (Table 5.6).* This type is a listing of all the finished products in which a component, subassembly, or assembly are used. This tool is useful when verifying the accuracy of a bill of materials because it provides an auditor with a simple tool to verify all the finished products with which a particular part is associated. Also, when a top-level where-used listing is used in conjunction with a master schedule, it is a useful tool in determining when, say, parts or components will be phased out or declared obsolete.

- *Costed bill of materials* The quantity per assembly of every component in the bill is extended by the cost of the components. The costs would include material, labor, and overhead.

TABLE 5.1   Single-Level Bill of Materials

Parent: 4000
Description: sailboat mast

Component	Description	Quality per	Unit of measure
6210	Mast head assembly	1	Ea.
6250	Lower spreaders	2	Ea.
6260	Upper spreaders	2	Ea.
1015	Boom assy.	1	Ea.

TABLE 5.2   Indented Bills of Materials

Parent: 4000
Description: 65 foot sailboat mast

Level	Component	Description	Units required	Unit of measure
1	6210	Mast head assembly	1	Ea.
2	2250	Light assy.	1	Ea.
3	1310	Anchor light assy.	1	Ea.
4	1410	Light bulb	1	Ea.
4	1798	Base	1	Ea.
4	1510	Clear plastic lens	1	Ea.
3	1890	Bracket	1	Ea.
3	1678	Running light assy.	1	Ea.
4	1410	Light bulb	1	Ea.
4	1798	Base	1	Ea.
4	3715	Red/green plastic lens	1	Ea.
2	1530	Forestay wire	70	Ft.
2	1610	Backstay wire	80	Ft.
2	2210	Wind speed assy.	1	Ea.
3	2220	Bracket	1	Ea.
3	2270	Speed indicator	1	Ea.
3	1320	Direction indicator	1	Ea.
2	3520	Shroud wire	400	Ft.
2	1582	Tangs	8	Ea.
2	3850	Topping lift	150	Ft.
2	3372	Turn buckles	8	Ea.
1	6250	Lower spreader	2	Ea.
1	6260	Upper spreader	2	Ea.
2	6333	Spreader light	2	Ea.
3	6480	Light fixture	1	Ea.
3	9310	Light bulb	1	Ea.
3	4475	Electrical wire	200	Ft.
1	1015	Boom assy.	1	Ea.
2	3333	Boom: 25 ft	1	Ea.
2	4710	Bails	2	Ea.
2	4950	Bracket	1	Ea.
2	1371	Main sheet system	1	Ea.

Note: The entire indented bills are not shown for brevity.

TABLE 5.3   Matrix Bill of Materials

	Parents		
Components	65-ft sailboat mast 4000	50-ft sailboat mast 6000	35-ft sailboat mast 8000
Mast head assembly	6210	8752	3719
Lower spreaders	6250	1395	1219
Upper spreaders	6260	5013	Not used
Boom assembly	1015	1313	9213

TABLE 5.4   Single-Level Where Used

Component: 1410
Description: Light bulb

Parents	Description	Units required	Unit of measure
1310	Anchor light assy.	1	Ea.
1678	Running light assy.	1	Ea.

TABLE 5.5   Multilevel Where Used

Component: 1310
Description: Anchor light assembly

Level	Parents	Description	Units required	Unit of measure
2	2250	Light assy.	1	Ea.
1	6210	Mast head assy.	1	Ea.
0	4000	65-ft sailboat mast	1	Ea.

TABLE 5.6   Top-Level Where Used

Component: 1310
Description: Anchor light assembly

Level	Description
4000	65-ft sailboat mast

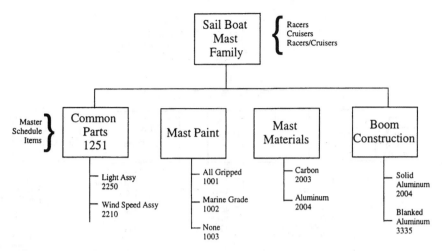

FIGURE 5.3 Modular bill of materials.

Bills of Materials Supporting Materials Planning

Bills of materials that support the materials planning process would include the following:

- *Modular Bills of Materials (Fig. 5.3).* The bill is arranged by common parts and product modules or options to facilitate the master scheduling and/or material planning processes. In the referenced figure, the sailboat mast is built for three markets: racing, cruising, and racers/cruisers. Certain options are common to all of these masts and are grouped and assigned a *pseudo part number* (1251). Other like options are grouped such as mast paint, mast material, and boom construction. This grouping allows a particular mast to be configured as customers define their needs. This topic will be discussed under "Structuring the Bill of Materials" and "Routings" in the last section of this chapter.
- *Planning (super) bills of materials (Fig. 5.4).* This bill of materials format expands upon the concept of a modular bill of materials. In the example, percentages of anticipated sales have been added to the various options, with the common parts being 100 percent. These percentages can be determined by market analysis. This information can then be used to drive the master scheduling and MRP II processes.
- *Transient (phantom, pseudo, or blow-through) bills of materials.* This structuring technique is used primarily for nonstocked subassemblies. Figure 5.5, which depicts a multilevel bill of materials for a light assembly, the light bulb (1410), base (1798), and the red/green lens (3715) are stored in the stockroom. These three parts are assembled to create the running light assembly (1678), which is immediately assembled with the bracket (1890) and anchor light assembly (1310) to create the light assembly (2250). In this scenario, the running light assembly (1678) is a transient part. To create a transient part, the following actions are taken:

Set the lead time to zero.

Set the order quantity to lot for lot.

Turn on a transient indicator in the MRP II System.

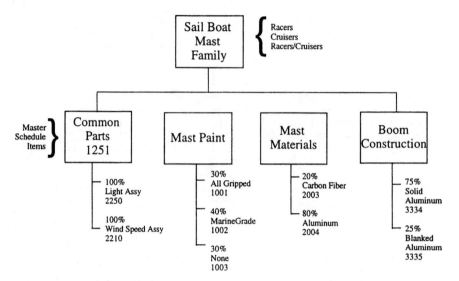

FIGURE 5.4   Planning bill of materials.

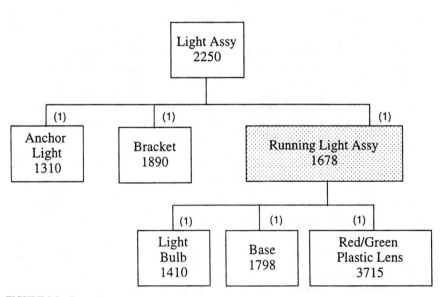

FIGURE 5.5   Example of transient part in a bill of materials. [*Note:* The running light assy. (1678) is a transient part.]

Creating a transient part allows the MRP logic to drive requirements straight through the phantom item to its components. This technique can be used for manufacturing cells where inventory is stored on the line to produce subassemblies that are consumed immediately in the manufacturing cell.

Information in a Bill of Materials Data Base

Information that is contained in a bill of materials database will vary by computer system and by company. As mentioned earlier, most companies maintain two sets of information within their bills of materials database: part-related information and structure-related information.

Part-Related Information. information regarding parts is typically stored in a file called an *item master, part master,* or *part record.* These files generally include the following information:

- *Part number.* A number that uniquely identifies raw material, fabricated parts, subassemblies, assemblies, and finished or top-unit products. In addition, some companies assign part numbers to items including maintenance items, tools, and operating supplies. A new part number is usually assigned when one or more of the following changes:

   Form. Configuration of an item by parameters uniquely characterizing the item such as shape, size, density, or weight

   Fit. The ability of an item to become an integral part of another item

   Function. The activities or actions that an item is expected to perform.

   When one of the above changes, the original part is no longer interchangeable and a new part number is assigned.

- *Part description.* A statement describing the form, fit, or function of the part. Many firms have adopted a standard, such as reverse engineering, to facilitate sorting by functional description. This technique incorporates a sequence of noun-adjective-adjective which allows sorting by noun type and then by a superior and subordinate adjective within each noun. An example of this type of sort is shown below:

   Belt, water pump, Detroit diesel engine

   Belt, water pump, Yanmar engine

   Connector, wiring, anchor light

   Connector, wiring, masthead light

   As opposed to:

   Anchor light wiring connector

   Detroit diesel engine water pump belt

   Masthead light wiring connector

   Yanmar engine water pump belt

- *Level code.* The level code indicates the position within the bill of materials database. APICS has established standards for numbering these levels: level 0 is the finished product or top unit; level 1 is assigned to all the components that go into the finished product or top unit; level 2 is assigned to all the components that go into the level 1 parts, and so on. This code is used for the following purposes:

  MRP II uses this code to determine when the bottom of a product structure has been reached so that the total demand for a particular part has been accumulated.

  Product costing uses this code to determine when a part represents the bottom of a product's parts structure. It then initiates the process of "rolling" the costs up the part's product structure, level by level, accumulating costs until the top of the part's product structure has been reached (level code is 0). Synonym is low-level code.

The item master (part master or part records) file may include additional information such as the following:

- *Scrap or shrinkage factors.* Factors applied against the quantity of a component required when 100 percent perfect parts are not consistently produced.
- *Source code.* Usually a one alphabetic character indicating the origin or source of the part. Typical source codes include the following:

  P for purchased

  M for manufactured

  E or B for either or both

- *Effective date and/or cumulative order number.* The date or cumulative order number that an engineering change is to become effective. The effective date and/or cumulative order number is usually assigned to the parent part number.
- *Engineering change stop date or cumulative order stop number.* The date or cumulative number assigned to a component part being phased out of production.
- *Effective change number.* A sequential number indicating the level or number of engineering changes processed for a given part.
- *Costs.* To obtain the total standard cost of the parent, the standard cost(s) of the component(s) is multiplied by the quantity per parent and then summed.
- *Units of measure.* These are conversion factors to facilitate various processes such as buying materials (purchasing), storing materials (stockroom), planning the use of materials (MRP II), and consuming materials (bill of materials). It is not uncommon to buy products and store materials in one unit of measure and plan and consume the materials in another unit of measure. For example, a $1.2 B supplier of electrical automotive components uses bubble wrap in such large quantities that the material is bought and stored in 8- by 6-foot rolls; however, the planned usage of the bubble wrap and the actual consumption of the bubble wrap are done in units of feet. It should be noted that conversion factors must be built into an MRP II system to maintain consistency and proper usage of these data elements.

Structure-Related Information.   The second set of information generally contained in a bill of materials database is structure- and usage-related data that describe the structural relationships of an item—that is, what components are linked to what parents and the number of times a component is used in the parent. Thus, one product structure record is required whenever two parts are linked together. For example, in Fig. 5.6, three

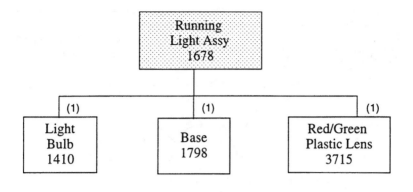

FIGURE 5.6   Product structure record.

product structure records would be required to describe the running light assembly (1678): one linking the light bulb (1410) to the running light assembly (1678), one linking the base (1798) to the running light assembly (1678), and one linking the red/green plastic lens (3715) to the running light assembly (1678).

BASIC CONCEPTS OF A ROUTINGS DATABASE

Topics discussed in this section include the following:

• Definition of a routings database
• Types of routings
• Information typically contained in a routings database

Definition of a Routings Database

A routings database is closely associated with a bills of materials database. Where the bills of materials database shows how a product is structured, the routings database contains information describing the sequence of operations that a product, assembly, subassembly, or fabricated part must go through to become a finished part.

The *APICS Dictionary* defines a *routing* as a set of information detailing the method of manufacturing a particular item. It includes the operations to be performed, their sequence, the various work centers to be involved, and the time standards for setup and producing the part. In some companies, the routings database also includes information describing tooling, operator skill levels, inspection operations, and testing requirements.

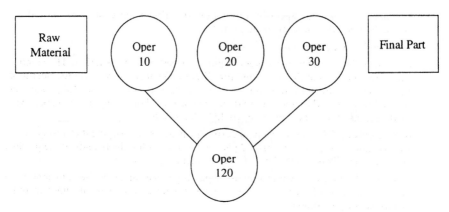

FIGURE 5.7   Alternate routing.

Types of Routings

There are numerous different types of routings including the following:

- *Alternate routings.* An alternative set of operations that produces an item identical to the item produced by the original routing. An example of an alternate routing, depicted as operation 120, is shown in Fig. 5.7.
- *Blanket routing.* Usually used for families of parts that use the same set of operations. One variable could be the size of the part that would impact the amount of material consumed, the standard times to perform the operations, and consequently, the standard costs. Each of the family members would have a different part number, consequently different amounts of material, standard operation times, and standard costs in the bill of material and routings. An example would be a company that manufactures truck rails. The truck rails are sold in 40-, 48-, and 52-foot lengths. These would all be processed through the same set of blanket operations.
- *Rework routing.* Rework is a non-value-added operation and normally would not be a permanent type of routing. However, in some situations in which a process is not in control, rework may have to be scheduled as a normal part of the operations sequence. An example of this could be a heat-treating operation in which the proper processing variables have not been established and the parts are produced with an out-of-spec bow in them. A rework operation to straighten the parts would have to be scheduled after the heat-treating operation.
- *Numerical control/computer numerical control/direct (distributed) numerical control routings.* NC/CNC/DNA routing instructions are fed directly into a machine tool controller via prerecorded coded information. The most sophisticated systems use DNC where individual manufacturing units are connected to a central computer that downloads instructions to the manufacturing equipment.

Information in Routings

As with the bills of materials database, the information contained in a routings database will vary by system and company. Information that may be found in a routings database includes the following:

- *Container(s) required.* Specific information describing the containers needed at a particular operation or work center.

- *Count point.* See *pay point.*

- *Crew size.* The number of workers required to perform an operation. The standard time should represent the total time for all crew members to perform the operation, not the net start-to-finish time for the crew. A crew size of less than 1.0 person may be used when a worker tends more than one machine. For example, if a worker were tending 2 machines, the crew size would be 0.5 person.

- *Inspection time.* The time consumed during the process of verifying that a component, subassembly, assembly, or finished part meets or is within the bounds of the product specifications. This is one element of manufacturing lead time.

- *Labor grade.* A class of workers whose capability makes them unique in their skill set or craft. Labor grades are normally associated with a particular job function (e.g., electrician or pipe fitter).

- *Load center.* See *work center.*

- *Manufacturing lead time.* The total time required to manufacture an item, exclusive of lead time for purchased component part(s). Elements of manufacturing lead time include the following:

Order preparation time

Queue time

Set-up time

Run time

Move time

Inspection time

Put-away time

- *Move time.* The time it takes to move a job from one operation to the next sequential operation to be performed. This is one element of manufacturing lead time.

- *Order preparation time.* The time required to analyze requirements and open-order status and to create the documentation necessary to release a purchase order or production order. This is one element of manufacturing lead time.

- *Operation.* A specific step in the manufacturing process that a component, subassembly, or assembly passes through on its way to becoming a finished part. Typically, a routing consists of multiple operations. For example, the operations to produce a truck rail include the following:

Operation 10: Shot blasting

Operation 20: Shearing

Operation 30: Blanking

Operation 40: Forming

Operation 50: Heat treating

Operation 60: Pressing

Operation 70: Cutting

Operation 80: Washing

Operation 90: Painting

Operation 100: Shipping

- *Pay point.* A point in the flow of material or sequence of operations at which production information for components, subassemblies, assemblies, or finished parts is reported. Information reported would include pieces completed and scrap.

  Pay points may be designated at the ends of lines or upon removal from a work center, but most often pay points are designated as the points at which material transfers from one department to another. Synonym: *count point.*

- *Put-away time.* The time required for moving material from the dock (or other location), transporting the material to a storage area, placing the material in a storage area, and moving the material to a specific location and recording this movement and the location where the material has been placed. This is one element of manufacturing lead time.

- *Queue time.* The time from when a job arrives at an operation until setup is initiated or the first part is prepared to run. This is one element of manufacturing lead time.

- *Run time.* The planned standard time to produce one or more units of an item in an operation. The actual time taken to produce one piece may vary from the standard, but the latter is used for loading purposes and is adjusted by dividing by the appropriate work center efficiency rate. For example, if the standard for an operation is 0.5 hours and the work center efficiency rate is 75 percent, the time used for loading would be 0.375 hours (0.50 hours times 0.75). This is one element of manufacturing lead time.

- *Set-up time.* The time required for a particular machine, resource, work center, or line to convert from the production of the last good piece of the previous lot to the first good piece of the next lot being manufactured. This is one element of manufacturing lead time.

- *Tooling data.* Specific data describing jigs, fixtures, or tooling needed at a particular operation or work center.

- *Utilization.*

  1. A measure of how intensively a resource is being used to produce a good or a service. Utilization measures actual time used versus available time. Traditionally, utilization compares direct time charged (run time plus setup time) to the clock time scheduled for the resource. This measure has led to improper conclusions in some cases.
  2. In the theory of constraints, utilization is measured as the ratio of actual time a resource is producing (run time only) to the clock time the resource is scheduled to produce.

- *Work center.* An area in a manufacturing facility where production is performed. It typically consists of one or more workers and/or machines with identical capabilities that can be considered as one unit for purposes of capacity requirements planning and detailed scheduling. Synonym: *load center.*

PRACTICAL APPLICATIONS OF BILLS OF MATERIALS AND ROUTINGS

Topics discussed in this section include the following:

- Structuring bills of materials and routings databases

- Using bills of materials and routings databases
- Developing and maintaining the accuracy of bills of materials and routings databases

Structuring Bills of Materials and Routings

Typically, bills of materials and routings databases are not created during a specific time period; rather, they evolve over time. The general phases a product may transition through during its life cycle could include the following:

- Concept
- Design
- Detailing
- Production
- Phase out or replacement
- Warranty or service

Bills of materials and routings databases generally are developed during the first four phases of the product's life cycle. During the concept phase, a salesperson could obtain a new idea from a customer, research and design personnel could come up with a new idea, or a new product idea could evolve from some other source. Typically, sketches are made to document the new product idea, and a high-level engineering parts lists is produced (this is sometimes called an *engineering bill of materials*). This information is passed to a design person, and a formal design (i.e., shape, dimensions, tolerances, and materials required) is created, part numbers are assigned, and the product starts to come to life. A design prototype could be made using stereolithography or some other means (clay, wood, etc.) to produce a physical model of the new product. At this point in the product's life cycle, manufacturing engineering and industrial engineering should be brought into the picture to provide input regarding the "ease of manufacturing and/or assembling" the product. Questions would probably be asked about the volumes of the product to be produced: If it will be a high-volume product, greater consideration would be given to automate the process that will produce the product; however, if it will be a low-volume part, consideration would be given to a more manual, labor-intensive manufacturing operation. Consideration will also have to be given to each part to determine if it will be purchased or manufactured. If it is to be manufactured, additional questions will have to be answered including:

- What types of machinery will be needed?
- How will the parts be transported throughout the manufacturing facility?
- How will the parts be loaded into the machinery?
- How much money will be allocated to automation?

At this point, the bills of materials and routings are beginning to evolve at a very high level.

All of this information will be given to cost accounting personnel, and the product's cost will be determined. Equipment and automation costs will be amortized over time according to company policy and a cost per unit consisting of labor, materials, and overhead costs will be developed. This information will be given back to the sales group, and management will incorporate the desired profit into the product cost to determine the selling price. This information will be reviewed with the customer, and if it is acceptable, the formal bills of materials and routings will be developed. Manufacturing engineering and industrial engineering will become heavily involved to add lead times, setup times, operation times, and so on, to turn the information engineering has been working with into formal manufacturing bills of materials and routings.

In addition to the above factors, it is important for a company to structure its manufacturing data to support both the manufacturing process and the type and variety of products the company sells.

Structuring Manufacturing Data by Manufacturing Process

The bill of materials in a process or repetitive environment will normally have very few levels, and the routings will tend to be relatively simple. In contrast, the manufacturing facility involved in all facets of assembly from molding and casting through subassembly and final assembly will have complex bills of materials and will require more operational steps to be included within the routings.

Structuring Manufacturing Data by Type of Product Sold

A company must make specific decisions on how manufacturing data are structured based upon the type of products it sells. For example, a company may elect to structure a bill of materials for every product sold, or it may elect to drop down a level in the bill and create bill of materials to represent product families or models and the various options and features offered to meet a customer's requirements. The former approach could be labeled a *generic bill of materials,* and the latter approach, a *modularized bill of materials.*

Generic Bills of Materials.   A graphic representation of a generic product structure is shown in the multilevel bill of materials in Fig. 5.8. The structure defines the relationship among various items comprising the product in terms of levels and parent item and component items relationships. The product structure can be defined by specifying four parent and component levels. The end item, the complete sailboat mast (4000), is at level 0 (APICS convention) and the mast head assembly (6210), lower spreaders (6250), upper spreaders (6260), and boom assembly (1015) are at level 1, and so on. The completed sailboat mast (4000) is a parent to the component boom assembly (1015), which is in turn a parent to the boom (3333), bails (4710), bracket (4959), and main sheet assembly (1371). Some of the parts are purchased parts and are never parents.

Modular Bills of Materials.   The second type of structuring for a bill of materials is called a *modular bill of materials.* This method is appropriate for companies that have a large number of finished products and choose to assemble the finished products to order. In the multilevel bill of materials for a sailboat mast (4000) just discussed, assume the mast manufacturer has decided to offer the customer the following choices:

- Five mast head assembly options
- Two types of lower spreaders
- Two types of upper spreaders
- Six boom assembly choices

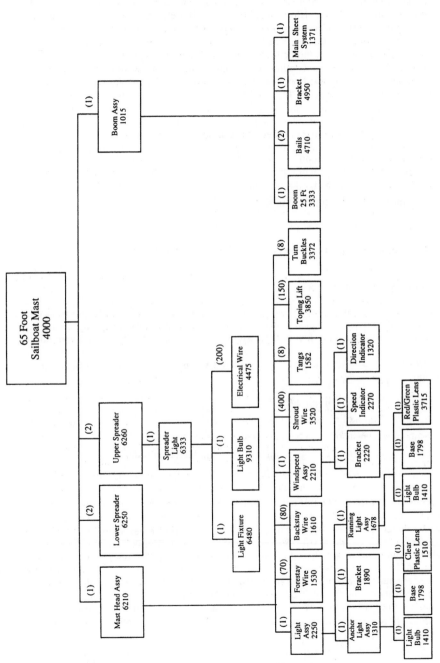

FIGURE 5.8 Generic bill of materials.

5.17

If the manufacturer created a separate bill of materials for each of these choices at the sailboat mast (4000) level, 120 (5 × 2 × 2 × 6) different end items would be required. This means 120 bills of materials would have to be created and maintained, 120 different forecasts would have to be prepared, and so on.

A simpler approach would be to use a modular bill of materials. In this approach all planning work is done one level below the end item sailboat mast (4000), at the mast head assembly (6210), lower spreader (6250), upper spreader (6260), and boom assembly (1015). Using this approach, only 15 items (5 + 2 + 2 + 6) would be involved in the planning process. Thus, when an order is received, the sailboat mast could be assembled quickly from component parts stored in inventory. The latter approach would reduce the amount of money invested in inventory.

An additional factor that must be taken into account when structuring the bill of materials is the trade-off between:

- Responding to a customer's requirements
- Maintaining an investment in inventory

Take, for example, a product that has the following lead times:

- Fabrication time: 2 weeks
- Assembly time: 1 week
- Final assembly time: $\frac{1}{2}$ week

The total lead time to build the entire product to customer order would be $3\frac{1}{2}$ weeks. If, however, the company decided to invest in inventory and to stock completed assemblies and assemble the final product to the customer's order, the lead time would be reduced to $\frac{1}{2}$ week.

Other trade-offs that need to be considered when structuring the bill of materials include:

- Complexity of the bill of material
- Number of bills of material to maintain
- Number of transactions to be processed
- Ease of converting a customer order into a manufacturing order
- Number of manufacturing orders released to the shop floor

Part Number Rules.   One last consideration to be made when structuring the bills of materials (and the routings) is the design of the part numbering system. This topic has been debated ad nausea over the years; however, experience has shown that the KISS principle (keep it simple, silly) is most appropriate for designing part numbering systems. Certain basic rules should be considered, including the following:

- *Use the minimum number of digits in the part number.* The more digits, the higher the probability of making an error during input. The controlling factor should be the total number of parts a company anticipates creating over the life of its products plus future product indicators. (A 6-digit part number will allow 999,999 part numbers, and an 8-digit part number will allow 99,999,999 part numbers.)
- *Eliminate the use of special characters such as #, @, *, and &.* Also, blank spaces should not be used within the part number (programmers can insert a blank space to facilitate reading a part number on the screen or on the hard copy, for example, 1578 2250, but the number should be keyed in as 15782250).

- *Eliminate the use of alphanumeric characters.*
- *Use a nonsignificant numbering scheme.* It is time-consuming and costly to change computer programs coded to make decisions on specific fields in a part number. For example, assume that the fourth and fifth digits are allocated to engineering changes and the sixth digit is allocated to the color of the product. It is then discovered that some parts have over 100 changes being made and that the marketplace demands more than 9 colors. Typically, dash numbers are added to the end of the part number to accommodate these changes, and computer programs must be changed accordingly.

  An example of the benefits of using nonsignificant part numbers is a multi-billion-dollar manufacturer of computers that converted from a 16-digit significant part number system to an 8-digit, random part number system with a check-digit scheme built into the part number. The company experienced a 70 percent reduction in data input errors!

- *Incorporate the use of a check digit.* This will allow a computer to automatically check the validity of the part number.
- *Eliminate synonym part numbers (i.e., using multiple part numbers to identify one part) and homonym part numbers (i.e., using one part number to identify multiple, dissimilar parts).*
- *Enforce the use of a single source when obtaining a new part number and part-related information.* This will minimize control and enforcement problems associated with part numbers.

If there is one guiding principle in the design of bills of materials and routings, it would be that the information in the bills of materials and routings *must* map exactly to the manufacturing process. Thus, in the example of the bill of materials for a sailboat light assembly in Fig. 5.9 and the example routing for a sailboat light assembly in Table 5.7, we should be able to walk out onto the manufacturing floor and see the following activities taking place:

- At operation 10, the light bulb (1410), base (1798), and the red/green plastic lens (3715) are assembled, producing the running light assembly (1678).
- At operation 20, the light bulb (1410), base (1798), and clear plastic lens (1510) are assembled, producing the anchor light assembly (1310).
- At operation 30, the anchor light assembly (1310), running light assembly (1678), and bracket (1890) are assembled, producing the light assembly (2250).
- At operation 40, the entire light assembly (2250) is tested.
- At operation 50, the light assembly is put into stock.

Using Bills of Materials and Routings

A manufacturing enterprise can, at a high level, be described by three major business processes as follows:

- Concept to market
- Order to cash
- Conflict to resolution

These business processes can be further broken down into subprocesses. The manner in which bills of materials and routings databases are used within some of these subprocesses will now be addressed.

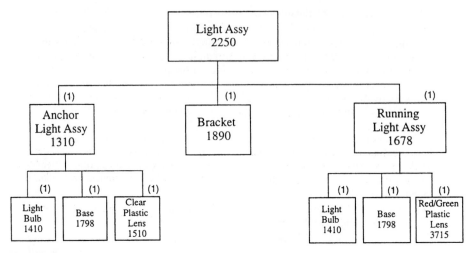

FIGURE 5.9   Example bill of materials for a light assembly.

TABLE 5.7   Routing for a Light Assembly (2250)

Part #	Part description	Operation #	Operation description
1410	Light bulb	10	Assemble to produce anchor lt. assy. (1310)
1798	Base	10	Assemble to produce anchor lt. assy. (1310)
1510	Clear plastic lens	10	Assemble to produce anchor lt. assy. (1310)
1410	Light bulb	20	Assemble to produce running lt. assy. (1678)
1798	Base	20	Assemble to produce running lt. assy. (1678)
3715	Red/green plastic lens	20	Assemble to produce running lt. assy. (1678)
1310	Anchor light assy.	30	Assemble to produce lt. assy. (2250)
1678	Running light assy.	30	Assemble to produce lt. assy. (2250)
1890	Bracket	30	Assemble to produce lt. assy. (2250)
2250	Light assy.	40	Test
2250	Light assy.	50	Put into stock

Designing Products.   Management may decide that a particular product is desirable to add to the company's product offerings. The product design department would be contacted to prepare preliminary sketches that could later be used to create the product via a computer-aided design (CAD) software-hardware system. As the product evolved, the product design personnel would eventually create the initial bill of materials, sometimes called an *engineering parts list.* The product design process typically is organized by function. Thus, for an automobile, a bill of materials might be created for the engine, the transmission, the axles, and so on. The bill of materials will contain all the components of these products for which the product design department wishes to maintain design control. Some additional unique characteristics of an engineering bill of materials may include the following:

- "As required" may be noted in some cases for the use of parts, components, and so on, used in the next level of the product structure.
- The entire product structure may be detailed by the product design function including the structure of parts that may be purchased since the "make-versus-buy" decision has not been made at this point in the business process.
- The product design function may consider a number of assemblies to be combined into one when the product is designed; however, when the product is manufactured or assembled, the assemblies would be created as individual units.

Selling Products. The sales department may become involved at different stages of the design process. The sales personnel may be key players in defining new products that customers desire. Once products are designed, the sales personnel are actively selling new and existing products.

A major manufacturer of trucks has over 30 branches spread across North America. The sales personnel at each of these branches typically will use bill of materials information for a number of purposes including:

- Determining the features and options to be offered to a customer
- Configuring a truck to meet customer's needs
- Costing and pricing the final truck configuration
- Determining service or replacement parts, service part kits, and so on, and the associated pricing

Planning for Production. Paraphrasing the *APICS Dictionary,* the materials planning function typically works with an MRP II system to determine when to replenish material and when to reschedule open orders and to establish and maintain valid due dates. The MRP II system typically uses the bill of materials in conjunction with inventory data and the master production schedule to determine the above information. The MRP II system uses the bill of materials to explode the master production schedule and determine gross and net requirements on a level-by-level basis. Capacity requirements planning can be done using information from the routing files such as work centers and standard operation times. In addition, pick lists identifying quantity and location in the stockroom of parts required on the manufacturing floor can be generated using the product structures in the bills of materials database and the operations maintained in the routings database.

The MRP II system can also use the bill of materials and routing information to "backflush" and reduce inventory at each operational step rather than at the end of the manufacturing process. This eliminates the need to report inventory movements at each operation. However, to effectively use backflushing, the accuracy of both the bills of materials database and the routings database must approach 100 percent. Otherwise, serious errors will occur in the inventory data maintained in the manufacturing system, causing material shortages and overages on the shop floor.

A major manufacturer of truck rails has an assembly plant in one state and a manufacturing facility in another state. The bills of materials are structured and maintained at the assembly plant with the completed truck rails as the top units. Demand from customers is received at the top unit level and is entered into the master schedule. High-level capacity planning is done utilizing information from the bills of material and routings, and the demand data is passed to the MRP II system where the top units are exploded using the bill of materials. Demand data are then derived for assemblies and subassemblies for the scheduling and order-release process. These data are then passed to the manufacturing plant at the assembly level to drive the master scheduling process at the manufacturing plant where the required assemblies are exploded via MRP II using the manufacturing plant's bills of materials and routings to produce planned and released orders for the subassemblies and component and purchased parts.

The truck rails start out as coils of steel and are blanked, formed, and heat-treated (with processes defined by the manufacturing plant's bill of materials) to create finished truck rail assemblies required by the assembly plant on the due dates specified in the manufacturing plant's master schedule. As these parts are completed, backflushing is done (using the manufacturing plant's bills of materials and routings) to relieve inventory from the manufacturing plant. The completed truck rail assemblies are entered into the assembly plant's inventory. As the finished truck rails are assembled, backflushing is performed again (using the assembly plant's bills of materials and routings) to relieve the finished truck rail's components from the assembly plant's inventory.

Manufacturing Products.   As the product moves from the product design process to the manufacturing process, the bill of materials will typically be structured by manufacturing engineering to map the way the product will be manufactured (as opposed to the product design function where the bill of materials mapped the manner in which the product is designed). Additional information is required by manufacturing engineering, such as operation and setup times, so that lead times can be calculated to assist with the executing of MRP II and scheduling of assemblies, subassemblies, components, and so on, which are performed during the materials planning process.

For example, a large manufacturer of computer products has opted to have two separate bills of materials: one for engineering and one for manufacturing. They have built a software interface between the two that "filters" the engineering bills to identify the missing information required by manufacturing. A bill of materials may not be transferred to the manufacturing bill of materials until all of the required information is in place. They have also developed an interface between engineering's bill of materials and the master schedule such that priorities can be set at the top unit level to work on structuring those manufacturing bills of material with close-in demand.

Processing Engineering Changes.   A cartoon in one of the trade journals had an engineer sitting at his CAD station designing a new product. His boss was looking over his shoulder. The caption under the cartoon said, "Let me know when you are far enough along so we can start making a few changes." Engineering changes are inevitable if a company wishes to remain competitive. Justifications for making an engineering change include the following:

- Reducing product costs
- Improving the product
- Simplifying the manufacturing or assembly process
- Complying with government regulations
- Facilitating the manufacturing or assembly process
- Correcting engineering errors

The bills of materials and routings databases are key, along with the MRP II system, in processing engineering changes against a finished product. Changes to the product structure are made in the bills of materials database, and changes to the manufacturing process are made in the routings database.

A major manufacturer of engines has its engineering-change control board meet weekly. The members of this board include representatives from the following functions:

- Drafting (chairman of engineering-change control board)
- Manufacturing engineering
- Purchasing
- Marketing
- Manufacturing plant (usually teleconferenced in)
- Engineering

Each proposed change is categorized by this group as emergency (e.g., environmental or government impact) and nonemergency. The emergency changes are generally immediately entered directly into the bills of materials and/or routings databases and phased into production via an effectivity date or cum number. Also, a quick, high-level cost analysis probably would be made to estimate the cost impact of the change.

The nonemergency engineering changes are further subdivided into those changes that do not have to be costed and those that have to be costed. For the former, the current level of inventory and any outstanding purchase orders are considered to determine if the change will be phased in when the inventory of the part being phased out has been consumed. Once this decision has been made, an effectivity date can be determined and entered into the bills of materials and/or routings databases.

For those engineering changes that have to be costed, the bills of materials and/or routings along with MRP II data and information from the manufacturing plant are evaluated to determine the cost impact of the change. Again, available inventory and incoming purchase orders, as well as the lead time to effect the engineering change (equipment may have to be modified or replaced) must be considered to determine an effectivity date that will be entered into the bills of materials and/or routings database.

As alluded to in this scenario, the *effectivity date* is a popular method of controlling the timing of phasing an engineering change into production. Once the engineering-change control board has determined when the change will be phased into production, the effectivity date IN in the bills of materials and/or routings databases is set to that date. Also, the effectivity date OUT of the changed part is set to that date in the bills of materials and/or routings databases. The MRP II system then checks these dates during an update run and automatically phases the changed part into production on the specified effectivity date. Consideration must also be given to notifying vendors and manufacturing operations of the change.

An example of the use of effectivity dates is shown in Fig. 5.10 and Table 5.8. Here the red/green plastic lens (3715) is being phased out on 5/10/95 and is being replaced by

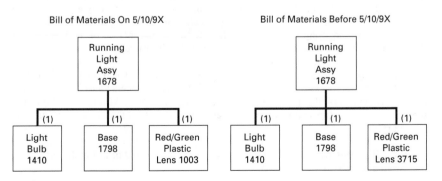

FIGURE 5.10   Effectivity dates.

TABLE 5.8   Bill of Material File

Parent	Description	Engineering change level	Effective date in	Effective date out
1678	Running light	2*	12/4/94*†	0
1410	Light bulb	1	12/4/94	0
1798	Base	1	12/4/94	0
3715	Red/green lens	0	12/2/94	5/10/95
1003	Red/green lens	0	5/10/95	0

*Note: Engineering change would be to 3 on 5/10/95.

†Note: This date would change to 5/10/95 on 5/10/95.

a red/green plastic lens (1003) on 5/10/95. MRP II would automatically take care of planning the materials requirements to meet these dates.

Another method of incorporating engineering changes into production is the *cum* (*cumulative*) *number.* Some companies control production via cumulative release of products into production. Thus, if the current cum number being released into production is 1000 and the engineering-change control board has determined that the engineering change will be incorporated at cum number 2000 and the current product rate is 500 per month, the change will be incorporated 2 periods into the future. If the production rate should change to 1000 per month, the engineering change will be automatically incorporated in the next period. The attractive feature of this method is that changes are incorporated with little human intervention. Other methods of incorporating engineering changes include using:

- Order numbers
- Batch numbers
- Serial numbers
- Lot numbers
- Recipe numbers

Determining Product Costs.   Accounting uses the same bill of materials that the manufacturing personnel use. Their major use of the bill of materials is to calculate labor, material, and overhead costs on a level-by-level basis starting at the bottom of the bill of materials (along with routing data) and summing these costs level by level to the top of the bill of materials to calculate a total product cost of each top unit. This information is used for budgeting purposes as well as to track performance of the business by the individual function and by the entire operation. The information is also used by management to develop pricing strategies.

Accounting also uses information from the bills of materials and routings databases to value work-in-process inventory. The quantities of part numbers located at each operation are extended by the unit cost (material, labor, and overhead accumulated through the particular operation) and summed to determine the total value of work-in-process inventory.

Costed Bill of Materials.   Table 5.9 is an example of a costed bill of materials generated from a route sheet.

TABLE 5.9 Costed Bill of Materials

Part No.: 2250
Description: Light assembly

Component	Description	Units required	Unit of measure	Unit cost	Price or content	Manufactured			
						Total direct labor	Direct labor	Total overhead	Overhead
2250	Light assembly	1	Ea.	101.91[17]	48.00[12]	36.00[14]	18.00[13]	17.91[16]	9.36[15]
1310	Anchor light assembly	1	Ea.	31.00[11]	17.50[8]	9.00[9]	9.00[9]	4.50[10]	4.50[10]
1410	Light bulb	1	Ea.	7.50[7]	7.50[7]				
1798	Base	1	Ea.	5.00[7]	5.00[7]				
1510	Clear plastic lens	1	Ea.	5.00[7]	5.00[7]				
1890	Bracket	1	Ea.	8.00[6]	8.00[6]				
1678	Running light assembly	1	Ea.	35.55[5]	22.50[2]	9.00[3]	9.00[3]	4.05[4]	4.05[4]
1410	Light bulb	1	Ea.	7.50[1]	7.50[1]				
1798	Base	1	Ea.	5.00[1]	5.00[1]				
3715	Red/green plastic lens	1	Ea.	10.00[1]	10.00[1]				

Note: The superscript numbers refer to steps defined in the description of a "Costed Bill of Materials."

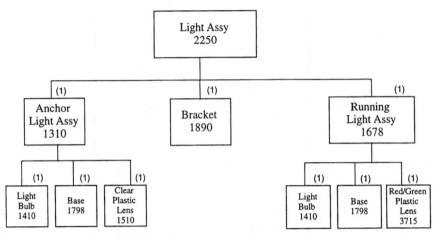

FIGURE 5.11 Bill of materials chart for the costed bill of materials example.

The quantity per unit of every component in the bill of materials is extended by the cost of the components. The costs include material, labor, and overhead. The example shows a costed bill of materials for the light assembly (2250) shown in the multilevel bill of materials in Fig. 5.11. The bill of material system would "explode" down the parts tree until it reached the bottom. Then it would "implode" back up the parts tree making the calculations shown in the following steps (the step numbers correspond to the superscript numbers on Table 5.9):

Example

Step 1. The purchase price and the unit cost of the red/green plastic lens (3715), the base (1798), and the light bulb (1410) are $10.00, $5.00, and $7.50, respectively. Since these are purchased parts, there is no direct labor or overhead costs associated with them.

Step 2. The purchased cost content of the running light assembly (1678) is $22.50, which is the sum of the purchase prices of the red/green plastic lens (3715), $10,00, the base (1798), $5.00, and the light bulb (1410), $7.50:

$$\$10.00/\text{part} + \$5.00/\text{part} + \$7.50/\text{part} = \$22.50/\text{part}$$

Step 3. The direct labor cost to assemble the red/green plastic lens (3715), the base (1798), and the light bulb (1410) for the running light assembly (1678) is $9.00/unit. The direct labor rate is $18.00/hour, and the production rate is 2.0 units/hour, or:

$$\$18.00/\text{hour} \times \frac{1 \text{ hour}}{2 \text{ units}} = \$9.00/\text{unit}$$

Step 4. The overhead and the total overhead for this operation is $4.05, which is the product of the overhead rate for this cost center, 45 percent, and the direct labor cost for this operation, or:

$$0.45 \times \$9.00/\text{hour} = \$4.05/\text{hour}$$

Step 5. The unit cost of the running light assembly (1678) is $35.55, which is the sum of the purchase content, $22.50/part, the total direct labor content, $9.00/part, and the total overhead content, or:

$$\$22.50/\text{part} + \$9.00/\text{part} + \$4.05/\text{part} = \$35.55/\text{part}$$

Step 6. The purchase price and the unit cost of the bracket (1890) is $8.00. Since this is a purchased part, there are no labor or overhead costs associated with it.

Step 7. The purchase price and the unit cost of the clear plastic lens (1510), the base (1798), and the light bulb (1410) are $5.00, $5.00, and $7.50, respectively. Since these are purchased parts, there are no labor or overhead costs associated with them.

Step 8. The purchased content of the anchor light assembly (1310) is $17.50/part, which is the sum of the purchase prices of the clear plastic lens (1510), $5.00, the base (1798), $5.00, and the light bulb (1410), $7.50, or:

$$\$5.00/\text{part} + \$5.00/\text{part} + \$7.50/\text{part} = \$17.50/\text{part}$$

Step 9. The total direct labor cost to assemble the clear plastic lens (1510), the base (1798), and the light bulb (1410) to produce the anchor light assembly (1310) is $9.00/unit. Assume a direct labor rate of $18.00/hour and a production rate of 2 units/hour:

$$\frac{\$18.00/\text{hour} \times 1 \text{ hour}}{2 \text{ units}} = \$9.00/\text{unit}$$

Step 10. The total overhead for this operation is $4.50, which is the product of the overhead rate, 50 percent, for this cost center, and the direct labor cost for this operation, $9.00:

$$0.50 \times \$9.00/\text{part} = \$4.50/\text{part}$$

Step 11. The unit cost of the anchor light assembly (1310) is $31.00, which is the sum of the purchased content, $17.50, the total direct labor content, $9.00, and the total overhead, $4.50:

$$\$17.50/\text{part} + \$9.00/\text{part} + \$4.50/\text{part} = \$31.00/\text{part}$$

Step 12. The purchased content of the light assembly is $48.00, which is the sum of the purchase prices of the running light assembly (1678), $22.50, the bracket (1890), $8.00, and the anchor light assembly (1310), $17.50:

$$\$22.50 + \$8.00 + \$17.50 = \$48.00$$

Step 13. The direct labor cost to assemble the running light assembly (1678), the bracket (1890) and the anchor light assembly (1310) to produce the light assembly (2250) is $18.00/unit (assume a direct labor rate of $18.00/hour and a production rate of 1 unit/hour):

$$\frac{\$18.00/\text{hour} \times 1 \text{ hour}}{1.0 \text{ unit}} = \$18.00/\text{unit}$$

Step 14. The total direct labor cost for the light assembly (2250) is the sum of the direct labor costs for the running light assembly (1678), $9.00, the anchor light assembly (1310), $9.00, and the light assembly (2250), $18.00:

$$\$9.00 + \$9.00 + \$18.00 = \$36.00$$

Step 15. The overhead for this operation is $9.36, which is the product of the overhead rate for this cost center, 52 percent, and the direct labor cost for this operation, $18.00:

$$0.52 \times \$18.00 = \$9.36$$

Step 16.   The total overhead for this operation is $17.91, which is the sum of the overhead for the running light assembly (1678), $4.05, the anchor light assembly (1310), $4.50, and the light assembly (2250), $9.36:

$$\$4.05 + \$4.50 + \$9.36 = \$17.91$$

Step 17.   The unit cost of the light assembly (2250) is $101.91, which is the sum of the purchased content, $48.00, the total labor content, $36.00, and the total overhead, $17.91:

$$\$48.00 + \$36.00 + \$17.91 = \$101.91$$

Service Products.   Eventually, parts will break or wear out. The information contained in the bills of materials and routings databases are retained so knowledge of how a particular product was built and the effective date is maintained in a product's history files. As customers require replacement parts, these files can be accessed to determine the proper parts the customer requires.

Processing Liability and Warranty Claims.   The manufacturer of heavy-duty truck brakes, mentioned earlier, must maintain a complete history of how each brake was manufactured. This entails maintaining the bill of material describing the parts used in the brakes via effective dates, and the routings describing the sequential steps used to produce the brake. The information is needed, along with the maintenance schedule of the product on which the brake was installed on. This information is used to prepare legal defenses for cases pending. Similar information is required to access warranty claims.

Accuracy of Bills of Materials and Routings

It is a generally accepted fact that the data contained in world-class bills of materials and routings databases should have an accuracy of 98 percent (or higher). But what does this mean?

Definition of Accuracy.   An *accuracy level of 98 percent (or higher)* means that 98 percent of a company's bills of materials and routings are 100 percent accurate and the remaining 2 percent of the bills of materials and routings have an accuracy of 98 percent or greater. The definition of *accurate bills of materials and/or routings* includes attributes such as the following:

- Having the right part numbers in the bill of materials database (i.e., a unique identifier must be properly defined for each component, subassembly, assembly, and top unit)
- Having the proper product structure in the bill of materials database (i.e., the "goes-into's" are properly defined)
- Having the proper quantities defined in the bill of materials database (i.e., the number of times a component or subassembly is used in its parent)
- Having the proper operation numbers, and the operations sequences in the routings database reflecting exactly how the products are manufactured and/or assembled on the shop floor
- Having the proper time standards, setup times, and labor grades or rates in the routings database

This begs the question, "How do you know the accuracy of your bills of materials and routings?"

Determining accuracy. There are a number of ways of determining the accuracy of bills of materials and routings including the following:

- *Disassembling a finished product.* Basically, a product is disassembled, and every assembly, subassembly, and component part is compared to the bills of material to verify part numbers, usage, units of measure, and so on. A manufacturer of computers forms a team of all the people using the bill of materials (e.g., sales, engineering, manufacturing, accounting, and service) and essentially takes a finished product and takes it apart assembly by assembly, subassembly by subassembly, and part by part and compares the results to the bills of material for the product being audited. An alternative to this approach would be to compare the bill of materials to the product structure as the product is built. This latter approach can also be used to verify that the routings map the manufacturing process. Either approach is a time-consuming and an expensive way of determining the accuracy of the bills of materials and routings. However, the determination could be done on a random basis, with the frequency being established according to the results of the audits.

- *Walking the line.* This method entails obtaining a hard copy of a routing for a particular product, determining when the product is going to be built, and physically following the product as it is built. The information on the hard copy is then verified against what actually occurs on the shop floor.

- *Tracing the causes of excess inventory.* This is an excellent area to enlist the help of the shop floor personnel. It is noted that whenever more parts are delivered to production than are needed or whenever the wrong parts are delivered, it is possible that the usage rates in the bills of material are incorrect or the bills of material are improperly structured. These occurrences should be reported by shop floor personnel and corrected by individuals responsible for maintaining the bill of materials database.

- *Tracing the causes of material shortages.* Checking with shop floor or stockroom personnel to determine which parts are chronically short will provide information that can be used to determine if the bill of materials is incorrect. The shortages could be caused by scrap occurring at earlier operations or by vendors' being late in delivering material; however, it could also mean that the bill of materials have incorrect usages or they are improperly structured.

- *Comparing standard costs of similar products.* Use the standard software costing modules to accumulate material and purchased costs of similar products and compare the results. This method will give an indication of how accurate the information in the bills of materials and routings databases is. This approach, unfortunately, identifies the problem after parts have been ordered, production schedules have been set, and promises have been made to customers.

- *Other approaches.* An additional way of monitoring the accuracy of the bill of materials is to simply perform spot-checks on the various data elements. The following data can be reviewed for correctness (many of these may vary due to company policy):

  Parts can either be purchased or manufactured. Because of capacity constraints or other reasons, a part may be both purchased and manufactured at the same time. The part source is coded as B for both or E for either.

  Units of measure for fluids need to be expressed as volumes such as gallons, pints, or ounces.

Costs may be in dollars per 100 units.

Commodity codes follow a certain specified format.

Descriptions follow a certain specified format.

Product codes follow a certain specified format.

Operation codes usually follow a specific format.

Whatever method or methods are chosen to determine the accuracy of the bills of materials and the routings, specific data should be chosen to be measured.

Selecting Data Elements.   Recently an accuracy study was conducted at a $1.6 billion heavy-equipment manufacturer. In addition to verifying that the proper part numbers were in the bills and routings, specific data elements were selected for verification. For determining the accuracy of the bill of materials, data elements verified included the following:

- Make-buy codes
- Quantities of usage
- Amount of usage (i.e., each, ounces, feet, etc.)
- Family codes
- Component part numbers used

For verifying the accuracy of the routings, data elements verified included the following:

- Labor codes or grades
- Machine codes
- Materials used (e.g., gloves)
- Operation codes
- Pay points.

Matrices were constructed with these data elements listed across the top and the part numbers to be verified down the side. Pass-fail indicators were entered into the matrices, and the overall estimated accuracy was determined for the bills of materials database and the routings database.

BIBLIOGRAPHY

Clement, J., A. Coldrick, and J. Sari: *Manufacturing Data Structures,* Maple-Vale Book Manufacturing Group, York, Pa., 1992.

Garwood, D.: *Bills of Material—Structured for Excellence,* Dogwood Publishing Company, Marietta, Ga., 1988.

Greene, J. H.: *Production & Inventory Control Handbook,* McGraw-Hill, New York, 1987.

Mather, H.: *Bills of Materials,* Dow Jones-Irwin, Homewood, Ill., 1987.

Wallace, T. F., and J. R. Dougherty: *APICS Dictionary,* 7th ed., American Production and Inventory Control Society, Falls Church, Va., 1992.

Veen, E. A. v.: *Modelling Product Structures by Generic Bills of Materials,* Elsevier Science Publishers, New York, 1992.

CHAPTER 6
PROCESS INFORMATION

Editor
Frank Gue
Partner, Industrial Education Services,
Burlington, Ontario, Canada

Process information (PI) is used in industries making products that are discrete (i.e., countable), made by assembling pieceparts and subassemblies, multilevel (i.e., having more than one level of assembly), and/or made either to order or to stock. Examples of such products would range from consumer electronics (high volume, low value) to heavy industrial equipment (low volume, high value). This does not exclude high-production makers of products such as soft drinks or pharmaceuticals; however, such manufacturers' process information is generally embedded in a plant layout and expressed in such units as gallons per hour. In these plants, product assembly synchronization is built directly into such things as the piping layouts and the chained feeding assembly and packaging lines.

A generic picture of how a manufacturer operates is shown in Table 6.1. Activities 4 and 5 will use the firm's on-file PI in varying degrees. Activities 6, 7, and 8 result in the creation of PI. Activities 9, 12, and 13 are made possible by existence of the PI. Process

TABLE 6.1 Business Activities of a Manufacturing Firm

1. Interpret customer requirements.
2. Negotiate the order.
3. Get the order.
4. Interpret the order.
5. Design the product.
6. Design the manufacturing process.
7. Plan the manufacturing process.
8. Interpret the manufacturing plan.
9. Build the product per plan.
10. Ship the product.
11. Bill the customer.
12. Administer field service and warranty matters.
13. Place details of the order in the company archives.

information occupies a vital position in the ability of the firm to operate day to day and to be an ongoing concern. Thus it is easy to see why all industries fitting the above product description use PI. In small firms making simple products, the PI will exist only in the minds of a few key people. Medium-sized firms will have varying degrees of computer support, from simple storage of PI for printing out when needed, to computer-based *materials requirements planning* (MRP) *systems* having varying degrees of integration with the financial and other branches of the firm. Larger firms making more complex products will have PI stored in digital form and will use comprehensive computerized *decision support systems* (DSSs) to assist the workforce to manufacture quality products on time at the best cost. Advanced plants increasingly will be linking their scheduled, exploded PI by wire or radio to production machines, providing part of the electronic instructions. This is a *computer-integrated manufacturing* (CIM) *environment,* in which the boundaries between the business activities become blurred, despite which all the listed activities must and do take place.

DEFINITION OF PROCESS INFORMATION

PI is the documentation, on either paper or computerized medium, of the resources needed to create a product and the sequence in which they are to be applied. Note that PI does not include the technical detail of the performance of complex processes.

Traditionally, process information has concentrated almost exclusively on the actual performance of the task. This has led to such wastes as the production of large stocks of faulty parts, followed much later by expensive and usually fruitless searches for what went wrong and whom to blame. In contrast, PI suitable for synchronized-flow manufacturing is based upon:

1. Technology, such as fast-reacting sales-tracking systems assuring prompt delivery of only those products desired by the customer
2. Factory organization such as the flexible work cell where the "customer" can detect faulty production 30 seconds after it has occurred
3. A rethinking of traditional wisdom, which has spawned the *economical order quantity* (EOQ) *system* in which a setup cost of zero leads directly to small-lot, stockless production

Process information supporting flow manufacturing enables the documentation of the parts, labor, tooling, and other resources, and their structure, required to manufacture a product. High-quality PI includes many non-cost-generating functions traditionally omitted from it, such as:

- Inspection, customer witness
- Process times (paint cure, anneal)
- Stock picking
- Subcontract intervals
- Upstream functions such as engineering design and drafting and customer drawing approvals
- Downstream functions such as shipment to the customer

Many of these flow-related items are omitted from the PI because cost accounting does not assign costs to them. However, accounting practices too have undergone dramatic changes in recent years, and it is recognized that accounting must be driven by manufacturing necessity rather than vice versa.

Process information is conventionally written for a quantity of *one*. Flow production planning and scheduling then explodes and multiplies the PI out to support a rate of production (for repetitive manufacture) or a *batch* [from one up, for high-value, made-to-order (MTO) goods]. A complex product may, of course, demand thousands of such things as rivets or laminations, and the PI must support this. These functions are dealt with elsewhere in this handbook; here we will study the PI itself.

Several comments in this section will show that the nature of PI, its appearance, and the way it is stored and used are changing rapidly under the influence of fast-evolving electronic data interchange among computers. This might be mistaken to mean that the importance of PI is diminishing equally rapidly. The reverse is true. With fewer and fewer people handling information that is moving ever more rapidly, there are two serious risks:

• Computerized mediocrity and obsolescence are such that PI could easily reflect the factory as it was some time ago simply because it is cheap to store and retrieve data but costly to find and revise it

• Storing, processing, and transmitting is so efficient that inaccurate data from sources such as the bill of materials can quickly spread throughout the system.

Manufacturing is moving toward reduced volumes of output paper that must, nonetheless, derive from accurate and detailed PI. As factories move toward CIM, accurate PI becomes an even more rigorous demand.

PI is usually written a page at a time. Each page describes the manufacture of one item (piece-part or assembly). The page is divided as follows:

• Header information containing administrative detail such as order number

• Labor information detailing routings, time values, etc.

• Materials bill

A "page" may, of course, have several sheets in the case of complex components or products.

Some PI is written with labor and materials bills blended, particularly where it is important that material be fed into the process partway through. This acknowledges that "a resource is a resource" and that the distinctions between labor resources and materials resources should diminish.

PI's CENTRAL PLACE IN THE ENVIRONMENT

Figure 6.1 is a model of a net-change information system in a manufacturer. PI is the documentation vehicle making blocks 2 and 14 work. Study of this model will reveal that blocks 2 and 14 either drive or are driven by every important function in the information flow. It must be realized, of course, that BOMP, or bill of materials processor, is a traditional term that now encompasses all resources, not merely materials. BOMP is the function that identifies, explodes, structures, and multiplies out all the detailed resources required to make the product. It is driven by the master schedule and final assembly schedule and is supported by the PI database maintained by technical personnel in box 14. From this, it can be seen that PI controls, initiates, or influences almost all that a manufacturing firm does. It can and should be a powerful integrating influence

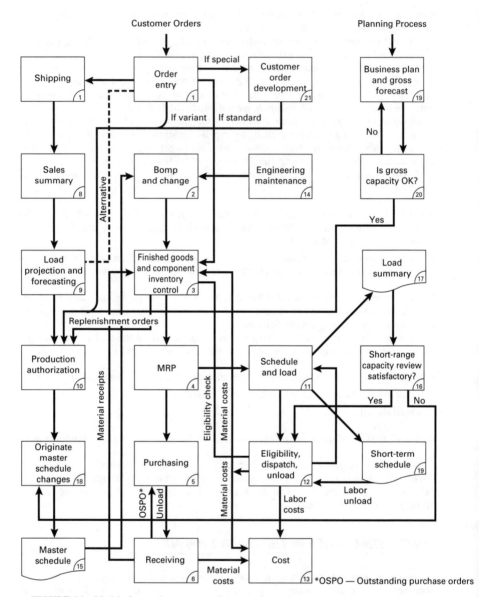

FIGURE 6.1   Model of a net change system for a manufacturer

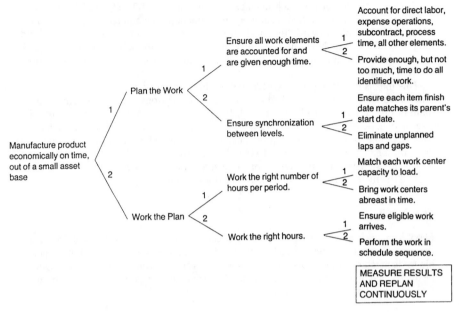

FIGURE 6.2 Broad-brush picture of manufacturing activities.

upon the operation of the firm and must not be delegated too low in the organization nor staffed by less than the best technical people.

Figure 6.2 is a broad-brush picture of manufacturing activities. Everything that must happen to produce economically and on time depends upon the top branch of the flowchart, plan the work. For successful manufacturing, everything below the top two items on the right depends upon high-quality PI. In total quality management (TQM) or similar umbrella philosophies, quality of planning ranks very high because it makes time-based, synchronized production possible. The core of this plan is the firm's PI.

RESERVATIONS AND WARNINGS

PI systems often depend upon hidden assumptions and call for too much, or too little, detail.

The Assumptions

Many requirements planning systems assume that:

1. Products should be highly standardized.
2. Runs should be long to get maximum economy.
3. Assembly should be done by drawing on ample parts stocks.
4. Parts should be made in large batches to optimize setup costs.

However, the lessons of such management practices as JIT, TQM, IRM, and synchronized production, are that customers are demanding customized products, which drives manufacturers toward "the ideal lot size of one." Therefore, they cannot afford long runs. They must have the capability of fast reaction to market signals and quick setups. They must "manufacture nothing which cannot be sold immediately at a profit" (Toyota Motor Co.).

This means that PI must be written with no bias toward such things as a "minimum order quantity"; it must not embed any arbitrary assumptions such as charging a minimum of one full sheet of plastic or steel. It must strongly support the concept of a lot size of one. A manufacturer would not, of course, make commodities like lamps in batches of one; however, if a traditional batch size is 50,000, a manufacturer could well drive for a batch size of 25,000 or 10,000. But nonetheless, the PI will be written for 1 lamp. This suggests that the writers of PI must assume a technical responsibility much beyond the mere clerical-administrative one often assumed.

The Detail

Flexible manufacturing systems (FMSs), U-cell layouts, and so on, reduce drastically the control demands once needed. PI must reflect this realistically by making it possible to dispatch one operation called "make" to cover numerous operations that used to be dispatched one at a time. However, the PI must not as a result become so abbreviated that the what-how much-who-where-when detail is lost.

THE INTERACTION OF PRODUCT STRUCTURE AND PI

PI must tie in closely with whatever structuring system is used to satisfy such marketing problems as options and configurations. Failure to integrate marketing, engineering, and manufacturing structuring is a major cause of high overhead, long premanufacturing cycles, and serious error. This is particularly true in firms specializing in manufacture-to-order (MTO) goods.

Marketing Versus Manufacturing Structuring

Most discussions of structuring deal with options available to customers and control of the resulting inventories, and so on. However, when an actual order reaches the factory, all these choices have been made, and the concern of the shop people is the unique structure of this order. The shop must know what goes into what to make what. PI must accurately portray these goes-into relationships. Upon this structure will depend all hope for synchronized production and traceability for U.S. Department of Defense (DOD) products and similar work.

Human- and Computer-Sensible Structuring

An ideal structure will do the following:

1. Clearly link each component with its parent ("where used") and with the resources required to make it ("where found").
2. Peg every item to its parent and through intermediate levels to the top level of the product.

3. Have numbers that are instantly readable by personnel and not demand a mental linking of "boxcar numbers." Letters and numbers should be an aid to the memory, assisting the shop personnel to recognize a language that is consistent from order to order.

4. Have identification that is computer readable and computer sortable.

5. Be flexible and tolerant in accepting changes.

6. Be robust, that is, not dependent upon artificial factors such as line sequence, order of citation, or date entered, etc.

7. Embed the level number of the part.

A Practical Structuring System

Fortunately, all of these demands can be met. The old Dewey Decimal System for classifying library books, the newer MRP indentation systems, and the much newer DOS or Windows directory systems using binary search[1] are examples.

One well-tried system, developed some time ago but closely related to the newer binary search, is the alphabetic symbolization system shown in Table 6.2.

TABLE 6.2 Alphabetic Symbolization

Level	Symbol	Description
0	M	The main assembly, final assembly, or master schedule item (example: a motor)
1	C	A component of M (example: a junction box)
2	CA	A component of C (example: a box, wall, or foot)
1	F	Another component of M (example: a stator assembly)
2	FR	A component of F (example: a core-coil assembly)
3	FRL	A component of FR (example: a stacked core)

This simple symbolized structuring technique (variously called the Symbolized Interval Chart and the Trail Code, as well as other names) is in addition to the usual engineering-drawing identifications, which often have few, if any, of the features of the "ideal" system above. The alphabetic symbolization system also provides one more degree of flexibility because the PI writer or engineer can use existing, unstructured drawings, customers' drawings, and so on, to work on a new order without having to originate drawing changes. Note that the level number shown is for illustration only, and it need not appear on the PI. A count of the characters in the symbol will tell a person or the computer what the level is.

A similar way of recording product structures is the indented parts list, a familiar document in all MRP systems. It contains much the same information, except that the parent-component relationship is not built into the identification, as it is in the symbolization scheme.

Modern computerized inquiry systems make it very easy to produce other useful sorts of reports generated from the PI file such as:

- Where-used listings showing all the parent products calling for a given item.

- Indented listings, amplifying the main where-used listing and showing all the parent-component relationships for a given item, up to the top level, indented to identify changes of assembly level.

- Planned-cost roll-ups in which a computer program compares the indented bill of materials against the standard cost files and costs out the labor and material and reports both the total cost of the finished item and the costs of all intermediate components and levels. Such a cost roll-up can be done on a simulation basis without requiring a customer order, or as part of processing actual factory orders. It is valuable for forecasting cost and monitoring. Such a facility is a vital component of advanced corporate functions such as determining cash flow of investments and inventory forecasting.

PROCESS INFORMATION AS A MODEL

The process information is a paper or digital model of a product or part. It is the medium by which engineering (product design) information becomes practical instructions on how the product is to be made in the plant. The first representation of this product model is created by engineers and draftspersons for an engineered product and is invariably one or some combination of documents going by many names, such as an *engineering drawing, process specification, parts list, bill of materials, test letter, design specification, electrical specification, recipe, blend sheet,* and *mix spec.* These original documents lean heavily toward what is to be made, very little toward how many, how, when, where, or by whom.

Some industries making semistandard products will use an estimating department to generate the original information for an order; this department draws on a bank of predetermined configuration combinations, almost invariably computer supported. The ideal origin for information for such products, of course, is the customer: He or she selects options and configurations from which the computer program creates engineering information directly.

Many firms, when reengineering their administrative and overhead processes, have questioned the need for separate engineering bills of materials and process information. They note that most bill of materials information has to be transcribed verbatim to PI, with attendant cost, delay, and error. They have found, in some cases, that most of their so-called drawing changes are actually changes in the bill of materials, not the graphic itself. Such changes need to be integrated tightly with manufacturing in the interests of time phasing the changes, phasing-in and phasing-out, release control, and sometimes public safety. Some firms either routinely or at least some of the time separate their materials bills from their drawings and convert them to PI, thus eliminating several complex and costly administrative procedures.

Combined with the engineering information in drawings and specifications, and exploded from the master schedule by MRP, the PI then forms a complete description of:

- What is to be made or done (name, drawing item, and issue number, etc.)
- How much is to be made or done (which is used by other elements of the DSS to identify factory loads and materials requirements out into the future)
- By whom it is to be made (which identifies skill demands and machine loads)
- From what it is to be made (raw materials, other pieceparts, etc.)
- Where (on what machines, in what facilities, by which subcontractors, etc.)
- How it is to be made (i.e., the sequence in which resources are to be applied.)

Note, once more, that this list does *not* include detailed specifications for highly technical processes.

Process information being discussed in this section supplies only information to make one item; other system elements do scheduling and system housekeeping such as summarizing all loads by plant location, by day, or by week, and so on. However, it bears reemphasizing that the vital functions shown in box 11 of the net change model (Fig. 6.1) are only as good as the PI on which they are based. Later an acceptable PI will be illustrated.

The Resources That Build up the Model

A resource is, quite simply, anything that is required to obtain a manufacturing result, which is usually (not always) the production of a usable part or a saleable product. The most common resources are:

- Labor-hours used in the plant, the drafting room, purchase department, or wherever
- Machine-hours used on a milling machine or a CAD work station
- Elapsed hours or process time, such as cure a finish, heat-treat, send out subcontract work
- Tooling required to make the product or part
- Raw materials and parts from stock
- Engineering drawings and specifications
- Bought-out parts, materials, and services
- The area of an assembly bay, since both area and time together determine the capacity of such facilities

Study of this list reveals that PI is far more than a bill of materials, a bill of labor, or some combination. For example:

- Firms can just as easily schedule completion of engineering designs and drawings as completion of work on a milling machine. A resource requirements (logistics) planning system need not know the difference between a buyer's desk and a lathe.
- Drawings and tools are resources too. They can and should be scheduled by an explosion from the bill of materials. Drawings can be produced "just in time" so that they are the latest issue. Tools can be treated as if they were parts in the MRP runs, complete with automatically generated "replenishment orders" to resharpen after 10,000 pieces.
- Outside suppliers can and should be treated the same as inside work stations. An outside supplier is just one of the work stations that happens to be owned by someone else. This leads naturally into the following subject of PI and its contribution to integration.

INTEGRATION AND PI

The hallmark of good systems is that they are integrated. In the case of PI, this means minimizing the differences among resources by removing artificial barriers that force us unnecessarily to treat as different the labor, materials, tools, drawings, process specifications, and so on, that make up a product. All the steps in the process should be included in scheduling—not merely those generating costs, but also such activities as engineering design, tool design, and drafting. Properly constructed PI enables a firm to generate clear, unambiguous information for the entire manufacturing team. This has enormous benefits such as eliminating informal manual systems for tools or drawings, improving relations with suppliers, reducing animosity among departments, providing a common language (based on time) that all members of the organization can speak in their routine work, and providing the basis for concurrent design. PI, then, is an important, central component of the systems of any manufacturing firm working toward a fully integrated environment.

INFORMATION SUPPORTING PI

PI does not stand alone but depends for its creation upon the existence of numerous sources of information, such as resources, dates, and dating.

Resources, Dates, and Dating

Among the most important components of this support system are (a) a resources file, (b) a scheduling template, and (c) a skeleton PI (where-used) file.

The Resources Files.   A record of data items such as a unique identification number, location, and capacity is kept in the resources file. The materials portion is usually subdivided into raw materials, parts, and perhaps other components divided more for accounting needs than for manufacturing convenience. The materials file is included in other sections of the handbook. Here we will discuss the labor (work center) file, the Monday dates file, the symbolized interval chart, and the skeleton PI file. These files are critical in any effort to meet the objectives to "manufacture economically, on time, out of a small asset base."

The Work Center File.   In time-based, synchronized manufacturing, virtually everything one does is based upon the interplay between demands upon resources and the capacity, over time, of those resources to meet those demands. Accordingly, PI is the meeting of these two: the demands and the resources. All work shown on the PI must pass through work centers that have been clearly documented and made available to the scheduling system. This documentation is kept in the work center file.

A work center is a place where certain work is done. Lathes, CAD machines, computer work stations, assembly benches, buyers' desks, and inspection stations are all work centers. A work center may consist of one or several closely related facilities or machines. A work center file contains one record per work center. Each record will contain, at minimum, the following items of data:

- A unique identification number, often consisting of a department number and a sequential number within the department
- A Company asset number
- Description (very brief, perhaps 20 to 25 characters)
- Some measure of capacity (hours per day, shifts, tons, etc.)
- A pointer to an alternative work center also capable of doing this work, if there is one

Additional information is needed as firms progress into labor requirements planning and other more sophisticated systems. The extended list below should not be considered a recommendation or requirement but merely an aid to the memory.

- A capacity profile extending into the future, reflecting staffing plans through time (just as an MRP system does with materials) (This type of profile will enable the firm to plan effectively around such things as shutdowns for maintenance or installation of new equipment.)
- Allocating an area for a large assembly work center where area and time, rather than time alone, govern capacity
- A never-exceed capacity figure
- Queue-control characters
- A multiplier by which estimated times are to be determined for scheduling purposes (Note the warning elsewhere in this chapter covering queuing and multipliers.)
- A major location identifier in multiplant firms if transit time between plants must be allowed for in the schedule

The Symbolized Interval Chart. Referring to the earlier broad-brush picture, Fig. 6.2, it is clear that PI must accomplish the following in the information in the upper branch, which is repeated here:

1. Account for direct labor expense operations, subcontractors, process time, and all other elements.
2. Provide enough, but not too much, time to do all the identified work.

These two points underlie much of this chapter.

The scheduling subsystem does the work contained in the next two components of the plan:

1. Ensure that each item's finish date matches its parent's start date.
2. Eliminate unplanned laps and gaps.

It is capable of doing this only if the first two items, contained in the PI, are accurate.

Coordinating the Parts

A Structuring Template. Implied in the net change model is the existence of an intermediate piece of time-based information, which is the structure of the product being made. The structure connects parts, subassemblies, and final assemblies in a coherent *goes-into network* that makes synchronized schedules possible. Equally important for some manufacturers—particularly those making high-value, low-volume products with long cycle times—is that the structure can be used as a scheduling template. Refer to Fig. 6.3, a scheduling template or symbolized interval chart.

In such a template, the branches are assigned time intervals. It is then an elementary exercise for the computer to connect these into a synchronized schedule similar to a PERT chart. But equally important, such a template makes it possible for the plant with long cycles to begin work on the earliest-wanted parts of a complex order long before the parts needed later have been designed. This frees manufacturing from one of its most severe constraints—the need to have complete information before production can be started. Firms using these techniques typically have scores of these templates in data storage. The PI writer, in consultation with engineering, decides which template, or which *same-as-except template,* is suitable and constructs the information structure on that template for a period of time.

①	②	③	④	⑤	
APP CLASS	MFG SYMBOL	INTERVAL DAYS	ADVANCE DAYS	COMPONENT NAME	
F	-M	5	0	INLET CYL ASSEMBLE	
F	R	4	5	INLET CYL COVER M/C	
F	RA	7	9	INLET CYL COVER FAB	
F	RAA	6	16	CYL DETAILS MAKE	
F	RAC	2	16	G.C. TEMPLATE MAKE	
F	U	6	5	STRUT ASSY FAB	
F	UD	8	11	STRUT RING ASSEM TACK &	
etc					
	etc				
		etc			
			etc		

FIGURE 6.3   Symbolized interval chart. (*Courtesy Power Generation Canadian Division, Westinghouse Canada, Inc.*)

Naturally, at times there is no prepared template that will fit the product precisely. However, experienced practitioners are able to readily identify—or revise—a model that is accurate enough for the purpose. Invariably it is found that the enormous benefits of synchronized production far outweigh any lack of perfection in the templates being used. Further, it is a simple matter to have the computer identify gross differences during the scheduling function, between the model being used and the actual product, and warn the user to take one of several kinds of rescheduling action.

Accordingly, it must be recognized that some kind of structuring model—for example, indented or symbolized—is also a vital part of process information, although it never appears as such at any given moment on the PI being created.

Scheduling or structuring templates should be avoided if the product is standardized, has a sufficiently high volume, and has a short cycle time to make the issue of complete information possible the moment it is required. Avoiding these templates in these situations is possible because the structure is fully and adequately portrayed in the PI itself. The scheduling program in effect creates a unique, this-order-only structure directly from the PI. Naturally, it is helpful if the program also writes out some key, symbol, or audit trail code to assist personnel.

Explanation of the scheduling template (see circled numbers on Fig. 6.3):

1. This is the *apparatus class,* or call name, of the model. More than one character may be needed.
2. The *manufacturing symbol* has been described elsewhere in this chapter. The characters -M are used at the start to force the main assembly to the top of the sort since the leading hyphen sorts first in ASCII code.
3. The *interval* is the expected time required to manufacture the item.
4. The *advance* is the number of days in advance of the final ship date this particular component must finish to remain on schedule.

5. The *component name* is written in a form similar to military stores' vocabulary—that is, the identifying noun (e.g., STRUT) is first, followed by modifiers as required. This method of expressing part names and operations has many advantages, such as facilitating the sorting of a list to bring together all the STRUTs or facilitating group technology work.

The Skeleton PI File.   On-file process information is simultaneously a great convenience and a big millstone, leading to long response times as the system searches through gigabytes of information. A skeleton PI is a little like an index file in a database program; it contains only "finder" and "structure" (or goes-into) information. It can be quickly searched for a called PI, which can then be accessed directly by the main system without further searching.

Combined Use of the Scheduling Template and the Skeleton PI File.   The use of the scheduling template with the skeleton PI file is usually necessary. Where prewritten, permanent PI is on file, it can be used 100 percent for wholly standard products such as industrial induction motors. The computer system explodes "PI on PI" down to the bottom level. The scheduling template is not needed for scheduling (even though the PI may be "symbolized" by the computer because it is such a convenient information device).

Where there is no permanent, prewritten PI, typical of some fully made-to-order (MTO) products such as large waterwheel generators, a template must be developed per order, and the skeleton PI file and the on-file PI are not used at all.

No PI explosion is done, and the computer fits the bits and pieces into the template as the information arrives from engineering and schedules them accordingly, not needing to know what comes between the top level and the bottom. However, many products use a mixture. Typically they seem like an MTO product at the top levels but a standard product at lower levels. The latter calls on-file PI for standard components. Products made in MRP shops that require a final assembly schedule (FAS) to create the customer's option combination typify this mixed mode. (As an aside, this is one of the major differences between factories that can use classical MRP and those that cannot.) Factories that cannot use MRP must, nevertheless, use good requirements planning to achieve synchronized production.[2]

ESTIMATING PROCESS INFORMATION

Process information can be viewed as a collection of estimates of what resources are required to produce a part or product. Efficient manufacturing depends upon the quality of these estimates. *Quality* does not imply impractical degrees of precision, as explained in the following discussion.

Estimating Labor

Labor time estimates for PI come from many sources: time studies, standard time formulas based on time studies, synthetic time systems, semiautomated methods involving videocameras or self-time-study by NC machines, and, often enough, personal guesses by qualified people.

There is a conflict between the need for time standards to schedule and estimate costs effectively and the need to control the overhead costs of developing and maintaining time standards. This problem can be eased by observing commonsense rules of thumb. Careful review of these suggestions will show that small-to-medium manufacturing enterprises (SMMEs) wishing to use good computerized systems need not despair merely because they do not have big industrial engineering departments. Small companies need not think that better endowed firms can get better standard time coverage and better scheduling at lower cost.

As in many situations in manufacturing, there is no exactly right way to develop time estimates; however, there are several ways that are "not wrong."

Pareto's Principle

According to this principle, in any array of numbers, a very few members of the array will account for those of the most importance—for example, 14 percent of inventory stocked items may account for 87 percent of dollar activity, and so forth. (This is not an "80-20 law." There is no such mathematical law.) Pareto's principle suggests that the work crossing a very few work centers or products in a plant may warrant time study but the majority can be subjected to a watch check or an intelligent estimate.

Accuracy Versus Precision

A precise time standard might have five significant figures—for example, 2.3456 hours to perform a certain operation. Such precision, or *closeness of measurement,* is very costly. The rule of thumb for machined parts is that the addition of one significant figure to a machined dimension (such as a diameter) doubles the cost of obtaining that dimension. Developing a time standard obviously must follow some rule. In most practical cases, what is wanted is not precision but accuracy—freedom from blunders. Seldom would it be essential to state the time value more precisely than 2.34 hours, quite precise enough for most purposes. All that said, however, it must be recognized that, in very high production environments yielding a high volume of low-value products, the expenditure or saving of a thousandth of an hour per piece may have important cost implications. In the manufacture of aluminum beverage cans, a 1 percent saving in metal can reduce the annual cost by scores of millions of dollars. Good judgment is needed in determining the optimal degree of precision in applying time standards.

Available Talent

The knowledge of experienced floor people can be of use in setting time values which are suitably accurate even if not precise. Labor times as used by experienced salespeople for bidding on jobs are often sufficiently accurate for shop purposes. If they are good enough to use to land jobs that make money, they may very well be good enough to use in managing the shop.

Number Sure to Be Wrong

One sometimes finds PI written without time values "because we don't have any standards for that operation." While no one in the firm may be in a position to give the "right" time estimate, an estimate of zero is sure to be wrong. In these situations, someone must make a suitable guess and be willing to stand by the guess and follow up with whatever corrective actions are possible and economical.

Fictitious Labor Content

Occasions arise when a number of parts should be marshalled, positioned for assembly, held awaiting purchased items, and so on. Most PI pages (see the definition of a *page* elsewhere) fit into our manufacturing systems better if there is labor associated with the material to be marshalled or obtained from an outside supplier, or subcontracted. Most systems—indeed, probably all computer systems— look for a labor operation to schedule. It is quite in order to provide a fictitious labor line reading, for example, "Draw from stores," or "Heat treat interval," or "Send out for keyboard assembly." It is merely necessary to code this labor line so that it trips the scheduling logic but does not trip any costing logic.

Queueing

Industrial experience worldwide shows that work-in-process is idle from 20 to 95 percent of the time. It is wise to leave queuing calculations to the computerized scheduling program and not build them into the PI. Every factory has its strong opinions for or against this or that way to provide for queuetime. However, some systems do provide features, sometimes called *multipliers,* that multiply the time value by some reasonable figure to approximate a queue time. The writer of PI may be asked to include this feature in the PI, but he or she should not volunteer to do so. Queuing is caused by factors entirely outside of the control and direction of the PI writer.

Accounting Drivers

Some firms diligently measure labor efficiency by dividing *the allowed time reported by the attendance time reported.* Progressive firms now understand that this, of all things to measure, is a poor one. Plants that do not pay on an incentive basis can spare themselves by not using this almost useless measurement. This is not to suggest that labor efficiency is unimportant, merely that reporting it this way and using it for "clubbing" supervisors or operators is not helpful. If a firm's PI supports labor efficiency measurements, an effort should be made to disconnect it. Recognize that a *standard time* is an estimate of what should happen when human and machine performance are "normal"; thus it is a very useful point of reference, and that is all.

HOW THE ESTIMATES SUPPORT THE SCHEDULING FUNCTION

Nonlabor Intervals

Many steps in the manufacturing processes, though very important to the scheduling function, carry no costs into the total product cost but nevertheless must be included in the PI. Examples of such nonlabor intervals are *heatruns* or *burn-ins*; annealing and case-hardening; curing of paint; and sending out for subcontract work. Every effort must be made to write a PI so the firm's computerized scheduling system can recognize a no-cost interval and schedule it properly without creating unwanted cost impacts. Some systems make this very easy by offering the PI writer a one-character "time code" that identifies for the computer the kind of time being called for, either chargeable or elapsed.

Overlap

Sequential operations for large quantities of parts (such as oriented-iron laminations for electrical apparatus) can result in the accumulation of large batches between operations. This can be avoided if the system overlaps operations. For example, begin operation 20 as soon as sufficient parts are on hand from operation 10. This overlapping is sometimes controlled by the PI and sometimes by the expert scheduling system. The PI writer must be knowledgeable about the system so that this can be done smoothly.

Batching

Some steps in manufacturing are necessarily done in batches such as one heat-treating furnace load. Labor writeups that simply list operations in sequence using the hidden assumption that parts can be processed one at a time break down here, forcing floor people to improvise around the faulty schedule. PI should be written to recognize batching by some computer signal in the labor line. This will be shown later.

Material Schedule Tie-In

Assembly of heavy equipment may take days or weeks, with costly subassemblies or purchased components not needed for some time after the assembly starts. The PI should provide the computer system with a specific instruction to "read" so that the scheduling system can date the material appropriately. For example, a $15,000 bushing called up on line 14 of the materials bill may not be required until operation 25 of the labor bill, three weeks into final assembly. The labor line for operation 25 might read, "Line 14, assemble...." The program then picks up the materials-wanted date from the labor written on line 25. Some newer systems are capable of handling mixed labor and materials bills, in which materials lines are interwoven with labor lines and take their dates directly from their position in the labor writeup.

Writing for Automated Assembly

Writers of PI that include automated machining or assembly operations are spared extensive instructions because the NC tape takes care of the moment-by-moment movement of parts and machinery. Nevertheless, some means must be found to carry the total time interval for the automated portion of the work into the PI. Otherwise the overall schedule and process coordination will suffer. Refer again to the net change model, which applies equally to automated or manual environments.

Estimating Materials

Units of Measure.   Depending upon the application there are three potential units of measure for materials: usage (square feet of plate steel), purchase (pounds of steel), and stores (sheets of steel). For any given material, all three units of measure may be different, although usually two will be the same. PI must state requirements in usage units. For example, plate steel is used by the square foot despite the fact that it may be bought by the pound and stored by the sheet. The DSS must be able to convert square feet to a dollar charge such as $/lb, for purchasing purposes. The writers of PI must observe the units of measure implied or shown on the engineering drawing. The conversion of these to stores or purchasing units must be left to the decision support system personnel who must have a table of units of measure with the necessary conversion factors and costs.

Such a units of measure (UM) table will contain possibly 50 to 100 UMs, such as PC for piece, GL for gallon, and BF for board foot. Each item in the table will have at least the following fields.

- Usage unit of measure: Square feet (SF)
- Stores unit of measure: Sheet (SH)
- Purchase unit of measure: Pound (LB)
- Cost per reference unit: Often cost per purchase unit ($/LB)
- Conversion factors from each unit to the reference unit: 0.258 SF of some steel equals 1.56 LB, from which the cost can then be computed. Materials control will state a "reference unit of measure" for a material that is the firm's common way of speaking about it, for example, lubrication oil, usually purchased and referred to "by the gallon" is often ordered and used by the ounce or drum. The reference unit of measure in the resources file would be "gal" with accompanying units of ounces and DRM and a conversion factor for each, so that the program can move smoothly from gallon to ounces or drums as requested for, say, costing usage.

Quantity Required.   Reasonably accurate materials call-ups are essential, especially in high-production environments because a small percentage error becomes very large when considering purchasing, inventory, or determining scrap dollars. Vague quantities like "as required" must be avoided. Avoid very large or very small numbers for the quantities; this can best be done by an adroit choice of units of measure. For example, units of measure such as HP (hundred pieces) are quite acceptable and should be used for items likely to run into the thousands for a given item such as rivets.

Fractional Quantities.   The quantity field in the PI must be able to include decimal or fractional quantities, often for reasons connected with option demands in marketing. Such materials requirements are usually in pairs. For example, one line will call for 0.6 of one cast-steel steam chest, while the next line is identical except that it calls for 0.4 of one cast-iron steam chest.

Materials That Can Be Omitted.   The process information is made up primarily of manufacturing instructions but it also contains vital scheduling and costing functions. However, each entry on the PI costs money to produce, handle, and dispose of. A single line of information on the PI triggers scores of messages in both electronic and hardcopy format that represent pure overhead with no saleable value added to the firm.

This suggests that many commonly used manufacturing materials can be simply omitted from the bill of materials because:

- They are used steadily in small quantities on most products—for example, whipping cord, or adhesives, lubricants.
- They are used in very large quantities but at very predictable rates—for example, weld rod in a fab shop or primer paint in a paint shop.

These latter tend to be included in hourly costing rates rather than separately in product cost. However, any of these "omittable" items must be included if they are infrequently used on special production runs. For example, primer paint might be omitted from the PI because it is used on all products and is charged to overhead, but a customer's special color paint will be missed entirely unless it is included in the materials bill of the PI so that MRP can pick it up.

Scrap Factors.   PI must state the engineered requirement but leave the calculation of yield and scrap to other segments of the integrated string of computer programs to determine cost. For example, steel collar 50-cm ID by 100-cm OD will require an engineered quantity of 100 by 100 cm of steel, which must appear on the PI, although the computer program may apply its scrap factor and charge the job with 113 by 113 cm.

However, sophisticated firms, mindful of the amazingly high cost of off-cuts in many first operations, may utilize the corners for gussets and the drop-out for other parts and charge the job for less than the 113 by 113 cm suggested above. Such programs require tight integration and electronic conversation among programs that can only be noted here. It is not the job of the PI to figure yield, nesting, or similar things.

Pieces From.   The better computer programs, with a little help from the PI and guidance from the designer, can "read," in some way, the materials line and apply some simple, rule-based artificial intelligence (AI) and compute the correct amount of material. A typical phrase to the program could be: "Make 2 from 100×120 of...."

Make From.   Material utilization, nesting, and similar programs, whether done manually or, more likely by computer, must be supported by the PI where feasible. A simple example would be the use of the "drop-out", the disk of scrap created when a ring is cut from a sheet of insulation, plywood, or steel. The designer can often apply this piece directly in the manufacture of a related part. This instruction might appear on the PI in some form, but it is not practical here to specify exactly how it should appear since this depends upon such external factors as the tooling, computer programs in use, and the product-costing policies of the firm. However, the simplest of write-ups is often the best, so line 21 of a bill of materials might well read, "Punching, rotor, make from drop-out of line 20," where line 20 is the stator punching for an electric motor.

Finding a Home for the Material.   PI must accurately state where each item on the materials bill is required in the process. Engineering drawings, as a matter of convenience, may call for items such as mounting bolts on the drawing of the item to be bolted to some assembly. In fact, however, the mounting bolts belong on the assembly drawing that calls for the item to be bolted to it. This forces the PI writer to depart from the engineering bill, using symbolized structuring and whatever else will help, to create bills that correctly reflect the location where the part is required rather than the location where some closely associated item is made. The shop is entitled to assume that all of the things, and only the things, listed in the PI's materials bill are needed to make the assembly on that page of PI.

Quantities Called up on a PI Page.   It has been pointed out that the PI is written for a quantity of 1. However, to make 1 steel pocket may require 6 machine bolts, 3 single-phase contactors, and so on. The burden of specifying the 6 machine bolts to create 1 steel pocket belongs to the person preparing the PI. But the determination that 36 machine bolts are required to make 2 tanks because each tank requires 3 bushing pockets, is done by "multipliers," in the bill of materials explosion routines in the BOMP, not by the PI.

MATERIALS CODING AND SKU NUMBERS

Every firm and government agency has its own strong opinions on how materials should be identified. There are proponents of highly significant materials codes. Westinghouse makes very effective use of a *basic material code* (BMC) *system.* In 10 digits it can express that a material in question is flat, hot-rolled, mild steel of a certain chemistry, 0.5 inch thick or the code can be used for an epoxy resin hardener, or a specific boxcar. Other authorities will insist that significant numbering systems lead into enormous, misdirected overhead costs and are, in the end, unable to retain their original significance. It should be emphasized that the PI must contain totally unambiguous materials codes. Any piece of material that differs from another piece in the slightest important way such as in diameter, chemistry, age, finish, and heat treatment must have its own unique *stock keeping unit* (SKU) *number.* In this the firm must be absolutely uncompromising. The standard commandment in this connection is that only items having the same form, fit, and function may bear the same SKU number.

In critical applications, such as some DOD jobs, the expiry of shelf life may require assignment of a different SKU number. For example, a certain parachute webbing must be used for the most critical application, personnel parachutes, within a certain number of months; thereafter it may be used for less critical applications such as a freight drop. Upon expiry of its first shelf life, it must receive a different, unique SKU number. The PI must be written accordingly. This PI section cannot deal with the inventory and accounting procedures necessary to control expiration dates and must simply emphasize the need for a unique identification.

The materials analysis and ledger-keeping programs that follow the BOMP programs must, of course, provide for permissible substitutions of materials and parts; but this is a dynamic, order-by-order function and the burden of substitution must not be imposed upon the PI.

These precautions are particularly vital where traceability of the product history is demanded by the customer. Department of Defense materiels and many civilian products such as aviation and utility-industrial turbines are subjected to this demand.

PROCESS SPECIFICATIONS AND MANUFACTURING PROCEDURES

In general, PI is not the place to include detailed, important instructions for complex or highly technical manufacturing. Heat treating, high-vacuum processing, clean-room processes, and similar processes unique to the firm or the product are typically written in other documents called by such titles as "process specification," "electrical specification," and "test letter." The PI, nevertheless, must accurately reflect the labor content of these processes and in particular must have some means of conveying to the scheduling system the elapsed time needed to, say, pull a vacuum, or burn in a circuit board, even when no cost is chargeable. Further, such documents are for resources and belong in the bills of materials.

PI AND THE SCHEDULING SUBSYSTEM

Woven throughout this discussion of process information, and in the background of virtually every part of it, is the fact that a firm's PI is the foundation upon which any system for time-based, synchronized manufacturing must be erected.

The Influence of PI on the Schedule

There are several points at which time moves from the background to the foreground and becomes the main consideration when constructing PI. These subjects center on how PI is issued and how it is constructed.

Timing the Release of PI

One objective of a modern system is to release as little paper as possible and as late in the process as possible. That is, information should be produced in small lots and just in time. Shop efficiency is greatly improved when PI is released at the last possible moment, which minimizes the amount of paper to be handled (and mishandled), filed (and misfiled), sequenced for dispatch (and resequenced, often in response to destructive expediting efforts), and issued with errors such as an outdated drawing sub. JIT treatment of PI also avoids the generation of a blizzard of change notices because what has not yet been issued can be changed cheaply at electronic speed within the computer. While timing the issuance of PI is not the direct concern of its writer, the writers should communicate often with systems people to ensure that what they write is suitable for any degree of information needed. The aim should be to issue properly prepared, eligible-to-run information one item at a time, with nothing whatever held on file outside the computer. Some firms are close to this ideal today, having replaced paper PI and lists with screen displays, one page (or even one operation) at a time.

HOW PROCESS INFORMATION IS CREATED

Traditional Methods

In the past, process information passed through many hands over many days. Salespeople obtained orders from customers specifying which options were to be incorporated; in some cases important customers for complicated machines supplied thick specifications to the manufacturer. Engineers and draftspeople created materials bills for their drawings. Technical clerks interpreted these bills, often revising them to repair such things as faulty structuring or outdated (or missing) materials numbers. Other experienced shop people routed these bills designing the manufacturing process through the plant that would produce the parts and assemblies described. Unusual manufacturing requirements, tooling needs, and so on were detoured to other specialists called *factory* or *manufacturing engineers,* which consumed still more time and effort. Time for each labor operation was estimated by industrial engineers. Purchased items awaited the attention of a buyer. Early computerized systems simply gave machine assistance to a few of the more routine of these functions, although enormous advances in coordinated scheduling were achieved very early in the 1960s. However, it typically could take 10 to 30 working days to create the PI for relatively straightforward engineered-to-order goods, and as much as a week for PI for standard parts and products for stock.

Reengineering the Creation of PI

We must bear in mind that all of the PI creation functions cited above still have to happen. Several things, however, have forced manufacturers to eliminate, automate, streamline, and improve the PI creation process, and they are described in the following paragraphs.

Computers and Software. Computers have become infinitely more efficient, user friendly, and inexpensive. It is now possible for one competent individual to perform, at a PC or work station screen, most or all of the PI creation functions cited above in perhaps a tenth of the labor time and a hundredth or less of the elapsed time. Determining whether some item is stocked and, if not, what to do about it now can take seconds instead of 2 days. It is also feasible to have the product designer and PI writer working at adjacent computer terminals so that manufacturing problems can be solved on screen before they become expensive trouble in the plant. This is *concurrent design,* that is, the design of the product concurrently with the design of the process.

Competitive Pressures.   Intense competition has made 30-day administrative intervals intolerable and the labor cost of doing them prohibitive.

Artificial Intelligence.   Rudimentary *artificial intelligence* (AI), in the form of rule-based expert systems, has completely eliminated several onerous, error-prone, time-consuming, drudge jobs such as performing "multipliers" for determining the quantity required at a low level after each of the goes-into quantities has been applied. AI has also eliminated the need to convert to units of measure and compute costs for an order.

Therefore, the present-day creator of PI should be one person who works continuously on a certain order until it is complete. He or she will work from standard computer order input information created in real time with direct interaction between the sales department and the customer. Such information captures, once and for all, the key front-end data that, in traditional systems, must be transcribed many times for sales, engineering, accounting, management, and others. They are supported by software that gives instantaneous access to all the requirements and resource information the firm owns. In 90 percent or more of the time, the recognition of demand, the finding and application of resources, the development of synchronized schedules, and so forth take place in the background, never appearing on screen. This enables the PI writer to concentrate on the technical, rather than the administrative problems of PI creation, such as the best process, best source, or exception conditions such as a supplier's promise that is too late to support delivery. These PI writers must be far more than clerks: They must be production engineers, willing and able to assume responsibility for successful manufacturing planning for their product. In the old way of doing PI, many people were responsible for many parts, and so no one was responsible for the quality of the PI. Today, full responsibility for the quick production of high-quality PI must ideally rest on one set of very broad shoulders.

The above brief description must be understood to be included in an ideal system. It is increasingly being approached by cutting-edge firms, but it is unlikely to be found in place 100 percent in any one of them. The individual practitioner must decide where in the spectrum between fully manual and fully automated the firm lies, recognizing that everything described in this chapter must be done somehow, and run on his or her own PI system with a blend of computer and manual components.

WHAT IS HIGH-QUALITY PI?

Viewed by the user—high-quality PI is easy to recognize. It is produced well before the first manufacturing activity is scheduled, and if followed exactly, will result in the production of the required quality product at the specified cost.

Written by Responsible People

This, once more, emphasizes that the PI writer must be a very responsible person who is well acquainted with several manufacturing disciplines such as requirements planning, synchronized production, storeskeeping, industrial engineering, tooling, purchasing, and quality planning and control.

Staffing for PI creation is therefore seen to be a critical activity in any manufacturing firm, particularly where the organizational pyramid has been flattened and broadened from what it perhaps was a few years before. Management must understand this criticality by careful selection, career planning, and backup of PI personnel. Management must find people with flexibility, a broad background, and willing assumption of responsibility—the key attributes of a PI writer.

PI STORAGE AND RETRIEVAL

PI is written to serve the exploded master schedule and the final assembly schedule (FAS). Most manufacturing is supported from a database of single item and subassembly masters that can be considered *permanent process information* (PPI), intended for repetitive use. A single call for a PPI from either a user or from the BOMP subsystem, retrieves the required PPIs and assigns an order number, an exploded quantity, and so on, and then writes the information into a different database. The database may be called *load ahead, outstanding orders, live load,* or some similar designation for live, dated operations and materials applications. This database is fast-moving and transient; it is unloaded to the cost system when work is done and reported.

However, most firms find, for reasons dealt with elsewhere in this handbook, that they also need a final assembly schedule. This is often custom built for a particular order. The PI for the final assembly schedule will occupy the top few levels, from -M partway downward in the structuring example shown earlier. This PI in support of the FAS will be written directly into the load-ahead database and will not be stored with the PPI.

The foregoing describes the high-value, low-volume end of the spectrum of assembled products. Long sequences of time-consuming operations upon only a few large, heavy, expensive parts generally require paper documentation for every part at several stages, to provide such things as an ID tag, or *traveller,* to attach to the part.

At the other end of the product spectrum, that is, the high-volume, low-value product, little or no shop paper is required. Product flows rapidly and is counted electronically. Bar-code labels and packing boxes may be included in bills of materials and supplied as part of the MRP explosion. At this end of the spectrum, the process information may merely reside in a shop book for occasional reference, completely lacking any order numbers or quantities; or more desirable yet, the PI may be callable on screen in the shop office if needed.

This reveals another central function of the PI and its associated subsystems. If the firm has succeeded in moving into a short-setup mode of manufacturing, inventory becomes a database of inexpensive, flexible, electronically stored PPI rather than expensive, fully manufactured, inflexible, physically stored hardware. In this way, PI moves out of the classification of an administrative overhead burden and into the status of being a strong support for small-lot, synchronized, JIT production which permits fast customer service.

PI AS AN AUDIT TOOL

The load-ahead database described above forms the ideal tool for auditing the firm's production planning and scheduling. It contains a large number of dated models, based upon labor and materials standards thought to be accurate as expressed in the PI, and scheduled using whatever algorithms the firm's computer program employs. Using the PI and product structure with a computer screen displaying actual results, it is easy to determine whether the four criteria for a sound plan ("account for direct labor," and so on) have been met. Some firms, in fact, have program enhancements that automatically detect and report errors of coordination, for example, mismatches between finish and start dates. This type of audit is essential and could be conducted once every few months, to ensure that programs have not begun to drift. Concerning manufacturing planning, there is a saying that battles are won before they are fought. Routinely auditing the firm's planning process is a means of ensuring the firm wins most of its manufacturing battles.

SPECIALIZED FORMS OF PROCESS INFORMATION

The Phantom Bill

This bill is used by firms operating mainly or wholly with MRP systems. MRP assumes that every item in a bill is stocked in a stores location and is to be withdrawn to be applied to a specific job. This may not be true where subassemblies are made and immediately consumed in the next process step, without physically passing through a storeroom. The MRP software in use in the firm will dictate how PI is to be identified as a phantom. These directions must be complied with, but will not conflict with anything written in this chapter. Firms manufacturing very high value, low volume, one-off products, such as power generation equipment, do not generally use MRP, although they all use requirements planning in the generic sense. Their bills will be nearly all phantoms in the sense that very few items will ever be stocked; all will be made to order, lot for lot.

Planning or Pseudo Bills

These bills will never be built but can be used to drive MRP beyond order lead time limits, which is usually necessary in most manufacturing businesses. One important feature of such bills is that they may call for decimal quantities of some items. See "Fractional Quantities" under "Estimating for PI" earlier in this chapter.

Kit Bills

These bills are used to collect such items as all the miscellaneous hardware needed to complete an assembly. Again, this is a fictitious assembly but is often a very convenient way of controlling the picking and dispatch of small, easily lost parts such as nuts and bolts. The PI for such an assembly must be structured exactly as if it were a normal assembly, and it is often both wise and convenient to have a labor line consuming production time and a descriptive term such as "pick stock" or "marshall parts," written on the item.

HOW TO CREATE PI

The following PI creation process is a general description. This will be followed by a detailed explanation of a specific example. Between these two views of PI creation, the reader will be able to steer a course that will suit his or her own environment. First are the three basic steps in the process.

Step 1.   Gather all relevant information, including:

- *Engineering drawings, specs, bills of materials, and so on.* Most particularly a clear and correct diagram or chart showing the structure of the product, that is, what goes into what to make what assemblies
- *A limiting facilities list showing all shop capabilities.* Lathe swings and bed lengths, heights to crane hooks, maximum surge generator voltage, boards per hour through wave soldering, burn-in room throughput rates, and so on
- *A flow process chart.* Showing in detail all operations, inspections, delays, and so on
- *Some source of time values for both productive labor and nonproductive process times.* An example of nonproductive time might be oven burn-in for an electronic chassis or paint drying time.

Step 2.   Write one page of PI for each single item and each subassembly, taking care to observe the structuring relationships explained above. The following step will deal with any one such page.

Step 3.   Assuming the system permits it, list on that page all operations and all materials, parts, drawings, and so on, required to manufacture the item or assembly. Conventionally the labor is at the top of the page. The labor and materials bills together must account for all the resources demanded for manufacturing the part—that includes specifications, drawings, and tools. Where the part goes through a *work cell,* that is, a single location having different machines doing sequential operations, it is necessary to work out in detail the times taken by suboperations such as "drive slot wedges." This assures that a time value reliable enough for production planning and costing can be developed for the entire operation, which might be "wind motor stator." While "wind stator" is all that may appear on the PI, a careful analysis might reveal that five or six suboperations may have gone into it. The list of labor operations must be correct and logical. This includes the following considerations:

- The sequence must be correct—drill before tap, and so on.
- Noncosted process times must be reasonable and also in correct sequence.
- Batching, as for heat treatment, must be flagged so that the scheduling subsystem can provide time accurately.
- All resource-consuming activities must be included, whether they are done in-house or subcontracted, and whether or not they generate costs in the accounts.
- Every advantage must be taken of opportunities that will minimize lost costs. For example, where operation sequencing is optional (mill first or drill first), position the operation first that is most likely to generate scrap.

COMPUTER-AIDED PROCESS PLANNING

PI creation can be laborious and repetitive. The alert PI specialist soon realizes that most of what he or she does is the same but different. For example, in many steel-fabricating shops, it will be found that perhaps 60 percent of pieceparts go through the sequence shear-pierce-bend-deburr-clean-primer paint and that 75 percent of pieceparts start out as rectangles. This suggests that, if these parts could be described to a computer program so that it could route the part to the right machines, assign time values, compute materials applications, and so forth, the labor to create PI could be reduced dramatically. This can, in fact, be done with *computer-aided process planning* (CAPP). This process has strong overtones of *group technology* (GT), and indeed the borders between GT, CAPP, and PI become more blurred as time passes. This drives us toward overall integration emphasized in the expression computer-integrated manufacturing (CIM).

CAPP is of two kinds: (1) *variant,* in which a standard drawing or other description of a part is assigned various dimensions to suit the job, and (2) *generative,* in which the part is described to a sufficiently intelligent computer program so that a suitable process can be developed automatically from scratch, without reference to any drawing. While CAPP is part of the CIM movement now developing, its software is still primitive and expensive except for the most elementary work. Variant CAPP on flat or noncompound curved parts is most likely to pay off. Generative CAPP, particularly if contoured (3D) work is involved, remains an alluring but immature technology that few firms so far have made pay off.

PI ILLUSTRATED

Refer to Fig. 6.4 for a parent subassembly in a product, and to Fig. 6.5 which is for one of the feeder items for that subassembly. The following is an explanation of the numbered features of process information in Figs. 6.4 and 6.5:

1. A computer-assigned serial number of use where bar-code unloading is not or cannot be used.

2. Shop order number, that is, the customer order number. The firm will be its own customer when the order is for stock replenishment.

3. Sub (of the shop order) is a means of splitting up very large orders into smaller separate orders for major components, to reduce the system's rippling effects. This is used only for high-value, low-volume products.

4. Apparatus code. This identifies the symbolized interval chart or scheduling template that was used for this order. Some special character, such as a hyphen, tells the programs that there is no template, that the information is complete, and that the programs must synthesize their own symbol string.

5. Symbol was discussed earlier; no effort is made to make the symbol significant, as by assigning R for *rotor.*

6. Level of this item in the product structure. In this example, the level is 2 since the symbol RA has two characters.

7. Product group (PG), that is, the product family within the company's business to which this order belongs. A firm may have one PG for new product, another for spare parts, another for a different product, and so on.

8. Quantity of this item needed to satisfy the top level of the order. This is the exploded quantity multiplied for each level of assembly. (The explosion and multiplying are done by the program, as explained earlier, not by people.)

9. Unit of measure, discussed earlier.

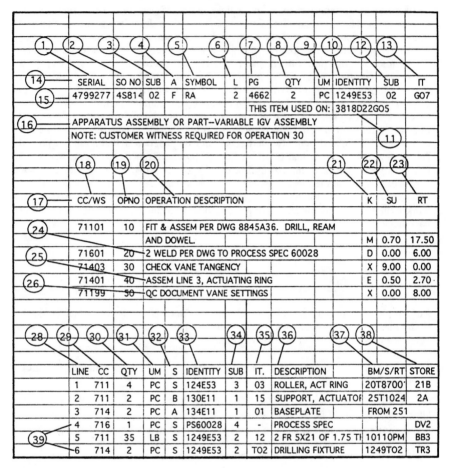

SERIAL	SO NO	SUB	A	SYMBOL	L	PG	QTY	UM	IDENTITY	SUB	IT
4799277	4S814	02	F	RA	2	4662	2	PC	1249E53	02	G07

THIS ITEM USED ON: 3818D22G05

APPARATUS ASSEMBLY OR PART--VARIABLE IGV ASSEMBLY
NOTE: CUSTOMER WITNESS REQUIRED FOR OPERATION 30

CC/WS	OPNO	OPERATION DESCRIPTION	K	SU	RT
71101	10	FIT & ASSEM PER DWG 8845A36. DRILL, REAM AND DOWEL.	M	0.70	17.50
71601	20	2 WELD PER DWG TO PROCESS SPEC 60028	D	0.00	6.00
71403	30	CHECK VANE TANGENCY	X	9.00	0.00
71401	40	ASSEM LINE 3, ACTUATING RING	E	0.50	2.70
71199	50	QC DOCUMENT VANE SETTINGS	X	0.00	8.00

LINE	CC	QTY	UM	S	IDENTITY	SUB	IT.	DESCRIPTION	BM/S/RT	STORE
1	711	4	PC	S	124E53	3	03	ROLLER, ACT RING	20T8700	21B
2	711	2	PC	B	130E11	1	15	SUPPORT, ACTUATOR	25T1024	2A
3	714	2	PC	A	134E11	1	01	BASEPLATE	FROM 251	
4	716	1	PC	S	PS60028	4	-	PROCESS SPEC		DV2
5	711	35	LB	S	1249E53	2	12	2 FR 5X21 OF 1.75 TH	10110PM	BB3
6	714	2	PC	S	1249E53	2	TO2	DRILLING FIXTURE	1249TO2	TR3

FIGURE 6.4   Example of process information. (*Courtesy Power Generation Canadian Division, Westinghouse Canada, Inc.*)

10. Drawing number on which this assembly is to be found. It is usually from the company's number series but may be a customer's drawing number. It contains 12 characters, which includes drawing issue number and BoM item number; serves most purposes; however, some customers, especially DOD and nuclear-related industries tend to have very long drawing numbers.

11. This is a cross reference to the parent item requesting this item on this order—for example, the single-level where-used reference.

12. This is the drawing sub number, or issue number, for this part for this order. It carries authority equal to that of the drawing number itself. Like the date, it must reflect the latest revision level and is critically important in controlling such procedures as phase in and traceability.

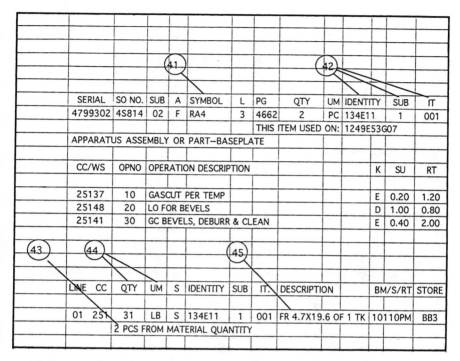

SERIAL	SO NO.	SUB	A	SYMBOL	L	PG	QTY	UM	IDENTITY	SUB	IT
4799302	4S814	02	F	RA4	3	4662	2	PC	134E11	1	001
						THIS ITEM USED ON:	1249E53G07				

APPARATUS ASSEMBLY OR PART–BASEPLATE

CC/WS	OPNO	OPERATION DESCRIPTION						K	SU	RT
25137	10	GASCUT PER TEMP						E	0.20	1.20
25148	20	LO FOR BEVELS						D	1.00	0.80
25141	30	GC BEVELS, DEBURR & CLEAN						E	0.40	2.00

LINE	CC	QTY	UM	S	IDENTITY	SUB	IT	DESCRIPTION	BM/S/RT	STORE
01	251	31	LB	S	134E11	1	001	FR 4.7X19.6 OF 1 TK	10110PM	BB3
	2 PCS FROM MATERIAL QUANTITY									

FIGURE 6.5 Process information for feeder items. (*Courtesy Power Generation Canadian Division, Westinghouse Canada, Inc.*)

13. Item (or subassembly) number within the bill of materials for this drawing.

14–16. These are the header information lines that supply the identification information and a limited amount of special nonlabor, nontechnical instructions that apply to this item only.

17. This is the line of titles for the labor bill columns.

18. Cost center/work station. Cost center is a departmental designation; work station is a particular place such as a machine, bench, group of similar machines, or work cell within that department.

19. Operation number. Many firms number operations as shown to leave room for possible additions when changes to the operation lineup become necessary.

20. Self-explanatory.

21. This is a key identifying the kind of time measurement being expressed by the process information. An array of keys would be: M = a measured time estimate (time-studied, synthetic, etc.); E = estimated (as from similar work or experience); D = a lower grade of estimate than E, that is, a best guess; X = elapsed time applied to the entire quantity, with no cost charged, for example heat treatment, inspection, or paint drying.

22. Setup time, that is, the time to prepare the workplace for the total quantity of the item.

23. Runtime, that is, time per piece.

24. The numeric digit 2 instructs the computer program to schedule this operation using a crew size of 2.

25. Line 3 instructs the computer program to schedule the material called for in line 3 of the bill of materials to be ready for operation 40 rather than for operation 10, which is the default required date.

26. Quality-control inspections are scheduled as normal operations, even though no cost is charged to the order for them.

27. Not used.

28. Self-explanatory.

29. The designation of the cost center (department) to which this material is to be delivered.

30–31. Self-explanatory.

32. This column shows the user which of four possible sources of materials applies to this line: S means get from stock; A, make for the order; B, bought outside, or E, expensed item (floor stock—not directly charged such as a weldrod). This source is assigned by the computer program and is for reference by employees.

33. This identifies the drawing and item that describes this resource; it is the where-found designation.

34–36. Self-explanatory, or described above.

37. This column contains one of four identifiers corresponding to the four possible sources explained under item 32, above. If the material is a stocked, or an expensed part, or stocked raw material, the stock keeping unit (SKU) number will be shown. If it is a self-made part for this order, the department from which it is to come is shown; if purchased, the company's purchase order number will appear.

38. This column shows the department number from which the part, material, tool, and so on is expected to be delivered.

39. *Note:* Included in this bill of materials are two items—a process specification number and a tool call-up number—that make it into a true "bill of resources." The computer system issues scheduled requisitions, to the tool room, drawing vault, and so on just as if these were machine shop or similar departments.

Any good requirements planning system can be designed to track such things as the number of times a drill jig has been used, and to requisition the toolroom's service for rebushing it after it has been used X number of times.

40. Not used.

41. Since this is a lower-level item called up by a parent, we would expect its symbol to be incremented as shown. The last digit, a numeric 4, is a tipoff that this item was recognized by the computer programs as an on-file PI which was then called, a manufacturing symbol (RA4), synthesized, blended with its parent, and thereafter treated as if it had been created by manual methods. If this item in turn has a lower level, the programs will repeat this process, yielding, say, a symbol such as RA47, and so on down to the lowest level.

42. This is the where-found drawing number called up by the parent item, materials line 3.

43. This is a program-generated reminder that the quantity shown will cut the two pieces required.

44. This unit of measure and quantity are what have been converted and computed, respectively, by the program in response to the description line noted in number 45 below.

45. This field was originated on the engineering bill of materials for the drawing. The computer programs incorporate a small expert system which analyzes this field and the SKU number beside it and decides how to use and convert the information for the inventory, purchasing, and other integrated runs, and present the information to the user of the PI in the most understandable way.

Reservations

In what follows, it must be understood that no one form of PI is universally suitable for all firms and products. The PI shown, however, is a useful point of departure for any firm because it is:

- In actual use
- Suitable for the product and environment defined at the top of this section
- Sophisticated but not too heavily dependent upon exotic artificial intelligence features, queuing, CAPP, and so on
- An example with several of the features explained in the preceding material
- A component of a tightly integrated, net change, closed-loop, bucketless, all-level-pegged system, and accordingly represents good practice in manufacturing decision support systems
- Oriented toward a process-layout factory but also applicable to FMS or work cell layouts (Process layouts will continue to be used where appropriate for some time to come.)

No one page of PI would be expected to show all these features, and the illustration may therefore suggest far more complexity than actually exists in any one page of PI.

The PI illustrated happens to be for heavy apparatus with a long cycle, high value, and low volume. However, the principles illustrated are generic and apply to any product fitting the "discrete product" definition at the start of this chapter.

There is no preprinted form for the PI. If one is desired, it is better to embed it in the computer software than to attempt to design and stock a separate form. Ordinary continuous-feed computer paper is cheaper than a special form and need not be scrapped when a format changes, and requires only a changeover in the computer. Further, the computer-generated form will probably serve as is, with no change whatever, when the PI system evolves into a paperless, on-screen, in-shop system.

Naturally, as data transmission and collection methods evolve, much of what is seen on this PI will be on screen displays rather than on hard copy. And as an aside, it should be noted that leading-edge firms are strongly questioning the need for the amount of paper generated by traditional systems. One outstanding indicator of this trend is the adoption of bar-code reading directly from the PI instead of the key entry used with the 80-column computer cards of the past.

For some years firms have used backflushing, in which the final delivery of a batch of product to the warehouse is taken as sufficient notice to relieve all parts and materials inventories leading up to that event. This is suitable for short-cycle products where the time-phasing error introduced is tolerable. Obviously, however, any such techniques require that the PI integrity be sufficient to support the degree of cost accounting rigor the firm may have adopted. In this connection, review the "quantities," "unit of measure," and related discussions that follow.

DATING PROCESS INFORMATION

Disagreement can be expected among operating personnel concerning the advisability of printing the required dates for the operations on the PI. The general principle that governs this is, "The scheduled date should be shown in only one place." If dates are shown in two places such as the PI and the short-term schedule, one can be sure that they will at times disagree. This causes confusion and errors in the shop, which will cause an out-of-synchronization situation. The operating rule that follows from the general principle above is that the date should be displayed only on the latest-produced piece of information. This ensures that the inevitable date changes entered into the system have the best chance of appearing on the information to which the shop has to work. Advanced firms, recognizing an opportunity to reduce redundant information, will use only one or the other of the two documents—the PI or the short-term schedule—but not both.

Sources of Data Items

The sources of information seen on PI are of three kinds:

- Entirely human
- Human, augmented by the computer programs
- Entirely from the computer programs

An example of an entirely human data source is the shop order number, although even here the computer programs can assist by, for example, replicating this number on successive pages or applying this number to on-file PIs called in for use on this order. An example of human but augmented by the computer programs is the quantity of a raw material to be applied to the order and its cost. The human input consists merely of specifying, for instance, the size of a piece of insulation needed to make one of some item. The programs do the necessary conversion for whatever the cost for a unit of measure and the quantity may be, for example, pounds for an order multiplied by cost per pound.

In a wholly computerized procedure, the computer recognizes that some item is on file as a repetitively used PI. The programs will call that PI; append it to the current order; multiply out the quantity required for the order; assign the shop order number; schedule the shop order; analyze and requisition the material; and blend it seamlessly into the order that called for it.

Progress in decision support systems for manufacturing plants consists to a considerable extent of driving more and more of the information flow into a wholly computerized system. However, it must again be pointed out that such systems demand and deserve an extensive monitoring and maintenance by personnel knowledgeable in shop practice and in touch with the steady flow of shop improvements, changes, and so on. On-file PI is cheap, quick, and convenient to use; but it is also voluminous, daunting to analyze, and "out of sight, out of mind." In addition, there is a very high risk of accumulating a large store of dated PI. Methods of guarding against this and doing something useful about it are outside the scope of this chapter; however, the practitioner is cautioned to give the subject the high-priority attention it deserves.

*PROCESS INFORMATION AND ENGINEERING CHANGES**

Inevitably, process information must be changed to accommodate outside influences such as customer and marketing needs, government regulation, and public safety and inside influences such as cost or quality improvement, product line enhancement or pruning, and new or changed models. PI changes range from routine ("To be incorporated when current parts inventories run out") to emergency ("All work-in-process is to be built to the new sub, fully traced and documented, with all product after Batch —— to be recalled, documented, and scrapped."). The PI system must incorporate a robust subsystem for accommodating this spectrum efficiently and with as little confusion as possible.

This subsystem is often called the *engineering change notice* (ECN) *procedure.* Personnel administering such procedures must understand that the company's financial health is at stake since reputation, cost of scrap, recall, or rework, and occasionally exposure to legal action can be involved. The PI and its control are usually at the heart of such activities.

It should be noted in passing that small-lot production, including small-lot issuing of information, is an enormous help in successful administration of the ECN procedure. Product or paperwork that has not yet been created and distributed in large lots need not be withdrawn, reworked, scrapped, or accounted for.

It bears repeating that, during ECN administration, even more than at other times, unique identification is mandatory. Among the main elements of this principle are that (a) if any part changes "form, fit, or function" as a result of the ECN, it must have a fresh part number, and (b) the issue number of the drawing must be religiously observed as having authority equal to that of the drawing number itself.

PI personnel must take a proactive approach to this very pervasive problem by ensuring that the materials control department understands what has taken place and is alerted to the numerous snowballing changes needed. Among these changes will be such things as reviews of inventory levels, decisions for disposition of stocks, revision to ABC classifications, adjustments to quantity figures where EOQs are in use, renegotiation of supplier contracts, notice to field service and repair departments, and much more.

During ECN administration, the PI function will be called upon to answer many important questions, such as where is this part used? What orders are open that use this part? How far along is the current batch? What is a feasible effective date? Most of these questions can be addressed by PI personnel who are the ones most likely to know what reports or database retrievals are needed. Close liaison with MRP planners is required to ensure that the new parts are called for in production neither too soon (causing fictitious shortages at assembly and unnecessary scrapping of old stock) nor too late (holding up production by genuine shortages).

The following checklist of items to be considered in administering an ECN should be consulted to ensure that nothing falls through the cracks. Any given ECN will hit only a few of them; nevertheless, all these bases should be touched each time, as each one is a source of potential difficulty if overlooked.

*This material on PI changes has been adapted from Kenneth W. Tunnell et. al., *Product and Process Information,* in Chapter 10, *"Production and Inventory Control Handbook,"* 2nd ed., McGraw-Hill, New York, 1987.

CHECKLIST OF ITEMS AFFECTED BY
ENGINEERING CHANGE

I. Inventories
  a. Finished goods
    (1) Warehouse
    (2) Distribution
    (3) Dealers
  b. Work-in-process
    (1) Major assembly
    (2) Subassembly
    (3) Parts production
      (a) Manufacturing
      (b) Subcontract
  c. Finished parts
    (1) Stores
    (2) Assembly area
    (3) Repair depots
    (4) Warehouse
    (5) Open orders with suppliers
  d. Raw materials
    (1) Stores
    (2) In process
    (3) Open order with suppliers

II. Industrial engineering
  a. Tooling
    (1) In process
    (2) Design lead time
    (3) Tool-making lead time
      (a) Materials
        (1) Stores
        (2) Open order or lead time
  b. Operation sheets
  c. Time standards
  d. Audiovisual production aids
  e. Make or buy
  f. Assembly-kit lists

III. Production control
  a. Production schedules
  b. Lead time
    (1) Engineering
    (2) Tooling
    (3) Methods, standards, kitting
    (4) Procurement
  c. Shop and machine loading
  d. Interchangeability and substitutions
  e. Classification of inventory
  f. Effective date
  g. Disposition of goods deleted or changed
  h. Rework orders

    i. Disposition of drawings, shop orders, and so on
    j. Where-used file
    k. Inventory class
    l. EOQ change

IV. Cost estimating and accounting
    a. Prices
        (1) Customer open orders
        (2) Open proposals
        (3) Future proposals
    b. Cost
        (1) Change of product cost
        (2) Obsolete parts and material
        (3) Tooling
            (a) Capital investment
        (4) Scrap
    c. Engineering
        (1) Design
        (2) Drafting
        (3) Clerical

V. Engineering
    a. Drawings
    b. Bills of materials
    c. Parts lists
    d. Product specifications
    e. Where-used file
    f. Handbook and instruction manual
    g. Schematics
    h. Customer requirements

VI. Sales
    a. Catalogs
    b. Price lists
    c. Handbook and instruction manuals
    d. Spare-parts provisioning
    e. Service centers and repair depots
    f. Products in the field (customers, dealers, etc.)
    g. Customer requirements and specifications

Clearly engineering changes can present a burdensome task to the entire manufacturing organization. Cost is always involved in design change, although the type and kind of change will dictate the order of magnitude. Therefore, the basic step in organizing for an engineering-change control system is to develop a strategy for evaluating changes.

Policy Development

Development of engineering-change policy will depend largely on specific product lines and methods of sales and distribution. The relationship of manufacturing and final delivery of the product to the customer is important to the policy. The answers to these questions will classify the problem at the start:

- Is the product manufactured to stock?
- Is the product distributed through warehouses and dealers?
- Is the product manufactured to stock and shipped directly from factory to customer?
- Is the product a standard item that is modified to customer specifications?
- Is the product manufactured completely to customer specifications?
- Is the product a commercial item or manufactured under government contract?

In most cases, these questions can be answered affirmatively. Moreover, in most plants the answers are different for various product lines. A standard engineering-change control system must apply to all product lines. Where a product is manufactured repetitively, regardless of whether the method is considered mass production, many changes can be incorporated in future production lots as opposed to the current production lot. The manufacturing group will hope for no changes at all during a production run. Although it is desirable to "freeze the design" during a production run, it is not always possible. Every effort must be made, however, to minimize changes during a production run. Only mandatory changes should be incorporated during a production run. Mandatory changes are those needed for function or customer requirements, which sometimes include essential quality and reliability improvement. All other changes should be incorporated in subsequent production runs.

Engineering-Change Considerations

Although we know that to freeze a design can result in a freeze in sales, we must be prepared to weigh the costs of change against the market probabilities. The total impact of change on the factory and customer deliveries must be measured.

These questions should be answered prior to approval of a change:

- Is the change necessary?
- What are the total costs of change?
- Can the change be incorporated in the next or subsequent runs?
- Will the change halt production? For how long?
- Will schedules and customer delivery be jeopardized?
- Have inventory positions been analyzed?
- If the change is requested for purposes of improving manufacturing methods, can the ease of manufacture balance the costs of change and schedule jeopardy?

Engineering-Change Classifications

Engineering changes should be classified or coded to indicate the extent and significance of change. An example of such a classification of change is shown below, from the U.S. Air Force-Navy Aeronautical Bulletin 445.

Class I Deviation.   Any change affecting fit, form, or function of an item or, more specifically, affecting one or more of the following configuration features:

- Contract specifications, price, weight, delivery, or schedule
- Contract reliability and/or maintainability

- Interchangeability
- Electrical interference to communications equipment or electromagnetic radiation hazards
- Safety, performance, or durability
- AGE/SE, trainers, training devices, or GFE

Class II Variations. Any change not falling within the class I category. Changes may be further classified to indicate incorporation policy.

Example 1

Mandatory. Must be incorporated into current production run.

Routine. Incorporate in next production run.

Example 2

Class A. Incorporate into all products including units in the field through revision AA1.

Class B. Incorporate into all unpacked units including units in assembly and sub-assembly.

Class C. Incorporate into all unassembled units.

Class D. Incorporate next time ordered.

Example 3

Class A. Scrap

Class B. Rework

Class C. Use up current materials

Class D. Next time ordered

Design Review Procedure

Engineering design or documentation changes occur more frequently in the early stages of production. Figure 6.6 shows a schematic of this procedure. It is not uncommon in some industries to anticipate these changes and to accept the problem. Many manufacturing companies maintain special areas where reasonably short runs are made as production pilot runs. During this stage of development, design and manufacturing methods can be tested and changes made at will. This pilot run can serve as the final design review before establishment of a baseline configuration. The policy provides for any change to be made during the pilot production run, which culminates in a complete design review and implementation of all changes. This point is frequently referred to as baseline design or configuration. After the establishment of baseline design, only mandatory changes affecting function and/or customer requirements may be incorporated.

Engineering changes can be requested from any department within the company and frequently from suppliers or vendors. The request for change is usually a printed form which, when properly approved, also serves as an engineering-change notice. *Engineering-change requests* (ECRS) are sometimes referred to as *engineering-change proposals* (ECPs). *Engineering-change notices* (ECNs) are sometimes called engineering-change orders (ECOs) or engineering-change authority (ECA).

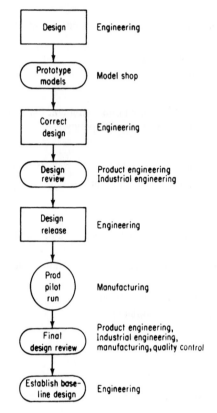

FIGURE 6.6   Pilot run and final design review procedure.

Design	Engineering
Prototype models	Model shop
Correct design	Engineering
Design review	Product engineering Industrial engineering
Design release	Engineering
Prod pilot run	Manufacturing
Final design review	Product engineering, Industrial engineering, manufacturing, quality control
Establish base-line design	Engineering

FIGURE 6.7   Multipart ECO system.

An ECR must have proper approvals, and then an ECN is initiated. Frequently, the same form with multicopies is used as the ECR and converted upon approval to an ECN. ECNs and ECRs must be numbered and logged for control. Should a request be rejected for any reason, the requester is notified and given an opportunity to represent his or her request at a higher level of management.

Figure 6.7 illustrates the format for a multipart ECO system, while Fig. 6.8 can be used both as an ECR and subsequently as an ECN. Figure 6.9 is an engineering authorization which is used for new-product release and an engineering-change order (ECO).

☐ Engineering channel request
☐ Engineering change notice
CM No. ________
Engineering change No. ________
Project No. ________
Sheet ____ of ____

☐ Class I (deviation)
☐ Class II (variation)

Dwg. no.

Drawing No. ________ Unit No. ________ Present revision ________

Rev. no.

Title ________

Reason for change	Type of Change	Effectivity	Material disposition
☐ Error	☐ Mandatory	☐ Immediate	☐ None
☐ Additional information	☐ Elective	☐ Next time ordered	☐ Use up stock
☐ Design improvement	☐ Routine	☐ (See remarks)	☐ Order as required
☐ Vendor required	☐ Emergency		☐ Scrap
☐ Customer required			☐ Rework
☐ Latest process			☐ Use elsewhere
☐ Clarification			☐ (See remarks)
☐ Cost reduction			
☐ (See remarks)			

Description of change From	To

Remarks

Change requested by ________	Approved by	Date
Date originated ________	Department head	
Effective date ________	Project engineer	
Change rejected by ________	Manufacturing engineer	
Reason ________	Director of engineering	
________	Quality control	
	Government agency	

Draftsman ________ Drafting supervisor ________ Checker ________
Date ________ Date ________ Date ________

FIGURE 6.8 Combined ECR and ECN.

Used on: _____ Drawing No. _____

Rev _____

Title: _____

D E S I G N :

1. Classification

☐ Class I ☐ New part ☐ -New assemblies

☐ Class II · Revision requiring no disposition of parts or assemblies

☐ Class III · Change to be made as soon as practical

☐ Balancing of parts required

☐ Class IV · Change to be effective immediately

Completed parts   Completed assemblies

☐ Use as is   ☐ Use as is

☐ Alter or scrap   ☐ Alter or scrap

E N G I N E E R I N G

2. The following parts are affected by the above change:

_____ _____ _____ _____ _____

3. Type of change (Give description and reason of change, special instructions, etc.)

☐ Design   ☐ Cost reduction

☐ Shop request   ☐ Sales request   S.O. _____

Description: _____

_____

_____

Reason: _____

_____

Prepared by _____ Date _____ Approved by _____ Date _____

P R O D E N G R

1. Estimated monthly requirement _____

2. Tooling information

☐ Tooling required   ☐ New   ☐ Alteration

☐ Tooling is available   ☐ Temporary   ☐ Permanent

☐ Tooling is not required

Remarks: _____

Approved by _____ Date _____

M E T H O D S   D E P A R T M E N T

1. Source

☐ Purchase part

☐ Shop part

2. Required tools

☐ Alteration   Date available _____

☐ New   Date available _____

3. Stock status

Completed parts

☐ Use as is

☐ Alter or scrap

Completed assemblies

☐ Use as is

☐ Alter or scrap

4. Material

☐ Standard

☐ Special

5. Special instructions

_____

_____

_____

_____

_____

_____

_____

_____

_____

_____

_____

_____

_____

Prepared by: _____

Date: _____

FIGURE 6.9 Engineering authorization.

Sample Engineering-Change Procedure

I. *Purpose:* To provide a procedure for processing and controlling engineering changes.

II. *Scope:* This procedure applies to all engineering changes and includes the procedure for requesting engineering changes.

III. Definitions:
    A. Document is any drawing, parts list, or product specification used to define a product.
    B. Deviation class 1 change is any change in fit, form, or function specifically affecting one or more of the following configuration features:
        1. Specifications, price, weight delivery, or schedule
        2. Reliability and/or maintainability
        3. Interchangeability
        4. Safety, performance, or durability

    C. Variation class 2 changes are all other changes not classified as class 1.
    D. Mandatory changes are those necessary to the function and operation of the product or specifically required by the customer. Mandatory changes must be incorporated in current production runs.
    E. Routine changes are those that do not necessarily affect function or operation and can be incorporated in the next or subsequent production runs. These changes can include those intended for cost reduction, product improvement, ease of manufacture, and quality improvement.
    F. Engineering-change request (ECR) is the form used for officially requesting a change.
    G. Engineering-change notice (ECN) is the authorization for changing engineering documents.

IV. ECR
    A. Any department may initiate an engineering-change request. The filled-out ECR form must include:
        1. Drawing number
        2. Title
        3. Reason for change
        4. Effectivity date
        5. Sign

    B. Department head must approve and sign ECR.
    C. Forward ECR to change control administrator (CCA).
    D. The control administrator will check the ECR and classify the change.
    E. The ECR shall be forwarded to the project engineer for disposition.
        1. If the request is rejected, the ECR with the engineer's reason for rejection is returned to the requester via the CCA.
        2. If the request is approved, copies of the ECR are distributed to industrial engineering, PIC, quality control, and the CCA.

    F. Industrial engineering reviews the ECR and evaluates costs, schedules, and technical feasibility. Considerations for cost include capital investment required, tooling, facility change, methods, and so on. These costs and considerations shall be defined and recommendations indicated.
        1. Copies of the ECR shall be forwarded to the CCA and the cost accounting and estimating group.

G. Production and inventory control will review the ECR and evaluate costs, schedules, and lead times. Cost considerations include all inventories affected. Effect of change on current schedules is evaluated, and effective dates are forwarded to the CCA and cost accounting and estimating.

H. Quality control reviews the ECR and evaluates costs, schedules, and quality considerations. Recommendations are made and copies are forwarded to the CCA and the cost accounting and estimating group.

I. Cost accounting and estimating reviews ECRs received from industrial engineering, PIC, and quality control and prepares a report and recommendation considering total cost of change. Cost consideration includes all inventories, capital investment, tooling, and so on. The summary report reflects new pricing and consideration for open orders and proposals and is forwarded to the engineering department with copies of ECRs from industrial engineering, quality control, and PIC.

J. The engineering department evaluates the cost and pricing reports along with recommendations from quality control, PIC, and industrial engineering and approves or rejects the ECR.
1. The controller and marketing department are to be consulted.
2. If the request is rejected at this step, the requester is advised.

K. Engineering assigns an ECN number to the ECR and forwards it to the CCA.

L. The CCA records the ECN number and releases it to drafting and engineering for processing.
1. Copies of ECNs are distributed to departments concerned (production control, manufacturing inspection, quality control, engineering, industrial engineering, etc.). The ECR procedure is shown in Fig. 6.10.

V. ECN

A. Upon receipt of the ECN, PIC will:
1. Issue appropriate stop-work orders.
2. Physically accumulate parts and materials, drawing shop orders, and assembly work orders for scrap, rework, or other dispositions.
3. Prepare inventory reports for the accounting write-off.
4. Place new orders or rework orders for items changed.
5. Determine available schedule times for materials, components, and so on.
6. Develop schedules and effective dates (adjust master schedules).
7. Communicate dates to sales.
8. Determine extent of tooling changes and obtain schedules.
9. Provide new machine loads as required.
10. Adjust inventory records including planned available balances.
11. Adjust where-used file.
12. Adjust interchangeability and substitution files.
13. Adjust inventory classification files.
14. Adjust EOQ values.
15. Establish follow-up dispatch plans.

B. Industrial engineering, upon receipt of the ECN, will:
1. Evaluate tool changes and establish tool schedules.
2. Prepare necessary tool stop-work orders.
3. Design new tools or changes.
4. Evaluate change or establish new methods and operation sheets.
5. Evaluate time-standard changes and implement new standards as required.

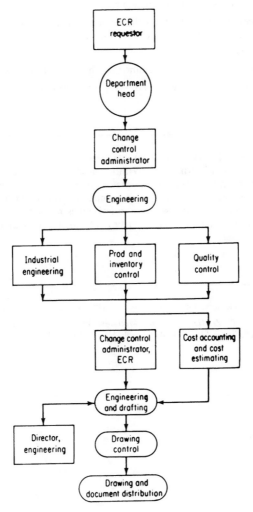

FIGURE 6.10   Simplified flowchart for an engineering-change system.

6. Determine make-or-buy policy as required.
7. Review and correct assembly kit lists.
8. Change audiovisual aids as required.

CONCLUSIONS

Although control of engineering changes is very difficult even in a class A MRP system shop, it is essential and can be performed effectively in many companies. Some of the essential elements of effective engineering control are:

- Well-defined engineering-change procedures
- Education programs to properly train all planners, expediters, schedulers, shop supervisors, and so on, in the proper use of the system
- Established effective dates
- Clear objectives for those who determine that changes will or will not be made
- Logs and reports to accumulate costs of scrap and rework of inventory

SUMMARY

Process Information (PI) and engineering-change systems are at the heart of the information system of a manufacturing firm. Within reason, any effort to render it both accurate (free from blunders) and sufficiently precise (containing dependable estimates) is well warranted. It requires staffing by very competent production specialists and support from tightly integrated subsystems. While it takes many forms and is sometimes invisible, its disciplines are essential to successful short-cycle manufacturing of high-quality, low-cost goods.

REFERENCES

1. Philip C. Murray: "Documentation Goes Digital," *Byte Magazine,* September 1993, p. 121.
2. F. S. Gue: *Push, Pull, ZI, JIT Production Methods; A Perspective,* 28th Annual International Conference Proceedings, APICS, Falls Church, Va., 1985, p. 116.

CHAPTER 7
CONTROL OF TOOLS AND NONPRODUCTION MATERIALS

Editor

Norman Hopwood

Chief Engineer, MACH System Consultants
Dearborn, Michigan

The tool control function seldom exists as a separate organization, even though specific sections or departments may be titled "tool control." As outlined in Table 7.1, tool control is a basic discipline in many manufacturing systems, beginning with the initial process planning, through project implementation, into production operations, and eventually to tool salvage or disposition.

Efficient control of tools and nonproduction material for manufacturing operations is essential for any competitive enterprise to survive. The practices and procedures necessary to achieve these goals are as varied as the range of tools and supplies involved. In the following discussion, an effort is made to describe good practice in generic terms. The reader should interpret the concepts broadly for his or her own individual applications.

DEFINITIONS

The diversity of manufacturing operations has generated a corresponding assortment of terms and definitions. To clarify the subject of tool control and nonproduction materials management, the following definitions will be used.

Tools

In the broadest sense, *tools* are the adjunct to materials, machines, and equipment that provide the means for a worker to generate wealth in the form of manufactured products. This definition may be extended to include operations in mining and/or refining when the product is a basic raw material for manufacturing processes. Tools are classified in a number of ways. The choice is subjective and depends largely on the segment of the manufacturing industry involved.

TABLE 7.1 Tool Control Functional Matrix

Activity	Production engineering support*	Tool control role
Product design	Establish manufacturing and assembly feasibility. Document functional requirements. Review design schedule.	Review special tool requirements. Identify potential cost and production problems. Establish tool commonality.
Facility specification and design	Determine operations sequence and equipment requirements. Establish specifications, and initiate design. Finalize process and design with preproduction tryout.	Minimize special design. Determine tool needs for production launch. Assess tryout experience, and establish needed changes.
Procurement	Identify potential sources, and evaluate quotations. Recommend sources and establish timing. Initiate expediting and quality follow-up procedures.	Determine maintenance requirements. Advise recommended fabrication sources. Improvise to handle delivery deficiencies.
Inventory management and disbursement control	Establish requirements based on planned production volumes. Clarify preferred stocking and replacement practices. Recommend tool cost accounting methods.	Review tool-handling and storage practices. Establish consumption cost control checkpoints. Assure design level and receiving inspection viability.
Production operations	Assess actual tool performance. Establish timing for ongoing product design changes. Finalize process sequence and equipment requirements.	Confirm recommended practices. Evaluate tool material and design alternatives. Finalize tool maintenance and replacement algorithms.
Recondition and repair	Consider alternative methods to improve durability. Coordinate adjustments to production schedules. Interpret operating experience to product engineering for potential design improvement.	Initiate design and materials changes to reduce wear and breakage. Recommend alternate tool change procedures. Update recondition and repair criteria.
Disposition	Concur in disposition of obsolete tools. Assure destruction of proprietary tools. Adjust tool history records.	Review salvage potential for obsolete tools. Establish rework procedure for salvageable tools. Determine potential for component reuse.

*This includes areas of manufacturing engineering, plant engineering, quality assurance, materials handling, and all other manufacturing support activities.

Design.   Tools are commonly classified as special, standard, or commercially available designs. *Specially designed tools* are unique to an enterprise's process and are supported by a graphic definition (drawings) for procurement and/or replacement. Their uniqueness may be attributed to product requirements, machine or equipment characteristics, or proprietary design features.

Standard tools have prespecified characteristics, usually described in a manual or other record maintained by the enterprise, which reflect industrial standards and provides the tool engineer with application parameters. Standard tools provide the obvious advantage of low cost, availability, and proven utility.

Commercially available tools have become generally accepted by particular users in the industry. They may reflect proprietary features, or they may be industry standard. From a tool control standpoint, they can be procured readily and require no further specification for their use or maintenance.

Expected Life.   Another defining characteristic of tools is their *normal life expectancy.* Life may mean how long they will last in use, how long they are applicable to a process, or the time to obsolescence.

Typical categorization includes the following: *Perishable tools* are consumed by use and/or necessary reconditioning. Obvious examples are the many different kinds of cutting tools, die inserts, abrasives, core pins, and other details subjected to higher wear, resulting in shortened life.

Durable tools, as the name implies, have an expected life beyond current production and are generally not directly a part of the processing operation. Their status may be attributed to accounting practices.

Accountability.   Tool control involves not just administrative responsibility but to some extent also includes financial accountability. This important aspect is reflected in the several groupings defined below:

- Expensed tools are perishable and as the name implies, are "expensed," or charged completely and immediately to a particular activity.

- Special tools are identified with a specific product or program and are eventually charged completely to it. Generally their useful life is associated directly with the production life of the product.

- Durable tools, by their nature, are not limited by the life of a specific product or program and are generally capitalized and depreciated over established time spans. Typically this depreciation period will range from 3 to 20 years.

Actuation.   Tools may be categorized by how they are actuated. Typical of such classes are:

- *Hand tools.* Tools that are held and actuated by hand are called *hand tools.* Generally, these are classified as common supply items but may include designed tools such as special wrenches.

- *Power tools.* Tools that are actuated by air, electricity, or hydraulics are called *power tools.* Although they may be power actuated, they are positioned and moved through the production process manually.

- *Portable tools.* As noted above, *portable tools* are manually cycled through manufacturing operations. It should be noted that portability may be enhanced by balancers, hoists, or other counterbalancing methods.

- *Stationary tools. Stationary tools* are fixed in one place, and work is normally brought to the tool. The tool is manually controlled. Many trim, assembly, and forming operations are done with such tools.

- *Machine tools.* Distinguished from all other tools, *machine tools* are self-contained, powered equipment.

Special tool control practices and procedures applicable to the above categories will be discussed later.

Nonproduction Material (Indirect Material)

As distinguished from tools, consisting of a wide variety of devices used to process the workpiece, there is a great variety of other nonproduction materials used indirectly to support manufacturing operations. These include the following:

Maintenance and Repair Materials.   Distinct from processing tools are those many components and materials that are required to maintain and repair manufacturing facilities. From a tool control standpoint, two issues are paramount: The cost of these items in inventory can become excessive because many replacement parts are expensive. However, they are essential for the continuity of machine and equipment operation. Shutdown losses may represent an even greater cost than tool inventory. Especially designated parts for machines and equipment require special consideration.

Supplies.   Supplies is another class of material vital to ongoing production operations. These can range from worker apparel to paper clips. A major portion of supply items may directly affect plant costs and efficiency and therefore require stringent control practices.

Bulk Materials.   Special attention must be given to those materials that are normally handled and stored in bulk. These include oils, greases, and other lubricants, gases, powders, paper, and fabrics. They involve a different set of controls, especially if they constitute a major portion of the items required by the enterprise.

Hazardous Substances.   As manufacturing processes become more sophisticated and many new materials are introduced into the plant environment, it has become important to recognize the danger of certain materials to workers' health and safety. Special inventory management and control are essential for hazardous material to conform with state and federal regulations.

Typically, these hazardous materials, including compounds that contain such materials, must be identified:

- To advise and train both production and maintenance personnel in proper handling procedures
- To track the hazardous material for the effects of aging and for volatility
- To establish appropriate emergency procedures for major accidents
- To consider storage location(s) and amounts at each site

Indirect Materials Management and Stores.   Under the functional control of materials management may be a broad array of shipping, handling, and storage items. This includes the availability, distribution, and repair of the many racks, dunnage, and packaging materials used with raw materials as well as finished products.

TOOL CONTROL FUNCTION

As noted in the introduction, tool control practices and procedures involve the entire manufacturing enterprise and may or may not be recognized by an organization title. Certain aspects of this type of control may vary widely in magnitude and importance from one enterprise to another.

Five distinct database systems are useful in the performance of the tool control function (Table 7.2). Because of tool control's pervasive nature, many of the data elements are common, so a combined data storage and retrieval program is desirable.

Database Design

The ubiquitous nature of the tool control function is obvious when facing the task of selecting computer system architecture and database design. The general characteristics and functional capabilities of a tool control database are described below, but they should be viewed finally in the context of information systems described in other handbook chapters.

Product Specifications and Design Data. Included in the database is all the product information necessary for the process planning function. Of particular interest to the tool control activity is the *assembly bill of materials.* In addition to a tabulation of the details of an assembly (process basis), a cross-reference table should be provided showing how many of each part are used in each assembly (volume and capacity requirements planning). In those applications where the process is directly associated with the product configuration, it is necessary to provide some sort of transition guide. Processes such as casting, forging, molding, and stamping not only shape the product but often determine its integrity and physical characteristics as well.

In the example of a cold-headed product, shown in Fig. 7.1, the progressive forming of the part essentially determines the shape of the tool detail and related tool design features (Fig. 7.2). Details of all part-shaping tools are identified along with associated die cases, sleeves, knock-out pins, and so on.

Manufacturing Information. The process information presented by the sequence of operations on a routing sheet for each part and assembly provides the initial basis for the tool control activities. The manufacturing process will include the requirements for all tools, machines, and related equipment. Inspection processes will provide comparable data for inspection and test operations. Similarly, materials-handling personnel will define appropriate materials specifications for packaging, containerization, and handling. The authorizations on the routing sheet provide a necessary and authentic cross reference of tools, gauges, and all other nonproduction materials. They will provide the basis for monitoring, design, and procurement.

TABLE 7.2 Data Storage and Retrieval Program

Database	Accessed by
1. Product specification and design data	Part nos.
2. Manufacturing information	Part nos.
3. Nonproduction materials data	Tool nos.
4. Procurement information	PO nos.
5. Design and application information	GT code

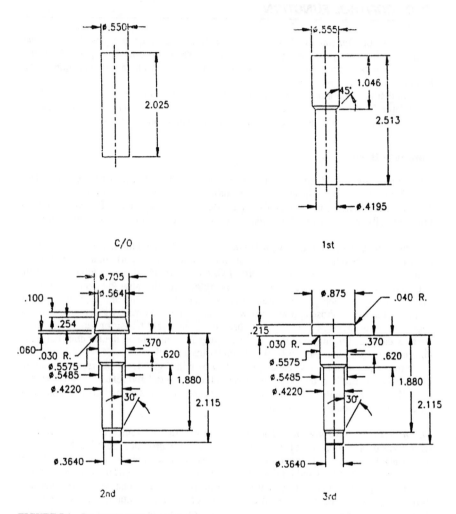

FIGURE 7.1   Progressive part-forming steps.

Nonproduction Materials (NPM) Data.*   The unique identification number assigned to each NPM item is the interface with the manufacturing system. This may consist of design drawing reference numbers, standard part designations, commercial item codes, or an inventory management stock code. The intent is to provide a viable system for tracking and reporting progress of all items and activities. The following information is needed:

- Design authorization, source, and progress and completion dates
- Number of parts and assemblies needed and recommended sources

---

*By permission of MASOTECH.

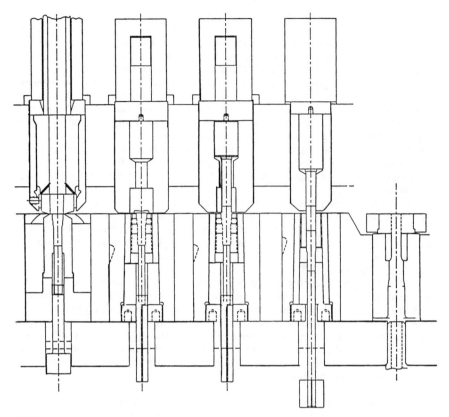

FIGURE 7.2 Die stages for part-forming (see Fig. 7.1).

- Materials procurement information, quantities needed, and source delivery promises
- Part and assembly operation assignments
- Initial setup requirements
- Stock status: on hand or in float
- Information for replacement parts, supplies, and support materials.

Procurement Information.   Procurement status is available by a tool or order number interfacing with the procurement system. Although some procurement data may be considered privileged with limited access, it is essential that purchasing information and status be available for the tool control function. However, often this service is isolated and placed in either the purchasing or inventory management group. The manner in which item costs are allocated to production operations is discussed in other chapters.

Group Technology Files.   Both part number and tool number files are necessarily organized by their unique item identification labels. The transition from part number to tool number data files may be accomplished in a variety of ways.

Typically, the identification labels may be inscribed on the items. They will also appear on the many documents used in engineering and manufacturing systems, including the design drawing that defines the item itself. These labels are used in the preparation of manuals, catalogs, parts lists, and so on. They are used as a basis for the necessary dialogue among the personnel associated with a product.

Although the sole purpose of a component or assembly "label" is to assure a unique identifier, it is common practice to include some significant meaning to the code. In the cold-heading process, for example, die inserts are used in common for a number of dies. A simple, but effective, group coding has been developed. Tool details are generally identified by the assigned heading machine. In this case, it is a 0.5-inch progressive header machine, and all details unique to this type of machine are in the 28xx series. To coordinate design and tool control, the more perishable parts of this tool are also given preassigned codes. For example, the third and fourth digits of all first-stage die inserts are the same.

Basic identification labels are usually numeric, but alphabetic codes are sometimes added to designate model, design level, component parts, and so on. Many coding schemes are used to catalog a variety of characteristics such as capacity and size. They can provide a useful guide through the necessary application parameters to make a proper choice. This type of coding often is based on industry standards, as shown for grinding wheels in Table 7.3.

While this type of coding facilitates communications in many transactions, it has practical limits in defining item characteristics. For example, such identification symbols are not compatible with the common NPM codes encountered in a typical tool control store. Often a secondary prefix code has to be added to establish that the item belongs to a more generic group known as *abrasives*. The technique for classifying the various characteristics of an item so that a "group" of items sharing the same characteristic can be quickly identified, cataloged, and retrieved has become a highly developed concept called *group technology* (GT).

Commercial GT Systems.   Comprehensive systems are commercially available for classifying and coding almost any universe of items. The supporting software provides a method of quickly isolating similar elements in a database. This permits the user to retrieve comparable items for new application studies, process planning studies, candidates for parametric design methods, and many other procedures that may benefit from group technology.

Group technology files can be easily interfaced to any or all of the databases described previously. They also provide a useful discipline for organizing a complex set of items, with assurance that the integrity of any item code is maintained. As an alternative to elaborate coding algorithms, and where a readable code is not essential, computer binary coding of group and class characteristics provides a significant advantage.

TABLE 7.3   Coding System

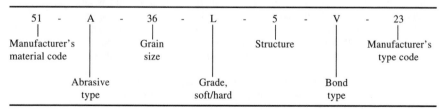

51	-	A	-	36	-	L	-	5	-	V	-	23
Manufacturer's material code				Grain size				Structure				Manufacturer's type code
		Abrasive type				Grade, soft/hard				Bond type		

Most readable codes are represented by 8-bit bytes in the computer, and 8 bits of binary code allow segregation of as many as 256 categories. For example, in a large materials list, the first bit could isolate metallic from nonmetallic; the second bit could distinguish ferrous and nonferrous; a third bit might separate symmetrical geometry from asymmetrical; and so on.

Decision Trees. Most computer-based group technology programs utilize algorithms based on binary decision trees, which provide a practical method for search and retrieval of database elements. Such utilities may be activated by a complete profile of the search object(s), or an interactive dialogue with the search program may be provided to progressively isolate those items with specified characteristics. An excellent example is that of an aerospace company that manufactures special avionic switches. These are complex devices, usually custom-built in small quantities to special order. Through effective use of interactive interview techniques and binary decision trees in their group technology system, company engineers can quickly establish an engineering parts list based on proven modules and meeting specified functional requirements. In turn, the manufacturing engineer can generate appropriate bills of materials, identifying types and numbers of subassemblies required in an assembly, as well as assembly sequence. These are preengineered subassemblies with known parts lists, processes, and tool requirements.

Use of such systems minimize:

- Reengineering of assemblies as a result of incompatible design
- Duplication of subassemblies through use of standard modules
- Redundancy in tools and NPM items
- Required lead time for manufacturing operations
- Tool control problems in design and procurement

An example of the cataloging and parts labeling is shown in Table 7.4.

In Tool Control activities, such capabilities provide an advantage in retrieving tool designs, application studies, and commonization programs. The decision tree approach allows all pertinent characteristics to be classified consistently, without duplication,

TABLE 7.4 Switch Catalog Number Including the Switch Definition

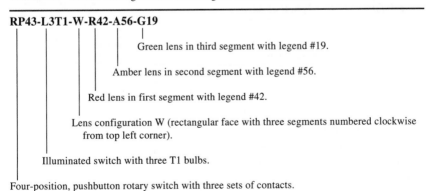

RP43-L3T1-W-R42-A56-G19

Green lens in third segment with legend #19.

Amber lens in second segment with legend #56.

Red lens in first segment with legend #42.

Lens configuration W (rectangular face with three segments numbered clockwise from top left corner).

Illuminated switch with three T1 bulbs.

Four-position, pushbutton rotary switch with three sets of contacts.

Source: By permission of CAM Software, Inc.

based on the best engineering application experience. Additionally, database search keys can then be formed using any combination of characteristics. Because of this power, the user may decide to use more than one GT base. One may be used to code item configuration characteristics and another for application characteristics or materials characteristics.

Item Identification.   Importantly, the unique individual identification code that must be assigned to each tool needed for design, procurement, or maintenance may or may not be based on such GT classification coding. As a general practice, it is recommended that only the code needed for the gross groupings of NPM management be retained in the tool identification number. For example, in a stores activity organized by types of inventory, one would expect to find all abrasive wheels in one general area, preferably identified by some unique group or class symbol. Stocking and disbursement operations would be facilitated by similar groupings for machine repair parts, cutting tools, apparel, or tool holders.

Considerations must be given to the preferred identification numbers, either that established by the user or by the industry standards organizations. Examples include ball bearings, tool holders, carbide inserts, limit switches, cylinders, electrodes, and fasteners. In these cases, an appropriate generic prefix code would be added to provide a general inventory category.

Use of Computer-Based Information Systems

As with all such systems, the benefits to be derived can be measured by the accuracy of the data provided and the discipline of timely entry. The casualness of the conventional informal system has been replaced by precision, speed, and better communication. This not only results in more efficient networking of information but also affords the opportunity for the expensive propagation of misinformation. In administering integrated systems, there are two functions that are especially critical to tool control but require rather conventional practices. These are review and approval of engineering designs and information and the necessary authorization of procurement and fabrication of tools and other NPM materials. Successful inclusion of tool control activities in a computer-integrated manufacturing system will depend on the smooth transition between the conventional practices and the computer system.

TOOL CONTROL PHASES

The interaction between available information systems will be described in the following discussion under subheadings associated with each phase of the manufacturing operation:

- Initial tool specification and design
- Process validation and initial procurement
- Inventory management
- Procurement guidelines
- Requisitioning and disbursement
- Tool change scheduling and monitoring
- Reconditioning and repair
- Research and development

Initial Tool Specification and Design

The process engineer has the responsibility of accurately defining the sequence of operations—that is, the routing—necessary to produce a finished component or assembly. Included is the responsibility for accurately describing the tools and accessories required in the production process. With this documentation, the tool engineer is expected to provide complete specifications for the possible design and initial procurement of tools. At this point, the tool control function starts. Preliminary decisions will be made regarding new versus existing tools and standard (commercially available) versus specially designed tools, in addition to decisions on the possibility of using tools that will be the same for similar product parts.

A good tool control practice involves a thorough screening of available tools, both standard and special, to avoid unnecessary duplication. The penalty for failing is redundant procurement and inventory with the associated added costs. In the case of expensed tools, there may be a further loss in not achieving procurement quantity discounts.

Essential to the success of this screening task is some form of group technology with the data processing hardware and database management software available. Use of an auxiliary classification number for cataloging design characteristics is recommended.

Once the need for a new design or modification of an existing design is established, a design source is selected. The choice is based on whether it is desirable to associate tool with machine or equipment design, retain a previous design group, or obtain one with known skills in specialty design. The tool control activity may contribute to this selection choice. If competitive bids are solicited, it is important that the design features desired are clearly defined in the request for quotation.

Design Validation.   Necessary revisions and changes to many tools will be indicated from the results of process validation and preproduction launch experience. Although the process engineer will be the judge of the process viability, it is the task of the tool engineer and the tool control activity to finalize the tool design and NPM specifications. They are responsible for obtaining usable tools with minimum delay and cost. It is at this time that need for a computer control system with its database becomes apparent. It should be noted that tracking the tool design, procurement, progress, and projected completion time is a vital part of using the computer database.

After the procurement of the initial complement of tools, immediate consideration must be given to tool, machine, and equipment maintenance practices. This becomes a part of the design validation phase. Replacement strategy should be established by tool control based on the history of similar tools. The projected needs based on experience and the importance of a component to equipment uptime.

Nondesign Tools.   Obviously, the tool control activity will also be involved with tools, supplies, and replacement parts that are not of special design. Tool control must have tool layout drawings for those operations that involve the multiple stations on a machine. The drawings must accurately depict all supporting details of the operation. In some organizations, these drawings will be maintained in lieu of the process sheet to portray all necessary tools and accessories. It is recommended that this tool layout be maintained under its own drawing identification number and also identified on the process sheet. It should not be included with machine or equipment drawings.

Figure 7.3 is the title corner of a tool layout drawing for an automotive steering-gear component. The rest of the equipment characteristics are shown in Fig. 7.4. Normally this type of reference data is accessed by tool control personnel, as needed, after reviewing the design drawing. When computer data systems become even more cost effective, it may be possible to store all layout information, including graphics, in an on-line database.

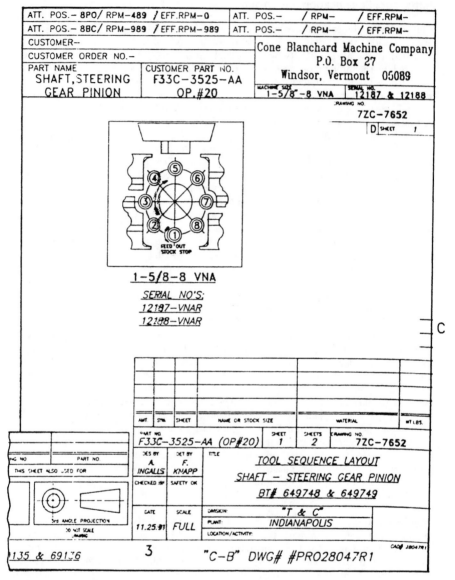

FIGURE 7.3   Title corner of drawing.

CHANGES

MACHINE COLLETS #G 7727
1.188/1.185 DIA. BORE (DULL SERRATIONS)

BALAS CAGE PUSHERS #P 11808

PICK-OFF COLLET #P 11383
1.145/1.142 DIA. BORE (SMOOTH BORE)

NOTE #1 - POS. #6-7 SPEC. .625 RISE CR. SLIDE CAM
     1ST - DWELL 70° (148 REVS)
     2ND - .625 R. IN 30° (.010 FD./63 REVS)

NOTE #2 - POS. #8 SPEC. .250 RISE CR. SLIDE CAM
     1ST - .250 R. IN 40° (.003 FD./84 REVS)
     2ND - DWELL 60° (127 REVS)

NOTE #3 - SPECIAL .938 RISE END-SLIDE CAM
     1ST - .938 R. IN 89° (.005 FD./188 REVS)
     2ND - DWELL 11° (23 REVS)
NOTE #5 - POS. #8 AUX. CAM - SEE LAYOUT# VN12322

NOTE #6 - POS. #4 SPECIAL DBL. RISE CR. SLIDE CAM
     1ST - .250 RISE IN 62° (.004 FD. IN 131 REVS)
     2ND - .030 RISE IN 30° (.0005 FD. IN 63 REVS)
     3RD - DWELL 8° (17 REVS)

MATERIAL SPECIFICATIONS		BRINELL HARDNESS	STOCK SPECIFICATIONS						
SAE-5115		175-225	SIZE-1.188 IN.			TOL.- -0.003 IN.			
COLD DRAWN			LENGTH-14 FOOT BAR			SHAPE- ROUND			

SPINDLE CHANGE GEARS		SPEED RANGE	SPINDLE RPM	FEET PER MIN.	GEAR CHART	FEED CHANGE GEARS		FEED RANGE	WORK REV'S	GEAR CHART
DRIVER	DRIVEN				81-120	DRIVER	DRIVEN			81-120
58	87		489	152	81-S99	41	23	LOW	211	81-F93

MAIN MOTOR SPECIFICATIONS	DEGREES IN WORK CYCLE	WORK CYCLE TIME	MACHINE IDLE TIME	TOTAL CYCLE TIME	PARTS PER HOUR GROSS
40 HP	100°	25.9 SEC.	2.1 SEC.	28.0 SEC.	128 PARTS

CYCLE TIME BASED ON : FORMING SPEED AND RECESS FEED.

CAMS	CROSS-SLIDE POSITIONS								MAIN END SLIDE CAM	AUX.	8TH AUX.	AUX.	AUX.
	1	2	3	4	5	6	7	8					
RISE		.281		SEE	.188	SEE		SEE	SEE		SEE		
FEED		.0014		NOTE	.0009	NOTE		NOTE	NOTE		NOTE		
TRAV.		.219		#6	.156	#1		#2	#3		#5		

B

FIGURE 7.4 Machine information.

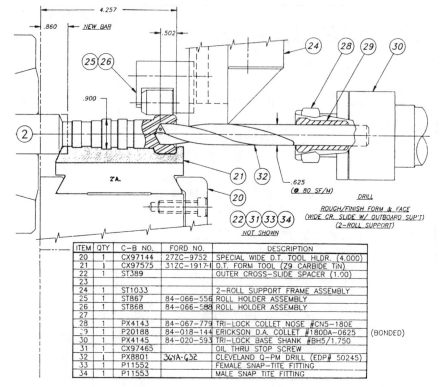

ITEM	QTY	C—B NO.	FORD NO.	DESCRIPTION
20	1	CX97144	27ZC—9752	SPECIAL WIDE D.T. TOOL HLDR. (4.000)
21	1	CX97575	31ZC—1917-I	D.T. FORM TOOL (Z9 CARBIDE TiN)
22	1	ST389		OUTER CROSS—SLIDE SPACER (1.00)
23				
24	1	ST1033		2—ROLL SUPPORT FRAME ASSEMBLY
25	1	ST867	84—066—556	ROLL HOLDER ASSEMBLY
26	1	ST868	84—066—588	ROLL HOLDER ASSEMBLY
27				
28	1	PX4143	84—067—779	TRI—LOCK COLLET NOSE #CN5—180E
29	1	P20188	84—018—144	ERICKSON D.A. COLLET #180DA—0625 (BONDED)
30	1	PX4145	84—020—593	TRI—LOCK BASE SHANK #BH5/1.750
31	1	CX97465		OIL THRU STOP SCREW
32	1	PX8801	36YA-G52	CLEVELAND Q—PM DRILL (EDP# 50245)
33	1	P11552		FEMALE SNAP—TITE FITTING
34	1	P11553		MALE SNAP TITE FITTING

FIGURE 7.5   Station information.

Figure 7.5 illustrates the tooling arrangement for station 2 of an 8-station machine. As can be seen, all design and application information is presented for this part of operation 20. Notice that variable data such as quantities, stocking practices, or recommended inventory levels are not shown but are maintained in the more dynamic nonproduction material database. For parts that use similar processes, the layout should include a table of the setups, instructions, and a tool list for each part.

Design or Process Change.   One of tool control's most difficult tasks is to maintain current tool assignments and design level of tools. Again, a suitable database program will facilitate this task especially as the product goes through the final preproduction process adjustments. The majority of changes at this point will probably be generated by the ongoing resolution of processing difficulties and the necessary modifications.

As the process matures, the majority of changes will be caused by changes in the product design and specifications. The change control and tracking algorithms incorporated in the tool control system should accommodate the different part changes. This may include changes in operating schedule dates and launch or cutoff dates of subsequent product levels. It is the responsibility of the tool control activity to manage these transitions with a minimum of delay and tool obsolescence.

Process Validation and Initial Procurement

Good manufacturing-engineering practice requires a reasonable tryout of the planned process, as well as the product design and its function. To the extent possible, all such preliminary evaluation should be realistic with actual tools, materials, and equipment. Tool control will play a critical role during this important phase of manufacturing planning.

Process Validation.   The general policy is to charge the supplier with the responsibility of obtaining the initial complement of tryout tools. If this is not the case, the tool control function will procure the tools needed for tryout and launch requirements. In either case, it becomes tool control's responsibility to know the quantities, design levels, and experience during the preliminary stage.

Tool control should monitor and document all tools that are broken by accident. These would not be a part of normal production experience. Abnormal wear or breakage that can be corrected by relatively minor design or material change or unexpected quality problems should be recorded. This record forms a basis for adjusting or setting initial production procurement quantities and design specification.

Adjustments will be simplified for standard or commercially available components. For specially designed components, where the design function is not subject to validation, the production launch quantities may be used to reduce the fabrication lead time and initial lot size.

Initial Procurement.   The tool control personnel will assist the tool engineer and the inventory manager to determine the varieties and amounts of tools needed to launch production operations.

With the resolution of the issues noted, the initial procurement quantities can be determined and the level of tool maintenance established. Reconditioning and repair procedures can also be determined. The optimum setup and float quantities must also be calculated. And finally, recommendations must be made for repair or disposal of the defective tryout tools.

Generally, the planned lot size is known at the initial procurement time. In these cases, tools and supplies may be *kitted*—that is, all necessary components for setup and processing of a production lot are packaged separately. It may be desirable to develop a detailed matrix record of tool usage for each product. Adequate quantities of common components are procured initially for such kitting.

Inventory Management

The investment in production parts, raw materials, and finished goods will exceed by several times the normal investment in tools and nonproduction materials. The just-in-time (JIT) concept has been applied to production materials to minimize storage space, handling costs, and investment. However, the practice has experienced mixed results when applied to tools and nonproduction materials. Reducing floats, reconditioning times, number of tool changes, and setup times have always been part of good tool control. JIT's effect has been on the production operations, and it has not had dramatic effect on tool inventories.

One relative measure of management's control of tools and nonproduction materials inventories has been the number of inventory turns per year. This is a ratio of the total inventory procurement cost for the year and the actual inventory cost at any one time. Any turnover ratio greater than 6 has been considered good. That is to say, average inventory is one-sixth of a year's consumption. Even this number may be misleading because large amounts of slow-moving or obsolete stock can be masked by extremely rapid procurement and disbursement cycles of many other items. Several management techniques for controlling tools and nonproduction materials can be provided by tool control personnel. These are discussed below.

Storage Strategy.   The mission of the tool inventory manager is to assure that tools and nonproduction materials are readily available for production operations. To ensure availability, clear specifications of the items involved must be provided. The tool control function advises the tool inventory manager where preferred stock storage locations are.

Types of Material.   The first consideration is the type of material. Tools and nonproduction materials that are used directly and frequently in production will be located in *expense cribs* strategically placed among the using activities. A reasonable balance should be achieved between available plant space, volume of material, and travel distance between storage and using site.

Reconditioning material is used for replacement, refurbishing, or setting up more complex tools. These should be stored at a site convenient to the reconditioning activity. If reconditioning is part of a tool room activity, the tool crib should be adjacent to it.

Often the tool control function involves inspection of worn production tool assemblies. The tool control function assesses the degree of wear, as well as what reconditioning steps are needed. Providing for these necessary services should be considered when determining storage of replacement parts.

A similar need arises when storing machine and equipment maintenance materials. In this case, the site of the maintenance department should be chosen based on the required number of maintenance workers and the skills, tools, and parts used. There are cases where materials used by specialty trades cannot be distributed in the plant and must be kept at a single site.

Bulk materials will generally be stored in one location and require special storage conditions. The materials will be delivered to each using location in drums, cylinders, barrels, or cartons to cover the daily or shift requirements. Salvage, disposal, and recycling of such containers becomes another consideration.

Usage.   A second factor in establishing a desirable storage strategy for tools and nonproduction materials has to do with the number and user's location.

Single-Use Material.   If a tool or a specific type of nonproduction material is used by one production activity, it should be stored near it. Alternatively, if usage is light, delivery short, and availability not critical, it may not be necessary to carry any inventory for such items.

Multiple-Use Material.   Proper tool control includes standardizing. Consequently, a number of cribs or storage areas will include the same items. It is the responsibility of the inventory manager to be aware of common part situation and consolidate the procurement of such items and provide distribution to the crib. If one using location uses most of an item, it is appropriate to designate it as a "master crib." It will be a single store location user, and other minor users will requisition their requirements from it. This efficacy may be offset to some degree because tool control may be unaware of abnormal usage.

General-Use Tools and Materials.   An effective alternative to the master crib strategy described is to establish a general stores. In addition to multiuse and general-use materials, the *general stores* is normally organized to act as a control point for procurement, distribution, and tool inventory management. Many single-use items may also be controlled by general stores until needed.

Plant management judgment is needed to determine whether a general stores within a single plant is desirable or whether it should be used for a multiplant complex. The decision will be based on volume, variety of tools, and materials. Similarity of participating plants, as well as preferred management organization, influence the decision.

Supplier Stores. It has become accepted practice to ask suppliers to maintain a contingent quantity of tools and indirect materials for guaranteed delivery. In return, the supplier expects a longer-term purchase commitment. The user may also ask for a fixed price. Such agreements become a factor in the establishment of inventory guidelines by the tool control and inventory manager.

Procurement Guidelines

Previously, the need for design and process validation was discussed, as well as the need for good procurement planning. A continuing longer-term outlook by tool control management is required at this point, considering the following factors:

> *Usage.* A good historical record is required. It is important that performance data that are usually expressed in terms of production quantity per tool unit, including number of regrinds or setups per tool, be recorded.

> *Float.* The quantity of tools required to fill the system is called the *float.* Float is an inventory factor only when the operation is initially tooled or when design changes require retooling.

Durable, long-lasting tools are required for setting up machines. Typically, these include tool blocks, rest blades, chucks, and so on. Another group of tools included in the float is nondurable tool assemblies such as sectional broaches, inserted-blade cutters, and die inserts. For these items one must include the tools presently installed, the preset quantities at the machine site, those being reconditioned, plus those in transit between the using site, refurbishing, and the inventory locations.

Design-Process Stability. Tool control is responsible for advising the inventory manager of pending process revisions, change studies being considered, potential product changes, and tool performance improvements.

Inventory Management. Separate from tool control and engineering is the discretion allowed the inventory manager concerning choice of supplier, procurement lead times, and costs. The inventory manager must consider the impact on plant performance if tools and materials are not available. The last is critical when applying a JIT policy to factory operations and its effect on subsequent users.

Requisitioning and Disbursement

The first consideration in establishing requisitioning and disbursing policies is to assure management that adequate financial controls are being applied. The following is a number of operating factors related to tool control.

Budget Control. Even small organizations must have tool and nonproduction materials control. To do this, a requisition form bearing an authorization signature is sent from the person requesting tools or materials to the inventory control. Unless tools have already been charged to the using group, the requisition enters the charge into the accounting system to provide a means of accumulating operating expense. The cost of certain tools and parts can be added to the machine costs. These costs may be capitalized as extending the machine's useful life and thereby altering its depreciable value.

Performance Monitoring.   The opportunity to monitor tool usage with the requisitioning procedure is important for the tool control activity. In many instances, abnormal tool usage may be detected within a day. Troubles caused by defective tools, out-of-specification workpieces, or improper machine operating conditions can be quickly identified and brought to the tool engineer's attention. Tool control practices should be such that this communication is made as direct as possible. Tool control can be alerted immediately when such problems demand emergency attention.

Tool Storage and Handling.   Plant economics may warrant using an automated storage and retrieval system (AS/RS) to achieve inventory density and minimize the need for disbursement personnel. Such systems normally require some type of box or tray packaging to facilitate tool handling. These packaging practices are also useful in manual stock handling. Customized trays and/or boxes are recommended for delicate and expensive tools such as carbide cutters (solid and tipped), gear and thread hobs, form broaches (spline or serration), and special mold inserts. Other tools may be protected by dipping, at least the finished end, in plastic. A further element of tool control is to make these tool containers of a size or capacity to hold one "setup complement" at the using site.

Replacement Part Control.   Accurate records of part usage not only provide necessary cost accounting information but also give the tool control activity invaluable insight into areas of needed improvement and potential cost savings. Some companies issue tags, or *tool checks,* to personnel working on machines and equipment. The tool check is used for signing out special maintenance tools and is returned by the storekeeper when the tool is returned.

Tool checks may also be used to assure that replacement parts are going to their assigned use and good practices are being followed. Some organizations require the return of a worn or equivalent tool to redeem the tool check.

Tool Change Scheduling and Monitoring

The most important reason for any tool control activity is to assure the proper application and use of tools in production operations. Inherent in this is the adoption of tooling practices that facilitate the adjustment and replacement of tools, the training of operating personnel in the necessary change discipline, and the maintaining of sufficient quantities of tools in the system so no compromise is necessary for maintaining production continuity. Establishing and adhering to suitable tool change schedules involve several essential system characteristics, as follows.

Preset Tools.   Consistent with conditions established in the design and procurement phase of the equipment, operating practices should be defined that minimize production losses due to tool change and adjustments. Many tools can be preset to exact dimensions, gauged, or made to fit other functional specifications. In addition to presetting capability, provision should be made, where possible, to allow continuing adjustment of the installed tool as ongoing production wear occurs.

Quick Change.   Closely allied with the preset philosophy is the use of tool blocks, mounting plates, and so on that help provide the rapid removal of worn tools and their replacement. As the quick-change concept has become popular, it has become good practice to provide quick-change features for major tool assemblies such as stamping dies. Obviously, applications at this level require adequate consideration in the early planning and design of machine tools and related automation.

Site Storage.   Because of delays in expediting the movement of tools from storage or reconditioning them, it is advantageous to include some tools at the site for near-term use. This procedure may require special benches and/or racks that setup personnel can use for making presetting adjustments prior to installation. For cutting tools, this facility may often provide all necessary bench accessories including special storage pockets for each tool. In complex tooling installations, part counters may be provided at the setup bench to indicate production piece-counts as part of a change schedule.

Production Monitoring.   Where analysis has indicated its necessity and value, certain parts of the operation cycle may be provided with instruments so the operator and/or support personnel may monitor production cycle conditions. Typically, a number of workpiece counters are provided to allow incremental tracking of specific tools. In-process gauges may be used to display critical dimension values for operating personnel. Power monitors are used to indicate abnormal energy needs caused by out-of-condition tools. These practices assure more consistent flow of worn tools to the refurbishing activity and less time spent in reconditioning broken or badly worn tools.

Integrated Tool Management.   With today's technology, it is both feasible and practical to incorporate many of the tool management functions described above into a computer-based facility interfacing other tool control systems, as well as machine and automation control systems.

A typical work site tool storage and setup station will have appropriate tool storage sockets provided for preset tools and holders and also a variety of accessories for tool setups. A number of tool positions on the machine can be monitored by production counters. A tool control system workstation can be included for entering tool performance data, to obtain tools, enter inventory data, or reconditioning status.

Establishing the Change Schedule.   Optimum tool change schedules are initially established from experience for similar tools and operations. The schedule is adjusted eventually on the basis of actual experience. Conditions that influence schedule changes are tool wear, workpiece quality, and production batch size.

Ideally, change schedules will coincide with normal production breaks such as shift changes, lunch breaks, or other relief breaks. Tools with a relatively long life expectancy should be scheduled accordingly. If a long setup time is needed for a tool, the decision of when to change may be very important.

If tools fail catastrophically, the schedule must consider tool cost and the loss of production. This is not like change cycles established by observing uniform tool wear patterns. The optimum schedule is based on workpiece quality, as well as reconditioning costs. If tool failure results in a damaged workpiece, the establishment of a fixed change cycle may be impossible. In this case constant observation of the tool by the operator is required. Quality monitors or meters monitoring the power used, reflecting processing difficulties, may be useful. Finally, the tool change schedule may be established to coincide with the end of batch lot quantities.

Tool Reconditioning and Repair

The proper restoration and/or reproduction of the original tool design characteristics is another major consideration for tool control. Skilled personnel, proper equipment, and suitable tool usage practices are all important ingredients of a viable refurbishing activity. Many of the procedures needed to maintain the tool will be established during the tryout and preproduction launch experience.

Tool Replacement Strategy.   Based on previous experience, an initial replacement strategy is chosen during the tool design phase. Machine access, quality requirements, and possible loss of production time are factors in determining how tools will be restored.

Simple Replacement of Perishable Tools.   Typically, these will include lathe tool inserts, drills, punches, electrodes, and rotary cutters. In this type of replacement, there is little concern about disturbing other tools, changing process dimensions, or obtaining access by maintenance personnel.

Modular Replacement of Tools and Toolholders.   Examples are drills, reamers, boring tools, plain grinding wheels, trim dies, and inserted-blade cutters (including broaches). Such modules can be assembled and preset, thereby reducing change time and reasonable assurance of maintaining process dimensions.

Installing a New Tool Assembly.   This type of tool restoration is done during scheduled breaks in production, and it may involve a major teardown of equipment and probably will require a significant effort to restore process dimensions and quality. Some examples would be large broach assemblies, multiple punch and die assemblies, mold patterns, and grinding wheel sets. The choices in these strategies will determine the quantity and makeup of the toolroom equipment required for restoring production tools.

Tool Inspection

Good tool control practices require not only an examination of tools going into production but also those worn tools coming from production. This latter examination provides early detection of needed changes in the tool design or material. Abusive practices and workpieces that are out of specification are important when considering the work required for restoration. The choices may be either to restore, adjust, or replace or a combination of all three. Restoration includes regrinding, polishing, and dressing of only slightly worn surfaces. Generally this represents good tool change practices.

Badly worn or broken details are usually the result of poor change schedules, although the vagaries of many manufacturing processes result in the damage to tool details. In almost all cases, tool adjustments are needed to restore setup dimensions. It is preferable to do this during the refurbishing activity, but in many cases it is done at the using site.

Salvage and Modification.   Significant tool economies can be had by modifying standard tools or by adapting broken tools. This is easier to do if the tool design characteristics are available in the tool database.

Disposition.   The tool control function is generally charged with disposing of unwanted or unusable tools. Tools used in the manufacture of restricted or proprietary parts must be disabled so they cannot be used. Tools that are unusable at the time of disposition may be scrapped in a conventional manner. Tool control analysts should determine if any useful parts have been removed for reuse.

RESEARCH AND DEVELOPMENT

Process improvement and productivity gains depend on active tool research and development programs. Essential to their success is an ability to identify and define potential improvement areas. The most effective method is to establish an adequate computer database so historical tool performances may be compared. Also performances with similar applications can be compared.

Tool control procedures should be established to record the following ongoing accumulation of tool and production experience:

- Tool life in product pieces per setup
- Total life of the tool
- Performance of the tool under different operating conditions
- Reconditioning costs per tool
- Change time for each production setup

Cost Performance

Tool cost information will provide the necessary planning support. The redesign and upgrade of components may be indicated based on the performance as compared with similar components. Comparable data should be accumulated for machine and equipment maintenance activities, including lost production time.

Safety Hazard Agenda

The need for accurate information about types and quantities of hazardous materials used has become increasingly important. For both safety and economic reasons, management must support ongoing studies to minimize the possibility of worker exposure. This can be a difficult inventory control problem to solve for hazardous materials.

SUMMARY

Whether the tool control functions, described in this chapter, are carried out by a separate tool control department or are the responsibility of each department, it is essential that they use established measures of performance that are checked on a regular basis.

Today's computer-integrated manufacturing (CIM) environment often is the opportunity for applying good tool control techniques. It is important, for competitive reasons, that employees are adequately trained to effectively use information systems in the management of tools and nonproduction materials.

It can be anticipated that the variety and speed of changes in manufacturing systems will increase rapidly to make manufacturing more profitable. Flexibility in machining and assembly facilities will demand responsive information systems that will maximize tool performance and minimize waste and obsolescence. The basic manufacturing processes are being supplemented continuously with new technology that requires support systems with greater sophistication and more extensive worker training. At the same time, greater care for employees' health and safety is being accommodated by the effective use of computer-based systems for tracking exposure to hazardous materials.

Finally, as with many of today's manufacturing support systems, the opportunity to gather volumes of operating data has never been greater. The practitioner must determine which data are pertinent and which can be further processed into meaningful information, and he or she must insist on computer assistance in analyzing important complex data relationships and presenting them to operating management for decision making.

CHAPTER 8
MANPOWER INFORMATION*

Editor

Henry H. Jordan, Jr., CMC, CFPIM
Chairman, Center for Inventory Management,
Sugar Hill, Georgia

Assistant Editor

Henry H. Jordan III, CMC, CPIM, CIRM
Professor, DeVry Institute,
Atlanta, Georgia

Contributors

Lloyd R. Andreas, CFPIM
Applications Manager, Marcam Corp.
Atlanta, Georgia

J. Thomas Brown, CFPIM
Principal Consultant, PowerCerv
Duluth, Georgia

Robert A. Leavey, CFPIM, CIRM
Atlanta, Georgia

Ernest C. Theisen, Jr., CFPIM
Consultant, Stone Mountain, Georgia

PLANNING AND CONTROL OF MANPOWER

A key factor in the success or failure of the manufacturing operation is the planning and control of manpower. It is certainly as important as having the right parts at the right time.

*The editors wish to acknowledge the contributors to the original version of this chapter: W. Neil Benton, Richard B. Black, Walter Cloud, Dr. Robert C. Klekamp, J. Clifford Kulick, Leo A. Smith, David D. Swett, and Dennis B. Webster. They also wish to acknowledge the contributors to the revision of this chapter in the second edition of the handbook: Joseph A. Carrano, Willard R. Hazel, and Robert W. Whittaker.

TABLE 8.1   Master Schedule

Product	Weeks							
	1	2	3	4	5	6	7	8
A 2001	20	20	20	20	20	20	20	20
B 1742	100		100		100		100	
C 4019	1500	1500	1500	1600	1600	1600	1700	1700
D 6730			10			10		

Master Production Schedule

Proper planning and control of manpower needs begin with the master production schedule (MPS) (see Table 8.1), which quantifies the products to be manufactured during specific time periods to meet the demands of customers. Through the use of time standards or historical profiles, the time-phased units of measure for each product are converted to man-hours or some equivalent meaningful factor for calculating manpower requirements.

Numerous factors directly or indirectly affect the development of the MPS and cannot be ignored if manpower planning and control is to be handled properly. These factors are shown in Fig. 8.1, along with the actions that follow as a result of the MPS.

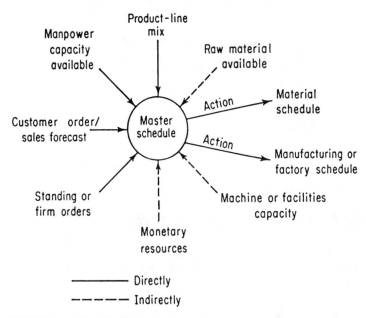

FIGURE 8.1   Master schedule input and output factors.

Manpower Capacity

The term *capacity* by itself can be misleading. In fact, calculations of both available capacity and required capacity must be made in manpower planning. *Available capacity* indicates the current availability of such resources as manpower, equipment, and facilities under normal operating conditions. *Required capacity* refers to the capacity needed to meet company goals of optimum customer service, inventory levels, and manufacturing efficiency in light of customer order/forecast requirements. Required capacity should be compared to available capacity to determine whether the latter should be, and can be adjusted to meet the forecasted demand.

In most companies, available manpower capacity is somewhat flexible because new hires assigned to open work stations or equipment can increase capacity while layoffs or departmental transfers can decrease capacity. In fact, many options are available to adjust manpower capacity:

- Working overtime
- Adding a second or third shift
- Hiring new employees
- Laying off employees
- Reducing the workweek
- Increasing subcontracting
- Reducing subcontracting
- Improving production methods

Successful manpower planning and control must also take into account the learning curve, the effect of adding new hires, quality of workers already in place, fatigue factor caused by working longer hours for extended periods, deteriorating equipment, and so on.

Customer Order and Sales Forecast

In those companies with large customer order backlogs, the development of an MPS and resultant manpower plan is eased somewhat because they are not subjected to the vagaries of forecasting.

When manpower planning is based on a forecast, in lieu of firm customer orders, it is important that the planning team understand forecasting techniques and their differing degrees of accuracy. Usually, by testing various techniques against historical demand, forecasting methods can be selected that give the "least wrong" results, thus minimizing the actual demand surprises that can force replanning of manpower requirements. Various forecast techniques are discussed elsewhere in this book.

Cyclical and Seasonal Considerations

Cyclical or seasonal sales patterns present a different challenge to manpower planning and control. A management decision must be made between a relatively stable workforce accompanied by fluctuating inventory levels and a fluctuating workforce with relatively fixed inventory levels. These decisions are usually dictated by the skill levels required to manufacture the product and the availability of workers with the corresponding skill levels in the communities surrounding the manufacturing facility.

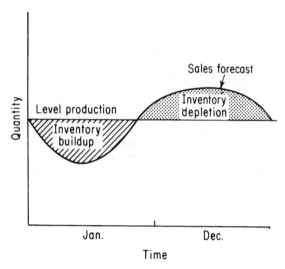

FIGURE 8.2 Level workforce.

Figure 8.2 shows an example of a level manpower plan versus a seasonal sales forecast. Production planned on the leveling method minimizes manpower fluctuations but accentuates inventory accumulation, as shown by the crosshatched area. The minimum manpower cost resulting from a constant level of production must be balanced against the increased cost of carrying inventory during the periods of slack customer demand.

Figure 8.3 illustrates a situation in which a trained labor force is readily available, or the labor skill required is low, resulting in low training costs. The planned production level is changed in a step manner to closely anticipate customer demand. An addition to the workforce would result in increased production; conversely, each decline would be accomplished via layoffs, shorter workweeks, or other decreases in available manpower capacity.

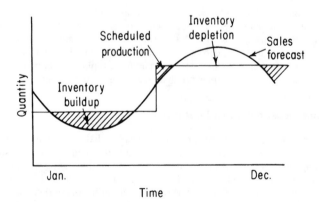

FIGURE 8.3 Variable workforce.

Some companies with the highly skilled labor needed to fabricate component parts and the easily available semiskilled labor used in assembly of the final product use both methods of manpower planning in a seasonal or cyclical environment. The skilled manpower is planned at the level rate, building up the less expensive component inventory during the off season, while the semiskilled labor fluctuates closer to the customer's demand for the finished product, thus keeping this more expensive level of inventory relatively low.

Product Line Mix

Variations in demand for different product lines made in the same plant must be taken into account in the manpower planning process. Variations to consider include skill levels needed to manufacture, material content, size of the product, high versus low volume, and contribution to profit. It is often necessary to regard each product line in the mix as a separate entity and to plan accordingly.

The problem of product mix is accentuated when the customer order forecast demands more capacity than can be made available. For example, suppose product line A demands 60 percent of the available capacity; product line B, 30 percent; and product C, 35 percent. Then current capacity has to be increased by 25 percent. If after all methods have been used to expand capacity, such as overtime, additional shifts, adding people, subcontracting, and so on, there is still a shortfall of capacity, then the alternative is to delay or stretch out customer order forecast requirements and quote longer lead times to customers. It might be feasible to load the available capacity with the higher-profit product lines and to fill out the balance with product lines in descending order of profit contribution. However, customer satisfaction and future product potential must be carefully weighed when this decision is made.

Standing Orders, or Firm Business

Many companies are fortunate to have firm customer orders covering long periods in the manufacturing cycle. This firm business, sometimes called standing orders, enables planners to assign manpower on a continuing basis to a core of work that is relatively permanent. This enables planning for a basically permanent workforce to handle the firm business, with the concentration of manpower planning performed on the other-than-firm segment of the business. Surges in the latter category are handled via overtime, temporary hires, additional shifts, and so on.

Control of Manpower

To control manpower requires monitoring, measuring, and comparing it with the manpower plan created earlier. Just as sales demand will vary around the manpower plan, so will production vary around the manpower plan. A certain amount of variation is considered normal, so it is wise to establish tolerances, or plus-and-minus ranges within which no change in manpower planning would be required. Any deviation from these predetermined ranges would trigger replanning via overtime, layoffs, and so on. Inherent in planning is the necessity to predict and prepare a manpower plan under conditions of great uncertainty. Successful control requires corrective action be taken as soon as possible when actual conditions fall outside the tolerances of the manpower plan. Numerous methods of reporting and measuring are used to compare actual performance against the plan. As part of an overall management information system, reports should be developed showing the number of employees, number of absentees, frequency of absenteeism, layoffs, transfers, new hires, types of skills, and skill levels.

Measures of productivity efficiency indicate output per unit of manpower. Measurement might be in dollars or units of output per man-hour, man-day, and so on. Other useful ratios are the number of direct to indirect man-hours, direct labor man-hours to idle man-hours, direct labor man-hours to machine-hours, overtime hours to straight-time hours, piece-rate workers to day workers. Each ratio measures actual performance against the plan, to trigger corrective action and bring results back to the planned norms. Without this type of comparison there would be no knowledge of either efficient or inefficient use of manpower. Under the philosophy of JIT, measurements of manpower *utilization* should be used with caution. Although they can assist in manpower planning, they should not be used to drive labor to produce unneeded inventories.

Long-Range Manpower Planning

Although most manpower planning is relatively short range, as compared to facilities planning, there is an important need for periodic long-range planning. This need is apparent where the demand for skilled labor is projected to increase but the available supply is constant or decreasing. This situation might require upgrading existing manpower through various training programs, such as apprentice programs to supply skilled toolmakers or machinists, formal on-the-job training programs, technical-school sessions, tuition-refund plans for technical training courses, etc. Attention to long-range manpower planning might dictate the relocation of a plant to an area with a surplus of the labor type required. Long-range manpower planning should be part and parcel of any company's projections which are greater than a year into the future. Resource profiles or *bills of labor* constructed for products or product families can incorporate requirements for manpower skills, and be used in long-range production planning to identify future needs.

MANPOWER LOADING

Manpower loading, also called *labor loading,* is a process that compares expected labor requirements with the available capacity of that labor. Many techniques are used in manpower loading but all perform three basic functions:

1. Estimate the manpower resources required to accomplish a specific production schedule. This production schedule may be a long-range production plan, a medium-range MPS, or a short-range schedule of manufacturing operations.

2. Project the manpower resources that will be available to meet the production schedule. This projection of manpower availability must span the time horizon stated in the production schedule and must include the labor skills specified in the requirements definition.

3. Provide visibility of current or anticipated imbalances between labor requirements and capacity. These imbalances are analyzed, and actions are planned to match labor resource availability and labor requirements for each period.

This process may seem familiar. It is just one of the forms of capacity or resource management. It is different from other forms of capacity management in that it specifically addresses only manpower capacity.

Effective management of the production process requires a knowledge of what labor skills are needed, how much labor is required to meet production objectives, when that labor is needed, and how much of the needed labor skills will be available. The techniques of manpower loading are used to assist the capacity planner in answering these questions, arriving at a sound manpower plan, and monitoring operations to ensure successful execution of the plan.

Manpower Versus Machine Capacity

Obviously, both labor and machine resources are essential for production. In terms of defining capacity and calculating projected load, these should be considered together. The relationship of manpower to machines needs to be viewed in terms of a single capacity unit, such as a work center, cell, or assembly line. The definition of these units has to be done at a level that supports the balancing of both manpower and machine capacity to meet production. The ratio of specific manpower requirements to machine requirements must be specified, with indications of what variables affect the overall capacity of the work center, cell, or line.

Manpower and Machine Data

The proper selection and definition of work centers for manpower and machine loading is crucial. The three-step procedure in Table 8.2 identifies those factors that indicate logical work center groups and define the work center's manpower and machine capacity.

Planning the Load

Many techniques can be used to project manpower requirements. The selection of the proper technique depends on the time horizon of the manpower plans being made, the type of production process, and data availability. Several commonly used techniques for manpower loading are presented here. This is, by no means, a complete list of all the techniques that have been successfully applied. However, most manpower loading techniques employ variations of the examples shown here.

Rough-Cut Manpower Loading

Rough-cut capacity planning can be used to provide early warning of long-range labor imbalances. It is not a technique for detailed manpower planning.

Rough-cut capacity planning verifies that adequate levels of the critical labor resources are available. This is accomplished by converting the production plan or MPS into requirements for labor and other resources using a *bill of resource* or resource profile.

The bill of resource shown in Table 8.3 specifies the key labor resources required to manufacture a fixed number of units of a specific item or a given mix of a family of items. The last column in the bill of labor shows the month in the production process during which that labor activity will most likely take place. The calculation of average standard hours used for a product group is typically accomplished by a weighted-average technique. This technique is demonstrated for assembly labor in Table 8.3. This

TABLE 8.2   Three-Step Procedure

Step 1. Identify the important resource attributes.		
	Manpower	Machine
Resource function	Labor type Operator Setup Inspector	Machine type Drill Mill Grinder
Resource rating	Skill level or grade	Size or speed
Alternative resource	Skill level or grade	Machine or work center

Step 2. Specify relationships between scheduled items and productive resources.		
	Manpower	Machine
Standard times	Setup labor hours Labor time per unit Teardown labor hours	Setup machine hours Machine time per unit Teardown labor hours
Planned allowances	Fatigue Delay	Adjustments Tooling changes
Efficiency factor	Labor efficiency	Machine efficiency
Actual performance versus standard times	Standard labor hours produced per hour worked	Standard machine hours produced per hour worked

Step 3. Estimate actual resources available in future periods.		
	Manpower	Machine
Gains or losses	Hiring or layoff plans Training plans Turnover percentage	Purchase plans Rebuild plans Divestiture plans
Availability	Absentee rate Holidays or vacations Training or administrative time	Repair downtime Preventive maintenance Fuel or power shortage
Utilization factor	Labor utilization	Machine utilization
Actual time worked versus scheduled	Production hours worked per hour scheduled	Hours operated per hour scheduled

product group is composed of four items whose projected product mix and standard hours are used to find the average standard for each labor type.

The rough-cut capacity plan is developed by multiplying the MPS quantities for each product group and the labor standards listed in the bill resource. An example of a plan for assembly labor, Table 8.4, shows the requirements for this labor type for each product group by monthly period, the total labor required, the projected labor available, and the projected difference between requirements and availability (Table 8.5).

TABLE 8.3 Bill of Resource Product Group A

	Average standard hours per 100 units	Month
Design engineers	10.8	1
N/C programmers	6.5	2
Machinists	30.0	3
Welders	12.2	3
Assembly	24.7	4

TABLE 8.4 Assembly Labor, Product Group A

Item	Product mix (A)	Standard assembly hours per 100 units (B)	A × B
1	0.20	27.6	5.52
2	0.13	31.4	4.08
3	0.42	21.3	8.95
4	0.25	24.6	6.15
	1.00		24.70

TABLE 8.5 Rough-Cut Capacity Plan for Assembly Labor

	January	February	March
MPS			
Product group A	14,400	17,000	15,000
Product group B	9,100	13,000	9,400
Manpower load hours			
Product group A	3,557	4,199	3,705
Product group B	1,911	2,730	1,974
Total	5,468	6,929	5,679
Available labor hours	6,350	6,000	6,100
Variance	+882	−929	+421

Capacity Requirements Planning

Capacity requirements planning (CRP) is a detailed, analytical approach for medium- to short-range capacity planning. It is as valuable as a manpower loading technique as it is for machine loading. The long-range, rough-cut manpower plans are not detailed enough to support the decisions which must be made concerning work assignments, the use of overtime, or reduction of shift hours. The distinguishing feature of CRP, then, is its attention to detail. Each item, including all subassemblies and component parts, is "backward-scheduled," and the required load is placed on the appropriate work centers in the proper time period.

Because of the detail involved, CRP is rarely performed manually. Generally CRP begins with the *materials requirements planning* (MRP) system output and loads the work centers shown in the routing file without considering capacity constraints (infinite loading). The load is assigned to the appropriate time period based on a calculated operation time for the lot and standard queue and transit times for the work center. The data required for this process come from the detail plant schedule or MRP, the routing file for each part, and the work center file for each load center. The output of CRP is a work center load profile that shows the load, time period, and source of that load.

Line Loading

In repetitive manufacturing and other flow-oriented production environments, manpower requirements over the short-term horizon can be developed from production schedules or individual line schedules. Detailed scheduling at an operations level is usually not necessary to determine manpower requirements. Instead, the manpower requirements will typically be a function of the product mix and the line speed or *daily going rate*. In short-cycle manufacturing, manpower requirements can often be easily calculated on a shift-by-shift basis. When line changeovers and throughput times cover several days, however, the identification of different labor skills and the timing of their requirements within the overall schedule will need to be defined.

Regression Analysis

In job shops where each part is engineered and produced to customer specification, it may be difficult to estimate labor requirements because of the variety of parts produced and the absence of historical data on a specific part. In fact, it is often necessary to estimate manpower requirements before the engineering department has completed the design process.

The experience gained in the past on parts with similar characteristics may be used to estimate requirements for a new part. This is done by using a technique known as *multiple linear regression*. By examining a representative sample of parts produced in the past, each with varying dimensions and characteristics, an estimating formula can be derived by using regression analysis that predicts the labor required to perform the major manufacturing operations. For example, a statistically significant relationship may be found that links four part variables X_i to the time Y needed for a drilling operation.

$$Y = T_0 + T_1X_1 + T_2X_2 + T_3X_3 + T_4X_4$$

where X_1 = alloy type code
X_2 = largest diameter
X_3 = number of holes
X_4 = weight of part

Multiple linear regression is used to derive estimates for the coefficients T_i, to verify statistically the validity of the variables and the overall predicting equation, and to estimate the range of expected errors.

Analyzing the Load

The steps in manpower loading covered thus far involve selecting appropriate capacity load centers, obtaining the necessary capacity data to define required and available capacity, and using these data with a production schedule to calculate the load on manpower resources. The next step in manpower loading is to compare the manpower capacity required with available resources. The imbalances must be analyzed to determine what actions need to be taken.

Graphing Techniques

The actual comparison of available manpower capacity to required capacity is best accomplished by using graphing techniques. In analyzing load problems, a picture is worth 1000 words and probably 10,000 numbers. The use of graphs makes analyzing the load easier, quicker, and more accurate because the planner can recognize the particular problem and separate true capacity problems from random variations. The particular technique used is not important. Some prefer bar charts while others favor line chart representations. The important point is to use some form of graph to assist in seeing the true load problems.

Period Versus Cumulative Loading

When a manpower load profile such as the one shown in Table 8.6 is analyzed, two basic questions must be answered: What are the capacity imbalances for each period? What is the total imbalance for all periods? Random fluctuations in load often create what appear to be serious problems.

On closer comparison of the cumulative capacity required versus that available in the example, the analyst observes that the level of manpower resources is actually well matched to the total requirements. The random variations in load can be smoothed by a modification to the schedule if necessary.

The best method for analyzing manpower is to use graphs for both cumulative and noncumulative loading. The two graphs in Figs. 8.4 and 8.5 illustrate this point. The first is a bar chart for the data previously presented in the load profile table for work center 760. Note in the first graph the magnitude of the load imbalances by time period. Obviously, the required hours in periods 29 and 32 exceed available capacity, and a rescheduling of at least part of this overload to periods 28, 30, and 31 is indicated. The second graph, which shows the cumulative load, indicates that there is no need for additional manpower since the total available additional manpower capacity is adequate.

Finite Scheduling

The availability of personal computers, more computing power, and advanced software has made finite scheduling and loading a feasible technique for short-term production

TABLE 8.6 Load Profile for Work Center 760

		Week Number				
	Past Due	28	29	30	31	32
Required man-hours	80	245	449	273	208	537
Available man-hours	0	360	360	360	360	360
Variation	+80	−115	+89	−87	−152	+177
Cumulative variation	+80	−35	+54	−33	−185	−8

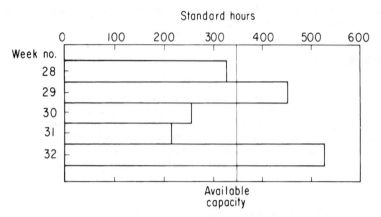

FIGURE 8.4   Manpower load profile.

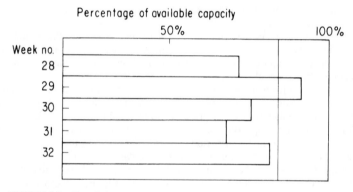

FIGURE 8.5   Cumulative manpower load profile.

management. These tools attempt to reconcile manpower and machine requirements with available resources in a manner that observes capacity constraints and other objective functions. Available manpower can be scheduled at a very detailed level to meet the manufacturing plan. Where the techniques discussed previously will identify imbalances between required and available manpower, finite scheduling will try to resolve the imbalances.

Manpower Load Control

Earlier we discussed the techniques of loading used in developing the manpower plan. The next step is to establish acceptable input and output performance ranges, to measure actual load inputs and outputs, and to take corrective actions when the limits are exceeded. Input/output control uses the manpower load plan to determine the average load expected to arrive (input) and the load expected to be completed (output) at each work center for each time period in the short range. For manpower controls the units used to measure input and output are standard man-hours.

TABLE 8.7   Input-Output Report for Work Center 124 in Standard Man-Hours

Week no.	Work-in-process beginning	Planned input	Actual input	Cumulative deviation (tolerance + 25)	Planned output	Actual output	Cumulative deviation (Tolerance + 25)
12	33	100	97	−3	100	94	6
13	36	100	102	−1	100	86	20
14	52	100	96	−5	100	91	29
15	57	100	109	4	100	95	34
16	71	100			100		
17		100			100		

Tolerance limits are set for acceptable variations in inputs and outputs by considering the degree of uncertainty (scrap, machine failures, etc.) in the manufacturing process. A statistical investigation of queue lengths can be an extremely valuable method for both setting planned queue lengths and determining the degree of variation considered as normal random occurrences. Actual queue lengths are monitored, and order releases are timed to keep queue lengths within established limits.

An input-output report is shown in Table 8.7. This report shows a situation in which the input to work center 124 is within the established tolerance limits. However, the output level is far below the planned level. The cumulative deviation of the actual to planned output is 34 standard labor hours, and the control limit is set at 25. The cause of this problem lies within work center 124, and corrective actions are needed to get the queue back into control and the actual output up to an acceptable level.

Direct and Indirect Labor

Most methods of manpower loading deal almost exclusively with direct labor. However, the amount of indirect labor used in many manufacturing operations is very significant, and because of increased automation, the trend is toward increased levels of indirect labor personnel. Good manpower management today must deal with planning and controlling indirect labor.

A common method used for indirect labor loading is known as ratio-trend analysis. In this method, the historical ratio between the number of direct and indirect workers in a plant or department is studied. A forecast of the future ratio is made that makes allowances for changes in organization or methods. In Table 8.8 the forecast of 320,

TABLE 8.8   Ratio-Trend Forecast—Inspectors

	Year	No. employees Production	No. employees Inspectors	Ratio Inspector:Production
Actual	−3	240	24	1:10
	−2	300	30	1:10
	−1	350	39	1:9
Forecast	Next year	320	36	1:9
	+2	280	33	1:8.5
	+3	270	34	1:8

280, and 270 direct production employees was derived by using the rough cut techniques previously described. The inspector forecasts of 36, 33, and 34, respectively, were computed by applying the forecast ratio to the direct production employee forecasts. This technique, although crude, is easy to understand and use.

A more analytical approach requires a study of all indirect labor jobs and the factors that affect them. The number of floor sweepers, for instance, is determined by the floor area to be cleaned, not by the level of production or the number of direct labor employees. The number of security guards required is a function of the number of unmanned shifts and the area to be patrolled.

When the number of indirect labor employees involved is small, note that the need for additional personnel is a step function. An example of this step-function behavior illustrates this point. Suppose each material handler is assigned to cover 10 machines. Presently, five material handlers cover 48 machines. If one or two machines are added, then the current level of five personnel should be adequate to handle the additional load.

TECHNIQUES OF WORK MEASUREMENT

To be proficient in planning and controlling production and inventory facilities, it is important to be able to schedule and evaluate plant operations. This can be accomplished only through the use of accurate time estimates. Thus it is important to know how to construct these time measurements and to realize their strengths and weaknesses.

Time estimates are used in two basic ways: for planning and evaluation. The planning estimate is used to schedule production and delivery dates, plan personnel requirements, plan for the arrival of incoming materials, and estimate costs. The evaluation estimate is used as a basis for wage-incentive plans or standard cost systems. For these reasons, the planning estimate may be called a *forecast,* and the evaluation estimate may be called a *standard.*

With all these different uses for time estimates, clearly any one measurement technique may not meet all the objectives required for each estimate. Various applications may require different accuracies in the estimates, and it is important to be able to select the tool that satisfies the intended need. However, analysis of the method should precede the application of a technique whenever it is to be used as a time standard.

A number of techniques have been developed. Methods are available that give highly accurate estimates where precision is required, and others give crude approximations where only ballpark figures are desired.

Estimates Based on Past Experience

This technique of obtaining time estimates is often used in practice but is rarely advocated in textbooks. Certainly, this method should not be employed unless time, resources, or needs permit no other technique to be used or unless the estimates need to be little more than approximate figures. Sometimes, however, even given these limitations, this technique may be the only way to obtain an estimate for an operation that has never been performed.

In the application of this procedure, past performances of similar jobs are often kept in the same file. Whenever an estimate of a particular task is needed, performance measures are available for reference for that or similar jobs. If a number of performance measures are available for the same task, an average or some other combination may be used, perhaps with some changes made based on modifications of other variables in the task. If there are no past records, an estimate of the time necessary for the task under consideration is often made by individuals familiar with the task, such as foremen or production personnel. Several of these people may discuss the task and arrive at a value judgment, or one individual may estimate the time.

Estimates from past experience should not be used for a critical, short-range purpose such as wage payments, but they may be very effective for highly repetitive, moderate, or long-range tasks, especially if the personnel are experienced and no better technique is available.

Stopwatch Time Study

One of the most common and accurate methods for obtaining time estimates is the stopwatch time study. Time study was originated by Frederick W. Taylor in the machine shop of Midvale Steel Company around 1881, but Ralph M. Barnes is often given credit for being a pioneer in the full development of this tool of management.

The objective of a time study is to develop a standard time for a particular task. *Standard time,* in this instance, is time (usually expressed in minutes per part) required to perform a task by a person possessing a moderate degree of skill, using a prescribed method, and working at a "normal" pace (i.e., a pace that will cause no harmful effects to the individual).

To obtain a standard time, some concept of a normal pace must exist, in order to arrive at a performance rating for the worker. In rating performance, one judges the performance as a percentage, in comparison to the expected performance of a trained individual working at the company's specified normal pace. For example, if a worker is judged to be working at only 80 percent of normal, the rating is 0.80; if the individual is working 20 percent higher than normal, the rating is 1.20. (Note, however, that the rating measures the worker's performance in terms of both speed and skill as contrasted to pace rating, which judges an individual's performance in terms of speed only.)

Also, tasks are not generally timed for a whole day, so other variables have to be considered in the estimate, such as personal needs and delays inherent in the task. The standard time allotted for a task must reflect these unavoidable delays and workers' needs that may be unrelated to the task.

The equipment used by a time-study analyst frequently consists of only a clipboard to which a decimal stopwatch and data sheets are attached. For the study, the analyst is positioned so as not to be distracting to the worker but where both the individual performing the task and the watch and board can be seen easily. Many variations in the method of conducting a time study exist (see Fig. 8.6a). This is one accepted procedure:

1. Observe and record job conditions.
2. Establish the elements of the job.
3. Time the elements.
4. Determine the normal time.
5. Calculate the standard time.

Step 1. Observe and Record Job Conditions.   The analyst should observe the job for a time and then discuss the task with both the supervisor and worker to become as familiar with the task as possible. All conditions surrounding the task should be recorded in a neat, orderly, and systematic manner, so the job could be reconstructed if the need arose.

Study No. ___10045___   STOP-WATCH OBSERVATIONS   Time began 1:30 Time ended 2:00
Production during study

No.	Description	*R	T	R	T	R	T	R	T	R	T	R	T	R	T	R	T	R	T	R	T	Ave. elem. time	Rating	Normal time	Allow	Std. time
				2		3		4		5		6		7		8		9		10						
1	Reach for assembled part and box - place box at side of paper and the part in the paper	120	03	100	21	110	38	100	56	120	74	100	92	100	12	100	35	100	52	80	72					
			3		4		4		3		3		3		5		3		3		4					
2	Wrap part	120	07	100	25	110	43	100	61	120	79	100	96	100	17	100	39	100	57	80	76					
			4		4		5		5		5		4		5		4		5		4					
3	Reach for box, Place wrapped part in individual box	120	11	100	29	110	47	100	64	120	83	100	99	100	23	100	43	100	61	80	79					
			4		4		4		3		4		3		6		4		4		3					
4	Close lid and aside individual box to carton	120	17	100	34	110	53	100	71	120	39	100	07	100	32	100	49	100	68	80	86					
			6		5		6		7		6		8		9		6		7		7					

Standard time - minutes/piece

Foreign elements

	Total	Average (hundreds of minutes) Average rating	Normal time
Element 1	3|5	35/10 ÷ 3.50	1.03	.0361
Element 2	4|5	45/10 ÷ 4.50	1.03	.0464
Element 3	3|9	39/10 ÷ 3.90	1.03	.0402
Element 4	6|7	67/10 ÷ 6.70	1.03	.0690

.1917 total normal time

Details of allowances —

Minimum delay   2%
Personal   4%
Fatigue   5%
Cleanup   1%
12%

Standard time = normal time + (normal time + allowances)
minutes/part

= .1917 + (.1917 × .12)

= 0.2147 minute/part

* R = rating, T = time   (a)

FIGURE 8.6   Stopwatch observation sheet. (a) Front.

Step 2. Establish the Elements of the Job.   For repetitive tasks, divide into "timetable" elements, and the elements may be described on the data sheets before the study begins. Elements should have definite beginning and ending points. Machine elements should be separated from worker-controlled elements. For nonrepetitive tasks, the job elements may be longer and not as easily anticipated as in the repetitive tasks. This may necessitate a "write as you go" type of study. Nonproductive and productive work should be separated.

Step 3. Time the Elements.   A number of observations should be recorded for each element. During these observations, the analyst should judge and record the worker's performance rating. For highly repetitive tasks, one rating may apply to an entire cycle; but for long or nonrepetitive tasks, a rating is generally applied to each element studied.

This step of the procedure is a sampling technique, and as such, enough samples must be taken to represent the population. Determining the number of samples is a statistical problem, but recognized texts dealing with management or industrial engineering practices give procedures, tables, or charts that can be used to determine the number of readings required for a desired level of accuracy.

Step 4. Determine the Normal Time.   Depending on how the rating procedure was performed in step 3 (by element or cycle), the ratings should be multiplied by the recorded time to calculate the normal time required for the task. If a rating is given for each element, the procedure should be to first normalize each element by multiplying the ele-

TiME-STUDY SHEET

Operation	Packing ball-stud scope mount			Oper. No.	46	
Mach. type	None	Mach. No.		Dept.	Final assembly	
Part name	Ball-stud scope mount	Part No.	1440	Operator	John Steele	
Study No.	10045	Analyst	James Smith	Date	5/20/86	

Elem No.	Left-hand description	Right-hand description	Machine element	Speed	Feed	Std. Time
		Written standard practice				
1	Reach for assembled part, grasp, and return, placing part on stack of tissue paper	Reach for individual box, grasp, and return, placing box at right side of tissue paper				
2	Wrap part in paper	Using the thumb, separate two layers of the paper and wrap the part				
3	Reach, grasp, and hold box	Reach, grasp, and hold box; transfer to the left hand and release; reach and grasp part, move part to box, position and place wrapped part in box				
4	Release and return, alternately aside individual box to carton, position and place box in carton	Close lid; alternately aside individual box to carton, position, and place box in carton				

Standard production – pieces/hour		Standard time —minutes/piece
Sketch of work place		Setup, tools, jigs, fixtures, gauges —

Legend:
1. Assembled parts in tote box
2. Individual boxes
3. Tissue paper
4. Cartons
5. Workman (seated)

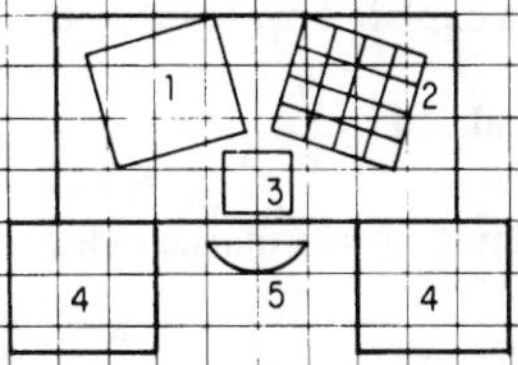

1 2 3 4 5 4

(b)

FIGURE 8.6 (*Continued*) Stopwatch observation sheet. (*b*) Back.

ment's recorded time by its rating and to then add all elements for the task, to obtain a total normal time for the task. If a rating is given for each cycle only, add the recorded times for all elements of the task and then normalize the total recorded task time by multiplying the total recorded time by its rating.

Step 5. Determine the Standard Time.   By using the normal time developed in step 4, allowances (usually expressed as a percentage of normal time) for rests, personal delays, and unavoidable delays are added to increase the normal time to the standard time for the task. The standard time is the estimate that is often used for scheduling and incentive-pay plans.

To recapitulate, the method and equations used to obtain the standard time from the recorded times of a task are as follows:

1. Recorded time $\times$ rating $=$ normal time
2. Normal time $+$ (normal time $\times$ allowances) $=$ standard time

Work Sampling

Work sampling, sometimes called *ratio delay,* is another method of direct observation for estimating the time to perform a task by using a sampling procedure. It can be used to develop allowances in time studies or to determine standard times for jobs. Work sampling has the advantages over other types of work measurement of being inexpensive, requiring little training for the observers, using no timing device, collecting data in simple terms, and simultaneously including many workers and machines in the data collection process. A high degree of accuracy may be obtained by using work sampling. In fact, sometimes it may be more accurate than methods using continuous observation.

The simplest work-sampling study consists of using a number of randomly selected observations and noting whether the individual on the task under study is either working or not; if the individual is working, a judged performance index is noted. The observations, therefore, are dichotomous and follow a binomial distribution. Frequently, a normal approximation to the binomial can be used, and normal-curve tables are searched to find the required number of observations for a desired level of accuracy. Any good reference text dealing with management or industrial engineering practices gives procedures or tables and charts which explain how to calculate the required number of observations.

The standard time for a job may be calculated by

$$\frac{\text{Standard time}}{\text{(time units/part)}} = \frac{\overset{\text{total time}}{\underset{\text{(time units)}}{}} \times \overset{\text{working time}}{\underset{\text{(percent)}}{}} \times \overset{\text{performance index}}{\underset{\text{(percent)}}{}}}{\text{total number of pieces produced}} + \frac{\text{allowances}}{\text{(time units/piece)}}$$

Of the estimates needed to determine the standard time, only the percentage of working time and the performance index must be provided by the work-sampling study. The total time can be found in the company's time-card records. The total number of parts produced can be obtained from production records. Allowances are the result of company-union negotiations or past practices and are readily available.

To determine the standard time for a task, do as follows:

1. Select the task(s) to be studied. Estimate the percentage of working time that can be expected to be observed on the task, from past records, if available. For this percentage, approximate the number of observations required for the desired accuracy level.

2. Divide the working time on each task into time increments, usually minutes, and number them consecutively. Using a random-number table, select the instants that an observation should be taken by choosing random numbers that correspond to the numbered time increments over the range of working times. The period of the sampling study should be long enough to allow the workers to become accustomed to the observer's presence and so less likely to feign activity and bias the results.

3. Begin making the observations as determined in step 2. Periodically check the percentages of working and idle times, and recalculate the number of readings that should be obtained.

4. Continue to collect data until the desired number of observations has been obtained. Calculate the standard time, using the equation given.

Predetermined Motion-Time Systems

The use of predetermined motion-time systems to calculate a time estimate is one of the most refined techniques of work measurement. As opposed to the techniques of time study or standard data, the time units are basic motions of much shorter duration in a predetermined motion-time analysis.

A number of predetermined motion-time systems have been formulated since the early 1940s. They are available under such names as *methods time measurement* (MTM), *motion-time analysis* (MTA), *work factor* (WF), *motor-time standards* (MTS), *basic motion-time* (BMT), and *Maynard operation sequence technique* (MOST). Generally, for these systems the times associated with the basic motions have been normalized, but no allowances have been added.

The basic motions contained in a predetermined motion-time system are very small elements upon which extensive time data have been collected and analyzed by such techniques as time-study and motion-picture analysis. To estimate a time for a task requires that the job be synthesized from the basic motions and the times accumulated for each of the motions included. Allowances are then added to determine the standard time for the task. In this manner, the methods and times for jobs can be specified even before the job is actually performed by an operator. The application of this technique necessitates the use of a well-trained analyst.

Standard Data

In the process of time-studying a number of similar tasks, it may become obvious that there are elements common to many jobs. If these elements are identical for each task, the time values obtained could be collected from all the jobs studied and averaged for a more accurate estimate than could be obtained from just the study of one task. This is exactly how standard data, or elemental times are developed. Data on elements common to a family of jobs are gathered, from which standard times may be synthesized for other tasks containing these elements. In effect, it is a form of predetermined time system, but the elements are not as minuscule and generally are developed within the framework of one plant's operations. However, some industries, such as the metalworking industry, have developed standard data for industrywide use.

Element types generally encountered during standard data compilation are (1) identical from job to job; (2) similar in nature, but the times vary because of differences in a particular variable (size, weight, etc.) involved in the task; and (3) times controlled by the physical or technical characteristic of the material and process.

Elements of the first type are easy to handle. To ensure that a representative time is obtained, a sufficient number are collected and averaged. Elements of the second type are a little more difficult. Sufficient studies have to be made to ascertain the relationship between the varying characteristic of the element and the performance time, so as to develop a series of time values that vary with the characteristic. Generally elements in the third group can be calculated from physical data such as the feeds, speeds, and depth of cut in the machining task discussed above.

Problems in Using Work Measurement Techniques for Production Control

A basic problem exists in using these methods of work measurement for production control. Except for the past-experience method, these techniques are used most often to determine standard times for incentive-pay systems. Time estimates for production control are also needed for planning and scheduling purposes. An incentive-pay system is generally set up so that an average-skill employee working at a normal pace will earn 25 to 30 percent incentive pay, that is, will be performing the task in 25 to 30 percent less time than the standard allows. Thus if the standard time is used for scheduling purposes, the jobs will be completed, on average, in 25 to 30 percent less time than the schedule permits and will greatly increase the likelihood of creating idle time on production facilities.

Before standard times are used for scheduling, therefore, the times should be adjusted to account for this discrepancy. This can be done separately by job, if it is known who the workers will be and their average performance indices; or by department, by using an average factor to account for the differences between the standard and expected times. Sometimes, however, this difference is ignored, the attitude being that the scheduling plan is so loose that this additional error will make little difference in the plan's overall effectiveness.

PRODUCTION PROGRESS FUNCTION

Anyone who has observed a repetitive task, whether it was simple, involving the performance of only a few operations, or complex, requiring many operations, probably noted the improved proficiency as frequency increased. That is, the operator has "learned" the task as he or she gained experience with it. The scale on which task proficiency was measured might have been based on any number of criteria, such as time to perform the task, accuracy of performing the task, or cost of performing the task. Nevertheless, the relationship between the proficiency measure and the number of times the task was performed probably appeared as shown in Fig. 8.7. In the typical learning curve, task proficiency is shown to be low initially, to increase rapidly as the task is repeated the first few times, and to continue to increase but at a slower and slower rate as the number of repetitions becomes greater. So the learning curve is typically exponential and can be represented by

$$Y = KX^n$$

where Y = proficiency measure
$\quad K$ = constant
$\quad X$ = cumulative number of task repetitions
$\quad n$ = exponent of curve

The phenomenon of the learning curve is familiar to individuals within the production planning and control organization concerned with the management of direct labor.

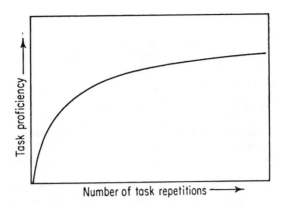

FIGURE 8.7   Typical learning curve.

It has long been recognized that human learning must be accounted for in setting time standards for manual operations, and a new employee should not be assigned to a paced task where the pace has been based on fully learned performance.

Human learning is not the only type of learning that should concern the production planning and control organization, however, because production processes, in the aggregate, also are subject to learning. Just as human performance tends to improve as individuals repeat tasks, so the performance of complete production processes tends to show improvement as time passes and manufacturing continues. This process improvement manifests itself as a decrease in the number of man-hours required to produce a unit of product. Although a large part of the improvement is the result of direct labor learning, a significant contribution to the total is made by improvement in supporting operations. For this reason, when reference is made to total-process learning, the phenomenon is sometimes called the *time-reduction curve, experience curve, startup curve, production progress function,* and *production-acceleration curve.*

A number of factors contribute to the ability of a manufacturing process to improve. If prior to production a large amount of effective engineering effort is expended on the problems of product design, tooling and equipment selection, work-method design, and personnel selection and training, then the opportunity for learning, or improvement, is reduced. Once production has begun, advances in the state of the art, tooling and work-method changes, quality improvements (resulting in less scrap, rework, and inspection), effective work-simplification programs, and human performance learning will all enhance process improvement. It is imperative that individuals using the production-acceleration curve as a planning tool understand that many factors contribute to the improvement.

Development of the Curve

The production progress function was first used for production planning in the airframe industry during the 1940s. The form of the equation used to model the improvement phenomenon was a negative exponential rather than the positive one given above, since the variable of interest was the number of man-hours required to produce each airframe. A variation of the original model commonly used today is

$$Y = KX^{-n}$$

where Y = cumulative average man-hours per unit after X units have been produced
K = number of man-hours required to build first unit
X = cumulative number of units produced
n = exponent of curve

A typical curve is plotted in Fig. 8.8. Note that in some applications of the progress function Y is defined as the actual number of man-hours required to build a unit after X units have been produced, rather than the cumulative average man-hours per unit. The definition of Y which should be used in a particular situation depends on the situation itself. Cumulative average man-hours are used here since its use is perhaps most common.

The model describes constant percentage reduction. Each time the cumulative production is increased by a constant percentage, the cumulative average man-hours per unit are decreased by a constant percentage. This characteristic can be illustrated as follows. Take any two points in production, say X_1 and X_2, where X_2 is greater than X_1. Define the ratio of X_2 to X_1 as the production ratio, and call this quantity C. Application of the model indicates that the cumulative average man-hours per unit at X_1 are $Y_1 = KX_1^{-n}$ and similarly at X_2 it is $Y_2 = KX_2^{-n}$. Next form the ratio of Y_2 to Y_1:

$$\frac{Y_2}{Y_1} = \frac{KX_2^{-n}}{KX_1^{-n}} = \frac{X_2^{-n}}{X_1^{-n}} = \left(\frac{X_2}{X_1}\right)^{-n} = C^{-n}$$

Since Y_2 is less than Y_1, the quantity C^{-n} lies between 0 and 1. Rearranging the previous equation gives $Y_2 = Y_1 C^{-n}$.

From this we see that if the production ratio between any two points in production is a constant C, then the cumulative average man-hours per unit at the second point will be a constant percentage C^{-n} of what it was at the first point.

In practice, the production ratio usually is $C = 2$. Thus each time production is doubled, the cumulative average man-hours per unit are reduced to 2^{-n} percent of the pre-

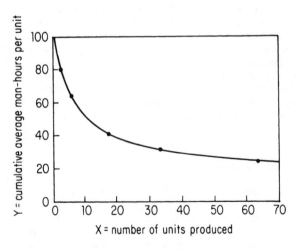

FIGURE 8.8 The production progress function.

vious value. Values of the exponent n for various percentage curves can be calculated quickly. For example, if the cumulative average time was reduced to 80 percent of its previous figure when production doubled, then $Y_2 = Y_1(0.80)$ or $C^{-n} = 0.80$. Since $C = 2$, $2^{-n} = 0.80$ and n is easily found to be 0.322. Values of n for several learning percentages are presented below for ready reference. Note that a learning percentage of P percent implies that when production doubles, the cumulative average man-hours per unit are reduced to P percent of the initial value, not reduced by P percent.

Learning percentage	n
95	0.074
90	0.152
85	0.234
80	0.322
75	0.415
70	0.515
65	0.622

The value of the constant K is defined as the number of man-hours required to manufacture the first production unit. This result is obtained in the following manner. Let Y_1 equal the cumulative average man-hours per unit after the first unit has been reproduced, that is, at $X = 1$. Note that the cumulative average time is equal to the unit production time when only 1 unit has been produced. Application of the model illustrates that K is equal to Y_1, which is the unit production time of the first unit.

$$Y = KX^{-n}$$

$$Y_1 = K(1)^{-n} = K$$

Example
The production progress function can be applied in the following situation. A firm has recently accepted a contract to build twenty 35-ft boats for a sport fishing charter outfit operating throughout the Caribbean. The first two boats have been completed, taking 7000 and 4900 man-hours, respectively. Estimate how many man-hours will be required to produce all 20 boats and how many boats will be completed before the man-hour requirement per boat is 3000 hours or less.

In approaching this problem, first determine the percentage learning in effect in order to know what value of the exponent n to use in the progress function equation. Since production has doubled from unit 1 to 2, the correct learning percentage can be determined by forming the ratio for the cumulative average time at unit 2 to the cumulative average time at unit 1:

$$Y_1 = \text{cumulative average time at first unit} = 7000 \text{ man-hours}$$

and

$$Y_2 = \text{cumulative average time after second unit} = \frac{7000 + 4900}{2} = 5950 \text{ man-hours}$$

so

$$\frac{Y_2}{Y_1} = \frac{5950}{7000} = 0.85$$

Thus the cumulative average time after unit 2 had been produced is 85 percent of what it was at unit 1, and the correct value of n is found in the table to be 0.234.

Now the total number of man-hours required for all 20 boats can be estimated. The total time required at any point in production is equal to the cumulative average time at that point multiplied by the number of units produced. Thus

$$T = \text{total time} = YX$$

$$= (KX^{-n})(X)$$

$$= KX^{1-n}$$

So the total time for all 20 boats is

$$T = \text{time for 20 boats} = K(20^{1-n})$$

$$= 7000(20^{0.766})$$

This equation can be solved directly if a scientific calculator is available or by converting to logarithms. Solution by logarithms is used here:

$$T = KX^{1-n}$$

$$\log T = \log K + (1 - n)(\log X)$$

$$= \log 7000 + 0.766 \log 20$$

$$= 3.84510 + 0.766(1.30103)$$

$$= 3.84510 + 0.99659$$

$$= 4.84169$$

$$T = 69{,}454 \text{ man-hours}$$

To find the production unit on which the time per boat goes below 3000 man-hours, we again use the total-time equation. The unit time for any particular unit X can be found by subtracting the total time at unit $X - 1$ from the total time at unit X. That is, unit time for $X = T_X - T_{X-1}$. To find the point in production where the unit time is equal to some specified number of hours, in this case 3000, we first guess at the point and then make successive unit-time calculations until the desired point in production is reached. This procedure is shown here, where the initial guess was that the unit time would be less than or equal to 3000 hours on unit 12:

$$T = KX^{1-n} = 7000X^{0.766}$$

Unit no.	Total time	Difference = unit time
11	43,934	—
12	46,962	3028
13	49,932	2970

Thus the unit time goes below 3000 man-hours on unit 13.

To get a close initial guess, take the first derivative of T with respect to X and solve for the value of X for which the derivative is equal to the desired number of hours. For the current example, the calculations would be

$$\frac{dT}{dX} = (1-n)KX^{-n}$$

$$= \text{estimate of man-hours required per unit}$$

$$3000 = (1 - 0.234)(7000)(X^{-n})$$

$$= (0.766)(7000)(X^{-n})$$

$$= 5362(X^{-n})$$

$$\log 3000 = \log 5362 - 0.234 \log X$$

$$3.47712 = 3.72933 - 0.234 \log X$$

$$\log X = \frac{3.47712 - 3.72933}{-0.234}$$

$$= 1.07782$$

$$X = 11.96 = 12$$

This method does not give an exact answer because X is a discrete rather than a continuous variable. But it becomes an increasingly better estimate as X increases, since the progress curve becomes flatter with increasing X.

This example demonstrates the type of planning information that can be obtained through application of the production progress function. Such information can be useful in scheduling production, estimating delivery dates and production budgets, and performing breakeven analyses and estimating man-hour requirements. The user may wish to actually draw the progress curve for the particular process for ready reference. This can be done rather quickly by calculating a few points on the curve and drawing the curve through these points:

Point in production	Cumulative average man-hours
Unit 1	$Y_1 = K$
Unit 2	$Y_2 = K \text{ (percent learning)}$
Unit 4	$Y_4 = K \text{ (percent learning)}^2$
Unit 8	$Y_8 = K \text{ (percent learning)}^3$
Unit 16	$Y_{16} = K \text{ (percent learning)}^4$
etc.	etc.

Note that if the progress curve is plotted on log-log coordinate paper, the resulting curve is linear with slope equal to $-n$. Many people may find the linear curve easier to interpret than the exponential one, and so at least consider using it.

For the example the progress curve can be plotted from the following data:

Point in production	Cumulative average man-hours
Unit 1	$Y_1 = K = 7000$
Unit 2	$Y_2 = K(0.85) = 5950$
Unit 4	$Y_4 = K(0.85)^2 = 5058$
Unit 8	$Y_8 = K(0.85)^3 = 4299$
Unit 16	$Y_{16} = K(0.85)^4 = 3654$

The curve is plotted on log-log coordinates in Fig. 8.9.

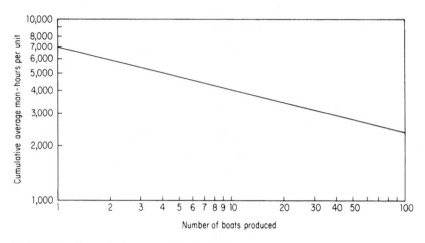

FIGURE 8.9   The production progress function, log-log.

Some Cautions in Applying the Production Progress Function

Probably the greatest problem that confronts the potential user of the production progress function is estimation of the correct value of n to use in the calculations. One common error is to assume that an n value which has been found to be appropriate for one industry or one class of products will be appropriate for other industries or other products. All too often the aerospace industry's characteristic improvement of 20 percent with its corresponding n value of 0.322 has been carried over to other applications with no justification for doing so. Several procedures can be used to estimate the value of n in any particular situation. A few are given here with the caution that each has its limitations and potential sources for error.

1. Assume n is the same as in previous applications with the same industry.
2. Assume n is the same as in previous applications with the same or a similar product.
3. *a.* Evaluate the status of production variables that affect the ability of the process to improve.
   b. Compare the current status of the variables with that existing during previous production of a similar product.
   c. Given n from the previous production situations, estimate the new n by comparison of (*a*) and (*b*).
4. Wait until 2 or 4 units have been produced, and estimate n from these data, as was done in the example.

Even if a good estimate of n has been obtained, there are several application errors to guard against. If elemental time data are used in calculating the expected value of K, so the model can be used before production begins, one must know whether the elemental data apply to a learned or unlearned process. If the data came from a learned process, perhaps the user should inflate the estimate of K as determined by the elemental data. Do not forget that the improvement percentage applies to the aggregate production process and that the same percentage may not apply to individual components of the process. Nor should it be assumed that multishift situations give the same results as single-shift operations in determining the value of X to use in the model calculations. Finally, do not ignore the effects of labor-force changes, production interruptions, or new-equipment installations, since these may result in a period of either relearning or unusually acceler-ated learning. If one is careful in estimating the values of n and K and keeps in mind the various factors that can affect production progress calculations, so as not to apply the model blindly, reliable information can be obtained for planning purposes.

ROBOTS IN MANPOWER MANAGEMENT AND CONTROL

Over the past three decades, robots have gradually moved in to the industrial environ-ment. Encouraging their growth have been advances in miniature computers, rising labor costs, and declining productivity. To offset these undesirable events management is using these "steel-collar workers" to make repetitive, time-consuming, and hazardous tasks more efficient and profitable.

Robotics Defined

The *APICS Dictionary* defines *robotics* as "replacing functions previously done by humans with mechanical devices or robots that can either be operated by humans or run by computer. Hard-to-do, dangerous, or monotonous tasks are likely candidates for robots to perform." A robot is a reprogrammable machine with multiple functions that can move devices through specialized motions to perform any number of tasks. It is essentially a mechanized arm that can be fitted with a variety of handlike fingers, grip-pers, vacuum cups, or a tool such as a wrench or welding rod.

Teaching a Robot

Advance capabilities have been designed into robots to allow vision, tactile sensing, and hand-to-hand coordination. In addition, some models can now be "taught" a sequence of motions of a three-dimensional pattern. As a worker moves the end of the robot arm through the required motions, the robot records this pattern in its memory and repeats them on command. This is analogous to "keyboard macros" that record your keystrokes and then play them back at the touch of a key.

If it is possible to automate or to make these types of tasks automatic, robots are good candidates since they are dependable, reliable, and efficient and can work without much supervision. There are currently about 300 types of robots ranging in price from simple single-axis robots costing a few hundred dollars to units in the hundreds of thousands with installations costing millions of dollars.

Applications and Implementation

Applications of robots involve tasks or processes that are tedious, repetitive, boring, or hazardous. Typical implementations of robots including welding, paint spraying, machining operations, loading and unloading, filling, parts picking and transfer, and inspection.

When a robot installation is considered, you should review the following implemen-tation guidelines:

1. Obtain top management policy guidance, active participation, and support in accor-dance with corporate objectives.

2. Prepare a short- and long-range plan of company automation needs and goals.
3. Perform a thorough industrial engineering study, identifying specific robot application needs.
4. Research the robot manufacturer's capabilities to meet application requirements.
5. Begin with applications where the risk of failure is lowest—that is, the most obvious and simplest application, with emphasis on operations which are physically hazardous.
6. Work with a robot manufacturer that understands the company's manufacturing operation and processes.
7. Educate manufacturing management and provide for their supervision in the use of robots. Achieve participation in selecting, developing, and installing the automated system. This will ensure acceptance and successful installation of robots.

Materials Management

Due to the high efficiency and almost perfect performance of robots, materials management—including MRP, inventory control, and materials handling—is critical to optimum production flow. The planning, movement, and supply of materials to the production line require exacting fulfillment of quantities, phasing, and timing requirements. Since robots usually do exactly what is expected, in terms of finite output and quality, material supply must be equally efficient, or else bottlenecks and delays will occur. Robot efficiency can be a major contributing factor in achieving significant reductions of work-in-process queues and increases in inventory turnover, which results in greater return on investment and profit.

Work Measurement and Efficiency

Compared to humans concerning work measurement and efficiency, robots offer exciting features such as exacting specifications, standard times, practically perfect performance, instantaneous reporting, and reduction in time and costs. In addition these tasks can be performed with 100 percent available active working time free of personal time and breaks.

Robots promote increased standardization of similar parts and processes, further increasing unit efficiency without demanding overtime or increased pay. Since their capacity is stable, scheduling and loading are always valid and dependable. It is essential that the surrounding work areas, supporting personnel, and equipment be made equally efficient to avoid an overload and promote a uniform increase in efficiency. The increased output, improved quality, and reduced labor costs are the primary advantages of an efficient operation.

Labor and Management

Robots are viewed by management quite positively as a way of establishing a competitive edge through reduced costs and prices. However, some general ground rules should be followed to promote a smooth interface with labor.

1. Present the personal advantages to the workers and union.
2. Forewarn workers and unions of installation to minimize apprehension and resistance.
3. Selling the foreman is essential to perpetuate the philosophy.

4. Publicize the fact that the robots are replacing hazardous, tedious, and uncomfortable human tasks.

5. Accomplish job elimination by normal attrition.

Experience has shown, especially in large corporations, that success was based on these ground rules. Labor, including unions, has realized that robotic installations have made the workers' lives less dangerous and more comfortable, meaningful, and enriched in general. Workers have also experienced greater job security and financial success. This has been made possible by robots being successfully welcomed into the company.

Robots and the Workers

Since robots take on many of the undesirable tasks of the workers and directly contribute to increased efficiency, the overall productivity (output divided by input) increases. Since more work can now be done with fewer workers, there may be a reduction in the workforce unless workers can be reeducated for other jobs or more demand created by lower costs and increased quality. Current estimates set worker displacement at anywhere from 1.7 to 6.0 employees per robot; the potential is especially high in repetitive industries. This idea has paved the way for many companies to maintain their competitive edge while promoting worker flexibility.

It will be just a matter of time before more sophisticated robots will be used for specialized assembly and touch-sensitive jobs. Some experts estimate that these robots of the future could replace as many as 3.8 million workers.

Robot Justification

Robots are expensive not only in their initial purchase price but with engineering changes and maintenance. However, not investing in new technology or automation can be even more costly, as you may lose your competitive advantage. Remember there are two types of businesses, those that are competitive and those that are out of business. Thus if robotics or automation will help your company be competitive, you may wish to perform a payback analysis.

The following modified basic payback formula from Chase and Aquilano may be of help[1]:

$$P = \frac{I}{L - E + q(L + Z)}$$

where P = payback period in years
$\quad I$ = total capital investment required in robot and accessories
$\quad L$ = annual labor costs replaced by the robot (annual wage and benefit costs per worker times the number of shifts per day)
$\quad E$ = annual maintenance costs for the robot
$\quad q$ = fractional speedup (or slowdown) factor
$\quad Z$ = annual depreciation

For example,

I = \$50,000

L = \$60,000 (2 workers at \$20,000, each working one of 2 shifts; overhead is \$10,000 each)

E = \$9,600 (\$2/hour × 4800 hours/year)

$q = +150$ percent   (robot works half again as fast as a worker)

$Z = \$10,000$

Then

$$P = \frac{\$50,000}{\$60,000 - \$9,600 + 1.50(\$60,000 + \$10,000)}$$

$$= \frac{1}{3} \text{ year}$$

At the Fort Worth General Dynamics plant, a computerized machine drills holes at a rate of 24 to 30 parts per shift with no defects. A human worker can produce only 6 parts per shift, with a 10 percent rejection rate. Even though the robot cost $60,000, it saved the company $90,000 the first year.

What Robots Cannot Do?

Even though there are many things a robot can do better than a human, and there will certainly be increasing sophistication with these unique workers, fortunately, there are still many things a robot will probably never be able to do. A talented and experienced human will still be required to peel a grape, catch a ball, cut hair with style, dance a ballet, kiss sensuously, and deliver a baby.

MAKE-OR-BUY ANALYSIS

The decision to make or buy is based on two basic considerations, which are separate and distinct and should be kept completely independent: reduced costs and additional capacity.

Reduced-Cost Consideration

If the supplier and the purchaser have nearly equivalent capabilities in terms of manufacturing processes, it is rarely cheaper to buy than to make. This may seem heresy to many accountants or purchasing executives, but it can be proved. The key factor, of course, is identification of fixed versus variable costs. Most large companies have high fixed costs as a result of rental or depreciation of equipment, salaries, taxes, and the like.

Make-or-buy decisions should be made on the basis of variable or incremental cost. In other words, ask how much extra it will cost to produce the units in question, never what the unit cost of producing the parts is, including full burden, administrative cost, and overhead.

Often one hears the phrase, "We can buy them much cheaper than we can make them," which may be true in a strict accounting sense. The following example, however, illustrates the principle involved. An article or part can be manufactured as follows:

Direct materials	$0.80
Direct labor	0.10
Factory overhead—fixed	0.40
Factory overhead—variable	0.05
General and administrative	0.60
Total factory cost	$1.95

The purchasing agent may easily locate a supplier who will furnish the part for $1.50. The vendor, while paying the same or even more for direct labor and materials and variable overhead ($0.95), can make a profit, since fixed costs may be much less as a result of limited overhead, general, and administrative expenses. The purchaser, however, may not be maximizing profits at this price because his fixed costs are ongoing.

Capacity Balance

Many firms purchase items they could make themselves, on the basis of balancing plant capacity. Cost is a factor here as is profit, but the decision is based on utilization of capacity in a long-term sense rather than a simple unit-cost concept. Firms must maintain a high utilization of equipment to keep costs low. Idle plant and equipment can be very costly. Therefore, where demand varies, wise management staffs and equips to a minimum point and absorbs fluctuations through purchase of fabricated items. This is an intelligent approach and is a real cost saver for several reasons:

- It cuts down on training costs for new employees—employees who produce the most scrap and are the least productive.
- It permits maximum output with minimum investment.
- It enables the plant to run with stable workforce and stable output.
- It reduces overtime.

The ability to level production by purchasing items depends on a company's ability to project production and predict shop loads accurately. The steps in the process are as follows:

1. Establish sales forecast or production needs for a period well in advance of purchase lead times.
2. Reduce sales and production forecasts to requirements for specific items of manufacture.
3. Use accurate work statements to project hours of work for each machine center of the plant.
4. Compare the workload for each section with optimum, stable levels desired for plant operations.
5. Contract with suppliers to furnish all items that would create excessive workloads.
6. Schedule and maintain machine loads for each machine center to dovetail with receipts of purchased items.

Other considerations in conjunction with make-or-buy decisions are quality-control requirements and diversification of supply to protect plant assembly schedules.

Quality Control

The production of items adhering to exact specifications requires time and organization. This fact should be seriously considered in make-or-buy decisions. A company may have gained a high degree of skill and in-plant experience that permits manufacturing items easily to exact specifications. A supplier who has not made a similar part may have difficulty initially in meeting specifications. It takes time to develop skills.

Diversification of Supply

Protection of assembly schedules through multiple sources can be a factor in the make-or-buy decision. Suppliers may be shut down by strikes over which a customer has no control. This dictates more than one supplier of critical items or splitting the requirements between the customer's own plant and a supplier. This approach may require some extra tooling but may be less costly than a production stoppage.

MULTIPLE SHIFTS AND OVERTIME CONSIDERATIONS

The question of whether to operate on a multiple-shift basis, to work overtime, or to expand single-shift operations is primarily economic. However, there are many other considerations, such as availability of labor, equipment, and supervision.

On one hand, there are series of continuous process-type operations such as in steel mills, refineries, and power plants where there is rarely any alternative to a full-time operation of three shifts, 7 days a week. Such operations are much more costly to shut down than they are to run on a continuous basis.

On the other hand, there are a few traditionally one-shift operations where no one would even consider working more than one shift. One is garment plants where the sewing machine operator has a machine which has been coddled and adjusted until it does everything just the way the operator wants it to—it "feels" right. No one else can run this machine, and only certain mechanics are allowed to put a screwdriver to it. That some stranger would come in and actually touch the machine at night is unthinkable.

In between these two extremes there is a larger body of industry where a change in shift operation as conditions vary may or may not be necessary and advisable.

Cost of Capital Investment

Where the cost of capital equipment is high, there are economic reasons why it must be operated at the highest possible degree of utilization. Textile factories are an example of this heavy investment in capital equipment.

The economics are simple. The depreciation costs are fixed, since the equipment will likely be obsolete in 5 to 10 years. With total fixed costs amounting to 30 to 40 percent on some operations, the equipment must operate no less than 24 hours per day since dropping two shifts will increase fixed costs to 40 to 50 percent.

Aside from the depreciation which must be carefully and accurately taken into consideration for cost purposes, there is, of course, the original cost of equipment acquisition. No company could afford to purchase three times as much equipment for a single-shift operation as the competitor who is using it on a three-shift basis. However, there are those operators, usually small, who have an abundance of fully depreciated equipment and therefore are not affected by original cost.

Availability of Equipment

When companies are forced to expand production on relatively short notice, often they cannot get additional equipment quickly enough. So they have no alternative but to run a second shift. This situation is frequently encountered when a single, specialized piece of equipment constitutes a bottleneck. Basically this is a short-term problem since in the long run additional equipment can be procured as warranted by other considerations.

Availability of Personnel

The availability of personnel may also affect decisions on shift operation. At times people may be available for first-shift work but not for second or third shifts. But there may be people available for second or third shifts but not the first. In this latter category are many people working at a second job, students who attend classes during the day, a parent who cannot leave the children except when the spouse or some other person who works days is available.

Availability of Supervision

Many times it is possible to recruit personnel for second- and third-shift work if adequate supervision can be provided. Where the technical qualifications required of supervision are high, this can be difficult.

Comparison of Quality and Performance by Shifts

In some plants and companies, performance relative to both quantity and quality is always higher on the second than on the first shift. Various explanations have been advanced for this. It has been said—facetiously, of course—that things are better on the second and third shifts because there are not so many members of management around to bother the workers. Strange as this may seem, there are good reasons why it is so. For example, the average experience may be higher on the later shifts if the company makes a practice of training on the first shift and putting more experienced workers on night. Obviously sometimes the reverse is true, and the new employees are all concentrated on the second shift. Or second-shift workers may be more professional in their approach to the job. Especially in banks where clearing activities are usually done at night to reduce float time, the best workers and highest performances tend to be at night. There may be fewer distractions at night, so workers can concentrate on the job at hand. Sometimes the second shift may not be loaded as fully, by having a smaller workforce or a smaller load per work station. Accordingly, there are fewer bottlenecks and problem areas.

INDUSTRIAL RELATIONS AND EFFECT ON MANPOWER

Industrial relations includes both the individual employer-employee relationships and the employer-union relationship. Although industrial relations is a highly specialized staff function, the primary responsibility for the effective use of the assigned workforce belongs to the line supervisor.

Employee Relations

The degree to which employee relations contributes to the successful operation of a company may be measured by the respect that labor and management have for each other. This respect is built up over the years by an intelligent and realistic approach to personnel administration and labor relations.

Selection and Training of Employees

The word *selection* as applied to new employees indicates that several applicants are available, and a selection can truly be made. If this is not the case in your company, examine carefully your wage levels, company policies, and working conditions. Supervisory training is more important than employee training. The ratio of supervisors to employees may average 1:10. Nevertheless, supervisory skills will provide a climate where 10 well-supervised employees will outperform 10 others.

The well-trained supervisor analyzes the employee-training requirements and lays out long-range plans. He writes job descriptions and checklists for new employees. He has a step-by-step procedure for introducing new employees to the job. This procedure should be coordinated with the personnel department.

Employee training does not stop with the new employee's understanding of his or her first job. He or she must be measured against known standards for each job. There is also the continuous task of training employees for transfer or promotion.

Collective Bargaining

The sessions where labor and management sit together to negotiate new labor agreements are known as the *collective-bargaining process.* But it is not just the session where new labor agreements are negotiated. It is any discussion throughout the year between management and labor of common problems. Any discussion between a supervisor and a worker in reality constitutes collective bargaining.

Wage and Salary Administration

Sound management practice dictates that the administration of wages and salaries should be standardized. A clock is a very poor tool to measure work performed. Two employees on the same job seldom turn out identical rates of production unless the production rate has been standardized in some way. Management realized this fact many years ago and so established a variety of piecework, incentive-rate, or bonus plans. These could be group or individual plans. They have one thing in common: Any change in material or equipment or method makes the old standard invalid. How much change? If you say "any change at all," it will take an army of industrial engineers to keep up with all the changes. If you say "any change that the supervisor determines is sufficient cause," you have a variety of incentive plans in effect at the same time.

Modern management practice tends toward measured-daywork systems. This puts the burden on the supervisor and on other management personnel to meet the standard. Management sets the standard without any negotiation with labor. The standard provides predetermined costs for budgeting and for pricing. No change of methods or materials will affect an employee's pay. Therefore, management can make changes that affect production rates at its own discretion. In addition, sound standards provide the data necessary for equipment and crew scheduling and lead to lower costs.

Records, Reports, and Research

Record keeping starts when a prospective employee applies for work. All application blanks should be retained. The applicant's files should be cross-indexed by name and job. Successful applicants will have added to their file copies of numerous government forms, health and insurance forms, union checkoff authorization, and so on.

However, suppose personnel turnover has become a problem in your company. Research is required, and some special reports should be issued for a stated time. Determine your plant's percentage of labor turnover by dividing the number of separations by the number of employees on the payroll, and multiply the answer by 100. Compute this percentage for a number of past periods. Plot the results on a graph. Analyze separately the reasons for employees being laid off and for voluntary separations. Make allowances for, but do not disregard, unavoidable separations. Set a goal for the labor turnover rate which will be acceptable. Change policies to correct the reasons for a high rate of separation. Measure progress toward the goal, and make special reports to management on this progress. Discontinue the reports when the goal is reached or when turnover is no longer a problem. The same approach should be applied to any other personnel problem.

Coordination with Industrial Relations

The impact of personnel problems on production output cannot be overemphasized. No attempt is made here to offer specific guidance to the production and inventory control manager in the solution of such problems. However, a yardstick is provided to measure the effectiveness of industrial relations in the company and thus act as a constructive force in the coordination of personnel actions affecting manpower.

ORGANIZATION FOR MANPOWER MANAGEMENT

Because of the need for quick response in today's competitive business environment, the effective management of manpower resources has become both increasingly complex and critically important. The most effective organization to manage manpower planning and control both specifically assigns responsibility for achieving results and inspires active participation and cooperation among line manufacturing, production and inventory control, sales, and finance functions. Whether its prime focus is a production planning committee or an individual manufacturing manager, the importance of coordination between the numerous interrelated responsibilities and functions outlined in the next section should be recognized.

Line and Staff Responsibilities for Manpower Planning and Control

Responsibilities for manpower planning and control can be divided into three important task areas: planning, acquiring and training, and control. The importance of the responsibilities within each area varies considerably depending on the company size, growth pattern, product design stability, cyclical pattern of business, types of manufacturing, and labor skills required.

Empowerment

Many companies on the brink of failure have found their salvation in a previously untapped source of ideas, innovations, and solutions, namely, the front-line workforce. When this vital segment of a company has been empowered to participate in problem solving, product improvement, and management decision making in joint effort with middle and top management, the results have been pleasantly positive.

The secret to successful empowerment is to change the line of communication from a top down form of directives to a free exchange of opinions, ideas, and even gripes on a horizontal level. Do not lose sight of the fact that listening is a vital element of communication.

Management must take the initiative in setting up an environment conducive to the free exchange of ideas. This can be as simple as a "walk around" in the plant to chat one on one with front-line employees, to regular communication meetings with free coffee and doughnuts, or lunch, in a relaxed atmosphere. Goals and actions should be arrived at jointly and implemented quickly to establish mutual trust.

Many problems are caused more by faulty systems than by human error, and the front-line personnel using the systems are generally more than willing to point out where the holes are and offer solutions. Management's key to successful empowerment is to be truthful, informal, and accessible. Positive results often come in gradual stages, and patience and persistence are needed for a successful program.

Using Consultants

A consultant may be called on to define any of the planning and control responsibilities previously outlined, recommend policy and organization structure, or even write operating procedures. In using a consultant, however, remember that in most cases he or she will not expound new truths but will more likely bring into the open the thinking within the organization, catalyzing it into meaningful policies or plans. Even with a reputable firm, a bitter experience can occur if the individual assigned to the project uses less than extreme care in evaluating the problem. Therefore, the choice is critical, and the client must make a comprehensive review of the qualifications of potential consulting firms. The following minimum considerations should guide the investigation:

1. Evaluate the background and experience of the consulting company's principals.
2. Compare the firm's experience with the project at hand.
3. Question former clients regarding work assigned, performance, personnel, action taken on the recommendations, and repeat work performed.

Upon completion of the preliminary investigation and prior to making a final selection, the client should request of one or more firms a written proposal clearly defining:

- The objectives of the assignment
- The work to be accomplished and the approach to be followed
- The involvement and coordination required of the client
- Possible difficulties that might hinder success in achieving the objectives
- The experience of the personnel to be assigned to the project and the role of each
- Statement of fees and the basis on which they are to be paid

It is important to realize in reviewing a formal proposal that the use of a consultant does not permit management to abrogate its responsibility for making decisions, adopting a course of action, and obtaining results.

MANPOWER DATA COLLECTION AND ANALYSIS

Effective planning and control of any manufacturing or service operation is impossible without information on the availability and utilization of its human resources. In today's rapidly changing, highly competitive business world, there is a growing need for improved manpower data collection and analysis capabilities. Those charged with making improvements in operational performance need a continuous, fast flow of highly accurate information on how the organization is using its employees and on how they are impacting the performance of the organization. Obtaining this information begins with the task of collecting the needed data.

While modern data collection and information processing technology has made it possible to track a wide variety of activities with virtually instantaneous speed, this data-handling power can result in tracking trivia if it is not properly focused and utilized. Many organizations have discovered too late that more data does not necessarily lead to better information and more effective management. Effective manpower data collection must accomplish three things: the collection of appropriate data, the accurate representation of current conditions, and the timely delivery of captured data to those who need it.

Designing the Data Collection System

The selection of the best data collection technologies, methods, and techniques for a specific situation will depend upon several factors:

- The types of production and service operations being performed
- The purpose or reasons for collecting the data
- The types of data being collected and their respective volumes
- The required degree of data timeliness and accuracy to support effective management

Process and Work Environment.   Designing the data collection and analysis system begins with an analysis of who we are as an organization, what we intend to be in the future, and the strategy we have selected to get us there. For example, a job shop operation with 100 employees wishes to continue supporting a group of customers whose main concerns are product quality and speed of delivery. In this company's targeted markets, price is typically not the primary factor in determining whether or not a customer chooses to place an order. Thus, production cost is not viewed as a critical success factor. The organizational culture encourages employee involvement in management, and there is a high degree of trust between labor and management. In this situation the approach to manpower data collection should focus on the effectiveness of quality-related activities and on time delays in engineering, production, and delivery processes. The system should be designed to involve employees in performing both data capture and analysis tasks.

Reasons for Collecting Manpower Data.   Listing and defining all the reasons for collecting manpower data is an essential first step in selecting and implementing an effective data collection system. When data collection needs are omitted, the design criteria for the system will be incomplete. This type of oversight may lead to expensive system modifications; or worse yet, the operation of multiple data collection systems that produce inconsistent and confusing information.

Types of Data Needed.   There are three general types of manpower or labor data commonly collected by organizations today:

1. Time and attendance data show the time for which an hourly employee is at work and is being paid. This type of data is typically used by payroll and human resource applications and may also be used by some cost accounting systems.
2. Job status data include the time actually spent working on tasks associated with a specific customer job or order. It may also include data on the number of units produced, the number of tasks accomplished, and the measurement of work results to a predefined set of standards. This data allows the organization to measure costs, efficiency, extent of completion, and the degree or level of quality achieved. This type of data is typically used by production control, customer service, incentive payroll, performance measurement, and quality-control applications.
3. Project status data are similar to job status data but are focused on tracking the current status, costs, and quality of work related to some ongoing program or project. This type of data may be used by project management, project costing, personnel evaluation, and quality-control applications.

Although presented here as separate data classes, in practice a single data collection system should be used to collect any or all of these classes of data in a seamless manner. Determining the many needs for manpower data is not a one-time occurrence. Conditions and needs change over time, and the data collection process should be reviewed periodically and fine-tuned when necessary.

Degree of Timeliness and Accuracy Required.   When the purpose for collecting data is clearly understood, it is possible to quantify the degree of accuracy and timeliness required. While many applications do not require immediate data input (for example, payroll applications typically require weekly input of manpower data), delaying the capture of data until it is needed often results in reduced data accuracy. Because this type of data loses its value rapidly if it is too old or inaccurate, many organizations have found it best to capture manpower data immediately and, if necessary, save it until it is needed.

There are three reasons to capture manpower data once, and only once—cost, accuracy, and consistency. Collecting basically the same data several times to feed different systems wastes not only time and money, it also leads to data errors and inconsistency in the information fed to management. If a job shop operation with a large number of hourly employees determines that controlling labor cost is key to their success, then a single data collection system should be designed to capture both time and attendance and job or cost data. Additional factors would have to be considered to determine if the system should also address other classes of data. Using data collected for payroll and production reporting purposes will virtually eliminate underreporting and overreporting. The fact that pay is affected if hours are not reported gives employees a real incentive to avoid underreporting work hours. On the other hand, production counts and efficiency measurements can be used to ensure that overreporting is not a problem.

When there is general agreement on the purposes for collecting data, the types of manpower data needed, and the degree of accuracy and timeliness required, the organization should proceed with determining the specific ways in which this data is to be captured, stored, and analyzed.

Data Collection Methods

While there are many ways to collect manpower or labor data, effective methods have three common attributes—they are easy to learn and use, they are constantly obvious to those who must enter data, and they are designed for quick and convenient use. Data collection methodologies that lack any one of these "ease of use" characteristics fall short of achieving optimum results.

Effective data collection systems are not always highly automated. While the use of computer technology is often a good idea, automation is desirable only if it makes life simpler and easier. Primary reasons for wanting to automate the data collection process include:

1. *To improve data accuracy.* Automating the data collection process makes it possible for the system to read and interpret data without human intervention and to validate the accuracy of the data near its source. Companies often find the level of accuracy achievable with automated systems greatly exceeds even the most disciplined manual approach. In fact, some system designs may not be feasible with the accuracy of data typically provided by manual data capture techniques.

2. *To improve the timeliness of available information.* Automating the data collection and analysis process makes it possible to greatly reduce the time lag between an event and the availability of information about that event. This timeliness of information is crucial to the effective management of operations in today's fast-cycle manufacturing operations. While many financial management systems work well with data that are a few days old, even a few hours' delay is far too much to properly manage shop floor operations for a high-speed, just-in-time factory.

3. *To reduce the cost of data collection and analysis.* Automating the data collection and analysis process makes it possible to manage large volumes of data in a more cost-effective manner. An automated data collection system may dramatically improve data accuracy and timeliness while being much cheaper to operate than the manual system it replaced. In addition to reducing the cost of capturing labor data, these automated systems also make it possible to store data in a more readily usable format, reducing the time and cost required for data access and analysis.

If automating the data collection process makes sense, an organization must still proceed with caution. The advantages sought in an automated data collection system will only be realized through a well-thought-out and properly executed system implementation. Ensuring that proposed procedures are complete and that the system will provide timely and accurate results is possible by performing a pilot test. A pilot of the system is performed by using the new system, or some reasonably similar approach, in one area of the operation. This pilot test can sometimes be performed manually before investing in automated data capture equipment. If the data collection process will not work on a small scale, it is very likely to produce high-speed garbage when applied to the whole organization.

On-line Data Capture. On-line systems record events as they actually occur via computer terminals or other electronic devices capable of capturing and transmitting the desired data. Given the capabilities of today's information technology, an on-line data capture system will likely be designed to update the appropriate database files immediately, even though the data may not be needed for several days or weeks. Since on-line data verification is usually performed, there is little if any additional cost to update the database immediately. The primary advantage of this approach is the ability to provide more thorough editing and improved data accuracy. For example, the system might verify that the shop order to which labor is being reported is a valid open order.

Sometimes the operator performing the work reports the initiation or completion of an operation, the time spent on a job, or the number of units completed. In other cases it may be the supervisor, crew chief, or timekeeper who is responsible for entering this task or event information into the system. With automated data capture capabilities, it is usually best to give the reporting responsibility to the individual operator closest to the origination of the data. If the task is performed by a team, the reporting responsibility may be rotated among team members, but it should always be clearly designated to one team member at all times.

Whether an organization requires a real-time or a periodic data capture system depends upon how the collected information is to be used and the additional cost of providing real-time computer systems and communication networks. As the cost of automated data capture technology continues to decline and the need for more timely and accurate information increases, more and more organizations are opting to replace their manual manpower data collection systems.

Data Capture Technologies and Techniques

Advances in computer technology have enabled organizations to capture, manipulate, and generate data at every level of their operation. The development of improved data capture technologies has played a central role in the development of this ability. Some of these data capture technologies still rely heavily on human input. Other forms of data capture technology are virtually automatic, requiring little, or no, human involvement.

Computer Terminals and Workstations.   Over the past two decades there has been an evolution on the shop floor from paper-based data collection, to dumb terminals, to intelligent workstations. Workstations in the factory today are based on the same powerful processors that have driven the PC revolution. These devices are often "hardened" to withstand a plant's harsh environmental conditions, and they may employ portable data collection terminals and other automated data acquisition devices. These shop floor systems allow manpower data to be stored and analyzed locally, uploaded to the corporate mainframe, or shared with other small computers over high-speed networks.

Data may be entered directly into the workstation via keyboard entry or through a number of other means. These include use of a mouse (point-and-click icons), touch screens, and bar-code input devices that can be directly connected to the workstation. In some cases, data may be entered into the information system via specialized terminal devices that are designed to handle a specific type of data entry. For example, there are terminal devices that are specifically designed to efficiently process a large volume of time and attendance transactions. Other data collection terminals are specifically designed to be located at each plant workstation for the entry of job status transactions. These terminals may be connected to a central processor or host computer via hard-wired data communications lines or via a wireless radio frequency (RF) connection. Using wireless RF terminals, workers can freely move about the plant or warehouse, yet their portable terminals are fully interactive with the host computer. If data must be provided to multiple applications residing on different systems, it may be necessary to connect the data capture system to a number of computers through a local-area or wide-area network.

Check Digits.   This technique for editing data as it is entered provides a way to catch most keyboard entry and transposition errors for predefined data elements such as employee number, part number, job number, and project number. Errors in recording this type of data are particularly insidious because they often create errors in two records, the one that should have been entered and the one that was entered erroneously. Most check digits involve the algebraic manipulation of the first $n-1$ digits of an n-digit number to obtain a correct value for the nth digit. For example, the computer takes the first five digits in a six-digit employee number and performs a predefined algebraic calculation. This calculation yields a value of 8. The computer will then refuse the entered number if any value other than 8 is entered for the sixth digit. A well-designed check-digit system can catch more than 99 percent of all data entry errors.

Bar Coding.   The most common form of automatic identification technology today is bar coding. This technology has proven to be an effective tool for capturing many types of data for a wide variety of applications and business situations. Bar codes can be printed along with human-readable text on employee badges, routing sheets, move tickets, and other types of documents used by people who perform manufacturing, logistical, engineering, clerical, maintenance, and administrative tasks. These bar codes encode machine-readable data that can be read by hand-held wands, human-operated laser scanners, or portable battery-operated units. In some situations fixed-position scanners can be installed to capture data automatically with no human action required. Bar-code reading devices are often configured to be used along with computer terminals and workstations to allow on-line verification of entered data. In many situations, bar coding offers the most accurate, timely, and cost-effective solution to satisfying at least some portion of the manpower data collection need.

Other Forms of Electronic Input.   Voice recognition is a "keyless" form of automatic identification technology that compliments the use of terminals and bar-code readers. While performing the same function, voice recognition is best suited to situations that require human input, that involve data that cannot be easily encoded and read by scanners, and that leave the operator's hands free to perform other tasks.

Other forms of automatic identification are currently in the product development and introduction process. These new technologies will provide the ability to read data in higher volumes and at greater distances than with prior data capture technologies. This new approach allows the system to continuously read and track special tags attached to employee badges. Thus, it is possible to continuously track the location of each employee in a real-time manner with no human actions required. While the impact of this evolving technology on the design and capabilities of manpower data collection systems remains to be seen, it will make the capture of some types of data faster, cheaper, and more accurate than ever before possible.

Analyzing Manpower Information

Capturing accurate and timely manpower data is only the beginning. Before it can be used, it must be converted from data into information. This conversion process involves structuring, summarizing, and analyzing the data to produce information valuable in solving some recognized problem, achieving a predefined objective, or supporting an ongoing business process or system.

Consider these examples. While employee attendance data is an essential input to the payroll system, the analysis of this data is also an important element in effectively managing many types of operations. To manage productivity and quality requires an understanding of how the organization's human resources are being deployed and how well they are currently performing. In engineering and other project-related functions, manpower data must be analyzed to determine which actions are needed to keep work proceeding on schedule. Virtually every type of operational management relies on the analysis of data related to the use of employee time and the conditions resulting from the performance of assigned tasks. While there are many ways in which manpower data may be analyzed, they all should have one thing in common—the objective of improving the organization's performance in achieving its mission.

When analyzing manpower information, we should begin by defining what we are trying to accomplish. In other words, clearly state the objectives of the affected organizational units, the objectives of the related business processes, and the objectives of this specific analysis. Next, we should determine which variables have a significant impact on the processes being analyzed. We should ask what information would be helpful in understanding the cause-and-effect relationships surrounding our objectives. Lastly, we should determine how we will measure these relationships and the types of data needed to compute and track them. For example, let us assume we are trying to reduce the cost of a manufacturing operation. We need to determine which cost elements and cost drivers are the most significant and which ones we are best able to control. State the way in which each data element will be manipulated and combined to produce performance measurements which will help us to reach our objectives. If we are also trying to improve the productivity of a process, we would first determine the variables with the greatest impact on productivity and then define exactly how this aspect of productivity is best measured. This should specify the exact form and format of the required manpower usage data and the exact form and format of the required production output data. If improving the quality of the process were also an objective, we would also need to determine the key variables, the best measures, and the specific data for achieving our quality objective.

As data are captured and performance measurements are analyzed, variations in the captured data will be observed. The analyst needs to record both positive and negative variations and the reasons for their occurrence if they are known. Any unusual conditions or circumstances should be noted and recorded as well. Over time, this type of tracking may begin to reveal trends in the measured data that are correlated to other events or conditions. This is how cause-and-effect relationships are discovered or verified and helps us to discover ways to better control and improve the performance of the process.

When the attribute being measured is some form of error condition or defective performance, it is often helpful to plot the measured data values on a logarithmic scale (Fig. 8.10). Since improvement efforts tend to reduce the occurrence of error conditions at a decreasing rate, it is easier to interpret what is going on in the process if we plot the measured data using a nonlinear scale as shown in the diagram below. By graphing the rate of reduction on graph paper with a logarithmic scale for the measured variable on the Y axis and a linear scale for time on the X axis, we observe a linear pattern that is easier for most people to understand and track. This form of graphical analysis continues to display a straight line with constant downward slope as long as the improvement process continues at the same pace. Changes in the slope of the line indicate a change in the effectiveness of continuous improvement efforts.

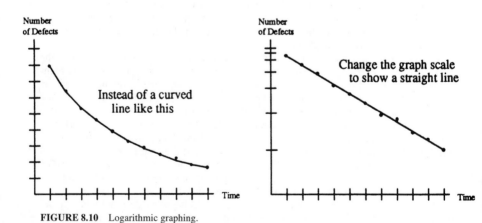

FIGURE 8.10   Logarithmic graphing.

A word of caution is needed for those who might believe the analysis of manpower data is always easy and straightforward. The determination of cause-and-effect relationships is often extremely difficult. Separating symptoms from their underlying causes when there is a chain of related events is almost always a challenge even for the most capable analyst. For example, the initial inspection of a labor usage report may indicate a problem. Our analysis may lead us to conclude that an observed drop in labor efficiency is due to poorly trained workers or unreliable equipment. However, the real reason for the apparent increase in labor usage may be a new engineer who has recently adjusted work standards. Since trends in manpower information often reveal only symptoms rather than underlying causes, we should probe each situation deeply. We should continue to question and analyze rather than accept the first explanation for the observed condition. As in the field of medicine, diagnosis of the real source of problems requires training and experience. If we fail to recognize the true source of a problem, it will usually lead us to actions that aggravate, rather than improve, the situation.

LABOR COST TECHNIQUES

Labor cost techniques, properly designed, provide timely and accurate information that management intelligently uses as a basis for decision making. That is, solutions to problems are derived from proper analysis and evaluation of facts provided by the technique and subsequently executed by the manager. These cost techniques provide management with the tools it requires to properly determine costs and evaluate product pricing, the return of investment, and profit.

Determining Labor Costs

Historically, estimators have had little black books in which they collected secret formulas, rules of thumb, and innumerable other devices for estimating labor costs. Management demanded estimates on which to base price quotations, plan personnel buildup, and schedule planned production. Any standard was better than no standard, so almost any figure could be used that seemed halfway reasonable. The conventional technique of the estimator was to explain why the estimate was wide of the mark. Changed methods or specification were a convenient alibi and were equally hard to prove or disprove.

Over time, considerable sophistication has been introduced to cost estimating, implying that accuracy is considerably improved and the results are much more reliable. This accurate cost estimating was made possible through the use of scientifically developed standard data, which became so developed that the term *estimating* was no longer appropriate. Rather, standard data applications superseded estimating per se and enabled a new level of significance and precision.

Today, due to the ever-decreasing amount of direct labor as a component of product cost, labor costs are being considered fixed in nature. An activity-based approach allows the labor costs to be charged to activities and subsequently assigned to products based on the amount of activity consumed by a product. This results in variances due to process, demand, and skill-level variations being applied directly to activities, not products. For example, the cost of testing is determined by the number of tests a product goes through. Product A requires 10 tests while Product B requires only 6. Knowing the total cost of all testing, the number of total tests, and therefore the cost to perform one test, each product can be charged for the specific number of tests it uses.

Standard Labor Costing

The accuracy with which standard data can be applied is entirely a function of how precisely an activity or method of production can be defined. If the exact method is known, the exact time is also known. When the number of unknowns increase, accuracy decreases since successive assumptions, whose validity are always subject to question, must be made.

To illustrate the method of cost calculation and the typical problems encountered, the following process may be useful. The development of costs for a single part is included with the understanding that the procedure would be the same for all parts and eventually for complete assemblies. The first step is to list the processes by which the part is made. This involves decisions as to whether a casting or raw stock will be used and a list of the operations and inspections necessary to produce the finished part. Here is a typical list of operations:

Operation	Machine or process
1. Cut raw stock to length.	Do-all saw
2. Turn to shape.	Engine lathe
3. Grind to final dimension.	Centerless grinder
4. Drill and ream.	Drill press
5. Plate.	Chrome plate process
6. Inspect	

The next step is to develop the detail for each operation to the depth necessary to apply data. To illustrate how this works, we consider operation 4, drill and ream, for the hypothetical part. We list the variables:

1. *Fixture.* If a tool drawing is available, exact data may be obtained of how the piece is placed and removed from the fixture and the type and number of clamps. This information together with the dimensions and weight of the piece makes possible an exact time value. If a fixture is to be used but no drawing is available, assumptions must be made about the fixture and the data applied on the basis of these assumptions, with a corresponding degree of uncertainty and loss of accuracy for the final result.

2. *Materials specifications.* If the precise material form of which the part is made is known, the exact drilling feed, speed, and time are known. However, if this has not been determined, an educated guess must be made and the data applied accordingly.

3. *Hole diameter and depth.* Usually this information is readily available, so an accurate time and cost can be determined if the material is known. However, for very rough standards, such as might be used for maintenance parts, any hole up to $\frac{1}{2}$ by $\frac{1}{2}$ inch might be considered as one standard and up to 1 by 1 inch as a multiple thereof, to reduce calculations and hence the time to arrive at the cost.

4. *Materials handling.* To arrive at a completely accurate standard, the type and size of container in which the parts are delivered for the operator should be known. If the data are not certain, assumptions based on the usual shop practices must be made.

5. *Lot size.* This factor has an obvious effect on the application of setup times and cost to a unit of product. It also influences the degree of proficiency operators can attain in making a particular piece. If there are few pieces, the operator may not develop his or her full production potential, especially if tooling and fixtures are complex.

When using standard data for calculations, consideration should be given to the degree of accuracy of the standard. The development of standards varies from using work measurement techniques, using historical data, and simply averaging actual performance.

Activity-Based Labor Costing

Labor costs consist of all the costs associated with the management and support of people in the organization. These labor costs include primarily salaries, fringe benefits, and the costs associated with supporting employees such as training and personnel. Labor costs are traced to and accumulated by activities. To determine the amount of labor cost for a specific product, the labor costs are assigned by the amount of the activity consumed by the product. For example, the labor content of engineering-change notice (ECN) processing activity is accumulated. The labor cost per ECN is then calculated. The labor cost is then charged to a product's cost by the number of applied ECNs.

Actual Versus Standard Costs

Actual cost versus *standard costs* is closely synonymous with saying *job-order* cost versus *standard costs*. Actual or job-order costs, without standard cost comparisons, do little from a control technique viewpoint. Actual costing implies identification of various costs with a job order and the collection of these costs to obtain the total cost for the job order. For factory labor, each operator records the hours worked for each job, which are accumulated to a specific job or order. When a job is finally completed and shipped, the costs are summarized and compared with an estimated budget or standard costs, when available. Subsequently, this information is useful in estimating future jobs, and a complete cost history is obtained. Job-order or actual costs can be used with or without standard costs.

Without standard costs, the job-order cost approach provides no frame of reference or anchor point to tell management where the performance was good or bad. Past information is available, and comparisons with estimates are possible and useful. However, there is no qualitative determination, that is, whether the performance was what it should be or could be and whether it was good or bad in an absolute sense.

Good labor standards are prerequisite to a standard cost system. Trying to install a standard cost system without them is to perpetuate an actual-cost-only system. Standards should be established on an engineered basis, with set standards separately identified. With labor standards available, they are naturally used for both control and cost purposes. This implies that operators will report time and units of production. The comparison of each individual's performance against the standard is made periodically for control purposes.

For controlling individual performance, it is usually advisable to segregate operation standards, which vary with the number of units processed, as opposed to setup standards, which vary per batch, per shift, or on some basis other than units produced. This prevents variances over which the individual operator has no control.

At times standards used for control purposes are applied on an "as-incurred" basis. This is the best way to determine and control the performance of individuals. For cost purposes, however, these as-incurred standards, such as setup, batch, and lot constant, must be included in unit standard costs.

Another significant difference between job-order and standard costs is in the way in which excess costs for delays, breakdowns, and so on are customarily handled. Under the job-cost system, excess labor costs usually get charged to the job being worked on at the time. This may produce significant variations in individual job costs. Under the standard costs system, there is usually provision for charging these activities as "off standard time." These charges find their way into overhead and are applied to all jobs rather than falling randomly to a particular job. Another problem involves differences in skill and effort of various individuals in the shop. Under the job-shop or actual-cost system, a new operator assigned to a job is unduly penalized. Under the standard cost system, a job has only one standard regardless of the person to whom it is assigned. Variance from standard or losses through failure to make standard are not all loaded onto a particular job but absorbed evenly by all jobs.

To summarize, standard costing is more refined than job costing because it establishes a "should-be" cost on an absolute level. It is also more equitable because excess costs for delays and substandard performance are absorbed by all jobs rather than by one or two jobs selected on a random basis.

Labor and Head Count Planning and Budgeting

The development of plans and budgets for direct manpower can be only as accurate as the ability to forecast the volume of production and product mix. Plans can be established in a number of ways, but the typical way is through the application of standards to accurate production forecasts. Other approaches are to develop plans by taking the trend of actual expenses for the past several time periods (months or years), and extrapolate the next period as a basis for an educated guess. This unscientific approach to planning needs no further analysis here since the techniques are fairly obvious and self-explanatory.

Plans for direct labor have several purposes and connotations for different people. The purposes of planning might be classified as profit planning and forecasting, forecasting manpower requirements, and control of manpower costs. Plans and budgets are planning and control tools, and every company should use them to maximize profits. Planning as related to profit planning starts with a sales forecast, which combined with selling prices results in the income plan. When all cost items, including labor, are deducted from income, a profit plan for the year is developed. The more detailed and accurate the sales forecast of quantities and mix, the more accurate the plan becomes. Operating with a plan or budget implies management's resolve to keep all costs in line with the plan. If the profit objectives are to be met, sales that fall off must be stimulated and costs that overrun the plan must be brought into line. Control mechanisms to keep management advised of each part of the plan are necessary if the planned results are to be realized.

The forecasting of manpower requirements is an outgrowth of the sales and profit plan. If increased sales are forecast and manpower needs are planned accordingly, management is given the lead time necessary to recruit and train personnel. Given the time necessary to develop people for each phase of the production process, a schedule for hiring and training can be developed to meet future needs.

Flexible Budgeting

The concept of planning used as a control mechanism is considerably more complex and introduces the ideas of a flexible budget. In this context, the flexible budget tells management how much manpower and associated costs are required for various forecast and production levels. Although a fixed budget, based on the forecast, works well when expected sales are realized, it lacks flexibility and hence usefulness when the volume becomes either more or less than the forecast. For example, if the volume of production is less than the forecast, the budgeted expenditures for manpower should be less. On the other hand, if sales and production increase, a comparison to the budget may be unsatisfactory because it appears that more labor is being used than anticipated, while in reality, the labor expended may be appropriate for the increase in sales.

The flexible budget is not directly related to the forecast and is only indirectly related to profit planning. More accurately the flexible budget reflects current performance and thus is more valuable as a control mechanism. Flexible budgets, which decrease as output decreases and increase when production increases, compare predicted performance against actual units produced and are more realistic and valuable as a control mechanism.

To be wholly effective and accurate, flexible budgets should be applied not only on units shipped or transferred to finished stock, but also on the actual production achieved at each operation during the production process. Otherwise, changes in work-in-process (WIP) inventories will distort the flexible budget and produce false readings. For example, if WIP inventory is reduced, the count of finished units produced will be too high. Conversely, if WIP inventories are being increased, much work will be accomplished without actually producing finished units. To illustrate the development of a manpower budget using standards and a production forecast, the following simple examples are used.

Assume the monthly sales forecast for the 5 products manufactured by a company are as follows: product A, 100; product B, 500; product C, 50; product D, 800; product E, 950. The standard cost sheet (Table 8.9) shows, among other things, the following

TABLE 8.9 Standard Cost Sheet

Standard cost calculation for product A			

I. Materials
   A. Steel sheet 1040 A   100 lb/unit
   B. Wire, copper no. 10 regular   50 ft/unit
   C. Paint, industrial enamel   0.50 gal/unit

II. Direct Labor

	Hours per unit	Rate per hour	Cost per unit
A. Cutting			
1. Do-all saw	0.2650	9.75	2.5838
2. Shear	0.4078	10.05	4.0984
3. Brake	0.2160	9.90	2.1384
B. Assembly			
1. Subassembly 1	0.5065	9.60	4.8624
2. Subassembly 2	0.7862	9.60	7.5475
3. Final assembly	1.6035	10.20	16.3557
C. Finish and pack			
1. Spray paint	0.1345	9.84	1.3235
2. Touch up	0.0756	9.45	0.7144
3. Pack	0.6300	9.30	5.8590

labor and materials requirements for product A. Similar cost sheets exist for products B, C, D, and E.

The application of the standards to the production forecast, simplified to illustrate the process, is shown in Table 8.10. The resulting calculations show the authorized manning for each department, based on the forecasted production requirements. Control reports that show the relationship of the forecast to the actual mix indicate the validity of the original budget.

The illustrated budget is valid, provided that the departments operate at standard, which, of course, is not always the case. If the actual productivity levels are substantially different from standard, the manpower figures can be prorated for planning purposes. For cost control the variance from standard may be highlighted.

Indirect Manpower Budgets

The term *indirect labor,* or *manpower,* is widely used in a number of different senses. In the narrowest sense it is labor that does not contribute anything to the value of the product. This includes materials handling, service personnel, inspection, and operations such as mold cleaning. This strict definition serves little useful purpose and seems to confuse the issue and budget concepts discussed here.

At the other extreme is the concept often associated with the aerospace and defense industries, where manpower is considered indirect if it cannot be identified with a given contract. Under this definition almost any function such as stockkeeping, maintenance, personnel, purchasing, and design can be classified as direct if the people perform their functions for only one contract. This definition is useful only for invoicing against a cost-based contract.

For budgeting and cost purposes, direct labor is any labor activity that can be applied specifically to a product, while indirect labor are activities supporting production, but not related to a specific product. These definitions result in some activities, such as inspection and materials handling between process, being classified as direct labor. Indirect labor typically includes maintenance workers, cleaners, stockroom workers, inventory control personnel, tool crib attendants, and clerical personnel. Some may argue that some manpower is more indirect than others, and this is true. Even indirect labor bears some relationship to specific products. But in a given instance, the relationship is not direct, and so it is correctly classified as indirect.

Applying Indirect Labor to Specific Products

Indirect labor costs usually find their way into the overhead cost for each department or factory. Overhead costs are applied to specific products by machine-hour, direct labor-hour, or some unit of production such as pounds or feet. Whichever basis is used, the overhead rate is determined, and the amount is applied to a product on the basis used, for example, the number of labor-hours used for a product.

The above approaches to indirect manpower budgets is an interesting exercise in algebraic addition and compares actual performance with the budget and with a planned profit. It shows why profit objectives may or may not be realized and in this sense is a control mechanism. However, it is not the complete answer to control since there is some indication of what management is actually getting of right amounts expended. Supervisory appraisal is the only assurance that control is maintained. A department may be well within budget but way out of line in relation to actual work accomplished.

The approaches currently being addressed to better control traditionally indirect costs lie in the areas of activity-based costing and physical control areas such as focused factories.

TABLE 8.10 Development of Manpower Budget: Direct Labor

Product	Cutting department			Assembly			Finish and pack			Total
	Saw	Shear	Brake	Subassembly 1	Subassembly 2	Final	Paint	Touch up	Pack	
A: 100	26.50	40.78	21.60	50.65	78.62	160.35	13.45	7.56	63.00	462.51
B: 500	—	—	—	—	—	—	—	—	—	—
C: 50	—	—	—	—	—	—	—	—	—	—
D: 800	—	—	—	—	—	—	—	—	—	—
E: 950	—	—	—	—	—	—	—	—	—	—
Total man-hours per month	753.25	835.56	685.60	940.36	1260.50	2580.36	436.12	350.48	1080.31	8922.54
Employees required	4.38	4.86	3.99	5.47	7.33	15.0	2.54	2.04	6.28	51.88
Manpower budget		13.23			27.80			10.86		

8.49

REFERENCE

1. Chase, Richard B., and Nicholas J. Aquilano, *Production and Operations Management,* Richard D. Irwin, Homewood, Ill., 1992.

BIBLIOGRAPHY

Andreas, F. J.: "The Learning Curve as a Production Tool," *Harvard Business Review,* January–February 1954.

Anthony, Robert N., D.B.A., and James S. Reece, D.B.A.: *Management Accounting,* 5th ed., Richard D. Irwin, Homewood, Ill., 1975.

APICS Dictionary, 7th ed., APICS, 1992.

Armstrong, M., and J. F. Lorentzen: *Handbook of Personnel Management Practice,* Prentice-Hall, Englewood Cliffs, N.J., 1982.

Baird, Lloyd S.: *Managing Human Resources,* Business One Irwin, Homewood, Ill., 1993.

Barnes, R. M.: *Motion and Study—Design and Measurement of Work,* 7th ed., Wiley, New York, 1980.

Beach, D., *Personnel—The Management of People at Work,* 4th ed., Macmillan, New York, 1980.

Brimson, James A.: *Activity Accounting,* Wiley, New York, 1991.

Bruns, William J., Jr., and Robert S. Kaplan: *Accounting & Management—Field Study Perspectives,* Harvard Business School Press, Boston, 1987.

Chase, Richard B., and Nicholas J. Aquilano: *Production and Operations Management,* Richard D. Irwin, Homewood, Ill., 1992.

Clark, J. T.: *Capacity Management, Part Two, 23rd Annual Conference Proceedings,* APICS, 1980.

Dickie, H. F.: "Six Steps to Better Inventory Management," *Factory Management and Maintenance,* August 1963.

Fogarty, Donald W., CFPIM, John H. Blackstone, Jr., CFPIM, and Thomas R. Hoffman, CFPIM: *Production & Inventory Management,* 2d ed., Southwestern Publishing, Cincinnati, 1991.

Hall, Robert W., H. Thomas Johnson, and Peter B. B. Turney: *Measuring Up: Charting Pathways to Manufacturing Excellence,* Business One Irwin, Homewood, Ill., 1991.

Kaplan, Robert S.: *Measures for Manufacturing Excellence,* Harvard Business School, Boston, 1990.

Krajewski, Lee J., and Larry P. Ritzman: *Operations Management: Strategy and Analysis,* Addison-Wesley Publishing Company, Reading, Mass., 1992.

McCormick, E. J.: *Human Factors Engineering,* 4th ed., McGraw-Hill, New York, 1976.

Niebel, B. W.: *Motion and Time Study,* 7th ed., Irwin, Homewood, Ill., 1982.

Pascale, Richard Tanner: *Managing on the Edge,* Simon & Schuster, New York, 1990.

Peters, Tom: *Thriving on Chaos,* Alfred P. Knopf, New York, 1987.

Rice, W. B.: *Control Charts,* Wiley, New York, 1955.

Robbins, S. P.: *Personnel: The Management of Human Resources,* 2d ed., Prentice-Hall, Englewood Cliffs., N.J., 1982.

Salvendy, Gavriel: *Handbook of Industrial Engineering,* 2d ed., Wiley, New York, 1991.

Vollman, Thomas E., William L. Berry, and D. Clay Whybark: *Manufacturing Planning and Control Systems,* 3rd ed., Business One Irwin, Homewood, Ill., 1992.

Wright, T. P.: "Factors Affecting the Cost of Airplanes," *Journal of Aeronautical Sciences,* February 1936.

SECTION 3

OPERATING THE PRODUCTION AND INVENTORY CONTROL FUNCTION

CHAPTER 9

MANAGING BY THE THEORY OF CONSTRAINTS

Editors

James F. Cox III, Ph.D, CFPIM
John H. Blackstone, Jr., Ph.D., CFPIM

Management Department,
Terry College of Business
University of Georgia, Athens, Georgia

The theory of constraints (TOC) is a systems approach to decision making which is built around the premise that "constraints determine system performance." As will be shown in this chapter, this knowledge allows anyone within any system to "think globally, act locally." By contrast, traditional cost-accounting-based decision making encourages people to think locally, in essence assuming independence between functions. In the sections that follow, we will demonstrate the superiority of constraint-based decision making. To date, TOC has been applied to performance measurement, to logistics, and to general decision making. In this chapter we concentrate primarily on logistics, although we do briefly discuss the other two areas.

THEORY OF CONSTRAINTS EVOLUTION

In the late 1970s, Dr. Eliyahu M. Goldratt, an Israeli physicist, developed a finite scheduling software package called *OPT (Optimum Production Technology)* that focused on scheduling operations based upon the constraint work center(s).[1] This software package was a major departure from traditional scheduling software that attempted to plan and control all operations at all work centers. Based on implementations of the OPT software in a number of quite different manufacturing environments, Goldratt identified several new logistics concepts and principles. In the early 1980s both the OPT and the just-in-time (JIT) philosophies were implemented in the United States. Both philosophies were described in the business literature as "synchronous" production based on the linking of all work flow to end items in the master schedule. While the term *synchronous* appropriately describes the flow of materials in the production process, it does not adequately describe the evolution and current development of either the theory of constraints (TOC) or just-in-time philosophies. Over the past 15 years, TOC has evolved in three separate but interrelated areas—performance management, logistics, and management skills.

OPT began with the principle that constraints determine flow through a shop. To maximize flow, the constraint must be utilized efficiently and must be buffered from disruptions occurring elsewhere in the shop. Nonconstraints have idle capacity and therefore do not need to be buffered.

Other control points in a system were identified, such as materials release, which must be limited to keep pace with the constraint to maintain a fixed level of WIP. As time passed, Goldratt recognized that structures like textiles, with few raw materials and many outputs, need a different control structure than products like a weapons system (such as a tank) with many components but few end-item variations. Later in the chapter we discuss product structures, control points, and planning and control systems.

Traditional cost accounting has been an ever-present obstacle to implementing the OPT philosophy and the logistics concepts.[2] In his paper "Cost Accounting: The Number One Enemy of Productivity" presented at the 1983 APICS International Conference, Goldratt criticized the use of traditional cost accounting in managing an organization.[3] To provide a valid performance measurement system linking local decisions to the organizational goal of making more money now and in the future, Goldratt[4] (and Fox[5]) designed three simple measures—throughput, inventory, and operating expenses and the five focusing steps of TOC. This was perhaps the first demonstration of how constraint-based logic permitted global considerations rather than the local decision making present under traditional cost accounting. Many of the TOC logistics and accounting concepts are described in the three versions of *The Goal* (1984,[6] 1986,[7] and 1992[8]) and in *The Race.*[9]

In the mid to late 1980s, Goldratt[10] developed two important general decision-making concepts—*the effect-cause-effect diagram* and the *evaporating-clouds* method. These two concepts provide the basis of the TOC management skills or thinking process area used by managers to answer three important questions.[11] Question 1: Of all the undesirable effects that can be addressed, how do I identify those few activities that are blocking the organization from accomplishing its goal of making more money? These few activities are called *core problems.* Question 2: Once a core problem is identified, what is a solution that everyone sees as a win-win solution? Question 3: Now that a truly acceptable solution has been identified, how do I implement the solution, ensuring that all parties are supportive of the changes?

While Dr. W. Edwards Deming is recognized as the father of *total quality management* philosophy, Dr. Eliyahu M. Goldratt is considered the father of the *theory of constraints* philosophy.[12] The TOC philosophy is based on the principle of focusing attention on those few elements (constraints) that control the performance of the entire system. A *constraint* is defined as anything that limits the performance of the system relative to its goal. Physical and policy constraints exist. Examples of physical constraints are a work center or department, a piece of equipment, or a raw material. Policy constraints include pricing policies that limit the market demand for a product, sales commission policies that encourage selling the wrong products, production measures that inhibit organizational performance, and personnel and staffing policies that promote conflicts. The management skills tools, such as effect-cause-effect diagramming and the evaporating-cloud technique, focus on identifying these core policy problems and on determining better solutions. We discuss management skills tools briefly in a later section.

TOC PERFORMANCE MEASURES

In the remainder of this chapter we first discuss TOC performance measures, then TOC applied to logistics, and finally TOC management skills. In each section we provide an overview, definitions, and an example.

Overview: The Traditional Accounting Concept of Product Costs

From a theory of constraints perspective, one of the most damaging concepts of traditional management decision making is the concept of product cost.[13,14] Product cost consists of those "variable" costs involved in producing an item, such as raw materials and direct labor consumed, plus those fixed costs, such as indirect labor and overhead, that are allocated to the product. Most managers feel that selling a product below "product cost" is sheer idiocy. But there are many situations in which a firm can have a positive cash flow and contribute to organizational profit from selling below "product cost." Consider the following: By spending $500 on materials, and with no increase in labor costs or overhead, a firm can produce a unit. The unit usually sells for $2000 and has a "product cost" of $1000. A school system has asked for an "educational price" of $750 each for 10 units. What are the cash flow and profit implications of this transaction?

Clearly, cash flow reflects a positive $2500 ($7500 revenue less $5000 expense). A quick answer to the question of profit is that profit is minus $2500 ($7500 revenue less $10000 expense based on the $1000 product cost). But a more considered answer is that the $500 fixed cost assigned to each unit using the product cost concept does not go away if this sale is declined. The correct logic is that products do not have profit, firms do. This transaction yields a plus $2500 contribution to organizational fixed costs and profits and therefore should be accepted.

Characteristics of an Organization

Chain.   Goldratt identified two organizational characteristics that had significant impact on managing an organization. One organizational characteristic[15] was that the various activities and functions were like the links of a chain and that, like a chain, an organization is only as strong as its weakest link. The weakest link, the constraint, could be in engineering, purchasing, marketing, sales, production, or somewhere else. To strengthen the chain, the weakest link must be strengthened. To improve an organization, the weakest function or activity must be strengthened. It makes no sense to strengthen the already strong functions. Traditional accounting measurements treat all activities or functions as independent and equally important. The TOC approach provides a new foundation for managerial decision making based on achieving the organizational goal of making more money. The major difference between TOC thinking and traditional thinking lies in TOC's focus on system throughput achieved at the constraint rather than the traditional view of achieving cost savings at all links. This TOC focus allows the organization to coordinate activities across functions to achieve the organizational goal—"to make more money now and in the future."[16]

Measurement.   The second organizational characteristic Goldratt recognized was the following: "Tell me how you measure me, and I'll tell you how I will behave. If you measure me in an illogical way,...I will behave illogically."[17] Goldratt recognized that most poor business decisions and actions are based on poor measures. Traditional measures were established in the 1920s. Since then, the business environment has changed; cost structures have changed. Organizational overhead was less than 10 percent of the cost of the product when cost accounting was created in the early 1900s; today overhead is over 50 percent of product cost in many companies. Direct labor was over 40 percent of product cost and was paid on a piece rate (a variable cost) in the early 1900s. Today direct labor is less than 10 percent of product cost in many companies and is paid on an hourly basis with a guaranteed minimum of weekly hours (a fixed cost).

TOC Performance Measurement System

The goal of most businesses is to make money now and in the future. Improvement is defined as movement toward the organizational goal. The TOC performance measures developed by Goldratt and Fox[18] are the following:

Throughput. The rate at which the system generates money through sales

Inventory. The money the system invests in things it intends to sell

Operating expense. The money the system spends in converting inventory into throughput

Throughput for a single item is equal to selling price minus raw materials expense. Goldratt's definition of raw material is similar to the economic definition of marginal cost, that is, those costs that vary directly when one unit more or less is produced. Summing all individual product throughputs provides organizational throughput. Organizational throughput must exceed organizational expenses in the long run for the organization to make a profit. Notice that this concept differs significantly from the accounting concept of *product cost.* The TOC focus is on *organizational profit.*

The Five Focusing Steps of TOC

The five focusing steps of TOC[19] are as follows:

1. Identify the constraint to the system.
2. Decide how to exploit the constraint.
3. Subordinate all else to the decision in step 2.
4. Elevate the constraint.
5. If in any previous step, the constraint is broken, go to step 1. Do not let inertia become the constraint.

The first and second steps of the five focusing steps *link* the measurement system to the logistics system. Prioritizing constraint production allows the constraint to make the most money for the organization. The third step, subordinate nonconstraints to the constraint's pace, is accomplished by releasing only enough materials at the gating operations to keep the constraint busy and by prioritizing nonconstraint tasks based on the constraints' needs. While *exploit* (step 2) means get the most from the existing constraint resource, step 4, elevate, means getting more of the constraint resources. Exploit, squeezing the most from the resource, is accomplished prior to spending money to get more of the constraint resource. Step 4 should be conscious and deliberate. Step 5 is a warning to continually check to ensure that the constraint has not shifted to another resource or a policy. Continual review of the organization and its environment is required.

An Example of Throughput World Thinking

Study a simple problem to identify how a business might be better managed by using the TOC measures and the five focusing steps. The example, Figure 9.1, is a simple company which makes four products—A, B, C, and D. Product A sells for $70 and has a 40 units per week demand; product B sells for $80 and has a 35 units per week demand; C for $90 and 30 units per week; and D for $100 and 25 units per week. There are 3 direct laborers working at 3 different work centers (WCs) who are each paid $12 per hour for 40 hours per week. The overhead rate is roughly 2.5 times the direct labor

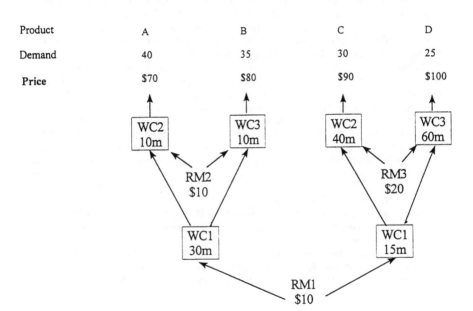

Product	A	B	C	D
Demand	40	35	30	25
Price	$70	$80	$90	$100

WCs 1,2,3 - 1 each
Each available 2400 min/week
Operating Expense $5,000/week
Setups on each WC = 60 minutes
Inventory is $200,000
Direct labor = $12/hour x 3 workers x 40 hours = $1440
Overhead is 2.5 x DL = 2.5 x $1440 =
$$\underline{3600}$$
$$\$5040 \approx \$5000$$

FIGURE 9.1 A simple firm. (Based on Goldratt's *Haystack Syndrome,* a well-known PQ example.)

cost with both totaling approximately $5000 per week. There are three raw materials—RM1 is used in all products and costs $10 per unit; RM2 is used in products A and B and costs $10 per unit; and RM3 is used in products C and D and costs $20 per unit.

To make products A and B, RM1 flows to WC1 and takes 30 minutes per unit processing time. The units then flow either to WC2 for combining with RM2 and processing time of 10 minutes per unit in making product A, or the units flow to WC3 to be combined with RM2 and processed for 10 minutes per unit for product B. To make products C and D, RM1 flows to WC1 for 15 minutes per unit processing. The units then flow either to WC2 to be combined with RM3 and processed for 40 minutes per unit in making product C or flow to WC3 to be combined with RM3 and processed for 60 minutes per unit in making product D. Setup time on WC1 is 60 minutes every time it changes from products A or B to products C or D (there is no setup from A to B or from C to D). When WC2 or WC3 change products, a 60-minute setup operation is required. Inventory (land, building, and equipment) is valued at $200,000. The information for this example is summarized in Fig. 9.1.

What is the net profit potential for this business? What is the profit if no resource constraint exists? Multiply the quantity demanded by the selling price minus raw material for each product and sum across products then subtract the operating expense. In Table 9.1, this solution is provided as $2650 profit per week—what a money-making machine! Can this be right? Can you make all four products? Probably not!

In many systems resource constraints exist. Check the production requirements to make the four products against the capacity at each WC. What are the production requirements for WC1 across the product line? WC2 across the product line? WC3? Do any WC requirements exceed 40 hours or 2400 minutes per week? WC1 requires 3075 minutes without any setup (remember, a setup is 60 minutes). With one setup, the firm needs 3135 minutes but only has 2400 minutes of capacity (40 hours a week). What of WC2's capacity requirements? 1600 minutes or 67 percent capacity required! And WC3? 1850 minutes or 77 percent required. What has been calculated is the capacity required, and in this case WC1's requirement exceeds 100 percent; therefore, step 1 has been executed in TOC—"*Identify the system constraint(s)."* The calculations are shown in Table 9.2, "Theory of Constraints Approach."

Now that the constraint has been identified as WC1, how can it be used most effectively? Which product(s) should be made? There are several alternative calculations in traditional accounting. You can compute each product's standard cost and identify which product gives the highest profit, next higher, and so on. Product A sells for $70, uses $20 in raw material, 40 minutes of direct labor or $8 per unit and $20 in overhead for a product cost of $48. Product A profit is $22 ($70 − $48). Following the same pro-

TABLE 9.1   Market Potential: What Is the Net Profit Potential?

Product	A		B		C		D		
Selling price	$70		$80		$90		$100		
Raw materials	20		20		30		30		
Contribution	$50		$60		$60		$70		
Demand	40		35		30		25		
Total revenue	$2000	+	$2100	+	$1800	+	$1750	=	$7650
Operating expense									$5000
Net Profit									$2650

TABLE 9.2   Theory of Constraints Approach: Step 1, Identify the System Constraint

WC	Product	Demand	Time per unit	Capacity required*
1	A	40	30	1200
	B	35	30	1050
	C	30	15	450
	D	25	15	375
				$\dfrac{3075}{2400} = 128$ percent
2	A	40	10	400
	B	35	0	0
	C	30	40	1200
	D	25	0	0
				$\dfrac{1600}{2400} = 67$ percent
3	A	40	0	0
	B	35	10	350
	C	30	0	0
	D	25	60	1500
				$\dfrac{1850}{2400} = 77$ percent

*Excludes setup time (SU).

cedure, product B's profit is $32.00, product C's profit is $21.50, and product D's profit is $17.50. Based on these calculations, you should make product B first, A second, C third, and D fourth. This calculation is provided in Table 9.3. Products are ranked from highest to lowest. Using these rankings, how much money can you make given that WC1 is the constraint?

Compute the capacity requirements to ensure that the 2400 minutes per week is not exceeded. If product B is made first, then 1050 minutes of WC1 capacity is required, product A is made second and 1200 minutes are required; a setup of 60 minutes is now required to switch to product C, and then 6 units of product C can be made for a total capacity used of 2400 minutes. Net profit is then calculated by subtracting operating expense (OE) of $5000 from the total contribution. Net profit is a *loss* of $540! Return on investment (ROI) is $[(52 \text{ weeks} \times -\$540)/\$200,000] = -14$ percent.

How can such a lucrative investment result in such a miserable failure? Maybe something is wrong with the logic! Cost accounting assumes average values for all WCs; yet one WC, the constraint WC1, controls throughput. What products are produced has no impact on labor or overhead costs. These costs are relatively fixed over the time horizon—only raw material costs vary based on what products and quantities are made. It seems logical that *throughput* should only consider the selling price minus raw material (true marginal costs). Note that production should be prioritized based on utilizing the constraint WC1 effectively, not on average resource costs.

Table 9.4 reviews the TOC approach to determining product mix, based on throughput per constraint unit. Recall that unit throughput is defined as the selling price minus the raw material cost.

TABLE 9.3 Conventional Cost Accounting Approach

Product	A	B	C	D						
Demand	40	35	30	25						
Selling price	$70	$80	$90	$100						
Raw materials	20	20	30	30						
Contribution	$50	$60	$60	$70						
Direct labor	$8	$8	$11	$15						
Overhead	$20	$20	$27.50	$37.50						
Product profit	$22	$32	$21.50	$17.50						
Rank	2	1	3	4						
WC1 capacity	30 m	30 m	15 m	15 m						
Make (units)	40	35	6	0						
Total capacity (min)	1200	+	1050	+	60 SU*	+ 90	+	0	=	2400 m
Total contribution	$2000	+	$2100	+	$360		+	0	=	$ 4460
Operating expenses										$ 5000
Loss										$−540

*SU = setup time.

TABLE 9.4 Theory of Constraints Approach: Step 2, Decide How to Exploit the Constraint

Product	A	B	C	D						
Demand	40	35	30	25						
Selling price	$70	$80	$90	$100						
Raw materials	20	20	30	30						
Throughput	$50	$60	$60	$70						
WC1 labor	30 m	30 m	15 m	15 m						
Throughput, WC1	$1.67	$2.00	$4.00	$4.66						
Rank	4	3	2	1						
WC1 capacity	30 m	30 m	15 m	15 m						
Make (units)	15	35	30	25						
Total capacity (min)	450	+	1050	+	60 SU*	+ 450	+	375	=	2385 m
Total contribution	$750	+	$2100	+	$1800		+	$1750	=	$6400
Operating expenses										$5000
Profit										$1400

*SU = setup time.

Throughput per constraint (WC1) unit for product A is $1.67 ($50 per 30 minutes); B is $2.00 ($60 per 30 minutes); C is $4.00; and D is $4.66. Based on prioritizing products by constraint contribution, 25 D's, 30 C's, 35 B's and 15 A's could be produced. These calculations produce a profit of $1400 per week and an annualized ROI of 36 percent (52 weeks × $1400/$200,000).

The product mix found in the table illustrates the second step, "*Decide how to exploit the constraint.*" The example company certainly improved its profit by focusing on the constraint. What product really contributes the most profit? Product D! Why not make only product D? The market demand for D is only 25. This is a market policy constraint probably strongly related to the price of $100. Could the company make more organizational profit by reducing the price slightly on part or all D products? Can the company encourage sales personnel to sell more of products D and C by structuring the sales commissions appropriately? What do sales personnel generally sell? Sales people probably promote those items that provide *them* the highest commission. Maybe your sales commission policies should be structured to support the goal of your organization—to make more money. That is, perhaps all sales commissions should be based on throughput per constraint unit.

The third TOC step is, "*Subordinate all else to the decision taken in step 2.*" Since the firm has a constraint, WC1, can you operate WC2 or WC3 at 100 percent utilization? No! What utilization should you expect? At WC2 56 percent and at WC3 77 percent. You cannot increase throughput by increasing WC's 2 and 3 utilizations.

The fourth TOC step is, "*Elevate the constraint.*" Now, how can you increase throughput? Suppose you can buy a $1500 fixture to reduce the setup time at WC1 to 30 minutes. Is it a good deal? You can save 30 minutes per week. You would make 1 more unit of A each week for a $50 increase in throughput. The payback is 30 weeks or $1500/$50—not a bad investment. How else might you increase throughput? If you could reduce the time per unit on WC1 for any product A, B, C, or D, you could make more A's at $50 per unit in throughput. You could also use overtime at WC1. You have made more of the constraint available by each of these actions. In contrast, what is the payback for reducing the setup time at the nonconstraints WC2 and WC3? Improvements at WC2 or WC3 do little to improve throughput.

The fifth and last step in TOC is, "*If in any of the previous steps the constraint is broken, then go to step 1. Do not let inertia set in.*" What would happen if you acquired a second of WC1 and kept producing at WC1's rate? You would build excess finished-goods inventory since there is no longer a resource constraint. What you should do now is produce at the market rate. Too many times companies become complacent, satisfied with their progress and resistant to new ideas or change. One fact is certain: The business environment is constantly changing—today's solution is tomorrow's problem. The only solution you should embrace is a process of continuous improvement.

TOC measures and the five focusing steps link the various organizational functions to achieve the organizational goal of making more money now and in the future. Top management should determine where the constraint should be for its company and develop a company strategy for moving the constraint to that resource. Marketing and sales efforts should be tied to the constraint through the exploit step. What products should a company make and sell to make the most money based on constraint usage? Does it have products that do not cross the constraint? Can it sell more of them? Engineering and employee improvement activities should focus on making the constraint more efficient. Additionally, a company should focus nonconstraint resources on how they might assist the constraint resource to be more effective.

THE THEORY OF CONSTRAINTS APPROACH TO LOGISTICS

Frequently the concepts of "product cost" and "product profit" lead to bad decisions.[20] A better, entirely consistent, holistic management philosophy is provided by the TOC measures and the five focusing steps. But to effectively implement this TOC philosophy requires linking the measurement area to scheduling in the logistics area. We therefore must first discuss how to manage constraint and nonconstraint resources.

Overview: Logistics and TOC

TOC's approach to logistics—drum-buffer-rope (DBR), buffer management, and VAT analysis—provides a methodology for managing the complete logistics system based on the constraint's capacity. Goldratt recognized two characteristics of logistics systems—dependent events and statistical fluctuation—whose interaction impacts the performance of the constraint and hence the entire logistics system.[21] His views on how to manage the logistics function to accommodate these two characteristics created TOC's approach to logistics. A simple production line will be used to introduce the problems of dependent resources and statistical fluctuation. *Dependent resources* or *events* means that a series of steps must be followed in completing a task—step 1 must be completed prior to step 2, step 2 prior to step 3, and so on. *Statistical fluctuation* means that activity times are not deterministic because deviations around the mean exist. The old manufacturing adage "Murphy is alive and well" is used to describe common statistical fluctuations. Murphy is worker absenteeism, lateness, and slowness, missing or damaged parts, machine breakdown, and so on. This dependent resources relationship among stations of the line creates a situation where lateness created or encountered at the first station is transferred to a late start at the second station, and possibly a late completion at the second station; this lateness could transfer throughout the remaining stations to lateness for the end item. Additionally, the late finish of the item at the first station also creates a late start for the next item at the first station. Recognizing this relationship, Goldratt devised several concepts and techniques that are useful in designing and managing logistics systems. In addition to the application of these concepts in manufacturing production and distribution environments, they apply to managing paperwork flows and in the planning and control of projects.

Lines.   First, we will define and illustrate several TOC terms to provide a better understanding of the causes of poor production process design and poor production management. Based on this understanding, the logic underlying the TOC concepts and techniques for line design, control points, scheduling, and so on are presented. In the *APICS Dictionary,*[22] a *line* is defined as "a specific physical space for manufacturing of a product that in a flow plant layout is represented by a straight line. This may be in actuality a series of pieces of equipment connected by piping or a conveyor system." A line can have an internal or external constraint. If market demand for the products produced on a line is less than the line capacity, then the market demand is an *external constraint.* If the piece of equipment with the least capacity in the line has production capability less than market demand for the product, then the line has an *internal constraint.* Our discussion will be limited to internally constrained lines. *Line capacity* is determined by the limiting operation or slowest resource in the series of resources in the line. This slowest resource, the constraint, determines the maximum throughput of the line. The line output may be less than maximum because of the dependence of the constraint on other resources.

Suppose that in a 6-station line, station 4 can only produce 3 units per hour while the remaining stations can produce 3.5 units per hour. This problem and its solution for a constrained line are depicted in Fig. 9.2*a* and *b*. Loss of throughput (less than 3 units per hour) can result from three different events related to the constraint:

1. The constraint is broken.
2. The constraint is starved.
3. The constraint is blocked.

First, when the *constraint is broken,* lost throughput results for the amount of time the constraint is down. (Actually this category includes any internal delays related to the

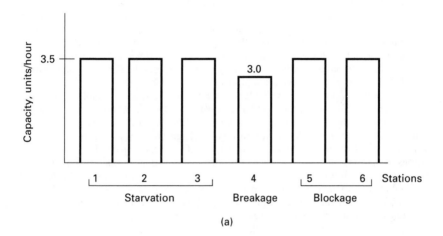

(a)

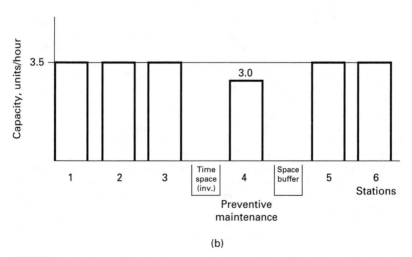

(b)

FIGURE 9.2 Design considerations for a constrained line, unbalanced. (*a*) Causes of lost throughput; (*b*) solutions to lost throughput

constraint, such as worker absenteeism, station setups, poor training of the constraint station worker, tool or material breakage, or scrap.) The way to reduce *constraint breakage* is to emphasize preventive maintenance (proper training, cross-training, setup reduction, etc.) on the constraint and when the constraint breaks, to get it fixed and running as quickly as possible.

Second, the constraint can be available to work but no work-in-process inventory (WIP) is available for processing by the constraint. This type of constraint idleness is called *starvation* and occurs when WIP is unavailable at the constraint because material was not released at the gating operation on time or a stoppage occurred between the first station and the constraint. A solution to constraint starvation is to provide a *buffer* of inventory in front of the constraint. This buffer is created by releasing material early at the gating operations to ensure its availability at the constraint when it is needed. In our example suppose that breakdowns at stations 1, 2, and 3 starve the constraint no more than 3 hours at a time. We could plan for a 3-hour buffer of inventory in front of station 4 for protection against Murphy striking at stations 1, 2, and 3. Space for up to 9 units (3 hours $\times$ 3 units per hour) of WIP storage in front of station 4 should be designed into the line layout. In practice, the constraint buffer should remain about two-thirds full to ensure adequate protection. This inventory buffer protects the constraint and system throughput from statistical fluctuation prior to the constraint.

Third, the constraint can be available to work but has no space available to place the completed units. This condition is called *constraint blockage* and occurs when a station (or stations) after the constraint is broken and WIP fills the buffers between the broken station and the constraint. A solution to this blockage problem is to provide a *space buffer* after the constraint to decouple the constraint from the impact of statistical fluctuations at stations after the constraint. In our example suppose that stations 5 and 6 block the constraint no more than 2 hours at a time. We could plan a space buffer of 2 hours, which is equivalent to providing a storage space for 6 units, directly after the constraint. The buffer behind the constraint is a space buffer and should be empty in most situations. When the space buffer is full, the constraint must stop since there is no place o put items after the constraint completes work on them. If the space buffer is usually full, then disruptions at nonconstraints after the constraint are jeopardizing throughput and the space buffer should be enlarged.

Collecting data on the percentage of constraint breakage, starvation, and blockage is useful in identifying and reducing the major sources of problems in a line. Breakages at the constraint can be reduced by a proactive preventive maintenance program for the constraint. The impact of stoppages at nonconstraints (starvation in front of the constraint and blockage behind the constraint) can be reduced by placing a buffer in front of the constraint (WIP inventory) and a space buffer behind the constraint (extra storage space). These three considerations have significant impact on the throughput of a line. Obviously, the size of WIP storage areas in front of and behind the constraint must be determined in planning the facility layout.

Some additional concepts and definitions[23] for constrained lines are shown in Fig. 9.3. Recognize that a constraint must exist in every line, whether the constraint is the product demand (external) or a work station (internal). All of the capacity of a constraint station should be viewed as *productive capacity* and scheduled to support throughput. In other words, in our internal constraint line example with station 4's capacity of 3 units per hour, the constraint should be scheduled to produce 24 units per day. Nonconstraints, by definition, have capacity greater than the constraint. Theoretically, given a deterministic world (no statistical fluctuation), a nonconstraint has productive capacity equal to the constraint capacity and additional capacity, which would be *idle capacity.* But with statistical fluctuations, some level of additional or *protective capacity* is needed so that when Murphy strikes at a nonconstraint, the nonconstraint has the

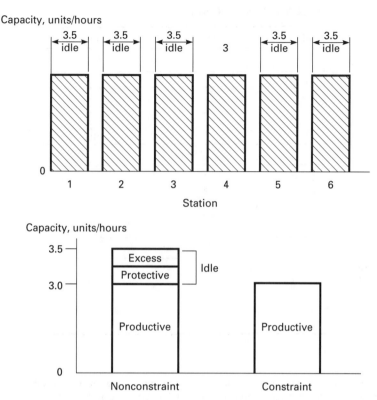

FIGURE 9.3 The relationship of productive, protective, excess, and idle capacity for non-constraint and constraint resources in a line.

capability to catch up to the production rate of the constraint. When two or more resources are linked together to produce a product and statistical fluctuations exist, then one approach to designing the line is to have more capacity (protective) at one resource (the nonconstraint) than the other (the constraint) to eliminate or reduce the impact of statistical fluctuations on the line throughput. *Excess capacity* is defined as that idle capacity above the amount needed for production and protection to support the constraint.

An example of protective capacity is given in Table 9.5, a simple two-station line. In stage 1, stations 1 and 2 have identical capacities of 3 units per day. Both have statistical fluctuation represented by having a daily capability of either 2 units or 4 units, equally likely. To eliminate the moderating influence of inventory, we will assume that no inventory exists between stations. Thus, the line in this example has an output equal to the smaller of the two stations' capability.

As stage 1 shows, the output of this balanced line is only 2.5 units per day despite the fact that each station has a capability of 3 units. In stage 2, the capacity of station 2 is raised to 3.5 units, resulting in a capacity of the line of 2.75 units per day. The increase in station 2 from 3 to 3.5 units per day represents protective capacity because it protects from the loss of output that occurred at stage 1. The stage 3 increase in line output from

TABLE 9.5 Protective Capacity

Stn 1	Stn 2	Line
	Stage 1	
2	2	2
2	4	2
4	2	2
4	2	4
		10/4 = 2.5
	Stage 2	
2	3	2
2	4	2
4	3	3
4	2	4
		11/4 = 2.8
	Stage 3	
2	4	2
2	5	2
4	4	4
4	5	4
		12/4 = 3

2.75 to 3 units per day comes about because more protective capacity is added to station 2. Were any further capacity added to station 2, beyond the 4.5 units per day in stage 3, it would be excess capacity. If inventory existed between stages, the protective capacity in station 2 would be more effective. Protective capacity and protective inventory are somewhat interchangeable. The more protective capacity there is, the less protective inventory is needed and vice versa.

In designing a line, a second approach to reducing the impact of statistical fluctuations is to buffer the system with WIP.[24] As WIP increases, the throughput increases but inventory investment (WIP level) and lead time also increase. WIP, like capacity, can be classified and defined by function—productive, protective, and excess. These concepts are illustrated in Fig. 9.4. For simplicity, assume that materials are moved between work stations once each hour. *Productive WIP* is the amount of inventory, measured in time units of the constraint, needed to support the constraint until material can get from the gating or first operation to the constraint. Nonconstraint station capacity is 3.5 per hour, station 4's (the constraint) capacity is 3 per hour. Let's assume WIP takes 3 hours to flow from the gating operation to the constraint operation. Productive WIP should therefore be 3 hours multiplied by 3 units per hour constraint consumption. In a deterministic world, this productive WIP level would maintain throughput until a unit can get from the gating operation to the constraint. *Protective WIP* is the amount of inventory, measured in time units of the constraint, needed to provide a given level of protection against statistical fluctuations prior to the constraint. The size and the frequency of statistical fluctuations significantly influence the amount of protective WIP needed to sustain throughput. If fluctuations are frequent but small, then the protective WIP level can be small. If the fluctuations are few but large, then the buffer should be larger. If the

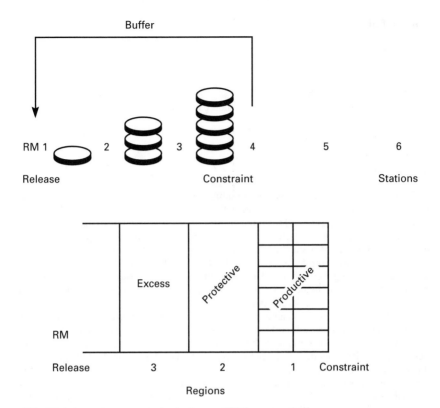

FIGURE 9.4 Productive, protective, and excess WIP in a constraint line.

fluctuations are numerous and large, then a serious problem exists. *Excess WIP* is any WIP in excess of productive and protective WIP. The lower the amount of WIP maintained in the line without threatening throughput, the more competitive the firm can be with respect to lead times, due date performance, and so on.

In traditional line design, line-balancing techniques are used to set capacity at all work stations at the same level. The assumption is made that processing times are deterministic. In reality, statistical fluctuations occur and cause serious disruptions to line throughput. One approach to maintaining system throughput is to buffer all work stations with WIP. In contrast, in designing a line using the TOC philosophy, the equipment would be selected to have one constraint work station and some idle capacity at other work stations. In this manner the nonconstraints have protective capacity, the ability to catch up to the constraint pace. Both protective capacity and protective WIP are used to reduce the impact of Murphy on the constraint. In contrast to the traditional approach, TOC balances the flow of the system at the constraint capacity and manages Murphy by providing strategically placed buffers (before and after the constraint) and protective capacity at nonconstraints. Using both protective capacity and protective WIP reduces the impact of statistical fluctuations significantly. Both protective capacity and protective WIP levels must be considered in designing a layout.

Control Points

Six *control points* exist in logical product structures.

1. The constraint
2. The first operation (gating)
3. Diverging points (points where a common part can be processed into one of several options)
4. Converging points (assemblies)
5. The last operation
6. The buffer

To control any logistics flow, these points must be controlled. The primary control point is the *constraint* of the system. All other points are planned and controlled based on the flow of materials to and from the constraint. By limiting the release of raw materials at the gating operations to the consumption of materials at the constraint, work queues and flow can be managed. Divergent operations occur where a common component (to two or more products) is input into a work center and the output is a distinguishing part among the products. The danger here is that material that should go to part A is used for part B and vice versa. Instructions as to which outputs should be produced must be given to divergent work stations.

A *convergent operation* is an assembly area where one or more nonconstraint parts are combined with constraint parts. Nonconstraint parts are planned to arrive at the convergent point early. In this manner, the constraint parts flow through the assembly without delay. The last operation or shipping point is managed to ensure that products reach the shipping area ahead of their due date. The constraint must be planned to exploit its capabilities; schedules for all related control points are then tied to the constraint schedule and its execution. The buffers are the planned time offsets between the release of materials and its arrival at the constraint, at the assembly area, and at the shipping areas. Buffers are planned time intervals for materials to arrive at a given work station ahead of schedule. The buffers reduce the impact of statistical fluctuation on key resources and on system performance. Planning and control by using the control points and buffers will be discussed in the next three sections.

DRUM-BUFFER-ROPE METHOD

Drum-buffer-rope (DBR) is a scheduling method that paces the flow of all materials to the capacity of the constraint.[25-27] Use the simple six stations discussed before to illustrate the DBR concept (Fig. 9.2).

The constraint to the line is identified as work station 4. The constraint is called the *drum,* and it determines the rate of throughput for the line. In our simple line the drum beat is 3 units an hour. The *buffer* is the amount of time material is released to the first work station ahead of its scheduled consumption at the constraint. This early release guarantees the material will be available for constraint consumption. The size of the buffer is measured in time. Suppose in the example that WIP is moved between work stations every hour. Then it would take material released at the gating work center 3 hours to move to the constraint station. Material should be released some 5 hours before it is needed at the constraint. We would expect to find 3 units at each of the first three stations plus 6 units at the constraint. If the transfer batch between stations is moved more frequently, then the constraint buffer could be smaller. The *rope* controls the amount of raw material released at the gating operations based on the drum schedule to ensure that the desired products are produced when required.

The rope is similar to the explosion and netting logic of an MRP system—the calculation of the amount of raw materials to be released to the production system. As the constraint processes a given number of units, the proper replacement quantity of raw material is released at the first station to maintain materials flow. If the constraint processes 2 units in a given hour, then 2 units are released to the gating operation. If the constraint processes 4 units in a given hour, then 4 units are released to the system. DBR provides the scheduling methodology to make a manufacturing system effective by loading the system with enough WIP to support the constraint capacity.

The more detailed example in Fig. 9.5 and Table 9.6 illustrates additional characteristics of DBR appropriate for a job shop environment.[28] Assume a company is in a make-to-stock environment with three products A, C, and E; five raw materials (RM) *a*, *b*, *c*, *d*, and *f*. There are six work centers (blue, green, cyan, red, magenta, and white) containing a total of eight workers. Blue WC has one machine with a setup time of 20

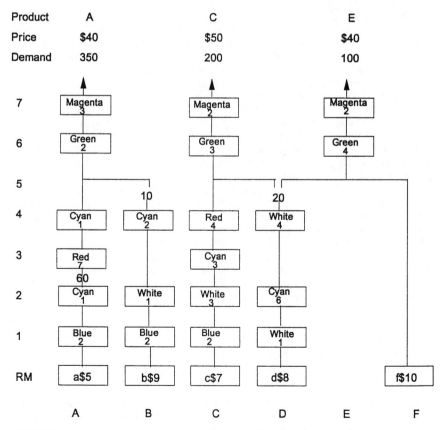

FIGURE 9.5 Physical product structure and work center information.

TABLE 9.6 Logical Product Structure and Work Center
Information

Work center	Number of machines	Setup time
Blue	1	20
Green	1	0
Cyan	2	10
Red	1	0
Magenta	1	10
White	2	30

minutes between different operations; the green WC has one machine with no setup time; cyan WC has two machines with a 10-minute setup time; red WC has one machine with no setup time; magenta WC has one machine with a 10-minute setup time; and white WC has two machines with a 30-minute setup time.

The part routings and bills of materials are combined to illustrate the flow of raw materials through WCs to assembly and then finished products. These structures are called *logical product structures.* The matrix notation A through F on the bottom horizontal axis and 1 through 7 on the vertical axis will be used to identify specific operations on various machines in part and product routings. Raw material a (RM a) is in the lower left corner and costs $5 per unit; RM b costs $9 per unit; and so on. Three products—A, C, and E—are displayed across the top of the figure with their weekly demands and prices. Product A has a weekly demand of 350 units and sells for $40, product C has demand of 200 units and a price of $50, while E has demand of 100 and sells for $40. Sixty units of WIP are located in front at the red WC awaiting operation A3; 10 units of WIP are located at the green WC (after operation B4) awaiting assembly operation A6; and 20 WIP units are (after operation D4) awaiting assembly at green WC to make products C and/or E. To make product A, 1 unit each of RM a and RM b are required. RM a is processed first at the blue WC for 2 minutes per unit processing time (operation A1 is performed); the second operation A2 is performed by cyan (1 minute processing time per unit); the third operation occurs at the red WC for 7 minutes processing time per unit, and so on. Product C is processed from 1 unit each of RMs c and d, which follow their respective parts routings and are assembled at operation C6 in green WC and continue along the routing until the product is completed at magenta WC after operation C7. Product E is composed of RMs d and f with these materials following their respective routings to completion (operation E7) of the finished product, at magenta WC. The steps in using the drum-buffer-rope scheduling process are:

1. Identify the constraint.
2. Decide how to exploit the constraint.
3. Construct a Gantt chart of the constraint schedule.
4. Decide on the appropriate sizes of the constraint, assembly, and shipping buffers for each product.
5. Subtract the appropriate constraint buffer from the beginning of the corresponding product constraint operation (on the Gantt chart) to determine the RM release schedule to support the constraint schedule.

6. Subtract the appropriate assembly buffer from the corresponding product constraint operation to determine the RM release schedule to support the assembly of non-constraint parts with the constraint part.

7. Add the appropriate shipping buffer to the end of the corresponding product constraint operation to determine the product shipment date for the shipping schedule.

8. For products that do not use the constraint resource (free goods), ship dates are determined based on the customers' requests. In scheduling free goods, care should be exercised not to create a temporary constraint.

9. Develop a schedule for parts production at divergent points (an operation in a part routing where two or more products can be made from the same common part) based on the constraint, shipping, and assembly schedules. The *divergent point schedule* defines which products are made from a common part or assembly.

10. All work centers that are not control points are instructed to work if work is available; otherwise wait. Work will arrive soon.

Remember that in order to plan and control any manufacturing environment, the control points must be planned and controlled. The next step is to apply the DBR scheduling steps to develop a weekly schedule for the control points in this example. To identify the constraint (step 1) for the three-product problem, multiply the weekly demand for each of the three products by the processing time per unit for each operation and sum the capacity requirements by work center. This capacity-required calculation is compared to the capacity available to determine which work center(s) is a constraint. The computations are provided in Table 9.7. The red WC is the constraint with the capacity required being 135 percent of what is currently available. Since you cannot make all the products required in step 2, decide how to exploit the constraint, and determine how much of each product to make. Using the red WC to work on product A earns approximately \$3.70 [(\$40 − \$15)/7 minutes] per minute in contrast to product C earning \$8.75 [(\$50 − \$15)/4 minutes] per minute. Product E does not use the red WC; therefore, you should be able to make its weekly demand of 100 units with your existing resources

TABLE 9.7 Identifying Constraints

Products	A	C	E	Resource utilization, percent
Demand	350 u/w	200 u/w	100 u/w	
Blue (1)	4 m/u	2 m/u	0 m/u	
	1400 m +	400 m +	0 m =	1800/2400 × 100 = 75
Green (1)	2 m/u	3 m/u	4 m/u	
	700 m +	600 m +	400 m =	1700/2400 × 100 = 71
Cyan (2)	4 m/u	6 m/u	6 m/u	
	1400 m +	1200 m +	600 m =	3200/4800 × 100 = 67
Red (1)	7 m/u	4 m/u	0 m/u	
	2450 m +	800 m +	0 =	3250/2400 × 100 = 135
Magenta (1)	3 m/u	2 m/u	2 m/u	
	1050 m +	400 m +	200 m =	1650/2400 × 100 = 69
White (2)	1 m/u	11 m/u	5 m/u	
	350 m +	2200 m +	500 m =	3050/4800 × 100 = 64

capacity. In calculating the number of units of C and A that can be made, all 200 units of C use only 800 minutes of constraint time, and the remaining 1600 minutes allow you to make approximately 225 units of A per week.

Once the constraint has been identified and the product mix determined, a detailed schedule and Gantt chart of the constraint should be constructed—step 3. Several equally good schedules are possible. (Any schedule having 200 C's, 225 A's, and 100 E's will produce the same profit as any other.) Since no setup is required at the red WC, batches approximately equivalent to daily demand can be made without creating a new constraint. Batches of 40 units will be scheduled at C4 alternating with batches of 48 units at A3. These batch sizes do not create a new constraint based on resource setup times at nonconstraints. By alternating small batches of each product on the constraint, materials flow through nonconstraints continuously. The timing of WIP arrivals at nonconstraints can create a temporary constraint if nonconstraints sit idle for long periods of time.

Since 60 units of WIP are in the constraint buffer of the red WC, 48 units should be scheduled for operation A3 first. The total processing time for the 48 units is 336 minutes. A word of caution concerning batch sizes should be provided. Two types of batches exist—process and transfer batches. The *process batch* is the number of units that are produced by a work center at one time. The *transfer batch* is the number of units that move between work centers at one time. The process and transfer batches do not have to be the same size. By using small process batches at nonconstraints and large process batches at constraints (if setups are significant), work flow is maintained (resulting in a reduction of lead time) while throughput is not sacrificed. Additionally, if the transfer batch is smaller than the process batch, consecutive operations on the same part can be overlapped to reduce lead times. In this example, small batches are scheduled at the constraint due to the absence of setups. In contrast, large process and transfer batches block the flow of parts through the facility causing idle time on nonconstraints and therefore create shifting and temporary constraints.

Given the Gantt chart and constraint schedule provided in Fig. 9.6 and Table 9.8, the supporting raw material release schedule can be constructed once the constraint buffer size has been determined—step 4. Three types of buffer exist: constraint, assembly, and shipping. For simplicity use an 8-hour buffer for each of them. The *constraint buffer* of 8 hours translates into releasing RMs scheduled to be processed on the constraint 8 hours prior to their processing—step 5. Because the transfer batch is small, overlapped processing occurs and WIP should arrive in the buffer a couple of hours before being processed. An *assembly buffer* is used when a nonconstraint part and a constraint part are joined. The assembly buffer ensures that the constraint part does not have to wait for the assembly operation. The assembly buffer should also be subtracted from the constraint schedule to determine RM release to support assembly operations with constraint

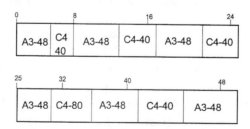

FIGURE 9.6   Gantt chart of red work center.

TABLE 9.8 Constraint Schedule for the Red Work Center (WC)

Product	Schedule for red WC	Quantity required	Processing time, hours	Approximate hour, start at red WC (hour)
A	A3	48	336 min≈5.6 hrs.	0
C	C4	40	160 min≈2.7 hrs.	6
A	A3	48	5.6	8
C	C4	40	2.7	14
A	A3	48	5.6	17
C	C4	40	2.7	22
A	A3	48	5.6	25
C	C4	80*	5.3	31
A	A3	48	5.6	36
C	C4	40	2.7	41
A	A3	48	5.6	44
				50

*80 units are scheduled instead of 40 units to ensure the 200 units of C (exploit step) are produced in this week.

parts (step 6). In this example, RM b, a nonconstraint part, is assembled to RM a, a constraint part, at operation A6. RM b should be released 8 hours before the matching RM is scheduled on the constraint. Similar logic controls the release of those RM d's to be mated with RM e's. Again the buffer should be large enough so that generally the parts will arrive half a buffer size ahead of the scheduled operation time. Products A and C are processed by the constraint resource, the red WC, and product E is not and is therefore called a *free good* (any product that has no internal constraint). Product E will be scheduled to be shipped in equal daily lots of 20 units.

In a make-to-stock environment, the *shipping buffer* is added to the constraint schedule operation to determine the ship date (step 7). For free goods, the *shipping buffer* is subtracted from the ship date to determine the RM release times (step 8). The results of subtracting the constraint and assembly buffers to determine the RM release schedule for the constraint products are provided in Fig. 9.7a. To take a small example from the figure, RM c is scheduled for operation C4 on the red WC at time hour 14. Release of RM c to the constraint buffer (8 hours) and RM d to the assembly buffer (8 hours) are scheduled for time hour 6 (hour $14-8$ hours = hour 6). The results of adding the shipping buffer to the constraint schedule operation are provided in Fig. 9.7b. The results of subtracting the shipping buffer from the ship date to determine raw materials releases for the free good E are provided in Table 9.9. The consolidated raw materials release schedule is provided in Table 9.10. The only other WC requiring a schedule is the green WC—a divergent point in the logical structures. (The green operations at C6 and E6 share a common material—RM d from operation D4. Unless these operations are carefully controlled, one may steal material from the other.) The schedule for the divergent point is derived from the shipping schedule of finished products which includes a common part (step 9). The green WC schedule for the common part is provided in Table 9.11.

By scheduling and monitoring the control points—the constraint, the gating, the assembly, the divergent and the shipping work centers and buffers—the entire logistics system can be managed. Instruct all other work centers to work when work is available; otherwise do not create work (step 10).

A make-to-order environment can also be scheduled using DBR. In a make-to-order environment, the ship date is a negotiated date between the customer and the master

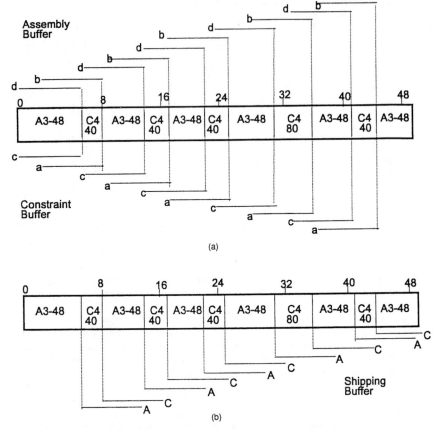

FIGURE 9.7   Gantt chart illustrating RM release and ship dates. (*a*) Raw materials releases for constraint and assembly buffers; (*b*) shipping due dates based on constraint buffers.

TABLE 9.9   Ship and Release Schedule for Product E (Free Good)

Product quality	Ship date, hour	RM, df	RM, release time, hour
E-20	8	20	0
E-20	16	20	8
E-20	24	20	16
E-20	32	20	24
E-20	40	20	32

TABLE 9.10 Consolidated Release Schedule for Raw Materials

Product	Raw materials	Quantity	Release time, hour
A	b	86	0
C	c d	40	0
A	a	36	0
E	f	20	0
C	c d	40	5
A	a b	48	8
E	d f	20	8
C	c d	40	14
A	a b	48	16
E	d f	20	16
C	c d	80	22
E	d f	20	24
A	a b	48	27
E	d f	20	32
C	c d	40	33
A	a b	48	36

scheduler. Suppose that a customer requests X units of a product Z by a certain date. The master scheduler must determine whether the ship date can be met. First, the master scheduler must determine whether product Z crosses the constraint. If not, it is a *free good* crossing only nonconstraints. Does the order create a new constraint? If not, use the shipping buffer size to negotiate a due date. If Z crosses the constraint, then the master scheduler must examine the current load on the constraint (the Gantt chart constraint schedule) to ascertain when the customer order can be processed on the constraint. Next, the scheduler backward schedules to determine RM release for constraint and nonconstraint parts. Is adequate time available to get materials to the constraint or assembly areas? If so, then the scheduler adds the shipping buffer to the constraint schedule of product Z to determine a realistic shipping date. If this DBR-determined ship date is less

TABLE 9.11 Divergent Point Schedule of Green Work Center (WC) for RM d

Product	Operation at green WC	Quantity	Product, ship time, hour	Raw materials (RM), release time, hour
E	E6	20	1	—
C	C6	40	5	—
E	E6	20	8	0
C	C6	40	13	5
E	E6	20	16	8
C	C6	40	22	14
E	E6	20	24	16
C	C6	80	30	22
E	E6	20	32	24
C	C6	40	41	33

than or equal to the customer request, then accept the customer order. If the customer wants the order sooner than normal DBR scheduling, the master scheduler must review the load on the nonconstraints and the priorities of other items in the shop. The scheduler may be able to expedite the order to the constraint buffer to get the part processed on the constraint sooner than under normal scheduling, or the scheduler may reduce the shipping buffer by expediting the order across the remaining nonconstraint operations. Using DBR, the scheduler can determine with a high degree of certainty the ship dates that can be attained.

Drum-buffer-rope has been successfully extended to distribution inventories[29] to reduce the need for detailed forecasts, to reduce finished-goods inventories significantly, to improve customer service, and to level the production requirements on manufacturing facilities. Additionally, it is being implemented in remanufacturing environments[30,31] and project management environments.[32]

Buffer Management

As previously discussed, the *constraint buffer* is defined as the amount of time between raw materials release and its scheduled processing time at the constraint; the *assembly buffer* is the amount of time between raw materials release and its scheduled assembly with a constraint part; and the *shipping buffer* is the amount of time between either constraint completion time and its shipping date for a constrained-flow product or between raw material release and its shipping date in the case of a free product. These buffers serve two purposes.[33] First, the buffer protects the *system* throughput and customer due date performance. Second, the buffer provides the necessary information for a process of continuous improvement.

Protection. A buffer is generally divided into three regions, each representing one-third of the buffer; region 1 represents one-third of the constraint schedule starting from the present moving into the near future; region 2 represents the middle third of the time buffer; and region 3 represents the recently released materials due for constraint consumption in the distant future. The constraint buffer protects throughput by ensuring that disruptions at preceding nonconstraints do not impact the constraint resource schedule. The amount of time in the buffer should allow ample time for the part to get to the constraint before the part appears in region 1 of the constraint buffer. When a hole appears in region 1 (an order is not present that is to be processed in the near time frame), the buffer manager locates the order by tracking backward through its routing to identify the work center currently holding the order. The buffer manager takes two actions. First, the buffer manager expedites the order by preparing each succeeding work center for its arrival. Second, the buffer manager tracks backward through the part routing to identify and record the source(s) of delay for the part. This action is discussed under the second purpose—a process of continuous improvement. As previously mentioned, if a part is missing from region 1, then the buffer manager should expedite the part to the constraint immediately. If the buffer manager is continually expediting, then the buffer is too small—not enough protection is provided for the schedule. Notice that buffer management is a proactive tool for identifying potential problems with the constraint schedule prior to their materializing. Most scheduling methods identify a schedule exception after the fact and therefore cause schedule disruption and possibly sacrifices system throughput.

Region 1 of the constraint buffer should have all scheduled orders in front of the constraint resource most of the time (a little expediting lets you know that the buffer is about the right size, as small as possible without disrupting the schedule). Region 2 should have about half of its scheduled parts present at the constraint; and region 3 may have some items present at the constraint. The assembly buffer ensures that constraint parts never wait on nonconstraint parts and its three regions are managed in a fashion similar to the constraint buffer. The shipping buffer protects due date performance by identifying which parts or products are falling behind schedule before it is too late to react. The shipping buffer is also divided into 3 regions, and orders are managed in a similar fashion. A major advantage in using buffer management is that the buffer provides protection from disruptions and ample time to respond to most situations before a problem arises. Preventing a problem from arising is much easier than having to solve the problem.

Buffer size determination is not as critical as one might think. Current lead time should be the maximum limit for the constraint buffer plus the shipping buffer. A good starting point for buffer sizing is five times the sum of the setup and processing times of the routing from RM to the constraint for the average order size. Similar estimates can be developed for the assembly and shipping buffers. Sum the constraint and shipping buffers, and compare this time to your current manufacturing lead time. If the time is approximately equal, then use this time as a starting point. If the times differ significantly, ask yourself why and use the larger of the two times as a starting point for the buffer size. Companies who are also implementing the use of small transfer batches frequently take their current lead time and divide it between the constraint and shipping buffer.

Divide the buffer into three parts. If parts are always missing from region 1 of a buffer, then the buffer is too small. Increase the buffer size. If parts are rarely missing from region 1, then the buffer is too big. Decrease the buffer size. Buffer size can be reduced significantly by eliminating the use of resource utilizations and efficiencies as performance measures at nonconstraints, by choking or limiting the release of RM at gating operations (release based on constraint consumption), reducing processing batches at nonconstraints (splitting operations), using small transfer batches (operation overlapping), and ultimately using buffer management as an information system to focus improvement activities.

Information System. The second purpose of buffer management is to provide information to be used in continuously improving *system performance.* If you know what work orders should be in front of the constraint, at the assembly area, and at the shipping dock and you know which orders are not yet there (holes in region 1), you can track back down the product routings to identify which operation, machine, setup, breakdown, and so on is jeopardizing the system performance. This activity is where improvement must take place to improve the production system. Buffer management should be used as the prioritization mechanism for just-in-time and total quality management techniques (preventive maintenance, setup reduction, lead time reduction, cross-training workers, statistical process control, etc.). For example, the machine with the longest setup time may not be the place where setup reduction is important. That machine may be and probably is a nonconstraint. Examine the example in Fig. 9.7 and observe that setup reduction at any work center does not improve throughput. What of preventive maintenance activities? Breakdowns on which machines are jeopardizing throughput or due date performance? If you can prevent breakdowns on the constraint, you can increase throughput. Remember—the machines with the highest downtime may not be the machines causing disruptions in region 1 of the schedule. The real question for focusing improvement is, "Where should we implement which technique to improve the bottom line of the company?" Buffer management provides this information— focused local improvement activities to bottom-line improvement is the key to competitiveness and profitability.

In implementing DBR and buffer management, companies have sometimes painted three rectangular areas on their floor (red, yellow, and green) to represent the three regions of the buffer. Others have used a rack with three shelves. Software for DBR scheduling, buffer management, and performance measurement is available from different vendors. Some firms use a Gantt chart to load their constraint resource and develop a shipping schedule then feed this shipping schedule in their MRP system as the master production schedule. Other modifications to the MRP logic are required to allow for deliberately overlapped scheduling, which usually does not occur in MRP. Some firms have developed a manual or spreadsheet scheduling system. Remember—only the control points need to be planned and monitored. In all instances, efficiencies and utilizations must be eliminated as performance measures at nonconstraints.

VAT ANALYSIS

VAT analysis[34] (Fig. 9.8) is the methodology used to describe the logical flows of raw materials to finished products. Bills of materials and part routings are combined to reflect the logical product flows through a plant's resources. Basic flows are classified by shapes including I, V, A, and T. These logical product structures provide information for plant design, staffing, planning and control, and information system design. Each logical product structure has control points that simplify production planning, scheduling, and control.

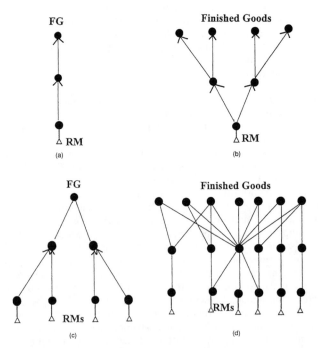

FIGURE 9.8   Logical product structures. (*a*) I structure; (*b*) V structure; (*c*) A structure; (*d*) T structure.

I Structures

We previously discussed a simple production line—which is the I-logical structure. The logical structure of the I flow line is provided in Fig. 9.8*a*. The flow line is the primary method of producing a large quantity of a standardized product at a low cost. This structure consists of a series of sequential operations where the first operation must be performed before the second, the second before the third, and so on. All products follow the same fixed sequence. The amount of work-in-process inventory is low, and parts move continuously from one operation to another along a direct route to product completion. The classical example of the I structure is the assembly line designed by Henry Ford. His motto was "you can have any color Model T as long as it is black." (Black paint dried the fastest.) The ideal I line is one that has none or only a few minor equipment setups to support product variation.

Primary control points for the I structure are the constraint, the gating work center, and the constraint and shipping buffers. The buffer sizes determine the amount of WIP on the factory floor and impact lead time directly. Measures of efficiency and utilization are important at the constraint while flow measures (performance to schedule) are important at nonconstraints.

General characteristics of an I structure include the following:

- High volume
- Standardized design
- Stable demand

I structures may be *continuous processes* (nondiscrete manufacturers) or *repetitive processes* (discrete products or services) and may be automated or manual. Different issues have to be addressed in each of these situations. Some issues related to an I structure include the adverse impact of statistical fluctuations and dependent sequences on line throughput, high capital investment, setup times, specialization of labor, wage differentials on line positions, and lack of flexibility.

V Structures.

A *V-logical structure*[35] (Fig. 9.8*b*) consists of a logistics flow where a few raw materials flow through fixed routings to produce one of many similarly finished products. A primary characteristic of a V structure is *product divergence*. At each divergent point, a decision has to be made as to what product is to be produced. Material misallocation is the dominant problem in V-logical structures. Open-ended and close-ended wrenches are representative of products produced on simple V structures.

The V structure can be thought of as a series of I structures with each product requiring the same sequence of operations and each emerging from a common raw material. A V structure starts from one or a few raw materials and diverges into different products as it proceeds through the sequence of operations. The V structure, illustrated in Fig. 9.8*b,* depicts the product line family. For a given unit of raw material, you can make product A *or* product B *or* product C. You do not get one A, one B, and one C from one unit of raw material. This is an important point since the major problem in a V structure is material misallocation. Material might be used to make product A when it should have been used to make product B. When forecasting is involved, it is not at all unusual to have excess A's on hand but no B's, and so on.

Primary control points for the V structure are the constraint, the gating work center, the divergent work centers, and the constraint and the shipping buffers. The divergent work center is scheduled to prevent material misallocation. The buffer sizes determine the amount of WIP on the factory floor and impact lead time directly. Measures of efficiency and utilization are important at the constraint while flow measures are important at nonconstraints.

General characteristics found with most V structures are the following:

- A few raw materials that diverge to many finished products
- Fixed routing (products follow the same operations sequence)
- Capital-intensive equipment
- Commodity-type products (metals, agricultural products, textiles, etc.)
- Capacity emphasis
- Misallocation of material at divergent points
- Planning and control information usually too late to be effective
- Poor performance measures of department efficiencies and utilization

Some business issues that emerge when V structures are used are that they are not cost competitive, they have low profit margins, their use results in reduced operating expenses, and they require capital-intensive equipment. Marketing issues in the use of V structures include the following: products are commodities, due date performance is generally acceptable, lead times are short, and finished goods are excessive. Production issues that arise in the use of V structures lead to local performance measures being used (since equipment is expensive, equipment utilization should be high), raw materials and finished-goods inventories are excessive, capacity is excessive, material is misallocated at diverging points in the logical structure, yield problems exist, and production control information is frequently late or useless.

A Structures.   An *A-logical structure*[36] (Fig. 9.8c) consists of a logistics flow where many raw materials, parts, and components are fabricated and assembled into a few finished products. A primary characteristic is *product convergence*—scheduling decisions have to be made prior to convergent work centers to ensure that parts are available when needed at the convergent points. Capacity misallocation is a dominant problem. Manual and electric pencil sharpeners are representative of products produced in simple A structures. An A structure is displayed in Fig. 9.8c. An A structure starts with several raw materials. Operations are performed on these raw materials in transforming them into parts. As additional operations are performed, these parts converge into subassemblies; these subassemblies converge into assemblies; and these assemblies converge into a *few* finished products.

Primary control points for the A structure are the constraint, the gating work centers, the convergent or assembly work centers, and the constraint, assembly, and the shipping buffers. The convergent work center is scheduled to prevent capacity misallocation to ensure the synchronization of parts flow into products. The buffer sizes determine the amount of WIP on the factory floor and impact lead time directly. Measures of efficiency and utilization are important at the constraint while flow measures are important at nonconstraints.

Characteristics found in most A structures include:

- The fabrication of several parts and subassemblies and their assembly into a few products
- Little or no standard assemblies across products

- Random part routings (a job shop environment)
- General-purpose equipment
- Resource capacity misallocated to the wrong part
- Resource efficiencies necessary in areas to sequence operations within each resource to reduce setups
- Low resource utilization but excessive overtime

Business issues are highly interrelated and cross business functions in an A structure. Issues include runaway operating expenses, excessive overtime, end-of-month expediting, poor due date performance, large amounts of work-in-process inventory, long lead times, and lack of synchronization of part arrivals at assembly points.

Jet engines, fork-lift trucks, cotton gins, and the fabrication of parts for ships, boxcars, and airplanes are common examples of A structures encountered in manufacturing. The manufacture of apparel, picnic tables, barbecue grills, Ping-Pong tables, pool tables, camping tents, back packs, and camping stoves by a small manufacturer may also be manufactured in A-structure routings.

T Structures.

A *T-logical structure*[37] (Fig. 9.8d) consists of a logistics flow where many subassemblies and assemblies are combined to make many different finished products. A primary characteristic is commonality of parts. Parts missing due to stealing when final assembly is scheduled is a dominant problem. VCRs and stereos are representative of simple T structures. A T structure is displayed in Fig. 9.8d. In a T structure, materials flow into common basic assemblies to provide dozens or even thousands of types of final products.

The first step in managing a T structure is to eliminate the need for parts stealing. Locked stockrooms, issues and receipts, and other control mechanisms must be implemented to increase inventory accuracy. Next the assembly buffers must be planned to ensure that parts are available when assembly is scheduled. Buffer management is critical to maintaining a supply of common parts. Primary control points for the T structure are the constraint, the gating work centers, the convergent or assembly work centers, and the constraint, assembly, and shipping buffers. The convergent work center is scheduled to prevent capacity misallocation to ensure the synchronization of part flows into products. The buffer sizes determine the amount of WIP on the factory floor and impact lead time directly. Measures of efficiency and utilization are important at the constraint while flow measures are important at nonconstraints.

Characteristics of a T structure include the following:

- Common subassemblies are configured into many finished products.
- There is commonality of parts and assemblies across products.
- Customer desired lead time (tolerance time) is less than manufacturing and distribution lead time, necessitating accurate forecasting.
- Considerable stores inventory (assemblies) exist between fabrication and assembly.
- Final assembly scheduling is based on customer orders.
- Operations are labor intensive at the end of the production process.
- A T structure can be on top of a V-structure, an A-structure, or a combination of structures.
- Parts routing can be fixed or random, based on the underlying structure.

- Misallocation of materials (assemblies) creates a major problem; Stealing common parts and subassemblies to complete a customer's order can have serious consequences.
- Large finished-goods inventory is used to cover most finished-product configurations.
- Poor due date performance is prevalent—some early, most late.
- Overtime is used excessively to expedite missing parts.
- Traditional measures (efficiency, shipping budgets) are used to track performance.

Automobiles with various engine types, automatic and standard transmissions, color selections, upholstery choices, stereo radio, tape or disc options, and deluxe trim packages translate into thousands of possible finished-product types. Household appliances such as electric food mixers, blenders, can openers, refrigerators, and stoves are examples of products manufactured in T-structure systems that accommodate the dozens of colors and options available. Microcomputers are also produced in T-structure systems to allow for the dozens of boards, chips, monitors, printers, modems, and so on that can be installed. The major issues that arise in the T-structure system are that due dates are frequently unmet (several products are early while several others are late); everything is expedited; lead time and work-in-process increases; and parts are often stolen.

Others

The logical structure concept can be extended to personal productivity (the independent resource), white-collar productivity (independent parallel resources and dependent resources), project management (divergent-convergent structures), and repair-remanufacture (disassemble and/or reassemble) operations. The control points for each logical structure can be used to plan and control these logistical flows effectively as a total system. By contrast, traditional management theory calls for planning and controlling all operations and all work centers.

The logistics paradigm shift impacts every organization whether service or manufacturing, whether profit or nonprofit, whether large or small. Consider the flow of paperwork through any business. Does paperwork (engineering design, purchase requisitions, equipment investments, etc.) take weeks and months to be processed? Go to the in-baskets of several employees, and determine the number of days (weeks) it would take to process the work. Examine the paperwork routings of this work. Does the paperwork have dependent relationships, that is, must the paperwork flow from one employee to another and yet another prior to completion? Is statistical fluctuation (Murphy) alive and well in all facilities? TOC can improve any business significantly by focusing on the critical operations in the flow of work.

MANAGEMENT SKILLS

Goldratt developed two basic types of decision-making concepts—the effect-cause-effect tree and evaporating clouds—to help managers think through problems to create a process of continuous improvement for their organization. The process of speculating a cause for a given effect and then predicting another effect stemming from the same cause is usually referred to as effect-cause-effect. Many times the process does not end there. An effort is often made to try and predict more types of effects from the same assumed cause. The more types of effects predicted—and of course verified—the more 'powerful' is the theory....Often times this process results in the cause itself being regarded as an effect thus triggering the question of what is its cause. In such a way, a logical tree that explains many vastly different effects can grow from a single (or a few) basic assumptions."[38] The *evaporating cloud* is a graphical technique used to define precisely a conflict and to identify its underlying assumptions. The purpose of the evaporating cloud is to challenge and break an assumption where the problem no longer exists.

The management skills area consists of a set of five tools for responding to three basic managerial questions:

1. *What to change?* The TOC tool: the current-reality tree
2. *Change to what?* The TOC tools: the evaporating cloud and future-reality tree
3. *How to cause the change?* The TOC tools: prerequisite tree and transition tree

Characteristics of an Organization

Like the previous two TOC areas, the management skills or thinking process area is also based on two major organizational characteristics. The first is based on Goldratt's recognition that there is an infinite number of problems to be solved in organizations and that management cannot solve all of these problems by developing detailed procedures for each application. He also found that most people who studied the first two TOC areas learned the specific logistics and cost accounting applications and implemented them successfully. They then wanted the next solution, and the next, and so on. Goldratt, in response, defined and developed a solution procedure that was robust enough to identify and solve any problem. This thinking process provides managers with a method for solving their organizational problems in an ever-changing environment.[39]

The second characteristic of the management skill area that was developed was based on the recognition that teaching solutions to problems prevents ownership of the solution and the problem-solving process. Therefore, TOC emphasizes using the Socratic approach to teaching and implementing solutions. The users must have ownership in the solution for it to be successful. Based on these two characteristics, Goldratt developed the five tools of his thinking process to assist managers in decision making.

The Three Management Questions

The first question is "What to change?" Every manager is overwhelmed by the vast number of problems to be solved. The *current-reality tree* (CRT) (a form of the effect-cause-effect diagram) is based on using logical rules to link *undesirable effects* (UDEs) to their underlying causes. Goldratt states that numerous UDEs are created by a few core problems. By identifying and addressing these core problems, the problems and their UDEs can be eliminated. Traditional management techniques focus on treating UDEs as if each were an isolated problem. The current-reality tree maps undesirable effects in the environment to the core problem(s) causing them.

The second question is "To what to change to?" The *evaporating cloud* (EC) and *future-reality tree* (FRT) are techniques for identifying, expanding, and testing solutions. The EC facilitates precisely defining a problem and the verbalization of the assumptions underlying the core problem so that actions to break assumptions can be easily identified and taken. The FRT is used to test the validity of the actions and expand these actions into a comprehensive plan. Causality is used to determine the consequences of taking actions prior to taking them. The primary purpose of the FRT is to identify pitfalls to the actions and to expand the actions into a plan prior to plan implementation.

The third question is "How to cause the change?" The *prerequisite tree* (PRT) and *transition tree* (TT) are useful in developing implementation plans. The PRT focuses on identifying obstacles that block achieving an objective. By identifying and sequencing these obstacles and formulating appropriate intermediate objectives to overcome these barriers, the overall objective can be attained. The TT provides a time line of the manager's actions at each stage in making the transitions from the current environment to each intermediate objective.

The following example uses the evaporating-cloud technique problem solving to solve an economical order quantity (EOQ) problem. The EOQ problem is usually expressed as shown in Fig. 9.9. The problem is to select an order quantity for an item experiencing a steady demand. As the order size increases, parts are held longer before they are used; hence holding costs increase. At the same time, as the order size increases, the number of orders per time period decreases; hence the order cost decreases. Total inventory cost is a single-turning-point formula with a minimum that occurs at Q*, the EOQ.

Now examine the EOQ problem as a cloud. The objective is to minimize inventory costs. To minimize setup costs requires large batches. To minimize holding costs requires small batches. These two prerequisites conflict. The traditional approach to dealing with this conflict is to compromise. The EOQ is a compromise that optimizes inventory costs. The evaporating-cloud technique tries to break the conflict by identifying an action to break an assumption.

The assumptions of the EOQ evaporating cloud are given in Fig. 9.10. The assumption Goldratt addressed in his drum-buffer-rope scheduling methodology is on → DD′: "'Batch' means the same in D and D′." "Batch" in D is the process batch. "Batch" in D′ is the transfer batch. The EOQ formulation assumes that the transfer batch equals process batch, but those quantities do not have to be equal. By choosing a large process batch and a small transfer batch, one can have the best of both worlds. (For purchased items, this is called a *blanket purchase order*; for manufactured parts, it is called *operation overlapping*.) The traditional compromise EOQ solution is far from optimal. There are numerous other assumptions of EOQ that are erroneous.

The evaporating-cloud approach was used to find a win-win solution. To test and implement the solution requires the other thinking process techniques.

Space does not permit a discussion of these five tools in depth. However, Goldratt[40] recently provided an overview of his management tools. Additionally, Goldratt pro-

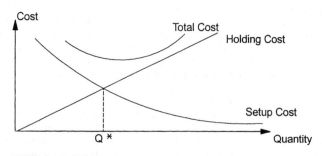

FIGURE 9.9   EOQ diagram.

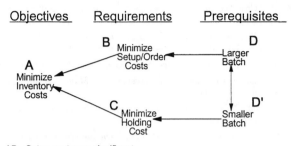

FIGURE 9.10 EOQ cloud diagram.

vided the steps and illustrations of the current-reality tree and evaporating cloud in his book *It's Not Luck.*[41]

Managers are faced with responding to these three different questions—what to change, what to change to, and how to bring about change. People generally confuse these questions and discuss one area while studying how to respond to another. In many cases when managers are trying to find a solution to a serious problem, they discuss why a given solution cannot be implemented. These three questions represent different aspects of the same problem, and these aspects must be addressed separately. However, identification of the real (core) problem, identification of a win-win solution, and implementation of this solution must be linked to ensure that the critical elements of the problem, its solution, and its implementation have been addressed.

SUMMARY

Three areas—performance measures, logistics, and management skills—represent the focal points of the theory of constraints. In addition to its early applications in the production function within manufacturing firms, the TOC has been variously applied in the engineering, purchasing, marketing and sales, and strategy functions and in such industries as health care, defense, airlines, and remanufacturing. Additionally, the TOC body of knowledge has been extended into project management, job shops, and repetitive, process, and distribution industries. All applications have the common characteristic of focusing attention of the constraint to achieving the organizational goal.

REFERENCES

1. Spencer, M. S., and J. F. Cox: "Optimum Production Technology (OPT) and the Theory of Constraints (TOC): Analysis and Genealogy," *International Journal of Production Research,* to be published.

2. Fry, T. D., J. F. Cox, and J. H. Blackstone: "An Analysis and Discussion of the OPT Software and its Use," *Production and Operations Management Journal* (1:2), spring 1992, pp. 229–242.

3. Goldratt, E. M.: "Cost Accounting: The Number One Enemy of Productivity," *Proceedings of the 26th Annual APICS Conference,* October 1983, pp. 433–435.

4. Goldratt, E. M.: *What Is This Thing Called Theory of Constraints and How Should It Be Implemented?* North River Press, Croton-on-Hudson, N.Y., 1990.

5. Goldratt, E. M., and R. E. Fox: *The Race,* North River Press, Croton-on-Hudson, N.Y., 1986.

6. Goldratt, E. M., and J. Cox: *The Goal: Excellence in Manufacturing,* North River Press, Croton-on-Hudson, N.Y., 1984.

7. Goldratt, E. M., and J. Cox: *The Goal: A Process of Ongoing Improvement,* North River Press, Croton-on-Hudson, N.Y., 1986.

8. Goldratt, E. M., and J. Cox: *The Goal: A Process of Ongoing Improvement,* North River Press, Croton-on-Hudson, N.Y., 1992.

9. Goldratt and Fox: op cit.

10. Goldratt, E. M.: *What Is This Thing Called Theory of Constraints and How Should It Be Implemented?* chaps. 3 and 4.

11. Ibid., chaps. 1 and 2.

12. Spencer and Cox: 1994, op cit.

13. Goldratt, E. M.: *The Haystack Syndrome: Sifting Information out of the Data Ocean,* North River Press, Croton-on-Hudson, N. Y., 1990.

14. Lockamy, A., and J. F. Cox: *Reengineering Performance Measurement: How to Align Systems to Improve Processes, Products, and Profits,* Irwin Professional Publishing, Burr Ridge, Ill., 1994.

15. Goldratt, *The Haystack Syndrome,* chap. 10.

16. Ibid., p. 14.

17. Ibid., p. 28.

18. Goldratt and Fox, op cit.

19. Goldratt, *The Haystack Syndrome,* chap. 11.

20. Fry, T. D., and J. F. Cox: "Local versus Global Performance Measures," *Production and Inventory Management Journal,* second quarter, 1989, pp. 52–56.

21. Goldratt and Cox, 1984, op cit.

22. Cox, J. F., J. H. Blackstone, and M. S. Spencer (eds): *APICS Dictionary,* 7th ed., APICS, Falls Church, Va., 1992, p. 26.

23. Goldratt, *The Haystack Syndrome,* chap. 18.

24. Ibid.

25. Goldratt, *The Haystack Syndrome,* part 3.

26. Schragenheim, E. M., and B. Ronen: "The Drum-Buffer-Rope Shop Floor Control," *Production and Inventory Management Journal,* third quarter, 1990.

27. Cohen, O.: "The Drum-Buffer-Rope (DBR) Approach to Logistics." In A. Rolstadas (ed.): *Computer-Aided Production Management,* Springer-Verlag, New York, 1988.

28. Goldratt, E. M.: Logistics and Engineering, Jonah Course, New Haven, Avraham Y. Goldratt Institute, 1988. This example is selected from this course material.

29. Sellers, P.: "The Dumbest Marketing Ploy," *Fortune* (126:7), October 5, 1992, pp. 88–94.

30. Guide, V. D. R.: "A Simulation of Present Production Planning and Control Versus Synchronous Manufacturing at a Naval Aviation Depot," University of Georgia, 1992.

31. Blackstone, John H., Jr., and Daniel V. Guide: "Drum-Buffer-Rope in a Remanufacturing Environment," *Proceedings of the International Society for Systems Improvement,* Detroit, February 1993.

32. Pittman, P. H.: "Project Management: A More Effective Methodology for the Planning and Control of Projects," University of Georgia, 1994.

33. Schragenheim, E. M., and B. Ronen: "Buffer Management: A Diagnostic Tool for Production Control," *Production and Inventory Management Journal,* second quarter, 1991.

34. Umble, M., and M. L. Srikanth: *Synchronous Manufacturing: Principles for World Class Excellence,* South-Western Publishing, Cincinnati, 1990.

35. Goldratt, E. M.: OPT Thoughtware Course, Milford, Conn., Creative Output, Inc., 1985.

36. Ibid.

37. Ibid.

38. Goldratt, E. M., *What Is This Thing Called Theory of Constraints?* p. 32.

39. Goldratt, E. M.: "What Is the Theory of Constraints?" *APICS: The Performance Advantage,* June 1993, pp. 18–20.

40. Ibid.

41. Goldratt, E. M.: *It's Not Luck,* The North River Press, Great Barrington, Mass., 1994.

CHAPTER 10
CAPACITY PLANNING

Editor

Ronald W. Bohl, CFPIM
Vice President, Jack Gips, Inc.,
Chagrin Falls, Ohio

Contributor

Charles J. Murgiano, CPIM
Principal, Waterloo Manufacturing Software
Twinsburg, Ohio

Manufacturing requires coordinated material and capacity plans to meet customer needs. *Materials requirements planning* (MRP) schedules orders to ensure that the right materials will be available when needed. It considers inventories, manufacturing orders, and purchase orders and plans additional orders when needed. Once material plans are generated, capacity planning assures that the necessary resources are available to accomplish the manufacturing orders that have been planned. There are several capacity planning tools used to assure these resources are available. The purpose of this chapter is to describe these tools and show how they are used to make valid capacity decisions in manufacturing companies.

DEFINITIONS

Manufacturing people must understand the capacity planning tools and effectively use them. Some companies misuse the tools because of inconsistencies in their definition of *capacity*. A manufacturing supervisor's definition of *capacity* is likely to be different than that of the manufacturing manager. The engineer who purchased the equipment may have a third definition. Accounting's definition may be based on a different unit of measure—earned hours. Any capacity planning team that includes these people will have difficulty in reaching an agreement on what capacity actions to take. The capacity management process fails because an agreement cannot be reached. It is therefore important to be specific about *capacity,* adding some adjectives to sort out the different views and provide common definitions. The terms defined below will be used consistently throughout this chapter.

Required Capacity

When manufacturing orders are converted to measurable units of capacity, such as standard hours, they can be used in predicting the need for capacity in different work centers over time. This statement of the resources needed to support the plan is called *required capacity.*

Demonstrated Capacity

The current rate of output of a work center that is accepted by the organization as its proven capability is called the *demonstrated capacity.* The conditions at the time the demonstrated capacity is measured such as product mix, current levels of manning, work schedules, and productivity levels must be identified.

Table 10.1 shows 8 weeks of historical output in standard hours in two different work centers. Over the past 8 weeks, work center A has demonstrated an average output of 356 standard hours. Work center B's output has been erratic. This may be due to unreliabilities such as equipment downtime, absenteeism, or tooling problems. It may also be a result of the way the work center was scheduled. These conditions helped determine the output that was generated. If they will continue to exist, the demonstrated capacities will apply to the future. If the conditions will change, someone must judge what will happen in order to determine the demonstrated capacities that the organization will accept and be willing to apply to future requirements.

Demonstrated capacity must be stated in the same units of measure as required capacity. For example, if the required capacity of a work center is stated in standard hours, then its demonstrated capacity must also be measured in standard hours.

Planned Capacity

Resources are often adjusted to meet changing requirements. Companies plan to add equipment, hire new operators, or add or reduce overtime. The predicted output of a work center in the future is called its *planned capacity.* Planned capacity is the demonstrated capacity plus or minus the expected results of known capacity adjustments.

Theoretical, or Maximum, Capacity

The maximum output a work center can achieve assuming the current product specifications, product mix, plan, and equipment is its *theoretical, or maximum, capacity.* This output is higher than the demonstrated capacity that could be achieved if specific capac-

TABLE 10.1   Historical Output, Standard Hours

Week	2/5	2/12	2/19	2/26	3/5	3/12	3/19	3/26	Total
				Work center A					
Standard Hours	320	400	370	365	410	300	330	355	2850
				Work center B					
Standard hours	190	0	245	70	0	220	170	55	950

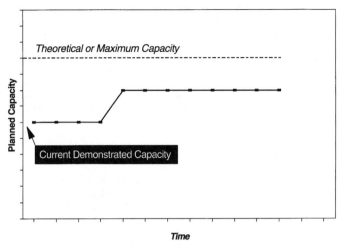

FIGURE 10.1   Capacity plan.

ity actions were taken. It is important to understand the capacity actions that are needed to achieve maximum capacity. Figure 10.1 is an example of the relationship between demonstrated, planned, and theoretical capacity in a work center.

Units of Measure

Capacity must be stated in a meaningful unit of measure that characterizes the workload. Most companies use standard hours to represent their required and demonstrated capacities. Measuring capacity in units of product when each runs at a different rate does not adequately describe the workload. That you produced 150 pieces yesterday and 300 pieces the day before is irrelevant unless the items were identical or consumed identical capacity. Otherwise, it makes sense to convert to a common unit of measure to represent the workload through a work center. Some companies choose to use a rate per hour as their standard. For example, one company measures its capacity in equivalent units (bottle size) per hour. Since they have varying bottle sizes that run at different rates, they have converted all of their capacity measurements to an equivalent bottle size. Different units of measure can be used in different work centers.

Efficiency, Utilization, and Productivity

Efficiency is stated as a ratio between standard hours earned and actual direct hours applied to the product. It measures how well a resource performs against its standards. *Utilization* is a measure of how intensively a work center is applied. This is the ratio between actual hours worked on production and the total hours the resource is scheduled to be available. *Productivity* is the product of the efficiency and utilization measures, or the standard hours earned in relation to the total hours the resource is scheduled to be available. It is used to help plan the capacity actions needed to meet the required capacity. As an example, a work center's required capacity is 12 standard hours greater than its demonstrated capacity. Its productivity factor is 80 percent. This means that the work center must be scheduled to run for 15 additional hours (12 divided by 0.80) to generate the 12-standard-hour difference.

Work Center

The *American Production and Inventory Control Society* (APICS) defines a *work center* as "a specific production facility, consisting of one or more people and/or machines that can be considered as one unit for the purposes of capacity planning and detailed scheduling."[1]

Capacity Planning Goal

Figure 10.2 describes the goal of capacity planning. The demonstrated capacity plus or minus the result of approved capacity actions equals the planned capacity. This must be equal to the required capacity. If the required and demonstrated capacities are equal, then no capacity actions are required. If demonstrated capacity is higher than required capacity, then some action should be taken to reduce the level of demonstrated capacity to the level of required capacity. If the demonstrated capacity is lower than required capacity, then actions must be taken to increase it. In either case, the most desirable action is usually to change the demonstrated capacity to meet the required level of capacity. If this cannot be done or is economically unfeasible, then the required capacity should be changed to equal the demonstrated capacity. This means rescheduling orders and changing plans because output is not adequate to accomplish them.

The process of adjusting capacities to meet the capacity planning goal is the essence of capacity management. The Seventh Edition of the *APICS Dictionary* defines *capacity management* as "the function of establishing, measuring, monitoring, and adjusting limits or levels of capacity in order to execute all manufacturing schedules; the production plan, master production schedule, material requirements plan, and dispatch list."[2] Capacity management hinges on the decision maker's acceptance of the common definitions. It is also based on some common assumptions. One of these assumptions is that demonstrated capacities and productivity factors based on several weeks' historical levels of efficiency, absenteeism, machine downtime, and product mix can be used to predict future levels of capacity. There are no guarantees that these factors will repeat exactly as time passes. Capacity management measures results against these forecasted assumptions and continuously adjusts actions to provide the expected results.

Capacity Actions

When there is a discrepancy between demonstrated capacity and required capacity, a *capacity action* is needed. The capacity action must be predictable, meaning that the outcome is fairly certain and measurable. Adding overtime, outsourcing work, adding equipment, and hiring additional people are all examples of predictable capacity

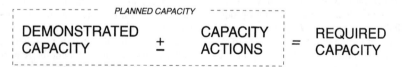

FIGURE 10.2   Capacity planning goal.

actions. Eliminating quality problems, reducing absenteeism, and equipment downtime, and improving efficiency will all increase capacity. These are desirable improvements, but it is difficult to predict the timing of their expected results. Only predictable capacity actions should be considered, particularly for short-term capacity decisions.

The choice of appropriate capacity actions also varies with time. The emphasis in the short term is to make decisions that allow order due dates to be met. The options are somewhat limited because of the need to take the action immediately. Short-term alternatives include working overtime, shifting the work to alternate work centers, or adjusting the workforce.

Medium-term decisions are made within the guidelines of an already approved business plan. The goal is to meet the production plan within the operating budgets derived from the business plan. Appropriate capacity actions in this time frame are to adjust the size of labor force, add or eliminate shifts, and establish or eliminate subcontract programs within the framework of the business plan.

Long-term capacity planning must consider the impact of new products, new markets, major product design changes, and new businesses. Appropriate capacity actions may include new plant and equipment. Regardless of the time frame, every capacity action requires an approval. The capacity planning system must provide the right information in the right form to achieve the goal of capacity planning.

CAPACITY PLANNING TOOLS

The capacity planning tools should improve resource decisions. They help to answer the following questions:

1. Are the schedules (required capacity) within the limits of the current demonstrated capacity?
2. If not, what are the size and time frame of potential capacity actions that can be taken to adjust the demonstrated capacities to meet the plan? What will they cost?
3. If there are no acceptable actions, what is the best set of plans that can be achieved within the capacity limitations?

Given this information, companies can make improved decisions to accomplish their plans at the most affordable costs. It is important to make these decisions far enough in advance to assure that the planned capacity will be available when the requirements show up. It is a mistake to wait until there is already a discrepancy between demonstrated and required capacity on the shop floor before taking action. This results in costly capacity actions or missed schedules that affect customer service.

Other symptoms of poor capacity planning are:

- High costs resulting from poor utilization of resources
- Overcommitted schedules causing missed deliveries and poor customer service
- Invalid priorities because more work is scheduled than can be accomplished
- Excess work-in-process inventory
- Longer cycle times and manufacturing lead times
- High raw materials and purchased-component inventories
- If resources are greater than required, excess idle time or poor efficiencies

The capacity planning tools that help resolve these problems are:

Resource requirements plans (rough-cut capacity planning)

Master production schedule summaries

Capacity requirements plans

Finite capacity plans

Capacity simulations

Input-output controls

Each of these tools helps accomplish the capacity planning goal at different planning levels. Time plays an important role in determining which capacity tool should be used. Figure 10.3 shows the relationships of the capacity planning tools and time.

The *resource requirements plan* is defined by APICS as "the process of establishing, measuring, and adjusting limits of long-range capacity. Resource requirements planning is based on the production plan. It addresses those resources that take long periods of time to acquire."[3] Because these decisions are often costly, they require top management approval. The resource requirements plan is therefore management's tool to accomplish the capacity planning goal.

The *master schedule summary* assures that the master schedules sum up to management's production plan. It is used regularly by the master schedulers to confirm that their master schedules have remained within the capacity limitations set in the production planning process.

APICS defines *capacity requirements planning* as "the process of determining in detail how much labor and machine resources are required to accomplish the task of production. Open shop orders and planned orders in the MRP II system are the input to capacity requirements planning, which translates these orders into hours of work by work center by time period."[4] This tool is a detailed representation of the workload in a work center. It is used to determine capacity constraints in the current materials plans.

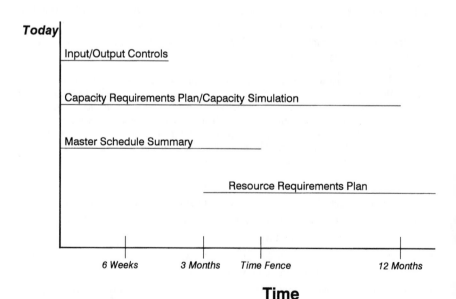

FIGURE 10.3   Capacity planning tools.

Finite capacity planning schedules fill the work centers' defined capacity limits in a given time period. It will never schedule more than these capacity limits. This tool uses much of the same data as capacity requirements planning but automatically adjusts the schedules to assure that the required capacities never exceed the demonstrated capacities.

Capacity simulation is used to generate alternative detailed capacity plans based on what-if scenarios. This tool is used to optimize resources by choosing the best possible plan.

Input-output controls are used to determine whether capacity is actually being delivered as planned. This tool measures actual input and output and compares them to planned input and output for a work center to see if they are within a specified tolerance. It is a vital part of the capacity planning system, helping to identify and resolve capacity problems in the short term.

CAPACITY PLANNING IN DIFFERENT MANUFACTURING ENVIRONMENTS

All manufacturing companies need to plan capacity. The tools they use depends on their environments. Table 10.2 shows some of the differences in planning in each of these environments that result in different approaches to capacity planning. The capacity planning goal is the same regardless of the environment. Required capacity must be equal to demonstrated capacity plus or minus the capacity actions. Capacity actions must have predictable results. The capacity planning tools must be understood and used by the organization.

RESOURCE REQUIREMENTS PLANNING (ROUGH-CUT CAPACITY PLANNING)

The *resource requirements plans* (RRP) are an integral part of the *sales and operations planning (S&OP) process*. The output of the S&OP is management's production plan. S&OP considers customer service goals, inventory and/or backlog strategies, financial goals, and manufacturing's capacities. The *resource requirements plan* (RRP) is used to assure that the production plan is achievable before it is passed to the master schedulers. Alternate production plans can be tested for their impact on capacities before the final plan is chosen and approved. The RRP must be quick and easy to generate to be effective.

Horizon

The resource requirements plan is a long-term capacity planning tool. Its time *horizon* is usually 3 to 24 months, but it should be at least as long as the lead time needed to approve and acquire the resources to meet the plan.

Responsibility

The resource requirements plan is top management's tool to adjust capacities in critical work centers to meet their changing business strategies. Resource requirements planning presents capacity linked to product families and highlights any resource variances. Due to the costs of the capacity actions, top management must be involved in their

TABLE 10.2   Capacity Planning in Different Environments

	Job shop or batch manufacturing	Repetitive manufacturing	Process or continuous flow
Manufacturing environment	Long lead times, many variations in rates and routings. Many different paths in manufacturing causing competition for work center capacities.	Dedicated lines, equipment, or facilities. Very similar routings (paths) and rates of flow. Shorter lead times. More synchronized work centers requiring less scheduling and reporting controls.	Dedicated facilities or lines of flow. High degree of automation. Highly reliable synchronized flow.
Capacity planning	Resource requirements planning, MPS summary, capacity requirements planning, and input-output controls used. Capacity planned in standard hours. Constraints involve both people and equipment. Product mix affects capacity. Constant capacity actions needed to balance required and planned capacity. Capacity simulation adds quality to resource optimization process.	Resource requirements planning, MPS summary, capacity requirements planning. Capacity planned in standard hours or equivalent rates of production. Capacity actions are tied to the entire line or facility. Capacity simulation offers less because alternate plans and their effects are more visual.	Resource requirements planning, MPS summary, finite capacity planning. Capacity planned in rates. Constraints involve equipment. Short-term capacity actions are usually nonexistent. Required capacity is often adjusted to meet capacity constraints. Capacity simulation offers few what-if alternatives to adjust capacity.

approval. If the capacity cannot be changed, then the production plan must be altered. It is the responsibility of top management to decide which product families should be affected.

Data Required

The sales and operations planning information is usually tied to product families. As management reviews capacity actions needed to support alternate production plans, it is important that the resource requirements plans associate capacity requirements with product families. The steps to follow when creating a resource requirements plan are the following:

1. Select product families.
2. Identify critical work centers.

3. Calculate product load profiles.

4. Calculate the resource requirements plans.

Selecting Product Families.   A typical make-to-stock or make-to-order product family consists of a logical grouping of end items. A typical assemble-to-order family consists of options, variables, and common parts included in a planning bill of materials. The great variety of choices must be taken into consideration using planning bills to account for the required resources. The number of product families between companies may vary but must include all of the demands that use the resources. Linking resources to product families lets management make product family decisions. The reports are easier to use and more acceptable to management.

Identifying Critical Work Centers.   Work centers that are first to become overloaded when schedules increase or to run out of work when schedules decrease are candidates to be critical work centers. Critical work centers are those in which:

- New equipment purchases are costly or require a long lead time to obtain.
- Subcontracting is costly and difficult to arrange.
- Skilled workers are not readily available.
- Bottlenecks exist under normal conditions.
- Alternate routings are not available or very costly.
- There is a proprietary or sole-source operation or process.

Critical resources may include nonmanufacturing work centers such as storage, engineering design, numerical control programming, tool design, documentation control, or outside suppliers for critical items.

Calculate Product Load Profiles.   A *load profile* is a statement of resources needed to produce one unit of a product family in each of the critical work centers. Resources can be defined in labor hours or equipment hours or both. Load profiles may be required for families that include service demands, experimental runs, specials, validations, and new products. Once a load profile is established, the RRP is generated by multiplying the family's production plan by the profiles. Similar to the term *load profile* are the terms *bill of labor, bill of capacity,* and *bill of resources.*

Table 10.3 shows examples of product load profiles. Each of the four families' profiles shows the hours required in the critical work centers to produce one unit of the family. Family A is composed of two end items X101 and Y202. The bill of materials for

TABLE 10.3   Product Load Profiles

Critical work center	Family			
	A	B	C	D
Blending	0.03	0	0.04	0.012
Press	0.08	0	0.12	0.022
Finish	0.05	0.055	0.23	0.036
QC test	0.021	0.02	0.07	0
Pack	0.015	0.015	0.03	0.01
Special process	0.076	0.055	0.060	0

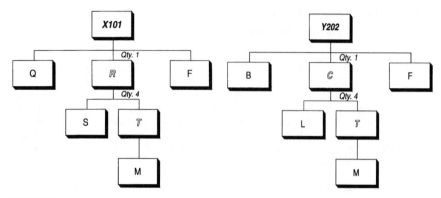

FIGURE 10.4 Bills of materials.

each of the items in the family is shown in Fig. 10.4. Items X101, Y202, R, C, and T are manufactured items that must be considered when developing the load profile for the family. Table 10.4 shows the routings for each of the manufactured items in the family. Six critical work centers have been identified. Each item's setup time in a critical work center is determined by dividing the setup time by the average lot size. This is added to the run time per piece to calculate the total hours required for the item. A weighted average of all the items is used to calculate the average resources required for one unit of the family in each of the critical work centers.

Looking at the previous load profile, the average resource required to produce one unit of product family A in the press critical work center is 0.08 hours. From the bill of materials and routings, manufacturing component T uses the press critical work center 0.019 hours of run time plus 0.001 hours of setup time per unit. The setup time is determined by dividing the 0.5 hour for setup by the average manufactured lot size of 500 units. The total required resource for T is 0.08 hour. This is the sum of the setup time and run time per unit multiplied by 4, the quantity needed on the bill of materials for end items X101 and Y202. The same process is used to determine the resource requirements in the remaining critical work centers.

Product family B shares the finish, QC test, pack, and special process critical work centers with family A, but it does not use the blending and press critical work centers. Its load profile considers this and generates the appropriate requirements for each work center.

If manufacturing lead times are lengthy, the resource requirements plan must be time phased. Lead time offsets in the load profiles accomplish this. Resource requirements plans are usually in monthly increments, so lead time offsets are set between months. More detailed capacity tools, such as capacity requirements planning, will specifically calculate the required capacity to the week or day it is scheduled. A load profile can be developed for a service parts family or an experimental family. It can be developed as above, using the routings of the specific service items or experimental orders.

Calculating the Resource Requirements Plan. Using the production plan for March in Table 10.5, the quantity for each family is multiplied by its load profile to generate the resource requirements plan. Family A's production plan for March is 3000. The resource required to produce one unit of Family A in the critical blending work center is as shown in the product load profile.

TABLE 10.4 Routings

Operation	Work center	Setup, hours	Run, hours
	Item X101—End item		
10	Pack	0	0.01
20	Ship	0	0
	Item Y202—End item		
10	Pack	0	0.02
20	Ship	0	0
	Item R—Subassembly (lot size 250)		
05	Finish	2.0	0.042
10	QC test	3.0	0.01
15	Spec process	6.0	0.035
	Item C—Subassembly (lot size 100)		
05	Finish	4.0	0.010
10	QC test	1.0	0.01
15	Spec process	5.0	0.042
	Item T—Manufacturing component (lot size 500)		
01	Weigh	1.0	0.003
02	Blending	1.5	0.0045
03	Press	0.5	0.019

TABLE 10.5 Production Plan Summary

Product family	January	February	March	April	May	June ...
A	2000	2500	3000	3000	3400	3600
B	4000	4000	4000	4000	3000	3000
C	700	700	700	800	1000	1000
D	8000	8000	9500	9500	9800	10,000

Multiplying 3000 by 0.03 equals 90 hours of resource required as shown in Table 10.6. Multiplying 3000 by 0.08 equals 240 hours of resource required in the critical press work center. This same calculation is applied to all the product families. Adding all the extended hours for the critical blending work center gives a total requirement of 232 hours in March. A comparison of the required capacity (232 hours) to the demonstrated capacity (245 hours) shows that there is enough capacity in blending to meet the production plan.

The critical press work center is overloaded. The required capacity is 83 hours, or 18 percent higher than the demonstrated capacity. Management must approve capacity actions to either increase the demonstrated capacity or reduce the production plan if the capacity actions are impossible or unacceptable.

TABLE 10.6 Resource Requirements Plan

Critical work center	Family				March	
	PP: 3000 A	PP: 4000 B	PP: 700 C	PP: 9500 D	Required	Demonstrated
Blending	90	0	28	114	232	245
Press	240	0	84	209	533	450
Finish	150	220	161	342	873	750
QC test	63	80	49	0	192	200
Pack	45	60	21	95	221	335
Special process	228	220	42	0	490	350

In practice, the resource requirements plans are generated for the same horizon as the production plan. Many companies use graphics to generate a picture of the comparison of required to demonstrated capacity over time. The graph of the critical press work center in Fig. 10.5 is a good example. The RRP reveals a capacity problem beginning in March and continuing through June. Specific capacity actions must be agreed on before the production plan is approved. Each critical work center has its own graph, enabling management to easily spot capacity problems that must be resolved.

A common dilemma in companies is whether to generate family RRPs, as we did above, or create RRPs at the master schedule level. Each MPS item's load profile is developed using its individual routing, including setup and run time, as above. The pro-

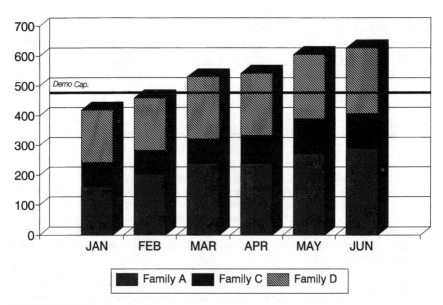

FIGURE 10.5 Critical work center, press.

TABLE 10.7   End Item Load Profiles

	End items					
Critical work center	X101	Y202	M405	N225	O807	N748
Blending	0.03	0.03	0	0	0	0
Press	0.08	0.08	0	0	0	0
Finish	0.05	0.05	0.035	0.075	0.08	0.03
QC test	0.022	0.02	0.02	0.015	0.025	0.020
Pack	0.01	0.02	0.01	0.01	0.03	0.01
Special process	0.059	0.092	0.065	0.030	0.055	0.070

TABLE 10.8   Resource Requirements Plan

Critical work center	End items		Total required, family A	End items				Total required, family B
	PP: 1500 X101	PP: 1500 Y202		PP:1000 M405	PP:1000 N225	PP:1000 O807	PP:1000 N748	
Blending	45	45	90	0	0	0	0	0
Press	120	120	240	0	0	0	0	0
Finish	75	75	150	35	75	80	30	220
QC test	33	30	63	20	15	25	20	80
Pack	15	30	45	10	10	30	10	60
Special process	89	139	228	65	30	55	70	220

duction plan must be broken down into specific MPS item requirements before multiplying by the MPS item load profiles. Tables 10.7 and 10.8 show the partial results of breaking up the production plan into individual end item plans, multiplying them by the MPS item load profiles, and generating resource requirements plans. Notice that the total hours required for the family are the same as in the resource requirements plan in which the family load profile was used. The advantages and disadvantages to this approach are summarized in Table 10.9. The key issue in determining the best level to calculate resource requirements plans is the ability to deal with changing product mixes within the families, precision, maintenance, and ease of simulation. Regardless of the technique, resource requirements planning is the right capacity tool used to assure that the production plan is achievable.

Results

The resource requirements plan shows that the critical finish work center is overloaded. When required capacity is greater than demonstrated capacity, the first choice is to try to increase the demonstrated capacity. The discrepancy in the critical finish work center starts at 123 hours in March and increases to 510 hours in September. Some alternative capacity actions are to:

TABLE 10.9 Load Profiles

Driven from families		Driven from end items	
Pros	Cons	Pros	Cons
Production plan alternatives are easily simulated.	It is more difficult to create and maintain family load profiles.	It is easier to load using existing routings.	More load profiles are required in the system.
Reports are focused on families.	When forecasted product mix changes, the family load profiles must be changed.	It is easier to accept.	Reports focus on end items rather than families.
The reports are simpler.		It is easy to simulate when a small number of end items exist.	Reports are more detailed.
Family load profiles are easier to use when there are a large number of end items.			

- Increase manpower by 1 person in March and 4 people in September. This assumes 160 standard hours of output per month times 80 percent productivity, or 128 standard hours per month per person. It also assumes that equipment capacity is not a limitation.

- Purchase new equipment that can perform the operation 70 percent faster than the existing equipment. The new equipment costs $1,375,000 and has a 6-month lead time.

- Subcontract the operation to an outside supplier at an additional cost of $0.035 per item.

Any of these, or a combination of all, will solve the problem. Management must evaluate the costs, benefits, and risks of the alternatives and determine which is most acceptable.

In the pack work center, the demonstrated capacity is higher than the required capacity. Appropriate actions include shifting people to another work center—work center press, for example—eliminating a shift, reducing or eliminating any subcontract program already in place, or reducing the labor force. Another possible solution is to change the required capacity by shifting some of the work from future months into months with low requirements. This, however, will have the negative impact of producing inventory earlier than needed. It can also adversely affect other work centers' capacities. These choices can be tested using the simulation, or what-if, capability of resource requirements planning to choose the best option.

The critical special process work center is definitely overloaded. This work center is already working at maximum capacity. The process is unique. The work cannot be shifted to another internal work center or to an outside supplier. Purchasing new equipment and hiring and training its operators soon enough to meet the load is not feasible. Since the demonstrated capacity cannot be changed to meet the required capacity, the required capacity must be reduced. This raises another important management decision. Should you reduce the schedule of product family A, which has the highest gross margin? Should you reduce product family B, on which the company's reputation is based? Should you delay introduction of the new product family C? This choice requires management's input. The inventory, customer service, and financial results of this decision must be carefully reviewed before the best plan is approved.

RRP provides management with valuable information about the impact of these plans on the resources in manufacturing. It avoids the tendency to release a questionable plan, order the purchase materials, release manufacturing orders, and then scramble to make it happen. It assures a good plan from the start.

MASTER PRODUCTION SCHEDULE SUMMARY

Purpose

The *master schedule summary* is a capacity planning tool that assures the end item schedules are in agreement with management's production plan. As the master schedules are updated, the master schedule summary identifies the differences between the production plan and the master schedules. These differences should be resolved before the master schedules are communicated to materials planners, manufacturing, and purchasing.

Horizon

The master schedule summary, like the production plan, is prepared in monthly increments. It extends out through the horizon of the master schedule.

Responsibility

The production plan is established monthly while the master schedules change daily. The master schedulers must respond to daily demand and supply changes but must also maintain the continuity of management's plan. The master schedule summary alerts the organization that the production plan is in jeopardy.

Data Required

There are three data elements needed to support the master schedule summary. First, there must be an approved production plan. Second, all master schedule items must be assigned to a production plan family. The third element is the master schedule itself.

Table 10.10 shows the master schedule for end item R123, a member of family D. A master schedule supply order for 4000 is scheduled in the week of 1/14. Another order is scheduled in the week of 2/11, another on 3/18, and one on 4/15. These orders are scheduled properly to meet total demand, represented by the forecast, customer orders, and safety stock. The master schedule orders for R123 are summed in monthly increments on the MPS summary report, Table 10.11. The MPS summary totals the end item schedules for all the items in the family and compares the sum to the already approved

TABLE 10.10 Master Schedule

Part No: R123 Safety stock: 1400 Lead time: 2 weeks Time fence: 8 weeks
Name: Master On hand: 2900 Lot size: 4000 Family: D
scheduled end item

		January				February			
	P/D	1/7	1/14	1/21	1/28	2/4	2/11	2/18	2/25
Forecast		0	700	1100	1100	1100	1100	1100	1100
Customer order		1500							
Available		1400	4700	3600	2500	1400	4300	3200	2100
MPS			4000				4000		
A-T-P		1400	5400	5400	5400	5400	9400	9400	9400

	MPS orders				Demand		
Date	Quantity	Order	Type	Date	Quantity	Customer	Order number
1/14	4000	M1001	Rel	Week 1	1500		C1001
2/11	4000	M5009	FPO				
3/18	4000	M9009	Plan				
4/15	4000	M9177	Plan				

TABLE 10.11 Master Schedule Summary, Product Family D

Item	January	February	March	April
R123	4000	4000	4000	4000
T456	1500	0	1500	0
S884	1600	1600	3200	3200
T773	3000	2500	500	2500
Total MPS	10,100	8100	9200	9700
Production plan	8000	8000	9500	9500
Percent monthly difference	+26.2%	+1.2%	−3.1%	+2.1%

production plan. If the discrepancy between the sum of the master schedules and the production plan for the family is outside a specified tolerance, two plans exist.

Results

The MPS summary report shows 26 percent more product scheduled in January than called for by the production plan. During the week, individual master schedule changes were made to accommodate changes in demand and supply. As these changes were made, the capacity reserved for the family was overcommitted. There are two possible solutions for this. Either the master schedules should be changed to equal the production plan, or the production plan must be changed. If the production plan is changed, because the master schedule changes are necessary or desirable, the resource requirements plan may need

TABLE 10.12   Master Schedule Summary, Product Family Airflow

Item	3/18	3/25	4/1	4/8	4/15	4/22	4/29	5/6
459C	0	19	10	10	30	10	10	0
656B	60	121	114	95	70	58	0	0
535C	50	10	26	30	20	0	20	0
133A	50	10	10	25	0	0	0	0
Total MPS	160	160	160	160	120	68	30	0
Production plan	160	160	160	160	160	160	160	180
Airflow family ATP	0	0	0	0	40	92	130	180

to be regenerated to identify the impact on resources. The MPS summary assures that management's plan is communicated to the rest of the organization.

Order Promising

Some make-to-order businesses use their master schedule summaries for order promising. Table 10.12 shows a master schedule summary with *available to promise*, or ATP. ATP is the difference between the production plan and the sum of the master schedule orders for the items in the family. Master schedules are planned to meet customer orders. In the figure there is no product available to promise until the third week of April. This is the first time capacity will be available to satisfy new customer orders. As new orders are accepted, master schedules are planned and deducted from the family's ATP numbers in the master schedule summary.

CAPACITY REQUIREMENTS PLANNING

Purpose

Capacity decisions on the shop floor require detailed information about the expected load in a work center. The status of work-in-process inventory must be considered when projecting the load for a work center. The *capacity requirements plan* (CRP) is the tool that identifies short-term discrepancies between required and demonstrated capacities. It is used by manufacturing and planning to adjust short-term capacities or level requirements to accomplish the capacity planning goal. Capacity requirements planning assumes that a work center's demonstrated capacity can be adjusted to meet fluctuating requirements. It provides visibility to evaluate the alternative actions to best utilize these resources. Since the capacity to handle the monthly requirements in the critical work centers has already been assured by management decisions resulting from resource requirements planning and maintained by master schedulers with the MPS summary, the CRP does not assume the availability of "infinite" capacity. Instead it calls for adjustments to resources already within an approved capacity plan.

Horizon

Capacity requirements plans are usually calculated in weekly increments. They extend through the horizon of the master schedules. They are typically used in the short term, roughly the first 3 months, to assure that the capacity planning goal is attained.

Responsibility

Management, in their planning, has not leveled the load for every work center from week to week nor identified minor capacity actions required to meet the schedules. It is the responsibility of manufacturing and planning to meet regularly, review the detailed capacity plans by work center, and take actions to meet these plans.

Data Required

There are a number of important data elements used in calculating the required capacity of a work center. A routing defines the sequence of operations in the manufacturing process and the work centers involved. The elements of lead time, move time, queue time, setup time, and run time are used to compute operation start and finish dates for every manufactured order. The shop order scheduling example in Table 10.13 shows the detail schedule for order number M7757. Operation start and finish dates have been calculated for every work center in item 8490's routing. The total setup and run time in standard hours is divided by the demonstrated daily capacity to arrive at the elapsed time for each work center. Sixteen hours of setup and run time are needed to perform the coating operation. The coating work center generates 8 hours of output daily. Therefore, 2 days of lead time are required from the start date of the setup to the completion of the quantity in coating to produce order M7757. This logic is applied to each operation to calculate schedules that can be met.

The 16 hours of required capacity in coating between 5/24 and 5/26 stems from the detailed scheduling of order number M7757. The total weekly required capacity is 200 hours, including the 16 hours from M7757 plus the hours required by all the other orders scheduled in coating during the same week. Table 10.14 shows the CRP details for the coating work center. Notice in the week of 5/20 that 16 hours of required capacity is generated by order number M7757.

Each week's required capacity is graphically represented in the bar chart in Fig. 10.6. Each vertical bar symbolizes the required capacity for the week. In the week of 5/06, 230 hours of capacity are required. The week of 5/20 shows the 200 hours represented

TABLE 10.13   Shop Order Scheduling

Item no. 8490
Order no. M7757
Order quantity: 3000
Order due date: 6/15/9X
Order start date: 5/10/9X

Operator	Work center	Move and queue, standard hours	Setup and run, standard hours	Daily demonstrated capacity, standard hours	Schedule start date	Schedule due date
10	Weigh	8	8	8	5/11/9X	5/12/9X
20	Compound	12	24	12	5/13/9X	5/17/9X
30	Tablet press	8	8	4	5/19/9X	5/23/9X
40	Coating	8	16	8	5/24/9X	5/26/9X
50	QC lab 1	48	12	6	6/8/9X	6/10/9X
60	QA release	12	6	6	6/14/9X	6/15/9X

TABLE 10.14   CRP Details, Work Center, Coating Department 10

Week	Hours	Part number	Order number	Type
5/20	16.9	1001	M1011	R
5/20	16.8	8162	M4234	R
5/20	11.3	2152	M6185	R
5/20	19.2	3894	M5344	R
5/20	14.6	9833	M7150	R
5/20	16.0	8490	M7757	R
5/20	23.1	1295	M2120	P
5/20	14.7	1443	M2875	P
5/20	8.5	6010	M7271	P
⋮	⋮	⋮	⋮	⋮
Total week 5/20 =	200			

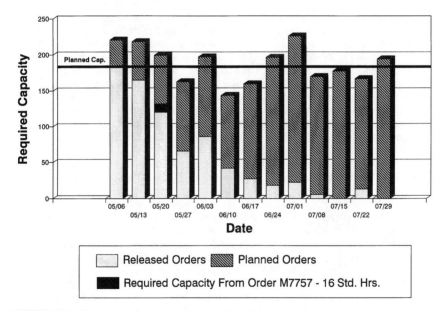

FIGURE 10.6   Capacity requirements plan, summary, work center, coating.

from the CRP details of Table 10.14. The dark horizontal line, set at 180 standard hours a week, represents planned capacity.

The report also separates the hours from released orders from those in a planned status. Planned orders must be considered in required capacity because they represent predicted needs. As operation completions are reported, capacity requirements are reduced. The critical data elements that support capacity requirements planning are the following:

Complete and accurate routings

Good work center definitions

Accurate move, queue, setup, and run times

Good shop scheduling logic

Accurate demonstrated capacities

Timely and accurate shop reporting

There are additional issues that affect the accuracy of the required capacity. *Parallel operations* in a routing occur simultaneously. For example, a company manufactures a batch of product and sends a sample to a quality-control laboratory for testing while the remainder continues through the next step in the process. The required capacity for two work centers, performing parallel operations is scheduled in the same time period.

Overlapping operations on a routing assumes that a portion of the lot size is started in a second work center before the entire lot is completed in the first. Operation schedule dates must reflect this logic. This logic places the capacity requirements accurately.

Campaigning is the manufacturing of multiple batches back to back through a work center to reduce the number of setups and cleanups. For example, a single batch of product requires 4 hours of setup time in the reactor work center. If five batches of the same product are campaigned through the reactor, then the setup time is still 4 hours. Each of the succeeding batches will use the setup of the first batch. Capacity requirements planning must recognize these issues when it calculates required capacities.

Some companies need to plan both equipment and labor capacities. Figure 10.7 shows the routing step of item G4550 in the L1 work center. The L1 work center contains six drill presses. It takes 2 hours of equipment time to set up one drill press to produce G4550 and 0.002 equipment hours to run each piece. Two people, working as a team, set up a drill press to produce G4550. Once the setup is completed, it requires only one-half of an operator's time to run the press because one operator runs two orders on two presses simultaneously. When order number M5542 for 1000 pieces of G4550 is scheduled, the required capacity in L1 is 4 equipment hours; 2 hours of equipment setup time plus 1000 pieces times 0.002 hours per piece of run time. The required capacity is 5 labor hours; 4 hours of setup time plus 1000 pieces times 0.001 hours per piece of run time. The scheduling logic should plan an elapsed time of 2 hours for setup plus 2 hours of run time for G4550 in L1. Stating requirements in both labor and equipment hours will identify capacity problems and actions involving labor or equipment in L1.

Many companies are training their people to be cross-functional so they can be moved to a number of work centers to help meet their plans. Capacity requirements plans should signal if equipment work centers are out of balance or if the total labor is a problem. For example, a company with seven packaging lines needs to know if any line has a capacity problem. Each line is defined as a work center. Individual routings specify the packaging line and the equipment setup and run time needed to produce each item. There is only enough labor to operate four of the seven packaging lines at any one time. Setting up a separate work center, called *packaging labor,* and including it on the routings will cause a CRP report to be produced for the labor resources required. Using

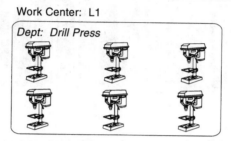

| | | Equipment | | Labor | |
Operation	Work Center	Setup Time (Std Hrs)	Run Time (Std Hrs)	Setup Time (Std Hrs)	Run Time (Std Hrs)
.	.	.	.	.	.
.	.	.	.	.	.
		.	.	.	.
40	L1	2.0	0.002	4.0	0.001
.	.	.	.	.	.

Work Center: L1

Dept: Drill Press

FIGURE 10.7   Routing file, item G4550.

parallel operation logic for the packaging line and packaging labor work centers will properly schedule the order. The capacity requirements plans can then show if any packaging line or total packaging labor has a capacity problem.

Results

The capacity requirements plan for the CNC work center in Fig. 10.8 reveals two problems. First, there is a short-term overload in weeks 6/06 and 6/13, including 109 hours past due. Figure 10.9 shows the same capacity requirements plan for the CNC work center in accumulative hours. This representation indicates that to be on schedule by the end of 6/06, the work center must perform at 161 percent of its demonstrated capacity. To catch up by week 6/13, the work center must perform at 134 percent of its demonstrated capacity for 2 weeks in a row. It also shows that the work center is balanced over the long run, meaning that management has set a good production plan. They did not, however, level the load each week. These detailed capacity requirements plans identify the weekly peaks and valleys and the need for actions to assure that week-to-week schedules are attained. The first alternative is usually to try to meet the plan before changing it. Short-term capacity actions such as working overtime, shifting the work to an alternate work center, or hiring temporary employees could resolve the short-term problem. The best choice should be made and documented.

The second problem occurs in the week of 8/22. There are 100 more required hours than demonstrated. The 2 previous weeks show available capacity. One decision might be to lower the demonstrated capacity by shifting people to other work centers in the weeks of 8/08 and 8/15, then increase it by returning them during the week of 8/22 to meet the requirements. Another decision might be to pull work forward from 8/22 into the 2 weeks and level the requirements. This decision must be made now, when there is enough lead time to schedule the materials appropriately. If you wait until the week of 8/08 to make this decision, it will be too late. The material will not be available to utilize the capacity. If the requirements are changed to level the load in this work center,

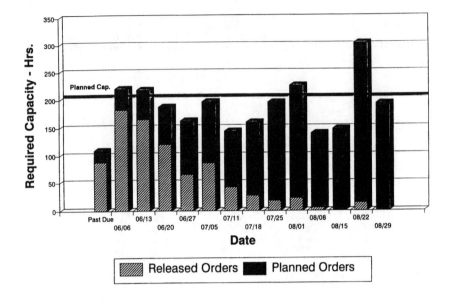

Date: 06/06/XX
Work Center: CNC

Week	Rel. Hrs.	Pld. Hrs.	Tot. Hrs.	Pld. Cap.	% Cap.
Past Due	88	21	109		
06/06	182	38	220	204	161%
06/13	165	54	219	204	107%
06/20	120	68	188	204	92%
06/27	66	97	163	204	80%
07/05	86	111	197	204	97%
07/11	42	102	144	204	71%
07/18	27	133	160	204	78%
07/25	18	179	197	204	97%
08/01	22	204	226	204	111%
08/08	5	135	140	204	69%
08/15	0	148	148	204	73%
08/22	14	290	304	204	149%
08/29	0	194	194	204	95%

FIGURE 10.8   Capacity requirements plan.

other work centers may be affected. Their capacity requirements plans should be reviewed to assure that a capacity problem does not exist.

FINITE CAPACITY PLANNING

Purpose

Finite capacity planning is a method of planning capacity that assumes capacity is fixed. The assumption of whether capacity is fixed, or finite, is the fundamental difference

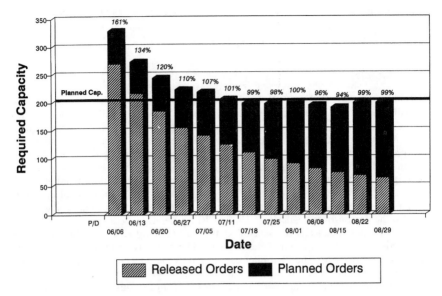

FIGURE 10.9 Capacity requirements plan, accumulative hours.

between it and capacity requirements planning. Capacity requirements planning effectively highlights the differences between required and demonstrated capacities. People must be able to reconcile the differences by agreeing to the necessary capacity actions. Given enough time and money, capacity can usually be changed. However, in some situations the ability to adjust demonstrated capacity is very limited. This is particularly true over shorter time frames. Finite capacity planning schedules requirements only to the limit of demonstrated capacity. It eliminates the need to reconcile the differences between the required and the demonstrated capacities.

Horizon

Finite capacity planning is limited to shorter time frames than resource requirements planning. Adding equipment, expanding a plant, or adding a new facility are long-term capacity actions. RRP is a better tool for choosing among these alternatives. In the short term they may not be feasible. If the demonstrated capacity is near or at the maximum or theoretical level, no capacity action to raise capacity can resolve the difference in the short term.

Responsibility

Finite capacity planning requires accurate demonstrated capacities. These become the upper limit to which the required capacity is adjusted. If a work center's demonstrated capacity changes, manufacturing must inform the capacity planning system. If extra capacity exists but is not reflected in the system, additional requirements will not be scheduled to use it. If the demonstrated capacity is lowered but is not changed in the finite capacity planning system, more required capacity will be scheduled than the work center can achieve. It is the responsibility of manufacturing to maintain the accuracy of the demonstrated capacities. The system itself will assure that no more work is scheduled than a work center can be expected to execute.

Data Required

The software classified as *finite loaders* are usually embedded in MRP II systems. Usually they run on the same computer hardware as the other MRP II modules. Much of the same data used in capacity requirements planning are used in finite capacity planning. What is different is how it uses the data. Finite capacity planning determines the required capacity just as CRP did. But it schedules the requirement by looking forward in time and assuring that capacity is available. It assigns no more work to a work center than it can be expected to execute in a given time period. It builds the operation schedule dates by proceeding sequentially from the initial operation to the final operation while observing capacity limits. The result is a level load or at least a load that does not exceed the demonstrated capacities. Under CRP, generating the load is a simpler task. Hours of required capacity are scheduled using a backward algorithm. Starting at the production due date, the resource requirement of each step is loaded backward in time. Since this approach assumes "infinite" capacity, the order in which the requirements are loaded is irrelevant. No company has infinite capacity, which is why CRP often appears to users as inadequate. Remember that CRP does not suggest this—it simply makes the difference between the required and demonstrated capacities visible. If capacity actions can be taken to meet the plan, then orders will be delivered when they are needed. If capacity actions cannot be taken, the required capacity must be changed.

Loading capacity finitely is more problematic. If capacity constraints exist and the requirement is loaded backward, it is possible for the start time of requirements to be set prior to the current date. Therefore, forward scheduling generates completion dates that closely approximate when production will actually be completed.

When planning finitely, the sequence in which requirements are loaded is extremely important. Requirements loaded first will have first access to resources while requirements loaded later may have to be pushed forward in time due to capacity constraints. Some finite loaders allow for a single priority rule to override the "first to load" method of allocating capacity. This helps to prioritize some orders ahead of others. Clearly, a single rule for finitely allocating demonstrated to required capacity will not fit all circumstances.

Differences with Capacity Requirements Planning (CRP)

Figure 10.10 shows the difference between a work center load using CRP and finite capacity planning. The demonstrated capacity is 500 hours a week. Capacity requirements planning has scheduled 630 hours in the week of 5/06, and as little as 400 hours in the week of 5/20. The capacity required is based on back-scheduling from the production due dates. If the capacity can be adjusted to meet the plan, order due dates will be met. The finite capacity plan assumes that the 500-hour limitation is fixed. Using the forward-scheduling technique, no week is overplanned. The due dates would be more realistic but based only on the finite capacity planning assumption that the customers are willing to wait until capacity is available. Since capacity cannot be increased to meet new requirements, the customer orders are pushed out into future periods.

Companies operating near or at maximum or theoretical capacity tend to have the conditions to better utilize finite capacity planning. In the short term, demonstrated capacity cannot be increased. Establishing a plan based on the assumptions of CRP

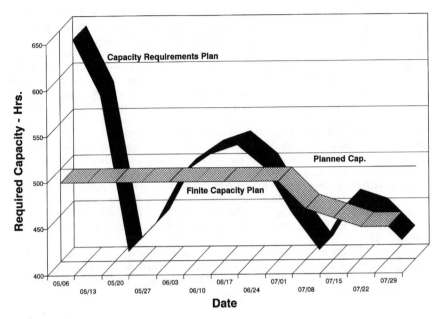

FIGURE 10.10   Capacity requirements versus finite capacity.

would require rescheduling. Finite capacity planning avoids this by rescheduling automatically. The order dates are then fed to other MRP II modules ensuring purchased material and components arrive on time. In cases where excess demonstrated capacity exists in all work centers, finite capacity planning looks like capacity requirements planning.

Since finite capacity planning assumes that the demonstrated capacity is fixed, lost capacity results in automatic rescheduling. A work center scheduled to satisfy 280 hours of requirements last week only achieved 200 hours because of some unplanned downtime, absenteeism, and a tooling problem. As a result, 80 hours must be added to next week's load. Capacity cannot be increased to 360 hours this week to make up the difference. Requirements will be automatically pushed out to accommodate the unexpected increase in the load. This may result in bumping many orders and in missed delivery promises. Finite capacity planning assumes that capacity limitations are real. The system cannot assume they are changeable, even under the pressure of meeting requirements. It demands a high degree of reliability from manufacturing to meet its weekly planned capacity and assure that schedules will not be automatically changed.

CAPACITY SIMULATION

Role of the Computer

The role of computers in capacity planning has steadily increased as computers have become faster, less expensive, and easier to use. An appreciation of the inherent complexity, yet iterative nature of capacity planning is important to understand when we see how these advances in computer technology have been applied. When planning capacity, a company's required capacity will almost never match its demonstrated capacity in every time period. A large part of capacity planning is spent considering alternatives for bringing the required and demonstrated capacities into balance. Rarely is there a single "right" answer. Each alternative can have subjective and hard-to-measure implications.

Once a capacity plan is approved and implemented, it can often change. Manufacturing may not always perform as scheduled, or the requirements can change. There is a need to regenerate capacity plans on a regular basis. Manually, this becomes difficult if not impossible. Suppose a capacity planner has three alternative actions that will result in balancing demonstrated with required capacity in a particular work center. The planner can schedule overtime, hire more operators, or outsource the operation. The predicted results of these alternatives on the work center may not be that difficult to simulate manually. But suppose the capacity planner needs to know the cost of each alternative and the impact each has on other work centers in the plant. There may be other constraints, such as tooling availability, allowances for equipment maintenance time, and labor training programs that must also be considered. The calculations required to provide the information that will lead to the right decision may be impossible manually.

Today's computer technology can assist people in capacity simulation. It excels at what-if capacity analysis. Drawing on insight obtained from the use of capacity simulation, people can quickly develop alternative capacity strategies, take the time to analyze the outputs, and choose the best alternative.

Comparison to Finite Capacity Planning and CRP

The software classified as "capacity simulators" are typically stand-alone products, marketed by companies who specialize in this technology. Capacity simulators usually require more detailed data than are contained in the traditional CRP or finite capacity planning systems. As a result, they offer users multiple options for planning capacity. Table 10.15 shows the comparison of capacity simulators, finite capacity planning systems, and capacity requirements planning systems.

The CRP scheduling principle places capacity requirements in time buckets using backward operation scheduling and making any discrepancy between demonstrated and required capacity visible for reconciliation. Finite capacity planning uses the forward-scheduling technique and places the required capacity into future time periods with the assurance that demonstrated capacity will not be overcommitted. Capacity simulation uses several different scheduling techniques to provide numerous capacity planning alternatives. The differences between demonstrated and required capacity are highlighted along with the cost of reconciling each alternative. The fundamental differences in most of the capacity simulators are the costs—the dollar cost of the recommended capacity action, the cost in late orders, or the costs in material expedites.

CRP and finite capacity planning use the data found in MRP II. Capacity simulators will start with the data contained in MRP II, but they usually require additional data. Multiple resource constraints, priorities, alternate routings, and costs must all be defined and maintained. Although CRP has the ability to use alternate routings, the decision rests in the hands of the capacity planner. Capacity simulators can automatically check alternate routings for available capacity. Capacity simulators are highly interactive. The data can be changed and easily tested with a simulation. In addition, the user has full control over the subset of the schedule they simulate. This allows for a portion of the schedule to be frozen or the horizon to be limited, which speeds the simulation process.

Another advantage of capacity simulation is the ability to reschedule automatically. Assume that a capacity plan is approved that requires the rescheduling of the required

TABLE 10.15   Comparison of Capacity Simulators, Finite Capacity Planning, and Capacity Requirements Planning

Characteristics	Capacity simulators	Finite capacity planning	Capacity requirements planning
Principle	Multiple scheduling techniques provide numerous alternative plans	Forward scheduling assuring no work center overloaded	Back scheduling making discrepancies visible
Detail level of data	High	Low	Low
Resource constraint	Multiple (labor, crews, equipment, tooling, etc.)	Work center	Work center
Routing alternatives	Automatic	No	Planner's choice
Handles capacity overloads	Makes visible, automatically pushes orders out	Never occurs	Makes visible
Handles capacity shortfalls	Makes visible, automatically pulls orders in	Makes visible	Makes visible
User interactivity	High	Low	Medium
Partial scheduling	Yes	No	No
Identification of costs	Yes	No	No
Rescheduling	Easier	Difficult	Manual
Handles scheduling complexities	Yes	Some	Some
Computing power requirements	High	Medium	Low
Integration issues	Many	Some	Few
Costs	Additional	Maybe embedded in MRP II	Part of MRP II

Source: Courtesy of Waterloo Manufacturing Software.

capacity. Using CRP, manual rescheduling is required. Finite capacity planning can automatically push orders out if demonstrated capacity is overloaded. But some of the capacity simulators can automatically push orders out, or pull orders in, to conform with the approved capacity plan. This assumes that the capacity simulator is integrated with the scheduling system. This saves work for the planning organization. Most of the capacity simulators include the complex scheduling issues found in some of the CRP systems. These include overlapping operation logic, parallel operation logic, and campaign logic. In addition, smaller time buckets, such as shifts, hours, or minutes, can be defined rather than the traditional days or weeks found in CRP.

One of the greatest attributes of capacity simulation is that it can vary the multiple constraints and scheduling techniques that provide alternate capacity plans. Users can prioritize criteria such as earliest due date or family groupings to limit changeover on setup or cleanup time. Priority can be applied to equipment constraints, labor constraints, tooling, or other resource constraints as well. Changing conditions on the shop floor, such as changes in standards, routings, queue times, planned capacity, and equipment and labor resources, can be simulated to identify potential problems before implementing. Different scheduling techniques, such as forward finite, forward infinite, and backward infinite, can be easily tested. For example, an initial capacity plan may show unacceptable levels of late work over a specific horizon. A planner could develop alternate what-if scenarios by simply changing the scheduling technique, the priority of the constraints, or a combination of both. Data would then be changed to reflect each of the scenarios, the capacity plan rerun, and the results saved. The planner would then compare the results of the alternatives, choose the best alternative, copy the saved plan into the actual plan, and automatically reschedule the orders to support the new plan.

Capacity Simulation Concerns

Although capacity simulation offers assistance in planning capacity, there are some concerns. Capacity simulation requires additional hardware and software to operate. The additional costs must be justified by its potential benefits. Capacity simulators can be implemented as stand-alone systems, or they can be integrated with existing systems. Most capacity simulators can extract the basic information from an MRP II system and then combine it with the additional data that are required. The additional data can be loaded manually unless system integration is developed. The source of production completion data must also be integrated with the capacity simulator.

Once a number of capacity alternative plans have been narrowed to one choice and the new plan is copied over on to the active file, the priority changes for manufacturing and purchasing must be quickly and effectively communicated. This can be difficult if MRP II needs to be updated manually to recognize the changes coming from capacity simulation.

Implementation

The key issues for the effective implementation and use of capacity simulation are the following:

- Defining where and when to use the tool
- Identifying and collecting accurate data
- Developing interfaces for downloading and uploading information to other systems
- Determining whether to maintain two sets of data (e.g., routing data) in both the MRP II and in the capacity simulator

- Defining how often you need to regenerate capacity plans
- Determining how to integrate it with MRP II and effectively communicate the new plan to manufacturing and purchasing
- Specifying to what degree you can afford change and effectively manage it
- Defining hardware requirements
- Selecting the capacity simulation software
- Developing education and training requirements
- Identifying the policies and procedures for operating and maintaining the system
- Justifying how the system will pay for itself

INPUT-OUTPUT CONTROLS

Purpose

APICS defines *input-output controls* as "a technique for capacity control where planned and actual inputs and planned and actual outputs of a work center are monitored."[5] When the actual deviates from the planned by a predetermined tolerance, immediate action is necessary. Input-output controls are a measure of work center performance. They deliver an early warning that capacity is not flowing as planned. This leads to capacity actions to return to the plan.

Horizon

Input-output controls are a short-term capacity planning tool. They usually cover the first 6 to 8 weeks of the planning horizon.

Responsibility

Input-output controls are used in combination with the capacity requirements plans during weekly capacity meetings. Materials planners, capacity planners, and shop supervisors review all the work centers that are out of tolerance from the plan. These meetings result in agreements on capacity actions and warnings given to related work centers that may also be affected.

Data Required

Table 10.16 shows the input-output report for the heat treat work center. The top half of the report refers to planned and actual hours of input for heat treat. The bottom half shows the planned and actual hours of output. There are 4 weeks, 4/08 through 4/29, of history and 6 weeks, 5/06 through 6/10, of future planned hours. The future planned input comes from CRP. The CRP is the projection of the required capacity in a work center. It is stated in standard hours. The planned output represents the planned capacity of the work center: demonstrated capacity plus or minus the agreed-upon capacity actions.

The heat treat work center has a planned queue of 450 standard hours. This equates to approximately 1 week's demonstrated output. The planned queue represents the normal expected amount of work available in heat treat. It is calculated from actual measurements taken over an extended period of time.

TABLE 10.16   Input-Output Controls, Heat Treat

Work center: Heat treat
Date: 5/6/XX

	04/08	04/15	04/22	04/29	05/06	05/13	05/20	05/27	06/03	06/10
	Tolerance ±75 standard hours (cumulative)									
Planned input	470	510	530	480	500	520	470	495	475	510
Actual input	455	500	535	490						
Accum. dev.	−15	−25	−20	−10						
	Tolerance ±90 standard hours (cumulative)									
Planned output	500	470	510	530	500	500	500	500	500	500
Actual output	520	500	490	525						
Accum. dev.	20	50	30	25						

Planned queue: 450 standard hours.
Actual queue: 415 standard hours

Tolerances of plus or minus 75 standard hours of cumulative input and plus or minus 90 standard hours of cumulative output provide boundaries for acceptable differences between actual and planned hours. If actual input or output differs from planned levels but remains within the specified tolerance, no capacity action is required. The work center is considered on schedule, and capacity is flowing as planned. If the difference is greater than the allowed tolerance, however, an exception message will be generated requiring immediate action. The tolerances are set to recognize that capacity does not always flow exactly as planned. The work centers that provide work to heat treat do not always perform at perfection. Unplanned equipment downtime, absenteeism, quality problems, tooling problems, and materials delivery problems can cause the flow of capacity to be interrupted. Planned capacity is also based on assumptions such as standard run times, standard setup times, and estimates of efficiency and utilization. The actual performance of a work center may vary from its standards. Output can vary for the same reasons. The output tolerance prevents overreacting.

As orders show up in the heat treat work center, actual input is recognized. For example, when order M200 is completed in a previous work center and arrives in heat treat, its capacity requirement is 12 standard hours: the standard setup time plus the order quantity times the run time. The heat treat work center will be credited with 12 standard hours of input. In Table 10.16, the 490 standard hours of input represents the total capacity requirement of all the orders that arrived in heat treat during the week of 4/29. As orders are completed, the work center will be credited with the same standard hours used in calculating the actual input. After completing order M200, heat treat will be credited with 12 standard hours of actual output, regardless of how long it may have actually taken. The 525 hours of actual output represent the sum of the standard hours of all the orders completed in heat treat during the week of 4/29. All of this data is taken from either the materials movement transactions or completion transactions reported on the shop floor.

Table 10.16 shows that the actual input compared to planned has varied slightly over the past 4 weeks. A cumulative input difference of 10 standard hours is reported. Likewise, the actual output exceeded planned output by 25 standard hours over the past 4 weeks. Both were within tolerance. The work center is on plan, and there should be no concern about meeting the planned input or output in the upcoming weeks.

The actual queue of 415 standard hours represents the sum of the available work in heat treat at the time the report was generated. The actual queue will increase when input is greater than output and will decrease when input is lower than output. When the actual queue differs from the planned queue by an amount greater than the specified tolerances, schedule attainment is in jeopardy.

Results

Table 10.17 shows the input-output reports for the quality-control laboratory and packaging work centers. Work flows from the QC laboratory directly into packaging. The actual input in the QC laboratory has been close to the planned input during the past 4 weeks. The actual output, however, is 265 hours below the planned output. This exceeds

TABLE 10.17   Input-Output Controls

Work center: Quality-control laboratory*
Date: 5/6/XX

	04/08	04/15	04/22	04/29	05/06	05/13	05/20	05/27	06/03	06/10
Tolerance ±125 standard hours										
Planned input	300	300	300	300	300	300	300	300	300	300
Actual input	280	320	340	295						
Accum. dev.	−20	0	40	35						
Tolerance ±100 standard hours										
Planned output	300	300	300	300	300	300	300	300	300	300
Actual output	260	245	190	240						
Accum. dev.	−40	−95	−205	−265						

Planned queue: 300 standard hours.

Actual queue: 595 standard hours.

Work center: Packaging*

	04/08	04/15	04/22	04/29	05/06	05/13	05/20	05/27	06/03	06/10
Tolerance ±50 standard hours										
Planned input	160	175	170	180	180	170	170	170	170	170
Actual input	135	140	90	130						
Accum. dev.	−25	−60	−140	−190						
Tolerance ±60 standard hours										
Planned output	150	170	160	175	180	170	170	170	170	170
Actual output	140	170	150	110						
Accum. dev.	−10	−10	−20	−85						

Planned queue: 100 standard hours.

Actual queue: 25 standard hours.

*Out of tolerance.

the tolerance of 100 standard hours resulting in an out-of-tolerance message. Work has been delivered to the QC laboratory as planned but was not completed as planned. The actual queue in the QC laboratory is 595 standard hours, well over the planned queue of 300 standard hours. A bottleneck has formed in the QC laboratory.

Conversely, capacity has not been delivered to packaging as planned. An out-of-tolerance message has been generated because the actual input was below the tolerance of plus or minus 50 standard hours. Packaging was able to meet their output plan for the first 3 weeks. In the week of 4/29, only 110 standard hours of output were generated. The lack of input finally resulted in packaging's missing their output plan. The actual queue is now only 25 standard hours, well below the planned queue. Packaging can no longer meet their capacity plan because of the input problem.

The input-output reports have identified the specific problem. Output must be increased in the QC laboratory. If capacity actions can be taken to accomplish this quickly, packaging will receive enough work to keep their people busy and meet their planned output. If output in the QC laboratory cannot be increased, the planned input must be lowered. There is no value in building a larger queue in the QC laboratory. Packaging should also lower its planned input and outputs and adjust their resources accordingly. Another solution could be to increase the output in the QC laboratory slightly and reduce the bottleneck over a longer period of time. The planned output of the QC laboratory and the planned input for packaging must be changed to reflect this decision. Then, the actual input and output can be measured against the revised plan. Regardless of the decisions, the input-output controls have identified the capacity problem early enough to take action and assure that schedules will be achieved.

CAPACITY STRATEGIES

Reserving Capacity

It has been common practice in some manufacturing companies to reserve materials for specific customers. Some companies have applied this reservation process to capacity. For example, a specific customer may require delivery in less than the full manufacturing lead time. The ideal situation would be to reduce the total manufacturing lead time to meet this customer's expected lead time. This may not be feasible in the short term, and the majority of customers may not require the shorter lead time.

There are two requirements to meet the shorter lead time for this customer. Material must be made available and capacity must be reserved. The materials are forecast and ordered using materials requirements planning. The capacity must also be forecast, reserved for this particular need, and later consumed with actual orders. Setting up a master scheduled item that represents a work center and forecasting the weekly amount of capacity that is to be reserved for the specified customer will provide a weekly *available to promise* (ATP). As actual customer orders are received, the master schedule is consumed and the ATP is lowered. As long as the ATP remains, capacity is available for the special customer. If the customer for this reserved capacity does not order, the capacity can be used for other customers or make-to-stock items. By reserving and managing this capacity, a company can assure quick delivery for a special customer without disrupting other manufacturing priorities. Attaching a routing to the MPS item will also put forecasted capacity requirements into the CRP and the input-output controls.

Load Leveling

APICS defines *load leveling* as "the spreading of orders out in time, or rescheduling operations so that the amount of work to be done in sequential time periods is distributed evenly and is achievable."[6] A work center that has a capacity limitation and cannot afford to lose capacity in any time period is a candidate for load leveling. Capacity requirements planning schedules "based on need" and does not attempt to even out the capacity requirements. Finite capacity planning assures that no more work is scheduled than can be achieved in a particular time period. It does not fill in the time periods where requirements are less than the capacity limit. It assures only that the limit is not exceeded. Load leveling requires scheduling the same amount of capacity in each time period. Orders may have to be rescheduled to accomplish load leveling. Capacity simulation is the best tool to level the load. Some simulators can automatically level work center loads. In the absence of a capacity simulator, manual rescheduling is the most common means to achieve load leveling.

Rate-Based Planning

The planners for the P1 assembly line plan and measure its capacity based on the number of units it can produce per hour. All of the units that cross the P1 assembly line use the same amount of capacity. The P1 assembly line's demonstrated capacity is 20 units per hour. The CRP report compares required capacity to demonstrated capacity in daily and weekly units. Capacity actions should be taken if differences exist. The capacity requirements plan shows that 1500 units are scheduled for next week. The P1 assembly line operates two shifts, 7 hours a shift, 5 days a week. Its demonstrated capacity is 1400 units per week: 20 units per hour $\times$ 14 hours per day $\times$ 5 days per week. The difference between required and demonstrated capacity is 100 units. Five hours of overtime need to be scheduled to meet the plan.

Establishing routings in units instead of standard hours will provide the CRP and the input-output controls in rates per hour. Rate-based planning is simply converting the requirements to an equivalent unit of measure that is accurate and fitting for the work center.

Transition to Manufacturing Cells

Many companies are improving their flows and restructuring their plants into manufacturing cells. A *manufacturing cell* is a configuration of equipment designed to produce a product or a family of parts. These cells should lead to synchronized operations, elimination of queues, elimination of move times, and improved visibility and reliability. Depending on the quality of the cells, capacity requirements planning may become unnecessary or may still be important but not necessarily for each work center within the cell. There may still be some part of the cell whose capacity is very dependent on the product mix. The items in the family may require different amounts of capacity in these work centers. Planning the entire cell on a rate-based planning concept could create a bottleneck within the cell. The routings should contain capacity data for the entire cell and capacity data for those work centers within the cell that need to be planned separately.

As companies improve their production flows, just in time and Kanban techniques can be used. A *Kanban* is a visual card or authorization to replenish consumed capacity or inventory. It works by signaling a part of the process to spend capacity and replace inventory when it is consumed by a downstream work center. It provides visibility of problems in production and creates a sense of urgency to resolve the problems and maintain the flow of capacity. Kanban replaces work orders and dispatch lists.

Although it is a very powerful execution and control technique, Kanban is not a planning technique. It cannot predict future capacity requirements; thus RRP is still needed to predict the load on manufacturing in the future. The master schedule summary is needed to assure that the schedules are equal to the production plan and that capacity has not been overcommitted to the customers. Planning for the entire cell using load leveling or rate-based planning techniques may still be necessary to adjust the short-term capacity requirements. Input-output controls used to expose bottlenecks are no longer needed. This tool is replaced with the physical input and output of Kanban.

CAPACITY PLANNING IN NONMANUFACTURING ENVIRONMENTS

Manufacturing companies are not the only organizations with a need to plan capacity. A local laundry may need to know whether overtime is necessary to accomplish the work they have accepted. A graphic arts company may contemplate hiring additional employees to meet their expected load. An engineering firm could question the purchase of more computer equipment based on their forecast. All of these nonmanufacturing companies have one thing in common: the need to plan capacity.

A capacity planning system using resource requirements planning and capacity requirements planning can be implemented in any of these firms. First, routings should be defined for each of the operations or activities. The estimated time required for each step must be determined. As customer orders are accepted, master schedules are created that use these routings to schedule capacity. Determining family load profiles from this routing data can lead to RRP reports. Other capacity concepts such as finite capacity planning, capacity simulation, load leveling, rate-based planning, and input-output controls can also be applied in nonmanufacturing environments.

STEPS TO EFFECTIVE CAPACITY PLANNING

Capacity Planning Forum

Capacity planning is effective only if there is an effective forum for making capacity decisions. It takes knowledgeable people who understand the capacity tools and data and who agree that capacity planning is important. They should meet regularly to discuss all levels of capacity planning.

Top management meets on a monthly basis in many companies to approve a production plan that considers manufacturing's capacities based on the RRP. Long-term capacity actions are made to assure that the resources are available to meet the plan. The master schedulers review the current master schedules to assure that they are in line with the production plan. The master schedule summary report is the tool that provides this assurance. The CRP and input-output controls are reviewed weekly. Representatives from planning and manufacturing should review the work centers that have problems and decide on the capacity actions to be taken. The effective use of any capacity meeting is based on the commitment to accomplish the capacity planning goal—that is, to assure that demonstrated capacity plus or minus the acceptable capacity actions match the required capacity.

The agenda at the capacity meeting should include a review of any work center with a problem. The first alternative should be to adjust the demonstrated capacity to meet the plan. Responsibility for taking the capacity actions must be defined. If these actions do not solve the problem, then the required capacity must be changed by rescheduling orders. Any capacity decision should be documented. One key to success is for manufacturing and planning to work together to solve the capacity problems. Computers cannot solve these problems, but people who are willing to make capacity decisions using the information from the computer can.

One common problem is the tendency to focus only on the short-term horizon. Effective capacity planning involves reviewing the entire horizon, recognizing problems in advance, and agreeing to the most effective alternatives to resolve them.

Policies, Procedures, and Performance Measures

Implementing capacity policy, procedures, and performance measures will assure that the philosophy of capacity planning endures over time. A capacity planning policy should include the following:

- The goal of capacity planning
- How to measure and maintain demonstrated capacity
- The predictable capacity actions that can be taken
- The time horizon of each of the capacity tools
- The frequency of each of the capacity planning meetings
- The attendees at each meeting
- The responsibility for the accuracy of the capacity information (defined by capacity tool)
- The documentation and follow-up process to assure that capacity planning is working effectively
- A good set of capacity performance measures

Some performance measures that help assure capacity planning success are as follows:

1. No critical work center's required capacity varies from its planned capacity by more than plus or minus 10 percent on a monthly basis.
2. The MPS summary report shows the master schedules are within plus or minus 7 percent of the production plan for each family.
3. The CRP reports show no work center with past-due requirements greater than 1 week's worth of demonstrated capacity.
4. The CRP reports show no work center with overstated requirements over a period of 4 weeks or more.
5. Input-output reports show less than 5 percent of all the work centers out of tolerance each week.

Capacity planning gives manufacturing a view of the future and helps them to make better decisions. The benefits of improved visibility can be significant. Improvements in meeting delivery promises, happier customers, increased market share, lower inventories, improved manufacturing efficiencies, improved utilization, less expediting, better use of outsourcing, lower transportation premiums, fewer or improved capacity expenditures, and lower costs can result with the effective implementation and use of capacity planning.

REFERENCES

1. *APICS Dictionary,* 7th ed., American Production and Inventory Control Society, Falls Church, Va., 1992, p. 54.
2. Ibid., p. 7.
3. Ibid., p. 43.
4. Ibid., p. 7.
5. Ibid., p. 22.
6. Ibid., p. 26.

BIBLIOGRAPHY

APICS Dictionary, 7th ed., American Production and Inventory Control Society, Falls Church, Va., 1992.

Gips, Jack, Richard Russell, Rod Morris, Richard Heard, and Craig Erhorn: "Capacity Planning," *American Production and Inventory Control Handbook,* 2d ed., APICS, Falls Church, Va., 1987.

CHAPTER 11
MANUFACTURING RESOURCE PLANNING

Editors

James W. Rice, P.E., CFPIM
Professor, University of Wisconsin-Oshkosh, Wisconsin

Michael F. Hatch, CFPIM
President, Hatch and Associates, Industry Consultants
Fond du Lac, Wisconsin

Manufacturing resource planning (MRP II) may be defined as an approach to managerial planning, execution, and control of a productive activity. MRP II was devised for manufacturing companies, but it is being applied more generally in nonmanufacturing industries such as service industries, utilities, and distribution industries. MRP II integrates, in a *closed-loop,* or *feedback,* manner, the forecasting of demand, production planning, production scheduling, and production activity control. MRP II is a philosophy for formal planning that provides a framework for the integration and implementation of managerial details covered elsewhere in this handbook.

MRP II involves integrating many data inputs by means of materials and capacity planning computations into various outputs of information. Most firms use special-purpose MRP II software that can relate the many information needs of all the functions and departments, including purchasing, accounting, payroll, distribution, marketing, engineering, production activity control, and general managerial planning, measurement, evaluation, and control. The involvement of so many users of the MRP II system requires a comprehensive policy development by management and the sophisticated understanding and execution at all levels of a company, which many users find difficult to implement. Some users find that "MRP doesn't work for us," which usually implies that their company does not have their management systems developed to the point that they are ready for a computerized management information system.

DEVELOPMENT OF MRP

Manufacturing resource planning evolved from *materials requirements planning* (MRP) when companies in the early 1960s began to apply emerging electronic computing technology to manufacturing management. Unlike the experience in accounting in which formal and consistent manual procedures were available to be computerized, manufacturing management was characterized by largely ad hoc informal procedures that were different for each company.

Early Development

MRP was initially called "processing the bill of materials," and BOMP (bill of materials processing) software was developed. The early developers were manufacturers of highly complex products. These products had many thousands of parts, subassemblies, and assemblies. The products had many steps or levels of manufacturing, necessitating multilevel bills of materials and typically many features, options, and accessories, perhaps some being partially customized. A large variety of service parts had to be stocked and supplied at many levels of the bills of materials. Often these products were part of a product family that shared a variety of assemblies, parts, and raw materials. People responsible for scheduling such products were in need of a managerial tool that would simplify and structure the process.

A good example of this product environment is the heavy construction and agricultural equipment industry such as the JI Case Company where in 1961 Joseph Orlicky developed material requirements planning. The JI Case Company manufactured a variety of heavy equipment for the construction industry, such as bulldozers, graders, and other earth-moving equipment, and farm tractors and a variety of agricultural implements. There was a great deal of commonality of parts within and across these product lines.

The initial task was to devise a logical system for materials and capacity resources management that could be computerized. Orlicky published the now-classic book *MRP—Material Requirements Planning* in 1975 which laid out the formalized computational logic for dependent-demand materials requirements planning. Oliver Wight published *Production and Inventory Management in the Computer Age* in 1974, which explained the shortcomings of informal systems and the rationale for developing formal, computerized materials and distribution requirements planning and control. Wight's book also outlined how MRP might be expanded into generalized logistics and resource management, which he called MRP II, as mentioned in the title of his 1981 book. The APICS (American Production and Inventory Control Society) launched an "MRP crusade" in the 1970s to publicize MRP, to educate practitioners, and to promote the development and implementation of MRP.

MRP Altered Management Practices

As the conceptualization of computerized production management information systems has expanded in the years since the Orlicky and the Wight books, many acronyms and initial-letter abbreviations have emerged to describe new ideas and to describe old ideas that have been rediscovered as useful. Today, the acronyms MRP and MRP I typically imply the basic materials requirements budgeting calculations as described in Orlicky's book, and MRP II is the broader concept suggested by Wight for the integration of data, computations, and policies that extend materials and capacity planning into comprehensive manufacturing resources planning and control. Managers who understand the logic and discipline of MRP recognize that it is an integrative approach that is not restricted to manufacturing, and hence the terms *managerial resources planning, MRP III, business requirements planning,* and others have been used, especially among consultants, to imply that it is a general approach to time-phased planning of the use of resources.

The earliest efforts toward computerizing manufacturing management sought to computerize individual company procedures. It was soon discovered that the approach should be reversed and that company management procedures should be altered to fit into MRP. Early resistance to MRP included contentions that "our company is different, and generalized MRP will not work for us." The evolution of MRP has shown that few companies are really "different" in the principles of management and that only small adjustments are necessary from company to company. Today, the nearly universal approach is to select from among commercial software packages that which best fits a particular company and, with minimal revision of software, to adapt company management procedures to be consistent with the software.

This has led to the benefit that MRP computer software has been developed to a high degree by vendors and is now sold "off the shelf" for implementation by knowledgeable users. However, it has likewise led to an error, especially by higher-level managers, of thinking that MRP is a computer system; some managers fail to understand that MRP is instead a management system that is computerized. Everyone in a company must understand and adhere to the MRP management system if the approach is to work. It is helpful to think of MRP as a spreadsheet budget of materials, capacity, labor, funds, and other resources needed to achieve a master production schedule. MRP is a bottom-up—instead of the traditional top-down, management model that is typically practiced in the United States—of data entry, information control, and management execution.

A popular theme of the 1970s and early 1980s was "how do we get top management to support MRP?" Thus management by intuition, imposed from a position of authority, was being displaced by a revised approach of formal bottom-up management based upon data and computer-generated information used by personnel at all levels of companies. Wrestling with evolving human resource issues within manufacturing was reflected by the popularity of "theory X and Y" and "theory Z" and "Japanese management techniques" of the 1970s and 1980s, and by total quality management (TQM) of the 1990s.

MRP As a Logistics and Capacity Management Information System

Key elements of MRP II implementation are the materials requirements planning (MRP), the capacity requirements planning (CRP), and the distribution requirements planning (DRP). At present, a distinction is made between MRP and DRP, although both can be visualized as essentially the same logic. The terms MRP and DRP will likely be merged into some new abbreviation as DRP becomes more widely implemented and understood. MRP can be thought of as beginning with the forecasted demand and the master schedule, which is the demand information that is given to manufacturing, enabling planning downward through the manufacturing bill of materials to basic inputs of raw materials and purchased parts. DRP can be thought of as planning upward from the MRP and master schedule levels through levels of distribution centers to the independent customer demand.

Effective with the 1992 APICS CPIM certification examinations, two examination modules "Materials Requirements Planning" and "Capacity Management" were merged into one examination called "Materials and Capacity Requirements Planning." The content of the former "Capacity Management" module was merged into the "Production Activity Control" examination, and capacity planning was merged with materials planning. This redistribution recognized the evolution of the basic MRP/CRP computations.

MATERIALS REQUIREMENTS PLANNING

Material requirements planning (MRP) was developed to provide a structured planning (and replanning) tool for manufacturing companies. In its most basic form, MRP is a set of calculations that accepts the *master production schedule* (MPS) as the input data and that computes planned order-start dates, due dates, and associated quantities for all required materials as a result. In addition to the MPS, data on inventory balances (on hand, on order), lead times, and *quantities per* (number of components per parent in the bill of materials) are required for all items to make the basic calculation. The structured bill of materials is the source of information for the parent-component link and the quantity per parent. The resulting schedule includes all items used in the product(s) and the supporting service and accessory items. All manufactured items and assemblies with direct labor or "touch labor" will have projected start dates and due dates calculated. They will also provide shop order quantities required or (to present the information in a different form) production rates per time period generated. All purchased parts and raw materials procured from outside sources will also have projected ordering dates, due dates, and quantities required.

In technical terminology, MRP is a *deterministic planning model.* That is, the results of each step in calculation are determined directly from the prior step without considering probability distributions for any of the variables. A probabilistic model would take into account such considerations. That approach is used where variables have a wide range of possible values. The deterministic MRP model is useful and sufficient for planning day-to-day manufacturing activities.

The MRP scheduling calculation is ordinarily done using the electronic computer and an appropriate MRP software package. In addition to the software, certain files are required on the computer. These files contain data that most manufacturing companies maintain whether they use MRP or not. First, a master production schedule file is required. This is a statement of all independent demand items including complete (end) products, accessories, service items, and engineering and research items. A due date and the quantity required on a particular date for each of these demand items are stated in the MPS. Second, an item master or part master file is required. This file is keyed by item or part number and contains all relevant data about each manufactured and purchased item. This is the source of on-hand balances and order status information. It is also the source of lead times needed to build or procure the product if these times are estimated. In practice, many people refer to estimated lead times as "plugged" lead times. The build lead time for manufactured items may be calculated from data in a routing or operations file, although this is optional. Third, a bill of materials file is needed from which parent-component relationships and the quantity of the component item required are available for each parent item. Again, most manufacturing companies already maintain all of this information in one form or another. Given these data, the basic materials planning calculation can be done.

The basic MRP calculation involves only simple arithmetic, but it is tedious and repetitive and best left to the computer in practical application. Manual calculation is performed by students of MRP so that they can gain a complete understanding of the step-by-step planning logic involved. The calculation is known as the *bill of materials explosion* since each bill of material scheduled is expanded into requirements for each item. The results are stored in a date and quantity requirements file on the computer. The bill of materials explosion is done at least weekly, and preferably on a daily basis. Some MRP software packages perform a real-time, transaction-driven explosion MRP calculation whenever a data change is entered.

Where MRP Is and Is Not Useful

MRP was designed for planning products that are complex enough to have more than two levels in the bill of materials. Nearly all manufactured products have more than two levels, making MRP useful. An exception to this is a single assembly operation of a collection of staged parts that have no intermediate subassemblies and no raw materials other than those used directly in the final assembly, and when there are no after-market service parts that require planning.

There are a limited number of companies and subcontract enterprises that devote nearly their entire effort to such simple assembly types of product. Examples include a company processing plastic pellets into trash bags or a company mixing a few chemical ingredients to produce a bulk product or a firm specializing in packaging items under contract, where the only components are the packaging materials and the items to be packaged. For these situations, MRP may not be useful because no product structures need to be exploded and netted, and other computer software approaches may be adequate and simpler. Even in these situations, however, the short-term scheduling features of MRP for materials and labor and capacity might prove useful.

THE COMPUTATIONAL LOGIC OF MRP

The core calculations of MRP are becoming easier to explain as everyone is becoming familiar with desktop computing and spreadsheets. The scheduled production for end items and service parts is given by the master production schedule. To determine the production requirements, MRP subtracts the independent-demand inventory that is on hand and on order. Knowing how many independent-demand items to produce, MRP calculates the net requirements for all components according to date of need. Using the manufacturing bill of materials, the quantity of component parts needed for any assembly or subassembly (parent) can be calculated by simply multiplying the number of components per parent.

A spreadsheet can be created for every product that a company produces, and the spreadsheet for every parent item can be linked to a materials requirement spreadsheet of every component subassembly or combination of items specified in the bill of materials, and so on down to all purchased components and raw materials. The result is a period-by-period budget for the planning time horizon of what independent-demand end items the company plans to produce and the timing of all of the resulting dependent-demand items that will be required to achieve the plan of the master schedule. The period ("time bucket") can be of whatever length is practical to the user. The planning horizon is the number of periods calculated and displayed.

Early computing systems used *regenerative MRP logic,* which reiterated all calculations once per week or less often and created huge stacks of paper output, causing companies to think in terms of monthly or weekly buckets. Advances in hardware and software now enable *net change MRP* to constantly update and display the present system status on a computer screen with each new data entry, allowing companies to think in terms of time buckets of 1 day or less and in terms of bucketless priority sequencing of operations.

Based on the spreadsheets of materials requirements, spreadsheets can be created for the capacity requirements plan that include labor, machine, capital, and requirements. A common procedure is to start with the master schedule to calculate the MRP, use the MRP to calculate the CRP, and observe whether sufficient capacity resources exist to achieve the MRP and CRP. If the tentative plan is not feasible, then the planner can simulate to iteratively revise the master schedule and recompute the MRP and CRP until a feasible plan is discovered. This trial-and-error approach is called *infinite planning* because each trial starts by assuming infinite capacity exists, without regard to the actual capacity of work centers. Future computing advances will enable operations research techniques such as linear programming to be built into the on-line computations to enable *finite capacity planning.* While some very small companies have used desktop computers and spreadsheet packages to calculate the MRP and while standard spreadsheets provide an excellent pedagogical approach, essentially all MRP users now purchase specialized MRP software, which provides more information with less effort.

COMPUTATIONAL ILLUSTRATION FOR XY COMPANY

The logic of materials and capacity resource planning (MRP-CRP) can be explained by means of a simple example, the XY Company, which produces only two products called X and Y. Although the illustration is intended to be simplistic, it illustrates many ideas of planning, scheduling, and control. The illustration emphasizes how the planner may inspect each calculation, whereas in commercial software the format is to use automatic planning within preset parameters and to use exception messages to minimize calls on the planner's time.

The principal inputs into the materials and capacity requirements planning calculations are as follows:

1. The product structure as given by manufacturing bills of materials
2. The product routings and time standards
3. The item master inventory files that describe materials
4. The master production schedule, which is the planned output schedule of finished goods

Product Structure, Bill of Materials, and Routing Input Data

Assume that product X and product Y have the product structures as shown in the tree diagram bills of materials of Fig. 11.1. To aid in visualizing, let X be a child's yoyo comprised of two rounded end pieces (component C3) held together by a center peg (component C4) to which a string (C5) is attached. Let product Y be a yoyo that differs from product X only in that the end pieces are elliptically shaped (component C8) for Y versus rounded for X. The production process routing involves shaping purchased blocks of wood (component C6) into the end pieces (either C3s or else C8s), which become WIP (work-in-process) inventory, which are routed to be shaped, bored, and sanded and then sent to the assembly operation. Purchased dowel stock (component C7) is sawed into pegs (C4s) and routed to assembly. The assembly department has a person cut string from a spool of string (component C5) and tie a knot into one end of the string, then insert the other end of the string and a peg (C4) between two end pieces (two C3s or C8s) and press the unit together.

A manufacturing bill of materials, the B/M, can be constructed from the above routing. Correct structuring of the B/M is critical to MRP, if it is to yield the correct information. Changes in routings or in operations or in policies of whether subassemblies might physically exist in inventory or whether intermediate steps are only transitory must be recognized by restructuring the B/M, and these changes usually will require part numbering and adjustments in the inventory item master record. Incorrect structuring of the B/M can lead to excessive data processing and misleading information. (Bill of materials structuring is reviewed in other chapters.)

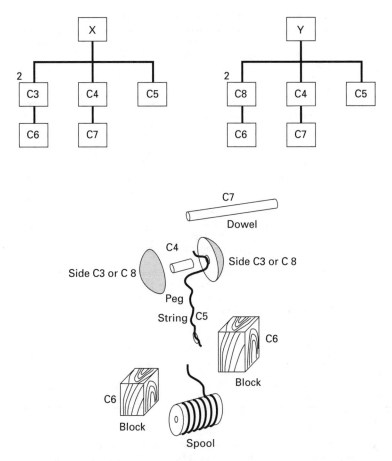

FIGURE 11.1 Tree diagram bills of materials.

Table 11.1 shows the indented manufacturing bills of materials that represent these routings.

Inventory Item Master File

The *item master* typically includes part numbers, item descriptions, primary and secondary vendors, prices, lead times, inventory balances, lot sizes, safety stocks, low-level code referencing the manufacturing bills of materials, and other information specific to each part number.

Part numbers are assigned to all purchased items and to all end items and to items in the intermediate steps of production for any item that might be inventoried or exist as work-in-process inventory. For the illustration of the XY Company, component C5 is a fraction of a spool of string rather than one cut string because string, once cut, is either used immediately or else discarded rather than accumulated as work-in-process. If the

TABLE 11.1   Indented Manufacturing Bills of Materials for Items X and Y

XY Company
Manufacturing Bill of Materials
Part 01

Part	Description	Quantity component per parent	Units of measure	Low-level code
01	Yoyo model X			0
05	String	0.75	Meter	1
04	Center peg	1	Each	1
07	Dowel stock	0.01	Each	2
03	End, round	2	Each	1
06	Wood block	1	Each	2

XY Company
Manufacturing Bill of Materials
Part 02

Part	Description	Quantity component per parent	Units of measure	Low-level code
01	Yoyo model X			0
05	String	0.75	Meter	1
04	Center peg	1	Each	1
07	Dowel stock	0.01	Each	2
08	End, elliptical	2	Each	1
06	Wood block	1	Each	2

operation were changed to prepare a stock of preassembled strings with buttons attached, then additional part numbers would be needed and the bill of materials would be restructured.

Master Schedule Input Data

The master schedule illustrated in Table 11.2 is the interface between the demand of the market and the plan of management for responding to the demand. In companies with DRP (a distribution requirements planning system), the master schedule is the link between the MRP and DRP. (Master scheduling is discussed in Chapter 12.)

TABLE 11.2   Master Schedule

Item	Week							
	1	2	3	4	5	6	7	8
Model X	75	95	85	65	65	65	300	60
Model Y	350	200	300	300	300	100	50	0

Typically, companies that lack MRP do not properly master schedule or plan; they simply react to customer orders. Such companies are often dominated by a sales philosophy that assumes that the production department should be "pounded on" to deliver whatever the customers ask for, as scheduled by the customers. Such philosophy is flawed in several respects. Unplanned, reactive production is generally more costly than planned production. And customers typically ask for unrealistic delivery dates when they distrust the abilities of producers to schedule.

Effective MRP allows effective managerial planning and control through cost-benefit analysis in managing the master schedule. Sales revenues increase through managed production and delivery. Costs are reduced by better management of capacity. Customers become more realistic in lead time negotiation when producers demonstrate reliability, and lead times usually shrink. Customer service increases while inventory levels decrease.

The master schedule lists by time period the planned production of every end item that the company makes. The master schedule includes all finished goods and also all component parts that have independent demand, such as service and repair parts. In a make-to-stock company, the master production schedule is usually developed to cover existing sales forecasts. In a make-to-order company, the master production schedule is designed to cover both backlog and forecast.

Explosion and Netting

An MRP spreadsheet is prepared for each item of the master schedule. If any component parts of product X or product Y were subject to independent demand (e.g., as service parts), then they too would be lines of the master schedule and would be planned within the MRP.

Table 11.3 depicts a materials requirements plan for product X as a planner might view it early in week 1. The row labeled "Gross requirements" is simply the row from the master schedule for the product. The table shows that a scheduled receipt exists of 20 units, representing a shop order to assemble a customer order for model X that was released 1 week ago and is due to be completed in week 1. The row labeled "Balance on hand" shows that the current week began with 70 units in finished-goods inventory and will end with 15: The 70 on hand plus the 20 to be received minus the 75 demanded will leave 15 units in stock. A planned order release exists for 80 units, which is a planned

TABLE 11.3 Materials Requirements Plan (MRP), Model X Product, Part 1

Low-level code 0
Lead time 1 week
Lot for lot
No safety stock

		Week							
	Past due	1	2	3	4	5	6	7	8
Gross requirements		75	95	85	65	65	65	300	60
Scheduled receipts		20							
Planned order receipts		0	80	0	0	0	0	0	0
Balance on hand	70	15	0	−85	−150	−215	−280	−580	−640
Planned order release		80							

order receipt in week 2, given a stated lead time of 1 week. Later period balances are negative because if no orders are released, then there will be a shortage of 85 in week 3, 150 in week 4, and so on.

Table 11.4 illustrates the effect of the scheduler's releasing the planned order for the current week, creating a shop order, to emphasize the distinction between a *planned order release, a planned order receipt,* and a *scheduled receipt.* It emphasizes that no inventory is created, and no resources are expended, by planned orders. The MRP logic is to provide a picture of the materials and capacity requirements of the planning horizon (8 weeks in this example) but to await specific action by the (human) scheduler up to the last possible moment. As soon as the shop order is released, the MRP converts the planned order release into planned order receipt. If a company always adheres to just in time, lot for lot, then the row labeled "Planned order receipt" would be redundant and could be eliminated from the software because a quantity would always be either a planned order release or a scheduled receipt.

Table 11.5 shows the plan for product X after it has been updated by running the MRP reschedule or "explosion" computer program. Planned orders for the item for weeks 2 through 8 are generated based on the current gross requirements, scheduled receipts, and on-hand balance. The order for 85 units will not be released until next week.

TABLE 11.4   MRP Model X Product, Part 1

Low-level code 0
Lead time 1 week
Lot for lot
No safety stock

		Week							
	Past due	1	2	3	4	5	6	7	8
Gross requirements		75	95	85	65	65	65	300	60
Scheduled receipts		20	80						
Planned order receipts		0	0	0	0	0	0	0	0
Balance on hand	70	15	0	−85	−150	−215	−280	−580	−640
Planned order release									

TABLE 11.5   MRP Model X Product, Part 1

Lead time 1 week
Lot for lot
No safety stock

		Week							
	Past due	1	2	3	4	5	6	7	8
Gross requirements		75	95	85	65	65	65	300	60
Scheduled receipts		20	80						
Planned order receipts		0	0	85	65	65	65	300	60
Balance on hand	70	15	0	0	0	0	0	0	0
Planned order release			85	65	65	65	300	60	

A planner using commercial software would see the initial computer screen to be like Table 11.5 rather than Tables 11.3 or 11.4 because the MRP assumes that the planner understands that the planner can override the system. Naive users, however, miss the point that the human is always in control and that the computer does not run the system but only suggests a good strategy. Daily changes in orders and production impact the system and cause the computer to revise the plans many times per day. This is called *system nervousness,* and it is a role of the planner to insulate other users from being confused by the dynamic, "nervous" nature of the system. Most software includes a *firm planned order* horizon within which the plan is locked in, and daily variables are not allowed to alter the agreed-upon plan.

A materials requirements plan is needed for each item in the master schedule. Table 11.6 is the MRP for product Y that follows from the master schedule. Tables 11.3 and 11.4 show that the *low-level codes* for products X and Y are zero, denoting that these are end items. The low-level code is defined as a component's structure level in the bill of materials; end items are level 0, parts comprising an end item are level 1, components of level 1 are level 2, and so on.

After the charts are prepared for all level 0 items, the planning proceeds to level 1 items, as shown in Table 11.7 for component C3. Because the bill of materials shows that each product X contains 2 of component C3, the planned order release of 85 units of X in week 2 becomes a gross requirement for 170 units of C3 in week 2, and so forth for each week. Similarly, each model Y product requires 2 of component C8 as shown in Table 11.8.

The gross requirements for component C4 in week 1 are 130 to build product Y; in week 2, they are 85 of C4 to build product X plus 300 to build product Y, totaling 385 of C4 in week 2, as shown in Table 11.9. The example illustrates the result of requiring a lot size minimum of 500 units each time that a shop order is released.

Table 11.10 illustrates a fractional quantity of component C5 per parent. For example, if string is purchased in spools of 1000 m and a 0.75-meter string is required for either model product, then the gross requirements for component C5 in week 2 are $0.75 * (300 + 86)$, or 288.8 m.

The planned order release of 1000 in week 5 illustrates that the planner may exercise judgment and not allow the planned balance on hand to fall to near zero despite a system policy of "no safety stock" programmed into the computer. Note here that most MRP software provides a unit-conversion option for actual ordering. In this case, if the planner uses that option, the planned order in week 5 would be displayed as 1 spool of string rather than 1000 m of string.

TABLE 11.6 MRP Model Y Product, Part 2

Low-level code 0
Lead time 1 week
Lot for lot
No safety stock

		Week							
	Past due	1	2	3	4	5	6	7	8
Gross requirements		350	200	300	300	300	100	50	0
Scheduled receipts		300							
Planned order receipts		0	130	300	300	300	100	50	0
Balance on hand	120	70	0	0	0	0	0	0	0
Planned order release		130	300	300	300	100	50		

TABLE 11.7   MRP Component Item C3 (Round End), Part 3

Low-level code 1
Lead time 1 week
Order lot for lot
No safety stock
Unit of measure, each

					Week				
	Past due	1	2	3	4	5	6	7	8
Gross requirements		0	170	130	130	130	600	120	0
Scheduled receipts									
Planned order receipts		0	160	130	130	130	600	120	0
Balance on hand	10	10	0	0	0	0	0	0	0
Planned order release		160	130	130	130	600	120		

TABLE 11.8   MRP Component Item C8 (Elliptical End), Part 8

Low-level code 1
Lead time 1 week
Order lot for lot
No safety stock
Unit of measure, each

					Week				
	Past due	1	2	3	4	5	6	7	8
Gross requirements		260	600	600	600	200	100	0	0
Scheduled receipts									
Planned order receipts		250	600	600	600	200	100	0	0
Balance on hand	10	0	0	0	0	0	0	0	0
Planned order release		600	600	600	200	100			

TABLE 11.9   MRP Component Item C4 (Center Peg), Part 4

Low-level code 1
Lead time 1 week
Order minimum 500
No safety stock
Unit of measure, each

					Week				
	Past due	1	2	3	4	5	6	7	8
Gross requirements		130	385	365	365	165	350	60	0
Scheduled receipts		500							
Planned order receipts			0	500	500	0	500	0	0
Balance on hand	120	490	105	240	375	210	360	300	300
Planned order release			500	500		500			

TABLE 11.10   MRP Component Item C5 (String, Spooled), Part 5

Low-level code 1
Lead time 1 week
Spool lot 1000 m
No safety stock
Unit of measure, m

					Week				
	Past due	1	2	3	4	5	6	7	8
Gross requirements		97.5	288.8	273.8	273.8	123.8	262.5	45	0
Scheduled receipts		20							
Planned order receipts		0	0	0	0	0	1000	0	0
Balance on hand	1350	1273	983.8	710	436.3	312.5	1050	1005	1005
Planned order release						1000			

In Table 11.11, the gross requirements for 760 of C6 in week 1 are caused by the planned order for 160 units of C3 plus 600 of C8. The gross requirements of level 2 items equal the planned orders for all level 1 parents of the component. The example assumes that C6 is a purchased item that is shipped in containers of 200.

It also illustrates the idea of expediting. The gross requirements in period 1 are greater than the availability, causing a planned order release to appear in the past-due column and a computer-generated message to expedite a purchase order for 600 units, in addition to the 200 already on order for delivery in week 1. In practice, this may cause an urgent call to the vendor to ship immediately 800 instead of 200, plus another 800 to arrive in week 2.

Table 11.12 illustrates fractional quantity-per for a component of the dowel stock. It is used in both end item X and end item Y at level 2, structured as a component of the center peg in each case (refer to the indented bill of materials in Table 11.1). A fraction of 1 length of dowel stock, 0.01, is cut off to make each center peg. Therefore, the quantity of dowels per center peg is stated as 0.01. Recall from the MRP in Table 11.9 for

TABLE 11.11   MRP Component Item C6 (Wood Block), Part 6

Low-level code 2
Lead time 1 week
Order multiples of 200
No safety stock
Unit of measure, each

					Week				
	Past due	1	2	3	4	5	6	7	8
Gross requirements		760	730	730	330	700	120	0	0
Scheduled receipts		200							
Planned order receipts		600	800	600	400	600	200	0	0
Balance on hand	60	100	170	40	110	10	90	90	90
Planned order release	600	800	600	400	600	200			10
Action Message: Expedite 600									

TABLE 11.12   MRP Component Item C7 (Dowel Stock), Part 7

Low-level code 2
Lead time 1 week
Order minimum 10
No safety stock
Unit of measure, each dowel
Yield, 100 cm per dowel

		Week							
	Past due	1	2	3	4	5	6	7	8
Gross requirements		0	5	5	0	5	0	0	0
Scheduled receipts		0							
Planned order receipts		0	10	0	0	10	0	0	0
Balance on hand	2	2	7	2	2	7	7	7	7
Planned order release		10			10				

the center peg that netting of requirements resulted in a planned order release of 500 in week 2 and 500 in week 3. These are multiplied by the quantity-per 0.01 and recorded in the gross requirements record for the dowel stock in weeks 2 and 3 as shown.

USE OF THE MRP OUTPUT INFORMATION

The MRP subtracts the available inventory, including on-hand and scheduled receipts, from the gross requirements to compute the net requirements. If the inventory data are wrong, then the calculated requirements are wrong and the errors are multiplied as the MRP is exploded down the bill of materials. Small data errors become large planning errors. The problem is difficult to manage because in practice it is difficult to achieve perfect inventory accuracy.

Inventory accuracy is often measured as the percent of items that are within a specified percentage tolerance of true balances. For example, if an "accurate count" consists of finding the actual inventory of a certain component within 1 percent of the data in the computer record and a random count of 100 part numbers finds 95 percent within 1 percent of predicted and 5 percent with larger error, then it is called "95 percent inventory accuracy."

A rule of thumb is that at least 95 percent accuracy is desired for effective MRP, while in practice many firms with MRP have great difficulty achieving anything near this level. Implementation of MRP usually begins with imposing strict physical controls on inventory and implementing a cycle-counting program to frequently count inventory, detect errors, find causes for errors, and improve controls in pursuit of eliminating causes for errors.

Pegging to Requirements

MRP enables management to respond to customer needs through the *pegging feature.* The illustration showed how gross requirements at each level are netted top-downward against on-hand inventory and scheduled receipts to compute the time-phased net requirements, which become the gross requirements for components one level lower in the bill of materials. The spreadsheets can also be traced bottom upward, known as *pegging*. At every level of the MRP explosion and netting, the requirements for components can be traced to their parents, and to higher parents, to determine which end item and customer order is causing which lower-level need. Thus, if an unavailability occurs for a raw material or component, the particular end order that is responsible for that component requirement can be traced. The relevant orders can thus be identified and deferred or expedited. Without MRP, "everything is late," and, lacking visibility, an order to replenish routine safety stock might share equal priority with a critical order to an important customer. With MRP, pegging provides the visibility to establish the correct priorities.

MRP AND THE MINIMIZING OF INVENTORY INVESTMENT

In principle, MRP is a lot-for-lot planning system that, if executed precisely, results in minimum inventory. The principles of MRP are consistent with just-in-time (JIT) and zero inventories (ZI), emphasizing minimal lot sizes and minimal safety stocks. MRP planning can be facilitated by production activity execution systems such as the Japanese *Kanban method.*

Cost relationships in Japan caused their industries to pursue policies of very frequent movement of small lots, with aggressive industrial engineering cost reductions, especially for model-change and setup costs. Common practice in the United States has generally emphasized calculating trade-offs among setup costs, holding costs, and stockout costs. This has caused firms to produce in batches based on lot-sizing formulas and to employ safety stocks instead of producing piece by piece or lot for lot.

Inventories are generally classed as being subject to independent demand at the finished-goods level, and dependent demand at all levels below that of end item. When MRP is integrated with distribution requirements planning, a DRP system has the effect of moving independent demand out to the distribution points nearest to the customers and creating dependent demand within the supply chain back to the master schedule and to the MRP. With DRP and MRP integrated, there may be little or no independent demand directly impacting the MRP.

Lot Sizing in MRP

The use of lot-sizing formulas within MRP software is purely optional, and they should be used properly and with discretion. Too many people in industry still believe that MRP is necessarily associated with producing in large lots or batches, resulting in excessive inventory. Most MRP software includes the option of specifying the time period of supply and the option of accumulating orders into lots. These options are useful in simplifying the ordering process for small, inexpensive category C items such as floor stock fasteners. (The designation of "category C" is from the ABC Pareto classification system.)

If lot sizing is not imposed upon the calculations, then the MRP computes net planned orders lot for lot, meaning just in time within the definition of the planning time bucket. Much study, mostly among academicians, has been devoted to how to best override the MRP lot for lot so as to combine the materials requirements over time into batch lots. The usual logic is to trade off holding costs against setup costs, perhaps also considering stock-out costs, by using various algorithms. An operations research method called *dynamic programming* in the form of the *Wagner-Whiten algorithm* is capable of an optimal solution to specific ideal data that are static in time. For real systems, simpler algorithms such as *part-period balancing* or others described by Orlicky (1975) are included in standard MRP software.

Users of the lot-sizing algorithms should recognize that the formulas like Wagner-Whiten or part-period balancing do not consider major costs such as work center congestion, expediting, queues of work-in-process inventory, customer service, and other factors that in total may be much more costly or important than setup and holding costs. People are still busy devising methods for multilevel lot sizing within MRP based on the oversimplified costs of replenishment, stock-out, and holding costs because the most important costs are difficult to measure and vary by company and situation. The manager should generally place little faith in lot-sizing formulas, especially those included in MRP software that the users are accepting on faith.

Another problem with lot-sizing algorithms in MRP is that the optimal lot size for parent items will likely result in nonoptimal lot sizes for components and vice versa. Again, when costs other than setup and holding are considered, the cost trade-offs can become very complex.

The result is that one should be skeptical of the lot sizes that may be computed by the MRP software. Management should have clear reasons for departing from lot-for-lot materials planning. A wiser philosophy is to adhere to the MRP logic of lot-for-lot production unless another action is clearly justified, and to pursue a just-in-time policy. A managerial philosophy of just in time tries to drive down setup costs and manage stock-out costs and so drives lot sizes toward lot for lot, and to a lot size of one, consistent with the basic MRP output.

Safety Stocks

Safety Stocks for Dependent-Demand Items.   As a general rule, safety stock should not be carried on dependent-demand items and planned with MRP. There are occasional exceptions such as items subject to difficult supply, quality problems, loss, theft, or similar causes of undependable availability. Such problems should be resolved by management action so that safety stocks can be eliminated. Eliminating safety stocks for dependent-demand items is a major advantage of using MRP, which reduces inventory investment.

Older references assumed that safety stocks for dependent-demand items should be based upon the same cost trade-offs as for independent demand: replenishment, stock-out, and holding costs. However, experience with MRP has shown that cost savings and profit opportunities occur that are much more important than trading off holding versus stock-out costs. These savings include the benefits of less facility congestion, reduced expediting, improved customer and supplier coordination, improved response flexibility, improved quality control, reduced investment in working capital, and other benefits that are not accounted for in theoretical formulas.

Because MRP provides the visibility to know how much stock is actually needed, it is better practice to reestimate demand frequently, maintain a realistic master schedule, focus on data accuracy, execute the MRP schedules, and depend less on safety stocks. The idea is that effective planning diminishes forecasting errors and thus the need for safety stocks.

Overplanning.   When safety stocks appear to be necessary within MRP, the computational logic of MRP includes a method called *overplanning* to create the effect of safety stocks without actually carrying safety stocks. In overplanning, the random fluctuation of demand for an item and all of its components is buffered within the gross requirements instead of with the use of safety stocks. The effect of overplanning is analogous to maintaining safety stocks by creating a calibrated amount of buffer inventory, but the advantage in overplanning is that the buffer inventory is dynamically keyed to the master schedule, which exploits the MRP logic to rapidly consume the excess inventory.

To understand overplanning, note that the customary practice of specifying the demand for each period by a single number is statistically incorrect; instead, each forecast should be expressed as the mean and standard deviation of the forecast.

To illustrate, assume in Table 11.13 that the gross requirements for periods 5 through 8 are composed of a forecast of 80 units for each period plus firm customer orders of 60 units in period 5, 50 units in period 6, 40 units in period 7, and 10 units in period 8. The forecast was simplistically stated to be 80 units per period, ignoring the standard deviation of the forecast. Assume that the forecast had a standard deviation of 5 units. In other words, the 95 percent confidence limits of the forecast were 70 to 90 units per period ("plus or minus two sigmas"). This implies that the gross requirements should be restated to be between 130 and 150 units in period 5, and between 120 and 140 units in period 6, 100 to 120 in period 7, and 80 to 100 in period 8.

Because the gross requirements in Table 11.13 failed to account for the standard deviation of forecasts, it failed to account for the likelihood that the gross requirements in each period were understated, and this error will likely result in stock-outs unless safety stocks are carried. To illustrate overplanning for the example in Table 11.13, assume that the target service level is 99.5 percent, meaning a 0.05 percent chance of stock-out, thus implying that there is a 99.0 percent probability that the actual demand in period 5 will be between 125 and 155 (plus or minus 3 sigmas, with sigma equal to 5 units). Demand is calculated similarly for the other periods as shown in Table 11.14.

At first glance, comparing the actual requirements shown in Table 11.14 with the numbers in Table 11.13, it looks like the gross requirements are overstated in every period, which might cause a huge buildup in inventory. However, a buildup does not happen because the MRP time-phased logic does not release all planned orders at once. Instead, if the planned order of 155 is released and the actual demand for that time bucket turns out to be only 130, then $155 - 130 = 25$ units, which shows up as excess scheduled receipts to be netted out against the gross requirements for period 6. This reduces the planned orders release of period 3 to $145 - 25 = 120$ to maintain a 99.5 percent service level. The MRP update for each successive period works the same way, and the safety stock is used up and reestimated with each planned order release.

Overplanning creates the effect of safety stock down the bill of materials to the sum of the lead times of all of the components of the parent that is overplanned. The total amount of buffer inventory remains under the control of the master scheduler and "dissolves away" when the master planner ceases to overplan.

TABLE 11.13   Table of Forecasts Plus Firm Orders

Lead time = 3

Time period	1	2	3	4	5	6	7	8
Gross requirements					140	130	110	90
Scheduled receipts								
On hand								
Planned orders		140	130	110	90			

TABLE 11.14   Overplanning Gross Requirements

Lead time = 3

Time period	1	2	3	4	5	6	7	8
Gross requirements					155	145	125	105
Scheduled receipts								
On hand								
Planned orders		155	145	125	105			

Push and Pull

A concept related to lot sizing is the meaning of the popular but ambiguous terms *push* and *pull*. Oliver Wight (1974) used *pull* to refer to the "bad" practices caused by lack of planning in the pre-MRP environment. Starting about 1980, some articles written about Japanese management techniques and Kanban systems defined *pull* as execution techniques that can lead to reduced inventories. Confusion thus arose, with *pull* going from "bad" to "good," and *push,* according to some writers going from "good" to "bad." A popular book on DRP defined DRP as a *push system,* leading to confusion by takers of APICS certification examinations who had been taught that DRP is *good* and *pull* is good, therefore DRP cannot be "push."

Presently, there seem to be two major meanings. In one context, *push* implies centralized decision making and *pull* implies decentralized decision making. Thus, planning (including MRP/CRP) is "push," and execution (including shop floor stock movement) is "pull." In another context, *push* means "supply" and *pull* means "demand." Because it is difficult to balance supply with demand, which means that some inventory usually is needed, some practitioners use *push* to mean production activity control with excess supply, larger lot sizes, queued work centers, and minimal idleness of capacity. These practitioners use *pull* to mean minimal supply, small lot sizes, unqueued work centers, and more occasions of idle capacity. The lot-sizing policies will affect the amount of work-in-process and the balances of capacity utilization. These are cost trade-offs that require management to study and make policy decisions for each MRP II environment.

In summary, so much confusion has arisen over the terms *push* and *pull* that it seems preferable to not use either term and to instead think in terms of *centralized* versus *decentralized planning* and in terms of *demand-driven* versus *supply-driven execution.*

INFORMATION OUTPUTS FROM THE MRP/CRP CALCULATIONS

A wealth of information useful to managers, employees, customers, and suppliers is automatically generated from the MRP/CRP planning run. This information is readily accessible, on-line, throughout the company and is the result of relatively few data inputs. If the more comprehensive MRP II approach is used, the scope of the information produced and its value to the firm is even more significant.

An important output of an MRP system includes complete information on current inventory balances, demand requirements, planned orders, open-order status, and recommended order action. This is available for all manufactured and purchased items throughout the planning horizon. This information is used to release and control orders. This activity is discussed in detail in the following section on *order action.*

Another very important function is communication with the firm's customers. When a customer calls to inquire about placing a new order or to check on an existing order for a product, service part, or accessory, the information is readily available from an on-line computer. The customer service representative can call up the item immediately on an inquiry screen to answer questions on the phone about availability of products or parts or about current schedule dates. This is done with consistent reliability. The ability to provide customers with quick and reliable information builds trust and confidence among the customers. This is one of the most meaningful benefits of an MRP system.

Some companies, particularly those that serve other manufacturers as *original equipment manufacturers* (OEMs), allow customers access to the manufacturing database through direct data communications. This is usually accomplished via modems and telephone lines, with the customers also using terminals at their own site. Such systems can also utilize touch-tone phones and voice response. Inventory data and other information are available to the customer on-line, and often customers enter orders directly. In general, this is known as *electronic data interchange* (EDI). The MRP database provides complete and timely data for this function.

The database also contains a requirements plan for all purchased materials. This information can be provided to suppliers to help them in their scheduling and capacity planning. It can also be used for negotiating long-term just-in-time contracts with suppliers. EDI can be used for communication with suppliers as well as customers.

Factory personnel are able to access information regarding open and planned orders, upcoming workloads, and the location and inventory status of needed items. This helps in meeting schedules and planning factory direct labor personnel levels and overtime. Maintenance personnel can access information that enables them to schedule preventive equipment maintenance with a minimum of downtime.

Sales personnel can inquire about items available to promise for customers and about the availability of options and accessories. In a make-to-order environment, sales engineers can check the available-to-promise capacity for quoted orders.

Financial planning personnel have ready access to the cash required to support the current production plan. Accountants have timely information on both historical and projected costs for all manufactured components, assemblies, products, and all purchased items. This information is generated from the cost roll-up function in MRP. This processing begins with purchased items at the lowest levels of the bill of materials and sums direct material (purchase) costs, direct labor costs, and any overhead costs used clear to the end item at the top. The component costs and totals are stored in the database at each level. As a result, all purchased and manufactured raw materials, parts, assemblies, and end products have a readily accessible cost structure. Often, more than one category of cost is used, and standard and actual costs are the two basic categories. Many software packages offer more than two.

The more comprehensive MRP II approach yields information for long-term capital planning for factory equipment, warehouse, and office facility requirements. It also provides information that helps in planning indirect labor and office staff requirements.

MRP Order Action

At the heart of the materials requirements planning process is the planning, release, and control of orders for manufactured and purchased items. After the MRP planning run, or "explosion," has been executed and planned orders have been generated for all items, the order review and release process can begin.

Historically, the planned order releases that were generated were distributed to planners in hard-copy form once per week (weekly MRP explosion) or each morning (daily MRP explosion). The computer output for the manufactured items went to the production control analysts, and the output for the purchased items went to the buyers or purchase planning analysts. Today, most software provides this information on-line via a video-display terminal with hard copy available on demand. Voice communication with the computer is also coming into use as a very efficient way to access information and perform certain transactions. While the weekly replanning run may be sufficient for some products, most companies today do daily (overnight) replanning or use the transaction-driven replanning option available in many MRP software packages.

Transaction-driven replanning explodes or replans all component items in a bill of materials on a real-time basis. Any time a transaction affects materials records in such a way as to require replanning, the replanning is done immediately by such methods as recalculation using an electronic spreadsheet. It is interesting to note that Joseph Orlicky, when he developed MRP in the early 1960s, originally envisioned MRP as a real-time, transaction-driven replanning process. Only in recent years with increased hardware processing speeds, more sophisticated software, and highly trained users has this become possible.

In any case, each user company must select a replanning frequency, from among the several options, that is appropriate for managing their products and components. Whatever the frequency of the replanning calculation, each item is assigned to an individual responsible for planning the item. A very small company may have only one or two planners. A large company may have several large departments of planners. In this case each planner is assigned a logical group of items (e.g., machined parts, subassembly, raw steel materials, or electrical parts). A number or name on the item master file, usually referred to as *planner number,* keys the item to a particular planner. This allows the MRP software to sort and display the items for the individual to whom they are assigned. Of course, any item can be accessed at any time by anyone if a need to do so arises.

After each planning cycle, the planner logs on to the system and brings up the requirements display screen. This is typically done each morning or at some designated time during the day. In most MRP software the requirements display screen for an item would be in the vertical format as shown in Table 11.15.

The prior examples in this chapter are shown in horizontal display format (time periods from left to right). This format is preferable for showing the MRP computations for instructional purposes. In actual practice, the vertical display format shown in this section is usually used. This allows up and down scrolling of requirement records throughout the planning horizon which many users find convenient to use. Some software packages do offer the horizontal display option as well.

In Table 11.15, the first gross requirement for a manufactured FRAME, MOTOR, A3, item 10175, is 22 units shown on 9/11/95. It is covered with a scheduled receipt (open shop order) for 22 units. The next gross requirement for 36 units is not yet covered. The projected start date that MRP has calculated for this order is 9/14/95, which is within the 5-day order review horizon window. Therefore, MRP has generated an action message to release (*REL) an order to cover it. The only order action required today for this item is to release an order for 36 units with a start date of 9/14/95 and a due date of 9/19/95. Note that orders are planned to cover only the requirement with no safety stock or lot sizing. In MRP this is known as *lot-for-lot ordering.* The item has a lead time of 3 days. Therefore, a due date of 9/19/95 has been offset 3 working days (not including the weekend) to determine that 9/14/95 is the start date. The software uses the 5-day order review horizon to generate order action messages today for all activity required during the 5 days following today's date. This is a parameter set by the planner or company policy. If we expand the planning horizon to 10 days, then a message would appear to release the 30-unit order to start 9/18/95, 3 days ahead of the 9/21/95 due date. With the 5-day order review horizon, the planner will not see this action message until 5 days have passed.

TABLE 11.15 Item MRP Requirements Display

Item: 10175
Desc: Frame, Motor, A3
Date: 09/08
OH Bal: 0
Lot size: 0
LLC: 1
Order review horizon: 5
Manufactured item lead time: 3
Safety stock: 0
Customer allocations: 0
Production allocations: 0

Date	Gross requirements	Scheduled receipts	Projected OH	Net required	Planned order receipts	Planned order releases	Order action
09/11	22	22	0	0	0	0	
09/19	36	0	0	36	36	36	*REL Start 09/14
09/21	30	0	0	30	30	30	Start 09/18
09/25	50	0	0	50	50	50	Start 09/20
10/18	30	0	0	30	30	30	Start 10/13
11/07	54	0	0	54	54	54	Start 11/02

Function keys:
Order release/review: F1   Peg to: F2   Next item: F3   Firm: F4   Page forward: F5   Quit: F6

Note that the MRP explosion has generated four additional planned orders shown on the screen. Paging forward to subsequent displays with the F5 function key would reveal additional planned orders as far out as the item has been planned throughout the planning horizon. The length of the planning horizon is set by the company using the software and typically would be in the range of 6 months to 2 years. The planner could firm up or release any of these planned orders if there were a specific reason to do so. Ordinarily orders are not released unless they come into the order review horizon. Orders released too early can result in excess inventory and other problems due to bill of materials changes, inventory adjustments, and so on. The orders may have to be modified or canceled and re-released if changes occur.

Often, planners elect to look at items by exception only. That is, on a given day, they routinely review only those items that have action messages in the order review horizon. Of course, any item can be called up at any time if necessary. Action messages are typically expedite, release, change, and cancel.

Assume that the planner decides to release the planned order for 36 units of the component. This is accomplished on most systems by calling up an order release display and reviewing the shop order. In the example, the F1 function key would be used to switch to the order release screen. All defaults should be on the display as in Table 11.16.

Note that the standard single-level bill of materials is read automatically from the database and displayed as the pick list. The standard routing is also read from the data-

TABLE 11.16   Shop Orders Release Display

Item: 10175
Desc: Frame, Motor, A3
Shop order number: 29546
Order quantity: 36
Start date: 09/14
Due date: 09/19
Order status: Planned
Pick list:

Item	Description	Quantity required	UM	Status code
10137	Base, frame	36	In	00
11286	Weldment, frame, side	72	Ea	00
10291	Screw, adjusting, frame	36	Ea	00

			Routing operations					
Operator	Department	Work center	Operation description	Std setup	Time run	Action setup	Time run	Status code
01	254	21	Assemble	2.30	42.72	0.00	0.00	00
02	276	03	Paint	0.10	3.30	0.00	0.00	00

Function keys:
Release order: F1   Return to requirements: F2   Change order: F3

base if routings are used. The dates and quantities are taken from MRP. Any of these data can be changed for this particular order if the planner decides to do so.

For a standard order release or after modification of the order, the planner need only touch the F1 key. The order for 36 units would be changed from planned to released status. The hard-copy shop order (or just a small card with a turnaround number in a "paperless" system) would be printed for distribution to the shop personnel. The on-line display of the open shop order would be available for all authorized personnel. Labor and materials may now be charged against the order until it is closed. The order would become a part of the prioritized departmental dispatch lists, also available on-line, after a shop rescheduling program is run (usually run with MRP).

If a shop floor just-in-time execution system featuring a visual record system—such as Kanban and manufacturing cells—is in place, procedures would vary somewhat. One advantage of these systems is that they usually have fewer "pay points" from which cost and movement data are reported back to the MRP database. They are also largely self-supporting once "primed" by incoming purchased materials and product schedules. Fewer, if any, actual MRP orders as described above need be generated to drive the system. As cost and movement data are reported from those fewer pay points, the MRP-generated shop schedule plays the important role of a plan against which execution is measured as opposed to actually driving it each step of the way.

Purchase orders and releases for suppliers are handled in a manner similar to that described for shop orders. The purchased materials planner views the requirements screen, heeds the action messages and any late-breaking information, and then releases, changes, cancels, or expedites quantities with suppliers accordingly. All companies will use the same basic procedures whether or not they practice just-in-time purchasing procedures. With just-in-time purchasing, the quantities are "releases" against long-term supplier agreements as opposed to complete purchase orders. Also, the order policy parameters in MRP are adjusted to reflect the smaller quantities and more frequent deliveries associated with just-in-time purchasing.

For an experienced planner working with well-designed MRP software, the entire process of order review and release may take only a few seconds for each item if the release follows the system recommendation for dates and quantity and uses the standard bill of materials and routing. MRP users find this is the case with the majority of items. If there are special problems such as shortages or late orders, additional time is required to analyze the situation and determine a course of action as in the following example.

Having completed the FRAME, MOTOR, A3 item review for the day, and probably for the next several days, the planner goes on to the next item. Software packages offer a variety of sequences in which items can be reviewed. Among those are item number order, description in alphabetic order, commodity type, supplier, purchase agreement number, shop department and work center, and type and date of action messages.

In this case, the next item for order release and review is the SCREW, ADJUSTING, FRAME, item 10291, shown in Table 11.17. This item has both independent demand by customers and dependent demand from more than one parent item. A safety stock of 200 is planned so that customer service orders can be filled and shipped immediately. The item happens to be a component of the motor frame just reviewed (see pick list in Table 11.16). Of the 95 units required on 9/14, 36 will be required for the shop order just released for the motor frame. But there is a more immediate concern with this item. As can be seen in Table 11.17, this is not a standard order release action. There are some special problems with the SCREW, ADJUSTING, FRAME requirements.

During the MRP planning run, all of the requirement sources are automatically consolidated according to order policy parameters established for the item. Forty units are allocated for customers, and 68 are allocated for production of parent items. *Allocated items* are those items required for open orders but not yet physically picked from the on-hand inventory. On-hand inventory is only 40 units, well below safety stock. There could be many causes for this low quantity such as an unusually high service demand or scrapped or lost parts. In any case, the planner is faced with an immediate shortage that needs to be filled inside the normal order lead time of 2 days. This has resulted in an expedite action and past-due message. Most critical are the 40 + 68, or 108, units required for customers and production. It is also important to replenish the 200 units for safety stock for future service demand, but this will take a lower priority. So, the 108 allocated units plus the 200 safety shown represent a gross requirement of 308 units. This amount less the 40 units on hand results in a net requirement of 268 units, needed now. The immediate need is indicated to the planner by the Expedite (compress lead time) and Past due (late) messages. In addition, there is a normal order release for 100 units within the planning horizon.

Note that lot sizing comes into play in this case. A multiple of 100 units has been determined because of processing requirements; so all orders are in multiples of 100. Also, the calculation convention used in this example for projected on-hand balance assumes that the order action indicated will be taken—that is, the planned orders will be released as indicated to fill the requirement. Safety stock is also used in the calculation of net requirements so that the projected on-hand balance is always at or above safety stock. Some systems handle these calculations slightly differently, but any MRP system will provide the same planned orders for release given the same gross requirements and planning parameters for the item.

The analyst's objective is to fill the shortage as quickly as possible and keep all production and service requirements on schedule. There are a number of ways to accom-

TABLE 11.17   Item MRP Requirements Display

Item: 10291
Desc: Screw, adjusting, frame
Date: 09/08
OH Bal: 40
Lot size: 0
LLC: 2
Order review horizon: 5
Manufactured item lead time: 2
Safety stock: 200
Customer allocations: 40
Production allocations: 68

Date	Gross requirements	Scheduled receipts	Projected OH	Net required	Planned order receipts	Planned order releases	Order action
Allocated	108						
Safety	200						
09/11	308	0	−268	268	300	300	*Rel
							* Expedite
							*Past due
09/12			232				
09/14	95	0	237	63	100	100	*Rel
							Start
							09/12
09/18	230	0	207	193	200	200	Start
							09/14
09/20	50	0	257	43	100	100	Start
							09/18
10/13	145	0	212	88	100	100	Start
							10/11
10/26	10	0	202	0	0	0	

Function keys:
Order release/review: F1   Peg to: F2   Next item: F3   Firm: F4   Page forward: F5   Quit: F6

plish this. While specific procedures may vary from company to company, following are steps that may be used:

1. Check the requirements display(s) for the component(s) of the SCREW, ADJUSTING, FRAME to determine stock available for SCREW, ADJUSTING, FRAME production. If stock is available, release an expedite order to replenish. Communicate with the factory personnel on this. Overtime may need to be scheduled.

2. Use the pegging option to check the parent of the component to see if there is any additional stock that can be "borrowed" temporarily to meet production requirements. Availability of parents of those items can subsequently be pegged in the same manner, working up through the bill of materials to the top. Ordinarily there would not be any safety stock unless some of the items were stocked service items.

3. If it is not possible to fulfill production and current customer requirements with the stock in-house, it may be necessary to contact suppliers and determine if the needed components can be brought in on an expedited basis.

4. Expediting is essentially compressing lead times. Lead times usually have some flexibility throughout the purchasing and production process. With an MRP database the information is readily available to identify points in the process where lead times need to be and can be compressed to meet the service and production schedules. In this case, lead time of the SCREW, ADJUSTING, FRAME itself, its components, or its parent items at some level above may need to be compressed. In the short term this is usually accomplished by rescheduling component items and arranging for overtime.

5. If all else fails, the master schedule dates for the service items and end products may have to be rescheduled forward. This means that customer items will be delivered later than promised, but if it is not done, the master schedule will be overstated.

There is nothing new about borrowing from service stocks or releasing expedite orders with the factory or with suppliers. With the MRP database, however, these functions can be done quickly in an orderly, managed fashion. Proper communications are accomplished on a timely basis, with everyone in the company working on-line with the same data. Whatever action is taken will be "cleaned up" automatically by the next MRP planning run. Any borrowed items or shortages will have new requirements generated, and any overages will be carried forward for future use.

Policies and procedures should be in place for each user company to govern the responses to problems. Usually, production control analysts and purchasing analysts can solve minor rescheduling problems and communicate with the factory about schedule changes and overtime to correct them so that products stay on schedule. If major changes arise, particularly those involving the master production schedule, the analyst is usually required to consult with the supervisor.

With up-to-date MRP software, the entire order release process can be automated to any degree as decided upon by the firm. Some companies choose to automatically release manufacturing and purchase orders on the date calculated by MRP. Others prefer review by an analyst prior to release. Today's software offers a variety of options.

PRODUCTION ACTIVITY CONTROL

The results of MRP are used by production control personnel to release orders to the shop floor. They are also used by purchasing analysts or buyers to release orders to suppliers. This order release and communications process can be automated to varying degrees, of course. The procedures may vary according to the shop floor execution system, such as the Kanban system.

In addition to the day-to-day process of order release, the MRP system can be used to provide medium- and long-term projections in the form of "planned orders." This information can be provided to suppliers to help them plan their production. It is important to note the old adage regarding the use of computers, "garbage in, garbage out." That is, the orders released and the schedules provided using MRP are only as good as the accuracy and integrity of the source data files the system uses for information. After scheduling comes rescheduling. In this step, the speed and accuracy advantages of the computer are most important. MRP software can recalculate the entire schedule in a relatively short time when changes occur in the master production schedule or the bill of materials, and as inventory recounts are done, and as scrap is reported. Production planners and buyers can act on the newly modified schedule and continue to meet planned product completion dates.

CAPACITY REQUIREMENTS PLANNING

The MRP provides a basis for planning other direct manufacturing parameters. People responsible for managing the shop floor need to know more than just the projected start dates and due dates for component parts and assemblies, or the daily rates of production of these. They need to have a reasonably accurate projection of other resources as well. Of these, manufacturing capacity is probably the most important. Capacity is usually measured in terms of either machine-hours or labor-hours. Both measures are used in many companies depending upon the particular operation being considered.

If we know the projected start date and due date for a given item, we know the time period during which we expect that item to be on the production floor. We know the projected quantity: how many are to be produced during that time frame. We need one additional factor: the hours of machine time per unit or labor-hours per unit. These can be provided from measured time standards, historical production records, estimates, or even reasonable guesstimates. Most companies have this information in one form or another so it is a simple matter to perform a multiplication and determine how many hours are required in a given time frame, say, a day or week, for that item. If we sum this for all of the items scheduled in the MRP, we have a total machine-hour or labor-hour requirement for the company. This can be projected in, for example, a bar-graph format showing total labor-hours required per day. Dividing by the average number of direct labor-hours per employee converts the graph to reflect the projected number of employees required. Other calculations can be done to determine overtime hours required at a given employment level and so on. This is very useful information for the plant management staff.

A routing or operations file needs to be in place to carry the capacity planning process to a work center or work cell level. This file contains a sequential series of production operations associated with each manufactured part or assembly. Using these data, the capacity planning calculation above can be performed for each work cell or work center. This will provide the first-line supervisor with useful short-term information to help in planning overtime and staffing. The logic provides a tool to plan scheduled downtime and maintenance and for moving or replacing shop equipment. Major facilities expansions or change can also be planned with the aid of MRP.

SYSTEMS CLASSES AND CONFIGURATIONS

MRP and MRP II systems can be classified in many ways. The most important overall classifications for the user are the type of product, service, and process to which the software is geared and the capacity of the available hardware systems for industries of various sizes. In outline form, we can classify by type of product, service, and process:

I. *Discrete manufacturing.* There are four categories, characterized by discrete, countable products and component parts:
   A. *Project.* One-at-a-time major projects such as construction, shipbuilding, and design of a new product.
   B. *Job shop.* Often a subcontract business that produces, traditionally in batch lots or job lots, a variety of individual parts and assemblies for, and designed by, other companies. Quantities may be ones or twos, or in the thousands or more.
   C. *Engineer to order or make to order.* Products designed and made to customer order and which therefore have some or a great deal of customizing such as special-purpose machine tools. Components are often produced in an in-house job shop environment.

D. *Repetitive.* Products produced in high volume from a standardized set of parts such as automobiles, appliances, and consumer electronics products. Usually associated with make-to-stock products that are forecasted.

II. *Continuous or process manufacturing.* Characterized by wet or dry product flow measurable by weight or volume. Examples are chemical and petroleum production and the early stages of food and paper processing.

III. *Service industry.* Characterized by providing a service that involves the expenditure of labor and/or the use of equipment to perform a task without a physical product delivered to the customer.

MRP and MRP II software may be designed primarily for use in one specific application, or they may be flexible enough to cover more than one. There are many packages that are specifically designed for project, job shop, make to order, repetitive, continuous process, and service operations. The job shop, make-to-order, repetitive, and continuous process operations are specifically MRP applications. Because many companies have some combination of job shop, make-to-order, and repetitive products there are comprehensive MRP software packages designed to accommodate all three. Continuous process MRP software is often found in a package separate from the others.

Project management software may be called *program evaluation and review techniques* (PERT) or *critical path method* (CPM), and operations software for service companies may have other names. Nearly all of these scheduling systems use the linked-network, time-phased planning logic that is the essence of MRP. PERT and CPM use nodes in place of items and activities in place of manufacturing operations and purchasing lead times, but the scheduling logic is basically the same as MRP.

There are three broad categories of hardware systems to support the MRP and MRP II software offerings:

1. *Microcomputers (PCs) and microcomputer networks.* These are used by smaller companies as the main data processing system. The network consists of a *file server* that is itself a microcomputer with a large data storage capacity and one or more microcomputers linked to the file server. Those additional microcomputers are located where needed throughout the company and act as stand-alone processors for the users as well as providing access to the central database on the file server. The MRP planning run can be done on the file server or on any designated microcomputer on the network.

2. *Minicomputers.* A larger company with more processing requirements may require a minicomputer as the main data processing unit. This offers greater processing speed, more main memory storage, and more secondary or disk storage than a PC network. PCs and PC networks can be linked to the minicomputers for *distributed processing.* When using a minicomputer the MRP planning run is done on the central minicomputer itself.

3. *Mainframes.* The largest companies may require a mainframe computer to meet their data processing needs. These are the most powerful of business application computers. They have processing speeds and data storage capacity far greater than minicomputers. Minicomputers, PCs, and PC networks can be linked to the mainframe for distributed processing. When using a mainframe, the MRP planning run is usually done on the mainframe itself. Companies requiring mainframe computers usually have multiple plants so that upper-level planning functions are sometimes done on the mainframe with requirements and then transmitted to the plants. The plants can then run an MRP plan for the items for which they are responsible.

The critical measures for selecting the appropriate hardware platform(s) and configuration are as follows:

1. Sizes of files, particularly the item master, bill of materials, routing, materials requirements, open-order operations, open-order materials, supplier files, and additional files required to support accounting, sales, distribution requirements and other functions

2. The expected number of users on the system from all departments at average and peak times

3. The number of transactions occurring each day during average and peak times for both inquiry and maintenance categories

4. Realistic future projections for all three of the above items

Table 11.18 summarizes the classes of MRP systems and gives an example of how a particular software package might look. It illustrates a typical MRP software package that provides for job shop, make-to-order, and repetitive manufacturing functions. It is available for either a microcomputer or minicomputer as the primary processing platform.

TABLE 11.18   Scheduling Software Analysis

	Primary processing platform		
Type of business	Microcomputer	Minicomputer	Mainframe
Project			
Job shop	X	X	
Make to order	X	X	
Repetitive	X	X	
Continuous process			
Service			

COMPUTER SOFTWARE SELECTION PROCEDURES FOR MRP

A wide variety of MRP and MRP II software is available in the marketplace. Many software companies offer complete production, operations, and financial management software packages. These include separate modules for MRP, inventory management, purchasing, production activity control, capacity planning, product definition (bills of materials and routings), order entry, distribution requirements planning (DRP), and others. They also include several modules to serve sales, engineering, accounting, and financial planning needs. These modules are often sold separately and can be installed at different times. Some modules are prerequisite for others. For example, inventory management and bill of materials modules are required, at minimum, before the MRP module can be used.

One task of prime importance is to choose a package of modules that provides a best fit for the organization. This alone is a major task and should be done carefully and methodically. From the 1970s through the early 1980s this was about all that was required for selection because there were fewer software packages. A specific software package ran on only one, or on a very limited number, of hardware platforms, and so selecting the software pretty much determined the hardware. Many of the packages were offered by companies that marketed both the software and the hardware. The offering of the complete hardware-software package is known as *bundling*. The hardware was typically a minicomputer for smaller companies and a mainframe computer for larger organizations.

Minicomputer models are now far more powerful in speed and memory capacity than the mainframes of only a few years ago. Powerful microcomputers (PCs) are networked together with a file server computer, providing users with processing power as well as central database access at relatively low cost. There has been a proliferation of software packages, with many designed specifically for particular types of operations such as repetitive manufacturing, job shops, process industries, and service industries. Many of these packages are "unbundled" from hardware—that is, they will run on a large number of different hardware platforms. This has been made possible by the introduction of new operating software that provides a very flexible interface between the hardware platform and the applications (MRP, etc.) software. Flexible hardware and software combinations are often referred to as *open systems*. For example, one operating software package that makes this possible is UNIX. Systems that use this software are often referred to as *UNIX-based open systems*.

This additional flexibility has made selecting a system somewhat more complicated, but the competition among hardware and software firms has also provided a price negotiation advantage for purchasers. If a company chooses unbundled software, the price of which can usually be negotiated, then there is a large number of hardware platforms from which to choose. This puts the system purchaser in the driver's seat during price negotiation for hardware and service contracts. Also, open systems make it possible to change from one hardware platform to another in the future, without a change in applications software. For those choosing a firm offering both hardware and software, that bundled package may have to be discounted significantly to compete. An advantage of the bundled approach is there is only one company to call if there is a problem, eliminating "finger-pointing" among supplying firms.

An additional consideration is the inclusion of a variety of user tools in today's software offerings. In general, these tools allow users, non-dataprocessing managers and practitioners who use the system regularly, to adapt the system to their needs. They can access the company database—if the security password permits for those data, of course—and design their own reports, screen displays, calculations, and comparisons and even add new data. This is accomplished through two general approaches, query programs and fourth-generation languages.

Query tools provide a simple way for users to quickly design custom reports and screen displays. Fields can be selected from the database, logical and arithmetic operations can be done in these fields, and the resulting information can be displayed, printed, or provided in synthesized voice output. *Fourth-generation languages* provide the more sophisticated user with an efficient tool to modify and tailor the software to better fit company needs. This avoids the tedious and time-consuming process in the data processing department of designing and programming software modifications with third-generation languages such as COBOL, PL-1, and RPG. One of the benefits of using these tools is reduced staffing requirements in data processing. The only caution is that the new tools may not be as efficient from a processing standpoint. But there is a considerable savings in development time, and users can get the information they need quickly. Data processing people can use the tools also, but, however they are used, policies, procedures, and controls governing their use should be in place.

Given these considerations, the steps for system selection, in broad terms, should be as follows:

1. Determine and document the organization's software requirements in terms of current and future needs. Consider interfaces between the MRP and MRP II system and

CAD/CAM, DRP, financial planning, accounting, order entry, quality management, and other software applications used by the company.

2. The most important consideration remains as always: selecting a software package that best fits those needs in unmodified form, often referred to as *vanilla form*. (See the section on rating MRP systems for details on this process.) In addition, consideration needs to be given to the capability of user tools and other methods of modifying the system, such as data processing support and outside programming services.

3. If an unbundled or open systems approach is used, select a hardware system that offers good reliability, service, and an upward migration path for growth. Current and projected data storage capacity needs, number of users, transaction volumes, and other processing requirements will dictate hardware specifications. A microcomputer network may be sufficient, or perhaps the more powerful minicomputer or mainframe will be required.

4. Provide for adequate education and training for users before and during implementation of the new system. (See the section on training and managing MRP users.)

A team of key employees should be selected to perform these steps. All user departments should be represented, such as accounting, sales, data processing, engineering, quality assurance, manufacturing, materials management, purchasing, distribution, and service. Ideally, people with professional certification in areas relating to resource management and computer systems should be part of the team. Examples of qualifications are the APICS certification, CPIM; purchasing, CPM; accounting, CPA or CMA; and professional data processing certification. It is often advisable to engage a consultant to guide the team through the process. The consultant should be experienced and knowledgeable in system selection and have a reputation for being independent and objective.

RATING MRP SYSTEMS

A formal rating system should be used when examining various MRP and MRP II software packages. The objective of the first phase is to narrow the choice of software packages to the few that will likely be suitable for your company. Basic questions at this first step are, Is the package geared to your type of business? Is it widely used and proven in the field? Is it appropriate for a company of your size, and will it handle your planned growth? Will it accommodate the necessary interfaces to other software? This initial culling of available offerings can be accomplished by studying literature from software suppliers, ratings in trade periodicals, and telephone discussions with software suppliers and other similar companies using the software. The help of an experienced, objective consultant might also be useful. No company has the time to look in detail at every software package on the market, or even a significant percentage of them. Some trade periodicals list as many as 50 packages in articles each year, and there are more than that number on the market. The objective of this first phase is to reduce the packages to be considered in detail to a manageable list, usually no more than 5 or 6.

The second phase of rating MRP systems consists of a detailed procedure. The MRP selection team members should use forms, preferably with numeric ratings by function and with room for notes, for each of the following three steps:

1. Initial software demonstration

2. Operating site visits at other organizations

3. A detailed benchmark comparison of the software

For the first step, the software supplier will provide a demonstration of the package for your team. This will be done either at the supplier's office or by bringing equipment into your office and setting it up there. This procedure will usually take one day. The software company representative will run brief demonstrations of each module your company would likely use. Often this will be done in the same sequence that an order moves through your company. For example, the demonstration will probably begin with cost estimating and sales functions and progress through engineering, MAP and scheduling, purchasing, receiving and stocking, capacity planning, production activity control, shipping, DIP, and after-market service. A similar demonstration will be provided for the financial and accounting modules and any others offered that would be of interest to your firm.

During this process, some software suppliers will use a special demonstration version of their software. This is an acceptable way to show the functions of the software in a short time as long as the version is truly representative of the actual package.

The purpose is to determine if it is applicable for the task and should be pursued further. Each member of the software selection team should indicate on each software package evaluation form whether the desired function is available and ask general questions and make any necessary notes. Plan adequate time for this step so that all modules under consideration can be addressed. Do not get bogged down in detail at this stage. Details will be examined later in step 3. After step 1, it will probably be possible to eliminate some of the contenders based upon their obvious inability to perform the functions required.

Step 2 involves visits to customer references of the remaining software suppliers to obtain answers to the questions, "Can this software help a company achieve its objectives?" "Are the users generally happy with the way it operates?" At least one visit should be made for each package remaining under consideration; two visits would be preferable. This step gives the selection team an opportunity to examine the use of the software and briefly interview day-to-day users of the package representing the various functional areas. Significant benefits and problems the company has experienced will come to light at this step. Team members should record their observations for later review.

You must anticipate that the software suppliers will refer you to their best sites, and those are exactly what you want to see. It sometimes becomes known that one or more companies are having significant problems with a software package. In most cases, this has nothing to do with the software package itself but is the result of poor planning, preparation, and training for the implementation of the software package and/or a lack of procedure and discipline in using it. In other words, the problems are often the fault of the user company and not the software although such companies will often blame the software. If the software is truly poorly written, incapable, or inappropriate for your business, and some are, the step-by-step process here should reveal this to the trained eye. It will probably be possible to eliminate one or more contenders based on the site visits.

The third and most important step in rating MRP software for selection is the benchmark test. Unfortunately, this step is often not taken, which can result in a wrong decision. This step answers the questions, "Can the program serve the need?" and "How well and efficiently does it work?" By this step the packages considered should be culled down to two or three at most. The benchmark test involves the members' of the selection team collecting sample data, entering the database, and performing typical transactions their company would perform during an actual hands-on use of the software. This process, usually done at the software supplier's site, will probably take 1 to 2 days. In some cases the required hardware can be set up at the potential customer's site, particularly where a PC network is the hardware being offered. The benchmark will involve several terminals or PCs to be used by team members from the various disciplines. A prepared numeric rating form, used by each team member, should include each functional step and room for notes. At this detailed level it is also important to record the number of key strokes (or button clicks if a graphical user interface is in use) and the time to complete each inquiry, maintenance, and transaction—literally, a stopwatch study of the software's efficiency. Remember that the transactions you are benchmarking here will be done many times, perhaps hundreds or thousands of times per day by the employees. Some software is very efficient to use while other packages are cumbersome or even difficult to use, and the packaged demonstration and the site visit might not reveal this. An example of this benchmark rating detail is shown in Table 11.19.

Prior to using the evaluation forms, enter the company's sample data into the database. This will include item masters, inventory balances, bills of materials, routings, customer orders, and accounts. Then each team member will perform a series of transactions and inquiries with the software. As shown on the evaluation form, a particular team member performs the following:

- Master schedule some items.
- Execute an MRP planning run.
- Release manufacturing and purchase orders.
- Run a shop reschedule.
- Do some stock receipts and issues against inventory balances.
- Post direct labor charges to jobs.
- Receive order quantities, and close orders.
- Ship and bill 2 items to customers.
- Check work center status and load.
- Run a new capacity plan, and check status for some shop projects.

These are transactions that are done every day in many companies. Of course, each company will include those transactions that are important for its use. In this case, a 0 rating means the function is nonexistent in the software, and a 3 means the function is excellent. Ratings of 1 and 2 are indicated to mean fair and good. Time to complete the transaction is recorded, and the number of key hits noted, if applicable. The team member is encouraged to make comments as he or she goes through the exercise of benchmarking the software.

The selection team should have enough information at the conclusion of the third step to recommend a specific package. The final phase will involve negotiation of the software price, service level, and selection and price of the hardware if the system is unbundled. If any serious problems arise during this process, it may be necessary to go back into one of the earlier steps and have another look at some of the other packages again.

The help of an experienced, independent consultant should be considered when rating software. Outside help will be of particular use in the first phase when narrowing down the wide selection of software on the market to a manageable number of packages. Beyond that, a consultant may be of help as a guide through the remaining steps of the rating process. With a knowledgeable selection team in place, the consultant would not necessarily have to be present at each demonstration, site visit, and benchmark test. A consultant's help in planning these activities and reviewing the results may be advisable. Remember, the consultant works for you, and it is your responsibility to plan his or her level of involvement within budget guidelines.

TABLE 11.19 Hands-on Software Functionality Analysis

		Rating						
	0	1	2	3	Time	Key strokes	Comments
4a. Master schedule items from (3). Run MRP, and review requirement records for the five MPS items and items 107368, 131612, 101130 (common) 594820, and 900001. **b.** Do requirements look right? **c.** Peg tos?								
5. Release purchase orders for items 100506, 131610, 101130, 102091 (add 500 units for customer), 101308 (add 1000 units for customer), and 141574.								
6a. Release MRP manufacturing orders for items 131615, 160517, 136929, 160501, and 594830. Review open-order materials and operations files for these. **b.** Availability check? **c.** Release 594823 and 594829 using alternate method of order release.								
7a. Run shop schedules (forward schedule). **b.** Review work orders.								
8. Receive purchased items 102091, 141574, and 101308 to stock.								
9a. Receive purchased items 100506, 131610, and 101130 directly to their respective shop orders for parents 131615 (100506 and 131610), 160517 (101130), and 136929 (101030). **b.** Enter cost updates from steps 7 and 8.								
10. Issue purchased items (in stock) 102091, 101308, and 142491 to shop orders for parents, respectively, 160517, 594823, and 160517.								
11. Post direct labor to jobs (see attached page on this) as follows:								

Item	Operation	Hours
131615	1001	0.2
131615	1001	0.2
160517	1001	1.0
160517	2001	14.0
160517	3001	5.0
160517	4001	2.0
160517	5001	1.0
136929	1001	0.1
594823	1001	0.4

12. Close manufacturing orders for 160517 and 136929 (see next item).								

TABLE 11.19   Hands-on Software Functionality Analysis (*Continued*)

	Rating						
	0	1	2	3	Time	Key strokes	Comments
13. Receive 160517 to its parent order 160501. Receive 136929 to stock.							
14. Check cost roll-ups at all levels for 160501 and 594822 for estimate, plan and actual.							
15. Add one 160501 to on-hand inventory.							
16. Ship and bill items 141574 and 160501 to the customer.							
17. Check work center status, workload, etc.							
18. Run capacity plan and review.							
19. Check project status for 160501 and 594822							

Source: Copyright © Hatch and Associates. Used by permission.

MRP CHECKLIST

A checklist should be developed by the company's project team when considering the installation of an MRP or MRP II system for the first time or when upgrading to a new system. The checklist should be reviewed periodically by management during the operation of the system. Following is a sample checklist of key items, in question (Q) and answer (A) form, with comments:

1. Customer Service

Q Can the program help meet schedule dates for products and service? How do we expect the system to help us accomplish this?

A. A properly managed MRP system provides a realistic picture of when make-to-order products can be shipped. For products and service items that are forecast and made-to-order stock, MRP provides a vehicle for controlling and maintaining customer-order fill rates at the desired level. Each user company should outline specific customer service objectives for each class of product. There should be a plan for using the MRP system to meet and perhaps improve on these objectives.

2. Quality

Q. What aspects of the system will help us maintain and improve quality?

A. The MRP database, which tracks all components and products from conception to service. The system also supports and complements quality-measurement information systems such as SPC.

3. Productivity

Q. How can the system help minimize any effort that does not add value to a product and creates waste in the production process and throughout the operational system of the company?

A. MRP is a structured way of managing information throughout the company from estimating, sales, and after-market service. This helps ensure that all personnel are working toward the objective of meeting the formal schedule and that labor and capacity are properly directed. Each user company should identify ways in which MRP can support continuous total quality improvement throughout the process.

4. Inventory Management

Q. How can we achieve the objective of a minimum inventory investment with maximum customer service?

A. The materials planning logic of MRP is itself a tool designed with the object of good inventory performance. Each user company must set policies and procedures for using the ordering, lot-sizing, and customer service functions to meet its objectives.

5. New Management Tools

Q. Will the MRP interface with and work in a complementary manner with Kanban, just-in-time shop floor execution systems, empowered teams, and process reengineering?

A. MRP provides a planning database that will support all of these. If the shop floor is to be reconfigured into a just-in-time work cell layout, perhaps through reengineering efforts, the MRP database will be changed to reflect this. The MRP formal planning process will then help achieve the productivity of the new approach. Work center parameters can be configured around work teams and/or manufacturing cells.

6. Just-in-Time Purchasing

Q. Will MRP help support just-in-time purchasing?

A. Generally, MRP systems accommodate the more frequent materials deliveries and smaller lot sizes, and they enhance the long-term supplier relationships that are characteristic of just-in-time purchasing efforts. Most MRP databases include software fields that can be used to tie individual items to one or more purchasing contracts. This permits an analysis of the delivery and product quality performance by suppliers. Techniques for analysis of prices, financial terms, and other considerations are available. Order and lot size parameters are flexible so that they can be adjusted for specific items and suppliers' contracts and planned orders can be generated for the proper quantities and time.

7. Interfaces

Q. Will MRP interface with systems in other functional areas such as CAD/CAM and financial planning?

A. One of the important considerations in selecting or upgrading an MRP system today is whether it will interface with CAD/CAM systems. Some systems will readily interface to several of these systems. This interface reduces duplication of effort in developing the item master and bill of materials. An interface to financial planning systems provides the integration of overall business planning sought in developing an MRP II system. Every MRP user should examine the possibility of adding these interfaces if they do not exist in the present system.

8. System User Satisfaction

Q. Does the MRP system respond with the important information needed by employees throughout the company?

A. This is a question that needs to be reviewed periodically. The system's ability to respond and furnish the information desired can be upgraded as new technologies become available.

The checklist that has been presented is general, but it does address key issues that most companies are concerned with in analyzing their manufacturing resources planning systems. Staff members of each firm should state their question in a manner that expresses their concerns and priorities and then seek answers to these questions.

TRAINING AND MANAGING MRP PERSONNEL

Many people throughout the organization will benefit from information generated by the MRP program. Employees in the order-entry department, materials management, scheduling, purchasing, engineering, and factory floor will have the responsibility for inputting, updating, and maintaining data to support MRP. Educating and training employees is crucial to the success of the system. First, they need a formal education. Then, in addition, they require a knowledge of production planning and control systems. There are a number of good sources for this: APICS certification courses offered by local APICS chapters and by the national society, technical schools, college and university courses in operations management, and customized education offered by consulting firms. It is important that these employees obtain a good understanding of the inputs, processing steps, and outputs of the MRP system. The company's specific MRP policies should be outlined as the first step of the process. New employees should be given this educational opportunity when they join the company.

Special training is necessary for the software in use. The software supplier of a new or upgraded package usually offers a training program as part of the package or as a separate purchase item. All users should have some formal training, and those responsible for data maintenance should have intensive training to ensure proper day-to-day use of the system. Periodic refresher courses are recommended, particularly if the company elects to install enhanced software revisions as they become available.

Managers and supervisors need to be very knowledgeable about using the formal system to take advantage of opportunities and to solve problems. Employees using the system will encounter situations on a day-to-day basis that require some guidance. For example, when a shortage is encountered on the shop floor, the supervisor should know how to locate the item or perhaps make a substitution. The operator could do this by making on-line inquiries using the production-activity control module and should do this with the least disruption to production. Necessary schedule and bill of materials changes occur because of requests from sales, engineering, or from customers. Employees and managers in production control and purchasing must have the knowledge to effect changes as smoothly as possible, using the MRP system as a tool.

EXECUTING MRP II

The execution of the basic MRP planning run and the subsequent day-to-day order release and control process are described in the MRP order action. The more comprehensive MRP II approach involves much more than production planning and control. Basic MRP begins with the master production schedule and produces planned start dates and due dates for all purchased and manufactured items. It can also provide labor and machine capacity planning data. The MRP II encapsulates the basic MRP but begins the planning process at a higher level.

The MRP II begins with a long-term business plan. This is a statement of objectives for all aspects of the business at an aggregate level. It includes the sales plan or forecast for new projected products and services as well as existing ones. It includes scenarios for new facilities, plant and equipment purchases, and retirement of old items. It has plans for all levels of personnel and their training and development. The business plan also includes consideration of new management approaches and systems (i.e., empowered teams, just in time, or enhanced information systems).

Production plans and budgets for all nonproduction-related areas are developed from the business plan. The production plan drives the budgets for all production-related items such as direct and indirect labor, cash for purchased materials, factory equipment purchases, maintenance schedules, and plant floor space requirements. A master production schedule to cover the production plan is generated. Rough-cut capacity plans may also be developed at this stage to test various master scheduling scenarios. Described thus far is an overview of the strategic planning phase of the comprehensive business planning process.

The tactical planning phase or central part of the process encompasses the basic materials requirements planning logic that is driven directly by the master schedule, and the development and maintenance of bill of materials, routing, and inventory status data. A detailed capacity plan is also generated at this stage.

The execution phase or operational output of the process is the actual order release and control of orders for the shop floor and for suppliers. The complete process, often referred to as the *closed-loop planning process,* is flowcharted in Fig. 11.2.

The most sophisticated MRP II user companies will have this entire process of business planning, financial planning, and manufacturing resources planning integrated and automated from the top down. This allows the organization to act on opportunities and changes in the business environment quickly and formally. What-if scenarios can be evaluated and the best plan implemented.

AUDITING THE MRP II SYSTEM

Measurement of success is critical. It is important to first measure and document current performance before installing an MRP or MRP II system for the first time or when upgrading to a new system. After implementation, the performance measures should be reviewed regularly as part of the company's management process. Strategic or tactical plans can be developed then and implemented to exploit the system to its fullest benefit by improving those measures.

When auditing an operational system such as MRP II, principal emphasis is placed on overall performance measures with only a limited number of numeric measurements. Only a few measures, such as inventory and bill of materials accuracy, stress specific

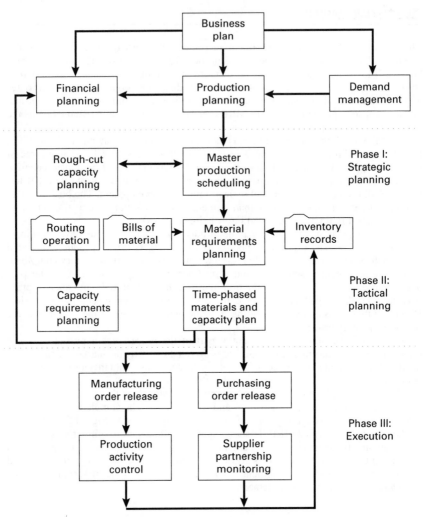

FIGURE 11.2   The closed-loop planning process. (*Copyright © Hatch and Associates. Used by permission.*)

accuracy measurements. This is a different perspective than that of familiar annual accounting audits that emphasize the accuracy of individual numbers and typically include an analysis of the accounting system.

Figure 11.3 lists some examples of important measurement ratios that can be used to document initial performance and then track that performance over the long run. Any of the ratios shown may be multiplied by 100 to represent them as percents.

An operating MRP system should provide all of these measures automatically without any additional data input except for the inventory, routing, and bill of materials accuracy measures. These will require periodic sampling and counting of data and

$$\text{Customer order satisfaction} = \frac{\text{total orders shipped on time}}{\text{total orders due}}$$

$$\text{Order booking performance} = \frac{\text{orders booked} - \text{orders booked outside lead time}}{\text{total orders booked}}$$

$$\text{Master production schedule execution} = \frac{\text{number of MPS orders completed}}{\text{number of MPS orders scheduled}}$$

$$\text{Shipping performance} = \frac{\text{total orders shipped on time}}{\text{total orders due} - \text{orders within lead time}}$$

$$\text{Quality performance} = \frac{\text{number of units accepted}}{\text{number of units delivered}}$$

$$\text{Inventory turns} = \frac{\text{cost of sales}}{\text{average inventory}}$$

$$\text{Inventory performance} = \frac{\text{beginning inventory} + \text{production} - \text{shipments}}{\text{beginning inventory} + \text{planned production} - \text{planned shipments}}$$

$$\text{Inventory accuracy} = \frac{\text{absolute value of book (on-hand balance)} - \text{actual count}}{\text{book (on-hand balance)}}$$

$$\text{Material availability} = \frac{\text{number of items short}}{\text{number of items needed}}$$

$$\text{Backlog performance} = \frac{\text{beginning backlog} - \text{shipments} + \text{bookings}}{\text{beginning backlog} - \text{planned shipments} + \text{planned bookings}}$$

$$\text{Bill-of-materials accuracy} = \frac{\text{number of BOMs correct}}{\text{number of BOMs checked}}$$

$$\text{Routing accuracy} = \frac{\text{number of routings correct}}{\text{number of routings checked}}$$

$$\text{Direct labor efficiency} = \frac{\text{standard or estimated hours per production unit}}{\text{actual hours per production unit}}$$

$$\text{Direct labor utilization} = \frac{\text{hours clocked on production work}}{\text{total hours in attendance}}$$

FIGURE 11.3 Ratios useful in MRP II performance audit.

inputting the results. The measurements shown here are specific to the operations part of the manufacturing resource planning system. There are other measures of overall company financial performance that an MRP II system can help provide, such as return on assets, return on shareholders' equity, and gross margin. Of course, departments such as sales, quality control, and purchasing will have more detailed performance measures for their day-to-day operations. The ratios given here are intended to be used as a management audit of overall MRP and MRP II system performance.

Following the proper implementation of an MRP II system, the company should see improvements in most or all of these measures. The values should be reported at least monthly for management review. Objectives can be set for performance improvement in specific areas and tactical plans developed to achieve the performance.

DISTRIBUTION REQUIREMENTS PLANNING

Distribution requirements planning (DRP) may be thought of as an upward expansion of the MRP logic from the master schedule through the distribution network to the ultimate customers. Above the master production schedule is the demand or shipping plan. For make-to-stock products, the plant's finished-goods inventory and therefore the customer's service level can be planned and controlled through the use of the DRP and MRP II.

When products are shipped to distribution warehouses rather than shipped directly to customers, there exists a customer shipping schedule, a warehouse inventory plan, and a warehouse receipt requirements plan besides the factory shipping plan. Management of these plans is often referred to as *distribution requirements planning* (DRP). DRP software is available that accepts the planned customer shipments from each warehouse

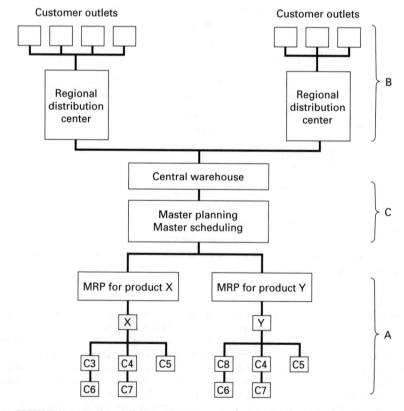

FIGURE 11.4 Linkage of MRP and DRP.

and the customers' desired service levels. From these data, factory shipping schedules are generated. DRP software enhances logic beyond the factory environment and provides a tool to manage warehouse distribution systems.

The logic of the distribution requirements planning calculations is nearly identical to materials or capacity requirements planning. Figure 11.4 illustrates: The MRP bill of materials A is a tree diagram of component requirements structured below the master planning and master scheduling. The DRP appears above the master planning and scheduling as an inverted-tree diagram B of the distribution flow. The master planning C may be thought of as long-range and policy management, and the master scheduling may be thought of as the daily response to the DRP within the requirements of the master planning.

Table 11.20 shows a numerical example to illustrate the linkage. The top part of the spreadsheet A is the data from the plant or central warehouse for product Y, which has collected the demands from regional warehouses RDC-10 and RDC-20. (These data are

TABLE 11.20 Plant Warehouse Serving Eastern and Western Regional Distribution Centers, Product Model Y

Lead time 1 week
Lot size pallets of 50
Safety stock 100

		Week							
	Past due	1	2	3	4	5	6	7	8
Demand from RDC-10		50	50	100	100	150	100	0	0
Demand from RDC-20		0	100	50	100	100	100	0	0
Other demand		80	80	80	80	80	80	80	80
Total demand on order		130	230	230	280	330	280	80	80
Planned receipt		0	350	200	300	300	300	100	50
Balance on hand	150	20	140	110	130	100	120	140	110
Planned plant order		350	200	300	300	300	100	50	

Plant warehouse planned plant order

	Week							
Item	1	2	3	4	5	6	7	8
Product X	75	95	85	65	65	65	300	60
Product Y	350	200	300	300	300	100	50	0

Master schedule

	Week							
Item	1	2	3	4	5	6	7	8
Model X	75	95	85	65	65	65	300	60
Model Y	350	200	300	300	300	100	50	0

identical to that generated by the DRP illustration in Chapter 20, "Distribution Requirements Planning.") Under this is shown the plant warehouse requirements for product Y for each week along with the plant requirements for product X (and for all other products shipped through the plant warehouse). Below this is shown the master schedule where for simplicity in this illustration, the quantity is shown to be equal to the plant warehouse demands. The result from the Chapter 20, "Distribution Requirements Planning," was used as the input for this example to aid the reader to see the connection between the DRP and the MRP logic. It shows the relationship between the logistics of independent and dependent demand.

Despite the numerical linkage of the DRP and MRP in these examples, it is apparent that the DRP is not simply connected by computer to the MRP. The interface between DRP and MRP is the master plan and master schedule, which illustrates the company decision for how to respond to the demand forecast and customer demands. The logic facilitates management ability to simulate the DRP and MRP decision, using trial and error, to create a visible plan for action. The plan that is decided upon in turn becomes the master schedule.

CONCLUSION

Manufacturing resources planning (MRP) systems represent a very important group of tools and techniques within the APICS body of knowledge that are central to formal professional planning and execution processes. When properly implemented and used by knowledgeable, trained personnel, MRP and MRP II can contribute to the substantial benefits of maximum customer satisfaction. They can provide a framework for planning and operating the entire business most effectively in this information age.

BIBLIOGRAPHY

Orlicky, Joseph: *MRP: Material Requirements Planning,* McGraw-Hill, New York, 1975.

Vollmann, Thomas E., Berry, William L., and Whybark, D. Clay: *Manufacturing Planning and Control Systems,* Richard D. Irwin, Homewood, Ill., 1991.

Wight, Oliver W.: *Production and Inventory Management in the Computer Age,* CBI, Boston, 1974.

———: *MRPII: Unlocking America's Productivity Potential,* CBI, Boston, 1981.

CHAPTER 12
MASTER PRODUCTION SCHEDULE

Editor
F. John Sari, CFPIM
John Sari & Company, Winston-Salem, North Carolina

The planning activities that go into creating the *master production schedule* (MPS) are very important for a manufacturing firm. The real importance of the MPS emerged in the mid-1970s as *materials requirements planning* (MRP) became more widely used and understood. It became obvious that a more formal tool had to be the "driver" of these powerful MRP systems. This tool is the MPS.

The American Production and Inventory Control Society's *Master Production Scheduling: Principles and Practice* offers a comprehensive treatment of the MPS.[1] It presents the MPS in a standard framework and examines eight companies relative to this framework. Each had developed effective approaches to master scheduling. This same standard MPS framework, which is shown in Fig. 12.1 is the framework for this chapter. A reprint of Chapter 2 of *Master Production Scheduling: Principles and Practice*, appears at the end of this chapter.

The *APICS Dictionary* gives the following definition:

master production schedule (MPS) (1) The anticipated build schedule for those items assigned to the master scheduler. The master scheduler maintains this schedule, and, in turn, it becomes a set of planning numbers that drives material requirements planning. It represents what the company plans to produce expressed in specific configurations, quantities, and dates. The master production schedule is not a sales forecast that represents a statement of demand. The master production schedule must take into account the forecast, the production plan, and other important considerations such as backlog, availability of material, availability of capacity, management policies and goals, etc. Synonym: *master schedule*. (2) The result of the master scheduling process. The master schedule is a presentation of demand, forecast, backlog, the MPS, the projected on-hand inventory, and the available-to-promise quantity.[2]

The length of this definition is understandable when one considers the many MPS interfaces and their tremendous importance in manufacturing companies.

It is assumed that the reader has a basic overall knowledge of manufacturing resource planning as well as access to *Master Production Scheduling: Principles and Practice*. This chapter does not attempt to duplicate that reference. The chapter does

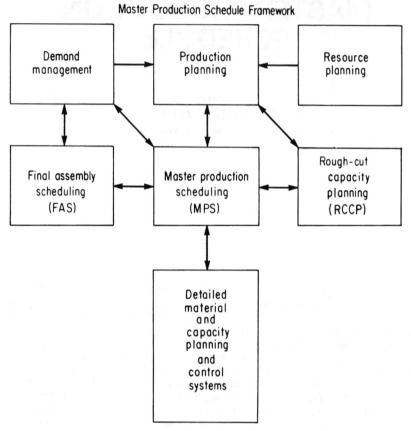

FIGURE 12.1   MPS standard framework.

provide a current, overall perspective of the master production scheduling process and outlines significant techniques that various companies utilize to implement and manage that process.

The reader may wish to read the reprint of Chapter 2 of *Master Production Scheduling: Principles and Practice* at the end of this chapter before proceeding.

PRODUCTION PLANNING (SALES AND OPERATIONS PLANNING)

Production planning is a formal management planning process that directly drives the MPS. Through production planning, the operating management reviews and revises aggregate rates of manufacturing for the various families, or classes, of products which comprise the business. The executive who has the profit-and-loss responsibility for the business operation—that is, the divisional president or general manager—presides over the formal production planning review meeting. Thus the sales and operations planning process truly represents top management's "handle" on the business.

The *APICS Dictionary* defines production planning as follows:

production planning The function of setting the overall level of manufacturing output (production plan) and other activities to best satisfy the current planned levels of sales (sales plan and/or forecasts), while meeting general business objectives of profitability, productivity, competitive customer lead times, etc., as expressed in the overall business plan. The sales and production capabilities are compared, and a business strategy that includes a production plan, budgets, pro forma financial statements, and supporting plans for materials and work force requirements, etc., is developed. One of its primary purposes is to establish production rates that will achieve management's objective of satisfying customer demand, by maintaining, raising, or lowering inventories or backlogs, while usually attempting to keep the work force relatively stable. Because this plan affects many company functions, it is normally prepared with information from marketing and coordinated with the functions of manufacturing, engineering, finance, materials, etc. Synonym: *sales and operations planning*.

production plan The agreed-upon plan that comes from the aggregate (production) planning function, specifically the overall level of manufacturing output planned to be produced, usually stated as a monthly rate for each product family (group of products, items, options, features, etc.). Various units of measure can be used to express the plan: units, tonnage, standard hours, number of workers, etc. The production plan is management's authorization for the master scheduler to convert it into a more detailed plan, that is, the master production schedule.

The Production Plan Versus the MPS—An Example

The production plan developed by operating management is the primary driver of the MPS, yet the two are distinctly different in many important respects. Using automobiles as an example, consider the hypothetical M-body family of cars seen in Fig. 12.2. The M-body family is one of several families produced by Acme Motors, yet it is distinguished from the others by several factors. The M body sells in a certain price range and thus competes in an identifiable market niche. All M cars share certain major components—chassis, body, engines, and so on. They are assembled in certain specified facilities.

Each month, Acme management formally reviews the M body, its status in the marketplace, and its production plan for the months ahead. The key to this plan is the marketplace. Historically, Acme knows that a 60-day dealer inventory of M bodies is desirable. A stock of this size provides a wide variety of product configurations, which, in turn, means customers usually can quickly get an M body that meets their needs. A 60-day stock is also financially manageable by Acme dealers. It provides a buffer between the sales rate and the production rate that does permit some leveling of Acme's labor force.

Every 10 days, dealers report sales statistics and inventory positions. Acme analyzes these and each month formally updates the M-body sales forecast. Using this forecast and the current inventory position, Acme calculates the days of supply of M bodies in dealer stock.

During periods when sales run heavier than expected, the days-of-supply number falls below the 60-day target. Acme management responds by scheduling assembly overtime within the constraints of major component supplies (engines, transmissions, chassis), labor contracts, and so on. If the strong sales situation appears to be long term, Acme considers other major capacity adjustments such as converting facilities to M-body production, and adding shifts. During periods of slow sales, Acme may respond with sales promotions, reduced-rate financing, temporary layoffs, and other moves to

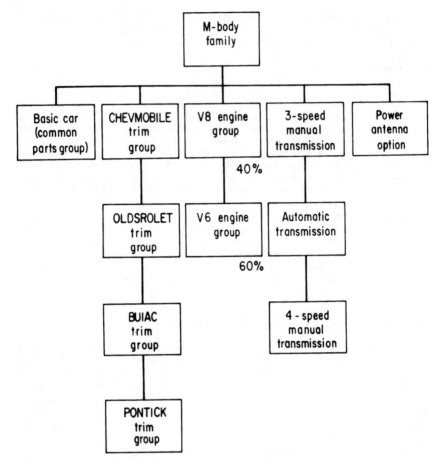

FIGURE 12.2   M-body family of cars.

adjust an 87-day dealer inventory downward. In either case, the desired adjustment to dealer inventory cannot be made instantaneously. Acme management is thus revising overall production rates for M bodies for the next few months to get back to the historical 60-day target.

Two major decisions typically result from this formal sales and operations planning process: (1) Agreed-to rates of manufacture for the family (the production plan), for example, 4000 units per week for the next 4 weeks because of materials constraints and 4400 units per week for the next 8 weeks, and so on, and (2) an agreed-to sales split that controls the amount of M-body output that will be Chevmobile, Oldsrolet, and so on.

These agreements drive the MPS process. The aggregate rates exactly define the numbers of common parts required. The forecasted mix of options is used to revise the master schedules for engine groups, transmission options, and so on. Master schedulers are responsible for this planning. They disaggregate the production plan and detail it in terms of the MPS items.

During production planning Acme executives discuss the M-body family, aggregate rates of sales and manufacture, and monthly plans. Master schedulers detail those plans in terms of specific MPS items, considering the weekly and daily rates of manufacture. They take into account such factors as desirable lot sizes and vendor sources that are not normally considered during production planning.

Business Planning Versus Sales and Operations Planning

Many manufacturing companies have formal annual business planning processes through which they set boundaries on the sales and operations plan and the production plan. The two processes are related, which is important to understand. It is also important to know the differences between the two and how ongoing sales and operations planning serves to support the business plan.

In general, the business planning process is more financially oriented than sales and operations planning and includes more far-reaching strategic implications. Business planning deals with investment planning, profit planning, asset planning, and capital planning. It includes products and market strategies such as market share, new-product planning, analyses of competition, distribution strategies, and product positioning to meet customer service objectives. Business planning is also concerned with major capital expenditures for new facilities, new technologies, new processes, and the like. These plans usually cover a 3- to 5-year planning horizon.

Certain aspects of business planning cover manufacturing plans. Aggregate inventory objectives such as planned levels and turnover objectives are included. Aggregate rates of manufacture are planned. Capacities required are planned, including overall workforce plans as well as needed plant and equipment.

The first year of a typical 3- to 5-year business plan generally represents the set of operating plans and budgets against which company performance is measured. Frequently there are midyear, or perhaps quarterly, reviews of operations. This budgetary aspect of business planning is the main area of overlap with the ongoing, monthly production planning process. The business plan can be viewed, in some senses, as establishing objectives, targets, and the strategies designed to accomplish them. The production planning process is then viewed as the ongoing review and refining of tactics necessary to meet the targets. Most businesses find themselves at variance with the operating plan and budgets at some time during the fiscal year. Continuous, midcourse adjustments are thus made through the sales and operations planning process.

Business plans can be distinguished from production plans in several important ways. Business plans are normally expressed in dollars whereas production plans are convertible to dollars but usually are expressed in other terms—units, tons, dozens, square feet, or other measures. Production plans also express monthly rates of manufacture by families of products whereas business plans often express annual objectives for the overall business, market segments, or other high-level groupings.

Sales and operations planning focuses on managing rates of manufacture to meet targeted inventory and/or backlog levels, which is only one aspect of business planning. Make-to-stock businesses target finished-goods inventory levels to maintain desired levels of customer service. Make-to-order businesses target backlog levels (all unshipped customer orders on hand, not necessarily past due) to maintain desired customer service levels. In the latter case, these are usually expressed as desired lead times to the customer, and there is a recognized need to offer competitive lead times. In both types of businesses, the aggregate forecast of sales normally drives the production plan. During periods of scarce capacity, the production plan drives the sales forecast. At times, it becomes necessary to revise targeted inventory and/or backlog levels because of marketplace or manufacturing conditions.

Sales and Operations Planning Formats and Mechanics

Figure 12.3 illustrates a typical production plan format and situation. The display shows 3 months of history in order to gain a better historical perspective and to clearly see how the current situation was reached. The 5-month picture in the future is shown here instead of the normal 12- to 24-month picture.

The original plan developed 3 months ago planned manufacture to exceed the forecasted rate of sales in order to increase inventory to a targeted position of 1 month's sales (or 30-day supply). Actual sales and manufacture for the last 3 months have varied somewhat from those planned. Sales have exceeded forecast by 19 units in the last 3 months, or approximately 5 percent (19/360). Manufacturing missed planned produc-

PRODUCTION PLAN WORKSHEET

Make-to-Stock · Target: One Month Inventory

Marketing

(Months)	-3	-2	-1	Today	Current	+1	+2	+3	+4
Forecast	120	120	120	Original	120	120	120	120	120
Actual	109	137	133	Revised	130	130	130	130	130
Difference	-11	+17	+13						
Cumulative difference		+6	+19						

Manufacturing

	-3	-2	-1		Current	+1	+2	+3	+4
Planned	125	125	125	Original	125	120	120	120	120
Actual	121	118	119	Revised	125	130	135	135	135
Difference	-4	-7	-6						
Cumulative difference		-11	-17						

On hand · Inventory

	-3	-2	-1		Current	+1	+2	+3	+4
Planned		106	111	116	Original	121	121	121	121	121
Actual	101	113	94	80	Revised	75	75	80	85	90
Difference		+7	-17	-36						

FIGURE 12.3 Production plan worksheet, make to stock. Target is 1-month inventory.

tion by 17 units, or 5 percent (17/375). Inventories thus are 36 units, or 31 percent (36/116), under plan.

The production plan worksheet shows the composite results of the sales and operations planning process. Sales and marketing have revised the sales forecast. A best-efforts manufacturing plan has been put forth by the manufacturing manager. Although materials and capacity constraints exist in both the current month and month + 1, the plan has been increased in month + 1. This is based on the expected resolution of a materials or capacity problem that was principally responsible for the manufacturing shortfall of 17 units over the last 3 months. Beginning in month + 2, manufacturing rates of 135 per month are being recommended to improve the inventory position. This strategy will not achieve the 1-month inventory goal by month + 4. To do so would require a significantly higher manufacturing rate than 135 per month. Judgment has suggested a course of action that, on balance, increases capacity and hiring but temporarily sacrifices target inventory goals. The key is that agreement was reached and communicated.

The example illustrates a typical compromise proposal that will not fully satisfy any one member of the management team. Sales may not be happy because of the inventory position. Manufacturing is being challenged since they have not consistently produced to plan in the past, and this revised plan calls for yet more output.

The example illustrates the formal process used to review sales and operations planning each month:

1. Sales forecasts are reviewed and revised.

2. Current inventory and/or backlog positions are documented.

3. Demonstrated capacities are documented.

4. Production rates are revised within the constraints of both materials and capacity availability.

5. Projected inventory and/or backlog positions are calculated and compared to targets. Financial projections are developed and reviewed.

6. Contingency plans are developed based on reasonable variations of sales and manufacturing from plans. For example, what are the optimistic and pessimistic alternatives?

7. Alternatives are presented for top management for discussion, review, and approval.

Note that in the example, substantial communication and preparation took place prior to the formal review for management approval. In most companies, this is the case. Middle management discusses and prepares alternatives for review and agreement. Usually, a formal planning cycle is defined in a policy that outlines the process, specifying the information that must be communicated by certain working days of the month to meet the formal review meeting schedule. On occasion, the top management approval meeting will initiate yet another plan revision.

Figure 12.4 illustrates a typical situation for a make-to-order family of products. In this example the target is expressed as a desired backlog level of 2 months. This could be expressed as a 2-month delivery lead time provided that all orders are delivered on a first-come, first-served basis.

Normally, make-to-order forecasts project bookings, or order receipt rates. The manufacturing plan expresses the projected rates of shipment since each product is produced in response to a firm customer's order. The time difference between the booking and the shipment is often expressed as a booking-to-shipment curve, or ratio. Figure 12.5 illustrates such a ratio. Of $10,000 booked this month, $2170 will ship this month, $1850

PRODUCTION PLAN WORKSHEET

Make-to-Order

Target: Two Month Backlog

Marketing

(Months)	-3	-2	-1	Today	Current	+1	+2	+3	+4
Forecast		30	30	30	Original	30	35	35	35	35
Actual		32	32	35	Revised		← NO CHANGE →			
Difference		+2	+2	+5						
Cumulative difference			+4	+9						

Manufacturing

		-3	-2	-1		Current	+1	+2	+3	+4
Planned		35	35	35	Original	35	35	35	35	35
Actual		33	32	33	Revised		← NO CHANGE →			
Difference		-2	-3	-2						
Cumulative difference			-5	-7						

Backlog

	Beginning Backlog				Backlog					
Planned		86	81	76	Original	71	71	71	71	71
Actual	91	90	90	92	Revised	87	87	87	87	87
Difference			+4	+9	+16					

FIGURE 12.4 Production plan worksheet, make to order. Target is 2-month backlog.

will ship in month + 1, and so on. This ratio, which varies according to marketplace conditions, is used to translate the bookings forecasts to shipment forecasts. Figure 12.6 depicts a consolidated format that includes both make-to-stock and make-to-order conditions. It combines the two previous examples of the production plan worksheets.

Note the shipments line that did not appear in the previous figures. Projected shipments appear as the marketing forecast line of the make-to-stock worksheet for the stocked portion of the family and, as noted, in the manufacturing planned line for the make-to-order portion. The shipments line consolidates these two.

Sales and Operations Planning Families and Units of Measure

It is sometimes difficult to define families for purposes of production planning. It is desirable to limit the number of families in order to streamline the top-management review process. However, this may be difficult to do in firms with diverse product lines.

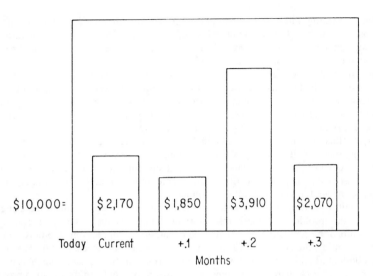

$10,000=	$2,170	$1,850	$3,910	$2,070
	Today Current	+.1	+.2	+.3

Months

FIGURE 12.5 Booking-to-shipment roles.

PRODUCTION PLAN WORKSHEET

Make-to-Stock and Order

Marketing	(Months)	-3	-2	-1	Today	Current	+1	+2	+3	+4
Forecast		150	150	150	Original	150	155	155	155	155
Actual		141	169	168	Revised	160	165	165	165	165
Difference			-9	+19	+18					
Cumulative difference				+10	+28					

Manufacturing

Planned		160	160	160	Original	160	155	155	155	155
Actual		154	150	152	Revised	160	165	170	170	170
Difference			-6	-10	-8					
Cumulative difference				-16	-24					

Inventory/backlog

Inventory	101	113	94	80		75	75	80	85	90
Backlog	91	90	90	92	Revised	87	87	87	87	87
Shipments		142	169	166		165	165	165	165	165

FIGURE 12.6 Production plan worksheet, make-to-stock and order.

The overriding objective is to structure families to facilitate marketing-manufacturing communications. On one hand, sales and marketing must be able to forecast marketplace demand. On the other hand, manufacturing must be able to translate proposed production rates to required capacities.

In many instances, such as the automobile M body noted earlier, the family structure serves both needs. Demand can be forecast for the M body because it serves an identifiable market niche. The planned production rate is straightforward in terms of planning needed capacity. In other instances, a communications gap exists. A hand-tool company with a family of wrenches in its product line including Allen, pipe, open-end, and socket wrenches illustrates the problem. The different wrenches require quite different manufacturing processes. It may be possible to adequately forecast the demand for wrenches. However, unless this demand can be translated smoothly to the expected mix of basic types of wrenches, manufacturing may be unable to determine staffing and equipment capacities needed to manufacture the product.

The unit of measure used to state the sales forecast rate and the manufacturing rate bears on this problem. In marketplace-oriented families such as the wrench family noted, units of measure such as "each" lose meaning. Dollars become the only common denominator in which communication can occur. In other instances, the family structure serves both marketing and manufacturing and permits units of measure such as units or each, pounds, tons square feet, dozens, and yards, to be used. Hours are an appropriate unit of measure in some businesses, especially with engineered-to-order products.

Marketplace-oriented families may require the use of *rough-cut capacity planning* (RCCP). To directly relate family rates of manufacture to needed capacities, RCCP load profiles that assume typical, or average, mixes are then used to determine rough-cut capacities. In similar fashion, even though some families may relate directly to some required capacities, RCCP may have a role in production planning. For example, the M-body family of cars might compete for stamping plant capacity with other families. Then RCCP would be useful in reviewing that competition for capacity.

DEMAND MANAGEMENT

Managing demand helps to manage supply. The capacity needed to meet current customer demand is lost when the wrong product is produced. Capacity is lost when excessive schedule changes ripple through a manufacturing process. MRP systems respond to forecasts of demand, and the better the forecast, the better the resulting customer service. MRP's rapid replanning ability must be controlled. The better managed the reaction to changing marketplace conditions, the better the overall performance in customer service, inventory, and productivity.

The activities that link sales and marketing to manufacturing and the needs of the marketplace to manufacturing plans are encompassed by the demand management process. *Demand management* is an umbrella term first publicized in the APICS text *Master Production Scheduling: Principles and Practice.* The current *APICS Dictionary* definition reads as follows:

demand management   The function of recognizing and managing all of the demands for products to ensure that the master scheduler is aware of them. It encompasses the activities of forecasting, order entry, order promising, branch warehouse requirements, interplant orders, service parts requirements.

The related definitions of *demand(s)* are:

demand   A need for a particular product or component. The demand could come from any number of sources, such as a customer order or forecast, or an interplant requirement, or a request from a branch warehouse for a service part, or for manufacturing another product. At the finished goods level, "demand data" are usually different from "sales data" because demand does not necessarily result in sales. If there is no stock there will be no sale.

dependent demand   Demand that is directly related to or derived from the bill of material structure for other items or end products. Such demands are therefore calculated and need not and should not be forecast. A given inventory item may have both dependent and independent demand at any given time. For example, a part may simultaneously be the component of an assembly and also sold as a service part.

independent demand   Demand for an item that is unrelated to the demand for other items. Demand for finished goods, parts required for destructive testing, and service parts requirements are examples of independent demand.

Several chapters of this book discuss aspects of demand management—forecasting, distribution resource management (of branch warehouse requirements), and sales order entry among others. The discussion that follows focuses on the important interfaces between the demand management functions and the other planning processes that compose the MPS framework. Figure 12.7 identifies these major interfaces.

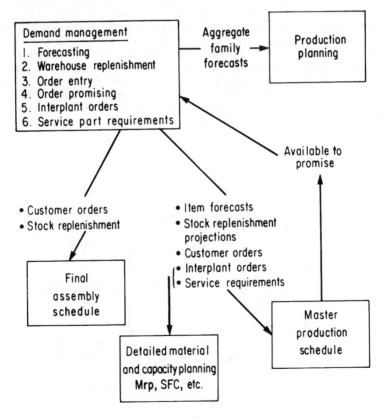

FIGURE 12.7   Demand management interfaces.

Forecast Interfaces: Aggregate Versus Item Forecasts

A *forecast* is a formal request from sales and marketing to manufacturing to have product or capacity available to meet perceived demand. With few exceptions forecasts are driving forces in MRP. Most firms rely on forecasts of expected business to plan major aspects of both materials and capacity, although some companies, such as defense contractors, have sufficient backlogs of firm orders with which to plan both capacity and materials requirements. Figure 12.8 describes the interface aspects of forecasts.

Aggregate family forecasts drive the sales and operations planning process. These forecasts, along with management decisions to increase or decrease inventories of backlog, establish the planned volume of production. Supporting item forecasts establish the planned mix through the MPS.

Good planning communications at this level require the two aggregation-disaggregation processes shown. The forecasting process should provide the ability to aggregate the item forecasts to ensure consistency with the family forecasts. Conversely, it is necessary to be able to disaggregate a family forecast into item forecasts. Companies derive forecasts both ways. Some begin at the item level and aggregate to the family. Others forecast the family and disaggregate to the items. Either way, it is important to have consistency.

A similar aggregation-disaggregation process exists between the production plan and the MPS. The agreed-to family rate of manufacture must be disaggregated to the item detail of the MPS. Superbills, or planning bills of materials, often serve this purpose. Bottom-up MPS summaries are used to aggregate the MPS to ensure that it agrees with the production plan within reasonable tolerances.

Forecasts of lower-level demands often interface directly to MRP, especially in companies with significant service-parts activity or interplant supply activity. Aggregate forecasts, usually expressed in dollars and/or hours, are used for sales and operations planning and RCCP. The item forecast detail may interface to the MPS but may also interface to MRP. MRP interfaces are needed with items that have both dependent (i.e., used on high-level items) and independent (e.g., service-parts sales) demands.

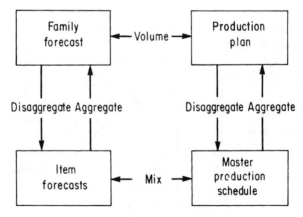

FIGURE 12.8   Forecast interfaces.

Forecast Interfaces: Forecast Consumption

In any given period, rarely does actual demand agree with forecasted demand, either in aggregate or by item. This fact, combined with the rapid replanning capabilities of MRP systems, leads to the need for forecast consumption—the process of replacing the forecast with customer orders, or other actual demands, as they are received. The examples that follow illustrate some of the issues.

In Fig. 12.9, an original sales forecast of 20 per month has been smoothed to 5 per week to present demand uniformly to the planning system. If no sales occur in period 1, that is, actual demand is less than forecast, the planning system requires some reasonable rules with which to proceed, or it may react too nervously. Figure 12.10 shows two possible solutions for 1 week later.

		Period							
		1	2	3	4	5	6	7	8
Forecast		5	5	5	5	5	5	5	5
Projected available balance	21	16	11	6	1	26	21	16	11
Master production schedule						30			

FIGURE 12.9   Smoothed forecast.

Today

Choice 1

			Period						
			2	3	4	5	6	7	8
Forecast			5	5	5	5	5	5	5
Projected available balance	21		16	11	6	31*	26	21	16

*Recommends reschedule out (De-expedite)

Choice 2

Forecast			10	5	5	5	5	5	5
Projected available balance	21		11	6	1	26	21	16	11

Master production schedule						30			

FIGURE 12.10   Forecast consumption alternatives.

Choice 1, dropping the unrealized forecast that has gone past due, will generate a reschedule-out (deexpedite) recommendation since the projected available balance of 31 in period 5 indicates the MPS quantity of 30 in period 5 is no longer needed. Choice 2, carrying forward the unrealized forecast into period 2, maintains the original projected available balance. No rescheduling action is recommended.

The choice of procedure is an important one. In any given period (week, month), demand would be expected to be less than forecast on half of the MPS items and exceed the forecast on the other half. Thus, there is a large potential for planning nervousness, that is, reschedule-in and reschedule-out recommendations. A master scheduler could spend quite a bit of time reviewing reschedule recommendations and deciding what, if anything, to do.

A visible, easily managed alternative to choice 2 is to define a cumulative forecast adjustment field that maintains a running total of the difference between actual demand and forecast. Figure 12.11 shows the operation of the forecast adjustment field after week 1 with no sales. If actual demands exceed the forecast over time, the forecast adjustment field will turn negative. In use, the forecast adjustment dampens reschedule recommendations to the master scheduler as actual demand varies from forecast. Thus, the forecast adjustment should be monitored and managed by a responsible individual in sales or marketing as well as the master scheduler.

A common rule is to consume forecasts within the forecast interval and not to expect them to be accurate in any smaller period. Many companies forecast monthly, spread forecasts weekly for scheduling purposes, yet consume forecasts quarterly. The cumulative forecast adjustment capability is especially useful for sporadic-demand items. It is frequently used for service demand for lower-level items handled by MRP in order to prevent excessive nervousness.

A forecast consumption process is required at several levels—in aggregate for production planning and at item levels in MPS and MRP. The MRP systems are capable of very rapid replanning. Forecast consumption processes permit people to exercise judgment and control.

Defined time fences (see the "MPS Mechanics" section) are another tool for managing the rate of change to schedules. Eventually manufacturing activity must react to changing marketplace needs. Time-fence policies define when and how.

Order-Entry and Order-Promising Interfaces: Available to Promise

The demand management function of order entry is the process of accepting and translating a customer order to the internal language and definition used by the manufacturer. This can range from translating a verbal description to a part number to a protracted

		Forecast adjust-ment	Period						
			2	3	4	5	6	7	8
Forecast		+5	5	5	5	5	5	5	5
Projected available balance	21	16	11	6	1	26	21	16	11
Master production schedule						30			

FIGURE 12.11   Forecast adjustment field.

engineering process. The order-promising function assigns delivery dates to the order. *Available-to-promise* (ATP) tools and procedures provide the necessary information to make good customer promises. ATP mechanics are discussed, with examples, in the "MPS Mechanics" section.

ATP tools essentially compare *actual* demands, not forecasts, to MPS items on hand or scheduled. The uncommitted portion of the inventory or planned production is "for sale." Time-phased ATP tools, frequently updated, provide up-to-date delivery possibilities. In the past, many companies quoted standard delivery lead times to their customers. These were reviewed periodically and changed with backlog conditions. ATP information is much more timely and better reflects the dynamics of customer orders.

Although the arithmetic of ATP techniques is quite simple, ATP status has become a sophisticated tool in practice. Firms producing optionalized products, for example automobiles, have ATP tools that can base the customer order promise on the gating option. For example, the engine and transmission ordered may have ATP status, but the requested sunroof option may not have ATP status to match.

Another adaptation of ATP tools involves promising an order with several line items. An order for a suite of office furniture might include desk, chair, credenza, and filing cabinets. Many of these could be optionalized products. The ATP status for the order reflects the ATP status for each line item. Transportation schedules become another consideration.

Capacity-managed businesses such as foundries (see the "MPS Environments" section) and engineered-to-order companies may base customer order promises on ATP capacity. Incoming orders are converted to capacity demands through an estimating process. These demands compete for ATP capacity with other demands.

Order-Promising Interfaces: Abnormal Demands

Closely associated with both consuming forecast with actual demands and ATP status is the need to manage abnormal demand conditions. Figure 12.12 shows the status of an MPS plan at the time an ASAP (as soon as possible) delivery order for 24 is received. Procedures and guidelines are needed to properly manage this type of situation. Clearly, a customer promise needs to be made since the 13 on hand will not satisfy the order for 24. Several important questions need to be addressed before that promise is made:

1. Should the future forecast be increased? Is this a new, continuing customer or source of demand?

2. Is this a truly abnormal demand? Should the order be treated as a one-time deviation (increase) to the forecast?

3. Is this order merely the forecast coming true? Is this item normally ordered in large quantities? This occurs if the normal practice is to spread the forecast uniformly while actual demand tends to be lumpy.

4. Should the total shelf stock be used to satisfy part of this order, or should some be held back to service other customers?

5. What is a realistic promise for this order? The portion of the order not shipped from on-hand inventory may be satisfied by the replenishment of 25 due to stock in period 5. Alternatively, it may be best to give this order full lead time in order to obtain enough product to satisfy this abnormal demand plus the forecast.

A procedure used in many businesses is to establish a maximum order size by item which can be satisfied from shelf stock. The intent of this guideline is to prevent depletion of on-hand stock by exceptionally large orders. To do so frequently leads to poor

		Period							
		1	2	3	4	5	6	7	8
Forecast		3	3	3	3	3	3	3	3
Production forecast									
Actual demand									
Projected available balance	13	10	7	4	1	23	20	17	14
Available to promise		13	13	13	13	38	38	38	38
Master production schedule						25			

FIGURE 12.12   Managing an abnormal demand: Promising an order for 24.

service levels for the normal customer order pattern. Maximum-order-size parameters are analogous to the demand filters used in some forecasting models. Demand filters are tripped when demand in a period differs from that forecast by a specified number of mean absolute deviations.

A reasonable set of rules is needed to manage unusual incoming demands. Normally, such rules are not unduly sophisticated. Computer logic and procedures are used to identify abnormal conditions. People make the final determination.

LONG-RANGE RESOURCE PLANNING AND RCCP

Two tools of contemporary capacity planning are considered parts of the overall framework of master scheduling. These are long-range resource planning and rough-cut capacity planning (RCCP). The *APICS Dictionary* provides the following definitions:

long-range resource planning   The process of establishing, measuring, and adjusting limits or levels of long-range capacity. Resource planning is normally based on the production plan but may be driven by higher level plans beyond the time horizon for the production plan, i.e., business plan. It addresses those resources that take long periods of time to acquire. Resource planning decisions always require top management approval. Synonyms: *long-range resource planning, long-term planning.*

rough-cut capacity planning (RCCP)   The process of converting the production plan and/or the master production schedule into capacity needs for key resources: work force, machinery, warehouse space, suppliers' capabilities, and in some cases, money. Bills of resources are often used to accomplish this. Comparison of capacity required of items in the MPS to available capacity is usually done for each key resource. RCCP assists the master scheduler in establishing a feasible master production schedule. Synonym: *resource requirements planning.*

In contemporary practice, long-range resource planning is associated most closely with the strategic aspects of longer-range business planning. Many companies develop annual business plans projecting several business objectives over a 3- to 5-year horizon. This exercise usually takes into consideration the following types of items:

1. *Financial plans:* Investment, profit, asset, and capital objectives and requirements
2. *Market and product plans:* Market strategies, product and technology plans, sales rates, customer delivery objectives, and so on
3. *Manufacturing plans:* Planned shipments, inventory and backlog levels, annual production rates, aggregate capacities, and so on.

The long-range resource planning aspects of this process are used to examine major capacity considerations, such as new facilities and overall staffing levels, which have significant capital budget implications. Computer-assisted techniques such as modeling, probability analysis, and financial analysis are sometimes used in this planning process. Periodic, less comprehensive plan updates may occur semiannually or quarterly.

RCCP is most closely associated with the ongoing production plan and/or the MPS. These planning horizons are shorter than those of the annual business plan and are usually more product specific. RCCP provides a reasonability test of capacity needed to accomplish these plans at intermediate levels of detail (i.e., more specific than the annual plan but less detailed than the routing-work center detail of capacity requirements planning). RCCP techniques vary among companies, but most involve two essential ingredients: identified critical resources and load profiles.

Critical resources are company specific. They normally include bottleneck factory processes, both equipment and labor, constraining supplier capacities, design or engineering capacities, quality assurance or test facilities, and so on, the critical few resources that truly dictate overall throughput rather than the large number of specific capacities.

Load profiles identify the loads placed on critical resources as production planning families of products or specific MPS items are planned. They are developed by summarizing the detailed routings used to produce the various components of a product and by analyzing cost data or labor reporting. Or they may simply be estimates prepared by knowledgeable individuals.

Through experience, companies develop a proper level of RCCP precision appropriate to their needs. Many companies perform RCCP at overall family rates of manufacture as stated in the production plan. Once satisfied, such companies proceed to develop detailed component plans through MPS and MRP. Other companies make a more precise RCCP analysis by evaluating item-specific plans as stated in the MPS before proceeding to the detailed component planning processes.

A tool manufacturer might illustrate this precision issue. A family of open-end wrenches could be rough cut as a family if all open-end wrenches followed essentially the same manufacturing process and generated similar loads for critical resources. However, a broader sales and operations planning family of wrenches that included both open-end and socket wrenches might be rough cut at an MPS item level since the different style wrenches impact on very different critical resources.

RCCP tools are designed to permit a rapid analysis of how reasonable the production plan and/or MPS is in light of demonstrated capacities. Highly interactive, computer-assisted RCCP is very desirable. What-if questions abound in most manufacturing companies, and RCCP is a major what-if evaluation tool. It is used whenever changes of consequence are proposed in production plans and/or the MPS. It is also used to evaluate high-impact customer orders in myriad other situations.

MPS ENVIRONMENTS

The overall framework for developing and controlling the master scheduling process is described at the beginning of this chapter. To repeat, the MPS is the *anticipated build schedule* that represents what the company plans to produce expressed in *specific configurations, quantities, and dates.* The master scheduler maintains this schedule, and, in turn, it becomes a set of planning numbers that drives materials requirements planning. The specific MPS approaches and techniques in use vary from firm to firm although the objective and purpose of the MPS remain the same.

One way to categorize this variety of contemporary master scheduling techniques is to examine the various competitive environments in which they are utilized. Current APICS terminology provides the following definitions:

make-to-stock product   A product that is shipped from finished goods, "off the shelf," and therefore is finished prior to a customer order arriving. The master scheduling and final assembly scheduling are conducted at the finished goods level. [*Author's note: Generally but not always true.*]

make-to-order product   A product that is finished after receipt of a customer's order. The final product is usually a combination of standard items and items custom designed to meet the special needs of the customer. Frequently long lead time components are planned prior to the order arriving in order to reduce the delivery time to the customer. Where options or other subassemblies are stocked prior to customer orders arriving, the term *assemble-to-order* is frequently used.

engineer to order   Products whose customer specifications require unique engineering design or significant customization. Each customer order results in a unique set of part numbers, bills of materials, and routings.

For purposes of this discussion, an additional category, *capacity managed products,* is added to the above in order to provide a more definitive breakdown of "make-to-order" businesses.

capacity-managed products   In businesses such as foundries and contract machine shops, capacities are planned prior to receipt of customer orders. Upon receipt of a customer order, capacity is committed to manufacture in order to meet the required date.

Implicit in these definitions is the competitive nature of the market. Companies must maintain an acceptable delivery lead time for the customer. Admittedly, in make-to-stock businesses, delivery off the shelf may not result solely from competitive pressure, but it certainly is a primary factor. Manufacturing processes, efficiencies, seasonality, load leveling, and other variables contribute to a decision to stock at various levels in anticipation of customer orders. Figure 12.13 illustrates the role of the MPS in controlling the competitive lead time offered to the customer. It depicts the level of completion through the manufacturing process at which the MPS stages materials and/or capacity prior to receipt of the customer order. The higher this MPS level, the shorter the competitive or delivery lead time to the customer.

Although any such generalization is subject to many exceptions, Table 12.1 describes commonly used MPS techniques in various environments. Where needed, the techniques themselves are described in the section "MPS Mechanics." The reader is cautioned not to assume that the techniques apply only in the listed environment since it is common to find many variations and clever uses of these various MPS techniques.

Multiple-level MPS processes are also common, for example, when a manufacturing facility logically breaks down into different processes. Bulk pharmaceutical manufacturing may have batch-process characteristics requiring one set of MPS criteria. The finishing or packaging process with line orientation is subject to another set of master scheduling considerations. In such circumstances, two separate but related, person-controlled "master schedules" may be in use.

A multiple-level or "two-level" MPS is utilized in assemble-to-order businesses where the production plan sets the rate of manufacture for the family, which also specifies the need for common parts. In addition, the second level, or option level, is also governed by the MPS because of the wide variation of end configurations and the difficulty of forecasting and scheduling at the end configurations level. This is discussed in more detail in the discussion of planning bills of materials.

Another multiple-level MPS example occurs with major subassemblies or component items subject to capacity or materials constraints. Although planning of such items normally occurs at MRP levels, it may be necessary to state a schedule with firm planned orders in order to recognize the constraints. This schedule then places significant constraints on the higher-level, possibly end item, MPS. Even though the lower-level item is technically an MRP item, it is given the same degree of attention and the same amount of human control as an MPS item.

Capacity-managed businesses—foundries, contract machining firms, and so on—are noted for their strong orientation to capacity management first, with secondary consideration for materials needs. Frequently, incoming customer orders are converted to capacity requirements and forward-scheduled based on both ATP capacity (load) and

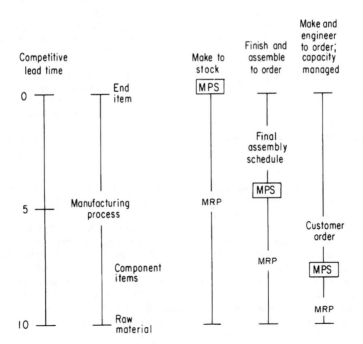

FIGURE 12.13   Role of MPS in controlling competitive lead times.

TABLE 12.1   MPS Techniques for Various Environments

MPS environments	MPS item	MPS techniques
Make to stock	End item	End item forecasts End item safety stocks End item bills of materials (BOMs)
Finish and assemble to order	Options, accessories, attach-ments, intermediates Common parts BOM	Option forecasts Planning BOM as aid Modularized BOM with or without end item BOM Phantoms and pseudo planning items Option overplanning (in lieu of safety stock) Available-to-promise materials
Make to order	Customer orders Management authorizations of: Long lead time component items Speculative items	Customer intelligence forecasts Replacement of authorizations with customer orders Customer commit fences Manufacturing cycle promising
Engineer to order	Customer orders Management authorizations of: "Generic" BOM Long lead time component items	Customer intelligence forecasts Engineering scheduling systems Engineering-manufacturing cycle promising Rough-cut capacity planning of both engineering and manufactur-ing capacities
Capacity managed	Capacity representations	Forward loading based on avail-able-to-promise capacity Raw-intermediate materials on order points or time-phased order points

customer request date. Materials needed are often secondary considerations. Many plastics businesses, for example, injection molding, are similar, especially those working with common compounds and other materials.

The concept of a master scheduling process, strongly oriented to capacity management with secondary consideration to material management, is perhaps another way to categorize various MPS environments. The early MRP pioneers tended to be job shop, assembled-products manufacturers who focused planning processes initially on materials needed and derived capacity needs from them. Repetitive manufacturers and process industries sometimes proceed in reverse fashion. With more dedicated, flowlike manufacturing processes, decisions on the use of capacity dictate the materials needed. In the more general-purpose job shop environment, the decision on what to make, stated in terms of materials needed, dictates capacities needed.

For some of these same reasons, process and flowlike industries often utilize operations research techniques, for example, linear programming, to optimize schedules for their facilities. Since these industries are usually capital intensive and normally less constrained by material considerations, their planning systems emphasize efficient utilization of facilities and capacity.

ROLE OF THE BILL OF MATERIALS IN MASTER SCHEDULING

There is a relationship between the structure and form of the bills of materials and the master scheduling approach within a company. Given the various categories of MPS environments outlined earlier, the format of the bills of materials most commonly in use is shown in Table 12.2.

The *APICS Dictionary* provides the following definitions:

end item　A product sold as a completed item or repair part; any item subject to a customer order or sales forecast. Synonyms: *end product, finished good, finished product.*

option　A choice or feature offered to customers for customizing the end product. In many companies, the term *option* means a mandatory choice—the customer must select from one of the available choices. For example, in ordering a new car, the customer must specify an engine (option) but need not necessarily select an air conditioner (accessory).

accessory　A choice or feature offered to the customer for customizing the end product. In many companies, this term means that the choice does not have to be specified before shipment but could be added at a later date. In other companies, this choice must be made before shipment.

attachment　A choice or feature offered to customers for customizing the end product. In many companies, this term means that the choice, although not mandatory, must be selected before the final assembly schedule. In other companies, however, the choice need not be made at that time.

modular bill (of materials)　A type of planning bill that is arranged in product modules or options. It is often used in companies where the product has many optional features, e.g., assemble-to-order companies such as automobile manufacturers.

planning bill of materials　An artificial grouping of items and/or events in bill of material format, used to facilitate master scheduling and/or material planning. It is sometimes called a *pseudo bill of material.*

super bill (of materials)　A type of planning bill, located at the top level in the structure, that ties together various modular bills (and possibly a common parts bill) to define an entire product or product family. The quantity per relationship of the super bill to its modules represents the fore-

TABLE 12.2　Format of Bills of Materials

Master scheduling environment	Bill of materials form	Engineering status
Make to stock	End item	Preengineered
Finish or assemble to order	Modular	Preengineered
Make to order	End item	Preengineered
Engineer to order	End item	Engineered to order
Capacity managed	End item (if there is one at all)	Engineered (if not a repeat order)

casted percentage of demand for each module. The master scheduled quantities of the super bill explode to create requirements for the modules that also are master scheduled.

common parts bill (of materials)   A type of planning bill that groups common components for a product or family of products into one bill of material, structured to a pseudo parent item number.

phantom bill (of materials)   A bill of material coding and structuring technique used primarily for transient (nonstocked) subassemblies. For the transient item, lead time is set to zero and the order quantity to lot-for-lot. This permits MRP logic to drive requirements straight through the phantom item to its components, but the MRP system usually retains its ability to net against any occasional inventories of the item. This technique also facilitates the use of common bills of material for engineering and manufacturing. Synonyms: *blow-through, pseudo bill of materials, transient bill of materials.*

pseudo bill (of materials)   Synonym: *phantom bill of materials.*

The sheer number of bill of materials terms here should forewarn the reader that there is much to consider in relating the MPS approach to the structure of the underlying bills of materials.

Modular Bills of Materials

Modular bills are the natural choice in firms producing products such as automobiles. Because of the very large number of possible end items in a family, end item needs cannot be effectively forecast. It is practical, however, to forecast and include in the MPS any options, accessories, and attachments. For similar reasons, such firms may not develop and maintain end item bills of materials. Since a particular configuration may be produced only once, a *one-time* bill of materials is constructed for the customer or final-assembly order. The one-time bill lists the options, accessories, and so on required to produce the end item and serves as the historical record of what was produced.

The groups of component parts that constitute the option and accessories bills of materials are often artificial groups. The power- and manual-steering options of an automobile illustrate the situation. Those related steering parts that are used on all cars of the family regardless of the power- or manual-steering choice are structured in a common-parts group. Those related solely to power steering (hydraulic pumps, hoses, etc.) are structured into power-steering-option bills of materials. Similarly, those related solely to manual steering go into a manual-steering-option bills of materials. This organization of the bills of materials often results in planning items—for example, common-parts group, or power-steering group—that cannot be assembled but can be planned as a matched set of parts. It requires a common-parts group *and* a power-steering group *or* a manual-steering group along with all other specified options, to actually assemble the completed product.

Many of the terms defined here developed in environments similar to this automobile example. The *super bill* type of planning bill is often used for forecasting options via percentage relationships. Specifics of super bills are discussed in the "MPS Mechanics" section.

Although modular bill concepts are generally discussed in the context of assembled products such as automobiles, machine tools, and industrial equipment, they can be useful in planning for a wide variety of products. Apparel manufacturers, for example, men's dress shirts, frequently produce large numbers of end items or stock keeping units (SKUs) because of the permutations of style, size, and color. Modular bills might be useful to plan common items such as yarn or thread and optional items such as dyes or labels. Specialty metals manufacturers may employ modular bill concepts to plan intermediate levels of metals in basic alloys and forms that they later fabricate or finish to customer specification.

The reader is cautioned to thoroughly study this relationship between the MPS approach and bill of materials structures. Bills of materials are cornerstone documents in a manufacturing company that have broad implications. Business procedures in addition to the master scheduling process that may be impacted by the structure of the bill of materials include the following:

- Order-entry and promising procedures
- Product costing procedures
- Invoicing procedures
- Engineering drawing systems and change procedures
- Forecasting processes
- Manufacturing instructions and documentation such as pick lists, material issue procedures, and routing or process instructions
- Bill of materials maintenance procedures

Custom, New, and Engineered Products and the Bill of Materials

Engineered-to-order firms, firms producing custom or special products, and firms introducing new products frequently utilize the bill of materials as a capacity planning mechanism and a type of project management tool. In many environments, new, custom, and engineered products evolve from previously produced products. It is often possible to categorize these with *generic* bills of materials, which are used for two purposes: (1) Generic bills identify major components, subassemblies, and materials needed to produce the product. Artificial part numbers are used for this purpose, along with estimated lead times based on past experience. (2) Again by using artificial part numbers, design and development activities, including both estimates of work required and estimated lead times, may also be incorporated into these generic bill structures. In many regards, such bill of materials structures resemble PERT or critical-path networks used to plan and control project activities. The critical path of a CPM network is analogous to the cumulative lead time path(s) of a bill of materials structure. These generic bills of materials serve as a planning element for both sales and operations planning and master production scheduling. The mechanics of the technique are discussed in the "MPS Mechanics" section.

A variation of this technique employs generic bills of materials along with generic routings and work centers. The bill of materials is used to identify major materials needed. Routings and work center relationships are used to describe design and development processes. Operations steps and associated work centers can be defined in the detail required—electrical engineering, mechanical, software, and so on. This approach permits standard MRP scheduling tools such as dispatch lists to be used to schedule various development activities.

THE FINISHING OR FINAL ASSEMBLY SCHEDULE

The *APICS Dictionary* provides the following definition:

final assembly schedule (FAS)   A schedule of end items to finish the product for specific customer orders in a make-to-order or assemble-to-order environment. It is also referred to as the *finishing schedule* because it may involve operations other than just the final assembly; also, it may not involve "assembly," but simply final mixing, cutting, packaging, etc. The FAS is prepared after receipt of a customer order as constrained by the availability of material and capacity, and it schedules the operations required to complete the product from the level where it is stocked (or master scheduled) to the end-item level.

Although not clear from this definition, the finishing or final assembly schedule is found in many make-to-stock as well as make-to-order companies. It is the specific schedule of end items to be produced. For make-to-stock businesses, this schedule replenishes finished-goods inventory. In make-to-order businesses, it states the specific schedule for satisfying customer orders.

The term *final assembly schedule* is in common use because many of the earliest companies to apply MRP techniques were assembled products manufacturers. The term *finishing schedule* is probably the better generic term and has gained acceptance in recent years. It better describes the many companies using MRP that do not produce assembled products, for example, textiles, metals, and chemicals. Synonymous terms include *packaging schedules, blending schedules,* and *line schedules.*

In many companies, the finishing schedule plays a role distinctly different from that of the MPS. The two plans are closely related, however, as the MPS provides materials for use in finishing and is used to plan aggregate finishing capacities. Despite this relationship, the identifiable differences are many.

Items Scheduled Differ between the MPS and the FAS

In many businesses, notably make- and assemble-to-order companies, the types of items scheduled in the FAS differ from those scheduled by the MPS. Capital equipment such as machine tools and automobiles are classic examples. Assembly schedules are often stated in terms of customer orders that define the precise configurations of end items to be produced. The MPS, however, is expressed in terms of a plan for the mix of product options, parts groups, subassemblies, or other lower-level component items. In such environments, the FAS is easily visualized as the relief mechanism for the MPS. Stated in terms of end items or customer orders defining end items, the FAS draws on and relieves the product options made available by the MPS plan.

Different Time Frames

To provide adequate forward visibility, cover cumulative manufacturing and procurement lead time, and plan needed capacities, the MPS may extend 12 or more months into the future. The associated finishing schedule may extend only a few days or weeks with firming of the schedule taking place at the very last possible moment in order to take maximum advantage of available materials and capacity.

Different Time Increments

The MPS and finishing schedule may be stated in quite different time increments. A typical MPS may be stated in weekly priorities (buckets) whereas the finishing schedule may be stated by shifts within the week, by day, by hour, or in other increments (e.g., the automotive industry states assembly schedules by the minute or less).

Control of Materials Issues

The finishing schedule frequently is used rather than the MPS to control the issuing of materials to specific finishing work areas or assembly line stations. A typical example is found in pharmaceutical manufacture with multiple packaging lines. The MPS provides both bulk and packaging materials without regard to packaging line while the packaging schedule controls the quantity and timing of materials issued to specific lines. In major capital equipment assembly, material is frequently issued directly to the proper manufacturing step or routing operation under the control of the assembly schedule.

In make-to-stock businesses utilizing end-item-oriented master schedules, the distinction between the FAS and the MPS may be unclear because both schedules represent statements of end items to be produced. Where a formal FAS is in use, it usually represents a refined MPS plan that considers specific assembly lines or finishing areas to be used, more specific timing of production, and control of the materials issue process. The MPS itself is usually not sufficiently detailed for these purposes.

Interfacing the FAS with the MPS

It is often necessary to create interfacing procedures between customer orders as entered and the underlying MPS in order to state or define the finishing schedule. A good example occurs in office furniture manufacture. A customer order specifies a catalog number that identifies a double-pedestal desk with a locking center drawer, specific drawer arrangements in each pedestal, a modesty panel, a certain finish for the top, and so on, which are only a few of several thousand possible configurations. Order-entry interpretation procedures, manual or automated, are used to translate the customer order to the product options (pedestals, drawers, desktops, locking parts, etc.) scheduled in the MPS. This interpretation process establishes the customer's actual demands, which are then used to calculate ATP dates from the MPS. The process also identifies component materials that must be issued to the assembly department in order to satisfy the order.

In other companies, for example, automobile manufacturers, the customer's order details a series of line items that specify the end item configuration. No catalog number or other permanent reference identifies the end item. The customer or assembly order itself serves as a one-time bill of materials. It is also the basis for historical records of what was produced, that is, warranty and necessary safety records for automobiles.

Because a wide variety of mechanics are used to state, plan, and control finishing and final assembly operations, significantly different requirements exist in different companies. Very sophisticated, computer-assisted tools are necessary in many firms. Manual schedules work well in others.

Anticipating Potential Delays

Preexpediting tools, such as the potential assembly delay report shown in Table 12.3 are frequently used for the near term to check availability of materials in the quantities needed to maintain trouble-free finishing operations. Such tools are used in lieu of physically staging materials prior to actual need. Even with MPS and MRP delivery performance of 95 percent and better (or much higher as demanded in just-in-time or synchronized production environments), near-term follow-up is needed to prevent materials shortages and improve assembly performance.

In the example, 30 of assembly 3503642 are to be assembled under manufacturing order 16649. This job is due to be issued (pulled) October 3 and requires 17 component items, 3 of which can cause potential delays—the motor, bracket, and bearing. *Potential* delays exist because the current on-hand balance will not cover this requirement plus all other requirements for the item in the specified 4-week horizon.

The follow-up message on the motor indicates that there is an existing purchase order on vendor 10124 that, if received on time, will cover this requirement. However, a vendor scheduler should be in contact with the vendor and working to ensure the deliv-

TABLE 12.3 Potential Assembly Delay Report

Assembly 3503642
Job 16649
Horizon, 4 weeks
Date 9/28/86

Component part	Description	On hand	Assembly quantity	Other requirements	Quantity short	Scheduled receipt	Quantity remaining	Date required	Vendor	
1012413	Motor	0	30	0	30	21413	80	10-3	10124	Follow up
1513164	Bracket	20	60	40	80	32141	60	10-3	Shop	Follow up
						32215	60	10-24	Shop	Reschedule in
207531	Bearing	35	30	30	25	31014	100	10-3	11028	Follow up

ery. Contrast this with the assumptions of MRP. Since the requirement is covered by a properly timed scheduled receipt, MRP assumes everything is fine and flashes no warning. In many companies, in the near term, that is usually not acceptable. People need to be actively working to prevent shortages on the factory floor.

The term *paper staging* is sometimes used for this process of anticipating potential delays. The technique only works, of course, with accurate on-hand and on-order records. If these records are not sufficiently accurate, physical staging or advance pulling usually results since it is the only true way to determine what material is actually on hand.

MPS MECHANICS

A large body of fairly standard MPS mechanics has developed as the master scheduling process evolved. The major techniques are discussed in this section.

Standard MPS Format

The standardized display or report format, as seen in Fig. 12.14, evolved from the MRP display, as seen in Fig. 12.15. Many early implementations of MRP simply drove a sales forecast into the projected gross requirements line of MRP as a way to state what was needed. This initiated the MRP process and did develop the component-materials plan much as it is done today. Before long, however, many people began to recognize the need to uncouple the sales forecast from the stated rate of manufacture. With MRP's rapid replanning capability, it was frequently impossible for the plant or suppliers to react to changes in plans caused by forecast changes. This uncoupling process sowed the seeds for some very important MPS mechanics.

The standard MPS illustrates the uncoupling as well as the basic information used to develop the MPS. Lines *A* and *B* of the standard MPS format provide two means to state forecasted requirements. Line *A,* the forecast, usually states independent demand forecasts for MPS items. Line *B,* the production forecast, states forecasts dependent on popularity of options, accessories, and attachments for a family (or model) of products. (See the treatment of planning bills of materials for additional discussion.) Line *C,* actual demand, summarizes current demand for this item.

Line *D,* the projected available balance, is the difference between total demand (both forecasted and actual) and total supply (on hand plus MPS on order). This triggers the logic-generating reschedule recommendations (expedite, deexpedite, cancel, etc.). The uncoupling of the sales rate from the manufacturing rate is very visible with the rise and fall of line *D.* For any number of valid reasons, the MPS may differ from the forecasted requirements for the item. Line *E,* ATP status, is the difference between *firm* actual demands (line *C*) and total supply (on hand plus MPS on order). Line *F,* the MPS, states the manufacturing and/or procurement rate in terms of released (inside manufacturing or supplier lead time) and firm planned orders.

Figure 12.16 illustrates the various calculations. The item is a stocked, purchased subassembly with two sources of demand. It is a product option used to produce parent items (winches) of certain configurations. As such, it has a production forecast, line *B,* representing this forecasted parent-item usage. It is also sold independently as a service or repair part and has an independent demand forecast, line *A,* representing this usage. Note that Fig. 12.16 displays ATP data as both a noncumulative and a cumulative number. A more complete explanation of ATP calculations appears later.

		1	2	3	4	5	6	7	8
A	Forecast				Independent demand forecast				
B	Production forecast				Dependent demand forecast				
C	Actual demand				Customer orders				
D	Projected available balance			Line D = (on hand + line F) − (line A + B + C)*					
E	Available to promise			On hand + MPS − actual demand of line C†					
F	Master production schedule			Released + firm planned orders					

*Assumes forecast consumption by actual demand.
†See sample calculations later in this section.

FIGURE 12.14   Standard MPS format.

Material requirements plan

	1	2	3	4	5	6	7	8
Projected gross requirements								
Scheduled receipts								
Projected available balance								
Planned order release								

FIGURE 12.15   Materials requirements planning format.

Firm Planned Orders

The *firm planned order* (FPO) is an item build or buy schedule that is fixed in both quantity and due date. Computer logic does not automatically change FPOs. Rather, the standard time-phased logic of master production scheduling and material requirements planning that calculates the projected available balance critiques the schedule of FPOs and recommends changes. Any change, however, is the responsibility of the master scheduler for that item. The FPO is the normal method of stating the MPS, and use of the FPO ensures a stable (not changed by the computer) MPS that may differ from the forecasted demand for the item.

By stating the MPS in terms of FPOs, the master scheduler has the opportunity to answer several important questions before actually changing either the quantity or the timing of the MPS: Is material available to support the change? Is capacity available to support the change? Is the change practical? Is the change too costly? Is there a real need to change the plan? (For example, if the recommended change results from actual sales differing slightly from forecast, there may be no real need to change the build plan.)

G 1 0 2 Gearbox		1	2	3	4	5	6	7	8
A	Forecast (service demand)		8			10			
B	Production forecast		0		4	12		15	
C	Actual demand		14		10	2			
D	Projected available balance	25	3	3	29	29	5	5	30	30
E	Available (noncumulative) to promise		11		28				40	
	Available (cumulative) to promise		11	11	39	39	39	39	79	79
F	Master production schedule				40				40	

FIGURE 12.16   Example of an MPS format.

Time Fences

Time fences are means of recognizing the degrees of stability required in the MPS. Frequently, they are merely statements of policy, as noted in the *APICS Dictionary:*

time fence   A policy or guideline established to note where various restrictions or changes in operating procedures take place. For example, changes to the master production schedule can be accomplished easily beyond the cumulative lead time, whereas changes inside the cumulative lead time become increasingly more difficult to a point where changes should be resisted. Time fences can be used to define these points.

In this context, time fences stipulate the time limits within which certain types of changes may occur to the FPOs composing the MPS. A typical policy statement is illustrated in Fig. 12.17.

Too frequently, time fences are established based primarily on cumulative lead times for both manufacturing and procurement of materials. In many companies, the constraints of capacity availability may be more severe than those of materials availability. A truly comprehensive time-fence policy reflects the firm's ability to flex capacity as well as materials availability. In many engineered-to-order companies, for example, engineering capacity is usually a major constraint, and the lead times required to make significant increases can be substantial. The same is often true in process- or capacity-managed businesses.

In addition to time-fence policy statements, some companies incorporate time-fence logic into their MPS formats. The *APICS Dictionary* provides the following helpful definition:

planning time fence   A point in time in the master production schedule. The master schedule planning horizon is divided into three regions. The demand time fence separates regions 1 and 2 and the planning time fence separates regions 2 and 3. Region 1 contains actual orders. Region 2 contains actual orders and forecast orders. Region 3 contains forecast orders and extends to the end of the planning horizon. The planning time fence represents a time period beyond which only forecasts of expected customer orders exist. Between the demand fence and the planning time fence

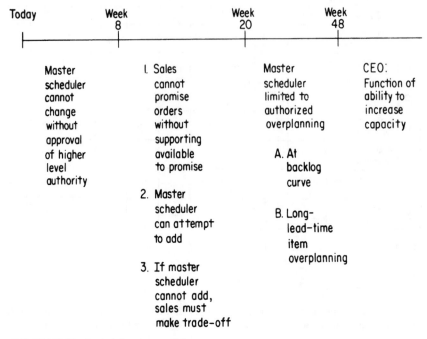

FIGURE 12.17   Typical time-fence policies.

actual customer orders replace the forecast quantities. Management of order acceptance depends on the manufacturing response strategies, make to stock, assemble to order, or make to order, being used by the firm and other management criteria. Synonym: *planning fence.*

Customer Order Promising: ATP Data

As mentioned in the earlier discussion of sales and marketing inputs to, and outputs from, the MPS, the ATP information is an important contribution to marketing-manufacturing communications and is critical to quality customer promises.

ATP status is calculated by comparing the *actual* demand to the on-hand plus MPS. Figure 12.18 shows a typical situation with a cumulative display of ATP data. Five are considered ATP in the current week (week 1). Although 23 are on hand, 18 customer commitments exist, 11 in week 1 and 7 in week 2, which must be satisfied from that 23. Customer commitments of 11 exist in weeks 3 and 4, which can be satisfied from the 40 scheduled due in week 3. This leaves 29 of the 40 available to promise plus 5 from previous weeks for the total shown of 34.

The MPS is stated with FPOs in order to cover forecasted demands for many months ahead. As time passes, actual demand materializes, but it rarely ever agrees exactly with the forecast. The ATP figure thus shows the current picture of product available to customers based on current customer commitments and current build plans. Many companies now rely on this information for quoting delivery dates instead of the older practice of quoting standard delivery lead times.

Many forms of make-to-order businesses routinely employ customer promising based on ATP data because they are continuously dealing with changing backlogs of

		Period							
		1	2	3	4	5	6	7	8
A	Forecast								
B	Production forecast		2	4	5	10	10	10	10
C	Actual demand	11	7	6	5				
D	Projected available balance	12	3	33	23	13	3	33	23
E	Available to promise (cumulative)	5	5	34	34	34	34	74	74
F	Master production schedule			40				40	

(Projected available balance leading value: 23)

FIGURE 12.18 Available-to-promise display.

customer orders scheduled for future shipments. Make-to-stock firms building to forecasts normally view on-hand shelf stocks as ATP. However, when they are back-ordered on an item or when customer orders are requested or scheduled for future shipment, make-to-stock firms require similar time-phased ATP information. It is important to protect existing customer commitments when new customer orders are promised.

Planning Bills of Materials

Although planning bills or super bills of materials were defined earlier, the use of the planning bill in master scheduling requires some additional discussion. Planning bills of materials are commonly found in companies that finish or assemble to order. In many instances, many possible configurations of end items that go into the assembly can be produced from a small number of subassemblies, parts groupings (modules), and common-component parts. Classic examples include automobiles, machine tools, and electronic equipment. Figure 12.18 shows a typical planning bill for the hypothetical M-body automobile family.

In most instances, planning bills grow out of the need to simplify forecasting problems. Often it is virtually impossible to forecast the finished end item configurations that will sell, but it is possible to forecast, with workable accuracy, the mix of product options, accessories, and attachments that will then be configured into the end item as specified by the customer order. The percentages of the planning bill detail this forecast of option mix. The term *two-level forecasting* is sometimes used to describe the process: Level 0 forecasts for the forecast family (M body), and level 1 forecasts for the percentage popularity of the product options (common-parts group, V8 group, V6 group, etc.).

The term *dependent forecast* is used to describe the forecast for a given option. For example, if the plan for the M-body family is 500 per week, then the dependent forecast for the 60 percent V6 engine group is 300 per week. Since 300 per week is calculated by multiplying by a percentage, it is termed *dependent* in the same sense that gross requirements for an MRP component are dependent demands calculated by multiplying quantity per relationships in a bill of materials.

Planning bills of materials are very powerful MPS tools. They have a number of purposes beyond simplifying the forecasting problem: They aid in sales and operations planning, reduce mismatched options, aid in rescheduling MPS options, aid order promising, and control forecast consumption for MPS options.

Aid in Sales and Operations Planning. Very often the planning families organized into planning bills are the same families reviewed by the sales and operations planning group. In the hypothetical M-body family of automobiles, the management group, faced with dwindling dealer stock, might agree to a rate of manufacture (production plan) that is designed to increase dealer stocks to a target level over time. This rate of production clearly must exceed the expected rate of sales by dealers during this period in order to increase dealer stocks. It is this agreed-to production plan for M bodies that is then used to drive the master scheduling of options through the planning bill of materials. It is for this reason that line *B* of the standard MPS format (Fig. 12.14) is often labeled the *production forecast.*

Reduce Mismatched Options. The option mix contained within the planning bill is reviewed frequently. Based on the historical mix, the mix of the current backlog, and marketing insight into future trends, these percentages are modified as needed. Any such changes immediately initiate the rebalancing of MPS options. Some companies have found it helpful to time-phase percentages in planning bills so that varying option mixes can be used at different times.

Aid in Rescheduling MPS Options. Over time, actual demand probably will occur in about the expected mix. In any given week or month, however, the actual mix will vary from the forecasted mix. As this occurs, appropriate rescheduling recommendations are made on those MPS options impacted. (The forecast consumption discussion that follows details some of the specifics of how this happens.)

Aid in Order Promising. Frequently, the planning bill is integrated directly into the customer promising function of order entry. In the M-body example, a customer or dealer order might call for a special model with a V6 engine, automatic transmission, and power antenna. The promise for the order would be based on the ATP conditions of the selected options. In concept, the gating or pacing ATP data would dictate the delivery date.

Control Forecast Consumption for MPS Options. A variety of techniques are used to control forecast consumption for MPS options with planning bills. Some common approaches are discussed here through a series of examples.

The classic example used in the literature is a hoist (Fig. 12.19), popularized by Orlicky, Plossl, and Wight.[3] With 2400 possible combinations of modules (options, features, attachments, etc.), planning bills are very useful for forecasting and master scheduling this product.

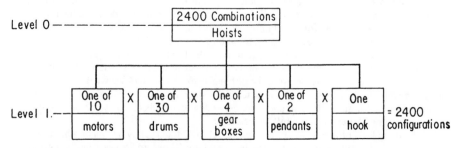

FIGURE 12.19 Hoist planning bill of materials.

Figure 12.20 illustrates the typical three-zone MPS of make- and assemble-to-order companies. The planning process involves setting a production plan (40 per month) for hoists that considers marketplace needs, desired backlog levels, staffing required, and so on. With a forecasted split of 50/50 between pendants 1 and 2 (P_1 and P_2), the second-level forecast for P_1 and P_2 becomes 20 per month, or 10 every other week, as shown. (The examples all assume 4-week months for simplicity.)

Zone 1 covers weeks 1 to 3, in which hoists are completely sold out. Second-level mix forecasts for P_1 and P_2 are no longer needed in zone 1 since actual backlog fully describes the P_1/P_2 mix. Zone 3 covers weeks 7 and beyond. There is no customer backlog beyond week 6, and the plan must be based on pure two-level forecasts. Zone 2 is in the middle, weeks 4 to 6, where the plan must deal with a mixture of backlog and actual demand. The actual demand indicates the 50/50 forecasted mix is not bad. Of 36 hoists sold through the fourth week, 19 used P_1 and 17 used P_2.

Three basic types of mechanics are used to control consumption of option forecasts. Type 1 planning bill mechanics (Fig. 12.21) explode the ATP data of the hoist family. In week 4 (zone 2), 16 of 20 hoists have sold, and 4 are available to promise to a customer. Of the 4 ATP hoists, a good estimate of option mix is 50/50, that is two P_1's and two P_2's. In week 2 (zone 1), this approach produces a zero second-level forecast, which is desirable. In week 8 (zone 3), it produces the desired 10.

This approach of exploding family ATP data is responsive to a changing mix of actual demand but does create the potential for "planning nervousness" with each sale in zone 2 of the MPS. In week 4, the original forecast of 50/50 has now been changed to a 45/55 percent split between P_1 and P_2. The combination of the remaining P_1 forecast of 2 and the actual P_1 demand of 7 totals 9. And 9 of 20 is 45 percent. A responsive MPS tool might recommend a reschedule or deexpedite of P_1 material in week 4 since the original forecast of 10 has been reduced to 9. The opposite is true in week 6 for P_1. The original forecast of 10 has been replaced by requirements for 11 (6 remaining forecast and 5 actual demand).

People who understand the probability theory of flipping coins prefer type 1 planning bills. Sixteen tosses have been made in week 4. Four tosses remain. The best estimate of results in those four tosses is a 50/50 split.

Type 2 planning bill mechanics (Fig. 12.22) consume option forecasts week by week with actual demand. Originally, all P_1 forecasts were 10. Since 7 sold in week 4, of the 10 forecast, 7 were consumed, leaving 3. In week 2, all 10 were consumed by actual demand of 12, and so on.

Type 2 mechanics must deal with the P_2 situation in week 2. Even though only 8 sold, the unconsumed forecast of 2 must be eliminated. Otherwise, the MPS would call for 10 sets of P_2 material, 2 of which are not required. Type 2 mechanics must also deal with situations in which forecasts and the actual demand do not fall in the same week.

Type 2 planning bills do a better job of protecting the original 50/50 forecast split than type 1 bills. The assumption made is that 20 hoists will sell 50/50 in the end.

Type 3 planning bills (Fig. 12.23) extend the thought process of type 2. For example, examine P_1. Type 3 mechanics recognize that through week 4, of the original 20 forecast for P_1, 19 have sold, and 1 unconsumed forecast remains in week 4. Through week 6, 24 of 30 have sold and 6 remain—1 in week 4 and 5 in week 6. Type 3 tries to hold to the projected 50/50 split on a cumulative basis. It potentially generates less MPS nervousness than either type 1 or 2. Type 3 is also slowest to respond to a changing mix.

Cautionary Notes on Planning Bills of Materials. Any discussion of planning bills would be incomplete if it did not include two notes of caution on planning bills. Planning bills work well under certain business conditions. Planning bills work well for families of products with reasonable sales volumes, fairly stable mix conditions, large

3 Zones

|←—— Zone 1 ——→|←—— Zone 2 ——→|←— Zone 3 —→|

Hoists		Period						
40 per month	1	2	3	4	5	6	7	8
Production plan/ MPS		20		20		20		20
Actual demand		20		16		8		0
Available to promise					44			

36

Pendant 1 (50%)	1	2	3	4	5	6	7	8
Forecast								
Production forecast		10		10		10		10
Actual demand		12		7		5		0
Projected available balance					24			
Available to promise			19					
Master production schedule								

Pendant 2 (50%)	1	2	3	4	5	6	7	8
Forecast								
Production forecast		10		10		10		10
Actual demand		8		9		3		0
Projected available balance					20			
Available to promise			17					
Master production schedule								

FIGURE 12.20   Three-zone MPS.

Hoists	Period							
40 per month	1	2	3	4	5	6	7	8
Production plan		20		20		20		20
Actual demand		20		16		**8**		0
Available to promise		0		4		12		20

Pendant 1 (50%)	1	2	3	4	5	6	7	8
Forecast								
Production forecast		0		2		6		10
Actual demand		12		7		5		0
Projected available balance								
Available to promise								
Master production schedule								

Pendant 2 (50%)	1	2	3	4	5	6	7	8
Forecast								
Production forecast		0		2		**6**		10
Actual demand		8		9		3		0
Projected available balance								
Available to promise								
Master production schedule								

FIGURE 12.21   Consuming MPS option forecasts, type I, explode family available to promise.

Hoists 40 per month		Period							
		1	2	3	4	5	6	7	8
Production plan			20		20		20		20
Actual demand			20		16		8		0
Available to promise									

Pendant 1 (50%)		1	2	3	4	5	6	7	8
Forecast									
Production forecast			0		3		5		10
Actual demand			12		7		5		0
Projected available balance									
Available to promise									
Master production schedule									

Pendant 2 (50%)		1	2	3	4	5	6	7	8
Forecast									
Production forecast			2		1		6		10
Actual demand			8		9		3		0
Projected available balance									
Available to promise									
Master production schedule									

FIGURE 12.22   Consuming MPS option forecasts, type 2, current period forecast consumption.

Hoists		Period							
40 per month		1	2	3	4	5	6	7	8
Production plan			20		20		20		20
Actual demand			20		16		8		0
Available to promise									

Pendant 1 (50%)		1	2	3	4	5	6	7	8
Forecast									
Production forecast			0		1		5		10
Actual demand			12		7		5		0
Projected available balance									
Available to promise						Σ 24 of 30			
Master production schedule			Σ 19 of 20						

Pendant 2 (50%)		1	2	3	4	5	6	7	8
Forecast									
Production forecast			0		3		7		10
Actual demand			8		9		3		0
Projected available balance					Σ 20 of 30				
Available to promise			Σ 17 of 20						
Master production schedule									

FIGURE 12.23   Consuming MPS option forecasts, type 3, cumulative forecast consumption.

numbers of customer orders for small quantities, and smooth customer demand patterns. As these conditions change, results become mixed.

Major customers who buy products in certain configurations—for example, a fleet buyer of automobiles that are all equipped with power steering—can disrupt a planning bill forecast which assumes a standard option mix. Lumpy demand patterns can vary substantially from the smooth pattern projected by planning bills. Planning families with small sales volumes or options with small percentage popularity are difficult to handle since any sale, in itself, represents a significant portion of the forecast and any variation from either forecast totals or mix will be significant.

The second cautionary note regards the general application of planning bills. Much of the literature describes planning bills as useful for planning families of assemble- or finish-to-order products—automobiles, hoists, and so on. Planning bills have also found use in many other planning situations. For example, when end items produced to stock are planned, aggregate forecasts of family sales can be apportioned to individual items by the percentages of a planning bill.

Another variation found in some companies is a planning bill that forecasts raw- and intermediate-materials needs in the intermediate to long horizon of the MPS. As these forecasted needs reach specified decision points or time fences in the MPS, the plans are converted to firm planned orders that define the specific end items to be produced. A firm making a family of hand saws might utilize this technique. Beyond some specified time, a planning bill could be used to forecast blade steels in some mix. As it came time to commit to specific end items, this planning bill would be replaced (consumed) by end-item-specific FPOs. Many process industries with relatively few common raw materials operate in a similar manner.

Option Overplanning

Option overplanning is a master scheduling technique used to manage a sophisticated form of safety stock. It is most commonly associated with finish- or assemble-to-order firms although, once again, variations on the technique also apply in other master scheduling environments.

Given the hoist with pendant 1 or pendant 2 options introduced earlier, Figs. 12.24 and 12.25 display the mechanics of option overplanning. Zone 2 of the MPS begins in week 4. This is the point at which the customer backlog curve declines. Customer orders on hand are less than the total number of hoists to be manufactured.

Only 20 pendants are required in week 4 since the overall production plan is set to produce 20 hoists, each requiring one pendant. The MPS, however, calls for a total of 22 pendants in week 4—10 P_1's and 12 P_2's. The excess of 2 represents a mix hedge in zone 2 of the MPS. This is the first point of exposure to possible variation in option mix demand.

In the fourth week, 4 hoists remain to be sold (20 hoists planned minus 16 firm customer orders). These appear as ATP hoists. Normally, these 4 would split 50/50 between P_1 and P_2. The number of ATP hoists for P_1, however, is 3 in week 4, since 7 actual customer demands exist for the 10 in the MPS. In week 4, similarly, 3 P_2's are available to promise (9 actual demands versus 12 in the MPS). The 2 extra pendants, that is, option overplanning, provide a 75/25 percent mix protection either way on the two pendants. Of 4 hoist orders, 3 could call for either pendant and sufficient components would be available. If perfect mix protection were desired, the MPS would read 11 in week 4 for P_1 with 4 available to promise and 13 in week 4 for P_2, also with 4 available to promise.

Figure 12.24 illustrates the management of option overplanning as hoist bookings materialize. Effectively, once 4 additional hoist orders are committed in week 4, zone 1

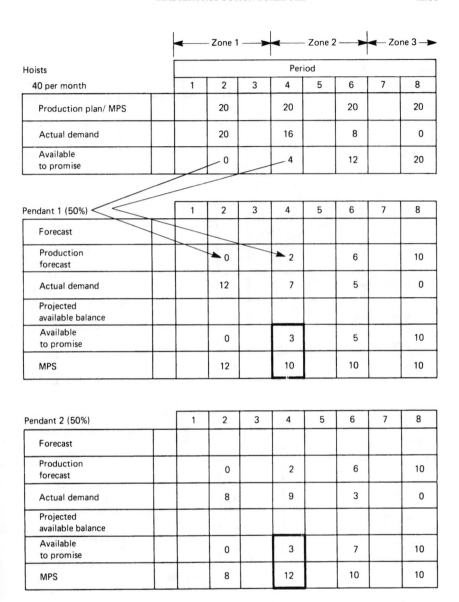

FIGURE 12.24   One example of MPS option overplanning.

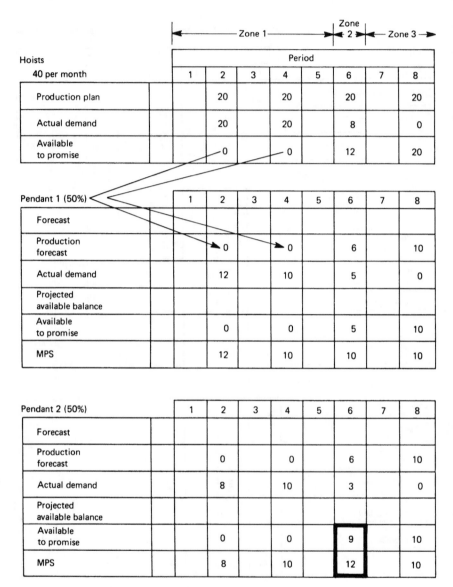

FIGURE 12.25 Another example of MPS option overplanning.

moves out and now includes weeks 4 and 5. In Fig. 12.25, of the 4 orders received, 3 specified P_1 and the other specified P_2. Under these circumstances, the extra two pendants visible in Fig. 12.24 are P_2's. Since these are obviously no longer required in week 4, the MPS is now changed in two positions: the 12 P_2's in week 4 of Fig. 12.24 are reduced to 10, leaving none available to promise, and the 10 P_2's in week 6 of Fig. 12.24 are changed to the 12 of week 6 in Fig. 12.25. Through this rolling-out process, the master scheduler attempts to maintain a measure of protection against customer order mix by managing extra options in the early periods of zone 2 of the MPS.

In the example, two extra (i.e., above the original forecast) P_1 options have been committed to customer orders in weeks 2 and 4. The master scheduler must now consider materials lead times and capacity constraints before increasing some future MPS plan to restore some option overplanning for P_1. Conceptually, the MPS plan would be increased in the period just beyond the cumulative lead time for P_1's.

Rolling the unused options forward as illustrated for the P_2 option creates the potential for planning nervousness within MRP. The original gross requirements pattern of 12 and 10 in weeks 4 and 6, respectively, has been changed to a 10 and 12 pattern on each component of the P_2 option. If some of these components are planned using discrete or lot-for-lot size rules, then a deexpedite or reschedule-out recommendation may result. As a practical consideration, however, this potential nervousness is often dampened by the MRP lot-sizing rules in use. For example, the change in the gross requirements pattern might have no effect on a component produced in lot sizes of 50.

Option overplanning has decided advantages over conventional MRP safety stock techniques. It is consciously managed by master schedulers whereas standard safety stock provisions are controlled automatically by computer logic. In periods of scarce capacity, for example, a person will react by cutting back on such overplanning. By contrast, standard computer logic without intervention will continue to plan to replenish safety stock and give safety stock equal priority to firm, committed customer requirements.

MRP safety stock logic also continuously attempts to maintain materials on hand and thus in inventory, unlike option overplanning techniques. A manufacturing company with a firm 12-week backlog (zone 1) of the MPS illustrates this difference. Components of a P_2 option with cumulative lead times greater than 12 weeks must be on order or in process to support P_2 option overplanning in week 13 of the MPS. Other components with lesser cumulative lead times may not even be on order. Standard safety stock logic, however, would try to maintain all specified components in inventory regardless of their lead times.

Most important, however, option overplanning in the MPS works to create safety stocks in *matched sets of parts*. To achieve the same effect by using MRP-level safety stocks, the safety stocks specified on the various component items would have to be carefully coordinated. In general, managing option overplanning in the MPS will more consistently create the necessary matched sets of parts.

Frequently, master schedulers who lack contemporary MPS tools resort to overstating the planning percentages in the planning bill of materials as a way to provide option mix protection. For example, one might specify 55 percent option forecasts on both P_1 and P_2 options in Fig. 12.24, totaling 110 percent. This forecasts a total of 22 pendant options for every 20 hoists planned. The shortcoming, however, in this approach is that it projects requirements at a 110 percent rate through *all* periods. By contrast, the option overplanning technique overstates the needs for P_1 and P_2 *only* in the early periods of zone 2.

On balance, option overplanning is a valid technique for managing safety stocks. Users of the technique should, however, be aware of its potential to cause MRP nervousness as well as the level of effort required by master schedulers to properly manage option overplanning.

Custom, New, and Engineered Products and the MPS

Earlier the use of generic bills of materials was discussed for firms producing engineered-to-order and custom products as well as firms managing significant amounts of new-product introduction. These generic bills are used to estimate levels of design and development activity as well as schedule that activity to meet required dates.

Both sales and operations planning and master scheduling have a strong capacity orientation initially. In the intermediate- to long-range planning horizon, the primary need is to plan adequate staffing capacities to meet expected business levels. Various categories of products and projects represented by generic bills are forecast. Expected rates of business are expressed with artificial family or item numbers in the production plan and MPS. Then MRP explosions of generic bills are used to calculate time-phased staffing requirements.

Customer orders, when received, are assigned the appropriate generic bill of materials. Assigned a completion date, the customer-specific bill is then used to schedule design and development activity. Long lead time items are customarily designed first. As the specifics of the design progress, the artificial part numbers of the generic bill are replaced by "real" part numbers. Routings and work center assignments are added by manufacturing or industrial engineering. In concept, the generic bill progressively evolves to the actual bill of materials for the product or project.

Conventional MRP logic is used with the progressing design to plan component material priorities. The generic bill of materials structure with estimated lead times that exists above the real components serves to time-phase priorities until the design is complete. Should customer-required dates change, MRP replanning is automatically initiated for all components and remaining development activities.

New-product development activities are often managed in a similar manner. Although new products are usually not ties to customer orders, the generic bill of materials structure serves as a project planning and control device.

Historically, PERT and CPM tools have been effective as *single-project planning and control tools,* although some now offer multiple-project capabilities. The generic bill of materials approach outlined above is effective because it is useful in the multiple-project circumstances found in many companies. In custom products manufacture, each customer order in-house is a "project" competing for common resources. MRP logic thus becomes useful in planning and scheduling that competition for capacity.

A GENERAL MASTER PRODUCTION SCHEDULING FRAMEWORK[1]

This is concerned with the actual practice of master scheduling by manufacturing firms. It seeks to define and generalize the present state of the art through a detailed analysis of the MPS systems at eight quite different companies. Before proceeding with the detailed descriptions of the eight systems, an overall framework is needed. First, we need to define *master scheduling* and the activities that are encompassed by the MPS function, and second, we need to define the relationship of the MPS function to the many other production planning and control activities that occur in manufacturing firms. This framework will be used in describing the operating features of MPS systems described here and in understanding the common elements in the practice of master scheduling in any firm.

Figure 12.26 depicts the elements in manufacturing planning and control systems that relate directly to master production scheduling. The arrows indicate the flows of

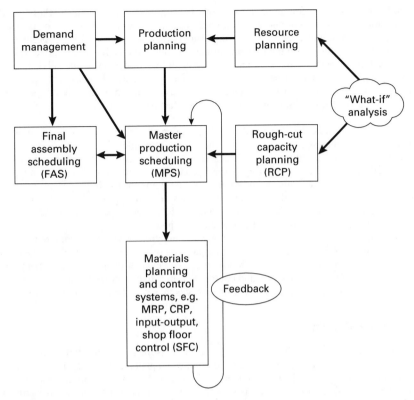

FIGURE 12.26 Relationship of master production scheduling to other manufacturing planning and control activities.

information among these elements. In this chapter, the activities contained within each of these elements are defined and discussed.

Demand Management

The *demand management block* shown represents the forecasting order entry, order promising, and physical distribution activities in a company. This block includes all of the activities that place demands (requirements) for products on manufacturing. These demands may take the form of actual and forecast customer orders, branch warehouse requirements, interplant requirements, international requirements, and service-parts demand. Clearly, some of these categories may take on more or less importance in particular companies. That is, the manufacturing output at some firms may be directed entirely at the replenishment of distribution warehouses, while at other firms the production output may be solely to satisfy individual customer orders. At still other firms, manufacturing may have to satisfy demand from both of these sources.

A key aspect of demand management involves the interfunctional coordination of various demands placed on manufacturing. That is, manufacturing needs to be closely coordinated with other functional areas within the company, for example, marketing and distribution, in processing detailed customer orders, in preparing forecasts of production requirements, and in coordinating the restocking of warehouses. This coordination is more than simply improving interfunctional communications. It is necessary to establish detailed computer databases and to clearly define functional responsibilities for transactions and updates to the databases. Examples include forecast data that are updated by actual customer orders, clear definitions of when a product is shipped, and how title passes for inventory moving from manufacturing work-in-process to finished goods.

Figure 12.26 indicates that the demand management activity influences three other manufacturing planning and control elements: production planning, master scheduling, and final assembly scheduling. The forecasts prepared as a part of the demand management activity are used in preparing overall production plans, as well as providing an estimate of the requirements for individual product items for use in preparing the master production schedule. Likewise, the order entry and order promising activities provide requirements information for individual products that is provided directly to the master schedule as well as to the final assembly schedule.

In a similar fashion, the demand management function serves to coordinate requirements from the field warehouse with the preparation of the master schedule or the final assembly schedule. Again, the particular interface between demand management and the other manufacturing planning and control activities may vary from company to company, and each of the related information linkages may take on more or less emphasis.

Production Planning

The production planning block in Fig. 12.26 represents the activities involved in preparing an overall production plan for the business. Such a plan represents a strategic "game plan" for the company, which reflects the desired aggregate output from manufacturing. In some firms, the production plan is simply stated in terms of the monthly or quarterly sales dollar output for the company as a whole, or for individual plants or businesses. In other firms, the production plan is stated in terms of the number of units to be produced in each major product line monthly for the next year. The units of manufacturing activities used in preparing the production plan vary considerably among companies. In addition to sales dollar output and the overall units per month for major product groupings, measures such as direct labor hours and pounds of product produced are also used.

The production plan is a top-management responsibility, representing management's control knob on the business. It provides guidelines and constraints within which manufacturing is expected to operate. The production plan represents an agreement between marketing, manufacturing, and finance as to what (in aggregate) will be produced and made available for sale to the customers. This agreement forms the basis for budgetary and market planning for the company. A change in one aspect of a company's strategic plans, such as the sales plan, the production plan, or the financial plan, necessarily means a change in the other two plans. Once the production plan is set, manufacturing has its task clearly defined—"to hit the production plan." In many firms, the production plan is a key yardstick for measuring the performance of the plant managers. Likewise, once the production plan is established and agreed upon by top management, sales has its work defined—"to make the sales budget." A sales budget that is not met (or is exceeded) means that unplanned finished-goods inventory (or excessive back orders) will be created.

The production planning activity at some firms is a highly structured process, often conducted on a monthly basis. This process often begins with the creation of a new sales forecast covering a year or more. Next, any increases or decreases in inventory or back-log levels are decided in order to determine total production requirements. Once the total demand to be placed on manufacturing is determined, the way in which manufacturing will meet this demand, that is, the production plan, can be decided. It is important to note that the production plan should equal the sales forecast in total over a designated period, perhaps a year. However, the timing of production may vary considerably from the sales forecast, creating planned increases (or decreases) in inventory levels. The steps involved in preparing the production plan occasionally take place over a period of several weeks or more, involving the top executives—the president, the vice-president of manufacturing, the vice-president of marketing, and the vice-president of finance.

The production planning block shown feeds directly into the master production scheduling activity. The production plan provides the guidelines within which the master production scheduling process takes place.

Resource Planning

The resource planning block shown represents the process of determining the long-range capacity needs of the business. This activity involves translating the long-range sales forecasts and production plans, covering the next 1 to 10 years, into the required manufacturing facilities. The time horizon considered reflects the lead time required to acquire new facilities. In some firms, the resource plan is stated in terms of the number of machine-hours required per year for individual machines and work centers to meet the planned annual production rate. At other firms the resource requirements may be stated in terms of the number of pounds of output required per year for specific manufacturing processes. Other measures are used as well.

The resource planning block is directly related to the production planning block. This indicates that resource planning sets the capacity limits within which the production planning activity must operate. To the extent that the resource planning activity is performed using the same units as those considered in production planning, improvement in communication and operation performance can result. Although not shown, the resource planning activity often provides the basis for the capital budgeting activities in a company.

Final Assembly Scheduling

The final assembly scheduling (FAS) activity serves as the basis for planning and controlling the final assembly and test operations in manufacturing. The preparation and execution of the final assembly schedule is separate from master scheduling. The master production schedule represents the *anticipated* build schedule for a firm's products, covering the time span between raw material acquisition and the delivery of the component items to the inventory just before final assembly. The final assembly schedule specifies the actual build schedule covering a time period that begins when all of the component items are available for final assembly and ends when the products are shipped to customers. Thus, it serves to accumulate necessary component parts and to schedule final assembly, testing, and packing operations.

The final assembly schedule represents a commitment to the production of specific end product configurations. If customer orders are not on hand for these items, they will become a part of the firm's finished-goods inventory. Thus, the decision of what items to put into finished-goods inventory becomes a part of the final assembly scheduling process. In make-to-order firms, where sufficient customer orders exist in an order backlog, the final assembly schedule is simply a commitment of when to produce each customer order.

In assemble-to-order and make-to-stock firms, it is desirable to hold off on the commitment of when to produce specific final product configurations until the latest possible moment that still allows time for order picking, final assembly, and test operations. By holding off as long as possible in firming up the final assembly schedule, component items can be used to produce actual customer orders as opposed to forecasts of what customer orders are likely to be received. Thus, excess inventories of finished products and assembly shortages at the same time are minimized. Because of the endless variety of final product configurations in most assemble-to-order firms, the assembly scheduling process is perhaps most critical in these companies.

The final assembly schedule is often stated in terms of the number of units of each end product catalogue item to be produced. However, in make-to-order firms the final assembly schedule may be stated in terms of individual customer orders, indicating all of the product units or assemblies that are required to ship a particular customer order. Another variant of the final assembly schedule is found in assemble-to-order firms. The final assembly schedule is frequently identified by an assembly order number and is stated in terms of the quantities of individual product options that are to be grouped together and assembled as a unit.

The final assembly schedule can serve an additional purpose in manufacturing firms where all of the items required to produce an end product are not under the control of the master production schedule. In many firms, inexpensive hardware items and short lead time components are scheduled and controlled via the final assembly schedule. Similarly, some component items are far too bulky or expensive to produce in advance of assembly; these items can sometimes be under the control of the final assembly schedule instead of the master production schedule, with timing carefully controlled by the final assembly schedule.

The flow of information into the final assembly scheduling block in Fig. 12.26 comes from two sources: demand management and master scheduling. Actual customer orders come from the order entry activity under demand management, and the production schedule for individual product configurations comes from the MPS function.

Rough-Cut Capacity Planning

The rough-cut capacity planning activity involves an analysis of the master production schedule to determine the existence of critical manufacturing facilities that are potential bottlenecks in the flow of production. Such analysis is typically made during the master schedule review or whenever adjustments are made to the master production schedule. Every firm has several critical steps in the production process that need to be carefully monitored as changes in the mix of products occur in the master schedule. At some firms, final assembly or finishing operations represent the critical operations to be closely watched. In other firms, the critical operation involves a key machine that is operating on a three-shift basis. At still other firms, the critical operation may be a vendor who supplies a key raw material not readily available from other sources. Rough-cut capacity planning identifies the impact of the MPS on these critical operations.

The rough-cut capacity analysis is typically performed much less frequently and covers a longer time span than the weekly shop load reports produced from capacity requirements planning (CRP) systems using shop floor control and MRP data. The rough-cut analyses also involve the use of simpler capacity planning techniques and far less detailed information than the CRP analysis. That is, rough-cut capacity planning typically involves the use of bills of capacity or simple planning factor estimates instead of time-phased MPR and routing file data. The simpler procedures, while less accurate, permit a quick analysis to indicate whether the MPS is feasible in view of the current capacity of the company. It also permits a rapid analysis of several alternatives that may be posed by top management in reviewing the master production schedule. Such an analysis sometimes leads to a decision to make changes in the master schedule in order to accommodate the capacity limitations of the key facilities, or a decision to change the MPS and to implement adjustments to capacity involving overtime, subcontracting, the alternate routing of work, employment level changes, and so forth. These changes are often planned over a considerable period of time, covering a quarter or more into the future.

The rough-cut capacity planning block is shown as feeding information into the MPS function. This reflects its basic objective of keeping the MPS realistic in terms of available capacity.

Master Production Scheduling

The master production scheduling block shown in Fig. 12.26 covers the variety of activities involved in the preparation and the maintenance of the MPS. The MPS represents a statement of the anticipated build schedule for a company's products. This schedule is stated in specific product configurations, and typically it indicates the quantity to be produced in weekly buckets during the next 6 to 12 months or longer. The product unit that is selected for master scheduling, however, varies considerably among firms. For example, in the make-to-stock company, the master schedule is often stated in terms of end product items. It can also be stated in terms of lower-level items like a major assembly or component part, or unpackaged bulk product. In some make-to-order firms, the actual customer order is used as the master scheduling unit. Assemble-to-order firms have a very complex problem in defining a master scheduling unit. In this case, their master scheduling unit may not be a buildable end item but rather units of a "planning" bill that facilitates the schedule of production and relies on the final assembly schedule to make a salable product. This could involve master scheduling at the "option" level if it reduced the number of items to be master scheduled. As an example, the master production schedule in an assemble-to-order firm may be stated in terms of customer options such as horsepower and rear axle gear ratios on trucks. One criterion in selecting the master scheduling unit is to minimize the number of items in the master schedule. By reducing the number of items considered in the MPS, improved forecasting accuracy and reduced administrative costs are gained.

The MPS represents a statement of production and not a forecast of market demand. That is, the planned production level may vary considerably from the actual pattern of market demand. The MPS reflects manufacturing's strategy (as stated in the production plan) for meeting the market demand, considering such factors as production capacity limits, raw material availabilities, and production economics.

Another characteristic of the MPS is that it represents a disaggregation of the production plan into individual product items. In particular, the MPS represents the *first* time that the production plan is desegregated into specific product units, while the final assembly schedule represents the *final* disaggregation of the production plan into specific buildable end products. This characteristic has two important implications. First, if the MPS represents disaggregation of the production plan, then the reverse must also be true. That is, the MPS must always aggregate back to the production plan in order for it to remain consistent with the overall business plan. Second, the MPS represents a *forecast* of what products will be built (anticipated build schedule), while the final assembly schedule specifies *exactly* what end products will be produced. The MPS represents a management commitment authorizing only the procurement of raw materials and the production of component items. The final assembly schedule represents a management commitment to deliver specific end products to either the customers or to the finished-good inventory.

This *firm planned order* is a key concept in master production scheduling. The firm planned order clearly separates the demand for a company's products from the schedule for producing the products. It makes it possible to manage the master schedule while accounting for capacity, demand, product mix, and other important variables. The firm planned order introduces stability into the schedule and provides the basis for account-ability in managing the schedule. In addition, it provides the communication link with the MRP system to explode component requirements.

The master scheduling block shown in Fig. 12.26 represents the focal point of all of the production planning and control activities shown. For example, demand management supplies all of the demand requirements and customer orders to the master pro-duction schedule. Likewise, production planning indicates the operating constraints within which the MPS function must work. Furthermore, the rough-cut capacity plan-ning activity indicates bottleneck work centers or production facilities that are likely to be road blocks in meeting the MPS. The MPS framework shown also indicates the flow of information away from the MPS activity. Scheduling information is provided for the preparation of the final assembly schedule. Finally, the MPS model shows the flow of information back from the MRP, CRP, and SFC systems to the master production sched-ule. This feedback is useful in indicating material and capacity unavailabilities, thereby keeping the MPS realistic.

What-If Analysis

Another element in the MPS model is *what-if analysis*. From time to time, top manage-ment may be concerned with the ability of the company to respond to certain changes in the production plan or the MPS. Sometimes these changes involve the addition of prod-ucts not currently included in the MPS. That is, marketing may want to know the impact on the current delivery commitments to customers if a large order is accepted, or if the delivery date on an order for an important customer is advanced. Likewise, a potential strike at an important supplier may be of concern to top management. Thus, an impor-tant element of the master scheduling system is the ability to simulate changes in the MPS or the production plan and to rapidly assess the effects of these changes.

Many computer-based MPS and production planning systems have the capability to answer what-if questions. Such systems have special features to ensure that the data files are not altered permanently to reflect the what-if analysis conditions but are returned to reflect the current conditions. Flexibility, rapid turnaround, and easy access to the data are all important in providing the capability.

MATERIALS PLANNING AND CONTROL SYSTEMS

Certain aspects of production planning and control systems have been deliberately excluded from the MPS model shown because they were not within the scope of this study. The materials planning and control systems block represents the MRP, CRP, shop floor control, input-output systems, and so on. While these systems are quite important in executing the MPS, they do not receive major emphasis in either the MPS framework or in its subsequent use in analyzing the practice of master scheduling at the eight firms reported in this book.

REFERENCES

1. W. L. Berry, T. E. Vollman, and D. C. Whybark, *Master Production Scheduling: Principles and Practice,* American Production and Inventory Control Society, Falls Church, Virg., 1979, 6th printing, September 1991.

2. James F. Cox, III, John H. Blackstone, Jr., and Michael S. Spencer, *APICS Dictionary,* 7th ed., APICS, Falls Church, Virg., 1992.

3. Joseph A. Orlicky, George W. Plossl, and Oliver W. Wight, "Structuring the Bill of Materials," *Production and Inventory Management* (13:4).

BIBLIOGRAPHY

APICS Training Aid—Master Scheduling, APICS, Falls Church, Virg., 1984.

W. L. Berry, T. E. Vollman, and D. C. Whybark: *Master Production Scheduling: Principles and Practice,* APICS, Falls Church, Virg., 1979, 6th printing, September 1991.

CPIM: *Master Planning Reprints Revised 1993,* APICS, Falls Church, Virg., 1993.

John F. Proud: *Master Scheduling: A Practical Guide to Competitive Manufacturing,* Oliver Wight Publications, Essex Junction, Verm., 1994.

F. John Sari: *The MPS and the Bill of Material Go Hand-in-Hand,* Richard C. Ling, Winston-Salem, N.C., 1981.

Oliver W. Wight: *Manufacturing Resource Planning: MRPII Unlocking America's Productivity Potential,* rev. ed., Van Nostrand Reinhold, New York, 1984.

CHAPTER 13
SCHEDULING TECHNIQUES

Editor
Timothy J. Greene, Ph.D.
Associate Dean for Research
College of Engineering, Architecture and Technology
Oklahoma State University, Stillwater, Oklahoma

Contributors*
Lloyd M. Clive, Ph.D., CPIM
Coordinator of Industrial Engineering Technology Programs
Center for Integrated Manufacturing
Sir Sandford Fleming College, Peterborough, Ontario

Stephen De Lurgio, Ph.D., CFPIM
Professor of Operations Management
University of Missouri, Kansas City, Missouri

Hank Grant, Ph.D.
Professor and Head, School of Industrial Engineering
University of Oklahoma

James Hunt
Manager Special Projects,
Arrowhead Metals, Ltd., Toronto, Ontario

Loading, scheduling, and shop floor control are so important to manufacturers and service providers that they have developed and implemented sophisticated, computerized systems for production control. While hospitals do not have production control departments, they do schedule operating rooms, laboratories, and other facilities. Similarly, radio and television broadcasters schedule commercials, and colleges and other schools schedule classes. Whatever their product or service, they face competition, necessitating looking into the future and gaining control over production, materials, and/or processes.

---

*The contributors wrote or edited portions of this chapter for earlier editions of the handbook.

TYPES OF PRODUCTION SCHEDULING

The type of loading, scheduling, and shop floor tools used is greatly affected by the performance measures employed and by the type of facility being controlled. Facilities that deal with a continuous medium (web, granular, liquid) require a different approach than those that deal with discrete batches (parts, components, jobs). In addition, the volume of materials being produced, the frequency, and the equipment's capabilities all affect the type of facility used and hence the control of that facility. The distinguishing feature of process production is that work flows through a fixed and continuous manufacturing process. This differs from a job shop, where work is processed intermittently by job, batch, order, or lot. Examples of continuous-process manufacturing are to be found in the chemical, food, and paper industries.

Intermittent Manufacturing

Intermittent manufacturing (or *production*) is defined in the *APICS Dictionary* as "a production system in which jobs pass through functional departments in lots." A plant with production of this type is usually called a *job shop*. A home kitchen can be thought of as a job shop, with the stove top representing one department, work counters a second, and the oven a third. The refrigerator can be considered as an inventory storage area for materials, either in work-in-process or in finished goods. Contrast this with a cannery where tomatoes are fed into one end of a processing line and continuously processed until they emerge from the other end in cans.

Anyone scheduling and controlling intermittent production is faced with several types of problems. One of these is the requirement for data on the status of the system. Such questions as these are common: "When will order 4763 be done?" "Is it behind schedule?" "How long will it take to make it?" "A machine is down, a product was scrapped, a key employee is absent. What does this do to our schedule?" "Why do you change the schedule so much?" And "Why didn't you tell us yesterday that we must work overtime today?"

An associated problem is that much of the data pertaining to the production system are not available, not readily available, unreliable, or reliable for only a short period of time. Thus, many decisions must be based on insufficient data, and consequently performance is often not what it could or should be. The cost of obtaining better data may be prohibitive. Another basic problem is deciding what to schedule and how to schedule it. Should products be scheduled, or should machines be scheduled? What about a combination of these? Should all products or all machines be scheduled or just a subset of them? Should departments or work centers be scheduled? What are the scheduling rules? How should they be applied?

There is little or no problem involved in determining the multitude of objectives for a production scheduling system. The problem is to achieve them. A good production scheduling system should give a smooth, efficient, profitable, low-overall-cost operation with minimum inventories of production materials, in-process materials, and finished goods. It should be reliable, deliver orders on time with minimal lead times, and have fast reaction times to sudden status changes caused by breakdowns, rush orders, late arrival of materials, and employee absences. Finally, it should give objective, clear-cut feedback of results.

Repetitive Manufacturing

Repetitive manufacturing is the production of discrete units, planned and executed by a schedule, usually at relatively high speeds and volumes, with the materials tending to move in a sequential flow. Typical repetitive manufactured products include electrical appliances, toys, and some types of clothing. The authority for production in repetitive manufacturing is the daily-run schedule, and the feedback information for control is the number of good and bad items that pass a control point.

Continuous-Process Manufacturing

Since work flows through a continuous manufacturing process, production control in this type of industry is often called *flow control*. The rate of flow can usually be varied, although there are processes in which the rate can be varied little if at all. The importance of production control and scheduling in a continuous manufacturing process is directly proportional to the ease and the amount by which the flow may be varied. If the rate of flow can be varied easily and significantly, management is more apt to vary it. The more it is varied, the more effort is required to keep the system under control, and the greater the need for the production control function.

There are different ways to vary the production rate in a continuous-process production.

- The line equipment may be operated for more or fewer hours.
- The line may be operated with more or fewer personnel.
- The line may be operated intermittently, with the personnel doing other work.
- The line may be operated in two or more stages by pulling the partially completed product from the line and accumulating an in-process inventory. After this inventory is built up to a certain point, the first phase of the process may be shut down and the second phase operated by feeding in the in-process inventory. The same personnel would be used in both phases.

Continuous-process manufacturing has an advantage over intermittent production in that *feedback*—that is, the comparison of what was scheduled versus what was actually produced—is easier. Since there is a "flow" of material, it is usually possible to utilize some means of automatically and continuously measuring the flow in terms of pieces, gallons, feet, pounds, and so on. Feedback, of course, is required in order to maintain the scheduling process. Generally, scheduling a continuous manufacturing process is easier than scheduling an intermittent manufacturing process. However, there is often enough difficulty so that computers and modern scheduling techniques have been successfully applied.

Project Manufacturing

Project production relates to the production of a unit or a small number of units that are managed by a project team. Paper machines, some large machine tools, marine diesel engines, and ships are all typical products made in a project production situation. The *program evaluation review technique* (PERT) and the *critical-path method* (CPM) are typical of the scheduling techniques developed for project production.

LOADING PRINCIPLES

There are two basic techniques for planning the control of a production system. One of these is loading; the other is scheduling. Of the two, loading is easier to do. But scheduling can give more control and is more detailed, although it is usually done for a shorter time period. A *load* is the amount of work assigned to a facility work center or operator, and *loading* is the assignment of work. Loading does not specify the sequence in which the work is to be done or when it is to be done. Loading is the aggregate assignment of jobs to specific entities. Inputs necessary for loading include:

- Routing
- Standard hours per operation or work center
- Gross machine- or man-hours available
- Efficiency factors
- Due date

Loading is closely tied to capacity planning in the sense that loading is the first indication that capacity levels need adjusting.

Steps in the Loading Procedure

Typically, the loading process can be considered a six-step procedure (Table 13.1). Steps 1 through 4 are managerial decision steps that usually do not change week to week or month to month. The last two steps are required on a periodic basis as an input to scheduling.

Step 1. The first step in machine loading is to choose the load centers. Some companies load by department only if all the machines in a department are interchangeable. When different machine centers within the department have different capabilities (as in a general machine department), the typical approach is to break the machines down into similar machine groups. All 24-inch boring mills, for example, might be included in the same group if jobs are interchangeable among the machines. If a screw machine is the same as others but has a milling cutter attachment, it should be identified so it can be singled out for a particular job. The trend is to group as many machines together as possible since doing so will reduce the complexity of the loading problem and tend to stabilize the load.

Step 2. The second step is to develop efficiency factors by *load centers* (also called *work centers*). A load center with two people is theoretically capable of 80 hours of production per week, but actual output might be considerably less than 80 hours if time is spent on setup work, indirect activities, or other non-value-adding activities. If they are

TABLE 13.1 Loading Steps

1. Choose load centers:
   a. Department
   b. Group
   c. Machine or workstation
	4. Choose loading method:
	   a. To infinite capacity
	   b. To finite capacity
	   c. Combination

2. Develop efficiency factors
   by load center.
	5. Load scheduled orders into
	   load centers.

3. Determine capacity by center.	**6.** Unload completed hours.

working on incentive, however, they could be turning out more than 80 standard hours of production.

Step 3. The third step is to determine the gross capacity by load center. This capacity is either human or machine dependent. A center is *machine dependent* if all machines have at least one operator assigned. A center is *human dependent* if there are more workers than machines and machines stand idle while all workers are busy. With the number of people or machines as an input, the gross capacity is the gross number of hours that the resources (people or machine) are available per planning period. The center's capacity is then the gross capacity times the efficiency factor.

Step 4. The fourth step is to choose the loading method, which may be either to *finite* or to *infinite capacity*. *Infinite capacity loading* means showing the work for a work center in the time period required, regardless of the work center's capacity. *Finite capacity loading* means putting no more work into a work center than it can be expected to execute.

Step 5. The fifth step is to load the scheduled orders into the load centers while at the same time considering the capacity and other restrictions.

Step 6. The sixth step is to select the unloading technique. *Unloading* is the process of removing the planned work from the work center load as jobs are partially or totally completed. Manual systems may require shortcuts, such as considering a job to be completed when the first lot of pieces is reported. This saves posting many partial lots and recalculating load balances, but the load is always understated by the number of hours remaining on jobs unloaded. Another shortcut relieves the load only when the last lot is completed, giving a load constantly overstated by the hours completed but not removed. The number of hours to be unloaded must equal the number of hours loaded for each job. For example, if 12 standard hours have been loaded and the job is completed in 9 actual hours, then 12 hours must be relieved from the load.

A work center load, based on the actual work orders released, is a good short-term technique for highlighting underloads or overloads on work centers and showing the need for overtime, temporary transfers, subcontracting, or other short-range adjustments. It is seldom adequate for long-term capacity planning.

Loading Concepts: Finite and Infinite Loading

Why use loading? The major reason is that it can predict some future events. A chart, instead of actual late orders, tells of an overload, and it tells this in advance. This same chart can warn of excess capacity before the machines and workers are idle. Therefore, loading is most useful to dispatchers, supervisors, and production schedulers planning shop work. Loading can be used to smooth the workload from month to month or between work centers. It is an aid in identifying the critical departments or machines and in judging the effect of breakdowns, rush orders, and new products. It is also useful for documenting the requirements for more or less capacity.

When using infinite loading to create the schedule, it is necessary to check the load to determine whether there is sufficient capacity available in the time period in which the work is required. Loading to finite capacity by operation is more complex than infinite capacity loading. A facility activity that does not go according to schedule may require that the load be recalculated, and therefore loads will fall in different time periods. Finite capacity loading also requires that the company establish priority for loading the jobs. In practice, finite capacity loading by itself is unsatisfactory since it assumes that present capacity is all that is available and does not show the time period in which overloads will occur if an attempt is made to meet desirable schedules. Without the latter information, action cannot be taken to improve the facility's performance in meeting customer requirements.

A good machine loading system involves a combination of both techniques. Orders are first scheduled and loaded to infinite capacity to see where overloads will occur, then rescheduled to level the load based on available capacity after corrective actions have been taken wherever possible.

An effective production capacity plan must extend far enough into the future to cover the time required for hiring and training the needed production and service employees, obtaining the necessary equipment and materials, and operating long enough at higher capacity to be worthwhile. The backlog of open orders in the machine load rarely covers this much lead time.

Companies have successfully used computer machine loads over longer planning periods to assist capacity planning. Forecasts of individual finished products to be manufactured during this period can be exploded into detailed requirements of production hours for each major work center. While actual production of individual items can be expected to vary greatly from such long-range forecasts, increases in one item will tend to be offset by decreases in another, and the aggregate hours will be reasonably accurate. Machine loads based on these aggregate hours will indicate developing trends toward underload or overload and will give dependable data on the average capacity required to meet the forecasted demand on manufacturing facilities.

The work may be assigned by the nature of the job. If the work can be done by more than one work center, it must be assigned to just one. If it can be done by only one work center, there is no alternative but that one work center. If the work is drilling a hole and there are three drill presses, assignment must either be made to one of them or the three of them can be considered as one work center. The work may be assigned on an individual job basis, but if the jobs are repetitive, they may be assigned on a standard basis by the use of routings. Standard routings show, for each part or assembly, all the operations that must be done to make that part or assembly. In addition to the operations required, the routings also usually show the facility that performs the operation and the standard time required to perform it. If standard routings are not available, someone must assign the individual jobs to the facilities and must estimate the work content of the assignments. This work content must be in terms that are comparable between jobs. Measures that may be used are hours, pieces, pounds, batches, gallons, and so on per hour, per shift, per day, and so on.

Work assignments must be accumulated by facility in order to calculate the load on each facility. One method is to use a ledger in which the job numbers and job loads are entered for each facility. When a job is completed, it is marked off. The jobs are then added periodically to obtain the load on the facility.

Another method is to accumulate the assignments in "buckets"—one bucket for each facility. The bucket may be a box, a file, a peg, and so on. A ticket is prepared for each job assigned to the facility and is placed in the box, in the file, or on the peg. A perpetual total of the facility load may be kept for each bucket. Job tickets, as they are added to the bucket, are added to this total. When completed and removed from the bucket, they are deducted from the total. If a computer is available, the buckets may be a computer file. If standard routings are available, these can also be kept in computer files. Then only the part numbers and the quantity need be entered for each job, and the computer can extend the quantities, make the assignments, and calculate the load.

OPTIMIZED PRODUCTION TECHNOLOGY

Optimized production technology (OPT) is a packaged computer software system that addresses the variability in an operational facility. Although the batch-size algorithms are proprietary, the general rules used to determine the various batch sizes are presented here.*

- Do not balance capacity—balance the flow.
- The level of utilization of a nonbottleneck resource is determined not by its own potential but by some other constraint in the system.
- Activating a resource (making it work) is not synonymous with utilizing a resource.
- An hour lost at a bottleneck is an hour lost for the entire system.
- An hour saved at a nonbottleneck is a mirage.
- Bottlenecks govern both throughput and inventory in the system.
- The transfer batch may not and many times should not be equal to the process batch.
- The process batch should be variable both along its route and in time.
- Priorities can be set only by simultaneously examining all the system's constraints. Lead time is a derivative of the schedule.

OPT provides a different perspective on the traditional methods of planning and scheduling, but it is more of a philosophy than a technique.

OPT has been compared to *materials requirements planning* (MRP), and it is claimed that the two conflict with each other. The two techniques are not mutually exclusive. The fundamental logic of time-phased orders still applies and is incorporated in OPT; however, the order in which the information is processed is different from that in traditional MRP systems. OPT begins with a model of the resources available and converts the conventional bills of materials, routings, and so on into a product-process network. By identifying the critical, or bottleneck, resources, it produces an optimum schedule for these resources.

OPT applies Pareto's law to the selection of orders and resources in that it schedules the orders by priority until most of the resources have been allocated. By working on the vital few first and not worrying about the trivial many until later, a solution is obtained faster. This schedule, which is like a master schedule to OPT, is then used to plan the use of the noncritical resources. Different parameters can be emphasized to improve operating efficiency, reduce inventories, or increase delivery performance, whichever is most critical. The noncritical resources are scheduled below capacity to allow for a safety capacity to exist at all times.

OPT recognizes only one goal for manufacturing: to make money. OPT's goal is simultaneously to reduce operating expense and inventory and to increase throughput (Fig. 13.1). OPT investigates five areas: variability, bottlenecks, setups, lot sizes, and priorities.

Variability

Most scheduling methods attempt to balance resources. The number of workers will be constantly adjusted to balance machine capacity with worker capacity, and the plans for

---

*Optimized production technology is a proprietary system of Creative Output, Milford, Connecticut.

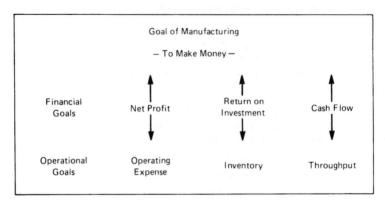

FIGURE 13.1   Goal of manufacturing

the subsequent work will utilize these resources at the capacity required to meet demand. It has been shown through mathematical simulation that a balanced plant cannot exist in the presence of variability. Variability in dependent work centers will cause schedules to be missed, resulting in decreased throughput, increased inventory, and increased operating costs. OPT rules are based on the realization that the constraints on an operation often exist outside the operation. The variability within an operation not only affects that operation but all subsequent operations, especially with bottleneck resources. Therefore, OPT's first rule is: *Do not balance capacity—balance the flow.*

Bottlenecks and Nonbottlenecks

A *bottleneck* is exactly as the term implies, a restriction or constraint in the flow of materials through a resource. A *resource,* in this case, is any element needed to make a product, whether it be a machine, a person, or space. A resource is considered a bottleneck when it is required to operate at 100 percent capacity to meet the present schedule. As the schedule changes or the product mix changes, different resources will become bottlenecks. To illustrate the interaction between bottlenecks, four different cases are presented in Fig. 13.2. They represent virtually all the possible combinations of interaction. In the examples, a certain product is manufactured that requires the use of two resources X and Y. This is the simplest case and can, of course, be expanded for multiple resources. Demand for this product places different time requirements on the two resources, and an imbalance occurs. X denotes a bottleneck resource that has a market demand of 100 hours per week; it also has a capacity of 100 hours per week. (The habit of demanding more from a resource than it is capable of producing will not be discussed.) Y denotes a nonbottleneck resource that has a market demand of 75 hours per week and a capacity of 100 hours per week. These two resources can only interact in four ways, as follows.

Case 1.   All product flows from X to Y. In this case, resource X has a requirement of 100 hours per week and is fully utilized, but resource Y has only 75 hours of work and is therefore underutilized. The output from X starves Y.

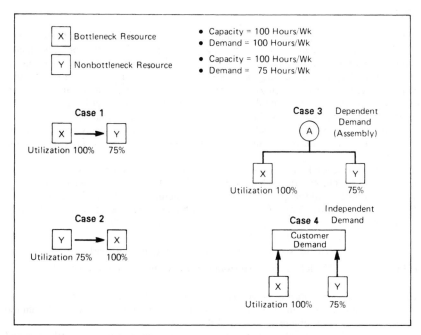

FIGURE 13.2 Interaction between resources.

Case 2. All product flows from Y to X, and X can again be utilized 100 percent of the time; however, if Y is activated 100 percent of the time, too much product will be produced for resource X. This will increase work-in-process inventory, consume resources, and not increase throughput. To balance the flow, Y needs to be activated only 75 percent of the time.

Case 3. X and Y both feed a common assembly area. Having worked through cases 1 and 2, we can see that X will be utilized 100 percent of the time to meet the market demand; however, activating Y 100 percent of the time will exceed the demand for this resource and will again build work-in-process in front of the assembly area.

Case 4. X and Y both feed independent customer demand and are not interrelated. Activating X 100 percent of the time is acceptable.

It is important that setups be saved at the bottlenecks since time spent not producing affects the entire system. The system will move toward larger batch sizes at the bottlenecks than traditional lot-sizing techniques would indicate. The cost of a setup at a bottleneck resource must also include the cost associated with a loss in throughput for the whole system and is therefore very high. However, at the nonbottlenecks there may be no gain in avoiding setups. Therefore, smaller batches are run. This does not increase throughput but can reduce inventory and operating expense. There are also advantages in maintaining the required workload below capacity in a nonbottleneck in order to avoid the possibility of constraining bottlenecks.

Lot Sizes

When the activity of a part moving through a production facility is viewed from the perspective of the part, there are only four stages in the job's life: setup, process, queue, and wait. Wait is the time that the part is idle in front of an assembly area waiting for another part. Typically, the setup and process times are a small portion of the total elapsed time. Some estimates place the percentage of active time at less than 20 percent; therefore, 80 percent of the time the part is waiting or in queue. In either case, the time a part spends in the production facility is determined by the bottleneck. The time that parts spend in the facility also determines the total inventory in the system. From this logic, the sixth rule is derived: Bottlenecks govern both throughput and inventory in the system.

The logic of rules 4 and 5 causes traditional lot-sizing rules to be very difficult to apply. As a batch moves through a facility, it encounters both bottleneck and nonbottleneck resources, and the question arises as to whether a batch should be considered of size one or infinity. Two different types of batches must be considered in manufacturing.

- *Transfer batch.* The lot size viewed from the standpoint of the part
- *Process batch.* The lot size viewed from the standpoint of the resource

The *economic order quantities* (EOQ) *model* maintains a balance between holding costs and setup ordering costs. In the case of a bottleneck, the setup cost is viewed from the perspective not only of the resource but of the entire system.

Since a batch moving through manufacturing will encounter both bottleneck and nonbottleneck operations, all with varying setup and run times, the parameters used in establishing a lot size for the batch must be examined for validity. Normally, batches launched on the shop floor are split, combined, and lap-phased to meet the demands of the schedules. The simplicity of EOQs cannot accommodate the complexities and reality of multiple work centers in a manufacturing environment, and it should not be expected that one batch size for a product moving through many work centers should always be the same. This can be stated clearly as OPT's eighth rule: *The process batch should be variable both along its route and in time.*

Priorities

Many rules exist to determine the sequence in which orders should be run. The most widely accepted rules consider the amount of time remaining to complete the order and the time available to complete the order, or the time of due date. MRP logic looks at the priorities of an item based on the required due date and the lead time offset of components. This initial rough cut does consider capacity constraints and results in a plan that requires reworking until feasible. In effect, MRP looks at the result of the priorities since two or more different jobs require processing at the same time. To satisfy capacity constraints, one job must be processed first and the subsequent job(s) delayed. Since delay has occurred, the lead time has been affected.

The lead time of a job is thus affected not only by the capacity of the various work centers but by the priority of other jobs. This leads to the ninth rule: *Priorities can be set only by simultaneously examining all of the system's constraints.* Lead time is a derivative of the schedule.

SCHEDULING PRINCIPLES

Inputs Necessary for Effective Scheduling

To do production scheduling, the production control department must know:

- What to make
- When to make it
- Where to make it
- How to make it
- What to make it of
- How much time is necessary to make it
- When it is due
- What is the availability of raw materials
- What are the expected machine maintenance and failure schedules
- What are the expected rework or scrap percentages
- What other items or demands are on the facility

Since production is often for inventory, sales forecasting is usually very important in providing input data to a production control scheduling system. Although the sales forecast may extend for planning purposes into the distant future, scheduling is usually done for only the near future of perhaps 1 or 2 months. Established company policy will usually require the product control department to schedule production to meet the requirements of the forecast. In some companies, however, production control is allowed to second-guess the forecast. Actually, there is some second-guessing in either case, in that production control may revise the schedule to use overtime or may increase the rate of production, if necessary, to meet the forecast or to meet actual sales.

Once production control knows what to make, it must know the materials required to make the product. That information should be available from a bill of materials. A bill of materials shows the structure of the product. Frequently, not even stock chasing begins until jobs have failed to meet their shipping date. A better approach is to establish schedule dates by operations and to review jobs that are due to ship this week and next week, as well as those that are past due, to determine what problems are causing delays. Table 13.2, "Production Schedule Review," shows this type of production schedule review, which can be very effective if used in conjunction with an operation scheduling system to detect delays. The sales department can then be informed which jobs will be shipped on time and which will not, thus providing it with the means of telling customers ahead of time if their jobs will not be shipped as promised.

Operation Time Scheduling

Table 13.3, "Scheduling Steps," lists the steps in scheduling operations. The first is to provide data for the scheduling system; this data must include the *operation sequence,* or *factory routing.* Figure 13.3 is a typical manufacturing order; it includes the operation sequence and shows the setup hours and processing times required. Processing times have been calculated by multiplying the quantity on the order (expressed in thousands) by the time figure shown in the column headed "Run hr/1000." This order is designed to

TABLE 13.2 Production Schedule Review

Customer	SO	Past due	This week	Next week	Nearest lot Location	Nearest lot Quantity	Next lot Location	Next lot Quantity	Remarks
Stalco	17,624	577			D 32	1,150			Will ship next week
Chambers	11,318			40	D 40	94			On salvage (?)
Trild Inc.	10,628		1,100		D 29	1,000		NA	Call complete
Morton	10,959		1,780	2,500	D 32	5,200			Balance 6040 stock
Padsing	11,003		7,000		D 22	7,500			OK
Pennbush	11,004			20,000	D 22	10,750	D 2	10,750	Will ship 10M balance 3/26
Stalco	11,008			7,000	D 40	8,240			OK

TABLE 13.3 Scheduling Steps

1. Provide data:
   a. Bill of materials
   b. Operation and routing sequence
   c. Standards, engineered or estimated
   d. Due dates

2. Develop system:
   a. Shop calendar
   b. Scheduling rules

3. Load facility.

4. Choose scheduling method:
   a. Back-scheduling
   b. Forward-scheduling

5. Schedule:
   a. Multiply order quantity by time per operation.
   b. Add transit time.
   c. Add allowance for delays.

6. Release work to shop; execute schedule.

7. Provide feedback to initial load and schedule.

Part name		Drawing No.	Used on			Date		Order		Qty.
Pinion spindle		E-17352	Frame assembly E-oo14			*wk. 21*		*2,950*		*5,000*

Material											
Steel bar stock −0.500″					Remarks						
Spec. A-407					Note thread is left-hand						

Dept.	Mach. group	Op. No.	Operation description	Set-up hr	Run hr/ 1,000	Run hr this lot	Man No.	Qty. comp.	Qty. scrap	Qty. salv.	Insp.
040	Truck	01	Draw bar stock from stores								
517	14	02	Make pinion spindle on screw machine	14.5	3.1	*15.5*					
319	18	03	Mill slot to B/P	1.3	9.5	*47.5*					
771	42	04	Tumble for burrs			*2.0*					
624	06	05	Drill hole for pin	0.2	4.C	*20.0*					
771	40	06	Degrease			*0.5*					
771	43	07	Plate − dull zinc			*4.7*					
009	04	08	Inspect			*AQC 405*					
040	Truck	09	Deliver to stock			—					

FIGURE 13.3 Typical manufacturing order.

travel with the work through the factory so that the operators can note their time and quantities directly on it. In some companies, this operation sequence is maintained on a master form, which can be reproduced when repetitive orders for the same product are run. In others, this type of routing is maintained in a computer file, which can in turn produce hard copy. When the manufacturing order is printed out, a card (traveler) may be made for each operation to be used by the machine operator to report the time. By itself, the traveling order does not usually provide the means to report an operator's time and quantity to the time keeping department.

Time standards, either engineered or estimated, are essential to any scheduling system. Since there will always be orders for new items that have to be scheduled into production before engineering standards have been developed, some means of estimating these standards in either the industrial engineering or the production control department is necessary. Accuracy is not vital, but consistency is important. Some simple scheduling assumptions are shown in Table 13.4, "Simple Scheduling Rules." These are oversimplified but illustrate the type of assumptions that must be developed before scheduling can begin.

Shop Calendar

Figure 13.4 shows a shop calendar used by many companies on which each working day is numbered consecutively; in some cases, the consecutive numbering covers a period of 4 years. This enables the scheduler to establish dates without correcting for weekends, plant shutdown periods, or holidays.

Block Scheduling

Many companies use general rules, such as the block-scheduling rules shown in Table 13.5, to estimate the amount of time required for each part. These save computation time but usually result in extremely long lead times. Table 13.6 shows two ways of scheduling the manufacturing order shown previously. Both cases show backward-scheduling

---

TABLE 13.4   Simple Scheduling Rules

---

1. Multiply hours per thousand pieces by number of thousands on order.

2. Round up to nearest 16-hour day (two shifts), and express time in days. Round down to nearest day when excess hours are less than 10 percent of total. Assume a minimum of 1 day for operation.

3. Allow 5 days lead time to withdraw stock from stockroom.

4. Allow 1 day lead time between successive operations within the same department.

5. Allow 3 days between successive operations in different departments.

6. Allow 1 day for inspection.

7. Allow 1 day to get material into stockroom.

8. Group parts with common setups together.

9. Inspect before major value-added operations.

JUNE

Wk No.	Sun.	Mon.	Tues.	Wed.	Thurs.	Fri.	Sat.
22	May 24	25 / 347	26 / 348	27 / 349	28 / 350	29	30
23	31	June 1 / 351	2 / 352	3 / 353	4 / 354	5 / 355	6
24	7	8 / 356	9 / 357	10 / 358	11 / 359	12 / 360	13
25	14	15 / 361	16 / 362	17 / 363	18 / 364	19 / 365	20
26	21	22 / 366	23 / 367	24 / 368	25 / 369	26 / 370	27

JULY

Wk No.	Sun.	Mon.	Tues.	Wed.	Thurs.	Fri.	Sat.
27	June 28	29 / 371	30 / 372	July 1 / 373	2 / 374	3	4
28	5	6 / 375	7 / 376	8 / 377	9 / 378	10 / 379	11
*29	12	13	14	15	16	17	18
*30	19	20	21	22	23	24	25

*Vacation weeks are subject to change.

AUGUST

Wk No.	Sun.	Mon.	Tues.	Wed.	Thurs.	Fri.	Sat.
31	July 26	27 / 380	28 / 381	29 / 382	30 / 383	31 / 384	Aug. 1
32	2	3 / 385	4 / 386	5 / 387	6 / 388	7 / 389	8
33	9	10 / 390	11 / 391	12 / 392	13 / 393	14 / 394	15
34	16	17 / 395	18 / 396	19 / 397	20 / 398	21 / 399	22

FIGURE 13.4 Shop calendar with numbered workdays.

13.15

TABLE 13.5   Block-Scheduling Rules

1. Allow 1 week for releasing order and drawing materials from store-room.

2. Allow 6 weeks for screw-machine operations.

3. Allow 1 day for each 400 pieces in the milling department; round upward to next full week.

4. Allow 1 week for drilling and tapping, burring, and similar operations using minor equipment.

5. When operations are especially short, combine within the same week.

6. Allow 1 week for inspection and delivery of completed material.

TABLE 13.6   Block Versus Operation Time Scheduling

Operation no.	Block scheduling		Operation time scheduling	
	Time allowed	Release date (Week)	Time allowed	Day
		37		402
01	1 week	38	5 days	407
02	6 weeks	44	12 days $T^* =$ 3 days	419
03	3 weeks	47	3 days $T =$ 3 days	425
04	1 week	48	1 day $T =$ 3 days	429
05	1 week	49	2 days $T =$ 3 days	434
06	1 week	50	1 day $T =$ 1 day	438
07			1 day	440
08	1 week	51	$T =$ 3 days 1 day	444
09			1 day	445
Date required		Week 51		Day 445

$^*T$ = transit time.

from the required date (week 51 or day 445). Block scheduling with completion dates by week numbers results in a total of 14 weeks' lead time. Operation time scheduling requires 44 working days, or about 9 weeks, to complete; in the computation, the transit time is added to the next operation. For example, operation 7 must be completed on day 440 to allow 3 days of transit time and 1 day of running time at operation 8. Transit time is used to cover the following elements:

- Time waiting to be picked up for movement out of the department—wait time
- Time actually in transit—move time
- Time waiting to be started at the next machine center—queue time

Setup time has also been taken into account. In operation 02, for example, 1 extra operating day is included because of the setup time required on the screw machine.

Backward- and Forward-Scheduling

There are two principal scheduling methods: backward- and forward-scheduling. *Backward-scheduling* starts with the due date and works progressively backward to a release date. This assumes that the finished date is known, and it computes the start dates. Backward-scheduling is becoming the most common approach, especially in batch manufacturing operations or operations in which parts are coming together for a subsequent assembly or kitting. Material requirements planning and just-in-time manufacturing now primarily use the backward-scheduling approach.

Forward-scheduling starts with either today's date or the first open time at the first operation, and computes the schedule date for each operation to determine the completion date. Forward-scheduling is most frequently used in companies such as paper and steel mills, where the product is bulky but requires few components. The scheduler will probably check the customer's order, and if the requested date and the required date are far enough away, he or she can see the order starting a reasonable time prior to the requested date so that there is ample time to complete the order by the required date. In essence the schedule is really combining backward-scheduling with forward-scheduling.

Backward-scheduling is typically used where components being manufactured that go into an assembled product have different lead times. After determining the required schedule dates for major subassemblies, the scheduler uses these as the required dates for each component and works backward to determine the proper release date for each component's manufacturing order.

Scheduling Similar Orders

Substantial advantages can be gained by processing similar orders in their proper sequence:

- Setup times on screw machines, punch presses, and so on can be reduced by running families of parts that require only minor changes to convert the setup.
- Cleanout and changeover times can be reduced by running lighter-colored batches of paints, chemicals, and so on, before darker ones.
- Raw materials can be saved by combining corrugate box sizes, textile patterns, and so on when cutting from continuous sheets.

Inventory records are usually coded to identify all members of the significant families or preferred sequences. Listings can be used for periodic review to ensure consideration of all items in the groups. The family or group can be considered as one item when determining (economic) order quantities. The total for the family is then distributed among its members so that all will run out or reach the reorder point at about the same time, and the family will again be ready for processing.

Scheduling Considerations

- Select the input to meet the planned production rate. If the facility is not actually producing to meet this plan, the amount of work released into starting operations should not exceed actual capacity.
- Keep backlogs off the shop floor wherever possible because they:

  Are more difficult to control.

  Make engineering changes more expensive to implement.

  Generate more expediting.

  Create physical problems (newer orders pile up in front of older orders that get pushed back into corners).

- Sequence orders based on latest requirements rather than on required dates established when the order was first released. The computer (which can compare changing inventory requirements for many items with production requirements) and the introduction of such techniques as critical-ratio scheduling make it possible to review and revise desired schedule dates periodically.
- Schedule only those items that the factory can make; planners or schedulers should not release orders for which raw materials, components, tools, or other necessary materials are not available. This will clearly define where the basic problem lies in getting work completed. There are some exceptions to this rule. Where a finished product takes 3 weeks to assemble and the missing component is one added at the last operation, assembly orders can be issued if the scheduler is confident that the missing component will be available when needed. In the drug, electronic, and similar industries, it is sometimes impossible to determine before a schedule is released whether the product can actually be produced.
- Schedule to a short cycle (weekly or even daily). This not only helps to get the latest and most accurate equipment dates on the orders scheduled but also assists in controlling the orders flowing through the factory. An interesting fallacy that has gained wide recognition is that the schedule period must equal the lead time. Even in the extreme example of a company with a 9-month lead time required for a sequence of 50 different operations, someone must make a decision, practically on a daily basis, as to which items will be started in the first operation. A firm 9-month starting schedule is not required. A weekly starting schedule based on the latest available information on customer requirements, inventory status, and facility workload is practical and effective.

Scheduling Assemblies

Two factors vital in scheduling assembly operations are component availability and assembly capacity rates. Parts flow must support assembly rates. Where components are common to many products, the order-point-quantity inventory control system is generally used. When unique to one product, a part in a complex assembly of many components with different lead times should be controlled by a materials plan.

Scheduled assembly rates can be held close to actual capacity since component availability is known. Staging or laying out sets of parts in advance of assembly should be held to a minimum. Increasing these advance supplies as a means of gaining information sooner on shortages is poor practice because:

1. Component inventories will be increased.

2. More space will be occupied.

3. Additional records for shortages of each kit will be required.

4. Components in short supply will become more critical.

5. Record errors increase through the shifting of components from one end product to another.

6. Stockroom workload increases.

7. Control of assembly priorities diminishes.

Scheduled assembly work should equal available capacity. Capacity usually varies with the mix of individual products requiring different assembly times. Line balancing is used to develop schedules of balanced loads of available capacity, utilizing the line flexibility by shifting work among workstations for economical assembly.

CRITICAL-RATIO SCHEDULING

Critical-ratio scheduling is a technique used for production scheduling to establish and maintain relative priorities among jobs. The priority is assigned based on a combination of when the completed job is required and how much time is required to complete it (see Fig. 13.5). The job farthest behind schedule is that which proportionately (1) has the earliest due date based on up-to-date knowledge of requirements and also (2) has the longest time left for its completion, based on knowledge of lead time and routing.

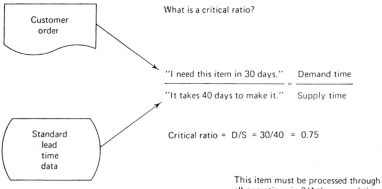

FIGURE 13.5 What is critical ratio?

Critical ratio converts the time relationship between the needed time and the available time into an index number:

$$\text{Critical ratio} = \frac{\text{available time}}{\text{needed time}} = \frac{(\text{due date}) - (\text{today})}{\text{lead time}}$$

The available time is the time until the order is due. The needed time is the total lead time required to successfully complete the order. This makes all jobs, at any point in the process, directly comparable, regardless of the date they are needed or the date they will be completed.

Critical ratio can be used in applications that require economic grouping or sequencing of jobs to minimize setup or changeover costs. This requires a two-step procedure. The first step groups or sequences like sets of jobs, as required, within specified delivery constraints. Then critical ratios establish the relative priorities of the respective sets. Critical ratio is a dynamic system, utilizing frequent feedback of both supply and demand information. In a stock-replenishment application, for example, regular reporting of updated on-hand balances enables the critical ratio to expedite those items for which demand is higher than normal. Equally important, the remaining items (for which demand is less than normal) are automatically "set aside" to permit critical jobs to move faster.

Critical-Ratio Applications

The critical-ratio technique can be incorporated into most production scheduling systems to:

1. Determine the status of a specific job.
2. Establish relative priorities among jobs on a common basis.
3. Provide the ability to relate both stock and make-to-order jobs on a common basis.
4. Provide the capability of adjusting priorities (and revising schedules) automatically for changes in both demand and job progress.
5. Permit dynamic tracking of job progress and location.
6. Eliminate the expediting functions of job progress lookup, redating of all associated documents, special hand-carrying, and so on by providing supervisors and dispatchers with proper job's sequences based on the most current information.
7. Provide basic data for overall queue control and manning decisions.

Critical-Ratio Meaning

The general available-versus-needed time relationship is developed as follows: If CR $>$ 1.0, the job is ahead of schedule. The date on which it will be available is earlier than the date on which it is required. If CR $=$ 1.0, the job is on time. If CR $<$ 1.0, the job is behind schedule (critical). Based on its standard lead time and normal rate of progress through the manufacturing process, it will take longer than the required date to obtain it. The lower the critical ratio, the more critical (further behind schedule) the job is.

Stock-Replenishment Formula

If the order for a stock item's replenishment due date (measured from today) is equal to the days of supply of stock remaining in inventory, assuming average daily usage, then the CR = 1.0. But the actual usage varies from the average. Critical ratio takes this into account. Whenever usage is below average, CR increases in value, and delivery of the job can be delayed by producing other, more critical jobs in the queue first. Conversely, whenever usage is greater than average, CR decreases in value, and the job moves faster through the process by taking a higher position in the queue.

Prior to implementing the formulas presented below, a decision must be made regarding the use of safety stock. Should the replenishment order be continuously monitored to time its arrival when:

On hand = safety stock?

On hand < safety stock but > 0?

On hand = 0?

The alternative selected would depend on the nature of demand (large, sporadic demands versus small, frequent demands) and the nature of the manufacturing process (flexible and responsive versus costly and time-consuming to make changes).

The critical ratio equation that includes a safety stock is:

$$CR = \frac{(OH - SS)/ADU}{LTR}$$

where OH = inventory on hand
    SS = safety stock
  ADU = average daily usage
  LTR = standard lead time remaining
    LT = total standard lead time for all operations

The equation for reserving a declining safety-stock balance is:

$$CR = \frac{[(OH - SS)(LTR/LT)]/ADU}{LTR}$$

This formula schedules the stock-replenishment order to arrive after some of the safety stock has been used but before the stock on hand falls to zero. The amount of safety stock reserved is directly proportional to the time remaining to complete the job (LTR/LT). It should be noted that LTR never reaches zero, so some safety stock is always reserved. Use of a proportional reduction is based on the ability of the critical ratio to accelerate delivery into stock if an unusually high variation in usage occurs. Note that this formula yields a higher CR than the first one and that a job becomes critical only when actual usage is greater than the sum of average usage plus the allowed safety-stock depletion.

For the case where no safety stock is reserved, a zero is substituted for safety stock in either of the above formulas. The result is the scheduled receipt of the order when OH = 0. This alternative would be satisfactory only if management were willing to accept a high level of stock-outs (although the duration of stock-outs would be relatively short).

For make-to-order items, the requirement date is equal to a predetermined delivery date rather than a calculated stock-depletion date (Fig. 13.6). The delivery date may be the customer's shipment date or, by explosion, the date that a component must be delivered to a stock point for use in a higher-level assembly. Frequently, this date must be delivered to a stock point for use in a higher-level assembly. Often this date must be changed between the original release date of the order and its completion date. All such changes must be kept current in order to calculate accurate critical ratios. The formula is:

Demand time = days remaining to required date, or (due date) − (today)

Required date, though subject to change, represents a "firm" commitment:
for assembly schedules
for customer shipments

Time is measured in working days.

FIGURE 13.6   Critical-ratio demand: make-to-order items.

$$CR = \frac{\text{due date} - \text{today}}{\text{LTR}}$$

where all days are working days.

The *standard lead time remaining* is the common denominator in all variations of the CR formula. It is defined as the expected elapsed time required for the job to pass through predetermined work centers from its present location to job completion. Since our concern is time remaining, not work remaining, the LTR is more than just the sum of setup and run times at all remaining operations. The LTR is equal to the total lead time minus the lead time for operations completed. The elapsed time, or standard lead time, for any specific work center is described by the formula:

$$LT = O + n[SQ + T] + \sum_{i=1} (SU_i + R_i)$$

where LT = lead time
   O = order preparation time
   n = number of operations required
   SQ = standard queue allowance for an operation
   T = standard transit allowance between operations
   SU_i = setup time for operation i
   R_i = operation processing time for operation i

All times should be in the same unit of measure.

In addition to knowledge of total lead times, which is required for every production and inventory control system, critical-ratio scheduling requires:

1. Knowledge of operation lead times
2. Elemental breakdown into queue, setup, and run times
3. Definition of *standard queue allowances*

Use of Queue Allowances

The optimum queue is the minimum amount of work that will satisfy the above objectives. It is sufficient that a standard (not necessarily an optimum one) be defined. The critical ratio can be used to:

• Sequence jobs (or economic groups of jobs) according to criticality
• Summarize the work in queue to determine whether delivery dates can be met
• Summarize the total shop load to determine whether changes in the overall production rate are necessary

Critical ratio operates by changing the relative positions of jobs in queue. It is effective to the extent that job sequence is variable and that individual jobs can be accelerated or delayed in the process. Critical-ratio queue and load analysis provide the basic information for controlling overall lead times.

Critical Ratio for Purchase-Order Follow-Up

While standard lead times for purchased items are generally known, there is frequently no elemental breakdown into checkpoints, comparable to production work centers, for reporting progress and determining the lead time remaining. Once such a breakdown is made, the same critical-ratio formulas used in production scheduling can be applied to purchase-order follow-up.

Some or all of the following checkpoints should have standard times associated with them and should have automatic feedback for status reporting:

• Requisition forwarded to purchasing
• Purchase order forwarded to vendor
• Vendor acknowledgment received; promised shipping date compared with lead time and LTR adjusted accordingly
• Vendor shipment made
• Order received
• Material inspected and approved
• In stock, available for use

Although critical ratio is a very powerful scheduling technique, we have seen that it is relatively simple and straightforward to use. Its biggest advantage is that it converts the time relationship between supply and demand into an index number that makes all jobs comparable. It can readily be used with a computer to handle a large number of orders.

SHORT-INTERVAL SCHEDULING

Short-interval scheduling is intended for the control of manpower-dependent processes in which (1) there is typically variation between jobs and (2) worker independence prohibits setting standard times. In essence, short-interval scheduling is an employee-by-employee, first-in-first-out queue system in which jobs are placed in the queue based on the scheduler's priority. The employee draws from the queue the next job to be processed, usually logging in when the job is started and when it is finished. This log provides feedback to the supervisor regarding employee performance. Employees can draw from a group queue or may have an individual queue.

Obviously, short-interval scheduling is scheduler dependent. The scheduler must determine who should receive that work on a very short time interval basis. In addition, the scheduler needs to have an intuitive feel for the expected operation time because the expected time has to be compared to the actual operation time in order to measure employee performance. The productivity of clerical activities can be improved 30 to 50 percent through the allocation, assignment, and control of work in small increments. Short-interval scheduling has also been applied to maintenance, mailrooms, tool and die making, construction, and similar nonstandardized activities. Other advantages include improved control of backlogs, better attention to job priorities, earlier detection and identification of problems, more equitable work distribution, and improved discipline. The system can be applied to short, repetitive operations that are reasonably uniform and constant in work content. Since the supervisor handles and distributes all work at frequent intervals and maintains the necessary control records, the supervisor must remain in the department almost constantly. The benefits of short-interval scheduling are that it:

- Reduces volume fluctuations by regulating all work coming into the system, controls backlogs by dispatching only the planned amounts of work, and regulates the sequence of processing
- Provides for handling nonroutine or exceptional work outside the system
- Identifies all operations and changes the sequence to get the best possible work flow
- Improves methods and layout to get the best possible performance
- Estimates or measures all operation times
- Determines the capacity of each work center and provides adequate, flexible staffing
- Determines the overall timetable for the entire process
- Determines the time interval for dispatching batches of work
- Establishes one or more dispatching points under a supervisor to release work in the proper amounts, time, and order
- Follows work-in-process to see that the schedule is being met

Forecasting and planning for work expected and manpower required for a future time period is necessary. Long-range forecasts by management provide overall manpower loads, space, and equipment requirements. Short-range forecasts by the supervisor provide the basis for day-by-day assignment and control of work, using the batch or tally systems. For project work, it is normal to plan months ahead. Short-interval scheduling relies on adequate work measurement techniques; however, precise work measurement is not necessary. Supervisors should know or develop the level of performance that they can expect from their people with the standards available.

Management should receive regular reports highlighting present performance and trends. Periodic audits of the system should be made by an independent function (systems department or controller's auditor) to be sure that the system is being used properly, that standards are up to date, and that service is adequate. The three types of short-interval scheduling systems in use are batch, tally, and project. Differences between the three types occur in length of scheduling increment, homogeneity of tasks to be performed, relative location of individual workstations, responsibility for recording work done, and degree of built-in control.

Batch System Short-Interval Scheduling

The *batch system* is the most positive. It includes, for each work center and work input station, the means for distributing batches of work to the employees, for keeping track of work assignments and completion, and for moving completed work to its next work center. At the input station, the scheduler sorts incoming work into convenient homogeneous batches approximating 1 hour in duration and attaches a batch ticket (Fig. 13.7) indicating to whom the work has been assigned and the number of units of work included. Batches are stored in trays or bins to be distributed in the desired priority. The employee initials the ticket and indicates the time that he or she completed the work.

The sign-out sheet (Fig. 13.8) shows the department's planned production target for the day. This provides a measure against which the supervisor can compare overall actual performance; it also indicates trouble spots developing either externally or internally. The supervisor notes the number of units of work assigned to each employee. At the end of each time period, the supervisor can determine incomplete assignments and distribute additional batches. The employees do not have to worry about work priority and can also be shown that work is being distributed fairly. As work batches are completed, the time period is noted on the sign-out sheet and the employee credited.

Tally System Short-Interval Scheduling

The *tally system* is used where employees work in scattered areas and/or where the work does not lend itself readily to batching. The work may go directly to the employee, or it may be received into an input station, sorted, and distributed. The supervisor controls the distribution of work to the individual employees. The backlog is kept at the work input station, where the supervisor may determine its quantity and assign priority. Unlike the batch system, the tally system requires that the supervisor review work accomplished during the day at the individual workstations. The tally system requires

		Date
Department		
Assign to		Card count
	Total	
Starting time	Stopped	Actual time

FIGURE 13.7 Batch ticket.

Department _____ Division _____ Unit _____ Supervisor _____ Date _____

Forecast and daily plan comparison

Starting carryover	Plan	Act.																		

Name	Hours received		Planned production			Ending carryover			Percent productivity			Hours required			Hours available			Out hours		
	Asgm't	Plan Act.	Plan	Act.	Diff.	Plan	Act.	Diff.	Plan	Act.	Diff.	Plan	Act.	Diff.	Plan	Act.	Diff.	C/O	Comp. Prod.	Plan Act.
	Assg'd																			
	Sched.																			
	Actual																			
	Assg'd																			
	Sched.																			
	Actual																			
	Assg'd																			
	Sched.																			
	Actual																			

Totals

Actual								C/O Comp. Prod.
Plan								Tot. Plan
Cumulative difference								

FIGURE 13.8 Sign-out sheet.

13.26

more diligent supervision. Spot checks of employees' tally sheets over long periods have revealed that actual productivity is often 10 to 15 percent less than that reported.

Project System Short-Interval Scheduling

The *project system* is used for controlling the work of professional staff personnel, including engineers, accountants, and researchers, and focuses on the major phases of the project in regard to accomplishing specific objectives. One day each week, individuals and their supervisors review the progress of work against the previous week's schedule, including project hours to date, hours remaining, and whether or not the project is on schedule. They plan the hours to spend on each phase of the project during the coming week. As the week progresses, the employee records the actual time spent each day on each phase of the project measured against successfully accomplishing specific objectives. Their supervisors periodically check the progress against the plan.

GANTT CHART SCHEDULING

The Gantt chart is a graphic method of scheduling activities. The horizontal axis is divided into time increments or production units. The vertical axis contains a row for each activity, employee, facility, or work station to be scheduled. Without a doubt, the Gantt chart principles are the most extensively used scheduling techniques. They may be used with a simple chart drawn on graph paper or with one dressed up in some of the commercial display panels available. The purpose here is to discuss only the principles, not the applications.

There are advantages to be found in the Gantt chart that can be found in none of the other techniques. These can be briefly stated as follows:

- A plan has to be made. Often this is the most important advantage of any scheduling technique.
- The chart shows the work that is planned and when it is to start and end. At the same time, it also shows the work that has been accomplished.
- Gantt charts are easy to work with and understand.
- The Gantt chart is dynamic. It shows a moving picture of what is being planned and accomplished.
- Gantt charts require very little space, considering the amount of information displayed.

Like most of the other scheduling techniques, the Gantt chart (Fig. 13.9) requires an understanding of a certain language, or set of symbols. These are illustrated at the bottom of the chart. The two inverted L's indicate when a task is to begin and end. The light line connecting these two L's shows what is to be accomplished. This line may be scaled in units of either time or production. The progress of the work is indicated by a heavy line. A "today" line must be placed on the chart to show when it was last brought up to date. In the example, a caret is used. Other symbols may be added to the chart as desired. For example, a crossed-out entry might indicate that a machine is down for repair.

There are two ways of entering information: Start with the present time and work *forward,* or start with some future date and work *backward.* The choice will depend upon the cost of the product as well as upon the availability of transportation, storage, and capital and other considerations.

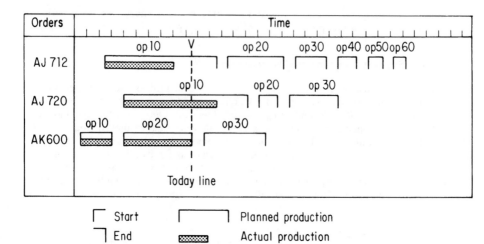

FIGURE 13.9   Schedule chart by order number.

For scheduling manufacturing, there are two choices in the way the chart is constructed. If getting production out is the important problem, the chart will be constructed in terms of manufacturing orders, as shown in Fig. 13.9. However, if keeping the machines loaded is of paramount importance, the chart should be constructed as shown in Fig. 13.10. Notice that in the former figure, the manufacturing orders are listed in the left-hand column, while in the latter the machines or work centers are listed.

In operating the chart, it is essential that information such as move orders or time cards be available to serve as *feedback* for updating the chart. Operating the chart successfully requires a person with a certain type of personality, a person willing to accept

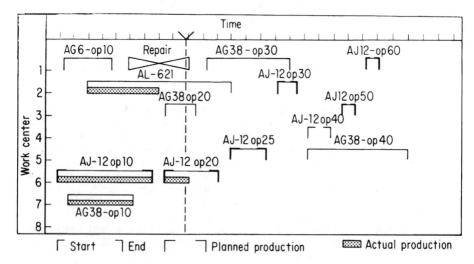

FIGURE 13.10   Schedule chart by work center.

changing conditions and able to work with details. Reading the chart is relatively simple. For example:

1. AJ720 is ahead of schedule.
2. AK600 is on schedule.
3. AJ712 is behind schedule.

You will notice in Fig. 13.10 that a number of jobs are shown for each work center. If each work center is staffed, the scheduler will probably want to keep all the vacant spaces filled, which will mean a more efficient facility. The scheduler will have to be flexible and willing to adjust the schedule from time to time. For example, it appears that order AG38, operation 20, is not going to be started before the time it is to be completed. This will require a rescheduling of the operations for AG38.

These are the basic principles of the Gantt chart. From here, one can make modifications to fit the particular situation.

LINE OF BALANCE (LOB)

The line of balance, Fig. 13.11, is a manual, graphic technique for planning, scheduling, and monitoring progress of simple to complex projects. These may be products assembled over a moderate time period against a firm schedule, a development program for a complex assembly, or a research and engineering project. The project is represented by a network showing the relationship in time among the various milestones (such as receipt of finished components or completion of testing) that make up the project.

The discipline required to set up the chart can help to ensure thorough planning. The schedule of activities can be developed accurately (depending on the accuracy of the due date or the required lead times) and the actual progress monitored. The technique permits showing the following simultaneously on one chart:

- Source of each component element (purchase, manufacture, assembly, test, etc.)
- Sequence of assembly, including subassembly, testing, inspection, packaging, shipping, and related activities
- Comparison of scheduled versus actual finished-product deliveries
- Comparison of scheduled versus actual component-element completions, showing present and potential shortages or delays

The technique is expensive to set up, increasing as the number of components and control points increases. It is inflexible and expensive to revise in terms of schedule changes, variation in elements, or revisions in elemental lead times. Analysis of project status requires accumulating data on all projects simultaneously.

LOB is a network planning technique similar to PERT, CPM, precedence lists, and so on, but it lacks their flexibility, versatility, and scope. A Gantt chart should be considered before applying LOB; it will be considerably less expensive and may produce equally good results. LOB has been most frequently applied to complex assemblies built for the U.S. Navy, whose contracts have required using the chart to report status to government inspectors.

Line-of-Balance Charts

Commercial and industrial applications of LOB as an operating technique are extremely rare. Its major application is in planning, scheduling, and controlling the production of

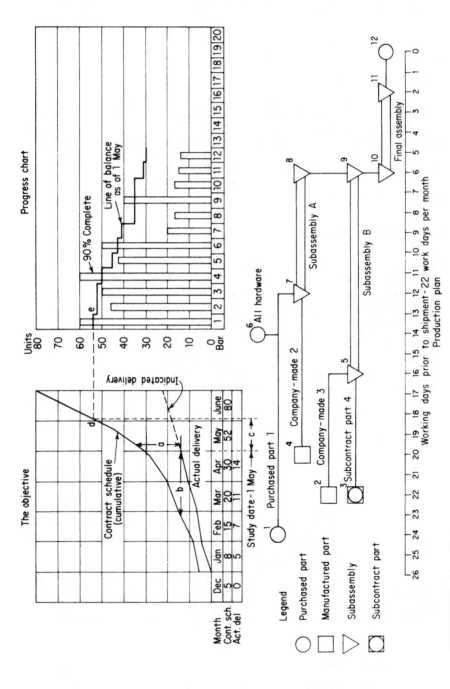

FIGURE 13.11 Line of balance.

complex, assembled products. An LOB chart consists of three sections: the production plan, the objective chart, and the progress chart. The lower half is the production plan; inaccuracies in it will be reflected through the LOB chart. It is a key-components product tree, with time represented on the horizontal axis. The length of each product tree bar denotes the lead time required to produce one batch of that component or assembly; the overall product structure length is the total product lead time. For example, purchased part 1 requires 12 working days' lead time (24 minus 12), and the total product lead time is 24 days.

To construct a production plan, first select those components (from the bill of materials) or events (from the route or process sheets) whose timely completion is important to the project. Relatively unimportant components are lumped together ("all hardware"). Second, obtain or estimate the lead times for each batch of the selected key components; these should be the most likely times, inclusive of processing, movement, and waiting times. Third, draw the chart by starting from the right with the completion day, week, or month as zero and working to the left, branching out as assemblies become subassemblies, and subassemblies become components. Fourth, connect all component horizontal lead time bars with a vertical line where subassembly assembly occurs, forming an interconnected network. Select a time scale in units suitable for effective monitoring. Fifth, mark the *start* of each key component or event line with a control-point number, commencing from the top left and moving to the bottom right.

Intermediate events should be given a number only if they are to be monitored. Always number the completion of the project. Symbols indicating the type of component (raw material, purchased part, manufactured part, subassembly, etc.) are helpful, and color coding increases the ease of interpretation. Descriptions of components or events can be shown on the chart. The selection of key components and events, the assignment of control-point numbers, and the use of descriptions must be dictated by the economics of over- or undercontrolling the project's progress.

Using Line-of-Balance Charts

The completed production plan could be used like a Gantt chart for monitoring one project by assigning specific dates to the horizontal time scale and recording actual progress on individual bars of the chart where few or no partial lots of the total order are expected at any control point. Where individual lots are scheduled over several periods, the Gantt chart is difficult to adapt, and the LOB progress chart makes it possible to record the control-point completion status against the schedule.

The upper left portion is the *objective chart*. It is the cumulative contract delivery schedule plotted vertically against the time plotted horizontally. The cumulative actual delivery schedule is plotted as the project progresses. The horizontal axis is divided into time intervals most closely approximating the delivery schedule. Frequently, both scheduled and actual deliveries in each interval are posted below this axis as a summary of project status. The vertical axis shows units of delivered end product.

The functions of the objective chart are:

1. To show the quantity of end product ahead of or behind schedule by the vertical gap between the two curves (*a*) and by the scheduled and actual totals summarized below the horizontal axis.

2. To show the number of time periods ahead of or behind schedule by the horizontal gap between the two curves (*b*).

3. To indicate the production rates by the slopes of the lines. Extending the actual line ahead on its historical trend can yield estimates of future production.

4. To provide the basis for drawing the line of balance on the progress chart where control-point completion status is measured.

The upper right portion of the figure is the *progress chart*. The length of the vertical bars represents the actual quantity of end product sets of each component or event completed at the study date. The bars are numbered horizontally for each control point on the production plan. The vertical scale shows end product sets (more than one component may be required per end product). The progress chart shares this scale with the object chart. The length of the bars increases as progress occurs at each control point. The most important benefit is the measurement of control-point status against plan and is obtained by striking the line of balance the minimum quantity of each control-point element required to support the end product delivery schedule as of the study date. To strike the line of balance:

1. Start with the study date (May 1 on the horizontal axis of the objective chart) and mark off to the right (*c* for control point 1) the number of lead time periods required for each control point in advance of end product completion. This lead time information is obtained from the production plan. For example, control points 8, 9, and 10 must be completed 6 working days in advance of shipment; control point 3, 2 months in advance, and so on.
2. Draw a vertical dashed line from the lead time termination until it intersects the cumulative delivery schedule as *d*.
3. From the point of intersection, draw a horizontal dashed line to the corresponding control point bar on the progress chart (*e*). This is the *balance quantity* or the minimum control point quantity required to support the end product delivery schedule.
4. Repeat this procedure for all control points on the production plan.
5. Join the balance quantities to form one staircase-type line of balance across the progress chart.

LINEAR DECISION RULES

Linear decision rules are an operations research-based modeling method for making aggregate decisions. Specifically, a linear decision model is a set of linear equations that, when solved, simultaneously provide either a single solution or a feasible solution space. The alternative ways to schedule production to meet fluctuation demand are:

1. Vary production to match the demand. The variation can be obtained by:
   a. Adding or subtracting people to the production force
   b. Working short shifts or overtime to vary the work hours of a constant labor force
   c. Subcontracting work to outside companies
   d. Some combination of *a*, *b*, or *c*.
2. Hold production constant and let inventories of products take care of demand fluctuations.
3. Hold production constant and let backlogs of unfilled customers' orders take care of fluctuations.
4. Some combinations of 1, 2, and/or 3.

Each of these major alternatives and subalternatives has costs associated with it. The problem of selecting that combination of alternatives which results in the lowest total cost of operations with relatively unknown future demand and performance is a formidable task. Linear decision rules have been developed that can give optimal (or near) solutions to this problem for certain well-defined assumptions about the related costs. An example will illustrate the form and use of a simple linear decision rule.

Company A manufactures glue, using a semicontinuous process. The amounts of regular payroll costs are known, as are overtime premium payments. The costs associated with hiring and laying off employees are shown in Table 13.7. Inventory-carrying costs are also studied and are determined to be as shown in Table 13.8. Negative inventory (back orders) is believed to be very undesirable, and high costs are associated with being out of stock. Two equations, shown in Table 13.9, are developed to yield minimum costs decisions on manpower and production rates for the glue company. Variables in Table 13.9 are defined as follows:

M = man-load, number of workers employed

I = inventory, gallons of glue in thousands

D = forecasted demand, gallons ordered in thousands

P = production, gallons of glue in thousands

TABLE 13.7 Costs of Hiring and Laying Off, Company A, Linear Decision Rule

Number of workers per month*	Total cost
1	$ 150
2	400
3	700
4	1,000
5	1,500
6	2,000
8	2,800
10	4,000
12	5,000
15	7,000
20	10,000
25	$13,500

*Net additions to (hired) or reductions from (laid off) the work force during the month.

TABLE 13.8 Inventory-Carrying Costs, Company A, Linear Decision Rule

Net inventory, thousands of gallons	Monthly cost
−200	$7,000
−150	5,000
−100	3,500
−50	2,250
0	1,600
50	1,000
100	600
150	400
200	450
250	800
300	1,250
350	1,900
400	2,800
450	4,000
500	$6,000

Using these two equations, simple calculations each month will determine the most economical man-load and production rate for the following months, based on forecasts of demand for the next 12 months. For example, suppose that the data at the end of December were the following:

$$\text{Man-load} = M_{\text{Dec}} = \text{workers}$$

$$\text{Inventory} = I_{\text{Dec}} = 300{,}000 \text{ gallons}$$

TABLE 13.9 Equations for Minimum Cost

$$M_{Jan} = 2.09 + 0.743\,M_{Dec} - 0.010\,I_{Dec} + \begin{cases} 0.0101\,D_{Jan} \\ +0.0088\,D_{Feb} \\ +0.0071\,D_{Mar} \\ +0.0054\,D_{Apr} \\ +0.0042\,D_{May} \\ +0.0031\,D_{June} \\ +0.0023\,D_{July} \\ +0.0016\,D_{Aug} \\ +0.0012\,D_{Sept} \\ +0.0009\,D_{Oct} \\ +0.0006\,D_{Nov} \\ +0.0005\,D_{Dec} \end{cases}$$

$$P_{Jan} = 153 + 0.993\,M_{Dec} - 0.464\,I_{Dec} + \begin{cases} 0.463\,D_{Jan} \\ +0.234\,D_{Feb} \\ +0.111\,D_{Mar} \\ +0.046\,D_{Apr} \\ +0.013\,D_{May} \\ -0.002\,D_{June} \\ -0.008\,D_{July} \\ -0.010\,D_{Aug} \\ -0.009\,D_{Sept} \\ -0.008\,D_{Oct} \\ -0.007\,D_{Nov} \\ -0.005\,D_{Dec} \end{cases}$$

Solving the two equations for January operating data gives the following:

$$\text{Man-load} = M_{Jan} = 82 \text{ workers (2 more than in December)}$$

$$\text{Production} = P_{Jan} = 426{,}000 \text{ gallons}$$

The inventory will increase by the difference between production and demand (426,000 − 380,000 = 46,000 gallons). The planned inventory at the end of January will then be 300,000 + 46,000 = 346,000 gallons. This can be calculated in one step, using the equation:

$$I_{Jan} = I_{Dec} + P_{Jan} - D_{Jan}$$

Some interesting observations can be made about the applications of such equations to the real business world:

- A practical management would want to test the effectiveness of the equations by simulating what would have happened if the equations had been used in the past and comparing this against the actual results.
- Because of the complexity of the mathematical equations, it is not possible to determine the effect on the decisions of changes in costs without deriving new equations.
- Factors not included in the original derivation might become important, and it may be difficult or impossible to include them in new equations.

- The equations assume a specific amount of production per worker. The actual number of people employed or the hours worked would have to be increased if this productivity were not met.

It is important to expand on the first observation. Linear decision rules can be applied to nearly any set of linear variables that are interrelated, but the model's results ignore any outside influences not captured by the model's variables; therefore, the results have to be tempered with logic. In addition, these models are very aggregate, not depicting variations due to time or outside perturbation. Hence, the results provide only general solutions, which may need to be adjusted.

Linear decision rules have real potential for assisting management toward controlling production-level changes on a traditional basis. The great danger lies in assuming that management can be relinquished to such rules and that the rules can handle all significant changes that may occur. The rules cannot! Applied properly, linear decision rules can improve control over production levels when compared to an intuitive approach. The results would certainly be more stable and consistent as long as no major variations occurred in those factors that affect the basic assumption used in the derivation of the equations.

SIMULATION

Digital simulation uses a mathematical model to represent a real or hypothetical physical system. A computer simulation model of a physical system provides a laboratory in which alternative designs can be explored and analyzed (see Chapter 36). Simulation is discussed in this section for loading and scheduling applications. The program, executed on the computer, is a replica of the manufacturing system and is controlled so that the system's behavior can be studied and analyzed. Decisions can be made concerning production alternatives. For example, adding a new lathe can be considered without disrupting the actual physical system.

Simulation depends on describing a system in terms acceptable to the computer language used. To do this, it is necessary to have a system-state description, which is typically characterized by a set of state variables included in the computer program that make up the simulation model. The various combinations of values that these variables can take characterize the unique states of the system. Sufficient variables must be defined to represent all of the pertinent details of the system. As the values of the variables are changed, the system effectively moves from state to state.

The process of building a simulation model consists of defining the state variables of the system and the operating procedures that cause the state variables to change over time. Simulation is then the process of moving the system from state to state according to the rules that characterize the operational procedures of the system.

There are two basic methods of managing the variable changes as they occur over time. The *discrete-event approach* makes the assumption that the system's variables change in value only at specific events. Each event, and the operating rules that cause the system's status variables to change in value, are incorporated in the computer program. The simulation moves through time from event to event, characterizing the system dynamics. The *fixed-time-interval approach* assumes that the system will be evaluated at regular, fixed time intervals. At the end of these intervals, the system status variables are updated according to a fixed set of rules, and then the system status is evaluated to determine if an event has occurred.

The discrete-event approach is used when the state variables change at irregular time intervals, such as in the manufacturing industry, which deals with discrete parts. The fixed-time-interval approach is typically used in systems having state variables of a continuous nature, such as those found in chemical process industries. Specially designed computer simulation languages provide many features for managing the updating of the state variables and advancing time. They also provide features for recording system performance statistics and for generating random numbers to introduce system randomness.

Simulation Languages

The lowest computer language typically used is Fortran or C++. This requires that the simulation process be coded, which is labor intensive. Higher-level languages, such as SLAM, SIMSCRIPT, SIMAN, and GPSS, facilitate simulation because they provide subroutines for time advancement, entity maintenance, and statistic collections. Higher-level simulation languages are designed for special purposes; MAP/I, SPEED, and MAST are three designed for the simulation of manufacturing systems. Some of the various computer simulation languages available are discussed in Chapter 36 on simulation.

Simulation Applications in Industry

Computer simulation has two important applications in industry, design and control. In design, the typical application is for analyzing a production system. Simulating a design is appealing because the components of the model are well detailed and have a one-to-one correspondence to the physical system. Because there are very few theoretical considerations, the model can represent many of the subtle system nuances; and with such a detailed model, the analyst can gain the confidence of the people using the simulator. Performance measurements, such as the number of parts passing through the system per day, can give an insight into the system's dynamic operation.

Some simulation languages can produce animations. This permits the simulation to be illustrated graphically on a computer terminal so the analyst can see the system in action and observe its interactions and behavior, a visual function beyond the scope of standard reporting technique. For example, TESS (a software program) provides animation, as well as model-building and output analysis capabilities, for the SLAM simulation language. When simulation is used as a control aid, it is used to generate and analyze possible production schedules. Since simulation models are based on very accurate predictions of system behavior, it is logical to use these powerful predictive techniques to develop precise schedules. Highly complex operating rules can be implemented in a model and then downloaded to the shop floor in the form of production schedules with operation start and end times.

LINE BALANCING

The term *line balancing* applies to assembly line operations in which a crew performs sequential operations. The objective of the balancing effort is to distribute the work as evenly as possible for maximum output and economy. In actual practice there are many kinds of line balancing (which is to say that the line-balancing principle may be applied to a number of varied operations). Consequently, there are several different approaches to line balancing, each being applicable to a particular set of conditions.

For lines to be balanced effectively, reliable predetermined time data should be available. The problem with using stopwatch time studies is that, when making changes and testing different line balances, one does not always have the time to study individual elements. Therefore, the method must actually be performed by someone and new time studies made to develop the correct standard time. The advantage of predetermined motion times, such as *methods time measurement* (MTM), is that the time for any conceivable method can be predetermined to develop the best line balance without a series of trial-and-error attempts. The savings in the time and effect of changes can be easily predicted. The following illustrates the use of a predetermined time standard applied to line balancing.

The two most common line types are *rigidly paced* and *spaced conveyor assembly lines* such as automobile assembly lines or the more flexible flat belts. The process of balancing these lines is basically one of determining the work content for each station of the line and organizing the work crew in the most effective manner. To accomplish this, the following steps are suggested:

1. Determine the output required per time period. It may be as small as an hour or as long as a day.
2. Determine the total man-hours work required per unit of output at standard operating efficiency.
3. Multiply the output required per period by the work standard to determine the total hours of work per period.
4. Divide the total number of hours in the normal work period at standard operating efficiency to find the number of people required to produce the necessary output.
5. Divide the total work per unit by the optimum number of people to arrive at the theoretical work cycle for each person per unit of output.

To further explain this, consider the following example. Assume a production requirement of 5000 pairs of heels per 8-hour shift. Assume 0.385 minutes per heel total true work. Total work required per shift is: $5000 \times 2 \times 0.385 = 3850$ minutes. With 480 minutes in an 8 hour shift, approximately 8 workers are needed. Divide the total work so that each operator on the line will have approximately a 0.0481-minute work cycle. There are several alternatives for balancing the line. All 8 members of the crew may be placed on the same side of the belt and perform the work sequentially with an approximate cycle time of 0.0481 minute. On the other hand, it may be desired to have 4 members on each side of the belt performing the same operation, having a cycle time of 0.0962 minute.

Some of the considerations that could have been used to determine which of these combinations to use might be as follows:

- *Difference in job rate.* Line feeders and line emptiers are often paid less than assemblers. Therefore, 2 people could have lower-paying jobs, reducing the total cost, other things being equal.
- *Long-cycle elements.* There may be an indivisible element longer than the desired work cycle. This requires that two identical work cycles be performed on the same or possibly on opposite sides of the belt.
- *Floor space and layout limitations.* Possibly, the belt is not long enough to have 10 people working on the same side, so the people must work on both sides of the belt.
- *Right- versus left-handedness.* In many cases, an element of work performed on one side of the belt with work coming toward the operator's left side may be completely different when the situation is reversed and the work approaches the right side.

Sometimes the operators can be trained to work either way, but in other cases extra movements and hence extra time may be involved.

Testing the Balance

With short, rigidly defined cycles, it is probably never possible to balance the line exactly; that is, not every operator can be assigned exactly the same amount of work. Therefore, since the pace is that of the slowest or longest cycle, there is a certain degree of imbalance that cannot be eliminated. To test the amount of imbalance and establish acceptable criteria for acceptance or rejection of the balance, the following procedure can be used. A rule of thumb is that the line balance is acceptable when the peak cycle, multiplied by the number of operators, is less than the total true work plus 25 percent.

Incentive Payment for Balanced Lines

The decision to accept or reject a given balancing solution should be made on the same basis, regardless of whether the operation is paid day work or is paid on an incentive basis. For lines of the type indicated above, the incentive payment, if any, must be paid on the basis of the peak cycle just as if everyone had the same amount of work. This is a group incentive system, and all members of the crew must produce the same number of units. One operator's pace cannot be different from another's except as caused by differences in assigned work over which the individual operator has no control whatsoever.

PROJECT MANAGEMENT WITH PERT/CPM

The original program evaluation review technique (PERT) was developed in the late 1950s as a method of planning and controlling the Polaris ballistic missile program for the U.S. Navy. At about the same time, the critical-path method (CPM) was developed by Du Pont, Remington-Rand, and J.E. Kelly in order to better manage chemical process plant shutdowns. PERT and CPM are graphic, network methods for organizing and scheduling projects that have activities of substantial duration—days, weeks, or months. Today there are many PERT/CPM computer software systems that are relatively inexpensive and include extensive graphic, cost accounting, decision support, and resource allocation modules.

PERT/CPM applications include managing the combined manufacturing lead time (that is, the critical path) for the purchase, fabrication, and assembly of products; the production of make-to-order tools and equipment, such as die sets and lithography plates; the design and implementation of new production information control systems; and the construction and move to a new facility. Some important project characteristics that assist in determining when to use PERT/CPM are listed below:

- The objective is to minimize times, costs, or resource idle times.
- The need is to know which events are on the critical path.
- The need is to coordinate many activities.
- There are complex activity interrelationships and interdependencies in parallel and in sequence.
- There is a need to meet contractual or promised due dates.
- There are long lead and activity times.

- There are limited resources involved in multiple activities or projects.
- Periodic reporting, budgeting, or billing based on project completion is required.
- Several different organizations (such as suppliers) are involved.
- There is uncertainty concerning activity times and delivery dates.
- There is a need for graphic representation of project progress, using Gantt, PERT, work center load profiles, cash flow, or percent completion charts.

Introduction to PERT/CPM Diagrams

Figure 13.12 illustrates three different project activity structures. All three structures are *activity-on-arrow (arc) diagrams,* in which the arrows represent activities and the nodes represent precedent relationships. Activities are specific tasks that require time and resources to complete. Frequently, several activities compete simultaneously for the same human or material resources; therefore, a rational method of allocating these resources is necessary. For an activity-on-arrow diagram, nodes (or milestones) mark the completion of all tasks preceding it. In Fig. 13.12c, for example, activity 3–4 cannot begin until activities 1–2, 1–3, and 2–3 are complete. Similarly, activities 2–4 and 2–3 cannot begin until activity 1–2 is complete.

Diagram Construction

The basis of product management using PERT/CPM are illustrated by a simple example of a wholesaler selecting, purchasing, and implementing a new finished-goods

(a) Parallel Activities (e.g. parallel assembly lines)

(b) Sequential Activities (e.g. a flow shop or repetitive processing)

(c) Interrelated Activities (e.g. a product scheduled through a job shop or project)

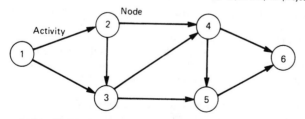

Activity (2-3) cannot begin until activity (1-2) is complete.
Activities (3-4) and (3-5) cannot begin until activities (1-2), (1-3), and (2-3) are complete.

FIGURE 13.12   Simple activity-on-arrow precedent structures.

inventory control system. Because the PERT/CPM diagram is the priority planning document that drives resource and capacity acquisition and allocation, a properly constructed network diagram is critical for successful project management. The following five steps are necessary in constructing a PERT or CPM network diagram.

Step 1: Define All Appropriate Major Milestones That Must Occur.   For the example, the following major milestones are identified:

1. Start project.
2. Select new system.
3. Complete operator training.
4. Install system.

Each of the four milestones has several activities that must take place to achieve the final milestone. In defining milestones, however, it is important to keep the level of detail the same for all. It is inappropriate to list a minor milestone such as "flowchart completed" with a major milestone such as "system installed."

Step 2: Define Activities.   It is necessary to define all activities that must be completed before each major milestone occurs and then rank them in approximate order of occurrence. In this simplified example, the following activities are defined:

1–2 Define the system and select a cost-effective, "canned" inventory control system.

1–3 Educate the operating personnel in the theory and tools of finished-goods inventory control systems.

2–3 Document the new system for clarity, maintenance, user reference, and standardization of procedures.

2–4 Install and check out the system, including the hardware, software, and interfaces to the new inventory control system.

3–4 Train the operators before going on-line with the new system.

To assist in identifying project activities, a hierarchical structure can be generated, as is done with a bill of materials. The bill of activities, or *work breakdown structure* (WBDS), shows low-level activities that are components of higher-level, general activities (Table 13.10).

Step 3: Define Precedence Relationships.   The precedence relationships that exist among events and activities need to be defined next. To define the precedence relationships, one must identify all activities that occur before each subsequent activity can begin. Those activities that are at the beginning or end of the project are the easiest to define. An initial pass at precedence can begin by using a simplified, indented activity list of work breakdown. However, network construction and revision are continuing processes requiring the same attention to detail, accuracy, and date integrity as a complex bill of materials.

There are several useful ways to display precedence relationships through *precedence-planning documents.* These include work breakdown structures, Gantt charts (Fig. 13.13), and precedence lists. A *precedence list* is simply a vertical list of all activities associated with each activity; a list of (1) all activities that *must be* completed *before* that activity can start, (2) all activities that cannot start until the activity is com-

TABLE 13.10 Work Breakdown Structure (WBDS) for Inventory Management Systems: Indented Activity Levels

1					INVENTORY MANAGEMENT SYSTEM SELECTION AND IMPLEMENTATION
	2				(1–2) System definition and selection
		3			Define desired system
			4		Define system requirements
				5	...
			4		Prepare functional specifications
				5	...
			4		Prepare system specifications
			4		Prepare system flowcharts
			4		Design forms and reports
			4		Define system computations
		3			Select best available system
			4		Analyze existing software
			4		Financial analysis
			4		...
			4		...
	2				(1–3) General education of operating personnel
		3			APICS certification classes
			4		Inventory management certification module
			4		...
				5	...
	2				(2–3) Documentation of new system
		3			...
			4		...
	2				(2–4) Installation and checkout of system
		3			...
			4		...
	2				(3–4) Systems training of users
		3			...
			4		...
				5	...

pleted, and (3) all other activities that are not affected. Just as the bill of materials is essential to MRP, the WBDS is essential in defining precedence, dependencies, project structure, and detailed work assignments. Gantt charts are useful for simple project or activity structures. Because they are so easily understood, they can provide operating personnel at all levels with graphic WBDS information, but they may not adequately represent the dependencies of a realistic project.

Step 4: Construct Diagram.   From these precedence-relationship aids, the network diagram can be constructed. The diagram can be either an activity-on-arrow (arc) diagram, which is also known as an *i–j diagram* (Fig. 13.14), or an activity-on-node diagram, also known as a *precedence diagram*. While activity-on-arrow diagrams can be slightly more difficult to construct than activity-on-node diagrams, their graphic representation of the project is easier to understand and use after construction. For this reason, the activity-on-arrow representation is chosen here. Activity-on-node diagrams (Fig. 13.15) are an efficient method of representing a network and are often used in computer software. This type of diagram has several advantages for the experienced PERT/CPM user that make it the preferred method. Fortunately, after understanding one

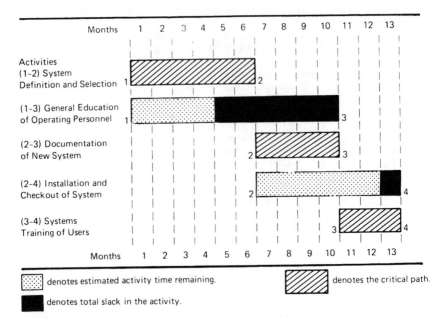

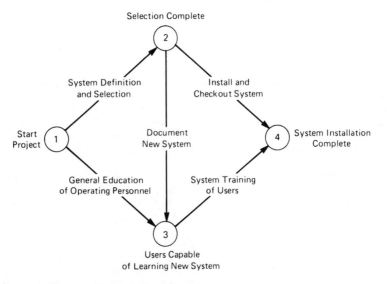

FIGURE 13.13 Initial Gantt chart of inventory control system project.

FIGURE 13.14 Activity-on-arrow diagram.

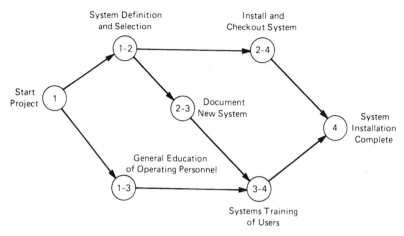

FIGURE 13.15 Activity-on-node diagram.

method, it is relatively easy to convert to the other. Constructing an activity-on-arrow diagram begins on the far left with a single start node. All initial activities that do not have other activities taking precedence emanate from the start node. At the end of an activity arrow, another node is constructed. Activities that must succeed the previous activity emanate from this node. Note that it is feasible that two or more activities connect two nodes (parallel activities). Also note that all activities that must precede an activity X must route through the node from which activity X starts.

Step 5: Estimate Activity Times. Once the precedence network is defined, project planning continues toward determining the critical path and critical resources. Before making these determinations, it is necessary to estimate activity times. To model the time relationships of a project, individual activity times must be estimated by people knowledgeable and experienced in each activity. The decision maker assumes that adequate resources (such as personnel, equipment, and material) are available for the activity, without regard to other activity demands.

PERT

CPM assumes deterministic values for activity times. PERT assumes a distribution for each activity time. For each activity in a PERT diagram, there is an estimated *most probable time.* But because of uncertainty, there is a *pessimistic estimate* and an *optimistic estimate* for each activity time. These times are not easily determined but are used to provide the planners with some understanding of the possible distribution of activity times that could occur.

The activity completion times are estimated by using objective or subjective data. When the activity times are relatively certain, a single activity time is estimated. CPM assumes a single, mean activity time ET_{i-j}. However, if the activity time estimates are uncertain, probability distributions are used, and the network diagram becomes a PERT diagram. Herein is the essential difference between CPM and PERT; CPM uses a single, mean activity time while PERT uses a probability distribution.

Specifically, PERT uses three estimates to calculate a mean activity time and a probability distribution; these are a, m, and b (defined in Table 13.11). These time estimates can be based upon objective historical data of similar tasks; if these are unavailable, subjective estimates are used. Some individuals have difficulty in estimating the times because they are subjective; however, it is far better to include a guesstimate of activity time ranges than to ignore variability.

From the three estimates (a, m, b), a mean activity time ET_{i-j} and a variance σ_{i-j}^2 can be calculated, using the assumption that the activity times form a beta distribution. The mean of the beta distribution is as follows:

$$ET_{i-j} = \frac{a + 4m + b}{6}$$

while the variance (the standard deviation squared) is the following:

$$\sigma_{i-j}^2 = \frac{(b - a)^2}{6}$$

The developers of PERT chose a beta distribution to represent activity times because, depending on a, m, and b, it can approximate a wide variety of other probability distributions. While few activity times theoretically match a beta distribution, most activities can be adequately represented by it from a practical standpoint. When an activity time can be better represented by another distribution (such as normal or exponential), it can easily be incorporated in the network. Table 13.12 for an inventory control project lists a, m, and b for each of the activities of this example. The mean and variance times for activity 1–2 are as follows:

$$ET_{1-2} = \frac{a + 4m + b}{6} = \frac{1 + 4(6) + 11}{6} = 6$$

$$\sigma_{1-2}^2 = \left(\frac{b - a}{6}\right)^2 = \left(\frac{11 - 1}{6}\right)^2 = 2.78$$

Using the PERT/CPM Diagram

Now that the PERT/CPM network diagram has been constructed and the associated activity times determined, the diagram can be used to analyze and control the project.

Activity Start and Finish Dates. There are several steps in calculating the project activities' start and finish dates. To distinguish between times and dates, a *date* is the day, week, or month on which an activity starts or finishes, while a *time* is the duration of the activity (such as ET_{i-j} and σ_{i-j}). In PERT/CPM calculations, one first works forward to calculate early start (ES) and early finish (EF) dates and then works backward to calculate late finish (LF) and late start (LS) dates.

Early start is the date an activity begins if all activities are completed in their expected times (ET). Similarly, *early finish* is the date an activity finishes if all activities are completed in their expected times. The first activities of a project begin on the

TABLE 13.11   Notation and Rules of PERT/CPM

---

i–j is used to identify activity i to j from start to finish. In this example, activity 1–2 is the "system definition and selection" activity.

Estimated by decision makers

a = an optimistic estimate of activity time. This or a shorter time will occur only 1 out of 100 times the task is completed.

m = the most frequent (modal) time to complete an activity. Out of 100 repetitions of the activity, this time will occur most frequently.

b = a pessimistic estimate of an activity time. This or a longer time will occur only 1 out of 100 times the task is completed.

Calculated activity times

ET_{i-j} = the expected (mean) time to complete activity i–j.

σ_{i-j} = the standard deviation of activity time i–j.

Calculated dates going forward

ES_{i-j} = the early start date of activity i–j = maximum EF of preceding (incoming) activities (see rule 2 below).

EF_{i-j} = $ES_{i-j}+ET_{i-j}$, which is the early finish date of activity i–j.

Calculated dates going backward

LS_{i-j} = the latest date on which activity i–j can be started without increasing the duration of the project = $LF_{i-j}-ET_{i-j}$.

LF_{i-j} = the latest date on which activity i–j can be finished without increasing the duration of the project. This equals the minimum LS of the successor (outgoing) activities of activity i–j.

Calculated activity and project times

TS_{i-j} = LS_{i-j} = ES_{i-j} = the total slack time of an activity. An activity can be delayed this amount without increasing the duration of the project.

ET_p = mean (expected) project time = sum of ET along critical path.

σ_p^2 = variance of project time = sum of the variances along critical path.

Network computational rules

Rule 1: All activities leading to an event must be completed before the event occurs and succeeding activities can begin.

Rule 2: When working forward in time at an event, always take the highest EF of preceding (incoming) activities as the ES for succeeding (outgoing) activities.

Rule 3: When working backward in time at an event, always take the lowest of LS of outgoing (successor) activities as the LF of incoming (preceding) activities.

TABLE 13.12   PERT Statistics for an Inventory Control System Project

Activities	a	m	b	Exp. times (ET)	σ^2 (ET)	Early start (ES)	Early finish (EF)	Late start (LS)	Late finish (LF)	Total slack (TS)
1–2 System definition and selection	1	6	11	6	2.78	0	6	0	6	0
1–3 General education of operating personnel	2	4	6	4	.44	0	4	6	10	6
2–3 Documentation of new system	1	4	7	4	1.00	6	10	6	10	0
2–4 Installation and checkout of system	2	5	14	6	4.00	6	12	7	13	1
3–4 Systems training of users	1	3	5	3	.44	10	13	10	13	0

first date of the project. In this case, it is assumed that the starting date is time zero, but in general the first period will be the shop calendar date. In Table 13.11, early starts 1–2 and 1–3 are both zero; therefore:

$$EF_{1-2} = ES_{1-2} + ET_{1-2} = 0 + 6 = 6$$

$$EF_{1-3} = ES_{1-3} + ET_{1-3} = 0 + 4 = 4$$

Activities succeeding events 1-2 and 1-3 cannot begin until all activities leading to them are completed:

Rule 1. All activities leading to an event must be completed before the event occurs and succeeding activities can begin.

Activities 2–3 and 2–4 can begin as soon as 1–2 is complete, while 3–4 cannot begin until both 2–3 and 1–3 are complete. The ES_{2-3} and ES_{2-4} are equal to the EF_{1-2}, which is 6; therefore:

$$EF_{2-3} = ES_{2-3} + ET_{2-3} = 6 + 4 = 10$$

Now that the EF_{2-3} is known, rule 2 is used to choose the ES_{3-4}:

Rule 2. When working forward in time at a node, always take the highest EF of preceding (incoming) activities as the ES for succeeding (outgoing) activities.

The ES_{3-4} is quite logically the maximum EF of all preceding activities. In this case, ES_{3-4} is 10 + 3, or 13. The EF_{2-4} is $ES_{2-4} + ET_{2-4}$, which is 12. Node 4, which is the project's completion, cannot occur until both 2–4 and 3–4 are complete; therefore, the EF of the project, denoted by EF_p, equals the maximum of either EF_{2-4} or EF_{3-4}. In this case, $EF_p = 13$ months since it is the largest value. The expected completion date of the project is the end of month 13. This completes the forward calculation of early dates. The next phase calculates the latest dates by working backward from the end of the project.

The backward calculation of the late start (LS) and late finish (LF) times is designed to determine how late the activities can start and finish without delaying the project's completion date.

LS_{i-j} = latest date on which activity $i-j$ can be started without increasing the duration of the project = $LF_{i-j} - ET_{i-j}$

LF_{i-j} = latest date on which activity $i-j$ can be finished without increasing the duration of the project = minimum LS of the successor (outgoing) activities of activity $i-j$

The LF and LS dates are important in identifying the critical and near-critical path activities and their completion dates. By convention, the late finishes of the project and the ending activities 2–4 and 3–4 are assigned the early finish EF_p of the project, in this case 13. Each activity terminating at node 4 (that is, 2–4 and 3–4) is assigned the LF of 13. These LFs denote that if activity 2–4 or 3–4 finishes later than 13, then the project will be delayed. Logically, the LS of each activity is LF–ET; for example,

$$LS_{3-4} = LF_{3-4} - ET_{3-4} = 13 - 3 = 10$$

$$LS_{2-4} = LF_{2-4} - ET_{2-4} = 13 - 6 = 7$$

The LF_{2-3} is equal to $LS_{3-4} = 10$. When a node has more than one activity leading back to it, then according to rule 3 of Table 13.11, the LF of activities leading into an event is the minimum of the LS of those activities leaving the event.

Rule 3. When working backward in time at a node, always take the lowest LS of outgoing (successor) activities as the LF of incoming (preceding) activities.

For example, LF_{1-2} is the minimum of $LS_{2-4} = 7$, and $LS_{2-3} = 6$; therefore, $LF_{1-2} = 6$. That is, if activity 1–2 is completed after month 6, then the project will be delayed. This procedure continues until all LSs and LFs have been calculated. Figure 13.16, the completed PERT/CPM diagram, gives the results for the example.

Slack and the Critical Path. The critical path (longest path) may be evident by inspection; however, it is typically more difficult to determine in a larger project. Total slack (TS) is used to identify the critical path. The difference between LS and ES or LF and EF is TS:

$$TS_{i-j} = LS_{i-j} - ES_{i-j} = \text{total slack time of an activity}$$

An activity can be delayed this amount without increasing the duration of the project.

For activity 2–4, this difference is $7-6$ or $13-12$, which is 1 month; therefore, activity 2–4 can be delayed 1 month without delaying the expected completion date of this project. In contrast, TS_{2-4} is $10-10$, or zero months. There is no slack in activity 3–4; therefore, a delay in this activity will delay the project. Logically, those activities on the critical paths 1–2, 2–3, and 3–4 have zero slack. The expected completion date of the project equals the sum of the ETs of these activities; $6 + 4 + 3 = 13$. Because these activities determine the project time, management should not permit their delay.

In a large project, there may be more than one critical path and several near-critical paths. For example, TS_{2-4} of activity 2–4 is only 1 month; therefore, the project will be delayed if activity 2–4 is delayed more than a month. Consequently, all activities should

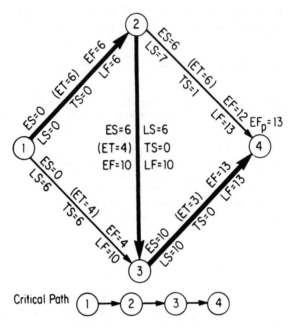

FIGURE 13.16   Completed PERT/CPM diagram.

be managed so as to minimize costs and meet project due dates. Also, if resources for an activity with considerable slack (such as activity 1–3) can be transferred to an activity on the critical path (such as 1–2), then the length and cost of the project may be decreased.

Probabilistic Estimates of Project Completion Dates.   Using the central limit theorem of statistical analysis, it is possible to estimate the probability distribution of project completion dates. The mean (expected) project completion is equal to the length of the critical path (or month 13). Because this is a mean, there is a 50 percent chance the project will be completed before this date and a 50 percent chance after this date. Just as in forecasting, a single quantity is much less useful than a range and its probability. Assuming that the activity times along the critical path are independent of each other, the central limit theorem denotes that the project's completion time approximates a normal distribution, with a mean ET_p equal to the critical path time and a variance σ_p^2 equal to the sum of the variances along the critical path.

$$ET_p = \text{mean (expected) project time} = \text{sum of ETs along critical path}$$

$$\sigma_p^2 = \text{variance of project time} = \text{sum of variances along critical path}$$

In the example,

$$ET_p = ET_{1-2} + ET_{2-3} + ET_{3-4} = 6 + 4 + 3 = 13 \text{ months}$$

$$\sigma_p^2 = \sigma_{1-2}^2 + \sigma_{2-3}^2 + \sigma_{3-4}^2 = 2.78 + 1.0 + 0.44 = 4.22 \text{ months}$$

Using these approximate relationships, it is possible to calculate probability estimates for project completion times. Using the characteristics of the normal distribution, there is a 68 percent chance that the project will be completed in approximately 11 to 15 months (that is, the mean plus and minus 1 standard deviation, or 13 plus or minus 2.05). Also, there is a 2.5 percent chance that the project will take more than 17.0 months (the mean plus 1.96 standard deviations). There is considerable uncertainty in the estimated completion times of this project because activity 1–2 has such a large variance. If the estimated time of this activity could be better defined (that is, have a lower variance), then the range of project completion times would be narrower.

Dependence of Critical Paths. In calculating the critical path's mean and variance, it was assumed that critical path 1–2–3–4 was the only possible critical path; however, path 1–2–4 has a very high probability of becoming critical. Path 1–2–4 is expected to be completed at the end of month 12; however, the variance of this path is quite high. In this case, the variance and standard deviation of path 1–2–4 are 6.78 (2.78 + 4.00) and 2.60 months, respectively. The probability, without showing the calculation here, that path 1–2–4 will take longer than 13 months is about 35 percent. Also, there is a 68 percent chance that path 1–2–4 will be completed in 9.4 to 14.6 months (the mean plus or minus 1 standard deviation) and a 2.5 percent chance that path 1–2–4 will take more than 17.10 months (the mean plus 1.96 standard deviations). Consequently, this path has a high probability of being the critical path and should therefore be monitored carefully.

ET_p and σ_p are only approximations because it is assumed that the critical-path time of 1–2–3–4 is independent of other paths; the independence assumption is theoretically wrong and at times misleading. The project duration depends upon the joint probability of completing all possible paths: 1–2–3–4, 1–2–4, and 1–3–4. Fortunately, some PERT/CPM software packages do not make the independence assumptions; they use the more complex and valid joint probability estimates of project completion times. From a management standpoint, it is important to understand the assumption of independent critical paths and to interpret it cautiously.

Because the uncertainties in a project are many and complex, the probability distributions of project and activity times may not be adequately represented by the simple joint probability rule. In such situations, Monte Carlo simulation has been found to be valuable. Computer simulations of projects is being applied more and more frequently, and specialized computer languages have been developed to assist in network simulations.

Dummy Activities. The construction of activity-on-arrow networks may require the introduction of artificial events and activities called *dummies*. For example, as shown in the diagrams in Fig. 13.17*a*, if two activities have the same beginning event 1 and the same ending event 3, then it is necessary to introduce a dummy event 2 and a dummy activity 2–3 to identify each unique activity. Dummy activities require no time

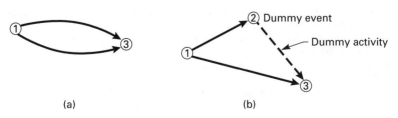

(a)   (b)

FIGURE 13.17 Dummy activity.

resources and are typically represented by dotted lines, as in Fig. 13.17*b,* or by thinner lines than those for the actual activities.

BIBLIOGRAPHY

APICS Certification Program Study Guide: "Capacity Planning and Master Production Scheduling," *Production and Inventory Management,* (20:2), 1979, pp. 85–102.

Bedworth, David D., and James E. Bailey: *Integrated Production Control Systems, Management, Analysis, Design,* 2d ed., Wiley, New York, 1987.

Berry, William L., T. L. Vollman, and D. C. Whybark: *Master Production Scheduling: Principles and Practice,* American Production and Inventory Control Society, American Production and Inventory Control Society, Washington, D.C., 1983.

Bestwick, P. F., and K. G. Lockger: "A Practical Approach to Production Scheduling," *International Journal of Production Research* (17:2), 1979, pp. 95–110.

Chase, R. B., and N. J. Aquilano: *Production and Operations Management,* 4th ed., Irwin, Homewood, Ill., 1985.

Colley, John Leonard: *Production, Operations, Planning & Control: Text and Cases,* Holden-Day, San Francisco, 1977.

Conway, R. W., W. L. Maxwell, and L. W. Miller: *Theory of Scheduling,* Addison-Wesley, Reading, Mass., 1967.

Crama, Yves: *Production Planning in Automated Manufacturing,* Springer-Verlag, Berlin/New York, 1994.

Dempster, M. A. H., I. K. Lenstra, and A. H. G. Kan Rinnoy: *Deterministic and Stochastic Scheduling,* Reidel, Boston, 1982.

Donovan, R. Michael: *Planning and Controlling Manufacturing Resources,* Amacom, New York, 1979.

Fogarty, D. W., T. R. Hoffman, and P. W. Stonebraker: *Production and Inventory Management,* 3d ed., South-Western, Cincinnati, 1991.

Fleming, Quentin W.: *Project and Production Scheduling,* Probus, Chicago, Ill., 1987.

Hall, Robert W.: *Attaining Manufacturing Excellence: Just-In-Time, Total Quality, Total People Involvement,* Dow Jones-Irwin, Homewood, Ill., 1987.

Harmon, Roy L.: *Reinventing the Factory II: Managing the World Class Factory,* Free Press, New York/Maxwell Macmillan, Toronto, Canada, 1992.

Hax, Arnold C.: *Production and Inventory Management,* Prentice-Hall, Englewood Cliffs, N.J., 1984.

Hershauer, J. C., and R. D. Eck: "Extended MRP Systems for Evaluating Master Schedules and Material Requirements Plans," *Production and Inventory Management* (21:2), 1980, pp. 53–66.

Holt, Jack A.: "A Heuristic Method for Aggregate Planning: Production Decision Framework," *Journal of Operations Management* (2:1), 1980, pp. 41–51.

Janson, R. L.: *Production Control Desk Handbook,* Prentice-Hall, Englewood Cliffs, N.J., 1975.

Landvater, Darryl V.: *World Class Production and Inventory Management,* O. Wight Publications, Essex Junction, Conn., 1995.

Migliore, R. Henry: *Production/Operations Management: A Productivity Approach,* Nichols/GP Publishing, East Brunswick, N.J., 1990.

Miller, Stanley S.: *Competitive Manufacturing: Using Production as a Management Tool,* Van Nostrand Reinhold, New York, 1988.

Pinedo, Michael: *Scheduling Theory, Algorithms and Systems,* Prentice-Hall, Englewood Cliffs, N.J., 1995.

Plossl, George W.: *Production and Inventory Control: Principles and Techniques,* 2d ed., Prentice-Hall, Englewood Cliffs, N.J., 1984.

Proud, J.F.: "Controlling the Master Schedule," *Production and Inventory Management* (22:2), 1981, pp. 78–90.

Riggs, J. S.: *Production Systems: Planning, Analysis and Control,* 4th ed., Wiley, New York, 1987.

Silver, Edward A.: *Decision Systems For Inventory Management and Production Planning,* 2d ed., Wiley, New York, 1985.

Silver, E. A., and R. Peterson: *Decision Systems for Inventory Management and Production Planning,* 2d ed., Wiley, New York, 1985.

Vollman, Thomas E., William E. Berry, and D. Clay Whybark: *Manufacturing Planning and Control Systems,* 3d ed., Irwin, Homewood, Ill., 1991.

CHAPTER 14
SHOP FLOOR CONTROL

Editor

William R. Wassweiler, CFPIM, CIRM

Manufacturing Industry Consultant,
Milwaukee, Wisconsin

An effective manufacturing system relies on two major components for operational success: realistic planning complemented by effective control over the execution of those plans. Shop floor control is that element of an MRP II system that is directly responsible for the activities required to execute the planned production for the company. It is the nervous system of the factory because of its responsibility to release work to the shop and receive feedback on the status of production activity. The principal function of shop floor control in addition to releasing orders and collecting status is monitoring and controlling lead times, establishing and receiving order priorities, planning capacity at each work center, and controlling queue time and work-in-process. In addition, it records performance of actual results to compare with standards and targets. Shop floor control is a critical element for a company's success since its actions impact cost and delivery lead time, two competitive factors that determine survival in a world market.

Shop floor control's major objective is to support the challenges facing manufacturing companies today with tools and techniques to produce products more quickly, to add value and lower cost, provide the capability of producing greater product variety, and improve product quality. Shop floor control (SFC) brings the entire manufacturing facility, including people, machines, materials, and tools together in an optimum relationship to execute the master production schedule. It controls shop priorities and work-in-process while providing acceptable customer service.

PRODUCTION ENVIRONMENT

Because of the dynamic nature of manufacturing today, SFC systems must be able to operate in a mixed-mode production environment. Shop floor control is required to support both process and product factory layout structures.

A *process* or *functional layout* (Fig. 14.1a) consists of organizing shop floor machines into work centers by the function of the equipment. As an example, drilling, boring, milling, and grinding machines would be grouped by common process characteristics. This layout organization is often referred to as a *job shop environment*. *Product layout* (Fig. 14.1b), as its name implies, refers to a layout that supports the production

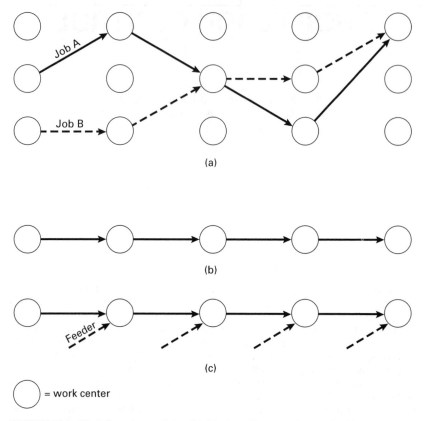

FIGURE 14.1 Work flow characteristics. (*a*) Job shop; (*b*) process flow production; (*c*) repetitive products.

flow of the product with a minimum amount of non-value-added materials handling. The production of high-volume or repetitive products dictate an assembly line layout (Fig. 14.1*c*) that is product oriented.

Within these environments, companies produce products that are made to order, made to stock, assembled to order, or engineered to order. It is not unusual for a company to have a product mix that requires it to operate in two or more modes of production using repetitive, intermittent, or project manufacturing techniques.

ENVIRONMENT CHARACTERISTICS OF CONTROL

Job Shop Control Characteristics

- Individual work centers scheduled
- Priorities assigned to each order
- Orders flowing between work centers in a variety of patterns

- Data tracked for each operation sequence number
- Orders released individually
- Materials-oriented MPS
- A "pick list" for each work order used to issue inventory
- Multiple levels in the bill of materials
- Lot size calculation possibly complex
- Lead times usually long

Process Flow Production

- Capital intensive
- Capacity-oriented master production schedule
- Work orders not required
- Master production schedule authorization to produce
- Few levels in the bill of materials
- Less complex lot sizes

Repetitive

- Mass production of discrete units
- Daily-run schedules used to authorize production
- Production runs given in MPS for specific time periods
- Data collection executed at key points in the flow
- Materials issue accomplished through *backflushing*
- Line balancing critical to production

SHOP FLOOR RELATIONSHIPS

Because of the impact on delivery performance and product costs, the SFC activities are tightly related to other business functions in the firm. As a consequence of downsizing and the development of cross-functional teams, the SFC group must work closely with accounting to reduce product costs, with design and process engineering to implement engineering changes and new methods, with quality control to meet product quality goals, with customer service to ensure timely product delivery, with the production department to achieve delivery and inventory objectives, and with plant maintenance to ensure meeting maintenance schedules without impeding customer service.

To achieve teamwork required by a cross-functional team, a company requires a seamless, integrated manufacturing system commonly referred to as *MRP II*. MRP II functions give SFC the ability to plan, schedule, and evaluate the effectiveness of shop operations. A key element of SFC is an information system that can present data promptly, concisely, and frequently so that action can be taken on time. For SFC to execute the MPS, it must operate within a closed-loop manufacturing control system (MRP II). The *closed loop* refers to a series of systems within a company that mutually interact through the integration of the software.

MAJOR ACTIVITIES OF SHOP FLOOR CONTROL

Shop floor control is responsible for managing the flow of shop orders from the moment that the order is released by the planning function and arrives in the factory system until that order is completed and disposed of. When the order is disposed of, the SFC system is no longer held accountable for that order. As far as it is concerned, the order is gone. To manage this flow, the SFC system relies on several interrelated activities:

- Order review and release
- Detailed scheduling
- Data collection monitoring
- Control feedback
- Order disposition

Each of these five activities is needed to manage the act of transforming the order from being a planned order (something that is written on paper) to a completed order. The schematic of this process and positioning of these five activities is summarized in Fig. 14.2.

DATABASE REQUIREMENTS

For the SFC computer program to generate the logic to release, prioritize, and track shop orders, specific data are essential.

Routing

The most important data required are for routing the product through the process (Table 14.1). It is the shop document that indicates how an item is converted to a finished part. A complete routing will contain the following information:

- How the item is produced
- Where the work is to be performed
- How much time is required to perform each operation
- The setup time, if any, required to ready the machine to produce the item
- The tooling required for each operation
- Type of labor required
- The sequence of the work
- How to machine and/or fabricate the item and a description of the activity or process

The routing is a process road map for an item, and it is the most critical piece of data to support SFC. The information contained in the routing is used to calculate lead times, costs, job status, and location control. Since routings chart the direction and sequence of work through the factory, it is essential that they be accurate but also be maintained up to date. Routings are typically used as *shop travelers,* which means that they accompany the work from start to finish.

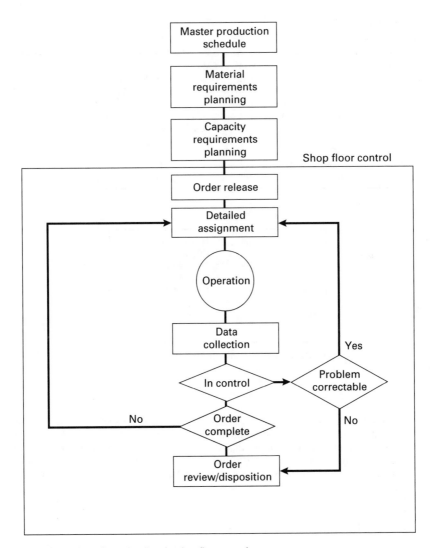

FIGURE 14.2   Information flow for shop floor control.

Work Center or Manufacturing Cell

The other piece of data critical to a shop floor control system is the characters of the work center. A *work center* is the specific location in the factory where the work is performed. A work center usually contains machines or equipment that are either identical or similar in capability or process. The purpose of the *work center file* is to assemble in one place all the relevant data (Fig. 14.3) related to a work center, such as information concerning cost, capacity, lead time, crew size, and function.

TABLE 14.1   Routing

Part number 8875

Operation number	Description	Dept.	Work center	Mach. number	Labor grade	Run HR/PC	Setup hours	Tools
010	Cut off	10	11	623	05	0.020	0.5	1012
020	Shape	10	12	127	05	0.030	2.10	601
030	Drill	20	21	500	08	0.060	0.20	500
040	Inspect	49	22		02	0.000	0.00	
050	Heat treat	H.T.	4		00	0.000	0.00	
060	Inspect	49	32		00	0.000	0.00	

Work center number	Hours per shift
Description	Efficiency
Capacity	Utilization
Setup hours	Number of operations
Machine hours	Labor rate
Queue time	Setup rate
Move time	Burden rate
Shifts worked	

FIGURE 14.3   Work center file.

A *manufacturing cell* is similar in concept to a work center except that the cell contains a small group of workers and different machines laid out and organized to provide a repetitive production flow for items that are similar. A cellular layout permits shorter cycle and setup times and also reduces materials handling and work-in-process. Cellular manufacturing is a positive method for reducing lead times and improving product velocity through the plant.

Bill of Materials

A bill of materials (see Chapter 5 on bills of materials) is a basic requirement for SFC, for it defines the components or ingredients of products to be produced. A parts list and pick list are created for each shop order from the bill of materials. This information, in conjunction with on-hand and on-order inventory records, determines materials availability and shortages for the start date of the shop order.

Tooling

The control of *tooling* is important for good schedule performance because tooling that is unavailable can be as devastating to shop performance as a materials shortage. Effective tool systems include location control, time remaining before the tool needs refurbishing, parts used on, need dates to support setup, and tool ownership status.

LEAD TIME DETERMINATION AND CONTROL

Shop lead time can be defined as the interval of time between planning the release of an order, work-in-process, until the order is completed. Shop lead times are either fixed or variable. *Fixed lead times* are determined on the basis of policy, estimates, or by past history. Fixed lead times are appropriate when it is impractical to calculate the lead time. *Variable* or *calculated lead times* are developed from *use factors* that affect the time a job is in process. These factors consist of the following:

- *Queue time* is the time a job is waiting for a setup to be made or a previous product to be processed. Typically, this element of lead time represents the longest segment.
- *Setup time* is that time required for preparing a machine or machines for production. Setup time is the time needed to produce the order.
- *Run time* represents the time the job is actually being worked on or in process.
- *Wait time* relates to the time a product waits before it is moved.
- *Move time* is the time for physically moving the material between work centers.

The data required to calculate lead times are stored in the routing and work center files. These data are retrieved periodically and fed to a lead time generating program that recalculates lead times and updates the part master record. This information is used to offset planned orders in the MRP. The lead time for an item will vary directly with its lot size—if the lot size is fixed, the time is constant regardless of the lot quantity.

A major objective in any factory is the reduction, or compression, of lead times. Product throughput times have a direct bearing on a company's ability to compete on price and delivery. The shorter the lead time, the lower the cost of work-in-process inventory and the faster the response to a customer's requirements. Taking a closer look at the elements of lead time, the setup, move, and queue factors stand out as non-value-added activities that increase cost and slow down production.

Creative approaches have been taken to reduce lead times such as the organization of machines and equipment on the shop floor into manufacturing cells and the use of *focused product operations* within a factory. Typically, a focused factory emphasizes its entire manufacturing system on a limited, concise, manageable set of products. Also, much has been done to reduce machine changeover time by applying setup reduction techniques such as single-minute-exchange of die (SMED), the goal of which is to maintain setup times of less than 10 minutes.

The reduction of lead time can be accomplished through many techniques that might compress shop time, but they may not be consistently cost effective. Subcontracting, the sending of production work outside to another manufacturer, might improve lead time by freeing up constraining, capacity-bound work centers but typically at a higher cost than the make-in-house standards. Subcontracting is characterized as a stopgap technique or a temporary solution. Other lead time reduction methods are listed here:

- Overlapping routed operations by sending material ahead to be processed (Fig. 14.4) prior to the completion of the entire lot will reduce lead times, generally without a serious cost increase.
- Running operations in parallel, rather than in series, must be considered when lead times are calculated for the manufacturing.
- Splitting a lot or work order and sending a partial order ahead will compress lead time. This technique is used primarily to expedite small quantities, but the non-value-added costs are duplicated on the balance of the lot to be processed.

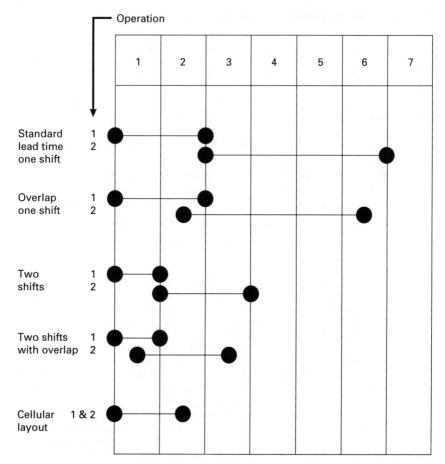

FIGURE 14.4   Scheduling techniques and the impact on lead time.

- Routing an item through an alternate operation step or using an alternate routing method can potentially reduce lead time. However, when an alternate routing is used, the work order will most likely incur an unfavorable cost variance since the standard routing is supposed to be the most cost-effective method.

Additional options are available to decrease lead times without incurring unfavorable variances such as the addition of a second or third shift for critical work centers and bottleneck operations when the capacity of one shift is insufficient to satisfy demand. Also, as discussed earlier, a cellular layout will definitely improve lead times and decrease non-value-added costs.

PRODUCTION ORDER RELEASING

The MRP is the mechanism in a manufacturing system that tells the shop floor what to make, how many to make, when the job must be started, and when it must be completed. The work order release cycle (Fig. 14.5) begins when an MRP planned order appears on the planning horizon requiring release based on its lead time. The focal point of all SFC systems is the order. Typically, a planner will review the MRP action message and tell the system to release the order or possibly amend the message with changes in the order quantity and the start and completion dates. After reviewing the demand and supply characteristics of the item, the system release logic checks the

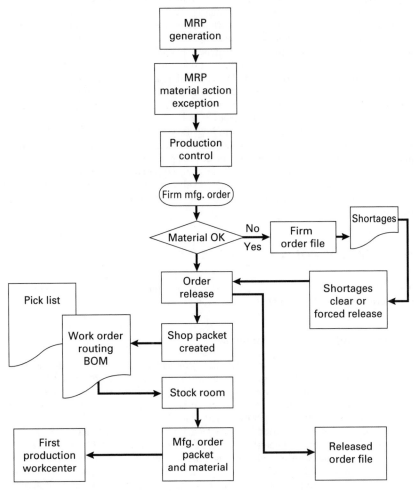

FIGURE 14.5   Work order release cycle.

availability of the components and materials required to produce the planned order quantity. If a shortage occurs on the materials pick list, the shop order will not be released and the shortage list will be updated. When material is available or on hand to support a shop order, the system will release the order with its required documentation, and the work order will be sequenced on the dispatch list for its first routed operation based on the priority rules used.

The need for specific shop documentation to accompany released work to the shop order depends on a company's manufacturing environment, process complexity, production reporting requirements, tooling and setup directions, and product specifications. As an example, engineer-to-order products typically require a drawing plus detail machine process information concerning speeds, feeds, and setup. A jet engine manufacturer would require documentation to support the records of the FAA's lot traceability requirements. Conversely, in a make-to-stock environment, no shop documentation may be required. Consider, for example, the production of garden tractors where paperless work order control is most appropriate.

A basic document released with a work order is the *pick list* or materials list which is sent to the stockroom. This facilitates the staging of materials support for the production of the work order item. After the material is pulled and the pick list is complete, the material and work order move to the first operation of the process. The exercise of picking and handling material to support work orders is an excellent example of a nonvalue-added activity that adds cost to the product and does not add value. Today, a common shop floor control practice is to stock material at its point of use, therefore eliminating the cost of the picking process.

Point-of-use material is relieved from inventory as a consequence of backflushing. *Backflushing* means reducing inventory balances as a result of reporting a completed quantity, either by operation sequence or at the completion of the item. When backflushing occurs at the completion of an item, the "exploded" bill of materials is used to facilitate the inventory deduction. If backflushing occurs at each or selected routed operations, the deduct logic selects components on the bill of materials that are tied to the specific routing operations.

PRIORITY CONTROL AND SCHEDULING

One of the most visible and action-oriented activities found in any SFC system involves the determination and assignment of operation priorities or schedules.

Backward- and Forward-Scheduling

A typical method used in most manufacturing companies entails backward-scheduling techniques. Backward-scheduling calculates operation start dates by starting with the MRP order due date and by working backward to determine the required start date and/or due date for each operation on the shop order (Fig. 14.6a). It is not unusual when backward-scheduling to find operation start dates falling into past-due time periods. This condition must be rectified through lead time compression tactics to keep the scheduling information in the system valid. Forward-scheduling logic is often used in conjunction with backward-scheduling when the start date is in the current time period. To use forward-scheduling techniques (Fig. 14.6b), begin with a known start date and work forward to determine a start and due date for each operation, which will give the completion date for the shop order. This approach to determining a shop order due date

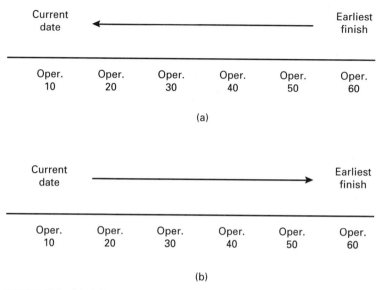

FIGURE 14.6   Scheduling techniques. (*a*) Backward scheduling; (*b*) forward scheduling.

is a convenient method for establishing a schedule, providing the order completion date is consistent with the master schedule and/or the customer's required date.

FINITE OPERATION SEQUENCING

Operation sequencing (Fig. 14.7) is a popular scheduling technique that uses simulation logic to determine the optimum run sequence of all work-in-process. Using a batch program, the released shop orders are sequenced to run in each work center based upon capacity, priority, existing workforce, and machine availability. This technique is frequently referred to as *finite loading* since the logic calculates run priorities within the finite capacity of each work center in order to level the load.

Rate-Based Scheduling

The use of work orders, along with the creation of shop paper and a pick list, is not always appropriate for repetitive or continuous production environments. Work orders are not a practical means of scheduling items that run continuously or are subject to long runs on equipment that might be dedicated to a few part numbers. Rate-based scheduling techniques are better suited to handle high-volume items based on a periodic production rate of a day, week, or month. The raw materials or components required for a rate-based product are stocked at the point of use. This facilitates backflushing the inventory that was consumed based on the number of reported completions. Schedule tracking and analysis consists of the cumulative quantities completed versus the cumulative quantities scheduled related to the production rate of the work center or assembly line.

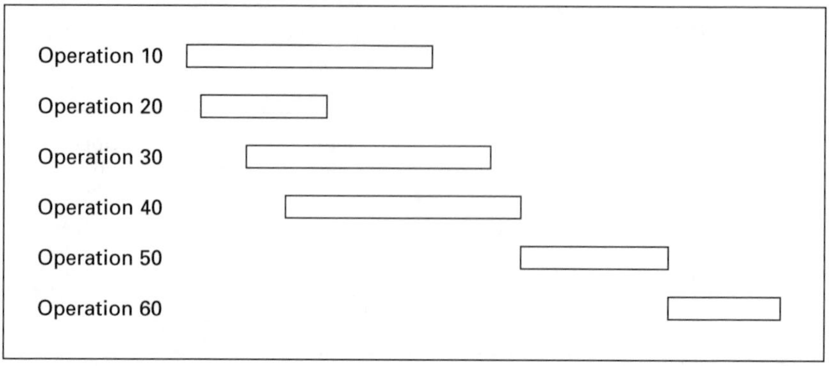

FIGURE 14.7   Operation sequencing.

DISPATCHING

The activity of dispatching involves the selecting and sequencing of available jobs to be run at individual work centers and the assignment of those jobs to workers (Table 14.2). In MRP II systems, operation priorities are determined using decision rules commonly referred to as *dispatching,* or *priority, rules.* The resulting priorities are essentially the orders ranked (the most important order is at the top while the least is located at the end of the list). The priorities are communicated to people in the system by means of a *dispatch list.* This list, which is usually produced daily, displays all of the shop orders at a work center that are either in process or waiting to be processed. The list, either a printed document or a real-time CRT display, ranks the jobs in priority sequence. The dispatch list is the starting point for the shop supervisor to assign shop orders to the operators. Experience has demonstrated that the simple priority rules are the most effective, especially when you consider that the rule is a fundamental means of communicating to the shop what is to be worked on and in what sequence to satisfy the requirements of the master schedule.

A popular technique for calculating a priority rule is the *critical ratio* (Table 14.3). Critical ratio calculates the priority index number by dividing the time to due date remaining by the expected work time remaining to finish the job. As the table illustrates, a priority less than 1.0 indicates a job is behind schedule, whereas a priority greater than 1.0 reflects an ahead-of-schedule condition, and a ratio of 1.0 points to an on-time schedule.

Another straightforward technique consists of calculating a start date and a required date for each routed operation on the shop order consistent with the MRP required date. For both of the priority rules discussed to be effective, the shop floor system must have the capability to calculate the lead time remaining with the data contained on the routing and information in the work center file.

TABLE 14.2 Dispatch List

Plant 03, Dept. 05, Mach. ctr., BH, Shifts worked 2.0, Capacity 83

Part no.	Part name	Order no.	Op. no	Oper. desc.	Priority	Qty. of op.	Qty. at Op.	Hours	Next location	Work rem.	Time. rem.
2093	Imp whl	438C34	020	Fin	0.436	142	142	11.1	0316NB	18.3	8.0
2161	Spinner	445C22	010	Turn	1.246	88	88	6.4	9395BQ	18.6	23.0
4639	Carrier	445B45	010	Turn	2.675	54	54	5.4	"Same"	8.5	23.0
4639	Carrier	445B45	020	Face	2.675	54		5.4	0305YE	6.3	23.0
1640	Retainer	441B22	010	Face	4.106	108	108	7.3	0305EG	10.4	43.0

Total hours in this machine center: 35.6

					Parts in previous work center						
2083	Imp whl	443C31	010	Turn	0.437	27	27	4.7	0316NBR	18.2	8.0
2035	Fw pilot	444C98	010	Semiturn	0.462	28	28	4.3	0316NBR	17.3	8.0
2083	Imp whl	446A09	010	Turn	0.742	250	250	15.4	0316NBR	24.2	18.0
2083	Imp whl	446A07	010	Turn	0.907	1234	1234	62.2	0316NBR	36.3	33.0
2093	Imp whl	446A10	010	Turn	1.388	141	141	11.1	0316NBR	20.1	28.0
5164	Retainer	445C90	020	Turn	2.006	98	98	6.1	0305BQ	11.4	23.0
2084	Impeller	444A44	010	Turn	99.999	10	10	4.1	0316NBR	10.4	XX.X

Total hours for this machine center in previous centers: 107.9

14.13

TABLE 14.3 Dispatching Rules

A. Critical ratio

$$\frac{\text{Time remaining}}{\text{Work remaining}} = \text{Priority}$$

Late:
$$\frac{\text{Part required in 30 days}}{\text{Work remaining on part 40 days}} = 0.75$$

Therefore, the job is required in three-quarters of its normal lead time.

On time:
$$\frac{\text{Part required in 30 days}}{\text{Work remaining on part 30 days}} = 1.0$$

When the work and time remaining are in balance, the job is on schedule.

Early:
$$\frac{\text{Part required in 30 days}}{\text{Work remaining on part 15 days}} = 2.0$$

When the work remaining is less than the need date of the part, the job is ahead of schedule.

B. Operation start date and required date

Work center 2010 Punch Press

Order number	Opt. seq.	Part number	Descp.	Start date	Req. date	Qty.
5589	010	213400	Plate	9/28/99	9/30/99	5000
9034	040	113907	Bracket	9/30/99	10/02/99	9990
2167	020	148866	Plug	10/02/99	10/05/99	8999

PRODUCTION REPORTING AND STATUS

Information in the SFC system acts as the major link between the planning system and shop floor control system. The information flows in two directions. The MRP system keeps the SFC system informed of any changes in the planned requirements, and in return the SFC system keeps the MRP aware of the progress of all orders through the system.

Data collection and monitoring involve the collection of the following information (Fig. 14.8):

- Current location of the order (including scrap replacements required)
- Current state of an order's completion

- Actual resources being used at each operation
- Actual material being consumed at each operation

This information is often collected in terms of hours, units, weight, volume, and costs. While the units are meaningful to people working in the system, the progress of the order is more easily understood by others in the firm if it is stated in terms of cost. The cost of an order is typically measured on the basis of actual dollars spent on materials, labor, and overhead rather than the established standard for these three costs required to produce the order.

Labor and materials variances (Table 14.4) are created when the standards are not achieved. Overhead variances occur when labor standards are missed because overhead is calculated as a percent of labor. The usual causes for variances relate to scrap, bill of materials errors, invalid routing times, rework, and the use of alternate materials and methods.

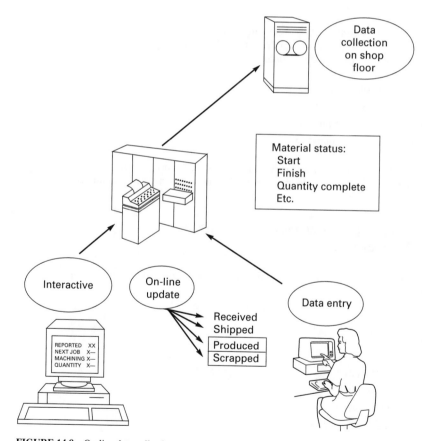

FIGURE 14.8 On-line data collection.

TABLE 14.4   Work Order Variance Evaluation

	Materials	Direct	Setup	Fixed	Variable	Total
Standard	$500.00	$75.00	$25.00	$100.00	$50.00	$750.00
Actual	700.00	50.00	10.00	60.00	30.00	850.00
Variance	(200.00)	25.00	15.00	40.00	20.00	(100.00)

Notes:
1. Assume order quantity of 10.
2. Items moved to inventory at $75.00 per piece.
3. Items cost $85.00 to produce.
4. Had an unfavorable variance of $10.00 per piece.
5. Materials and labor and overhead variances can and often do offset each other.

Once the information has been collected, it must be reviewed. This is done by comparing the actual progress with the expected or planned progress. Progress is measured along several different dimensions:

- State of completion
- Cost incurred to date
- Amount of scrap produced
- How near to the due date

Ultimately, the purpose of monitoring is to identify those orders with the largest gaps between actual and desired levels of performance so corrective action can be taken.

DATA COLLECTION AND REPORTING CONSIDERATIONS

The following is a list of places in the system where data collection and reporting should be considered:

- Job issue
- Order acceptance
- Operation start
- Materials move
- Scrap and rework
- Inventory receipt
- Operation completion
- Order close
- Integration with payroll

MEASUREMENTS FOR CONTROL

The following performance criteria can be used to develop valid shop floor yardsticks to measure the effectiveness of production.

Scrap

The amount of material produced outside an item's engineering and quality specifications is a valid measurement of the necessary operator skill, the production process, and/or the design for manufacturing. As a result of work-in-process accounting, scrap rates may be expressed in unfavorable materials variance costs and should be analyzed and remedied.

Rework

Keeping track of the amount of rework by item is a meaningful method for reducing the non-value-added costs of salvaging defective materials (Table 14.5).

TABLE 14.5   Rework Report

Order number	Part number	Quantity	Operations	Problem
538C27	6081	50	20	ECN
235A56	7050	1	70	Tooling
478B21	3011	6	40	Operator error

Queue Time

The period of time a job waits at a work center before it is processed is significant. Queue time, as discussed earlier, represents needless work-in-process that increases a company's inventory investment and inflates lead times. A queue measurement must be based on work that is either on or behind schedule since work that is ahead of schedule could be waiting as a result of order deferment from the master production schedule.

Labor and Materials Variances

As discussed earlier, labor and materials variances generated by a standard cost system may indicate the accuracy of the standard times on a routing and the accuracy of the bills of materials.

Schedule Performance

An excellent index of performance is, comparing for a time period, the number of shop orders completed by the due date to those that are past due (Table 14.6). But for this report to have meaning and assist in curing the cause of missing schedules, it is necessary to answer questions relating to why performance was not 100 percent. The late-order report provides the direction for remedial action.

TABLE 14.6 Late-Order Report

Order number	Part number	Quantity	Due date	Work rem.	Time rem.	Queue time	Problem
438C34	2093	142	9-16	18.3	8	14.6	Late tooling
443C31	2083	27	9-17	17.2	16	14	Machine down
446A09	2083	250	9-19	24.2	18	19.3	Machine down

Statistical Process Control (SPC)

SPC can control product quality by monitoring and analyzing process outputs by statistical techniques. Feedback can be used to maintain and improve process capability.

Efficiency

Efficiency is measured, usually in percent, of the actual output to the standard output expected. It is the ratio of the actual units produced to the standard number of products expected in a time period.

Productivity

Productivity is an overall measure of the ability of a given process to produce a product. It is the actual output of production compared to the actual input of resources. As the output increases with a decrease in resources, such as labor and machine-hours, productivity increases.

Setup Reduction

In those cases where setup costs and time account for a fairly large percentage of the total cost or lead time, a program must be put in place to reduce changeover time. Single minute exchange of die (SMED)[1] is an excellent program for reducing setup time and cost.

ORDER DISPOSITION

This stage in an SFC system includes all of the activities needed for transferring a shop order out of work-in-process. Manufacturing is completed, and costs are accounted for. Order disposition has three major objectives:

- To relieve the SFC system of the responsibility of the order
- To provide information for dispersing the product either by shipping or storing
- To provide the rest of the firm with order completion information on which to evaluate performance of the process

When this stage is completed, the SFC system is no longer responsible for the order. The orders can be disposed of in one of two ways. In the case of acceptable orders, the items become part of the firm's inventory stocks. Such items are now treated as assets by the accounting system, and they are available for filling customer orders. In case the material is scrap, the items in the order can be disposed of to one or more "profit-and-loss" accounts. If there is no recoverable salvage value, the cost of the scrapped items can be charged off to a salvage account such as scrap expenses.

After the completion of order disposition, the management can evaluate against standards the performance of both the operations management system and the conversion process. These are factors to be considered for evaluation:

- The amount of resources used (e.g., number of labor-hours used, amount of machine-hours used)
- The materials used for the order
- The number of setup hours used
- The cost of tooling used
- The date on which the order was completed
- The amount of rework or scrap generated by the order
- The number of units completed compared with the number started

Finally, order disposition is important because it is the last chance for everyone involved in the conversion process to examine orders and to understand what happened to them. Once the order is closed out, it is no longer of interest to the SFC system, and people involved in the SFC system tend to forget about it. However, before the order is closed out, it is useful to study it and see what problems it encountered and why. This is an important step in such programs as total quality management and just in time.

PULL SCHEDULING

With pull scheduling, work moves between operations in response to demand from the immediate downstream work center. To understand this logic, examine the three work centers illustrated in Fig. 14.9. Here work center A feeds work center B which, in turn, feeds work center C. Under a pull-scheduling system, when work center A has finished its work, it goes idle unless there is a demand from work center B. In a sense, work center B "pulls" production from work center A. Once the work is taken from work center A, then the people at this work center can start building more items (again obeying the rule that once they finish building the next order, they must wait until demand from the downstream work centers removes the completed items).

FIGURE 14.9 Example of pull scheduling.

Pull scheduling is very attractive for several reasons. Scheduling is simplified; operators only build what is required when it is required. When an order arrives from a downstream work center, the operators know that there is a real demand driving that order. Problems become immediately apparent. If operators experience a breakdown at work center C, ultimately work center A and B will become idle. These idle work centers indicate that there is a problem somewhere in the system. Finally, when a problem occurs, the bottleneck is not loaded with extra work. If there is a breakdown at work center C, no excess inventory builds in front of the affected work center. As a result, the life of the people working at work center C is simplified. All they have to worry about is getting the work center back up. They do not have to worry about clearing out any excess inventory that has built up in front of their work. However, implementing a pull-scheduling system is not easy. It requires that there be strong linkages between the various work centers. Work center A should support only a handful of other work centers, and they should be known in advance.

Pull scheduling demands good planning. The work released to the SFC system by the planning system should ideally be level and balanced. Once the schedules are implemented, opportunities for the customer or marketing to intervene in the system (by asking for orders to be moved up or by asking for changes in the quantity or mix of orders) must be strictly controlled. In short, the benefits offered by pull scheduling come at a price.

CAPACITY EVALUATION

Even though the material is available, while important, it is not enough by itself to ensure that manufacturing orders released to the shop floor can be considered feasible. In addition to available material, there must be adequate capacity available to produce the order. In the capacity evaluation stage, the capacity required by the order is compared with the capacity available. That is, capacity is available, but it is not being used to process other orders. At this stage, a judgment must be made. If there is not enough capacity, the release of the order can be delayed until the time that the necessary capacity becomes available. Why is this such an important step in the order review and release process? Because if the order is released to the transformation process when there is not enough capacity, then all that would have been accomplished would simply be the overloading of the operations management system. The result would be a longer lead time, greater lead time variation, and greater confusion among the conversion process operators trying to identify which orders they can or cannot work on because of a lack of capacity.

It is a general shop floor control rule that operators should work only on those orders for which there is capacity rather than working on any orders released by the planning system. Orders released by the planning system simply indicate what the planning system wishes to process. It is the intent, but the level of capacity available determines what can actually be processed.

Before leaving this section, one question should be addressed: If the planning system is supposed to assure the SFC system access to adequate capacity, why is it necessary to check actual capacity levels? The answer to this question is in the different orientations of the planning system and the SFC system. The planning system sets capacity levels *in advance*. It tries to set expected capacity levels available. However, at any time, the amount of capacity that is available may vary greatly from what is expected. There are a number of factors that may account for this:

- People may be absent because of illness, vacation, jury duty, or other similar commitments.
- Equipment may not be available because of unanticipated breakdowns or planned preventive maintenance.
- Problems may exist with estimated processing times. Jobs may take longer and consume more capacity than planned.
- Priorities may change. Equipment capacity may be allocated to orders that are now considered to be urgent, thus taking that capacity away from other orders.

LOAD LEVELING

In many SFC systems, the orders recommended for release by the planning system are not always released immediately upon arrival. Instead, these orders are often accumulated (backlogged) for a short period of time and released to the shop floor at a controlled rate so as to level the resulting load. The objective of load leveling is to smooth out the peaks and the valleys of the load. *Peaks* are those periods where the demand on capacity exceeds the capacity available. *Valleys,* in contrast, are those time periods in which the demand generated by arriving orders is far less than the capacity available. The problem with peaks is that there is too much work resulting in increased queue times on the shop floor and increased lead times. In contrast, during the valleys, lead times drop drastically because capacity is not a problem. When effects of peaks and valleys are combined, the overall result is too much lead time variance. Ideally one would prefer to remove the excess demand from the peaks and move it to those periods where excess capacity is available. This rearrangement of workloads by changing the time at which the work is released is the responsibility of the load-leveling activity of order review and release function in the organization.

SCHEDULED MAINTENANCE

Preventive maintenance is important because all equipment and tooling is subject to wear and tear that daily operations place on them. Machines break down frequently, but the amount of preventive maintenance affects the frequency of breakdowns. The more often that preventive maintenance is done, the longer the periods between breakdowns will be on average. When equipment or tooling breaks down, their productive capabilities are temporarily lost to the manufacturing process. One rule with which most shop floor personnel are familiar is "machines and tools always break down when they are needed most."

The intent of scheduled maintenance is to reduce the risk of machine breakdowns, especially breakdowns taking place when the products are really needed. Scheduled maintenance is considered part of "detailed scheduling" because preventive maintenance activities often compete with manufacturing orders for access to tools and equipment. When preventive maintenance is being done on a piece of equipment, it is effectively depriving access to that specific machine.

What is involved in preventive maintenance? Typically, preventive maintenance includes such activities as lubrication, inspection, and the periodic overhaul of tools and equipment. It also includes replacing used parts with new or refurbished parts.

FUTURE DIRECTIONS FOR SHOP FLOOR CONTROL

There is no doubt that the future direction of SFC will be tied directly to advances in computer and programming technology in addition to advances in process automation. Developments such as group technology, flexible manufacturing systems, automatic storage and retrieval systems (AS/RS), bar coding, manufacturing execution systems, and client-server technology may influence the characteristics and organization of the production process. The changes introduced by these developments have resulted in reduced setup times, reduced manufacturing lead times, and enhanced ability to produce a greater variety of products without affecting production efficiency. As a result, these developments have offered manufacturing firms new opportunities to improve their profit by changing the production process.

REFERENCE

1. Shigeo Shingo, *A Revolution in Manufacturing, the SMED System,* Productivity Press, Stamford, Conn., 1985.

BIBLIOGRAPHY

Melnyk, Steven A., and Philip L. Carter: *Production Activity Control: A Practical Guide.* Homewood, Ill., Dow Jones-Irwin, 1987.

Melnyk, Steven A., Philip L. Carter, David M. Dilts, and David M. Lyth: *Shop Floor Control,* Homewood, Ill., Dow Jones-Irwin, 1985.

Milwaukee APICS Chapter: *Shop Floor Control.* Training Aid Published by APICS, 1972.

Wassweiler, W. R.: "Materials Requirements Planning—The Key to Critical Ratio Effectiveness," Production and Inventory Management, September 1972, pp. 89–91.

————:"Shop Floor Control," *American Production and Inventory Control Society 20th Annual Conference Proceedings,* Washington, D.C., 1977, pp. 386–394.

————:"Fundamentals of Shop Floor Control," *American Production and Inventory Control Society 23rd Annual Conference Proceedings,* Los Angeles, Calif., 1980, pp. 352–354.

————:"Tool Requirements Planning," *American Production and Inventory Control Society 25th Annual Conference Proceedings,* Chicago, Ill., 1982, pp. 160–162.

————:"Production Activity Control," *The MGI Management Institute,* Harrison, N.Y., 1984.

————:"MRP II In Perspective," *APICS—The Performance Advantage,* vol. 4, no. 1, 1994, p. 47.

CHAPTER 15

PRODUCTION PLANNING AND SCHEDULING FOR PROCESS FLOW MANUFACTURERS*

Editors

Sam G. Taylor, Ph.D.

Professor, College of Business
University of Wyoming, Laramie, Wyoming

Steven F. Bolander, Ph.D.

Professor and Chair of Department of Management
Colorado State University, Fort Collins, Colorado

There is a growing consensus that planning and scheduling systems should be tailored to the needs of a particular manufacturing environment. This chapter offers an approach to production planning and scheduling quite different from the MRP paradigm presented in the previous chapters. While this chapter emphasizes process industries, it should be noted that some repetitive manufacturing firms have similar planning and scheduling system requirements.

We begin this chapter by briefly examining the characteristics of process flow manufacturers. Next we develop a systems framework for process flow manufacturing. This is followed by an example that illustrates a scheduling approach called *process flow scheduling* (PFS). We then present three basic principles for process flow scheduling. We conclude the chapter with a brief comparison of process flow scheduling and other approaches to scheduling.

---

*A majority of the material in this chapter is taken from the book, *Process Flow Scheduling: A Scheduling Systems Framework for Flow Manufacturing*, by Sam G. Taylor and Steven F. Bolander. This material is used with permission from the American Production and Inventory Control Society.

FLOW MANUFACTURING ENVIRONMENTS

The *APICS Dictionary*[1] defines *process manufacturing* as "production that adds value by mixing, separating, forming, and/or performing chemical reactions. It may be done in either batch or continuous mode." One segment of the process industries are the process flow manufacturers. Flow manufacturers are characterized by plant layouts in which all products follow a similar, fixed sequence of operations (routing). For example, all production in a potato processing plant follows a sequence of potato washing, skin removal, cutting, blanching, frying, freezing, and packaging. Thus all potato products have the same fixed routing through the plant. Note, however, that plants with fixed routings may employ either batch operations, continuous operations, or a mixture of batch and continuous operations.

Another segment of the process industries are job shop manufacturers. Job shops are characterized by variable product routings. For example, a specialty chemical plant may have a variety of batch reactors, mixers, and other process equipment. Moreover, in this example plant each specialty chemical product has its own particular processing requirements. These unique requirements are met by a routing specific to the product. Since the routings may vary from one product to the next, the plant has *variable product routings*. The planning and scheduling needs for process industry job shops are best met by MRP systems, which are covered in other chapters in this handbook.

Flow manufacturers tend to sell high volumes of a relatively small number of products. These products are often quite similar to competitors' products. This low level of product differentiation leads to a marketing strategy that places a greater emphasis on product availability and price in flow manufacturing than in job manufacturing. Flow manufacturing products have relatively few design changes, low unit values, and relatively high transportation costs. Typical flow manufacturing products are food, beverages, paper, primary metals, petroleum, commodity chemicals, and commodity ceramics.

The manufacturing environment for flow manufacturers directly reflects the needs imposed by the marketing environment and business strategy. Costs are minimized by using high-volume, dedicated equipment arranged *in process trains* or *production lines*. Often highly automated, specialized equipment is employed. This equipment is relatively expensive to purchase, but it has low variable operating costs and yields low unit costs when production volumes are high. A principal weakness of flow manufacturing is its lack of flexibility.

There is often a strong relationship between the variety of products manufactured and the process layout. This relationship is shown in Fig. 15.1, which shows a product-process matrix. Horizontal positions on the matrix show the degree of product differentiation. Vertical positions show process layouts ranging from job shops to flow shops.

Most industries tend to fall on the principal diagonal of the product-process matrix. Notice that process industries tend to fall in the lower right portion of the matrix while fabrication and assembly industries tend to fall in the upper left. Exceptions certainly exist. For example, pharmaceutical and specialty chemical manufacturers are in the upper left quadrant while container manufacturers are in the lower right.

Materials may move through flow manufacturing lines continuously or in batches; however, families of similar products are often produced on the same process train or production line. Thus continuous-flow operations often schedule blocks of time for different products on the same process train. This gives rise to production lots, which are very similar to production batches. There is often no reason in flow manufacturing operations that all units in a particular lot must complete an operation before the lot can begin processing at the next operation in the process train. This flexibility facilitates job overlapping, which, in turn, leads to low work-in-process inventories and fast throughput times.

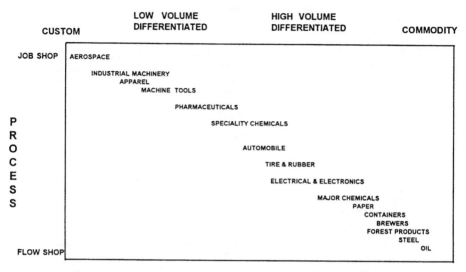

FIGURE 15.1 Product-process matrix.

Since the products of flow manufacturers have low levels of differentiation, product availability is often an important priority. The need for high product availability is achieved by producing products to stock and storing finished goods in warehouses in principal demand centers.

SYSTEMS FRAMEWORK

A planning and scheduling systems framework for flow manufacturing is shown in Fig. 15.2. The framework is hierarchical with long-range resource requirements plans governing the intermediate-range production plans, which, in turn, govern the short-range operating plans.

Forecasting

The forecasting module provides the necessary demand forecasts that drive the resource requirements plans, production plans, and operating schedules. Long-range forecasts give estimates of aggregate annual demand over the economic life of the facility. These forecasts may be developed using life-cycle analysis, econometric models, and market surveys, and they generally include a major dose of managerial judgment.

Intermediate-range forecasts develop estimates of monthly or quarterly demand by major product families for the next annual budget cycle. Intermediate-range forecasts may be developed using regression models, seasonally adjusted exponential smoothing models, and sales force estimates. Again a good dose of managerial judgment is often required.

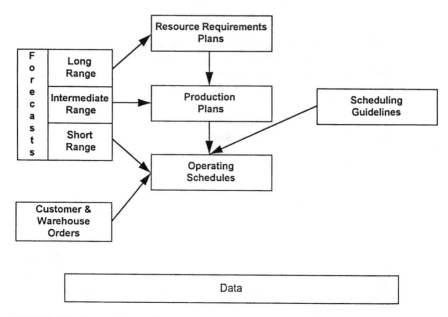

FIGURE 15.2   Systems framework.

Short-range forecasts are an important input for the development of operating schedules for both manufacturing and distribution. Short-range forecasts estimate daily or weekly demand over a period of 1 to 3 months for each selling location. Short-range forecasting techniques include exponential smoothing, moving averages, sales force estimates, and use of available sales order data. These forecasts, like the others, also benefit from managerial input. Additional information on forecasting systems may be found in a book by DeLurgio and Bhame.[2] Particular care must be exercised in all forecasts to distinguish between sales goals and sales forecasts.

Resource Requirements Plans

Resource requirements planning (RRP) develops resource acquisition plans. Resource requirements plans might include strategic plans for building a new plant or expanding an existing plant, long-term contracts with suppliers for major raw materials, labor contracts, energy supply contracts, purchase and implementation of new information systems, and a disposal plan for waste materials. The time horizon for resource requirements plans should cover at least the lead time for acquisition of resources and extend over the economic life of the assets. Resource requirements plans are generally the responsibility of senior management who are assisted by their planning staffs and operations managers. These strategic decisions must be closely coordinated with strategic marketing and financial plans and have a major impact on the long-range success of the firm. Decisions made at this top level of the planning systems hierarchy constrain the lower-level production plans and operating schedules by specifying upper limits on the available plant capacity.

Production Plans

Production planning develops resource utilization plans. Although Fig. 15.2 shows but a single box for production plans, a company may have several production plans covering different time horizons and varying in scope. For example, in a multiplant environment, annual and quarterly aggregate production plans may be developed at the corporate level as well as at each plant. In addition, more detailed production plans may be developed monthly at each plant. Production plans are usually tied closely to the annual and quarterly budgeting process. Production plans address a variety of problems that are often specific to a particular manufacturing environment. Production plans give close attention to meeting forecasted product demands at the minimum cost. Table 15.1 summarizes some major production planning issues.

Assignment and Allocation Decisions.   The first two issues listed in Table 15.1 concern assigning products to production facilities. These issues apply only in manufacturing environments where there are multiple plants or multiple process trains that can produce one or more of the products. These assignment decisions may be influenced by technical feasibility, cost, quality, customer service, and labor considerations. Some firms employ formal optimization models to help develop these plans. For example, the use of linear programming in the aluminum industry is presented by Bradley, Hax, and Magnanti.[3]

The next two production planning issues listed in Table 15.1 concern allocation of demand to plants and process trains. These issues apply only in manufacturing environments where multiple plants or multiple process trains are assigned to produce the same product. In the case of allocating demand to plants, the decision often involves specification of a sourcing plant for each of the company's products for each warehouse or customer demand center. Allocation decisions are influenced by capacity, cost, quality, customer service, and labor considerations. Many firms in the petroleum, paper, food, and chemical industries use linear programming to assist in developing these plans. Examples of the use of linear programming in petroleum industry production planning are given by Aronofsky, Dutton, and Tayyabkhan.[4]

Matching Production to Demand.   The next production planning issue concerns how to meet seasonal demands. One basic strategy, called the *chase strategy,* adjusts the production rate to meet demand. An alternative strategy, called the *level strategy,* uses a

TABLE 15.1   Production Planning Issues

- What products will be produced in each plant
- What products should be produced on each process train
- How demand should be allocated among plants
- How demand should be allocated among process trains
- How seasonal demand should be produced
- How aggregate production should be matched to demand
- How maintenance requirements should be met
- How much raw materials will be needed

---

level (constant) production rate and builds inventory during the off-season to help meet demand in the peak season. Often the least-cost strategy is a combination of the chase and level strategies and is called a *mixed strategy*. The best strategy minimizes the combined costs of production rate changes and inventory holding costs. Some firms use electronic spreadsheets to evaluate alternative seasonal production strategies. Others use formal optimization techniques such as linear programming. An example of the use of linear programming for seasonal production planning is given for the Quaker Oats Company by Bolander, Heard, Seward, and Taylor.[5]

Another production planning issue concerns the operating strategy for reducing production output. When demand is less than capacity, a process train's production overtime must be less than its capacity, or inventories will build. One strategy for cutting production is to throttle the output rate so that the production rate equals the demand rate. An alternative strategy is to run the process train at capacity, which is its most efficient rate. However, this strategy requires that a process train be shut down periodically to reduce inventories and bring production back in line with demand. Taylor gives a procedure for comparing the throttled and shutdown operating strategies.[6]

In other environments demand may exceed the firm's total productive capacity for a group of products. In this situation capacity must be expanded or demand reduced. In the intermediate range period covered by production plans, major capacity expansions are generally not feasible. However, depending on the environment, capacity may be expanded by overtime, additional shifts, process debottlenecking, subcontracting, or product exchanges. If capacity cannot be expanded in an economic and timely manner, then demand will need to be reduced by raising prices, pruning products, or putting customers on allocation.

Major Interfaces.   Production plans must also be coordinated with the plans of other operating groups. Two major interfaces are with maintenance and purchasing. Maintenance sometimes requires the shutdown of an entire process train, thus creating a period with no production. Purchasing departments often determine raw materials requirements from the production volumes specified in the production plan.

While the production planning decisions discussed above present interesting individual problems, the real production planning challenge is to simultaneously optimize all of the issues that are relevant to a particular manufacturing environment. While quite effective optimization approaches have been developed for individual problems, only limited success has been achieved in simultaneously optimizing all the production planning issues that apply in most manufacturing environments. In practice, most companies decompose very large production planning problems into a series of smaller production planning problems. Hand calculations, spreadsheets, simulation models, and optimization models are used along with managerial judgment to develop and then integrate these production plans.

Scheduling Guidelines

The scheduling guidelines shown in Fig. 15.2 consist of priorities, targets, rules, and procedures. These guidelines help provide direction for the scheduling process.

Priorities.   Priorities evolve from business strategies and specify the relative importance of service, cost, inventory, and quality objectives. These priorities help resolve scheduling conflicts. For example, a scheduler may need to decide whether to accept a rush order. However, the scheduler has a dilemma. Producing the rush order will disrupt the least-cost production sequence and increase manufacturing costs. Priorities give the answer. If the business strategy emphasizes fast delivery, the scheduler should accept the order. On the other hand, if the business strategy emphasizes low costs, the scheduler should defer or decline the order. Performance measurement systems should reflect these competitive priorities, and schedulers must be aware of these priorities.

Targets.   Targets typically originate as part of the production planning process. Targets may include (1) minimum and maximum inventory levels, (2) production run lengths, (3) campaign cycle lengths, and (4) production sequences. Two common targets in make-to-stock environments are planned minimum and maximum values for each finished, intermediate (work-in-process), and raw materials inventory. The minimum inventory values are *safety stocks*. These provide a buffer against supply disruptions (e.g., machine downtime) and requirements variations (e.g., forecast error or variations in downstream requirements).

The maximum inventory values may be *hard* or *soft constraints*. Hard constraints are based on equipment constraints, such as tank capacity, or on product constraints, such as shelf life. Alternatively, the maximum inventory may be a soft constraint. For example, an item's peak planned inventory generally occurs at the end of a production run. This peak inventory is the sum of the item's safety stock and its peak cycle stock. If exceeding the planned peak does not create major problems, the resulting maximum inventory is a soft constraint.

Another target concerns run lengths or, equivalently, lot sizes. Lot sizes can also be classified as *hard* or *soft*. A hard lot size may evolve from equipment constraints such as the size of a batch reactor or minimum run lengths needed to achieve acceptable quality levels. Soft lot size or run length targets are more flexible than the hard constraints. Classical lot-sizing models yield soft lot sizes. When setup (changeover) costs are significant, a trade-off exists between setup costs and inventory carrying costs. Short run lengths result in frequent setups and correspondingly high setup costs. Conversely, long run lengths result in high inventories and high carrying costs. Classical lot-sizing models calculate target lot sizes that minimize the sum of setup costs and inventory carrying costs. Dividing the resulting lot sizes by item production rates gives the corresponding "optimal" target run lengths. However, the resulting target run lengths can readily be shortened or lengthened, thus creating a soft constraint. Mathematical models for lot sizing are presented in many texts, including a book by Salomon[7] and this handbook.

The next target concerns the frequency an item is produced. Cyclic schedules are often used when a single machine or production line produces several products. These production cycles have different names in different organizations. We use the term *campaign cycle*; however, others use the terms *schedule wheel, product wheel, rotation schedule,* or simply *campaign*. Guidelines help the scheduler decide (1) the approximate length of the campaign cycle and (2) whether to produce a product every cycle or to skip some cycles. This scheduling problem is commonly known as the *multiproduct lot cycling problem* or the *economic lot scheduling problem*. It is discussed in such books as Brown,[8] Hax and Candea,[9] Magee and Boodman,[10] and Silver and Peterson.[11]

Another common target is the production sequence. Natural production sequences often exist in process industry manufacturing. Examples are light to dark colors, wide to narrow widths, and low to high molecular weight. If production schedules use these natural production sequences, setup costs can be minimized and product quality improved. In other situations, production sequences can affect setup costs, but process technology may not establish a readily identifiable optimum production sequence. Here a sequencing algorithm that minimizes the setup costs should prove helpful. Several texts—including Baker,[12] Hax and Candea,[9] and Morton and Pentico[13]—give sequencing algorithms for a variety of scheduling environments.

Rules.   While scheduling rules may be broken, they are somewhat firmer than the pre-viously discussed targets. There is no clear distinction between targets and rules; how-ever, *targets* tend to be developed by production planners and schedulers, and *rules* tend to be set by management and involve considerations with a significant impact on other functional areas. Examples of scheduling rules are (1) overtime must be less than 8 hours per week, (2) schedules are frozen for a 3-day horizon, (3) no changeovers are allowed on Sunday, and (4) the switch from product X to product Y should be made on day shift.

Procedures.   Scheduling procedures define how schedules will be developed and com-municated to line workers and operating management. Generating schedules requires a blend of scheduler and computer tasks. Some commercial scheduling systems have commands to help schedulers build or modify schedules. Examples of *commands* are adding, deleting, extending, and replacing scheduled activities. Some vendor systems provide special algorithms to help generate and modify schedules. For example, algo-rithms might balance inventories of items within a product family or run a product fam-ily until an item in another family reaches its minimum planned inventory. Some software vendors provide expert systems capability to assist in building schedules.

All scheduling systems must include procedures for conveying the authority to pro-duce to the line operators. In most process flow scheduling systems, the authority to pro-duce is the *production schedule*; however, some systems use *work orders*. Some plants use both schedules and work orders. These plants have some process areas that are flow shops and other areas that are job shops. The flow shop areas control production with schedules, and the job shop areas use work orders.

In addition to the above, scheduling procedures are needed that specify the following:

1. Scheduling frequency
2. Schedule time intervals ("buckets")
3. Schedule horizons
4. Responsibilities for various scheduling tasks
5. Sources and updating of scheduling data
6. Techniques for linking the production plan with the production schedules

Operations Scheduling

Production scheduling develops operating schedules in sufficient detail that the sched-ules can be executed by the direct labor workforce. Although Fig. 15.2 shows only one box for operating schedules, more than one schedule may be developed for a particular operation. For example, a higher-level schedule may be developed by days for a 1-month horizon and another, more detailed, schedule developed by the hour for a 3-day horizon.

Scheduling involves the use of the production plan, scheduling guidelines, and data to generate schedules for each process unit in a plant. In addition, inventory levels are projected for all materials. The development of a schedule often begins with a computer-generated schedule that is produced using a spreadsheet or commercial scheduling pro-gram. However, most situations require a scheduler to modify the computer-generated schedule. This usually involves a trial-and-error simulation of alternative schedules until a satisfactory schedule is obtained. Scheduling software assists the scheduler in this process by both simulating and evaluating alternative schedules.

Production scheduling is primarily concerned with creating a feasible schedule. However, schedule optimization is not totally ignored. The production schedule is constrained by the production plan, which is often developed using formal optimization techniques or simple trial-and-error methods to minimize costs. Production schedules are also constrained by scheduling guidelines. These guidelines may incorporate some optimization when calculating targets for minimum inventories (safety stocks), run lengths, campaign cycle lengths, and production sequences. Thus schedule optimization is accomplished by passing optimized targets from the production plan and scheduling guidelines to the detailed scheduling process. In addition, some formal or trial-and-error optimization is sometimes included in the schedule generation process.

Production schedules include more product, process, and time detail than production plans. Schedules also consider additional rules that may have been ignored in developing production plans. The end result of scheduling is a detailed plan that unit operators can execute. Exception messages report violations of scheduling rules and targets. Problems are resolved by referring to the competitive priorities, which specify the relative importance of service, cost, and quality objectives. Schedule performance may also be measured in terms of changeover costs, inventory carrying costs, and projected customer service levels.

Data

The foundation of the scheduling systems framework as shown in the systems framework given in Fig. 15.2 is a database that supplies inputs for the other modules. This data include sales histories, inventory status, resource availability, and production activity data. Sales histories are used by the forecasting modules to generate statistical forecasts. The planning and scheduling modules require data on the current inventory status of all input and output materials. This data must include on-hand balances by stock keeping unit. Additional stock status data may include age, shelf life, lot-tracking information, allocated quantities, and any scheduled receipts.

Another data category is resource availability. All resources that can constrain production plans and schedules need monitoring. These resources may include process unit (or machine) hours, labor-hours, and energy requirements. In certain circumstances, less conventional resources must be considered, such as emission, effluent, and exposure limits on waste and toxic substances.

Production activity data quantify the amount of input materials and resources required to produce an output intermediate or finished product. For example, a production activity for a bottling operation might show that in order to make 1 bottled drink, 12 ounces of drink, 1 bottle, 1 cap and 0.3 seconds of machine capacity are required. Production activities combine data that an MRP system separates into the bill of material and routing files.

This concludes the brief overview of a planning and scheduling systems framework for process flow manufacturing. The following example will illustrate detailed scheduling calculations for a type of scheduling called *process flow scheduling* (PFS). The purpose of this section is to illustrate typical scheduling calculations with a simple example. It begins with a description of a hypothetical company's process flow. Next a flowchart is presented for the scheduling procedures, and then a numerical example of each scheduling step is given.

POLYGOO MANUFACTURING

The United Chemical Company manufactures three grades—A, B, and C—of a viscous liquid called Polygoo. Each grade is sold in 1-gallon cans and 5-gallon pails. The products are designated by grade and package; thus, A1 is grade A in a 1-gallon can, and A5 is grade A in a 5-gallon pail. Similarly B1, B5, C1, and C5 designate the other finished products.

The products are shipped daily from a plant warehouse in truckload and carload quantities. The demand has no seasonality and does not vary by day of week. The forecasted daily demand is shown in Table 15.2.

Figure 15.3 gives the process structure for the Polygoo process train. The triangles represent inventories, and the rectangles represent operations. Production begins when the feed stock *F* is withdrawn from inventory and processed in the stage 1 reactor. The reactor operates 24 hours a day, 7 days a week. The reactor production rate for all grades is 100,000 gallons per day. Bulk Polygoo is stored in large tanks that buffer stage 1 reactor operations from the packaging operations in stage 2.

Product quality considerations determine the minimum production run lengths. Grade switches are made by changing the reactor temperature and pressure, which in turn affect the molecular weight of the Polygoo. These grade switches, which are made without shutting down the reactor, generate off-specification transition material. This transition material may be upgraded to meet product specifications by blending it with a sufficient quantity of prime (high-quality, on-specification) material. Consequently, to meet product specifications, each grade requires a minimum run length of 1 day to blend off the transition material.

The second-stage operation is packaging. Here bulk products are withdrawn from the storage tanks and packaged in 1-gallon cans or 5-gallon pails. Thus, in Fig. 15.3, product A1 is produced by combining inventory A with inventory 1 (1-gallon cans) in the packaging operation. The other products are produced in a similar manner. The packaging line, which is cheaper to operate than the reactor, is only operated 1 shift per day, 7 days per week. The packaging line operates at a rate of 100,000 gallons per shift. It can therefore fill 100,000, 1-gallon cans or 20,000, 5-gallon pails in 1 shift. Grade changes can be accomplished without washing out or shutting down the packaging equipment. However, when the container size is changed, the line must be shut down for a 4-hour setup. This setup is performed after the normal 8-hour shift and does not affect the line capacity.

The bulk inventories of A, B, and C between stages 1 and 2 are needed for several reasons. First, a surge capacity is needed because the reactor produces 24 hours a day while packaging only consumes 8 hours a day. The surge capacity provides a temporary storage of bulk material between the reactor and packaging processes. Second, this buffer protects the reactor against unscheduled downtime on the packaging lines. Without a buffer between the reactor and the packaging lines, the reactor would have to shut down when the packaging line breaks down. Because of limited reactor capacity and a large capital investment in the reactor, such a shutdown would be unwise. Finally,

TABLE 15.2   Product Demands

Product	Volume, units	Volume, gal	Percent of total
A1	30,000 cans	30,000	30
B1	20,000 cans	20,000	20
C1	10,000 cans	10,000	10
A5	4,000 pails	20,000	20
B5	2,000 pails	10,000	10
C5	2,000 pails	10,000	10

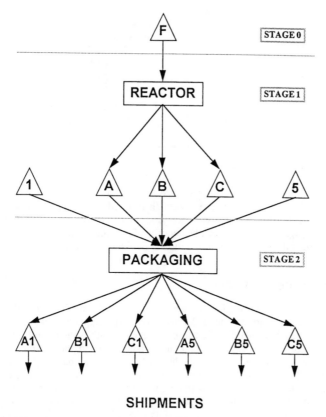

SHIPMENTS

FIGURE 15.3 Polygoo process flow.

the bulk inventories can be used to decouple the reactor and packaging schedules. This allows the flexibility to schedule each stage with different lot sizes and in different sequences.

Target Inventories

We will assume that management has established target minimum and maximum levels for each plant inventory. The feed stock is received in 1,000,000-gallon quantities and stored in three 500,000-gallon dedicated tanks. Accordingly, the feed stock inventory has a maximum level of 1.5 million gallons. A planned minimum 2-day feed stock requirement (200,000 gallons) is used to buffer the plant against supply variations.

The bulk products are stored in 320,000-gallon tanks, with one tank for each grade. In order to leave an operating cushion, the planned maximum inventory for each grade is 300,000 gallons. A planned minimum of 1 day's average requirements is used for bulk inventories. This translates to 50,000 gallons for grade A, 30,000 gallons for grade B, and 20,000 gallons for grade C.

The finished-goods inventories are stored in packaged-goods warehouses. Safety-stock levels have been established for each product using a statistical analysis of

TABLE 15.3   Safety Stocks

Product	Minimum inventory
A1	100,000 gallons
B1	70,000 gallons
C1	40,000 gallons
A5	15,000 pails
B5	12,000 pails
C5	12,000 pails

demand variations, target customer service levels, and production frequencies. These safety stocks, shown in Table 15.3, establish planned minimum inventories. There is excess packaged-goods warehouse space, and no maximum levels are placed on finished-goods inventories. However, the benefits of minimizing inventory are recognized, and finished-goods inventory minimization is a scheduling objective.

Production Campaign Cycles

A *production campaign cycle* is a sequence of production runs in which all major products for a process unit are produced. A Polygoo reactor campaign cycle involves the production of grades A, B, and C. The campaign cycle length is the period of time needed to cycle through all grades. Some companies visualize a campaign cycle as a schedule wheel. Figure 15.4 shows sample schedule wheels. The campaign cycle length is the time required for 1 revolution of the wheel, where the faster the schedule wheel is turned, the shorter the campaign cycle length and the lower the inventories. The wheel is turned to the right; thus, the production sequence for the Polygoo reactor schedule is A, B, C; and the Polygoo packaging schedule is A1, B1, C1, A5, B5, C5. So, all products are produced in each cycle.

The minimum campaign cycle length for the reactor is controlled by the minimum production run length for the lowest volume grade. Grade C constitutes 20 percent of total demand, and since the minimum-grade run length is 1 day, grade C can be pro-

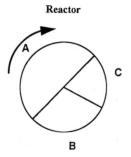
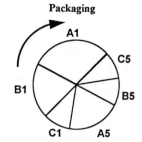

FIGURE 15.4   Schedule wheels.

duced no more frequently than once every 5 days, which in turn sets the minimum campaign cycle length. This calculation may be formalized by

$$T_{Rmin} = \frac{T_{Cmin}}{F_C} = \frac{1}{0.2} = 5 \text{ days}$$

where T_{Rmin} is the minimum campaign cycle length, T_{Cmin} is the minimum run length for grade C, and F_C is the fraction of production time devoted to grade C. Since the production rates are the same for all grades, F_C is calculated from C's percent of total demand. The target run lengths for grades A and B are found by:

$$T_{Amin} = F_A T_{Rmin} = (0.5)5 = 2.5 \text{ days}$$

$$T_{Bmin} = F_B T_{Rmin} = (0.3)\,5 = 1.5 \text{ days}$$

The reactor schedule wheel in Fig. 15.4 illustrates the target run lengths and production sequence for the reactor.

A campaign cycle for the packaging line produces all six products. Manufacturing practices require a minimum packaging run of one shift for each product. Accordingly, the minimum campaign cycle length for packaging, T_{Pmin}, is found from the product with the minimum packaging run length. Products C1, B5, and C5 are tied for the lowest-volume product. Any of these could be used to calculate the minimum campaign cycle length. Product C1 will be used:

$$T_{Pmin} = \frac{T_{C1min}}{F_{C1}} = \frac{1}{0.1} = 10 \text{ days}$$

where T_{C1min} is the minimum production run length for product C1, and F_{C1} is the fraction of packaging time devoted to C1.

Using the minimum packaging campaign cycle length, target production run lengths for each product may be calculated from the following:

$$T_i = F_i T_{Pmin}$$

where T_i is the target run length for product i, and F_i is the fraction of packaging time devoted to product i. This calculation results in the following target production run lengths:

$$T_{A1} = 3 \text{ days} \qquad T_{B1} = 2 \text{ days} \qquad T_{C1} = 1 \text{ day}$$

$$T_{A5} = 2 \text{ days} \qquad T_{B5} = 1 \text{ day} \qquad T_{C5} = 1 \text{ day}$$

The production sequence is also important in packaging. Setups may be minimized by grouping package sizes together. Consequently all 1-gallon products will be scheduled in one group, and all 5-gallon products in a second group. Thus, a typical packaging campaign sequence would be A1, B1, C1, setup, A5, B5, C5, setup. The target run lengths and sequence are illustrated by the schedule wheel for packaging in Fig. 15.4.

Scheduling

A flowchart for scheduling tasks is given in Fig. 15.5. The scheduling procedure begins by developing a forecast, which is used to reverse-flow the process schedule; that is, schedule in the direction opposite from the materials flow needed to produce the prod-

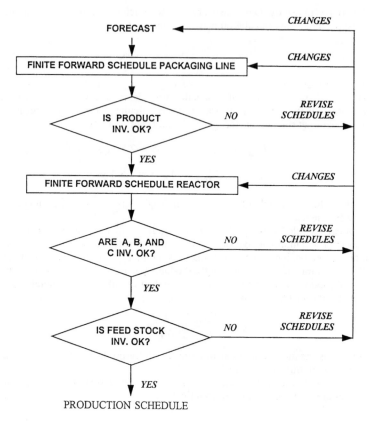

FIGURE 15.5   Scheduling flowchart.

uct. This forecast is used to help set target run lengths as described above. Next a trial schedule for the packaging line is proposed, as shown in the Gantt chart at the top of Fig. 15.6. The production run lengths for the Gantt chart use the target run lengths depicted in the schedule wheel in Fig. 15.4. Using the trial production plan and the demand forecast, finished-product inventory projections are calculated with the resulting inventories, as shown in the Gantt chart, in Fig. 15.6. The supporting calculations are given in the *production demand inventory* (PDI) *record* of Table 15.4. Note that the quantities in this record are expressed in thousands. Beginning inventories are shown in period 0.

The *period row* in each record gives the day associated with each column. The production row entries are obtained from the Gantt chart and the packaging rate of 100,000 gallons per day for all products. The demand row entries are obtained from the forecasts of daily demand.

The last row in a PDI record is inventory. The beginning inventory is shown in period 0. The inventories in subsequent periods are calculated by adding the current period's production to the prior period's ending inventory and subtracting the current period's demand. Rather than display the PDI records, it is often easier to work with inventory line graphs as shown in Fig. 15.6.

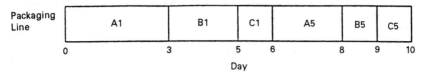

Polygoo Packaging Schedule

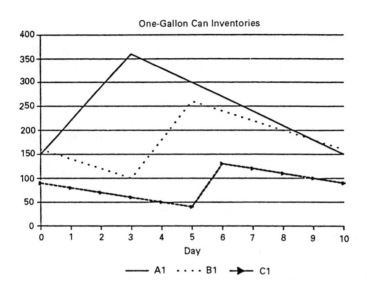

One-Gallon Can Inventories

A1 ···· B1 ➤ C1

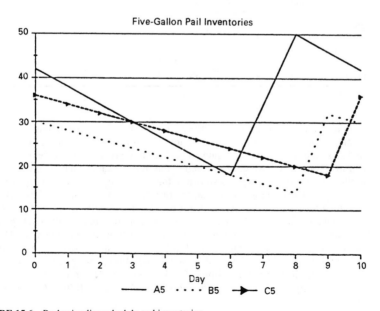

Five-Gallon Pail Inventories

A5 ···· B5 ➤ C5

FIGURE 15.6 Packaging line schedule and inventories.

TABLE 15.4 Polygoo Packaging Schedule, Production Demand Inventory Record

Product A1

Period	0	1	2	3	4	5	6	7	8	9	10
Production		100	100	100							
Demand		30	30	30	30	30	30	30	30	30	30
Inventory	150	220	290	360	330	300	270	240	210	180	150

Product B1

Period	0	1	2	3	4	5	6	7	8	9	10
Production					100	100					
Demand		20	20	20	20	20	20	20	20	20	20
Inventory	160	140	120	100	180	260	240	220	200	180	160

Product C1

Period	0	1	2	3	4	5	6	7	8	9	10
Production							100				
Demand		10	10	10	10	10	10	10	10	10	10
Inventory	90	80	70	60	50	40	130	120	110	100	90

Product A5

Period	0	1	2	3	4	5	6	7	8	9	10
Production								20	20		
Demand		4	4	4	4	4	4	4	4	4	4
Inventory	42	38	34	30	26	22	18	34	50	46	42

Product B5

Period	0	1	2	3	4	5	6	7	8	9	10
Production										20	
Demand		2	2	2	2	2	2	2	2	2	2
Inventory	30	28	26	24	22	20	18	16	14	32	30

Product C5

Period	0	1	2	3	4	5	6	7	8	9	10
Production											20
Demand		2	2	2	2	2	2	2	2	2	2
Inventory	36	34	32	30	28	26	24	22	20	18	36

The projected finished-product inventories can now be checked against their target minimums and maximums. In this example the projected inventories are above their minimums, and there is no maximum, so scheduling proceeds to the next stage. If projected inventory levels were unacceptable, the trial packaging schedule or the forecast would need to be revised. This is shown in the scheduling flowchart in Fig. 15.5 by the check "Is product inventory OK?" and the first "No, Revise schedules" branch.

Next, a trial schedule for the reactor is proposed, and bulk inventories for A, B, and C are checked. This procedure is similar to that just presented for the packaging stage. The Gantt chart at the top of Fig. 15.7 shows the trial reactor schedule. The corresponding PDI records are presented in Table 15.5, and the related inventory line graph is given in Fig. 15.7. Note that the demand for bulk Polygoo depends on the packaging schedule. Thus, the number of gallons of A demanded in day 1 is calculated by $1 \times$ (A1 production in day 1) + ($5 \times$ A5 production in day 1) = (1×100) + (5×0) = 100,000 gallons.

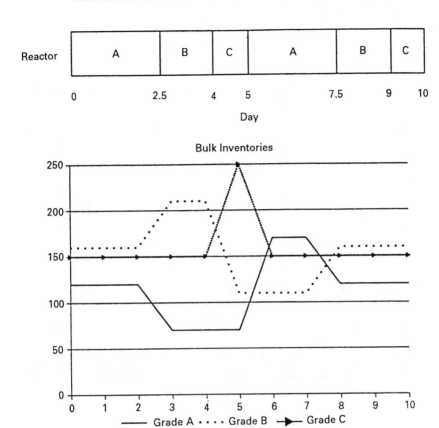

FIGURE 15.7 Reactor schedule and bulk inventories.

The inventories in the PDI records are now checked against their maximums and minimums. Alternatively, the plots of the PDI inventory rows shown in Fig. 15.7 may be used. If the bulk inventories are not within their prescribed bounds, it will be necessary to revise the reactor schedule, the packaging schedule, or the forecast. This was shown in the scheduling flowchart in Fig. 15.5 by the check of A, B, and C inventories and the second "No, Revise schedules" branch. Since all inventories for the example are within their limits, scheduling can proceed to the final step.

Scheduling the feed stock in stage 0 is the last step. The demand for feed stock is calculated from the production schedules for A, B, and C. Thus, the demand for F in period 1 is calculated from $1 \times$ (A production in period 1) + $1 \times$ (B production in period 1) + $1 \times$ (C production in period 1) = $(1 \times 100) + (1 \times 0) + (1 \times 0) = 100,00$ gallons.

When projected feed stock inventories fall below the planned minimum, receipts of feed stock are scheduled. A *receipts demand inventory* (RDI) *record* for feed stock is given in Table 15.6 and shown as a graph in Fig. 15.8. The calculations begin by projecting the inventory in period 1. The demand of 100 is subtracted from the 200 in inventory at the end of period 0. This gives a trial inventory of 100, which is below the

TABLE 15.5   Reactor Production Demand Inventory Record

Quantities expressed in thousands

Grade A

Period	0	1	2	3	4	5	6	7	8	9	10
Production		100	100	50			100	100	50		
Demand		100	100	100	0	0	0	100	100	0	0
Inventory	120	120	120	70	70	70	170	170	120	120	120

Grade B

Period	0	1	2	3	4	5	6	7	8	9	10
Production				50	100				50	100	
Demand		0	0	0	100	100	0	0	0	100	0
Inventory	160	160	160	210	210	110	110	110	160	160	160

Grade C

Period	0	1	2	3	4	5	6	7	8	9	10
Production						100					100
Demand		0	0	0	0	0	100	0	0	0	100
Inventory	150	150	150	150	150	250	150	150	150	150	150

TABLE 15.6   Feed Stock Requirements Schedule

Feed stock

Period	0	1	2	3	4	5	6	7	8	9	10
Receipts		1000									
Demand		100	100	100	100	100	100	100	100	100	100
Inventory	200	1100	900	900	800	700	600	500	400	300	200

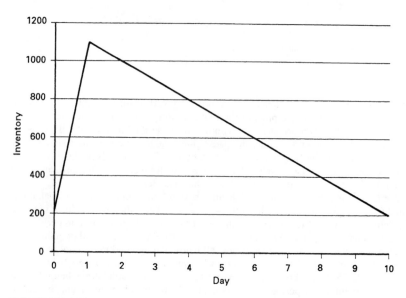

FIGURE 15.8   Feed stock inventory.

minimum inventory level of 200. A receipt of 1000 is then scheduled in period 1. This brings the inventory in period 1 to 1100. Similar calculations are performed for subsequent periods, and the resulting inventory is plotted.

Note that the above calculation for the feed stock supplier is based solely on materials. The feed stock supplier must check to verify that there is adequate inventory or capacity to meet the raw materials requirements of Polygoo. If the requirements can be met, the schedule is complete. If not, earlier schedules will need to be revised as shown in the scheduling flowchart in Fig. 15.5. Since stage 0 schedules materials before capacity, a materials-dominated scheduling approach, which will be discussed later in this chapter, is used.

The materials-dominated scheduling of feed stock contrasts with the processor-dominated scheduling exhibited by the scheduling of stages 1 and 2. In these stages, the processor and its related capacity were scheduled first by scheduling the production campaign cycles. Following this processor schedule, materials inventories were checked to ensure feasibility of the schedule. Both materials and capacity are needed to produce the product. However, determining the scheduling order identifies the relative importance of materials versus capacity and, therefore, where the company places its emphasis.

Summary of Polygoo

Polygoo illustrates simple process flow scheduling calculations. While this example is representative of the logic and calculations used in PFS systems, it should be recognized that many variations exist. Since stages were scheduled from last to first, Polygoo illustrates reverse-flow scheduling. Moreover, processor-dominated scheduling with finite forward-scheduling was used in stages 1 and 2 for the reactor and packaging operations while materials-dominated scheduling was used in stage 0 for the feed stock.

The example illustrates a scheduling logic much different from MRP logic. PFS scheduling logic uses the *process structure* to guide scheduling calculations while MRP uses the *product structure* (bill of materials) to guide scheduling calculations. Also note that for Polygoo, both materials and capacity were reconciled in each stage before proceeding to schedule the next stage.

Many process industry firms and some repetitive manufacturers use PFS logic for scheduling all or part of their operations. While some firms use custom software, other firms use commercial finite scheduling software. Many of these PFS implementations use logic similar to that illustrated above for Polygoo.

PROCESS FLOW SCHEDULING PRINCIPLES

The Polygoo example given in the previous section illustrates but a single method for scheduling a process flow manufacturing facility. The Polygoo example is valuable because it provides a numerical illustration of scheduling procedures for process flow manufacturers. However, many other scheduling variations are used. These variations are conceptually captured in the three principles for process flow scheduling, presented below.

Process Structure Guides Calculations

The first process flow scheduling principle is as follows:

Scheduling calculations are guided by the process structure.

This principle is the dominant concept underlying all PFS systems. A classification procedure and terminology are needed to define process structures. Figure 15.9 illustrates a proposed classification and terminology. A *process structure* consists of process units, stages, and trains. A *process unit* performs a basic manufacturing step, such as polymerization, mixing, or packaging. Process units are combined into *stages,* with stages being separated by inventories. Processes that are not separated by inventories are best combined into a single stage that can be scheduled as a single entity. Separating different stages with inventory allows these stages to be scheduled somewhat independently. Finally, stages are organized into process trains. A *process train* is a fixed, sequential series of process stages in which a family of products is produced. No material is usually transferred from one process train to another, although process trains may use common raw materials and produce common products. We emphasize *usually* here because a few exceptions to this nontransfer-of-materials rule exist.

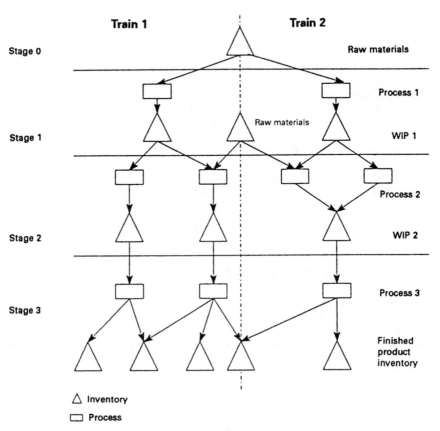

FIGURE 15.9   Process structure.

Stage-Scheduling Alternatives

The second PFS principle specifies alternatives for scheduling single stages:

Stages are scheduled using processor-dominated scheduling (PDS) or materials-dominated scheduling (MDS) approaches.

To operate a process stage, schedules are required for both the processing unit and the materials. If the processing units are scheduled before the materials, processor-dominated scheduling has been used. Processor-dominated scheduling was illustrated by the way the packaging and reactor stages were scheduled for Polygoo. Gantt charts were used first to propose trial processor schedules; then inventories were checked to determine if the proposed schedule was feasible.

The alternative stage-scheduling logic is materials-dominated scheduling. MDS begins by developing materials plans for all items produced in a stage. When inventory of an item falls below its target minimum value, a replenishment batch is scheduled. After scheduling all the materials for a particular stage, the processors for the stage are scheduled and then checked to verify that sufficient capacity is available. If there is insufficient processor capacity, the materials schedules must be revised and the processor schedules checked again. A simple example of the MDS approach was illustrated for the feed stock stage in the Polygoo example.

The selection of PDS or MDS for a given stage depends on the particular scheduling environment. In general, PDS should be used when (1) capacity is relatively expensive, (2) the stage is a bottleneck, or (3) setups are expensive. Conversely, MDS should be used when (1) materials are relatively expensive, (2) there is excess capacity, (3) setup costs are negligible, or (4) the stage consists of a set of processing units that operates like a job shop.

Process Train Scheduling Alternatives

The third PFS principle specifies alternatives for scheduling process trains:

Process trains are scheduled using reverse-flow scheduling, forward-flow scheduling, or mixed-flow scheduling.

The first principle of PFS requires that the process structure be used to guide scheduling calculations. However, process stage schedules can be linked together in many ways to form a process train schedule. Figure 15.10 shows an example of a process structure for a simple three-stage system. There are the three alternatives for scheduling, as follows.

Reverse-Flow Scheduling.   Reverse-flow scheduling builds a schedule by proceeding backward through the process structure, scheduling one stage at a time. In the reverse-flow scheduling flowchart shown in Fig. 15.11, scheduling begins with the last stage, stage 3. Either PDS or MDS can be used for stage scheduling; PDS will be used in this example. First a Gantt chart is used to create a trial schedule for processor P_3. Downstream finished-product inventories are then checked. The inventories may be displayed as a line graph of inventory versus time. A separate plot is needed for each finished product; however, several inventory plots can be displayed on one graph by using symbols or by color coding different products. If the trial schedule yields unacceptable inventory levels for one or more products, a new schedule must be proposed and inventories checked. When a satisfactory schedule has been obtained for stage 3, the scheduling computations move to stage 2.

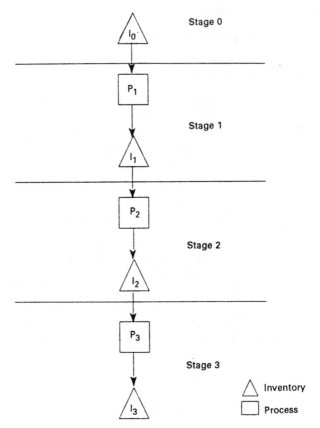

FIGURE 15.10   Multistage system.

A similar processor-dominated scheduling procedure is used for stage 2. First, a Gantt chart is used to schedule P_2, and inventories are then checked with line graphs. If a problem (such as an inventory level below its target minimum level) surfaces, the schedule of P_2 is adjusted. Alternatively, the downstream schedule for P_3 or the forecast for the finished products may be revised.

When a satisfactory schedule is obtained for stages 2 and 3, stage 1 is scheduled. The procedure used in stages 2 and 3 is repeated for stage 1. Finally, the raw materials inventories I_0 are checked. If supply problems surface, the previously developed schedules and inventory projections must be revised.

Since the schedule was constructed by proceeding against the materials flow from finished products to raw material, it is called *reverse-flow scheduling*. This example also illustrates the use of processor-dominated scheduling at each stage. It should be noted that reverse-flow scheduling can be used with MDS, PDS, or a combination of the two.

Forward-Flow Scheduling. An alternative procedure, *forward-flow scheduling,* begins with the initial processing step and forward-schedules through the process struc-

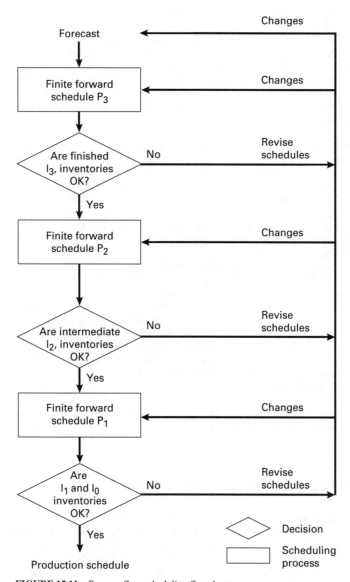

FIGURE 15.11 Reverse-flow scheduling flowchart.

ture. Therefore, it schedules in the same forward direction that materials move through the process train.

Initial observation suggests that forward-flow scheduling is the least likely alternative to occur. However, firms that are severely limited in some way by the availability of key materials are likely candidates for using this approach. Plants that process by-products produced by another plant or food companies that are dependent upon a short harvest cycle are examples of situations in which forward flow scheduling makes sense. As with reverse-flow scheduling, the forward-flow schedule can be created using PDS, MDS, or a combination of approaches.

Mixed-Flow Scheduling.   *Mixed-flow scheduling* combines forward- and reverse-flow scheduling concepts. Consider again the simple three-stage example process structure illustrated in Fig. 15.10. However, suppose that in this case process P_2 requires an expensive piece of equipment that is also a bottleneck. Efficient operation of the plant requires efficient utilization of this bottleneck process. To efficiently use the bottleneck P_2, it is scheduled first (see Fig. 15.12) using a Gantt chart. This PDS schedule pushes production into the buffer inventory represented by I_2. Stage 3 can now be scheduled using either PDS or MDS. We have chosen to illustrate MDS, which first develops a materials plan for I_3 and then schedules the processor P_3.

The inventory I_2 is a reconciliation point. The PDS schedule for P_2 pushes production into I_2, while the schedule for P_3 pulls materials requirements from I_2. If the resulting inventory for any item in I_2 is below its minimum or above its maximum, adjustments will be required in the schedules for P_2 or P_3. Alternatively, the forecasted demand for the finished product I_3 may be modified. Stage 1 and the raw materials in I_0 may be reverse-flow-scheduled after achieving an acceptable schedule for stages 2 and 3. Since mixed-flow scheduling combines forward- and reverse-flow scheduling, forward-scheduled production from an upstream stage must be reconciled with downstream materials requirements at some time in the process structure. This reconciliation point is where *push* meets *pull*.

The three principles presented here form the foundation for all process flow scheduling systems. It should be noted that PFS is a general approach to scheduling, not a rigidly defined technique. Accordingly, these principles can be implemented in many ways.

COMPARISON OF SCHEDULING PARADIGMS

Those of you who have spent some time in the production and inventory management field have seen a variety of planning and scheduling systems emerge in the past 25 years. Paramount among these are materials requirements planning (MRP), just in time (JIT), theory of constraints (TOC), and process flow scheduling (PFS). Each of these systems is, in its own right, a valuable system for companies to consider. However, since it is unlikely that any of us would make the claim that all manufacturing environments are the same or that any approach has universal application, it is apparent that companies must select and match the systems. It is our firm belief that planning and scheduling systems must be tailored to a firm's manufacturing environment and to its competitive strategies. Therefore, this chapter will examine each system and where it might best be applied. In doing this, there will be no attempt to explain the techniques; the reader is referred to other chapters in this handbook for the details of these approaches.

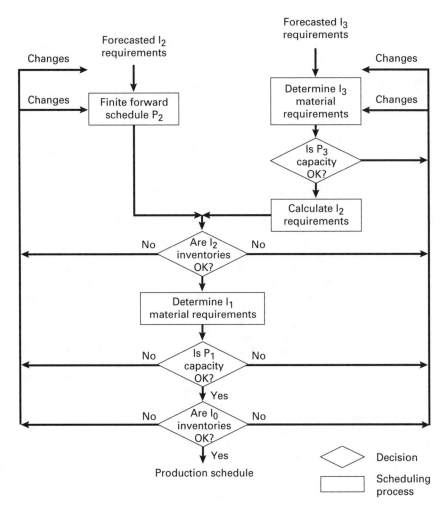

FIGURE 15.12   Mixed-flow scheduling flowchart.

Scheduling Frameworks

MRP was developed primarily through the 1970s and expanded upon in the early 1980s. It is founded upon a master schedule of order due dates (customer or replenishment orders) that is backward-scheduled through the bill of materials and offset for lead times in order to develop recommended materials release dates for each part in the bill of materials. It is a widely used and accepted approach for many industries. However, these industries are concentrated in the middle to upper left of the product-process matrix as shown in Fig. 15.1. MRP is used in job shop environments with little application in process or continuous manufacturing. Two exceptions do exist: Process industries that operate batch processes often exhibit characteristics similar to job shop environments and can use MRP. Pharmaceutical companies provide a good example. Second, many flow manufacturing companies will use the MRP logic to order purchased materials needed to support production plans and schedules. This application of MRP logic uses a simple two-level bill of materials and does not require a complete MRP system.

JIT was developed and implemented during the late 1970s and 1980s. It is founded upon an attempt to limit materials inventories within the manufacturing system while production is linked directly to demands. Product demands provide the pull mechanism that authorizes materials movement throughout the manufacturing system. JIT is used primarily in repetitive manufacturing operations that exhibit continuous-flow characteristics producing discrete units, that is, in the middle of the product-process matrix. In addition, JIT requires quick setups. Continuous-flow manufacturers that produce nondiscrete units generally do not use JIT scheduling techniques, although some might argue that pipelines and surge tanks between operations are merely forms of inventory limits, similar to kanbans in the JIT approaches. However, since products are typically produced to stock, their schedules are not directly linked to demand. Moreover, continuous-flow manufacturers may either push or pull product through downstream or upstream operations. In other words, the pure JIT logic may be broken in many continuous-flow environments.

TOC emerged in the late 1970s with much of its concept development in the mid-to-late 1980s. Its structure is founded upon identifying the constraint and then scheduling the constraint to maximize its throughput. All nonconstraint operations are then subordinated to the constraint schedule. TOC applications have been concentrated in areas similar to MRP, in the middle to upper left of the product-process matrix. However, it is important to note that constraint identification and throughput maximization is a common activity in most process and continuous manufacturing operations. Subordination of nonconstraints is another issue. It is common for most continuous-flow manufacturing to decouple major operations with inventory. This allows them to run these operations more independently of upstream or downstream operations, thus breaking the subordination. Therefore, complete application of the TOC approach is relatively rare in most flow manufacturing.

PFS, first documented in the late 1980s and early 1990s, is a malleable concept that can be shaped to meet the needs of many different manufacturing environments. Companies in the lower right quadrant of the product-process matrix are more likely to use PFS concepts. Typical characteristics of plants using PFS are:

- Similar routings leading to a flow of materials through a series of process stages.
- Production is often scheduled to meet forecasted demands rather than individual customer orders.
- Production is authorized by the schedule.

It is also interesting to note that within the PFS structure, MRP, JIT, TOC, and other techniques may be used to schedule individual process steps (stages). They may even be used in combination; that is, MRP schedules one stage, and TOC schedules another stage, with inventory decoupling the two schedules. A variety of combinations are possible and have been documented in earlier writings.[14]

A closer look at a number of detailed issues reveals contrasts in each of these approaches. One must also recognize that this contrast is only a summary of issues and is not meant to be an in-depth analysis. The following issues will be evaluated: scheduling procedures, usage domains, scheduling calculations, capacity, production, authorization, and cost analysis.

Scheduling Procedures

The four frameworks mentioned above use different approaches for scheduling. PFS schedules processes using processor-dominated scheduling or materials-dominated scheduling. Generally both materials and capacity are scheduled for a process stage before scheduling begins for the next process stage. These process schedules are linked together using one of the following scheduling strategies: reverse-flow scheduling, forward-flow scheduling, and mixed-flow scheduling.

In contrast, MRP systems schedule all materials before checking capacity. Materials scheduling begins by setting due dates for all end item orders. Start times are calculated next by using the lead times to schedule backward from the due dates. Product structures are then used to determine the materials needs from the next lower level in the bill of materials (a bill of materials explosion). Scheduling proceeds in this manner until all levels are scheduled. Following the development of the materials schedule, capacities are checked using the materials schedule's due dates, processing times for individual operations, and routings for each part. If problems are found, the materials schedule is revised.

TOC is similar to MRP, but it does not directly use order due dates. Schedule dates at the constraint operation, rather than the end item order due dates, drive the TOC schedule. These schedule dates are, however, linked to the order due dates. Lead times of operations upstream from the constraint operation are added to a time buffer in front of the constraint to determine the timing of releasing materials to the gateway operation. In this sense TOC backward-schedules from the constraint operation to up-stream operations. On the other hand, downstream operations and materials priorities are driven by the availability of materials from the constraint operation. Material is processed on a first-come, first-served basis as it is received from the upstream constraint operation. Variations from the above description exist.

JIT systems use a materials pull, backward-scheduling strategy. However, JIT systems do not use lead times, work orders, or formal schedules. Instead, downstream empty kanbans (cards, squares, shelves, etc.) authorize upstream operations to produce. The overall production lead time is controlled by the number of kanbans, but lead times are not used to determine a production schedule.

Usage Domains

The use of either the process or the product structure for guiding scheduling calculations affects the choice of a scheduling technique. Process flow scheduling uses the process structure and applies in flow manufacturing environments. Although the process flow may be complex, there must be a discernible, directed flow through one or more process trains in a PFS system. In contrast, MRP fits best in job shops. Each order in a job shop can have its own routing. Thus there is no discernible directed flow on which to base PFS scheduling calculations. On the other hand, MRP systems model job shops quite closely by giving each unique part its own routing. MRP systems can be used for flow manufacturing environments; however, other frameworks are generally more efficient and effective.

TOC is similar to MRP in its focus on product structures, and we therefore find also most applications of TOC in job shop environments. However, TOC's use of product structures differs somewhat from MRP's use of bills of materials. Since the focus of TOC is on constraints and the subordination of nonconstraint schedules to the constraint's schedule (the drum and the rope), TOC fits better in flow environments than does MRP. Unfortunately, the literature of TOC does not clearly explain how to make this adaptation to flow manufacturing environments.

JIT systems strive for a continuous flow, and, like PFS, these systems work best in manufacturing environments with consistent, well-defined process flows. As material flows become more variable, JIT will still work, but more inventory is required. JIT systems require manufacturing processes that can quickly change over from one product to the next. Lot sizes are ideally quite small, and production sequences are easily changed.

Guiding Scheduling Calculations

The first PFS principle states that scheduling calculations are guided by the process structure. MRP and TOC systems use the product structure (bill of materials) to guide scheduling calculations and differ in this regard from PFS systems. JIT systems, on the other hand, do not have any scheduling calculations. However, the flow of kanbans and materials is guided by the process structure.

Capacity

Each of the four frameworks has a different approach for dealing with capacity. PFS schedules each process using either process-dominated scheduling or materials-dominated scheduling. In either case, both capacity (equipment and labor) and materials are generally scheduled for a process stage before the next process stage is scheduled. This results in a process-by-process reconciliation of materials and capacity.

MRP initially assumes infinite capacity is available. It is only after the initial material schedule is created that one reviews the capacity load and manually intercedes to alter either the materials schedule or the available capacity. In this regard, MRP uses a materials-dominated scheduling approach.

JIT also uses a materials-dominated scheduling approach. JIT does not pay any real attention to capacity except during the design of the line and in production planning where an upper limit may be placed on the number of order kanbans. During the design phase, excess capacity is built into the production line to handle demand variations. Thus when a JIT line is operating, capacity is secondary to the signals for materials movement.

TOC uses a capacity treatment more closely aligned to PFS than to MRP or JIT. Most TOC examples use a materials-dominated scheduling approach to finitely schedule materials on the constraint. However, TOC does not preclude the use of processor-dominated scheduling for the constraint. In either case, the objective is to maximize constraint throughput while maintaining level product flow to avoid creating temporary bottlenecks.

TOC schedules only materials at stages considered nonbottlenecks. This follows from the assumption that throughput is limited by a single constraint and that nonconstraints will not have any capacity problems. This assumption must be challenged in many flow shops. The initial design of many flow shops balances capacity among the processes within a process train. Under these conditions, the existence of a single constraint may not be valid. For example, when running product A, the constraint may be in process I; however, when running product B, the constraint may shift to process II. In this situation, scheduling should check capacity at both constraints using a PFS approach.

Authority to Produce

After a schedule is developed, it must be communicated to unit supervisors and line workers. The four frameworks all use different methods for authorizing production. PFS authorizes production by issuing a production schedule. Only the *frozen* part of the schedule is executed. Periods further out provide a look ahead, but new schedules are issued before periods beyond the frozen schedule need to be executed. MRP releases production orders to workstations identifying what must be produced along with start dates, due dates, materials needed, and so on. Production is authorized in a JIT system by an empty kanban. TOC authorizes work at the constraint by the release of a constraint schedule. Nonconstraint activities are authorized by a first-come, first-served prioritization of work and an attitude of work if and only if there is work to do.

Costs

Most implementations of all four scheduling frameworks do not directly incorporate costs or optimization in their scheduling calculations. Optimization and cost considerations are factors in process design and in developing production plans. On the other hand, scheduling is concerned primarily with finding an acceptable, feasible solution—one that meets demands without violating too many guidelines. However, some scheduling guidelines, such as lot size targets for PFS systems, are based on optimizations performed as part of the earlier production planning process.

Application

So, which framework best fits your manufacturing environment? Fortunately, you are not constrained to using just one framework. Thus one part of your plant may be able to use JIT. If so, do it. JIT, which is simpler than the other frameworks, should be used if it fits your environment. Another part of your operation may need to operate as a job shop; you should probably use MRP here. Finally, you might want to optimize the use of a bottleneck process with a finite forward-scheduling technique. All these techniques may be combined into one unified system using PFS concepts to link the three processes together.

Process flow scheduling provides a new framework based on the scheduling practices of many firms. It is a flexible framework that can be molded to fit most—if not all—flow manufacturing environments. This flexibility allows firms to customize their scheduling systems for specific circumstances. Process flow scheduling allows firms to break from the MRP philosophy of *one size fits all*. PFS systems exploit the flows in a process structure to simplify scheduling calculations and to improve the resulting schedules. Additional information and 10 brief case examples of the use of PFS are presented by Taylor and Bolander.[14]

REFERENCES

1. J. F. Cox, J. H. Blackstone, Jr., and M. S. Spencer (eds.): *APICS Dictionary,* 7th ed., APICS, Falls Church, Va., 1992.

2. S. A. DeLurgio, and C. D. Bhame: *Forecasting Systems for Operations Management,* Business One Irwin, Homewood, Ill., 1991.

3. S. P. Bradley, A. C. Hax, and T. L. Magnanti: *Applied Mathematical Programming,* Addison-Wesley, Reading, Mass., 1977.

4. J. S. Aronofsky, J. M. Dutton, and M. T. Tayyabkhan: *Managerial Planning with Linear Programming in Process Operations,* Wiley, New York, 1978.

5. S. F. Bolander, R. C. Heard, S. M. Seward, and S. G. Taylor: *Manufacturing Planning and Control in Process Industries,* APICS, Falls Church, Va., 1981.

6. S. G. Taylor: "Optimal Aggregate Production Strategies for Plants with Semifixed Operating Costs," *AIIE Transactions* (12:3), 1980, pp. 253–257.

7. M. Salomon: *Deterministic Lot Sizing Models for Production Planning,* Springer Verlag, New York, 1991.

8. R. G. Brown: *Decision Rules for Inventory Management,* Holt, Rinehart and Winston, New York, 1967.

9. A. C. Hax and D. Candea: *Production and Inventory Management,* Prentice-Hall, Englewood Cliffs, N.J., 1984.

10. J. F. Magee and D. M. Boodman: *Production Planning and Inventory Control,* 2d ed., McGraw-Hill, New York, 1967.

11. E. A. Silver and R. Peterson: *Decision Systems for Inventory Management and Production Planning,* 2d ed., Wiley, New York, 1985.

12. K. R. Baker: *Introduction to Sequencing and Scheduling,* Wiley, New York, 1974.

13. T. E. Morton and D. W. Pentico: *Heuristic Scheduling Systems,* Wiley, New York, 1993.

14. S. G. Taylor and S. F. Bolander: *Process Flow Scheduling: A Scheduling Systems Framework for Flow Manufacturing,* APICS, Falls Church, Va., 1994.

CHAPTER 16
JUST-IN-TIME CONCEPTS: SCOPE AND APPLICATIONS

Editor

Robert W. Hall, Ph.D.

Target Editor-in-Chief
Association for Manufacturing Excellence
Indiana University, Bloomington, Indiana

The purpose of using just in time (JIT) is to eliminate waste from processes, thereby reducing the elapsed time to complete them. Just-in-time methods can be applied to all kinds of processes, large and small, and its use is not limited to manufacturing. Insightful people have used the just-in-time concept for centuries, but the popularization of the Toyota Production System enabled people to see how powerful JIT can be. The name is misleading because it suggests that the concept begins and ends with materials arriving just in time for use. But JIT timing of materials flows is a result, not a cause. Well applied, the JIT concept catalyzes many kinds of improvements in quality, product design, maintenance, and other system components—even in selling.

Under the name *JIT,* the concept has been applied mostly to production and shipping. Under other names—*reengineering, time-based competition, reducing time to market, Quick Response, and even "concept to cash"*—the JIT concept has been applied to almost every kind of process: Order fulfillment (only part of which is production), new product and service development, customer acquisition, and service of existing customers. All processes may include supplier organizations.

The major benefit of JIT techniques is not better production control, but the simplification of the processes themselves so that they flow smoothly. Achieving short lead times requires technical and personal mastery of operations, individually and collectively, which implies leadership, dedication, imagination, coordination, teamwork—that is, significant human development. Those who progress in implementing the JIT concept change themselves. Managers who regard the JIT concept as just another technique to install find "it" to be something else that does not work.

The balance of this chapter discusses basic JIT concepts. Although the human aspects are the key to successful implementation, they are not the focus of attention.

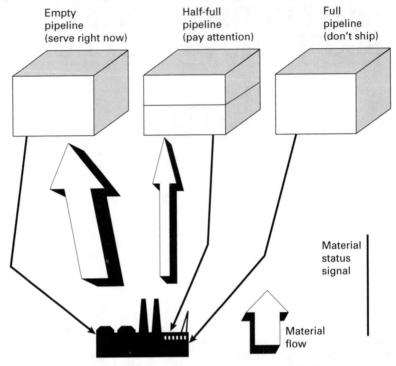

FIGURE 16.1   Basic concept of a pull system. The thin lines represent information status fed back to the supply point. The heavy lines represent materials moved forward for customer use. In this example, the empty container is an urgent message to fill it up. The 40 percent full one asks for attention, and the full one is ignored.

PROCESS OVER PROCEDURE

The primary objective of JIT is to remove waste from processes. All else is secondary. A pull system of flow control, defined in Fig. 16.1, is commonly identified with JIT. However, a pull system is only one aspect of overall visibility, which is vital to JIT, built into the design of processes themselves. Visibility is useful both for controlling processes and for triggering improvement of them. Effective visibility leads to rapid, inexpensive correction of operating conditions, using either automated systems or human ones. The primary consideration is improvement. Well done, the JIT process links into as large a menu of improvement techniques as one has the ability to implement. The defining performance measurement of JIT is lead time, but reducing lead times also requires improvement of many other indicators because the objective is total improvement, not making trade-offs, such as adding people or equipment, to reduce the lead times.

A pull system starts with the customer, or with a primary using operation, such as final assembly in production. Whether pull signals are simple or complex, materials are replenished at approximately the same rate they are used. A water glass in a high-service restaurant illustrates a simple pull system at work. No sooner does a sip diminish the water level than a server tops off the glass again. This simple system fulfills the three basic functions of a pull system used for process improvement:

1. *Replenishment is triggered by the customer.* The trigger may be actual use, as by sipping water, or the signaling of strong intent to use. In the restaurant, a diner's steak is started before the salad is delivered. In a production setting, sending a kanban card back to the supply operation when a container starts to be used signals intent to consume all the contents of the container.

2. *Discipline limits the amount of materials in a pipeline.* In the case of the water, a glassful is the maximum waste. If the restaurant patron never takes a sip, the glass is never refilled. Any pull system that stimulates process improvement restricts the maximum amount of inventory that can accumulate. When the using operation ceases to consume, production of supplies stops. But limiting the inventory in itself minimizes only one type of waste, and the system should stimulate more improvement than that.

3. *Communications and visibility are promoted.* The next operation is the customer—an internal customer. One should pay attention to all customer needs, just as a waiter should pay attention to more than filling a glass, but watching it keeps him or her attentive. Likewise, a production operator should pay attention to more than the next operation's demand signals. Fast feedback on defects or other inadequacies promotes many other kinds of improvement. But if visibility of the next stage of the process stimulates improvement, creating visibility of all relevant processes, including those of the end customer, stimulates much more.

The objective of JIT is to streamline a process—to change and improve the process itself, not to install a control pull system on a process undeveloped for it. Improvement is multidimensional: delivery, cost, quality, customer satisfaction, and so on. All these are related to the primary performance dimension that would be improved by JIT, which is lead time, often called *cycle time.*

Lead time is the elapsed time between two different events that may be unique or that may recur. *Cycle time* is the time between events that recur, such as the time between finishing parts on a machine or the time between completion of units on an assembly line. The cycle time of an assembly line producing cars at 60 jobs per hour is 1 minute between cars, which means that all assembly work must fit within 1 minute of time available at the average station. Actual work cycles may be multiples of 1 minute because workers or (in rare cases) machines can move along the line for various distances, but the work cycles must synchronize with 1 minute.

Cycle times are a key element in regularly making detailed improvement. In repetitive manufacturing, events recur, and knowing the *planned cycle times* (often called *tact times*) between units is part of developing the schedule for upcoming production periods. Decentralized workers use planned cycle times to plan the optimal work cycles within each station, while all the stations synchronize—assuming that workers develop the ability to regularly revise and improve their own work in detail. During execution, the ability to see at any moment how actual performance compares with the plan becomes part of the visibility system.

Lead times (as elapsed process time) come in a variety of forms. The lead times for some common materials used in production processes are as follows:

1. *Throughput time, or time to flow through the production process.* For this increment to be meaningful, the entry and exit points need to be clearly defined. In the case of assembly, at least two subtypes of throughput time are useful:

   a. *Time the materials are waiting to be used, from entry of material into the process until it is consumed in assembly.* This is frequently estimated as the amount of WIP on hand divided by the rate of use (or multiplied by the cycle time of use).

   b. *Time for materials to move along the assembly process.* In the automotive case, it is the number of hours of cars on-line from initial body weld until line-off of the finished car.

2. *Supplier lead time, or the actual times for materials to be transformed by suppliers and to arrive from them.*

3. *Planning lead times.* Planning can add considerably to lead times.

4. *Customer lead times.* The time between customers signifying that orders are firm until they receive the orders and are satisfied with the product and service performance that they represent.

One objective of JIT is to minimize the length of time in which a schedule is firm. That is the opposite of holding a big backlog of actual orders or striving for a perfect forecast in hopes that the perfect plan will then zip materials through production itself in hours. If planning lead times are long, the process is inflexible to change. If customer lead times are long, fast materials flows had to have been achieved at the expense of customer satisfaction.

More broadly, the objective of JIT is to reduce all kinds of lead times, not to decrease one lead time by increasing those elsewhere, or by trading off cost, quality, or any other significant dimension of process performance. "Reducing the time to correct errors," or "reducing the time to prevent errors (correct a process before it goes out of control)," are two maxims among JIT practitioners that suggest how reducing lead times relates to quality improvement, and quality improvement is a subject in itself. Well done, the JIT concept stimulates overall improvement of the processes to which it is applied.

Process improvement has many dimensions. Organizations serious about process improvement have a large number of performance indicators. When a change is made, performance by some measures may fall off temporarily because of learning, but that period should not last more than a few weeks. Long term, performance should improve by all significant indicators with no trade-offs between significant performance indicators, as illustrated in Fig. 16.2.

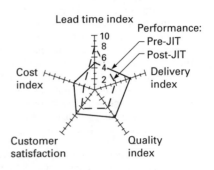

FIGURE 16.2   The objective of JIT is to improve the processes to which it is applied on all dimensions, not by reducing only a single class of lead times or by only reducing inventory levels.

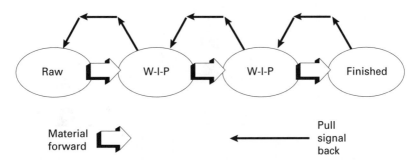

FIGURE 16.3 Simplified diagram of flow in a standard routing using a pull system. (1) If each of the workstations adjoin each other in a cell, the pull system is a one-piece transfer system. (2) If two stations are within sight of each other but do not adjoin, the pull system consists of simple kanban squares, or the equivalent. If a square is empty, fill it; if it is full, stop. (3) If two stations are out of sight of each other, circulation of a fixed number of standard containers between the stations serves as the simplest pull system, an empty container being a signal that it should be filled for return. (4) If for some reason, containers cannot circulate exclusively between two points, then it is necessary to construct a pull signal system using cards or some other marker of demand that is one level of abstraction removed from the process itself.

Often the goal of lead time reduction is quantified. An example is the reduction of throughput time to no more than two times the cumulative times of all operations. Said differently, the idle time (or queue time) of materials in process should be equal to no more than the amount of time value-added work is being performed on it. This level of "value-added ratio" is only possible if materials are processed by one-piece flow in the line.

Production in cells, or *one-piece flow,* or just standard flow paths with a pull system does not happen by itself. Process design comes first. With thought and effort, flow paths can be standardized to some degree, thus working toward the conditions in Fig. 16.3. With one-of-a-kind work and nonstandard routings, a pull system will be an improvisation far short of the ideal case. However, the objective is still to improve the total process on as many dimensions as possible. The techniques used to stimulate improvement of repetitive, in-line work are only one manifestation of visibility systems.

POWER OF PROCESS VISIBILITY

Visibility systems can be applied to all kinds of processes. For example, 10 years ago a company called Inductoheat developed a form of JIT for a job shop environment using visibility principles. Since the products were custom engineered, few components followed a standard routing, so a pull system linking a sequence of work centers was impractical.

Instead, visibility was created in part by hanging up a final assembly schedule so that all fabrication workers could see it. All shop paper for each part contained the assembly job number for which that part was destined. The workers determined the priorities needed to finish each part in time for it to reach final assembly on the date posted. Shop workers who executed the fabrication operations could understand directly what needed to be done and when. They learned a lot just by looking. The basic concept is illustrated in Fig. 16.4.

Furthermore, the workers were authorized to contact design engineers or others directly whenever a question arose. No management intermediaries held meetings about

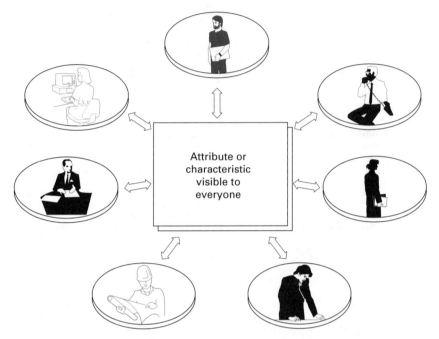

FIGURE 16.4 Visibility characteristic. Anything that can be seen by all humans within view of the process and who are paying attention. If everyone can see the same thing, no supervisory description or interpretation is needed. That in itself is part of the process.

errors or misunderstandings. The shop workers could learn a great deal just by asking too. The shop floor virtually ran itself.

In the Inductoheat case, as in all others, the visibility system was not separate from the basic methods by which work is done and by which people relate to each other. The work of supervisors was much diminished, and several transferred into other jobs.

The kanban system used in repetitive operations, briefly described in Fig. 16.3, is one method to improve process visibility by promoting observation of the operations served. In the ideal case, each workpiece serves as a pull signal, or visibility marker. The presence or absence of a part indicates what must be done next, and that basic principle can be incorporated by simple automation sensing the presence of a part. One level of abstraction removed from the workpiece itself, kanban signals can be transmitted by containers, cards, lights, or other markers. In general, the less abstract the system, the more it has been simplified, which is another way of stating that old adage, "Simplify, then automate."

The details of pull system visibility are usually illustrated with a kanban card system. Each card represents only one standard container holding a fixed number of parts of a given type. Limiting the number of cards between any two points strictly limits the maximum inventory that can accumulate between them. Applying such a discipline to an entire system limits the maximum amount of inventory that can accumulate in the system. Limiting the amount of inventory in the system increases the visibility of all kinds of problems. The basic idea is to run at a level that puts just enough stress on the system that, at a minimum, there is no room to be lax. Even better is making visible a steady stream of small problems that suggest how to tighten the process further.

The major objective of kanban is to prompt continuous improvement and process standardization in any way: product design, machine capability, work procedure, materials transport, layout, operator flexibility, instrumentation, automation, and so on. A kanban system with excess inventory in process is no more than a variant of an order-point system. A kanban signal can be used for more than a flow of materials. Where materials are processed repetitively, tools, consumable supplies, test data, machines, and people also operate by a repetitive pattern. One of the more popular variants is a "production" kanban signal used to communicate from the output side to the input side of a large production operation. (A large paint system and a big heat-treat furnace are two examples.) Kanban systems have also been applied to tooling and consumables.

But the general concept of visibility is not restricted to production and logistics. It is useful for nonmanufacturing operations as well. The concept: Turn any process in itself, including the people in it, into a self-regulating system. In the broad sense, manufacturing processes include quality, personnel, maintenance, shipping—everything needed to deliver the product offering to the customer. The concept also applies to any kind of process such as: (1) new-product (or process) development and launch, (2) customer acquisition, and (3) customer service.

Visibility is the practical side of creating a system that is self-organizing. A number of prescriptive visibility techniques listed in Tables 16.1 and 16.2 are only a start. The principle of visibility is to keep communication as simple as possible. "Broadcasting" through visibility of the process itself should require near-zero added effort to encode routine information. Reception is instantaneous. Interpretation is immediate. Information waste is minimal.

A few principles of maintaining visibility are as follows:

- Communicate using the process itself to minimize the level of abstraction.
- Maximize the use of unwritten, unspoken communication.
- Simplify documentation. Capture necessary data correctly the first time.
- Minimize delay when acting on information. Minimize interpretation time.

In practice, one cannot improve visibility without improving the process it describes. It is possible to overdo visibility—overwhelm the senses with too many signals—but that rarely happens. When it does, the process begs for simplification. Most common are processes developed with little thought for visibility and therefore without constant stimulus for continuous improvement.

The first characteristic to look for in any plant or any other functioning process is visibility. If any observer can quickly begin to comprehend the system, the people doing the work are genuinely empowered to operate the process and improve it. Where visibility is absent, someone must supervise—that is, figure out what to do, tell the workers to do it, then follow up to be sure they did it.

WORKPLACE ORGANIZATION, OR 5S

Just in time begins with the basics of visibility, often called *5S*, which comes from five Japanese words beginning with an S sound, but goes back further to alliterative reminder words long used by military units as checklists when preparing for inspection. 5S is so simple that it is easy to dismiss it as trivial, but it is powerful. Unfortunately,

TABLE 16.1   List of Visibility Techniques: Manufacturing

None of the items on this "starter list" are hard to grasp. They are difficult to apply primarily because of behavioral reluctance to give up control and because process simplification takes work.

- 5S practices should be in place. All unnecessary items should be removed from the workplace. Standard locations should be available for all equipment, tools, supplies, and materials, and so on. Workplaces should be clean.

- Make layouts of a process for maximum visibility of a process from any location in it or around it. This is one reason for using U lines, J lines, and signs that explain what each area does.

- Immediately needed operational instructions should be easy to see and immediately at hand. (Instruction sheets should be hanging within view. Necessary manuals should be at hand in standard locations. If instructions are transmitted by computer, any operator can call up the needed instruction with no delay while working. Documentation check-offs should be in standard location, and writing pens kept with the documents.)

- Quality status markers and charts should be within easy view. A system should be in place for immediate feedback of quality problems to the probable source. For example, a defect should be taken to the location where it was made. This correction should be made promptly and rapidly.

- Pull system markers, such as cards, should be used where applicable. Standard inventory or materials locations should be clearly marked. Standard containers should be used and color coded.

- Schedules, backlogs, shipment status, or overall quality status should be within view from anywhere on the factory floor. This allows everyone, not just managers, to plan work in advance.

- Trouble boards, trouble lights, and status lights should be incorporated into the system. Such systems have been referred to as *andons,* a Japanese term meaning "a signal lamp." Anyone can quickly understand what part of a process is or is not running, and perhaps why.

- Up-to-the minute completion status should be available. Production goals versus completion counts should be posted where everyone can see them. Also, improvement project goals versus status, including suggestions and actions taken to implement them, should be posted.

- Maintenance status markers and check-offs should be used for machines, tools, instruments, or anything on which regular maintenance is needed.

- A personnel location board should be used, as well as a training and qualification status board.

- Financial data should be posted regularly.

5S is often called "housekeeping." This is misleading because it implies that 5S is something to be done apart from value-added work—cleanup tasks. Actually, 5S is incorporated into all work practices.

In 1980, when questioning a Toyota supplier, Tokai Rika, on how the company had established JIT production, the vice president who led the effort confided that at least half the benefit was considered to be from 5S. But before 5S, much less JIT, could be implemented, the leaders of the company had to demonstrate to the entire workforce that they trusted them both to operate and to improve shop processes. Such an emotional change is no easier in Japan than anywhere else.

TABLE 16.2   List of Visibility Techniques: Project and Administrative Processes

The more abstract the work, the bigger the challenge to communicate through visibility.

1. *Create work flows wherever possible.* Identify documents or files that are the focus of work. Organize them for repetitive processing. Restrict the volume of work in process, just like materials in JIT factory operations. Example: Color-code insurance claim files so that all functions to be performed in a day are finished that day. Flow the work through a cross-functional cell instead of passing them department to department.

2. *For major projects, create "war rooms."* Use blackboards, flip charts, and similar media easily visible to everyone working in the area in the normal course of work.

3. *In projects, work toward clarity of data and status when making milestone decisions.*

4. *Create visible layouts (often called open-office layouts).* Locate people as close to the action as possible. Minimize the number of closed cubicles needed for private meetings. A large "bullpen" is noisy and conducive to irrelevant communication, such as sports talk; however, in a layout of closed cubicles, no casual but relevant information is ever gained by just observing. Design layouts so that needed information is easily communicated.

5. *Locate near each other those people who should work together.* For example, locate staff who should serve production on the shop floor or close to it and visible from it, if possible. Likewise, co-locate key members of design teams to maximize visibility and face-to-face communication. All this presumes cross-functional teams.

6. *Have regular, frequent, short team status meetings.* For example, schedule morning meetings. (Meetings are kept short by having no chairs.)

7. *Post meeting schedules where everyone must see them regularly.* Limit the number and duration of formal meetings by limiting the space in which to hold them. Rule of thumb: A person spending more than one-third of his or her time in meetings cannot be prepared for them.

8. *Make files easily accessible, and establish a file discipline.* For example, in engineering design, keep master drawings or models centrally visible (even if done by computer) with a system for keeping them current. Simplify configuration management.

9. *Develop visibility discipline in systems.* For example, when a detail drawing is opened in a CAD network, "flags" show relevant changes from the configuration master. When it is closed, it must "report" to the master. Work procedures and process system design should incorporate this kind of visibility discipline into daily work.

Once the behavioral preparation is made, the steps of 5S are:

1. *Clearing and simplifying (seiri).* Remove from each workstation and from the general work floor everything not needed in the near future. "Everything" includes materials, tools, supplies, instructions, instruments—even spare machines and personal items. This is the first step in reforming daily work practices, and the workers themselves are the only ones who know what is really needed, and then some decisions are difficult. Where different workers and different shifts use the same work areas, they must agree on the issues, so they have to discuss what they are doing. In addition, the action will bring up issues beyond their control—like what to do with materials on "quality hold."

2. *Standardizing locations (seiton).* Create a place for everything and keep everything in its place. Locate anything needed regularly where it can be found quickly without search. Keep items used at the same time together—like the tools and accessories

used for a quick setup. Store anything that is rarely used or that is never needed quickly. One of the most common examples is a silhouette-marked tool storage board.

While this is all common sense, it is the second stage in reform of daily work habits and the first stage of instituting a visibility system. Since everyone who works in the same area must agree on the layout, they must also agree on how to standardize their work procedures—correct methods of work—so this reform goes much deeper than merely making the plant look neat.

3. *Cleaning (seiso).* Removing dirt, dust, and foreign materials improves cosmetics and morale, but the most important reason for cleaning is that it improves quality and safety, whether in an iron foundry or in a class 10 clean room. Those who regularly clean their areas thoroughly must also know their workplace in detail—one of the most important reasons for a rule that everyone cleans his or her own workplace. In due course, the workers will suggest and implement methods to prevent the workplace from becoming contaminated in the first place.

4. *Work habits (shitsuke).* Learning to practice 5S does not occur overnight. Everyone slips up now and then. One of the more practical ways to think of it is that teamwork should become so ingrained that everyone tries to leave the workplace in better condition than when he or she arrived. When an individual allows 5S to degrade, his or her coworkers will tell him or her. When disagreement about work processes arises, coworkers will talk about it without delay so that variations do not show up in physical evidence.

5. *Participation (seiketsu).* Many of the problems that prevent 5S from progressing are not on the shop floor but originate elsewhere. For example, an engineering change is not clear, quality requirements of the customer are not interpreted the same way, or a supplier makes an error that must be corrected on the shop floor. Therefore, 5S is not merely a shop floor consideration. Staff and executives must perform their jobs well to make 5S a reality.

Success with this system depends on executives' or leaders' setting examples. This is done in a small way by the Disney organization where the rule is that any associate who first sees a piece of trash in a theme park picks it up, even if his or her job is CEO. Just as important, by resolving the problems that are far removed from the shop floor or other direct work areas, the staff and executives support 5S, and therefore the improvement process. When all this starts to come together, it leads to visual control systems in production and elsewhere. Such an organization is achieving the necessary teamwork to operate by a "JIT system" that is appropriate to develop the type of work flow suitable to various kinds of work in which they engage.

SCHEDULING IMPROVEMENT CYCLES

In manufacturing job shops, it is frequently said that no two orders are alike and that, if work is customized, almost all jobs do differ in the details. However, no business thrives if each job is a learning experience that has not been built upon what was done previously. Learning fast and improving work quickly should be an enduring aspect of JIT. Developing a flow process, then expecting it to run for a long time without further tinkering, leads to stagnation—and the demise of the JIT concept.

Improvement cycles are repeated cycles of improvement and learning. In school, class sessions and semesters are examples of development cycles with deadlines. They stimulate learning when otherwise we would never get around to it. The purpose of improvement cycles in business is similar. The Toyota Production System is still the best example of scheduling improvement cycles. A major schedule change occurs once a month. A new assembly rate and model mix is forecasted for each assembly plant. (To change each month, equipment, layout, and workers—the total production process—must develop great flexibility to resume a high level of efficiency under different loads.)

At Toyota, major schedule patterns stated in monthly time buckets are then broken down into weeks, days, and takt times. A *takt time* is the planned time allowable between completion of each vehicle model, subassembly, and part. The takt times for parts are calculated by exploding the parts quantities needed, then dividing the time allowed in which to make them by the quantities required. Every activity needed to make each part must be accomplished within this takt time. Toyota workers then plan how to organize each workstation to do that. So do the workers at their supplying plants in Japan, but not in foreign countries.

This schedule is not executed exactly to plan. Each day the Toyota assembly plants make the mix of actual domestic orders that arrived the day before. Only about a week of domestic orders and a month of export orders are in backlog, so the daily pattern varies, and the major changes are by the month. This system sets up an improvement cycle. Every month there is reason to revise many workstations, and a few are adjusted each day. The workers themselves develop most details of next month's layouts and procedures using the tact times that are issued with the schedules.

While they do try to improve the process any time they can, the system stimulates improvement at regular intervals. The monthly schedule change is a good time to implement a backlog of suggestions, and likewise it prompts the staff to have improvement projects ready for implementation. This combination of schedule cycles, visibility, and teamwork stimulates continuous improvement—perfection of the current operation. Different cycles of major product and process change are needed to make more radical changes. As an example of this in production, a few plants make major architectural changes once a year, corresponding to major maintenance cycle turnarounds.

So how does one begin to set up an improvement cycle? A good cycle covers a natural work cycle for a plant, which should be tied to a natural work cycle for all operations including those of the customer acquisition process. (The Inductoheat Company initially determined that 2 weeks was a good work cycle because one team usually had a 2-week interval between completing customer orders ready for shipping. After efficiency improved, they cut the interval to 1 week.)

A good way to start mentally is by grouping operations into major processes: Order fulfillment, product development, customer acquisition, and service. As now done, what is the natural work cycle for each process? If the natural interval for all processes is not the same, or at least compatible, they do not integrate. An initial goal of improvement is just to achieve better time integration. (A common imbalance problem is sales cycles' prompting order closures at times that dump orders into the fulfillment process in indigestible heaps. The customers are not well served, and the operations scrambling displaces time better spent on improvement.) A time interval that makes a good improvement cycle should also be the schedule cycle.

PRODUCTION SCHEDULING

A system of scheduling must plan a process in its current condition. A mixed model assembly schedule that calls for components in small lot sizes is of little use if the production process has bottlenecks and the operations have long setup times. JIT may stimulate the streamlining of a process, but merely implementing a system of scheduling changes nothing by itself. On the other hand, if setup times are cut and lot sizes reduced, the process capability will be wasted if the scheduling system continues to call for large lot size production. Lead times remain long, and much of the waste remains in the system.

The production planning system must be flexible enough to keep up with smaller lot sizes and shorter lead times as that capability is advanced. If the system consists of rigid MRP software with weekly time buckets and lead time offsets, it no longer describes reality if the total throughput time drops to less than a week. Many companies have found that a production planning system designed for a process that no longer exists inhibits further progress.

Determining the software package to use for a particular case warrants a lengthy, in-depth discussion in itself, and thus this discussion will not be attempted here. However, many MRP packages are now not only capable of considerable systems integration but are also sufficiently flexible to allow removal of features no longer needed, such as detailed shop floor reporting or stage-by-stage inventory reporting. Software with this integration capacity and flexibility is best.

After first understanding the JIT concept, use the schedule to promote the development of processes beyond their current state by calling for challenging lot sizes and short lead times. Anticipate that the needs of planning will change not once but several times. Select a computer package that can change with the process. A few packages can even adapt to guiding the shop floor in the production of units in a lot size of one where each unit has some unique feature. (In that case customer engineering becomes a production process with a takt time just like a shop floor operation.)

If a process is capable of being reduced to small lot size repetitiveness, the planning system may prepare the operations to function by a pull system in an upcoming schedule segment. The most vital part of that planning, which is now frequently omitted, is the development of tact times for detailed planning of each workstation to execute that schedule. All lot size planning does not have to be executed by a single centralized system. The workers do some of the detail work because they are close to the detail. They may also keep the pipeline inventory down to minimum levels. A central planning system calculates the lot sizes and pipeline stock necessary for delivery from suppliers, depending on the state of the processes used by a number of suppliers. Planners who have been accustomed to detailed shop lot size planning may find this frustrating at first. They must learn to create planning data that enable the workforce to do their own planning. That is just one of the switches that make the JIT system challenging.

BIBLIOGRAPHY

Arai, Keisuke, and Kenichi Sekine: *Kaizen for Quick Changeover,* Productivity Press, Portland, Oreg., 1992. (Originally written in 1987.)

Campbell, John Dixon: *Uptime: Strategies for Excellence in Maintenance Management,* Productivity Press, Portland, Oreg., 1994.

Hall, Robert W.: *Zero Inventories,* Business One Irwin, Burr Ridge, Ill., 1983. (Contains details on scheduling and Kanban systems.)

———: *Attaining Manufacturing Excellence,* Business One Irwin, Burr Ridge, Ill., 1987.

———: *The Soul of the Enterprise,* Harper/Collins, New York, 1993. (Contains a chapter on improvement cycles.)

Hirano, Hiroyuki: *JIT Implementation Manual: The Complete Guide to Just in Time Manufacturing,* Productivity Press, Portland, Oreg., 1990. (This is a very large book valuable for details on development of cells and for ideas on process analysis forms.)

————: *5 Pillars of the Visual Workplace,* Productivity Press, Portland, Oreg., 1994.

Johansson, Henry J., Patrick McHugh, A. John Pendlebury, and William A. Wheeler: *Business Process Reengineering: Breakpoint Strategies for Market Dominance,* Wiley, New York, 1993. (Has examples that broaden the JIT concept to the entire business.)

Nikan Kogyo Shimbun: *Visual Control Systems,* Productivity Press, Portland, Oreg., 1991.

Ohno, Taiichi: *Toyota Production System: Beyond Large Scale Production,* Productivity Press, Portland, Oreg., 1988. (Originally written in Japanese in 1978.)

Nakamura, Shigehiro: *The New Standardization: Keystone of Continuous Improvement in Manufacturing,* Productivity Press, Portland, Oreg., 1993.

Sekine, Kenichi: *One-Piece Flow: Cell Design for Transforming the Production Process,* Productivity Press, Portland, Oreg., 1992.

Shingo, Shigeo: *Study of Toyota Production System,* Japan Management Association, Tokyo, 1981. (The classic, original "green book" on JIT. A later, smoother translation is available from Productivity Press, Portland, Oreg.)

————: *A Revolution in Manufacturing: The SMED System,* Productivity Press, Portland, Oreg., 1991.

Suzaki, Kyoshi: *The New Manufacturing Challenge,* The Free Press, New York, 1987.

————: *The New Shop Floor Management,* The Free Press, New York, 1993.

Shonberger, Richard J.: *Building a Chain of Customers,* The Free Press, New York, 1990.

Swartz, James B.: *The Hunters and the Hunted: A Non-Linear Solution for American Industry,* Productivity Press, Portland, Oreg., 1994.

CHAPTER 17

COORDINATING NUMERICAL AND PRODUCTION CONTROL

Editor

Carl Watkins

President, Manufacturing Information and Control Systems
Eugene, Oregon

Computer numerical control (CNC) *machinery* is causing a worldwide revolution in manufacturing. A slow but relentless shift from manual machines to CNC machines has changed the way products are produced and has consequently changed the equation for competitive production. Over the past 20 years, computerized machine tools have cut parts of better quality, in less time and at a lower cost. During that same time, computers have found their way into virtually all aspects of manufacturing companies. *Automation systems* for production control have been developed to solve specific information control needs. Computer networks now have capabilities to link these applications and their data files in expanding configurations known as manufacturing execution systems (MESs). Through this approach, production and inventory control systems can now be integrated with planning and management systems to improve overall company performance. The shop floor can be integrated with the total company automation system, communicating important information with the other sections of the company.

COMPUTER NUMERICAL CONTROL

CNC machines produce a wide variety of parts in large quantities with greatly improved quality. By adding computers to metal-cutting machines to control motorized drive tables, or cutters, it is possible to repeatedly execute certain cutting motions. Accuracy and reliability have resulted. From their introduction, the computers that control the cutting motions and activities on these machines, however, have not been standardized. The features of the control quickly became a competitive point among machine tool manufacturers. While most controls use some form of what is known as *G* and *M codes* (G01 is a linear move, M07 is coolant on), there is no real standardized code either. Early machine and control manufacturers included Bunker-Ramo, Moog, Kearney & Treaker, Bendix, Cincinnati, and Warner & Sweasey.

At first, the code to control the cutting movements was entered directly into the control. This was very tedious and error prone, so punched-tape readers were added that could read the output from teletype punches. This was an improvement, but it was still required that the part programmer do endless calculations and then type in individual codes. Programming errors often resulted from typing errors, calculating errors, or damage to the tape. This eventually led to the development of computer-assisted part-programming systems, and they acquired the name *computer-aided manufacturing* (CAM).

COMPUTER-AIDED MANUFACTURING

The first computer-aided manufacturing systems were based on a method of computer code manipulation known as *language programming*. This entailed the creation of computer language statements that were then converted into the previously described G and M code statements that the CNC understood. The idea was that it would be easier for a person to work with a familiar language than the cryptic codes used by the machine. These language-based CAM systems were a distinct improvement, but it still took a long time to learn the language, and constant practice was required to maintain proficiency. One big advantage of language systems was their minimal use of *random-access memory* (RAM). On computers at that time, a total RAM of 16K was typical. The first programming language system was Automatically Programmed Tools (APT), and it was used by the Air Force and several defense contractors including IBM. IBM was the first to offer APT commercially, but it was quickly followed by other companies offering CAM systems. MDSI was an early CAM industry leader with Compact II, available on a time-share basis on-line. McDonnell Douglas offered UniAPT, Moog had Slo-Syn, and Warner & Sweasey provided Cuts.

COMPUTER-AIDED DESIGN (CAD)

At the same time CAM system programmers were developing languages, computer applications were finding their way into the design world. *Computer-aided design* (CAD) *systems* automated the creation of new-product design and drawing. They have all but replaced the manual drawing board. CAD systems are based on a database structure, however, rather than a language structure. Lines and arcs are stored in a database that includes a starting point and an ending point, as well as other attributes.

LINKING CAD AND CAM

The computer-aided design information is the same information required by the CAM systems for development of the tool path. Naturally, people wanted to use CAD information in the CAM system, so links between CAD and CAM were developed, and the term *CAD/CAM* came into use. Unfortunately, because of the difference in system structure—database versus language—this was not an easy task. Some manufacturers still needed to have a person look at plotted drawings and manually enter data into a CAM system, even though both CAD and CAM were from the same manufacturer.

McDonnell Douglas offered UniGraphics with UniApt, Schlumberger acquired Applicon and linked it to Compact II, GE offered the CALMA system, Computervision introduced its own CAD/CAM system, and IBM offered CATIA from Dassault and CADAM. Other major players include Integraph, Gerber, Autotrol, CIMLink and MCS. Some large manufacturers, such as GM and Boeing, set out to develop their own in-house systems. These systems were the mainstay of the industry for many years, but they are gradually being replaced or updated.

IMPACT OF THE PERSONAL COMPUTER ON CAD/CAM

The personal computer revolution has fostered development of CAD and CAM systems that are more closely integrated. At the same time, companies specializing in CAD and others specializing in CAM have grown in prominence. While each has their strengths and weaknesses, many vendors now offer very capable products that are light-years ahead of systems sold as recently as 5 years ago, and these new systems sell for a fraction of the cost. CAM systems are now developed using databases designed specifically for the task of organizing data into sequential tool paths. Faster computers and continuing improvements in system capability now make it possible to program parts in a few hours or even minutes—a task that not too long ago would have taken days. Just a few years ago, in fact, it was common for machines to be sitting idle waiting for part programs. CAD/CAM has eliminated this problem for manufacturers of all sizes. CAD and CAM systems are now affordable and are actually essential to the profitable operation of any size machine shop. Popular CAD systems include AutoCAD, CADKey, MicroStation, Velum, and MicroCADAM. Popular CAM systems include SmartCAM, MasterCAM, CAMAX, and Esprit.

CAD, CAM, and automated systems for *computer-aided engineering* (CAE) analysis make it possible to quickly design better parts and create the necessary part processing programs. When needed, it makes sense to move these programs to the CNC machine tools as quickly as possible, and with a minimum of errors. Originally, this move was done with the paper tape using a teletype and punch reader. Gradually, the move came to be made by a direct connection with a serial port on the computer. Serial communication moves part programs without manual input errors or problems associated with punched tape. Not surprisingly, it has led to more elaborate systems of part program communication.

DISTRIBUTED NUMERICAL CONTROL (DNC)

Distributed (or *direct*) *numerical control* (DNC) *systems* have been used for a number of years to improve part program communication to CNC machines. The benefits are faster program downloading and uploading, elimination of input errors, ability to work quickly with more complicated part programs, and increased productivity. The CNC operator handles more information about the machining processes than just part programs. Until now CNC operators received drawings, setup sheets, routing sheets, and tooling specifications in a paper packet. These paper packets were prone to the same handling errors as punched paper tape.

Manufacturing automation is in full swing all over the world, and computerized systems are finding their way into virtually every corner of the production environment. Companies are working on, and succeeding at, reducing the time taken between product development and market release because published studies show that delay in product introduction is the single biggest cause of lost revenue and profit.

CAD, CAM, and CAE were among the first software applications to lower hardware and software cost. Also, a wide variety of application-specific programs have joined the parade. Most of us are familiar with systems for job estimating, tool tracking, *statistical process control* (SPC), manufacturing resource planning (MRP), electronic data collection, tool path verification, and many others, but one software niche that has remained undeveloped is DNC.

As noted, DNC transfers the part programs coming from the programming department to the computer control on the machine tools. On the surface, this would appear to be a simple task. In fact, there are many opportunities for mistakes to occur between the part design drawing and the manufactured part. Originally, CNC operators would read a part program and enter it manually using the control keypad (manual data input). This opportunity for a nightmare of typos was replaced by punched tape. This was an improvement and many controls were equipped with tape readers, but tape storage and handling became a problem. It is difficult to tell if a tape is the latest revision or if it is in good enough condition to go through the reader, or if tapes from one machine can be used to run another.

As the price of personal computers continues to drop, CAM systems for programming tool paths have become commonplace. The computers on which these systems run have serial communications ports designed so that data can be sent to another automated device. The NC machine control was an obvious application for personal computers, and soon these controls were being equipped with RS232 serial port connections. Now, in fact, if you want to order a tape reader with a machine control, it is usually an add-on, and the serial port is a standard feature. So DNC systems were developed to connect multiple machine controls to the serial communication ports on PCs.

Early on, tape readers and serial ports added to machine controls did not follow any standard communication protocol. This resulted in an endless variety of ways to connect the 25-pin connectors. It often seemed as if manufacturers were competing to see who could come up with the most unusual configuration. Some even used the amount of voltage in certain wires to indicate protocols to the control. Specialists developed businesses to hook up machine tools. Eventually, most DNC companies developed a library of attachment cable formats and associated communication protocols so that they could hook up to almost any machine control. A few older controls have been difficult to hook up, and only a couple of persistent DNC vendors can do all types of controls. CIMNET from JNL Industries, Greco Systems, Minifile, and Highland Technologies' Shoplink are the leading DNC systems.

Initially DNC products were little more than elaborate switch boxes used to send part programs to various machines. Features have been added that improve the operator's ability to download and upload part programs when needed. For instance, if they make program changes, they can send the changes back to the program library where "compare" utilities allow the programmer to compare changes with the original program. The programmer can decide to save the changed program as the final authorized version or keep the original. DNC terminals were added to put more control on the shop floor. Terminals usually consist of small keypads with LCD displays of a few lines. Other features included part program editors, daily activity logs for each machine, and methods of spoon-feeding large part programs.

To communicate with order machines that do not have a serial port, *behind the reader* (BTR) *boards* were developed to bypass the tape reader. They can receive information serially, then simulate the reader to provide codes to the control. Some BTRs are specific to a certain control, while others are generic and can be configured for various controls. This latter are helpful should a BTR break down, as you can have a spare on hand. CIMNET and Greco are leading BTR vendors.

It is fairly common for a DNC vendor to physically connect all machine tools into a system of branching serial cables that move part programs to machines. This is an important first step, but there are numerous important differences in the way vendors have implemented this technology. For instance, some vendors provide a way to reload binary exec files (the CNC operating system) into a machine control should the memory be erased. Without this facility, reloading an exec file can take hours.

MULTITASKING AND OTHER METHODS

Another method is *multitasking* by which some systems can simultaneously communicate from the part program library to more than one machine. In contrast, suppose a machine control has limited memory and the *spoon-feed* option is used to feed data gradually into the control's memory. Then the system cannot communicate to more than one port at a time, so no other part programs can be sent to any other machines while this spoon-feeding is taking place. Long delays are caused as production machines and operators wait for their next job.

DNC PROPRIETARY HARDWARE

Debate has arisen regarding the use of "proprietary hardware" from DNC vendors. This is based on the availability of low-priced PCs that can be used on the shop floor to replace the keypad terminals. Originally, these proprietary terminals were an economical answer to put control of the part program downloads out where operators could get to them. But now it may be cheaper to use a 386- or 486-chip-based PC. If the PC breaks down, it can be switched out with minimal inconvenience, especially if the DNC system has the ability to reload the configuration into memory.

Depending on the circumstances, a specifically designed hub or an add-on communication card with multitasking capabilities for up to 16 ports can offer better communication capabilities than a PC. This is because DOS and Windows serial communications are limited by the number of ports they can use.

DNC AND COMPUTER NETWORKS

Another DNC system uses computer networks. Some system vendors now offer products that actually run on a network. This means that a PC terminal that is truly a "node" on the network can be placed by a production machine or a group of machines. Using a network node means that the operator has access to a variety of information on the network. In comparison, if the DNC system is not on the network, the operator has access only to files on the DNC system file server. This DNC server in turn communicates with the company network where part programs and other files originate. The difference may seem small, but it has a significant impact on how the system can be used. On a network node, the operators can retrieve more than part programs. They can get setup sheets, routing sheets, part drawings, and tooling information from anywhere on the network. Instead of relying on a packet of paper sheets and drawings, they can look on the computer screen and locate all the necessary information. This is where manufacturing really starts to be productive, but without a way to control available information, it is only a start. CIMNET and Shopnet both have versions that run as network servers.

MANUFACTURING ISOLATION

Networks are becoming commonplace in most businesses, and they have been around long enough to become almost essential for administration, accounting, order processing, inventory control, and most information-handling tasks. They also are becoming the primary method of intracompany communication, starting with e-mail. Typically, the manufacturing sectors of companies have not been part of this network connection. The CAD systems are sometimes hooked in, but the CAM system almost never is, and having the shop floor on-line is extremely rare. There are many reasons cited for this circumstance. For instance, the information is different, the perception is that there is no need for other departments to see what is going on out on the floor, the machine operators have no need for other data, or production does not want other departments to introduce errors into their data. For whatever reason, the production department and its equipment are isolated within most companies—an island of separate information and communication.

Another reason manufacturing divisions have been left out of the network revolution is that often the people providing network application software to the accounting department and the sales department do not understand the needs of manufacturing. Unfortunately, there is little communication coming from manufacturing departments regarding their needs because people in manufacturing often think in terms of communicating to CNC machines that are not networked.

NETWORKS FOR MANUFACTURING

CNC machine operators have used computers longer than most employees of manufacturing companies. On the other hand, machine operators are often the last to be offered the use of new computing equipment and technology. This should change significantly because of the rapid changes in the way people think of and use computers. Manufacturing companies of all sizes are using computers for more tasks to improve productivity, responsiveness to market opportunities, and product quality. The results are improved competitiveness and increased company strength. Until recently, DNC systems were developed for a specific segment of the production environment, with a limited scope. These systems served one primary, important function—quickly getting the part program code into the machine control with a minimum of errors. The scope of DNC is about to change significantly.

GRAPHIC USER INTERFACE

The computing world has changed in the last few years, and those changes are beginning to influence the direction of DNC systems. For the average user, the biggest change in computing is in the *graphic-user interface* (GUI—pronounced gooie). This term refers to how you interact with what you see on the screen to get the computer to do what you want. For years computer operators were required to learn cryptic instructions that are typed on command lines. Users had to know certain commands just to get started with the operating system. Application software required even more extensive learning and practice, requiring typed-in text instructions. It is no wonder that many people avoided using computers.

Digital photographs are an important new capability for computer networks. "A picture is worth a thousand words," and when it reduces machine downtime and material scrap, it can be worth thousands of dollars. CIMNET's Viewer supports numerous file formats for graphics, forms, and text.

New GUI eliminates the need to type commands and learn many application-specific instructions. The increasingly popular Windows operating system GUI, and Motif in the Unix world, as well as the MAC interface, are examples. Using a pointing device, typically a mouse, to indicate selections and a button to press for confirmation, is a much simpler way than typing an entire command to make the computer respond correctly. This has two very important implications for the future of DNC systems.

The first big benefit for DNC system users is that the machine operators and part programmers can move files to and from machine controls with only a few points and clicks of a mouse. This is not much different from the way DNC commands are given with dedicated shop floor terminals, but it is just as easy. Where the dedicated terminal had a button for "download," the new systems use standard PCs as terminals with a similar download button on the screen. Using PCs as terminals is the second important benefit. Instead of offering a single application on limited hardware, a PC can do a multitude of things. This makes all the difference in the world in DNC.

DNC, as we have seen, is the solution for the problems of paper tape, which in turn was the solution for the problems of manual data input. These problems resulted in errors on the machine. Torn or incorrectly labeled paper tape wasted machine time at the least and *crashed* a machine at the worst. A well-chosen and correctly installed DNC system can successfully prevent these problems. But there are similar problems involved with the other uses of paper forms on the factory floor. Copies of part programs, drawings, or tooling sheets can be outdated, difficult to read, or incorrectly filed. Repeated blueprinting can be expensive. Job packet information, or travelers, can be slow in moving design changes to the shop floor and even slower in responding to errors or changes initiated by machine operators.

Part programs are integral to the total information package an operator needs in order to make good parts. But they are only a small portion of the complete information required. Part drawings, setup instructions, and tooling and routing sheets are also required. Computers have been the source of improvements of many manufacturing activities. CAD systems have improved design activities, and CAM systems have improved part program and CNC process development. Computerized MRP systems have helped optimize equipment usage, and bar-coded inventory tracking systems have smoothed work flow and reduced inventory. Application programs are now influencing virtually every page of information supplied to the machine operator. It makes sense that if all this information resides on computers, the operators' information ought to be available immediately, on their computer.

When computers are networked together, with a well-run communication protocol, users are immediately provided with the latest, essential accurate information. Networks help companies communicate better by making it easy to give out information and get information back. Of course, networks do not run automatically, but they are getting more independent all the time. Networks can run well with proper planning, installation, training, and support. Once on-line, most users do not know how they got along without their network. On the other hand, some companies use networks only to archive data from various applications. Getting the most from a network requires learning to use it, which takes time, thought, and cooperation.

With all the manufacturing information resident on computers and networks available to transport it to the shop floor, why are so few companies taking advantage of the "paperless factory"? One answer has to do with ease of use, but a second reason is the users' unfamiliarity with computerized networks and their benefits. Maybe the best way to explain those benefits is with a hypothetical example.

THE FUTURE OF DNC

Bob, who operates the CNC milling machines, arrives at his workstation and powers it up on a typical Monday morning. In a few seconds he is presented with a screen displaying several small pictures, or icons, that he knows accesses computer programs he may need. He clicks on one icon that presents a GUI specifically designed for machine operators. He types in his password and is immediately presented with a list of three jobs he will be working on that day. He clicks on the job at the top of the list and is given an electronic folder listing relevant files associated with this particular operation. Also listed are the part number, job number, and order number that identify this folder. First Bob clicks on the part drawing file and the view button. The latest CAD drawing from the design department is displayed on his screen. It is a part he has done before, but it includes some minor changes indicated by a link box, or a small square in red lines meant to call attention to a section of the drawing.

He clicks on the link box, and a second drawing appears with more detail and a note number. He clicks on the note number, and a small box appears indicating he should notice a change in the surface finish. Bob closes the viewer. *Closes* is a term used in the Windows environment that means he has clicked on a line button in the upper left hand corner of the screen. The result is that the viewer window goes away.

Back at his original folder screen, Bob clicks on the part program and views the text listing of code. He locates the section where a second finish cut has been added to the program. He returns to the folder and views the tool listing to verify that the tool is in the correct tool-holder position. Satisfied that everything is in order, he sets up the machine as instructed and returns to the workstation. Closing the viewer and folder windows he chooses a DNC button and clicks on download. Turning to the machine tool control, the part program is loaded and ready to run, so he dry-runs it and then proceeds to start cutting the first part.

Confident that it will run without any problems, he goes back to the computer and calls up a listing of folders in his queue. He clicks on his next job folder, and a new listing of relevant files is presented. Bob proceeds to prepare the second mill for its assigned operation. This second mill is used for specialized machining, and he notices that he will be running a more complicated job including swarf cuts. Checking the part drawing and notes, he learns that this job will require special fixturing and that a similar part has already been made. The folder includes a fixture graphic file, which he selects. A digital photograph appears showing the particular fixture, and he reads a note about the setup and where it is stored. Another file listed in the folder indicates that a voice message from the previous operator is also saved. He clicks it on and hears a lengthy recording about the best way to secure the part and how to get the digital caliper on the correct measurement point. As an added precaution, Bob calls up the tool path simulator and runs through a materials removal sequence to see how the cutter will travel relative to the proposed fixture.

Based on what he sees, Bob is concerned that one of the drilling operations will interfere with the fixture by using the specified drill and collet. Knowing that he has a longer drill of the same diameter, he goes to the part program editor and makes changes to the file. Satisfied everything will run properly, he downloads the file and starts the job. As required by QC, he uploads the modified part program to the upload directory and leaves an e-mail message asking the programmer to look at the modified file.

Bob returns to the first part, which is now finished with its cycle. At the computer he clicks on the icon for SPC. He takes several part measurements using the digital calipers, and he prepares to load the next billet. Once he has completed the required number of cycles for this job, at the workstation he indicates that the job is complete. This closes the folder for his queue. He clicks on teardown and prepares the machine. As Bob makes his indications, the system tracks the work flow of each job and part leading to final assembly. This link to the inventory control and production scheduling programs provides Bob's company with the information necessary to manage resources accurately. Direct machine monitoring on critical machines supplies data on cycle time per part, tool wear, and labor allocation.

The next job in Bob's queue is a new job that has not been made in production quantities. He views the part drawing and the part program, the tooling sheets, and the setup information. He notices that in one area a separate tool is used to fit through a gap to rough an area. This will slow the production cycle per part considerably. Using a different roughing cutter with a smaller diameter allowing a faster feed rate, he can eliminate two tool changes. Additionally, several interruptions for tool retractions will be eliminated. In the viewer window of the part drawing, Bob clicks on redline and chooses circle. He clicks on two points, and a circle is drawn where he wants to make the change. He then selects note and writes a short message. He saves the redline file, which is automatically linked on the network to the part drawing without actually changing the original. Next, he returns to the operator screen and clicks on the voice icon. Using a small handheld microphone, he records a detailed message about what he thinks would improve the cycle time for this part to be produced in large quantities. Finally, he clicks on e-mail and is presented with a list of people on the network with whom he normally communicates. He clicks on his supervisor, Fred, and the part programmer, Jim. He writes a short note indicating that he has added a voice message to the folder and asks them to review it. When he saves the message, he knows that their workstations will flash their screens indicating they have a message.

Fred is in his office reading when his computer beeps to tell him a message is waiting. He clicks on the message from Bob and immediately pulls up the folder. In the viewer, he looks at the redlined area, reads the note, and in another view window looks at the tool listing. On the network, he clicks on another icon that initiates a video conference with Jim. Fred and Jim each have video cameras and speakers attached to their workstations, which support network video conferences with up to four people. Fred opens a window containing the video image of Jim. Jim has done the same, and they are both looking at a screen with each other's image, as well as the part drawing and the tool path graphic. After a few minutes, they decide that Bob's idea is a good one. Over a lot size of 430 pieces, many hours of machine time will be saved.

They close down their conference, and Jim pulls up the part program in the CAM system. Selecting the particular section of tool path to modify, he changes the tool and recreates the roughing cycle. He saves the file as the latest revision and clicks on the icon that archives the new file in the document manager. He pulls up the appropriate folder where he substitutes the latest part program. Jim gives the folder a new revision number and clicks on the distribution icon of his information manager screen. He replaces the newly revised folder in Bob's queue and uses e-mail to notify Bob of the new folder. He adds a message, 15 minutes after Bob first put his suggestions on the network, of thanks for a job well done.

This may have sounded far-fetched, but every software and hardware feature described is currently available today, at surprisingly affordable prices. What seems unrealistic is the prospect of getting from where most of us are now to this idealistic situation. Paper is still the primary means of communicating, and some DNC systems still have problems with lost data, cryptic communication protocols, slow baud rates, and machine compatibility. Even now, many companies still use punched tape or transfer part programs by using serial ports on their programming station hooked to A-B switch boxes. Uploading an operator-modified part program is a big hassle, maybe not technically but logistically, for the people who later must deal with it. How do you document this procedure for ISO 9000 compliance, let alone make sure it gets saved in the correct directory?

And what about the current state of networks in most companies when they have a variety of systems by different vendors? The design department has their Lantastic system, while sales and accounting are on Novell, or perhaps a mainframe. The data collection system is a proprietary system, and inventory tracking is 10-Base-T. PCs are mixed with Unix and Macs. Just getting e-mail to work is a big challenge. And that is just the hardware.

Working out a way for everyone to work together is as big an implementation issue as physically installing the equipment. Making the changes necessary to get to a smoothly functioning automated environment may seem more trouble than it is worth. But there is no question that production situations like the one just described will eventually be the standard operating procedure. If you don't think so, imagine trying to compete with Bob, Fred, and Jim's company on a regular basis. A few companies are now very close to making this a reality, and many are moving in that direction.

PLAN FOR A PAPERLESS FACTORY

The first step is to have a plan for total company automation—an automation plan that starts with implementing one system at a time and that eventually coordinates all systems so that they will work together on the same or compatible equipment. Because most of us have been solving one pressing problem after another, just recognizing that this plan is a possibility is a revelation to many people. The development of *open systems* makes this possible, and standardization makes open systems possible.

The "paperless factory" of the future will have a network terminal for each machine operator. All types of files and information will be accessible immediately when needed. Data about the production process will be collected in real time and used to optimize performance. Data collection for SPC and inventory control will link to network terminals throughout the factory floor. Immediate reaction to trends toward accurate parts will improve quality and production levels.

Most manufacturing companies now have CAD and CAM systems where practical, and are in the process of adding DNC, SPC, and inventory-tracking, work flow management, or MRP. Many times, two networks are functioning side by side on the factory floor, with the information from one totally separate from the other. Just as CAD and CAM system vendors have learned how to communicate and now work on the same hardware and networks, other information systems will learn to be compatible.

MANUFACTURING EXECUTION SYSTEMS

A new term, *manufacturing execution system* (MES), is being used to describe software systems where coordination and integration between various applications are established. There has been confusion about where MES fits into the manufacturing automation picture. MES is a very general term that describes the linking of manufacturing planning systems and factory floor control systems. It can include systems for managing everything from chemical processing mixtures, to assembly line sequencing, to discrete part tracking. There is no doubt that expanding the scope and use of information, eliminating redundant data, and looking at the larger manufacturing-production picture offer greater efficiencies. In a sense, MES is akin to *computer-integrated manufacturing* (CIM), another general term for tying together design and production application systems such as CAD, CAM, and CAE.

SELECTING AND PURCHASING EQUIPMENT

The problem is, how do you buy an effective CIM system or an MES system? Most manufacturing processes are too complex to tackle all at once. Manufacturing needs to be very specific about what application software systems do and how they work. Parts need to meet exacting tolerances, so companies are buying what are known in the MES world as "point solutions" to solve specific problems. A point solution can be DNC, for instance, or CAD, CAM, SPC, or inventory tracking. From there, the manufacturer builds a networked, integrated system for processing manufacturing information.

The companies that have implemented "enterprise-wide" MES are typically very large, multiplant operations that pay consultant integrators to build customized systems. The results have been favorable, and more companies are considering implementing MES. But they can be expensive and demand a great amount of implementation and training. They may even require a complete reengineering of the company. Smaller companies will logically start with point solutions.

DNC FOR COMMUNICATION WITH THE MANUFACTURING FLOOR

Communicating with CNC machines has been the stumbling block when trying to network the factory floor. The DNC industry grew up around the need to effectively get part programs to the CNC control. The result was that DNC systems were often nonstandard proprietary products dedicated to specific tasks. In the new networked factory, DNC systems must be compatible with the other networks in the company if for no other reason than to get better use of an expensive investment in computer equipment. When choosing a DNC system, keep all your automation options open, as in open systems. Some of the important criteria for selecting a DNC system are the following:

1. The DNC system should work on an industry standard operating system such as DOS, UNIX, Windows, NT, OS/2, and the hardware that supports such systems. This can be a low-priced DNC starter system with minimal functionality, but it needs to be upwardly compatible with network upgrades.

Preferably, the DNC system should work on multiple platforms and operating systems because many companies have a variety of such systems in-house already. Unix systems are prevalent in the manufacturing industry because Unix supports more information-handling capability, but Novell networks are quickly gaining acceptance due to their lower cost. A good DNC system should support both.

2. The DNC system can communicate with all the CNC controls in the plant. This is no small feat, and the measure of a DNC system vendor's success is often tied directly to his or her success in hooking up all types of controls. It should transfer data to the control at the maximum rate the control will accept, without transmission errors. Stipulate this in the purchase order.

3. The DNC system should be capable of handling a variety of data in a wide variety of ways. This means simultaneous, real-time, multitasking communications to all CNCs on the network. In other words, can any operator request a download at any time, even if someone else is currently spoon-feeding a large program? This also means reloading the binary exec program for the machine control if power fails and computer memory is lost. Essentially, the DNC capability should be powerful enough that any part program can be run at any CNC machine whenever wanted. Do not assume that all DNC systems are the same because they all have different features, and some are better than others.

MICS, THE MES POINT SOLUTION

A *manufacturing information control system* (MICS) is an MES that emphasizes integration of the factory floor by extending the company network through a DNC. An MICS makes the paperless factory possible by providing the machine operator all the information necessary to make a part. This includes part programs through a DNC, but it also includes part drawings, setup, routing and tooling sheets, digital photos, data collection, and bar-code tracking.

The InfoMaN screen from CIMNET's Folders (Fig. 17.1) product shows the basics of MICS data handling. Files from various application systems such as CAD, CAM, or a tool manager are selected and added to the electronic folder. CIMNET Folders' WorkMaN screen (Fig. 17.2) is easy for the machine operator to use. As a workplace module, it mirrors the process now happening with paper. Operators view files for their next job, download and/or upload files with DNC features, and report on machine activity. Larger-than-normal "buttons" support touch screens. Machine monitoring with CIMNET's FactMaN (Fig. 17.3) records the activity of each machine and reports the results in bar or pie graphs. Monitoring can also be linked directly to the control to record spindle on-off or cycle start-stop.

An essential part of an MICS is the collection of information from the shop floor. This includes monitoring machine usage so production management will know immediately what stage of a job is completed. It also reports on the amount of time each machine has been used for setup, cycle time, teardown, cleanup, and downtime.

In our hypothetical job shop, the supervisor, Fred, can periodically check the current status of each machine and get a report showing how much time is spent on each task. He can ask (query) the system for the usage of machine groups and the status of a particular machine tool's queue of folders. He can monitor quality-control SPC data for a machine or cell or automatically rearrange a group of machine's queues based on updated information from an MRP system.

The primary function of MES, and particularly MICS, is the coordination of data. The different applications described above potentially generate hundreds of files every

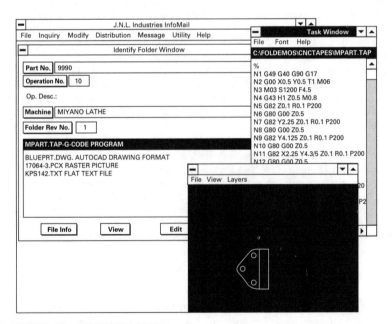

FIGURE 17.1 CIMNET InfoMaN screen.

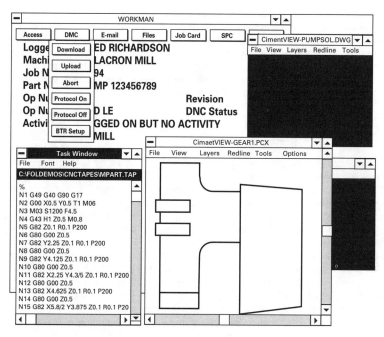

FIGURE 17.2   CIMNET WorkMaN screen.

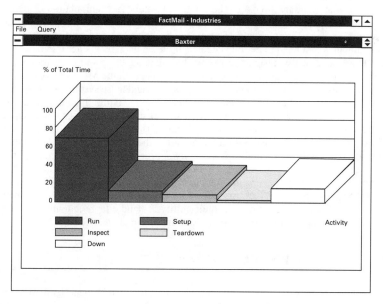

FIGURE 17.3   Machine monitoring.

day. While this replaces an equal number of pieces of paper, it can still be overwhelming. Many people who work in the production department where there isn't a computer system have little time to use their skills because they are looking for pieces of paper, searching for files, organizing information, copying documents, and carrying them to other workers. A good MES is designed to eliminate many of these tasks and make others easier. One of the basic purposes of such a system is to handle lots of data. Without a way to handle volumes of files quickly, the benefits are lost.

RELATIONAL DATABASES

The key to handling the growing mountain of data generated by software application programs is a *rational database management system,* commonly called an RDBMS. The RDBMS is able to create an information link, through a "pointer." The system assigns attributes to the data, and locates them in its native directory and/or subdirectory. It does not actually copy the data files, so redundant data is not created. This is very important because redundant data will quickly fill up memory storage devices, especially if graphic files are included.

The major advantage of a RDBMS is the speed with which it can find data files. A scheme called *index–sequential-access method* (ISAM) is used to access information. This access method allows the computer to sort information by multiple-key fields, or indexes. This kind of search, called *binary,* can be changed according to your needs. The alternative is to search files *linearly,* or one at a time in sequence. With limited numbers of files, the difference in speed is negligible, but with 1000 items in a list, the binary search is 50 times faster, and with a million items, it is 25,000 times faster.

Relational databases that can be customized to your needs are readily available. DBase IV, Paradox, and Fox Base are well-known examples. But these require a database programming expert on staff, and even then, customizations must be made in the fourth-generation language (4GL) of the relational database. Manipulation of data by such a system requires significantly more computing time, disk access time, and disk space, and also it performs slowly. These drawbacks are caused by instructions for search commands that need to be translated each time a data item is accessed.

An RDBM specifically designed for shop floor data handling and written in a third-generation language, such as C, handles more data faster. Some MES vendors use off-the-shelf databases as the foundation for their products, and these systems are applicable where file size and number are expected to remain small. To minimize use of network computing resources, they will require a network workstation to be a fast 486 computer with a large hard drive so files can be saved locally. This can cause problems because data files can be modified at one station but not all of the others. The important point to understand is that with files coming from many sources, an information management system is essential.

Another type of file management system is based on *flat file technology.* Although not an MES, these products help organize information in a Windows environment. Without a RDBMs structure, however, their ability to handle large amounts of data is limited. These can be used where file quantities are minimal and file size is small.

DIRECT BENEFITS: WHAT IS THE PAYBACK?

Conceptually, it is hard to disagree that an MICS system can be beneficial. What are these benefits specifically? Mostly, the benefits are based on work being performed more effectively. MES vendors typically claim an average savings of approximately 25 percent of the time it takes to complete standard tasks without the MES. There are a number of ways this can be calculated, but direct cost savings for manufacturers may result from improved machine utilization and the elimination of scrapped or reworked parts. If production machine operators can find information quickly and know that it is correct, they can complete machine preparation much faster. Digital photographs of setups will typically decrease setup time by 50 percent. Documents are prepared and distributed faster, allowing more care to make sure information is correct. A reasonable result is an additional hour of production from each machine per shift.

Another benefit, not easily estimated, is improved response time to market changes or customer needs. A company can do a better job overall. For instance, if the MRP system is scheduling jobs with unreliable data, the benefits are significantly reduced. Errors and delays caused by paper handling can quickly render a tight schedule inaccurate.

Industry is growing aware of the need to use our resources, materials, people, and machines much more effectively. Getting an extra hour a day from only 3 machines can save $37,500 a year assuming a burden rate of $50 a day for each machine working 250 days a year ($50/day/machine × 250 days/year × 3 machines). An MICS supporting 3 machines should require only about a $15,000 investment, installed. This includes 3 shop floor workstations on a network and training the operators. Also the reduced scrap and rework costs will improve the direct monetary benefits.

OPPORTUNITY FOR REENGINEERING

"Reengineering the corporation" refers to the process of making basic changes in the way a company gets its jobs done. Rather than trying to continuously improve established ways of working, the company as a whole steps back and rethinks their whole process. A company can often eliminate wasted tasks, introduce new technologies, improve responsiveness to customers, and ultimately become more competitive and profitable. This is not without much effort and energy by everyone involved. It usually requires a cooperative atmosphere that begins with a "buy-in" for all employees and contributions by the company leaders, extending through the whole organization. It is a long-term process with many steps and a clear picture of where the company wants to go. Adding an MICS to the production capability is an opportunity to start the reengineering process. In the implementation of an MICS project, a company can move from old ways with ancient paper-oriented methods to new technologies with a paperless factory.

As easy to install as any software product appears to be, you should always plan for training and implementation. Any time a new process replaces an old one, there can be resistance. Computers are frightening to some people, and operators especially must feel confident that they will not make mistakes. No one wants to be responsible for a botched job, particularly when it involves expensive parts within tight tolerances. Allocate plenty of time for everyone to understand the system and their role in it before going on-line. Vendors and their VARs should offer several levels of training ranging from training disks to in-house custom training classes.

Ideally, information within a company should be accessible to everyone who needs it. Creating such an environment is a process that will take time and effort. The MES is the way of the future for manufacturers, whether it is a collection of point solutions or as a single system implemented company-wide. Manufacturing companies are making improvements necessary to respond quickly to market changes. This means carrying minimal inventory and building to sales as much as possible. Automated order entry tied directly to production with JIT part supply lines linked to CAD/CAM/CAE and DNC can produce parts faster than ever before. Concurrent engineering virtually begs for such a networked communication environment. Add to that systems for resource planning, SPC, and numerous other systems from process simulation to cost analysis. It is now possible to truly optimize the functioning of an entire company.

WHAT WILL THE FUTURE BE LIKE?

One trend is clear: Computers and software applications are spreading throughout manufacturing, as well as almost every other aspect of our lives. More and more information and data will be available, to the extent that it can be overwhelming. A proactive attitude can make the challenge of dealing with all this data manageable, and DNC, MICS, and MES systems can help. In fact, they will probably be essential. While some aspects of the scenario described, such as video conferencing, are a long way off, eventually these tools will come into wide use. A true concurrent engineering environment will require the active use of such tools. Manufacturing is an integral part of the product development cycle. Current publicity for an "information superhighway" is just an indication of where we are headed technologically. Manufacturers should be prepared to travel that road.

SECTION 4

INVENTORY CONTROL

CHAPTER 18
INVENTORY CONTROL RECORDS AND PRACTICES

Editor
Gerald A. Sanderson, CFPIM, CIRM
President, Gerald A. Sanderson, Inc.
Roeland Park, Kansas

The practical aspects of managing and controlling inventory involve more than order-quantity formulas and inventory planning models. A successful inventory management process translates techniques into daily tactical responses to customer demands and business needs. This requires an understanding of how inventory functions support business objectives. The inventory investments affect the profits, return on assets, and customer service. Additionally, the physical aspects of storing and handling inventory present logistical problems. Maintaining accurate and timely inventory information is critical to successful planning and execution. Planning systems, formed by bringing the functional elements of inventory management together, depend on reliable and complete information. This chapter discusses inventory management concepts using basic terminology and simple examples. Chapter 19, "Inventory Control Theory," in this handbook will cover the mathematics and statistics that relate to inventory planning and scheduling.

INVENTORY FUNCTIONS

Understanding the purposes of tracking inventory leads to an appreciation of how to control and physically manage this investment. The major concern about inventory should be to have the right investment that meets strategic business objectives. Inventory is frequently the gauge used to make judgments about the effectiveness of a firm's planning, manufacturing, and control. Companies often compare inventory levels and turnover rates. However, making direct comparisons assumes that all companies have the same business strategies and are managed in the same way. Comparing industry averages can lead a company to mediocrity.

The basic reason for controlling inventory is to establish a buffer between the variations in supply and demand. Inventory can decouple these forces and contribute to the efficient flow of products through the plant. Marketing provides a sales forecast that frequently varies from the actual customer demands. Manufacturing experiences schedule changes because the sales forecasts do not always match the customer's actual demand. Sometimes component shortages come from machine breakdowns, absenteeism, and supplier delivery problems. Economic and political situations can make continuity of supply very difficult to achieve. Available production capacity may not be sufficient to meet peak seasonal demands, forcing the company to produce before there is a need. Lot sizes, inventory cost, lead times, and quality influence a manufacturer's ability to produce efficiently and effectively.

Six Functions of Inventory

Inventory should fulfill six functions that work to decouple supply and demand and cushion the impact of some variations that occur in the business. These functions are buffer, anticipation, hedge, transportation, lot size, and lead time inventory. If inventory does not accomplish at least one of these functions, it becomes excess and waste. Inventory exists because a company usually cannot produce exactly what the customer wants immediately. A discussion of each function will explain the areas of variation and waste that are the fundamental cause of excess inventory.

Buffer Stock Inventory.   This inventory helps decouple the impact of the variations in both the demand and supply of materials, products, and components. *Safety stock* is another name for buffer stock. Buffer stock should cover the differences between actual demand and the sales forecast, or between the actual supply time and the planned lead time.

The graph in Fig. 18.1 shows an example of both demand and supply variation and how inventory can help to prevent stock-outs. Safety stock should reduce stock-outs and shortages and contribute to achieving a high level of customer service. The sawtooth-shaped inventory-level lines of the demand and the supply variability examples start at the same points. The slope of the inventory level shows the rate of change in the demand or sales. When the inventory reaches the order point, an order would be issued to replenish stocks within the lead time of four periods. After receiving the replenishment lot size, the inventory increases sharply.

The demand rate variability part of the graph shows a change in the rate of demand but no change in the replenishment lead time. When the rate of demand increases, shown by the change in the slope of the demand line, the safety stock covers the additional requirements. Conversely, because demand slows and the replenishment order arrives within the lead time, safety-stock inventory does not get used. Typically, a company should expect to use the safety stock about one-half of the time.

Frequently, especially on purchased materials, significant variations occur in the lead time, and deliveries become unreliable. The graphic of supply variability shows the stock-replenishment time taking longer than the planned lead time. Demand stays at a constant rate. If the delivery time takes longer than planned, the safety stock becomes safety time supply and prevents a stock-out. When inventory is a buffer for the variation in lead time that causes late deliveries, it is frequently called *safety time supply.* A discussion about figuring out the buffer-stock quantity and time supply comes in a later section of this chapter. Figure the amount of buffer stock directly by measuring the variability in the demand quantity or supply lead time.

Anticipation Inventory.   Some manufacturers have to accumulate inventory ahead of known future events because the requirements cannot be met with the available production capacity. This anticipation inventory is often used to decouple the impact of

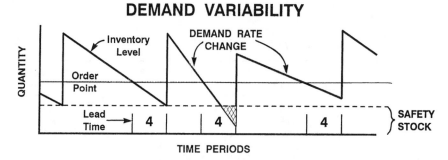

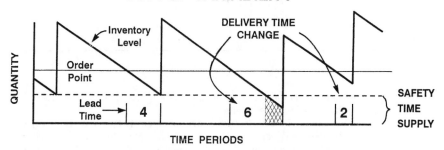

FIGURE 18.1 Buffer-stock inventory.

seasonal sales, promotions, or planned interruptions in supply. Generally, the types of supply interruptions are plant shutdowns for vacations, model changeovers, strikes, construction, maintenance, and other known events.

Table 18.1 illustrates an example of a plant with a maximum capacity of 2000 units per period. The low point of unit demand is 500, and the high is 4000. Additionally, a scheduled plant closing appears in period 10 because of construction. Here, the strategy is to build up enough inventory to meet the demand in every period. Forecasted demand in periods 5 and 6 exceeds capacity. In "anticipation" of the demand, production is planned in periods 2 and 3. The inventory in periods 2 through 5 is anticipation inventory. Inventory projected in period 9 is maintained in anticipation of the shutdown for plant construction in period 10.

Hedge Inventory.   The function of this inventory is to help the business overcome random future events that are uncontrollable. Hedge inventory is frequently confused with anticipation inventory because both involve positioning the company to respond to a future event. But the difference is the amount of control and the degree of certainty present during the decision process. Hedge inventory can help the management team carry out business strategies and protect the company against threatening situations or risky opportunities. Reasons for building a hedge inventory include a possible strike at a critical supply source or political instability of a country that exports critical raw materials.

Demand is very unpredictable when introducing a new product. Buffer stock should meet the "normal" variations in the expected demand, but management may want to have additional inventory to ensure that customer demand gets filled during this critical

TABLE 18.1   Anticipation Inventory

Production capacity = 2000 per period
Beginning inventory = 1000 units
Plant construction in period 10

Period	Demand forecast	Production schedule	Projected inventory
1	500	0	500
2	500	2000	2000
3	1000	2000	3000
4	2000	2000	3000
5	3000	2000	2000
6	4000	2000	0
7	2000	2000	0
8	1000	1000	0
9	1000	1500	500
10	500	Plant down	0

time. Purchasing extra inventory because of rumors of an expected price increase is a frequent application of hedging inventory.

Another distinguishing characteristic of hedge inventory is that management judgment dominates the decision processes. Anticipation inventory should be based on a known seasonal pattern of requirements, known capacity, and predictable events. The amount of buffer stock should depend on the measured variation of supply and demand. However, a rumored transportation strike may force a management decision on how much hedge inventory to purchase to keep the plant operating. This is a direct management decision.

Hedge inventory decisions and control depend largely on documentation and follow-up by management. Management should specify the purpose of the hedge inventory, the inherent assumptions, and the duration of the decision. Hedge inventory implies significant risks and uncertainty. Management should evaluate these decisions routinely to avoid excess inventory. Every decision should include a plan of how to phase out the hedge inventory when the reasons for it pose no future risks.

Transportation Inventory.   This inventory, sometimes called *pipeline stock,* is the materials and products in transit between locations in a distribution system between plants or to customers. The function of this inventory is to relocate inventory to the point of need. The value of the transportation inventory can be considerable for many companies. Controlling and planning for this inventory must take into consideration the factors of time, distance, and mode of transportation.

Transportation inventory is calculated primarily as a function of the in-transit time between locations. Table 18.2 illustrates how in-transit time affects inventory investment. A key variable in the formula is the in-transit lead time because the other elements of annual demand, unit cost, and annual time periods should remain relatively constant. Using faster modes of transportation normally reduces the in-transit lead time but could also increase distribution costs. A company could reduce the in-transit time by using airfreight instead of rail service. Transportation inventory would likely decrease, but transportation costs could increase significantly. Therefore, the level of transportation inventory should reflect the costs of transportation. Management should evaluate the

TABLE 18.2 Transportation Inventory

Annual demand	$= 20,000$
In-transit lead time	$= 10$ days
Unit cost	$= \$50$ per unit
Annual time periods	$= 250$ days

$$\text{Annual demand} \times \text{unit cost} \times \frac{\text{in-transit lead time}}{\text{annual time periods}} = \text{Average transportation inventory}$$

$$20,000 \text{ units per year} \times \$50.00 \text{ per unit} \times \frac{10 \text{ days}}{250 \text{ days}} = \$40,000 \text{ per year}$$

total costs related to the trade-off between inventory-carrying costs and transportation costs when deciding how best to manage this inventory function.

Lot Size Inventory.   Lot size inventory is frequently called *cycle stock* because it relates to the inventory quantity used between replenishment cycles. The function of lot size inventory is to minimize the total costs of carrying the inventory and the costs of procurement. The trade-off is between the costs to carry the inventory resulting from the lot size and the costs of procurement that occur for each order.

Procurement costs include ordering, preparation, setup, changeover, and cleanup costs. Decreasing these costs of replenishment should lead to smaller lot sizes and a decrease in the inventory investment. This is why reducing setup cost is so important in the application of value-added manufacturing processes.

As a rule, the lot size inventory should approximate one-half the size of the replenishment quantity when usage is stable and consistent over time. Figure 18.2 illustrates the relationship between the quantity of the lot and the resulting average inventory. Immediately after the receipt of the order quantity, the lot size inventory is at a maximum; and just before the receipt, it is at its low point. It is generally assumed that the demand rate will on average be constant. Divide the order quantity by 2 to obtain the average inventory.

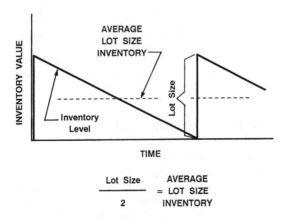

FIGURE 18.2 Lot size inventory.

A large order quantity distributes the replenishment costs over more units and keeps unit costs low. However, the resulting larger lot size inventory increases inventory-carrying costs. The opposite occurs by making the lot sizes small; inventory investment and cost are lower, but more frequent ordering results in higher fixed costs per unit. The inventory replenishment section, later in this chapter, discusses these cost relationships thoroughly. Lot size inventory also has the function of conserving limited capacity. This happens when the time to produce all the items and make the planned setups exceeds the total time available. Producing larger lot sizes can result in fewer setups and save time.

Lead Time Inventory.   Work-in-process in a manufacturing company is a good example of this type of inventory. When lead times are long, the quantities of inventory tied up in the manufacturing process can be significant. This inventory results from the amount of time it takes to produce the order quantity. The function of this inventory is to decouple manufacturing operations and the different orders on the shop floor. Lead time inventories are semifinished goods waiting between operations, moving between operations and in queues, staged in front of operations. This type of inventory also includes the materials maintained during setup and run times.

Long lead times for purchased materials influence inventory differently. A supplier may encounter all the same inventory considerations and functional issues, but the results may be manifested in their order quantities and delivery reliability. These factors affect the customer's buffer and lot size inventory levels. Longer lead times generally increase the possibility for poor delivery, requiring more buffer stock. Reducing setup times, queues, and move times results in shorter lead times and decreases in inventory levels. More discussion on the elements of lead time will come later in this chapter.

Summary of Inventory Functions

The function of inventory is to compensate for a wide range of situations faced by a manufacturing company. Buffer stock lessens the effect of variations between the demands of forecasts and customer orders and the timing between planned and actual supply. If capacity is limited, inventory accumulated in advance can cover the expected demand using anticipation inventory. Inventory can also help a company overcome situations of high risk and little control by creating hedge inventory to help reach strategic objectives. The function of transportation inventory is to maintain the flow of goods through the distribution system at reasonable transportation costs. Lot size inventory should decouple the fixed ordering costs and free capacity by requiring fewer setups to produce large lot sizes. Lead time inventory should decouple manufacturing operations and allow time for production and scheduling. These techniques, when applied to the total inventory, provide management with ways to estimate how inventory levels should change. All inventory should be maintained for one or more of these inventory functions; otherwise, the inventory is a waste of important resources.

PERPETUAL AND PERIODIC INVENTORY

Financial inventory accounting relies on either a perpetual or periodic method to evaluate or track inventory. A perpetual inventory system records inventory transactions as they occur and reports the results regularly. Most manufacturing businesses, except those that are very small, use a perpetual inventory method. Alternatively, a periodic inventory accounting system uses a count of the actual inventory balances. The physical inventory figures are required for checking the perpetual inventory and to determine

TABLE 18.3 Inventory and Profit

	Expected gross profit	Ending inventory increased	Ending inventory decreased
Beginning inventory	$ 5,000,000	$ 5,000,000	$ 5,000,000
Receipts	6,000,000	6,000,000	6,000,000
	$11,000,000	$11,000,000	$11,000,000
Ending inventory	− 4,000,000	↑− 5,000,000	↓− 3,000,000
Disbursements	$ 7,000,000	$ 6,000,000	$ 8,000,000
Sales revenue	$10,000,000	$10,000,000	$10,000,000
Gross profit	$ 3,000,000	$ 4,000,000	$ 2,000,000

the status of the business over monthly, quarterly, or yearly periods. The financial value of inventory is a key factor when figuring the profitability of the business. The equation:

Beginning inventory + receipts of inventory − ending inventory = disbursements

is the way to compute the cost of goods sold for company profit.

Receipts are all additions to inventory, including materials purchased and the labor and overhead added during production. *Disbursements* are the costs of the products sold to customers.

In a periodic inventory system, a physical inventory at the end of each period determines the value of the inventory on hand and consequently the cost of goods sold. The cost of all purchases and the production payroll and expenses during this period are added to the beginning inventory. Subtracting the disbursements from total sales revenue gives the gross profit for the business.

Using a periodic system for financial accounting obscures what is happening to the business between the periodic inventory counts; however, perpetual inventory accounting does not necessarily eliminate the need for an annual physical inventory. Any manufacturing company with ongoing inventory accuracy problems usually requires an annual physical inventory. The annual physical inventory is a check on the reported profits of the business. Table 18.3 shows how the annual physical inventory can impact the profit of the company. A mismatch between the physical inventory count and the perpetual inventory balance affects profitability. Problems with inventory accuracy and control, exposed by the physical inventory, show on both the company's profit-and-loss statement and the balance sheet.

ABC ANALYSIS

Most inventory situations involve controlling many different kinds of items, with each having a different impact on cost. The physical characteristics of items can be a major concern because of short shelf life, special storage (refrigeration), space, and materials handling. ABC Analysis is a tool that management uses to categorize materials and components into workable groups. The small A item group contains the items that have the most significant impact on the inventory investment. In contrast, the large C item group consists of items that usually have little consequence on the investment. The ABC Analysis is the application of Pareto's principle of analysis and segregation to the inventory investment.

In 1896, Vilfredo Pareto studied the distribution of wealth in Italy and found that the control of a large amount of the wealth was in the hands of very few people and that conversely, the vast majority of the population had only a small amount of the wealth. He later found this phenomenon existed in many situations. For inventory analysis, this means that the A item group is where 80 percent of the investment is concentrated in 20 percent of the different inventory items. The B and C item groups represent 20 percent of the investment but 80 percent of the inventory items. The focus should be to concentrate inventory management resources on the A items—the 20 percent that will likely have 80 percent of the financial impact on the inventory investment. The remaining 80 percent of the items should be divided into B and C groups. The B category usually represents 30 percent of the items and 15 percent of the value; the C category is 50 percent of the items and 5 percent of the value. Any particular inventory distribution will be managed according to some variation on this general rule, but the rule is an excellent starting point when deciding how to categorize the aggregate inventory. Other categories to identify special inventory situations, like discontinued or obsolete items, are frequently added to the ABC groupings.

ABC Analysis Technique

Table 18.4 uses 10 items to explain the technique:

Step 1 is to calculate the annual usage in terms of dollars for each item.

Step 2 is to divide the annual usage in dollars by the total annual usage in dollars for all the items. This gives the percent of total value that each item number represents.

Step 3 sequences the parts from high to low by annual dollar usage.

Step 4 accumulates the percentages.

Management then decides which items go into the A, B, and C groups. After adding any special inventory categories, management should have a good profile of the inventory investment.

Figure 18.3 shows the result of the analysis in graphic form. Any group of inventory items will likely show some difference in the way the three groups break down in relationship to number of items and dollar value. Some companies add an additional group for special items like obsolete or discontinued items written off the financial books and carrying no inventory value. Each group classification gives management an opportunity to apply specific inventory policies to better control the inventory investment and functionality.

ABC Application

The A items should receive the most attention from management. Management should frequently review the inventory function of this group. Most of the time and resources of the inventory management team should be directed to these high dollar impact inventories. For A items, the inventory record accuracy should be the best, lot sizes the smallest, and lead times the shortest. Management should use the best and most detailed inventory management techniques on this important group that could involve using statistical analysis to set buffer-stock levels. There should be special efforts to reduce lot

TABLE 18.4   ABC Analysis

Step 1

Item	Unit cost		Unit usage		Dollar usage	Percent usage
1	4.40	×	1250	=	5,500	1.1
2	1.50		2000		3,000	0.6
3	.35		20000		7,000	1.4
4	20.00		5000		100,000	20.0
5	15.00		2000		30,000	6.0
6	.15		10000		1,500	0.3
7	150.00		2000		300,000	60.0
8	25.00		1000		25,000	5.0
9	200.00		100		20,000	4.0
10	2.00		4000		8,000	1.6

Total annual usage = $500,000

Step 2

$$\text{Percent annual usage} = \frac{\text{dollar usage for item}}{\text{total annual usage in dollars}} = \text{percent usage}$$

$$= \frac{5500}{500,000} = 1.1 \text{ percent}$$

Steps 3 and 4

Item	Dollar usage	Percent usage (step 3)	Cumulative percent (step 4)	ABC class
7	300,000	60.0	60.0	A
4	100,000	20.0	80.0	A
5	30,000	6.0	86.0	B
8	25,000	5.0	91.0	B
9	20,000	4.0	95.0	B
10	8,000	1.6	96.6	C
3	7,000	1.4	98.0	C
1	5,500	1.1	99.1	C
2	3,000	0.6	99.7	C
6	1,500	0.3	100.0	C

sizes and lead times and more frequent checks to compare the actual inventory balances with the records. These *cycle counts* help to ensure that the inventory records are both accurate and timely. Frequently a company will plan to receive A items at the point of use and just in time for consumption or sale. The A items should be checked more frequently than others and reviewed by higher management. This helps management keep hands-on control and better understand the inventory investment.

Conversely, the B and C items should receive less attention because most of the inventory management resources should be assigned to the A items. Planning the B and

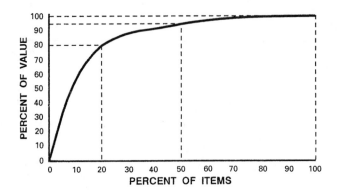

CLASS	ITEMS	PERCENT ITEMS	PERCENT DOLLARS
A	7 and 4	20.0	80
B	5, 8 and 9	30.0	15
C	10, 3, 1, 2 and 6	50.0	5

FIGURE 18.3   ABC Analysis curve.

C groups should be more routine and take less time. This requires carrying some additional B item inventory and even more C items. Some companies stock heavily on C
items so they do not run out of materials. The value of this inventory is usually very low
so the risk of financial loss is minor. These companies use simple and easily managed
methods, like the two-bin system, to take care of stock replenishment. Other inventory
groups that might become discontinued and obsolete should be routinely analyzed with
the purpose of reducing their impact on the inventory investment. ABC Analysis provides management the means to selectively apply inventory policies and processes to
the parts and components that will likely have the most impact on the business.

ABC Analysis has other applications. Ranking items in high to low sequence,
according to unit cost, is a way to identify expensive items with high unit cost. It may
be appropriate to use secured storage and tighter control procedures to reduce theft or
improve record accuracy for these high-unit-cost items. This type of analysis can guide
cost reduction efforts to bring down the unit price of materials and components.
Extending the annual usage in units by the storage cube for each can give management
an overview of possible warehousing problems and help when planning storage areas.
The ABC Analysis process applies in many situations, including the establishment of
buffer, lot size, and lead time inventory policies.

Summary of ABC Analysis

ABC Analysis is a valuable tool for inventory management. It directs attention to the
items that should receive the most control. The technique helps management apply the
resources of time and talent where it will have the greatest benefit.

Materials and components in the C item group still require planning and control, but
they use less time and effort than the other item groups. This may require carrying more

buffer stock or ordering larger lot sizes. For the C group, additional inventory reduces planning time while still maintaining appropriate service levels. This frees time for more detail planning of critical A and B class components and assemblies.

ITEM CODING

Every different item in the inventory should carry an identifier that distinguishes it from all the others. These identifiers are usually called *part* or *item numbers*. There are many schemes to construct item codes, each with advantages and disadvantages. Companies rarely change their item coding scheme because of the amount of work and complexity involved. However, it is still important that a policy is in place that details the authority and rules concerning the issuing of item codes.

Item Code Examples

The variety of item coding schemes is overwhelming.

Nonsignificant Codes.   These codes have nothing in them that would help a person know what the code is identifying. The code does not describe the part. The advantage of this type of approach is that assigning a code is simple and each identifier is unique. Numbers are usually used when a coding system is based on nonsignificant identifiers. The code numbers can be assigned automatically in random or sequential order.

Significant Coding Systems.   Significant coding systems include some key characters in the identifier that gives the user information about the items. Some or all of the characters, numeric or alphabetic, tell the user about the part. As an example, 1 alphabetic position in an item code can carry 26 different meanings. Coding systems that have significance in the item identifier require more controls and management concerning their assignment and use in a company.

Mnemonic Codes.   Mnemonic codes use alpha characters arranged to jog the memory. Consider an item coding scheme for a company that manufactures children's wagons and tricycles: WG036RS and TC024SM. These codes identify a wagon (WG) that is 36 inches long and customized as a red special (RS) and a tricycle (TC) with a 24-inch wheelbase that is a standard model (SM).

Numeric Codes.   "Significance codes" can also be developed with numeric characters. For a manufacturer of glass containers, the numeric code 0210008 could mean smoke glass (02), square shape (100), in the 8-ounce (08) size. The extreme of significance is probably using the item's name or description as the item code. Taking the idea of significance to this level of detail can limit the flexibility and expansion of the item coding system.

Random Codes.   Part numbering scenarios range from the completely random assignment of numbers and letters to every digit's carrying a special meaning. The prudent approach would be to find a compromise between the two extremes that works well for all involved. Most everyone in a company will use item codes. Consider the person who picks materials in the warehouse, the operator on the shop floor, and planners and order-entry personnel who use the item codes daily. An example of a compromise on the significance of the item coding system is the identifier 045732. The first two numbers of the item number designate a group of items like glass containers, plastic containers, or closures (lids, caps) or other grouping. The remaining digits 5732 are unique non-significant numbers assigned sequentially.

Code Expansion

The system should be expandable. Establishing an item coding system based on the extensive use of characters that have specific meaning can limit flexibility when adding new item identifiers. The coding system should be expandable and allow for new items added to the business over time. Item codes that use characters with a high degree of significance to the user can inhibit expansion by reducing the potential number of unique item codes.

Uniqueness.   Each item should have a unique identifier. It makes little sense to have the same item code for two physically different items. When the fit, form, or function of parts is different, they should have different item codes. Parts that have only slight differences might have some segment of the item's number remain the same, but different characters should be used as a suffix to maintain part separation and uniqueness.

Brevity.   Use as few alphanumeric characters as possible. An item coding policy that requires 10 or more characters significantly increases the difficulty of remembering and using the part numbers. For long part identifiers, it is common to find groups of significant digits separated by dashes. A telephone number is a good example. The last four digits of your phone number identify your home or office. The other numbers include a three-digit prefix that identifies the zone in your city or type of service. The area code that positions a person within North America may also key to special telephone services. For manufacturing control and usefulness, staying in a general range of 7 to 10 characters, with some significance, seems operable in most situations. When the item code is too short, expansion can become a problem.

Significance.   Each item code should have some significance. Item codes assigned sequentially or randomly can result in part numbers that are difficult to use. They usually require referring frequently to the item master records for identification. Item coding systems that use blocks of alphanumeric characters to identify item groups helps people to be more productive and efficient. However, part identifier systems that are completely significant can run out of unique numbers.

Usability.   The item code should be usable for all parts of the information system. It should not be necessary to enter dashes to separate characters of a long part number when processing inventory transactions. Entering dashes reduces efficiency and presents opportunities for data errors. A similar problem arises when item identifiers use a combination of numeric and alpha characters for numbers and letters. The alpha character O is easily confused with the numeric digit zero, and the lowercase L can be confused with the number one, and S can be confused with a five. Avoid these and similar characters in item identifiers. If dashes or other alphanumeric symbols are essential to a part numbering system, it is a good rule to always place them in the same position in the identifier. This helps eliminate confusion.

Modern inventory management systems can ameliorate many problems related to processing long and complex item codes. Most good inventory systems check item numbers against the item master database before updating records. The key to an effective and efficient item coding system is to be sure that they are easy to use, yet flexible for the long term.

Bar Coding

A *bar code* is an item identifier made from a series of lines of various thicknesses and spacings that can be read by an optical reader and transmitted electronically to a data collection device. The best example of a bar code is the *Universal Product Code* (UPC) in grocery stores. For inventory management, bar coding items and documents can improve productivity. Information can be transcribed faster and more accurately for transmission directly to the information system. Both accuracy and speed improve dramatically.

A bar code can include much more information than just a unique item identifier. Included in the bar codes can be lot or batch numbers for tracing and selecting material. Current bar-code technology can instantly scan and transmit several pages of information unique to an inventory item. However, except for a few elements of information, the bar code needs to be processed through computer software that will translate the code into readable data. Many handheld bar-code readers can carry out this task conveniently.

Phantom and Pseudocodes

Sometimes special item identifiers are set up to help the scheduling and planning functions of production. The names for these item codes are *phantom* and *pseudo codes*. Phantoms usually reflect a manufacturing stage of an item that requires scheduling; however, it is not something made with the intention of being stocked in inventory. Phantoms are used mainly in scheduling and reporting. An example of a phantom is the item code for a tank of a formulated mixture, with a short shelf life, which immediately goes into several different sizes of final containers. The mixed ingredients and the final packaged products all have normal item identifiers. A phantom item code identifies the tank of formulated product. Formulated product in the tank requires scheduling but is not placed in inventory storage after completion. Phantom item codes are convenient for reporting and data entry. For example, reporting the use of the ingredients going into the phantom item (the tank of formulated product) avoids entering the quantity used for each final package size. Finally, reporting the use of the phantom, after filling the formulated product into the final container sizes, further simplifies reporting.

The *pseudo item code* aids scheduling and planning but unlike a phantom, items cannot be produced. Consider the example of a manufacturer of colored marking pens. A pseudo item code is set up to represent the total sales forecast of all marking pens. A planning bill converts this aggregate forecast into item forecasts for each color pen. The item code for the marking pen family is a pseudocode. Its purpose is for helping to plan inventory, although it is not a stock item.

INVENTORY REPORTING AND PHYSICAL CONTROL

The database of a good planning and control system is important for effective reporting and control of inventory. Management is responsible for the physical handling and storage of inventory to keep materials in usable condition, secure against damage and theft. The management is responsible for tracking and control of inventory and for providing proper storage facilities.

Inventory Database

An important information file in the inventory management system is the *item master record* that contains basic information for managing the inventory. This database is the

TABLE 18.5 Item Master Information

Item number	Drawing number
Item description	Item ABC class
Unit of measure	Freight codes
BOM low-level code	Weight/cube
Revision number	Family name/group
Make or buy	Planning fences
Item status	Storage requirements
Order policy	Gateway work center
Yield	Forecast codes
Lead time	Available to promise
Buyer or planner name	Post deduct
Safety stock	

repository for the item codes that identify all the inventory items and also contains much of the information needed for planning and scheduling. Table 18.5 shows the data likely to appear on the item master record. The basic information is needed for developing the plan for materials replenishment. Information in the item master and the inventory stock status records is essential for materials and capacity planning and execution.

The *inventory stock status record* illustrates the dynamic information needed for inventory control. It includes inventory balances by location and the status of open and firm planned orders. This information may reside in several files within the information system. Table 18.6 lists the typical information found for each part number in the stock status databases.

The *quantity on hand* is the total physical inventory. It is often further segregated into the categories of *available, allocated, on hold,* and *nonusable* inventory. The *available inventory* is the quantity remaining after removing allocated and nonusable stock. *Allocated inventory* is the quantity of the on-hand inventory designated for use on open

TABLE 18.6 Stock Status Information

Inventory data	Open-order status
Stock/bin location	Order numbers
Quantity on hand	Quantity on order
Quantity allocated	Expected receipt dates
Quantity on order	Order dates
Quantity on hold	Supplier/work center
Lot or serial number	Responsibility
Unit cost	Deliver to location

orders scheduled for release to manufacturing or purchasing. *On-hold inventory* is usually stock that cannot be immediately used because of some special situation—stock may need to be held for inspection, engineering disposition, or information from a supplier. Different inventory management systems may either include or exclude the on-hold inventory when computing the available balance and allocating inventory for open orders. *Nonusable inventory* includes rejected and obsolete material that is not usable yet remains as part of the total quantity on hand. The available-inventory figure and the order point are used to tell when to replenish inventory. When computing the net requirements for *material requirements planning* (MRP), the available inventory should include scheduled receipts (open orders) on the date due.

An *open-order status* file provides management the information for scheduled receipts that are due to arrive on future dates. The analysis of these dates during the MRP process frequently lead to action messages that recommend when to order more stock or to expedite, delay, or cancel an order. The accuracies of the scheduled receipt dates are primary requirements for an effective MRP system. Table 18.7 shows how the inventory status can change over time. New orders for parent items cause allocations; receipts to stock will increase the on-hand balance; negative projected available stock will result in new scheduled manufacturing receipts. Allocations are relieved when the store's personnel issue the components needed for manufacturing orders.

Inventory Transactions

Inventory balances change as new demands are generated and supplies are received. Purchasing orders, manufacturing orders, and sales orders are the three types of orders used in the inventory management system. A *purchase order* authorizes procurement of materials and components from an outside supplier. Usually the supplier will provide all the materials and labor and produce and ship the materials to its customers. A *manufacturing order* is authorization to convert raw materials and semifinished goods into products ready for sale. *Sales orders* represent demands from customers that trigger the issuing of manufacturing orders or delivery from stock.

Items made by manufacturing usually have a bill of materials and routing that specify the materials, labor, equipment, and operations needed to carry out production. Actions convert a manufacturing planned order to a scheduled receipt, which creates an

TABLE 18.7 Inventory Transactions

Part number: 16-443-2234							Order quantity: 5000		
Name: Steel bearing							Lead time: 5 days		
Classification: B							Order-point: Time phase		
Unit cost: $57.85							Safety stock: 50		

	Ordered		Received		Issued		Balance	Allocated		Available
Date	No.	Qty.	No.	Qty.	No.	Qty.	On-hand	No.	Qty.	Qty.
6/20							3900			3900
6/22							3900	MFG-840	3000	900
6/24							3900	MFG-930	1000	−100
6/24	PO-321	5000					3900			4900
6/29					MFG-714	3000	900	MFG-840	−3000	4900
6/30			PO-321	5000			5900			4900

allocation of the materials and components listed in the bill of materials. Inventory issued from stores reduces "allocations" and "on-hand" inventory simultaneously.

Sales orders for products on hand trigger the disbursement of finished-goods inventory to customers. Manufacturing orders generate requirements for production. Purchase order receipts add to inventory. Most activities surrounding these orders either add or subtract to the physical inventory records. Adjustments for scrap, rejects, and receiving or disbursement errors are also additions or subtractions to the inventory balances.

Other transactions change the location or category of the inventory but do not affect the on-hand balances. Transferring materials in and out of inspection or moving inventory between stock or bin locations are inventory transactions that usually do not change the on-hand balances. Yet each change results in the possibility of an error's occurring. Minimizing the number and type of inventory transactions is important for maintaining timely and accurate inventory stock status information. Setting up "special" inventory transactions can add confusion and complexity to the reporting processes. Using transactions that only add, subtract, and adjust the inventory helps simplify the reporting process.

INVENTORY STORAGE CONSIDERATIONS

Proper storing and securing of inventory begins with making a layout of the storage facilities and then deciding how and where to locate every inventory item. Some inventory items need special handling to ensure proper stock rotation and also need protection against pilferage or spoilage. Since inventory has value, it must be secured to discourage theft and unintended usage. Sometimes securing the inventory may involve keeping stock in safes, locked cabinets, or fenced storage areas.

Location Designator

A good inventory location system tells where to store items by giving a general location and a specific bin within the location. A storage facility can be divided according to whether it has shelving, storage racks, open areas for bulky items, and refrigeration or cold storage.

Good location designator systems identify the storage point in three-dimensional space. This method is effective when using pallet racks and shelves for storage. Visualize an area containing 10 rows of pallet racks or storage shelves 20 sections deep and 4 levels high. One column would have 80 bin locations (20 sections times 4 levels). The total number of locations is 800 (80 bins times 10 rows). Each bin location could have a unique designator that describes its location using 5 characters. The first 2 values identify the row (1 to 10); the next 2 tell the section or column in the row (1 to 20); the final digit gives the level (1 to 4) in the section. An inventory item with a location designator of 10-13-3 means it can be found in the tenth row, thirteenth section, on the third level. Sometimes materials are stored on the floor in open stock locations. The first two characters of the location designator would identify the general floor area, and the other digits could identify the row in which the item can be found. Open storage of this type works best by storing materials of the same type in the same rows.

Fixed Locations

When an inventory item has been assigned a designated location where it must be stored, it has a *fixed location*. This type of stocking system is usually easy for people to remember and reduces transactions related to moving stocks. However, using fixed locations can lead to a waste of storage space because the locations are kept available even when there is no inventory.

Random Locations

When warehouse space is limited, storing inventory in random locations will usually give the best solution. This method allows for storage in any open bin anywhere in the warehouse. The disadvantage of this method is that similar or the same items might be anywhere in the warehouse. Therefore the time and distance to find and pick stock is often longer than it would be using fixed locations. Random location depends on an accurate stock locator system to keep track of where everything is in the warehouse.

The number of transactions and volume of movement can vary significantly among different inventory items. Fast-moving items should be in locations that are easily accessible and close to the using area. This requirement favors the use of fixed storage locations. Locating the fast-moving items on the lower levels of the storage racks makes picking easy and quick. The slow movers go on the top levels of the racks and less accessible locations. Random storage works well for slow movers. Most warehouses use a combination of storage techniques. Fixed storage areas can be identified for groups of items with similar characteristics. Within these fixed areas, a random location system can help to use the available space effectively.

Special Handling

Some inventory items need special handling and storage because of safety, spoilage, pilferage, or their physical characteristics. As an example, when storing chemicals, it is sometimes necessary to store them in separate locations to avoid contamination and potential safety hazards. Many items need to be kept in cool or refrigerated areas to prevent spoilage and to prolong their shelf life. Stock rotation can be critical in maintaining the longest shelf life possible and avoid costly inventory losses.

Sometimes inventory needs to be traceable so it is controlled in storage by lot or serial number. This is especially true for the pharmaceutical and other health-related products. Frequently the ingredients used in manufacturing need to be traceable, and companies need to document every movement and transaction including supplier's name, date received, lot numbers, quantities, and other information. Good lot control requires an inventory system that includes transactions by lot number, location, and item number. The item master record should include the special storage or handling requirements. This information should also appear on orders and reports related to storing, moving, and using these materials.

Security

Some inventory items require more secure storage than others. The procedures for receiving, storing, and disbursing precious metals and other costly items should command special attention. A slight inventory loss could cause a significant financial loss and require adjustments to the inventory.

Some inventory items seem to attract thieves because they are popular items and easily sold for cash. Most consumer products and appliances fall into this category. Some items that seem to have no "street value" can suddenly become a security issue.

Gasoline prices were high in the 1970s, and rumor persisted that by attaching a magnet to an automobile's gas line, mileage would be significantly improved. A company who sold powerful magnets to their customers suddenly experienced rampant pilferage and eventually put them in locked storage! More routinely, items need secure storage for safety and regulatory concerns, especially for items like drugs and alcohol.

Providing secure storage may involve using vaults, fencing, and locked storerooms. Special authorization is required to obtain materials from these secured locations. Bonding employees does not deter theft 100 percent. The bonding agent usually does some investigative work to learn about the trustworthiness of the warehouse personnel. The bond only ensures the company against financial loss. Bonding does nothing for the physical security of the inventory and is often limited to a specific maximum amount and usually applies to specific people. The bonding agent reimburses the company for financial loss, but only after the employee is legally found guilty of theft. Management should concentrate on proper controls and accountability as the best approach to inventory security.

INVENTORY RECORD ACCURACY

Maintaining high inventory accuracy is important not only for the financial controls of the business but also for the quality of the planning and execution of manufacturing operations. Both reasons are equally important yet are frequently confusing. A financial officer, thinking in terms of dollars, might say inventory accuracy is very good and cite a small dollar adjustment for the last physical inventory. Manufacturing might respond that accuracy is poor because shortages and excesses occur frequently. Each has a different purpose and measurement of inventory record accuracy.

Table 18.8 shows the different viewpoints. Note that a small financial difference in total inventory dollars can still represent a substantial financial risk. This risk and financial loss come from part shortages, missed schedules, and ineffective operations. Both item and dollar accuracy are important. Poor item accuracy is a clear signal that a large financial inventory adjustment will likely occur soon. Beyond inventory adjustments, shortages, and excesses, poor inventory record accuracy leads to poor decisions and destroys integrity and confidence in the planning and control systems.

At the item level, inaccurate inventory increases purchasing and expediting costs. The A items that should receive more management attention may be overlooked while others receive more follow-up than necessary. Figure 18.4 illustrates how poor inventory stock status information, primarily inventory record accuracy, affects the integrity of the planning process. The master production schedule, bills of materials, and inventory stock status are the drivers of the materials requirements planning process. The quality of the MRP reports depends on the joint accuracy of these drivers. Even if the accuracy of the drivers meets class A requirements of a minimum 95 percent performance, the quality of the MRP at level one is only 86 percent. This is derived by multiplying the chances that the three drivers are accurate ($0.95 \times 0.95 \times 0.95$) to get the cumulative probability of the accuracy of the MRP (0.86).

The quality of the MRP report depends on the joint accuracy of the drivers. Planned orders generated by the MRP at a parent item level drive the demands at the component level. At level 2 the MRP is driven by the same 95 percent performance for the inventory stock status and bills of materials. But, the planned orders from level 1 MRP are only 86 percent reliable. These performance factors determine the probability of accurate MRP output for level 2 ($0.95 \times 0.95 \times 0.86 = 0.77$) of 77 percent.

TABLE 18.8 Inventory Accuracy

Item	Class	Book balance	Cycle count	Error	Tolerance	Accuracy	Dollar adjust
1	A	100	100	0	0	Yes	$ 0
2	A	249	250	−1	0	No	−250
3	A	300	300	0	0	Yes	0
4	B	152	150	2	3	Yes	+ 120
5	B	172	175	−3	3	Yes	−150
6	B	640	650	−10	13	Yes	−300
7	B	320	320	0	6	Yes	0
8	C	4202	4000	202	126	No	+ 101
9	C	4400	4500	−100	132	Yes	−40
10	C	8950	9000	−50	268	Yes	−10

Total value book balance = $194,981 $−539

Class	Tolerance	Aggregate performance
A	None	Unit accuracy $= \dfrac{10 - 2}{10} \times 100 = 80.00$ percent
B	±2%	
C	±3%	Dollar accuracy $= \dfrac{194{,}981 - 539}{194{,}981} \times 100 = 99.72$ percent

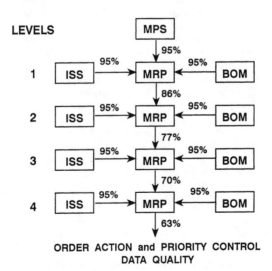

LEVELS

ORDER ACTION and PRIORITY CONTROL
DATA QUALITY

FIGURE 18.4 Interactive performance. (BOM = bills of material, ISS = inventory stock status, MPS = master production schedule, MRP = material requirements plan.)

As the process continues through more levels, the integrity of the plan continues to disintegrate. The cumulative effect of inaccurate inventory, along with the other two drivers, can make MRP useless. Additionally, the class A standard of 95 percent is not sufficient for effective MRP planning.

PHYSICAL INVENTORY

Once each year, and sometimes more frequently, companies usually take a physical inventory to verify the correctness of their financial records. An inventory audit assures the company that profits and tax liabilities are correct. The annual physical inventory usually entails a production shutdown to conduct the counts. Taking physical inventory can be a massive task requiring many people for several days. Typically, personnel from accounting, materials planning, inventory control, engineering, and manufacturing are involved in the process. Preparation for a physical inventory requires training and organizing the counters, obtaining clerical supplies, and organizing and identifying inventory items.

Physical counts are recorded on serial numbered *count cards*. Before the actual counting begins, all item identifications and their storage locations must be verified. Teams of internal auditors verify the accuracy of the counts and observe the proceedings for irregularities, especially for the high-value A items. Finally, after recording, collecting, and entering the counts from the count cards into the data processing system, the physical and the book balances are compared.

When the information system reports big differences between the book balances and the physical counts, the items should be counted again. At some point, the physical inventory gets "validated," and adjustments are made to reconcile the books with the physical counts.

Taking an accurate physical inventory is difficult. Frequently the people who conduct the counts are not familiar with the inventory items, locations, units of measure, or item identification. Furthermore, the desire to complete the counting quickly so that manufacturing can resume operations can lead to recording inaccurate information. One problem with taking a physical inventory is identifying the cause of errors and taking corrective action. The time between physical inventories can be quite long. People do not remember situations that happened months ago so tracking errors and discovering why they happened is very difficult. The number of items that need reconciliation is usually high, and frequently, time limitations may rule out proper investigation. What usually happens, except on the A item discrepancies, is that an arbitrary inventory adjustment is made to match the physical count. Only a few discrepancies undergo analysis to identify problems and corrective actions.

CYCLE COUNTING

Supplementing, and frequently replacing the annual physical inventory, is the effective use of cycle-counting procedures. *Cycle counting* is an ongoing process of monitoring current inventory so that counts are always correct. Trained teams identify what items to count, do the counting, make the adjustments, and find the cause of any errors. These team members are very knowledgeable about the location and flow of inventory, the inventory transactions, and how the system operates. Cycle counting all the inventory items during a year might not be possible, but the A items should be counted several times. Frequent counts during the year make it easier to identify and correct the causes of inconsistencies in inventory counts. Cycle counting concentrates more on finding and eliminating errors than it does adjusting book balances.

Counting Frequency

ABC Analysis is a helpful guide for deciding the frequency of counting different items. The A items that represent about 80 percent of the inventory value but only 20 percent of the items should be counted several times during the year. The B items get counted less frequently than the A items. C items are counted once a year or less. The frequency of counting depends on the number and importance of errors. In some situations a B or C part is an A item for cycle-counting purposes because it has a history of accuracy problems causing serious consequences for manufacturing and customer service.

Control Group

Start the cycle-counting process with a group of items that represent a cross section of inventory types with frequent transactions. The purpose of this control group is to identify and correct basic problems related to processing inventory transactions. A control group is a manageable number of items that can be counted and reconciled daily. Achieve a high degree of accuracy with the control group before cycle counting the other inventory items. Focus the control group counting process on finding the primary causes of inventory errors and eliminating them. The full cycle counting program starts after correcting most of the causes of problems identified by using the control group. In this way, the cycle counts should remain accurate after making any needed adjustments. Stop the control group counts after identifying and correcting the inventory problems. If old or new problems begin to occur, control group counts can be put into effect again.

What and When to Count

The ABC Analysis is a guide for selecting what items to count and when to count them. A high level of accuracy, with little tolerance, is important for the A items because it affects the financial integrity of the business. Counts might be conducted daily, weekly, or monthly for these high-dollar items. On the other extreme are C items that might not get counted more than once or twice every 1 or 2 years. Wider tolerance between the actual count and the book record is usually acceptable for this group. The C items are frequently high-volume parts, like nuts and washers, and they are difficult to count.

Another count frequency criteria besides high unit cost is short shelf life. Also critical components that have a history of inaccurate counts should be counted more often.

Perhaps the most efficient way to select items for cycle counting is to take the counts just before new stock gets put away into storage. The quantity of inventory on hand should be at a low level. This, naturally, makes counting much easier and quicker. An effective way to select and count items that have a fixed stock location is to go through the warehouse and record the number of empty stock locations. When picking items, the warehouse personnel can take "free counts" by reporting when the last item is picked from a location. The inventory quantities for these locations are zero, and the records should agree.

After deciding what to count and how often, it is possible to estimate the resources needed for the cycle-counting program. Table 18.9 helps when estimating resource requirements, organizing the count team, and conducting counts.

TABLE 18.9 Cycle Count Frequency

Inventory class	Number of items	Count frequency	Number of counts	Inventory value
A	1,000	6	6,000	$4,000,000
B	1,500	3	4,500	750,000
C	2,500	1	2,500	250,000
Other	100	.5	50	0
Totals	5,100		13,050	$5,000,000

Hours per count = 0.75, counts per day = 52.2, time required = 9788 hours, counts per person/day = 10.67, personnel required = 4.89 people, hours per person/year = 2000, days per year = 250.

Management decides the number of cycle counts to take for each inventory class. The A items are counted more frequently than the B or C items. In the example, the estimated number of counts is about 13,050 with 50 percent of them taken for the high-inventory-value items. Management should know the time and resources it takes to establish an effective cycle-counting process. If it takes 75 percent of an hour (45 minutes) to count and reconcile an item, it will take 9788 ($0.75 \times 13,050$) hours to complete all the cycle counts in the example. Assuming a person works 2000 hours per year, it will take 4.89 people (9788/2000), making about 10.67 counts ($4.89 \times 10.67 \times 250$) to complete the task.

These time estimates can be used, along with other information, to project the costs related to a cycle-counting process. Comparing the resources required for cycle counting to the costs of inaccurate data, the benefits and payback become very attractive. When the cycle-counting process obtains a high degree of accuracy, the number of counts should be decreased. Companies that achieve a high level of inventory accuracy often stop cycle counting, but they use control groups periodically as a way to monitor and maintain performance.

Appropriate tolerances on the count accuracy must be determined for each group. The A items may have little or no tolerance when comparing the book balance to the physical counts. The B items could have a tolerance of 1 percent, and the C items 2 percent or higher. Setting the tolerance is a management judgment. Consider the nature of the items and the relative difficulty for obtaining an exact count. Compare the difference between the book balance and the physical count to see if it is within the established tolerance. If the difference is within the tolerance, consider the count correct for the item.

To determine the inventory accuracy as a percentage, divide the number of different stock items that are accurate by the number of stock items counted and multiply by 100. Example:

$$\frac{85 \text{ bins of bolts were accurate}}{100 \text{ bins of bolts were counted}} \times 100 = 85 \text{ percent}$$

To find the dollar record accuracy, multiply each item's unit costs by its positive or negative error. Then compare the net total inventory dollar adjustment for all items.

Cycle-Counting Steps

Conducting a cycle count is a six-step process (Fig. 18.5). Central to the cycle count is establishing an inventory accuracy goal that is challenging and attainable, keeping in mind that 100 percent accuracy is the ultimate objective. Significant improvements in

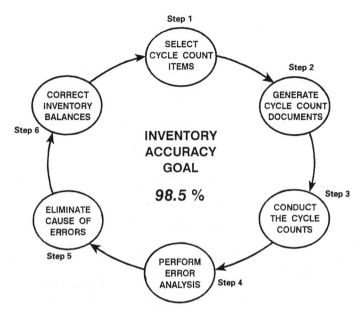

FIGURE 18.5   Cycle-counting steps.

inventory record accuracy come from finding the cause of inventory discrepancies and eliminating them.

Step 1.   Conducting a cycle count starts with selecting the items that should be counted. Many computerized inventory management systems include a data field that contains the last cycle count date for each item and its count frequency. Add the time of the count frequency to the last cycle count date. When the date equals or is earlier than the current cycle count, the item should be counted. List and review all the items scheduled for the cycle count. During this process, you may reschedule some item counts to a later date as a way of smoothing out the workload. Sometimes you may add items known to have chronic accuracy problems to the count list.

Step 2.   Generate the documents used to record the physical counts for this select list of items. Count sheets show the item codes, descriptions, and spaces to record the counts. The document should give the location and book quantity of the inventory items. Knowing the storage locations helps the counters find and identify the items quickly. Having the book inventory quantity on the report helps the counters avoid counting errors. If the cycle count is significantly different than the book balance, the counter can double-check it immediately.

Good housekeeping in the warehouse helps make cycle counting an efficient and effective process. There are fewer count errors when the inventory items are neatly arranged for easy identification and counting. Have every item counted a second time, preferably by another person. If the same person repeats the counting, he or she should do the counting in a different way, for example, counting by groups or starting from the back and working to the front. Variety in the way the count is conducted breaks the routine and helps detect counting errors. When the counter is satisfied with the accuracy of the count, record the quantity on the cycle count document. If the book balance and the cycle count do not match, take a recount to be sure.

Step 3. This step involves the analysis of the completed physical counts. Compare the counts by location to the book balances by location. If the difference is within the established tolerance, the item is designated as correct and no adjustment should be made to the book balance. If an item does not fall within the agreed-upon tolerance, it is a problem requiring corrective action. Before any record adjustments, count the item again. During the second count, it is important to check other storage locations, especially the points of use of the items. Make every reasonable effort to find all the inventory and get an accurate count.

Step 4. This step of the process begins after rechecking the counts for all items that are out of tolerance. These inventory items undergo a detail audit to find the cause of the error. An audit trail listing the transaction between the last and the current cycle-counting dates is a valuable tool to help find the cause of the problems. An audit trail gives the type of transactions, document numbers, quantity, and the person who processed the transaction. When an audit report lists the transactions for an item by date sequence, a running of the changes to inventory will help spot problems. Discovering the cause of errors is detective work that takes patience and curiosity. A good cycle-counting staff should find the root cause of errors for over 90 percent of all inventory discrepancies. Inventory errors can be the result of poorly designed forms, untrained personnel, carelessness, or poor document control.

Step 5. This step in the cycle-counting process is communicating the cause of errors to the person(s) responsible for the problem. Telling someone that he or she made a mistake is not a pleasant task, but it is essential to take corrective action. Yet, when the people responsible for inventory accuracy understand the importance to the company, they want to know about the problems so they can improve their performance and take pride in their accomplishments.

Step 6. The last step in the cycle-counting process is to correct the inventory balances so that they match the cycle count results. This inventory adjustment is a documented transaction that includes supporting documentation. If the error is traceable to a specific document, like a purchase order or a materials picking ticket, the adjustment should tie to this document. This ensures that the accounting function can charge the appropriate accounts. For example, a mistake on a purchase receipt makes the inventory wrong, but it also causes problems with accounts payable. Finally, update the date of the last cycle count, and compute the level of record accuracy and post it for all to see.

Attitude and Action

Companies that achieve a high degree of inventory accuracy have little patience with errors. They assign responsibility for accuracy and timeliness to those who work with the inventory, and they hold them accountable. Management makes sure those responsible have the needed resources, training, and support for success. Measuring and reporting performance should be done weekly and summarized monthly. Emphasis centers on finding out the cause of the inventory inaccuracies and making the changes that prevent the error from occurring again. The objective is to have accurate and timely information for planning and daily decisions. By fulfilling this objective, the accuracy of the financial records is assured.

FINANCIAL CONSIDERATIONS

Inventory managers should understand the financial aspects of inventory. This includes the classification of inventory for accounting purposes, analysis of aggregate inventory, recording the movement of inventory, the cost to carry inventory, and the basic approaches to assigning a dollar value to the inventory. An effective inventory management process recognizes the financial implications of the inventory investment and how it influences the profitability of the company.

Inventory Classifications

Inventory reporting generally follows the flow of goods through the company and reflects the way value is added during manufacturing. The terms used to describe these classifications can vary considerably between companies and industries. *Purchased raw materials* and *components* are inventory items that have had no value added by the company. These materials become *finished goods* by being processed through various stages of manufacturing. The inventory value of purchased raw materials and components should represent at least the purchase price of the items.

Work-in-process describes inventory that is between production stages. Scheduled receipts for a manufacturing order are a typical example. During the production process raw materials and other components are withdrawn from inventory and processed. Labor and overhead are charged to the work orders for these items. During this period, production is not complete and the items are not usable. *Subassemblies* and *intermediates* describe items at a stage of manufacturing where they get combined with other components and subassemblies to make new subassemblies. *Semifinished goods* and *final subassemblies* are terms frequently given to items that are ready for the last assembly step as schedules dictate. *Finished goods* is the last classification of inventory. These are goods ready for sale to customers. Finished goods have all the value added and carry the full costs of materials, labor, and overhead.

Aggregate Inventory Analysis

Most basic financial inventory reports show the dollar value of inventory by classification. It is possible to learn more after separating the inventory into classifications by departments or product lines. Comparing reports over time frequently reveals trends and track changes. Inventory levels could be high because of low sales or unusually large purchases or increased production. These reports help identify inventory changes caused by anticipating demand and supply. Aggregate inventory analysis helps management guide operations with an inventory plan.

A significant deviation from the inventory plan can cause a swing in the profits. Low inventory levels can suggest customer service problems, stock-outs, and late shipments. An effective inventory plan by department and product line can get management closer to the cause and lead to corrective action.

Return on Assets

One important measure of financial performance is the percent *return on assets* (ROA) that includes the inventory investment. Inventory is usually the most significant part of assets for most manufacturers, perhaps second only to their fixed investments in plants, warehouses, office facilities, and equipment. The return-on-assets calculation brings together the profit-or-loss statement and information found on the balance sheet. *To figure the return on assets, divide the net profit of a company by the value of its assets,* and then multiply the fraction by 100 to give a percent. Figure 18.6 illustrates these calculations.

On the balance sheet side, the $7,000,000 total inventory is the sum of the finished goods, the work-in-process, and the semifinished and raw materials inventory accounts. Current assets include total inventory plus cash and accounts receivables. The fixed assets, plants, equipment, and real estate, plus the current assets, give the total assets of $7,500,000 for the company in the example.

The cost of goods on the profit-and-loss statement side comprises direct labor, factory overhead, and materials costs. Other expenses are added to the cost of goods to get the total costs of $30,000,000. Subtracting the costs $30,000,000 from sales $32,000,000 gives a profit of $2,000,000.

Compute the profit margin by dividing the profit $2,000,000 by the sales revenue of $32,000,000 and multiply by 100 to obtain 6.25 percent. Similarly, compute the asset turns by dividing sales revenue $32,000,000 by the total assets $7,500,000. Calculate the return on assets by multiplying the profit margin 6.25 percent × 2.67 percent by the asset turns. Dividing the $2,000,000 profit by the $7,500,000 total assets is a direct way to calculate the ROA of 16.7 percent.

An important factor for managing the inventory investment is understanding how inventory influences the rate of return on the total assets of the company. Decreasing the inventory investment will usually increase the return on assets and enhance the financial effectiveness of the business. Lower inventory investment results in lower costs to carry inventory and other expenses that further improve company financial performance.

Inventory Turnover and Day's Supply

The faster raw materials can be converted into finished goods and sold, the lower the inventory investment and the higher the return on assets. The speed with which inventory moves through a company is a gauge of the effectiveness of sales and manufacturing. There are several ways to compute this inventory movement. The most common method is the *inventory turnover rate,* which compares sales to the average inventory during a period.

When calculating inventory movement, the sales figures should reflect the cost of goods sold, which should be on the same cost basis as the inventory investment. *Inventory turnover* is a measure of the number of times the average inventory investment is "consumed" during a year. Dividing the annual costs of goods sold by the average inventory gives the inventory turnover rate. As an example, inventory turns twice when the volume of cost of goods sold in one year is $10,000,000 and the average inventory investment is $5,000,000.

To compute the *day's supply of inventory,* divide the number of days in a year by the inventory turnover rate. If an inventory turns twice a year, the day's supply is about 182. This method of calculating the rate of inventory movement overstates the real rate of inventory movement. This is so because the calculations do not account for when and how value is added during the production processes.

Inventory Flow Analysis

Recall the discussion earlier in this chapter that states that managing work-in-process is an inventory function. *Inventory flow analysis* includes an estimate of how much value is being added during production for each inventory class. Figure 18.7 illustrates these computations. Purchased raw materials and components carry only their purchase value

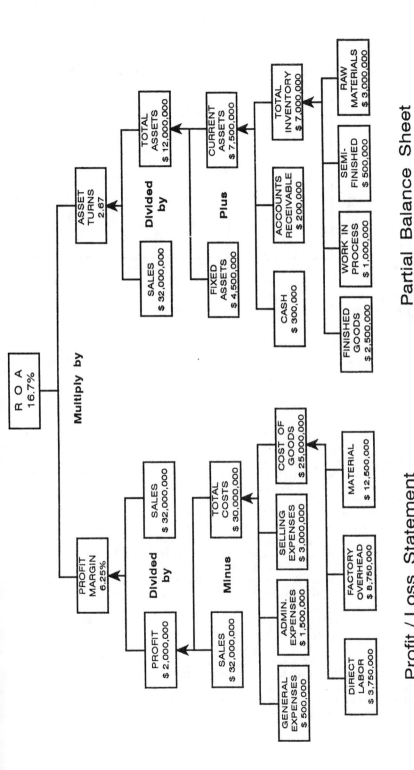

FIGURE 18.6 Return on assets.

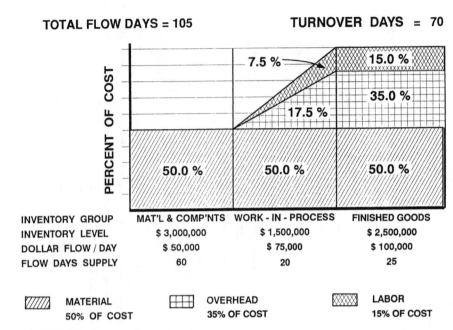

FIGURE 18.7   Inventory flow analysis.

of the cost of goods sold. Manufacturing adds value with labor and overhead while converting purchased raw materials and components into subassemblies or semifinished goods. This increases the value of these inventory classifications. Finally, at the end of finished-goods stage, all the value has been added and the products are ready for sale. Inventory flow analysis uses the daily flow of cost for each inventory class used in goods when figuring the day's supply or flow. This method is a better measure of inventory movement than the traditional day's supply figure.

When calculating inventory turnover or inventory flow analysis to determine past performance, the historical inventory and cost of goods sold are frequently used. However, using the cost of goods based on sales forecasts could be a way to project inventory turns and flows for future periods. Other ways to project inventory include using the average inventory for the immediate past quarter and annualize the cost of goods sold for the quarter. The selection of the data may vary, but the methods of computation are the same.

Not all companies compute inventory turns and flow the same way, so care should be taken when comparing the performance of different companies. Inventory movement is usually different between industries because of the differences in products, processes, and services to the customers. Comparison within an industry group can also be misleading. Having the highest inventory turns is not a guarantee of a competitive edge. Different accounting methods, marketing strategies, and manufacturing capabilities may have dramatic effects on inventory turnover. In addition, inventory turnover can be calculated in a variety of ways that can make interpretation and comparison difficult.

Inventory-Carrying Costs

These costs are generated in the storing and handling of inventory. In addition, there are costs for financing the inventory investment and for paying taxes and insurance premiums. Some inventory is amenable to spoilage, obsolescence, and pilferage, adding additional costs to the risks of having inventory.

Storage and handling costs are frequently the largest cost segment of inventory-carrying costs. Suitable storage may include refrigeration to keep products fresh and locked areas to secure high-value items. The cost of renting or building a warehouse facility is not a trivial expense. Even fully depreciated storage facilities have an implied cost related to the market value of the space, especially when using it for more productive purposes. Handling equipment moves inventory from place to place. Handling equipment costs include those for forklifts, storage racks, conveyors, automatic retrieval systems, and other equipment. Add to these costs the wages of the people that staff and manage the warehouses and storage operations.

The interest component of inventory-carrying costs usually relates to the cost of borrowing money. Yet some companies are debt free and finance all their investments from internal funding. These companies should use opportunity costs or their expected internal rate of return for the cost of financing their inventory investment. *Opportunity costs* can be found by asking the question, "How much could be earned by investing the money elsewhere?" The *internal rate of return* is what a company expects to receive for the money invested in plant and equipment. Sometimes the commercial prime rate guides the decision for the amount of interest expense companies assign to inventory carrying costs.

Obsolescence, damage, spoilage, and theft are often significant inventory costs. Some inventory items naturally attract theft and loss from unauthorized employee use. Changes to product specifications frequently lead to obsolete components and finished goods that are no longer usable or saleable. Quality problems and product recalls can significantly affect inventory carrying costs. Tracking some of these costs can be difficult. When spoilage and damage occur, an inventory adjustment can keep the stock balances correct; the accounting department usually has these records. The losses from theft can be more difficult to obtain but frequently show up during cycle counting or the annual physical inventory.

Some states and cities levy a property tax on business inventory. In addition, most companies insure their inventory and the storage facilities for losses from fire and potential disasters. Include all these types of costs when figuring the cost to carry inventory.

Inventory-Carrying Cost Percentage

It is possible to calculate a general inventory-carrying cost percentage that can be useful when making inventory decisions. Table 18.10 shows how all the inventory costs elements can be combined to make a percentage that can be used to estimate future inventory costs. This percentage helps management evaluate the impact on profit by a particular level of inventory. The inventory-carrying cost percentage is frequently used to evaluate the trade-off between the cost of setup and the carrying cost created by the lot-size decisions.

The inventory-carrying cost percentage is an average, so when averaging is appropriate, use it. Adjust percentage to fit specific applications. Use ABC Analysis as a guide by adjusting the percentage to be sure the A items have the correct inventory-carrying cost factor.

TABLE 18.10 Inventory-Carrying Costs

	Range of percent	
Cost	Low, %	High, %
Interest	10.0	14.0
Insurance and taxes	3.0	5.0
Damage and shrinkage	0.5	3.0
Obsolescence and shelf life	1.5	4.0
Storage and handling	5.0	10.0
	20.0	36.0

Example calculation for storage and handling		
Warehouse rent	$190,000	Average inventory = $8,000,000
Personnel	150,000	
Maintenance	30,000	
Utilities	30,000	$\dfrac{\$400,000}{\$8,000,000} \times 100 = 5$ percent
Total	$400,000	

Inventory Valuation Methods

Standard cost is probably the most popular method for valuing inventory. When comparing item standard costs to actual cost, differences usually result. The profit, based on standard costs, is usually adjusted by this variance. If the calculation is favorable, that is, the actual costs are less than the standard cost, decrease the cost of goods by the favorable variance amount. Other costing methods can give different results. *Last-in, first-out* (LIFO) assumes that the newest inventories get used first. Therefore, the remaining inventory carries the older costs and the most current costs will be passed on to the cost of goods sold. Conversely, *first-in, first-out* (FIFO) assumes the oldest inventory gets used first so that the remaining inventory has the value of the most current costs.

Note that the *physical movement* of the inventory can be based on FIFO while simultaneously the *valuation* of the inventory can be based on LIFO. It is not necessary that the inventory movement match the method of valuation. A pharmaceutical product with a very short shelf life can be valued using standard cost, but the physical control of inventory movement follows a FIFO policy.

Other ways to cost the inventory include using average and actual costs or some hybrid methods. Changing costing systems usually requires the approval of the Internal Revenue Service because of the impact on profits and related taxes. Considering tax liability, using LIFO when materials costs are increasing (inflation) will pass these costs on to the cost of goods more quickly and show lower profit for the company. Lower profit means the company pays less in taxes. The reverse is true when using the FIFO accounting method. Here, the higher costs show in the inventory and the lower costs go to the cost of goods.

The different ways of valuing inventory sometimes make it difficult to compare the inventory performance between companies. An inventory valued at LIFO will be higher at times than the same inventory valued under FIFO. Inventory-carrying costs can differ dramatically as well. Many judgments that management makes about inventory levels and materials flow are based on financial considerations. Companies that take comfort in knowing their inventory turns are the "industry average" make a mistake. They ignore the fact that "average" companies struggle to survive and many eventually fail in today's competitive markets. Seek out those companies that show outstanding performance, and learn how they do it. Then adopt the ideas that make sense for your business.

Concern for inventory levels is critical for improving the financial well-being of the enterprise. Inventory management affects profit by reducing costs and investment in inventory, factors that relate to the return on assets. Reducing inventory decreases inventory-carrying costs and increases profits. Inventory reduction decreases the total investment. A combination of cost and inventory reduction can make a significant improvement in the return on assets for most companies.

Measuring Inventory Performance

View inventory levels as an important part of the business plan when implementing strategies to achieve the objectives of the enterprise. Evaluating inventory performance should focus on trends of continuous improvement. The level and flow of inventory reflects the effectiveness of demand and supply strategies. Inventory levels are the direct result of these two factors. Inventory reduction comes from increasing sales (demand) or reducing production and procurement (supply). Trying to improve inventory performance without recognizing the supply and demand relationships usually leads to less than satisfactory results. Monitor the inventory levels against the inventory plan. Developing the inventory plan from the demand and supply strategies should be the goal.

Inventory record accuracy and timeliness are important when making decisions about planning and scheduling operations. Measuring the accuracy of the inventory should begin by evaluating product groups using ABC Analysis and establishing reasonable tolerance when comparing book balances to physical counts. The tolerance for A items should be very small in comparison to the C items. First, bring the accuracy up to the goal based on the established tolerance. Next, tighten the tolerance or increase the goal. Inventory record accuracy should be 98 percent or better before the formal planning system can work effectively. Publish the inventory performance in a place so that all can see.

Inventory provides a buffer between variations in demand rates and supply reliability. Establish safety stock with the idea that about one-half of the time, the sales forecast or procurement lead time is greater than forecast or plan. Safety stock should be used during about one-half of the replenishment cycles. This principle suggests that safety stocks could be too high if the inventory level does not go below the safety-stock level during about one-half of the replenishment cycles. The same idea applies to inconsistency in supplier delivery timing. If, on an item basis, the inventory never goes below the safety stock, then more than likely the buffer stock is too large. On balance, the safety stock should be needed during one-half of the replenishment cycles. The infrequent use of finished-goods safety stock is an indication that inventory is too high. For a make-to-stock company, check the established safety-stock levels and reduce the item service factors.

Inventory investment is caused by the unpredictability of demand and supply. Reducing inventory arbitrarily by cutting its level could increase costs. True inventory reduction comes about by eliminating the causes that require inventory. Work on making demand and supply more predictable, or have sufficient capacity to meet peak demand, keep lead times short, and lot sizes small. Finally, accurate inventory information becomes even more critical when inventory levels decrease after removing the waste.

ELEMENTS OF INVENTORY REPLENISHMENT

Determining what to order, how much, and when is an essential function of production and inventory management. Replenishment stock should be ordered when the inventory on hand plus on order reaches a level equal to the amount used during the replenishment lead time, plus the amount allowed for the variation in demand and supply. The inventory functions of buffer stock, lead time, and lot size become active during the ordering decision.

Replenishment Lead Time

Each activity that occurs during the replenishment lead time should be segmented into the elements of *queue, setup, run, wait,* and *move times.*

Queue time is the period a replenishment order sits in a work center before work begins.

Setup time describes the time needed to get ready to do the work. For manufacturing, setup time covers all the activities between production of the last good piece of the previous order to the first good piece of the new replenishment order. Setup for purchasing involves the time to review the order, select a supplier, and place the order. In the broadest sense, setup time is all the time for the activities to prepare to purchase or produce an item. Manufacturing setup time usually consumes production capacity.

Run time is the time when value is being added while manufacturing an order. Run time usually varies in relation to the quantity of the lot size.

Wait time is the time an item sits until it gets moved to the next operation.

Move time is the time it takes to move the item to the next operation. For a purchased item, the wait and move times can represent the in-transit time between the suppliers and the manufacturer.

When estimating the replenishment lead time, identify all the activities, and then break each into the five elements of lead time. The queue time is usually the longest of the elements. For manufactured items, queue time is the time work-in-process inventory sits idle and accumulates cost but no value.

Table 18.11 describes both manufacturing and purchasing lead times separated into activities and elements. Establish lead time by segmenting the time into activities and elements. This disciplined approach will yield better lead time estimates and the detail needed for reducing the waste of time and money.

To avoid a stock-out, enough stock should be on hand to cover the usage that could occur during the replenishment lead time.

Example

The lead time for an item is 15 days, and normal usage is 40 per day. If the normal usage is always correct, a replenishment order should be placed when the available inventory

TABLE 18.11   Lead Time Activities and Elements

Manufactured

Activity		Lead time elements				
	Setup	Run	Move	Wait	Queue	Total
Review		0.5			1.5	2.0
Pick materials		0.5	0.5	0.5	2.0	3.5
Produce	0.5	2.0	0.5	0.5	7.5	11.0
Inspection	0.5	0.5	0.5		2.0	3.5
Totals	1.0	3.5	1.5	1.0	13.0	20.0

Note: Lead time = days.

Purchased

Activity		Lead time elements				
	Setup	Run	Move	Wait	Queue	Totals
Review		0.5			1.5	2.0
Vendor fab				10.0		10.0
Transit time			5.0			5.0
Inspection	0.5	0.5	0.5		1.5	3.0
Totals	0.5	1.0	5.5	10.0	3.0	20.0

Note: Lead time = days.

(on hand plus open orders) reaches 600 (15 days times 40 units). Ordering earlier than 15 days in advance could cause excess inventory; yet ordering later might cause a stock-out. Avoiding either situation depends on the accuracy of the usage per day and the planned lead time. Buffer stock, as safety stock or safety time, should absorb most of these variations.

PROBABILISTIC APPROACH TO ORDERING

If an order can always be filled from the inventory on hand, the *service index* is said to be 100 percent. If it cannot be filled, it is a *stock-out*. The relationship between the service index and stock-out index is illustrated in Fig. 18.8 and expressed by the equation:

$$\text{Service index} = 100 \text{ percent} - \text{stock-out index}$$

Usage and lead time both vary, so to simplify, consider *the frequency of quantities used during lead times* as shown by the distribution A on the figure. It has been shown that, in practice, the distribution can be represented by a normal curve. As you can observe by moving the *order-point quantity line* up and down, you can change the service and stock-out indexes. As you would expect, the lower the line, the greater the service index. The order-point quantity can be defined as follows:

$$\text{Order point} = \text{usage during lead time} + \text{safety stock}$$

where safety stock equals safety factor times the standard deviation.

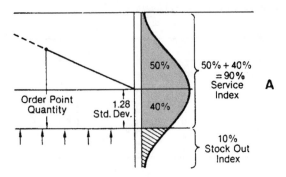

FIGURE 18.8   Service and stock-out index.

The steps for measuring demand variability are shown in Table 18.12.

Step 1.   Obtain the numeric error between the forecast and the demand for a representative number of periods: Column 3 − column 2 = column 4.

Step 2.   Square the numeric error as shown, column 6.

Step 3.   Calculate the standard deviation σ for the distribution of errors:

$$\sigma = \sqrt{\frac{\text{sum of squared errors}}{n - 1}} = \sqrt{\frac{\Sigma \text{ squared errors}}{n - 1}}$$

$$= \sqrt{\frac{4298 \text{ (column 6)}}{12 - 1 \text{ (column 1 } - 1)}} = 19.77$$

Step 4.   Select a safety stock and customer service index. For example, management wishes to be sure of serving the customer 90 percent of the time. Refer to the previous figure, and you will see that the customer will be served 50 percent of the time if there is no safety stock. For a service level of 90 percent (50 percent + 40 percent), the order point must be lowered 1.28 standard deviations as shown at A on Table 18.13.

Step 5.   The order point as stated before is as follows:

Order point = usage during lead time + safety factor × standard deviation

$$= 250 + (1.28 \times 19.77)$$

$$\approx 275$$

Mean Absolute Deviation (MAD) Application

When managers considered using the standard deviation for calculating order points, it was thought that doing so was too tedious for practical applications, so a shortcut estimate was derived using the *mean absolute deviation* (MAD). Some authorities, how-

TABLE 18.12 Measuring Demand Variability

(1) Period	(2) Forecast	(3) Demand	(4) Numeric error	(5) Absolute error	(6) Squared error
1	250	240	−10	10	100
2	250	245	−5	5	25
3	250	255	5	5	25
4	250	264	14	14	196
5	250	272	22	22	484
6	250	225	−25	25	625
7	250	278	28	28	784
8	250	235	−15	15	225
9	250	273	23	23	529
10	250	230	−20	20	400
11	250	261	11	11	121
12	250	222	−28	28	784
Total	3000	3000	0	206	4298

Standard deviation

$$\sqrt{\frac{4298}{12-1}} = 19.77 \text{ units}$$

Mean absolute deviation

$$\frac{206}{12} = 17.17 \text{ units}$$

TABLE 18.13 Safety Stock and Customer Service

	Service factors		Service levels
	(1) Standard deviation	(2) Mean absolute deviation	(3) Probability of avoiding stock-outs
	0	0	.50
	.68	.85	.75
	.84	1.06	.80
	1.04	1.40	.85
A	1.28	1.61	.90
	1.41	1.76	.92
	1.56	1.95	.94
	1.65	2.06	.95
	1.75	2.18	.96
	1.88	2.35	.97
	2.05	2.56	.98
	2.33	2.91	.99
	2.58	3.23	.995
	3.08	3.85	.999

ever, consider extensive calculations no longer a problem with the arrival of computer power on the industrial scene. However, there are enough people using MAD to make it worthwhile discussing.

The relationship between MAD and the standard deviation is:

$$\text{Standard deviation} = 1.25 \text{ MAD}$$

To determine the order point using MAD, follow the steps given in Table 18.13 and below:

Step 1. Obtain the absolute errors by subtracting the values in column 2 from those values in column 3 to obtain the numeric errors in column 4.

Step 2. Change all negative signs in column 4 to positive signs as shown in column 5, absolute errors.

Step 3. Sum all the absolute errors in column 5, and divide by 12.

$$\frac{206}{12} = 17.17$$

Step 4. Instead of selecting the service factor for standard deviations, use the service factor for MAD, column 2 on the previous table.

Step 5.

$$\text{Order point} = \text{usage during lead time} + \text{safety stock}$$

$$\approx 250 + (1.61 \times 17.17) = 277.64$$

$$\approx 278$$

Stock-Out versus Safety Stock

The relationship between the probability of a stock-out and the quantity of safety stock needed is not direct as shown for the previous example (Table 18.14).

Increasing the probability of avoiding a stock-out by 5 percent from 85 to 90 percent requires an increase of about 4.74 (5 units) while increasing the probability of avoiding a stock-out of 5 percent from 90 to 95 percent requires an increase of safety stock by 9.49 (10 units). The cost of avoiding stock-outs increases dramatically with an increase in the probability of avoiding stock-outs.

TABLE 18.14 Probability of Stock-out versus Safety Stock

Probability of stock-out, %	Probability of avoiding a stock-out, %	Service factor		Standard deviation, units
15	85	1.04×19.77	=	20.56
				4.74 units
10	90	1.28×19.77	=	25.30
				9.49 units
5	95	1.76×19.77	=	34.80

Stock-Out Exposures

The chance of a stock-out increases when the inventory gets low before a new receipt. Figure 18.9 shows how the frequency of being exposed to stock-outs can influence the amount of safety stock to carry in inventory. The solid line represents the inventory levels with an ordering cycle of twice a year for a quantity of 100 units. This exposes the item to a stock-out twice a year. The dotted line shows an order cycle of 10 times a year. The chance of stocking out by ordering 10 times a year is 40 percent greater than an order cycle of twice per year. Lot sizes can affect the amount of buffer stock inventory because more buffer stock is needed when more exposures are likely.

Assume that management decides that they do not want a stock-out of any item more than once a year. The frequency of replenishment for one product is 10 times a year, and its standard deviation of forecast error is 20. The implied service level comes from subtracting the stock-outs allowed from the annual exposures and dividing the answer by the annual exposures. This calculation gives a service level of 90 percent, that is, a stock-out is allowed during 10 percent of the replenishment cycles. On Table 18.13, find .90 in the column service levels, and then find the service factor of 1.28 to the left, under standard deviation. Multiply the standard deviation of the forecast error by the service factor to get the safety-stock quantity.

If the order cycle is twice per year with one stock-out allowed, the implied service level is .50 and no safety stock should be required. This is because of the assumption that the forecast errors give a normal distribution and the chances of overselling or underselling are equal. Establishing safety-stock inventory based on stock-out exposures relates to the incident of a stock-out and not the magnitude of the stock-out.

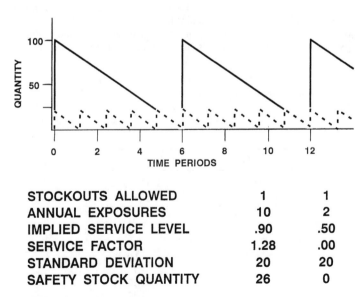

STOCKOUTS ALLOWED	1	1
ANNUAL EXPOSURES	10	2
IMPLIED SERVICE LEVEL	.90	.50
SERVICE FACTOR	1.28	.00
STANDARD DEVIATION	20	20
SAFETY STOCK QUANTITY	26	0

FIGURE 18.9 Stock-out exposures.

Management Decision

Applying the idea of buffer stock begins with management deciding the level of customer service they want to provide. They should consider the cost of carrying the buffer
stock and how many stock-outs are acceptable. Eliminating stock-outs entirely would
require an exorbitant quantity of safety stock and is, at least statistically, impossible to
achieve.

Do not make the mistake of treating all the items in a group as if the demand and lead
time errors will be the same. Inventory policies like "carry 4 weeks' supply of safety
stock on the A items" is evidence of this approach. As a rule, only apply *safety-stock*
procedures to finished goods and purchased items. For finished-goods stock, use either
a quantity or time supply. Lead time variations are more common for purchased materials and components, so safety time usually works best.

Avoid safety-stock components and assemblies manufactured in-house. Adjust any
variations by solving the internal operation problems that caused them. Adding safety stock
to manufactured items usually hides problems and confuses priorities on the shop floor.

Safety time supply can be determined by dividing the safety-stock quantity for an item
by its average daily usage. If the calculated safety stock is 50 and the daily usage is 5, the
safety time supply is equivalent to (50 items/5 items per day = 10 days) 10 days' supply.
Management seems to deal with the idea of time supply more readily than quantity. In
addition, the idea of safety time is dynamic and adjusts better to increases and decreases
in future-period forecasts. Apply safety time by figuring out when a net requirement
occurs for an item and then shifting the net requirements forward by the safety time.

Forecast and Replenishment Lead Times

Many companies measure the differences between actual and forecast demand monthly,
but the replenishment lead times rarely align with the forecast interval, and buffer stock
should cover only the variation in usage *during the replenishment period.* Refer to Table
18.15 and the example calculation. Consider how to align the differences in demand
over a period of four weeks (monthly) with a replenishment lead time of eight weeks.
The forecast error over four weeks needs adjustment to reflect what would likely hap-

TABLE 18.15   Forecast Interval and Lead Time

$$\text{Adjustment} = \sqrt{\frac{\text{lead time}}{\text{forecast interval}}}$$

Forecast interval = 4 periods

Lead time periods	Safety-stock adjustment
1	.5
2	.71
3	.87
4	1.00
5	1.12
6	1.22
7	1.32
8	1.41

pen by measuring the error over an eight-week interval. Make an acceptable adjustment by taking the square root of eight weeks lead time divided by the four-week forecast interval. Then multiply the adjustment (1.41 = square root of 8 divided by 4 for the example) by the number of standard deviations (service factor) needed for a given service level.

Example. Determine the safety stock for the following situation (the MAD was calculated as shown in previous example):

Desired service level	98 percent
Mean absolute deviation from previous example	17.17 units
Service factor (see Table 18.13)	2.56
Forecast interval	4 weeks
Lead time	8 weeks

Calculations. Forecast interval and lead time adjustment:

$$\sqrt{\frac{8 \text{ weeks}}{4 \text{ weeks}}} = 1.41 \text{ weeks}$$

$$\text{Safety-stock units} = 17.17 \text{ units} \times 2.56 \times 1.41$$

$$= 62 \text{ units}$$

To convert the results into an equivalent amount of time supply, divide the 250 units per 4-week period forecasts by 62 units of safety stock. This gives a time supply of approximately 1 week.

Order Point. Adding the buffer stock to the usage during the replenishment lead time will give the order point for an item. Continuing with the safety-stock example, use a weekly 62.5-unit forecast, a lead time of 8 weeks, and a safety stock of 62. The order point is 562 units ($62.5 \times 8 + 62$). When the on-hand inventory and the quantity of the open orders equals the order-point quantity, it is time to order a replenishment lot size. At this time the quantity of the available inventory (on hand plus on order) should be enough to cover most of the requirements until the receipt of a new replenishment order. The order point compared to the on-hand balance plus the open orders answers the question of what to order and when.

ECONOMIC ORDER QUANTITIES

If the *order quantity* is the most economical quantity, it is referred to as the *economical order quantity,* or EOQ. To determine if order quantities are economical, the total yearly cost must be calculated. The *total yearly cost* is composed of three components:

1. *Ordering costs for year.* The costs involved with procuring the inventory for a year. This would include setup and ordering costs.

2. *Carrying costs for year.* The cost of storing the inventory for a year. Referred to most frequently as *carrying costs.*

3. *Inventory cost for year.* The cost of the inventory carried during the year. This last factor is often ignored because, as you will see, it does not affect the solution.

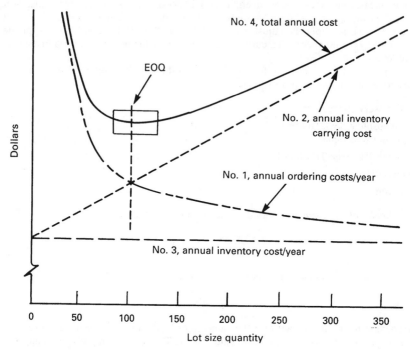

FIGURE 18.10   Economic order quantity, graphical solution.

These various costs versus lot size can each be represented graphically as shown on Fig. 18.10. The lines on the graph are numbered to agree with the equations which are developed here.

Curve No. 1: Ordering Costs

Cost of getting the inventory = number of orders per year

× cost of placing an order, $ per order   (18.1)

The number of orders per year is the quantity used per year divided by the order quantity. For example, if 400 items are used per year and 200 are ordered at a time, then two orders would be placed. If 100 are ordered, four orders would be placed. The smaller the order, the higher the number of orders that have to be placed. The number of orders per year is determined by this equation:

$$\text{Number of orders per year} = \frac{\text{quantity used per year}}{\text{quantity in order}}$$

$$= \frac{Y}{Q}$$

where Y = quantity used per year, units per year
Q = quantity ordered, units per order

The cost of procuring the inventory for a year is the number of orders placed times the cost of procuring the order quantity:

$$\text{Ordering costs (\$ per year)} = \frac{Y}{Q} \times C$$

where C = cost of ordering one order

This equation is shown by a line on the graph of costs versus quantity. The procurement costs go down as the order size increases and the number of lots decreases. This is a strong incentive for ordering large quantities.

Curve No. 2: Carrying Costs

Carrying cost for a year (\$ per year) = average inventory on hand (units per year)

$$\times \text{ cost (\$ per unit)} \times \text{ carrying cost (percent of unit cost)} = \frac{Q}{2} \times U \times I$$

where U = unit cost for each item, \$ per unit
I = carrying cost, stated as a percentage of the unit costs per year

The term I reflects the cost of money.

The cost of keeping the inventory goes up as the order quantity increases, which is what you would expect. This is an incentive to obtain small quantities.

Curve No. 3: Cost of Inventory

Cost of inventory per year = yearly demand (units per year) $\times$ cost of each unit (\$ per unit)
$$= YU$$

Curve No. 4: Total Yearly Inventory Cost

The three costs, when added together, give the total yearly inventory cost (TYIC):

$$\text{TYIC} = \frac{YC}{Q} + \frac{QUI}{2} + YU$$

The total yearly inventory cost curve is illustrated on the diagram by the typical *bathtub curve*. The curve may be plotted by adding the three cost increments, as shown. The objective, of course, is to find the order quantity on the horizontal axis, which is beneath the lowest point on the total yearly inventory cost curve. By coincidence, a vertical line through the lowest point on the bathtub curve coincides with the intersection of the ordering cost and carrying cost curve. The cost of the inventory YU, which is a horizontal line on the graph, has no effect on the order quantity. This explains why the value of the inventory is often omitted from some EOQ equation developments.

You should now have some insight into ways of solving the EOQ problem. Find the order quantity where the total inventory cost curve is the lowest or where the carrying and ordering costs intersect. The first calls for a calculus solution, and the latter a simultaneous equation solution.

Calculus Solution

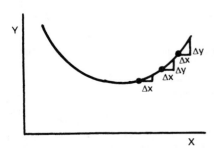

FIGURE 18.11 Calculus solution.

The minimum point on the total yearly inventory cost is where the slope of the line is zero (Fig. 18.11). The slope of a line, like the slope of a hill, is stated as the vertical distance traveled in a certain distance. As shown by three points on the curve, the slope becomes less until it reaches the bottom of the curve.

The slope in calculus is designated by a small part of y called Δy over a small part of x, Δx. When the Δy and Δx become infinitesimally small, they are called dy and dx. Because the TYIC is on the y axis and the quantity is on the x axis, the slope may be stated as $d(\text{TYIC})/dQ$. This is called the *first derivative* in calculus (unless you are familiar with the subject, you may have to take the next steps on faith or refer to a basic calculus text):

$$\text{TYIC} = \frac{YC}{Q} + \frac{QUI}{2} + YU$$

Find the first derivative of TYIC with respect to Q:

$$\frac{d(\text{TYIC})}{dQ} = -\frac{YC}{Q^2} + \frac{UI}{2} + 0$$

We are particularly interested in the point where the slope, or first derivative, is zero:

$$\frac{d(\text{TYIC})}{dQ} = 0$$

$$0 = -\frac{YC}{Q^2} + \frac{UI}{2}$$

Solving for Q:

$$Q = \sqrt{\frac{2YC}{UI}}$$

The Q in the equation is an incorrect description because it is not *any* order quantity but the most *economical* quantity. Therefore, it should be called the *economical order quantity* (EOQ):

$$\text{EOQ} = \sqrt{\frac{2YC}{UI}}$$

It is interesting that the value of the inventory YU became zero when the first derivative was taken. This result points out again that the value of the inventory has no impact on the answer, which is why it is left out by many people.

This equation, or a slight modification of it, is the one used by the majority of companies using EOQs. It is also the equation that appears in the computer software packages.

Example. A company has the following information about an electric relay they sell to computer manufacturers:

Unit cost $U = \$0.80$ per unit

Yearly demand $Y = 60,000$ units per year

Value of $I = 30$ percent

Ordering costs $= \$200$ for each order

$$\text{EOQ} = \sqrt{\frac{2 \times 60,000 \times 200}{0.80 \times 0.30}}$$

$$= 10,000 \text{ units}$$

Simultaneous Equation Solution

As noted, the point (quantity) where the procurement and carrying costs intersect is the same as that found by the lowest point on the TYIC curve. The intersection means that the procurement and carrying costs are equal:

$$\text{Ordering costs} = \text{carrying costs}$$

$$\frac{YC}{Q} = \frac{QUI}{2}$$

$$Q^2 = \frac{2YC}{UI}$$

$$Q = \sqrt{\frac{2YC}{UI}}$$

or

$$\text{EOQ} = \sqrt{\frac{2YC}{UI}}$$

This solution may be easier to accept by those who feel insecure with calculus. It also points out the contest between the procurement and carrying costs.

Tabular Solution

The tabular method may be considered an extension of the simultaneous equation method because the quantity where the carrying and procurement costs are equal is found by tabulating these costs for various quantities to find when they are equal.

Table 18.16, "Economic Order Quantity, Tabular Solution," shows the EOQ calculated by trial. Listed are six different order quantities and their resulting total cost. The calculations begin by taking the order quantity column 1, and multiplying it by the unit cost to get the order value, column 2. Average annual inventory is the order value divided by 2, column 3. Multiply this average annual inventory by the inventory-carrying cost percent to get the annual inventory-carrying cost dollars, column 4.

The next step is to determine the annual ordering cost. Divide the annual demand by the order quantity to calculate the number of orders per year, column 5. Multiply the orders per year by the cost to place an order to get the annual ordering costs, column 6.

TABLE 18.16   Economic Order Quantity, Tabular Solution

Annual demand (Y) = 500 Units

Unit cost (W) = $2

Order cost (C) = $4

Carrying cost percent (I) = 20 percent

$$EOQ = \sqrt{\frac{2YC}{IU}}$$

(1) Order quantity	(2) Order value	(3) Average annual inventory*	(4) Annual inventory-carrying cost	(5) Number of orders per year	(6) Annual order cost	(7) Total cost
25	$ 50	$ 25	$ 5	20	80	$85
50	100	50	10	10	40	50
100 = EOQ	200	100	20	5	20	40
125	250	125	25	4	16	41
250	500	250	50	2	8	58
500	1000	500	100	1	4	104

*The average annual inventory is justified only if the carrying costs increase and decrease with the inventory quantity.

As the final step, find the total cost, column 7, by adding the annual inventory-carrying cost, column 4, and the annual order cost.

As an example, an order quantity of 25 multiplied by a $2 unit cost gives an order value of $50. Dividing $50 by 2 gives the average annual inventory value of $25. Multiplying this by 20 percent gives an annual inventory-carrying cost value of $5. Next, divide the annual demand of 500 units by the order quantity 25; which gives 20 orders annually. Multiply the orders per year by the $4 per order to obtain an annual ordering cost of $80. The total annual inventory cost for an order quantity of 25 is $85 (the sum of the $5 annual inventory-carrying cost and the $80 annual ordering cost).

The table shows six different order quantities and their resulting total cost. As the order quantity increases, the annual inventory-carrying cost increases, but the annual ordering cost decreases. The total cost column shows a decrease for the first three order quantities increases but then increases for the last three order quantities. As shown, when the annual inventory-carrying cost equals the annual ordering cost, the total cost will be at its minimum. This lowest total cost order quantity is called the *economic order quantity* (EOQ). This is reached when the order quantity is 100. Calculate the EOQ directly using the EOQ formula shown.

Nomograph Solutions

When many hundreds of inventory items are being controlled, the methods described for obtaining EOQs may not be convenient. Consequently, companies have developed nomographs and tables. These are easy to understand and use.

EOQ IN PRACTICE

The larger the order quantity, the higher the inventory-carrying cost and the lower the ordering cost. The EOQ is the point where these two costs are equal.

EOQ Sensitivity

A previous EOQ graph shows that the total cost line is almost flat around the EOQ point. This fact gives the flexibility to choose an order quantity close but not equal to the EOQ without appreciably increasing the total cost. This is typical of all EOQ calculations and a fact frequently missed when deciding the order lot size and reconciling the practical application problems. This flatness of the total cost curve is the result of how the square root in the EOQ equation affects the data used in the calculation. This situation gives some latitude concerning the accuracy of the annual demand, unit cost, ordering cost, and the inventory-carrying cost percent data. For instance, if the data should be off by 100 percent, the EOQ is understated by only 40 percent. Precise data are not critical when using the EOQ to help in deciding the lot size. There are practical considerations when deciding lot sizes. For example, a tumbler can handle 5000 parts so a lot size of 5500 parts is too large. If an operator can make 200 parts in a shift, don't order 210 if you can help it.

Working with a series of lot sizes within a reasonable range of minimum total cost gives flexibility to using the EOQ in daily operations. The basic EOQ formula is the basis for an economic analysis of order policies. The EOQ depends on the assumptions that demand is fairly constant throughout the year and that items need to be ordered in batches or lots. It is better to start with an economic analysis of the lot size first and then modify it to better fit daily operations.

Simultaneous Receipt and Use

The trade-off between the cost to order and the cost of carrying inventory should be a basic first step for deciding lot sizes. There are other factors to consider before deciding the lot size. Frequently an order gets received in small quantities over a period instead of all at once. Some of these receipts are consumed simultaneously as new stock comes into inventory. The trade-off analysis needs an adjustment to account for the rate of inventory buildup and the rate of usage.

This situation would reduce the storage space requirement and consequently the cost of carrying the inventory. An EOQ equation that considers this situation is the following:

$$EOQ = \sqrt{\frac{2YC}{UI\,(1 - w/r)}}$$

where w = rate at which product is being used
r = production rate

Fixed and Variable *I* Values

The cost of carrying the inventory in the EOQ equation was assumed to be for the average inventory. This is not realistic for all situations if the storage space cannot be used for some other purpose. To overcome this problem, some companies have modified the EOQ equation to include a fixed and variable factor I_v and I_f.

$$\text{TYIC} = \frac{YC}{Q} + \frac{QUI_v}{2} + QUI_f + YU$$

$$\text{EOQ} = \sqrt{YC/U\,(I_v/2 + I_f)}$$

What Should the Value *I* Be?

It is often difficult to determine *I* in practice. Some would argue that *I* should be related to money borrowed by the firm while others have argued for the rate of return on a company's money. Some authorities believe *I* should be a management control factor and increased or decreased to accomplish management's objective.

Grouping similar items is a way to save ordering and setup costs and gain capacity. some ordering costs are unique to an item, and some are common to all items in the group. The principle is to reduce the ordering costs that are common to the entire group.

Purchase Discounts

Purchase discounts influence ordering decisions because the unit cost depends on the quantity ordered. Purchase discounts can change the results of the economic lot size calculation because of the savings generated by the discounts. When the lot size reaches the discount quantity, the unit cost is reduced, which changes the inventory value and total product costs. Getting the lowest unit costs is sometimes the only consideration when deciding the lot size. This approach frequently leads to a poor decision from a total cost basis.

Table 18.17, "Purchase Discounts," shows how the EOQ and discount options should be evaluated. In comparison, the EOQ gives a lower inventory-carrying cost, but the discount option gives even greater savings in total item cost and ordering cost. The total costs line shows a net savings of $660 from the discount option. A trade-off must account for the unit discount savings, and the added inventory costs from purchasing the

TABLE 18.17 Purchase Discounts

	EOQ option	Discount option	Change
Annual demand	500	500	
Ordering cost	$ 16.00	$ 16.00	
Inventory-carrying cost	20%	20%	
Purchase discount		5%	5%
Purchase prices	$ 50.00	$ 47.50	−$ 2.50
Order quantity	40	200	160
Number of orders per year	12.5	2.5	−10
Average inventory units	20	100	80
Average inventory value	$ 1,000.00	$ 4,750.00	$3,750.00
Annual costs			
Item total cost	$25,000.00	$23,750.00	−$1,250.00
Inventory-carrying cost	200.00	950.00	750.00
Ordering cost	200.00	40.00	−160.00
Total costs	$25,400.00	$24,740.00	−$ 660.00

larger discount quantity. In general, when considering purchase discounts, the order quantity, average inventory, and carrying cost will increase. Simultaneously the item's annual total cost and ordering cost will decrease.

Purchase Discounts and Cash Flow

First judge purchase discounts based on the total annual costs of the purchase price, inventory, and ordering costs; then evaluate the change in total inventory investment. The example seems to support a decision to take the discount and save $660 annually. However, the average inventory investment will increase from $1000 to $4750, an increase of 375 percent. How will this and other similar decisions impact cash flow? Is the 17.5 percent return on the added inventory investment ($600 divided by $3750) adequate? Does the warehouse have the storage facilities for the larger order quantity? Are there risks of obsolescence or shelf life? Taking the practical considerations into account is often the most difficult part of the decision.

Varying Lot Size

A lot size can be a fixed order quantity each time or a variable quantity that changes to reflect requirements over time. Some lot size decisions are one-time events related to highly perishable or seasonal items with high inventory risk. A variety of formulas and methods to calculate lot sizes abound in most textbooks on production and inventory management. While calculating the economic trade-off of setup, inventory, and other costs is a good first step, the economic quantity needs modification to account for the realities of daily operations.

As an example, minimum quantity restrictions can increase or decrease order quantities. Orders may need to be in specific quantity multiples that lead to rounding off the order quantity to meet the requirement. Maximum order quantities can be the result of limited storage and handling capabilities. Yields cause adjustments to calculated order quantities for some items. Increase the lot size for items that consistently experience production problems that affect yields. To yield 100 units if the expected loss is 5 percent, the lot size should be at least 106 (100 divided by 0.95 and rounded up).

The availability of materials and a probable product phase out also affects lot size decisions. Tool-and-die life is frequently an important consideration when shop floor operations are involved. The regularity with which a tool or die wears out or needs maintenance may decide the lot size quantity. If a die needs sharpening after producing 7000 parts, it makes sense to make the lot size an even multiple or fraction of 7000. This avoids additional setups or the premature scheduling of small lot sizes that will increase costs.

Despite the many factors that influence the order quantity, the best approach is to strive for the smallest lot size possible. Small lot sizes mean lower inventory levels and carrying costs. If quality problems occur, small lot sizes mean fewer items to inspect and parts to rework. Small lot sizes shorten the replenishment cycle and give manufacturing and purchasing more flexibility responding to customer requirements. Once management settles on the lot size, there is usually some latitude to increase or decrease it, yet not affect the costs significantly.

An order quantity converted to an equivalent time supply is easier and more flexible to apply in daily operations. Just divide the lot size quantity by the average daily usage to get the time supply of the order quantity. When it is time to order, add the net requirements over the days' supply to calculate the order quantity. There are more sophisticated time supply techniques, such as part period balancing and the Wagner-Whitin algorithm, but they involve many calculations. Yet with the availability of the desktop computer and spreadsheet programs, these sometimes laborious calculations are no longer a problem.

TIME-PHASED ORDER POINT

When the projected demand is level over the planning horizon, it is possible to calculate the order point by using average demand during lead time and adding safety stock. Then when the available inventory is less than or equal to the order point, order the planned lot size. However, when the forecast of demand is not level over time, use a *time-phased order point* to plan the replenishment. Table 18.18, "Time-Phased Order Point," shows requirements for different quantities and periods and the application of principles discussed earlier.

The calculation of net inventory shows the reduction of the 800 beginning inventory by the gross requirements for each period, which leaves a projected inventory of 700, 600, 500, and so on. A scheduled receipt for 600 is added in period 6 as available inventory. In period 9 all the available inventory is consumed and the remaining net requirement of 400 triggers a need for stock replenishment and inventory analysis. The first step, shift for safety time, moves the net requirements forward by 2 periods to meet the inventory policy for buffer stock. Next calculate the first planned order receipt for 2200 by adding the requirements of the next 4 periods. This process repeats for period 11, 15, and so on. When these planned order receipts are offset by the 6 periods of lead time, they become planned order releases.

The report shows that the planned order release of 2200 should be issued in period 1. This will allow it to arrive by period 7, meeting the safety time plan and the gross requirements. In general, the time-phased order point uses the same calculations as the materials requirements plan. The major difference is that the gross requirements are independent—driven from a forecast instead of bills of materials. Analysis of the report shows that besides the need to place an order for 2200, the scheduled receipt in period 6 needs expediting to maintain the two periods of safety time.

The reason for using the time-phased order point is that the gross requirements change significantly in many planning periods. The time-phased order point handles seasonal and sporadic demand patterns very well. The safety time supply and lot sizes are dynamic and adjust to the discrete demands in each period. Planned orders that appear in the first period signal that the item is at order point. Analysis of the scheduled receipts of open orders can lead to adjustments that avoid stock-outs or excess inventory.

INDEPENDENT DEMAND

The demands for some items, especially finished goods, are often forecasted. Forecasts may be a combination of mathematical models, historical information, market analysis, and management judgment. Requirements for finished goods are usually independent of factors directly controlled by production and inventory management. Statistical and time-phased order points are appropriate ways to plan the replenishment of this type of demand. For manufactured items, the master scheduling function will likely plan the replenishment of these independent demands.

TABLE 18.18 Time-Phased Order Point

Demand = discrete by time period	Lot size = 4 periods' supply
Lead time = 6 periods	Demand periods 17–20 = 100
Safety time = 2 periods	Demand periods 21–28 = 200
	Beginning inventory = 800

Time-phased order-point report

Time period	1	2	3	4	5	6	7	8	9	10	11	12	13	14	15	16
Gross requirements	100	100	100	100	200	200	200	200	600	600	600	600	300	300	300	300
Scheduled receipts						600										
Plan order release	2200				1200				400				800			
Projected inventory	700	600	500	400	200	600	2600	2400	1800	1200	1800	1200	900	600	700	400

Time-phased order-point calculations

Time period	1	2	3	4	5	6	7	8	9	10	11	12	13	14	15	16
Net inventory	700	600	500	400	200	600	400	200	−400	600	600	600	300	300	300	300
Net requirements							400	600	400	600	300	300		300	100	100
Shift for safety time									600	600	300	300	300	300	100	300
Plan order receipt							2200				1200				400	
Action messages	A					B										

A = Release order for 2200 units to be delivered in period 7.
B = Expedite scheduled receipt by 1 period (below safety time supply).

18.51

DEPENDENT DEMAND

Determining the demands for subassemblies, components, and other materials used in manufacturing depend on the quantity per parent item as shown in the bills of materials. Their requirements depend on the scheduled quantity for the parent item. Historical usage and statistical forecasting techniques are not necessary for assemblies and components and can cause serious supply problems if used. The dependent-demand items should be scheduled using the principles and techniques of materials requirements planning.

Materials Requirements Planning

All the items that are below the end item (finished goods) in a product structure are potential points for planning stock replenishment and inventory. *Materials require-ments planning* (MRP) is an excellent tool for deciding what, how much, and when to order dependent-demand items. An effective MRP process can also maintain order priorities by recommending action to keep replenishment orders in line with requirements. Sometimes planned lot sizes can generate excess inventory because they are out of synchronization with all the levels of the product structure.

Consider an item that uses one component for each parent item. If the parent lot size is 100 and the component's lot size is 137, a remnant of 37 components will result. This remnant is excess inventory. Synchronizing the lot sizes by changing the component lot size to 100 or 200 may improve the likelihood that all the inventory is eventually used. Lot size remnants have no function and may be a waste.

The effectiveness of the MRP process depends on the accuracy of the master schedule and bills of materials. In addition, the accuracy of the inventory stock status is crucial for good planning. Inventory information must include accurate and timely inventory balances, reasonable lead times, and correct due dates on open orders. Recall the discussion on interactive performance earlier in this chapter and the rapid deterioration as planned orders from one level decides the requirements for the next level. Inaccurate data simply becomes more inaccurate for each new planning level. MRP is an information-driven system designed to plan and control inventory. It is sometimes called a *push system* because the planning of requirements and execution of orders uses schedules offset by lead time into the future. MRP usually works best when product structures are complex and requirements change frequently.

DEMAND PULL METHODS

Contrasting with the MRP process is a *pull system* that triggers order action only when there is a demand for use or stock replenishment. These systems depend on a highly visible inventory and usually do not rely heavily on system information. A signal, received from a user, triggers the issue of materials. This signal is frequently a kanban (card) that authorizes a supplying workstation to provide a standard quantity of parts. Pull systems feature execution and provide little planning information. Controlling the number and quantity on the kanbans is the key to managing inventory levels. A kanban accompanies each fixed quantity of parts. When the container, box, skid, or pan is empty, the kanban goes to the supplying work center as an authorization to replace stock.

Other simple inventory replenishment systems include using *two bins* and *visual reviews* to trigger order action. With a two-bin system, one bin should contain sufficient inventory to cover the demand during lead time and the safety stock. The order quantity is also equal to one bin. When a bin is empty it causes an order to be placed for a replacement of the bin quantity. The order should arrive before the inventory in the second bin is gone. Visual review methods require physically checking the inventory on a regular cycle. When the inventory goes below a visual order point (box quantity, line on a container, parts in a bag, etc.), it is a signal to issue an order for stock replenishment. These systems are very useful to simplify the process by eliminating paperwork. They work effectively for the large number of parts in the C item group that have little influence on inventory investment.

SUMMARY

The proper management and control of inventory levels and transactions are important for the success of any business. Inventory is an element in many business decisions. Timely and accurate inventory information is critical for these decisions. When the inventory data are accurate and timely, both top management and operations management can make and execute their plans with confidence.

Excess inventory is often used as a way to escape from disciplined management practices and to cover up problems. The inventory investment in most companies is substantial so top management should demand a high return on this investment. Every item in inventory should add value to the business by fitting into one of the six functions of inventory:

- Buffer
- Anticipation
- Hedge
- Transportation
- Lot size
- Lead time

It is important to use the distribution pipeline efficiently when positioning products for sale to customers. Using the inventory generated by the lot size and replenishment lead time information should give lower product cost and more efficient production.

Conversely, every effort should be made to reduce inventory costs by removing the causes such as poor forecasting, uncontrolled lead times, high ordering costs, insufficient capacity, and inaccurate inventory information. Less inventory means fewer items to store and to cycle count. It also means reduced inventory-carrying costs and the many problems related to physical control. Inventory planning and control is an intricate dichotomy. Having excess inventory can help a company be highly competitive and profitable. Yet too much inventory can produce exactly the opposite results. The responsibility of inventory control personnel is to constantly pursue the objective of getting the maximum benefits from the least amount of inventory.

BIBLIOGRAPHY

Fogarty, D. W., J. H. Blackstone, and T. R. Hoffman: *Production and Inventory Management,* 2d ed., South-Western Publishing, Cincinnati, Ohio, 1991.

Vollmann, T. E., W. L. Berry, and D. C. Whybark: *Manufacturing Planning and Control Systems,* 3rd ed., Business One Erwin, Homewood, Ill., 1992.

Sanderson, G. A.: *Inventory Management: A Managerial Perspective,* MGI Management Institute, White Plains, N.Y., 1992.

————: *Basic Techniques of Inventory Management,* MGI Management Institute, White Plains, N.Y., 1992.

————: *Successfully Managing the P&IC Function,* MGI Management Institute, White Plains, N.Y., 1989.

————: "Breaking Through the Class A Barrier," *APICS 34th International Conference Proceedings,* 1991, pp. 633–636.

CHAPTER 19
INVENTORY CONTROL THEORY

Editor

Robert G. Brown, CFPIM

President, Materials Management Systems, Inc.
Thetford Center, Vermont

A homemaker maintaining kitchen inventories and a shopkeeper ordering to restock shelves tend instinctively to reorder when current stock levels are "low." The homemaker and the shopkeeper will select a quantity that will last a "reasonable" length of time. They will order products they obtain from the same source at the same time. In general, small-business managers apply the same inventory principles that the shopkeeper and homemaker use. The procedure works because managers are in direct contact with both the demand side and the supply side of the business. The operations are small enough that some inefficiency is tolerable.

In a large corporation usually the marketing department knows about the demand side of the business and tries to influence it. The production side of the business is made up of a different set of people with quite different loyalties. The people in this side know how things can be purchased or manufactured. There is imperfect communication between marketing and production. The resulting delay and ambiguity in transmitting plans and decisions from one to the other increase the uncertainty that has to be buffered, just as if the ordering lead time were longer.

A 10 percent reduction in the investment required to run a large business can represent several millions of dollars of capital. The purpose of inventory models is to sharpen up the instinctive decisions made by individuals in small businesses so that large businesses can run efficiently. The term *inventory* has many different meanings in different audiences. In some discussions *inventory* means a list of products, and *stock* is the amount held of any one product. To the financial press and boards of directors, *inventory* means a total capital sum invested in stocks. To a warehouse manager, *inventory* may mean pallets and cartons that have to be moved, put on shelves, picked, and shipped. This chapter conveniently distinguishes among three related concepts:

1. *Inventory control* means keeping records of issues and receipts of the book records of what is in stock. *Cycle counting* is pertinent to inventory control to assure that the records reasonably reflect the physical stock. This topic is covered elsewhere in this handbook.

2. *Inventory management* means budgeting planning factors for how much to produce (EOQs) and when to produce (order points). This topic is covered in the first section of this chapter, after identifying what parts of the total inventory investment are subject to inventory management.

3. *Inventory scheduling or planning* uses information from inventory control about stock status and information from inventory management about safety stocks and lot sizes to generate orders to replenish stock. This topic is covered in the last section of this chapter.

TYPES OF INVENTORY

Inventory management is concerned with only part of the total capital invested in inventory: safety stock and working stock. Planning or scheduling is concerned, in addition, with stabilization stock. Pipeline inventory and *slow-moving and obsolete stock* (SLOB) are part of the total investment, but these contributions to the requirements for capital are outside the discussion in this chapter.

Safety Stock

Inventory decisions are made a lead time in advance of the time when the materials will be available. The consumer's lead time for shopping at a retail store is essentially zero, so the consumer does not need a safety stock at all. The current intense interest in *supply-chain management* (*vendor-managed inventory, trading partners, quick response,* and quite a variety of similar buzzwords) is an effort to shorten the effective lead time and thus cut down on the investment in safety stock. Some of the implementations merely push the safety stock back to the supplier where there is less value added and there is a broader spectrum of information about the needs of all customers. Other implementations improve the whole supply chain by accurately sharing current, complete information about stock status and requirements.

The decisions about when to produce (purchase or manufacture) materials are based on a forecast. The more accurate the forecast, the less safety stock is required. An important feature of supply-chain management is that the customer provides the supplier with the best possible time-phased information about future requirements. This was also the motivation behind the flap over MRP and MRP II—to provide accurate information up the logistics pipeline about "lumpy" lot-sized withdrawals from stock.

In some industries the uncertainty is buffered by making the customer wait for his or her order to be filled. It is impractical to make a customer wait for service parts to repair equipment, and the demand is inherently uncertain. A good forecast will identify secular growth (up or down) and seasonal profiles where present. But there is always an unpredictable residual uncertainty. Safety stock can buffer that uncertainty over a lead time. The next section of this chapter covers the principles behind decision rules to establish how much safety stock to carry to balance expense against investment.

Working Stock

There have been some attempts to replenish inventory on the basis of the *sell-one, order-one principle.* That may work well for locomotives and mainframe computers, but it won't work for eggs. As long ago as 1906 Wilson[8] at Bell Labs documented that in manufacturing, there is a setup cost associated with beginning to make a batch of a product. If a quantity is produced that is sufficient to last for more than current needs, then there is an inventory, which is called *working stock.* The bigger the average batch, the more working stock and the fewer setups per year. There is an economic balance between acquisition costs (a generalization of manufacturing setup costs) and the holding costs for the working stock. The problem is simple enough that graduate students can solve it every year, and the answer has just enough mathematics (a square root) to make it look important. The essential structure of the decision rule for how much to produce at one time is described in the next section.

Stabilization of Seasonal Stock

Some businesses have a pattern of peak demand at some part of the year with a much lower rate of demand during the slack period. For example, canning of seasonal crops is often a source of summer employment for students and faculty. The peak may be artificially induced by promotions. Not all industries have the capacity to produce at current rates of demand during the peak season. Producing materials early builds up a *stabilization stock,* that is, a capital investment in lieu of the alternative of investing in more production capacity. There exists an optimal amount of investment in inventory and machinery in relation to the expense of overtime and hiring and training costs. These concepts are discussed in the last section of this chapter.

Pipeline Inventory

It takes lead time to produce material. The lead time may be for purchasing from a supplier, for manufacturing, or for moving stock from the point at which it is produced to the warehouse from which it will be sold. The average capital investment in pipeline inventory is the length of the lead time multiplied by the rate of usage at the output end. In general, shorter lead times require more expensive methods (including more effort to control manufacturing processes and to negotiate with the principal suppliers). If such expense does reduce the length of lead time, the capital invested will be smaller. Changes in pipeline inventory are outside the scope of this chapter.

There Is Inevitably Some SLOB

The storage of slow-moving and obsolescent stock is inevitable. Whether or not the circumstances that made a radical change in requirements were foreseeable at the time the decision was made to acquire stock, they are sometimes not foreseen. Cyclical engineering changes, competition, the economy, and government regulations are expensive, if not impossible, to forecast well. Therefore the actual demand that occurs after stock is in place may differ widely from the forecast used to decide to produce stock. One could, of course, start a rumor that the material is in short supply. Management of SLOB requires some ingenuity in finding ways of disposing of it to retrieve some of the money spent without disrupting markets for active products. How to do that is outside the scope of this chapter.

DECISION RULES

In the 1940s H. Ford Dickie[5] of the General Electric Company preached the concept of ABC Analysis with decision tables to fine-tune decisions about when and how much to produce. He noted that if the list of products were sorted in descending sequence by the value of annual usage, relatively few items at the beginning of the list (perhaps 5 to 10 percent of all the products) accounted for 50 percent of the total annual volume. These are the *class A products.* Because there are relatively few of them, management intervention and review are not very expensive. Furthermore the aggregate value is so large that intervention to improve operations is worthwhile.

The bottom half of the list, called *class C products,* has the lowest value of annual usage and, in total, represents perhaps 5 to 10 percent of the annual value of sales. There are too many *class C* products for it to be practical to do much review and modification, and the total value is small enough that approximating procedures do not waste a lot of corporate resources.

In the middle of the list, the *class B products* account for almost half the products and almost half the value of annual sales. There are enough products that some routine procedures are required and enough value that the procedures should produce good results.

It is important to recall that in the 1940s the most advanced data processing equipment available to industry was the punched-card tabulator. It was practical to set up decision tables that said the safety stock or the order point should have certain values (perhaps expressed in weeks of supply) where the value was different for classes A, B, and C. Another set of tables expressed the production quantity (in months of supply) with different values for the three classes. If you were careful not to drop the deck of punched cards on the floor, it was straightforward (but oh, so tedious!) to sort and gang-punch the decision tables into the product records.

In today's environment the punched card has been replaced by computers, and even the corner grocery has a personal computer that can calculate averages and square roots and logarithms (in spite of Admiral Grace Harper who said the business has no use for logarithms). One can get much finer control by using decision rules that compute results from a variety of characteristics of each product to give different recommendations for how much to order and when to replenish stock.

Inventory management is concerned with two decisions: how much to order (lot quantities) and when to order (order points that involve safety stock). The theory and practice deal with long-term averages to trade expenses for capital investment. In general, a higher investment in either working stock or safety stock reduces some associated operating expense. The motivation for planning *how much* to produce and *when* is to tend toward increasing corporate return on investment (Fig. 19.1).

EOQ Equation and Theory

The theory[6] of economical order quantities seeks to balance the expense of acquiring each lot or batch of materials against the capital investment to hold the resulting working stock. The hundreds of papers in the literature make (tacitly or explicitly) an assumption under each of five item characteristics. The basic model looks for the minimum total cost. Let A (dollars per lot) be the acquisition cost for each lot. If the lot quantity is Q (pieces) and annual usage is S (pieces/year), then the annual total cost of acquisitions or setup is AS/Q dollars per year. Assume that the average working stock is $Q/2$ pieces, each is worth v (dollars per piece), and the annual carrying cost is r (dollars per dollar per year). Then the cost to hold the average inventory is $rvQ/2$ dollars per year.

The total cost is $C = AS/Q + rvQ/2$. The cost is a minimum when the lot quantity is the following:

$$Q = \sqrt{\frac{2AS}{rv}} \quad \text{pieces}$$

This expression is very "robust." Consider any factor in the expression that is off by a factor of 2—double to half the real value. Using the square root, the resulting lot quan-

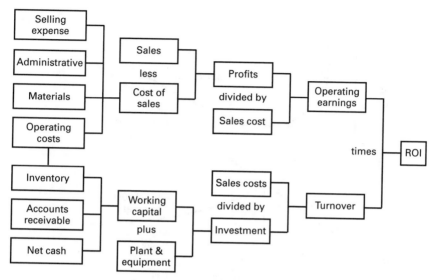

FIGURE 19.1   ROI flowchart.

tity will be between 70 and 140 percent of the theoretical optimum lot. If the lot quantity used is larger than the optimum, the holding costs will be high, but that cost is offset by a decrease in acquisition costs so that the total cost is no more than 6 percent above the theoretically achievable minimum.

Because the cost curve (Fig. 19.2) is quite flat near the minimum, it makes sense to limit the computed value by maximum or minimum time supplies or quantities. Of course, it would not make sense to require that all products be ordered at least four times a year but be maintained at a level never less than a 90-day supply. It does not make sense to express the EOQ to more than perhaps two significant digits: Use 2800, not 2761.3 pieces. In simple situations it may be advisable to have a decision table, such as Table 19.1, that expresses the quantity to buy as one of a finite set of time supplies based on ranges of the value Sv of annual (or monthly) usage.

Acquisition or Setup Cost.   The default assumption is that it costs A dollars each time a lot or batch of a product is produced (purchased or manufactured). Industrial engineers frequently study the setup cost for manufacturing operations in minute detail. If the values do not come readily to hand (as may be the case for purchasing rather than manufacturing), one can easily infer the true costs by examining past ordering practice. The economical balance of acquisition and holding costs is so sensible that people will usually produce in nearly economical quantities.

Look at past orders for a representative sample of products. Tabulate the approximate time that the order quantities last against the value of annual usage. Plot a scatter diagram on log-log paper (Fig. 19.3). The points will tend to cluster around a line of central tendency with a slope of $-\frac{1}{2}$. The intercept of that line gives an estimate of the ratio of the acquisition cost to the carrying charge A/r.

The example clearly shows a predilection for limiting the lot quantities to a year's supply. The acquisition cost is $A = \$40$ for a carrying charge $r = 0.24$.

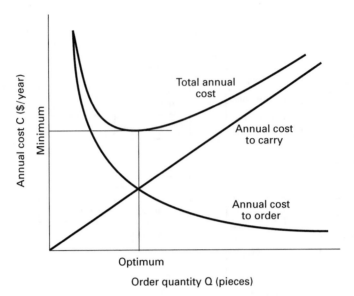

FIGURE 19.2   Acquisition, holding, and total cost.

TABLE 19.1   Simple Ordering Table

Carrying charge (fraction) per year: 0.240
Cost to process an order: $25

	Value of monthly usage	Order months' supply
Over	4400	0.5
1100 to	4400	1.0
400 to	1100	2.0
120 to	400	3.0
31 to	120	6.0
8 to	31	12.0
3 to	8	24.0
Under	3	36.0

Where several products contend for a common production facility, there may be a major cost incurred when changing from one family of products to another and a much smaller cost for changing from one product to another within a family. Thus, in general, it is wise to consider the whole group as an item where usage is expressed in a common unit of measure like dollar values or man-hours to produce. Compute the standard EOQ for that aggregate, and express it as a time supply—the interval between changing from one family to another.

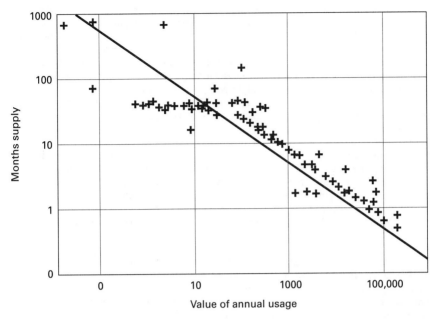

FIGURE 19.3   Estimating cost to acquire.

When there are several products to be considered as a family group, the expression for the interval between making that group is given by the following:

$$T = \sqrt{\frac{2(A + \Sigma\, a_i)}{r\, \Sigma\, v_i S_i}}$$

where A is the major changeover cost for the family and a_i are the minor changeover costs for members of the same family. The management policy variable is the carrying charge r dollars per dollar per year, as v_i and S_i refer, respectively, to the unit value and the annual usage of the ith item in the family. If annual usage for the most popular product in a family is many times greater than annual usage for the least popular product, it may be marginally economical to make enough of the slow-moving products to cover several cycles.

Storage or Holding Cost.   The default assumption is that the cost to hold working stock is a carrying charge (dollars per dollar per year) times the average investment in working stock. Some papers in the literature make an inaccurate assumption that the average working stock is half the lot quantity. In the case of some bulky products, the space occupied may be of more concern than the dollar investment.

It can be shown that if you want to contribute to maximizing the corporate return on investment, the carrying charge used for EOQs should be equal to the current rate of return on assets employed. More advanced financial analysis may increase the carrying charge if the particular inventory is much more risky than the average investment. For example, one corporation charges a much higher rate on finished goods in the field than raw materials at the factory. The raw materials have a wider range of possible applications as requirements change. You might want to lower the carrying charge if inventory is more liquid than the average investment—that means you have the way to lower the average inventory permanently and not replenish stock that has been consumed.

It makes sense to use the carrying charge as a management policy variable. A large increase in the rate makes inventory look relatively expensive. The result would be to make many more small lots, which might be a good thing during a recession where the extra work can cause some of the more skilled employees to be retained and the short runs allow the flexibility to make whatever customers happen to order.

Rate of Delivery to Stock. If the lot quantity Q is delivered to stock essentially all at one time, then a first approximation to the average working stock is $Q/2$ pieces. If new stock is produced into inventory at an annualized rate P which is less than twice the annualized rate of sales S, then the average working stock is $0.5Q(1 - S/P)$. Obviously the annual actual production is equal to the annual sales. The rate P is based on the rate of production while you are producing. Then the simple EOQ becomes $Q = \sqrt{2AS/rv(1 - S/P)}$ with an obvious extension to the case of groups of related products.

Unit Value. The default assumption is that each unit in inventory has a standard cost used in calculating the value of the investment. In a country with very high inflation, the standard unit cost for the next order may be very different from the current cost. The practical way to handle that is to increase the carrying charge by the rate of inflation. When there is a one-time opportunity to buy now at a cost that is much lower than the cost on the next order (promotional prices, tooling changes), a good rule of thumb is to increase the months of supply ordered now by 1 month for each 2 percent of anticipated price rise. The same rule of thumb works well when a supplier offers a quantity discount for buying a larger quantity than the conventional theory would call for.

Usage Rate. The original EOQ theory was based on a known annual rate S of consumption. Some of the elaborate extensions of the theory consider cases in which there is a known trend in the rate of consumption, a known seasonal pattern in consumption, or a known degree of random variation in consumption. There is also the case of mandated engineering changes for health and safety where any stock left on hand at the time of the change becomes SLOB.

The theory can be simplified with no practical consequences and applied to running a business (whatever the consequences in having a thesis approved). Work out the standard EOQ based on an annualized rate of usage S. Convert the quantity Q into a time supply $T = Q/S$. Order in quantities q_t that cover the forecast for T periods, starting at the time t when you place the order.

There is one place where the simple theory for deterministic demand can be improved. When there is random variation in usage around the forecast, it is necessary also to invest in safety stocks. The decision rules for computing the proper level of safety stock take account of $N = S/Q$ the number of times per year when replenishment stock will be ordered. The image is that stock is low just prior to receipt of the next lot, which is when there is exposure to running short. The larger the value of N, the more safety stock will be required.

George Gerson[6] has developed explicit forms for the interdependence between frequencies as a result of lot quantity decisions and the safety stock. These expressions are nonlinear equations that cannot be solved in closed form. Extensive simulations show that if the lot quantity is "large" compared to the standard deviation of forecast errors, the difference between using the interdependent model and two independent models is trivial in terms of consequences to the business.

Therefore a practical approach is to compute the EOQ in the usual way. Compare the result to the standard deviation of forecast errors. For an expensive, slow-moving product, it may appear economical to order a small quantity. However the standard deviation of errors in forecasting lumpy demand for a slow-moving product may be large. Simply round up the quantity Q if necessary to be at least as large as the standard deviation. This result is not the theoretical optimum solution, but the difference is small compared to the costs of computing what the optimum is.

Safety Stock

Procedures to trigger replenishment orders are discussed later in this chapter. In general, all procedures compare what is available (on hand and due in) with an order point. The *order point* is a forecast of usage over the lead time plus a safety stock to cover some of the demand that exceeds the forecast during the lead time. This section will look at decision rules to recommend the right level of safety stock for each product.

In a naive inventory system the safety stock may be expressed as weeks of supply based on some forecast. Even if it is, the consequences of alternative values for the number of weeks must be calculated based on expressing safety stock as the product of a safety factor k and the standard deviation σ of errors in forecasting demand over a lead time. The safety factor k is a pure number, generally in the range of 0 to 4. The standard deviation σ is expressed in pieces (per lead time) and generally is computed in the course of generating a forecast of demand.

Some inventory systems continue to base safety stock on the *mean absolute deviation* (MAD) rather than the standard deviation. I developed the MAD during the 1950s not because it was in any sense theoretically correct but pragmatically because the primitive computers could not handle numbers as large as the squares of other numbers and could not (in reasonable time) take square roots. If the distribution of forecast errors is exactly normal, then the standard deviation $\sigma = 1.25$ MAD. The actual ratios turn out to range from 1.0 to 1.5, so the estimated standard deviation can be 25 percent too high for some products and 25 percent too low for others. In an era of intense concentration on getting the forecast accuracy improved by another 5 percent, that margin of error is too large to be acceptable.

A related note about exponential smoothing used in forecasting: The reason the smoothing constant α was set at 0.1 was that on those punched-card machines, it was far faster to move the wires over one position on the plug board and add than to try and multiply. It was nearly a decade later that modeling of actual time series showed that in many cases the value 0.1 is in fact nearly optimal.

Lead Times. One can observe lead times by noting the time when a transaction triggers a replenishment order and the time when the resulting stock is on hand ready for use. Such lead times will vary from order to order. Often the variation is small compared to the average. Then it makes sense to plan the future orders to arrive in just about the average time. When there is a finite interval between opportunities to order, the lead time used in planning safety stock should include that interval.

There have been several attempts to postulate models of the variability in lead time. All of them give the wrong answer because they leave out one essential factor. The objective is to calculate a value for σ, that is, the standard deviation of demand during a lead time. This is a measure of the dispersion of a joint distribution of demand and of lead times. It is essential to consider the covariation. Suppose you are one of many customers who order from a common supplier. When demand is high, you and the other customers order more. The workload swamps the supplier, who is then late in filling these orders. Demand goes up, the lead time goes up. Consider another situation in which you order whenever you like, but the supplier waits until you have ordered a full truckload before shipping. When you have high demand, you get delivery quickly.

The first example illustrates positive correlation, the second negative correlation. It is dangerous to assume that the two distributions are statistically independent. There are two courses of action. In most industrial situations the best procedure is to postulate a planning freeze period that is equal to the longest reasonable actual lead time and to plan production and safety stocks on the basis of that freeze period.

An alternative is to measure the correlation between variation in demand and variation in lead times. When you trigger a replenishment order, make a note of the demand to date. When the material comes into stock, compare current demand during a lead time. You can measure the standard deviation of that series of observations, which is the exact value of σ without any theoretical approximations.

Some suppliers take the attitude, "I will not carry any inventory merely to oblige a customer. If a customer wants my product, he or she should order it far enough in advance so that I can go out and buy the raw materials, machine them, and deliver the product." When the supplier is another company, you can shop around for better terms. When the supplier is your own factory, this method allows manufacturing to cut into the total profits. Inventory carried as raw or semifinished materials has the smallest possible value added and the widest possible range of potential uses as requirements change. If manufacturing demands that marketing carry finished-goods inventory to buffer uncertainty over a long lead time, then that strategy will produce the greatest value added and the least flexibility in alternative uses.

It is prudent to carry buffer stocks at various stages so that the planning lead time for the next stage is only the time to produce from that intermediate inventory. If you have a long manufacturing cycle time to produce bulk product and a relatively short cycle to package it in a variety of customer forms, it makes sense to carry a buffer stock of bulk, with safety stocks based on the long manufacturing cycle but with demand aggregated over many different end formats so that the standard deviation of forecast error is relatively low. Then plan packaging, with the very uncertain demand pattern, over a short lead time from the bulk material.

Investment.   The planned investment in safety stock is $kv\sigma$ where v is the unit value (standard cost) used to accumulate financial statements about the value of inventory. The larger the safety factor k, the larger the investment.

Expense of Filling All Demand.   Customers generally get a large fraction of demand satisfied from stock available at the time the demand arises. That stock is a combination of safety stock, working stock, and stabilization stock. Occasionally total demand for a product exceeds the forecast during the lead time by more than the safety stock provided. Customers manage, one way or another, to get the rest of their demand satisfied. If they will wait for a backorder to be filled or take their business elsewhere, the expense incurred is proportional to the amount by which total demand exceeded forecast plus safety stock. If you can satisfy the order by some form of expediting (short-dated orders on the source, flying stock from an alternative location, substitution, or cannibalization), the expense incurred as customers get all their demand satisfied is probably more nearly proportional to the number of times you run short rather than the amount by which you run short.

If there are N opportunities to run short, just prior to arrival of a replenishment order, the expected number of shortages is $i\Sigma NF(k)$ where F is the probability that there will be a shortage given that the safety factor has the value k. The expected value of demand that gets lost or back-ordered is $Nv\sigma E(k)$ where E is the partial expectation, which Howard Raiffa calls the *linear loss function* and IBM calls the *service function*. It is not usually tabulated in books on statistics. It is the integral under the upper tail of $F(k)$ from k to infinity.

The tables in Table 19.2 are derived from a computer rational approximation to the normal distribution function developed by Peter Strong.[2]

Form of the Probability Distribution. The analysis depends critically on the form of the probability distribution used to calculate F and E. There is a great difference between a symmetrical distribution like the normal and a skewed distribution like the exponential or Poisson.

Decision Rules. The decision rule to compute the value for the safety factor k can be derived by minimizing an expression for total cost subject to a constraint, which could be considered in terms of a Lagrange multiplier.[3] When the expense is proportional to the number of shortage occurrences:

$$\text{Minimize } \sum NF(k) + \lambda(B - \sum vk\sigma)$$

where λ is the Lagrangian to make the total inventory investment equal to the constraint B. The rule is to select a value of the safety factor k so that the probability density

$$p(k) = \frac{rv\sigma}{N \times \text{MPV}}$$

where MPV is a *management policy equivalent* to the imputed marginal cost of a shortage. The effect of this rule is to give somewhat larger safety factors to the slow-moving class C products. You do not want to have to expedite cap screws. Take your chances on the few high-value class A items for which intervention is worthwhile and there is usually another lot in process that can be moved up in the schedule if needed.

When the expense is proportional to the amount of demand back-ordered, then:

$$\text{Minimize } \sum NF(k) + \lambda(B - \sum vk\sigma)$$

The resulting rule is to select a value of the safety factor k so that the probability

$$F(k) = \frac{1}{N \times \text{MPV}}$$

where the management policy variable MPV has the dimensions of years per shortage occurrence. The effect of this rule is to give larger safety factors to the popular class A products. The safety factor for some slow-moving class C products may in fact be 0 on the ground that the working stock covers a sufficiently high proportion of total demand.

Exchange Curve. Because of the nonlinear form of these decision rules, especially when E and F are based on the normal distribution, it is not practical to have management pick a fill rate and compute the safety factors directly. Treat either MPV as a parameter, and generate a series of values of the investment, the number of shortages, and the expected value of back-ordered demand. Some managers prefer to read a graph of investment versus expense, others are more comfortable with a table.

When management can point to a row in the table (Table 19.3) or a point on the graph (Fig. 19.4) of the exchange curve that seems to produce sensible results in terms of investment, shortages, and backorders, that point determines the value for the MPV, and safety factors can be computed for individual products.

TABLE 19.2 Approximations to the Normal Probability Distribution

Safety factor k	Probability density $p(k)$	Probability $F(k)$	Partial expectation $E(k)$
0.00	0.39894	0.50000	0.39655
0.25	0.38667	0.40224	0.28414
0.50	0.35207	0.30988	0.19609
0.75	0.30114	0.22769	0.13009
1.00	0.24197	0.15912	0.08281
1.25	0.18265	0.10561	0.05047
1.50	0.12952	0.06657	0.02938
1.75	0.08628	0.03987	0.01628
2.00	0.05399	0.02267	0.00856
2.25	0.03174	0.01223	0.00426
2.50	0.01753	0.00623	0.00200
2.75	0.00909	0.00299	0.00089
3.00	0.00443	0.00135	0.00038
3.25	0.00203	0.00057	0.00015
3.50	0.00087	0.00023	0.00006
3.75	0.00035	0.00009	0.00002
4.00	0.00013	0.00003	0.00001

Function R	Probability density $p^{-1}(R)$	Probability $F^{-1}(R)$	Partial expectation $E^{-1}(R)$
0.3162	0.682	0.481	0.175
0.1778	1.271	0.911	0.547
0.1000	1.664	1.260	0.879
0.0562	1.980	1.580	1.200
0.0316	2.252	1.879	1.505
0.0178	2.494	2.141	1.773
0.0100	2.715	2.355	1.989
0.0056	2.920	2.532	2.158
0.0032	3.110	2.691	2.303
0.0018	3.290	2.859	2.449
0.0010	3.461	3.050	2.620
0.0006	3.623	3.259	2.826
0.0003	3.779	3.466	3.060
0.0002	3.928	3.643	3.291
0.0001	4.072	3.776	3.489

TABLE 19.3   Example of an Exchange Curve

Policy variable	Safety stock	Number of shortages	Backorder value
7400.000	471,106	7.52	625,662
10500.358	566,934	4.86	360,309
14899.664	645,269	3.34	231,524
21142.136	713,594	2.41	161,273
30000.000	775,147	1.82	120,608
Current	859,008	5.17	448,517

Policy variable	Safety-stock weeks	Fill rate	
		Lots, %	Value, %
7400.000	1.62	97.80	95.85
10500.358	1.95	98.58	97.61
14899.664	2.22	99.02	98.47
21142.136	2.46	99.30	98.93
30000.000	2.67	99.47	99.20
Current	2.96	98.49	97.03

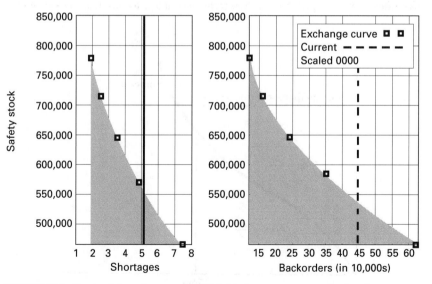

FIGURE 19.4   Graphs of the exchange curves. Minimize shortage occurrences for given investment.

Stratification. The perceived expense will be different for different kinds of products within a single corporate inventory. Current, captive, critical service parts justify an inventory investment that is quite different from past-model, commercial standard, trim parts. The analysis of values for the management policy variable should be carried out independently for different ways of describing the importance of a group of products to the marketing mission.

ORDERING PROCEDURES

Some of the literature on lot quantities is more about scheduling a time-phased series of replenishment orders than about inventory management to develop planning factors. The search for a dynamic way of finding the best lot quantity to order now seems to focus only in the requirements from now forward on the assumption that you have reached order point and have to order something. This analysis conveniently overlooks the problem of deciding what the order point is, taking account of safety stock to cover the uncertainty over the lead time.

The principal techniques are the *least unit cost,* developed in Germany for IBM's PICS package, and *part-period balancing* developed in the United States by DeMatteis and Mendoza[4] for IBM's PICS package (Fig. 19.5). There is a curious symmetry between these rules.

Consider a graph of cumulative usage, which is not a straight line because usage is planned to occur at different rates in the future. One rule finds a lot quantity such that the area above the curve is equal to Ar/v. The other finds a coverage time such that the area under the curve is equal to Ar/v. The Silver-Meal[11] algorithm seeks a coverage period such that costs per unit time are a minimum. The Wagner-Whitin[12] approach uses dynamic programming. Unlike the three techniques above that just look at how long the

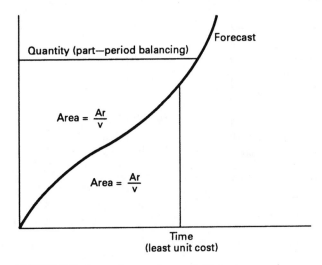

FIGURE 19.5 Least unit cost and part-period balancing.

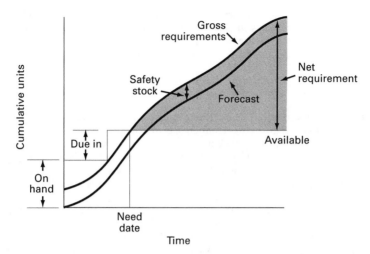

FIGURE 19.6   Graph of cumulative planning requirement.

proximate order quantity will last, this approach looks at total requirements over the planning horizon. Consider covering those total requirements in N lots for $N = 1, 2, 3,\dots$. For a given value of $N,$ find the lot quantities that minimize the number of piece-months of inventory. Then consider the acquisition costs for N lots, and find the value of N that minimizes total costs.

Extensive simulation with a variety of demand patterns shows that none of the more elegant dynamic ways of scheduling achieves savings in total annual costs (over thousands of products in the inventory) that are enough lower than the simple method to pay for the extra costs of computation.

It is convenient to discuss ways of planning a string of "notional" orders to cover requirements over the planning horizon in terms of a graph like the one shown in Fig. 19.6. The vertical axis is in cumulative units. The horizontal axis represents time starting as of the most recent information about stock on hand. Start by plotting the cumulative forecast of requirements. Move that line up to represent safety stock (or to the left to represent safety time). The resulting line is called *cumulative gross requirements.*

Plot stock on hand along the vertical axis. If there is some work-in-progress, add the quantity due as of the date due. The resulting line is cumulative gross available stock. Since available stock usually does not increase after some time in the future and the requirements will continue to grow with time, there will be a point where the two graphs cross. The corresponding time is a *need date,* the latest time when additional supplies can arrive without eating into safety stock (which is provided to cover unforecasted variation in demand during the lead time or freeze period). The amount by which requirements exceed available stock past that need date is called *cumulative net requirements.*

Production Forecast Versus Market Forecast

The forecast in the previous figure may be a good estimate of what will be sold of a particular SKU (stock keeping unit) or a product at a stocking location such as a field warehouse or distribution center. The requirements to produce will be offset to the left to allow for the lead time to get material from the production source to the stocking location. Production requirements will also net out actual stock in the system compared with planned safety stock to increase or decrease the amount to be produced to bring stock into line with the plan.

Pull Versus Push

Traditional pull procedures for replenishing stock wait until available stock is below an order point—the cumulative gross requirements over the freeze period—and then place an order on the supplier. Since stock is usually slightly below the order point when the order is triggered, there is slightly less than planned lead time available before the need date. Since the supplier is bombarded with lot-sized orders, his or her demand can be quite lumpy and hard to predict, so he or she may not have quite enough on hand to fill all the orders and someone's order may be back-ordered.

Contrast that with a push system in which the supplier can always see stock status and requirements everywhere. That makes it practical to have the right quantity of the right product in the right place at the right time. It also means that the supplier can anticipate requirements and ship some stock a few days before it is needed rather than a few days after it is needed. Good supply-chain management[1] requires that the customer side of any inventory keep the supply side informed of true time-phased requirements.

Each of the following techniques for scheduling future production can be accommodated in most *manufacturing resource planning* (MRP) systems. The choice among techniques is more a matter of pragmatic accommodation to the operating environment than any theoretical model of economics.

Net Requirements by Period.   Where the purpose of "ordering" is to keep the supplier informed, the best technique is to state net production requirements by period. The supplier should have some latitude in deciding how much actually to send, based on his or her actual supply and the requirements for his or her other customers. Provided that the supplier keeps each customer's net requirements covered without too much advance cover, everyone will be happy and the total systems cost will be low.

Fixed Time Supplied.   In many manufacturing operations, there are sound reasons for ordering in discrete lot quantities. It makes sense to start from the economical order quantities developed under inventory management in order to balance acquisition and holding costs. If requirements vary over time (growth and seasonal profiles), it is better to order an economical time supply in quantities that cover the actual forecast from the point at which each lot will arrive in stock.

Fixed Lot Quantities.   There may be constraints on possible quantities, possibly because of the packages in which major raw materials come, or the production of one shift, or the capacity of a heat-treat facility. In this type of situation, you can order in integral multiples of the practical increment or rounding quantities that come close to the economical order quantity.

Fill 'er Up.   If materials are stored in a silo or other facility with finite capacity, it makes sense to order enough to bring available stock up to the capacity of that facility. If practical, choose a storage tank that has a capacity consistent with the economical order quantity.

Fixed-Interval Review.   The supply tender may visit oil rigs in the North Sea only once every 5 days. It does not make sense to order a 3-day supply of anything. Order enough to last until the next opportunity to order. For slow-moving products, the economical quantity may last much longer than the interval between opportunities to replenish stock.

Allocation. If you purchase a number of products from a single supplier, it makes sense to order all the materials you need at one time. The interval between orders from that supplier can be calculated from the economical time interval for a joint family. The quantity ordered for any one product should be sufficient to last until at least the next opportunity to order. If you replenish your own field warehouses or the stock held by a customer from whom you get reliable time-phased requirements, it makes sense to replenish stock in full truckloads. The mix of products in a trailer or a railcar or a shipping container can be calculated to cover net requirements through the same period of time to all customers or destinations for each product.

Production Rates. There are many manufacturing processes where one wants to schedule a rate of production rather than a series of discrete lots. Using Fig. 19.6, visualize a line that can pivot around available stock as of the end of the freeze period. The slope of the line represents the rate of production. A slope that is too low will not cover gross requirements through the planning horizon. A slope that is too high will generate extra stock not required by the visible requirements.

A starting point is a line that is just tangent to cumulative gross requirements sometime within the planning horizon. That production rate can be modified to a pair of rates chosen from a finite family of feasible rates. The early rate is perhaps higher than the average rate, and the late rate is tangent to the cumulative gross requirements. The intersection of these two rates is an estimate of the time when you will plan to change from one rate to the other.

The area between the line(s) representing production and the cumulative gross requirements is the stabilization stock, sometimes called the *anticipation stock*. This inventory is a capital investment in inventory in lieu of a capital investment in sufficient capacity to produce a current requirement during the peak season.

SIMULATION OF MODELS

Simulation can be a powerful tool to investigate the consequences of alternatives. Many kinds of simulation are possible. The choice among them should be dictated by what you are trying to learn. One class of simulations looks at the dynamics over time. They are especially useful when you are concerned about how long it will take for a change in policy to take effect or when you are concerned about events like a temporary shortage just prior to the arrival of a replenishment order.

Within dynamic simulations are what Goode and Machol call *single-thread simulations* where you follow one product over time, possibly repeating the experiment with the same initial conditions, and vary the controls.[7] The purpose here is largely to trace the logic of the control system. When the single-thread models have proven to be acceptable, then a *full-load simulation* can process large groups of products. In the latter case, the measures are aggregates of the number of orders placed, the average total inventory, the number of times a shortage occurs, the total amount of the shortage until it is cleared, and so on.

Before you start on a full-load simulation, write a report to management that says, "I recommend this procedure over that one because the true measure of performance—which is significant in our business—is much better." Then plan a simulation to collect data relevant to that choice. Do not try to collect everything just because you have a computer, since doing so may generate data but very little information.

A very different approach to simulation is to use a mathematical model of the steady-state consequences of alternatives. Here the purpose is to make a strategic choice among alternative decision rules and, having made that choice, make a tactical choice of the value of the management policy variable. Bear in mind that any simulation will tend to prove the hypothesis that the designer had in mind when he or she set out to design the simulation.

REFERENCES

1. C. Billington: "Strategic Supplychain Management," *OR/MS Today* (21:2), April 1994, pp. 20–27.

2. R. G. Brown: *Decision Rules for Inventory Management,* Holt, Rinehart & Winston, New York, 1967.

3. R. G. Brown: *Advanced Service Parts Inventory Control,* Materials Management Systems, Thetford Center, Vt., 1982.

4. J. J. deMatteis and A. G. Mendoza: "The Part-Period Algorithm," *IBM Systems Journal* (7:1), 1969, pp. 30–46.

5. H. F. Dickie: "ABC Inventory Analysis Shoots for Dollars, Not Pennies," *Factory Management and Maintenance* (5), 1951.

6. G. Gerson and R. G. Brown: "Decision Rules for Equal Shortage Policies," *Naval Research Logistics Quarterly* (17:3), pp. 351–358.

7. H. H. Goode and R. E. Machol: *System Engineering,* McGraw-Hill, New York, 1957.

8. R. Mennel: "Early History of the Economic Lot Size," *APICS Quarterly Bulletin* (2:2), April 1961, pp. 19–22.

9. F. Raymond: *Quantity and Economy in Manufacture,* McGraw-Hill, New York, 1931.

10. E. A. Silver: "Inventory Control under a Probabilistic Time-Varying Demand Pattern," *AIIE Transactions* (10:4), December, 1978, pp. 371–379.

11. E. A. Silver and H. Meal: "A Heuristic for Selecting Lot Size Requirements in the Case of a Deterministic Time-Varying Demand Rate and Discrete Opportunities for Replenishment," *Production and Inventory Management* (14:2), 1973, pp. 64–74.

12. H. Wagner and T. Whitin: "Dynamic Version of the Economic Lot-Size Model," *Management Science* (5), 1958, pp. 89–96.

CHAPTER 20
DISTRIBUTION REQUIREMENTS PLANNING

Editors

Quentin K. Ford, CFPIM
President, Manufacturing Control Associates, Inc.
Palatine, Illinois

James W. Rice, Ph.D., CFPIM, P.E.
Management Consultant
Eldorado, Wisconsin
and Professor Emeritus, University of Wisconsin
Oshkosh, Wisconsin

Ralph D. Tileston
Vice President, Manufacturing Control Associates, Inc.
Palatine, Illinois

Distribution requirements planning (DRP) was first developed as a technical method for planning the distribution operations of manufacturing companies. As a result of experience with this method in manufacturing companies, DRP has been extended to most types of distribution operations and processes. DRP enables the coordination of logistics among multiple organizations, even where the manufacturing and distribution operations are in different organizations or corporate structures. The DRP concept is the enabler of an integrated supply-chain process, in which the critical problem is to balance the use of assets and operational costs while providing world-class service to customers. DRP improves key performance for such activities as customer service, inventory management, purchasing, manufacturing effectiveness, and profit maximization.

DRP uses *time-phased planning* techniques that are very similar to MRP as used in manufacturing. By using the same time-phased planning technique in both distribution and manufacturing, many of the problems that have traditionally haunted manufacturing and distributing are greatly reduced and in some cases eliminated. The DRP management philosophy is to manage distribution as the supply-chain extension of manufacturing, even when separate companies are involved. DRP enables a partnering between traditional adversaries—manufacturing and distribution—and encourages them to operate as one. Traditionally, they *were* separate organizations. This separation frequently resulted in organizational conflicts, inefficiencies, and cost penalties from different processes, systems, and even conflicting goals.

The extension of computer-based distribution requirements planning into a broader managerial approach for distribution resources planning and control is called *DRP II*. This is similar to the extension of materials requirements planning (MRP) into a broader process of manufacturing resources planning and control, called *MRP II*. New terms and abbreviations are emerging as companies learn how to integrate the logistics of production and distribution with the assistance of computer-based information systems, and to integrate MRP II with DRP II into a united logistics management information and control process.

DRP's Basic Concept

DRP does the planning of materials movements into, within, and out of a distribution network. DRP makes materials available so that inventory can be "pulled" through the distribution network to provide *just-in-time* responses to customer demand.

Time-Phased Planning

Time-phased planning is the essential ingredient of both DRP and MRP. DRP is becoming the standard technique for planning distribution replenishment. Capacity planning techniques can be used to determine the transportation, warehouse, and other logistic resource requirements. Using the DRP logistics information, management can make overall distribution resource plans to support the future business strategies of the company. Just as MRP enabled the development of *just in time* (JIT) for manufacturing, DRP facilitates the evolution of a JIT philosophy in distribution and other nonmanufacturing environments. This occurs because both MRP and DRP provide an operational definition of what is "just-in-time."

DRP plans the movement of materials into, within, and out of a distribution network. The system was developed to improve the overall asset performance of distribution networks. Goals are to improve the performance of product delivery to the customer, and to do so with less total inventory and lower total distribution costs.

A major function of DRP is to plan the movement of materials within the distribution network. This encompasses the planning of replenishment orders by either the manufacturers or suppliers, to the time that the materials are consumed by the customer. As a result, DRP plans all the replenishment actions needed to keep inventory within management-defined levels at all points in the distribution network.

Primary Goal of DRP

The primary goal is to maintain a well-balanced inventory at all appropriate locations within the network. In today's just-in-time environment, this means a lean and trim inventory that can be rapidly deployed to meet actual demand throughout the distribution network. For any company involved in distribution or other nonmanufacturing activities, DRP enables improved performance of the inventory investment, materials distribution resources, and working capital.

Distribution Planning Link

DRP is the distribution planning link in a company and provides information for management as to what action steps are needed to ensure that materials in the distribution network are going to be in place to meet the business plan. When the business plan cannot be executed because of unavailable materials, DRP and MRP information indicates this in advance, which allows the planner to revise, where possible, the planned materials movements or as a last resort, request a change in the business plan.

In the past, extra inventory was carried throughout the supply chain so managers could respond to whatever events might occur, regardless of the business plan. In the past, when profit margins were greater and international competition was less, excessive inventory and overinvestment in working capital were commonly employed to cover an unwillingness or inability to plan. Economic conditions, worldwide competition, and today's customer expectations have rendered that strategy noncompetitive.

Transparent View of Distribution

For DRP to function, the system must enable observation of the movement of materials through the supply-chain network. Knowing the planned movement of each *stock keeping unit* (SKU) throughout the supply chain gives a person enhanced information for dealing with sources of supply to establish and maintain a JIT flow of material. This results in measurably improved customer service.

Just in Time

The objectives of just in time include:

- Deliver products on schedule in the quantities that customers need
- Deliver perfect quality using no unnecessary lead time
- Eliminate waste
- Develop worker productivity
- Continue the quest for improvement

Inventory management must use time-phased planning for a company to fulfill these objectives. Planning plays an important role in making the materials resources available in the near future for the processing. This planning process is called *MRP* in manufacturing and *DRP* in distribution. A prerequisite for JIT distribution is that time-phased replenishment planning of DRP must exist. DRP is the means for planning materials and logistic resource requirements so that they are in place to meet customer's requirements as they occur. DRP provides the best chance to achieve just-in-time distribution. Without DRP, distribution must rely on random chance or on level demand, which by definition, is not just in time.

ILLUSTRATION OF DRP LOGIC

The computational logic of distribution requirements planning is very similar to that of materials requirements planning. Each has similar data inputs. In MRP, the inputs are the product structure bills of materials, accurate inventory balances, and a master production schedule. In DRP, the inputs are the distribution network (product) structure, accurate inventory balances, and a schedule of daily or weekly planned demand for each product at each location in the network.

DRP Example

The following example describes the way DRP is calculated and emphasizes how a production planner, not the computer, is in charge at each step. In practice, the planner does not need to intervene at every step. DRP software computes conditions within predetermined management parameters and lists only the exceptions so that the planner or scheduler can examine them. For example, the computer software uses a "firm, planned order horizon," which is the number of planning periods into the future within which the computer cannot initiate or reschedule a planned order. If the computer program detects a need to change or reschedule an order within the firm order horizon, it creates an exception message for the planner. This message identifies that a condition exists so the period ending balance does not agree with preset guidelines, which the computer cannot correct by rescheduling or by creating orders. Exception messages are generated by a computer for all items in the DRP and sequenced by priority for the planner. The priority sequence is from most critical, for those locations not having enough inventory, to the least critical for those locations having too much inventory.

Distribution Network Structure

Figure 20.1, model of product, illustrates the warehouse relationships for a company's distribution network. This figure is very similar to graphic bills of materials used in MRP. Assume that many retail outlets in the western part of the country are supplied from two distribution centers called DC 1 and DC 2. DC 1 supplies the northwest region, and DC 2 supplies the southwest region. The retail outlets in the northeastern part of the country are supplied by DC 3, and DC 4 will supply the southeast. Assume that DC 1 and DC 2 are in turn supplied from a western regional distribution center named RDC 10 and that DC 3 and DC 4 are supplied from an eastern regional distribution center named RDC 20.

Assume that the two regional distribution centers are supplied with many products from manufacturers and primary distributors. To simplify this example, however, confine the illustration to logistics of one product, Y. Product Y is manufactured by a company, staged in its plant's central warehouse, and then is distributed according to the DRP from RDC 10 and RDC 20.

DRP Calculations

The examples of DRP used in this chapter are all stated in weekly time periods. Any planning period may be chosen, such as days or hours, according to the company's reaction ability. The most workable time period is usually in weeks. The periods need represent only specific planning durations. Immediate periods might be days and later on, weeks, and distant periods might be months or calendar quarters. A system might be "periodless," meaning that the planning record columns may denote shipping sequences instead of time spans. The time horizon is related to the reaction capability of the supply network, and the choice of 8 weeks in this example was arbitrary.

Table 20.1, represents a time-phased replenishment plan for product Y. DC 1 serves many retailers with numerous products, and DC 1 maintains a DRP plan for every product that it distributes. The DRP plan shows the demand week by week, either forecasted or known; what goods are actually in transit with a firm, scheduled arrival date; what the on-hand inventory balance is for the item; and what are the planned orders for each week.

For this example, the accumulated demands from all outlets are 10 units of product Y in the current week, 10 units in week 2, 20 units in week 3, and so on. The table shows that the current inventory at DC 1 is 50 units of product Y. It also shows that 10 units

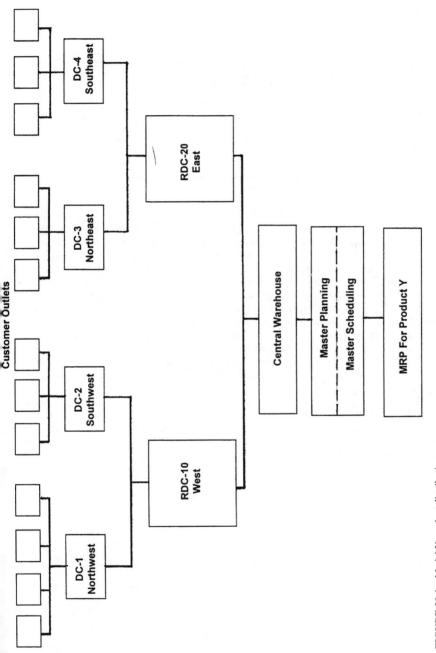

FIGURE 20.1 Model Y product distribution process.

20.5

TABLE 20.1   Distribution Requirements Planning Record for DC 1

Model Y product
Distribution Center: DC 1
Serving northwest cities
Lead time: 1 week; lot size: units of 10 each; safety stock: 10 each

		Weeks							
Activities	Past due	1	2	3	4	5	6	7	8
Forecast		10	10	20	30	40	60	70	70
In transit		0	0	0	0	0	0	0	0
Planned receipt		0	0	0	0	0	0	0	0
Balance on hand	50	40	30	10	−20	−60	−120	−190	−260
Planned order		0	0	0	0	0	0	0	0

are planned to be shipped out during the current week, leaving 40 units in inventory at the end of the week. Ten units will be shipped in week 2, and 20 in week 3, leaving 10 in inventory at the end of week 3, meaning that week 4 begins with 10 units on hand.

The record in Table 20.2 is given for illustration purposes only; today's software will automatically calculate planned orders as long as the planning time period is beyond the firm, planned order horizon. The "Planned Order" row shows clearly how the DRP record is a planning document. It shows that week 4 is scheduled to begin with 10 units on hand, with anticipated shipments to customers of 30 units for the week, of which 20 would not be shipped because of stock-out. The demand in week 5 would further reduce the balance on hand to −30, and so on. These negative balances will accumulate in the planning record until the planning system decides how to correct the anticipated negative balances. A decision most likely will include consideration of lot sizing, safety stocks, inventory financing, shipping schedules, supplier schedules, and various other factors.

Table 20.3 is a revision of Table 20.2, and it shows that the planner anticipates releasing an order for 30 units in week 3, which will arrive at DC 1 in week 4 and which will remove the anticipated negative balance that was shown before. It is different from in transit because they are only tentative plans at the present. They do not become in transit until converted to in transit by being placed on a pick list and a transaction is

TABLE 20.2   Second Distribution Requirements Planning Record for DC 1

Model Y product
Distribution center: DC 1
Serving northwest cities
Lead time: 1 week; lot size: units of 10 each; safety stock: 10 each

		Weeks							
Activities	Past due	1	2	3	4	5	6	7	8
Forecast		10	10	20	30	40	60	70	70
In transit		0	0	0	0	0	0	0	0
Planned receipts		0	0	0	30	0	0	0	0
Balance on hand	50	40	30	10	10	−30	−90	−160	−230
Planned orders		0	0	30	0	0	0	0	0

TABLE 20.3   Third Distribution Requirements Planning for DC 1,
After Planning for Full Horizon

Model Y product
Distribution center: DC 1
Serving northwest cities
Lead time: 1 week; lot size: units of 10 each; safety stock: 10 each

Activities	Past due	Weeks							
		1	2	3	4	5	6	7	8
Forecast		10	10	20	30	40	60	70	70
In transit		0	0	0	0	0	0	0	0
Planned receipt		0	0	0	30	40	60	70	70
Balance on hand	50	40	30	10	10	10	10	10	10
Planned order		0	0	30	40	60	70	70	0

entered into the process notifying the database that the first planning record materials were picked.

The past-due column identifies quantities of materials that were on last period's pick list and that were not received by the distribution center as scheduled or quantities that are a priority replenishment on the current pick list. A priority replenishment is created when actual demand has exceeded forecast by enough quantity to reduce the on-hand balance below the safety stock or when the on-hand balance falls below the safety-stock quantity prior to the arrival of the next scheduled shipment (calculated by using the in-transit lead time). In addition, the in-transit orders are late. Table 20.3 is a further revision, showing the current plan for DC 1 after the planning system creates orders for the rest of the planning horizon on the basis of just-in-time replenishment.

Table 20.4, shows a distribution plan for DC 2, which serves retail outlets similar to those served by DC 1 but in a different geographic area. It shows that DC 2 has 10 units of product Y on hand, and last week it picked an order for 20 units that are in transit and are scheduled to arrive at DC 2 in the current week. Ten on hand plus 20 in transit minus 5 demanded equals 25 in stock at the end of the current week. Future demands will be served by orders planned to be released for 40 units in week 2, for 50 units in week 4,

TABLE 20.4   Distribution Requirements Planning Record for DC 2,
After Planning for Full Horizon, Showing Impact of Varying Demand

Model Y product
Distribution center: DC 2
Serving southwest cities
Lead time: 1 week; lot size: units of 10 each; safety stock: 10 each

Activities	Past due	Weeks							
		1	2	3	4	5	6	7	8
Forecast		5	10	15	30	50	70	50	30
In transit		20	0	0	0	0	0	0	0
Planned receipt		0	0	40	0	50	70	50	30
Balance on hand	10	25	15	40	10	10	10	10	10
Planned order		0	40	0	50	70	50	30	0

and so on. Almost all of the computer software that is in place today will replace the negatives in each time period as they are encountered. However, for discussion purposes the examples just given illustrate the basic workings of the DRP logic. Later, there will be a further discussion on how this is done today in conjunction with better, more current computer software.

The eastern distribution centers, DC 3 and DC 4, are clones of the western distribution centers. Table 20.5 illustrates the resupply of DC 3, where 10 units of safety stock are planned, the expected demand is constant, and all shipments must be lot sized on pallets of 20 units. Since DC 3 has a lower volume of total dollars of throughput, the lead time and lot size are greater. These values reflect a biweekly replenishment cycle that offsets the higher transportation costs of weekly shipments.

Note that the current balance on hand is 5 units and it is projected to be 5 again in week 2, which is less than the planned safety stock of 10 units. However, this condition does not result in an automatic signal to expedite an order since safety stock is permitted to randomly fall below a target level, as long as there are not planned stock-outs.

Table 20.6 depicts a seasonally cyclic demand at DC 4. Note this plan clearly identifies the pull nature of DRP by shipping varying quantities as demand changes. This

TABLE 20.5   Distribution Requirements Planning Record for DC 3, After Planning for Full Horizon

Model Y product
Distribution center: DC 3
Serving northeast cities
Lead time: 2 weeks; lot size: units of 20 each; safety stock: 10 each

		Weeks							
Activities	Past due	1	2	3	4	5	6	7	8
Forecast		30	30	30	30	30	30	30	30
In transit		60	0	0	0	0	0	0	0
Planned receipts		0	0	40	40	20	40	20	40
Balance on hand	5	35	5	15	35	15	25	15	25
Planned orders		40	40	20	40	20	40	0	0

TABLE 20.6   Distribution Requirements Planning for DC 4, After Planning for Full Horizon, Showing Seasonal Demand

Model Y product
Distribution center: DC 4
Serving southeast cities
Lead time: 1 week; lot size: units of 10 each; safety stock: 10 each

		Weeks							
Activities	Past due	1	2	3	4	5	6	7	8
Forecast		20	30	40	50	60	50	40	30
In transit		50	0	0	0	0	0	0	0
Planned receipts		0	0	50	50	60	50	40	30
Balance on hand	5	35	5	15	15	15	15	15	15
Planned orders		0	50	50	60	50	40	30	0

keeps the total distribution chain in balance with demand and thereby sends realistic requirements to the manufacturing site through the master production schedule.

Regional Distribution Centers

The two western distribution centers are supplied by a regional distribution center called RDC 10. Table 20.7 shows how the planned orders from DC 1 and DC 2 are summed for the total demand upon RDC 10. Observe in Table 20.8 that even with a policy of maintaining no safety stock at RDC 10, significant safety stock is still in place as a result of lot-sizing policies.

Demand from Two Regional Distribution Centers

The demands from the two regional distribution centers, RDC 10 and RDC 20, are supplied by the central warehouse, along with other forecasted demands of the plant, as

TABLE 20.7   Effect of Combined DC Demand

Model Y product
Distribution center: DC 1 and DC 2
Serving western cities

Activities	Past due	Weeks							
		1	2	3	4	5	6	7	8
Total forecast		15	20	35	60	90	130	120	100
Total in transit		20	0	0	0	0	0	0	0
Combined planned receipts		0	0	40	30	90	130	120	100
Combined balance on hand	6	65	45	50	20	20	20	20	20
Combined planned order		0	40	30	90	130	120	100	0

TABLE 20.8   Distribution Requirements Planning Record for RDC 10
Replenishment Requirements for Two Distribution Centers

Model Y product
Regional distribution center: western RDC 10
Serving distribution centers DC 1 and DC 2
Lead time: 1 week; lot size: units of 50 each; safety stock: none

Activities	Past due	Weeks							
		1	2	3	4	5	6	7	8
Planned replenishment orders for DC 1		0	0	30	40	60	70	70	0
Planned replenishment orders for DC 2		0	40	0	50	70	50	30	0
Total planned orders		0	40	30	90	130	120	100	0
In transit		0	0	0	0	0	0	0	0
Planned receipts		0	50	50	50	150	100	100	100
Balance on hand	10	10	20	40	0	20	0	0	100
Planned order		50	50	50	150	100	100	100	0

TABLE 20.9 Distribution Requirements Planning Record for Central Warehouse, Input to Manufacturing's Master Production Schedule

Model Y product
Central warehouse
Serving eastern (RDC 20) and western (RDC 10) regional distribution centers
Lead time: 1 week; lot size: pallets of 650 each; safety stock: none

Activities	Past due	Weeks							
		1	2	3	4	5	6	7	8
Planned orders for RDC 10		50	50	50	150	100	100	100	0
Planned orders for RDC 20		100	50	100	100	50	100	100	0
Other demand		80	80	80	80	80	80	80	80
Total demand		230	180	230	330	230	280	280	80
Planned receipt		0	650	0	650	0	0	650	0
Balance on hand	300	70	540	310	630	400	120	490	410
Master production schedule for plant		650	0	650	0	0	650	0	0

shown in Table 20.9. The central warehouse demands are communicated to the production operations and are supplied to the plant's master production schedule. Note the MPS in week 6 calls for a shipment of 650 into the central warehouse. This order is generated because of the planner's overrides at RDC 10 and RDC 20. Without these overrides, there would not be a requirement in week 6. When the forecast at the DCs for weeks 7 and 8 appear in the planning horizon, the MPS will be adjusted to balance supply with demand. This example illustrates how DRP collects random demands from many customers served by the distribution centers, which in turn are served by the regional distribution centers, which are served by the central warehouse. It further illustrates how random demand is gathered into time-phased, scheduled, dependent demand.

In principle, the network may contain any number of primary and secondary distribution centers tied together in any way. Considerations among facilities include trade-offs, investments, dependability of customer service, safety-stock, inventories, and information processing costs.

PLANNER'S ROLE

In any system such as DRP, there has to be a human overseer and the capability to deal with unusual situations. In the case of DRP that role is filled by the planner. It is the job of the planner to enhance and enable the performance of the DRP system.

The Planner's Judgment

Analogous to the DRP for the western centers are the demands from the eastern distribution centers as shown in the DRP planning record for DC 3. The DRP record for seasonally cyclic demand for DC 4 are served by RDC 20, as shown in Table 20.10. Note that the planner entered an order larger than necessary to be released in week 6. This illustrates that a planner may exercise judgment and override the entries posted by the computer near or at the end of the planning horizon. The planner decides that the projected demands for 100 in week 5 and in week 6 are indicated by continuing demand in weeks 7 and 8. At first glance, this appears to cause excess inventory toward the end of

TABLE 20.10   Model Y Product Record

Model Y product
Regional distribution center: eastern RDC 20
Serving distribution centers DC 3 and DC 4
Lead time: 1 week; lot size: units of 50 each; safety stock: none

					Weeks				
Activities	Past due	1	2	3	4	5	6	7	8
Planned replenishment orders for DC 3		40	40	20	40	20	40	0	0
Planned replenishment orders for DC 4		0	50	50	60	50	40	30	0
Total planned orders		40	90	70	100	70	80	90	0
In transit		0	0	0	0	0	0	0	0
Planned receipts		0	100	50	100	100	50	100	100
Balance on hand	100	20	30	10	10	40	10	130	230
Planned order		100	50	100	100	50	100	100	0

the horizon. However, the point to remember is that the planned orders will not be released for some weeks, and until then no inventory is created. Also as the DRP is updated and forecast data enters the DRP system, it will replan the order by moving it out, leaving it where it is, or moving it in closer depending on how the forecast compares to what is anticipated. At time period 1, the planner is only alerting the distribution planner and manufacturing's MPS to a possibly more realistic future other than "zeros."

The Planner's Changing Role

The MRP/DRP time-phased planning software has continued to improve from its initial development in the mid-1960s (MRP) and the mid-1970s (DRP). Improvements in the software have been principally directed toward giving the computer the ability to do all of the routine computations, such as planning orders and detecting anomalies in the status of each SKU during a time period. Anomalies are noted by the computer and tested for a series of conditions and listed on an exception report for the assigned planner.

The example just discussed illustrates that DRP is a plan-ahead technique that is a management system based upon computerized information but continually supervised by planners. That is, DRP is a management system, not a computer system.

Exception Reports

Table 20.11 is a generic example of the exception messages in priority sequence. Exception reports are sorted by preestablished priority before they are printed (or put into the planner's electronic mail). Priority is determined by sequencing each exception from highest to lowest by both importance and urgency. For instance, the planner should review an SKU that will be out of stock within the in-transit lead time and take corrective action. The planner should do this prior to looking at an SKU where the on-hand balance will fall below the safety-stock quantity within the firm, planned-order time horizon.

When the planner calls up an exception message from the priority list, all exception messages for that item will be given to the planner at the same time. In this way the planner can review all of the problems that the computer has detected since the last time the

TABLE 20.11 Generic Examples of Exception Messages, In Priority Sequence

Priority	Message
1.	Stock-out is during period 1.
2.	Stock-out is within firm planned order horizon.
3.	BOH is less than 25 percent of safety stock.
4.	BOH is less than safety stock within the firm planned horizon.
5.	BOH is greater than maximum within the firm planned horizon.
6.	BOH is greater than maximum beyond the firm planned horizon.
7.	No usage has occurred in last 12 months.
8.	No usage has occurred in last 24 months.
9.	No usage has occurred in last 36 months.

planner manually reviewed the item. After the planner has reviewed the exception messages and has taken corrective action, he or she enters the action taken against each message into the computer database or log, and this becomes part of the history and also part of the anomalies for which the computer tests during each update.

Role of DRP Planners Today

The role of a planner has undergone major redefinition as a result of the improvements made in a number of MRP/DRP software packages. The role of the planner has become one of controller. This redefinition has shifted the planner from the routine tasks of planning orders to that of fixing the anomalies detected by the computer and examining the parameters used by the computer to detect these anomalies. The fixing that the planner has to do can cover several areas and can vary from very simple to very complex. As a result, each fix can take a short time or last hours. It could be as simple as a 30-second phone call confirming that the message should be ignored, or as complex as having to reset several ordering and forecasting factors to enable the computer to plan the time-phased requirements with fewer anomalies.

Planning Parameters

The things the planner must consider include the following:

- Selection of lot size algorithm
- Selection of safety-stock algorithm
- Adjustment of safety-stock factor
- Lead time algorithm
- Adjustment of a component of lead time
- Assignment of item to appropriate inventory (ABC)
- Selection of forecast algorithm
- Adjustment of forecast factor

Cornerstones of DRP

DRP is supported by the same three basic legs that MRP operates on. In MRP, they are the bill of materials, accurate inventories, and a realistic master production schedule. In DRP, they are the distribution network bill, accurate inventories, and realistic and current forecasts of demand.

FUNDAMENTAL CHARACTERISTICS OF DRP

Figure 20.1 illustrates the nature of distribution networks. While just in time is achieved to a great degree, the dispersed geographic nature of distribution networks and the associated heavy capital costs of transportation usually preclude moving materials in small, lot-for-lot replenishment quantities. The relationship of reimbursement and distribution points is similar to the *component-parent relationships* established in a bill of materials. In effect, each item that is sold from a distribution point has passed through a structured network.

The figure illustrates the *source and distribution relationships*. Just as a bill of materials defines distinct relationships between parents and components, so too must the relationship for each *stock keeping unit* (SKU) be defined. This means that a primary source must be defined for every level within an item's distribution network. However, alternative sources may be handled by making them sublevels or by using the alternate bill concept in the same way alternate component materials are handled in MRP. While multiple sources exist, a proportionate split of requirements is made in order to pass needs down to the next level. This can be handled in a way similar to the use of planning bills in MRP systems.

Need for Accurate Inventories

It is obvious that the need for accurate inventories is the same for DRP as it is for MRP and that the same techniques apply for establishing and maintaining inventory accuracy.

Distribution-Dependent Demand

The example shows how the distribution structure can be described in the same way as a product structure for the bill of materials. It shows how the bill of materials can be expanded to include the distribution network. Beginning with the final distribution point and the stock keeping unit as the highest level, each lower level identifies the replenishment source for the final distribution point. The lower level would identify any subsequent levels until the entry point of the item into the network is identified. This product structure identifies the distribution network for that particular item, and it is the distribution bill of materials. This structure can become the extension of the manufacturing bill. This new expanded product structure provides a way to cascade requirements back to reimbursing points and manufacturing.

Distribution of Time-Phased Planning

Time-phased planning techniques (MRP and DRP) are far superior for planning dependent-demand items than any other method. One of the first steps in designing manufacturing replenishment planning systems for distribution is to recognize the dependent-demand nature at all network replenishment points. An argument has been made that in larger distribution networks, the lumpy demands of individual distribution points would tend to offset each other and smooth out demand at a replenishment point. In reality, this does not occur. Although for some items the demand is smoothed through offsetting demands, that is a random exception and is not widespread. Experience has shown that in the larger networks, lumpy demand becomes more pronounced rather than less. Also, the higher-volume items exhibit a greater magnitude of lumpy demand than lower-volume items, which was an unexpected phenomenon, and makes the need for DRP much more important than was originally thought. Experience, again, has shown that when demand increases significantly, lumpy demand becomes amplified. As a result, DRP is a better tool than others and provides a much more precise plan at a time when the need for accurate and precise plans becomes critical. Unless planned, significant demand changes can place available quantities out of balance with requirements because of the lag time needed to adjust supply. The most effective way to avoid this lag is to antici-pate the demand change in the DRP process.

These observations about the organization of distribution networks and the nature of demand lead to the conclusion that the time-phased planning method is both applicable and necessary in distribution. Therefore, DRP is the starting point for manufacturing control of a company involved in both distribution and manufacturing. DRP develops as a near-accurate set of dependent-demand requirements to be passed on to the manufac-turing master production schedule.

TECHNIQUES WITHIN DRP

The discussion so far has been on the generic logic and objectives of DRP. The next sec-tion will discuss some specific techniques and considerations in implementing a system.

Demand Management and the Development of Forecasts

Because of the inherent self-correcting capability of time-phased planning, the accuracy of the demand forecast is not as critical as needed for other replenishment systems. Many people believe that accurate prediction of demand is more essential with time-phased planning than with other systems, but experience has shown this is not true. The frequent updating allows DRP to employ simple forecasting models and simple mathe-matics. Exponential smoothing with trend and perhaps seasonal capabilities is generally adequate. The need for less accurate forecasting is a result of the capability of time-phased planning to frequently (at least weekly) determine when materials are needed to prevent shortages. Therefore, if an SKU exceeds planned demand, then the new plan will call for the next replenishment to occur sooner. And if actual demand has been less than planned, replenishment will be delayed to meet that changed demand.

The ability to respond to differences at the consuming end of the product manufac-turing and distribution cycle identifies DRP time-phased planning as a pull system. Some practitioners have focused on the centralized planning concepts of DRP and have called DRP a push system. DRP is therefore a pull or push system depending on one's perspective.

One of the key benefits of DRP II and MRP II is the coordination that is accom-plished by having formal plans that are synchronized within all functions of the busi-ness. The downward demand planning process provides a means for integrating an item's planned demand with the business objectives. The demand management pyramid seen in Fig. 20.2 is an example of the relationships of levels of planning from broad

FIGURE 20.2 Demand management pyramid.

business plans down to individual stock keeping units. The pyramid relationship establishes the concept of multihierarchical levels of planning and forecasting. This concept identifies that each level of planning and/or forecasting is constrained by the outer limits set by the level above.

Development of Override Capabilities

The need for applying management judgment arises at all levels within the demand management process. A demand management system needs to provide for overriding the calculated demand. These judgment overrides should be applied through a number of techniques. As a result, the demand management system used in DRP provides a number of ways in which overrides may be inserted into the demand planning.

Monitoring Forecast Performance

Monitoring planned demand involves adapting techniques developed by quality-control professionals. The monitoring of planned demand should be measured in two ways:

1. It should be determined if the error is cumulative by the planned demand being biased too high or too low.
2. The occurrence of significant single-period errors should be tracked.

If it is a cumulative error, then an overall adjustment of the planned item demand should be made upward or downward, and the correction should bring the demand back into line.

The occurrence of a significant, single-point error spike requires more analysis. There are two possible causes for demand to spike, and the analysis must determine the cause. First, determine if the spike is caused by demand that varies from the plan because the demand is very lumpy and the statistics were artificially smoothed. Second, determine if some extrinsic effect is impacting the item demand so that the planned demand needs to be changed.

Future planned demand should not be changed as long as the actual performance is within the plan's acceptable range. The acceptable range limits are set by considering the customer's desired service level and the budgeted amount of inventory investment. Each SKU is monitored and performance evaluated for a significant period of time, generally 1 year.

Selection of Demand History

A demand history should be kept at the same level of detail as that maintained in the plan. Records should cover the actual performance as well as the planned demand history. Historical records of actual and forecasted demand need to cover at least three planning cycles, generally 3 years to be statistically significant.

Ability to Tailor to Individual SKUs

Demand for individual items often changes their behavior patterns independent of the behavior patterns of other items. A demand management system needs to provide the ability to adjust the planned demand of individual items. When this occurs, properly conceived overrides provide for modifying the planned demand to reflect the needs of the operation.

The highest level for an item's planned demand is the *item master schedule* for DRP. The pyramid demand management technique enables it to be derived directly from the business and sales plan of the company, the same as in an MRP environment.

Replenishment Planning

Replenishment logic uses standard time-phased planning (MRP) logic but explodes the transit lead times back through the distribution network and the bill of materials. It uses standard shipping and location safety-stock quantities to plan shipments over the planning horizon of the DRP system. As can be seen from Table 20.12, "Finished-Goods Inventory Planning Report, A," everything is in balance for this item at this distribution center, except that an in-transit shipment of 1152 units is overdue by 9 days (as noted in the exception message at the foot of the table). The exception message was caused by a parameter set in the computer: "If any in-transit inventory is late beyond 5 working days (Monday through Friday), it is critical and the planner has to find out why the materials have not been received." It may be that the materials have been delivered but have not been entered in the DC's records, or it may be that the shipment was lost. Whatever the reason, it is the responsibility of the planner to see that appropriate corrective action is taken.

Table 20.13, "Finished-Goods Inventory Planning Report, B," indicates that it is now 4 weeks later than the previous display and an exception message has been received by the planner that distribution center DC 0243 is going to be out of stock in week 4 on this item. The computer software is informing the planner of this because the "firm,

TABLE 20.12 Finished-Goods Inventory Planning Report, A

Distribution center: 0243
Division: 004
Product: 00270-VS
Size: 400
Group: Btl
Package: 12-500
Planner: KLL

Shipping quantity	Safety stock	FPO fence	Current BOH	Lead time	Singles per			
					Carrier	Case	Tier	Pallet
576	889	6	855	PT 2 / IT 1 / PA 1		12	288	576

	Past due	April 4	April 11	April 18	April 25	May 2	May 9	May 16	May 23	May 30	June 6	June 13	June 20	June 27
Demand		437	437	437	437	402	402	402	402	516	726	726	726	645
In-transit	1152													
Planned receipts				576	576		576	576		576	1152	576	576	576
Planned BOH		1570	1133	1272	1411	1009	1183	1357	955	1015	1441	1291	1141	1072
Firm planned orders				576		576	576							
Planned orders			576						576	1152	576	576	576	576

	July	August	September	October	November	December	January	February	March	April	May	June	July	August
Demand	1270	1620	2139	1944	2081	2672	1473	1684	2231	2071	1903	3602	1432	1827
Planned receipts	1152	1728	2304	1728	2304	2880	1152	1728	2304	1728	2304	3456	1728	1728
Planned BOH	954	1062	1227	1011	1234	1442	1121	1165	1238	895	1296	1150	1446	1347
Planned orders	1152	1728	2304	1728	2304	2304	1728	1728	2304	1728	2304	3456	1152	1728

Exception messages:
Past due in-transit: A0322706 0279 1152 03/25

20.17

TABLE 20.13 Finished-Goods Inventory Planning Report, B

Distribution center: 0243
Division: 004
Product: 00270-VS
Size: 400
Group: Btl
Package: 12-500
Planner: KLL

	Carrier	Singles per		
	Carrier	Case	Tier	Pallet
		12	288	576

Lead time		
PT	2	
IT	1	
PA	1	

Shipping quantity	Safety stock	FPO fence	Current BOH
576	889	6	868

	Past due	April 25	May 2	May 9	May 16	May 23	May 30	June 6	June 13	June 20	June 27	July 4	July 11	July 18
Demand		437	402	402	402	402	516	726	726	726	645	318	318	318
In-transit														
Planned receipts				576	576		576	1152	1728	576	576		576	576
Planned BOH		431	29	203	377	−25	35	461	1463	1313	1244	927	1185	1444
Firm planned orders			576	576		576	1152							
Planned orders								1728	576	576	576	576	576	

	July*	August	September	October	November	December	January	February	March	April	May	June	July	August
Demand	318	1620	2139	1944	2081	2672	1473	1684	2231	2071	1903	3602	1432	1827
Planned receipts		1728	2304	1728	2304	2304	1728	1728	2304	1728	1728	4032	1152	1728
Planned BOH	1126	1234	1399	1183	1406	1038	1293	1337	1410	1067	892	1322	1042	943
Planned orders	576	1728	1728	2304	2304	2304	1728	1152	2304	2304	2304	2880	1728	1152

Exception messages:

Out-of-stock condition in week 5.

Below safety stock in weeks 1, 2, 3, 4, 5, and 6.

Spike note: Demand in previous week exceeded forecast by 540 (124 percent).

*Partial month.

20.18

planned order horizon" is six time periods, and an unusually high, actual demand has occurred in recent weeks that is consuming the weekly forecast plus safety stock. Because of the established DRP management parameters, the computer cannot create a planned order within the *firm, planned order horizon,* and the planner has to determine what is the appropriate corrective action. This could be as simple as planning to ship enough stock in the next replenishment, to ignoring the message because the salesperson may tell the planner that a customer has decided to order less frequently in larger quantities to save on transportation costs and therefore the data on near-term, future demand is overstated. In each instance, the planner must investigate to find the cause and take corrective action.

Table 20.14, "Finished-Goods Inventory Planning Report, C," depicts the status of the same SKU 4 weeks later, and the planner has now received an exception message that this item's planned, on-hand balance will exceed the maximum allowed inventory level in week 2. The computer display tells the planner this because the firm planned order horizon is still 6 weeks, and within that time frame, the planned on-hand balance is going to exceed the safety stock plus shipping quantity. Because the established DRP parameters do not allow the computer to change a planned order within the firm planned order horizon, the planner, notified by the exception, determines what the appropriate correction action is. This could be as simple as moving the next firm order to a later shipping date, or finding out that a critical customer has been shut down for the last 2 weeks and is just preparing to make up an order that will return the on-hand balance to the normal range.

The productivity of the planner has been increased severalfold by using the computer to create the routine planned order and shipment schedule changes, which allows the planner to work on those items that are true exceptions. The authors know of an instance in which one planner, while responsible for over 25,000 SKUs, was occupied less than 25 percent of the time with exception messages requiring corrective actions.

Pareto in DRP

Table 20.15, "DRP Lot-Sizing and Safety-Stock Matrix," demonstrates the use of the Pareto ABC concept to identify the relationship between distribution centers and SKUs. The matrix assigns a Pareto class value to each distribution center and item, which can in turn be used to set standard shipping quantities and safety-stock quantities. When an SKU appears on exception lists with some regularity, this matrix gives the planner a reason to adjust the values of either safety stock, shipping lot size, or both. These adjustments enable the planner to set the MRP/DRP system so that it can handle a high percentage of the SKU's planning without the need for intervention.

Servicing Special Marketing Efforts

Special marketing efforts can be divided into two main topics, special promotional efforts or changes in customer location. Both can be effectively handled by a DRP. Promotional efforts can be incorporated through "overrides" done by capable individuals. A customer's moving to a new location can be handled by a person's previous experience and the override capabilities by first moving the demand to another DC location. The planner working directly with the customer can apportion part or all of the actual demand to the new DC. By using the apportioned demand, a new period-by-period prediction can be created for the new DC. At the same time the period-by-period demand for the first DC can be reduced. All of this can be done through the use of overrides.

TABLE 20.14 Finished-Goods Inventory Planning Report, C

Distribution center: 0243
Division: 004
Product: 00270-VS
Size: 400
Group: Btl
Package: 12-500
Planner: KLL

Shipping quantity	Safety stock	FPO fence	Current BOH
576	889	6	1027

Lead time: PT 2 IT 1 PA 1

Singles per:

Carrier	Case	Tier	Pallet
	12	288	576

	Past due	May 16	May 23	May 30	June 6	June 13	June 20	June 27	July 4	July 11	July 18	July 25	August 1	August 8
Demand		402	402	516	726	726	726	645	318	318	318	318	405	405
In-transit														
Planned receipts				576	1152	1152	576	1152		576		576		576
Planned BOH		625	223	283	709	1135	985	1492	1175	1433	1116	1374	969	1140
Firm planned orders		576	1152	1152	576	1152								
Planned orders								576		576		576		

	August*	September	October	November	December	January	February	March	April	May	June	July	August	September
Demand	810	2139	1944	2081	2672	1473	1684	2231	2071	1903	3602	1432	1827	2104
Planned receipts	576	2304	2304	1728	2880	1152	1728	2304	2304	1728	3456	1728	1728	2304
Planned BOH	906	1071	1431	1078	1286	965	1009	1082	1315	1140	994	1290	1191	1391
Planned orders	576	2304	1728	2304	2304	1728	1728	2304	2304	1728	3456	1728	1728	1728

Exception messages:

Planned BOH exceeds maximum stock level in week 7.

Cum. error note: Cumulative forecast exceeds cumulative actual by 53 percent.

*Partial month.

TABLE 20.15 DRP Lot-Sizing and Safety-Stock Matrix

Item class	Class of distribution center				
	A	B	C	D	E
A	2 weeks MAD 1 week FCST	1 month MAD 2 weeks FCST	2 months MAD 1 month FCST	3 months MAD 2 months FCST	3.75 months MAD 4 months FCST
B	1 month MAD 2 weeks FCST	2 months MAD 1 month FCST	2.5 months MAD 1.5 months FCST	3 months MAD 2 months FCST	3.75 months MAD 4 months FCST
C	2 months MAD 1 month FCST	2.5 months MAD 1.5 months FCST	3 months MAD 2 months FCST	3.75 months MAD 4 months FCST	4 months MAD 6 months FCST
D	2.5 months MAD 1.5 months FCST	3 months MAD 2 months FCST	3.5 months MAD 4 months FCST	4 months MAD 6 months FCST	4.5 months MAD 8 months FCST
E	3 months MAD 2 months FCST	3.5 months MAD 4 months FCST	4 months MAD 6 months FCST	4.5 months MAD 8 months FCST	5 months MAD 12 months FCST
F	3.5 months MAD 4 months FCST	4 months MAD 6 months FCST	4.5 months MAD 8 months FCST	5 months MAD 10 months FCST	5.5 months MAD 12 months FCST

Note: MAD = mean absolute deviation; FCST = forecast.

Allocation Control and Planning

The allocation method retains the inventory in replenishment centers and material is pulled to the distribution points in response to actual demand. This can be done by production materials schedulers.

First, run the item's DRP without standard lot size shipping quantities to determine if inventory can be maintained at the replenishment centers. If so, then you need not take further action. If not, remove safety-stock quantities from the item's DRP. If you can now maintain inventory, then you need not take further action. If, however, you cannot maintain inventory levels, assign transportation to the item to reduce transit lead time. Removal of these and other constraints one by one from the DRP calculations has the effect of pulling the materials, as required, and maintaining the greatest share of inventory in central or regional replenishment centers.

Experience has shown that removing shipping quantity lot sizes will alleviate the problem in about 75 percent of the cases. Safety stock remedied the situation in 15 percent of cases, and faster transportation, another 7 percent. When the manufacturing source cannot keep up with the demand on a prolonged basis, the balance has to be solved through management intervention and other means such as additional suppliers or subcontract sourcing.

The need for an allocation is detected by an inventory shortage within the firm, planned order horizon. The firm, planned order horizon is usually defined systemwide, but the system should have the ability to lengthen the firm, planned horizon by item.

INTEGRATING DRP WITH OTHER PLANNING

DRP integrates with other production planning processes at two levels. First, at the master planning level, DRP enters aggregate product demand into sales and operations planning. Second, at the master production scheduling level, DRP enters specific planned replenishment orders for delivery to the distribution network. These deliveries are usually from the manufacturer to the central or plant warehouse.

Sales and Operations Planning (S&OP)

DRP is integrated with *sales and operations planning* (S&OP) in two ways, depending on two limiting factors of manufacturing: manufacturing capacity or materials available. When a manufacturer is limited by production capacity, the S&OP process compares forecasted demand with the available manufacturing capacity. If the manufacturing capacity cannot satisfy the demand, the sales plan is adjusted to fit within the capacity limits. If demand and capacity match, the only action required by the S&OP management is approval of the plan. When there is excess capacity, management must choose to either not use the full capacity or build to inventory.

When production is limited by materials available, the planned replenishments are used in the *capacity requirements planning* (CRP) *process* to determine the manufacturing capacity required. Manufacturing initiates plans to have manufacturing capacity available to manufacture the needed replenishment. In a materials-driven situation, excess capacity is always available, but there are not enough materials available to build inventory. Therefore, the need for the trade-off between capacity and inventory is not viable.

Master Production Scheduling (MPS)

Planned shipments ultimately become demands on the manufacturer in the form of replenishment requirements for the distribution network. Planned replenishments for the distribution network are used by the master scheduler to construct a manufacturer's master production schedule. Table 20.16, "Master Production Scheduling Chart," is an example of how all of the planned replenishment shipments become the input to the manufacturing master production schedule. If there are no capacity constraints established by the S&OP process, the planned orders can be passed directly through to the master production schedule. However, if there are constraints, the master scheduler will have to adjust the orders before inserting them in the master production schedule.

If there is not enough to handle the planned orders, the master scheduler will have to reduce the quantity ordered. The DRP planners will be requested to reduce the number of items or product forecast so that the orders will not exceed the capacity constraints. In this way, the DRP/MRP process can be brought back into equilibrium. If the manu-

TABLE 20.16   Master Production Scheduling Chart

	Production weeks					
	1	2	3	4	5	6
Sum planned shipments	250	0	650	0	450	0
Written work orders		600				
Firm planned orders					600	
Planned work orders						
End-of-week balances	705	1305	655	655	805	805

Note: Safety stock = 600.
Beginning balance = 955.
Standard finishing quality = 600.

facturer is a different company, the set of requirements is conveyed to it. The MPS becomes the requirements for the manufacturer's materials requirements plan. After the purchasing organization makes a contractual commitment, the replenishment requirements are usually released directly with the manufacturer's master scheduling function.

The manufacturer's master scheduler constructs a master production schedule that ensures that the product will be manufactured and delivered to the customer's distribution network on time. The master scheduler sees to it that the total demand put in the MPS is equal to the S&OP plan.

Pick Lists

Pick lists that are generated by the DRP list the quantity of all items to be picked for shipment to each replenishment warehouse. The *pick list date* is the scheduled shipping date minus the item needed for picking. Before being released for picking, each item is checked for sufficient on-hand inventory. Only items with sufficient inventory are included in the pick lists. Items that are short are listed on a separate section of the pick list. The pick list also includes items that have sufficient quantities on hand for the next scheduled shipment. This gives warehouse employees the option of filling transportation facilities efficiently without upsetting inventory control.

The pick list is organized so that warehouse employees have the information for making detailed operating decisions in the same way that manufacturing department employees have sufficient information to make on-the-scene manufacturing decisions. With the pick list organized as shown in Table 20.17, "Saturday's Distribution Pick List," the warehouse people can maximize vehicle utilization without a negative impact on customer service. The information in the pick list "Past due (PD) plus week 1" column tells the warehouse employees the minimum amount needed to replenish a warehouse (DC) to keep each SKU at the acceptable level. Warehouse employees know the maximum amount that they can ship without upsetting the equilibrium of the DRP inventory. This maximum replenishment quantity is obtained by adding the quantity in the week 2 column to the quantity in the past-due plus week 1 column on the pick list.

The past-due column is the absolute minimum quantity that needs to be shipped to the DC to avoid the strong possibility of a customer's being shorted. The information in the past-due column could also be used when warehouse people know that they do not need to use the standard means of transportation to replenish the DC. The pick list shows the warehouse people the minimum, maximum, and preferred quantities to be shipped

TABLE 20.17 Saturday's Distribution Pick List

Review cycle days: 05; pick days: 05; in-transit days: 02;
put-away day: 02; next scheduled ship date: 04/16

Part numbers	Case description	PD + week 1	Week 2	Past due
92-30292	24/1000			
92-30416	144/100			
92-30752	50/10/10	4C		
78-46166	72/100	36C		
78-44112	24/500	60C		
80-10003	10/4/25		60C	
62-06261	50/10/10			
51-82152	24/500	72C	36C	72C
51-81047	72/30			
50-90031	72/100	36C		24C
47-46138	50/10/10			
47-46297	24/500			
47-03604	72/100	24C		
31-05758	144/100			
30-05263	20-5/20ML	10C		
27-66977	20-5/50ML	7C		

Note: C = cases; run date: 04/05.

to the DCs to keep the DRP process in equilibrium. By organizing the pick list as shown, warehouse personnel have the information needed to make discretionary decisions in the *distribution execution system* (DES) to maximize the productivity of the warehouse and of the transportation.

Scheduling Shipments

Using a pick list and planning data from DRP makes scheduling shipments a routine activity. The shipment schedule between central and plant warehouses and regional DCs and DCs triggers the issuing of the pick list. The pick list is sent to the issuing warehouse in sufficient time for materials to be picked and to meet the shipment schedule. The materials are picked as previously described, loaded on a transport vehicle, and shipped per schedule. Unscheduled shipments can be accomplished by issuing an "exception." The shipping department will decide what transportation to use to meet the customer's need. When the need for the exceptional shipment occurs, arrangements will be made by a DRP planner via phone. The DRP system's feedback is a report of what is loaded on the transport and notice that it has departed. DRP keeps track of the quantity of each item in transit until a receiving entry moves the quantity to on hand. DRP will also show *in-transit past due* once the database transit time has elapsed.

Broadening DRP into DRP II

Just as the manufacturer's materials requirements planning became the basis for manufacturing resources planning (MRP II), so too has DRP formed the basis of distribution resources planning (DRP II). In manufacturing activities, MRP is used as a basis for planning manufacturing operational activities, so the distribution function can use DRP as the basis for distribution planning operational activities.

DRP materials transactions provide the basis for determining the resources needed for each time period. The transaction's information shows the quantity and time for the movement for all SKUs. The planned receipts and issues for each time period and location provide the information for calculating the labor needed. The inventory balances at the beginning and end of a period provide the basis for calculating the space requirements at each stocking location within the distribution network. This information can be used for simulating the transportation resources requirements.

Vehicle Load Planning

The pick list for releasing shipments to a distribution point may be converted to the amount of transportation space required by applying *a cubic load value* for each SKU that is stored in the database. The total cubic volume can be calculated for each type of transportation resource selected for the specific need. The physical characteristics of each type of transportation is on file so the most cost-effective one may be chosen. As shown in the previous table, alternate transportation resources can be listed on a pick list.

This vehicle summary would include all the types of vehicles that are an option for shipping between each replenishment and distribution point. A summary of vehicle requirements is produced for each distribution point and replenishment point. Table 20.18, "Distribution Center Transportation Requirements," is an example of how the transportation requirements are summarized using the pick list for shipping quantities. The distribution resource database contains the transportation measurements required for each SKU. Multiplying the SKU standard cubic load value by the quantity on the pick list determines space requirements for each product listed. Summarizing the total space requirements for each pick list provides the transportation department with information to select the most cost-effective method for shipping to a particular distribution center.

Transportation Resources Requirements Planning

Materials included in the DRP schedule will determine the transportation requirements for going to each distribution center. This allows the shipping department latitude for consolidating several weeks' shipments. A summation of all materials movements can

TABLE 20.18   Distribution Center Transportation Requirements

	Past Due + Week 1			Week 2			Past Due		
	Weight	Cube	Pallet	Weight	Cube	Pallet	Weight	Cube	Pallet
Truck: 20 ft	9.5	9.3	10.6	15.3	14.3	16.1	3.1	3.2	3.7
Truck: 40 ft	5.1	5.0	5.6	8.2	7.6	8.5	1.7	1.7	1.9
Truck: 45 ft	5.1	4.1	4.9	8.2	6.3	7.4	1.7	1.4	1.7
Railcar: 50 ft	2.4	3.0	3.7	3.8	4.6	5.6	0.8	1.0	1.3

Note: weight = metric tons; cube = cubic feet; pallets = number of standard pallets: 40 × 48 inches.

be entered in a database to schedule the total transportation requirements. A simulation using planned orders, through the total DRP horizon, and the distribution resources database will assist in determining the needed future transportation resources.

Storage Resources Requirements Planning

For simulating storage space requirements, the planned inventory balances can be converted to cubic storage requirements. The storage requirements can be calculated for each period's planned inventory balance. Space requirements can be calculated for each stocking location in the distribution network.

Distribution Labor Resources Requirements

To determine labor requirements, the planned receipts and issues per period for each distribution location must be known. The labor resources requirements can be calculated in a fashion similar to the vehicle and space requirements described. For labor resources, the required time for the receipt and issue of each item is maintained in a *labor database*. From this data, the labor resources requirement can be calculated. The materials movements and planned shipments for each warehouse can be converted with a labor database to labor requirements. These are all adaptations of capacity-planning techniques that are used in conjunction with MRP.

DRP II CONCLUSIONS

Broadening of DRP into DRP II is accomplished by using the materials plans generated by DRP to calculate the distribution resources needed to handle the materials movements and storage operations specified by the DRP. There are only three types of resources needed to operate a distribution network: vehicles, storage space, and labor. The basis for determining the requirements of all three of these resources is the amount of materials each will be required to handle in a time period.

The potential of DRP II is being realized today in industries where it had been predicted for many years. Representative companies that have demonstrated the usefulness of DRP II include leaders in their industries such as a broad product line distributor, a major pharmaceutical products manufacturer, a distributor, a large Canadian health-care products company, a specialty music and video distributor, a leading children's products distributor, and a large world-class electronic manufacturer. The power of DRP supports aggressive business strategies.

The present stage of DRP's development has just scratched the surface of its potential use in manufacturing, distribution, retail, and utility businesses. Software and hardware technology advances such as electronic data transfer and data encoding, communications via satellite, and lower-cost and improved data processing methods have become primary enablers in DRP implementation.

DRP II is an integrated logistics system that can provide solutions to meet the needs of distribution resources planning and replenishment. DRP generates the planned shipment and stock status for each location within the distribution network. This information is then used to calculate materials and transportation requirements for each location which is then available for the system's full planning horizon, which typically is 1 year.

DRP provides a planning structure for computer simulation that can extend the resources requirements plan as far into the future as the business requires. DRP II, in practice, has proven to yield many benefits. It may lower the total inventories by as much as 80 percent and increase customer service levels into the upper 90 percents. DRP enables the following benefits: increased management control, lower transportation costs, and lower costs of warehousing, labor, and overhead. It provides a direct tie into manufacturing. The balance and mix of inventory at each distribution and replenishment point is improved.

Manufacturers that use a distribution network find that an integrated system of DRP and MRP is required to achieve a significantly enhanced performance level. DRP combined with MRP yields a fully integrated manufacturing and distribution system that will enhance the profits and returns on investment.

Public utilities, in a new competitive environment, are now beginning to use the DRP technology to plan requirements and movements. The industry has just come to the realization that materials needs can and must be planned and that most of their materials needs are dependent and therefore require time-phased planning rather than reorder-point control. This industry is in the same state of awareness and development that the retail industry was in in the early eighties. Materials planning is active in the utility industry as it faces many of the same problems that manufacturing and to an even greater extent retailing faces. Supplier-customer "partnering" relationships have a significant opportunity to apply DRP and DRP II technology. The need to plan across multiple organizations makes DRP the technology of choice to facilitate partnerships.

BIBLIOGRAPHY

Ford, Quentin: "Distribution Requirements Planning & MRP," *APICS 24th Annual International Conference Proceedings,* 1981, pp. 275–278.

————: "DRP/MRP: Distribution JIT," *APICS 30th Annual International Conference Proceedings,* 1987, pp. 672–676.

————: "Retail DRP JIT," *APICS 35th Annual International Conference Proceedings,* 1992, pp. 452–456.

Hanson, Paul C.: "MRP/DRP...Where Does That Demand Come From?" *APICS 34th Annual International Conference Proceedings,* 1991, pp. 338–340.

Martin, Andre J.: "Distribution Resource Planning (DRP II)," *APICS 23rd Annual International Conference Proceedings,* 1980, pp. 161–165.

————: "Distribution Resource Planning, Distribution Management's Most Powerful Tool," Oliver Wight Limited, Essex Junction, Vt., 1983.

————: "Integrating the Supply Chain: Key to High Velocity Customer Response," *APICS 35th International Conference Proceedings,* 1992, pp. 483–484.

Moody, Patricia E.: "Distribution Requirements Planning: Getting Closer to the Customer," *APICS 33rd International Proceedings,* 1990, pp. 504–506.

Turner, Jerry R.: "DRP: Theory and Reality," *APICS 33rd International Conference Proceedings,* 1990, pp. 545–549.

SECTION 5

PRODUCTION AND INVENTORY CONTROL SUPPORT FUNCTIONS

CHAPTER 21
LOGISTICS PLANNING

Editor
William T. Walker, CFPIM, CIRM
Supply Chain Management, Hewlett-Packard
Rockaway, New Jersey

The PIC professional should be knowledgeable about effective logistics. Inbound materials flow from suppliers to the factory, and outbound finished goods flow from the factory to distribution centers and customers. This chapter explains how to physically connect supply with demand using motor freight, airfreight, and ocean freight for both domestic and international shipments. The chapter presents a process framework for planning logistics that addresses the following four topics:

1. How is freight physically packaged for transport?
2. What organizations are involved in a freight movement?
3. Where are the logistics cost trade-offs?
4. When do legal and regulatory issues become important in logistics planning?

A detailed accounting of freight rates, carrier routes, and duty classifications is beyond the scope of this chapter. Rather, the focus here is on a planning process, grounded in practitioner experience, that leads to consistent, predictable, and cost-effective results.

PACKAGING FREIGHT FOR TRANSPORT

A *unit load* is a full pallet of product. Most often, a unit load is some quantity of the same *stock keeping unit,* or SKU, stacked in layers onto the pallet. Occasionally, the unit load may consist of multiple SKUs on one pallet to save transportation cost at the expense of extra handling in shipping and receiving. The dimensions of length, depth, height, weight, and quantity per pallet are fundamental to developing a logistics plan for the SKU. In many parts of the world dimensions are expressed in metric rather than English units. For later reference, note that 25.4 millimeters (mm) equals 1.00 inch, and 2.2 pounds equal 1.0 kilogram.

Defining a Unit Load

The unit load can differ substantially from both the product designed in engineering and the product ordered through sales. This is because value-added transformation may occur within the logistics channel. For example, parts with a limited shelf life, like batteries or software, might be added in final distribution. Or subassemblies might be combined to form the final product at the distribution center in a strategy to minimize duty cost. Or instruction manuals and line cord sets localized for English, French, Italian, Spanish, or German might be added to the generic computer product just before shipment to a reseller. Or printers might be transported in bulk packaging from Japan and individually boxed for customer shipment at the distribution center in Europe. It is important to visualize how the SKU flows along its entire supply chain before finalizing the details of the unit load.

Start by thinking about how the product is packaged for consumption by the end customer. Identify where along the supply chain this packaging is to be applied. Will the supplier put finished goods into a shipping carton that will carry the product all the way to the customer in an attractive box ready to place on the retailer's shelf? Or will the product be transported in bulk packaging, then individually boxed at the wholesaler's warehouse? Such decisions ultimately come down to volume-driven trade-offs between product packaging costs and transportation costs. The SKU configuration is assigned a unique number; where product packaging changes within the logistics channel, the SKU number must also change. Generally the SKU definition used for logistics will be different from both the manufacturer's in-house product number and the customer's product ordering number. For example, a manufacturer's master scheduled item 3900-60 is imported as SKU number F3900-80001 and distributed to customers as product F3900A.

Value Added in Distribution

The logistics practitioner should think through the supply chain routing from the lowest-level supplier to the highest-level end customer, making note of the operations performed within each distribution center. This exercise should be completed prior to finalizing any packaging designs in order to facilitate the flow of unpacking, repacking, and inserting material. Only by conceptualizing how and where the product might change within distribution (see Fig. 21.1) can customer satisfaction, the pipeline inventory investment, and the total logistics cost structure be optimized. SKUs are routed through distribution centers for one of four reasons, as discussed below.

First, freight can be consolidated. Inbound freight, sourced from multiple suppliers for example, will flow into a freight *consolidation center*. Here, the inbound SKU loads are combined onto a single pallet or into a single container for consolidated transport to the next destination. The concept of consolidation applies to all modes of transportation including feeder flights of smaller aircraft into major airport hubs and feeder sailings of smaller ships into major container ports. The benefit of freight consolidation is the lowering of transportation cost between the city of origin and the city of destination due to freight volume leveraging. Consolidation does not alter the definition of the SKU.

Second, cross-docking points can be considered. A *cross-docking facility* consists of many receiving docks and many shipping docks on the opposite sides of a building. Container loads and truckloads, carrying many different SKUs, arrive from various consolidation points. At this point of route switching, the container loads are split, merged with other partial loads, and consolidated anew into trailers and containers bound for the next destination. The benefit in cross-docking is the combination of reduced transit time

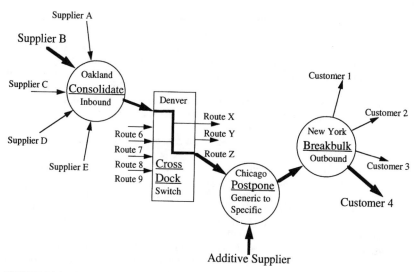

FIGURE 21.1 Four distribution operations.

to reach a final destination and the reduction in inventory investment because product is kept moving. Transit time is reduced because the unit load can approach the city of final destination by a direct path without miles of overshoot. Cross-docking does not alter the definition of the SKU.

Third, the SKU can be redefined in a *postponement center*. Generic product is shipped to the postponement center where additional materials are added, transforming the SKU into a customer-specific product. Country localization is one example where keyboards and line cords and foreign language documentation are added to make the SKU country specific. Other value-adding examples include filling operations for product with a limited shelf life or the insertion of software on floppy disk or CD-ROM just prior to shipment when the life cycle of the added part is short, causing inventory to be at a high risk of obsolescence. Postponement can also be used in the sense of shipping generic product to the distribution center based on a forecast, then localizing the product into specific flavors based on actual customer orders. An example is the selection of one of five disk drives for a generic personal computer where carrying finished goods on all five models is expensive and has a high mix risk. Postponement provides flexible, responsive delivery, but the definition of the SKU changes.

Finally, distribution centers can provide breakbulk processing for outbound shipments. *Breakbulk* is the opposite of consolidation where container loads and pallet loads are separated into individual product shipments outbound to customers. The distribution center may also perform the packout process of boxing the SKU for final delivery; here the quantity of the packaged SKU may change, and other materials may be added to the shipping carton. This distribution concept applies to all modes of transportation including short-hop air flights from a central hub and smaller ships off-loading a few containers from an ocean freighter for drop-off along the coastline. Cost savings in transportation and handling along with shortened delivery cycle times are the benefits of a breakbulk distribution operation.

Cartons, Master Cartons, and Pallets

Product is packaged for shipment to the end customer in one of two places: the supplier or the distribution center. Either the supplier places each individual product into a shipping carton, or the distribution center receives product in bulk and packs product into a shipping carton. The carton protects the product during transit and may provide attractive advertising of the product on the retailer's shelf. Smaller products can be arranged together as two packs, or four packs, or six packs, and so on for easy consumption by customers. Bulk pack is a scheme that trades off lower transportation cost from the supplier to distribution against higher tooling costs for packaging plus the labor cost at the distribution center for the packout operation.

Small SKUs can be combined into cases, or master cartons, for ease of palletization. A master carton might hold 10, 24, or 50 units of the same SKU. The design of the master carton should optimize the dimensions and weight of the unit load, while at the same time make it easy to present individual SKUs to the retailer for sales. For example, master cartons may be slit open or be placed on gravity-feed rollers for ease of unloading.

The unit load is built from cartons or master cartons stacked onto a wooden pallet or a plastic slipsheet. Stacking should be done in such a way that no part of the carton overhangs the pallet footprint. Also, the pallet is more stable when rectangular cartons can be stacked in an interlocked fashion. The total number of cartons or master cartons that can be stacked on a single pallet is determined by the total gross weight of the load and by the total height of the unit load. Some guidelines suggest holding the total load weight to about 1100 pounds (500 kilos) and restricting the load height to about 42.5 inches (1080 mm) including the pallet thickness.

Slip sheets are surfaces of thick plastic upon which cartons or master cartons can be stacked. A slip sheet serves the same handling purpose as a wooden pallet. A $3 slip sheet may be compared with a $15 pallet and can save the nearly 5 inches (125 mm) of pallet thickness for loads where container height clearance becomes critical. However, slip sheets have the disadvantage of requiring specially equipped forklift trucks at every shipping dock, cross-dock, and receiving dock along the route where the unit load will be handled. The special fork attachment grabs an edge of the plastic sheet and slips it over the fork, pulling the cargo along with the sheet.

For additional protection of the freight, a unit load is usually assembled with cardboard corner guards and a cardboard, or plywood, top cap as shown in Fig. 21.2. These precautions help to keep the individual cartons from being crushed. The entire load is then covered with shrink-wrap both to keep the load intact and to protect it against moisture. Unit loads shipped as airfreight can experience extreme handling conditions. The airlines use *air pallets,* which are metal frames that slide onto the floor of an aircraft; the dimensions of an air pallet accommodate the footprint of six side-by-side pallets arranged two by three. Air pallets waiting outside an aircraft will be subjected to rain during loading and unloading. Also, cargo handlers tend to climb on top of palletized goods during their stacking and tie-down operations; individual product cartons may not be able to handle the additional weight without crushing.

Labeling Requirements

All carton, master carton, and palletized unit loads should display bar-coded labels for ease of identification and tracking. Such labels should be printed with boldface characters of sufficient font size that the label can be easily read and scanned. In a warehouse many SKUs will look similar with SKU numbers differing by only a few digits. Make maximum use of readable bar codes for reliable physical distribution. A *readable bar*

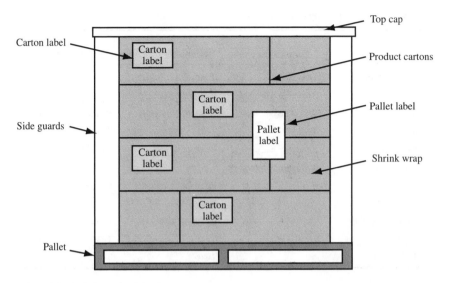

FIGURE 21.2   Palletized unit load.

code means that the equivalent text is printed just above or just below the bar-code lines and spaces. Clarity in labeling can help prevent costly mistakes.

Label information should be placed on the side, not the top, of each carton and master carton. This makes the carton label visible through the shrink-wrap after the cartons are palletized. When a label is on the top of a carton, the whole pallet has to be disassembled to read the label information. Table 21.1 lists the information content for each type of label. Pay attention to those data elements that need to be carried through from the product label to the carton label to the master carton label to the pallet label. One important example is the country of origin where customs officials will be checking the paperwork against the packaging and product labels. The SKU number, UPC, and description are the primary means of identification used by materials handlers during a freight movement and in the warehouse.

Always include a date code or date code embedded within a serial number. A date code can facilitate first-in, first-out stock rotation for SKUs with limited shelf life. The date code is also the primary means for separating bad product from good product within a warehouse. Avoid mixing date codes for the same SKU at the pallet level. Distribution centers want to manage their stock by pallet and not by the individual carton. Materials handlers should be able to quickly spot the date code on the label.

Dimensions and Weight Considerations for Containerization

Standard pallet dimensions vary widely around the world. The United States uses a 48-inch by 40-inch pallet while Europe uses 1200 mm by 1000 mm. Another standard, the *Euro pallet,* is 1000 mm by 800 mm. The Euro pallet is an expensive but sturdy wooden pallet built to exact specification. Euro pallet users are expected to return an empty Euro pallet each time they receive a loaded Euro pallet; this requires a complete reverse logistics path to return the empties.

TABLE 21.1 Continuity of Label Information

Data element	Carton label	Master carton label	Pallet label
Country of origin*	Text	Text	Text
SKU number*	Readable bar code	Readable bar code	Readable bar code
UPC	Readable bar code	Readable bar code	Readable bar code
Description	Text	Text	Text
Date code*	Readable bar code	Readable bar code	Readable bar code
Serial number*	Readable bar code		
Quantity per		Readable bar code	Readable bar code
Weight per		Text	Text
Tracking number		Readable bar code	Readable bar code
Ship from address		Text	Text
Ship to address		Text	Text

*On the product.

Many suppliers in the Far East use nonstandard pallet dimensions; they build the pallet footprint to exactly match the stacked load. This practice optimizes freight cost at the expense of warehousing cost. Freight costs go down because more product will fit into an ocean freight container. Warehousing costs go up because some racking systems and gravity-feed systems do not accommodate nonstandard dimensions. The distribution center ends up repalletizing the unit load and incurs additional expense to dispose of used pallets.

Footprint dimensions determine the total number of pallet stacks that can be loaded onto a truck bed or into a container. For example, using North American pallets in Europe means that only 9 pallet footprints will fit onto the bed of a standard-width lorry versus an expected 10 pallet footprints. This results in a higher per-unit freight cost. The undercarriage construction of the pallet can also be a critical cost factor. Some warehouses use racking systems that use two steel beams in place of a complete floor or shelf to carry the weight of the palletized loads. If the spacing between the runners, or the orientation of the stringers, underneath the pallet are not compatible with the racking beams, then the load will be repalletized by the distribution center at an additional cost.

The unit load height dimension is determined from the following considerations. Unit loads should be designed for stacking at least 2 high. This 2-high stack, each of which includes the height dimension of the pallet and the thickness of top cap, should clear the vertical door jam dimension of a standard container allowing vertical clearance for a pallet jack. Table 21.2 shows some typical dimensions that are used for international ocean freight containers and for domestic (U.S.) motor freight trailers. A 20-foot container can hold 20 pallets when stacked 2 high; a 40-foot container can hold 40 pallets when stacked 2 high. Airfreight container dimensions vary widely. Airfreight forwarders assemble air pallets by arranging the pallet loads from their customers three pallets across by two pallets deep by two pallets high, covering the freight with plastic sheeting, and securing the freight to the pallet with a rope webbing.

The total weight of a unit load is also important. Weight is the fundamental freight cost driver. The customer pays freight on the product, its packaging materials, and the

TABLE 21.2 Typical Container Dimensions

	20-ft dry freight container		40-ft dry freight container		45-ft-high cube container	
	Metric	English	Metric	English	Metric	English
Interior length	5.919 m	19' 5"	12.051 m	39' 6.5"	13.582 m	44' 6.5"
Interior width	2.340 m	7' 8"	2.340 m	7' 8"	2.347 m	7' 8.2"
Interior height	2.380 m	7' 9.5"	2.380 m	7' 9.5"	2.690 m	8' 10"
Door width	2.286 m	7' 6"	2.286 m	7' 6"	2.340 m	7' 8"
Door height	2.278 m	7' 5.5"	2.278 m	7' 5.5"	2.584 m	8' 5.7"
Tare weight	1,900 kg	4,189 lb	3,630 kg	8,003 lb	4,110 kg	9,061 lb
Payload	22,100 kg	48,721 lb	27,397 kg	60,401 lb	28,390 kg	62,589 lb
Cubic capacity	33.0 m³	1,165 ft³	67.3 m³	2,377 ft³	85.7 m³	3,026 ft³

container. An empty wooden pallet can weigh 50 to 60 pounds, and the *tare weight,* or unloaded weight, of a 40-foot container can be 8000 pounds. Do not load more than 1100 pounds (500 kg) onto a single pallet. A container loaded with heavy pallets may exceed the maximum payload limit of the container or the over-the-road gross weight limit of the trailer. When pallets are stacked, the upper pallet tends to crush the master cartons of the pallet below. When the load shifts dynamically, especially in airfreight, this crushing effect gets much worse. One guideline suggests that packaging and palletization is properly designed for transportation dynamics when four identically loaded pallets can be stacked statically without the bottom pallet showing signs of crushing. And there are important safety reasons to limit unit load weight. Wooden pallets that are weakened and damaged by usage or are dissimilar in construction tend to wobble when stacked. Bracing is often needed within a container.

ELEMENTS OF THE LOGISTICS NETWORK

The logistics practitioner buys services from numerous commercial logistics organizations. The variety and complexity of organizations required for moving freight are driven by the mode of transportation and the need to move freight internationally. Fully integrated logistics services are available for a price. Other approaches include supplementing in-house logistics expertise with specific third-party capabilities. In order to plan for the purchase of the right level of services, the practitioner should have a good understanding of the kinds of logistics organizations involved in moving freight domestically (see Fig. 21.3) and internationally (see Fig. 21.4).

The Carrier

Transportation companies, called *carriers,* provide the means of moving freight from the supplier's *point of origin* to the customer's *point of destination.* There are several legal forms for a carrier as related to operating rights and pricing policies. These legal forms include common carrier, contract carrier, exempt carrier, private carrier, and independent carrier. *Common carriers* provide scheduled transportation services for commercial customers at a fee subject to the limitations of its operating authority. All

LAND TRANSPORT

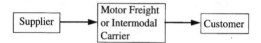

AIR/SEA TRANSPORT

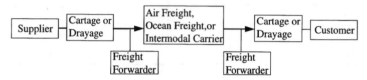

FIGURE 21.3   Domestic logistics.

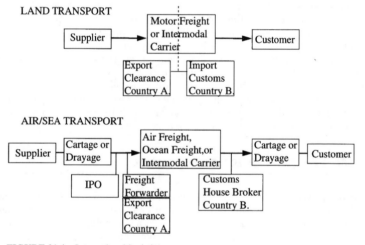

FIGURE 21.4   International logistics.

the other legal forms involve business arrangements for irregular schedules, for specific service area exemptions, for privately owned transportation services, and for owner-operator independent transportation. Carriers are classified by their mode of transport, that is, motor freight, rail freight, ocean freight, and airfreight. A transportation company makes its profit by moving the weight of freight over some distance. The heavier the freight and the farther the distance, the more profit made by the carrier.

The Freight Forwarder

The *freight forwarder* provides a logistics service by arranging for the transport of goods. A freight forwarder is able to consolidate shipments of less-than-container load volumes to obtain full-container load rates. The forwarder uses this volume leverage to obtain lower carrier rates for air and ocean freight and takes a profit on the margin. Freight-forwarding companies are specialized by the mode of transportation and are located in the major port cities along the routes they service.

Freight Forwarder and Carrier Selection

Effective logistics planning involves doing some research to discover the best solution. The largest forwarders, carriers, and port authorities advertise in the trade magazines such as *Inbound Logistics, Traffic Management,* and *Export Today. Purchasing Magazine* runs an annual *Transportation Sourcing Guide,* and the *Thomas Register* is available on the Internet for a price. Federal Express and United Parcel Service have *home pages* on the Internet that describe their small-parcel services and provide convenient real-time tracking of a shipment from door to hub to hub to door. Do not overlook the possibility that a key supplier or another division is already moving a large volume of freight through a particular forwarder or carrier; this is an excellent place to leverage from for established routings and rate structures.

1. The first cut at selecting transportation services comes down to the geography between origin and destination and to the required mode of transport.

2. Evaluate potential freight forwarders and carriers on more than just the cost of their services. Talk to their senior management, and visit their local motor pool or terminal or hub. Ask about their current customer base and plans to open or close facilities that will impact future freight movement. Get a first-hand look at their process documentation, methods of employee training, degree of union representation, serviceability of equipment, investment in technology, and quality-defect tracking.

3. Take the time to understand the structure of the rate tariff. The forwarder and carrier will want to see a forecast for freight volume. Make sure that the carrier you select services the entire geographical area and already has substantial business between the origin and destination cities. If not, select another carrier. Make sure that the freight forwarder selected conducts substantial business in airfreight or ocean freight as required for both the origin and destination cities. If not, select another forwarder. If the rate tariff seems high, ask what might be done to make the freight movement less expensive. Perhaps a small change in the dimension or weight of the unit load will make a large difference in cost. Perhaps extending the transit time by 1 or 2 days will also make a large difference in cost. Make sure that costs gets quoted door to door to avoid the surprise of hidden extras. Whenever possible, play into preferred processes and high-volume routings.

4. Track the delivery performance of the forwarder and carrier on a routine basis. Deal with any issues such as late pickup, goods damaged in-transit, missed deliveries, delays through customs, lost pallets, or mistakes on bills of lading immediately. Set high expectations, and demand timely proof of corrective action.

The International Procurement Organization

An *International Procurement Organization,* or IPO, can be an effective intermediary within a foreign country for sourcing logistics services. Because the IPO is generally located in the same country as the supplier, the IPO can resolve business issues related to local law, insurance, currency exchange, and language and culture difficulties for the customer at a reasonable cost. The IPO can recommend carriers, brokers, and freight forwarders with the added advantage of being able to easily visit their management. In addition, some IPOs have traffic specialists and can assist in shipping document preparation and shipment tracking. The IPO makes its profit by charging an uplift percentage on the value of goods exported.

The Customs House Broker

Customs house brokers make their profit by providing a service to expedite the importation of goods through customs. The broker is responsible for preparing customs documents and for clearing the physical goods through the customs process. The broker may also provide temporary *bonded warehousing*. The customs authority allows imported goods to be stored in a bonded warehouse without payment for duties until such time as the goods are physically removed from the warehouse. Customs house brokers must be licensed by the customs authority. In the United States they are licensed by the U.S. Treasury Department.

U.S. Customs Service

In the United States, customs is a branch of the Treasury Department. The *U.S. Customs Service* regulates the movement of carriers and freight entering and exiting the country. It collects all duties, taxes, and fees owed on freight imported from foreign countries, and it enforces certain export control laws of the United States. In addition, the U.S. Customs Service enforces laws to prevent illegal trade, and it protects the country from the importation of hazardous materials.

Import Administration

The United States *Import Administration* is part of the U.S. Department of Commerce. The Import Administration implements antidumping and countervailing duty laws, participates in the negotiations for fair trade, and implements the law regarding foreign trade zones. The Import Administration is influential in the international agreements including GATT and NAFTA, which determine the duty rate structure paid on goods imported into this country. Duty is a significant incremental cost factor with international trade.

Export Administration

In the United States the *Bureau of Export Administration* is under the auspices of the U.S. Department of Commerce. The Export Administration oversees export licensing and export policy. It does this by acting to restrict the flow of goods and technologies that could significantly contribute to the military force of other nations to the detriment of national security. The Export Administration places certain licensing and administrative requirements on all exported goods. Statistics on all exports are reported to the Bureau of Census, which is also part of the Department of Commerce. These administrative activities are an incremental cost for international trade.

LOGISTICS COST TRADE-OFFS

The transportation industry offers a bewildering assortment of services, rate tariffs, and terms and conditions. Basic information about the type of cargo, the weight of the cargo, the distance and terrain to be traveled, and the allowable time for transport should be understood when planning logistics. Use the following questions to begin:

1. Is this shipment a one-time event or expected to be repetitive?

2. Will this freight be shipped as common cargo, or will it require special handling, because it is perishable or refrigerated or it contains hazardous materials (HazMat)?

3. Based on the cubic volume and weight of the shipment, which one of the following types of service is appropriate: small parcel, less than truckload (LTL) and less than container load (LCL), full truckload or full container load, or bulk shipment?

4. Is standard in-transit time acceptable, or is expedited delivery required?

A combination of transportation modes may be appropriate, see Table 21.3.

Common cargo is handled according to its size and weight: small parcel, *less than truckload* (LTL), full container, and bulk. The basic modes of transportation include motor freight, rail freight, airfreight, and ocean freight. The customer can pay for standard delivery or for more expensive expedited delivery, which often involves some form of airfreight. Some carriers combine transport modes to offer interesting intermodal alternatives resulting in faster turnaround at a reduced cost relative to airfreight. For example, the intermodal combination of motor freight with rail freight using roll-on/roll-off trailers can save 2 days' transit time when moving cargo from the northeast United States to the south. And the intermodal combination of ocean freight with air-freight can save 5 days over straight ocean freight when moving cargo from Singapore to Rotterdam.

Motor Freight and Intermodal Rail Freight

The initial transportation leg from the supplier and the final transportation leg to the customer is usually made by motor freight. One exception is the factory or distribution center serviced by a railroad siding. The number of additional transportation modes to connect the supply with the demand is then a function of weight, cube, in-transit time, and terrain. International shipments between countries that are not connected by a land mass necessitate the use of ferries, ocean freight, or airfreight.

The easiest and most frequent situation is setting up a motor freight carrier for a domestic shipment. A freight forwarder is not required for motor freight. However, there is a choice of motor freight carrier depending on whether the freight is to be transported to a local intrastate destination or to a long-haul interstate destination. The supplier contacts the carrier's dispatcher at the local terminal location with responsibility for pickups within the supplier's geographical area. The dispatcher schedules the next available pickup and routes the freight through to its destination terminal. When the freight arrives at the originating terminal, it is consolidated with other shipments before being transported to its final destination. The destination terminal dispatcher schedules delivery of the freight to the customer within the destination terminal's geographical area.

Some suppliers operate their own fleet of trucks and can deliver the goods factory-direct to the customer. A *milk run* is a fixed delivery schedule maintained by an independent trucking firm where each day of the week one truck makes pickups at each of several parts suppliers and ends with one delivery to the factory. Where a factory's suppliers are located in close proximity, a milk run can be less expensive than using common carrier services. Trailers are often returned to their terminal empty; this is called *deadheading*. It is sometimes possible to coordinate the transportation of outbound freight with the carrier for inbound freight who is returning empty.

TABLE 21.3   Combining Airfreight with Ocean Freight to Fill the Pipeline

---

Situation: A company supplies its Amsterdam distribution center with computer peripherals manufactured in Taiwan at a landed cost of $115 each. The peripherals are individually boxed and come to the distribution center 18 units per pallet. The pallet dimensions are 1000 mm wide $\times$ 916 mm deep $\times$ 1168 mm high. A full pallet load weighs 155 kg. Door-to-door freight has been quoted by freight forwarder MSAS at $3.30/kg and 6 days for air movement and by freight forwarder Kuehne & Nagle at $0.48/kg and 24 days for an ocean movement through Rotterdam. In preparation for a new-product announcement, the company needs to build up inventory in the distribution center at a minimum rate of 200 units per week for a 4-week period.

Airfreight delivered week 1:
  Transport 1 air pallet of 3 $\times$ 2 $\times$ 2 high unit loads. The total number of units per shipment equals 216. The total weight per shipment equals 1860 kg. The total airfreight cost is $6138.

Airfreight delivered week 2:
  Transport 1 air pallet of 3 $\times$ 2 $\times$ 2 high unit loads. The total number of units per shipment equals 216. The total weight per shipment equals 1860 kg. The total airfreight cost is $6138.

Airfreight delivered week 3:
  Transport 1 air pallet of 3 $\times$ 2 $\times$ 2 high unit loads. The total number of units per shipment equals 216. The total weight per shipment equals 1860 kg. The total airfreight cost is $6138.

Ocean freight delivered week 4:
  Transport 40 pallets in one D40 ocean container. The total number of units per shipment equals 720. The total weight per shipment equals 6,200 kg. The total ocean freight cost is $2,976.

Cash invested in pipeline inventory:
  3 flights $\times$ $115/unit $\times$ 216 units/flight equals $74,520 for 6 days.

Cash invested in pipeline inventory:
  $115/unit $\times$ 720 units/container equals $82,800 for 24 days.

Average investment in pipeline inventory:

$$\frac{(\$74,520)(6 \text{ days}) + (\$82,800)(24 \text{ days})}{648 \text{ units} + 720 \text{ units}} = 1779 \text{ dollar-days per unit}$$

Average freight cost per unit:

$$\frac{\$18,414 \text{ airfreight} + \$2976 \text{ ocean freight}}{648 \text{ units} + 720 \text{ units}} = \$15.64 \text{ per unit}$$

For long-haul freight, such as freight that crosses the United States, two or more carriers may be in strategic partnership "handing off" the freight from one to another in order to span the total distance. Local freight terminals at each end of a route are interconnected by a network of strategically located freight distribution centers. Here the motor freight carrier performs consolidation and breakbulk operations to better service the geographical area. The point-to-point movement of freight from distribution center to distribution center is called a *line haul*. Motor freight carriers may provide regional service as does Viking Freight System, which services the western United States, or full domestic service as does Roadway Express, which services all 50 states plus Canada and Mexico. Sometimes motor freight will involve an international shipment passing through customs, such as at the border crossing from the United States into Mexico at Laredo, Texas, or the border crossing from Malaysia to the duty-free zone in Singapore at the Johor Causeway. In Europe especially, motor freight may involve taking a ferry ride between the continent and the United Kingdom or Scandinavia.

In North America a few of the larger long-haul carriers combine motor freight with rail freight to offer intermodal service with faster delivery at a reasonable cost. Such a service eliminates having to deal directly with the nuances of rail freight and provides more reliable rail delivery than could be scheduled by the small customer. Straight rail freight is also attractive for high-bulk shipments like automobiles and construction machinery or tanker car movement of liquids and gases.

Airfreight

Shipping cargo by airfreight involves "hand-offs" between several organizations that are usually transparent to the shipper. An airfreight transaction is begun by contacting a freight forwarder with offices in the airports at both ends of the routing. The supplier arranges the *cartage,* or local motor transport, to move the freight from the factory to the forwarder. The freight forwarder accepts the freight from the supplier, consolidates the freight for shipment, prepares the legal and customs paperwork, schedules the shipment with the carrier, transfers the freight to the carrier's agent, and notifies the destination office of when to expect the arrival of the shipment. At the destination airport, the freight forwarder or customs broker accepts the freight from the carrier's agent, may warehouse the freight until inspected and released by customs, performs breakbulk services, examines legal and customs paperwork, and arranges for cartage or local motor transport to the customer. The carrier owns and operates the fleet of aircraft along with the air pallets and air containers used by that airline. The carrier's agent performs loading and unloading operations of properly palletized or containerized freight with the aircraft. The port authority owns the runways, tower, gates, and hangers contracted out to the airlines. Specific arrangements may vary.

Airfreight is carried by different classes of aircraft. Passenger aircraft carry only a small tonnage of freight in the belly of the plane. Freighter aircraft can carry only freight tonnage, and "combi" aircraft can trade off some of the passenger seating for an extended cargo bay. The passenger and cargo flights scheduled out of a particular airport determine the *uplift capacity* for that airport. In some remote parts of the world, flight schedules can significantly limit the volume of freight that can be flown in or out of an airport. In addition, hazardous air cargo materials are limited to freighter aircraft, which are routed through a more restricted selection of cities.

Ocean Freight

An ocean freight transaction is begun by contacting a freight forwarder who has offices in the ports at both ends of the routing. The supplier arranges the *drayage,* or local motor transport, to move the goods to the forwarder. The freight forwarder accepts the cargo from the supplier, consolidates the freight for shipment, prepares the legal and customs paperwork, schedules the shipment with the carrier, transfers the freight to the stevedore company, and notifies the destination office of when to expect arrival of the shipment. At the destination port, the freight forwarder or customs broker accepts the freight from the stevedore company, may warehouse the freight until inspection and release by customs, performs breakbulk, forwards legal and customs paperwork, and arranges for drayage to the customer. The carrier owns and operates the shipping fleet along with all oceangoing containers used by that carrier. Ocean containers are carefully scheduled and maintained. A customer who continues to use a container more than 48 hours past a specified time will pay a demurrage fee to the carrier. The stevedore company performs loading and unloading ship operations of properly containerized freight with the ship. The port authority owns the docks, drydocks, cranes, and warehouses that are contracted out to the shipping lines.

Commercial ocean shipping schedules are organized into *slow lanes, fast lanes,* and *conference lanes.* Slow lanes differ from fast lanes by the type of ship, the number of ports of call, and the number of days' transit time from the port of origin to the port of destination. Fast-lane ocean freight utilizes faster vessels servicing fewer ports, but it is more expensive than slow-lane ocean freight. A conference lane is the scheduling of ships from two or more ocean carriers to provide regular service among a set of seaports. Each of the ocean carriers agrees to the same rate structure from the port of origin to the port of destination; the customer does not get to specify which ocean carrier makes the shipment. For example, ships from the Maersk Line, Hapag-Lloyd, and SeaLand might all service the same conference lane. Secondary ports are then serviced by small feeder ships making container pickups and deliveries up and down the coastline from a major harbor such as Hong Kong.

Inbound and Outbound

Inbound freight is the interconnection of the supplier base to a single customer such as a factory or distribution center. Inbound freight can be broken into A, B, and C classifications, as shown in Table 21.4, for freight cost management. Pareto techniques are useful for managing the A and B classes of inbound. Freight costs can be rank-ordered from highest to lowest by supplier, by carrier, and by route. Duty costs can be rank-ordered by commodity or by country of origin. These simple analyses will draw attention to opportunities for freight cost reduction. A number of suppliers may be within half a day's drive of the customer's site. Here it may pay to contract a reliable independent trucker for less cost than a common carrier to make a daily or twice-a-week pickup from each supplier for a single delivery to the customer.

Outbound freight is the interconnection of a single factory or distribution center to its customer base. The customer base can be quite large, with shipments to any one customer being infrequent and unpredictable. With outbound freight the carrier should be asked to guarantee the maximum transit time for delivery anywhere within a geograph-

TABLE 21.4   Inbound Freight

Freight class	Class description	Freight management
A	High cube and weight Frequent delivery Few suppliers	Closely managed high freight costs Consolidate at the supplier Use preferred carriers and specify routings
B	Less than truckload Frequent delivery Many suppliers	Medium freight costs Group suppliers by common carriers LTL rates lower cost than single parcel
C	Small parcel Infrequent delivery Many suppliers	Medium to low freight costs Hard to leverage favorable rates Single-piece minimums by zone

ical zone. Actual delivery performance should be measured continuously by the customer and fed back to the carrier. When the total volume of outbound freight within a zone is large, the best freight rates will be based on total tonnage rather than on the box count.

Transit Time versus Inventory versus Cost Trade-offs

There is a fundamental logistics trade-off to be made among transit time, freight cost, and pipeline inventory. One end of the spectrum is next-day airfreight where the turnaround is 1 day, the freight cost is 7 to 10 times the cost of ocean freight, and the pipeline inventory is a few pallets for 1 day. The other end of the spectrum is slow-lane ocean freight where the turnaround time is 35 days, the freight cost is the cost reference, and the pipeline inventory is 40 pallets per container for 35 days. Transit time considerations include the type of service requested, the mode of transport, the carrier's schedule frequency, the routing of the transport, export license and import customs clearance time for international shipments, and restricted routings and schedules for HazMat shipments. Table 21.5 lists some typical transit times.

Primary freight cost drivers include the mode of transportation, the weight of the shipment, and the distance traveled. Secondary drivers include the need for expedited service, the cube of the freight, IPO uplift, insurance, cartage or drayage, forwarder documentation fees, customs brokerage fees, and container service charges (see Fig. 21.5). Freight rates are quoted in dollars per kilo (kilograms of freight where 1 ton equals 909 kilos). It costs a fixed dollar amount to move a container from point A to point B whether the container is full or empty. The transportation industry capitalizes on this by offering both full-container load rates and less-than-full-container load rates, or LCL rates. Freight forwarders make their margin by charging the customer LCL rates but paying the carrier the lower full-container rate. Expect to pay additional small or fixed fees for documentation handling, customs processing, terminal fees, and container service charges.

A *tariff* is a published collection of rates, rules, and regulations that govern a particular transportation movement. Tariffs define freight rates both by lane, or route taken, and by the type of commodity transported. Historically motor freight common carriers were required to file their tariffs with the Interstate Commerce Commission for interstate

TABLE 21.5 Typical Door-to-Door Freight Transit Times

From	To North America— San Francisco and Oakland	To Europe— Amsterdam and Rotterdam	To Asia/Pacific— Singapore
North America New York	5 days—motor freight 2 days—airfreight (coast to coast)	16 days—ocean freight 6 days—airfreight	24 days—ocean freight 7 days—airfreight
Europe Frankfurt	18 days—ocean freight 7 days—airfreight	2 days—motor freight and ferry (within Western Europe)	22 days—ocean freight 7 days—airfreight
Asia/Pacific Singapore	20 days—ocean freight 6 days—airfreight	22 days—ocean freight 7 days—airfreight	5 days—airfreight (within Southeast Asia)

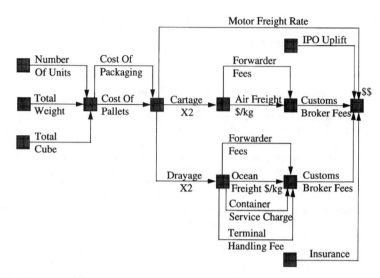

FIGURE 21.5   Freight cost drivers.

transportation services and with each state organization for intrastate transportation services; the tariff then became a matter of public record. But, the ICC was abolished with transportation industry deregulation. Always ask the carrier to explain the tariff. Motor freight rates are quoted per hundred weight, abbreviated cwt, meaning the load weight is divided by 100 and multiplied by the rate. For example, it costs $99.20 to transport 500 pounds on a tariff rate of $19.84 cwt. Full truckload rates of 10,000 pounds (4545 kilograms), and above, are more economical than less-than-truckload rates.

While tariffs are defined around tonnage and distance, there is a minimum fixed charge for a common carrier to move even the smallest package. Small-parcel services like Federal Express, United Parcel Service, and DHL exploit this minimum charge by moving small packages domestically within 24 hours and internationally within 48 hours. The small-parcel services have both a maximum weight and a maximum width plus length plus height dimension restriction on their shipments. Packages that exceed either limit will have to be moved by an LTL carrier.

Pipeline inventory investment is driven by the cube, or cubic volume, of freight per shipment, by the frequency of shipment, and by the in-transit time (see Fig. 21.6). The relative investment of two pipeline inventory alternatives can be compared by computing the dollar-days per alternative; the lower the dollar-days, the smaller the investment. Pipeline inventory also drives a set of secondary warehousing costs. This cost is related to the number of units delivered all at once in a container shipment and the cost premium for incremental warehousing capacity and materials-handling staff to receive that delivery. For example, 2 air pallets per week delivered to the warehouse will require a receiving capacity of 24 pallets per shift, a maximum storage capability of 12 pallet footprints (stacked 2 high within the warehouse), and a pipeline inventory investment of 24 unit loads. On the other hand, two D40 ocean containers delivered to the warehouse once every 4 weeks would require a maximum receiving capacity of 80 pallets per shift, a maximum storage capacity of 40 pallet footprints (stacked 2 high within the warehouse), and a pipeline inventory investment of 80 unit loads.

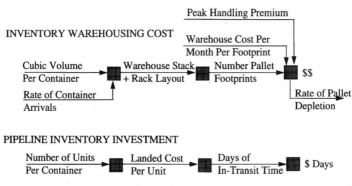

FIGURE 21.6 Pipeline inventory cost drivers.

LEGAL CONSIDERATIONS

The terms and conditions of logistics are one of the key considerations in the contractual agreement between a supplier (seller) and a customer (buyer). The transfer of title for the goods, the risk of loss during transport, and the liability for paying freight and duty are all open to negotiation between the parties.

Incoterms

Incoterms is the set of international standards for trade terms generally accepted around the world. Incoterms define the point of delivery, the transfer of title, the freight cost liability, the party responsible for import-export paperwork, and the insurable risk of loss between the seller and the buyer (Table 21.6). Incoterms are defined and maintained by the International Chamber of Commerce; the ICC can be contacted through their home page on the Internet. The full set of 13 Incoterms specify relative risk and cost trade-offs between seller and buyer from the time the goods leave the seller's shipping dock via local cartage to the forwarder through export clearance to in-transit by sea or air to docking through customs via local cartage, till the time the goods reach the buyer's receiving dock.

Part 3, Section 2, of the Uniform Commercial Code, the UCC, used in the United States also defines certain delivery terms that are applicable to domestic motor freight. FOB-Origin is called a *shipment contract*. Under FOB-Origin, title for the goods is transferred at the place of shipment, and the buyer is responsible for the cost and risk of transport. FOB-Destination is called a *destination contract*. Under FOB-Destination, title for the goods is transferred at the place of destination, and the seller is responsible for the cost and risk of transport. The UCC terms are consistent with the Incoterms.

The transfer of title is accomplished through a bill of lading. Freight costs can be prepaid to the carrier before pickup or collect to the carrier upon receipt. Freight forwarders can arrange for cargo insurance to cover the risk of loss during transport. It is usually very expensive to insure an individual shipment. So the value and irreplaceability of the goods should warrant such insurance. Many shipments go uninsured. A common approach to insure frequent freight shipments over a regular route is an open policy written to cover an entire shipment plan; premiums for such a policy will be much less expensive than the premium to insure the loss on individual freight movements.

TABLE 21.6   Example Incoterms

Term	Seller's responsibility	Buyer's responsibility
Ex works (EXW)		Buyer bears all cost and risk to destination including loading at seller's dock.
Free on board (FOB)	Seller bears cost and risk for export documentation and loading at a mutually agreeable port.	Buyer bears cost and risk to final destination.
Cost, insurance, and freight (CIF)	Seller bears the cost, but not the risk, to the port of entry (ocean freight).	Buyer bears risk during transit and unloading once goods are accepted by the carrier.
Carriage, and insurance paid (CIP)	Seller bears the cost, but not the risk, to the port of entry (airfreight).	Buyer bears risk during transit and unloading once goods are accepted by the carrier.
Delivered duty paid (DDP)	Seller bears all cost and risk to destination including payment of freight and duty.	

Commercial Invoice

The *commercial invoice* lists the goods shipped with the price to be paid by the buyer. A typical invoice includes the following information: invoice date, invoice number, supplier's name and invoice to address, invoice due date, customer's order number, item, description, quantity shipped, unit price, amount due, freight payment method, and terms of payment. For international shipments additional information may be included on the invoice: country of origin, HTS classification, carrier, waybill number, shipping method, terms of delivery, and date shipped.

Packing Slip and Box List

The *packing slip* and *box list* are documents providing detailed itemization of the contents of each carton, master carton, pallet, and container being shipped. The list typically includes the following information: supplier invoice number and customer order number, item part number or stock keeping unit, destination city, ship date, total box count or pallet count, and total shipment weight. For export by airfreight, a box list may include the house airway bill number, the master airway bill number, the carrier, the flight number, the estimated time of departure, and the estimated time of arrival. For export by ocean freight, a box list may include the bill of lading number, the carrier, the vessel name, the estimated date of departure, and the estimated date of arrival.

Bill of Lading

A *bill of lading* is a carrier's contract and receipt for the freight that the carrier agrees to transport, from a port of origin to a port of destination, with delivery to a designated person. The bill of lading details the following: the shipper, the consignee, the party to be notified, a description of the goods, country of origin, weight, cube, box count information, routing instructions to the destination point, the vessel name when shipped by ocean, and all charges. The shipper *consigns* the goods to the carrier, meaning that title for the goods passes to the carrier. The *bill of lading paper* serves as the receipt for the goods; in the case of a freight loss, the bill of lading is the basis for filing a freight claim.

Waybill

The *waybill* describes the shipment and routing instructions and identifies the shipper, the consignee, and the destination. Waybills are useful for tracing lost freight and for tracking the progress of a freight movement. A *master air waybill* (MAWB) lists the airline, flight number, estimated time of departure (ETD), and estimated time of arrival (ETA). A *house air waybill* (HAWB) itemizes each of the customer pallets loaded on an aircraft, and it can be used to prevent a freight forwarder from unstacking and restacking a pallet, which sometimes leads to damaged cartons.

Letter of Credit

For international trading, where the seller may be unsure of the buyer's credit rating, it is common practice to finance the transaction through a *letter of credit*. The letter of credit is issued from a domestic commercial bank, called the *issuing bank*, for the buyer. It authorizes the seller to draw drafts against the buyer's credit at a second, foreign bank that is convenient to the seller. The second bank is called the *confirming bank*. The letter of credit promises payment from the issuing bank to the confirming bank upon proof of delivery of the goods. Letters of credit should be carefully drafted to anticipate any delays in shipment and to make the proof of delivery as straightforward as possible. If the slightest error occurs with the commercial invoice or other proof-of-delivery documentation, the letter of credit will not be paid. A letter of credit involves a processing fee, interest due for each day the money is borrowed, and a currency exchange fee.

EDI and Laser Scanning Technology

Two technological trends are revolutionizing the overhead in logistics. The first, related to logistics documentation, is the utilization of *electronic data interchange* (EDI) to move toward paperless transactions for bills of lading, letters of credit, commercial invoices, customs clearances, and so on. The second, related to physical identification, is the application of *laser scanning technology* to provide, within a credit-card-sized memory device, a definition of the physical attributes of each item within a container. This technology is a level of information integration well above bar-coded label tags.

REGULATORY CONSIDERATIONS

In addition to the structuring of tariffs for freight rates, four other areas of government regulation impact the global flow of goods through a logistics network. The areas are import duties, export licensing, hazardous material transportation, and environmentally responsible packaging.

Import Duty

Throughout time, the industrialized nations of the world have established treaties regulating world trade. In such treaties a *duty* is a tax on imported goods that creates a trade barrier against the foreign production of specified commodities. This is a protection for the domestic production of those same commodities. GATT, the General Agreement on Tariffs and Trade, is the foundation or starting point for the system of import duties used by the United States and many other industrialized nations. A number of other specific treaties between trading countries overlay the GATT provisions with sets of duty preferences specific to the exporting country, the type of goods, and the time frame of the preference. The Maastricht Treaty defines the customs provisions of the European Union. NAFTA, the North American Free Trade Agreement, establishes a 15-year timetable to achieve duty-free trade among the United States, Canada, and Mexico.

The *duty rate,* expressed as a percentage of an import's declared value, is based on the duty classification of the import and the country of origin. The duty owed to customs is then the multiplication of the duty value of the goods times the applicable duty rate (see Fig. 21.7). An import shipment is said to be *liquidated* when the duties on that shipment are paid to customs. In some cases liquidation will occur indirectly by having a customs house broker clear the freight and pay the duty; the broker is then reimbursed for the duty payment and processing fees by the customer.

The *duty value* of the goods is the price shown on the commercial invoice with adjustments. In the United States the price used for duty payment is the *free-on-board* (FOB) price. In Europe the price used for duty payment is the *costs insurance and freight* (CIF) price at the point of entry into the European Union. There may also be a one-time adjustment for a *duty assist.* When the customer pays for production materials or production tooling used by the foreign supplier to manufacture the imported product, the customer creates an assist that is dutiable. The commercial invoice for the first production shipment that uses the customer-supplied materials or tooling should have a separate line item for the value of the assist. The duty rate for the assist is the same percentage as the duty rate for the goods.

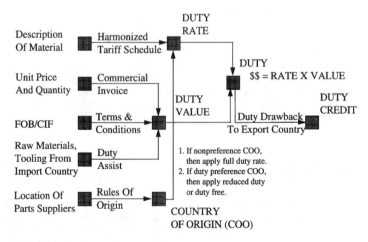

FIGURE 21.7   Import duty calculation.

Duty Classification. Any product, part, or material imported into a country will require a duty classification. In the United States the duty charged on imported goods depends on how the goods are classified under the Harmonized Tariff Schedule, HTSUS, also known as Schedule B. The classification number 8543.90.9500 is one example of an HTSUS designation; there are tens of thousands of duty classification codes specified by the government for every imaginable kind of material and product that passes through customs. It is the responsibility of the shipper to properly classify goods. Sometimes the Harmonized Tariff Schedule is open to interpretation. While the shipper can choose the classification code with the most favorable duty consequence, U.S. Customs is constantly monitoring and may challenge the shipper to substantiate the classification. The first time a customer imports goods under a new HTSUS code, U.S. Customs may audit the customer on that classification.

The Maastricht Treaty defines the European Union as a *customs union.* This means that once goods are imported into a member country of the union, those goods can be reexported to another country within the union without paying additional duty. In the European Union, goods are classified under the Combined Nomenclature. Generally, the first six digits of both the Combined Nomenclature and the HTSUS are the same, 8543.90, for example. However, certain subtleties can occur country to country, particularly within the last four digits. There are two methods of paying duty in the European Union. Under the *duty drawback method,* duty is paid at the time of import, and any intent for reexport must be stated. If the goods are later reexported outside the European Union, for example, to Russia, then a duty drawback credit is issued when the goods leave the customs union. Under the IRP method, all goods are imported into the customs union duty free. Duty within the European Union is paid at the time of sale. Or, upon reexport, the goods pass duty free outside the customs union.

Country of Origin. The *country of origin* (COO) is of critical importance in determining the duty paid on imported goods. Once the duty classification is established, the country of origin is used to determine which of several duty rates should apply. All duty preferences are based on country of origin. A *duty preference* means that the duty rate for that country is significantly reduced, perhaps even to the point of being eliminated. The physical product is required to be labeled with its country of origin. And COO information must appear consistently on each level of packaging label including the carton, the master carton, and the pallet. COO information is recorded on the commercial invoice and on the bill of lading.

Duty Preference. The country of origin determines those duty classifications eligible for special tariff treatment. The worldwide *General System of Preference* (GSP) is designed to benefit underdeveloped nations by reducing or eliminating duties on goods exported from the GSP country. GSP designations are reviewed annually by the United States and the other industrialized countries, and they may be changed or eliminated at any time. Such reviews look at the recent economic development of the lesser-developed country and at the actual volume of exports by product grouping. Major trading blocks around the world maintain trade acts and treaties that grant other specific duty preferences. When a product is manufactured or assembled from component parts sourced largely from other countries, the country of origin is not obvious. There must be a "substantial transformation" of the foreign material and local content of up to 60 percent to qualify for duty preference. *Substantial transformation* means changing the form of the materials—for example, using plastic resin pellets to manufacture the plastic cabinet parts of a television set. Goods that qualify under GSP will require a Form A attachment from the supplier with each commercial invoice. Duty preference can make a big difference in the landed cost of an import (see Table 21.7).

To be eligible for duty-free status under NAFTA, goods from the United States, Canada, and/or Mexico must have 50 to 60 percent local regional content. Two types of analysis can be documented to gain NAFTA eligibility for a product: regional value content and tariff shift. Under *regional value content,* the specified percentage of the product's value has to originate within a NAFTA country. The *tariff shift method* requires that nonoriginating materials be classified under one tariff provision prior to processing and be classified under a different tariff provision after processing. A *certificate of origin* is used to document a NAFTA-eligible import. At the present time NAFTA implementation requirements are documentation intensive.

Duty Drawback.   In some situations dutiable raw materials and purchased parts are brought into country B from country A for the production of a dutiable product that is then reexported back into country A. The concept of duty drawback eliminates the double duty taxation that would occur in this situation. The final-assembly plant declares

TABLE 21.7   Landed Cost with a Duty Preference

Situation: An assembly plant in California has a choice between buying a power supply module from a supplier in New Jersey for $85 per unit FOB—Origin or buying the same module offshore, through an IPO, from a supplier in Malaysia for $75 per unit FOB-origin. The import duty classification is 8504.40.0000. The power supply module is packed 12 units per master carton, with 18 master cartons per pallet. Each module weighs 5 pounds. Current market demand is running about 4000 units per month.

Delivered cost for the domestic supplier:		Landed cost for the international supplier:	
Unit price of module	$85.00	Unit price of module	$75.00
Total units per shipment:	3888	Total units per shipment:	3888
Freight		Freight	
Cost of 18 new pallets	$270.00	Drayage into Singapore	$50.00
Motor freight New Jersey to	$3,100.00	Cost of 18 new pallets	$325.00
California;		Ocean freight Singapore to	$1,800.00
20,520 pounds total		California; D20 container	
		Container terminal fees	$300.00
		Drayage to customer	$225.00
		Forwarder document fees	$100.00
		IPO	
		1.5 percent uplift	$4,374.00
		Duty	
		Customs processing fees;	$75.00
		Malaysia/Singapore border	
		Duty free into Singapore	
		U.S. Customs broker fee	$125.00
		5.9 percent normal duty into	
		United States	
		2.0 percent duty GSP Malaysia	$5,832.00
Total freight	$3,370.00	Total freight and duty	$13,206.00
Total freight per unit	$0.87	Total freight and duty per unit	$3.40
Landed cost per unit	$85.87	Landed cost per unit	$78.40

itself the importer of record. While the final-assembly plant pays duty on the imported component at the time of their import, the final-assembly plant can file for a duty drawback when the finished product is exported. One disadvantage of the duty drawback method is the level of tedious documentation and parts inventory tracking required by customs. Another consideration is the cash flow that is tied up with import duty payments from the time of the parts import until the time of product export.

Export Licensing and Classification

Export licensing is used by the United States and other governments as means of exerting national security control over the proliferation of chemical, missile, and nuclear technologies into the hands of enemies. Any product, part, raw material, or repair part leaving the United States needs to be classified for export and will require an export license. Product originating in the United States that moves country to country is considered a *reexport*. Reexports require the same degree of export licensing.

The *export classification control number* is called the *ECCN code*; 3A96 is an example of an ECCN. An export license depends on both the sensitivity of the technology to national security and the country of destination for the export. Certain countries of the world, and certain companies that front to those countries, are embargoed from receiving exports. These countries and companies are listed in the Table of Denial Orders, which can be found in the Export Administration Regulations.

There are two types of licenses: general export and individual validated. A *general export license* covers technology items considered to be nonsensitive and allows export into all but denial countries. The designation 3A96G indicates a general license on the example ECCN. An *individual validated export license* covers sensitive technology going to specific countries. An individual validated license should be applied for on an as-needed basis; goods cannot be shipped until the authorization is granted. Authorization can take a couple of weeks for a general license or months for an individual validated license.

The exporter is responsible for verifying that the customer is legitimate and knows the intended use of the goods being exported. The exporter must verify that the customer is not listed on the U.S. government Table of Denial Orders. The exporter must know the address of the customer, the end use of the export, and the intent of the customer to modify the goods or to resell the goods. The exporter should verify that the supporting documentation from the importer matches the information on the export license.

The Bureau of Export Administration requires the shipper to report export statistics, called *EXSTATS* and *SEDs,* to the Bureau of Census. EXSTATS is an automated reporting system required on airfreight and motor freight exports. SEDs, or Shipper Export Declaration, is a requirement for ocean freight exports and special situations like mailed exports. These forms request the following information: the origin, the consignee, the export reference number, the waybill number, the export license, Schedule B classification, the country of destination, the port of export, and the product description, quantity, weight, and value.

Transportation of Hazardous Materials

A *hazardous material* (HazMat) is legally classified as having the potential to endanger the public. The U.S. Department of Transportation (DOT) is responsible for the transportation of hazardous materials for all modes of transport. The International Air Transport Association (IATA) publishes the *Dangerous Goods Regulation* for air transport. HazMat freight requires special arrangements including the use of specialized shipping containers and strict adherence to labeling. Routings for HazMat freight are designed to separate passenger movement from cargo movement by restricting the type of vessel or aircraft used, by limiting the location of ports for departure and destination, and by controlling the time of day of freight movement through populated areas. Examples of HazMat freight include, but are not limited to, flammable, explosive, radioactive, magnetic, infectious, toxic, and corrosive materials. Freight forwarders and carriers handling HazMat shipments are expected to be registered with the appropriate government agencies, like DOT. They must comply with all HazMat regulations and train their personnel in the proper use of all personal protective equipment.

Environmental Issues with Packaging Materials

Environmental protection laws seek to regulate certain heavy metals from being introduced into solid waste management. Corrugated cardboard packaging materials that are incinerated can cause polluted air emissions. Plastic packaging materials buried in landfills can leach pollution into the groundwater. Other commonly used plastic materials may not be biodegradable. A typical unit load contains wooden pallets, plastic shrink-wrap, plastic or metal banding, a plywood or cardboard top sheet, cardboard corner guards, paper labels, corrugated product cartons, adhesive tapes, plastic bags, and poly-styrene or polypropylene for product cushioning. The majority of this material is discarded by the customer upon receipt of the product.

Toxins and carcinogenic agents come primarily from printing inks and color pigments added to corrugated cardboard and from heat stabilizers used in the chemical formation of packaging plastics. Such restricted heavy metals include cadmium, hexavalent chromium, lead, and mercury. Environmental programs seek to reduce the source of problem materials. Where that fails, reuse and recycling of packaging material is favored over outright disposal. Plastic cushion parts are to be stamped with an identification symbol that defines the type of plastic and the recycled content of the part. Corrugated material is overprinted with the recyclable symbol when appropriate.

While it is expected that the supplier will ensure the use of environmentally responsible packaging, the burden for the removal of *dunnage,* or used packaging materials, is often the responsibility of the logistics organization. In some cases a complete reverse logistics path will have to be established to recover dunnage from the customer's site and ship it to a specified location for waste processing. The recycling and reuse of pallets and slip sheets is also an important consideration for environmental protection.

SUMMARY CHECKLIST

The PIC practitioner will find that each new freight shipment is a little different from the last. However, the logistics planning process that connects the supplier with the customer, whether inbound or outbound, whether domestic or international, is a common process. This chapter has detailed the steps in the logistics planning process. Table 21.8 puts the steps into an easy-to-use checklist.

TABLE 21.8 Logistics Process Planning Checklist

Item	Consideration
☐ Unit load length plus depth	Truck bed; racking system floor
☐ Unit load height	Container door jam maximum height
☐ Unit load weight	Container over the road maximum payload
☐ Value of cargo	Duty cost; insurance coverage
☐ Import duty classification	Duty cost; duty drawback; duty assist
☐ Country of origin	Duty preference; COO documentation
☐ Export license classification	Export license restriction; denial list
☐ Commercial invoice	Customs clearance
☐ Freight forwarder	Freight tariff
☐ Bill of lading	Transfer of title; shipment tracking
☐ Mode of transport	Freight cost; transit time
☐ Transportation route	Freight cost; transit time
☐ Terms and conditions	Transfer of title; freight payment; insurance
☐ Ship from	The supplier
☐ Ship to	The customer
☐ Hazardous cargo	Restricted routings
☐ Perishable cargo	Shelf life
☐ Environmentally responsible packaging	Requirement for reverse logistics; recycle pallets

BIBLIOGRAPHY

Hickman, Thomas K., and William M. Hickman, Jr.: *Global Purchasing: How to Buy Goods And Services In Foreign Markets,* Business One Irwin, Homewood, Ill., 1992.

International Chamber of Commerce: *Incoterms 1990,* ICC Publishing, New York, 1990.

Purchasing Magazine Staff: *A Supplement To Purchasing—Transportation Sourcing Guide 96,* Cahners Publishing, Highlands Ranch, Col., September 21, 1996.

United States International Trade Commission: *Harmonized Tariff Schedule of The United States (1995),* Washington, D.C., 1995.

CHAPTER 22
CUSTOMERS, SALES, AND SERVICES

Editor

John E. Martin, CFPIM, CIRM
Curriculum Manager
IBM Solutions Institute
A. J. Watson Education Center
Brussels, Belgium

Since the last edition of this book, there has been a worldwide awakening to the concept of quality. We have seen quality presented, described, emphasized, and eschewed in many ways using different terms: *quality function deployment, house of quality, total quality management,* and *business process reengineering.* Here in the United States we have even seen a national quality incentive formed with the creation of the Malcolm Baldrige National Quality Award. On an international scale, the industrialized world has embraced the *ISO 9000 framework.* Most recently, there has been something of a grassroots revival concerning quality. This revival is a focus on the concept of *return on quality* (ROQ).[1] In the ROQ concept, quality is a function of purpose, not a function of process. However, this chapter is not about quality. Rather, this chapter is about the experts on quality—the experts who led the reawakening, redefinition, and refinement of quality concepts and the final arbiters of quality: the *customer.* After all, it is the customer who defines quality and price and what is important in the marketplace.

CUSTOMERS, PRODUCTION, INVENTORY, AND MARKETS

With the tempo of today's complex and dynamic world, it is fairly easy to lose an appreciation for the basic simplicity of economic theory, whether that theory is Marxian, laissez faire, or something else. To better understand customers, one should understand the basic components of economics. According to the Nobel Prize–winning economist, Paul Samuelson:

> Economics is the process of people and society choosing, with or without the use of money, how to employ scarce productive resources that could have alternate uses, to pro-

duce various commodities and distribute them for now or in the future, among various people and groups in society.[2]

Fundamentally, what Samuelson has described is a perpetuating system with four components:

- *Production.* The means for making goods and services (commodities). An automobile manufacturer has the means for producing automobiles. A travel agent has the means for producing vacation packages. A fast-food shop has the means for producing hamburgers. *Production* represents the means for generating the *inventory* of goods or services necessary to replenish the **supply side** of the economic equation.
- *Inventory.* This is the available pool of goods or services (commodities) that is brought to a *market* for the *customer* to purchase. *Inventory* can be in the form of automobiles, vacation packages, or hamburgers. *Inventory* is used to satisfy the **demand** generated by *customers.*
- *Market.* This is where **supply** and **demand** meet. It is the outlet for the *inventory* where the *customer* comes to purchase. This can be a dealership for automobiles, a restaurant for hamburgers, or a travel agency for a vacation package.
- *Customer.* This is the factor that completes the economic cycle. The *customer* (people, society) acquires, or consumes, *inventory,* or **supply.** In exchange for goods and services, the *customer* trades either currency (a capital society) or other goods and services (a barter society).

The above defines what economics is. It is also important to understand what economics is not. Economics is not a system that works one way for products and another way for services. Supply and demand logic works the same for vacation packages and automobiles. Economics does not apply a filter for differentiating customers. Any customer with a means of exchange (barter, currency) can compete with any other customer for goods and services.

It is important to keep in mind what economics is not in order to appreciate that it is a mechanism, a mechanism that is indifferent. If the supplier understands the customer and the product or service supplied, it will be up to the supplier to make a difference in the product. One way to do this is through customer service activities, which is the central theme of this chapter.

HISTORICAL PERSPECTIVE

Economics is as old as the human race. The economic cycle was started when two human beings decided to barter for each other's goods. Whether they actually consummated the exchange is not as important as the fact that they met and at least negotiated terms for an exchange. Figure 22.1 depicts this economic engine that has basically remained unchanged through the millennia.

In a nomadic barter economy, the hunter traded goods with the gatherer. As civilizations became more agrarian, a feudal economy developed. This feudal economy depended on colonization, and then exploitation of the land and its inhabitants. In the mid-eighteenth century, the industrial revolution displaced feudal operatives. The industrial revolution changed the base from land to capital. Capital made it possible for entrepreneurs to generate more and more goods and services (*inventory*) from their enterprises (*production*). Most importantly, the industrial revolution allowed enterprises to think of their *markets* and *customers* in global terms; a true world economy!

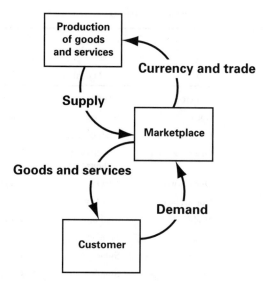

FIGURE 22.1   Basic economic system.

Customers, production, inventory, and markets have changed dramatically in the progression to the industrial revolution. Table 22.1 demonstrates the distinct shifts that have occurred as one economic system was displaced by another.

WHO IS YOUR CUSTOMER?

In any economic system, a customer is needed to buy the goods and services produced. The customer determines how productive resources are to be employed. This determination is made with money or trade. The exchange medium is not important. What is important is the effect. By buying or trading for my product, that customer is giving me the incentive to make more—that is, to repeat the process and ultimately compete again for additional customer dollars.

The central question, then, is, "Who is *your* customer?" This is perhaps the toughest question for any enterprise to answer. In fact, this is not a single question but rather a conglomeration of related *who, what, where, why, when, how,* and *how much* qualifying interrogatories:

- *Who* are my customers?
- *Where* are they located?
- *What* do my customers value in my product and service?
- *How* can I make a difference in my product's or service's quality?
- *Why* do my customers come to me for products or services?
- *How much* will my customers pay?
- *When* will my customers need more product or service?
- *How much* will my customers need?

TABLE 22.1   Historical Shifts in Economic Systems

	System characteristics		
Enterprise characteristics	Hunter-gatherer	Feudal	Industrial
Self-sustaining level	99 percent	50 percent	1 percent
Market penetration	Local	Regional	Global
Method of production	Make an "extra"	Craft construction	Mass production
Number of customers	One to several	Hundreds to thousands	Thousands to millions
Number of products	One or two	Several	Hundreds to thousands
Availability	Constrained	Limited	Varies
Personalized service	High	Medium to high	Low to medium
Quality measures	Utility	Product "signature"	Warranties, guarantees
Competition	None	Some	Intense
Product or service distribution	Simple	Simple	Complex
New-product introduction	Function of evolution	Some	Required to compete
Legal considerations	None	Few	Varies
Trade constraints	None	Few	Many

For the hunters-gatherers, the *who* question was easy. Their customer was quite likely another family member or another village member. In most cases, the customer was known personally. But today, this question is not so easily answered. As an example, consider a manufacturer of automotive after-market parts, say, spark plugs. Customers (*who*) can be represented by:

- Large U.S.-based automakers
- Foreign automakers
- New-automobile dealerships
- Used-automobile dealerships
- Automobile repair shops
- Automobile parts wholesalers
- Retailers who carry repair parts
- The do-it-yourselfer

The point to be made here is that after answering the *who, what,..., how much* questions, completely different and even radically different profiles will emerge for the customer groups. If we were to look again at the spark plug manufacturer through the eyes of two different customers, an automobile manufacturer and a do-it-yourselfer automobile mechanic, the contrasts can be quite dramatic, as shown in Table 22.2.

TABLE 22.2 Customer Profiles

Profiling question	Customer 1	Customer 2
Who are they?	Automobile manufacturer	Do-it-yourselfer
Where are they located?	Several facilities	Millions of homes
What do they value?	Minimal inventory investment	Variety of "tune-up" products on retailers' shelves
How can you make a difference?	Timely delivery	Price
Why do they buy?	Total service	Availability when needed
How much will they pay?	Varies according to several factors	"Close" to what they paid last year
When will they need more?	Every week	Twice a year
How much will you need?	Millions of units	8–16 units

THE ULTIMATE CUSTOMER: A SUMMARY

Although the basic logic of economic systems has remained fundamentally unchanged over the millennia, the complexities introduced by customers, products, and markets have added multiple dimensions to these economic systems. A customer who used to buy from a supplier based solely on his or her price may now be buying based upon a combination of several value factors. Likewise, the suppliers who counted on price to differentiate their product now must understand the customers' new value systems. This means that getting to know your customers is not a one-time-only task. Rather, it is an iterative process that must keep pace with the customers' constant refinement of their value systems.

COMPETITIVE FACTORS

Despite the evolution from barter- to feudal- to industrial-based economics, the basic business purpose of the enterprise has remained the same: to provide the right product or service of the right quality, to the right customer at the right time and in the right quantity. However, as we saw earlier, today's customers and enterprises are conducting business in a complex and highly variable environment. As an example, consider the automotive after-market supplier who both buys and sells on an international basis. Figure 22.2 shows the scale and complexities involved in competing in a global economy.

This global economic model has added customer profile factors of which manufacturers must be aware. Although distance and time remain major influences, a foreign consumer may also introduce additional dimensions, particularly to the *what do they value* and *how to make a difference* factors:

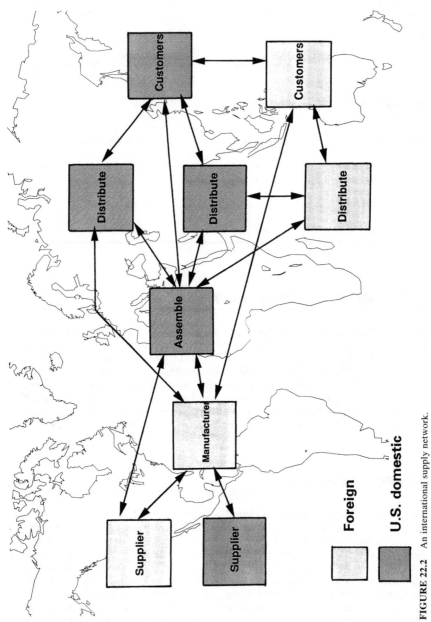

FIGURE 22.2 An international supply network.

- *Language.* Should the product carry labeling in the language of the country? In a country with several dialects, is there a neutral dialect or accepted language for labeling?

- *Culture.* Are there aspects of this product that will appeal to the culture of these consumers?

- *Religious.* Does this product carry religious sanctions?

- *Ethics.* Does this product imply a compromise of ethics or moral issues endemic to these consumers?

Logistics

Although economists can view the world in terms of the supply and demand cycle, business enterprises have realized that current market operands demand an approach that is sensitive and cognizant of the variables of time and distance. The demands of time and distance have given enterprises a different focus—a *logistics focus.* This logistics focus is a total quality management focus that represents the following activities:

- Procurement (purchasing) obtains the right materials and services through negotiating supplier contracts, fostering supplier partnerships, and being the primary supplier interface.

- Production and inventory control plans and monitors the levels of inventories and production.

- Distribution delivers products and services to customers.[3]

This logistics view of the enterprise sees the process as a logical progression of value-added steps. First, procure resources necessary to make up the product or service. Then manufacturer or assemble or package the product or service. And, finally, distribute the ware via the appropriate channels to the proper marketplaces.

Supply-Chain Management

The interaction of the distinct logistics processes has led to the view that supply and demand is an interconnected *supply chain,* or *pipeline.* Figure 22.3 depicts this supply-chain, or pipeline, concept. Each segment adds value to the service or product it provides to its customer—the next downstream process. Each customer, in turn, provides, in return, payment to its supplier or suppliers—the preceding upstream process. Because every segment adds the proper value at the proper time, the ultimate consumers obtain the product and product value they ordered. However, simply knowing who the ultimate customer is does not bring an assurance of an ability to fully address the ultimate customer's quality measures. As we saw in Fig. 22.2, a manufacturer who is part of an international supply network can be many miles and many levels removed from the ultimate customer. To assure that customers receive what they expect, organizations that are part of the supply chain must all work to manage the movement of goods and services along that chain.

Supply-chain management starts with an understanding of roles and contributions: Who must do what and when, in order to satisfy the customer. As on a stage, a "role" demands a level of interaction and dependency on another role or roles. This implies a level of understanding of the other functions in the supply chain. The producer must understand how the supplier procures raw materials, and how the distributor brings the goods to market.

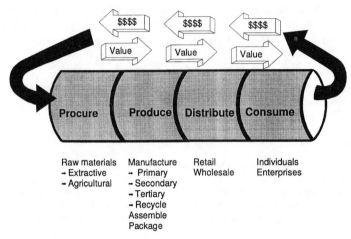

FIGURE 22.3 Supply-chain management.

TABLE 22.3 Roles within the Supply Chain

Product or service values added	Supplier	Manufacturer	Distributor
Product availability	◑	◑	●
Product quality	◑	●	◑
Product mix on shelves	○	○	●
Post-sales service	○	◑	●
New-product features	◑	●	○
Product selection	○	●	○
Product price	◑	●	◑

Note: ● = major role.
◑ = secondary role.
○ = minimal or no role.

These roles and contributions can be shown as a two-dimensional table with the links of the supply chain on one axis and the value-added components along the other axis. Table 22.3 uses, as an example, the automotive after-market parts supplier who is distributing through a retail automotive repair supply. As shown in the table, in most cases, each of the three links in the supply chain (supplier, manufacturer, and distributor) has either a major or secondary role in contributing product or service value.

Design for Logistics

Most links in a market's supply chain must forecast what their customers will buy. Then, based upon this forecast, an enterprise will make plans with their vendors to procure the goods and/or services necessary to complete the delivery of the product or service to their customers. Within the context of logistics, an enterprise's customer is the next direct link downstream toward the ultimate consumer. Using this same logistics perspective, an enterprise's vendor is the next direct link upstream in the supply chain.

Forecasting is an anomaly. With its roots in mathematics, it is, indeed, a science. But when most people think of a science, they think of a discipline that is exact and accurate—a process that delivers a product that is precise to within minuscule tolerances. Yet we all know that the first rule of forecasting is, "Forecasting will deliver an answer that is wrong." Furthermore, in addition to providing a wrong forecast, the forecasting science will provide a range of forecast error. In other words, forecasting will deliver a wrong answer along with a measure of how wrong that answer is!

Enterprises should not stop forecasting, but they should be aware that they are relying on a tool that was designed to treat a symptom—the symptom of unknowns. Because I do not know what my customers will be buying, I will rely on a forecast with a 95 percent accuracy to tell me what my customers will be buying. Should we, either as enterprises or customers of enterprises, be satisfied with 95 percent? To help answer that question, let's consider an example that demonstrates the impact of 95 percent.

A particular company is an extractor and supplier of a raw material that is used exclusively in a consumer goods product. This raw material enters the supply chain through the company and ultimately goes through four more supply links before it is ultimately made available to the customer, a retail distributor (see Fig. 22.4).

To demonstrate the impact of 95 percent forecast accuracy, assume that all six supply links are forecasting the demands of their respective customers. The extractor company is forecasting the demand of the refiner, the refiner is forecasting the demand for the initial manufacturer, and so on. Ultimately the retail distributor is trying to forecast the customer's demand for the consumer good. Now make another assumption that all six segments in the supply chain are forecasting at a 95 percent accuracy level. Since the forecasting error for the consumer good at the retail outlet is the cumulative errors of forecasts of all the supply links, theoretically, it is possible for a customer of the retail distributor to be faced with a $.95^6$ probability of finding this consumer good on the shelf. This equates to 74 percent, less than 3 out of 4. As a customer, when was the last time

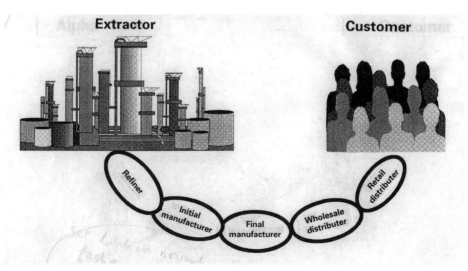

FIGURE 22.4 The impact of 95 percent correct.

you were satisfied with a retailer who found what you were looking for only 75 percent of the time?

This 95 percent scenario was contrived to demonstrate a point. Those enterprises who wish to meet and exceed their customers' expectations will need to move beyond probabilities as a determinant of their service levels and approach the service challenge as businesspeople, not bookies.

The P:D Ratio

Most consumers would not be satisfied with a 75 percent service level and would seek typical consumer remedies: buy a substitute product, buy the same product from another supplier, or maybe even go without the product. So, where does that leave the enterprise? To find a better forecaster? Purchase a better forecasting package? Perhaps, at least in those situations where better forecasting is possible. Alternatively, enterprises can look for ways to eliminate the need for forecasting.

One business approach begins with an understanding of the $P{:}D$ ratio.[4] P is the total time for an enterprise to produce their goods or services from placing an order with their vendors, until supplying the goods or services to satisfy a customer order. D is the customer's lead time—that is, the time between the customer's generation of an order and the customer's expectation of delivery (Fig. 22.5). Any enterprise with a $P{:}D$ ratio greater than 1 is forced to forecast what their customers' demand will be. Therefore, if enterprises want to minimize, perhaps even eliminate, the dependency on forecasting, the options as defined in Table 22.4 are available.

Understanding the $P{:}D$ ratio is important for several reasons. One reason is that once you understand the logic behind production P and distribution D factors, you are in a position to effect changes. Second, gaining an understanding of this logic demands cross-functional analysis. Product differentiation, for example, requires input from engineering and sales. As you will see later in the discussion of organizations, cross-functional or horizontal communication has been identified as a key enabler of improved customer service.

Competitive Factors: A Summary

One of the economic systems' complexities is that they are now global in nature. This has introduced time and distance as factors to be considered. The disciplines of logistics and supply-chain management have evolved to help with this reckoning. Both these dis-

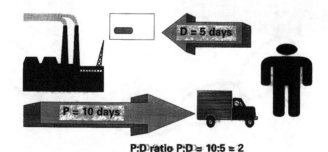

P:D ratio P:D = 10:5 = 2

FIGURE 22.5 P:D ratio.

TABLE 22.4   Alternatives to Forecasting

| | Responsible department | | |
Choice	Manufacturing	Engineering	Sales
Reduce P time: Qualifying questions: 1. Can my suppliers reduce their lead times? 2. Can I reduce my intransit time? 3. Can I effectively graduate to an assemble-to-order environment?	X	X	
Extend D time: Qualifying question: 1. Can I differentiate the value of my products such that my customers will wait?		X	X
Add safety stock: Qualifying questions: 1. Will the incremental inventory investment generate an adequate return? 2. Is the increased service level necessary to market growth and retention?	X	X	
Establish vendor relationships: Qualifying question: 1. Are there certain economies of scale that I can help my vendor exploit?	X	X	X

ciplines are based upon enhancing product or service delivery to the customer through closer relationships among the different components of the supply chain: procurement, production, and distribution. The *P:D* ratio was discussed as a tool for analyzing the effectiveness of an enterprise's supply chain.

THE COOPERATIVE OPERATIVE

A logistics perspective has allowed a manufacturer to stratify and evaluate the operational economics of their enterprise from a logistics standpoint. Basically, enterprises must ask themselves:

- Do I try to retain direct control over various links of the supply chain through vertical integration, or do I depend upon effective supplier and customer linkages?
- If I do not want complete vertical integration, what stages of the supply chain will I trust to others?

These questions are profound. To demonstrate the logic of this problem, let's consider leather shoes. Figure 22.6 depicts the supply chain for leather shoes. Enterprises involved in leather shoes have a choice. To what degree do they employ vertical integration as a competitive weapon? An enterprise that is completely vertically integrated

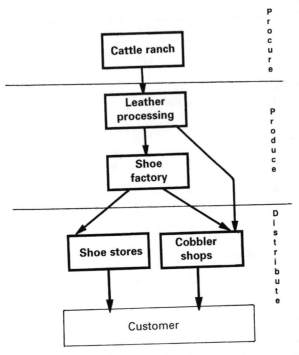

FIGURE 22.6   The leather shoe supply chain.

would own everything from the cattle ranch to the cobbler shops. Conversely, an enterprise may choose to compete only in specific supply links, for example, just raising the cattle or just selling the shoes. This do-I-make or do-I-buy trade-off question, from a logistics standpoint, can be analyzed in several dimensions as shown in Table 22.5.

Vertical Integration versus Supplier Development

Based upon the evaluations presented in Tables 22.4 and 22.5, establishing vendor relationships does present tremendous potential for four reasons:

1. All enterprise departments are potentially involved. This involvement will breed success.
2. Vendor relationships fit well into the supply-chain management philosophy. Earlier we talked about logistical roles, i.e., the procurer, the producer, and the distributor. Effective fulfillment of a role is a function of understanding all roles.
3. Decisions are not the result of a single, perhaps inbred, company process.
4. Decisions are not driven solely by corporate financial analysis.

Traditionally, customers and vendors have functioned in relationships that, at best, could be described as "toleration out of necessity." For customers, this meant establishing policies and practices that were designed under the premise that vendors were not to

TABLE 22.5   Make or Buy

Vertical integration "make"	Supplier development "buy"
Lower transaction costs but higher overhead costs because of capital investment required	Higher transaction costs that are offset through efficient linkages in the supply pipeline
Possibly prohibitive switching costs due to capital equipment requirements	Switching costs proportional to number of supplier linkages
Benefits balanced against entire company	Benefits balanced against total supply-chain network
Internal decision process	Cooperative, consensus decision making

be trusted. This untrusting attitude contributed to the practice of keeping many sources of supply for a particular item. Having many sources would allow a customer to nego-tiate their requirements and leverage one vendor against another in order to get the best deal. Likewise, and it was to be expected, vendors established what amounted to coun-termeasures and counterpractices that viewed the customer with the same degree of apprehension. Relationships with customers were not based on trust. Rather, they were based almost solely on the terms and conditions of the purchase order or the contract. These adversarial attitudes resulted in both customers' and vendors' having to establish procedures that allowed them protection against the other and dictated recourse in the event of nonperformance.

Deming has argued and demonstrated that the competitive position of an enterprise is enhanced not so much by price and productivity as by quality. His "chain reaction"[5] in Fig. 22.7 shows price and productivity as effects, not causes, of competitive health.

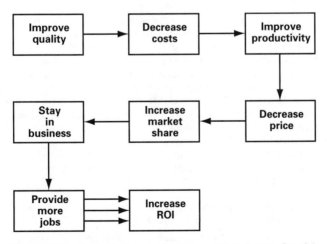

FIGURE 22.7   Deming's chain reaction. (*Source: W. E. Deming,* Out of the Crisis, *Cambridge, Mass., 1986, M.I.T. Press, p. 3.*)

Based upon Deming's and others' works on quality, many industries have reevaluated their relationships with their vendors and customers. This reevaluation has allowed customers and vendors to ask questions such as the following:

Customer:

- "Why must I maintain a veritable stable of 'available' suppliers? Why not maintain a few 'qualified' suppliers? Certainly, with fewer supplier contacts, I should be able to cultivate closer and perhaps even more personal vendor relationships. Additionally, with fewer contacts, administrative costs should be less."
- "For years I have been doing this activity to add value to my product. Would it be easier and more economical for my supplier to do this? Would they be willing to do this?"

Vendor:

- "Why not let my customers see my production facilities? I believe that my product is of world-class quality. If I show my customer how I run my business, perhaps my customer will favor me with more business."
- "If I can package my product differently, the cost of my product will be lower and my product will be more acceptable to my distributor's customer. I wonder if my distributor would be willing to accept this packaging?"

It was answers to these and other introspective questions that finally allowed vendors and customers to realize that service is the sum of a complex and intricate network of relationships. Actually, as was shown earlier, service is a chain of relationships. The stronger the chain, the stronger the service. Conversely, if there is any weak link in the chain, overall service to the final customer is compromised.

Time As a Competitive Advantage

Earlier we identified the universal factors that give every enterprise the opportunity to establish a competitive position; delivering the right *product* or *service,* in the right *quantities,* of the right *quality,* at the right *time.* Of these *"right" linkages* (see Fig. 22.8), *time* has been identified as a factor of growing influence. All other factors being equal or nearly equal, consumers will purchase what is available now. Additionally, studies have shown that in introducing a new "right" product, there is a direct correlation between total lifetime product revenues for that product and the amount of time that elapses between product introduction and the entrance of competitors. Being a sole supplier of a new product for 6 months can add 33 percent to the revenue potential for that new product over its lifetime.[6]

Recognition of *time* as a strategic link has precipitated the development of time-based competitive strategies, notably *just-in-time* (JIT) and *quick response* (QR). At a macro level, these strategies have two central themes:

1. Time is a critical resource. Although we cannot control time, we can decide how time should be allocated and how we can optimize its use.
2. There is truth to the adage that "a chain is only as strong as its weakest link." This led to the realization that every link in the supply chain needed to look for ways to strengthen any other link.

Manufacturer   Customer

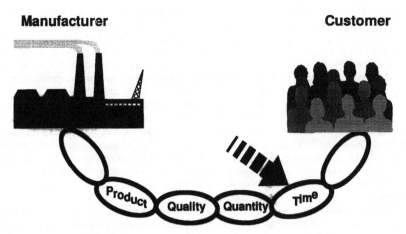

FIGURE 22.8   The "right" linkages.

In seeking ways to strengthen the supply chain, suppliers have modified their views to be more universal, to look beyond the next mile marker that represents their immediate suppliers and customers. This has led to questions and approaches like the following:

- "What is important to my customers' customers?"
- "How can I help my suppliers' suppliers?"

The analysis spawned by these and other questions helped form a new, cooperative basis for the contracting and procurement of goods and services. The foundation of this cooperative base is the sharing of business processes previously reserved for each member's internal organization. Examples of these shared processes could include the following:

- Communications
- Strategies
- Market objectives
- New opportunity exploration

By operating outside the traditional organizational boundaries, enterprises recognized opportunities to reduce overall operational costs through improved communication and minimized duplication of both direct and indirect resources. Two examples of this cooperative contracting would include *vendor-managed inventories* and *vendor source marking*.

Vendor-Managed Inventories

In a typical buyer-seller relationship, ownership of purchased inventory passed from manufacturer to retailer based upon FOB terms. As an example, consider a manufacturer who distributes directly to a retailer. FOB terms might specify retail ownership once the inventory is shipped. Or ownership could transfer once the inventory is unloaded at the retailer's facility. This was the old model. A new model that is a direct challenge to this ownership plan is the vendor-managed inventory model. Although there are several variations, these variations basically revolve around the concept that the manufacturer will manage the inventory in the retailer's facility. In other words, the retail establishment is basically viewed by the manufacturer as just another finished-goods stocking location. As such, the manufacturer retains responsibility for keeping those stocking locations replenished. In some manufacturing-retailing relationships, this ownership issue has been pushed to a new dimension where ownership does not pass from the manufacturer to the retailer *until the inventory is sold to the consumer by the retailer!*

So why would a manufacturer be willing to entertain such a concept? What would motivate a manufacturer to, in effect, increase their finished-goods position and ultimately their inventory investment? While an initial analysis may suggest that this ownership arrangement is risky for the manufacturer, further analysis shows that there are factors that can not only mitigate the risk of increased inventory but offer the opportunity for improving overall enterprise performance. The logic at work here is fairly simple. If more inventory is followed by more sales, the net impact on both the P&L statement and balance sheet can be positive.

To demonstrate the potential of vendor-managed inventory, consider the following business scenario. A manufacturer of automotive after-market parts sells to consumers through a major discount store retailer. The manufacturer and retailer have decided to implement a vendor-managed inventory program for certain products. Basically, the way this program works is that the manufacturer will have sole responsibility for deciding when to replenish the retailer's stock. The manufacturer will have visibility into the retailer's inventory position through direct access to its point-of-sale data. As part of this arrangement, the manufacturer will retain ownership of the inventory until purchased by the consumer. Additionally, the manufacturer will be the sole supplier for certain after-market products and will have preferred retail shelf space for certain products.

The analysis provided below, identifies some of the potentially immediate benefits to be realized from this vendor-managed inventory program:

To the Ultimate Consumer:

- Higher satisfaction because of better inventory availability

To the Retailer:

- Lower operational cost through the following:
  Reduction or elimination of inventory management activities
  Reduced inventory investment
  Reduced procurement activities
- Reduction in lost sales due to stock-outs
- Increased sales through better inventory availability

To the Manufacturer:

- Increased sales through the following:
  Enhanced supplier status
  Reduction in lost sales due to retail stock-outs
- Reduced operational expense due to reduced order-taking time

The benefits listed above are just the beginning. As a manufacturer and a retailer nurture and grow their relationship through earned trust, additional benefits may begin to accrue over the long term. Areas that have the potential for returning additional benefits include the following:

- Eighty to eighty-five percent of customer data enter the retail organization through the point-of-sale activity. The manufacturer will have access to all of these data and will be able to learn more about their ultimate consumer.
- Both will have the opportunity to involve each other in decisions that affect delivery to the ultimate customer. For the retailer, this may mean consulting with the manufacturer on the design of a new product or the redesign of an existing product. For the manufacturer, this may mean the opportunity to explore different ways of assuring better quality at lower costs.

Vendor Source Marking

Perhaps the best demonstrable example of supply-chain management lies in the development and use of vendor price and product source marking. Although bar-coding technologies made the concept economically feasible, it was not the technology that spawned the concept. The concept was born of the recognition that there are some fundamental economic operatives in supply-chain management:

Price Marking Economies.   Numerous studies have looked at the logistical challenges of product price tagging. Although the grocery industries, thanks to acceptance by the consumer, have been able to institute shelf-marked prices, other industries still face the challenges of having to attach retail price tags to each sales unit. As an example, garments, whether hanging or flat, must have price tags applied before retail display. Within the supply chain, there are basically four opportunities for price tagging the merchandise: in the manufacturers' plants, in the manufacturers' distribution centers, in the retailers' distribution centers, and in the retailers' stockrooms. In looking at the opportunities, there are economics that will argue for different tagging points:

- *Just in time.* "What are the imperatives for doing this operation now? Can I delay this activity until later? Will a delay improve my ability to serve my customer and reduce my costs?"
- *Cost.* "From an overall cost perspective, where is the best point in the logistics pipeline to add price tickets?"
- *Responsibility.* "Whose responsibility is retail price marking?"
- *Quality.* "Are there quality issues that can be obviated depending upon where tags are applied?"
- *Type of product.* "Are there certain SKUs or SKU families that can be price marked by the manufacturer? Are there certain SKUs that are best left for the retailer?"

In the final analysis of these factors, when retailers reviewed their individual operations and relationships with suppliers and consumers, it was shown that *type of product, cost,* and *quality,* Fig. 22.9, were the major arbiters.

- *Type of product.* For certain stock items, it makes sense to contract with the manufacturer to add the price tickets. These products have a retail price behavior that typically can be accurately forecast enough into the future to allow price marking far in advance of the actual retail display.
- *Cost.* Studies have shown that having a retailer put a price tag on a garment costs 10 times as much as having the price put on the garment as part of the manufacturing

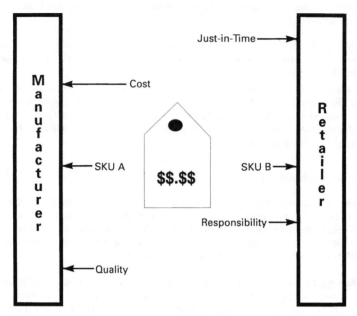

FIGURE 22.9   The logic of price marking.

process. The reason? Done by the retailer, tagging is a very labor intensive process. Done by the manufacturer, tagging is seen as a simple, repetitive process that lends itself to automation. Due to economies of scale, the manufacturer is in a much better position than the retailer to automate processes.

- *Quality.* Adding price tags to a garment as part of the manufacturing process eliminates a step requiring a person to handle an item. Reducing hands-on steps reduces the opportunities for mishandling and consequently diminished quality.

Product Source Marking Economies.   Consider the movement of produce from the fields to the consumers' cupboards. As an example, corn is an edible product from the time it ripens in the field. Those of you who have brought it right to the kitchen from your garden can testify that taste and quality are best at this time. However, because few of us have the opportunity and convenience to pick corn right from the field, suppliers of corn are faced with two major challenges:

1. Add convenience to the product. This means packaging and distributing corn in a variety of forms to appeal to a variety of consumers' palates; fresh frozen kernels, fresh frozen on the cob, fresh in the husks, whole kernels in the can, cream style in the can, or as a corn chowder.
2. Retain the essence of quality. Depending on how the corn is packaged, quality can be measured in several ways. Considering fresh frozen kernels, consumer quality values can be summed up as follows:
   - It should taste like fresh corn.
   - It should look like fresh corn.

The point is, that despite the differences in convenience packaging, the product remains corn whether it is in the field or in the kitchen. Therefore, in moving the product from the field to the consumer, we should be able to attach a universal product identifier that makes this product recognizable as "corn" to all the logistics segments in the supply chain—farmer, coop, processor-packer, wholesaler, and retail distributor. This early source marking of products means a reduced chance of error through reinterpreting or recoding a product and reduced administrative costs through relabeling product.

The Cooperative Operative: A Summary

The evolution of supply-chain management has seen the redefinition and redeployment of responsibilities across the supply chain. Vendors and producers have used comparative advantage to help determine where a value-added function should be performed. This has led to a more cooperative than adversarial relationship between links in the supply chain. Two strategies that have consistently been able to demonstrate improved quality at a lower cost are vendor-managed inventories and vendor source marking.

CUSTOMER SERVICE

As we have seen, it is the objective of every enterprise to get the right product or service in the right quantity and of the right quality to the right customer at the right time. This objective is a constant, whether the enterprise deals in vacation packages or automobiles. Of course, how this objective is carried out will vary tremendously from industry to industry. After all, if I am in the market for a vacation package, I will not expect it to be marketed and delivered like hamburgers.

With the recognition of supply-chain management as a competitive tactic, enterprises in the same market have realized that all the right objectives can be delivered. What's more, these objectives do not have to be delivered like the competitors'. Enterprises can appeal to customers' changing perception of quality. In addition to products and service, customers now buy expectations. And what happens if expectations are not met? Consider the following data:

- An average customer who has a complaint tells 9 or 10 people about it. An average customer who has a complaint resolved satisfactorily only tells 5 other people.
- For every complaint, there are 19 other dissatisfied customers who did not bother to complain.
- It takes 5 to 10 times more resources to replace a customer than it does to retain an existing customer.
- A customer must have 12 positive experiences to overcome 1 negative experience.
- Most companies spend 95 percent of service time redressing problems and only 5 percent trying to figure out what went wrong in the first place.
- For those companies that make an effort to do something about customers' complaints, more than half their efforts actually reinforce the negative reactions and make the customers more frustrated.[7]

Customer Service As Measurements

Central to an effective logistics operation is customer service. But just what is customer service? Well, in its most basic form, customer service is a series of measurements that indicate responsiveness to customer demand. A typical customer service measurement might include product availability, which is an indicator of the percentage of customer orders that were filled complete. Other measurements might include service call response time, length of service call, cancellation rate, or a multitude of others that are defined by the product or service being distributed.

Customer Service As a Department

Many organizations make use of a customer service department to deal with customer inquiries or complaints. In the earlier apparel price marking scenario, the retailer's customer service function would be responsible for determining the source of a price marking error:

- Was the price applied by the manufacturer or the retailer?
- When was this price applied to this garment? Was the price correct at that time?
- Is this a right price but the wrong tag?
- Was the supplied price right, but wrong when applied?

Based upon the answers to these questions, customer service may be required to interact with several functional areas that may be across several vendor companies.

Customer Service: A Quality Improvement Function

This third definition does not imply that customer service is not a department. Nor does it imply that customer service is a series of ineffectiveness measurements. This definition means that to be truly effective, customer service must be more than a department that establishes and tracks measurements. Customer service must look for ways to improve products and services. Using Shewhart's PDSA cycle,[8] this process would appear as shown in Fig. 22.10. Using the previous example of a price marking error, an effective customer service approach would include:

- Baseline goals for correct price marking
- Measurements to allow analysis of price marking
- An understanding of the entire price marking process
- A historical analysis of price marking errors
- Development of processes or procedures for minimizing recurring instances of price marking errors

Customer Service As a Way of Doing Business

By blending measurements, people, and quality-improvement incentives, customer service becomes more than a department, more than a postscriptive reaction to information. Rather, customer service becomes a way of doing business, a prescriptive agent of change. Figure 22.11 depicts the relationships of customer service departments in a supply chain. Note that unlike a typical business function, as accounts payable, it has become extremely difficult to point to customer service as a discrete point in time. Rather, as shown in the figure, customer service needs to be viewed as many points of interaction within the closed-loop process of logistics supply-chain management.

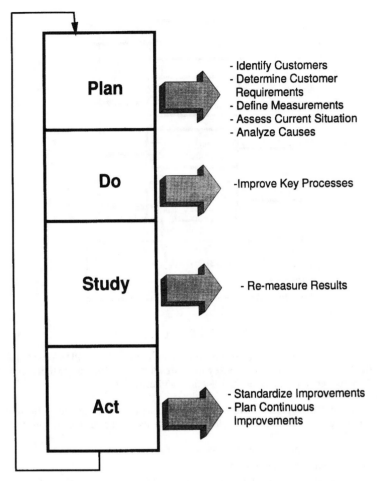

FIGURE 22.10 Shewhart's PDSA cycle. (*Source: W. A. Shewhart,* Statistical Method from the Viewpoint of Quality Control, *Dover Press, New York, 1991, p. 45.*)

Types of Customer Service

Earlier a *customer* was defined as the next downstream process in the supply chain. This means that every link in the supply chain is servicing a group of customers. But this also means that there will be differences in how customer service operates and is measured. A wholesale distributor will service their retail store customers differently than the retail store will service their consumer customers. This is because each of these different customer groups has different service requirements.

Enlightened and empowered enterprises, those who recognize that they must serve their customers, have established effective performance measurements as a way of monitoring and improving customer service. To be effective, measurements must directly or

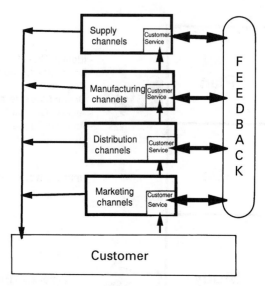

FIGURE 22.11   The closed-loop logistics supply chain.

indirectly support the customers' requirements as defined in the PDSA cycle (see Fig. 22.10). The following are common key measures for each of the major logistics supply-chain components: procurement, production, and distribution.

Procurement Measurements.   Procurement measurements indicate how effective product and services are procured and deployed. The procurement cycle includes the following:

- Establishing a supplier network
- Sourcing a procurement request
- Purchasing the required product or service
- Receiving or inspecting the purchased product or service
- Salvaging rejected product

Procurement cycle measurements are stratified as follows:

- *On-time delivery.* Used to evaluate the delivery effectiveness of suppliers or the overall procurement function. Common measurements might include the following:
  Percent of on-time deliveries
  Percent of early deliveries
  Number of stock-outs caused by late deliveries
- *Supplier quality.* Used to evaluate supplier quality performance or, more globally, an entire supplier network. Common measurements here might include the following:
  Percent of nonconforming materials
  Percent of certified parts
  Percent of total vendors that are certified

- *Total cost effectiveness.* Used to evaluate how well the enterprise's capital is being deployed. Measures here might include the following:

  Prices paid compared to target prices

  Gains and losses from forward-buying activity

  Purchase orders issued without firm prices

Production Measurements.   Procurement has committed enterprise capital to an investment in raw and component materials and/or services. It is production's responsibility to add value to that investment by transforming materials and/or services into the salable products demanded by the enterprise's customers. Production measurements are indicators of the efficiency and effectiveness of that transformation process.

- Efficiency measures are used to gauge the transformation of labor, materials, and equipment inputs into output product.

  Labor efficiency = standard hours earned / actual hours worked

  Machine efficiency = standard hours earned / actual hours worked

  Percent scrap produced

  Inventory turns

- Effectiveness measures are used to gauge how well schedules and plans are executed.

  Release reliability = (on-time orders released/total orders released) $\times$ 100

  Plan performance (machine capacity, labor-hours)

  Data accuracy (inventory, bills of materials, routings)

Distribution Measurements.   Production has salable units that must be delivered to the customers. Distribution measurements are indicators of how "well" these units are delivered.

- *Service level.* Percent of customers' orders shipped complete and on time.
- *Shipment error rate.*
- *Inventory turns.*
- *Order cycle time.* Indicates the average amount of time required to process an order; from time of customer order entry until time of shipment:

$$\frac{\text{Total order cycle time}}{\text{Orders scheduled}}$$

- *Customer returns.* Indicates the return percentage of product:

$$\left(\frac{\text{Return dollars}}{\text{Total sales dollars}} \right) \times 100$$

Customer Service: A Summary

To be competitive, an enterprise's customer service function must operate as a quality-improvement process. To do this requires a blend of people, measurements, and a quality incentive. This interaction allows customer service to be prescriptive in its ability to influence quality changes up and down the supply chain, both inside and outside the immediate enterprise. Thus, customer service functions within a closed-loop supply chain.

ORDER PROCESSING

Phrases that are fashionable today include *customer oriented* or *market driven* or *delighting the customer.* In some cases, while customers might initially feel flattered that they are the center of attention, reality quickly returns when they have to call their vendor and ask "Where's my order?" or "What you sent me is not what I ordered." In response, vendors might say, "We shipped your order 10 days ago. You should have it by now." Or "We shipped based upon what your order specified." Earlier we talked about the fact that economics is as old as the human race. It is also likely that conversations similar to these are as old as human speech.

In contrast to these exchanges, there are organizations who have delighted customers—Federal Express's promise, "When it positively, absolutely has to get there overnight." Motorola's six sigma improvement process is another example. Dell Computer Company has revolutionized the PC market by direct-mail selling. To better understand why, on one hand, some organizations continue to have the "tough" conversations with their customers while others consistently strive to please their customers, let's look at a generic order-management cycle (Fig. 22.12).

The Order-Management Cycle

At a macrolevel, all order-management cycles have 10 steps that populate the three basic phases of the order life cycle; preorder, order, and postorder. While order-management cycles are different for products and services and vary from industry to indus-

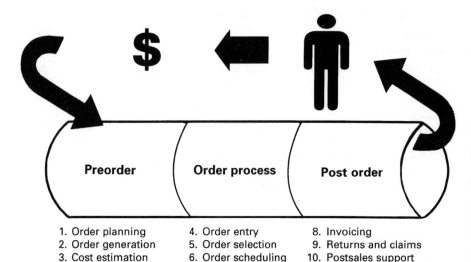

Preorder	Order process	Post order
1. Order planning	4. Order entry	8. Invoicing
2. Order generation	5. Order selection	9. Returns and claims
3. Cost estimation and pricing	6. Order scheduling	10. Postsales support
	7. Order fulfillment	

FIGURE 22.12 The order-management cycle.

try, all enterprises perform these 10 steps in some fashion. Also depending on industry and product, certain activities may fall under different steps.

Information Linkages

It is also important to understand that without certain information, these order steps and phases become very disjointed. Figure 22.13 provides a generic data flow model of the order cycle and shows how business functions contribute to the definition and flow of this information.

Preorder Activity. Some activities, called *preorder activities,* take place prior to the actual acceptance of an order by an enterprise. This planning is needed to support the order process, and it occurs at both a strategic and operational level.

Step 1. Order Planning. All enterprises must do some level of planning and sales forecasting prior to actually handling a "live" customer order. For manufacturers, capacity and production plans must be put into place to support the sales forecast. For retailers, merchandise inventory planning must be done. Additionally, for both retailers and manufacturers, step 1 is where new-product introduction is planned.

Step 2. Order Generation. The placement of customers' orders is the actual marketing activity that generates interest. The sales department makes contact with both existing and prospective customers. Sales contact can be in several forms. A sales representative can meet with the customer, either personally or over the phone. Alternatively, contact can be made via product or service brochures, multimedia advertising, or product or service catalogs. Part of the order-generation process may involve the negotiation and establishment of specific terms and conditions for sales transactions. In some cases, an order acknowledgment may be generated and sent to the customer.

Step 3. Cost Estimation and Pricing. For custom products, costing and pricing can be quoted based upon a customer inquiry. For standard products and services, costs and prices are reviewed regularly. Typically, pricing reviews and quotes require input from all functional areas in the enterprise.

Order Processing Activity. These activities actually constitute order fulfillment, that is, getting the product or service into the hands of the customer.

Step 4. Order Entry. Once the customer has ordered the product or service, the internal mechanics of the actual order processing activity are set in motion by entering the customer's order into the enterprise's order system.

Step 5. Order Selection and Prioritization. Based upon customer interest, this is the process of deciding which orders to accept and which orders to decline. For custom products or services, there is typically a formal process for reviewing open opportunities. Deciding not to accept an order or to discontinue marketing efforts is a real, conscious effort and can be based upon a number of factors. Reasons for disengaging may include the following:

- *Risk.* An evaluation has indicated that profit, enterprise prestige, or litigation factors do not make the opportunity worth pursuing.
- *Enterprise strategy.* The customer has requested a product or service that is not aligned with the enterprise's product or service strategy.

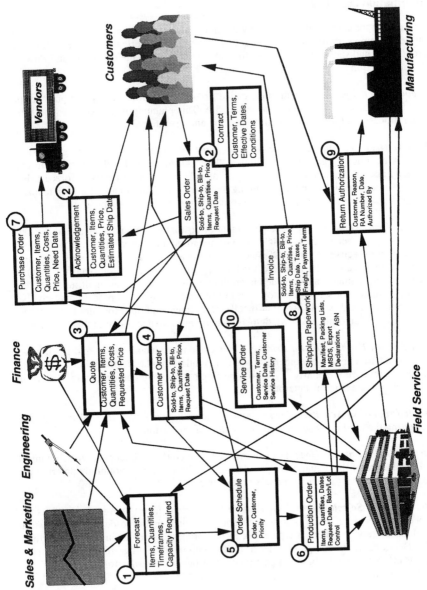

FIGURE 22.13 Order processing forms.

22.26

For standard products or services, decisions not to engage may be somewhat less conscious. An enterprise with an extremely popular product may experience demand that far outstrips their ability to supply. Customers faced with a significant wait may choose to buy elsewhere. Although it could be argued that in this case the customer decided to disengage, in reality, the enterprise's unwillingness or inability to meet the customer's demand was a decision to reject a certain portion of customer demand.

Step 6. Order Scheduling. Once entered into the order system, orders are scheduled and assigned an operational and production sequence. Scheduling may be internal to the enterprise, or it may involve negotiation with the customer.

Step 7. Order Fulfillment. This is actually a series of subprocesses very specific to the product, but generically, it covers the steps of the logistics supply chain:

* Procurement of raw materials, components, or supporting services
* Production and/or packaging of the product or service
* Distribution to a retail outlet or direct to the end customer

Postorder Activity. These are the "follow-through," and in some cases the "fall-out," steps of processing an order.

Step 8. Invoicing and Shipping Papers. There is no "typical" way of invoicing. Invoicing can be effected along several time lines:

* Invoices can be delivered after the product or service is delivered.
* Invoices can accompany the delivery of the product or service.
* Invoices can be multiphased—for example, 10 percent with order, 70 percent upon delivery, and 20 percent at the conclusion of the warranty period.

Likewise, shipping paper will vary based upon the following:

* Nature of the businesses involved
* Nature of the products involved
* Contractual agreements
* Location of the shipper in relation to the customer

Step 9. Returns and Claims. All enterprises are faced with some level of returns or customer inquiries, which can be considered "cost of doing business." For some markets, a 5 percent return could be considered world class, while for others, 5 percent might be considered disastrous. Regardless of the percentage, returns and claims have an impact on administrative costs, scrap, transportation expenses, and customer relationships.

Step 10. Post-Sales Service. Depending upon the product or service, this final step could cover a myriad of activities including the following:

* Ongoing maintenance on either an on-site, field support basis or on a carry-in basis
* Physical installation

- Training
- Release upgrade

Role of Inventory in Customer Relations

The order-management cycle encompasses the planning of the delivery of the product or service, the actual delivery of the product or service, and the follow-up with the customer concerning that delivery. Central to this cycle is inventory. In this central role, inventory generates a fundamental trade-off decision process involving the customer and inventory—the cost of carrying excess inventory versus the cost of a lost customer sale (see Fig. 22.14). This trade-off analysis is not trivial. On one side of the equation is inventory. It is tangible. It can be planned. It can be quantified. With strong suppliers and processes, it can be controlled. Therefore, something that is measured can typically be managed. Opposed to inventory in the equation is customer service and the potential for a lost sale.

Customer service in the form of meeting customer expectations is not a tangible component in the equation. Typically, being intangible, this side is somewhat less man-

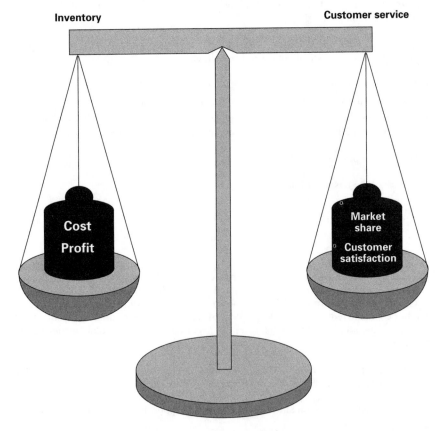

FIGURE 22.14   The inventory versus customer service evaluation.

ageable. So, what we have is a situation where we are trying to rationalize between two choices; one somewhat predictable and manageable and the other very unpredictable and fundamentally unmanageable. So how does one make a rational analysis of what could be thought of as a Jekyll-Hyde situation? One way is to look at the investment economics and mathematics of safety stocks.

Customer Service and Safety Stocks

Inventory is an anomaly when viewed from different perspectives within an organization:

- *Message from the shop floor:* "We need a steady supply of raw materials and WIP so that we can keep people busy and equipment utilized."
- *Message from sales:* "We need maximum levels of finished-goods stocks so that we can provide maximum service to our customers."
- *Message from finance:* "As an investment, we need to minimize our inventory dollars."

From a balanced perspective, it is clear that inventories have a dynamic and complex role in an organization. As an asset (the sales view), inventories can be sold and turned into a receivable, that is, a more liquid asset. As a resource (the shop floor's view), inventories are necessary in order to fuel the production engine. On the other hand, too much inventory is a liability (the finance view) because it has the potential to produce a low return investment. This trade-off relationship is shown graphically in Fig. 22.15.

To quantify this trade-off relationship, let's look at a business example. A mass merchandiser sells refrigerators at a price of $1000 per unit. These refrigerators are purchased for $600 per unit. Sales of refrigerators average 10 per day. Average replenishment time from the supplier is 10 days. In light of variable demand, the merchandiser tries to decide the level of safety stock to maintain. Table 22.6 provides the additional economics behind this problem.

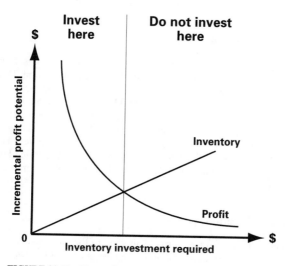

FIGURE 22.15   The profit and inventory trade-off.

TABLE 22.6   Incremental Contribution of Safety Stock

Reorder point	100	337	574	811	1048
Standard deviations	—	1	2	3	4
Risk of stock-out	50%	15.9%	2.3%	0.135%	0.003%
Service level	50%	84.1%	97.7%	99.999%	99.99997%
Average monthly demand	200	200	200	200	200
Lost sales potential	100	32	5	0.27	0.006
Lost profit potential	$40,000	$12,800	$2,000	$108	$2.40
Potential incremental profit gain	—	$27,200	$10,800	$1,892	$105.60
Incremental inventory investment required	—	$142,200	$142,200	$142,200	$142,200
Return on inventory investment	—	19.13%	7.59%	1.33%	0.07%

From this analysis, it appears that maintaining a reorder point of 337 is a worthwhile investment for three reasons:

1. It improves service level from 50 to 84.1 percent.
2. It generates an additional $27,200 in profit.
3. It returns over 19 percent on the inventory investment.

Investing in safety stocks beyond this level gives mixed results:

- A reorder point of 574 improves the service level from 84 to 97.7 percent, but only returns 7.59 percent on the additional inventory investment.
- A reorder point of 811 increases the service level from 97.7 to 99.999 percent and returns 1.33 percent on the additional inventory investment.
- A reorder point of 1048 increases the service level from 99.9 to 99.99997 percent and returns 0.07 percent on the additional inventory investment.

Safety Stock: A Diminishing Return

The above example demonstrates the diminishing contribution of safety stock, both from a customer service level and an inventory investment standpoint. However, recall that customer expectations are not easily quantifiable. As an example, assume the merchandiser decides to maintain a reorder point of 337. This means that potentially, 5 customers a month will not be able to buy a refrigerator. By itself, in consideration of the other economics, this is probably a reasonable trade-off. But, what if any or all of these 5 shoppers tell their friends of the merchandiser's inability to deliver? Has there been an impact on future sales beyond the 5 calculated as part of the service level-inventory evaluation? This potential impact on future sales is a real component of service level and needs to be considered.

Order Processing: A Summary

Order processing is the enterprise's critical linkage to the customer. It is here that the enterprise has many opportunities to "delight the customer" as the customer's request is addressed by the order-management cycle. The order-management cycle itself is a process that involves preorder, order, and postorder activities. The basic function of the order-management cycle is to plan the delivery of product or service, deliver the product or service, and gain feedback from the customer on the delivery. Central to the effective control of the order process is information.

ORGANIZING FOR SALES AND SERVICE

Management is the process of planning, directing, and controlling the deployment of resources necessary to deliver a product or service. Effective employment of this process depends to some degree on how the enterprise is organized. There are many different types of organization models, which can be collapsed into three basic configurations as shown in Fig. 22.16.

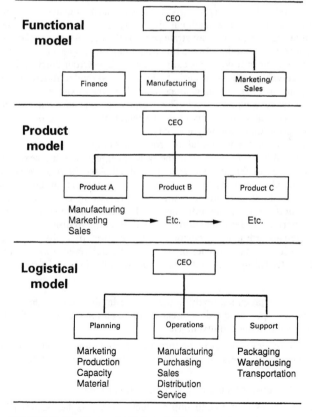

FIGURE 22.16   Basic organization models.

Organization Models

- *Functional model.* Alignment of resources and upward communication lines are based upon business functions. Departments are aligned and grouped into divisions based upon the similarity of functions; manufacturing, marketing, and finance.
- *Product model.* Enterprises with multiple products or services may choose to organize according to the product model. Here, the enterprise groups functions underneath products. Product A and product B would both have their own manufacturing facilities and marketing organizations.
- *Logistical model.*[9] In this model, the organization seeks to integrate the total logistics process by combining physical distribution and materials management. Orientation is strategic as well as operational.

Horizontal versus Vertical Organization

The obvious difference among the three models is "where functions are aligned." For example, in the traditional functional model, marketing and sales are very prominent in the alignment. However, in both the product and logistical models, marketing and sales, based upon the informal pecking order implied by an organization chart, are farther down in the hierarchy. In fact, in the logistical model, marketing and sales, traditionally next-door neighbors in the organizational hierarchy, are not even in the same division. This logistical model serves to demonstrate perhaps the biggest, but not so obvious, difference in organizational models. In the functional model, people understand their function as a discrete point in time. Sales calls on customers. Order entry records the sale, and accounts receivable collects the cash. In the logistical model, functions are still seen as a discrete point in time, but more important, they *are linked horizontally to other upstream and downstream processes.*[10] The operative here is horizontal. Because every functional area can expect to be involved at several points in the order-management cycle, every function must not only understand the order cycle but also must have an organization that facilitates horizontal, or cross-functional, communication.

As shown in Table 22.7, every time the order progresses to the next step, there is the potential to have a different business mix involved. Also, in most cases, the key role will change. This changeability has important implications in the design of an order processing system. First and foremost, the order processing system must provide up-to-date and accurate order status information. This lets everyone, including the customer, know where the order is and allows proper planning to proceed so that the order will be completed according to the customer's expectation. In addition, the design must consider the type of orders and types of service being delivered. Based upon the types of service, the order filling step could vary dramatically. Types of service include the following:

- *Retail.* Includes shipments directly to the retail establishment. Orders can be based upon the retailers' purchase orders or can be more automatic, as described earlier, in the form of vendor-managed inventories.
- *Distribution.* Provides services in the form of consolidation, deconsolidation, kitting, pricing, and a host of others that the distributor's economies of scale can accommodate.
- *Repair.* Includes repair of a product or component or the manufacture of repair parts.
- *Direct mail.* Includes activities to ship product directly to the customer based upon either a catalog or other home-shopping service aid.

TABLE 22.7   Processing Orders Through the Enterprise

Step		Business function					
	Sales	Marketing	Customer service	Purchasing	Finance	Manufacturing	Distribution
1. Order planning	○	●	○	○	○	●	○
2. Order generation	●	○	○				
3. Pricing	○	●	○	○	○	○	○
4. Order entry	○	○	●			○	○
5. Allocate order	○	●	○		○	○	○
6. Schedule order	○	○	○	○		●	○
7. Order fulfillment			○	○		●	●
8. Order invoicing	○	○	○		●		○
9. Returns/claims	●		○		○	○	○
10. Post-sales service	○		●			○	○

● = plays a key role.

○ = plays a secondary role.

Source: B. P. Shapiro, V. K. Rangan, and J. J. Sviokla, "Staple Yourself to an Order," *Harvard Business Review,* July–August 1992, pp. 113–122.

Organizing for Sales and Service: A Summary

Effective sales and service is a function of effective organization. Effective organizations were shown to be those organizations that facilitate cross-functional or horizontal communications. Three different organizational structures—functional, product, and logistical—were explored.

TOOLS, TECHNIQUES, METHODS, AND THE FUTURE

Every time a customer's order is passed on to the next step in the order cycle, the customer is passed along also. This has care-and-handling implications for any future developments in supply-chain management.

Mass Customization

One new development, mass customization,[11,12] could have profound implications. This approach, which is already being employed by some enterprises, seeks to deliver a product or service using a dynamic network of relatively autonomous operating units. Each operating unit has a specific task or series of tasks for which it is responsible. Tasks in a mass customization framework may not be executed in the same sequence every time as in a typical serial mass production system. The determination of what tasks are needed and when they are to be executed is driven by the customer's wants and needs. Table 22.8 compares the widely used mass production approach with this new mass customization concept.

TABLE 22.8   Mass Production versus Mass Customization

	Mass production	Mass customization
Change conditions	Periodic and/or forecastable changes in market demand	Constant and unforecastable changes in market demand
Workflows	Serial, linear flow of work executed according to plan	Customer or product unique value chains
Key organizational tool	Standardized, dedicated production process	Loosely coupled networks of modular, flexible processing units
Control system	Centralized, hierarchical command system	Centralized network coordination, and independent processing control

Source: A. C. Boynton, B. Victor, and B. J. Pine, II, "New Competitive Strategies: Challenges to Organizations and Information Technology," *IBM Systems Journal* (32:1), 1993, pp. 40–64.

Product Configurators

Based upon the current organization experiences, mass customization results in greater variability and quality of products at affordable prices and is an achievable and demonstrable strategy for business enterprises in the twenty-first century. One tool already in place to support mass customization incentives are product *configurators*. These software tools are designed to quickly and accurately configure not only the customer's product but also the manufacturing steps necessary to make and ship the customer's product. In effect, the configurator, based upon the features and options requested by the customer, customizes the order requirements necessary to produce to the customer's request.

Computer Networking

This chapter opened with a preamble about quality and stated that since the last edition of this book, a commitment to achieving high-quality results in product or service industries has developed as a major force in manufacturing. Actually, there is a second force that has gained momentum over the last 5 to 10 years: computerization. The computer's role in the supply chain has progressed from that of an information keeper to that of a planner, to actually guide the execution of the plan. The computer and information services have had tremendous influence across all facets of the supply chain.

- *Electronic data interchange* (*EDI*), that is, electronic linkages, handle orders, acknowledgments, advanced shipping notices, and actual invoices and payments between all levels of trading partners.
- *Robotics* are assuming more and more responsibility for the repetitive, more mundane tasks, both on the shop floor and in the warehouse.

- *Bar coding* has already transformed the grocery industry and is making an impact in other areas of the retail sector and on the shop floor. Bar-code-based warehouse management systems have demonstrated an ability to maintain accurate inventories, by part and by location, to the 99.9 percent level.

- *Radio-frequency equipment* has made it possible to provide real-time, accurate information in all kinds of environments, from laboratories to extremely harsh manufacturing environments.

- *Advanced communication technologies* have made it possible for organizations to collect massive amounts of data and to offer these data to other organizations on a subscription basis.

- *Automated identification technologies* have taken information gathering to new levels of automation. Radio frequency/ID and voice and imaging systems are among the most promising technologies.

Reengineering

As an enabling model, reengineering has been shown to return tremendous benefits to those organizations that follow the reengineering tenets. As a methodology, reengineering is truly nonpartisan. It can be applied to any enterprise in any sector, and it can be applied across all functions within an enterprise. In their landmark work,[13] Hammer and Champy give examples of many organizations that have reengineered operations and have realized results in all areas of their logistics functions:

- *Procurement.* Ford Motor Company reduced their payables department from 500 to 125 by simply changing their business procedures from "pay when invoice received" to "pay when goods received." Currently, Ford is exploring a new concept of "pay when goods used." IBM Credit Corporation, by cross-training specialists into generalists, was able to reduce their credit-issuance process from 7 days to 4 hours.

- *Production.* Kodak has added concurrent engineering to their new-product development processes and has reduced new-product development from 70 weeks to 38 weeks.

- *Distribution.* Bell Atlantic has reduced their hookup service time for new customers from 15 days to 3 days. This reduction was accomplished by re-creating installation processes that were independent and could be initiated as soon as the required information was available and precedent activities were completed.

As a quality-improvement technique, reengineering has demonstrated that it indeed is an application of the return-on-quality approach that was discussed earlier in this chapter. By definition:

> Reengineering is the fundamental rethinking and radical redesign of business processes to achieve dramatic improvements in critical, contemporary measures of performance, such as cost, quality, service, and speed.[14]

It is obvious that reengineering focuses on purpose, not on process. This fits quite nicely with logistics where the focus is outward on delivery (purpose), not inward on functional turf (process).

Benchmarking

Many companies have improved performance through budget extrapolation. "If I improve sales by x percent over last year, then I should be able to improve profit by y percent." This technique can work, but it is a linear and gradual approach. Another technique that has gained acceptance because, like reengineering, it can return dramatic, even exponential results is benchmarking:

> Benchmarking is the search for industry best practices that will lead to superior performance.[15]

Xerox Corporation initiated competitive benchmarking in 1979 as a way to examine its unit manufacturing costs. Xerox's benchmarking activities were against its own Japanese subsidiaries and other Japanese copier manufacturers. Xerox eventually went on to benchmark all aspects of their operations. Their experiences and results have been well documented and have led to a formal, working definition of benchmarking.

Not so obvious in this definition, and in the Xerox experience, is that companies can and should benchmark companies outside of the industry. As an example, Xerox, a manufacturer, benchmarked its distribution functions against L.L. Bean, a direct marketer.

Tools, Techniques, Methods, and the Future: A Summary

This section explored the new enablers that can lead to enhanced performance in the areas of sales and customer service. Computers and methodologies are the key enablers.

SUMMARY

This chapter has looked at customers, sales, and service from the standpoint of the supply chain. That is, customers are not just the people shopping in the retail outlets; rather, customers are the people immediately upstream from your enterprise. This supply-chain view has provided new models for enterprises to follow. Cooperation between customers and vendors has allowed technologies to be developed and economies of scale to be exploited. Through all of this resurgence, reawakening, and revival, three key factors have been identified:

1. *Horizontal view.* Enterprises must view their organizations, their logistics systems, and their industry on a horizontal plane. Communications must flow across enterprise functions.

2. *Technology.* Technologies will continue to serve strategic, tactical, and operational incentives.

3. *Time.* We have shrunk distances, mastered technologies, and discovered new methodologies. Time has remained an unmastered constant. However, we do have control over how time is allocated.

REFERENCES

1. D. Greising: "Quality: How to Make it Work," *Business Week,* August 8, 1994, pp. 54–59.

2. P. A. Samuelson: *Economics,* 9th ed., 1973, McGraw-Hill, New York, p. 3.

3. APICS: *CIRM Logistics Student Guide,* Falls Church, Va., 1991, p. xi.

4. H. Mather: "Design for Logistics," *Production and Inventory Management Journal,* APICS, Falls Church, Va., first quarter, 1992, pp. 7–10.

5. W. E. Deming: *Out of the Crisis,* M.I.T. Press, Cambridge, Mass., 1986, p. 3.

6. J. T. Vesey: "The New Competitors: They Think in Terms of 'Speed to Market,'" *1991 International Conference Proceedings,* APICS, Falls Church, Va., pp. 274–277.

7. M. N. Sinha: "Winning Back Angry Customers," *Quality Progress,* American Society for Quality Control, November 1993, pp. 53–56.

8. W. A. Shewhart: *Statistical Method from the Viewpoint of Quality Control,* Dover Press, New York, 1991, p. 45.

9. D. J. Bowersox, et al.: *Logistical Management,* Macmillan Publishing, New York, 1986, pp. 303–320.

10. B. P. Shapiro, V. K. Rangan, and J. J. Sviokla: "Staple Yourself to an Order," *Harvard Business Review,* July–August 1992, pp. 113–122.

11. B. J. Pine, II, B. Victor, and A. C. Boynton: "Making Mass Customization Work," *Harvard Business Review,* September–October 1993, pp. 108–119.

12. A. C. Boynton, B. Victor, and B. J. Pine, II: "New Competitive Strategies: Challenges to Organizations and Information Technology," *IBM Systems Journal* (32:1), 1993, pp. 40–64.

13. M. Hammer, J. Champy: *Reengineering the Corporation: A Manifesto for Business Revolution,* Harper Collins, New York, 1993.

14. Ibid., p. 32.

15. R. C. Camp: *Benchmarking: The Search for Industry Best Practices That Lead to Superior Performance,* Quality Press, 1989, p. 10.

BIBLIOGRAPHY

APICS: *CIRM Logistics Student Guide,* Falls Church, Va., 1991.

Bowersox, D. J., et al.: *Logistical Management,* Macmillan Publishing, New York, 1986.

Boynton, A. C., Victor, B., and Pine, B. J., II: "New Competitive Strategies: Challenges to Organizations and Information Technology," *IBM Systems Journal* (32:1), 1993.

Camp, R. C.: *Benchmarking: The Search for Industry Best Practices That Lead to Superior Performance,* Quality Press, Cold Springs, N.Y., 1989.

Delavigne, K. T., and Robertson, J. D.: *Deming's Profound Changes: When Will the Sleeping Giant Awaken,* Prentice-Hall, Englewood Cliffs, N.J., 1994.

Deming, W. E.: *Out of the Crisis,* M.I.T. Press, Cambridge, Mass., 1986.

Greene, J. H.: *Production and Inventory Control Handbook,* 2d ed., McGraw-Hill, New York, 1987.

Greising, D.: "Quality: How to Make it Work," *Business Week,* August 8, 1994, pp. 54–59.

Hammer, M., and Champy, J.: *Reengineering the Corporation: A Manifesto for Business Revolution,* Harper Collins, New York, 1993.

Karten, N.: *Managing Expectations,* Dorset Publishing, New York, 1994.

Kuczmarski, T. D.: *Managing New Products: The Power of Innovation,* Prentice-Hall, Englewood Cliffs, N.J., 1992.

Mather, H.: *Competitive Manufacturing,* Prentice-Hall, Englewood Cliffs, 1988.

———: "Design for Logistics," *Production and Inventory Management Journal,* APICS, first quarter, 1992, pp. 7–102.

Miller, J. G., et al.: *Benchmarking Global Manufacturing,* Richard Irwin, Homewood, Ill., 1992.

Pine, B. J. II, Victor, B., and Boynton, A. C.: "Making Mass Customization Work," *Harvard*

Business Review, September–October 1993, pp. 108–119.

Robeson, J. F. (ed.): *The Distribution Handbook,* 3d ed., The Free Press, New York, 1985.

Samuelson, P. A.: *Economics,* 9th ed., McGraw-Hill, New York, 1973.

Semich, J. W.: "Information Replaces Inventory at the Virtual Corp.," *Datamation,* July 15, 1994, pp. 37–42.

Shapiro, B. P., Rangan, V. K., and Sviokla, J. J.: "Staple Yourself to an Order," *Harvard Business Review,* July–August 1992, pp. 113–122.

Shewhart, W. A.: *Statistical Method from the Viewpoint of Quality Control,* Dover Press, New York, 1991.

Sinha, M. N.: "Winning Back Angry Customers," *Quality Progress,* American Society for Quality Control, November 1993, pp. 53–56.

Stratton, A. D.: *A Quality Transformation Success Story from Storage Tek,* Quality Press, Cold Springs, N.Y., 1994.

Vesey, J. T.: "The New Competitors: They Think in Terms of 'Speed to Market,'" *1991 International Conference Proceedings,* APICS, pp. 274–277.

Vondle, D. D.: *Service Management Systems,* McGraw-Hill, New York, 1989.

CHAPTER 23
FORECASTING SYSTEMS AND METHODS

Editors

Stephen A. De Lurgio, Ph. D., CFPIM
Professor of Operations Management
University of Missouri, Kansas City, Missouri

James I. Morgan
Business Science Specialist, Retired
The Dow Chemical Company, Midland, Michigan

Carl D. Bhame, CFPIM
Vice President
American Software, Atlanta, Georgia

This chapter develops *systems* and *methods* for forecasting the demands for one to several hundred thousand items. To forecast for many items, highly automated, but interactive, systems are required. These systems provide forecasts and planning data for short-range manufacturing planning and long-range marketing and financial planning systems. Forecasting systems exist so that organizations have the right product or service, in the right quantity, in the right location, at the right time. However, having the right product available for customer demands is not necessarily always a short-range tactical activity but, rather, is often a strategic process of developing new products. Thus, forecasting systems should support daily operational control and ongoing strategic planning.

It is important to distinguish between the terms *forecasting methods* and *forecasting systems*. A forecasting method is a statistical or subjective technique for generating a forecast. In contrast, a forecasting system is an integrated computer-based information system that supports the functions of demand database management, forecasting, user interface, system control, and maintenance as defined in Table 23.1.[1] However, most advertised statistical forecasting software packages are simply implementations of the forecasting module and do not include the other functions defined here.

There are at least two forecasting functions in most organizations: the routine forecasting of existing products using integrated systems and the nonroutine forecasting of new or major product groups or technologies. These two different forecasting activities

TABLE 23.1   The Modules of a Forecasting System

I. Demand Data Module
System input and output of local and remote demand data
Demand capturing
Logical filtering (demand versus supply or shipments)
Special event filtering (promotions, price changes, product introductions)
Initial outlier detection, adjustment, classification

II. Forecasting Module
Forecast mode selection
Outlier detecting, adjustment, classification
Reasonableness test
Final forecast
Error measures
Tracking signal control

III. Managerial Interface and Interaction Module
Graphic-user interface
Graphical presentations
Management forecast input
User help
Management feedback
User notepad
Expert advisory menu

IV. Output Module
File generation
Routine batch reports
Ad hoc reports
Exception reports

V. System Control and Maintenance
Navigation and system control of modules
Input-output control between modules
Simulation control
Database updating and maintenance
Detection of system malfunctions and bugs

VI. Database module
Actual demand history
Adjusted demand history
Promotional profiles
Seasonal profiles
Item and group hierarchical structures

Source: S. A. De Lurgio and C. D. Bhame, *Forecasting Systems for Operations Management,* Irwin Professional Publications, Burr Ridge, Ill., 1991.

support different types of decisions and are sometimes managed by different departments. This chapter discusses the methods and systems that are important to all corporate decisions, immediate (1 to 28 days), short (1 month to 1 year), medium (1 to 3 years), and long range (3 to 20 years). First forecasting systems will be discussed, then methods.

FORECASTING SYSTEMS

Good forecasting systems are much more complex than good statistical forecasting software. Figure 23.1 illustrates the interrelationships between the modules of a forecasting system. This is a computer-based system that:

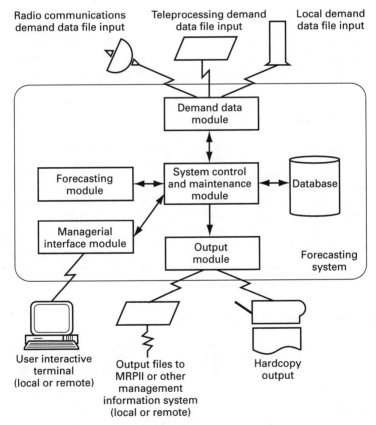

FIGURE 23.1   The modules of a forecasting system. (*Source: S. A. De Lurgio and C. D. Bhame,* Forecasting Systems for Operations Management, *Irwin Professional Publications, Burr Ridge, Ill., 1991.*)

- Automatically selects correct seasonal, trend, linear, and nonlinear forecasting models
- Provides a graphical user interface to ease use by a variety of managers
- Processes thousands of demand and forecast records intelligently and quickly
- Captures and maintains at least 36 months of demand data
- Provides monthly forecasts for 1 to 3 years into the future for all SKUs
- Groups items with low demand to achieve good group forecasts
- Generates hierarchical reports for several levels of management
- Integrates information for operations, marketing, and finance
- Highlights exceptions when they occur[1]

The following paragraphs will clarify the modules of forecasting systems summarized in Fig. 23.1 and Table 23.1.

Demand Data Module

The *demand data module* captures and processes demand before it is input to the demand database and automatically checks to ensure that the data has not been put in incorrectly or affected by very unusual events. Unusual values, called *outliers,* are highlighted and exceptions are reported.

Forecasting Module

The *forecasting module* selects a good forecasting model for each item or product group managed by the firm. In addition, the forecasting module generates forecasts for product-line groups and low-demand items. The forecasting modules of most, if not all, systems use univariate methods, sometimes called *intrinsic methods. Univariate methods* use only time or past product demands to forecast future demands. Consequently, no external variables such as GDP, income, or competitor prices are used in most forecasting systems. Such external variables are used in *multivariate models* such as regression analysis or econometric methods. Few comprehensive forecasting systems routinely use multivariate methods in forecasting; however, these more advanced methods are part of most statistical forecasting software. Nonetheless, this is one of the cutting-edge developments in forecasting systems.

Managerial Interface and Interaction Module

The *managerial interface and interaction module* is the user's interface to the forecasting system. It should provide a good graphic-user interface, screen displays, and navigational aids, thereby facilitating manager interaction with the forecasting system.

Output Module

The *output module* generates routine periodic batch reports and output files, including exception reports. These exception reports are important because they identify situations requiring human intervention in the forecasting and inventory management processes.

Database Module

The *database module* holds actual demands, adjusted demands, seasonal information, and special events (i.e., outlier and promotional) data for each item and group. This database can be quite large because it contains this information for a minimum of 36 months. Also, additional data, such as 12 or more monthly forecasts and the performance of past forecasts of all items and groups, are stored in this database. The database is updated periodically, typically every week or month. Until the recent reductions in the cost of digital and optical storage devices, many firms did not maintain adequate databases. However, with the low cost of data storage, there are few, if any, excuses for not maintaining a sufficiently large database.

In addition to the many characteristics of forecasting systems mentioned above, the system should do the following:

- Be able to forecast daily, weekly, 4-week, monthly, quarterly, annual, and other data.
- Maintain at least 3 and preferably 5 years of demand data.
- Allow subjective and objective user overrides of forecasts and past demands.
- Capture and model past and future marketing promotions.
- Detect out-of-control situations through the use of *tracking signals* and demand filters. These topics are developed later in this chapter.
- Derive seasonal factors for groups.
- Facilitate the combining of low-volume items into effective groupings.
- Forecast accurately.

This last characteristic is sometimes overlooked. When a system is bought or developed, the accuracy of its statistical methods should be benchmarked. Unless the software has a proven record, the developer's generalized statements concerning system accuracy are sometimes unreliable. A system should have significant intelligence built into the forecasting methods so that it detects the correct demand patterns (e.g., trends and seasonality).

Selecting Forecasting Systems

The selection of a forecasting system can be a complex endeavor; consequently, it is important to do the following:

- Apply the principles and procedures of good system development processes.
- Familiarize yourself with the principles of forecasting systems as presented in De Lurgio and Bhame,[1] Brown,[2] APICS,[3] and statistical forecasting methods in De Lurgio[4] and Makridakis, Wheelwright, and McGee,[5] Hanke and Reitsch,[6] and Goodrich.[7]
- Create a system specification committee to oversee the development and selection process.
- Involve all users in the development process.
- Select a well-respected user as a project team leader.
- Benchmark the system's accuracy, flexibility for expansion, compatibility with existing systems, and other considerations developed above.

- Use outside or inside consultants prudently in the system design process.
- Do not overlook the importance of a user-friendly database system to support the effective managerial use of forecasts and demand information.
- Run the new forecasting system in parallel with the existing system until the "bugs" have been driven out.
- Do not be seduced into buying a low-cost unsophisticated forecasting system. The return on investment from a good, higher-cost system may be extraordinary, while the return on investment from a mediocre, lower-cost system may be negative.

Problems to Avoid with Forecasting Systems

The following problems occur so frequently that they should be highlighted.

- *No demand database exists.* Most firms do not capture actual demands but instead capture shipment data. Shipments frequently do not reflect demand but only the lower of supply or demand. The shipped quantity may be low because of product shortages, delayed shipments, substituted products, or transshipments. The old adage, *garbage in, garbage out* (GIGO) applies very well to forecasting systems. Demand has to be captured!
- *Past outliers and promotions obliterate true demands for a product.* For example, because marketing promotes a product in different months of the year, the product appears to have no seasonality when, in fact, it does. The unusually low or high values of a month should be adjusted in the demand database; this is why actual and adjusted demands are maintained as shown in Table 23.1.
- *Only one demand file is maintained.* It is very important to maintain several demand records, including recorded demand, adjusted demand, outliers, and a promotional history. For example, as mentioned above, past promotions and outliers affect sales in abnormal ways. Consider the situation in which promotions during April increase demand by 4000 units while decreasing demand in the following month, May, by 1000 units. The increase and decrease should be part of the adjusted demand history by decreasing the inflated April and increasing May values. Also, the system should keep a separate file of past promotional effects so these can be used to predict future promotional effects. Thus, we see at least three records are necessary: actual demand, adjusted demand, and promotional effects.
- *Attempting to forecast dependent demands.* Despite well-known principles to the contrary, some firms continue to forecast dependent demands; instead, forecast independent demands and calculate dependent demands. For example, a manufacturer-distributor with *regional distribution centers* (RDCs) supplied by factories should forecast demands for each product at the retail level if possible. Then, using *distribution requirements planning* (DRP), the dependent demands can be accumulated back to each supplying RDC and factory.
- *Not detecting turning points.* Detecting the demand variations of product life cycles (i.e., introduction, growth, maturity, and decline) is an important function of a forecasting system. A good forecasting system should detect when the forecasting process is out of control. The tools to do this are based on statistical process control methods of Shewhart, using methods developed by Brown[2] and others. In addition, the statistical tools of tracking signals and demand filters are an essential part of a good forecasting system; these are studied in the latter part of this chapter.

FORECASTING METHODS

Effective PIC planning requires methods for reducing the uncertainty of the future. A necessary part of uncertainty reduction is forecasting. The term *forecasting* is used here to denote the process of arriving at an estimate of the future. While uncertainty reduction is possible, it is not possible to eliminate all future uncertainty, and some error will always exist. This chapter develops several different forecasting methods. A rich variety of forecasting methods has been developed in statistics, econometrics, engineering control, system dynamics, inventory management, marketing research, and technological planning. The International Institute of Forecasters (IIF) and the International Society of Forecasters (ISF) and the International Association of Business Forecasting (IABF) and their journals integrate the many related disciplines involved in the application and development of forecasting methods.[8]

Considerations in Forecasting

Realizing that we must forecast to plan, what do we need to know about forecasting? Obviously there are questions of why, what, and how; but also such questions as the frequency, time horizon, precision, and what constitutes a good forecast.

Why Forecast? Forecasts are necessary because planning lead times require forecasts. The longer the lead time of the decision, the longer the forecast.

What to Forecast? Forecast independent demands; do not forecast dependent demands. A more precise answer is: "Forecast all independent demands that are needed to plan the future." This covers such things as product demands, supplier uncertainty, costs, prices, and lead times.

In every system, there is an uncontrollable *triggering event* that initiates action in the rest of the system. In an inventory or production scheduling system, the triggering event is demand for items in the form of an order or requisition. Accurate forecasts of these demands yield decisions that maximize system effectiveness. The location or geographical area of demands is another determinant of what to forecast. Each area yields another SKU that should be forecast. Clearly, adding the location of independent demands (i.e., adding SKUs) to the "what" definition significantly increases the number of items to be forecast.

Another aspect of forecasting is the time period. Should annual, quarterly, monthly, weekly, or daily demand be used in the system? In general, the time period used in forecasting should be that used in planning. If the plan requires quarterly data, then quarterly forecasts should be made. Because of the recent developments in quick-response, continuous replenishment, just in time, and supply-chain management systems, there has been a movement to weekly time periods, particularly in the wholesale and retail industries.

How to Forecast? Here, the following questions should be answered:

What are the different methods?

How are these methods applied?

Which are the practical methods?

What are the limitations of each method?

While there are many good methods, no universal method has been developed that is good for all time series.

The ideal way to estimate future demand for a product is to first determine the customers' demand, their uses for the product, how much they need for each use, how and when each customer will order, and any other relevant information. Then develop a model to relate the demands to those factors. However, because of the vast number of factors and interrelationships, a complete causal model is rarely, if ever, possible. Good causal models, however, have been developed and used effectively in many practical situations.

Some Distinctions between Forecasting Methods

Forecasts or Predictions.   In estimating demand, it is useful to consider two types of factors generating the future. One type has generated the demand in the past and is expected to repeat; the other types are the factors that will influence demand for the first time. Brown refers to estimates of the first class as *forecasts* and the estimates of the second class as *predictions.*[9]

Examination of the past should reveal the repeating patterns of demand. Univariate models provide one way of anticipating the future on the basis of these repeating patterns. These techniques assume that the relationships of the past will continue into the future, an assumption that is not always true. However, the effects of new causal factors are not predicted by univariate analysis. For both repeating and new factors, knowledge, experience, judgment, and intuition are important in forecasting.

Single-Point or Frequency Distribution.   A forecast should not be a single value but, instead, a frequency distribution. A *frequency distribution,* or *probability statement,* is an essential part of a forecast and may be nothing but an estimate of the highest and lowest values of demand. Whenever a range is given, a probability statement should be given. A forecast should be stated as an expected value (i.e., mean) and an estimate of the variation about that value (e.g., a standard deviation). For example, if the forecast is 1000 and the standard deviation of that estimate is 300, then the forecast can be stated as an expected demand of 1000 with a 34 percent chance of 700 to 1000 and a 34 percent chance of 1000 to 1300. The 34 percent chance is the characteristic plus or minus 1 standard deviation from the *normal distribution* (ND).

Repetitive or One Time.   Another distinction is whether the forecast is made once or repetitively. Univariate methods become more important with repetitive or periodic forecasts because these methods are easily implemented in more or less automated forecasting systems. Fortunately, there are many useful methods for one-time forecasts such as management science and marketing research.

Long, Medium, Short, or Immediate Range.   The selection of a forecasting method is influenced by the length of the planning horizon. While *long* and *immediate* are relative terms, the following definitions of forecasts are typical: immediate (1 day to 1 month), short (1 month to a year), medium (1 to 3 years), and long range (3 to 20 years). In some situations, an estimate of sales 1 year hence may be considered short range, whereas an estimate of the operation of a particular machine for 1 year is considered long range. The techniques of estimation used in both cases are usually different. Finally, very long range estimations are inherently less objective, and thus they are based more on subjective predictions of future events.

Qualitative (Subjective), Extrapolation, or Causal (Scientific).   The distinction between these concepts is often one of degree. A qualitative estimation is based primarily on subjective judgment or other nonquantitative characteristics. When judgment and experience are the only possible sources of information about the future, then subjective methods are better than scientific estimates based on unrealistic assumptions. However, when past demand patterns or relationships repeat regularly, then extrapolation or causal estimations are more valid. Extrapolation methods cast forward (i.e., forecast) past patterns or relationships that are expected to repeat in the future. Similarly, causal methods cast forward the past causal relationships into the future. They attempt to model the factors that cause a variable (e.g., sales) and the ways in which these relationships change with time. However, because of their complexity, number of causal factors, and the lack of scientific methodology, time, or resources, it is seldom possible to make a complete causal model. Consequently, a scientific causal study may not always be successful, and it is almost always quite expensive. In fact, for short-term forecasts, extrapolations (e.g., time-series and noncausal regression models) are normally more accurate than causal models.

Outline of Methods

There are many forecasting methods; in fact, the literature on forecasting methods is so voluminous that all methods cannot be surveyed in this chapter. The following outline, however, summarizes the spectrum of forecasting methods.[10]

I. Univariate (intrinsic, extrapolation, and time-series) methods
  A. Univariate analysis
   1. *Persistence or momentum.* The same value that occurred last period will occur next period (this is called a *highly autocorrelated series*).
   2. *Trend.* The trend of the past data is fitted to a mathematical curve by least-squares or other techniques. It is assumed that future values will follow the same trend. These trends may be short or long range, linear or nonlinear.
   3. *Seasonal.* Patterns recur with a known periodicity because of weather or artificial conventions. Frequently, these seasonal patterns can be identified easily using a variety of methods. These seasonal methods include the simple method of using the actual value of last year: July, year 1, is used to predict the actual value of the next year, July, year 2. However, there are more general methods, which will be discussed later.
   4. *Cyclical.* These methods are similar to trend methods except that cycles are examined and are assumed to hold for a very limited number of future periods. Cyclical variations are recurrent but with no known period; thus, they are very difficult to forecast.
   5. *Smoothing or averaging methods*
     a. The arithmetic average of all past data gives the estimate for the next period.
     b. The moving average of some recent values give the estimate. Data are smoothed over a finite number of the recent periods.
     c. A weighted average of all or part of past data gives the estimate. Exponential smoothing fits into this category.
   6. *Autoregressive.* An estimate is developed from an autocorrelation function that relates the estimate to a finite number of preceding actual values.

7. *Random.* A probability distribution is obtained from past data or estimated subjectively; then, estimates of future values are obtained by Monte Carlo simulation methods.

II. Multivariate (causal and extrinsic)
These scientific methods develop multivariate and causal models of factors influencing a time series.

  A. *Regression methods.* A mathematical equation relates the forecasted variable to current or past values of other variables. Example, $Y_{t+3} = f(X_t)$ or $Y_t = f(X_t, Z_t)$. The first equation is an example of a leading time series; X_t predicts the value of Y three periods hence, that is, Y_{t+3}. For example, the second equation relates Y to two coincident values, as new-home sales Y to incomes and mortgage rates X and Z.

  In these examples no assertions are made that the relationship is a true causal one; accurate predictions are sought without formal assertions of cause and effect.

  B. *Causal and econometric methods.* Cause-and-effect models such as econometric methods are used to model the simultaneous causal relationships between several variables—for example, the demand for books at a bookstore as related to the demographics and economics of the surrounding area. In such cases one seeks to not only predict but also to explain a variable.

III. Qualitative techniques

  A. Guesses based on intuition.

  B. Estimates based on experience, judgment, and commonsense reasoning.

  C. *Historical analog.* The characteristics or behaviors of some other variable (e.g., a related product) are useful in estimating the demand for a new product. These techniques are especially valuable when no historical data are available.

  D. Methods using the consensus of panels of people including the Delphi method and a variety of marketing research techniques.

IV. Other methods

  A. *Combining methods.* Weighted or unweighted averages of any of the above methods can be combined into a composite forecast. Considerable research has shown that typically, the average of several good forecasts of an item is more accurate than any one of those forecasts.

  B. *Artificial neural networks and expert systems.* There is growing body of knowledge regarding the use of artificial intelligence in the development of forecasting methods.

The technique used in a particular situation depends on many factors. One is the ability to interpret the factors influencing the variable in question. Available historical data and what data can be generated are also important. The time and resources available to make studies are another.

How Frequently to Forecast?

This question does not have a universally applicable answer. In repetitive situations, two possibilities exist: periodic updates or updates only when some new data are available. The best approach is to periodically update forecasts when monthly or weekly quantities are aggregated but to update immediately when a very unusual event occurs.

For example, in real-time control systems, supporting quick-response or continuous replenishment systems, it may be necessary to adjust a forecast when the new demand (new history) is significantly different from the expected. Thus, prior to a periodic update, an item is looked at when some new action is required. There is considerable art or trial and error to ensure that updates do not make the system too nervous to random variations. Tracking signals, which are discussed later, assist in effective updating.

With periodic systems, a balance must be made between the benefits and costs of a new forecast. Because a forecast is by nature inaccurate, it is often of little benefit to update a forecast just because new data are available, especially when the new forecasts may be expensive to obtain. Such tools as ABC inventory analysis can be helpful in determining how frequently to forecast—often for A items and less often for B and C items.

How Often Should Data Be Updated?

Information systems may give a lag between a transaction and its recording in the demand database. Time is necessary to assemble, condition, and aggregate data. This information lead time can result in failure to identify important changes in demand that may make forecasts (based on "old" data) unreliable. Today, the information lead time can be reduced by improved information systems. Nevertheless, the cost of the information system must be balanced against the strategic benefits received from more timely data.

What Time Horizon to Forecast?

The time horizon to forecast is dependent on planning lead times. Unless seasonality or supply capacity is important, inventory control forecasts generally are short term—one to three periods in the future—and production planning forecasts, especially when supply constraints or seasonality are present, may be over a medium term, say, 12 to 36 months. Facilities planning forecasts are of even longer time, say, 3 to 10 years in the future. Some methods are generally better for the short-term forecasting (simple time series), others for medium term (time series with trend and seasonality), and still others for longer term (multivariates causal models). Forecasts for all time horizons do require judgment, with judgment typically being most critical to longer-term forecasts.

How Accurate Are Forecasts?

Table 23.2 provides a self-explanatory summary of forecasting methods along with the considerations discussed previously. Consider the relative accuracy of different forecasting methods. Important to the question of accuracy is the value of the decision being made. With important decisions such as the management of high-value items (e.g., a jet airplane or ocean vessel), it is important to be precise in demand forecasts. However, with unimportant decisions, accuracy is not as important. Such tools as ABC Analysis can be helpful in determining how precisely to forecast. Concentrate on the big decisions with more sophisticated methods; use less sophisticated methods on the small. In fact, the most important decisions might be based on several different forecasting methods, especially where the forecasts support the same conclusions. The level of accuracy can be controlled using different trip points on demand filters and tracking signals, as discussed below.

TABLE 23.2 Comparison of Forecasting Methods for Management

Methods	Horizon length (a)				Accuracy at each horizon (b)				Cost (c)				Data period used (d)				
	Immediate (<1 month)	Short (1–3 months)	Medium (3 months–2 years)	Long (>2 years)	Immediate	Short	Medium	Long	Very low ($0.10)	Low ($10)	Medium ($100)	High ($1000)	Days	Weeks	Months	Quarters	Years
Univariate:																	
Simple smoothing	•	•			H	M	L	V	•				•	•	•		
Complex smoothing	•	•	•		H	H	M	L	•	•			•	•	•	•	
ARIMA	•	•	•	•	H	H	H	L		•	•		•	•	•	•	•
Multivariate:																	
Multiple regression		•	•	•	H	H	M	L	•					•	•	•	•
Single-equation econometric		•	•	•	M	H	H	M		•					•	•	
Multiequation econometric			•	•	L	H	H	M		•					•	•	•
MARMA	•	•	•	•	H	H	H	M		•	•		•	•	•	•	•
Qualitative:																	
Delphi			•	•	M	M	M	M			•					•	•
Market research			•	•	M	H	M	M			•				•	•	•
Panel consensus			•	•	V	L	L	V			•	•			•	•	•
Historical analogy			•	•	M	M	M	M			•	•			•	•	•

H = high accuracy.
M = medium accuracy.
L = low accuracy.
V = very low accuracy.

Weekly	Monthly	Quarterly	Yearly	Item-level plan	Production plan	Aggregate plan	New-product plan	Strategic plan	Very low	Low	Medium	High	Use of external and subjective data (h)	None	Trend	Seasonal	Cyclical	Explanatory	Low (<36)	Medium (36–48)	High (>48)
•	•			•	•							•	No	•					•		
•	•			•	•	•	•					•	No	•	•					•	
•	•			•	•	•	•	•			•	•	No	•	•	•					•
	•			•	•	•	•			•			Yes	•	•		•		•	•	
	•	•		•	•	•	•	•		•			Yes	•	•	•	•		•	•	
•	•	•		•	•	•	•	•		•			Yes	•	•	•	•		•	•	
•	•	•		•	•	•	•	•			•	•	Yes	•	•	•	•				•
	•	•		•	•	•						•	Yes subjective	•		•	•		•		
	•	•		•	•	•	•					•	Yes	•	•	•	•		•	•	
•	•			•	•	•						•	Yes subjective	•		•	•		•		
•	•	•		•	•	•						•	Yes subjective	•	•	•			•	•	

What Is a Good Forecast?

In general, a good forecast has low error and low bias, the best model having the lowest forecast error and lowest bias. The error in forecasting is the difference between the actual and forecasted value:

$$\text{Error} = \text{actual} - \text{forecast}$$

Bias occurs when several consecutive errors are consistently above or below zero. This is very undesirable because the model is consistently underforecasting or overforecasting, and thus errors accumulate. The problem of bias is often overlooked; however, in inventory control and customer service, bias is important as it can cause serious understocking or overstocking. In some other situations it is not a serious matter. Other important considerations in selecting a good model are *richness* (does the forecast resemble the past and expected future, capturing the essential behavior of the series?), parsimony (are there few parameters to estimate?), and understandability (can the forecast be readily interpreted and explained?). However, the most important characteristic of model validity is the ability to accurately forecast the future (i.e., low forecast errors). To better understand this concept, study forecasting error statistics.

FORECAST ERROR STATISTICS

When forecasting, a model is fitted to past data to help select a best model. Note, however, that the error in fitting past values is frequently lower than the error in forecasting future values; thus, we must be cautious in choosing one model over another. It is forecast errors that should be minimized, not the fitted errors. Most forecasting methods assume that an actual value equals some explained pattern plus some unexplained randomness embodied in the error term:

$$\text{Actual} = \text{pattern} + \text{error}$$

The model attempts to identify that pattern yielding a minimum of forecast errors. An error is that which cannot be explained. Thus, in mathematical terms, this basic error equation is the following:

$$e_t = Y_t - F_t \tag{23.1}$$

where e_t = forecast error for period t
Y_t = actual sales for period t
F_t = forecast sales for period t

To measure model accuracy, it is necessary to have statistics that reflect errors over time, not for just one period. There are several ways of measuring errors including the *sum of errors* (E), *mean error* (ME), *mean absolute deviation* (MAD), and *standard deviation of errors* (called the *residual standard error,* RSE), *mean percent error* (MPE), *mean absolute percent error* (MAPE). These are shown in Table 23.3 where two forecasts of the same demand are illustrated.

Measures of Forecasting Accuracy

Because errors can be positive or negative, the sum of the forecast errors SE$_t$ fluctuates around zero. It is used to test bias and to ascertain whether the forecast system is out of

TABLE 23.3   Error Statistics for Two Models

	Y_t	F_t	e_t	e_t^2	$|e_t|$	PE_t	$|PE_t|$	F_t	e_t	e_t^2	$|e_t|$	PE_t	$|PE_t|$
			Model 1 (unbiased)							Model 2 (biased)			
1	53	49	4	16	4	7.5	7.5	50	3	9	3	5.7	5.7
2	55	52	3	9	3	5.5	5.5	52	3	9	3	5.5	5.5
3	56	60	−4	16	4	−7.1	7.1	54	2	4	2	3.6	3.6
4	58	59	−1	1	1	−1.7	1.7	57	1	1	1	1.7	1.7
5	59	55	4	16	4	6.8	6.8	55	4	16	4	6.8	6.8
6	50	55	−5	25	5	−10.0	10.0	45	5	25	5	10.0	10.0
Sum			1	83	21	1.0	38.6		18	64	18	33.3	33.3
			ME =	MSE =	MAD =	MPE =	MAPE =		ME =	MSE =	MAD =	MPE =	MAPE =
Mean			.167	13.83	3.5	.167	6.4		3	10.67	3.0	5.6	5.6

control. The other error measure that is used to detect bias is the mean error (ME_t). Other measurements that estimate the dispersion of the errors about a mean of zero are the *mean absolute deviation* MAD_t and the *mean squared error* MSE_t. Measures that estimate the relative magnitude of the errors are the percent error (PE_t), mean percent error (MPE_t), and mean absolute percent error ($MAPE_t$). In the discussion that follows, it is assumed that there are n actuals and forecasts and therefore n error terms. The statistics in Table 23.4 can be used to measure model accuracy. (Table 23.4 gives the error measures using the results of Table 23.3.)

These measures of fit denote the following: the sum of errors SE for model 1, which is (1), is considerably less than that of model 2, which is (18). Thus, model 1 is less biased than model 2 in Eq. (23.3). Model 1 has a mean error ME of .167 while model 2 has a value of 3, again, confirmation of the slight bias in model 2. Thus, the errors of model 1 are centered on approximately zero. The mean absolute deviation MAD denotes that the absolute average error is 3.5 and 3.0, respectively; thus model 2 has less dispersion about zero than does model 1. If the distribution of errors is symmetrical, 50 percent of the errors are above this value and 50 percent are below. Note, however, that in general, absolute errors are not necessarily symmetrical even if the ME is zero. The sum of squared errors SSE and mean squared errors MSE provides similar information as that of the MAD—model 2 is more accurate than model 1 because lower values of these error measures denote higher accuracy. In addition, the residual standard error RSE measures the dispersion of values about the mean error of zero, in this case 3.72 versus 3.27 for models 1 and 2. Assuming that the errors are approximately normally distributed, the most common assumption, then the RSE can be used to generate the usual confidence intervals about the mean error of zero.

Other measures of Table 23.3 use percentages as intuitive measures of accuracy. The percentage error PE measures the ratio of the error to actual. The MPEs again confirm that model 2 is slightly biased. The average error for model 1 is 0.16 percent while that of model 2 is 5.6 percent. Just as is true for the mean error ME, the mean percentage error MPE varies about zero because positive errors are offset by negative errors. While the MPE is useful in detecting bias, remember that with no bias (i.e., an MPE of zero), the MPE is misleading when extremely high positive errors are offset by extremely low negative errors. In contrast, because absolute values are used in the MAPE, the positive and negative errors do not offset each other. However, the MAPEs confirm that model 1 is less accurate than model 2. Model 1 has an MAPE of 6.4 percent while that of model 2 is 5.6 percent. Thus, these relative measures confirm that model 2 is the more accurate model having slightly less error dispersion.

TABLE 23.4 Error Measures for Two Models

	Model 1	Model 2	Equation number
Sum of errors			
$\text{SE}_t = e_1 + e_2 + \cdots + e_n = \sum_{t=1}^{n} e_t$	1	18	(23.2)
Mean error			
$\text{ME}_t = \sum_{t=1}^{n} \dfrac{e_t}{n}$	.167	6	(23.3)
Mean absolute (error) deviation			
$\text{MAD}_t = \sum_{t=1}^{n} \dfrac{|e_t|}{n}$	3.5	3.0	(23.4)
Sum of squared errors			
$\text{SSE}_t = \sum_{t=1}^{n} e_t^2$	83	64	(23.5)
Mean squared error			
$\text{MSE}_t = \sum_{t=1}^{n} \dfrac{e_t^2}{n}$	13.83	10.67	(23.6)
Residual standard error			
$\text{RSE}_t = \sqrt{\sum \dfrac{e_t^2}{(n-1)}}$	$\sqrt{13.83} = 3.72$	$\sqrt{10.67} = 3.27$	(23.7)
Percentage error			
$\text{PE}_t = \left(\dfrac{Y_t - F_t}{Y_t}\right)(100)$ (period 1)	$\left(\dfrac{4}{53}\right)100 = 7.5$	$\left(\dfrac{3}{53}\right)100 = 5.7$	(23.8)
Mean percentage error			
$\text{MPE}_t = \sum_{t=1}^{n} \dfrac{\text{PE}_t}{n}$	.16	5.6	(23.9)
Mean absolute percentage error			
$\text{MAPE}_t = \sum_{t=1}^{n} \dfrac{|\text{PE}_t|}{n}$	6.4	5.6	(23.10)

Cautions in Using Percentages

When using percentages or ratios, one must be cautious because extremely small denominators in Eq. (23.8) yield extremely high percentages or ratios, sometimes in the millions (remember that the limit of division by zero is infinity). This problem is prevalent in forecasting whenever the actual value in a time period is very low. Thus, the use of percentage measures has to be monitored for low denominators. While one would hope that such low actual values are detected as outliers and therefore adjusted, frequently this is not the case.

Other Error Measures

There are many other measures of forecast error. Some measures are generated for making comparisons; some are calculated as part of the iterative process of identifying and diagnosing better models. These other error measures and references are listed in Table 23.5.

TABLE 23.5   Other Error Measures

Error statistic	See listed references
Autocorrelation (ACF): used to detect repeating patterns in a single series of errors	Later in this chapter
Cross-correlation (CCF): used to detect correlations between two series over time	Later in this chapter
Durbin-Watson statistic (DW): used to detect patterns in a series of errors	References 4, 5, 6, 7
Coefficient of determination $\overline{R}^2$: used to measure model accuracy	References 4, 5, 6, 7
Schwarz Bayesian information criteria (BIC): used to determine the best from competing models.	References 4, 5, 6, 7
Akaike information criteria (AIC): same use as BIC	References 4, 5, 6, 7
Theil's U statistic (U): used to compare accuracy of a model to a naive model	Reference 5
Demand filter: used to detect outliers	Later in this chapter
Trigg and Leach tracking signal (TST)	Later in this chapter
Cumsum tracking signal (TSC)	Later in this chapter
Backward cumulative tracking signal: tracking signals for out-of-control cumulative errors	Reference 2

Fitting Versus Forecasting

There is an important distinction between the process of fitting a model and forecasting with a model. The process of fitting involves using past data to select a model and its coefficients. In contrast, the process of forecasting involves using a model to forecast unknown future values. This simple sequence is (1) *fit* a model to past data and (2) use that model to *forecast* future data.

The Principle of Parsimony.   As is true in most forecasting situations, the fitted and forecast accuracies can differ. Sometimes the forecast accuracy is the same or better than the fitted accuracy. Unfortunately, most often, the forecast accuracy is inferior to that of

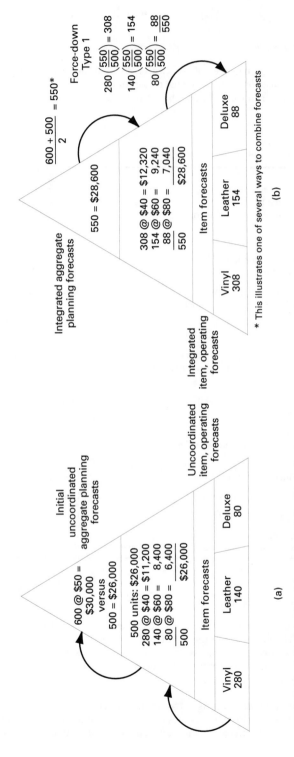

FIGURE 23.2 (a) Initial roll-up forecasts; and (b) force-down forecasts.

fitted accuracy, sometimes by very little and other times dramatically so. This occurs sometimes because one is misled and chooses a model that fits the past data best without regard to how well this model will fit in the future. When one has modeled patterns in the past that are not expected to repeat in the future, then one has *overfitted* the model. To avoid model overfitting, one should choose simple models that capture the essence of the repeating patterns of the future *and* past. This objective is related to the *principle of parsimony*. This principle states that a model that is simpler but nearly as accurate will always out-perform the more complex model when actually forecasting. Consequently, we should seek simple, but effective models, not complex models that fit the nonrepeating patterns of the past.

The best test of a forecast technique is to fit a model to some past data and then try it out on another group of past observations. This may not be possible if there is little past data available. If there is sufficient past history, then it is good practice to develop a forecast model on the first half and then test it on the second half. This is simple enough, but it seems as if few forecasters bother with this simple test. Other considerations in selecting a good model are *richness* (does the forecast resemble history, capturing the essential behavior of the series?), parsimony (are there few parameters to estimate?), and simplicity (can the forecast be readily interpreted and explained?).

Aggregation of Forecasts

If many items at different levels of detail are forecast, then an important consideration is whether the sum (aggregate) of the forecasts of a group of items is equal to the independent forecast of the group as a whole. If planning in an organization is integrated or if for some reason a forecast for the total is believed to be superior, it may be desirable to "force" the various subforecasts to equal the total, so that there is internal integrity. A number of approaches can be used to force consistent numbers up and down the hierarchy. Muir[11] and De Lurgio and Bhame[1] discuss some methods and special considerations. Figure 23.2 illustrates an example of the level of detail necessary to forecast in a hierarchical production-distribution environment. The method used in the figure is one of several that yield good, consistent forecasts. Because of variance reduction, forced forecasts are often better than individual item forecasting. The variations of one item are offset by variations of others.

PRACTICAL FORECASTING METHODS

The forecasting methods that have found widest application in production and inventory control utilize historical data. They are based on the assumption that the past history of a time series has information about future values. History tends to repeat itself in that patterns observed in the past will often recur in the future. By careful analysis of the past, one can observe these patterns and thus predict the future. A glossary of the symbols used in describing the methods is given at the end of the chapter.

The following sections present a variety of forecasting methods based on the general categories of moving average and regression analysis. In the following sections are presented some forecasting methods based on measuring how a time series is changing over time. Then an integrated approach to forecasting that considers error measurements, moving averages, equation fitting, and change measurements is presented.

Smoothing and Averages

Many common forecasting methods come under the general category of moving averages. Since most time-series experience variations in demand (called *errors* or *noise*), better estimates are generally possible by smoothing the history through averaging. These techniques *average,* or *smooth,* past data in some way. Remember that *smoothing* and *averaging* are synonyms.

Simple Averages

The general formula for calculating an average of n periods (where, for example, $n = 12$ for a 12-month average) is:

$$A = \frac{Y_1 + Y_2 + \cdots + Y_n}{n}$$

$$= \frac{\sum_{i=1}^{n} Y_i}{n} \tag{23.11}$$

where Y_i = sales in period i. Because of its ease of understanding and application, this method is used often. However, how should one determine n? Also, importantly, this method is not suitable when there are systematic, repeating patterns such as trend, cyclical, or seasonality in the data.

Simple Moving Averages

A *moving average* is an average taken many times over a period that moves with time. For instance, the forecast for a given month might be the average monthly sales over the pervious 6 months rather than the last 36 months. This moving of the base period makes the forecast respond more rapidly to demand than if one used the full 36 months in the database. In mathematical terms, a moving-average forecast is:

$$F_{t+1} = A_t = \frac{Y_t + Y_{t-1} + \cdots + Y_{t-n+2} + Y_{t-n+1}}{n}$$

$$= \frac{\sum_{i=t-n+1}^{n} Y_i}{n} \tag{23.12}$$

where A_t = average through period t

F_{t+1} = forecast for period $t + 1$

Y_t = sales in time period t

Y_{t-1} = sales in time period $t - 1$

In practice, the moving average for a period can be calculated by taking the previous average, adding the proportionate part of the latest value, and subtracting the proportionate part of the oldest observation as shown below:

$$A_t = A_{t-1} - \frac{Y_{t-n}}{n} + \frac{Y_t}{n} = A_{t-1} + \frac{Y_t - Y_{t-n}}{n} \tag{23.13}$$

In practice, there are two types of moving averages, *trailing* and *centered*. The formula above is based on a trailing moving average. However, for analytical purposes, such as correlating one time series with another, centered moving averages are used often. In this type of average, the referenced time period is the *middle period* of the average. For instance, the formula for a 3-month centered average is:

$$A_t = \frac{Y_{t+1} + Y_t + Y_{t-1}}{3} \tag{23.14}$$

Also, special adjustments are needed for centered moving averages for even-numbered periods. Obviously, centered moving averages cannot be used for direct forecasting because the actual values of period t and greater are unknown. For a stationary series (i.e., having low correction), a long-term moving average gives the best results. Here a 12-, 15-, or even 18-month moving average can be used. Examples of products suitable to this approach might be soap, flour, or washing machine parts.

However, when changes in demand level are expected, short-term moving averages are better models of these changes. Three-month moving averages might be better for products such as popular CD recordings, software, books, or dye (color) stocks. Common examples are stock prices and the weather, which are best predicted with a 1-day moving average (i.e., the weather tomorrow will be the same as today). Also, note that moving averages do not capture or model trends or seasonality of demand patterns.

Weighted Moving Averages

The simple moving average gives equal weights to past data. For instance, Eq. (23.12) can be written:

$$A_t = \frac{1}{n} Y_t + \frac{1}{n} Y_{t-1} + \cdots + \frac{1}{n} Y_{t-n+1} \tag{23.15}$$

where $1/n$ is the weight given to each value.

As is always true, the sum of weights is 1. With this average, each past period is assumed to be equally important. In many situations, especially if the time series is not stationary, it may be desirable to give more weight to the most recent data. For instance:

$$A_t = 0.7Y_t + 0.3Y_{t-1} \tag{23.16a}$$

might be used to make a weighted forecast based on two periods of history. In this case, more weight is given to Y_t, the more recent actual. In more general terms, this forecast formula can be written as:

$$A_t = \alpha Y_t + (1 - \alpha)Y_{t-1} \tag{23.16b}$$

where α is a weighting factor.

For an n periods average, the general equation is:

$$A_t = w_t Y_t + w_{t-1} Y_{t-1} + \cdots + w_{t-n+1} Y_{t-n+1}$$
$$= \sum_{i=1}^{n} w_{t-i+1} Y_{t-i+1} \tag{23.17}$$

where w_t is a weighting factor for time t, and:

$$w_t + w_{t-1} + \cdots + w_{t-n+1} = 1$$

In inventory forecasting, a particular type of weighted moving average, exponential smoothing, has been used extensively. Exponential smoothing is supported by an extensive body of literature and is discussed in detail later in this chapter.

Seasonal Factors

Where seasonality can be measured, better forecasts are possible by modeling this seasonal pattern. For series with regular, repetitive variations over L periods ($L = 12$ for seasonal monthly data), a *seasonal multiplier,* or *factor* (S), can be used in an equation such as:

$$SF_{t+1} = F_{t+1} S_{t+1} \qquad (23.18)$$

where SF_{t+1} = seasonally adjusted forecast
F_{t+1} = unadjusted (i.e., nonseasonal) forecast
S_{t+1} = seasonal multiplication factor

Alternatively, seasonal influences may be additive. Thus, forecasts can also be adjusted by an additive factor:

$$SF_{t+1} = F_{t+1} + S_{t+1} \qquad (23.19)$$

where S_{t+1} is the seasonal additive factor. The choice between Eqs. (23.18) and (23.19) depends on whether the seasonal influence is multiplicative—for example, June is 50 percent higher than the average month or additive where June is 50 units higher than the average month.

There are several methods for determining a seasonal adjustment factor, the most common method being the ratio of the actual demand in a period to the average demand over the full seasonal cycle. That is:

$$S_{t+1} = \frac{Y_{t+1-L}}{SA} \quad \text{(multiplicative)} \qquad \text{or} \qquad S_{t+1} = Y_{t+1-L} - SA \quad \text{(additive)}$$

where Y_{t+1-L} = demand in period $t+1-L$
SA = average demand during a full seasonal cycle
L = seasonal-length period

A seasonal factor obtained in this way is simply one estimate of the seasonality. More accurate seasonal factors can be estimated by averaging several estimates for a specific period (e.g., a specific month or quarter).

A major problem with the use of seasonal factors is that several seasons of history are needed to obtain reliable estimates. Further, the existence of trends, other cyclical factors, and random factors can complicate the determination of seasonal factors. Therefore, it is important to ascertain that seasonality really exists and that the use of seasonal forecasts will significantly improve the forecasts. Subjective estimates may exaggerate the magnitude of seasonality. Also, what appears to be seasonality may actually be induced by control mechanisms. See Harrison,[12] De Lurgio and Bhame,[1] or Brown[2] for a discussion of seasonality in forecasting and some methods for making seasonal estimates. There are several methods for testing the significance of seasonality, of which the analysis of variance is the most common. Of course, the simplest seasonal forecasting model is:

$$F_{t+1} = Y_{t+1-L}$$

$$F_{\text{July year 2}} = \text{Actual}_{\text{July year 1}}$$

That is, the forecast is the actual demand for the same period last year.

Census Method II

One of the best-developed moving-average techniques is the X-11 version of the Census Method II procedure. This method was developed by the Bureau of the Census to forecast economic time series. It is often called the *Shiskin decomposition method* (for Julius Shiskin, the statistician responsible for its development).[13] This method was an outgrowth of Census Method I, which was the computerization of standard methods of time-series analysis.

Method II takes fuller advantage of the electronic computer capabilities, adding many adjustments and other features. The method is not feasible without a computer because of the number of steps required. We do not give a detailed presentation here. Croxton and Cowden,[14] or Dagum,[15] and Makridakis, Wheelwright, and McGee[5] give detailed discussions. In any case, software for executing the method is available on a number of computer systems. Thus, the user is spared the necessity of doing the multitudinous calculations.

Basically, the method assumes a demand series Y composed of four components:

$$Y = T * C * S * I \tag{23.20a}$$

where T = trend component
C = cyclical component
S = seasonal component
I = irregular component

It decomposes the series into three components:

$$Y = TC * S * I \tag{23.20b}$$

where TC is the combined effect of trend and cycle components. The components are estimated by the following steps:

Step 1. Estimate TC component via a moving average of Y.

Step 2. Estimate SI as ratio of Y to TC.

Step 3. Adjust SI for extreme points (find extreme points and smooth by moving average).

Step 4. Estimate S by an averaging of SI.

Step 5. Estimate TCI by ratio of Y to S.

Step 6. Estimate I by ratio of TCI to TC.

Several steps are repeated more than once for refinements. The procedure provides models of trend, cyclical, and seasonal factors that can be the basis for a forecast. For example:

$$F_t = TC_t * S_{t-L}$$

where F_t is the forecast.

Plots of the trend-cycle curve are useful in tracking trends and estimating turning points. Figure 23.3 shows the raw, seasonally adjusted, and trend-cycle curves for a time series. Because of the heavy computer requirements, the method is not used routinely in automated forecasting systems. However, this is a cost-effective method for groups. It is also limited to products with sufficient history (at least 3 years of monthly data). Its principal uses in production and inventory planning are in monthly forecasting for seasonal product groups over the coming year and in analyzing trend and seasonal factors for use in other forecasting methods.

Extensions and adaptations to the X-11 procedure have been developed. Levenbach and Cleary[17] summarize the *Seasonal Adjustment—Bell Laboratories* (SABL) *decomposition program* that has alternative methods of smoothing, summarizing, and displaying data. In addition, the X-11 ARIMA is a popular method. See also Dagum[15] which develops the method called X-11 ARIMA method. Several X-11 computer codes are in the public domain.

Exponential Smoothing (Exponentially Weighted Moving Averages)

The use of exponential smoothing in inventory forecasting was introduced by R. G. Brown.[9] This method is a moving-average forecast which requires minimal data storage.

Basic Model. In essence, exponential smoothing is a moving average with declining weights for past actual values. The weights are set so that they decrease back in time. The basic formula of this method is:

$$\text{Forecast}_t = \alpha * \text{demand}_{t-1} + (1 - \alpha) * \text{forecast}_{t-1} \qquad (23.21a)$$

where the forecast of period t equals a weighted moving average of the past demand and its forecast and α (i.e., alpha) is a smoothing constant between 0 and 1. For illustrative purposes, assume the previous forecast (i.e., average for period $t - 1$) is 100 and the most recent demand (i.e., in period $t - 1$) is 120. A new average can be used as a forecast for the next period (i.e., period t). A particular firm wants to take advantage of the latest demand to generate a new forecast. How much weight should be assigned to the latest demand and how much to its forecast? The weight assigned to each is determined by α and logically its complement, $1 - \alpha$.

An alternative view of exponential smoothing can be made by rearranging the previous relationship as follows:

$$\text{Forecast}_t = \text{forecast}_{t-1} + \alpha(\text{demand}_{t-1} - \text{forecast}_{t-1}) \qquad (23.21b)$$

In this case the choice of alpha is determined by how much of the error should be added to (or subtracted from) the previous forecast.

As both of these formulas illustrate, the value of alpha determines how much weight to give to the new experience—the higher the value, the greater the weight. Using either formula, if alpha is 1, all the weight is given to the latest value while ignoring the old average. If alpha is 0, the latest actual value is ignored. Assuming an alpha of 0.25, the new forecast in this example is:

$$\text{Forecast}_t = 100 + 0.25(120 - 100) = 100 + 5 = 105$$

Mathematically, the relationship is:

$$F_t = \alpha Y_t + (1 - \alpha)F_{t-1} \qquad (23.22)$$

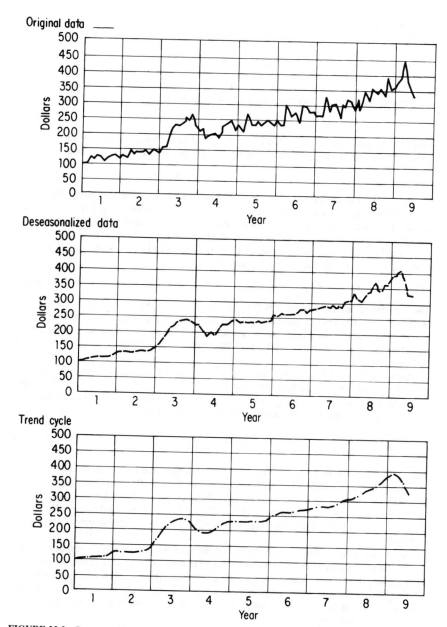

FIGURE 23.3 Decomposition of time series by the X-11 method.

where F_t = forecast for period t

F_{t-1} = exponentially smoothed average through $t - 1$ (previously calculated average)

Y_{t-1} = actual demand in current period t

α = smoothing constant ($0 \leq \alpha \leq 1$)

The preceding relationship can be rearranged to give:

$$F_t = F_{t-1} + \alpha(Y_{t-1} - F_{t-1}) \tag{23.23}$$

which is the basic equation of simple exponential smoothing. Then one can take this value of F_t as the old average in the calculation for the next time period. That is:

$$F_{t+1} = \alpha Y_t + (1 - \alpha)F_t$$

Thus, one of the principal advantages of a simple exponential smoothing over other types of moving averages is that only three values have to be carried from period to period. To make a forecast for the next period, all that is necessary is the value for α (the smoothing constant), the more recent actual information, and the last forecast.

When Eq. (23.23) is applied successively backward in time to some initial average F, the exponential smoothing model becomes:

$$F_{t+1} = \alpha Y_t + (1 - \alpha)Y_{t-1} + (1 - \alpha)^2 Y_{t-2} + \cdots + (1 - \alpha)^{t-1}Y_1 + (1 - \alpha)^t F_0 \quad (23.24)$$

The *exponential* part of the name is derived from the exponents of $(1 - \alpha)$. Since α is less than 1, the coefficients of the past-demand terms decrease going back in time. Since $(1 - \alpha)$ is the factor that causes the coefficients to decrease, $(1 - \alpha)$ is sometimes called the *discount rate*. Also the coefficients of Eq. (23.24) sum to 1, so the model is a weighted moving average.

As we can see when comparing Eq. (23.15) and Eq. (23.24), the weighting or smoothing factor is related to n, the number of periods in a moving average. Since the relationship is inverse ($\alpha \sim 1/n$), small α values should be used where large n values are effective. Brown relates α and n using the approximate formula:

$$\alpha = \frac{2}{n + 1} \tag{23.25}$$

Hence, if a 12-month moving average were used, then the last 12 past values have a weight of 1/12, or 0.08333 (and 0 for values older than that), and the equivalent exponential smoothing model would have a smoothing constant of $2/(12 + 1) = 0.154$. The weights in Eq. (23.24) would be 0.154, 0.130, 0.110, 0.0932, and so on, decreasing exponentially. Figure 23.4 illustrates the weights for some representative smoothing constants.

Another way of understanding the significance of the smoothing constant is to compare what proportion of the total weight is given to a specific number of periods. A value of 0.5 gives over 90 percent of the total weight to data from the last 4 periods, whereas a value of 0.1 gives the same proportion of weight to data from the last 22 periods. The necessary information to start such an exponential smoothing forecasting system includes the following:

1. Some initial estimate Y_0 (usually an average of historical data)

2. A value for the smoothing constant α

Because of the difficulty of choosing alpha and because of the possibility that varying values of alpha may be appropriate at different times, several methods have been

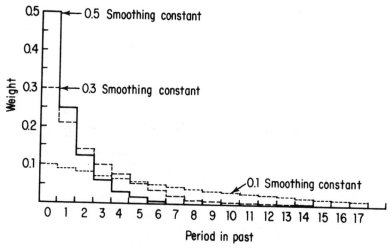

FIGURE 23.4 Exponential smoothing.

developed that allow alpha to change based on certain criteria. Some of these methods are discussed later. Bretschneider and Gorr[18] illustrate the relationships of some of the newer approaches.

The initial estimate can be one data point or an average. Because of decreasing weight, the influence of the initial estimate on the forecast decreases with time; therefore, the initial choice is not overly critical. One way of starting a system is to assume an alpha of 1 for the first period (all the weight is applied to the only piece of history Y_0, an alpha of $\frac{1}{2}$ after the second period, an alpha of $\frac{1}{3}$ after the third period, and so on until the alpha is no longer greater than the long-term desired smoothing constant. In mathematical terms:

$$\alpha = \frac{1}{n} \quad \text{if } \alpha > \alpha' \quad \text{otherwise} \quad \alpha = \alpha' \qquad (23.26)$$

where n = number of periods of history

α' = long-term (steady-state) smoothing constant

As with the number of periods included in a moving average, the smoothing constant in exponential smoothing can be varied by series type. For a relatively random, level series, α could range from 0.1 to 0.15, corresponding to 18- to 12-period moving averages, while for series with sharp level changes such as ramp and step functions as in Fig. 23.5, α may vary from 0.2 to 0.5, equivalent to 9- to 3-period moving averages.

Low alphas are often appropriate with shorter periods (day or weeks, compared to quarters or years) because they have relatively greater fluctuations than longer periods. Likewise, individual SKUs may have greater relative fluctuations than aggregate items and so call for smaller smoothing constants.

The figure shows the response of the simple exponential smoothing model to several standardized inputs. The *impulse* might represent the effect of random noise (e.g., large outlier). The simple model reacts proportionally to α in the next period and then resumes tracking the true value. The *step* and ramp examples illustrate *nonstationary* (i.e., nonconstant mean) *series*. The speed of the response of the simple model is directly proportional to the value of alpha. In the case of *ramp* or *trend,* the simple

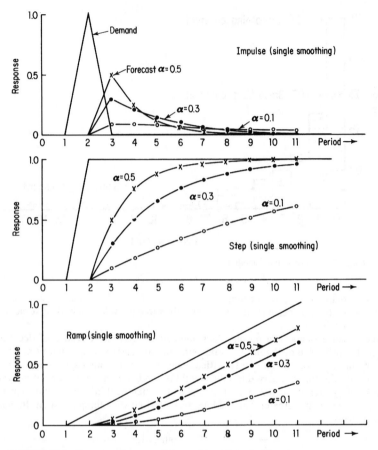

FIGURE 23.5 Response of exponential smoothing of standard inputs.

model eventually has the correct slope but always lags the true value, the lag being inversely proportional to alpha.

A careful examination of the response to various inputs and smoothing constants suggests that if α could be adjusted or updated, the model might more closely track the underlying series. Several different approaches to adapting alpha have been researched and will be discussed later in this chapter.

Multiple Exponential Smoothing

Because the simple exponential smoothing model lags when there is trend and seasonality, higher-order models have been developed and used. The most popular approaches of higher-order models are those developed by Brown,[16] Holt, and Winters.[19]

Brown's Double Exponential Smoothing.[16] Brown's double exponential smoothing model computes the difference between single and double smoothed values and adds this to the single smoothed value together with an adjustment for current trend. Brown's model is implemented with the following set of equations (S_t' denotes a single smoothed value, and S_t'' denotes the double smoothed value):

$$F_{t+m} = a_t + b_t m \qquad (23.27)$$

where F_{t+m} = m period ahead forecast
$\quad a_t$ = smoothed value as of time t
$\quad b_t$ = estimated trend
$\quad m$ = number of periods into the future

$$S_t' = \alpha Y_t + (1 - \alpha) S_t' - 1 \qquad (23.28)$$

$$S_t'' = \alpha S_t' + (1 - \alpha) S_t'' - 1 \qquad (23.29)$$

$$a_t = S_t' + (S_t' - S_t'') = 2S_t' - St_t'' \qquad (23.30)$$

$$b_t = \frac{\alpha}{1 - \alpha} (S_t' - S_t'') \qquad (23.31)$$

Holt's Two-Parameter Trend Model. Holt's two-parameter double exponential smoothing model, as the name implies, differs from Brown's model in that it allows the use of a second smoothing constant to separately smooth the trend. Holt's model further adjusts each smoothed value for the trend of the previous period before calculating the new smoothed value. Holt's two-parameter trend model can be implemented with the following set of equations:

$$F_{t+m} = S_t + b_t m \qquad (23.32)$$

where F_{t+m} = m period ahead forecast
$\quad S_t$ = smoothed value as of time t
$\quad b_t$ = estimated trend
$\quad m$ = number of periods into the future

$$S_t = \alpha Y_t + (1 - \alpha)(S_{t-1} + b_{t-1}) \qquad (23.33)$$

where α = normal smoothing constant.

$$b_t = \delta(S_t - S_{t-1}) + (1 - \delta)b_{t-1} \qquad (23.34)$$

where δ = trend smoothing constant.

Note in Eq. (23.33) that the smoothed value from period $t - 1$ is adjusted by the trend from that period. This eliminates some of the natural lag of the process. The normal smoothing constant α is then used to adjust the resulting value for the error in the previous period. The second smoothing constant δ is used to smooth out the trend in Eq. (23.34). This has the effect of removing some of the random error that would otherwise be reflected in the trend adjustment.

There are two basic questions to be answered with Holt's model. These are: What smoothing constant(s) should be used? and how should the exponential smoothing process be initialized? In starting the forecasting process, initial values are needed for both S_1 and b_1. For S_1, Y_1 can be used, which is the observed value for period 1. The initial trend estimate is a little more difficult. Some possible values are the difference between the first two observed values, some average of the observed slope for the first several periods, or an estimate of the series slope from a plot of the data. Any of these methods may work well if the data are consistent from period to period. However, if the data are not well behaved, that is, they show a significant drop at some point when the general trend is upward, inclusion of such irregularities in the initial slope estimate can require a lengthy period of time to overcome their impact. In such instances, it would be better to estimate the longer-range trend slope from the data plot.

Winters's Modified Model.   Winters developed a model to account for seasonality and trend while still using relatively simple exponential smoothing techniques.[19] It consists of a multiplicative seasonality factor and an additive trend factor, each smoothed separately. This model is an extension of the Holt's two-parameter model and is often referred to as the *Holt-Winters model*. Its form is shown in Eq. (23.35). The forecast for *m* periods in the future is:

$$F_{t+m} = (S_t + mb_t) S_{t-L+m} \qquad (23.35)$$

$$S_t = \alpha \frac{Y_t}{I_{t-L}} + (1 - \alpha)(S_{t-1} + b_{t-1}) \qquad (23.36)$$

where I_{t-1} = seasonal factor
$\quad\ b_{t-1}$ = trend factor

The trend factor is updated by:

$$b_t = \delta(S_t - S_{t-1}) + (1 - \delta) b_{t-1} \qquad (23.37)$$

where δ = smoothing constant ($0 \leq \delta \leq 1$). The seasonal factor is updated by:

$$I_t = \gamma \frac{Y_t}{S_t} + (1 - \gamma) I_{t-L} \qquad (23.38)$$

where γ = smoothing constant ($0 \leq \gamma \leq 1$) and, as before, L = length of the season. One advantage of using seasonal and trend factors in an exponential smoothing model is that one can forecast one or more seasons, often with great accuracy.

With this model, the problem of choosing a smoothing factor is threefold, since theoretically values for α, δ, and γ must be selected. In practice, however, since trend and seasonality are not subject to step changes very often, smoothing factors between 0.1 and 0.2 are often assigned based on experience. Some popular software has been programmed to select the best smoothing constants from 27 different combinations of the three parameters. Finally, many software packages choose the optimal parameters, based on the minimization of the mean squared error. However, when high values of smoothing constants (i.e., greater than 0.6) are selected, forecasts can become unstable when outliers occur.

Outliers and Tracking Signals.   In general, the selection of a smoothing constant should be based on which constant gives the lowest error by one of the statistics mentioned earlier, typically, the mean squared error. In practice, however, a plot of mean squared errors versus the smoothing constant often gives a curve with a flat minimum, as in Fig. 23.6. Thus, at times several values of smoothing constants yield nearly identical results.

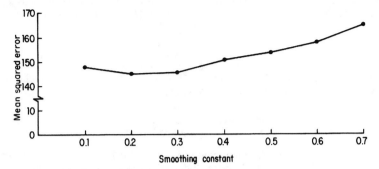

FIGURE 23.6 Error related to smoothing constant.

Exponential smoothing can be used to generate a type of mean absolute deviation using smoothed values. Its calculation is:

$$\text{MAD}_t = \eta|e_t| + (1 - \eta)\text{MAD}_{t-1} \tag{23.39}$$

where MAD_t = mean absolute deviation at period t
η = smoothing constant $(0 \leq \eta \leq 1)$
$|e_t|$ = absolute value of e_t

In most practical systems, $\eta = 0.1$ (assuming no radical swings in absolute deviation).

Another related statistic is the *smoothed-average deviation* (SAD). It is calculated similarly as:

$$\text{SAD}_t = \eta e_t + (1 - \eta)\text{SAD}_{t-1} \tag{23.40}$$

Here again a practical value of η is 0.1.

In measuring the suitability of a particular model for a particular time series in a multiple forecasting environment, the assumption is made that the errors actually are independent random values, normally distributed with zero mean. If this assumption is granted, then control limits can be estimated for these errors. To do this, some measure of how the system is following or tracking the actual data is needed. If the above assumption is made, MAD can be shown to approximate (or at least be proportional to) the root-mean-square error, and it could be included as one factor in such a tracking signal. If the random-error assumption is correct, the sum of such errors SE_t should also oscillate around zero. If, however, some change has occurred in the basic character of the series, SE_t will accumulate above or below zero. Therefore, the ratio of Eq. (23.41) will measure the relative cumulative error:

$$\text{TSC}_t = \frac{\text{SE}_t}{\text{MAD}_t} \tag{23.41}$$

This ratio is commonly called a *tracking signal cumulative* (TSC). The most commonly used control-limit values are ±4.0. If TS passes these limits for, say, two consecutive periods, SE is reset to zero. If, within some short time (say, 6 time units), the same control value is again violated, then it is likely that the basic series has undergone a change in character. If no further violations are observed in this period, it is assumed that some short-term aberration affected the series. In a similar way, the tracking signal using the ratio of MAD and SAD (called the *tracking signal MAD*) can be calculated by:

$$\text{TSM}_t = \frac{\text{SAD}_t}{\text{MAD}_t} \tag{23.42}$$

Here the theoretical limit of the ratio is ± 1.0. When errors are not autocorrelated, the approximate ± 2 *sigma tracking signal limit* (TSML) is:

$$\text{TSML} = \frac{2.4\eta}{[\eta(2-\eta)]^{0.5}} \tag{23.43}$$

For $\eta = 0.1$, this is ± 0.55. A similar control-by-exception system to that above would serve to warn of changes in the characteristics of the series. The tracking signals above should be used with another controlled device, the demand filter, Eq. (23.44).

   Demand filters.   The *demand filter* is the simple ratio between a recent error and either the MAD or *residual standard error* (RSE). This ratio is used in a simple t test of an error. A ratio above 2 or 3 RSE is indicative of an outlier:

$$t_t = \frac{e_t}{\text{RSE}_t} \tag{23.44}$$

Adaptive models.   Research in exponential smoothing forecasting systems has led to the development of models in which the smoothing factor is not constant but is adjusted based on current performance of the model. Some representative adaptive systems that have been used in actual situations are discussed here.

Trigg and Leach modification.   A simple modification of single smoothing has been proposed by Trigg and Leach.[20] They point out that since the SAD/MAD ratio has limits of ± 1.0, its absolute value could be used directly as an adaptive smoothing constant. In their evaluation of the response of such a system, they show good results for step and ramp functions. The response, or rather overreaction, to impulses suggests that this method should not be used where large random fluctuation may be encountered. They also suggest that, because of the magnification of effect, this adaptive α can be used only in the equation for single exponential smoothing. Simulation done by Gardner and Dannenbring have shown that trend-adjusted models are more accurate and stable than adaptive models under a wide variety of situations.[21]

BIVARIATE AND MULTIVARIATE MODELS

Many series have patterns correlated with time or with some other series. These correlations may yield mathematical curves or relationships that can be used for forecasting. The most commonly used statistical approach to curve fitting involves *regression by maximum-likelihood criterion*. Other chapters cover this subject, so it is only discussed briefly here. A more detailed presentation is given by Draper and Smith,[23] Pindyck and Rubinfeld,[25] and others.[4–6]

   Curves fitted by maximum-likelihood regression have the property of least squares. The fundamental concept of least squares involves selecting the coefficients of an equation so that the sum of the squares of the deviations of the fitted values from the actual values is minimized.

Least-Squares Time-Series Analysis

Two types of least-squares curve fitting are commonly used in forecasting systems. In one type, called *autoregression,* the predicted value is related to past values of another variable. In the other, the predicted value is related to time. Least-squares methods are most commonly used to fit these types of curves; however, other techniques are also used, and some are mentioned here. Fortunately, regression analysis software is very common in spreadsheets, and other data analysis packages are available for almost any computer.

Autoregression. The basic concept of autoregression is to correlate a current value of a time series to previous values. The most obvious relationship of this type is $Y_{t+1} = Y_t$; that is, the forecast is the last value of the series. Other common relationships are:

$$Y_{t+1} = Y_t + \theta_0 + e_t \qquad \text{where } \theta_0 \text{ represents a trend}$$

$$Y_{t+1} = \theta_0 + \phi_1 Y_t + e_t \qquad \text{constant and autoregressive term}$$

$$Y_{t+1} = \theta_0 + \phi_1 Y_t + \phi_2 Y_{t-1} + e_t \qquad \begin{array}{l}\text{constant and second-order autoregressive} \\ \text{terms, i.e., } Y_t \text{ and } Y_{t-1}\end{array}$$

The general linear autoregressive equation is:

$$Y_t = \theta_0 + \sum_{i=1}^{p} \phi_i Y_{t-i} + e_t \qquad (23.45)$$

where p = the number of past-value terms (order of autoregression).

The coefficients may be obtained by the linear multiple-regression techniques; however, frequently a nonlinear least-squares procedure should be used when the least-squares errors are themselves highly autocorrelated. Seasonality can be introduced into an autoregression function by having one of the terms include an actual value from the previous seasonal cycle.

Time-Dependent Correlations. The spectrum of possible models in which a time series can be related to time is limited by the forecaster's ability to formulate the model and solve for its coefficients. A discussion of some of the more common models follows.

Linear. The most familiar model is the linear, or straight-line, model:

$$Y_t = a + bt + e_t \qquad (23.46)$$

In this equation, the coefficient b represents the linear trend. The equations (called *normal equations*) for determining the coefficients are easily applied using spreadsheets. This model may also be used for a nonlinear series if the data can be transformed to a linear form. For instance, if:

$$Y_t' = a + bt + e_t$$

where Y_t' is some transformation of Y_t such as taking logarithms or some power transformation such as squares or square roots. For example:

$$Y_t' = \log(Y_t) = a + bt + e_t \qquad (23.47)$$

With this model projections can be made by extrapolating the model in time beyond the given data set. Care must be taken in this extrapolation, however, because the confidence interval widens as the curve projects in time. Figure 23.7 is an example of a fitted curve that is projected in time.

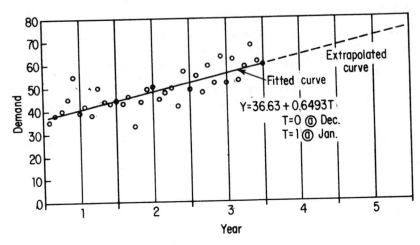

FIGURE 23.7   Extrapolation of fitted linear curve.

Polynomials.   Polynomials in time are sometimes helpful but are much more sensitive to minor fluctuations in data. The general equation is:

$$Y_t = a_0 + \sum_{i=1}^{M} a_i t^i \tag{23.48}$$

where M = number of time-dependent terms. If $M = 1$, then the linear Eq. (23.46) of the previous section results. If $M = 2$, then a second-order equation of the form $Y = a_0 + a_1 t + a_2 t^2$ results. The second-degree equation can be used if there is accelerating trend. For example, first, second, and third-order polynominals are:

$$Y_t = a_0 + a_1 t$$

$$Y_t = a_0 + a_1 t + a_2 t^2$$

$$Y_t = a_0 + a_1 t + a_2 t^2 + a_3 t^3$$

The coefficients of each term can be determined by the linear multiple-regression techniques shown in Chapter 35. Note that the term *linear* here refers to the model structure and not the variables. Care must be taken in using these equations as they can give extremely unrealistic forecasts in long-range projections because exponents above 2 will yield extremely high or low values for high values of t. Their use should be based on a thorough appraisal of the past data, and long-term forecasts should be checked for reasonableness.

Trigonometric Relationships.   Trigonometric relationships such as:

$$Y_t = a \sin \omega t + b \cos \omega t \tag{23.49}$$

can be effective methods for fitting seasonal or cyclical patterns. These methods are commonly called *Fourier series analysis* and are used in several item-level forecasting systems. They can be used to represent cyclic, or recurrent, patterns when these appear to be the dominant factors. The parameter $\underline{\omega}$ gives the period of the cycle. These methods are more fully developed in De Lurgio and Bhame,[1] and Brown.[16] As mentioned, these are particularly effective in modeling the repeating patterns of seasonality.

Exponential Relationships. One family of commonly used curves involves the use of the exponential function *e*, or exp. The most common equation is:

$$Y_t = a \exp bt = ae^{bt} \tag{23.50}$$

where *a* and *b* are coefficients and *e* is the base of the natural logarithm ($e = 2.71828...$). This equation assumes that the series is growing at a constant rate of exp $(b) - 1$. For a growing series, *b* will be positive; for a decaying series, negative.

This equation may be linearized by the natural logarithm transformation:

$$\log Y_t = \log a + bt \tag{23.51}$$

Hence the formulas for the linear model may be used to obtain a fit by substituting log Y_t for Y_t. The resulting coefficients are log *a* and log *b*. Figure 23.8 is an example of a fitted curve. This curve can also be expressed by:

$$Y_t = aB^t \tag{23.52}$$

where $B = \exp b$. The linearization form is then:

$$\log Y_t = \log a + t \log B \tag{23.53}$$

These constant-rate growth curves are primarily for trend forecasting. Care, however, should be exercised in using them for too long a forecast horizon.

Technological Growth Curves

S-Type Growth Curves. A family of curves has the characteristic that systematic variations in the rate of change is of prime consideration in modeling growth. As is common in many systems, the growth rate declines as the level approaches a limit. These curves are sometimes called *S curves* because they usually start with a small slope (when plotted on constant scale paper), sweep upward in the midarea, and flatten out as they approach a maximum value. Their first stage represents a period of experimentation; the second stage, the rapid exploitation of the product; and the third, the leveling off of growth with the saturation of demand. They are also sometimes referred to as *asymptotic growth curves* because each approaches an upper limit. Such curves are very important in modeling product and technology life cycles as developed in Martino[24] and Girifalco.[25]

The two most common types of *S* curves are the *Gompertz curve* (see Fig. 23.9):

$$Y_t = ka^{b^t} \tag{23.54}$$

and the *Pearl-Reed*, or *logistics, curve:*

$$Y_t = \frac{1}{k + ab^t} \tag{23.55}$$

For the Gompertz curve, *k* is the upper limit. For the logistics curve the upper limit is $1/k$. Their main difference is the point of inflection, the Gompertz reaching the inflection earlier.

Since neither curve can be linearized directly, they cannot be solved directly by linear-regression techniques. One approach to solution involves splitting the historical

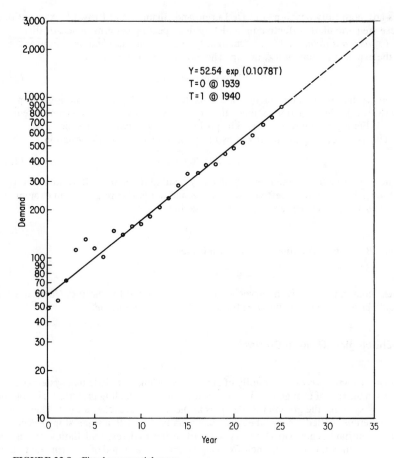

FIGURE 23.8   Fitted exponential curve.

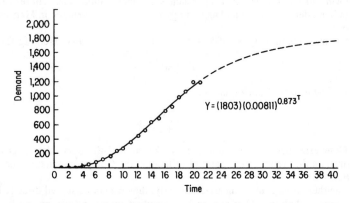

FIGURE 23.9   Fitted Gompertz curve.

data of N values into three equal parts and taking partial totals of the appropriate function of the data. For the Gompertz, the function is the natural logarithm:

$$S_1 = \sum_{i=1}^{N} \log Y_i \qquad S_2 = \sum_{i=N_1+1}^{N_2} \log Y_i \qquad S_3 = \sum_{i=N_2+1}^{N} \log Y_i$$

where $N_1 = N/3$ and $N_2 = 2N/3$. For the logistics, the function is the reciprocal $1/Y_i$.

The coefficients for the Gompertz can then be obtained by solving the following equations:

$$b^{N_1} = \frac{S_3 - S_2}{S_2 - S_1}$$

$$\log a = \frac{(S_2 - S_1)(b - 1)}{(b)(b^{N_1} - 1)^2}$$

$$\log k = \frac{S_1 \times S_3 - (S_2)^2}{(S_1 + S_3 - 2 \times S_2)N_1}$$

For the logistics, a and k are substituted for $\log a$ and $\log k$, respectively, in the above equations.

Another approach for determining the Gompertz curve coefficients is to first transform the equation to the form:

$$\log Y_t = \log k + b^t \log a \tag{23.56}$$

Then select an arbitrary value of b (some value between 0 and 1), and take a regression between $\log Y_t$ and b^t, calculating the sum of squares of the residuals or errors. Repeat, using other values of b, until a value is obtained that gives the lowest sum-of-the-squares values. The values of k and a are coefficients obtained by this regression.

For the Pearl-Reed model, first transform the equation to:

$$\log \frac{1 - kY_t}{Y_t} = \log a + t \log b \tag{23.57}$$

Then select a value of k (an approximate upper bound on k is the reciprocal of the highest data value), and take a regression of the left-hand term of the equation versus t. Repeat the iterative process with different values of k until no significant reduction in the sum of the squares of the residuals is obtained.

Care must be taken in the use of fitted curves. Data should include history of the item from its inception. There should be reason to believe the growth rate is varying with time and that the series is apt to reach a saturation point. For a fuller discussion of the use and fitting of these curves, see Croxton and Cowden,[14] Cleary and Levenbach,[26] Girifalco,[25] and Martino[24] who discuss general types of growth curves useful for long-term and technological forecasting.

Use of Regression Models

Some points need to be emphasized on the use of a fitted curve, particularly in regard to data selection and model projection. A careful perusal of the time-series data before regression analysis may eliminate causes of later difficulty. When a rough plot of the data is examined to determine a tentative relationship, outlier data should be investigated, then adjusted, eliminated, or smoothed. Such data might be early information with an obviously different trend or individual points that are outliers.

The base period (*time span* on which the regression is based) of the historical data can have a major influence on the coefficients obtained. The inclusion of one additional data value may give different coefficients if that data point is unusually high or low. To get away from the ambiguity of base-period selection, although not completely away from the problems, a moving–base-period fit can be used. For example, a regression may be done each period by using the last n periods as the base period. Another approach to selecting a base period is to take a regression for all possible base periods and then measure the fitted and forecast errors as discussed in DeLurgio.[4]

When regression models are projected into the future as a forecasting mechanism, two major factors should be considered in regard to the confidence placed in the extrapolated points. First, how good is the model at fitting the past? This can be judged by measures such as those discussed in the error statistics section. Even if the correlation is excellent, extrapolation of the fit is into an area of widening confidence limits (Fig. 23.10). A second factor to consider is the relationship of the forecast extrapolation period to the base period. Intuitively, you should not project more than one period if you only had two periods' data. (Hopefully, you would not project anything at all!) Similarly, if you had a model that gave a good fit for a long period (60 to 96 periods), you would project it for 6 to 12 periods with reasonable confidence. You might be more confident still if you had used 48 periods (of 60) to build the model and had good results predicting the remaining 12 points of the history.

In using curves, especially growth curves, for longer-range forecasting, it is helpful to compare the curve for an item with the curve for the set of which the item is a part, for instance, comparing the curve for apple sales and the curve for fruit sales. It is quite possible to fit curves in which the growth of apple sales is greater than the growth of fruit sales so that in some future period the forecast demand for apples is greater than the forecast demand for fruit. Judgment is continually called for in forecasting.

The discussion so far has assumed, for the most part, the use of linear-regression techniques in curve fitting. This approach uses a least-squares criterion. While it often

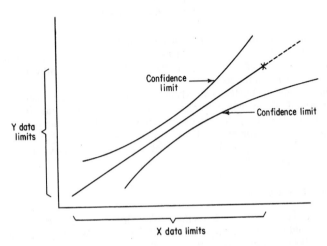

FIGURE 23.10 Confidence limits of fitted curve.

is, this criterion is not necessarily always the best. For one thing, least-squares fits may give undue weight to unusually high or low values (outliers). As a result, a number of other mathematical approaches to curve fitting are used. Two of these approaches come under the headings of "linear programming" and "nonlinear programming."

Linear Programming Curve Fitting

Techniques of linear programming may be used to fit linear-coefficient curves by criteria other than least squares. Linear programming techniques are well developed, and software packages are readily available in spreadsheets. The trick is to formulate the criterion and its restrictions in such a way that a standard linear programming algorithm can be used to determine the coefficients. One criterion amenable to this approach is the minimization of the sum of absolute errors. To use this criterion for the linear curve $Y = a + bt$, each historical value is assumed to be determined by:

$$Y_i = a + (b - c)i + d_i - g_i \qquad (23.58)$$

where a, b, c, d, and g are coefficients. The latter two coefficients represent the error and thus are different for each period. The doubling of the coefficients (b and c) is necessary because of the nonnegativity constraint in linear programming. If only positive coefficients are desired, c would be removed. A similar argument explains the double-error terms d_i and g_i. In both cases, only one coefficient will be greater than zero for any solution.

The linear programming model is then:

$$\text{Minimize} \sum_{i=1}^{N} (g_i + d_i) \qquad (23.59)$$

subject to the above set of equations and to all coefficients being greater than or equal to zero. Another criterion is to minimize the maximum deviation (minimax). The objective here is to minimize d subject to all coefficients being greater than or equal to zero, where d is the maximum deviation. The equations for the linear curve are:

$$Y_i = a + (b - c)i + d - f_i$$

$$Y_i = a + (b - c)i - d + g_i$$

Again, double coefficients are necessary where both positive and negative coefficients are possible. Also note the necessity for doubling the number of equations to allow for a negative maximum deviation. The particular nature of this criterion calls for extra judgment in the use of curves derived from it for forecasting.

Another feature of regression by linear programming is the ability to add constraints to any variable. As noted, the coefficients can be selectively limited to positive values. In addition, the coefficient values may be bounded, the regression line may be forced through the origin (0, 0) by elimination of the free term a, or any other constraint of the variables that can be expressed as a linear inequality may be used. This makes the two regression schemes based on linear programming very flexible indeed. Klein[27] and Bracken and McCormick[28] give a more detailed discussion on curve fitting by linear programming.

Nonlinear Programming Curve Fitting. For the fitting of curves in which the coefficients are nonlinear and also for cases where a nonlinear criterion is used, several nonlinear programming techniques have been used. See Bracken and McCormick,[28] Wilde and Beightler,[29] and Draper and Smith[22] for an introductory discussion. Nonlinear techniques are more complicated mathematically and are not as standardized as linear programming, so we do not delve into them here.

Causal Models

Causal models are a subset of multivariate models that attempt to model true cause-and-effect relationships.[4,23,30] When developing causal models, it is important to distinguish between two concepts, prediction and explanation. In forecasting, we are almost always interested in the model that predicts most accurately. However, causal models are valued for their ability to explain the change in one variable as a function of a change in another variable. Many forecasting studies have shown that simple predictive models provide more accurate forecasts than more complex causal models. Thus, one might ask why, in the context of forecasting, are we interested in causal models?

Almost every time series is influenced by many causal factors, although it may not be known exactly how. The most rigorous models are those modeling the cause-and-effect relationships between the forecast variable and causal factors. Construction of such models involves examining the system for the true underlying causes for demand and then building equations composed of the relationships between the forecast variable and the causative factors. Such models are expensive; consequently, the value of the forecast has to justify the effort.

For cases in which explicit causative models are not feasible and for cases in which causal relationships are believed to exist but their exact nature is not known, regression techniques are commonly used to fit good predictive equations that are not purported to be true cause-and-effect relationships. These techniques are used also to relate time series in which "nonsense" correlations exist. That is, one series may be useful in predicting another even though there is no theoretical basis for the relationship. In such cases one should be cautious in using these relationships, but they are nonetheless useful on some occasions. The relationship should be periodically reevaluated to see whether it is still valid.

Linear Least Squares.   Causal techniques utilize past relationships between the forecast variable and one or more causal factors. A simple example is the fitting of the curve:

$$Y_t = a + bX_t + e_t \tag{23.60}$$

by least-squares techniques. Here Y_t is the value of a time series for period t. For this equation, the equations to determine the parameters are:

$$a = \frac{\sum X^2 \sum Y - \sum X \sum XY}{n \sum X^2 - (\sum X)^2}$$

$$b = \frac{\sum Y - na}{\sum X} \tag{23.61}$$

where the summations are over periods 1 to n. The value of the variable X_t may be smoothed or adjusted before the fit is made.

Any number of variables can be included in a regression relationship. Likewise, more than one term could be included for each variable (a variable could have both a linear and squared term). A problem with using this approach is determining which variables and terms to include. Stepwise regression techniques that selectively analyze the significance of each term are helpful in determining which factors and terms to include in the equation. However, stepwise methods are inadequate when the purpose of the study is to fit causal models. Methods for fitting multiple-variable and multiple-term equations are discussed in Chapter 35.

When forecasting with Eq. (23.60), it is assumed that future values of Z_t are available. This situation is generally not possible; nevertheless, forecasted values, with their increased uncertainties, are often available, particularly when provided by government or research agencies. In this latter situation, however, the relationship might better be identified by using the historical forecasts rather than the actual values. When many variables are involved, such as in the national economy, it is necessary to use sets of regression equations (which are not necessarily linear). Many techniques in the field of econometrics have been developed to handle sets of simultaneous equations.[4,23,30,34]

Leading Series. Rather than relating two coincident variables, it is advantageous to relate a forecast variable to past values of the independent variable, such as:

$$Y_t = a + bX_{t-3} + e_t \tag{23.62}$$

This is a *lead-lag relationship*. As with the equations mentioned in the preceding section, multiple variables and terms may be included in the equation. Both current and leading variables may be included in the same equation.

With this type of relationship, we must find useful *leading series*. The Department of Commerce has extensively studied time series that affect the national economy in its search for leading series. It publishes the commonly referenced *Index of Leading Indicators* plus many other time series that might be leading indicators. Also many computer databases have series that can be tested for lead traits. Recently many governmental, nongovernmental, public, and private institutions have provided econometric and industry-specific data on information networks such as the Internet and CD-ROMs at no cost.

Correlation Measures, ACFs, and CCFs

The question of how to detect lead-lag relationships is one that has been asked for at least a century. Earlier textbooks suggested the use of graphs on tracing paper where one series is superimposed on another. Fortunately, we have the computer-age equivalent of this through the use of the extensive graphics capabilities in spreadsheet and statistical software. Correlation coefficients, as developed in Chapter 35, are important tools in forecasting. The correlation coefficient measures the degree of association between two variables. The *autocorrelation coefficient* (ACF) measures the degree of association between Y_t and Y_{t-k} where k can vary over any finite range, but it is often analyzed from 1 to two or three multiples of the seasonal length. For example, with monthly data, a high correlation of Y_t with Y_{t-1} might indicate a trend or *random walk* in the series. A high correlation of Y_t with Y_{t-12} would most likely indicate seasonality in the series. Several references develop the use of ACFs and CCFs in greater detail.[4-8,23,34]

An equally powerful correlation measure is the *cross-correlation function* (CCF), which is used to detect correlations between two series over time. The CCF(k) measures the correlation between values of Y_t and Y_{t-k}. For example, if the CCF(3) is statistically significant while other CCFs are not, then this is indicative of the relationship expressed in Eq. (23.62).

CHANGE ANALYSIS

In forecasting, we have an interest not only in the current level of the variable but also in how the level of the variable is changing over time. Measurement and analysis of differences, rates of change, growth rates, and trends are an integral part of many forecasting methods. These measures are part of the general approach called *change analysis.*

Trends can be estimated using a variety of methods. In many situations, particularly in long-range forecasting, an estimate of a growth rate may be more important than the actual time-value estimates. Also, the rate-of-change curve for one variable may be a leading indicator of the movement of another variable. In general, the evaluation of differences and rates of change can give early warnings of significant changes in a variable.

Change Measurement

Changes may be measured a number of different ways:

Formula		**Example**
Difference = (absolute change)	current − base	$110 - 100 = 10$
Relative = (proportionate ratio)	$\dfrac{\text{current}}{\text{base}}$	$\dfrac{110}{100} = 1.1$
Relative percent = (proportionate percent)	$\dfrac{\text{current}}{\text{base}} \times 100$	$\dfrac{110}{100} \times 100 = 110$ percent
Proportionate change = (differential ratio)	$\dfrac{\text{current}}{\text{base}} - 1$	$\dfrac{110}{100} - 1 = 0.1$
Percentage change = (differential percent)	$\left(\dfrac{\text{current}}{\text{base}} - 1\right) \times 100$	$\left(\dfrac{110}{100} - 1\right) \times 100 = 10$ percent

All the ways of measuring change or growth involve some relationship between two values: current and base. Many of the comments that follow apply to each of the different ways. Change analysis can be applied not only to raw historical data but also to conditioned data (e.g., smoothed data or deseasonalized values).

Differencing.   *Successive differencing* of the history of a time series is when the base measurement immediately precedes the current measurement. Differencing helps in specifying parameters to certain forecasting models and can give guides to making subjective forecasts of the series. The first difference of a time series at any time t is:

$$D_t = Y_t - Y_{t-1} \tag{23.63}$$

The second difference, which is first differences of first differences, is:

$$D_t^2 = D_t - D_{t-1} \tag{23.64}$$

$$= Y_t - Y_{t-1} - (Y_{t-1} - Y_{t-2})$$

$$= Y_t - 2Y_{t-1} + Y_{t-2}$$

Similarly, higher differences can be generated.

A plot of the first differences can tell much about the series. Values that are consistently above zero may indicate a trend. A forecast model should consider this trend. If the first differences are randomly above and below zero, with the deviation following a normal distribution, then the series is said to be *stationary*. Runs of positive and/or negative values are indicative of serial or autocorrelation.

Second differences measure changes in trends. They indicate an accelerating or decelerating growth. In addition, it is effective to consider seasonal differences such as:

$$D_t^S = Y_{t-S} \quad \text{for monthly data} \quad D_t^{12} = Y_t - Y_{t-S} \tag{23.65}$$

Note that the differences between nonseasonal second differences [Eq. (23.64)] and seasonal second differences below:

$$D_t^2 = Y_t - Y_{t-2} \tag{23.66}$$

Relative Change. If historical data are available for a time horizon over which there is some growth, then growth might be more meaningful if it were modeled using relative changes rather than differences. The relative change from one period to a value i periods past is:

$$\text{ROC}_{t:i} = \frac{Y_t}{Y_{t:i}} \tag{23.67}$$

where ROC is the relative change, sometimes called *rate of change,* and i is the lag. The ROC may also be expressed as a percentage by multiplying it by 100. The use of ROC is more common than it is thought to be; for example, whenever logarithms are used, coefficients represent the rates of change.

Periodic Change. If the series is periodic, such as monthly or quarterly, then the difference between the current value and the corresponding value one seasonal period ago is of interest. For instance:

$$D_{t:L} = Y_t - Y_{t-L}$$

where L is the seasonal period (that is, $L = 12$ for monthly data). The corresponding ROC equation is:

$$\text{ROC}_{t-L} = \frac{Y_t}{Y_{t:L}} \tag{23.68}$$

Corresponding period evaluations are common in that they give a quick reading of the instantaneous growth rate, and they cancel the effects of seasonality.

Growth Rates. The proportionate change is sometimes called the *growth rate*. It is related to the relative change (rate of change) by:

$$g_t = \text{ROC}_t - 1 \tag{23.69}$$

It may be expressed as a percentage by multiplying it by 100.

If the data are yearly, then g_t is an annual growth rate. If the data are monthly, then the following equation gives a simple annualized growth rate:

$$g = 12g_t = (12)(\text{ROC}_t - 1) \tag{23.70}$$

If data were quarterly, then 4 would be substituted for 12. The above equation does not consider compound growth. The compounded annualized growth rate is:

$$g = \text{ROC}_t^{12} - 1 \tag{23.71}$$

Growth rates derived from the above equations are essentially instantaneous. A long-term growth rate can be derived by the linear-regression (least-squares) method by relating logarithms as in Eq. (23.47) to time. For example, a least-squares growth rate can be derived from the coefficient b fitted to Eq. (23.47) when logarithms to the natural number e are used. The resulting growth rate is:

$$g = (\exp b) - 1 \tag{23.72}$$

Care must be taken in using growth rates calculated by regression equations. Extreme values may distort the results. Also, using different ranges of historical values can give dramatically different results. Techniques of exclusion, discounting, or averaging can be used to adjust for extreme values. Splitting the data in different time horizons and calculating growth rates for each horizon can often alleviate distortions caused by time-horizon selection. The growth rate for an eyeball fit can be obtained by estimating the slope and constant from two points on the fitted straight line.

Rate-of-Change Analysis

The plotting of different ROC curves over time has proved to be a useful tool in anticipating cyclical changes in a time series and in comparing two time series. In these analyses, there is a constant time interval from the current and the base measurements, so a running comparison is made. Any time interval may be used, but the most common ones are the last period and the corresponding period 1 year ago.

Essentially two components are involved in an ROC analysis: the method of averaging the raw data and the period of the lag. Since the method of averaging can vary and the period of lag can vary, certain terminology is commonly used to identify a particular rate-of-change curve. The format is source identification/lag period, where the source identification refers to the type of moving average. For a simple trailing moving average, a number is used that gives the periods in the average. A moving average of 1 is the raw data. Thus a 1/12 rate of change for monthly data is a comparison of the current month to the 12-month previous value (same month last year). Other common curves are:

$\dfrac{1}{1}$ current period to previous period

$\dfrac{3}{12}$ trailing 3-period average to trailing 3-period average 12 periods ago

$\dfrac{12}{12}$ trailing 12-period average to trailing 12-period average 12 periods ago

For monthly data, a 12/12 rate of change is a moving year-to-year comparison. For quarterly data, a 4/4 rate of change is also a moving year-to-year comparison. A 3/3 rate of change for monthly data is equivalent to a 1/1 for quarterly data. To remove the volatility of the 1/12 curve while maintaining its currentness, some smoothing method may be used. One approach is a trailing 3-month moving average of the 1/12 curve.

ROC curves can give early warnings of changes in the basic movement of a time series. A downward movement indicates a declining growth and thus may be a warning of continued decline. The point at which a curve levels after an upward movement should be noted.

Some analysts use the point B at which the 1/12 curve crosses the 12/12 curve as a warning signal. Figure 23.11 shows a trend cycle curve, TC/12, with a 12/12 curve. The

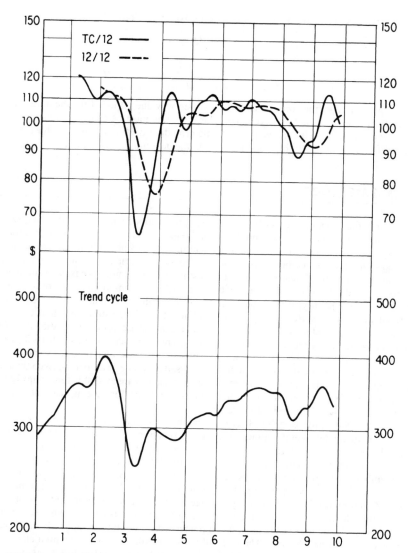

FIGURE 23.11 Rate-of-change curves with corresponding trend-cycle curve.

TC/12 is a smoothed alternative to the 1/12 curve. Downward cross points are noted in years 3, 5, 6, 8, and 10. Years 3 and 8 cross points did give some leads on subsequent downturns. The year 5 cross point was at the trough of a minor dip.

A comparison of the TC/12 curve with the trend-cycle curve shows that generally the peaks and valleys of the two coincide. However, the TC/12 peaked in late year 7, some 5 months before the trend-cycle curve.

ROC values can also give some simple forecasting methods. For instance:

$$F_{t+1} = (Y_t)(\text{ROC}_{t+1-L:1})$$

$$= Y_t \, \frac{Y_{t+1-L}}{Y_{t-L}} \tag{23.73}$$

This equation takes the forecast as the latest period value adjusted for the 1/12 ROC value for the same period one cycle ago. However, one must be cautious in using such a relationship because it can result in extreme growth or decline when the values in the numerator are abnormally high and the term in the denominator is abnormally low.

ARIMA METHODS

In general, the techniques described so far have just assumed a model and then analyzed the fit of the time series to that model. Box and Jenkins[31] have developed a unified forecasting system that includes the empirical determination of not only model parameters but also a model. The method also provides estimates of confidence limits for forecasts.

The Box-Jenkins philosophy is that forecasting models should be based on summary statistics of the historical data rather than unverified assumptions (e.g., preselected models). Consequently, these models are derived empirically; that is, the models are arrived at through systematic procedures of identification, estimation, and diagnosis.[4,5,6,7,23,31] The methods developed by Box and Jenkins are commonly called *ARIMA* (for *autoregressive integrated moving average*). The approach requires at least 30 values of history (preferably more) for good results. The method also requires some experience in subjectively evaluating statistics and in setting model parameters. Even though the method is complex, many computer software packages are available that simplify its use, and the most recent software applications for SKU forecasting use automated expert systems to select the best models.

The methods proposed by Box and Jenkins combine several techniques in an approach to model specification, parameter estimation, diagnostic checking of the model, and subsequent forecasting from the specified model. Basically, a time series will depend on the length and type of "memory" inherent in the series. Some series "remember" only their prior values (autoregressive). Others remember shocks or random noise values (moving averages). Still others remember both and so are a combination of autoregressive and moving averages. The techniques proposed attempt to determine which type or types of memory are exhibited by a time series and then specify the model using the least number of parameters (parsimonious parameterization) that adequately describes the data. The residual portion (differences between predicted values in the past and actual series data) is then used to characterize the unpredictable nature of (the "random noise" affecting) the series. With the model specified and the noise characterized, both point forecasts and confidence limits may be projected.

Moving Average

The moving-average model assumes that the time series has a mean μ and that all values are distributed about this mean. The simplest moving-average model is:

$$Y_t = \mu + e_t - \theta_1 e_{t-1} \tag{23.74}$$

where, as before, e_t is the forecast error. And θ (theta) is the moving-average coefficient. While this equation is analogous to the basic exponential smoothing equation, it allows the coefficient to be positive or negative. The above equation is called a *first-order moving-average process* and is abbreviated MA(1). The model can be extended to include any number of terms. Its general equation is:

$$Y_t = \mu + e_t - \sum_{i=1}^{q} \theta_i\, e_{t-i} \tag{23.75}$$

where q is the order (number of terms). Fortunately, q is rarely above 2, that is, there are rarely more than two θ_i's. The above equation is symbolized by MA(q). In contrast to the moving-average models discussed earlier, the coefficients do not necessarily sum to 1.

Autoregression

The autoregression model is an extension of the general autoregression equation:

$$Y_t = \theta_0 + \sum_{i=1}^{p} \phi_i\, Y_{t-i} + e_t \tag{23.76}$$

where e_t is the error term, p is the order (number of terms), and θ_0 and ϕ are coefficients much as in a linear-regression relationship. Fortunately, p is rarely greater than 2. Equation (23.76) is notated as AR(p), a p-order autoregressive model. A first-order autoregressive model, an AR(1) model is:

$$Y_t = \theta_0 + \phi_1 Y_{t-1} + e_t \tag{23.77}$$

Autoregression-Moving Average

Combining the two models gives:

$$Y_t = \theta_0 + e_t + \sum_{i=1}^{p} \phi_i\, Y_{t-i} - \sum_{i=1}^{q} \theta_i\, e_{t-i} \tag{23.78}$$

The general notation for the above is ARMA(p, q).

Achieving Stationarity

The ARMA model is meaningful only if the data are stationary. A series is stationary if its statistical properties do not vary over time (i.e., it has a constant level and variance). A stationary series thus tends to wander more or less uniformly about some fixed level with a constant standard deviation. The Box-Jenkins method provides a model-building approach to converting most nonstationary behavior into stationary behavior. Box and Jenkins do this integration through the process of differencing as in Eqs. (23.63) to (23.66). In some cases when variance nonstationarity exists, it may be necessary to do a prior transformation (such as taking the logarithms or power transformations) before the differencing process is attempted.

The need for differencing can be detected by calculating the autocorrelation function of the variable with itself for a range of lagged time periods. Many computer programs automatically generate a graph (*correlogram*) of the autocorrelation functions for visual examination. If their autocorrelations dampen to zero, there is little gained by differencing. If the autocorrelations are all the same sign, then there may be a trend that can be removed by differencing. The general notation of the integrated model is:

$$\text{ARIMA } (p, d, q) \times (P, D, Q) \tag{23.79}$$

where p = degree of nonseasonal autoregression
   d = degree of nonseasonal differences
   q = degree of nonseasonal moving average
   P = degree of seasonal autoregression
   D = degree of seasonal differences
   Q = degree of seasonal moving average

In general, the degree refers to the number of terms.

In most practical cases, the derived degrees of autoregression, differencing, and moving averages will be small, typically of an order of 0 to 2. The MA(1) and AR(1) models then become special cases. For instance, MA(1) is equivalent to ARIMA (0, 0, 1), and AR(1) is equivalent to ARIMA(1, 0, 0).

Confidence Limits

An advantage of the Box-Jenkins method is that it provides formulas for setting the confidence limits of forecasts of m-period ahead forecasts.[4,31] These formulas are based on the variance of the errors. They reflect changing confidence as the forecast horizon increases. Because these are difficult to develop and are sometimes part of computer software output, they are not developed here.

ARIMA Model-Building Steps

There are three principal steps in a Box-Jenkins analysis: identification, estimation, and forecasting. In the identification, or specification step, summary statistics of autocorrelation and partial autocorrelation relationships are generated. These statistics may indicate that differencing or other transformations of data should be made. The step can then be repeated with data transformed by one or more degrees of differencing. The statistics also indicate appropriate degrees of autoregression and moving-average specification. The purpose of this step is to tentatively identify an initial model and its appropriate differencing, autoregression, and moving-average structure.

The second step is to estimate the parameters in the tentative model via a minimization-of-errors or maximum-likelihood method. The estimated errors are then checked by goodness-of-fit criteria (i.e., are they normally and independently distributed). If necessary, reidentification and reestimation may be done until a model and parameter are achieved that meet requirements of being stationary and having low error. The final step is the forecasting by using the derived model. Evaluation of forecasting results may require further iterations of the previous steps.

ARIMA Extensions

The Box-Jenkins methods described so far handle the relationship of a variable with itself; however, there are methods for including the effects of external variables through techniques of multivariate ARIMA. Here, multiple-regression techniques are integrated with ARIMA techniques using MARMA methods, see Box, Jenkins, and Reinsel,[31] De Lurgio,[4] and Makridakis, Wheelwright, and McGee.[5]

IMPLEMENTING A FORECAST

This chapter has introduced forecasting methods and systems. We have discussed some of the more practical methods with some mention of how they are applied and their limitations. In this section, we expand on these latter two subjects by discussing the problems of implementing a forecasting procedure.

In developing a forecasting system, we must answer the questions stated earlier in this chapter. In addition, we must determine the importance of subjective estimates in the forecast. Another concern is that the product of forecasting is often the understanding of relationships rather than the particular numbers involved; that is, in modeling, the insights provided by the analysis are often more important than the actual numbers.

Influences of Subjective Factors

Rarely is forecasting completely objective. No matter how sophisticated the methods, there is much subjective judgment in determining which method and data are best. This is one reason why proven forecasting systems are so valuable when acquiring new systems; others have spent many years improving these systems.

Should causal-multivariate methods be used instead of univariate methods? In many cases, this question is answered by the cost effectiveness of using multivariate techniques, and the cost effectiveness is often influenced by the number of forecasts that must be made. When there are predictor variables that provide cost-effective and more accurate forecasts of a predicted variables, then the benefits from using causal methods are so high that this capability should be included in the system. When multivariate methods are not used routinely, they can be used selectively on important items.

One of the most intriguing areas of forecasting is how to combine subjective considerations (such as special knowledge about a new customer or other kinds of marketing intelligence) with a scientific forecast. Often this can be done by including additive special-knowledge factors in the forecast. For example:

$$F^* = F + SK \tag{23.80}$$

where F^* = forecast after special knowledge
F = forecast before special knowledge
SK = special-knowledge factor

There is danger, however, in overdoing special knowledge, especially when forecast deviations are a part of the forecast system. This danger can be overcome by including the special-knowledge factor if the factor is, say, greater than some measure of the forecast error. For example:

$$\text{If } SK > k \times RSE \quad \text{then } F^* = F + SK$$
$$\text{else } F^* = F$$

where RSE = residual standard error
k = control factor (such as 1.5)

One practical way to combine nonstatistical and statistical predictions is to see whether the single-value prediction falls within plus or minus some control limits (in the quality-control sense) of the statistical forecast. The control limits are best derived empirically. If the initial forecast falls outside the control limits, then the forecaster is asked to reevaluate the estimate. Figure 23.12 shows the comparison of a statistically derived forecast with a prediction.

There are several ways of combining forecasts including simple averages, weighted averages, and regression analysis.[4,32] The combining of forecasts has been studied in considerable detail. Interestingly, many studies have found that a simple average of two

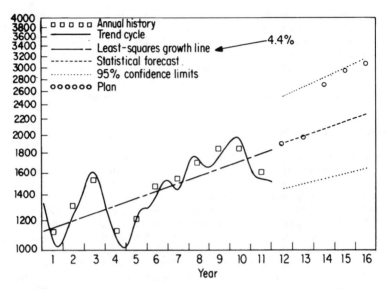

FIGURE 23.12   Comparison of predicted plan with statistically derived forecast.

forecasts is as effective as other combining methods and most often better than using either single forecast.[32,34] When forecasting accuracy is paramount, then several accurate forecasts should out-perform a single forecasting model.

Comments about Sophisticated Methods

The question of model sophistication plagues novice and expert alike; are more sophisticated methods worth the effort? Do they forecast better? The general answer is that more sophisticated *systems* are almost always worth the effort; however, more sophisticated *methods* may not always be worth the effort. Forecasting research has shown that if a method models the relevant demand patterns, then it will be an effective method, possibly the most cost-effective approach. Also, we should note that the terms *more and less sophisticated* are relative terms, dependent on the sophistication of the analyst; thus, a good study of the forecasting methods of this chapter is necessary before one's assessment of "more or less sophisticated" has meaning.

Unsophisticated methods fail to furnish a clear explanation of phenomena under investigation; nevertheless, they are desirable in a first look at a problem. Even sophisticated models yield unreliable results if they are employed without careful planning, without understanding the phenomena, and without understanding the technique of analysis.

A look at the management science literature on forecasting—especially that on forecasting competitions—shows that simpler approaches frequently serve as well or almost as well as more sophisticated methods. However, these simpler methods must include the relevant demand patterns of randomness, trend, and seasonality. Elaborate models are worthwhile only if they are fully understood and adequately researched.

Choice of Method

The requirements of a good forecasting method are as follows:

- Fulfillment of its intended purpose
- Clearly presented assumptions
- Ability to model underlying trend and seasonal patterns of the series
- Estimation of probabilities and ranges of errors
- Easily understood
- Detection of out-of-control situations
- Accurate forecasts

The various methods have their advantages and disadvantages. The basic simple exponential smoothing and simple moving-average models do not model trend or seasonality. Because they include relevant demand patterns, Winters's, ARIMA, Fourier series analysis, and other decomposition methods are viable forecasting methods. In general, curve-fitting methods are used for longer-range forecasts. Long-range forecasts are better fitted to yearly rather than weekly or monthly data because of the increased randomness that tends to appear in shorter periods. Fitted curves can, of course, be adjusted by seasonal factors.

When many items are forecast at the same time, consideration must be given to whether the same method is used for all items or different methods are used for various classes of items. The concept of ABC Analysis is important in addressing this choice. Even when the same method is used for many items, questions arise as to whether each item will have its own parameters in its equations or whether some parameters can be used for many items. For instance, common seasonality and/or trend factors may be used for many items. All time-series models are limited by the basic assumption that historical patterns will continue in the future.

The ultimate criterion as to which is the best forecasting technique or parameter in a forecasting model isn't which gives the best forecast by some error criteria but rather which minimizes the production and inventory planning and control costs. These do include inventory, production, and customer service costs along with system costs—the costs of forecasting. The costs of forecasting include the cost of developing, testing, and selling the technique as well as the cost of use and maintenance. The cost versus the value of the forecast is often overlooked, but it is extremely important. However, the cost of forecasting systems development and maintenance have declined considerably in recent years.

Recent Computer Advances

The computer has had a dramatic effect on the development of forecasting methods. Methods that were formerly prohibitive because of costs or resource requirements are now feasible. Many new methods have been developed including the use of Expert Systems, Artificial Neural Networks, and powerful simulation routines. One advance has been the development of forecasting software that can easily interface with the production and inventory control system. These easy interfaces are the result of pervasive standardization of operating systems, databases, and graphic-user interfaces.

Another development has been computer programs that automatically try out different methods on historical data. Many software companies offer these packages, and many companies now have developed their own. However, most manufacturers who develop their own programs lag the state-of-the-art software available from vendors. The state-of-the-art forecasting systems can very rapidly simulate how well a given technique works with actual data. These simulations assess the forecasting accuracy of several models. The automated selection methods are important because there is no single forecasting method that can effectively handle all types of data.

In addition, these software packages provide effective graphic-user interfaces that facilitate the interaction of the analyst with the forecasting process. The analyst can provide the intervention of human judgment, an extremely important part of an effective forecasting system.

Special-Event Modeling.   Recent advances in forecasting systems have included and improved the capabilities for modeling the impact of special events such as promotions and deals. These methods include procedures known as *intervention and impact analysis.*[1] Because promotions are used frequently by many manufacturers, distributors, and retailers, the demands for their products vary significantly from normal demand patterns. As mentioned earlier in this chapter, the modeling of such abnormal, but often repeating, patterns is very important in achieving accurate forecasts and effective decisions. The purchasers and developers of forecasting systems should ensure that these capabilities exist in their software systems.

SUMMARY

The following points summarize the factors to consider in the search for techniques:

- There are no infallible ways to forecast the future. No technique works for all situations, and more than one technique may work for a given situation.
- A forecast should recognize that there is no certainty. Therefore, a forecast is expected to be wrong on occasion. Even though there is uncertainty, one should use good methods.
- Conditions change so that one must have some way of adapting forecasts to these changes.
- Even though many forecasting techniques may be statistically sound, there is judgment in:

   Use of techniques and results

   What data to use

   How data are conditioned

   The forecaster is more important than the method.

- The forecaster should not be technique oriented.
- Precision is seldom important in a forecast.
- Elements that determine the best method include:

   Purpose

   Cost versus benefit

   Timeliness

Another difficulty is that people tend to ignore the fact that some mathematical method is used in developing a computer-derived forecast. They become result—rather than method—oriented. Because they do not have to perform the calculations themselves, they often do not understand the method. More important, they may not understand the limitations of the method and thus the limitations of the results. Finally, the results from a computer depend on the input data with the GIGO (garbage-in, garbage-out) principle in effect. Conditioning sales history by computer can be an extremely difficult job.

GLOSSARY OF SYMBOLS

The following is a list of the mathematical symbols used in this chapter, with a brief definition of each. Indexes, coefficients in equations, and intermediate values used in simplifying formulas are not included.

A	=	Average for all n periods
A_t	=	An average as of time period t
a_t	=	Smoothed value as of time t
ai	=	Coefficients in regression modes
b_t	=	Estimated trend for period t
C	=	Cyclical component in a time series
d	=	Order of differencing in ARIMA models
D_t	=	First difference for period t
D_t^2	=	Second difference for period t
e	=	Exponential using natural number
e_t	=	F_{it} = Fitted error or forecast error for period t
SE_t	=	Sum of errors through period t
F_t	=	Forecast for period t
F^*	=	Special-knowledge adjusted forecast
g_t	=	Growth rate at period t
I	=	Irregular component in time series
I_t	=	Seasonal index for Winter's model
K	=	Safety or significance control factor
k	=	Upper limit of S curve
L	=	Time periods season in cycle
M	=	Number of terms in equations
m	=	Forecast horizon
N	=	Number of periods in history
n	=	Number of periods in series
P	=	Order of autoregression in ARIMA models
MAD_t	=	Mean absolute deviation (MAD) at period t
q	=	Order of moving average in ARIMA models
SAD_t	=	Smoothed-average deviation (SAD) at period t
T	=	Trend at period t

$\text{ROC}_{t;i}$ = Rate of change for period t for lag i

S = Seasonal component in time series

S_t = Seasonal adjustment factor for period t

S'_t = Single smoothed value for period t

S''_t = Double smoothed value for period t

SA = Average demand over a seasonal cycle

RSE = Residual standard error of forecast errors

SK = Special-knowledge factor

t = Time period

t_t = t value of demand filter

T = Trend component in time series

T_t = Trend estimate for period t

TC = Trend cycle

TS_t = Tracking signal at period t

TSC_t = Tracking signal cumulative

TSML_t = Tracking signal limit

TSM_t = Tracking signal based on MAD at period t

w_t = Weighing factor for period t

X_t = Independent variable (external factor) in period t

Y = Actual demand

Y_t = Actual demand in period t

Y'_t = Transformed demand in period t

α = Smoothing constant

α' = Long-term demand smoothing constant

β = Discount rate = $1 - \alpha$

γ = Seasonality smoothing constant

δ = Trend smoothing constant/equation coefficient

η = Error smoothing constant

μ = Mean

σ = Standard deviation

ω = Cycle period in sinusoidal functions

ϕ = Autoregression coefficients

θ = Moving-average coefficients

θ_0 = Constant in ARIMA model

REFERENCES

1. S. A. De Lurgio, Sr., and C. D. Bhame: *Forecasting Systems for Operations Management,* Burr Ridge, Ill., Irwin Professional Publications, 1991.

2. R. G. Brown: *Advanced Service Parts Inventory Control,* 2d ed., Thetford, Vt., Materials Management Systems, 1982.

3. "Master Planning Module," *CPIM Certification Study Guides,* Falls Church, Va., American Production and Inventory Control Society, 1994.

4. S. A. De Lurgio, Sr.: *Forecasting Principles and Applications,* Irwin Publishing, Burr Ridge, Ill., 1997.

5. S. Makridakis, S. C. Wheelwright, and V. E. McGee: *Forecasting Methods and Applications,* John Wiley & Sons, New York, 1983.

6. J. E. Hanke and A. G. Reitsch: *Business Forecasting,* Allyn and Bacon, Boston, 1995.

7. R. L. Goodrich: *Applied Statistical Forecasting,* Business Forecast Systems, Belmont, 1989.

8. *Journal of Forecasting,* Wiley & Sons, Limited, Chichester, United Kingdom and *International Journal of Forecasting,* Elsevier Science Publishers, Amsterdam, *The Journal of Business Forecasting,* Flushing, New York.

9. R. G. Brown: *Statistical Forecasting for Inventory Control,* McGraw-Hill, New York, 1959.

10. D. M. Georgoff and R. G. Murdick: "Manager's Guide to Forecasting," *Harvard Business Review* (64), January/February 1986, pp. 110–120.

11. J. W. Muir: *The Pyramid Principle, American Production and Inventory Control Society,* 22d Annual Conference Proceedings, Washington, D.C., 1979, pp. 105–107.

12. P. J. Harrison: "Short-Term Sales Forecasting," *Applied Statistics* (14), 1965, pp. 102–139.

13. J. Shiskin, A. H. Young, and J. C. Musgrave: U.S. Bureau of Census, *The X-11 Variant of the Census Method II Seasonal Adjustment Program,* Tech. Paper no. 15, Government Printing Office, Washington, D.C., 1967.

14. F. E. Croxton and D. J. Cowden: *Applied General Statistics,* 2d ed., Prentice-Hall, Englewood Cliffs, N.J., 1955.

15. E. B. Dagum: *The X-11-ARIMA Seasonal Adjustment Method,* Statistics Canada, Ottawa, 1980.

16. R. G. Brown: *Smoothing, Forecasting and Prediction of Discrete Time Series,* Prentice-Hall, Englewood Cliffs, N.J., 1963.

17. H. Levenbach and J. P. Cleary: *The Beginning Forecaster: The Forecasting Process through Data Analysis,* Lifetime Learning Publications, Belmont, Calif., 1981, pp. 248–274.

18. S. I. Bretschneider and W. L. Gorr: "On the Relationship of Adaptive Filtering Forecasting Models to Simple Brown Smoothing," *Management Science* (27), August 1981, pp. 965–969.

19. P. R. Winters: "Forecasting Sales by Exponentially Weighted Moving Averages," *Management Science* (6), March 1960, pp. 324–342.

20. D. W. Trigg and A. G. Leach: "Exponential Smoothing with an Adaptive Response Rate," *Operational Research Quarterly* (18), March 1967, pp. 53–59.

21. E. S. Gardner, Jr., and D. G. Dannenbring: "Forecasting with Exponential Smoothing: Some Guidelines for Model Selection," *Decision Sciences* (11), 1980, pp. 370–383.

22. N. P. Draper and H. Smith, Jr.: *Applied Regression Analysis,* 2d ed., Wiley, New York, 1981.

23. R. S. Pindyck and D. L. Rubinfeld: *Econometric Models and Economic Forecasts,* McGraw-Hill, New York, 1991.

24. J. P. Martino: *Technological Forecasting for Decision Making,* 3rd ed., Amsterdam, North Holland, 1993.

25. L. A. Girifalco: *Dynamics of Technological Change,* Van Nostrand Rheinhold, New York, 1991.

26. J. P. Cleary and H. Levenbach: *The Professional Forecaster: The Forecasting Process through Data Analysis,* Lifetime Learning Publications, Belmont, Calif., 1982, pp. 78–88.

27. M. Klein: "Rational Approximation via Minimax Linear Programming Regression," *Proceedings of the 23d National Conference of the Association for Computer Machinery,* Brandon Systems Press, Princeton, N.J., 1968, pp. 79–84.

28. J. Bracken and G. P. McCormick: *Selected Applications of Nonlinear Programming,* Wiley, New York, 1968.

29. D. J. Wilde and C. S. Beightler: *Foundations of Optimization*, Prentice-Hall, Englewood Cliffs, N.J., 1967.

30. H. J. Cassidy: *Using Econometrics*, Reston Publishing, Reston, Va., 1981.

31. G. E. P. Box, G. M. Jenkins, and G. C. Reinsel: *Time Series Analysis Forecasting and Control*, 3d ed., Prentice-Hall, Englewood Cliffs, N.J., 1994.

32. P. Newbold and T. Boe: *Introductory Business and Economic Forecasting*, Southwestern, Cincinnati, 1994.

33. S. Makridakis and R. L. Winkler: "Averages of Forecasts," *Management Science* (29), September 1983, pp. 987–999.

34. C. W. J. Granger and P. Newbold: *Forecasting Economic Time Series*, Academic, New York, 1977.

35. C. C. Holt: *Forecasting Seasonal Trends by Exponentially Weighted Moving Averages*, Research Memorandum 52, Office of Naval Research, Washington, D.C., 1957.

BIBLIOGRAPHY

Abraham, B., and J. Ledolter: *Statistical Methods for Forecasting*, Wiley, New York, 1983.

Aiso, M.: "Forecasting Techniques," *IBM Systems Journal* (12), 1973, pp. 187–209.

Anderson, O. D.: *Time Series Analysis and Forecasting—The Box-Jenkins Approach*, Butterworth, London, 1976.

Anderson, T. W.: *The Statistical Analysis of Time Series*, Wiley, New York, 1971.

Armstrong, J. S.: *Long-Range Forecasting: From Crystal Ball to Computer*, 2d ed., Wiley, New York, 1985.

Ascher, W.: *Forecasting: An Approach for Policy-Makers and Planner*, Johns Hopkins, Baltimore, 1978.

Bails, D. G., and L. C. Peppers: *Business Fluctuations: Forecasting Techniques and Applications*, Prentice-Hall, Englewood Cliffs, N.J., 1982.

Bean, L. H.: *The Art of Forecasting*, Random House, New York, 1969.

Bloomfield, P.: *Fourier Analysis of Time Series—An Introduction*, Wiley, New York, 1976.

Bowerman, B. L., and R. T. O'Connell: *Time Series and Forecasting: An Applied Approach*, Duxbury Press, North Scituate, Mass., 1979.

Brillinger, D. R.: *Time Series: Data Analysis and Theory*, Holt, Rinehart and Winston, New York, 1981.

Bulter, W. F., R. A. Kavesh, and R. B. Platt (eds.): *Methods and Techniques of Business Forecasting*, Prentice-Hall, Englewood Cliffs, N.J., 1974.

Chambers J. C., S. K. Mullick, and D. D. Smith: *An Executive's Guide to Forecasting*, Wiley, New York, 1974.

Chatfield, C.: *The Analysis of Time Series: An Introduction*, 2d ed., Chapman & Hall, New York, 1980.

Chisholm, R. K., and G. R. Whitaker, Jr.: *Forecasting Methods*, Irwin, Homewood, Ill., 1971.

Cleary, J. P., and H. Levenbach: *The Professional Forecaster: The Forecasting Process through Data Analysis*, Lifetime Learning Publications, Belmont, Calif., 1982.

Dauten, C. A., and L. M. Valentine: *Business Cycles and Forecasting*, 5th ed., Southwestern, Cincinnati, 1978.

Draper, N. R., and H. Smith: *Applied Regression Analysis*, 2d ed., Wiley, New York, 1981.

Eby, F. H., Jr., and W. J. O'Neill: *The Management of Sales Forecasting*, Lexington Books, Lexington, N.Y., 1979.

Enrick, N. L.: *Market and Sales Forecasting—A Quantitative Approach*, Krieger Publishing, Huntington, N.Y., 1979.

Fels, R., and C. E. Hinshaw: *Forecasting and Recognizing Business Cycle Turning,* National Bureau of Economic Research, Columbia University Press, New York, 1968.

Fildes, R., and D. Woods (eds.): *Forecasting and Planning,* Saxon House, Farnborough, England, 1978.

Firth, M.: *Forecasting Methods in Business and Management,* Edward Arnold Ltd., London, 1977.

Fuller, W. A.: *Introduction to Statistical Time Series,* Wiley, New York, 1976.

Georgoff, D. M., and R. G. Murdick: "Manager's Guide to Forecasting," *Harvard Business Review* (64), January/February 1986, pp. 110–120.

Gilchrist, W.: *Statistical Forecasting,* Wiley, New York, 1976.

Gordon G., and I. Pressman: *Quantitative Decision Making for Business,* 2d ed., Prentice-Hall, Englewood Cliffs, N.J., 1983.

Granger, C. W. J.: *Forecasting in Business and Economics,* Academic, New York, 1977.

Granger, C. W. J., and P. Newbold: *Forecasting Economic Time Series,* Academic, New York, 1977.

Gross, C. W., and R. T. Peterson: *Business Forecasting,* 2d ed., Houghton Mifflin, Boston, 1983.

Hanna, E. J.: *Multiple Time Series,* Wiley, New York, 1970.

Harrison, P. J., and C. F. Stevens: "A Bayesian Approach to Short-Term Forecasting," *Operational Research Quarterly* (22), 1971, pp. 341–362.

Harvey, A. C.: *The Econometric Analysis of Time Series,* Halsted Press, New York, 1981.

Hirsch, A. A., and M. C. Lovell: *Sales Anticipations and Inventory Behavior,* Wiley, New York, 1969.

Hoff, J. C.: *A Practical Guide to Box-Jenkins Forecasting,* Lifetime Learning Publications, Belmont, Calif., 1983.

Intriligator, M. D.: *Econometric Models, Techniques, and Applications,* Prentice-Hall, Englewood Cliffs, N.J., 1978.

Introduction to Sales Forecasting, STSC, Inc., Rockville, Md., 1985.

Jenkins, G. M.: *Practical Experience with Modelling and Forecasting Time Series,* Gwilym Jenkins, Lancaster, United Kingdom, 1979.

Jenkins, G. M., and D. G. Watts: *Spectral Analysis and Its Applications,* Holden-Day, San Francisco, 1968.

Jones, H., and B. C. Twiss: *Forecasting Technology for Planning Decisions,* Macmillan, New York, 1978.

Kendell, M.: *Time Series,* Hafner Press, New York, 1976.

Klein, L. R., and R. M. Young: *An Introduction to Econometric Forecasting and Forecasting Models,* D.C. Heath, Lexington, Mass., 1980.

Levenbach, H., and J. P. Cleary: *The Beginning Forecaster: The Forecasting Process through Data Analysis,* Lifetime Learning Publications, Belmont, Calif., 1981.

Lewis, C. D.: *Industrial and Business Forecasting Methods,* Butterworth, Sevenoaks, Kent, England, 1982.

Lewis, C. E.: *Demand Analysis and Inventory Control,* Saxon House/Lexington Books, Lexington, Mass., 1975.

McLaughlin, R. L.: "A New Five Phase Economic Forecasting System," *Business Economics* (5), September 1975, pp. 49–60.

McLeod, G.: *Box-Jenkins in Practice,* Gwilym Jenkins, Lancaster, United Kingdom, 1983.

Makridakis, S., and S. C. Wheelwright (eds.): *The Handbook of Forecasting,* Wiley, New York, 1982.

Makridakis, S., and S. C. Wheelwright (eds.): *Forecasting,* North-Holland, Amsterdam, 1980.

Makridakis, S., and S. C. Wheelwright: *Interactive Forecasting, Univariate and Multivariate Methods,* 2d ed., Holden-Day, San Francisco, 1978.

Makridakis, S., S. C. Wheelwright, and V. E. McGee: *Forecasting Methods and Applications,* 2d ed., Wiley, New York, 1983.

Malinvaud, E.: *Statistical Methods of Econometrics,* 3d ed., North-Holland, Amsterdam, 1980.

Michael, G. C.: *Sales Forecasting—A Managerial Approach,* Longman Group, London, 1975.

Montgomery, D. C., and L. A. Johnson: *Forecasting and Time Series Analysis,* McGraw-Hill, New York, 1976.

Moore, G. H.: *Business Cycles, Inflation and Forecasting,* 2d ed., Ballinger, Cambridge, Mass., 1983.

Muir, J. W.: "Without a Forecast You Have Nothing," *American Production and Inventory Control 25th Annual Conference Proceedings,* APICS, Washington, D.C., 1982, pp. 554–557.

Murdick, R. G., and A. E. Schaefer: *Sales Forecasting for Lower Costs and Higher Profits,* Prentice-Hall, Englewood Cliffs, N.J., 1967.

Nelson, C. R.: *Applied Time Series Analysis for Managerial Forecasting,* Holden-Day, San Francisco, 1973.

Nerlove, M., D. M. Grether, and J. L. Carvalho: *Analysis of Economic Time Series,* Academic, New York, 1979.

Nickell, D. B.: *Forecasting on Your Microcomputer,* Tab Books, Blue Ridge Summit, Pa., 1983.

O'Donovan, T. M. (ed.): *Short-Term Forecasting: An Introduction to the Box-Jenkins Approach,* Wiley, New York, 1983.

Pankratz, A.: *Forecasting with Univariate Box-Jenkins Models; Concepts and Cases,* Wiley, New York, 1983.

Parzen, E.: *Empirical Time Series Analysis,* Holden-Day, San Francisco, 1970.

Pindyck, R. S., and D. L. Rubinfeld: *Econometric Models and Economic Forecasts,* McGraw-Hill, New York, 1981.

Plossl, G. W.: "Getting the Most from Forecasts," *Production and Inventory Management* (14), 1973, pp. 1–15.

Rao, P., and R. L. Miller: *Applied Econometrics,* Wadsworth, Belmont, Calif., 1977.

Rao, V. R., and J. E. Cos, Jr.: *Sales Forecasting Methods: A Survey of Recent Developments,* Marketing Science Institute, Cambridge, Mass., 1978.

Rothermel, T. W.: "Forecasting Resurrected," *Harvard Business Review* (60), March/April, 1982, pp. 139–149.

Sales Forecasting, The Conference Board, New York, 1978.

Singhvi, S. S.: "Financial Forecast: Why and How?" *Managerial Planning* (32), March/April 1984, pp. 32–41.

Smith, B. T.: *Focus Forecasting Computer Techniques for Inventory Control,* CBI Publishing, Boston, 1978.

Spencer, M. H., C. G. Clark, and P. W. Houget: *Business and Economic Forecasting,* Irwin, Homewood, Ill., 1961.

Stekler, H. O.: *Economic Forecasting,* Praeger, New York, 1970.

Sullivan, W. G., and W. W. Claycombe: *Fundamentals of Forecasting,* Reston Publishing, Reston, Va., 1977.

Tersine, R. J.: "Logic for the Future: The Forecasting Function," *Managerial Planning* (31), March/April 1983, pp. 32–35.

Theil, H.: *Principles of Econometrics,* Wiley, New York, 1971.

Thomopoulos, N. T.: *Applied Forecasting Methods,* Prentice-Hall, Englewood Cliffs, N.J., 1980.

Vandaele, W.: *Time Series Models for Business Decisions,* Academic, New York, 1983.

Wheelwright, S. C., and S. Makridakis: *Forecasting Methods for Management,* 4th ed., Wiley, New York, 1985.

Wolberg, J. R.: *Prediction Analysis,* Van Nostrand, Princeton, N.J., 1967.

Wonnacott, R. J., and T. H. Wonnacott: *Econometrics,* 2d ed., Wiley, New York, 1979.

Woods, D., and R. Fildes: *Forecasting for Business,* Longman, New York, 1976.

CHAPTER 24
PURCHASING*

Editor

John M. McKeller, D.B.A., CFPIM

Director of Education,
The National Association of Purchasing Management
Tempe, Arizona

This chapter is a collaborative effort between the National Association of Purchasing Management (NAPM) and the American Production and Inventory Control Society (APICS). Both organizations encourage interested readers to engage in a comprehensive review of the many aspects of organizational buying. However, the purpose of this brief chapter is merely to acquaint the reader with fundamental purchasing concepts and methods. The chapter presents the reader with basic information regarding the strategic importance of the purchasing function, the elements of the purchasing process, and the tasks associated with the execution of that process. Resources for a more complete review of purchasing are available through both NAPM and APICS.

PURCHASING DEFINED

No organization is so self-sufficient that it is capable of meeting all its needs for goods and services with internal resources alone. Therefore, whether or not they are "for-profit" enterprises, all organizations must engage in some form of buying activity. The word *purchasing* is used to characterize the *process* of buying. In its organizational context, the *purchasing process* usually includes the identification and definition of a need, identification and selection of a supplier, negotiation of price and terms, and any subsequent tasks that assure delivery and supplier payment. The term *purchasing* is often used to identify one of many corporate functions. However, it is still most frequently used to identify a specific department that has been delegated the responsibility for executing the tasks associated with the process of buying.

---

*Material in this chapter is from various National Association of Purchasing publications and is used by the courtesy of the National Association of Purchasing Management.

PURCHASING'S ROLE IN THE ORGANIZATION

Purchasing is a critical function within any organization. For manufacturing firms or service firms that consume large quantities of materials and supplies, purchasing should play an indispensable role in managing the external linkages in the supply chain. In practice, the purchase of raw materials and products used in manufacturing has long been regarded as purchasing's primary role. However, areas in which purchasing has not traditionally been active provide enormous opportunity for cost savings. These nontraditional buys include such items as travel services, consultancy agreements, utilities purchases, information services, employee benefits, advertising, and contracts with motor carriers. Unfortunately, in executing its customary role in the replenishment of production resources, purchasing has been typically identified as an overhead expense. In reality, purchasing must be a value-adding function helping to integrate the organization and its suppliers in order to cost-effectively meet the needs of the final customer.

Although purchasing has recently been identified in some circles as a "fast-track" function for eager executives,[1] recognition of the importance of purchasing is still not universal. A report issued by the Center for Advanced Purchasing Studies (CAPS) determined that most chief executives "view the purchasing function as very important to the overall success of the firm."[2] In spite of this recognition by senior management, the same report suggests that purchasing is frequently underutilized as a resource in the development and execution of business strategy.[2] Evidently some organizations still mistakenly regard purchasing as basically a clerical function.

Fortunately, such erroneous attitudes have largely been replaced by a recognition of the enormous value and competitive advantage that can be achieved through the proper management of the purchasing function[3] and the active engagement of purchasing in the pursuit of organizational goals.[4] In fact, many organizations have even discarded the term *purchasing* in favor of more inclusive formal titles such as *materials management, supply management,* or *procurement.* These more encompassing functional titles may represent a corporate department with responsibility for the management of transportation, stores, receiving and receiving inspection, supplier accounts payable, and inventory control in addition to those tasks associated with the purchasing process itself. Regardless of the terminology used to identify it as a corporate function, effective management of the supply channel is now regarded as one of the most important ways to achieve competitive advantage in the marketplace.[5]

THE STRATEGIC IMPORTANCE OF PURCHASING

Strategic Planning Defined

To appreciate the important role that purchasing should play in a firm's long-term business strategy, it is necessary to reflect for a moment on just what "strategic planning" itself should be. Essentially the term *strategy* may be defined as "the art and science of combining the many resources available to achieve the best match between an organization and its environment."[6] Strategic planning, therefore, is a process by which a firm's managers evaluate the organization's external and internal environment and determine answers to questions such as the following:

- What is our present business, and what should be our future business(es)?
- What do we do very well now or what should we be doing very well in order to provide us with an advantage over our competitors?
- What are the attributes that do or should differentiate us (our products, services) from others in our business(es)?
- How should we be organized to meet the requirements of our present and future business(es)?
- What are the constraints that must be overcome in order to excel in our business(es)?

As a result of this question-and-answer process, a "strategic plan" is developed that specifies the organization's long-term goals and defines what is to be done in pursuit of those goals—that is, just how the organization will achieve the "best match" between itself and its environment. The ways in which that "match" is to be accomplished through the development and execution of a firm's strategic plan has been the subject of much debate over the last decade. One recommendation suggests three potentially overlapping strategies by which a firm may excel beyond its competitors: overall cost leadership, differentiation, and focus.[7]

Overall Cost Leadership.   Firms with the lowest costs can position their products more competitively in the marketplace. Since product costs are lower, these firms are able to offer products at lower prices and/or obtain better profit margins from the sale of their products. Furthermore, the ability to produce products at a very low cost helps to keep new competitors from entering the firm's market. Combined with close attention to customer wants and product quality, this strategy has helped to create the tremendous turnaround in the fortunes of U.S. auto producers.[9]

Differentiation.   The ability to set the firm's products or services apart from those of competitors may be accomplished through better quality, better or more product features, excellent customer service, or a variety of other combined additions or improvements to product or service attributes. A key to this strategy is for the firm to provide customers with products or services that are not only different than the competitors' products or services but that provide more value to the customer because of those differences.

Focus.   The essential aspect of this strategy is the firm's conscious decision to center their efforts on a specific "buyer group, segment of the product line, or geographic market."[9] This allows the firm to become more effective and efficient because they can converge their efforts on a more concise customer group.

Of course this brief model is not the only advice available to company executives. Senior managers have also been advised by other well-regarded authorities to pursue a variety of diverse strategic initiatives. They have been told to achieve total quality management,[10] to reduce cycle times in all business processes,[11] and to "reengineer" their organizations,[12] and they have been cautioned to ignore old models of "strategic fit" and thereby leverage their resources "to reach seemingly unattainable goals."[13] Regardless of the specific strategic philosophy pursued by management, the incorporation of the purchasing function in the development and execution of any strategy will help to ensure its success.

PURCHASING'S ROLE IN CORPORATE STRATEGIES

With its ability to manage sources of supply, purchasing can assist in controlling and reducing costs, help to differentiate the firm's products, and assist in keeping the organization "focused."

Controlling Costs

A company's *cost of products sold* (COPS) represents the total investment the company has made in producing the product. For U.S. firms, about 30 to 80 percent of a product's cost is composed of the costs that companies pay for materials used to manufacture those products. Of course, costs do vary among industries. Consequently these figures represent a wide range of the average percentages. But whatever the percentage, the cost of purchased materials and parts is usually a significant proportion of COPS. Therefore, firms must pay close attention to the cost of purchased materials in order to achieve "overall cost leadership" or to "differentiate" their products based upon the price paid by the final customer. The early design phase of a product is the most effective point at which to influence product costs. Purchasing plays an important role in actively developing suppliers who can assist in the product design process.

Because the total cost of purchased materials extends well beyond the price paid to suppliers, a "price-only" focus is a misguided strategy for either management or purchasers. Although hidden costs such as those associated with poor quality, late deliveries, field failures, rework, or customer dissatisfaction do not show up directly on the accounting ledger, they still reduce the company's bottom-line profits and market flexibility. Through their ongoing efforts to identify, qualify, and develop a cost-effective, high-quality supplier network, purchasing has a tremendous ability to impact both the apparent and hidden factors of product cost.

Product Differentiation

In both the service and the manufacturing sectors, one of the most frequent routes to differentiation is through the application or incorporation of new technology. Purchasing is well positioned to assist in the identification and evaluation of new technologies. Because of continual interaction with outside suppliers, purchasing is often aware of recent innovations in electronics, communications, transportation, and manufacturing methods. Such information may be incorporated in the development of new or different products and services to achieve a marketplace advantage.

Maintaining Focus

The concept of "focus" has taken on an extended meaning in this time of "reengineering" and "outsourcing." Companies may develop strategies that include both a focus for their marketing efforts and an internal, process focus. This "internal focus" may include a reexamination of what the organization does and then a decision to outsource what is not considered a "core competency." Once again, purchasing's view to the outside can provide enormous help in the identification, selection, and contracting of outside service providers.

With their eyes and ears turned toward the outside world, buyers are quick to learn of new technologies, better sources of supply, methods of reducing lead times, alternative materials, and marketplace benchmarks in both price and service. Firms that fail to incorporate supply management considerations in their strategic planning process do so at considerable risk to their long-term goals. Assurance of high-quality supplies at reasonable cost cannot be taken for granted. Buyers have the potential to make a significant contribution to the accomplishment of any corporate strategy through their ability to impact the factors of speed, quality, cost effectiveness, and the integration of recent technology. Therefore, purchasing should play a proactive role in the development and execution of corporate strategy.

ORGANIZATION OF THE PURCHASING FUNCTION

The manner in which the purchasing function is organized within a company's overall structure varies among firms. This variety is further extended when a firm has multiple sites. Historically, the function has been organized according to the tasks to be performed. That is, a purchasing manager performs the management activities, buyers perform the actual buying activity, expediters follow up on open orders, and other personnel perform the necessary clerical tasks associated with the purchasing process. In manufacturing companies, purchasing has been regarded for many years as a function performed within a materials management organization. A typical organizational chart for a materials management organization is shown in Fig. 24.1. However, the reporting structure and organization of the purchasing function has recently undergone substantial changes in many firms. Traditional hierarchies and distinct areas of specialization are sometimes replaced by process-focused commodity management teams that include personnel from various organizational functions.

The Purchasing Process

As with many business processes, organizational buying processes vary among firms and even within firms. While usually similar in most aspects, processes may differ because of the nature of the purchase or the type of buying methods employed. The order in which tasks are performed in the purchasing process will also vary according to the nature of the purchase and the extent to which the buying organization has embraced the philosophy of strategic supply management. The "traditional" purchasing process examined here is only a model used to simplify a review of the many tasks associated with purchasing.

Traditional Purchasing Process. A traditional purchasing process includes the following primary activities:

- Identification of the need
- Description of the need
- Identification and evaluation of potential supply sources
- Preparation and solicitation of bids or quotes
- Evaluation of bids or quotes
- Supplier selection
- Negotiation of contract terms
- Preparation and issuance of the contract (purchase order)
- Follow-up on the order and/or expediting if required
- Receipt and inspection of goods

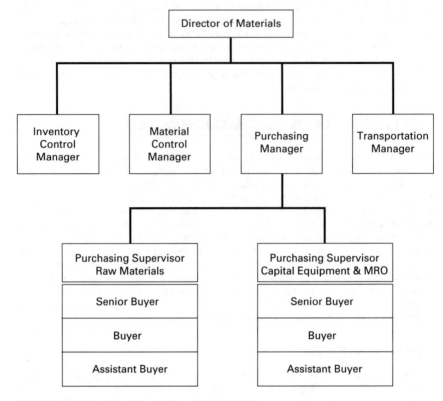

FIGURE 24.1 Materials management organizational chart.

- Review of the invoice and clearance for payment
- Maintenance of the records concerning the order

While each activity in this process is important, some of them merit a more thorough review than others. Furthermore, as previously noted, there are advanced purchasing processes that often improve purchasing effectiveness and efficiency by eliminating some of these steps. References to more advanced purchasing methods will be explored within the context of the activities associated with the traditional process.

Identification of the Need.   Professional purchasers must consider the type of commodity required and the frequency with which it is needed. Both factors significantly influence the acquisition process. Organizational requirements can generally be grouped into the following commodity categories:

Raw materials. These are items that the company will transform in some way in their manufacturing process. Examples of raw materials include sheet metal, steel tubing, paint, wire, tubing, chemicals, and resins.

Parts and components. These are finished or semifinished goods that the company will incorporate into their products. Examples of these items include machined castings, electronic components, pumps, motors, belts, wire harnesses, lenses, and molded plastics.

Services. These are intangible items (primarily a purchase of labor, either physical or intellectual). Examples of services include consulting, janitorial, legal, facilities maintenance, transportation, software development, and bookkeeping.

Capital goods. These items are company assets. They have a long useful-life expectancy, they are usually high-dollar purchases, and their value for tax purposes is depreciated over time. Capital goods may be either single-purpose or multipurpose items. Examples of capital goods include machinery, buildings, automobiles, fork-lifts, data processing equipment, and manufacturing equipment.

Maintenance, repairs, and operating supplies (MRO). This category of needs consists of maintenance, repair, and operating supplies. Included in this group are items such as adhesives and solvents consumed in manufacturing, machine lubricants, spare parts for production or facilities equipment, and general supplies used throughout the firm.

Resale. This designates those items that are purchased as finished goods to be resold as distinct products or as accessories to the firm's primary products. Examples include "bright stock" canned goods that are purchased without labels and then labeled and sold under the buying company's name or items such as accessories for computers and stereo equipment.

Packaging. This group of needs includes any material used to contain or to enclose and protect the company's products during transit to the customer. Examples include molded foam, plastic shrink-wrap, corrugated boxes, and glass or plastic containers.

Nontraditional purchases. This group is so named because it has not usually been incorporated into the responsibilities of the purchasing department or function. Nontraditional purchases may include transportation services, consultancy agreements, service contracts, benefits administration, educational services, insurance coverage, travel services, and utilities purchases. This list is not all inclusive. The potential for adding value through purchasing involvement with nontraditional buys remains largely unrecognized.

Beyond these classifications, organizational needs may be further categorized according to the frequency or timing of the required purchase:

Recurring or repetitive. Such as ongoing production requirements

Periodic or seasonal. Such as holiday goods or agriculture-related items

Episodic or nonrepetitive. Such as a situation that creates the need for legal services or a discrete capital asset purchase

These categories of organizational needs create distinct sets of circumstances that the purchaser must consider in fulfilling a requirement. The supplier used, the type of contract awarded, the length of contract term, and the price negotiated are just a few of the many variables that are dependent upon the type and frequency of the purchase to be made.

Purchase Requisitions

A traditional purchasing process begins when a user or "requisitioner" determines that there is a need that should be satisfied through a purchase from an outside source. The requisitioner (or user) then creates a *purchase requisition* (PR or "req") and forwards the requisition to purchasing for action. A traditional purchasing process uses two basic types of requisitions to communicate needs to the purchasing department—a standard purchase requisition or a traveling requisition. The *standard, or single-use, requisition* should be used to request discrete or nonrepetitive purchases. A *traveling requisition* is used in manual purchasing processes as a more efficient means of communicating repetitive requirements.

Standard Requisitions. The information displayed on a standard requisition form should be clear and complete. These forms generally require that the user provide the following information:

* A purchase requisition number for identification
* The date the requisition was completed
* The requisitioning department's name
* An account number to be charged
* The name and a thorough description of the material, part, or service to be purchased
* The unit of measure and quantity
* The date the item is needed ("need date")
* Any unique packaging or shipping instructions
* A "ship-to" location
* Signatures of the requestor and approval signatures if required by company policy

Standard purchase requisition forms vary among firms. Figures 24.2 and 24.3 are typical examples of these forms.

Traveling Requisitions. These documents are used in traditional purchasing processes to communicate requirements for repetitively purchased parts or materials. The use of traveling requisitions (TR) reduces the paperwork and time associated with making repeat purchases. Traveling requisitions are usually cards that identify the part or material to be purchased and list previously purchased quantities, prices, dates of purchase, the suppliers used, and prices paid. A TR is both a means to communicate current requirements and a historical record of purchases (see Fig. 24.4). The using department most often maintains TR files in their area. When a need arises, they send a TR card to purchasing with information regarding the quantity required and the date it is needed.

Description of the Need. When a description of the need is being developed, tremendous benefits can result from collaboration and teamwork among the requestor, the buyer, and frequently the supplier. It is the buyer's responsibility to verify that a need actually exists and to help determine if the most cost-effective means of satisfying that need have been identified. The systematic techniques of *value analysis* (VA) is one method that can be used by the team to maximize the value of a particular material, part, or service.

The VA method asks, "What is the function to be performed by the material, part, or service?" Once the function is identified, the next question is, "What is the value of this function?" After the function and its value have been identified, it then becomes the team's responsibility to determine how to match the value of the function with the cost of providing it. Such systematic exploration of the association between value and cost often leads to creative and more cost-effective alternatives to the original part, material, or service that was requested.

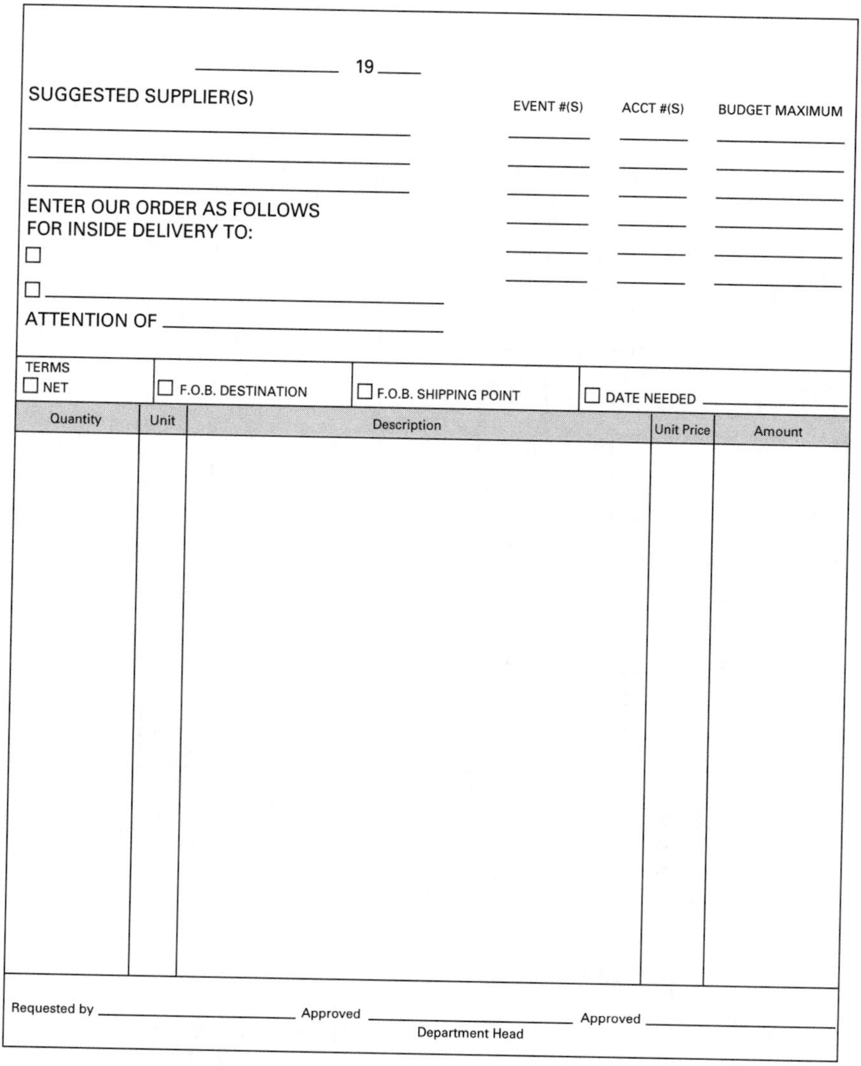

_____ 19 ____

SUGGESTED SUPPLIER(S)

EVENT #(S)   ACCT #(S)   BUDGET MAXIMUM

ENTER OUR ORDER AS FOLLOWS
FOR INSIDE DELIVERY TO:
☐
☐ _____
ATTENTION OF _____

TERMS
☐ NET   ☐ F.O.B. DESTINATION   ☐ F.O.B. SHIPPING POINT   ☐ DATE NEEDED _____

Quantity	Unit	Description	Unit Price	Amount

Requested by _____ Approved _____ Approved _____
Department Head

FIGURE 24.2 Standard requisition form. (*Source: NAPM.*)

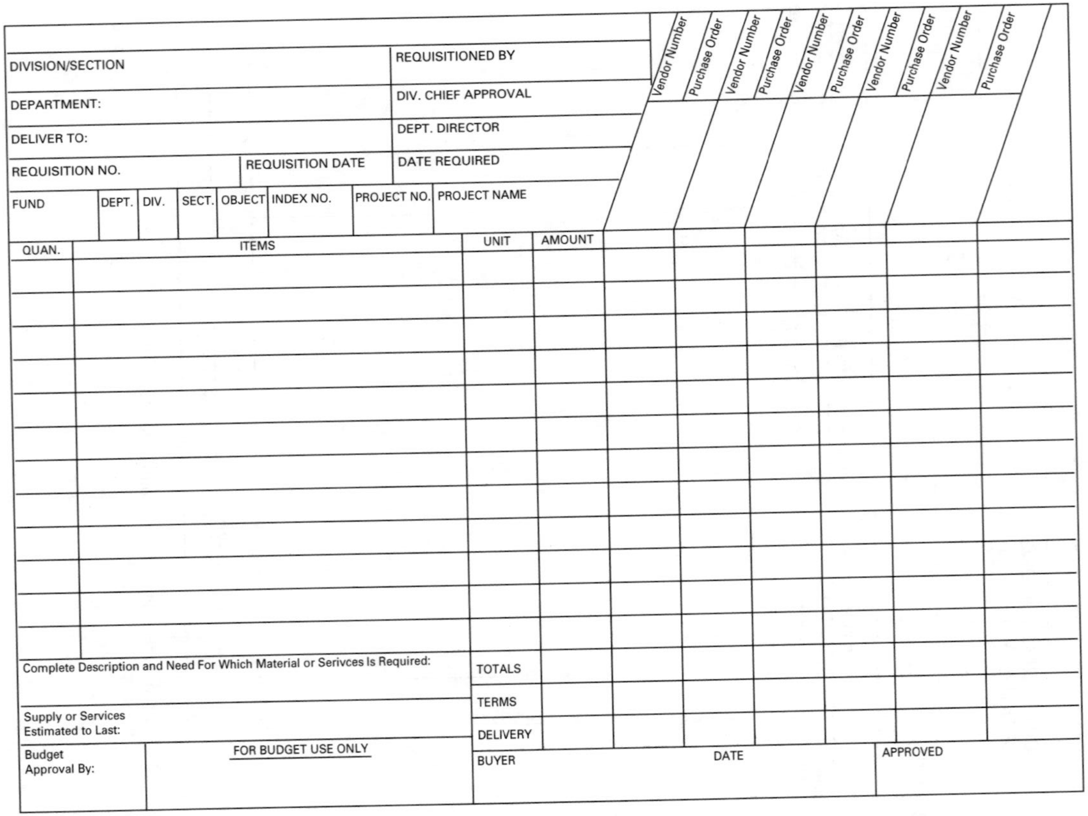
DIVISION/SECTION
REQUISITIONED BY
DEPARTMENT:
DIV. CHIEF APPROVAL
DELIVER TO:
DEPT. DIRECTOR
REQUISITION NO.
REQUISITION DATE
DATE REQUIRED
Vendor Number
Purchase Order
Vendor Number
Purchase Order
Vendor Number
Purchase Order
Vendor Number
Purchase Order
Vendor Number
Purchase Order

FUND	DEPT.	DIV.	SECT.	OBJECT	INDEX NO.	PROJECT NO.	PROJECT NAME

QUAN.	ITEMS	UNIT	AMOUNT

Complete Description and Need For Which Material or Serivces Is Required:
TOTALS
Supply or Services
Estimated to Last:
TERMS
DELIVERY
Budget
Approval By:
FOR BUDGET USE ONLY
BUYER
DATE
APPROVED

FIGURE 24.3 Purchase requisition. (*Source: NAPM.*)

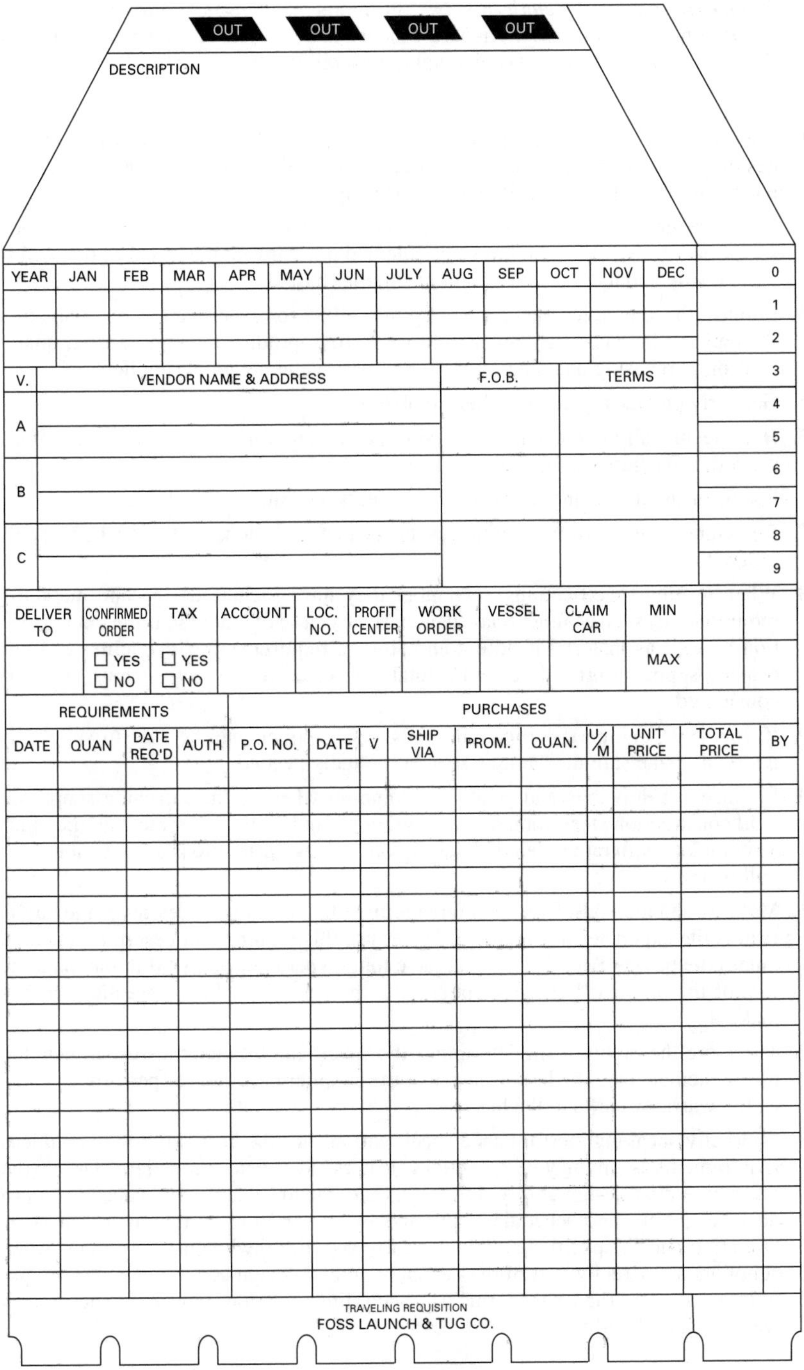
OUT OUT OUT OUT

DESCRIPTION

YEAR	JAN	FEB	MAR	APR	MAY	JUN	JULY	AUG	SEP	OCT	NOV	DEC

0 1 2 3 4 5 6 7 8 9

V.	VENDOR NAME & ADDRESS	F.O.B.	TERMS
A			
B			
C			

DELIVER TO	CONFIRMED ORDER	TAX	ACCOUNT	LOC. NO.	PROFIT CENTER	WORK ORDER	VESSEL	CLAIM CAR	MIN
	☐ YES ☐ NO	☐ YES ☐ NO							MAX

REQUIREMENTS				PURCHASES									
DATE	QUAN	DATE REQ'D	AUTH	P.O. NO.	DATE	V	SHIP VIA	PROM.	QUAN.	U/M	UNIT PRICE	TOTAL PRICE	BY

TRAVELING REQUISITION
FOSS LAUNCH & TUG CO.

FIGURE 24.4 Traveling requisition. (*Source: NAPM.*)

The Proper Definition of Requirements.   From his many years as a practitioner, educator, and consultant, Professor Richard Pinkerton, Ph.D., has developed a list of 16 "tips" regarding the way to maximize value through the proper definition of requirements.

1. Buy standard "shelf item" products whenever possible. In other words, do not design a component, etc., unless the need dictates this. Custom goods always cost more both in preparation and ownership changes.

2. Use commercial standards as determined by industry associations and government specifications bureaus whenever possible. Do not reinvent the wheel as this will be more costly and reduce your potential supplier base.

3. Employ the Integrated Purchasing System (IPS) for specification determination. This allows the necessary input from marketing, production, engineering, quality control, purchasing, installation-service, finance and potential suppliers.

4. Get early purchasing and supplier involvement.

5. Have technically competent purchasing personnel work with engineering. When needed, use a purchasing engineer.

6. Focus on suitability and the best buy concepts, not simply "the best."

7. Remember, the final customer makes the ultimate decision, not those who make the product.

8. When writing specifications, remember they must include design and marketing requirements, such as functional characteristics, ease of manufacturing, and inspection as well as material handling and storage requirements. Scheduling and purchasing-supplier procedures and total life-cycle cost factors must also be considered.

9. If you write unique specifications, only one supplier may be able to supply the material; make sure the "unique spec" is actually needed.

10. Engineering drawings and prints are common when buying machine shop work (and construction steel, foundry castings, etc.), and while very practical, they must be complete with rather detailed descriptive written instructions as to what the part will be used for.

11. Material and method-of-manufacture specifications may be necessary if the buying firm is the expert for this material. Never use this requirement description method unless the buying firm does in fact have long experience and skill in the manufacture of the product. Let the supplier have the final say when suggesting "how to make it."

12. The more the buying firm determines the specification, materials used, manufacturing method, etc., the less responsible the supplier becomes for performance, that is, the warranty shifts to the buyer.

13. Generally speaking, performance specifications are the best way to communicate requirements assuming your potential suppliers have been screened for state-of-the-art engineering design ability, integrity, manufacturing skill, and capacity to produce to quality and schedule requirements. A variation of this approach is the "function and fit specification" under early supplier involvement programs where suppliers are actually part of the design team and design components that are part of larger systems (hence the term "fit") according to various objectives such as cost, weight, and reliability.

14. A combination of the above may be appropriate (i.e., an engineering drawing with performance specifications and some components would be "branded" and samples to show colors).

15. Do not forget to include OSHA and other product safety liability regulations in the requirements.

16. Spend time and effort on requirement determination based on "ABC" inventory analysis and other total cost factors (i.e., buy generic paper clips in bulk at the lowest price over the phone or by fax).*[14]

Evaluation of Bids or Quotes.   This is accomplished by developing a matrix to help compare the elements of all the information submitted by suppliers. A brief example of this concept is shown in Table 24.1. When comparing supplier quotations, it is vital to remember that *total cost*, not price alone, should be the deciding factor. Assuming that each supplier quoted is already "approved" (see Supplier Selection), consider quality-related factors, terms of sale, discounts offered, lead times, and any other attribute of supplier or product performance that will influence the total cost. If a supplier has not been previously approved, there is an additional cost associated with the tasks necessary to qualify the supplier prior to any contract award. For instance, the obvious "low bidder" shown in Table 24.1 is "M. Co." However, this basic quote comparison does not identify any additional costs or savings that should be attributed to each of the suppliers before awarding a contract.

TABLE 24.1   Quote Comparison for PN 123456

Supplier	Price	Quantity	Lead time	Shipping terms	Payment terms
ABC Co.	$1.59 ea.	10,000/mo.	2–3 days	FOB dest.	1%10N30
XYZ Co.	$1.87 ea.	10,000/mo.	7 days	FOB dest.	None
M. Co.	$1.46 ea.	10,000/mo.	next day	FOB dest.	2%15N30

Supplier Selection

An excellent supplier base is mandatory in order to successfully satisfy an organization's materials, products, or service requirements. The creation of such a group of high-quality, cost-effective suppliers cannot be approached haphazardly. One of the most important functions of purchasing is to employ a rigorous, systematic approach in the identification, evaluation, and selection of the most qualified suppliers. In a traditional purchasing process, these steps may be completed (if at all) only after the quote evaluation process. However, more progressive organizations first identify commodities or products that are of strategic importance and then engage in a comprehensive process required to prequalify the best suppliers. The steps outlined in Fig. 24.5 define a thorough process used in the identification, evaluation, and selection of suppliers.

---

*Courtesy of Professor Richard L. Pinkerton.

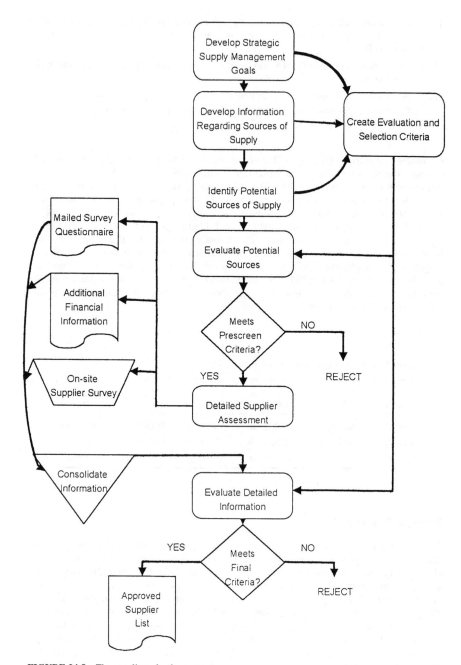

FIGURE 24.5 The supplier selection process.

Develop Information Regarding Sources of Supply

The purpose of this first step is to gather as much information as possible regarding potential suppliers, current suppliers, the market characteristics for the commodity, and any other data that may be of importance. Seek to determine who are the "best-in-class" suppliers. Use this benchmark information to help create overall evaluation criteria.

Sourcing Information. The first place to search for information regarding existing and potential suppliers is within existing purchasing files or with individuals in the technical departments. Outside the buyer's own organization, the availability of information is dependent upon the potential supplier's status as a private company, a public company, a subsidiary of a larger corporation, or a foreign-owned enterprise. Information sources exist regarding each of these types of company.

Public Companies. Standard and Poors provides reports on thousands of companies and Moody's has information regarding corporate histories, mergers, acquisitions, financial data, locations, and products. Published sources such as *Conover-Mast Purchasing Directory, Directory of Corporate Affiliations, MacRae's Blue Book,* and the *Thomas Register* are also available. In addition, trade magazines, manufacturers' catalogs, promotional literature, and even the *Yellow Pages* can offer information regarding sources. Access to numerous computer-based information services exists at local libraries or just about anywhere with a computer and a modem.

Private Companies. Since private companies are not required to publish information regarding their finances and performance, these companies present the bigger challenge in the information search process. Of course, the best source of information regarding a private organization is the company itself. Although they are usually reluctant to reveal any financial data, most will provide adequate information for initial assessment purposes. However, other resources are available for the determined buyer and for more detailed assessment purposes. Government agencies such as the Federal Bureau of Industrial Economics branch of the Commerce Department and local and state economic development boards are also information resources.

Published sources of information such as trade articles and newspaper reports can be accessed in local libraries or through numerous online, computer-accessed information services. More extensive computer-accessed supplier locating methods are currently being developed for the Internet. Although still in its infancy, this new computerized method will eventually provide buyers with immediate access to almost limitless information concerning potential suppliers.

Foreign-Owned Companies. The international nature of today's business corporations assures that many foreign-owned enterprises must disclose information in the United States according to applicable laws. In addition to what may be found within the United States, there are other information sources. For example, the U.S. Commerce Department's International Trade Commission can provide materials or research guidance. Another information resource that is similar to Dun and Bradstreet is *Kompass,* a directory of foreign companies.

Networking. In addition to formal sources, informal networking should not be overlooked as a means of information gathering. Frequently the details of both public and private firms' operations and customer relations are not found in published sources. It is important to network with individuals and organizations familiar with likely supplier candidates. Personal contacts such as communications with colleagues in professional organizations (APICS, NAPM, AMA) or persons who are the company's competitors and customers may reveal previously hidden information.

Market Information.   An understanding of the nature of the market for the commodity is essential in developing a sourcing strategy. The technology utilized, the level of current and expected demand, the number and size of available suppliers, where the commodity or product is in its life cycle, and the possibility of its obsolescence or substitution are all important considerations. Additionally, in the case of manufactured products, factors affecting the individual constituents of the product must be similarly assessed. These would include pricing and availability for raw materials, components, and any specialized labor required for production.

IDENTIFYING POTENTIAL SOURCES OF SUPPLY

A list of possible sources can be developed after reviewing the data assembled during the information-gathering step. These early steps in the supplier evaluation and selection process do not require an intimately detailed analysis of the supplier's operation or financial status. The purpose is to identify the extent of available sources and then broadly select the most appropriate candidates for further review. This step in the process is only meant to create a list of potential suppliers who appear to be the most likely candidates and therefore merit further assessment efforts.

Neither existing suppliers nor potential new sources should be excluded from the initial evaluation since the ultimate goal is to find the best match between the organization's needs and the supplier's attributes. At this point there are still many questions to be answered but a manageable list of supplier candidates can be developed. More detailed assessments using mailed surveys, site visits, and a formal financial analysis will take place later in the process.

Preliminary Selection Criteria

The specific criteria used to develop the preliminary selection list is dependent upon the supply strategy previously identified for the raw material, part, or product. However, early evaluation criteria should examine supplier characteristics such as the following:

- Company size
- Cost competitiveness
- Domestic versus international organization
- Financial health
- Local or national service
- Location
- Manufacturer or distributor
- Market share
- Market reputation
- Performance history
- Quality reputation
- Recommendations from other customers
- Single or sole source

CREATE EVALUATION AND SELECTION CRITERIA

The list of possible criteria used to select suppliers is almost limitless. However, any criteria that influence four key results are those generally regarded as most important.

Cost

- Active value engineering program
- Capacity utilization
- Cost containment programs
- Current profit, sales, and historical trends
- Environmental impacts of production
- Financial stability
- Hazardous waste creation and disposal
- Labor contracts
- Manufacturing capabilities
- Union contracts
- Productivity
- Operating results
- Product cost analysis
- Planned capital investment and historical trend

Delivery

- Capacity utilization
- Consignment opportunities
- EDI or other computer-based order processing systems
- JIT capability
- Lead times
- Location
- Logistics system
- Order processing times

Quality

- Results of quality system assessment (ISO 9000 or customer-designed survey)
- Baldrige criteria performance
- Warranty policies
- Quality history
- Market preference
- Management attitude

Service

- Technical support
- Response times
- Design and development capabilities
- Field service support
- Consignment, kanban, or other supplier stocking services

The development of evaluation and selection criteria is an iterative process. Preliminary goals for a supplier base are developed in the course of charting the organization's supply management strategy. However, these original goals may have to be modified to accept the realities of the marketplace.

DETAILED SUPPLIER ASSESSMENT

Survey Questionnaires

The purpose of a mailed survey questionnaire is twofold: (1) It provides additional information used in evaluating the company's potential to become a supplier, and (2) it helps identify additional questions to be answered during an on-site visit to the supplier's facility.

Survey Design and Content

Mailed surveys are a standard element in the supplier assessment process used by numerous companies. Those organizations that have not developed a survey instrument should consider alternatives to "reinventing the wheel." It is quite likely that examples of surveys used by current suppliers, customers, or other companies can easily be obtained, evaluated, and modified if necessary.

If a decision is made to develop a custom survey instrument, the seven examination categories defined in the *Malcolm Baldrige National Quality Award* provide an excellent basis for areas of inquiry and should be considered:

1. Leadership
2. Information and analysis
3. Strategic planning
4. Human resource development and management
5. Process management
6. Business results
7. Customer focus and satisfaction

Free information regarding the Baldrige award criteria may be obtained from:

Malcolm Baldrige National Quality Award
National Institute of Standards and Technology
Route 270 and Quince Orchard Road
Administration Building, Room A537
Gaithersburg, MD 20899-001

Detailed Financial Information

Survey questions regarding the potential supplier's financial status and history should be included in the mailed survey questionnaire. Ask the company to provide information such as the following:

- Present ownership and history (buyouts, mergers, acquisitions, etc.)
- Historical trends in profitability, stock prices, and gross revenue
- Financial ratios and comparisons with the ratios of other companies in their standard industrial classification (SIC) category
- Dunn and Bradstreet and/or other financial rating data
- Market share data
- Any other information that helps to assess their present and future financial status

On-Site Facility and Quality System Assessment

There are numerous reasons that an on-site supplier facility and quality system survey are important. An on-site survey allows the personnel from the buying organization to:

- Assess any potential risks associated with doing business with the supplier
- Communicate mutual expectations for doing business
- Begin to establish a working relationship
- Identify opportunities to improve efficiencies
- Evaluate the supplier's potential to provide "certified" products
- Identify opportunities for the transfer of technology
- Help to initiate necessary changes [15]

Exactly what should be done during an on-site supplier assessment is a matter to be defined well before the actual visit. One source for guidance in what to look for can be found in the ISO 9000 series of quality system standards. These criteria provide a solid basis for the assessment of a supplier's quality system. The original intent of the ISO 9000 series of quality system standards was to provide a means by which the buying organization could be confident that a supplier had met minimum standards for an acceptable quality-assurance process. Therefore, the use of a supplier assessment method that follows the 20 elements of ISO 9001 is appropriate.

Regardless of the guidelines used, a supplier site survey should be well planned and systematically executed. One industry expert suggests the following steps to assure that a thorough site survey is completed. [16]

Step 1. Identify your needs to the supplier. Prior to any site visit, review other companies' manuals and existing standards such as the AIAG Guide and ISO 9000 to help develop your expectations. Develop your own standards, or adopt an existing standard. However, remember that your requirements must reflect the needs of the final customer. Document the standards that you have adopted or created, and update them periodically. Another aspect of this step is the development of a site survey and evaluation instrument. This is a guide for those who perform the survey. It should list the areas and issues to be investigated and provide a measurement system to record the investigator's observations.

Step 2. Share your needs with the supplier. This can be done by providing a copy of your company's quality standards for suppliers. Personal discussions or conferences with suppliers should also be used to communicate your needs.

Step 3. Survey the facility. Team up with the supplier's personnel, and put emphasis on the supplier's quality system. Use the site survey instrument as a tool to record observations and evaluation scores while actually walking through the supplier's quality, production, and management systems. This will help to quantify and document the results of your findings.

Step 4. Analyze the results of the survey. Together with the other personnel who participated in the survey, identify areas in which the supplier did not meet your company's standards. Seek to find the "root causes" for these deficiencies, and assess their potential impact on product quality. Discuss possible alternative ways in which the supplier can eliminate these deficiencies and meet your company's expectations.

Step 5. Develop a corrective action plan. Once the root causes of the supplier's deficiencies have been determined and suggested alternatives have been evaluated, try to select the "best" alternatives. Document a solution for each deficiency identified, and assign responsibility for implementation of the solution. A timetable for completion should also be documented.

Step 6. Implement the corrective action plan. Follow-up on the supplier's progress toward the implementation of the corrective action plan is essential. The supplier should be able to verify improvements made according to the established timetable. The plan may be altered by mutual agreement as circumstance requires, but any completed improvements should be institutionalized to assure that the original deficiency does not recur.

CREATE APPROVED AND QUALIFIED SUPPLIER LIST

As the steps in the supplier selection process demonstrate, professional purchasers do not wait until an organizational need is identified before they find a source. Because suppliers are recognized as an extension of the firm's manufacturing capability, the supplier selection process is viewed as an integral part of the firm's supply management strategy. The creation of an *approved supplier list* (ASL/QSL) is one consequence of this proactive strategy. Therefore, it is important to understand that the list is a result of a rigorous process. It is not an independent entity to be easily or arbitrarily amended and therefore should remain under the specified control of a company function or department.

Supplier Categories

In addition to designations such as "approved" or "qualified," organizations frequently have other categories for suppliers. Each category must be defined and have specific criteria by which suppliers are included or excluded from it. These criteria include those used in the original supplier identification and selection process and additional criteria by which ongoing supplier performance is evaluated (see Supplier Rating Methods). A typical list of supplier categories is shown in Fig. 24.6.

Supplier "Partners." These are suppliers with whom there are close, cooperative working relationships and long-term agreements [see Strategic Supplier Relationships ("Partnerships")].

Progressive firms have recognized that the adversarial buyer-supplier relationships of the past are far less effective than relationships built on a spirit of cooperation and collaboration. The terms *partnership* or *alliance* are frequently used to identify such close relationships between buying and selling firms. These partnerships are characterized

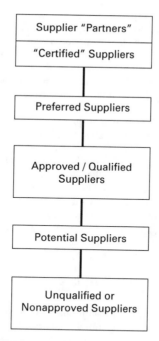

FIGURE 24.6 Supplier categories chart.

by a willingness to share information and to work toward mutually beneficial goals. They require trust, communication, and a solid belief by both parties that the relationship will continue. This supplier category usually represents only a small percentage of all suppliers.

"Certified" Supplier. This term is somewhat more ambiguous than even the term *partner.* Its connotations vary widely among companies. In most instances, a *certified supplier* has continuously demonstrated the ability to ship products of such consistently high quality that receiving inspection is unnecessary. In essence then, it is the parts that are supplied which are really "certified" by the buying organization. The ability to provide nearly defect-free parts and materials is usually one criteria for supplier partners (see "Supplier Certification").

Preferred Suppliers. This category is applied to those suppliers who consistently meet expectations for quality, delivery, service, and cost.

Approved or Qualified Suppliers. This category usually represents newly designated suppliers, those who have had little history with the buying organization or those with whom the buying organization has only infrequent or limited transactions.

   While the previous designations are shown in a hierarchy of upward progression, there is no reason to require or assume that every supplier become a partner or that all its products become certified. It is completely appropriate for some suppliers to remain in the approved or preferred categories because the buyer-supplier relationship may not warrant the additional effort and resources required to create a true alliance or partnership.

The approved or qualified suppliers listing can be either an impediment or an asset in managing the supplier base. Since the purpose of a list is to preidentify those companies with which the organization chooses to do business, such a list does constrain the sourcing alternatives available to purchasing. However, as long as the purchasing function remains actively involved in the source identification, qualification, and selection process, the approved suppliers list is far less an impediment than an asset. The ability to readily identify highly capable suppliers when needs arise is an important asset for all company functions. The speed of response to requirements is increased, and there is assurance that important variables such as quality, delivery, cost, and technology have already been established for the prospective supplier.

ASL Categories.   An *approved supplier list* (ASL) is more useful when divided by product categories. These may include the general categories such as production materials, capital equipment, and services and more specific categories by type of product or service. A computerized listing with keyword searchable data is very effective in assuring ease of use by everyone in the organization. The ASL should include a company profile of commodities and products offered, as well as general business information such as locations, telephone numbers, and sales personnel.

NEGOTIATION OF CONTRACT TERMS

Negotiation is a process of conferring with others in the pursuit of a mutually acceptable agreement. The subject of negotiation has provided content for an endless number of books and seminars, and it is beyond the scope of this section. However, there are 5 *P*s of negotiation that are important to remember.[17] These are preparation, purpose, people, process, and performance.

Purpose

Have a plan for what you want to accomplish. If you do not know where you are going, any road will get you there. Most often a buyer's objectives in a negotiation are to ensure the receipt of quality products, ensure on-time deliveries, ensure a fair and reasonable price, and develop the basis for a continuing business relationship.

Preparation

Of the volumes that could be written about negotiation, perhaps the most significant is the importance of preparation. Preparation is the most important aspect of any negotiation. Know your needs, your products, your supplier, and your supplier's needs.

People

Recognize that only people negotiate. Although we often speak in terms of "company A negotiating with company B," the fact is that it is the companies' personnel who are really negotiating. Therefore, in addition to readily apparent factors of availability and market demand, there are other forces that sway people's actions in a negotiation. All the factors that influence people such as status, titles, peer groups, time, reciprocity, authority, and association with others are likely to be meaningful considerations.[18]

Process

Negotiation is a process. Rather than a single act, negotiation involves a series of steps in which both parties should try to recognize each other's needs, find areas of agreement, and develop alternatives in areas of disagreement.

Performance

One key to ensuring performance is to negotiate an agreement that is genuinely acceptable to both parties. A lopsided contract will only be half-heartedly performed by the party who felt they lost the negotiation. Even well-balanced contracts should include a clear method for resolving any disagreements that occur after the ink has dried. Once a mutually agreeable contract has been executed, each party should monitor the other's adherence to the agreement.

PREPARATION AND ISSUANCE OF THE CONTRACT (PURCHASE ORDER)

The preparation of a *purchase order* (PO) can be accomplished manually, through an automated process, or through electronic means. Purchase orders are usually multipart forms. As demonstrated by the examples provided in Figs. 24.7 and 24.8, purchase-order forms vary among organizations. Whatever the format, a properly executed PO should contain at least the following information:

- PO identification number
- Date the PO was issued
- Buying company name and address
- Ship-to address (destination)
- Billing address
- Supplier's name and address
- The quantity ordered and the unit of measure
- The dollar value per unit of measure and total order
- A description of the part, product, service, or raw material to be purchased
- Delivery schedule required
- Method of shipment
- FOB point and freight payment terms
- Payment terms (discounts)
- Buyer and/or supplier part number identification and revision level
- Signatures required for authorization

The *Uniform Commercial Code* requires that transactions for goods with a value of $500 or more be in writing to be enforced. However, many companies disregard this fact and choose not to send "hard-copy" POs to their preferred suppliers unless significant dollar values are involved. EDI systems, blanket orders and releases, or simple telephone orders are used in place of paper POs.

PURCHASE ORDER

THIS NUMBER MUST APPEAR ON ALL INVOICES, PACKING SLIPS, PACKAGES & CORRESPONDENCE

ORDER DATE	F.O.B.	SHIP VIA	TERMS	DELIVERY/PERFORMANCE DATE

SELLER:

NAME ____________________

ADDRESS ____________________

____________________ ZIP ________

SHIP TO:

NAME ____________________

ADDRESS ____________________

____________________ ZIP ________

[ ] CONFIRMING ORDER [ ] CHANGE ORDER [ ] TAXABLE [ ] NON-TAXABLE

PLEASE ENTER OUR ORDER AND FURNISH GOODS OR SERVICE SPECIFIED BELOW IN ACCORDANCE WITH TERMS OF THIS PURCHASE ORDER INCLUDING THOSE TERMS AND CONDITIONS PRINTED ON THE REVERSE HEREOF.
If this is a change order, this order affects only the following, all other terms and conditions of the original contract remain in effect until contract completion.

ITEM	QUANTITY	U/M	PART NUMBER	DESCRIPTION	UNIT PRICE	TOTAL

BILLING INSTRUCTIONS: SEND AN ORIGINAL AND ONE (1) COPY OF INVOICE TO:
INCLUDE PURCHASE ORDER NUMBER ON ALL INVOICES. INVOICES WITHOUT PURCHASE ORDER NUMBER WILL BE RETURNED.

ACCEPTANCE OF THIS ORDER IS EXPRESSLY LIMITED TO THE TERMS AND CONDITIONS OF THE ORDER. SEE REVERSE SIDE FOR ADDITIONAL TERMS AND CONDITIONS.

BY ____________________

PURCHASING AGENT

FIGURE 24.7 Purchase order. (*Source: NAPM.*)

Follow-Up on the Order and/or Expediting If Required

While all buying firms expect performance to the terms of a purchase contract, life is not always so simple. In some organizations individuals are designated as "expediters" or those personnel whose major responsibility is to stay in contact with suppliers in order to ensure delivery performance. In cases of immediate requirements, the buyer may have incurred additional costs for a "quick turnaround" by the supplier. Therefore it makes sense to keep track of the supplier's progress toward completion of the order.

Receipt and Inspection of Goods. The first inspection of the goods shipped to a buyer takes place at the receiving dock. Personnel in the receiving department check the packing slip against open POs to verify that the type and quantity of materials match what was ordered. In addition, they check the goods for any visible signs of damage done in transit. After the goods have been conditionally received at the dock, they may undergo further inspection by incoming quality control personnel. Although industry trends con-

MA	Exp.	Loc.	Dept.	Job	Phone #		Est. Cost	

SUPPLIER COPY

Required by

601 Rayovac Drive
Madison, WI 53711-2497
P.O. Box 44960
Madison, WI 53744-4960

PRINTED WITH
SOY INK

RECOVER

RAYOVAC®

Exp. Approval Auth.

Date   Page

Purchase Order No. and Line No. must appear on all Packages, Packing Slips, Shipping Paper, Bill of Lading, Invoices and Correspondence.

To:

Deliver
To:

Please Enter Our Order for the Following Subject to the Conditions Below:

Item	Item I.D.	Description and Specification	Order Qty.	Unit	Price
		VOID			

☐ TAXABLE   ☐ TAX EXEMPT   Explain Tax Exempt Qualification:

Please Note
1. Invoice in DUPLICATE to RAYOVAC CORPORATION, P.O. Box 44960, Madison, WI 53744-4960 on date of shipment.
2. Original Bill of Lading or Express Receipt must be attached to the original invoice.
3. Packages and Bundles must be securely wrapped and marked showing contents, Part Number, Purchase Order Number, and Line Number.
4. All Goods are subject to our inspection and test upon arrival, notwithstanding prior payment to obtain discount.
5. This order must not be billed at prices higher than previously invoiced without our permission.
6. This order is subject to the terms and conditions on the reverse side hereof.
7. Vendor agrees to notify RAYOVAC before making changes in the physical characteristics, manufacturing process or chemical composition of the product.

CONTACT TRAFFIC DEPARTMENT IF UNABLE TO USE SPECIFIED ROUTING. CALL 608-275-4464

FIGURE 24.8 Purchase order. (*Source: Rayovac Corp.*)

tinue to reduce or eliminate receiving inspection, in many organizations it is still the only method available to help verify that the goods received meet the expected quality requirements.

Review of the Invoice and Clearance for Payment. In a traditional purchasing process, the accounts payable personnel must match the packing slip, the purchase order, and the supplier's invoice in order to release payment for the goods received. This is an auditing function to ensure that the packing slip quantities, invoice prices, and other terms all match with the original contract. More advanced purchasing processes have eliminated such cumbersome and cost-adding tasks through the application of computer technology or consolidation of supplier billing methods.

Maintenance of Order Records. It has been customary for purchasing departments to retain copies of closed orders for both their value as historical records and for access if needed in legal or tax matters. Closed order files may be cross-referenced by supplier and purchase-order number. In commercial purchasing organizations, these files are rarely maintained on-site for more than 1 year and generally are not maintained in any location beyond 5 to 7 years.

Alternative Purchasing Processes. There are several disadvantages inherent in the traditional purchasing process, which is often burdened with paperwork, approval cycles, excessive lead times, file maintenance, and multiple tasks that add no value to the purchase. Furthermore, the process is somewhat disengaged from other business processes in the organization. To encourage greater efficiency and effectiveness in the purchasing process, alternative processes are frequently used. These alternatives may be used in conjunction with existing traditional methods, or they may replace those methods entirely. However, not all of these methods are interchangeable, and they are most effective when used for repetitive purchases. The following are a few of the most widely accepted alternative purchasing processes.

Blanket Orders. There are numerous instances when the issuance of individual POs can be more costly than the actual items to be purchased. In those circumstances where small, repetitive purchases are required, a buyer may elect to use a *blanket order* covering a single product or numerous items over an extended period of time. While the blanket order contains the same basic information as a regular purchase order, delivery times and quantities are not identified. The terms *as required* or *upon release to buyer* are inserted in the agreement instead. Once the blanket order has been awarded, the buyer then issues *releases* against the order, which signals the supplier to ship the required quantities as noted on the release.

Systems Contracts. A *systems contract* is a more efficient extension of a blanket order. The benefit of a systems contract is in the elimination of additional paperwork and administrative processing. For example, a systems contract may be awarded for a family of products such as office supplies. Requisitioners then merely check the catalog of products offered by the supplier and phone in their order. When the order is delivered, the signed packing slip becomes a supplier record of the delivery and an invoice for accounts payable.

Computerized Applications. Computer software companies have developed on-line systems that simplify the steps in the purchasing process to reduce or eliminate many of the paper documents required in traditional systems. Although software varies among the many providers, most computer-based on-line purchasing systems will include the ability to do the following:

- Create requisitions
- Provide on-line approvals as required
- Create purchase orders
- Track purchase orders
- Compile supplier histories
- Compile part or product buy histories
- Provide audit trails
- Produce order status and supplier performance reports

The ability to perform *electronic data interchange* (EDI) functions such as electronic invoicing and payment may also be included with some software packages. In addition, other software systems are available that expand these EDI capabilities to include access to multiple catalogs of information regarding available suppliers and products. Computerized requisition and order placement systems may be used to replace the traditional hard-copy purchasing systems or simply interface with existing methods.

SUPPLIER MANAGEMENT

The management of a high-quality, cost-effective supplier base is an essential purchasing function. The first step in this ongoing process is the development of a supply management strategy. This strategy must be consistent with and supportive of the organization's comprehensive business strategies (see "Purchasing Role in Corporate Strategy"). The next element in supply management is the identification, evaluation, and selection of the best suppliers (see "Supplier Selection"). Once these suppliers are selected, various methods are then used to continuously manage their performance. Among the many methods employed in supplier management, a few of the more important include supplier rating, supplier certification, and supplier partnerships or alliances.

Supplier Rating Methods

As part of the supplier management process, many firms use performance metrics and other criteria to place suppliers in various categories (see "Supplier Selection"). These categories may then be used to help determine the type and quantity of business conducted with a supplier. The most frequently utilized performance metrics include historical part or product quality statistics, on-time delivery performance, cost containment performance, and service performance.

Historical Part or Product Quality Statistics

The most commonly monitored quality statistics concern the supplier's performance in providing almost defect-free parts or products. Most organizations have replaced the concept of *acceptable quality levels* (AQL) with a commitment to zero defects. Statistical records are maintained and monitored for all parts and products. Routine receiving inspection is conducted on those parts that have not been certified for direct shipment to the point of use, and some type of periodic audit is performed on those parts and products previously certified (see "Supplier Certification"). All firms should require suppliers to maintain an excellent average level of quality performance as a condition of continued business.

Supplier Certification

Because supply management practices such as "lean manufacturing" or JIT require minimal on-hand inventories, buyers must have the ability to ship parts or products directly from the supplier to the point of use on the manufacturing floor. In a lean manufacturing system, receiving inspection is a cost-adding activity that wastes time and resources. Therefore, the quality of a supplier's parts and products must be assured at the supplier's facility. This is one important factor that has led to the practice of supplier certification.

The meaning of the term *certification* has become muddled because of the many ways in which it is now used. For example, the term *ISO 9000 certified* is often used to identify companies whose facilities, processes, and procedures have been registered as in compliance with one of the three ISO 9000 quality system standards (9001, 9002, or 9003). While companies may display a "certificate" that attests to the fact that they have succeeded in meeting ISO 9000 standards, this certificate does not guarantee that they are qualified to ship products directly to the buyer's manufacturing floor. To clarify the context in which the term *certification* is used here, the following definitions apply:

- A *certified supplier* is one who has demonstrated the continuing ability to provide virtually defect-free parts and products so that no further routine inspection by the purchasing organization is required.
- *Supplier certification* is a process by which a supplier's quality system has been determined capable of consistently producing virtually defect-free parts or products.

Supplier Certification Goals

The following is a list of frequently cited goals that individual companies choose to pursue through supplier certification:

- Improve product quality.
- Develop best-in-class supplier base.
- Provide for small lot sizes of required materials.
- Eliminate all non-value-adding activities.
- Achieve the lowest total cost of materials.
- Develop strategic supplier relationships (partnerships).
- Provide for continuous improvement of the quality and supply management systems.

Improve Product Quality

Because supplier certification requires suppliers to achieve a C_{pk} greater than 2.0, the process of certification has a direct impact upon part or product quality. (C_{pk} is a measure of the ability of a process to produce consistent parts or products.) In addition, other quality-related improvements such as the elimination of rework, scrap, and defects are operational objectives that contribute to improved overall quality. The elimination of receiving inspection also reduces costs since such inspection is no longer necessary.

Develop Best-in-Class Supplier Base

The process of certifying suppliers requires firms to develop and utilize formal supplier evaluation and survey methods. This helps to ensure that only the best possible suppliers are retained in the firm's supplier base. Supplier certification also helps to foster the move toward single-sourced items, which reduces the overall number of suppliers and the resources necessary to manage them.

Provide for Small Lot Sizes

Minimal on-hand inventory is one of the factors that help achieve the cost benefits associated with lean manufacturing or JIT techniques. While working through the supplier certification process, buying and supply firms can cooperate in establishing more effective, efficient processes that will allow the production and shipment of smaller lot sizes.

Elimination of All Non-Value-Adding Activities

For many firms, supplier certification extends well beyond part or product quality issues. Certified suppliers are expected to continuously improve their business processes to seek out and eliminate non-value-adding activities. Improvements are achieved through the use of such techniques as the introduction of EDI, consolidated billing, elimination of inspection, reductions in overtime, and the continual monitoring of the supplier's quality system.

Achieve the Lowest Total Cost of Materials

The supplier certification process requires the up-front use of techniques such as *value analysis engineering* (VA/VE) and *quality function deployment* (QFD). These customer-focused analytical techniques combined with statistical methods such as *design of experiments* (DOE) and *statistical process control* (SPC) help to ensure product quality and conformance to target costs.

Provide for Continuous Improvement

Quality and cost control cannot be viewed as one-time-only events. The supplier certification process results in a mutual agreement between buying and supplying organizations to constantly monitor manufacturing methods, materials employed in manufacture, and quality-monitoring systems.

THE PROCESS OF CERTIFYING A SUPPLIER

Supplier certification is a process, not a program. Programs have a flavor-of-the-month connotation while a process is ongoing and constantly improved. Supplier certification must be just one element in a firm's companywide procurement and quality system. It is not a purchasing or quality-assurance department program and cannot succeed as an independent activity delegated to a few employees.

Supplier certification is not a stand-alone activity. As previously noted, certification is only one element in a well-constructed supply management system. Therefore, the certification of suppliers proceeds in phases:

- Strategic analysis and preselection
- Capability assessment
- Quality systems development
- Part or product certification
- Partnership or alliance

One of the most frequently cited reasons for the failure of certification efforts is the inability to involve all the corporate functions necessary to make it happen. Any time certification is delegated solely to purchasing or quality assurance, it is doomed to fail. Many other functional areas within an organization must be responsible for assisting in the design and implementation of the process. As an ongoing process, supplier certification demands that each function incorporate the tasks and attitudes required for its success. Some of the most important company functions and a few of their responsibilities include the following:

Marketing
- Determine customer expectations.
- Communicate customer requirements.
- Provide forecast information.
- Provide new-product directions.
- Identify field problems.

Quality Assurance and Control
- Provide historical data.
- Establish reporting requirements.
- Establish rating system.
- Assist in setting specifications.
- Monitor supplier quality.

Receiving
- Assist in information systems development.
- Maintain delivery record.
- Establish materials-handling procedures.
- Assist in developing certified and noncertified materials-handling procedures.

Production
- Provide packaging and lot size recommendations.
- Provide assembly specifications.
- Provide nonconforming materials information.
- Monitor process controls.

Purchasing
- Provide leadership.
- Communicate plans and goals with suppliers.

Accounting
- Help identify and quantify components of total cost.
- Help develop cost-of-quality models and tracking systems.
- Establish supplier payment terms.

Human Resources
- Assist in the management of change.
- Redefine job duties and descriptions.
- Help provide training.

Engineering
- Establish specifications with suppliers.
- Utilize concurrent engineering methods.
- Develop and maintain accurate bills of materials.

In many organizations there is frequently a need to educate and convince management of the benefits to be derived from a well-functioning supplier certification process. One means of accomplishing this is to compare the present supply quality system (one without certification) with the proposed quality system (one with certification) and present this analysis to management. To accomplish this, the following activities are essential:

- Develop flowcharts of existing and proposed systems.
- Identify non-value-adding current activities.
- Determine the costs of quality for the organization.
- Develop a cost-of-ownership profile for materials.
- Identify customer-driven requirements for certification.
- Determine industry benchmarks.

The use of deployment flowcharting (process mapping) will help to analyze what is currently being done and illustrate the extent of non-value-adding activity.

Financial Justification for Certification

The total cost of materials is greatly affected by an organization's overall costs of quality. As part of their total quality management (TQM) efforts, firms often determine that it is useful to track and evaluate their company's costs of quality. These include the cost of activities designed to prevent defects, activities that appraise or inspect products, the costs of defective products during the manufacturing process, and the costs associated with defective products that reach customers.

Published reports suggest that the cost of quality in a manufacturing organization can be as high as 60 percent of sales, and yet most financial executives underestimate this reality.[19] Therefore, efforts to identify the costs of quality can provide the basis by which the required resources for supplier certification are financially justified.

Part or Product Certification

The actual process of certifying a part or product can be accomplished in a series of five steps:

- Secure management commitment and supplier commitment for necessary resources and involvement.
- Verify that the product design meets customer needs and apply value analysis principles in determining specifications and key control characteristics.
- Verify the manufacturing process and sequence, and develop control plans.
- Evaluate performance to the plans using statistical methods to establish C_{pk}, and improve processes to meet minimum C_{pk} levels. Then monitor delivered product quality until criteria for certification have been met.
- Monitor and maintain supplier performance through the review of SC and C_{pk} data, regular audits, and close communication regarding changes or problems.

In each of the many steps toward certification outlined here, there are numerous "devilish details" that either assist or undermine efforts toward certification. However, the single biggest contributor to success or failure may be how well your organization can manage change. For some companies, the functionally integrated, quality-focused, strategic nature of the certification process may require changes in personnel, resource allocations, manufacturing methods, job descriptions, information technologies, and many, many other aspects of the business. These changes are often difficult. But in the future, there will be two kinds of companies: those who have eliminated all non-value-adding costs in their supply systems and those who no longer exist.

Strategic Supplier Relationships ("Partnerships")

A critical component in the supplier certification process is *early supplier involvement* (ESI) in the design and development of parts or products and the manufacturing process used to produce them. Because it often addresses the root cause of supplier quality problems, this up-front supplier involvement is also an essential characteristic in successful supplier partnerships. Many quality issues are in reality design- or process-related issues that can be avoided by incorporating the supplier's expertise early in the development process. Such early supplier support can help assure that both design and process specifications are appropriate for continuous high-quality production.

The term *partnership* can represent both a legal entity and a way of doing business. In a legal sense, a partnership is a form of business ownership in which two or more parties accept both joint liability for the acts of the partnership and a shared interest in the profits of the partnership. The joint-liability aspect of a partnership has encouraged many organizations to abandon their use of the term when it is only intended to signify a close, cooperative way of doing business.

Partnerships in business are characterized by a mutual willingness to share information, resolve problems, cooperate in product development, and avoid acting in one's self-interest only. These are long-term relationships that require considerable resources in time and personnel. Therefore, they are usually confined to a small percentage of the total number of an organization's suppliers. Professor Lisa Ellram has identified "five phases in the development and evolution of purchasing partnerships" outlined in Fig. 24.9.[20]

PURCHASING AND THE LAW

A thorough examination of the law regarding the commercial purchase of goods or services is well beyond the scope of this chapter. However, it is important to define and review several key legal terms and concepts that must be addressed in the daily perfor-

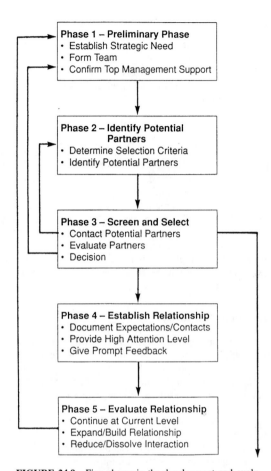

FIGURE 24.9 Five phases in the development and evolution of purchasing partnerships. (*Source: Lisa Ellram, "A Managerial Guideline for the Development and Implementation of Purchasing Partnerships,"* International Journal of Purchasing and Materials Management, *August 1991, p. 4.*)

mance of a professional buyer's duties. The following is a brief overview of several important legal terms and definitions.[21]

- The Uniform Commercial Code (UCC)
- Agency and actual versus apparent authority
- A contract
- An offer
- Acceptance
- Counteroffer
- Purchase order

UCC

The *Uniform Commercial Code* is a set of standards for commercial transactions (sales and contracts) that has been adopted by all the states except Louisiana. The intent of the code is to "simplify, clarify, and modernize the law governing commercial transactions."[22] Article 2 of this code applies to the "transactions in goods" and therefore has the greatest importance to purchasers.

Agency Law

The term *agency* is used to define the relationship that exists between a buyer (agent) and his or her employer (principal) when that employer designates the buyer to act on the company's behalf. The law recognizes the buyer as an agent (purchasing agent) of the company by whom he or she is employed. As an agent, the buyer is not personally considered a legal party to any agreement between the buying and selling firms. However, as an agent, the buyer has the power to conduct business with suppliers and to conclude agreements for the purchase of goods and services required by the company. As an agent, the buyer is obligated to represent the company (the principal) with diligence, care, and loyalty. The company also has an obligation to the buyer to be certain that he or she has received clear instructions regarding the buyer's scope of work, duties, and level of authority.

Actual Versus Apparent Authority

The concepts of actual versus apparent authority are important because both types of authority create legal obligations for the company and have legal consequences for both buyers and the firms they represent. *Actual authority* is that granted by the principal to the agent (buyer). *Apparent authority* is that which occurs when someone is allowed to act in a manner that gives others reason to believe he or she is a legitimate agent of the principal.

Consider a situation in which a buyer has actual authority for up to $25,000 in purchases. A buyer who then commits to purchase $50,000 of goods has acted outside of his or her actual authority. However, because the seller relied upon the "apparent authority" of the buyer, the company is still committed to the contract. Such a situation can also arise when engineers or other members of the organization place orders with suppliers even though the organization has not granted them the formal authorization to do so.

Buyers must also be aware that the issue of apparent versus actual authority is an important consideration when dealing with salespeople. Most salespeople are called "representatives" for very good reason. They are not legal agents and can really do no more than seek orders that must be approved by the company they represent.

A Contract

The term *contract* may represent three different things in various combinations:

1. A series of acts by two or more parties expressing their concurrence
2. The legal relations resulting from the acts of the parties, always including the relation of *right* in one party and *duty* in the other
3. A physical document executed by the parties as a fact in itself and as lasting evidence of their having performed other necessary acts expressing their intentions[23]

In essence, a contract is a promise or a set of promises between two or more parties. Contract law recognizes that both parties have a duty to perform that promise or set of promises. If the contract is breached, that is, if one of the parties does not fulfill a promise, then the law provides a remedy for the party for whom the promise was not fulfilled. A contract must result from a mutual assent or approval of two or more parties. The most common way in which this binding legal relationship (contract) is formed is through the process of offer and acceptance.

An Offer

An *offer* is a conditional promise in which an offeror agrees to be legally bound if the offeree agrees to the performance outlined in the offer. The *offeror* is the individual or individuals making the offer, and the *offeree* is the individual or individuals to whom the offer is made. For example, an offer is made when a potential purchaser (the offeror in this case) agrees to be bound to pay a purchase price if the seller (the offeree in this case) agrees to sell goods meeting certain specifications. Conversely, an offer is made when a seller (the offeror in this case) agrees to be bound to sell to the purchaser (the offeree in this case) certain goods in exchange for a specific price.

Acceptance

Acceptance is the act of agreeing to be bound by the terms of an offer.

Counteroffer

The person who receives an offer need not accept it. If she or he changes the terms of the proposed contract, the proposed changes constitute a *counteroffer*. The counteroffer is both a rejection of the initial offer and a proposed new offer.

PURCHASING ETHICS

The legal aspects of purchasing are immensely important to buyers. However, the legality or illegality of an act does not always represent its ethical context. The subject of ethical behavior is critically important to professional buyers and goes well beyond considerations of legal versus illegal behavior. As agents for their organizations, professional purchasers are responsible for the expenditure of great sums of money, communication of proprietary information, and the commitment of their own and the supplier's company resources. Such enormous responsibilities require a code of conduct that exceeds that required by the law alone. Along with their colleagues in marketing and sales, professional purchasers are the intermediaries between their organizations and the outside world. Therefore, the maintenance of public trust must be a vital priority.

Many organizations have established their own codes of conduct for their employees and their buyers. Some of these codes of conduct reflect the same principles outlined by the members of the National Association of Purchasing Management (NAPM) in their *Principles and Standards of Purchasing Practice*. This is a code of ethics that all NAPM members are pledged to uphold in the execution of their professional duties. It is a recommended standard of conduct for anyone involved with organizational purchasing, and it is an appropriate selection with which to conclude this chapter.

Principles and Standards of Purchasing Practice

Loyalty to your organization

Justice to those with whom you deal

Faith in your profession

From these principles are derived the NAPM standards of purchasing practice (domestic and international):*

1. Avoid the intent and appearance of unethical or compromising practice in relationships, actions, and communications.

2. Demonstrate loyalty to the employer by diligently following the lawful instructions of the employer, using reasonable care and only authority granted.

3. Refrain from any private business or professional activity that would create a conflict between personal interest and the interests of the employer.

4. Refrain from soliciting or accepting money, loans, credits or prejudicial discounts and the acceptance of gifts, entertainment, favors, or services from present or potential suppliers that might influence, or appear to influence, purchasing decisions.

5. Handle confidential or proprietary information belonging to employers or suppliers with due care and proper considerations of ethical and legal ramifications and governmental regulations.

6. Promote positive supplier relationships through courtesy and impartiality in all phases of the purchasing cycle.

7. Refrain from reciprocal agreements that restrain competition.

8. Know and obey the letter and spirit of laws governing the purchasing function and remain alert to the legal ramifications of purchasing decisions.

9. Encourage all segments of society to participate by demonstrating support for small, disadvantaged, and minority-owned businesses.

10. Discourage purchasing involvement in employer-sponsored programs of personal purchases that are not business related.

11. Enhance the proficiency and stature of the purchasing profession by acquiring and maintaining current technical knowledge and the highest standards of ethical behavior.

12. Conduct international purchasing in accordance with the laws, customs, and practices of foreign countries, consistent with United States laws, your organization's policies, and these Ethical Standards and Guidelines.

NOTES

1. "Purchasing's New Muscle," *Fortune,* February 20, 1995, pp. 75–83.

2. William Bales and Harold Fearon: "CEOs'/Presidents' Perceptions and Expectations of the Purchasing Function," *CAPS Report,* 1993, p. 6.

Source: National Association of Purchasing Management, adopted January 1992.

3. Keki Bhote: *Strategic Supply Management,* Amacom, New York, 1989.

4. Michiel R. Leenders and David L. Blenhorn: *Reverse Marketing,* The Free Press, New York, 1988.

5. "The Car Makers' Recovery Stakes," *The Economist,* October 29, 1994, p. 73.

6. Jon L. Pierce and Randall B. Dunham: *Managing,* Scott, Foresman, Little, Glenview, Ill., 1990, p. 170.

7. Michael E. Porter: *Competitive Strategy,* The Free Press, New York, 1980, p. 35.

8. "The Car Makers' Recovery Stakes," *The Economist,* October 29, 1994, pp. 72–73.

9. Michael E. Porter: *Competitive Strategy,* The Free Press, New York, 1980, p. 36.

10. David A. Garvin: *Managing Quality,* The Free Press, New York, 1988.

11. George Stalk, Jr., and Thomas M. Haut: *Competing Against Time,* The Free Press, New York, 1990.

12. Michael Hammer and James Champy: *Reengineering the Corporation,* HarperBusiness, New York, 1993.

13. Gary Hamel and C. K. Prahalad: "Strategic Intent," *Harvard Business Review,* (67:3), May–June 1989, p. 65.

14. Richard Pinkerton: *Techniques for Cost-Effective Buying,* University of Wisconsin, Management Institute, Seminar Notebook, Sec. 4, 1994, pp. 16–20.

15. Mohammed O. Ezzat: *Supplier Certification: Guidelines for Implementation,* University of Wisconsin, Management Institute, Seminar Notebook, Sec. 5, 1994, p. 4.

16. Mohammed O. Ezzat: *Supplier Certification: Guidelines for Impiementation,* University of Wisconsin, Management Institute, Seminar Notebook, Sec. 5, 1994, pp. 7–12.

17. John M. McKeller: *Negotiating and Contracting,* University of Wisconsin, Management Institute, Seminar Notebook, Sec. 6, 1994, pp. 1–20.

18. Robert B. Cialdini: *Influence, The Psychology of Persuasion,* Quill, New York, 1984.

19. Michael Ostrenga: "Return on Investment Through the Cost of Quality," *Journal of Cost Management* (5:2), 1991, p. 37.

20. Lisa Ellram: "A Managerial Guideline for the Development and Implementation of Purchasing Partnerships," *International Journal of Purchasing and Materials Management,* August 1991, p. 4.

21. James Broderick, Michael P. Erhard, and John M. McKeller: adapted in part from *Contracting and Negotiating,* University of Wisconsin, Management Institute, Seminar Notebook, 1994.

22. Michael P. Erhard: *Contracting and Negotiating,* University of Wisconsin, Management Institute, Seminar Notebook, Sec. 2, 1994, p. 1.

23. James Broderick: *Contracting and Negotiating,* University of Wisconsin, Management Institute, Seminar Notebook, Sec. 3, 1994, p. 10.

BIBLIOGRAPHY

Burt, David N: *Proactive Procurement: The Key to Increased Profits, Productivity, and Quality,* Prentice-Hall, Englewood Cliffs, N.J., 1984.

Dobler, Donald W., David N. Burt, and Lamar Lee, Jr.: *Purchasing and Materials Management: Text and Cases,* 5th ed., McGraw-Hill, New York, 1990.

Leenders, Michiel R., and Anna E. Flynn: *Value-Driven Purchasing,* Irwin, New York, 1995.

Leenders, Michiel R., Harold E. Fearon, and Wilbur B. England: *Purchasing and Materials Management,* 9th ed., Irwin, Homewood, Ill., 1989.

Raedels, Alan R.: *Value-Focused Supply Management,* Irwin, New York, 1995.

CHAPTER 25
WAREHOUSING AND STORAGE

Editor

James A. Tompkins, Ph.D.
President, Tompkins Associates, Inc.
Raleigh, North Carolina

The profession of planning and managing warehouse operations is indeed a critical one. With over 300,000 large warehouses and 2.5 million employees in the United States, the warehousing industry has costs equaling over 2 percent of the gross national product. Unfortunately, only recently has the field of warehousing begun to receive the attention its fiscal stature deserves. Even so, the recent emphasis given to warehousing has been primarily technological, resulting in innovations in materials-handling and materials storage equipment. What is still lacking is a concerted effort to educate and train managers to plan and manage warehouse operations effectively.

Warehouse operations are often mistakenly thought to exist in a static environment, where conditions and requirements rarely change and where warehouse planning entails the one-time activities of building a structure and providing equipment. Similarly, warehouse management is thought to be merely the supervision of a few simple, highly repetitive tasks. On the contrary, warehouse operations exist in a dynamic environment. The continual demands for greater product proliferation and better customer service have combined to create warehousing conditions and requirements that rarely remain constant for long. Consequently, warehouse planning is, in fact, a continuous activity, and warehouse management is a series of critical interactions among the warehouse managers, workers, and users.

In addition to being a dynamic profession, warehousing is a challenging one. Perhaps the greatest challenge confronting the warehouse professional is the need to alter the image attached to warehousing by companies and by society. In fact, over the past few decades, the warehousing function has been the "whipping boy" for the manufacturing and marketing functions of most firms simply because few managers have identified the impact that more efficient and effective warehouse operations can have on the total system.

WAREHOUSING DEFINED

Warehousing is simply holding goods until they are needed. The functions of a warehouse are to:

1. Receive the goods from a source.
2. Store the goods until they are required.
3. Pick the goods from the storage area when they are required.
4. Ship the goods to the appropriate user.

Whether the goods are received from an internal or external source and shipped to an internal or external user, or any combination of the two, is insignificant. If the primary functions of an activity are receive-store-pick-ship, then that activity is a warehouse, regardless of its position in a company's logistics, and the tools and techniques presented in this chapter can be successfully used to plan and manage that activity.

VALUE OF WAREHOUSING

Does warehousing an item add value to that item? The traditional school of thought will conclude that, no, warehousing does not add value to a product; in fact, warehousing is strictly a cost-adding activity that is often a necessary evil. In firms that follow this school of thought, warehousing costs are typically classified as indirect costs, overhead, burden, other operating expenses, and so on. Often, these cost categories are "spread out" over the direct costs of the firm in such a way that the cost of warehousing is no longer distinguishable.

The true value of warehousing lies in having the right product, in the right place, at the right time. Thus, warehousing provides the time and place utility, or the availability, necessary to give materials in the proper form true value. The objective of a firm should not be to sell products but to get the products into the hands of the consumer so that the consumer will pay for the products. Consequently, form utility without availability is worthless. From this view of value, warehousing should now project a different image in your mind. Perhaps the greatest challenge of the warehousing professional is to help others understand the value and role of warehousing in their firms.

WAREHOUSING OBJECTIVES

The primary objective of warehousing is to maximize the effective use of the warehouse resources while satisfying customer requirements. The keywords in this objective, which must be delineated to give the objective true meaning, are *warehouse resources* and *customer requirements*. The resources of a warehouse are space, equipment, and personnel. To understand fully the importance of using space within the warehouse effectively, you must know the cost of space within the warehouse. Most warehouse managers have some knowledge of the cost of building or obtaining new space, but surprisingly few know the cost of maintaining the space (taxes, insurance, maintenance, and energy). A warehouse whose available cubic space is used ineffectively is annually losing a considerable sum of money in operating costs.

The equipment resources of a warehouse include data processing equipment, dock equipment, materials-handling equipment, and storage equipment, all of which combine to represent a sizable capital investment in the warehouse. If you wish to obtain an acceptable rate of return on this investment, you must scrutinize the use of each piece of equipment to guarantee that it is being used most effectively. Often, the personnel resource of the warehouse is the most neglected resource, even though the cost of this resource is usually the greatest. Approximately 50 percent of the costs of a typical warehouse are labor related. A great deal of care must be taken when planning and managing a warehouse to encourage high labor productivity, good labor relations, and worker satisfaction.

Customer requirements are simply the demand to have the right product in good conditions at the right place, at the right time. Therefore, the product must be accessible and protected. If a warehouse cannot meet these requirements adequately, then the warehouse does not add value to the product and, in fact, very likely subtracts value from the product.

Based on the assessments of a warehouse's resources and the customers' requirements, the following set of objectives defines the primary objective more clearly:

- Maximize effective use of space.
- Maximize effective use of equipment.
- Maximize effective use of labor.
- Maximize accessibility of all items.
- Maximize protection of all items.

Although all warehouses are unique, the types of problems faced in planning and managing warehouses are not unique. Consequently, a definite method can be followed to address these problems in all warehouses, regardless of location, size, type of warehouse, type of product stored, and the like. This science of warehousing is the focus of this chapter.

SPACE PLANNING

The warehouse manager of XYZ Company submitted the annual capital-budgeting report for his department to the plant manager. In it was a request for an allocation of $500,000 in the next fiscal year to expand the company's warehouse. The warehouse manager justified the requested expansion by citing the generally overcrowded conditions that resulted in lost or misplaced stock, storage of obsolete materials because of poor stock rotation, and poor labor productivity. After reviewing the plant's capital-budgeting report, the warehouse manager confronted the plant manager demanding to know why the proposed warehouse expansion had received little consideration. The plant manager retrieved a file containing the warehouse manager's capital-budgeting reports for the preceding 5 years. Each report proposed a warehouse expansion. Each year, the justification was the same. Each year, the proposed expansion was rejected.

The plight of this warehouse manager is all too common in the warehousing industry. As long as warehouse management continues to back up warehouse expansion requests with opinions, those responsible for capital-budgeting decisions will turn a deaf ear to the requests. To win the capital-budgeting battle, warehouse management must present justification in the form of a quantitative assessment of warehouse space requirements and a statement of the economic impact of operating with and without the requested space. Then, and only then, can the capital-budgeting decision makers objectively compare the proposed warehouse expansion with alternative capital investments.

Space-Planning Method

Space planning is the part of the science of warehousing that is concerned with making a quantitative assessment of warehouse space requirements. The space-planning method consists of the following general steps:

Step 1. Determine what is to be accomplished.

Step 2. Determine how to accomplish it.

Step 3. Determine space allowance for each element required to accomplish the activity.

Step 4. Calculate the total space requirements.

Space Planning for Receiving and Shipping

The most neglected areas of a warehouse are the receiving and shipping docks. Unfortunately, the most important functions of a warehouse occur on the receiving and shipping docks: transfer of control of merchandise between the warehouse and carrier. If these transfers of control are not accomplished in an efficient, safe, and accurate manner, then the warehouse cannot meet its objective of satisfying customer requirements, regardless of the quality of the other aspects of the warehouse. An important prerequisite of efficient, safe, and accurate receiving and shipping activities is allowing enough space to perform these activities.

The first step in space planning for receiving and shipping operations is to define the materials that will be received or shipped. This explanation should be in sufficient detail to determine the size of unit loads, throughput, materials-handling equipment required, and time to process. After the materials to be received or shipped have been defined, the requirements for the receiving or shipping dock bays can be determined by answering two questions: (1) How many dock bays are required? and (2) How should the dock bays be configured?

How Many Dock Bays Are Required? The three most common techniques of determining the number of receiving or shipping dock bays a warehouse requires are the following:

- Guessing
- Waiting-line analysis
- Simulation

Of these techniques, only simulation will consistently result in an accurate assessment of the number of dock bays required for a typical warehouse. Unfortunately, guessing is used most often. The guess is usually based on some historical experience of the guesser, such as the number of dock bays used in the old warehouse or in other warehouses in the area. Although guessing may very well result in the correct answer, success can usually be attributed to luck rather than knowledge. Waiting-line analysis, or queuing theory, is often suggested as the correct technique for determining the number of dock bays required if the time between carrier arrivals and the time to service the carriers at the warehouse vary randomly. However, this rarely is the case in most warehouse operations. Instead of being random, carrier arrivals usually follow a pattern, resulting in waiting-line analysis providing an inaccurate determination of the number of dock bays required.

Simulation is the recommended technique for most warehouses because carrier arrivals and service times are not random. Contrary to what complicated statistical models and computer programs imply, simulation is a straightforward, simple tool. Simulation results are based on actual truck arrivals and load-unload times that are used to develop a distribution model. From this model, either manually or using a computer program, simulated truck arrivals and processing times are generated that test the validity of a given number of dock bays. Unfortunately, simulation will not result in an unequivocal answer to the dock bay question. Simulation does, however, reveal how dock performance will vary with different numbers of dock bays, and it gives valuable data upon which one can base sound management decisions.

How Should the Dock Bays Be Configured? The first issue in determining dock configuration is the type of dock required. Two basic types of docks exist: *90° docks* and *finger docks*. Figure 25.1 illustrates dock configuration. With a 90° dock, the truck

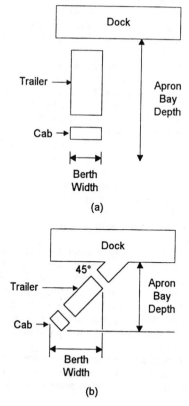

FIGURE 25.1 (*a*) 90° docks versus (*b*) finger docks.

(trailer and cab) is positioned at the dock so the angle between the truck and the dock is 90°. At a finger dock, the angle between the truck and the dock is less than 90°. For example, for a 45° finger dock, the angle between the truck and the dock is 45°. The differences between 90° docks and finger docks lie in the amount of space required for dock operations inside and outside the warehouse. A 90° dock requires less width (the distance parallel to the building) and more depth (the distance perpendicular to the building) than a finger dock. Therefore, a 90° dock requires less inside warehouse space and more outside space than a finger dock needs. Since space inside a warehouse is typically more expensive than space outside a warehouse, 90° docks are more popular than finger docks. When outside space is at a premium, however, due to the shape of the warehouse site or the need to expand, finger docks become a more attractive dock configuration.

The second issue in determining dock configuration is the proper *berth width* of dock bays. The most common berth widths found in warehousing today are 10 and 12 feet. Naturally, the greater the berth width, the more inside warehouse space occupied by the dock. Because inside space is expensive, berth widths of 10 feet are very popular. Unfortunately, minimizing the berth width results in trade-offs between outside apron space and safety. Maneuvering trucks into a dock bay becomes more difficult as the berth width decreases. To compensate for this loss of maneuverability, the dock must have additional apron space to allow positioning of the truck.

The most overlooked vehicle interface requirement in warehouse planning is the direction of vehicle travel about the facility. The direction in which vehicles travel around a warehouse has a significant impact on the efficiency of carrier spotting and the space requirements of that activity.

Trucks should enter a dock area in a counterclockwise direction of travel to allow the truck to back into the dock berth in a clockwise direction of travel. Clockwise backing enables the truck driver to clearly see the rear of the truck as it turns into the dock berth. Conversely, when backing counterclockwise, truck drivers must rely on rearview mirrors to guide their approach to the dock. At first glance, this issue may appear trivial; however, experience has shown that counterclockwise backing requires that the apron bay depth be approximately 20 feet greater than for clockwise backing.

Inside the warehouse, the receiving and shipping docks consist of the space needed to enter and exit the carrier, a travel aisle, and the staging areas. The first component of the receiving or shipping dock space is the area occupied by the dock-leveling device. The amount of space required will vary according to the type of leveling device used. Generally, temporary inside dock-leveling devices will occupy 3 to 7 feet, measured from the dock face, while permanent inside dock-leveling devices will require 4 to 10 feet of inside warehouse space.

The second component of the receiving or shipping dock space is an aisle located between the back edge of the inside dock-leveling device and the staging area. This aisle allows unloading-loading personnel and equipment to enter and exit the carrier and to travel to the appropriate staging area. The dock maneuvering aisle should not be a main warehouse aisle. Travel in this aisle should be restricted to dock personnel and equipment actively servicing carriers. The dock maneuvering aisle should be approximately 4 to 6 feet wide for manual materials handling, 6 to 8 feet wide for powered handtrucks, and 8 to 10 feet wide for forklift trucks.

Staging areas should be located adjacent to the dock maneuvering aisle. The receiving staging area serves as a depository for the materials unloaded from the carrier. The shipping staging area serves as an accumulation point for the merchandise that comprises a shipment.

Specifying accurately the optimum amount of receiving staging space or shipping staging space is a very difficult task. Unfortunately, an incorrect amount of space will reduce greatly the efficiency and effectiveness of the receiving or shipping operation.

The impact will be particularly severe if too little staging space is provided. Too little staging space will lead to dock congestion that will inevitably cause lost materials, damaged materials, split shipments, and erroneous shipments. The more uncertain the receiving or shipment workload is throughout the day, the more flexible and larger the receiving or shipping staging area must be.

The last step in the space-planning process for warehouse receiving and shipping functions is to determine the space requirements for the warehouse office, a quality-control hold space, trash disposal, storage of empty pallets, and a truckers' lounge.

Space Planning for Storage Activities

Storage space planning is particularly critical because the storage activity accounts for the bulk of the space requirements of a warehouse. Inadequate storage space planning can easily result in a warehouse that is significantly larger or smaller than required. Too little storage space will result in a number of operational problems, including lost inventory, inaccessible materials, poor housekeeping, damaged materials, safety problems, and low productivity. Too much storage space will breed poor use of space so that it appears that all the available space is really needed, resulting in higher space costs in the form of land, construction, equipment, and energy.

The first step in storage space planning is to define the materials to be stored. Again, sufficient detail is required to determine unit load sizes, maximum and average inventory levels, throughput, and anticipated storage means. The amount of inventory that is maintained is dependent on the storage philosophy used. The two major storage philosophies are *fixed-* or *assigned-location storage,* and *random-location storage.* In fixed-location storage, each item is assigned a specific storage location. A given item will always be stored in a specific location, and no other item may be stored in that location, even though the space may be empty. When random-location storage is practiced, any item may be assigned to any available storage location. An item in location A one month might be stored in location B the following month, with a different item stored in location A. If fixed-location storage is used, each item must be assigned sufficient space to store the maximum amount of the item that will ever be on hand at any given time. For random-location storage, the maximum quantity on hand at any time will be the average amount of each item.

Which storage philosophy is better? Unfortunately, an unequivocal answer to this question does not exist. Choosing one storage philosophy over another means making a number of trade-offs. Table 25.1 presents a qualitative comparison of fixed and random storage.

TABLE 25.1   Comparison of Storage Philosophies

	Philosophy	
Criteria/Philosophy	Fixed-location storage	Random-location storage
Use of space	Poor	Excellent
Accessibility to materials	Excellent	Good, if there is a good materials-locater system; poor otherwise
Materials handling	Good	Good

Fixed-location storage trades space efficiency for easy accessibility to material; random-location storage trades accessibility to material for space efficiency. The only general conclusion that can be drawn is that the poor use of space by fixed-location storage is a big factor. Compared to random-location storage for the same materials, fixed-location storage will generally require 65 to 85 percent more space.

Once the storage philosophy and the planned inventory levels have been determined, the next step is to identify, evaluate, and select the best storage method. Storage alternatives are evaluated based on the space costs of that alternative. To determine the space costs of a storage alternative, the space requirements of the alternative must be calculated. The space requirements of a storage alternative are directly related to the volume of material to be stored and the use-of-space characteristics of the alternative. The two most important use-of-space characteristics are aisle allowances and honeycombing allowances. *Aisle allowance* is the percentage of space occupied by aisles within a storage area. The amount of the aisle allowance depends on the storage method, which dictates the number of aisles required, and on the materials-handling method, which dictates the size of the aisles. Figure 25.2 shows the calculation of the aisle allowance for shelving storage with manual storage and retrieval of material.

Honeycombing allowances are the percentage of storage space lost because of ineffective use of the capacity of a storage area. Honeycombing is illustrated in Fig. 25.3. Honeycombing occurs whenever a storage location is only partially filled with material. The unoccupied area within the storage location is honeycombed space. Honeycombing may occur horizontally and vertically. For example, Fig. 25.3a presents a top view of a bulk storage area in which material can be placed three units deep. Because the bulk storage area is full, no honeycombing occurs. In Fig. 25.3b, however, two units of product A and one unit of product B have been removed, leaving three empty slots. No other items can be placed in these slots until the remaining units of A and B have been removed (otherwise, blocked stock will result), so these slots are horizontal honeycombing losses. Figure 25.3c is an elevation view of a bulk storage area in which material can be stacked three units high. Here again, the storage area is full, and no honeycombing occurs. In Fig. 25.3d, however, one unit of product A and one unit of product B have been removed, leaving three empty slots. To avoid blocked stock or poor stock rotation, no other units can be placed in these slots until remaining units of A and B have been removed. Consequently, the empty slots are vertical honeycombing losses.

Determining the aisle and honeycombing allowances is essential for calculating space standards for the storage alternative(s) under consideration. A *space standard* is a benchmark defining the amount of space required per unit of product stored. The idea of space standards is not new. In the 1940s, the U.S. Navy became interested in such standards in the design of submarines. The Navy determined that it takes 1.86 ft^3 of space to store 1 ft^3 of product in a submarine. In the 1960s, the National Aeronautics and Space Administration (NASA) became interested in space standards in the design of space vehicles. NASA determined that it takes 1.50 ft^3 of space to store 1 ft^3 of product in a space capsule. In today's warehouses, it takes between 3 and 6 ft^3 to store 1 ft^3 of product. The example that follows (with Fig. 25.4) is an example of how this standard is calculated.

Example: Space Planning for a New Storage Area. Commodity A, to be stored by the LMN Warehouse, requires special environmental control. A special area must be established to house the maximum quantity of commodity A expected ever to be on hand. A storage analysis chart has been completed. It shows the maximum storage requirement for the next 3 years as 300,000 cases. Commodity A is to be stored on pallets and may be stacked 3 pallets high. One alternative storage method is bulk storage areas 2 pallets deep. Given the following data from the storage analysis chart, how much space should be allocated for the storage of commodity A?

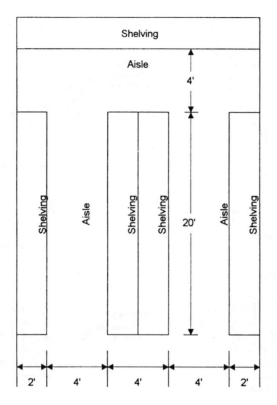

total area$= (2 \text{ ft.} + 4 \text{ ft.} + 4 \text{ ft.} + 4 \text{ ft.} + 2 \text{ ft.}) \times (2 \text{ ft.} + 4 \text{ ft.} + 20 \text{ ft.})$
$= 16 \text{ ft.} \times 26 \text{ ft.}$
$= 416 \text{ ft.}^2$

aisle area$= (16 \text{ ft.} \times 4 \text{ ft.}) + (20 \text{ ft.} \times 4 \text{ ft.}) + (20 \text{ ft.} \times 4 \text{ ft.})$
$= 64 \text{ ft.}^2 + 80 \text{ ft.}^2 + 80 \text{ ft.}^2$
$= 224 \text{ ft.}^2$

aisle allowance$=$ (aisle area $\div$ total area) $\times 100$
$= (224 \text{ ft.}^2 \div 416 \text{ ft.}^2) \times 100$
$= 54\%$

FIGURE 25.2   Aisle allowance calculation.

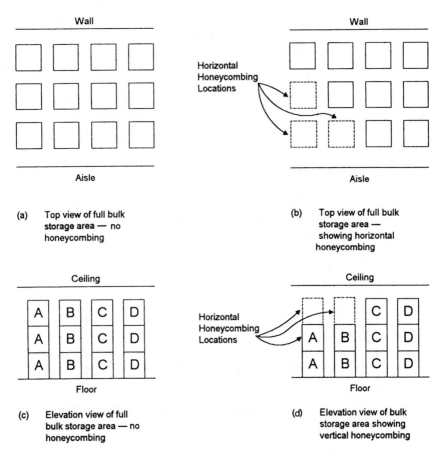

(a)   Top view of full bulk storage area — no honeycombing

(b)   Top view of full bulk storage area — showing horizontal honeycombing

(c)   Elevation view of full bulk storage area — no honeycombing

(d)   Elevation view of bulk storage area showing vertical honeycombing

FIGURE 25.3   Honeycombing.

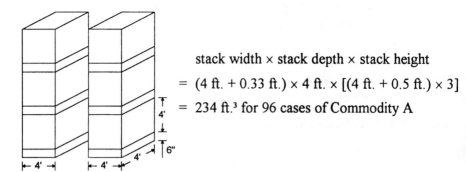

stack width × stack depth × stack height

$= (4 \text{ ft.} + 0.33 \text{ ft.}) \times 4 \text{ ft.} \times [(4 \text{ ft.} + 0.5 \text{ ft.}) \times 3]$

$= 234 \text{ ft.}^3$ for 96 cases of Commodity A

FIGURE 25.4   Total space required for one 3-pallet-high stack of commodity A.

- Case size = 2 ft $\times$ 1 ft $\times$ 1 ft (height) = 2 ft^3
- Palletized = 48 in $\times$ 48 in pallet $\times$ 4 tiers high = 64 ft^3

Step 1. The aisle allowance (AA) for the proposed bulk storage method has been estimated from a proposed layout to be 10 percent. The expected honeycombing allowance (HA) has been calculated to be 36 percent.

Step 2. The pallet height is 6 in, and the clearance between stacks should be 4 in. The total space required for one 3-pallet-high stack of commodity A is therefore shown in Fig. 25.4.

Step 3. The inclusion of allowances for aisles and honeycombing results in the following space standard:

$$\frac{234 \text{ ft}^3}{(1 - AA)(1 - HA)(96 \text{ cases})} = \frac{234 \text{ ft}^3}{(1 - 0.10)(1 - 0.36)(96 \text{ cases})} = 4.23 \text{ ft}^3 \text{ case}$$

Step 4. The total storage space required for the maximum anticipated volume of commodity A, using the proposed storage method, is:

Total storage space required = 300,000 cases $\times$ 4.23 ft^3/case

= 1,269,000 ft^3, or 94,000 ft^3, having a clear stacking height of 13.5 ft

The space calculations do not include areas for receiving or shipping docks, plant services, or personnel services.

It is important to grasp the fundamental objectives of space planning: (1) Emphasize the importance of documenting quantitatively warehouse space requirements, and (2) present a scientific approach by which warehouse space requirements can be quantitatively documented. To grasp one objective and not the other is equivalent to grasping neither. To understand the importance of warehouse planning and not to grasp the method is to have the desire without the know-how. To understand the method of quantitative space planning and not its importance is to possess the know-how without the desire.

EQUIPMENT PLANNING

The equipment that performs the receiving, shipping, and storage activities has a direct bearing on space planning. Therefore, to plan space properly, the equipment occupying the space must also be properly planned.

Warehouse Equipment Planning Method

Effective equipment planning must follow an equally rigorous method as space planning. The general steps to this method are the following:

Step 1. Specify what functions the equipment must perform.
Step 2. Identify equipment alternatives.
Step 3. Evaluate the equipment alternatives.
Step 4. Select the equipment.

The first step in the equipment-planning method is to define the functions the equipment must perform. What must the chosen equipment be able to do to accomplish the desired objective? This question is crucial, and it must be thoroughly answered before

TABLE 25.2   Typical Information Required to Specify Equipment Capabilities

Objective of equipment	Typical questions that must be answered
Unload incoming truck shipments.	What types of trucks will be serviced? What types of unit loads will be handled? How heavy are the unit loads that will be handled? What combination of unit loads might be found on a given shipment? Where will the unit loads be deposited after unloading? What constraints in maneuvering space must be met? Is lifting capability required? To what heights? What productivity rates must be achieved? What other activities will this equipment be required to perform?
Place materials into storage racks.	What type of storage rack will be used? What type of unit load will be handled? How heavy are the unit loads that will be handled? How high must the unit loads be lifted? From where will the unit loads be obtained? What constraints in storage aisle width must be met? What constraints in maneuvering space outside the storage area must be met? What other activity occurs simultaneously in the operating area of this equipment? What other activities will this equipment be required to perform?
Retrieve materials from storage rack.	What types of loads will be retrieved? Full unit loads? Full cases? Individual pieces? How much do the loads that will be retrieved weigh? What type of storage rack will be used? How high off the floor is material stored? What constraints in storage aisle width must be met? What constraints in maneuvering space outside the storage area must be met? What order-picking philosophy will be used: zone picking, full-order picking, simultaneous picking of multiple orders? Where will the materials be deposited after retrieval? What productivity rates must be achieved? What other activities occur simultaneously within the operating area of this equipment? What other activities will this equipment be required to perform?
Load materials into carriers for shipment.	What types of loads will be handled? Unit loads? Loose cartons? What combination of loads? How heavy are loads that will be handled? From where will loads to be handled be obtained? Is lifting capacity required? How much? What types of carriers will be loaded? What maneuvering space constraints must be met? What productivity rates must be achieved? What other activities must this equipment perform?

one begins to identify alternatives. Failure to adequately specify the work the equipment must accomplish and its minimum capabilities will often result in selection of equipment that fails to solve the real problem.

Unfortunately, no standard guidelines exist that guarantee a thorough specification of desired equipment capability. What is desired of the equipment will vary not only from warehouse to warehouse but also from activity to activity. Although each circumstance will require different answers to different questions, the types of questions that will allow adequate specification are virtually the same for all activities within a warehouse. Table 25.2 lists the types of questions one might have to answer before specifying equipment.

The next step is to identify specific equipment alternatives that meet the specifications decided upon. The intent should not be identifying the specific make or model of each alternative but rather to identify generic categories of alternatives. One must first compare the various generic equipment alternatives (pallet rack versus cantilever rack versus drive-in rack versus flow-through rack versus bulk storage) to identify the best storage alternative.

Unfortunately, choosing the best equipment alternatives is easier said than done because of the enormous variety of warehouse equipment on the market today. The number of combinations of equipment that can be made to achieve a certain goal is virtually limitless. A great deal of ingenuity and foresight is often required to predict the impact of integrating several types of equipment into a warehouse system.

A proper evaluation of warehouse equipment alternatives includes both a quantitative comparison and a qualitative comparison of the alternatives, such as flexibility, reliability, or maintainability. The quantitative comparison is typically accomplished by performing an economic evaluation of equipment alternatives, that is, by identifying and estimating the relevant costs of each alternative over its useful life. Relevant costs are usually divided into two categories: *investment costs* and *annual operating costs*. Investment costs are incurred to obtain the equipment, and they occur on a one-time-only or periodic basis. Annual operating costs are the recurring expenses that keep the equipment in operation.

Qualitative issues can be derived by considering the following attributes that might be considered important:

- Ability of the equipment to fit into and serve warehouse operations
- Versatility and ability to adapt to day-to-day changes in products and fluctuations in productivity requirements
- Flexibility (ease of changing or rearranging the installed methods)
- Limitations imposed by the equipment on the flexibility and ease of expansion of the layout, buildings, or both
- Use of space
- Safety and housekeeping
- Working conditions and employee satisfaction
- Ease of supervision and control
- Availability of trained operators
- Frequency and seriousness of potential breakdowns
- Ease of maintenance and repair
- Volume of spare parts that must be stocked
- Quality of product and risk of damage to materials

- Ability to keep pace with productivity requirements
- Personnel problems: training capability, disposition of unnecessary workers, job description changes, and union contracts or work practices
- Potential delays from required synchronization and peak loads
- Supporting services required
- Time required to complete installation, training, and debugging

The final step of the equipment-planning process is to select the specific equipment. The selection process is as follows:

1. Sell management on the proposed equipment, and obtain approval for any capital appropriations required.
2. Compose detailed specifications of the equipment required.
3. Identify vendors who can potentially provide the equipment.
4. Prepare and distribute a vendor bid package.
5. Receive and evaluate the vendors' bids.
6. Select and order the equipment.

Equipment and vendor selection should never be based solely on a low invoice bid. Other factors specifically related to vendor selection are the availability of the equipment, installation and debugging services provided, warranties, and the reputation of the manufacturer and its local representative.

Warehouse Equipment Alternatives

The purpose of this section is to introduce the major classifications of warehouse equipment. Because this is a broad topic to which entire books and periodicals are dedicated, our discussion merely attempts to lay a foundation upon which a more extensive knowledge of warehouse equipment can be built.

Dock Equipment.   Several kinds of dock equipment are used within the warehouse. They are dock levelers, bumper pads, dock shelters, and dock lights.

Dock Levelers.   Dock levelers can be broadly classified into two major categories: internal dock levelers and external dock levelers. *Internal dock levelers* may be portable or permanently installed. Portable dock levelers, commonly called *dock boards,* are fairly inexpensive dock levelers because they can be used at more than one dock door. Consequently, fewer dock levelers are required. Dock boards are commonly used on docks where the amount of dock activity is felt to be insufficient to justify permanent dock levelers. The major drawbacks of dock boards are lack of convenience, safety hazards, and limited capacity.

Permanent internal dock levelers solve the major inadequacies of dock boards. One dock leveler is permanently installed at each dock bay, allowing maximum convenience and safety. Permanent dock levelers can typically service a wider range of differences in height between the dock and the carrier but are more expensive than dock boards.

The two common types of *external dock levelers* are truck levelers and lifting docks. A *truck leveler* is installed in the dock bay well outside the warehouse. It raises or lowers the truck bed to match the height of the dock. The major drawback of truck levelers is maintenance costs. The truck leveler is subjected to the weather outside the warehouse and to physical contact with the truck.

A *lifting dock* is essentially a lift table that is raised and lowered between the dock height and the carrier height. When a truck arrives, the lifting dock is raised to the truck bed, material is loaded onto the lifting dock, the lifting dock is lowered to the dock height, and the material is removed from the lifting dock.

Bumper Pads. Bumper pads are installed on the face of the dock bay to cushion the impact of the truck's hitting the dock as the truck is backed into position. The absence of bumper pads can be disastrous. For example, a 40,000-pound load traveling at 4 miles per hour hits a dock with an impact of 150,000 pounds of force. This force is enough to bend reinforcement steel buried 6 inches into the concrete surface. Eventually, the concrete around the dock door will begin to flake and crack. If $4\frac{1}{2}$-inch-thick bumper pads are installed on the dock face, however, that same 40,000-pound load traveling at 4 miles per hour will hit the dock with only 3,000 pounds of force.

Dock Shelters. Dock shelters, installed on the outside face of the dock door, shelter the dock from the weather. When the truck backs up to the door, the dock shelter engages the rear of the trailer and forms a seal around the trailer. Wind, rain, snow, dust, or other elements of the weather cannot enter through the open dock door. Slippery floors, heat or cooled-air loss, and uneven airflows do not occur.

Dock Lights. Dock lighting is critical to efficient dock operations. A common way to supply light inside the carrier is to use a swivel floodlight that is attached to the inside wall of the dock and swings into the carrier. These floodlights are typically explosion proof. If they are hit, they simply bounce out of the way.

Storage Equipment. A variety of storage equipment exists to meet the needs of warehouse operations.

Pallet Rack. A pallet rack is a rigid structure consisting of upright frames, load-bearing crossarms, and bracing that is specifically designed for pallet storage. The pallet is set down on the load-bearing crossarms. The pallet rack can also be decked, usually with plywood or wire mesh, so that loads other than pallets can be stored there. The three critical factors to consider when specifying a pallet rack are the weight capacity, the width of the pallet rack opening (the distance between upright frames), and the height between the load-bearing crossarms. These factors must be compared to the size of the load to be stored.

Cantilever Rack. A cantilever rack consists of a series of upright frames with load-bearing arms attached at one end to the upright frames. This kind of rack is similar to a pallet rack except the front upright columns are missing, making a cantilever rack much more versatile than a pallet rack.

Drive-In/Drive-Through Rack. A drive-in/drive-through rack is a rack structure where the forklift truck is actually driven into or completely through the structure to store or retrieve pallet loads. A truck enters the *drive-in rack* structure from one side and then backs out of the structure from the same side. When the lift truck enters one side of the *drive-through rack,* it could potentially exit from the other side. Using a drive-in rack results in a *last-in, first-out* (LIFO) storage system. Using a drive-through rack, on one side of which material is typically placed in storage and on the other side of which material is removed from storage, results in a *first-in, first-out* (FIFO) storage system. A drive-in/drive-through rack is primarily used to approximate bulk storage for unit loads that allow very limited or no stacking.

Flow-Through Rack. Flow-through rack is a series of vertical columns and horizontal load supports with conveyors mounted to the horizontal supports such that a load—either pallets or cartons—enter the rack at one end and travel to the other end. A flow-through rack maintains a FIFO inventory system, and the rack is used to approximate bulk storage for unit loads with limited or no stackability. Because materials are placed in storage at one end of the rack and retrieved at the other end and because the fluctuations do not occur in the same aisles, coordination problems between the materials storage and order-picking functions are minimized.

Sliding Rack or Shelving.   The rack or shelving can be mounted on guide rails or tracks, giving the rack or shelving mobility, which means that several rows of rack or shelving need only one aisle. The location of the aisle can be altered by sliding the rack or shelving along the guide rail or track. This storage system is highly space efficient because the aisle allowance required is extremely small. The rack can be electrically, mechanically, or pneumatically powered. The shelving is typically manually powered.

Portable Rack.   In the portable rack category is a wide range of devices used to bulk-store pallet loads or other unit loads in such a way that the material does not bear the weight of other loads stacked above it.

Shelving.   Shelving is a common storage device for small items, usually in cartons. However, if the space available on a given shelf is not effectively used, an overall poor use of space may result.

Drawer Storage.   Drawer storage is an excellent alternative to shelving storage. Instead of placing materials on shelves, one puts them in drawers that can be sized and divided into compartments to match the size of the material being stored. Drawer storage is primarily used when a great variety of items is being stored and when throughput is fairly low.

Carousel Storage.   Carousel storage is an alternative to drawer storage when the throughput of the materials being stored increases. A horizontal carousel consists of a series of bins hanging from an overhead support and circulating around the support. Material in a carousel is brought to the *order picker,* not the other way around. Therefore, material can be retrieved at a rate greater than that for shelving or drawer storage. A vertical carousel is similar except that it uses the height of the building more efficiently.

Automated Storage/Retrieval System (AS/RS).   Automated storage/retrieval systems consist of a series of materials-handling and materials-storage devices integrated to form a single, coordinated storage organism. Unfortunately, the barrage of nomenclature created by AS/RS manufacturers and vendors has effectively disguised the various types of systems. Table 25.3 presents a simple classification scheme by which any AS/RS can be categorized.

Materials Handling.   Because of the broad range of equipment in this category, we will cover only the two most common warehousing materials-handling alternatives: humans and lift trucks. Humans are still the most common materials-handling alternative used in warehousing today. People are most effective when handling occurs infrequently, when areas are confined and congested, and when materials have diverse

TABLE 25.3   AS/RS, Three-Characteristic Classification Scheme

Characteristic	Alternatives	Type of AS/RS
Weight of unit load	Less than 500 pounds	Miniload AS/RS
	Greater than 500 pounds	AS/RS
Function performed	Full unit loads in, full unit loads out	Unit load AS/RS
	Full unit loads in, partial unit loads out	Order picking AS/RS
Location of operator	Operator rides S/R device	Human-aboard AS/RS
	Operator at central control console	End-of-aisle AS/RS

shapes. A person is an inefficient machine, having a low power-to-weight ratio. (The average male is limited to regularly handling loads that weigh not more than 35 pounds.) This inefficiency is made up for by the ability to do two or more things at once. Humans require little capital expenditure but have significant annual operating costs.

Lift trucks are the workhorse materials-handling devices in warehousing today. Lift trucks can be broadly classified as either counterbalanced trucks or reach trucks. The basic *counterbalanced lift truck* has as a fulcrum the front wheels of the truck. The truck is made stable by a counterweight behind the fulcrum that exceeds the weight of the load being lifted. Because of this counterweight, the standard counterbalanced truck is relatively large and requires a fairly wide aisle in which to make right-angle turns for storing or retrieving material.

The *reach truck* was designed to reduce the required aisle width and to increase the efficient use of space. A reach truck replaces the counterweight with outrigger arms that ride in front of the truck to provide truck stability. The center of gravity is no longer behind the forks but is extended underneath the forks. The absence of a counterweight enables a reach truck to operate in an aisle 2 to 3 feet narrower than that of a counterbalanced truck.

The desire to achieve even better use of space led to the attempt to eliminate the need to make right-angle turns within storage aisles. The result of this effort was the *sideloading truck*. The mast and forks of the sideloading truck are perpendicular to the direction of travel of the truck. The need for right-angle turns in the storage aisle is eliminated; therefore, the aisle width must be only slightly wider than the width of the load handled. Sideloading trucks are highly specialized; however, they are not capable of doing much outside the storage area. In addition, upon entering an aisle, the sideloader has access to only one side of the aisle. If a sideloader places a unit load in storage and then wants to retrieve a load on the other side of the aisle, it must leave the aisle, turn around, and reenter the aisle. To solve this problem, the *turret truck* was designed. The turret truck is a counterbalanced truck whose forks can rotate 90° left and right of the travel direction. It does not have to make right-angle turns into the storage rack, so both sides of the aisle can be accessed without its leaving the aisle to turn around.

The variety of lift trucks available is virtually limitless. The specific truck chosen by a given warehouse depends solely on the needs of that warehouse.

Equipment is one of the primary resources of a warehouse. In most cases, equipment represents the largest percentage of capital investment in the warehouse, even greater than that in building and land. Consequently, the planning of warehouse equipment should occupy a representative percentage of the warehouse management's attention. The challenge now is to keep abreast of future developments as they occur so that a talent for identifying potential equipment alternatives can be developed.

PERSONNEL PLANNING

Despite the great strides that have recently been made in warehouse mechanization and automation, warehousing is still a labor-intensive industry. Labor accounts for approximately 50 percent of the costs of operating a typical warehouse. Yet, labor productivity in a warehouse is often much lower than that in a manufacturing environment where large sums of money are continually spent to measure, track, and improve labor productivity. The classification of warehouse personnel as *indirect labor* has led many firms to ignore this group's tremendous potential for productivity improvement and cost reduction.

Planning Warehouse Staff Requirements

Warehouse personnel planning must begin with the determination of actual warehouse staff requirements. Only after the number of people who will work in the warehouse has been determined can the personnel-related aspects of the warehouse be planned. There are three general steps to planning warehouse staff requirements:

Step 1. Determine the tasks to be performed.

Step 2. Determine operating and clerical personnel requirements.

Step 3. Determine administrative personnel requirements.

Operating tasks are the activities that cause the physical movement of materials into, through, and out of the warehouse. *Clerical tasks* are the activities required to accurately record and report both the physical movement of materials into, through, and out of the warehouse and the effort required to achieve that movement. *Administrative tasks* are the activities required to plan, direct, and control the physical movement of materials into, through, and out of the warehouse.

Each of the major functions of a warehouse, receive-store-pick-ship, consists of operating, clerical, and administrative tasks. To define the operating tasks of a warehouse as simply the receiving operating task, the storage operating task, the picking operating task, and the shipping operating task does not adequately specify the operating personnel required for each task. Such a definition is too general. Instead, each task within each function of the warehouse must be defined. The objective is to define each task in such a way that the amount of labor required to perform each task can be assessed. For example, the defined activities for a truck-receiving operating task might be the following:

1. Spot the carrier.
2. Chock the truck wheels.
3. Check the truck seal.
4. Open the truck doors.
5. Unload the material.
6. Palletize or containerize the material, as required.
7. Stage material.
8. Close the truck doors.
9. Unchock the truck wheels.

Assuming that the labor required to perform each of these activities for one truck can be determined and that the expected volume of truck receipts can be estimated, then the total operating labor required for the task of receiving trucks can be determined. Once the labor requirements for each task activity have been determined, steps can be taken to combine the individual task activities into specific jobs. For example, it may be that the person who spots the carrier, chocks the truck wheels, checks the seal, and opens the truck doors is not the same person who palletizes or containerizes the material and unloads and stages the material.

It is usually a good idea, and often a requirement in some union warehouses, to explicitly define each warehouse job in writing in the form of a job description. A key to the effective design of jobs is to avoid a job description that is too narrow and restrictive. This is not to suggest that everyone should be allowed to do everything or is even capable of doing everything. On the contrary, a job description should emphasize the specific, primary, and related tasks for the accomplishment of which the job exists. The job description should be presented to employees for their review at the time they are hired or assigned to a job.

Once the individual warehouse tasks have been defined, the labor required to perform each activity must be determined. These activities will then be grouped into specific jobs to determine the number of workers required. The number of clerical personnel depends on the level of computerization and paperwork. In a real-time warehouse control system environment, very few, if any, clerical personnel are required because all actions are performed and verified by the operator. The transaction records are updated in a matter of seconds via radio-frequency transmission. If clerical work is required, the number of personnel can be determined in many ways.

The four most common methods of determining the labor requirements of operating and clerical tasks are the use of historical data, work sampling, time study, and predetermined time elements. Of these methods, predetermined time elements are felt to be the most practical in measuring warehouse operations. *Predetermined time elements* are a compilation of time standards that are usually based on long-term study or work sampling. The U.S. Department of Agriculture (USDA) has compiled a comprehensive set of predetermined time elements for a wide variety of warehouse operating and clerical activities. This set of predetermined time elements can be used to establish the staff requirements for a very high percentage of the tasks that take place in a typical warehouse.

The nature of administrative tasks makes it very difficult, if not impossible, to use quantitative techniques to determine the labor requirements for them. Historical experience has usually been the basis on which administrative staff levels have been determined. Many companies have established ratios for determining administrative staff levels. Yet, when companies with such ratios are examined, no common denominator in seemingly similar situations can be identified. Unfortunately, we do not have an acceptable solution to this dilemma. We can, however, offer one maxim: It is easier to add than to eliminate administrative personnel.

Planning Warehouse-Personnel-Related Areas and Services

Wherever people are employed, certain personnel-related areas and services must be provided. Warehouses are no different. The personnel-related areas and services of interest in a warehouse are:

Warehouse offices

Food services

Lavatories

Locker rooms

Office space must be provided for all warehouse employees engaged in clerical and administrative tasks. Private space should be allocated based on the following scale:

Position	Square feet
Senior executive	300–400
Junior executive	200–250
Supervisors	100–175
Staff personnel	100–150

General office space should consist of approximately 100 square feet for each clerical employee to work in the area. Aisles and corridors should be 4 feet wide in the private office area of the warehouse and 6 feet wide around the general office area.

The need for food services within a warehouse can become a critical factor if this need is not recognized before the warehouse is built. The Occupational Safety and Health Administration (OSHA) has ruled that food may not be eaten nor may any beverage be consumed in any place where toxic substances are present. The OSHA definition of a *toxic substance* is extremely liberal and encompasses almost any material found in a warehouse. Therefore, the picnic tables on the receiving docks of many warehouses are illegal. Warehouse food service areas generally take the form of a segregated lunch area with vending machines. The area required for a vending machine food service should conform to the following scale:

Number of persons using area at any given time	Square feet of area required per person
25 or less	13
26–74	12
75–149	11

The Occupational Safety and Health Act defines very clearly the lavatory requirements in a warehouse. From a warehouse design viewpoint, the important initial considerations are the following:

1. Separate facilities shall be provided for each sex, not to be farther than 200 feet from the location where workers are regularly employed.

2. The number of water closets for each sex shall be determined by the following table:

Number of persons	Minimum number of water closets
1–9	1
10–24	2
25–49	3
50–74	4
75–100	5

One additional facility is required for each additional 30 persons.

3. Where more than 10 men are employed, the number of water closets given in the table above may be reduced by one for each urinal provided. The number of water closets must remain at least two-thirds of the number specified in the table above.

4. At least one sink with adequate hot and cold water shall be provided for every 10 employees, or portion thereof, up to 100 persons; for over 100 persons, one sink for each additional 15 persons must be provided. A sink will be at least 24 inches wide and shall have an individual faucet.

OSHA requires that separate locker rooms be provided for each sex whenever it is the practice to change from street clothes to working clothes. If locker rooms are not provided, OSHA requires that facilities be provided for hanging outer garments. Although it is desirable to locate locker rooms for the convenience of the employees, they should, if possible, be away from the primary flow of materials and in a location that provides good ventilation. Mezzanines or locations along an outside wall are often good places for lavatories and locker rooms.

LAYOUT PLANNING

The last phase of the warehouse planning process is the development of a warehouse layout that improves upon good space, equipment, and personal planning. The result will be an efficient and effective warehouse plan. Before layout planning can begin, however, the specific objectives of a warehouse layout must be determined.

Objectives of a Warehouse Layout

As noted, the first step in any planning process is to define what is to be accomplished, that is, the objectives to be achieved. The objectives of a warehouse layout are the following:

1. To use space effectively
2. To allow the most efficient materials handling
3. To provide the most economical storage in costs of equipment, use of space, damage to material, and handling labor
4. To provide maximum flexibility in order to be able to meet changing storage and handling requirements

Layout-Planning Method

All layout planners, regardless of the particular circumstances in their warehouses, face the same problem: How can we arrange and coordinate the physical resources of the warehouse to most effectively and efficiently utilize those resources? At this point in the warehouse-planning process, the inputs into the layout-planning process—space, equipment, and personnel—have already been determined. Therefore, the layout-planning method consists of just two steps:

Step 1. Generate a series of warehouse layout alternatives.
Step 2. Evaluate each alternative against specific criteria to identify the best warehouse layout.

Generating warehouse layout alternatives is akin to generating warehouse equipment alternatives in that it is as much an art as it is a science. The quality of the layout alternatives will depend largely on the skill and ingenuity of the layout planner.

Unfortunately, layout planners often either lack creativity or do not attempt to express their creativity. Many layout planners approach the problem with a preconceived idea about what the solution should be. They tend to bias the layout-planning process toward that preconceived solution. As a result, creativity is stifled. Often, the layout chosen for a new warehouse looks exactly like the layout in the old warehouse. The generation of layout alternatives thrives on the creativity of the layout planner, yet many layout planners withhold this basic and essential ingredient. The generation of warehouse layout alternatives should proceed as follows:

1. Define the location of fixed obstacles.
2. Define the location of the receiving and shipping functions.
3. Locate the storage areas and equipment, including required aisles.
4. Assign the materials to be stored to storage locations.

Defining the Location of Fixed Obstacles. Some objects in a warehouse can be located only in certain places, and they can have only certain configurations. These objects should be identified and placed in the layout alternative first, before objects with more flexibility are located. Some fixed obstacles are building columns, stairwells, elevator shafts, lavatories, sprinkler system controls, heating and air-conditioning equipment, and, in some cases, offices. Failure to consider the location of these types of items first will prove disastrous. The warehousing corollary to Murphy's law states, "If a column can be in the wrong position, it will be."

Define the Location of the Receiving and Shipping Functions. Often, the configuration of the warehouse site will dictate the location of the receiving and shipping functions. When this is not true, however, the receiving and shipping location decision becomes an important one. Should the receiving and shipping functions be located together or in different areas of the warehouse? In most cases, the receiving and shipping functions should be located together. Figure 25.5 is used to justify this statement.

Warehouses A and B are identical in size. Warehouse A has three receiving dock bays located on the opposite side of the building from three shipping dock bays, and warehouse B has three receiving and three shipping dock bays located on the same side of the building. When receiving and shipping are located on opposite sides of the building, the average travel distance for a product that is received, stored, picked, and shipped is 600 feet. Because receiving and shipping are located together in warehouse B, it would be logical to store items with the highest throughput close to receiving and shipping, and items with the lowest throughput farthest from receiving and shipping. The average travel distance to receive, store, pick, and ship a product in warehouse B will typically be much less than 600 feet; it might be closer to 300 feet. As a result, warehouse B is superior to warehouse A with respect to the amount of materials handling required.

In addition, the use of materials-handling equipment is generally more effective in warehouse B than in warehouse A. Effective use of materials-handling equipment is defined as the percentage of time the handling equipment travels loaded. In warehouse A, material is received and then placed in storage. After the load is stored, the equipment returns to the receiving area empty (called *deadheading*). When the same material is to be shipped, the shipping materials-handling equipment deadheads into the storage location, retrieves the material, and moves it to the shipping area. As a result, maximum effective use of the materials-handling equipment in warehouse A is 50 percent, and actual effective use is typically closer to 25 percent. In warehouse B, material is received and placed in the proper storage location. Because receiving and shipping are located together, the materials-handling equipment can now move directly from the storage location in which the received material was just stored to a storage location containing an item to be shipped. Therefore, the materials-handling equipment deadheads to the storage location, retrieves the material, moves it to the shipping area, and then deadheads back to receiving. In this case, maximum effective use of the materials-handling equipment is approximately 75 percent, with actual effective use about 35 percent.

In addition to the materials-handling advantages discussed above, warehouse B possesses greater flexibility. The increased flexibility lies in the fact that the number of dock bays actually dedicated to receiving or to shipping in warehouse B can vary from zero to six, to adjust to volume fluctuations. In warehouse A, however, the physical location of receiving and shipping makes adjustments very difficult, if not impossible.

One potential problem in locating the receiving and shipping activities together is the possibility of receiving what you ship and shipping what you receive. Care must be taken to segregate received goods from goods to be shipped. Perhaps the best way to accomplish this is to locate the receiving and shipping offices and the truckers' lounge between the receiving and shipping dock doors. This physical barrier will effectively

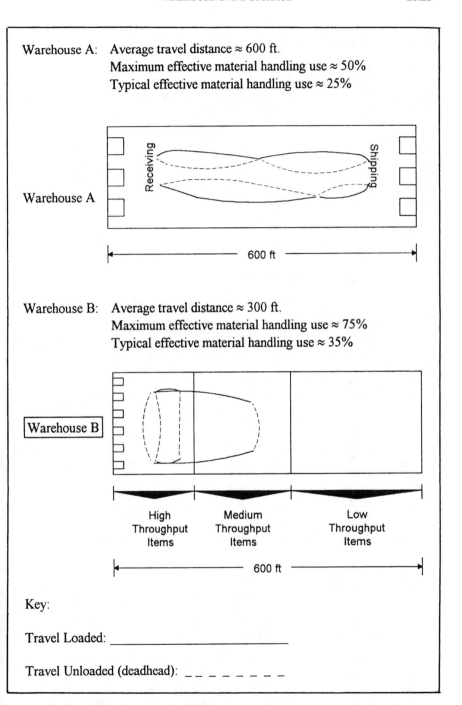

Warehouse A: Average travel distance ≈ 600 ft.
Maximum effective material handling use ≈ 50%
Typical effective material handling use ≈ 25%

Warehouse B: Average travel distance ≈ 300 ft.
Maximum effective material handling use ≈ 75%
Typical effective material handling use ≈ 35%

Key:

Travel Loaded: _____

Travel Unloaded (deadhead): _ _ _ _ _ _ _ _

FIGURE 25.5 Comparison of receiving and shipping area locations.

separate the two activities while still allowing the materials-handling and flexibility advantages of having receiving and shipping located close together.

Locate Storage Area Aisles and Equipment.   The types of storage areas and equipment to be used will dictate the configuration of the storage layout and the aisle requirements. Be sure to make allowances for the fixed obstacles in the facility. Main warehouse aisles should connect the various parts of the warehouse. The cross aisle at the end of the storage area may need to be wider than the aisles within the storage area, depending on the type of materials-handling equipment used. For example, a sideloading fork truck that can operate with a 7-foot-wide storage aisle may require 12-foot-wide cross aisles at the ends of the storage aisles to allow maneuvering into and out of the storage aisle. An effective warehouse layout is also dependent on a number of warehouse storage philosophies. Each warehouse layout alternative should be evaluated based on these warehouse layout philosophies:

How frequently materials are stored

Similarity of the materials stored

Size of the materials stored

Special characteristics of the materials stored

How Frequently the Materials Are Stored.   An Italian economist named Pareto once stated that 85 percent of the wealth of the world is held by 15 percent of the people. On closer examination, Pareto's law actually pertains to many areas other than wealth; one of these areas is warehousing. In a typical warehouse, it is not unusual to find that 85 percent of the product throughput is attributable to 15 percent of the items, that another 10 percent of the product throughput is attributable to 30 percent of the items, and that the remaining 5 percent of the product throughput is attributable to 55 percent of the items. Consequently, the warehouse contains a very small number of highly active items (often called *A items*), a slightly larger number of moderately active items (often called *B items*), and a very large number of inactive items (often called *C items*).

The warehouse layout philosophy on popularity suggests that the warehouse should be planned around the small number of highly active items that constitute the great majority of the activity in the warehouse. The popularity philosophy maintains that the materials having the greatest throughput should be located in an area that allows the most efficient materials handling. Consequently, high-turnover items should be located as close as possible to the point of use. In a warehouse, the points of use are typically the receiving and shipping activities. If the receiving and shipping activities are located together, then materials should be assigned to storage locations as previously shown in warehouse B.

Similarity of Materials Stored.   The basic premise of this philosophy is that items that are commonly received and/or shipped together should be stored together. For example, consider a retail auto parts distributor. Chances are good that a customer who buys a spark plug wrench might also require a condenser, points, and spark plugs. Because these items are typically sold (shipped) together, they should be stored in the same area. Similarly, an exhaust system tail pipe should be stored in the same area that the mufflers, brackets, and gaskets are stored.

Similar types of items might also be stored together. They will usually require similar storage and handling methods, so their consolidation in the same area results in more efficient use of space and more efficient materials handling. Caution should be taken whenever items are so similar that storing them close together might result in order picking and shipping errors. Examples of items that are too similar are two-way, three-way, and four-way electrical switches. They look identical but function quite differently. Storing these items close together will inevitably result in order picking and shipping errors.

Size of Materials Stored. The warehouse layout philosophy on size offers a number of guidelines for developing warehouse layouts. The size philosophy suggests that heavy, bulky, hard-to-handle goods should be stored close to their point of use. The cost of handling these items is usually much greater than that of handling other items. That is an incentive to minimize the distance over which they are handled. In addition, if the ceiling height in the warehouse varies from one area to another, the heavy items should be stored in the areas with a low ceiling and the lightweight, easy-to-handle items should be stored in the areas with a high ceiling. The size philosophy also asserts that the size of the storage location should fit the size of the material to be stored. Do not store a unit load of 10 cubic feet in a storage location capable of accommodating a unit load of 30 cubic feet. A variety of storage location sizes must be provided so that different items can be stored differently. This issue is one of the major drawbacks of most shelving: The cubic space available on a given shelf is generally ineffectively used. In addition to looking at the physical size of an individual item, one must consider the total quantity of the item to be stored. Different storage methods and layouts will be used for storing two pallet loads of an item than will be used for storing 200 pallet loads of the same material.

Special Characteristics of Materials Stored. The warehouse layout philosophy on special characteristics indicates that some materials have certain attributes or traits that restrict or dictate the storage methods and layout used. Oddly shaped and crushable items, subject to stocking limitations, will dictate special storage methods and layout configurations to effectively use available cubic space. Hazardous materials such as explosives, corrosives, and highly flammable chemicals must be stored in accordance with government regulations. Items of high value or items commonly subject to pilferage may require increased security measures such as isolated storage with restricted access. Contact between certain individually harmless materials can result in extremely hazardous reactions and/or significant product damage. For example, the storage of carbon steel products in contact with stainless-steel products causes the physical properties of the stainless steel to deteriorate.

Specific criteria should be established for each warehouse layout philosophy. Then, each layout alternative should be quantitatively evaluated against these criteria and against any other qualitative factors of importance, using the techniques previously presented. The warehouse layout that achieves the best overall balance among all factors should be chosen. Remember, however, that warehousing exists within a dynamic environment; therefore, the layout chosen as best today may not be so as conditions change. The extent and timing of changing requirements in the future should be forecast and a warehouse master plan established to effectively compensate for the changing mission of the warehouse.

MANAGING THE RECEIVING AND STORAGE FUNCTIONS

Receiving and storage are the functions responsible for taking control of the merchandise to be handled in the warehouse. The objectives of the receiving function are to efficiently and accurately complete the transfer of control from the source of the merchandise to the warehouse and to prepare the merchandise for storage. The objective of the storage function is to hold, protect, and track the received material until someone requests the material. The purpose of this section is to identify the activities and techniques used to accomplish these objectives and to set forth a number of guidelines for identifying deviations from sound receiving and storage practices so that management can work to realign actual performance with desired performance.

Managing the Receiving Function

Receiving is perhaps the most important function performed in a warehouse. Because it is the first function performed, deficiencies in the efficiency, effectiveness, and accuracy of the transfer of control can destroy an otherwise successful operation. If the right materials in the right quantities are not properly accepted and reported, then the warehouse objective to satisfy customer requirements cannot be met.

To be able to manage the receiving function, one must first identify the kinds of activities that must be performed to receive material. Then, a set of desired performance standards must be established for the receiving function so that receiving deficiencies can be recognized and corrected.

All warehouses share a common set of activities that must be performed if the receiving function is to be accomplished. The differences in the receiving functions from warehouse to warehouse lie in the order in which and the extent to which these basic activities are carried out. In fact, how the activities are performed may vary from one shipment to another in a given warehouse. The following paragraphs describe the basic receiving activities that should be performed in all warehouses.

Spot the Carrier. When a carrier arrives at the warehouse, how does the responsible warehouse employee decide with which dock door the carrier should be aligned? This decision may be insignificant in a small warehouse with only several receiving dock bays. However, carrier spotting in a larger warehouse can be a significant issue. If a warehouse has 30 receiving dock bays, with which one should a given truck be aligned? If the wrong decision is made, material might be unloaded at one end of the warehouse only to be stored at the other end. Materials handling will be extremely inefficient in a case like this. Therefore, a decision process should be in effect that ensures that carriers are spotted properly. Methods commonly used to spot carriers include specifying choices of receiving dock bays in the shipping instructions on the purchase order, assigning a dock bay to the carrier at the warehouse security gate as the carrier arrives on site, or having the carrier drop the trailer in a staging area and allowing a dock attendant to spot the carrier using a shuttle vehicle.

Chock the Carrier Wheels. Chocking the carrier wheels is not only good safety practice but is also required by law. Truck wheels that are not chocked will inevitably cause truck movement during unloading, creating a safety hazard, perhaps even causing fatal injury to workers.

Check the Seal and Open the Carrier Doors. Depending on the type of carrier and the physical characteristics of the dock, it might be necessary to open the carrier doors before the truck is completely positioned at the dock. In this case, the carrier wheels should be chocked after the seal has been checked and the doors opened. If a shipment is supposed to be sealed and the seal has been broken before arrival at the dock, the warehouse has the right to reject the load and should not hesitate to do so if other irregularities are suspected. Precautions taken at this point can avoid even greater problems associated with filing claims against the carrier and/or vendor after the shipment has been completed.

Palletize or Containerize the Material, as Appropriate. Consolidate the materials into as large a unit load as feasible to maximize materials-handling efficiency. If the truck driver is to assist in unloading the truck, provide him or her with the necessary equipment and instructions to build a unit load that can remain intact throughout the receiving and storage functions.

Unload the Material. Whenever possible, use mechanization to unload carriers. Mechanization allows more material to be unloaded in a shorter period of time than manual handling does. Unload the material in a logical and orderly fashion so that any required inspections and receiving rallies can be efficiently and accurately performed.

Prepare a Receiving Tally. The extent to which the materials received must be counted will vary according to the type of material, the manner in which it is packaged, and the specific desires of warehouse management. For example, one shipment might consist of palletized loads of sealed, well-marked, bar-coded cartons. Preparation of the receiving tally might only entail scanning the number of pallet loads received and verifying against the *advanced ship notice* (ASN). Another shipment, however, might consist of pallet loads of unmarked cartons. In this case, preparation of the receiving tally might involve breaking down each pallet load, opening each carton, and counting its contents. Past experience with the material, the carrier, and the vendor should be weighed in deciding how the receiving tally should be prepared.

Reconcile the Receiving Tally against the Carrier's Bill-of-Lading, the Vendor's Packing List, and the Purchase Order. The receiving tally is compared to the carrier's bill of lading to verify that the carrier has delivered what the carrier will be paid to deliver. The receiving tally is compared to the vendor's packing list to verify that what was actually received is what the vendor said was shipped. The receiving tally is compared to the purchase order to verify that what was actually received corresponds to what was desired. If there are significant discrepancies between the receiving tally and the bill of lading, packing list, or purchase order, a discrepancy report should be initiated and the proper authorities consulted before any portion of the shipment is accepted. This manual process is rapidly becoming extinct with the advancement of automatic identification and electronic transfer of information.

Prepare a Receiving Report. The receiving report serves as a formal record and notification to the appropriate parties that the materials listed in the receiving report have been received. Receiving reports are commonly distributed to accounting, purchasing, quality control, and the party who initiated the request for the material.

Segregate the Goods into Usable and Nonusable Categories. Damaged or defective material should be physically separated from acceptable material. Otherwise, unacceptable material will be mistaken for acceptable material and will proceed into the warehouse system. Often, quality-control inspections will be required to identify unacceptable goods. Efforts should be made to expedite the performance of such inspections so that valuable receiving buffer space is not crowded with a backlog of material requiring inspection.

Dispatch the Goods Received. Once the disposition of the material has been determined—whether it is acceptable or unacceptable—the removal of the material from the receiving area should be expedited. Many warehouses do an excellent job of dispatching accepted material, but they do a poor job of disposing of rejected material. The longer rejected material remains in the receiving area, the greater the probability of its finding its way into the warehouse system. Vendors should be promptly notified of material to be returned and should be expected to retrieve this material within a reasonable amount of time.

To properly manage the receiving activities, one must identify deviations from acceptable performance and initiate actions to correct the deviations. Before deviations from acceptable performance can be defined, however, acceptable performance must be defined. Several basic characteristics of a good receiving system are as follows. By monitoring the receiving function for adherence to the following requirements, one can easily recognize unacceptable performance:

- Flow of materials through the receiving function should be essentially straight line.
- The receiving workload and flow of materials should be continuous and uniform.
- Receiving activities should be consolidated.
- Materials handling should be efficient.
- Only the correct materials should be received.
- Paperwork should be processed quickly and accurately.
- The receiving function should be able to handle exceptions.
- A receiving performance reporting system should be followed.

Managing the Storage Function

The storage function maintains effective control over all materials in the warehouse until the materials are released for shipment. Effective control involves (1) properly storing the materials to ensure maximum use of space, protection of the product, and adequate accessibility to the product; (2) tracking the location of the materials at all times; and (3) maintaining accurate inventory records for all materials until they are released for shipment. Tracking the location of materials is accomplished by adopting a materials location system. A materials location system can be a manual system, a computerized system, or a combination of the two.

Having materials in storage in a warehouse but not knowing exactly where each item is stored, is equivalent to not having the materials at all. Lost material equals no material. Consequently, steps must be taken to track the location of each item throughout its stay in the warehouse. Material location systems fall into three basic categories: memory systems, fixed-location systems, and random-location systems.

Memory Systems.   Tracking the location of material by a memory system depends on the recall of the individuals responsible for placing material in and retrieving it from storage. Memory systems work well if the following restrictions are met:

- Only one person works within a given storage area.
- The number of different items stored in that area is relatively small.
- The number of different storage locations in that area is relatively small.

If any of these restrictions are not met, then the memory system will be disastrous.

Fixed-Location Systems.   In a fixed-location system, each stock-keeping unit is assigned a specific and unique location in storage. A particular item will always be stored in its assigned location, and no other item may be stored in that location, even though that location may currently be empty. In a fixed-location system, the location of every item is always known.

Random-Location Systems.   Random-location systems allow material to be stored in any location currently available in the storage area. Each storage location is given a unique name or address. When an item is randomly placed in the storage area, the address of the specific location into which it is put is recorded for future reference. Maintenance of random-location system records may be either manual or computerized. The greater the number of storage locations and SKUs makes the manual system very labor intensive. A random-location system may work in the following manner:

1. When an item is received, the stock location records are checked to determine if any of the item is currently on hand and, if some is, to find its location.

2. If a location contains that item and if sufficient space remains, the newly received material is stored in that location and the stock location record for that item is updated to reflect the new quantity stored in the location.

3. If no location contains the item or if there is insufficient space in the current location, the newly received material is placed in any available storage location.

4. The stock location record for that item is updated by recording the address of the storage location in which the material is stored and the quantity of material stored in that location.

5. When retrieval of the item is desired, the stock location record is queried to determine the address of the storage location in which the item is stored.

6. The material is located, the quantity desired is removed from the location, and the stock location record is updated by adjusting the recorded inventory level in the storage location.

The majority of the work will inevitably be accomplished by the computer. The operator merely acknowledges and verifies the information given by the computer.

Random-location storage with a properly designed and maintained material location system is a highly space efficient storage system, with good control of and accessibility to material. However, if the material location system is not properly designed or maintained, the random-location system is equivalent to a memory system.

Management of the storage function often boils down to identifying and correcting deficiencies in the maintenance of the material location system. A number of guidelines can be followed as a major step toward maintaining an effective material location system:

Keep the material location system simple. The material location system must be completely understood by all the personnel required to use it. If the warehouse employees do not understand the system, it will surely fail.

Do not move, place in storage, or withdraw from storage, any material without valid instructions. Violation of this law of warehousing is the primary cause for the downfall of most material location systems.

Keep the material location system records current. The material location system records must be kept current. This is easily achieved with a real-time radio-frequency system. If records are entered manually, ensure that it is kept up; otherwise, material will be in storage without location records. Such material is, in effect, lost, and it is unavailable to users. Issued material must be promptly subtracted from the material location records. Otherwise, the records show that the material is still on hand, is occupying space, and is available to users.

Report and rectify discrepancies in the material location system records. Human errors are inevitable in a manual system, but much less in a real-time RF system. The fact that errors occur, however, does not mean that they cannot be corrected once they do occur. Warehouse employees should not be reluctant to report errors discovered while performing their jobs. Errors must be reported and corrected; otherwise, the integrity of the system will be compromised, and the system will fail.

The most efficient means to maintain accurate inventory records is a technique known as *cycle counting*. Cycle counting entails spreading the verification of inventory levels throughout the fiscal year, instead of doing so at one or two points during the year as with a *physical inventory*. This way discrepancies in inventory records are discovered on a timely basis to allow effective investigation and correction of the causes of discrepancies. The result of a well-planned and well-executed cycle-counting system is confidence in the inventory records. In addition, because the comparison of actual inventory levels with inventory records occurs continually, it is more likely that the causes of discrepancies can be traced and corrected.

MANAGING THE PICKING AND SHIPPING OPERATIONS

The receiving and storage functions serve the purpose of accurately and safely transferring control of merchandise to the warehouse. The primary reason the warehouse exists, however, is to get the merchandise into the hands of its customers. If the merchandise cannot be extracted from storage and transferred to the customer, then customer requirements will not be satisfied. The act of extracting materials from storage is called *picking* (or *order picking* or *order filling*). The act of transferring control of the merchandise from the warehouse to the customer is called *shipping*.

Managing the Picking Function

The effectiveness and efficiency of the picking function are directly related to the effectiveness and efficiency of the storage function. If personnel do not know where an item is stored, then the task of removing that item from storage is difficult. Consequently, the first step in developing a sound picking function is to develop a sound storage function, complete with a good materials location system and accurate inventory records. In addition to a sound storage function, a good picking system depends on a good information system, which tells the order picker what items are to be picked, where the items are located, how much of each item is to be picked, and in what order the items are to be picked. The output of the information system that contains these instructions is the picking document: either a pick sheet or a display on a *radio data terminal* (RDT).

There are essentially three ways to pick material to fill customer orders. One way is to have one order picker—human or mechanical—pick all the material on a given customer order. This is called *discrete picking*. In this case, the picking document is in the form of a standard customer order, a prerouted customer order, or a prerouted and preposted customer order. When the customer order is filled, the order picker picks the next customer order. The second way to pick is to have multiple order pickers pick only a portion of a given customer order. This is called *zone picking*, and the picking document is generally a prerouted customer order for the items to be picked by each order picker. Again, when one order is filled, the pickers begin with the next order. The third type of order picking is called *batch picking*. This is similar to discrete order picking as it requires only one order picker. The difference is that multiple orders are batched together and picked concurrently. The use of different kinds of picking documents for the three methods of picking are discussed in the following sections.

One Order Picker Picks an Entire Order Using a Prerouted Customer Order. A *prerouted customer order* is simply a standard customer order that has been altered to sequence the items to be picked according to their location in the warehouse. With a prerouted customer order, backtracking of order pickers is eliminated because each item is picked the first time it is passed. The total distance traveled by the order picker is reduced. If the distance traveled per customer order is reduced, the productivity of each order picker is increased. As a result, fewer order pickers are needed for a prerouted-customer-order picking system.

To further improve productivity, the picking document should only direct the picker to a location where material is on hand. This is now a *prerouted and preposted customer order*. Preposting is the act of verifying the on-hand status and updating the inventory records of the requested items of an order before the picking document is produced. If an item is not on hand, then it is omitted from the picking document. If the quantity on hand is lower than the quantity ordered, then the picking document reflects the quantity the order picker can expect to find. Preposting is most effective in warehouses with cycle-counting systems where material location and inventory records are maintained at a level of 98 to 99 percent accuracy.

One Order Picker Picks Only a Portion of an Order Using a Standard, Prerouted, or Prerouted and Preposted Customer Order (Zone Picking). The benefit of zone picking is minimizing order picker travel by maximizing the number of picks along the travel path. In a system in which one order picker picks an entire order, the order picker typically spends a high percentage of time traveling from one storage location to another. This is true even when the picking document is prerouted because the items on a given order may be scattered throughout the warehouse. In a zone picking system, however, an order picker picks all the items for each customer order that are stored within the zone of the warehouse assigned to that order picker. Consequently, the order picker spends a much larger percentage of time actually picking items.

In zone picking, however, time and space must be allocated for the consolidation of the individual portions of a customer order into a complete order. The time required to consolidate the individual portions of a customer order can be minimized by using an auto identification sortation system. When order consolidation is relatively easy and quick, zone picking will likely be much more productive than picking the customer's entire order.

A number of guidelines will assist in establishing and maintaining an effective picking system, although the importance of these guidelines and the extent to which each can be applied naturally depends on the circumstances of each particular warehouse.

Pick more than one order at a time. Regardless of whether order pickers pick entire customer orders or practice zone picking, they should pick as much material at one time as possible. Picking material for more than one customer order at one time reduces the amount of time spent traveling.

Avoid the use of checkers. A *checker* verifies that the order picker picked the proper quantity of each item requested on the customer order. Many warehouses use checkers to verify 100 percent of the customer orders filled, resulting in higher operating costs. Train the pickers to do it right the first time. When using a real-time warehouse control system to direct the order pickers, the checking function occurs when the item is picked, eliminating the need for checkers.

Measure, instead of count, when appropriate. It is a proven fact that human beings cannot count. If you place 200 marbles in a hat and ask 10 people to count them, the answers are likely to range anywhere from 190 to 210. Quantities of material can often be estimated within acceptable limits by measuring the weight, volume, or length of material.

Managing the Shipping Function

The primary objective of the shipping function is to efficiently and accurately transfer control of merchandise from the warehouse to its customers. Sound receiving, storage, and picking functions will go for naught if the product is not released to the customer in good condition and on a timely basis. Shipping is composed of a series of basic activities. The extent to which each of these activities is performed varies according to the particular circumstances of each warehouse.

Accumulate and pack the order. As material is picked from storage, it must be consolidated and containerized, as appropriate, to ensure that all the items of a customer order are shipped to the proper destination. Packing operations should strive to create the largest unit load that can be handled, not only on the warehouse dock but also at the customer's dock. Combining merchandise into unit loads increases materials-handling efficiency and usually improves use of space within the carrier.

Check and stage the customer orders. Before the customer's order is shipped, it must be checked and staged on the shipping dock. Checking the customer order at this point in the warehouse system is not the same thing as using checkers to verify order picking accuracy. In checking a customer order before shipment the objective is to determine that all containers to be shipped have been accumulated. The objective is not to verify that the right quantity of each item has been picked. Checking the order before shipment is necessary to ensure that the individual items in an order have not become separated during the process of accumulating and packing the order.

Reconcile the shipping release and the customer order. Make sure that what the warehouse claims it is shipping is what the customer ordered.

Spot and inspect the carrier. The process of spotting the shipping carrier is identical to spotting carriers at the receiving dock. To ensure efficient carrier loading, the carrier should be spotted at a dock bay with good access to the staging area from which the carrier is to be loaded.

Load the carrier. If more than one customer order is to be shipped on the same carrier, care must be taken to load the carrier in a way that facilitates unloading the customer orders in the sequence in which the customers will be visited by the carrier.

Release the Carrier. The packing list accompanying the shipment must be reconciled against the carrier's bill of lading to ensure that the carrier accepts responsibility for delivering all of the items that the warehouse claims to be shipping. Otherwise, the processing of a customer's claims that what was received was not what was ordered will cause many problems.

To manage the shipping function, one must define acceptable shipping performance so that actual performance can be monitored against the standards. Deviations of actual performance from the acceptable performance standards indicate the need for management action aimed at eliminating the causes of the deviations. Additional requirements of a sound shipping function include the following:

- Goods should be handled so that they are delivered on time and safely.
- Shipping documents should be prepared so that they clear the warehouse of the accountability for the merchandise shipped.
- Shipping documents should contain all the information needed to fulfill the warehouse's invoicing and other fiscal responsibilities.

- Shipments should enhance the company's relationship with its customers. What the customer does see, however, is the output of the shipping function.
- There should be a shipping performance reporting system.

LOSS CONTROL

A *loss* is an unplanned expense resulting from the degradation of personnel, products, or property. A *personnel loss* happens each time an employee is injured. A *product loss* occurs when damage, fire, pilferage, or any other act reduces the value of materials. *Property losses* take place when fire, vandalism, or any accident degrades property. The planning and the management action required to avoid or minimize these losses is called *loss control*. Warehouse loss control should be approached from both a planning and a regulatory perspective.

The planning perspective of loss control is on the limitation of losses by anticipating their causes. By making loss control an integral part of the warehouse-planning process, losses may be minimized. The regulatory perspective of loss control is on compliance with established industry regulations as a way to minimize losses. Organizations like the Occupational Safety and Health Administration, the American National Standards Institute, and the National Fire Protection Association have established regulations and standards applicable to warehouse activities, equipment, and physical facilities.

Four critical areas must be addressed in developing an effective warehouse loss control program. These areas are (1) personnel safety, (2) fire prevention and protection, (3) theft and pilferage prevention, and (4) product damage and contamination prevention.

Personnel Safety

Personnel safety is enhanced by the careful planning of every activity in the warehouse with which personnel may have contact. Standard operating procedures should be established that spell out the dos and don'ts of each activity and that serve as regulations the warehouse employees are expected to obey. The causes of warehouse personnel accidents and injuries are infinite, so an attempt to compile an exhaustive set of guidelines for the elimination of the causes of personnel losses is an exercise in futility. Experience has shown, however, that a great many personnel accidents and injuries can be avoided by enforcing a few basic personnel safety rules.

Unless an accident is reported, the chances of finding and eliminating its cause are remote. Not only should all actual accidents be reported, but so should all near misses. The following are some guidelines to reduce the occurrences of accidents:

- *Promote good housekeeping.* Poor housekeeping breeds personnel accidents.
- *Store materials according to standards.* An item should be stored in the warehouse using the same storage and handling methods each time it is handled.
- *Dispose of waste in a timely fashion.* Scrap begets scrap, and damaged material begets damaged material. Letting these materials lie around the warehouse causes unsafe working conditions.
- *Effectively mark aisles and maintain their integrity.* Aisles are for personnel and materials-handling travel, not for materials storage. To have materials protruding into the warehouse aisles will inevitably lead to personnel and/or materials-handling

equipment hitting the materials. The result will be employee injuries, not to mention damage to the material.

- *Have adequate lighting.* The "Dark Ages" are over; we can no longer expect warehouse employees to work in a dark warehouse. Lighting costs money, but the personnel injuries caused by inadequate lighting are much more costly.

Fire Prevention and Protection

Perhaps the quickest way to end a business is with fire. Fire not only can destroy products and property but it can eliminate one's ability to continue doing business. A very high percentage of businesses damaged by fire never resume operation. Consequently, fire prevention and protection are of paramount importance to warehouse management. The issue of fire prevention in a warehouse boils down to one basic question: Is smoking permitted in the warehouse? Smoking is, by far, the primary cause of warehouse fires. Approximately 85 percent of all fires in the industry are started by cigarettes. If smoking is permitted in the warehouse, then there will inevitably be fires. If smoking is not permitted in the warehouse, then the potential for fire is significantly reduced.

The most common method of fire protection used in the warehousing industry is the automatic sprinkler system. Automatic sprinkler systems are classified as either dry or wet systems. In a dry system, typically used in an unheated warehouse, the piping system is filled with air. When the sprinkler head is activated, the air is released and then water flows through the piping to the head. With a wet system, water is stored in the piping system to be released immediately upon activation of the sprinkler head.

The fire protection system in the warehouse should comply with local, state, and federal regulations. The warehouse's insurance underwriter should be relied on to document the type and extent of fire protection needed.

Theft and Pilferage

Industrial theft and pilferage is one of the fastest-growing "industries" in the United States today, meaning billions of dollars in costs to industry each year. The problem is particularly prevalent in the warehousing industry because individuals have daily access to finished goods that are highly susceptible to pilferage. Warehouse security should be emphasized during the planning of the warehouse. Some of the questions that should be asked are the following:

- Should the perimeter of the warehouse be protected by a fence?
- Does outside lighting illuminate the areas where security breakdowns are possible?
- Have the number of entrances and exits been minimized, and have access areas for warehouse employees, office employees, visitors, and docks been effectively separated?
- Has employee parking been separated from truck and trailer parking?
- Are storage areas subdivided and protected to the extent necessary for the types of materials stored?
- Are waste containers and trash accommodation areas separated from dock and storage areas?
- Have electronic protection systems, such as sound detectors, microwave sensors, electronic eyes, and closed-circuit television, been fully considered?

- Are critical areas adequately protected?
- Have windows, roof hatches, outside ladders, skylights, ventilators, manholes, and storm drains been designed with security in mind?

Product Damage and Contamination

Warehouse management must continually emphasize the importance of following established materials-handling procedures. When activities are performed that do not conform with these procedures, then the employees must be reeducated on the proper procedures.

The extent of product damage and contamination in a warehouse is closely tied to the quality of housekeeping. If aisles are cluttered and storage areas disorderly, then product damage will result. Proper warehouse planning will eliminate much of the potential for product damage. The kinds of questions that must be addressed when planning the warehouse to minimize product damage include the following:

- Are aisles properly planned for materials-handling maneuvering?
- Are doorways, passageways, and ramps planned to allow ease of movement of the product handled?
- Have the product storage methods been properly planned to prevent product crushing and product falls?
- Has the compatibility of materials to be stored close together been investigated?
- Have products been properly protected from moisture, severe temperatures, leakage, and staining?

PERFORMANCE REPORTING SYSTEMS

At the foundation of any management system is the ability to identify deviations from acceptable levels of performance. Once actual performance is judged to be unacceptable, management actions can be taken to realign actual performance with the standard desired. To determine whether actual performance is acceptable or not, one must first define acceptable performance and then be able to compare actual performance with this definition.

The primary objective of a warehouse is to maximize effective use of the warehouse's resources while satisfying customer requirements. According to this definition, then, the performance of the warehouse activities are acceptable as long as customers are happy. Right? Wrong! While this statement is essentially true, the effort the warehouse must expend to keep customers happy is equally important to the determination of its level of performance. The emphasis of this section is placed on developing sound warehouse labor and space performance reporting systems.

Labor Performance Reporting Systems

Many warehouse managers are under the mistaken impression that they already have a labor performance reporting system. In reality, however, these reports are typically the output of an activity reporting system, not a labor performance reporting system. Activity reporting merely reports what was done. It is difficult to evaluate performance because many factors are involved. A labor performance report, however, provides the necessary information about what should have been done.

The first step in developing a labor performance reporting system is to determine the standard amount of labor required to perform all the activities of the warehouse. The tools to calculate these labor standards have previously been discussed. Once labor standards have been determined for all the activities performed, the standards form the foundation for an effective labor performance reporting system. The output of the labor performance reporting system is a comparison of actual labor requirements with standard labor requirements. Large sums of money and time should not be spent to guarantee that the time standards are accurate. The benefits of time standards can be realized even if the standard is not completely accurate. The important statistic to note in interpreting time standard performance data is the trend of the data over time. The goal should not be to obtain 100 percent performance over the standard but rather to develop a consistent improvement in performance over time until an acceptable level of performance is reached. When a labor performance reporting system is installed, the initial level of performance may be much lower than 100 percent. Over time, performance may improve until labor reaches a level that proves difficult to surpass. This level of performance is consistent with the potential of the individuals performing the task and should be considered the acceptable level of performance, even though it may still be well below 100 percent performance against the standard. The goal now is to maintain future performance at the established acceptable level. When performance drops significantly below this level, then management actions should be initiated to identify and correct the causes of the decline.

There is no need to adjust the standard so that the acceptable level of performance equals 100 percent performance against the standard. As a matter of fact, it is often advisable to remove any connotation that there is a 100 percent level of performance. Otherwise, performance over the 100 percent level of performance according to the standard might be stifled if employees take the position that they need not perform beyond "perfection."

Labor standards also allow management to quantitatively determine the labor requirements of the warehouse. Where labor standards do not exist, management must rely on historical experience and judgment to anticipate future labor requirements. Requirements determined this way are very often difficult to sell to those who must approve increases in the labor force. However, if standards of a labor performance reporting system are the basis for projections of future manpower requirements, they usually are not contradicted.

Use-of-Space Reporting Systems

The principle behind a use-of-space reporting system is very similar to that of a labor performance reporting system. The primary tool used to develop an effective space performance reporting system—the space standard—has been discussed. Space standards should be developed for each category of material stored in the warehouse. How material is classified depends on the kind of storage used for an item and its specific storage characteristics.

The primary value of a use-of-space reporting system is in capacity planning. The reporting system serves as an early warning that a space problem is developing. Actual use of space above 100 percent of the space standard indicates that the actual space being lost to aisle allowances and honeycombing is less than that expected for the type of storage method being used. As honeycombing losses decrease, materials accessibility will generally also decrease. Therefore, predictions can be made that blocked stock exists, that material is infringing on the warehouse aisles, and that the maintenance of a first-in, first-out inventory system is suffering. The objective of the use-of-space report-ing system is to anticipate such problems before they develop so that management actions can be taken to avoid them. As projections of future inventory levels are made, they should be compared with the applicable space standards to verify that sufficient space exists for the expected volume. Future space requirements should be monitored to allow sufficient lead time to develop and evaluate alternative strategies for accommo-dating the material to be stored. Otherwise, overcrowding will eventually occur. The labor required to keep the warehouse operating will usually increase, housekeeping will suffer, safety of employees will be compromised, and product damage will increase.

CONCLUSION

Although warehouses vary in size and activity level, the approach to plan, manage, and improve warehousing practices are applicable for any institution that receives, stores, picks, and ships material. The information presented in this chapter gives you the sci-ence of warehousing. Combining the science with the art of warehousing, gained from experience, will allow the warehousing industry to improve the performance of the time and place utility, known as *customer service,* and consequently improve the image of warehousing. In addition, the cost of warehousing, both equipment and operating costs, will steadily decline, allowing for the betterment and success of the company.

CHAPTER 26
QUALITY ASSURANCE

Editor

Bill Winchell, J.D., P.E.
Associate Professor, Manufacturing Technology
Ferris State University, Big Rapids, Michigan

Today, many of the product development planning functions take place using teams with members from appropriate departments. This procedure is called *simultaneous engineering*. Characteristic of simultaneous engineering is the near-parallel development of the design, business, and manufacturing processes. This contrasts with past practices of waiting until the design was nearly complete before developing the manufacturing process. Results show a drastic reduction in the time it takes to bring a product to market. Also designs and processes are stronger and more likely to meet the needs of the customer and user because of the input from the various diverse groups that are on the team.

Many companies transferred quality functions, such as inspection, to manufacturing to better match responsibility with the ability to control results (Fig. 26.1). In many organizations, this change brought about dramatic improvements in quality. No longer did a manufacturing operator wait for a quality inspector's approval. If there was a problem obvious to the manufacturing operator, it was usually addressed promptly and quickly solved.

In general, the activities in the quality system are concerned with the following:

1. Converting the needs of the customer or user to a product or service according to specifications

2. Controlling both business and manufacturing processes so that products and services consistently meet specifications

3. Continually improving both products and services by strengthening the processes producing them

4. Focusing on preventing problems rather than on correcting mistakes

5. Assessing how well the business and manufacturing processes are meeting requirements

Organizations that have an effective quality-assurance effort can demonstrate improvements in customer satisfaction coupled with upward trends in internal process

I. PREVENTION

A. Validation of Design
1. Failure mode analysis
2. Failure prevention analysis
3. Test & Calibration procedures
4. Calibration equipment
5. Product testing-design
6. Product testing-prod. processes
7. Insp. proc., prototype, & 1st art.
8. Analytical analysis
9. Field tests
10. PG tests
11. Prototype build
12. Design review
13. Release and validation
14. Drafting
15. Design

B. Process
1. Process/matl. capability studies
2. Process control
3. Process design

C. Problem Management
1. Scrap/rework reduction
2. Warranty reduction
3. Feedback of Q/R & failure information
4. Warranty chargeback comm.

D. Packaging & Handling

E. Service-Dev. Field Diagnostic Proc., Owners & Shop Manuals, Ser. Bulletin

F. Mgmt. & Engrg. Unrelated to Above
1. Management
2. Vendor audits
3. Quality/reliability training

II. APPRAISAL

A. Inspection & Testing
1. Inspection-direct-100%
2. Inspection-direct-less 100%
3. Quality audits
4. Inspection-indirect
5. Set up for inspection & test
6. Material for inspection & test
7. Review test & inspection date
8. Receiving insp. & storage
9. Lab accept. testing-receiving insp.
10. Lab accept. testing-prod. area
11. Outside lab services
12. Field testing
13. Reliability testing

B. Tool & Equipment
1. Maint. & Calib. test & insp. equip.
2. Gages; test fixture cost & maintenance
3. QC/reliability equipment cost
4. Design & devel. of qual. measurement & control equipment

C. Mgmt. & Engrg. Unrelated to Above
1. QC/reliability planning
2. Procedure audits
3. Engrg. review & shipping release
4. QC/reliability training
5. Management

QUALITY SYSTEM

III. FAILURE

A. Internal
1. Scrap
   a. Division responsible
   b. Vendor responsible
2. Rework
   a. Division responsible
   b. Vendor responsible
   c. Direct labor sorting
   d. Reinspection
3. Loss of prod. & cost due to QR/ problems

B. External
1. Warranty
2. Recall campaign
3. Customer complaints
4. User complaints
5. Returned matl. proc. & repair
6. Salaries related to prod. liability
7. Product liability costs
8. Field service
9. Civil penalty for lack of due care
10. Scrap-division resp. at assembly plant

C. Mgmt. & Engrg. Unrelated to Above
1. Management
2. Material review committee

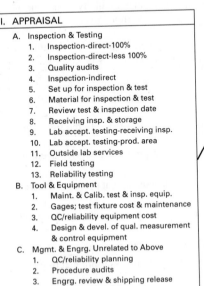

FIGURE 26.1 Quality system activities in a typical company.

quality. Such progress normally is not possible without equivalent improvements at suppliers. Producing high-quality products or services that fully meet the needs of customers has now become a prerequisite for doing business in the highly competitive marketplace.

QUALITY: WHAT IS IT?

In the past, the meaning of *quality* focused on the factory floor. If the product was approved by the inspector, it was considered "good quality." Tolerances often were not met, and if the inspector did not want to overlook the errors, then "written deviations" were processed by management for approval. Those making decisions on quality usually did not have contact with the customer or user and only became part of the loop if the product was rejected when it was received. Unfortunately, customers often tolerated poor quality to keep their production lines running.

Strong foreign competition offering better quality has changed this in the past decade. Sales by domestic companies slowed during the 1980s because of this foreign competition. Improved quality became the only way to regain sales momentum for the domestic companies. Thus, the focus of product quality assessment and acceptance changed from the factory floor to the customer or user. This change is slow and arduous to implement and requires altered thinking and management. For most companies, the change in focus is only partially complete and is still under way. The bottom line is that quality is now widely recognized as important in satisfying the needs of the customer or user.

Customer Focus

The *American Society for Quality Control* (ASQC) defines *quality* as "the totality of features and characteristics of a product or service that bear on its ability to satisfy given needs." It can be inferred from this definition that the "driver" of quality is to meet the needs of the customers or users. Also important is that deciding whether the quality desired has been achieved depends upon the perception of the customer or user. Once the customer's or user's needs are learned, the features and characteristics of a product or service can be determined in general terms. Subsequently, these can be translated into specifications and drawings. Processes can be selected to match the tolerances required.

Often laboratory and field tests are done prior to production, to validate that the customer's or user's needs will be met. Quality measures are also developed prior to shipping to predict how well the customer's or user's needs are met. A system is also required to determine the customer's or user's perception of the product or service produced. Often, these perceptions are tracked periodically for a substantial part of the product life cycle. In this way, durability and reliability problems can be recognized.

Taguchi Loss Function[1]

Variability is present in everything that is produced. A target or nominal dimension for variability is desired, however, and a tolerance is allowed about this target or nominal dimension because of variation. Each part produced will vary slightly from the target value. If the dimension of each part is charted as shown in Fig. 26.2a, it will produce a *histogram*. The random variation of the histogram can be smoothed to form the *normal curve* (Fig. 26.2b), also called the *bell curve* because of its shape. The curve illustrates

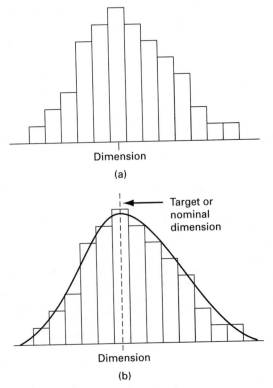

FIGURE 26.2 Illustration of variability found in nature. (*a*) Histogram; (*b*) normal curve.

the variation that is always present, and the wider the base of the curve, the more variation is present.

The *Taguchi loss function,* in simplistic terms, states that less variation lowers the cost of the product when considering the expenses during its entire lifetime. This concept recognizes that much more is spent on the product by the user servicing the product than is spent by the company in scrap and rework before it is shipped. There is widespread belief in this concept. Many studies, such as those made at Ford on automatic transmissions and at Sony on TV sets, strongly support this concept.

The Taguchi loss function has important implications in the application of tolerances. No longer is it sufficient to just meet tolerances because lifetime costs can be drastically reduced by a continuous effort to minimize variation about the target or nominal dimension regardless of the tolerance.

It is extremely difficult to establish tolerances that are necessary to meet a customer's or user's needs, which is a good reason to reduce variation despite meeting tolerances. Usually, it is a major challenge to just determine the proper target or nominal dimension needed, let alone the tolerances. Of course, tolerances will continue to be valuable in assuring process capability on difficult processes and to evaluate the *stackup* of parts to assure that they can be readily assembled.

Figure 26.3 illustrates a typical curve for a part having too much variability to consistently meet specifications. Parts extending beyond the tolerance, as shown in the

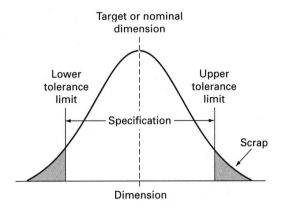

FIGURE 26.3   Illustration of variability extending beyond tolerance.

shaded area, should be reworked or scrapped before shipping. Even more significant is that the farther away a part is from the target or nominal dimension, even though it is within specification, the more it is expected to cost the customer or user to service. Figure 26.4 illustrates a typical curve for a part with much less variation but well within specifications. To achieve this curve, each part produced will consistently meet specifications. The average cost during the lifetime of the product is expected to be much less.

This relationship has important implications as it affects customer satisfaction. A product having less lifetime cost to the user will help produce satisfied customers and more repeat sales. It is projected that the additional profit generated over the long haul by repeated sales will be greater than the cost of minimizing a product's variability.

Before Shipment

Quality cannot be improved after shipment except by costly and often widely publicized recalls. Whether the product or service will meet a customer's needs should be estab-

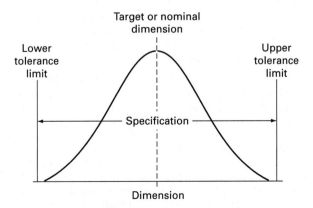

FIGURE 26.4   Illustration of variability well within tolerance.

lished before then. Studies show that product design and the planning occurring around it have the largest effect on quality; about 80 percent of the impact. The rest, by and large, is attributed to manufacturing activities. For many companies, a significant degradation occurs in quality during shipping and handling both in-plant and after delivery to the customer.

Simultaneous engineering has assured the timely input from pertinent disciplines and has vastly improved both the product and process design. But it is difficult to determine standards of quality for evaluating a process that agrees with the customer's or user's needs. Although standards are improving, they remain challenging to most organizations. Effective quality standards are vital for fine-tuning processes as products are made.

CUSTOMERS: THEIR NEEDS

Customers and users usually do not care about dimensions or specifications because, for the most part, they have their own perceptions as to what the product should be like. Quality is judged by comparing the actual product to what they think it should be like. Often there is a difference in the expectations of the product brought about by individual preferences. A real challenge to an organization is to provide a design that accommodates the differences in expectations or needs by potential customers.

Customer Satisfaction

The way a customer or user feels about a product or service is called *customer satisfaction.* Most organizations strive for high customer satisfaction. Driving the desire for high customer satisfaction is that a happy customer will typically share this satisfaction with 5 other prospective customers. On the other hand, an unhappy customer tells of their dissatisfaction to many more—typically 35 or more. This network of information, good and bad, is felt by many organizations to have a dramatic effect on future sales.

Four factors subconsciously influence the way a customer or user feels about a company's product or service. The four factors are illustrated in Fig. 26.5. Together, the four factors help the customer or user form a perception about the quality of a product or service. When a perception is formed, each factor is not weighted equally in the mind of a customer or user. The specific influence of each factor varies greatly depending on the individual and the situation:

1. *Function* is about how well the product or service does the job that is perceived to be necessary. For a microwave oven it may be, "Can it heat soup in less than 2 minutes?" Also of concern may be, "Can it perform this function consistently during the life of the product without servicing?"

2. *Use features* concern how well the user interfaces with the product or service. For the microwave oven, it may be how user-friendly the controls are perceived to be.

3. *Perception features* are about how the product appeals to the customer or user. A technical enthusiast may be attracted to the product if the microwave oven has all of the latest technology. Others may be attracted if the oven is perceived to match the decor of the kitchen.

4. *Price* concerns the perceived value to the customer. In most situations, this is a trade-off with the other factors. In tight economic times, a microwave oven with simple controls and a low price may be the best perceived value for some. Likewise, in robust economic times, the opposite may be perceived.

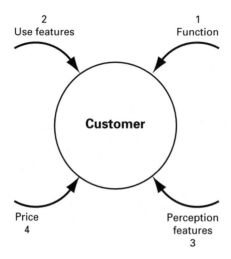

FIGURE 26.5   Customer perceptions of quality.

Perceptions about customer satisfaction are widely sought by companies through surveys. These surveys may be conducted by mail or telephone solicitations. Results are aggregated and summarized, and they furnish valuable feedback for the continuous improvement of business and manufacturing processes within an organization. Often these surveys are done by outside firms, and competitors' products are evaluated as well. Comparison to a competitor's product often furnishes a valuable benchmark for how well the customer's expectations are being met in the marketplace.

External Customers

Customers and users outside the organization are considered *external customers*. One could conclude that the perceptions of external customers are the bottom line of customer satisfaction. What they think about the product or service provided could make the difference between the long-term success and failure of a company.

Internal Customers

On the other hand, *internal customers* are within the organization that is providing the products or services. Everyone in the organization is both a supplier to others and a customer of someone else. Input is received from others, and after it is processed, it is given to the next internal customer. This is continued many times until delivery is finally made to an external customer. The collective effectiveness of each person in the internal chain determines whether the needs of the external customer and user will be met.

In some companies, this internal relationship is formally recognized by teams of employees that perform a process that accepts input from other processes that serves as internal suppliers. After the team completes its process, they pass it to their internal customer, which is another team of employees performing a process. Quality measurements are made as each team completes its process. The product is progressively checked to determine if it meets the needs of the next process done by an internal customer. Also, the quality needs of the external customer are determined at regular intervals as the product is produced.

LIABILITY CONSIDERATIONS

Today the responsibility of a company to a customer extends beyond delivery of a product or service. Years ago this was not true because "let the buyer beware" was the law. Today, most products have warranties spelled out in agreements between the manufacturers and the customers. Additional liability may be imposed by regulations of the legal system. A company typically bears a large burden for the safety of a product, especially while it is being used. The liability for the safe use of a product has been found by law to extend far into the lifetime of a product. The court judgments and settlements in these lawsuits could be of such a magnitude to virtually threaten the future existence of a company. An important quality-assurance activity is to help provide product designs that are safe to use and thereby make it possible for a company to avoid the liability for accidents. Typically, this requires product analysis, design reviews, and extensive product durability testing.

Warranty

This type of liability imposed on the manufacturer could be of two types: expressed and implied. *Expressed warranties* are typically representations made by the seller in the warranty agreements, such as that the cost of a vehicle's repairs will be covered during the first 36,000 miles or for 3 years, whichever comes first. This is null and void when the product is misused. Courts also have found that representations in advertisements must be honored by the seller.

Implied warranties are those liabilities of a seller that are not formally stated or written but may be imposed by a court. For example, in the past, items were sold "as-is," with no expressed warranty. However, courts are now finding, in many situations, that there is an obligation owed by the seller of a product. In doing this, courts are recognizing that there is an implied warranty of "fitness-of-use" for products. Often these court findings are made into laws, such as the "lemon laws" adopted by many states to provide a resolution of situations where a product is not fixed in a timely fashion.

Negligence

A manufacturer must take reasonable and prudent care when designing or processing a product. If an accident occurs after the product is delivered because reasonable and prudent care was not exercised, a court may find that the manufacturer is liable for damages incurred. An example of lack of reasonable and prudent care may be when something is repaired but there has been no check made to assure that the repairs were made correctly.

Product Liability

Most people would agree that product liability is the most burdensome one placed on the seller of a product. *Strict liability* occurs where a defect causes a product to be unreasonably dangerous while it is being used. The defect may be either a design or processing defect. It also may be unknown to the seller prior to delivery. Even more burdensome, it may be only a single occurrence in an entire production run and may occur any time during the product's lifetime. If harm occurs because of that defect, the seller may be liable for the damages despite all the precautions taken. Often huge judgments or settlements are reported for product liability claims concerning accidents involving motor vehicles and other consumer goods.

IMPORTANCE OF RELIABILITY

More than ever before, customers and users expect a reasonably trouble-free performance during a product's lifetime. Often, the choice of whether to purchase again from a company is based upon the experience with a product currently owned or used. Also, a potential customer that is new to a company may rely on the opinion of others who use their products. For any company, sales influenced by past experience help assure future success.

Reliability

In simplistic terms, *reliability* is the probability that a product will survive without failure over a certain period. For new light bulbs the reliability may be 0.98 for 200 hours. This means that 98 percent of the bulbs will burn for at least 200 hours. A curve, described as a *bathtub curve* because of its shape, is often used to describe the failure pattern of products over their lifetime. A typical bathtub curve is shown in Fig. 26.6.

Failures when the product is just entering into use are usually very high. This phase is called the *infantile failure period*. Often these failures are due to manufacturing problems. Certain products, such as computers, are cycled through this period at the factory prior to delivery. In this way, customers and users are not exposed to these high failure rates. The next phase is called the *constant failure period*. Failures during this phase are usually very low and reflect what may be expected during the normal lifetime of the product. Many causes of the failures in this phase are inherent in the design.

The last phase is called the *wearout period* when the product reaches the end of its useful life and should be recycled. Failures during this phase continue to climb, and costs to make repairs become excessive. To assure a reliable product requires formal analysis, design reviews, extensive product durability testing, and often field testing.

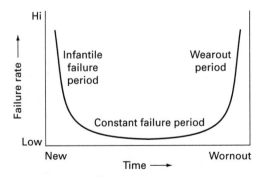

FIGURE 26.6 Bathtub curve illustrating failures during the lifetime of a product.

Maintainability

Once a repair of a product being used is necessary, it should be fixed quickly and economically. *Maintainability* is a measure of the ease of returning the product to performing its useful function. Maintainability is the probability of fixing a product within a particular time. For example, 0.8 may be the maintainability for fixing a problem in 16 hours, which means that 80 percent of the problems of this type can be repaired in 16 hours or less. Obviously, a customer or user desires that a failed product be repaired as quickly as possible and at a reasonable cost. The time for repair depends upon many things such as the availability of replacement parts and the location of service sites. Assuring effective maintainability requires up-front planning and an effective logistics system for the lifetime of the products.

MANAGEMENT OF QUALITY

The responsibility for the management of quality extends throughout the entire organization and thus must be orchestrated by the top individual in the organization. Not only must the current quality activities be stabilized and coordinated but continuous improvement must be sought. That improvement can be obtained by focusing on three factors—the organization, business and manufacturing processes within the organization—and individuals. Many companies feel the way to accomplish this is through strategic planning and a long-term outlook.

Strategy

In many companies, planning begins with strategic planning by top management. The approach differs among companies, but it generally starts with a vision of what the company should be like 5 or 10 years from now. From this, the mission of the company is developed. Then long-term strategy and tactics are developed to achieve the vision. From this, much more specific plans are developed. These specific plans typically address manufacturing, marketing, financing, and product development. The plans are short to medium range in nature. Quality is not usually dealt with separately as it is in other activities such as JIT, but it is included as a vital part of the specific plans. The specific plans typically deal with improving the organization and business and manufacturing processes within the organization. The strategy and detailed plans are often fine-tuned to reflect changing conditions. Thus, continuous improvement is brought about in an effective manner.

Culture

In the past, most companies were driven primarily by production targets. So quality was of secondary importance, which made customers and users dissatisfied. Many companies have embarked on a cultural change to produce satisfied customers by meeting strategic plans. The focus of these companies is changing from production targets to customer satisfaction by dealing with the following factors on an equal basis:

1. Timing of delivery of products and services
2. Quality of products and services as delivered and used during their lifetime
3. Cost of products and services, both when delivered and when used, so as to reflect value in the eyes of customers
4. Product and service appeal in the eyes of the customer or user

Most organizations have concluded that the following characteristics are needed in the new culture:

1. A focus on the customers and their needs must be adopted by all the individuals throughout the organization.

2. Judgment of product quality can be made only through the perceptions of the customer and the user. In effect, perceptions by the customer and user are the reality concerning product quality.

3. The organization must consider and respect its employees, and this attitude in turn will carry over to produce satisfied customers.

4. Every effort must be made to develop a workforce with exceptional motivation.

5. The organization must stress safety. This includes personnel, facilities, and products as well as the community in which it resides.

6. Preventing problems from happening must be given high priority. This requires a cooperative organization and excellent business and manufacturing processes, as well as trained individuals.

7. Self-directed work teams must be used throughout the organization. Teams usually work out more innovative and effective solutions to problems than do individuals or management.

8. Every employee should be part of the problem-solving and continuous improvement effort. There should be total involvement by all employees to assure "buy-in" by everyone.

9. Decisions concerning manufacturing or business processes should be made by those directly involved. Those closest to a problem typically produce the best solution.

10. Every employee must be able to speak the truth without fear of punishment or retribution. Open discussion of all the issues is absolutely vital to any continuous improvement effort.

11. There must be trust among individuals in the organization.

12. Management should facilitate the efforts of self-directed work teams. They should act as leaders or visionaries and not attempt to manage the team's efforts.

Many believe that it will take a long time for organizations to fully incorporate these characteristics into their company culture. But they also believe that the effort to make the transition is absolutely necessary to assure the future viability of an organization.

Quality System

The American Society of Quality Control defines a *quality system* as "the collective plans, activities, and events that are provided to ensure that a product, process or service will satisfy given needs." Thus, the goal of the quality system is to assure that the product or service meets the needs of the customer or user.

All departments in an organization have a role in making the quality system work. An effective quality system must be orchestrated so that all parts act collectively and in unison. Fiefdoms or power bases in an organization counter the smooth operation of a quality system and must be eliminated to assure success. Quality activities exist in marketing, product development, suppliers, materials, manufacturing, and service. When operating alone, these quality activities can cause conflict. Working together, the activities can easily accomplish the common quality goals of the organization. Directing and facilitating the smooth operation of all the activities is the role of management.

Self-directed, cross-discipline teams that cut across department lines but have a common interest in quality have helped immensely in achieving harmony in the quality system activities. For example, a product development team may be led by a member from product development and include part-time members from marketing, materials, manufacturing, major suppliers, and service. A member from the quality organization may advise others on the team regarding quality issues.

Organization

Many companies use a quality council and teams for managing their quality system and pursuing needed improvements. *Quality council* members of the quality council include the top manager in the organization and the heads of the functional areas. In this manner, the key decision makers in an organization are brought together with a common purpose—operating and improving the quality system. Allocation of resources can be agreed upon within the council so its efforts are enhanced. Figure 26.7 shows a typical organization of this type.

The quality council is the driver of the quality system and acts as a facilitator for the teams that are carrying out the activities for needed improvements. It also provides the vision and assistance to the teams so desired actions happen. In a sense, each member of the team acts as an agent for the customer to motivate the organization to improve customer satisfaction. Many companies feel that the main reason for a quality council is to assure customer focus. Other important reasons given are to remove artificial barriers among departments and to foster consensus in the company's direction.

Use of Quality-Cost Techniques.   Some companies use quality-cost techniques to help members of the quality council focus on needed improvements in the quality system. These techniques can be used to define the existing quality system in terms of cost. Through reviewing the cost relationships, inconsistencies are found that often lead to

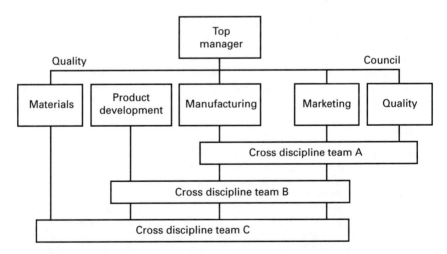

FIGURE 26.7   Organization to operate and improve activities in quality system.

significant improvements. For example, one study showed that despite the high cost or product quality validation tests, the relevant warranty cost remained high. Adjustments in testing priorities brought about much lower warranty costs.

Teams. In many companies quality and improvement activities are handled by teams of part-time members. These teams are organized and facilitated by the quality council to achieve organizational objectives. The quality council determines priorities for team efforts. The purpose of the teams is to sustain needed activities and to implement desired changes.

One person may be a member of several teams and also perform regularly assigned duties in their function area. Cross-discipline teams may be most effective where activities and improvements cross departmental boundaries. When team goals are short range in nature, ad hoc teams are formed and disbanded when the job is done.

Audits

Audits scheduled at periodic intervals can be described as a critique of the quality system and its activities, processes, or products. These audits can be helpful in identifying opportunities for improvement that are not obvious to management or those who are directly involved. Often audits are classified as first-party audits, second-party audits, and third-party audits. *First-party audits* use auditors that are employed by the company being audited. When the audit is performed by a customer, it is said to be a *second-party audit*. A *third-party audit* is performed by an independent agency not attached to the company or the customers.

Auditing for a company's registration of its quality system that is to meet a standard, such as ISO 9001, is done by a third party. Recognition of this registration by customers may eliminate the need for second-party audits by each customer. In this case, audit expense may be substantially reduced for both the company and its customers.

Audits can also be viewed as of three types: product audit, process audit, and system audit:

A *product audit* centers on the product delivered to the customer. It is usually done by taking the customer's viewpoint. The location of the audit varies. It may be in the plant just before shipping, at railheads, distributors, or warehouses. The specific audit is a detailed examination of the product. It may include a visual examination, measurements, performance testing, and durability testing.

Process audits focus on business and manufacturing processes. They are intended to verify that the process, operators, tools, gauges, and equipment are functioning correctly. In accomplishing this audit, there is a detailed examination of the input, processing, and output of the process. Also evaluated is whether requirements are lacking or unclear. Procedures and work instructions must reflect the requirements that will result in meeting the customer's needs.

Systems audits are very broad. They critique the business processes in a company and their relationships. Often these critiques extend to the supplier base. They include an evaluation of management, systems, procedures, and operations. A systems audit often includes both a product and process audit. The audits are often quite complex, usually requiring cross-discipline teams to accomplish. The registration process to a standard, such as ISO 9000, can be classified as a systems audit.

There are usually many products, processes, and systems in a company, and an audit, because of time limitations, can critique only a few of them. Therefore, it is necessary to carefully choose representative items to audit. This choice is usually not made on a random basis, but rather, it is based on a preconception of the auditors as to where the audit would be most effective. For these items, small samples are taken to conserve time, and, even though the sample sizes may not be statistically significant, opportunities for improvement can be effectively identified.

STANDARDS

Not being aware of the standards with which a product or quality system has to comply could be disastrous for a company. An international marketer is faced with thousands of standards for the various countries with whom it conducts business. Sorting through this array of standards to find those that apply is a formidable task.

If a product does not meet an appropriate standard, it may be unsalable. Even worse, if sold, the company may be liable for regulatory fines and huge legal settlements for the harm that is done. Standards are sometimes defined by the various laws and statutes of countries. For example, in the United States, standards may exist at the federal, state, and local government levels. Often standards are set under the guidance of organizations—for example, the ASME, ANSI, ASQC, and the International Organization for Standardization in Geneva who coordinates the various ISO standards.

Product Technical Requirements

Standards exist for many business and industrial needs and cover a very broad subject. Product standards may involve processing, testing, identification, packaging, shipping, and installation. Also these standards can cover size and strength characteristics, as well as performance requirements, safety, and reliability. Other standards relate to the environment and are met with product warnings, labels, and instructions.

ISO 9000 Quality Standards

An international quality system standard, ISO 9000, is being widely used for third-party registration. A third-party registration is performed by an independent auditor, called a *registrar,* who is not attached to the company being audited or its customers. The independent auditor doing the registration has met stringent requirements to become a registrar.

The ISO 9000 standard originally became available in 1987. The standard was developed under the auspices of the International Organization for Standardization in cooperation with representatives from many countries. By the end of 1993, over 40,000 companies worldwide were registered as being in conformance to the standard. Several thousand of these registered companies are in the United States. It is interesting that several industry groups have adopted this standard, as well as the U.S. Department of Defense. This standard is experiencing increasing popularity in the international marketplace.

Registered companies are recognized as meeting at least minimal requirements for the management of their quality-assurance system. Recognition of this registration by customers, in effect, can qualify a company to supply products or services without any further action. Companies that are some distance from each other can be confident of doing business together without further quality audits. In this way, a barrier to world trade is removed. Also potential audit expense is substantially reduced for both the company and its customers.

The ISO 9000 standard is actually three standards, so the choice of which application depends on the type of company being registered. ISO 9001 is for a full-service company that does design, development, production, installation, and servicing of a product. For a company doing just production, installation, and servicing but not design and development, ISO 9002 would be applicable. ISO 9003 has few applications since it is designed for companies performing only final inspection and testing. There are other ISO 9000 standards that are guidelines for the proper application of ISO 9001, 9002, and 9003. These include, for example, help in applying the standards to generic situations, services, process industries, and software. Other guidelines are available in the ISO 10000 series for auditing and measuring equipment applications.

MEASURING QUALITY

Deciding whether quality has been achieved depends upon the perceptions of the customers or users. This is because the "driver" of quality is the needs of the customers or users.

Prior to Delivery

It is critical in the product or service design phase that the customer's or user's needs are properly reflected in the specifications and drawings. Laboratory and field tests prior to production can verify whether needs will be met by the proposed designs. User clinics can also be of help.

Once an effective design is found, quality measures can be specified to determine that the product will conform to the design. In this way, the measures can help predict how well the customer's needs are met during production prior to shipping. If customer perceptions can be predicted before the product is delivered, needed corrections may be possible before the customer receives it.

Quality measures in production can be a dimensional measurement, performance test data, or durability test data. The first two quality measures tend to confirm early in the product's life cycle that needs are met. Durability tests, or accelerated life testing, can help predict satisfaction with the product later in its life cycle. Because satisfaction is important for the entire life cycle, durability tests are growing in importance.

After Delivery

After the product is shipped, actual perceptions about meeting needs can be sought. Perceptions are found by companies through direct contact, as well as surveys. Surveys may be conducted, for example, by mail or telephone. Results furnish valuable feedback for the continuous improvement of business and manufacturing processes. Surveys may be conducted by outside firms so that the competitor's products are evaluated at the same time. Comparison to a product of a competitor gives useful information as to how well customer expectations are being met in the marketplace.

ANALYSIS TOOLS

There are many tools that are used for analyzing quality issues to come up with better solutions. The most popular ones are discussed here. Other tools for your applications can be found in the references at the end of the chapter. For convenience, the tools are listed in two groups: *design phase* and *production phase*. Those in the design phase seem to be most effective when designs and processes are still being planned and changes do not require large cost for revamping facilities or equipment. On the other hand, tools in the production phase have been effective after planning has been completed and facilities and equipment are installed. Depending upon the application, a tool in the production phase may be very useful in the design phase and vice versa.

Design Phase

Benchmarking.   *Competitive analysis* is more commonly called *benchmarking* today. In simplistic terms, a benchmark is a reference point to which actual results can be compared. For a company, the reference point is what is being achieved by other companies. Benchmarking can concern the relationship of a company's product to the similar product of a competitor. Thus, specifications can be compared by laboratory analysis and by dissecting the competitor's product. Also, how well the customer's or user's needs are met may be found by conducting surveys.

Benchmarking can concern the relationship of a company's process to another company's similar process. Usually this comparison is not made with a product competitor but with a company known to be best in working with a certain process. An advantage of this comparison is that visits can be made to view an excellent process without competitive concerns. Often, benchmarking produces valuable targets for both planning products and processes. Knowing that these targets were achieved by either a competitor or another company provides an important reality check.

Quality Function Deployment (QFD).   This method helps ensure that the customers' and users' needs are provided for in the design of the product, as well as in the processes involved. Typically, the QFD consists of four matrices with the output of one matrix being the input for the next, as shown in Fig. 26.8. The first matrix translates the customer's or user's desires into their needs. Then, the second matrix converts their needs into product design features. The third matrix translates the product design features into process requirements. Finally, the last matrix converts process requirements into process control requirements.

A cross-discipline team usually handles the development of the matrices and translations involved in QFD. Through the discussion taking place, team members become customer focused. Output from the various matrices can be used to develop customer surveys, design the product and processes, and specify appropriate process controls. With QFD, meeting the needs of the customer and user is greatly enhanced.

Potential Design Failure Mode and Effects Analysis (DFMEA).   A DFMEA is a methodical way of reviewing a product design for potential failures that can occur when in the hands of the customer or user. The goal of a DFMEA is to identify and eliminate in the product design potential failure modes and their causes. If they cannot be fully eliminated, the objective is to minimize the risk of those failure modes and causes that remain. A cross-discipline team usually handles the development of the DFMEA. Figure 26.9 shows a typical DFMEA.

Potential failure modes are often identified through brainstorming. For each potential failure mode, the cause and effect are agreed upon by the team. Then, the probability of occurrence, seriousness of the failure, and likelihood of exposing the customer are estimated by the team. Corrective action is sought for each of the potential causes of failure. The estimate is redone including the corrective action to see what progress has been made by the team. Output from the effort could result, for example, in one or more of the following:

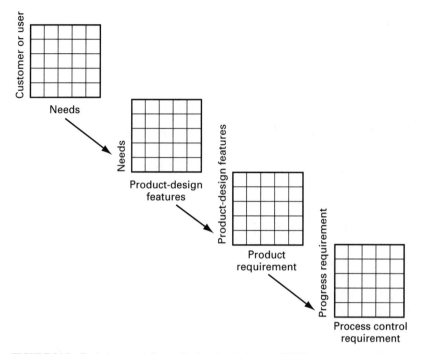

FIGURE 26.8   Typical approach for quality function deployment (QFD).

1. Redesign of the product to be safer in the customer's hands
2. Redesign of the business and manufacturing processes to minimize the potential for design failures ever reaching the customer or user
3. Adding validation tests prior to production so that failure modes can be predicted and addressed before exposing the customer or user
4. Adding inspection and tests in the production processes to sort out marginal products that may fail in the customer's or user's hands
5. Supplying the customer with appropriate instructions and warning labels

Potential Process Failure Mode and Effects Analysis (PFMEA).   The goal of the PFMEA (Fig. 26.10) is to identify and eliminate potential failure modes and their causes during the manufacturing process. Like a DFMEA, if that goal cannot be achieved for all potential failures, then the objective is to minimize the risk of those remaining failures that occur. That risk could be for the customer, or user, or the plant personnel facilities as the product is produced. A necessary input to the development of the PFMEA is the applicable DFMEA.

As can be seen, the PFMEA is very similar to a DFMEA. The steps taken in processing a PFMEA by a cross-discipline team are also similar to those for a DFMEA. In addition, the general outputs from a PFMEA are similar in nature to those listed for a DFMEA. But the specific findings normally do not duplicate each other because the DFMEA focuses on the product design while the PFMEA focuses on the manufacturing process.

System			FMEA number 1234
x Subsystem			Page 1 of 1
Component 01.03/Body closures	Design responsibility Body Engineering		Prepared by A. Tate - X6412 - Body Engr
Model year(s) vehicle(s) 199X/L/on 4dr/Wagon	Key date 9X 03 01 ER		FMEA date (Orig.) 8X 03 22 (Rev.) 8 X 07 14
Core team T. Fender-Car Product Dev., C. Childers Manufacturing, J. Ford-Assy Ops (Dalton, Fraser, Henley Assembly Plants)			

Item function	Potential failure mode	Potential effect(s) of failure	S e v	C l a s s	Potential cause(s)/ mechanism(s) of failure	O c c u r	Current design controls	D e t e c	R. P. N.	Recommended action(s)	Responsibility and target completion date	Action results				
												Actions taken	S e v	O c c	D e t	R. P. N.
Front door L.H. H8HX-0000-A	Corroded interior lower door panels	Deteriorated life of door leading to: • Unsatisfactory appearance due to rust through paint over time	7		Upper edge of protective wax application specified for inner door panels is too low.	6	Vehicle general durability test veh. T-118 T-109 T-301	7	294	Add laboratory accelerated corrosion testing.	A. Tate-Body Engrg 8X 09 30	Based on test results (Test No. 1481) upper edge spec raised 125 mm.	7	2	2	28
• Ingress to and egress from vehicle • Occupant protection from weather, noise, and side impact • Support anchorage for door hardware including mirror, hinges, latch and window regulator		• Impaired function of interior door hardware	7		Insufficient wax thickness specified.	4	Vehicle general durability testing—as above	7	196	Add laboratory accelerated corrosion testing. Conduct design of experiments (DOE) on wax thickness.	Combine w/test for wax upper edge verification. A. Tate-Body Engrg 9X 01 15	Test results (Test No. 1481) show specified thickness is adequate.	7	2	2	28
					Inappropriate wax formulation specified.	2	Physical and chem lab test— Report No. 1265	2	28	None.						

- Provide proper surface for appearance items—paint and soft trim

							Sev	Occ	Det	RPN
Entrapped air prevents wax from entering corner/edge access.	5	Design aid investigation with nonfunctioning spray head	8	280	Team evaluation using production spray equipment and specified wax.	Body Engrg & Assy Ops 8X 11 15	Based on test, additional holes will be provided in affected areas.	7	1	3	21
Wax application plugs door drain holes.	3	Laboratory test using "worst-case" wax application and hole size	1	21	None.						
Insufficient room between panels for spray head egress.	4	Drawing evaluation of spray head access	4	112	Team evaluation using design aid buck and spray head.	Body Engrg & Assy Ops 8X 09 15	Evaluation showed adequate access.	7	1	1	7

FIGURE 26.9 Design failure mode and effects analysis.

26.19

Item Front Door L.H./H8HX-0000-A **Process Responsibility** Body Engrg./Assembly Operations **Prepared by** J. Ford - X6521 - Assy Ops

Model year(s)/vehicle(s) 199X/Lion 4dr/Wagon **Key date** 9X 03 01 ER 9X 08 26 Job #1 **FMEA Date (Orig.)** 9X 05 17 (Rev.) 9X 11 06

Core Team A. Tate Body Engrg., J. Smith-OC, R. James-Production, J. Jones-Maintenance

Process function requirements	Potential failure mode	Potential effect(s) of failure	S e v	C l a s s	Potential cause(s)/ mechanism(s) of failure	O c c u r	Current design controls	D e t	R. P. N.	Recommended action(s)	Responsibility and target completion date	Action results			
												Actions taken	S e v	O c c	D e t	R. P. N.
Manual application of wax inside door	Insufficient wax coverage over specified surface	Deteriorated life of door leading to: • Unsatisfactory appearance due to rust through paint over time	7		Manually inserted spray head not inserted far enough.	8	Visual check each hour— 1/shift for film thickness (depth meter) and coverage	5	280	Add positive depth stop to sprayer	MFG Engrg 9X 10 15	Stop added, sprayer checked on line	7	2	5	70
To cover inner door, lower surfaces at minimum wax thickness to retard corrosion		• Impaired function of interior door hardware								Automate spraying	Mfg Engrg 9X 12 15	Rejected due to complexity of different doors on same line				

Potential Cause(s) of Failure	Occ	Current Process Controls	Det	RPN	Recommended Action(s)	Responsibility & Target Completion Date	Action Results	Sev	Occ	Det	RPN
Spray heads clogged: • Viscosity too high. • Temperature too low. • Pressure too low.	5	Test spray pattern at start-up and after idle periods, and preventative maintenance program to clean heads.	3	105	Use Design of Experiments (DOE) on viscosity vs. temperature vs. pressure	Mfg Engrg 9X 10 01	Temp and press limits were determined and limit controls have been installed—control charts show process is in control $C_{pk} \approx 1.85$	7	1	3	21
Spray head deformed due to impact.	2	Preventative maintenance programs to maintain head.	2	28	None						
Spray time insufficient.	8	Operator instructions and lot sampling (10 doors/shift) to check for coverage of critical areas	7	392	Install spray timer	Maintenance 9X 09 15	Automatic spray timer installed—operator starts spray, timer controls shut-off—control charts show process is in control $C_{pk} \approx 2.05$	7	1	7	49

FIGURE 26.10 Process failure mode and effects analysis.

Design of Experiments (DOE) and Taguchi Methods.[2]   When planning an experiment, the objective must be carefully defined. For example, an objective may be to find out what variables have a major effect on a quality characteristic. The plan for reaching the objective is called a *design of experiment* (DOE). The classical method of experimentation is changing just one variable at a time and holding all other variables constant. This process takes many computer runs and a long time to accomplish. Modern DOE concepts allow several variables to be varied at the same time and usually many fewer test runs. Thus, a needed objective may be determined in a more timely manner.

An important use of DOE in product development is *parameter design.* Each parameter has a nominal, or target, value and a tolerance about the target value. Taguchi methods find the most appropriate nominal or target value and tolerance that will achieve design goals. The premise behind parameter design is that variation in performance is affected much more by some variables than by others. Also, the amount of variation can possibly be changed by choosing a more appropriate nominal or target dimension.

Tolerances can be increased on those variables that do not affect variation in performance, thus lowering manufacturing costs. Tighter tolerances may be needed on variables that have a large effect on variation of performance. In this way, the quality of the product design can be more consistent and meet customer and user needs better.

By Taguchi methods, nominal or target dimensions and tolerances may be selected so that the performance of the product is little affected by variation in the manufacturing process or variation in conditions where the product is used. When this occurs, the product design is said to be "robust," or "insensitive," to variation.

Production Phase

Process Flow Charts.   The various steps in a process can be shown in a process flow chart. Because this helps in understanding the process, it is usually the first step in trying to make an improvement. A process flow chart also helps in deciding what should be improved and how it will be done. Figure 26.11 shows a typical process flow chart. A detailed process flow chart can identify the following:

1. Where materials and parts originate
2. The sequence of using the parts and materials
3. The sequence in which the operations are performed
4. Where inspection and testing are performed
5. Where completed materials are delivered
6. The method for handling scrap and rework

Pareto Analysis.   Often the second step in seeking an improvement is making a *Pareto chart,* which is a bar chart in which the bars are arranged in decreasing order of magnitude. A Pareto chart provides direction as to what action will result in the greatest impact. The chart was named for an Italian who in the late 1800s found that most of the wealth in his country was owned by a few people. His finding is often called the *20–80 concept* today. The concept states that 20 percent of the categories account for 80 percent of the observations. See Fig. 26.12 for a typical Pareto chart.

For this chart, it appears that pursuing numbers of cracks in a part may lead to the highest benefit for the time invested. Cracks account for 80 percent of the problems. Yet, it is one of five kinds of defects, or only 20 percent of the defects. Often, that which

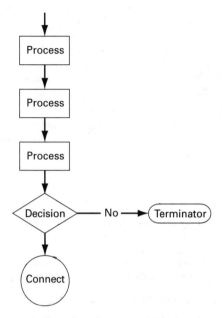

FIGURE 26.11   Process flow chart.

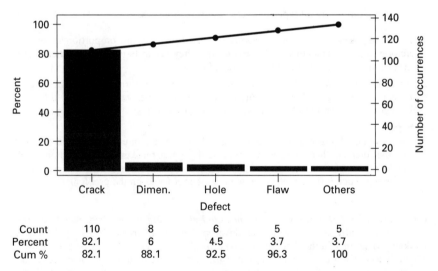

	Crack	Dimen.	Hole	Flaw	Others
Count	110	8	6	5	5
Percent	82.1	6	4.5	3.7	3.7
Cum %	82.1	88.1	92.5	96.3	100

FIGURE 26.12   Typical Pareto chart for analysis of nonconformances.

Defect type	Mon	Tues	Wed	Thurs	Fri	Total
Cracks	19	23	20	18	30	110
Hole	2		1	2	1	6
Flaw	1	1	1	1	1	5
Dimension 190-210 mm		1	1	1	1	4
Dimension 15-20 mm	1	1		1	1	4
Surface finish			1	1	1	3
Missing material			1		1	2
Total	23	27	24	25	35	134

FIGURE 26.13 Attribute check sheet.

accounts for 20 percent of the categories is called the "vital few." The remaining 80 percent of the categories are called the "trivial many."

Check Sheets. The next step taken is usually to collect data using check sheets. Before the type of check sheet is designed, the following issues should be dealt with:

1. What may be learned from the data?
2. Based on the answer to question 1, what is the best format for the check sheet so that the data can prove this assertion? (All check sheets are custom-made for the specific situation at hand.)

There are three general types of check sheets, as follows:

1. *Attribute check sheet.* This is normally used to assess the proportion of defects among categories and to seek the reasons that they occur. Figure 26.13 indicates that cracks in a product are the major source of defects.
2. *Variable check sheet.* This is often used to seek more information about a specific defect. Figure 26.14 shows that the occurrence of cracks varies as metal thickness changes. The metal thickness used in lot A seems to result in the least number of cracks.
3. *Location check sheet.* This is used to find if failures are more prevalent in one area of a part than another. The check sheet is really a general sketch of the part on which the locations of defects are marked. Figure 26.15 indicates where the cracks are occurring. Such information could lead to a better focus on the problems.

Cause-and-Effect Diagrams. The *cause-and-effect diagram* is often called the *fishbone diagram* after its shape. It was developed in Japan in the 1960s by Professor Ishikawa. The lines in the diagram link an effect with the possible causes of the effect. Major causes of a problem could be materials, methods, human beings, machines, measurements, or the environment. Many factors of possible causation are usually listed under each major cause in such a diagram. In this way, the diagram helps people analyze a problem. One of the potential factors may be the root cause. Figure 26.16 shows a cause-and-effect diagram that was prepared for cracks.[3] There are 18 factors that may be causing cracks, and 1 of the factors may be the root cause of the problem.

Cracks	Mon	Tues	Wed	Thurs	Fri	Total
Metal thickness						
Lot A	1	2	1	0	3	7
Lot B	4	5	4	4	6	23
Lot C	5	5	5	6	7	28
Lot D	4	7	4	5	7	27
Lot E	5	4	6	3	7	25
Total	19	23	20	18	30	110

FIGURE 26.14   Variable check sheet.

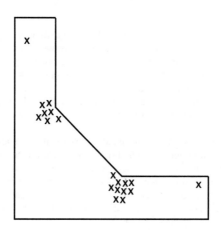

FIGURE 26.15   Location check sheet.

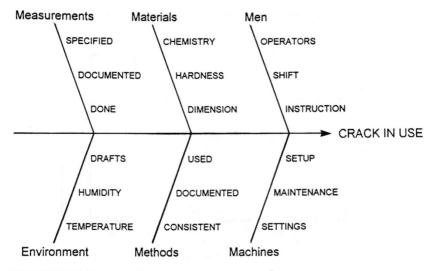

FIGURE 26.16   Cause-and-effect diagram (Ishikawa diagram).[3]

Stratification Diagrams.   This type of diagram helps focus on the cause of problems. It is a bar chart that stratifies the breaks by the number of defects caused by similar potential contributors. Potential contributors to the problem may be shifts, plants, machines, or operators. Figure 26.17 illustrates a stratification chart for three different suppliers. It appears that supplier B may have the fewest defects if equal amounts have been received from each supplier.

Scatter Diagrams.   These diagrams show how one variable relates to another. In Fig. 26.18, the two variables, TEMP and DIM, show a strong relationship between each other. One would expect that if TEMP were increased, DIM would also increase. However, in another situation (Fig. 26.19), it appears that no relationship exists between the two variables. Thus, it is difficult to predict what value of DIM will result from raising TEMP.

Histograms.   These charts present a great deal of data usually in an easy-to-understand visual format. A variable histogram, as in Fig. 26.20, shows how often something occurs for different dimensions on the X axes. The data are grouped by class interval. In this case each class interval, the width of a bar, is 2.5 mm wide. The number of class intervals for a set of data is often determined arbitrarily, but a rule of thumb indicates that there should be between 10 and 15 class intervals for a set of data. The cell midpoint is at the center of the class interval and represents the average value of the bar.

Control Charts.   A *control chart* is a visual comparison that shows by a graph how well a process is performing versus control limits. Data for the control chart come from the production process. The control limits are calculated from the production process data. It is important to understand that specifications do not enter into making up the initial control charts since control charts are not intended to evaluate how well tolerances are being met. The objective of a control chart is to reduce the variation found in the process.

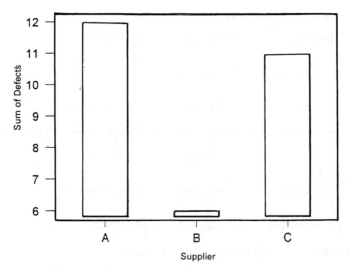

FIGURE 26.17   Stratification chart.

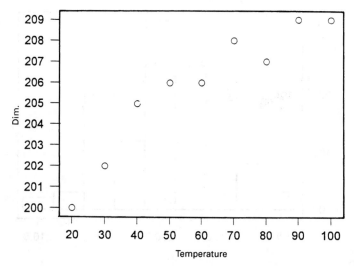

FIGURE 26.18 Scatter diagram showing the relationship between the TEMP and DIM.

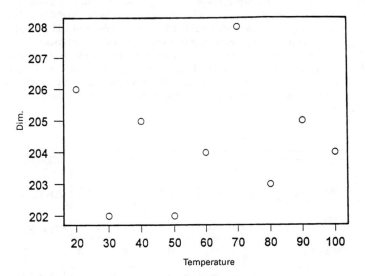

FIGURE 26.19 Scatter diagram showing no relationship between the TEMP and DIM.

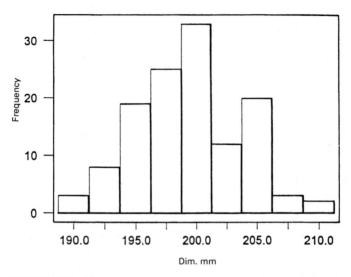

FIGURE 26.20   Histogram.

Data to determine how the process is performing consist typically of taking five measurements, called a *rational subgroup,* at regular intervals during production. For variable data, the average and range are calculated for each subgroup and plotted on the control chart, as shown in Fig. 26.21. Control limits are calculated using the laws of probability. In the United States, the limits are located three standard deviations above and below the subgroup averages, so that there are only 3 chances out of 1000 that a subgroup will fall outside of the control limits if only random variation is present. Random variation is inherent in the basic process and cannot be changed without altering the basic process.

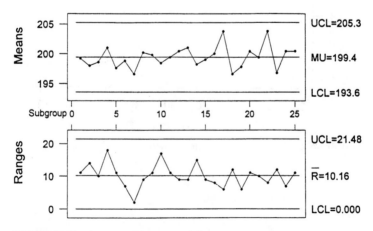

FIGURE 26.21   Average and range control charts.

With this construction of control charts, process variation can be separated into two types, as follows:

1. For *random variation,* subgroups fall within the upper and lower control limits. A process that has only random variation is in a state of statistical control. To reduce variation further requires altering the basic process or design of the product, which requires action by responsible management. The production operators cannot accomplish this improvement. Note that the process charted has only random variation.

2. For *assignable variation,* subgroups fall beyond the upper and lower control chart limits. In this case, the variation is not entirely random but due to *special causes.* Frequently, this variation may be eliminated by the operators of the process producing the part. For example, variations may be eliminated by adjusting the process.

A control chart enables a person to recognize that a special cause is present. However, the chart does not indicate the specific cause. The cause of the variation must be pursued separately, and until it is found, it will continue to cause variation in the products.

To solve the problems of special causes, the responsibility for maintaining control charts has been turned over to production operators. The operators are assigned the charting responsibility for critical variables. Often charts are prepared using direct measurements from the process and computer software that produces the chart. If assignable variation is indicated, the operators are also responsible for seeking the special causes and correcting them promptly. In this way, personnel who are responsible for quality can control quality. Quick solutions are obtained, resulting in reduced overall variation and more consistent quality. Additional reduction in variation requires reducing randomness in the process. The amount of random variation is the amount between the control limits as shown on the control chart. It is also clear that the variability can be reduced only by management's altering the process or the design of the product.

Control charts have also found applications for improving business processes. These improvements become possible when a sizable random variation is identified. This is a signal that the basic system needs changing to achieve more consistent quality.

REFERENCES

1. Phillip J. Ross: *Taguchi Techniques for Quality Engineering,* McGraw-Hill, New York, 1988.
2. Phillip J. Ross: *Taguchi Techniques for Quality Engineering,* McGraw-Hill, New York, 1988.
3. K. Ishikawa: *What Is Total Quality Control?* Prentice-Hall, Englewood Cliffs, N.J., 1985.

BIBLIOGRAPHY

Automotive Industry Action Group (AIAG): *Potential Failure Mode and Effect Analysis,* AIAG, Southfield, Mich., 1993.

American Supplier Institute: *Quality Function Deployment QFD,* ASI Press, Allen Park, Mich., 1988.

———: *Total Quality Management,* ASI Press, Allen Park, Mich., 1989.

Boothroyd, G., and P. Dewhurst: *Product Design for Assembly Handbook,* Boothroyd Dewhurst, Inc., New York, 1987.

Burr, John T.: *SPC Tools for Operators,* ASQC Quality Press, Milwaukee, Wis., 1989.

Campanella, Jack (ed.): *Principles of Quality Cost*, 2d ed., ASQC Quality Press, Milwaukee, Wis., 1990.

Deming, W. E.: *Out of the Crisis*, The M.I.T. Press, Cambridge, Mass., 1986.

Gitlow, Howard, Shelley Gitlow, Alan Oppenheim, and Rosa Oppenheim: *Tools and Methods for the Improvement of Quality*, Irwin, Homewood, Ill., 1989.

Grant, Eugene L., and Richard S. Leavenworth: *Statistical Quality Control*, 6th ed., McGraw-Hill, New York, 1988.

Juran, J. M. (editor in chief): *Quality Control Handbook*, 4th ed., McGraw-Hill, New York, 1988.

Juran, J. M., and Frank M. Gryna: *Quality Planning and Analysis*, 3rd ed., McGraw-Hill, New York, 1993.

Miles, L. D.: *Techniques of VA and VE*, 2d ed., The Miles Value Foundation, Washington, D.C., 1972.

Moran, John W., Richard P. Talbot, and Russell M. Benson: *Guide to Graphical Problem Solving Processes*, ASQC Quality Press, Cold Springs, N.Y., 1990.

Ott, Ellis R., and Edward G. Schilling: *Process Quality Control*, McGraw-Hill, New York, 1990.

Peach, Robert W.: *The ISO 9000 Series Handbook*, 2d ed., CEEM Information Services, 1994.

Salvendy, Gavriel (ed.): *The Handbook of Industrial Engineering*, 2d ed., Wiley, New York, 1993.

Winchell, William: *Continuous Quality Improvement: A Manufacturing Professional's Guide*, SME, Detroit, Mich., 1991.

CHAPTER 27
COST ANALYSIS AND CONTROL

Editors

Nancy Weatherholt, Ph.D., CPA
Associate Professor
Henry W. Bloch School of Business and Public Administration
University of Missouri-Kansas City, Kansas City, Missouri

David W. Cornell, Ph.D., CPA, CMA
Associate Professor
Henry W. Bloch School of Business and Public Administration
University of Missouri-Kansas City, Kansas City, Missouri

The purpose of this chapter is to present basic cost accounting information used by many organizations today. Accountants within an organization must provide timely and relevant information for internal decision making. Cost accounting systems have remained virtually unchanged throughout this century. The accounting information systems were developed primarily to serve the purpose of inventory valuation for external reporting requirements and have been based on labor-intensive production processes. However, major changes in technology and production practices have made new ways of collecting, combining, producing, and evaluating accounting information for decision-making purposes necessary.

This chapter presents a summary of some of the accounting concepts involved in the production and inventory control function. The topics are presented in an abbreviated manner, as a complete discussion is prohibited because of space limitations. The chapter begins with basic cost information and how it is used in the accounting process. This discussion is followed by an overview of how these cost concepts are used in accounting for planning and control. The chapter concludes by examining new cost concepts being employed by accountants as they strive to keep accounting information useful.

COST BASICS

This section presents basic cost information. It focuses on what they are, their classification in the accounting process, estimating techniques currently in use, and how accountants allocate costs to units produced.

Definitions

The glossary at the end of the chapter presents definitions that will be used throughout. A *cost* is a sacrifice made to acquire or create something. Costs are classified as either *assets* or *expenses* depending on whether they have a probable future economic benefit to the organization. An *asset* is a cost with a probable future economic benefit, such as the purchase cost of an automobile. An *expense,* on the other hand, has no future economic benefit, such as charges for utilities.

The classification of costs within a manufacturing environment is more complex, however. All costs related to the process of manufacturing a product are considered assets of the company until the product is sold. This is done to accurately determine the cost of a good manufactured and the resultant net benefit to the company from the manufacture and sale of the product. Therefore, for example, utility charges paid for by a manufacturing plant are assets of the company until the product is sold.

The concept is best understood by thinking of costs "attaching" to the good as it is produced. A portion of the utilities bill paid for by the manufacturing plant is systematically attached to each of the goods produced. This is accomplished by first determining a *cost driver* for the cost, then using that cost driver to determine an *application rate*. The cost driver is the event or activity that causes the cost to be incurred. Direct labor-hours have typically been used as a cost driver because of the correlation between direct labor-hours worked and costs incurred. The application rate is determined at the beginning of the year by estimating the total cost and dividing by the estimated total units of the cost driver, as shown below.

$$\text{Application rate} = \frac{\text{estimated total cost}}{\text{estimated number of units of cost driver}}$$

For instance, if it is anticipated that $10,000 of utilities for the plant will be incurred at the plant and that 100,000 direct labor-hours will be utilized, the application rate is 10 cents per direct labor-hour ($10,000/100,000 direct labor-hours). If 5 direct labor-hours are spent on a unit of product, 50 cents of utility cost would be attached to the product.

Additional costs such as direct materials costs and direct labor costs are incurred and attach to the cost of the goods as the goods move through production. The good is available for sale when it is finished and all of its costs are accumulated and attached to it. All of the costs of production are considered assets at this point since they were incurred to produce something with future economic benefit to the company. The future economic benefit is, of course, the company's ability to generate cash by selling the product in the future.

When that product is sold, the costs attached to the product are transferred to an expense account because the product no longer has a future benefit to the company since it no longer belongs to the company. Instead of having the product and its associated cost as an asset, the company now has cash. The difference between the sales price and the total accumulated cost of the product is the *gross profit*. This relationship is shown below:

$$\text{Gross profit} = \text{sales price} - \text{accumulated manufacturing costs}$$

The gross profit is therefore the net benefit to the company as a result of the manufacture and sale of the product.

Costs are attached to the goods produced by the company through the use of a *cost accounting system*. The system usually consists of two stages:

- In the first stage costs are accumulated in a deliberate manner, often by department.
- In stage 2, the accumulated costs are either traced directly or allocated to specified cost objects, which are usually units of the product passing through the department.

Categories of Costs

Table 27.1 reflects the various relationships among many of the terms defined in the glossary. Many of the names relate to the same cost, yet are necessary to provide information for analyzing the cost in different ways for management's control. For instance, costs are separated into *variable costs,* that is, those that change in total in direct proportion to changes in a related cost driver, versus *fixed costs,* that is, those that do not change in total when a related cost driver changes. These classifications can be useful for management in determining how costs will change with a change in the quantity of the product produced. This calculation can be helpful when contemplating strategic decisions such as a change in how a product is marketed.

Cost Estimation

Cost estimation techniques are used to separate costs into their fixed and variable components. Companies use several methods to estimate variable and fixed costs, but *account classification* is the most common procedure. Costs are assigned to certain accounts coded as fixed or variable for analysis. The primary benefit of account classification is its ease of use. A limitation is its heavy reliance on the classification of the cost as variable or fixed, based on one or just a few observations at a single-activity level.

Regression analysis is also used for cost estimation. Activities that *drive* costs, or cause costs to be incurred, are identified and data are collected on each. A cost function is estimated based on these data. This analysis procedure assumes cost behavior can be approximated by a linear function. While this method provides insight into past cost behavior, it does not specify optimal levels, nor does it necessarily include all relevant variables.

Another method of cost estimation is the *conference method,* whereby individuals involved in the production process are asked to estimate costs. The problem with this method is that experts' judgments vary. Engineering studies are useful, but they are an expensive undertaking. They are most beneficial when the underlying process has a distinct relationship between outputs and inputs. Direct physical observation of the pro-

TABLE 27.1   Relationship of Costs

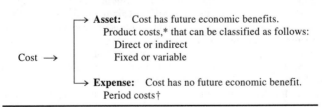

*Examples of product costs include manufacturing labor, materials used in the production of the good, and factory overhead (e.g., utilities).

†Examples of period costs include general administration and marketing.

duction process can lead to standards developed in physical terms, such as number of units, which can be converted to dollars by multiplying the appropriate unit prices.

Some limitations are inherent to all cost estimation techniques. The distinction between fixed and variable costs depends on the time period relevant to the analysis. In the short run, most costs are fixed—that is, commitments have been made that cannot easily be changed. In the long run, however, virtually all costs can be considered variable. Additionally, certain costs do not fit neatly into either category. For example, direct labor costs might vary directly with units produced until a certain production level is attained, at which time costs might increase dramatically as an entire shift has to be added to accommodate the additional production.

TWO TYPES OF PRODUCT COSTING SYSTEMS

There are two methods of accumulating costs for a product, or attaching costs to the product: *job order* and *process costing*. The difference between the two rests in the ease of identifying the specific costs associated with each individual good being produced:

- A job order costing system is used when a large, specific item or a small batch of product passes through the production process as a distinctly identifiable *job lot.*
- Process costing is used with production lines where the goods are generally not individually identifiable.

Job Order Costing

In a job order costing environment, the various costs of production are easily tracked to the individual good. Materials can be tracked through the use of requisition order forms, which specify the quantity and cost of the materials requested and the job for which they will be used. Labor time spent and hourly rate for the job are accumulated either electronically or by time tickets. Those costs that cannot be traced directly to a cost object are jointly referred to as *overhead.* Overhead is usually applied to the cost object on the basis of one or more cost drivers, similar to the process described. Table 27.2 shows an example of the application of overhead to a job.

Process Costing

The other common type of costing system is a *process costing system,* which is used when goods are produced in a continuous manner through a sequence of processes, such as in the chemicals, oil, and lumber industries. This method arrives at broad, average unit costs, not distinguishing among individual units of product. It is simpler and less expensive than job order costing systems.

In process costing, a *cost of production report* is usually prepared for each department for a time period. A summary of the flow of units through each department is prepared first. To do this, equivalent whole units are computed.

The formula for determining the number of equivalent whole units is as follows:

Equivalent whole units = (number of units) × (percent complete)

For example, eight 1-gallon cans of paint each 25 percent full would equate to two equivalent whole units. These eight cans contain a total of 2 gallons of paint evenly distributed among the cans. If the paint had instead been poured into one can at a time, it

TABLE 27.2 Example of Job Order Costing

Direct product costs*	
Direct labor:	
100 hours at $20 per hour	$2,000
Direct materials	1,500
Factory overhead costs†	200
Total cost of the product	$3,700

Direct costs are those costs of manufacturing that can be directly traced to the item being produced.

†*Factory overhead* is applied to the units produced based on the anticipated cost of the various items comprising factory overhead and the anticipated number of units of the cost driver to be used during the year. *This example assumes direct labor-hours is the cost driver.*

Indirect labor (supervisors)	$40,000
Indirect materials	20,000
Utilities	12,000
Depreciation	8,000
Total anticipated factory overhead	80,000
Number of estimated direct labor-hours	÷ 40,000
Factory overhead rate	$2/DLH
Number of direct labor-hours on the current product	× 100
Factory overhead applied to the good	$200

would have completely filled two 1-gallon cans. Table 27.3 illustrates how process costing works.

INVENTORY SPOILAGE

While "abnormal" spoilage is expensed in the current period under both types of systems, normal spoilage is treated differently depending on the system used:

- In a process costing system, an equal cost of normal spoilage per unit is allocated to all units passing inspection.
- In a job order system, normal spoilage that occurs during a particular job is added to that job. Normal spoilage that occurs as part of general production is added to the cost of all jobs by including it in overhead costs.

CLASSES OF INVENTORIES

Regardless of the method of costing chosen, three different inventory accounts are used:

- The value of the *raw materials inventory account* represents the cost of goods purchased from other manufacturers that will eventually be used in the production system. These costs have not yet been attached to a product being produced. An example of this are the tires purchased by a company to produce automobiles. The cost of the tires is classified as raw materials inventory until the tires are installed on the automobile frame.

TABLE 27.3   Example of Process Costing

Determination of equivalent units

	Physical units	Percentage*	Equivalent units completed
Beginning inventory	10,000	75	7,500
Units started	100,000	100	100,000
Units in process	110,000		107,500
Ending inventory	(5,000)	40	(2,000)
Units completed	105,000		105,500

Determination of the total costs	
Materials	$900,000
Labor	1,100,000
Overhead costs	110,000
Total manufacturing costs	$2,110,000

Determination of the average cost per unit produced	
Total manufacturing costs	$2,110,000
Equivalent units of production	÷ 105,500
Average cost per unit of production	20

*The percentage of the beginning inventory and the percentage of the number of units started during the year is the percentage completed during the year. The ending inventory percentage is the amount to be completed on those units.

Not all of the units started during the year were completed even though they are indicated as 100 percent complete. Therefore, the ending inventory equivalent units is reduced by the percentage not completed.

Another way of looking at this is, 75 percent of the 10,000 units in the beginning inventory were completed (7500), 100 percent of 95,000 units started were finished (95,000), and 60 percent of 5000 units started but not finished (3000), which yields the same total of 105,500 equivalent units.

- The *work-in-process inventory account* reflects the costs attached to the units put into process but not yet completed. Continuing the automobile example, the cost of the tires is transferred to work-in-process inventory when the tires are attached to the frame of the automobile.
- The *finished-goods inventory account* is the amount of costs attached to those goods completed but not yet sold. This occurs when the automobile is complete and is driven out of the assembly plant.

Finally, when the automobile is sold, the costs attached to the automobile are expensed and thereby netted against the sales price to determine the net benefit to the company of manufacturing and selling the automobile.

PLANNING AND CONTROLLING OPERATIONS IN THE SHORT TERM

An important role of management is to adequately plan and control a company's operations over time. This planning must be done both for the short term and the long term.

The use of budgets, standard costs, and cost-volume-profit analysis are commonly used techniques for the short-term planning and controlling of a company. Each of these methods is discussed below.

Budgets

Budgets enable companies to plan their operations and therefore anticipate and alleviate, mitigate, or prevent many problems prior to their occurrence. They also enable companies to identify deviations from the plan early and thus take corrective action before the problem gets out of control. The budgeting process begins with a planning phase in which the projected performance of the organization and each of its subunits is determined. This provides each subunit with a goal toward which to strive during the year. Actual performance is then measured against the budget as the year progresses, and any variances are investigated. Corrective actions to bring the unit back into budget compliance may be taken as a result of the investigation, or the budget may be adjusted if it is determined that the variance was caused by a factor outside of the control of the unit. Regardless of the action taken, management of the company, through the use of budgets, was made aware of the situation earlier than otherwise possible.

Feedback is an important component of an effective budgeting system. Results of one period should be used to help determine projections for the following period. Additionally, budgets should be attainable and flexible in order to maximize the effectiveness of their use.

The *master budget* is the budget for the entire company. It represents the summation of the budgets of all the individual units comprising the company. The *sales budget,* which is prepared first with the assistance of the marketing staff, represents the starting point of the budgeting process. It is the cornerstone upon which all budgets will be based.

Using the sales budget, the *production budget* is constructed from which the anticipated beginning and ending inventory balances can be determined. The production budget determines the number of physical units the company will produce. This number is then used to determine the budgets for the inputs to production, including direct materials, direct labor, and various overhead amounts. A *budgeted income statement,* as well as budgets for marketing and administrative expenses, is developed from this information.

A *flexible budget* recognizes that there may be various levels of production. A normal volume level is determined, and fixed costs are considered constant thereafter at that level. It is assumed that variable costs will change in direct proportion to the fluctuations in volume. The budget is adjusted to the actual level of performance achieved during the period. Then the adjusted budget amounts are compared with actual costs as the basis for determining variances from budgets.

Standard Costing

Flexible budgets provide a means whereby standard costs can be compared with actual costs and the variances examined for causes and corrective action where necessary. Standard cost accounting has been used for decades by many companies to isolate deviations from the anticipated costs of the goods produced. However, standard cost accounting has diminished in importance because of advances made in technology and the manufacturing processes during the past decade. A brief discussion of standard costing follows.

A *standard* is a prespecified measure of both the quantity and the cost of a particular input given an expected level of output. For instance, given an anticipated 10,000 units of production, the standard for direct labor is 2 hours per unit at a cost of $10 per hour. Standards are established during the budgeting process for each of the inputs—materials, labor, and overhead—to a production system. The standards are the goals the company would like to achieve for each of the inputs. The difference between the goal and the actual input is used to judge the performance of the production team.

There are two basic variances, price and quantity (sometimes referred to as *efficiency*), which can be calculated for each of the three inputs. The formulas for the variances are shown in Table 27.4, and they are used later to examine a hypothetical situation. The information in Table 27.5 indicates that the company is $180,000 over budget for the level of activity at which it is operating. Variance analysis provides management with information from which it can proceed in its investigation of the reason the company is over budget.

The results indicate several areas of potential concern for management. For instance, examining the direct materials variance analysis, which is labeled (A) in the table, it is evident that the company is using more material in production than anticipated. This is reflected in the unfavorable variance of $132,000. This variance is partly offset because the company was able to acquire the material for less than the budgeted amount, as reflected in the $66,000 favorable price variance. Labor (B) and variable overhead (C) variances are similarly favorable from a price standpoint and unfavorable from an efficiency standpoint.

Management must use the results of the variance analysis judiciously. As an example, in the table it appears that the purchasing department should be rewarded for buying materials at less than the budgeted price and thereby outperforming the budget, while the manufacturing division should be penalized for not keeping within budget.

TABLE 27.4   Standard Costing Variance Analysis Formulas

Direct materials variance analysis:
  Materials purchase price variance (MPPV) = AQPx(SPM − APM)
  Materials quantity variance (MQV) = SPMx(SQP − AQU)
    Total direct materials variance = MPPV + MQV

Direct labor variance analysis:
  Wage rate variance (WRV) = AHLx(SWR − AWR)
  Labor efficiency variance (LEV) = SWRx(SHL − AHL)
    Total direct labor variance = WRV + LEV

Analysis of variable overhead variances:
  Spending variance (SV) = FBOH − AOH
  Efficiency variance (EV) = SOHRx(SHL − AHL)
    Total overhead variance = SV + EV

where AHW = actual hours of labor
     AOH = actual overhead
     APM = actual price of materials
     AQP = actual quantity purchased
     AQU = actual quantity used
     AWR = actual wage rate
   FBOH = flexible budget overhead (budget adjusted to standard hours)
     SHL = standard hours of labor for level of production
   SOHR = standard overhead rate
     SPM = standard price of materials
     SQP = standard quantity for the level of production
     SWR = standard wage rate

TABLE 27.5 Example of Standard Costing Variance Analysis

	Standard	Actual
Assumptions:		
Raw materials used per unit	5 pounds	6 pounds
Cost per pound of material	×$12	×$11
Units of production	×11,000	×11,000
Total raw materials costs	$660,000	$726,000
Labor-hours per unit	4	5
Labor rate per hour	×$20	×$18
Units of production	×11,000	×11,000
Total labor costs	$880,000	$990,000
Overhead rate per labor-hour	$2	
Labor-hours per unit	×4	
Units of production	×11,000	
Total overhead	$88,000	$92,000
Total costs	$1,628,000	$1,808,000

A. Direct materials variance analysis:

Materials purchase price variance $= [(11,000)(6)]($12 - $11)$ $66,000

Materials quantity variance $= ($12)$

    $[(5 \times 11,000) - (6 \times 11,000)]$ $-132,000$

       Total direct materials variance $-66,000$

B. Direct labor variance analysis:

Wage rate variance $= (11,000 \times 5)($20 - $18)$ $110,000

Labor efficiency variance (LEV) $= ($20)$

    $[(4 \times 11,000) - (5 \times 11,000)]$ $-220,000$

       Total direct labor variance $-110,000$

C. Two-way analysis of variable overhead variances:

Spending variance $= (11,000)(5)($2) - $92,000$ $18,000

Efficiency variance (EV) $= ($2)$

    $[(11,000)(4) - (11,000)(5)]$ $-22,000$

       Total overhead variance $-4,000$

         Total variance $-$180,000

However, further investigation may reveal that the purchasing department is able to beat the budgeted purchase price by simply buying goods of an inferior quality. This fact can have two results for the company. First, the purchasing department is under budget, which is good from a company-wide perspective. Second, the manufacturing department may have to reject a higher than normal amount of the raw materials or spend more time than normal trying to work with the inferior materials. This makes the manufacturing division's results look bad in comparison to the budget and may cause the company to be less profitable. Therefore, the purchasing department, which initially looked good based upon the variance analysis, may actually be causing the company to be less profitable. Variance analysis is therefore only a starting point for the investigation of budgeted differences and must be followed up with further investigations. The preceding analysis considered only variable overhead and ignored the analysis of fixed overhead. Fixed overhead can also be analyzed, which is generally done by computing a spending and production volume variance. The fixed overhead spending variance is caused by costs exceeding or being less than the standards allowed. The production volume variance occurs from producing at a level different than that used to establish standards. In this case fixed costs are effectively spread over more or fewer units.

Some companies have discontinued computing efficiencies, believing that the data are often too late to effect change when needed. Additionally, the concept of efficiencies has been attacked by some as contributing to misguided decisions by management.[1] Specifically they can lead people to pursuing activity and production as ends in themselves rather than as means to an end. Also, it is believed that standards keep people from relentlessly pursuing means of reducing costs. Though some companies have moved away from an emphasis on standard costs, they are still useful to aid in determining budgets and assessing performance in many instances.

Cost-Volume-Profit Analysis (Breakeven Analysis)

Cost-volume-profit analysis (often referred to as *breakeven analysis*) is also used for short-term planning. It provides management with a rough but sensitive analysis tool for assessing the effect of what changes in unit cost of sales will have on operating income in the short run. Because many costs are essentially fixed for the short run, the primary uncertainty is the number of units that will be sold.

The simplest case addresses the question of how many units must be sold during the period that total revenues are equal to total costs and the company therefore "breaks even." This type of analysis requires that costs be classified as either fixed or variable. Fixed costs do not vary as volume of output varies during a given period. They typically include factory support and maintenance costs, depreciation, property taxes, research and development costs, and advertising expenditures. Some fixed costs are committed costs while others are determined periodically during the budgeting process. Variable costs vary directly with fluctuations in volume levels during the period. They include direct materials, direct labor, and certain overhead and marketing costs.

Breakeven concepts can be easily understood using graphic analysis, as shown in Fig. 27.1. Since fixed costs do not vary in total with production, they are shown as a horizontal line throughout the range of sales. Variable costs are constant on a *per-unit basis,* and therefore change *in total* as the sales level increases. Total variable costs therefore start at zero when sales are zero and go up proportionately with an increase in sales. Total cost is simply the summation of fixed and variable costs and appears as a line parallel to the variable-cost line but starts at the intersection of the fixed-cost line and the *y* axis.

Sales revenue varies proportionately with units of sales, starting at zero and increasing with units sold. The sales revenue line and the variable-cost line look similar. However, the sales line is steeper, indicating a higher amount per unit because the sales price per unit is greater than the variable cost per unit. The breakeven point occurs at the intersection of the sales line and the total cost line. Any level of sales to the left of the breakeven point results in a loss, and any level of sales to the right yields a profit. The amount of profit or loss is the difference between the sales and total cost lines.

Management may also be interested in the impact of changing the relative cost structure of its manufacturing process. For instance, variable direct labor costs may be reduced by increasing the investment in equipment, which results in a fixed depreciation charge. Figure 27.2 gives a graphic depiction of how these changes might affect the

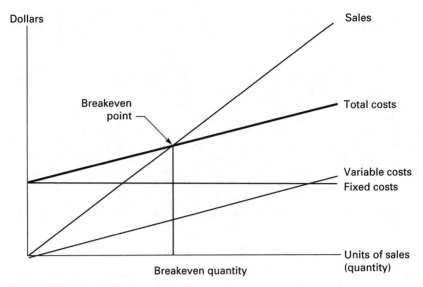

FIGURE 27.1   Graph of breakeven analysis.

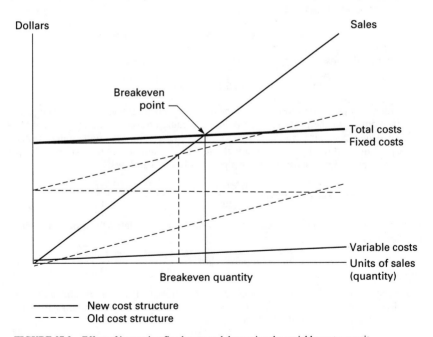

FIGURE 27.2   Effect of increasing fixed costs and decreasing the variable cost per unit.

breakeven point. The original cost structure is shown in dotted lines, and the new structure is in solid lines. The increase in fixed costs causes the total cost line to shift upward, while the decrease in variable costs causes the total cost line to be not as steep as it was previously.

As drawn, the change in the cost structure has the impact of shifting the breakeven point to the right, indicating that more units must be sold to break even. The difference between the sales and the total cost lines indicates a greater contribution margin per unit. This implies that losses will be greater to the left of the new breakeven point and net income will be greater to the right of that point. It must be remembered that these results reflect only one possible combination of changes in the cost structure and that the results cannot be generalized for all changes. The relative magnitude of the increase in fixed costs and decrease in variable cost per unit can change the results. For instance, it is possible to graph similar changes in such a manner that the breakeven point actually shifts to the left, indicating a lower breakeven point. Calculating actual amounts required gives a better understanding of how changes in the cost structure will affect profits. The derivation of the breakeven equation is relatively easy. Operating income is the difference between sales and the cost of the units sold:

$$\text{Operating income \$} = \text{sales \$} - \text{variable costs \$} - \text{fixed costs \$}$$

The costs of the units sold can be separated into fixed and variable, as discussed previously, yielding the following:

$$\text{Operating income \$} = \text{sales \$} - (\text{fixed costs \$} + \text{total variable costs \$})$$

By definition, the breakeven point occurs when operating income is zero or when sales revenue generated from the sale of units produced is equal to all costs of the units. In equation form, the breakeven point occurs when:

$$0 = \text{sales \$} - (\text{fixed costs \$} + \text{total variable costs \$})$$

Rearranging the above equation yields:

$$\text{Fixed costs \$} = \text{sales \$} - \text{total variable costs \$}$$

The breakeven point therefore occurs when sales minus total variable costs is equal to the fixed costs. It is helpful to further reduce the equation by examining sales and variable costs on a per-unit basis. Total sales is equal to the number of units times the sales price per unit, and total variable cost is the number of units times the variable cost per unit. The equation can be rewritten on a per-unit basis as follows:

$$\text{Fixed costs} = (\text{units})\left(\frac{\text{sales price}}{\text{unit}} \right) - (\text{units})\left(\frac{\text{variable cost}}{\text{unit}} \right)$$

Rearranging this equation to factor the units sold out of the left-hand side of the equation results in:

$$\text{Fixed costs} = (\text{number of units sold})\left(\frac{\text{sales price}}{\text{unit}} - \frac{\text{variable cost}}{\text{unit}} \right)$$

The question generally being addressed in breakeven analysis is, "How many units must be sold to break even?" The answer to this question is derived by rearranging the equation such that it solves for the units sold, as shown below:

$$\text{Number of units sold} = \frac{\text{fixed costs}}{\text{sales price/unit} - \text{variable cost/unit}}$$

As can be seen from this equation, if fixed costs or variable costs decrease or if the selling price increases and other costs remain constant, the number of units required to be sold to break even is reduced.

The denominator of this equation, selling price minus variable costs per unit, is referred to as the *unit contribution margin*. The unit contribution margin is the increase in profit that results from selling an additional unit. It is the "contribution" of a single unit's sale to the profit of the company. The breakeven equation can be rewritten substituting the unit contribution margin in the denominator as follows:

$$\text{Number of units} = \frac{\text{total fixed costs}}{\text{unit contribution margin}}$$

The concept of unit contribution margin is useful in answering questions about the relationship between sales volume and profitability. For instance, what level of unit sales must be achieved to reach a target operating income level? This question can be answered easily by simply adding the desired profit level to the above formula. This results in the following equation:

$$\text{Number of units sold at breakeven point} = \frac{\text{fixed costs \$} + \text{target operating income \$}}{\text{unit contribution margin \$/unit}}$$

The levels of each of the variables can be modified to determine the effects of deviations from expected levels. Table 27.6 includes examples of the use of these equations. It also provides a numerical example of changing the cost structure of the firm by increasing fixed costs and decreasing variable costs, as discussed above.

Assumptions of Cost-Volume-Profit Analysis

Several assumptions underlie the use of cost-volume-profit analysis:

- One product is considered in isolation, and a given sales mix remains constant.
- Total revenues and total costs are estimable and linearly related during the relevant time period and over the relevant quantity range.
- The level of sales during a period is equal to the number of units produced during that period (there is no change in inventory levels during the period).
- The selling price is independent of the amount of the product that is sold.
- Over the relevant time period, total fixed costs are constant and total variable costs vary directly with volume over the relevant range of output.
- Volume is the only cost driver.

In spite of these assumptions, many of which are violated in practice, cost-volume-profit analysis is effective as a low-cost heuristic.

The breakeven technique has been criticized in recent years as leading to product proliferation.[2] Specifically, since certain fixed costs such as indirect labor and support staff increase as product diversity and complexity increases, they are not truly "fixed" unless the product mix remains constant. Hence, cost-volume-profit analysis should be used cautiously unless it can be determined that product proliferation will not likely result.

TABLE 27.6   Example of Breakeven Concepts

Assume the following facts:

Sales price per unit	$50
Variable costs per unit	$30
Total fixed costs	$100,000

The breakeven formula is as follows:

$$\text{Number of units} = \frac{\text{total fixed costs}}{\text{unit contribution margin}}$$

$$= \frac{\$100,000}{\$50 - \$30} = 5000 \text{ units}$$

To reach an operating income level of $250,000:

$$\text{Number of units} = \frac{\text{fixed costs} + \text{target operating income}}{\text{unit contribution margin}}$$

$$= \frac{\$100,000 + \$250,000}{\$50 - \$30} = 17,500 \text{ units}$$

The company's income statement would appear as follows under both assumptions:

	5000 units	17,500 units
Sales	$250,000	$875,000
Variable costs	150,000	525,000
Fixed costs	100,000	100,000
Operating income	$ 0	$250,000

If fixed costs were increased to $150,000 and the variable costs were reduced to $25 per unit, the breakeven point would be 6000 units, but the profits at 17,500 units would be greater.

$$\text{Number of units} = \frac{\$150,000}{\$50 - \$25} = 6000 \text{ units}$$

	6,000 units	17,500 units
Sales	$300,000	$875,000
Variable costs	150,000	437,500
Fixed costs	150,000	150,000
Operating income	$ 0	$287,500

OPERATIONS PLANNING AND CONTROLLING
FOR THE LONG TERM

Long-term planning, often referred to as *strategic planning,* often involves decisions about new investments. There are numerous capital-budgeting techniques available to management for making these decisions. Because of the long-term nature of the investment and the resultant cash flows, some of these methods use discounting techniques to account for the difference in the timing of the cash flows. This discounting reflects the time value of money, which must be understood prior to examining the capital-budgeting techniques.

Time Value of Money

Any long-term decision should consider the impact of interest rates on the various components considered in the decision. Interest rates are generally specified in financing contracts and are therefore explicit in the decision process. However, the "cost-of-capital" concept implies that there is an interest rate component in all business decisions regardless of whether financing is involved. The cost of capital for an organization is the cost of the funds used in its operations. This cost is determined by the capital structure of the organization, which consists of its particular mix of debt and equity. Any decision to use money should be weighed against other uses of the money, such as paying off debt or returning funds to investors in the form of dividends.

A dollar earned today is more valuable than a dollar earned a year from today. This difference in value is caused by the fact that the dollar earned today can be invested to earn interest and therefore "grow" during the year to an amount in excess of a dollar. There is a direct relationship between the amount a dollar increases in value and the interest rate and time horizon. An increase in either the interest rate or the time horizon will increase the value of the dollar at the end of the specified period.

Present and Future Value of a Lump Sum. The future value of an investment is equal to the amount invested plus the interest accrued on that investment over the time horizon. For instance, $10,000 invested at 6 percent for 1 year earns $600 of interest and yields a future value of $10,600. This can be written as:

$$\$10,000 + (\$10,000 \times 6\%) = \$10,000 \times (100\% + 6\%) = \$10,600$$

If the money is not withdrawn from the investment, $636 of interest will be earned during the second year and the investment will be worth $11,236. The interest earned in the second year is $36 greater than that of the first year because interest is earned on the unpaid interest of $600 from the first year ($600×6 percent = $36). The value at the end of the second year can be determined as follows:

$$\$10,600 + (\$10,600 \times 6\%) = \$10,600 \times (100\% + 6\%) = \$11,236$$

or

$$\$10,000 \times (100\% + 6\%) \times (100\% + 6\%) = \$11,236$$

The future value of an investment can therefore be calculated by multiplying the present value by 100 percent plus the interest rate, or 106 percent in this instance, for each period the investment is held, which was twice in this example. Generalizing this results in the following formula:

$$FV_{\text{single payment}} = PV \times (100\% + i)^n$$

where PV = present value or payment
    FV = future value
     n = investment horizon
     i = interest rate.

As in any formula, if one of the four variables in the equation is unknown, it can be calculated from the other three. The formula for the present value of a payment received in the future could be determined by dividing each side of above equation by $(1+i)^n$, which yields the following formula:

$$PV_{\text{single payment}} = \frac{1}{(100\% + i)^n} \times FV$$

Future Value of an Annuity.   Payments are often made over time instead of in a single lump sum. The stream of equal payments is called an *annuity,* and the formulas for determining the present and future values can be derived from the formulas for single-sum payments. Since an annuity is in essence several lump-sum payments, the future value of an annuity is simply the summation of the future values of each of the payments, as shown below:

$$FV_{\text{annuity}} = PMT_1(100\% + i)^{n-1} + \; + PMT_2(100\% + i)^{n-2} + \cdots + PMT_n(100\% + i)^0$$

where n = total number of payments
  PMT_n = payment made in a specific year

If the amounts of the payments are all equal, the formula can be rewritten as follows:

$$FV_{\text{annuity}} = PMT(100\% + i)^{n-1} + PMT(100\% + i)^{n-2} + \cdots + PMT(100\% + i)^0$$

Since the payments are all equal, they can be factored out of the equation to arrive at:

$$FV_{\text{annuity}} = PMT[(100\% + i)^{n-1} + (100\% + i)^{n-2} + \cdots + (100\% + i)^0]$$

Multiplying each side of the equation by $100\%+i$ yields the following:

$$(FV_{\text{annuity}})(100\% + i) = PMT[(100\% + i)^n + (100\% + i)^{n-1} + \cdots + (100\% + i)^1]$$

Subtracting the last equation from the previous equation results in the following:

$$FV_{\text{annuity}}\,i = PMT[(100\% + i)^n - 1]$$

Dividing the results by i results in the future value of an annuity equation, which is:

$$FV_{\text{annuity}} = PMT \times \frac{(100\% + i)^n - 1}{i}$$

Using this equation, the future value of $10,000 per year for 5 years with an 8 percent interest rate would yield $58,666:

$$FV_{\text{annuity}} = \$10,000\, \frac{(100\% + 8\%)^5 - 1}{8\%} = \$58,666$$

Present Value of an Annuity. The present value of a series of payments is the sum of the present values of the individual payments to be received each year. This can be shown as:

$$PV_{annuity} = \frac{PMT_1}{(1 + i)^1} + \frac{PMT_2}{(1 + i)^2} + \cdots + \frac{PMT_n}{(1 + i)^n}$$

where n = number of years in which payments are made
PMT = payment made in a given year

If the payments are equal and the interest rate i is held constant, the equation can be reduced to:

$$PV_{annuity} = \sum_{t=1}^{n} \frac{PMT}{(1 + i)^t}$$

where t = time period
PV = present value of a stream of payments (FV) to be received in equal amounts at year end, discounted at rate i

This formula is not convenient for computational purposes, however. If the payments and interest rate are unchanged over time, the computational formula can be derived in a logical, two-step process. First, the *future value* of the annuity of cash flows is determined, and second, that amount is then discounted back to its *present value*. The process therefore starts with the future value of an annuity formula as developed above:

$$FV_{annuity} = PMT \times \frac{(1 + i)^n - 1}{i}$$

where $FV_{annuity}$ = future value of the payments (In the above example, the future value of five annual payments of \$10,000 each discounted at 8 percent was \$58,666.)
PMT = equal yearly payment
i = interest rate, which is constant over time

The result from that equation is entered in the equation for the present value of a lump sum, which was shown as:

$$PV_{single\ payment} = \frac{1}{(100\% + i)^n} \times FV$$

where $PV_{single\ payment}$ = present value of a single payment received in the future
FV = single payment made in the future

This formula is for a single sum, however, while we are determining the present value of an annuity of payments. In order to convert this single-payment formula into an annuity formula, we simply use the future value of the annuity instead of the future value of the single payment. The formula would appear as follows:

$$PV_{annuity} = \frac{1}{(100\% + i)^n} \times FV_{annuity}$$

where $PV_{annuity}$ = present value of an annuity of payments
$FV_{annuity}$ = future value of an annuity of payments

Continuing the previous example, to find the present value of five $10,000 payments discounted at 8 percent involves two steps. First, we determine the future value of the payments, which was done above with the result of $58,666. Next, we discount this amount back to the present value, as shown below:

$$PV_{annuity} = \frac{1}{(100\% + 8\%)^5} \times \$58,666 = \$39,927$$

We therefore changed the present value of a *single-payment formula* into the present value of an *annuity formula* by substituting the future value of an annuity for the future value of a lump sum in the present value formula. Algebraically, this process can be shown by substituting the formula for the future value of an annuity into the present value of a single-payment formula, which yields the following:

$$PV_{annuity} = \left[\frac{1}{(100\% + i)^n} \right] \times \left[PMT \, \frac{(100\% + i)^n - 1}{i} \right]$$

which condenses to:

$$PV_{annuity} = PMT \left[\frac{(100\% + i)^n - 1}{i(100\% + i)^n} \right]$$

This can be simplified by multiplying the numerator and denominator by $1/(100$ percent $+ i)^n$, as shown below:

$$PV_{annuity} = PMT \left[\frac{(100\% + i)^n - 1}{i(100\% + i)^n} \right] \times \frac{\dfrac{1}{(100\% + i)^n}}{\dfrac{1}{(100 \text{ percent} + i)^n}}$$

$$= PMT \times \frac{1 - \dfrac{1}{(100\% + i)^n}}{i}$$

The last formula is easy to work with computationally. Carrying our previous example forward, the present value of five $10,000 payments discounted at 8 percent is $39,927, which would be calculated as follows:

$$PV_{annuity} = \$10,000 \times \frac{1 - \dfrac{1}{(100\% + 8\%)^5}}{8\%} = \$39,927$$

An example of how payments are allocated between interest and principal reduction is shown in Table 27.7. Most financial calculators and computer software spreadsheet programs have built-in functions for solving these time value of money problems.

Time value of money concepts are very important for many of the decisions made both in personal and corporate financial planning. An example of the former is, "How much money do I need to deposit in the bank today to pay for my child's education, which will begin 10 years from today and last for 4 years?" An example of the latter is, "Should the company invest in a new project that has a certain cost today but will return a given cash flow over the next 10 years?" This type of question is answered using capital-budgeting techniques.

TABLE 27.7 Time Value of Money Concepts: Annuities

The present value of an annuity formula is as follows:

$$PV_{annuity} = \frac{1 - \dfrac{1}{(1 + i)^n}}{i} \times payment$$

An example of how to calculate the present value of an annuity is shown below using the following assumptions:

PV =	present value:	????
n =	term of the investment:	5 years
i =	interest rate:	6 percent
Payment =	annual payment, if any,	$10,000

$$PV_{annuity} = \frac{1 - \dfrac{1}{(1 + 0.06)^5}}{0.06} \times 10,000 = \$42,123.64$$

The present value of five annual payments of $10,000 each discounted at 6 percent is therefore $42,123.64. This implies that if you placed $42,123.64 in a bank account earning 6 percent per year, you could withdraw five $10,000 payments from the bank, after which the checking account would have a zero balance. The following table summarizes the activity in the checking account:

Date	Payment	Interest earned	Change in balance	Balance
Deposit	42,123.64			42,123.64
First year	(10,000.00)	2,527.42*	(7,472.58)	34,651.06
Second year	(10,000.00)	2,079.06	(7,920.94)	26,730.12
Third year	(10,000.00)	1,603.81	(8,396.19)	18,333.93
Fourth year	(10,000.00)	1,100.04	(8,899.96)	9,433.97
Fifth year	(10,000.00)	566.03	(9,433.97)	0.00

*Interest earned is computed by multiplying the amount in the bank by the interest rate, or $42,123.64×6 percent = $2,527.42.

Capital-Budgeting Techniques

Capital budgeting is the process companies use to make investment decisions. These investments generally require current cash outlays for the investment, followed by cash inflows resulting from the investment. The decision process involves comparing the cash inflows to the cash outflows to determine if the project is "profitable" to the company. The problem with this type of analysis is that, as noted before, one should not compare cash spent today to cash to be received 10 years from today without recognizing the time value of money.

It is therefore inappropriate to simply compare the total cash paid out to cash received as a result of the investment. Two capital-budgeting techniques, *net present value* (NPV) and *internal rate of return* (IRR), use time value of money concepts to compare cash spent today to cash received in the future by incorporating the impact of interest on the cash flows. Two other techniques, *payback* and the *accounting rate of return,* do not consider the impact of time on the decision.

Net Present Value. The net present value technique of capital budgeting uses the company's cost of capital to discount the cash flows related to an investment. The formula for determining the net present value is the following:

$$\text{NPV} = \sum_{j=0}^{n} \text{present value of cash flow}_j$$

where j = period in which the payment is made, with 0 being the present time or the initial cash outlay at the start of the project
n = last period in which cash is either paid or received

Cash outflows are entered as negative numbers, and cash inflows are entered as positive numbers.

In essence, the net present value technique converts all present and future cash flows to current dollars by taking their present value at the company's cost of capital and then sums them to arrive at either a positive or a negative number. The fact that the cash flows are discounted at the company's cost of capital means that the projects undertaken must yield at least that rate of return. Any return above that rate results in a positive NPV and, therefore, a positive decision, while a return that is less than that rate results in a negative NPV and, therefore, a negative decision. Table 27.8 has an example of the NPV technique.

Internal Rate of Return. The internal rate of return for an investment is the interest rate required to equate the present value of its expected cash inflows with the required cash outflow(s). This rate, once determined, is compared with a *hurdle rate* (preferably the cost of capital), and the project is acceptable if the rate exceeds the prespecified hurdle rate. This method is considered to be inferior to the net present value method in situations in which the following conditions exist:

- Some projects are mutually exclusive or have different lives.
- There is more than one internal rate of return (which can result when there exists an interleaving of positive and negative cash flows during the project's life).
- The hurdle rate does not equal the firm's cost of capital.

In these instances, the net present value method provides a superior ranking of acceptable projects.

Payback Method. The net present value technique and the internal rate of return just discussed consider the time value of money on long-term capital investment decisions. The payback method does not use time value concepts but instead determines how quickly a company will recover its initial capital investment. For example, if the initial outlay is $8,000,000 and the projected cash inflows are $3,000,000 at the end of each of years 1 and 2 and $4,000,000 thereafter, then the payback period is 2.5 years. The decision rule used in this analysis is a predetermined acceptable recovery period. For instance, one might decide to accept any projects with a payback period of less than 3 years. Given this acceptance rule, the project in the example above would be accepted because it pays back the investment in less than 3 years.

TABLE 27.8 Example of Capital Budgeting Using the Net Present Value Technique

Assume the company is considering an investment with the following cash flows:

Original investment	$200,000
Cash inflow each year	$55,000
Life of the project	5 years
Cost of capital	11%

Net Present Value. The net present value would be determined as follows:

$$NPV = \sum_{j=0}^{5} \text{present value of cash flow}_j$$

$$NPV = -\$200,000 + \$49,550 + \$44,639 + \$40,216 + \$36,230 + \$32,640$$
$$= \$3,275$$

The NPV is positive, and the project would therefore be profitable to the company and should be undertaken. This implies that the project yields more than an 11 percent return, which is the minimum that the company requires on its investments.

Internal Rate of Return. The internal rate of return on the project would be determined as follows:

PV	−$200,000
Payment	$55,000
n	5
i	11.65 percent

The project should be undertaken since the internal rate of return is greater than the company's cost of capital (11.65 percent > 11 percent).

There are many detractors of this method because it ignores both the time value of money and any cash flows that occur after the period of initial recovery. However, it is being used in the current competitive environment by companies with short product lives. When product life cycles are extremely short, discounting techniques are less relevant and the primary concern becomes one of recovering the cash outlays quickly.

Accounting Rate of Return. The accounting rate of return method also ignores the time value of money. The return is computed as the average annual income generated by the project divided by the average investment in the project. Table 27.9 presents an example of the accounting rate of return and contrasts it with the internal rate of return. Note that the numerator of the accounting rate of return equation ($50,000 in the table) is income based, not cash flow based as in the internal rate of return method. The two methods may result in different decisions due to the fact that the two methods examine different variables. For instance, if the company has a decision rule to accept projects with a return greater than 6 percent, it would reject the project shown in the table if the accounting rate of return method were used. However, the company would accept the project if the internal rate of return method were used. That the two methods often yield conflicting results causes concern over the validity of the methods.

The cause for the discrepancy is that the accounting rate of return ignores the time value of money and uses an accounting-based income number instead of cash flows.

TABLE 27.9   Accounting Rate of Return

Assume that a project with an initial cost of $1,000,000 would generate a net positive cash flow of $250,000 for 5 years. The investment would be depreciated over the 5-year periods, resulting in $200,000 of depreciation each year, as shown below:

Cost of the equipment	$1,000,000
Useful life of the equipment	÷5
Depreciation per year	$200,000

Income from the investment is the difference between the net positive cash flows and the depreciation expense:

Net positive cash inflows	$250,000
Depreciation	200,000
Net income	$50,000

The accounting rate of return is calculated as follows:

$$\text{Accounting rate of return} = \frac{\text{average annual income}}{\text{average investment}}$$

$$= \frac{\$50,000}{\$1,000,000} = 5\%$$

The internal rate of return would be calculated as follows:

PV	−$1,000,000
Payment	$250,000
n	5
i	7.93%

Because of these weaknesses, many argue against using the accounting rate of return in capital-budgeting decisions. However, it is still used in practice because it is easy to use and it sometimes yields results compatible with one of the discounting methods. Additionally, the compensation of some managers is based on the *return on investment* (ROI); hence, they are comfortable with making decisions on that basis.

NEW COST CONCEPTS

The cost techniques discussed above have been in use for decades. While these techniques are still valuable to management, there are several relatively new concepts regarding costs and their role in the current international business environment. These techniques came about because the "old" techniques do not always provide management with the information required to adequately control operations and compete in the new global economy. The next section of the chapter reviews *target costing, life-cycle costing, super-variable costing,* and *activity-based cost management.*

Target Costing

Target costing, or *price down/cost down,* is a concept that was borrowed from Japanese companies during the 1980s. U.S. companies, operating in a post-World War II growing economy, had priced their products on the basis of cost plus a desired profit margin. Japanese companies, recognizing the competitive nature of the marketplace they faced, determined that the best way to gain market share was to calculate *first* the price that would garner that market share, then to determine the cost at which the product needed to be produced in order to yield a desired profit.

Target costing has been used primarily by companies in assembly-oriented industries. Over 90 percent of the actual cost of a product is usually determined during the design phase.[3] The target cost of the product, determined from profit targets, engineering estimates, or a combination of the two methods, should be a feasible though not easily achievable amount. It often includes not only projected production costs but also estimates of research, development, and distribution costs.

Cross-functional teams work together from the inception of the product design, iteratively working through the design process such that the product ultimately can be produced as inexpensively as possible. Various manufacturing issues are addressed during the design phase including the cost of an engineering-change order, the choice of a better product material, and whether a common component can be designed and used across different models. Accounting considerations during this phase include determining what variables should be monitored during the product's life so that resources are being used most effectively. When should new technology be added, and how should managerial control information be integrated with the financial control information needs of the company?[4]

After the product design process is complete, efforts begin to keep production costs as close to the target cost as possible. Management of the Japanese companies ensure that employees understand how their tasks affect the overall performance of the organization. They place more importance on direct performance measures such as the amount of scrap due to error, the required setup time, and the percentage of defective products requiring rework.[5]

Life-Cycle Costing

The product life cycle as discussed in the marketing literature is generally partitioned into four stages: start-up, growth, maturity, and harvest. *Life-cycle costs* are those costs incurred by the producer during the four stages of the product life cycle. Costs incurred by consumers are not included in the amount but are included in an amount referred to as the *whole-life cost.* It is estimated that as much as 85 percent of a product's total life-cycle cost is determined early in the life cycle, so a substantial amount of the total cost can be reduced by striving to minimize cost during the design and testing phases prior to production.

Certain guidelines have been suggested to effectively implement a cost system for managing costs from a life-cycle perspective[6]:

- The company should be organized along product, not functional, lines.
- Whole-life costs must be considered, not just product life-cycle costs.
- Any decisions should include only relevant costs.

- The company should invest heavily in premanufactured subassemblies and labor, and investments should be expended during the early phases of the life cycle to minimize overall whole-life costs.
- Target costing should be the norm, not standard costing, since the focus should be on reducing costs, not controlling costs.
- The compensation of factory personnel should be tied to the product's success over the entire life cycle to reinforce a whole-life cost perspective.
- Efforts should be directed to ensure that all employees support the system and are continuously educated in how to increase its effectiveness.

Activity-Based Cost (ABC) Management

What Is Activity-Based Costing?   Many companies that have adopted newer manufacturing techniques during the past two decades noticed that the existing cost accounting system did not complement the changes being made elsewhere in the organization. Coupled with the technology improvements, making advanced cost systems feasible, led to the widespread consideration of *activity-based costing* (ABC) *systems* during the 1980s.

In the past, most companies applied overhead to the product on the basis of direct labor-hours or dollars. When direct labor was a significant portion of the total product cost and when the other inputs were proportionate to direct labor, product costing in this manner produced few distortions. Over time, direct labor has decreased with improvements in technology, so other cost drivers now play a more significant role in the determination of total product cost.

Using traditional costing systems can lead to cross subsidization of products. In particular, large products and high-volume products often bear some of the cost that should have been absorbed by the small products and low-volume products. Low-volume products reflect higher costs under an ABC system because batch-level and product-sustaining level drivers are identified and used as well as unit-level drivers in the application of overhead.[7] Table 27.10 provides an example of this.

The top section of the table uses direct labor-hours to allocate the overhead costs, which is how overhead has conventionally been applied. As can be seen, product B absorbs most of the overhead cost simply because more direct labor-hours are expended in its production. Product A, on the other hand, has very little overhead applied to it because only two direct labor-hours are incurred for its production. This method is easy to implement but provides misleading results largely due to its simplicity. The reason the results are misleading is that while product A absorbed only 2 hours, or 12 percent, of the direct labor-hours, it absorbed 33 percent of the machine-hours, 20 percent of the number of setups, and 50 percent of the number of parts. Each of these percentages is higher than the percentage of direct labor-hours upon which the allocation of overhead costs was based. Product A therefore received less than its appropriate share of the overhead costs incurred.

The ABC system attempts to avoid this problem by using additional and more appropriate cost drivers to allocate overhead costs. The cost drivers are those activities that cause costs to be incurred. Using more cost drivers results in a more accurate allocation of costs to the goods being produced. The second panel of the previous table uses the ABC system to allocate overhead. The system is more complex, using three different cost drivers for allocating cost instead of simply using direct labor-hours as was done in the conventional method. The ABC system resulted in more overhead cost being applied to the low-volume product A than did the conventional method. The higher cost represents a truer picture of the costs incurred to produce both product A and product B.

TABLE 27.10 Example of Activity-Based Cost Management

Assumptions				

	Levels of activity by product			
	Product			
	A	B	Total	Cost
Unit-level costs:				
Direct labor-hours	2 hours	15 hours	17 hours	$340
Machine-hours	1 hour	2 hours	3 hours	600
Indirect materials costs				20
Total unit level				960
Batch-level costs:				
Number of setups	1	4	5	300
Product-sustaining costs:				
Number of parts	2	2	4	400
Total overhead costs				$1,660

Conventional System

Overhead is applied based on the number of direct labor-hours expended on each product under the conventional approach. In this example, the overhead application rate is determined by dividing the total overhead cost of $1660 by the 17 direct labor-hours to arrive at an overhead application rate of $97.65 per direct labor-hour. Product B absorbs the bulk of the overhead costs because more direct labor-hours are spent working on that product, as shown below.

	Product A application		Product B application	
	Method	Amount	Method	Amount
Overhead application:				
Cost driver: direct labor-hours	2		15	
Rate	×$97.65		×$97.65	
Allocation of costs		$195.29		$1,464.71
Total allocation of costs		$195.29		$1,464.71

Implementing ABC in an Organization.   Input from all functional areas is required to effectively implement an ABC system. Information needed includes the following:

- Consumers' demands
- What processes are used to make the products
- Which products place the greatest demands on scheduling
- Inspection and materials movement
- What the customers' buying and payment patterns are

The various functional areas can use the system's output for different purposes such as performance evaluation, pricing decisions, and design costing options.

TABLE 27.10   Examples of Activity-Based Cost Management (*Continued*)

Activity-Based Costing System

Activity-based costing allocates overhead costs in a manner that more closely reflects the reason those costs were incurred. The first step in the process is to determine the "cost drivers," the activities that result in costs being incurred. In this example, it is assumed that the cost drivers are direct labor-hours, number of setups, and number of parts for unit-level, batch-level, and product-sustaining costs, respectively. The second step is to determine the overhead application rate for each of the drivers, which is shown below:

	Unit level	Batch level	Product sustaining
Aggregated activity cost	$960.00	$300.00	$400.00
Cost driver	÷17	÷5	÷4
Application rate	$ 56.47	$ 60.00	$100.00

The third step in the process is to allocate the overhead costs on the basis of the cost drivers to the products.

	Product A application		Product B application	
	Method	Amount	Method	Amount
Unit-level costs:				
Cost driver: direct labor-hours	2		15	
Rate	×$ 56.47		×$ 56.47	
Allocation of unit-level costs		$112.94		$847.05
Batch-level costs:				
Cost driver: number of setups	1		4	
Rate	×$ 60.00		×$ 60.00	
Allocation of batch-level costs		60.00		240.00
Product-sustaining costs				
Cost driver: number of parts	2		2	
Rate	×$100.00		×$100.00	
Allocation of costs		200.00		200.00
Total allocation of costs		$372.94		$1,287.05

An *activity* is defined as a process or set of procedures that cause work to be performed to convert resources into outputs. The initial analysis involves identifying activities performed within the organization. These represent what an organization does, such that if changes are deemed necessary, they can be implemented at the activity level. Examples of activities include order processing, billing a customer, scheduling a delivery, and making a sale. Identifying specific activities assists in determining the factors that drive costs. Activities should be partitioned into those that are value added and those that are non-value added. For example, are any activities performed to support product diversity? Can some activities be performed more efficiently? How much is the company spending on quality costs? What are the total costs of obtaining raw materials and moving them?

After identifying many of the organization's activities, the cost and effectiveness of the activities should be determined. Each type of resource that is traced to an activity is included in the activity cost pool. Each activity cost pool is then traced to the cost objects (products, services, customers) by means of an activity cost driver. In general, as the number of identified drivers increases and is incorporated in the cost system, accuracy of product costs increases as well. When determining the activity drivers to be used, certain questions should be considered, such as the following:

- How easy is it to obtain the needed data? The benefit in added accuracy should exceed the cost of obtaining the data.
- How does actual usage of the activity correlate with the usage implied by the cost drivers?
- A question that is vital, though often overlooked, is, "Will the selection of a particular driver induce undesirable behavior on the part of employees?"[8]

Whereas traditional costing systems use one or more unit-level cost drivers to assign overhead costs to products, ABC systems identify and use unit, batch, and product-sustaining drivers for cost assignment. Certain activities and resources consumed related to setup, ordering, and materials movement are related to the number of batches produced, not necessarily to the number of units produced. Other activities and resources consumed are to sustain a product line and are not directly related to the number or units or batches produced. A well-designed ABC system identifies these activities and the best cost driver to assign the related costs to products so as to not penalize high-volume products and subsidize the lower-volume products produced. In general, activities and related resources consumed to sustain a facility should be assigned to a general and administrative expense, not allocated to the products.

Though many proponents of ABC systems exist, some detractors voice concerns as well. For some companies, the benefits of designing and installing an ABC system might not exceed the associated costs. Additionally, as an ABC system is implemented and certain activities are identified as non-value added and eliminated, it is not clear that the related spending by the organization decreases. In some cases, excess capacity is just created. Hence, for an ABC system to be maximally effective, management must consider carefully the implications of its use. Most advocates of ABC systems indicate that they are not just product costing systems but overall management systems.

GLOSSARY

asset   A cost incurred that has a probable future economic benefit to the organization.

cost   The sacrifice or effort incurred to obtain or create an object.

cost driver   An item whose change causes a change in the total cost of a related **cost object.** For example, as the number of setups increases, the total cost of the product being produced increases.

cost object   An item for which a distinct measurement of costs is desired. It may be a product, service, project, department, or any other item.

direct labor variance   The portion of the variance between standard costs and actual costs caused by direct labor. It is the total of the wage rate variance and the labor efficiency variance.

direct materials variance   The portion of the variance between standard costs and actual costs caused by direct materials. It is the total of the materials purchase price variance and the materials quantity variance.

direct product costs   Costs that can be identified specifically with the related product.

expense   A cost incurred that has no probable future economic benefit to the organization. These costs are charged against income in the period in which they were incurred.

fixed costs   Costs that do not change in total when a related cost driver changes.

indirect product costs or factory overhead costs   Costs that cannot be identified specifically with the related product and are therefore attached to the product based on a systematic and rational basis using the related cost driver.

labor efficiency variance   The portion of the variance between standard costs and actual costs caused by the number of hours of direct labor required to complete production being different from the standard number of hours.

materials purchase price variance   The portion of the variance between standard costs and actual costs caused by the purchase price of materials being different than the standard cost.

materials quantity variance   The portion of the variance between standard costs and actual costs caused by the quantity of materials used to produce a product being different than the standard amount.

period costs   Those costs that are not attached directly to the product and are instead expensed in the period in which they are incurred.

product costs   Those costs that are directly traceable to the product.

unit contribution margin   The net benefit, or "contribution," to the company from the sale of one additional unit of product. It is the difference between the sales price of the unit and the variable costs incurred in its production and sale.

variable costs   Costs that change in total in direct proportion to changes in a related cost driver.

variable overhead efficiency variance   The portion of the variance between standard variable overhead cost and actual variable overhead cost caused by the difference between the actual units of the cost driver and the standard number of units of the cost driver.

variable overhead variances   The portion of the variance between standard costs and actual costs caused by variable overhead. In a standard two-way analysis, it consists of the variable overhead spending variance and variable overhead efficiency variance.

variable overhead spending variance   The difference between the actual variable overhead and the amount of overhead budgeted based on the standard rate per unit of cost driver.

wage rate variance   The portion of the variance between standard costs and actual costs caused by the difference between the standard wage rate and that actually paid to workers.

REFERENCES

1. Eliyahu Goldratt and Jeff Cox: *The Goal,* North River Press, Great Barrington, Mass., 1986.

2. Robert S. Kaplan and Anthony A. Atkinson: *Advanced Management Accounting,* Prentice-Hall, Englewood Cliffs., N.J., 1989.

3. Michiharu Sakurai: "Target Costing and How to Use It," *Emerging Practices in Cost Management,* Warren, Gorham & Lamont, New York, 1992.

4. David M. Dilts and Severin V. Grabski: "Advanced Manufacturing Technologies: What They Can Offer Management Accountants," *Management Accounting,* March 1990, pp. 50–53.

5. Robert A. Howell and Michiharu Sakurai: "Management Accounting (and Other) Lessons from the Japanese," *Management Accounting,* December 1992, pp. 28–34.

6. Michael D. Shields and S. Mark Young: "Managing Product Life Cycle Costs: An Organizational Model," *Journal of Cost Management* (5:3), 1991, pp. 39–52.

7. Robin Cooper, "Activity-Based Costing for Improved Product Costing." In Barry J. Brinker (ed.): *Handbook of Cost Management,* Warren, Gorham & Lamont, New York, 1992, pp. B1–B50.

8. Ibid.

SECTION 6

INFORMATION SYSTEMS

CHAPTER 28

COMPUTER HARDWARE SELECTION AND ACQUISITION

Editors

Paul R. Rouse, CPIM
Consulting, IBM Corporation
Allegon, Michigan

Janet L. Cohen, CPIM
IBM Corporation
Milwaukee, Wisconsin

For manufacturers and businesses in general, the selection of computer hardware is no longer a stand-alone decision. As the price of computer hardware has declined and its performance has improved, hardware at times becomes secondary compared to the software one chooses to run the business.

The selection and acquisition of computer hardware for an enterprise's information system must be consistent with its business goals and objectives. It should support the company's strategic plan. In fact, an additional strategic plan should be developed for information systems to support the business's strategic plan. This plan should provide for the ongoing acquisition of computer technology to support the growth and changing needs of the business.

The APICS Systems and Technology certification course stresses the link between computer systems and business strategy, with many references to effectively linking the two. Even though new technology is critical to companies, those companies with superior strategy *and* execution are the ones that will surpass their competition.

SYSTEM REQUIREMENTS DOCUMENTS

The first step in the selection is a thorough understanding of the business's strategic plan, after which a *systems requirements document* is developed. The requirements document should specify the functional characteristics of the enterprise information system.

For example, if one intends to implement just-in-time techniques, the information system should have the support of just-in-time manufacturing and the ability to "backflush" materials and labor as one of its functions.

There are a number of different ways to develop a requirements document. Some companies establish an internal team with members from each functional area to specify these requirements. Others engage outside consultants to define the system requirements. The most effective method seems to be a combination of outside consultants working with internal functional representatives, to form a team to create and execute a *requirements survey*.

Requirements Survey

The requirements survey is normally conducted over a period of days by interviewing key representatives from different function areas of the business such as purchasing, materials management, warehousing, and engineering. The survey identifies problem areas, critical business processes, and information flow, while also identifying desired improvements or changes such as reengineering the processes. The requirements survey is limited to the process and information flow, and it does not specify computer hardware or software.

Information Systems Steering Committee

Regardless of how it is developed, the functional requirements document should be approved by the *information systems steering committee*. An information systems steering committee is typically composed of senior management from each of the functional areas of the enterprise. The chief executive officer should serve as the chair, to ensure that the needs of the business are met. The purpose of the steering committee is to oversee all information systems requirements and assure that the requirements identified are in line with the business's plans and objectives. The key reason is to ensure that the business gets the computing power needed to meet the demands of future operations.

Several noted manufacturing experts have written that it is imperative for top management to become involved in the technology plan. Their involvement ensures that a link is made between the computer system selected and the needs of the business as defined by the corporate strategy.[1]

As computer technology expands, manufacturers are having to rely more on computer experts to take the place of the industrial engineer. Computer experts have a monumental task of understanding and controlling their technology, so it is essential that upper management makes sure that the computer system enhances the business policy.[2] Companies can no longer afford to allow their data processing departments to be the sole caretakers of information systems and technology. Data processing experts should help analyze the technology and provide standards and guidance. However, the information gathered in the computer is of vital importance to the business and should be accessible to those who need that information to make day-to-day decisions.[3]

APPLICATION SOLUTIONS

Once the steering committee has approved the requirements document, the team should investigate possible application solutions to meet the requirements. At this time, software should be the *only* consideration—that is, how the needs of the business are satisfied by the software's function—and not the computer hardware on which it runs.

Software Packages

To meet the team's requirements, packaged software will be the most cost-effective choice over the long term, so it should be evaluated first. A company may request proposals from software vendors as a means of narrowing the choice of possible solutions.

Custom-Designed Software

Some companies may choose to develop custom-designed software to meet their information requirements if packaged software does not come close to meeting their needs. The most common solution is the selection of a package that can be customized to meet unique business requirements.

Hardware Selection

Once the software package is chosen or the decision to develop in-house software is made, the choice of hardware becomes more obvious. Packaged-software vendors should prepare a recommendation of the hardware configuration. During the development of software, the hardware sizing should be performed with the assistance of the chosen hardware vendor. Consideration should be given to the ways of shortening the software development time while ensuring quality.

Solution Benchmarks

Regardless of the software solution, companies should perform a *benchmark study* to determine if the solution is an improvement. Benchmark procedures typically identify the critical information functions and compare the current processes with simulated, new software.

Pilot Implementation

When all of the critical information processing functions have been simulated and approved, a pilot implementation should be made. Pilot implementations typically are carried out in a smaller and more easily controlled environment to determine if there will be implementation problems for the enterprise. Problems encountered during the pilot implementation should be resolved, and modifications should be made to avoid these problems during a broad-based implementation.

Cost-Benefit Analysis

When the software solution has been chosen and the benchmark comparisons have been performed satisfactorily, a detailed *cost-benefit* analysis is developed that includes both tangible and intangible benefits. Keep in mind that many managers see a *head count* as an easy way to identify cost savings. Though this makes sense, the typical company does not reduce its head count immediately upon implementing a new software package. Rather, personnel may find they have time freed up to analyze the computer data, time they may not have had in the past.

A cost-benefit analysis will be needed to request capital appropriations required for computer hardware, software, and services. The company executives and/or board of directors will decide whether to lease or purchase the hardware. If the decision is made to purchase the hardware, an accelerated depreciation schedule should be considered because of the rapid changes in computer technology. For example, computer hardware frequently becomes obsolete in less than 5 years. Typically a discounted cash flow analysis is performed to aid in the decision of whether to lease or buy equipment.

COMPUTER HARDWARE OVERVIEW

Computer hardware is classified into four categories depending on whether the central processing unit is a mainframe, midrange, personal, or networked system.

Mainframe Computers

Mainframe computers are large centralized computer systems. These systems are typically used for applications that are computer intensive or that require large databases. They have a great deal of flexibility in meeting information processing requirements, but this flexibility brings complexity that makes it more difficult to change the system as the business's requirements change. An extensive systems support staff is normally required for mainframe systems. Frequently, firms that have mainframe systems are plagued with large backlogs of maintenance projects.

Some companies with mainframe computer systems requirements are finding it beneficial to outsource, or subcontract, for computing services. *Outsourcing* means that another company maintains, manages, and operates the computer systems at a guaranteed service level. An example of a guaranteed service level would be the following:

- The system will be available from 6:30 a.m. until 12:00 a.m.
- During the time the system is available, it will be up 99 percent of the time.

Midrange Computers

Midrange is a term used to describe those computers that have processing speed and power between the mainframes and the personal computers. In the last few years, midrange systems have increased in power and capability to the point that there is little difference between the mainframe and midrange computers except in the total computing cost. The largest single factor in the total cost of computing is in the cost of the technical support personnel. Usually a midrange system requires fewer costly technical support personnel.

Personal Computers

These efficient small computers are used for such applications as word processing, spreadsheets, filing, and faxing. They can operate alone, or they can be combined to form a network.

Networked Computers

Networked computers are typically personal computers tied together in a network to share computer resources. With the advent of cheaper and more powerful small computers, many companies are considering "downsizing" or "right-sizing" their computer systems from mainframes to either midrange or networked computers. Networked computers are increasing in popularity; however, many companies are finding that the total costs of networked processors are, in fact, higher than the other alternatives. Network costs are often higher because of the highly skilled technical personnel required to maintain them. Although networked processors do provide considerable flexibility, they also require more maintenance because of the increased number of processors needed to update and back up the files.

NETWORKS

There are two types of networks: internal and external. *Internal networks*, otherwise known as *local area networks* or *LANs*, usually cover a distance of less than 1 mile. The most common LANs are *Ethernet, Novell*, and *Token Ring*. Cabling for these networks commonly uses twisted-pair wiring, which is relatively inexpensive. It is the same wiring that is used for analog telephones. *External networks* provide information processing over *wide area networks* (WANs) or long distances. External networks are more costly because they typically require modems or digital service units and leased telephone lines.

Technology is constantly changing, and it is expected that the capabilities of networks will improve greatly in the next 10 years. At the present time, a new type of WAN exists that allows for a wireless connection to a host computer. This type of connection facilitates the move toward mobile employees, who are not tied down to a specific office. Sales and order-entry personnel will be the biggest group to benefit from this. If sales personnel carry a laptop computer, they can be connected without wires to a computer at the company's headquarters. They can enter sales orders directly into the company's order-entry system. The manufacturing facility will have instant access to the most up-to-date order information. This will allow the manufacturer to meet strategic plans for delivering products quickly to the market. The direct, wireless connection can save from 10 to 48 hours from the time it required in the past when updates were typically written at the end of the day and posted the following day, or sent from a remote office to the central computer. The faster the manufacturing facility receives order information, the faster they will be able to respond to a customer's request.

HARDWARE ACQUISITION

Computer power has increased, especially in the "smaller" computers. Thus many people are claiming that computer networks will eventually replace the mainframe and the midrange computer systems. One of the theories behind these claims is that LANs are not as costly as midrange or mainframe systems. On the surface that appears to be true, but the total cost of computing should be investigated carefully before making a decision to use only networked personal computers.

The majority of a midrange or mainframe's costs are known up front and include hardware, software, application, and support. Many of the costs for LAN-based systems are hidden, and they do not become known until the LAN system is up and operational.

Even though the LAN system is properly secured and protected, the costs of supporting the updates for individual personal computers can become staggering. However, if a company has already invested extensively in personal computers for mainframe or midrange workstations, the prospect of making better use of these becomes clearer with a technology known as *client-server*.

CLIENT-SERVER

Client-server is a computer buzzword of the nineties, and like many buzzwords, it has more than one meaning. Basically, *client-server* means that some type of computer is used as a workstation (client), while another, more powerful computer contains information that must be shared by two or more of the clients and therefore "serves" the clients' computing and/or storage needs.

Each client workstation is usually a personal computer that interacts with the server (which could be another, more powerful PC, or a midrange or mainframe computer) by passing electronic messages. The client passes a message to request something from the server, and the server replies to that request. A basic tenet of client-server is the transparency of where the data comes from (location) and the independence of hardware or software platforms. As everything else in the computer world today, the definition and function of client-server are constantly changing.

FAX AND EDI

Other examples of external networks include *facsimile* (fax) and *electronic data interchange* (EDI). The use of fax has become increasingly widespread, to the point that many companies fax their purchase orders and other important documents rather than mail them. Some companies even fax documents to other departments within the same building. In some cases, fax is considered the poor person's EDI since the time it takes to deliver a document is reduced from days to minutes. However, with fax, one does not reap the full benefits of EDI, which will be explained in the following paragraphs.

With advances in technology in the early 1990s, fax has become even more commonplace. For example, the hardware and software technology exist to allow you to send a purchase order directly from your purchasing departments to your vendor's fax machine rather than to a printer, therefore eliminating the paper, handling, and mailing costs and at least a day or more of time. It stands to reason, then, that the reverse is also possible—to receive a faxed purchase order directly into your software. A more common way of receiving information directly into your application software would entail the use of electronic data interchange, or EDI.

ELECTRONIC DATA INTERCHANGE

Electronic data interchange has evolved over the years as a more efficient and error-free method of business communications than fax. EDI is prevalent in the automotive and retail industries, where current information for schedules or blanket purchase orders are critical. According to the *APICS Dictionary,* EDI is "the paperless (electronic) exchange of trading documents, such as purchase orders, shipment authorizations, advanced shipment notices, and invoices, using standardized document formats."[4]

As shown in Fig. 28.1, EDI consists of a "sender," company ABC, with some type of computer system. Their business system creates some documents, but instead of

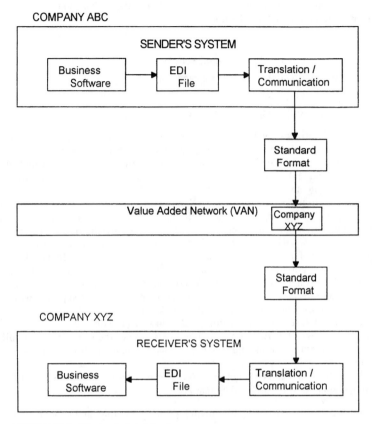

FIGURE 28.1   Electronic data interchange.

printing them, the system puts them in a file to be handled by the EDI software. The EDI software then *translates* the documents into a standard format that connects to the value-added network (VAN), using a *modem,* and sends the transactions to the mailbox of the "receiver," company XYZ, where they wait until the receiver is ready to pick them up.

When the receiving company is ready, their computer system dials up the value-added network, accessing company XYZ's mailbox and using their EDI communications software and a modem, to bring the documents down to the receiving company's system. Those documents are then translated from the standard format into a format that company XYZ's computer understands, and finally the transactions are entered electronically into the receiver's business system, as if someone had entered them via a keyboard.

The key to a successful EDI system is using the standardized format, which is governed in the United States by the *American National Standards Institute's* (ANSI) *Accredited Standards Committee (ASC).* The specific standard used in the United States is called X12. The X12 standard guarantees that a receiver of information will know exactly what type of document is being sent and where each piece of information is located in the file that is sent. When sending documents, such as purchase orders, via EDI, the actual data are sent as a series of records called a *file.* One of the first pieces of information in that file is the type of transaction that file contains, given as a document number. A purchase order is document number 850 in the X12 standards. Some other documents defined for EDI are the following:

810   Invoice

820   Payment order and/or remittance advice

830   Planning schedule with release capability

840   Request for quotation

860   Purchase-order request for change

EDI normally utilizes a value-added network to transmit information from one company to another and back again. Those companies doing business electronically are called *trading partners*. The VAN functions as an electronic post office, which allows companies to send and receive information when it is most convenient (and cost effective) for them to do so.

It is possible to use EDI without a VAN, as some small suppliers may be forced to do when dealing with a large customer. Without a VAN, a personal computer is used with communication software supplied or recommended by the trading partner. The benefits of using a VAN become obvious when doing business electronically with more than one customer, if trading partners use different communications software. The chore of sending a set of purchase orders via personal computer to different suppliers can be replaced by the business system sending sets of transactions to a VAN, which then distributes a set of transactions to the respective trading partners. As a supplier to multiple companies, all doing business electronically, the key to success is finding a format that all will accept when sending transactions. EDI allows you to do that.

One point to consider: Electronic mail and EDI are not the same. The main difference is in the actual translation of data into a *common format*; electronic mail is free formatted text.[5]

The benefits of EDI can be staggering. A regional transportation company listed the following as *some* of the benefits they realized:

Materials cost was reduced by eliminating printing, mailing, and paper handling.

Labor cost was reduced since fewer people were entering data.

Human errors of manual entry were reduced.

EDI allowed faster response time.

EDI allowed transcontinental tracing and tracking.

EDI improved customer relations due to the availability of up-to-date information.[6]

The decision to implement EDI, like any other business decision, should be supported by upper management and implemented by the users, not the data processing staff. When the people affected by the potential benefits are involved in making the decisions, they will make sure it works and become invaluable employees in the process. Besides, without the system users' support for a change, they may continue to do business the "old way" and therefore increase costs, rather than reduce them, as EDI normally does.

COMPUTER PERIPHERALS

In addition to central processing units or computers themselves, there are a number of other computer components necessary to complete the system. The components common to most systems are as follows:

Disk drives are used for the storage of data on easily accessible magnetic media.

Computer terminals allow on-line access to the data on the system.

Printers of many varieties are used to produce reports, bar codes, MICR-encoded checks, and all kinds of external communications.

Magnetic tapes or diskettes are used to copy data from the disk drives for back-up purposes. Tape is the most economical and widely used form of backup for large volumes of data.

There are many different types of disk drives available, but the type of drive is not as important as the capacity of the drive. Because of the rapidly changing disk storage technology, the cost is decreasing dramatically while the speed and capacity are improving. The most important consideration in selecting disk drives is that there is enough capacity to store the information required and provide for expansion. Companies frequently buy computer systems that do not have adequate disk storage, so they are forced to purchase more capacity before they had planned.

Computer Terminals

Just as there are many different types of disk drives, there are also many types of computer terminals. These are classified as either *programmable* or *nonprogrammable* *workstations*. Personal computers are the most frequently used programmable workstations. There has been a dramatic increase in the use of programmable workstations because of their increased functions and power. Some functions can be performed directly on the programmable workstation without using the main computer system.

Color displays on workstations, if the software is available, take advantage of using color to aid data entry and highlight errors or abnormal conditions. Studies have shown that there is less eye-strain for the user of color displays.

The number of different types of printers is confusing. It is recommended that the system use *both* high-speed, high-volume printers and low-speed, low-volume printers. The low-speed printers can be used as workstation printers located near the users of the system.

Bar Codes

In today's manufacturing environment, many people are using bar codes on printed documents, which allows for very accurate and speedy data collection. Most modern manufacturing systems provide for bar-coded data collection. Special consideration must be given to the capability of the printer if it will be using bar codes since not all printers can print bar codes. Laser printers are frequently recommended because of their high-quality output.

Magnetic-Tape Drives

The importance of adding a magnetic-tape drive to the system is that it allows the rapid backup and restoration of data on the disk drives. Backup and restore procedures can be performed either selectively or for an entire system. Typically, once a backup or restore procedure has started, the data are unavailable until the backup or restore procedure is complete. Therefore, in applications where the availability of the data is critical, high-speed, high-capacity tape drives should be selected. Diskettes are usually used to back up or restore small amounts of data so the lack of speed is not an important factor.

SYSTEM ARCHITECTURE

Computer hardware systems are typically implemented in one of four general systems architectures:

Centralized
Distributed
Departmental
Cooperative

Centralized Architecture

In a centralized architecture system, the processing unit is located at a central location and personnel using the computing services are either at the same location or they are using a terminal at a remote location connected to that system. The primary processing in this case is done at the one location.

Distributed Architecture

The computing resources are distributed to various locations, and it is common to communicate between locations with computing resources.

Departmental Architecture

Major functional areas have their own computing resources and typically communicate to a headquarters level.

Cooperative Architecture

Using a cooperative architecture, processing for different functions is performed on various types of computers. For example, part of a function may be performed on a personal computer, while the database may reside on a file server, and other data may be obtained from a centralized mainframe. It is difficult to establish good response time if one is trying to run an on-line, real-time manufacturing system communicating via phone lines to a remote centralized system.

DATA COLLECTION AND CONTROL

Automated data collection and control has been an issue that businesses have struggled with for many years. Bar coding has become a standard in many industries, such as the automotive industry and retail distribution. There are a number of different bar-coding schemes in use. Code 3 of 9 (or 39) has become the standard of the Automotive Industry Action Group (AIAG), and it is therefore the most commonly used bar-coding scheme in manufacturing. The most common applications of bar codes are time and attendance reporting, job and labor reporting, inventory reporting, and warehouse picking and shipping. The use of bar codes for data collection is becoming more common because of its reliability, lower cost, and accuracy.

Bar-Code Readers

There are many different types of bar-code readers, but the most common ones are wands, slots, and laser guns. There are also many different types of bar-code printers in use including impact printers, thermal printers, and laser printers. The laser printers produce a high-quality bar code, faster and more reliably than the other technologies. They also have a tendency to cost more, but they are more flexible.

Radio-frequency transmission devices for bar-code data collection are becoming more practical and common. For instance, it is not at all unusual to see hand-held data collection terminals or mounted data collection devices being used by a forklift truck operator. Some radio-frequency systems are regulated by the Federal Communications Commission (FCC) and require a license. Often radio-frequency data collection devices are subject to interference from other electronic devices that can introduce errors into the system. Much has been published by APICS in this area, and the person interested in using data collection equipment can find additional valuable details in the bibliography.

Advances in Data Processing

Some advances in these technologies are voice recognition, voice coding, multimedia presentations, the use of image and vision systems, and rapid prototyping. For example, stereo lithography is used to rapidly produce solid models for an engineering prototype. Another example that has appeared recently is the use of multimedia personal computers to show a video of setup instructions on a production floor. Voice, "time reporting," is beginning to be promoted by many time-and-attendance software vendors. The use of computers and advanced technology by manufacturers is just in its infancy. We will see many new advances in the near future.

REFERENCES

1. Wickham Skinner: "Manufacturing—missing link in corporate strategy," Systems and Technologies APICS Readings for CPIM, *Harvard Business Review*, Sept. 1991, p. 5.
2. Wickham Skinner: "Manufacturing—missing link in corporate strategy," Systems and Technologies APICS Readings for CPIM, *Harvard Business Review*, Sept. 1991, p. 7.
3. M. E. Porter and V. E. Miller: "How information gives you competitive advantage," Systems and Technologies Readings for CPIM, *Harvard Business Review Reprints*, Sept. 1991, pp. 103–114 (Reprint 85415).
4. James F. Cox III, John H. Blackstone, Jr., and Michael S. Spencer: *APICS Dictionary*, 7th ed., American Production and Inventory Control Society, Falls Church, Va., Jan. 1992, p. 15.
5. William K. Riffle: "EDI: Let's Look at the Basics. What Can It Do For You?," *APICS: The Performance Advantage*, vol. 3, no. 6, June 1993, pp. 26–28.
6. G. J. Udo and Trish Grant: "Making EDI Pay Off: The Averitt Express Experience," *Production and Inventory Management Journal*, vol. 34, no. 4, 4th quarter 1993, pp. 6–11.

BIBLIOGRAPHY

Fuller, Jr., T. H.: "Have Gun, Will Travel—Does Technology Lead Strategy or Vice Versa?" *APICS 1990 Conference Proceedings,* CPIM Systems and Technologies Reprints, pp. 113–123.

Kulonda, D. J.: "Competing Through Manufacturing: The Role of Manufacturing Systems," *APICS 1987 Conference Proceedings,* CPIM Systems and Technologies Reprints, pp. 182–185.

Lee, W. B.: "Technological Options for Computer Integrated Manufacturing," *APICS 1986 Conference Proceedings,* CPIM Systems and Technologies Reprints, pp. 196–200.

Lopez, D. A. and Haughton, D. A.: "World-Class Manufacturing Northwest Electronics Companies: Distressing Results for Technology and MPC Applications," *Production and Inventory Management Journal,* vol. 34, no. 4, 4th qauarter 1993, pp. 56–60.

"Putting expert systems to work," S&T APICS Readings for CPIM, *Harvard Business Review.*

Shuh, L. J. and Todd, A. C.: "An Executive Perspective: Planning Today for the Information Needs of the Future," *APICS 1986 Conference Proceedings,* CPIM Systems and Technologies Reprints, Falls Church, Va., pp. 257–260.

Stauffer, R. N.: "Lessons Learned in Implementing New Technology," *Manufacturing Engineering Magazine,* June 1988.

CHAPTER 29
SOFTWARE IMPLEMENTATION

Editor

William M. Grauf

Client Manager, J.D. Edwards World Solution Company
Oak Brook, Illinois

This chapter outlines a method for implementing business software systems that is especially appropriate for enterprise-wide and MRP II systems.

INSTALLATION VERSUS IMPLEMENTATION OF SOFTWARE

To install software means simply to load it on the computer. Installation is typically only one small task within a system implementation project plan. In contrast, when software has been *implemented,* it is being used to run the business. A fully implemented software system can enable a business to achieve certain objectives and benefits. However, the business will operate differently than it did without the software, and the behavior or the manner in which the business operates on a day-to-day basis must change to take advantage of the software's capabilities. The number of behavioral changes will depend on the objectives and scope of the implementation. If the software is an enterprise-wide system, then most employees and processes will be affected in one manner or another. Often greater discipline and accuracy will be required.

An *implementation method* is an approach to project management that is a combination of techniques, activities, and organization. A method allows the project team to take advantage of the developer's experience and thereby avoid some of the errors that might have otherwise been committed. Using the method will also typically jump-start the team because they will have a template or outline to help develop the timeline and identify activities for completion. Many large software and consulting firms have developed methods for use with their clients. The best methods are based on solid experience and are no more complex than the project objectives require.

IMPLEMENTATION: MULTIPLE SUBPROJECTS OR PATHS

An implementation plan consists of many subprojects or paths. The paths, described below, must often support and interface each other:

1. The *management plan*, or *operating plan*, is where the behavioral changes that will improve a company's performance take place, as discussed in many of the preceding chapters. For example, cycle counting and monthly sales and operations planning meetings should be started early in the project. Both are prerequisites to achieve the type of dramatic return on investment most companies are seeking.

2. The *system implementation plan* is more directly tied to the application of the software to support the business. The methods of many software companies concentrate on this plan with minimal attention given to the operating plan.

3. The use of a *technical plan*, or *network plan*, has become more prevalent with the migration toward client-server technology. This plan may include the preparation of the environment, installation of software and hardware, cabling, operating system and database issues, communications, data conversion, interface to other software, and modifications.

4. An *education plan* should be developed separately, but it should be tightly coordinated with all three plans. It should cover all education and training for business concepts and techniques, problem solving and facilitation skills, change management concepts and techniques, technical training, software training for the project team, and detailed training for the end users on a combination of software and new company procedures.

An implementation of paperless shop floor control could involve all four plans or subprojects. The software may support backflushing and other techniques to reduce the number of transactions and the need for paperwork. Before these techniques may be effectively applied, the bill of materials and processes must be simplified. This is part of the management plan. To understand the need for simplification and how backflush functions within the software is all part of the education plan. Typically there are several levels to this plan, including conceptual education, training on the software, and end user training that integrates the company's procedures with the use of the software. The data collection requires that equipment and software be installed on the shop floor. Communications with the main business system must also be established. Everything must be thoroughly tested so that disruptions are minimized when the system goes live.

The above plans are linked to the system implementation plan. Parameters within the software are set to match the way the company wants to run the business, as established through the management plan. Then the software is integrated into the business processes so that procedures may be defined for the end users. Only when everything has been tested, users trained, and data converted is the system ready to go live. The software implementation plan coordinates these activities so that they all come together just prior to that point.

This chapter will prescribe a system implementation and education plan, as illustrated by a project time line shown in Fig. 29.1. (This chapter represents only the system implementation and education plans, as the technical plan is the purview of the information systems department.)

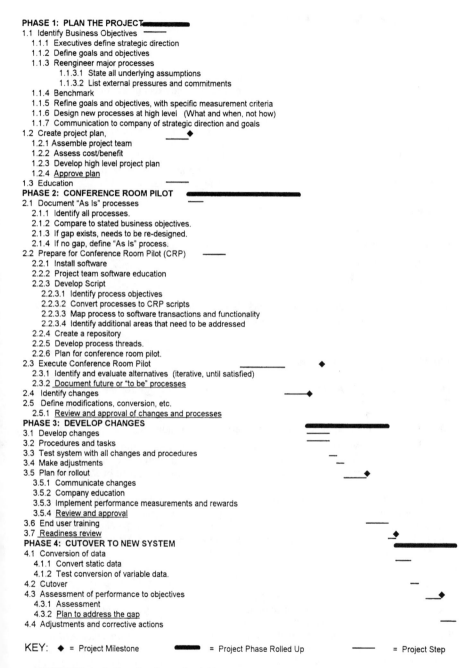

PHASE 1: PLAN THE PROJECT ▰▰▰▰
1.1 Identify Business Objectives ▬▬
  1.1.1 Executives define strategic direction
  1.1.2 Define goals and objectives
  1.1.3 Reengineer major processes
      1.1.3.1 State all underlying assumptions
      1.1.3.2 List external pressures and commitments
  1.1.4 Benchmark
  1.1.5 Refine goals and objectives, with specific measurement criteria
  1.1.6 Design new processes at high level (What and when, not how)
  1.1.7 Communication to company of strategic direction and goals
1.2 Create project plan,   ◆
  1.2.1 Assemble project team
  1.2.2 Assess cost/benefit
  1.2.3 Develop high level project plan
  1.2.4 Approve plan
1.3 Education ▬▬
PHASE 2: CONFERENCE ROOM PILOT ▰▰▰▰▰▰▰▰▰▰
2.1 Document "As Is" processes ▬▬
  2.1.1 Identify all processes.
  2.1.2 Compare to stated business objectives.
  2.1.3 If gap exists, needs to be re-designed.
  2.1.4 If no gap, define "As Is" process.
2.2 Prepare for Conference Room Pilot (CRP) ▬▬
  2.2.1 Install software
  2.2.2 Project team software education
  2.2.3 Develop Script
      2.2.3.1 Identify process objectives
      2.2.3.2 Convert processes to CRP scripts
      2.2.3.3 Map process to software transactions and functionality
      2.2.3.4 Identify additional areas that need to be addressed
  2.2.4 Create a repository
  2.2.5 Develop process threads.
  2.2.6 Plan for conference room pilot.
2.3 Execute Conference Room Pilot ▬▬▬▬ ◆
  2.3.1 Identify and evaluate alternatives (iterative, until satisfied)
  2.3.2 Document future or "to be" processes
2.4 Identify changes ▬▬◆
2.5 Define modifications, conversion, etc.
  2.5.1 Review and approval of changes and processes
PHASE 3: DEVELOP CHANGES ▰▰▰▰▰▰
3.1 Develop changes ▬▬
3.2 Procedures and tasks ▬▬
3.3 Test system with all changes and procedures ▬
3.4 Make adjustments ▬
3.5 Plan for rollout ▬▬◆
  3.5.1 Communicate changes
  3.5.2 Company education
  3.5.3 Implement performance measurements and rewards
  3.5.4 Review and approval
3.6 End user training ▬
3.7 Readiness review ◆
PHASE 4: CUTOVER TO NEW SYSTEM ▰▰▰▰▰▰
4.1 Conversion of data ▬
  4.1.1 Convert static data
  4.1.2 Test conversion of variable data.
4.2 Cutover ▬
4.3 Assessment of performance to objectives ◆
  4.3.1 Assessment
  4.3.2 Plan to address the gap
4.4 Adjustments and corrective actions ▬

KEY: ◆ = Project Milestone   ▰▰▰▰ = Project Phase Rolled Up   ▬▬ = Project Step

FIGURE 29.1   Project time line and activities.

PHASE 1: PLANNING THE PROJECT

Make a Commitment

Management support is mandatory for the project to be successful. In fact, the executives must lead the way through the process of change. The executive team needs to create a vision for how the company will look in the future, which is often called the *future state*. They must also clearly define a set of measurable goals. The vision and goals must be communicated often. This communication takes many forms beyond just signing the check. Some of the communication will be formal while some will be more symbolic or informal. Executive expectations, benefits, and objectives must be clearly stated. The executive team should take the form of a steering committee to review the project status periodically. The executive sponsor and steering committee must also:

- Identify and assemble the project team.
- Communicate the vision, goals, and objectives.
- Provide the project team with the resources needed to achieve those objectives.
- Establish boundaries for the change.
- Remove barriers for the project team.

The project team will do most of the work, but without the steering committee's guidance and assistance, success will be more difficult to attain.

Identify Business Objectives

Define the Strategic Direction. Executives establish a strategy for the project, as in the following example:

Goals Provide the best customer service in our industry.

Objectives New-order cycle time will be 48 hours or less, with less than 1 percent backorders and 2 percent returns. This will cause sales to increase by 5 percent, or $5,000,000, with a net profit of $700,000.

A cost-benefit analysis or project justification should be developed to truly recognize the potential benefits and the cost of any delays to the project's timely completion. Include an analysis of the potential resistance to the changes and the cost of reducing that resistance. For an excellent, easy-to-understand discussion of this type of analysis, see *MRP II: Making It Happen,* by Thomas F. Wallace.[1]

Define Goals and Objectives. A statement of purpose should be developed that includes the goals, objectives, and scope, as well as the reasons why the changes are required. It should establish rough parameters such as the following: *Implementation will include all aspects of the order fulfillment process including order entry, EDI, projection planning, shop floor control, and distribution. System must interface with the current telemarketing and financial software. The system will eventually be implemented in all three plants but piloted in the Chicago plant first.* This type of statement informs the project team of what they should focus on and what they need to accomplish. False assumptions have submarined and sidetracked many a project.

Reengineer Major Processes.   Many companies want to combine the software implementation with reengineering. The software is viewed as a technology that enables dramatic improvement to the business performance. *Business process reengineering* has been defined as "the fundamental rethinking and radical redesign of business processes to achieve dramatic improvements in critical contemporary measures of performance, such as cost, quality, service, and speed."[2] How can those objectives be achieved? If the order process currently requires 15 people in 5 departments to accept and schedule an order, how could the process be modified so that the order needs to go to only 3 people and take less time? The project team will test various alternatives during the conference room pilot design, but what changes and improvements can be identified at this point? For instance, could orders be processed through EDI and only exceptions handled by a person? At this point, the process details would not be finalized, as this will occur in the conference room pilot design (phase 2), but major changes like this will have an impact on the project plan and team thinking.

The reengineering of business processes requires creativity, out-of-box thinking, and inductive logic; otherwise, the exercise becomes a simple matter of incremental improvements as opposed to radical change. To encourage creativity, companies have used benchmarking, education, outside assistance, and various other techniques. An enlightened and impassioned executive may often produce excellent results and lead a motivated project team. Objective facilitation from an outside observer frequently proves invaluable in this type of session. The team must explore new technologies, ideas, and techniques, which may come from their competitors. For truly dynamic results, however, the team should study other industries or organizations as well. Long-standing rules and policies must be challenged. While this plan may appear to be strictly reengineering oriented, in actuality it resembles MRP II, ISO 9000, JIT, and TQM, all of which concentrate on processes. The notable difference is that reengineering strives for radical, or "order-of-magnitude," change.

Create Project Plan

Develop a High-Level Project Plan.   The project plan should include a rough timetable to the cutover time. In addition, it should contain a well thought out project plan that considers the various subprojects and the resources to complete the project in a timely manner. While it may be implemented locally, the plan must be developed from a global perspective, first. It must focus on improving and integrating the individual processes. The big picture must be known before anything is done with the pieces. The following example will explain the process.

For competitive reasons, a company wants to reengineer their order-fulfilling process and apply for ISO 9000 certification as quickly as possible. They also recognize the need to purchase and implement business software and eventually move toward a more just-in-time environment. While this is a full agenda, many "experts" would have the company complete the reengineering of the order-fulfilling process first and then purchase and implement the software. This would allow software to be selected that closely fits the reengineered processes. The ISO 9000 and JIT would come much later.

It makes sense to simplify business processes prior to automating them. However, doing so does not mean the whole reengineering project must be completed prior to the selection of software, which will arbitrarily limit the choices based solely on features and functions. A focus on features and functions tends to overcomplicate the project. Instead, the two projects should be accomplished in parallel, so that the fine-tuning of the processes may be completed based on system function. This approach consumes far less time and fewer resources because it minimizes duplication of effort and adds structure in difficult situations. If software is to be selected, it should be done after the high-level reengineering and strategic planning have been completed so that the software will support the company's strategic initiatives. Slight adjustments in the business processes would allow a less complex software system to be used and so reduce the overall cost and implementation effort. Optimization of one project will usually not produce optimal results for the whole. Figure 29.2 represents a time line for both approaches.

The ISO 9000 certification and short cycle manufacturing (just in time) should be planned for early on, rather than sequentially. Most of the work can be done later or in parallel. In this manner, all of the major system changes are integrated prior to implementation, and considerable time may be saved in testing the software's parameter settings. Most software packages will support this process-oriented implementation, although this order of activities usually requires some amount of flexibility from management. The modules and training are developed around functions, so only pieces of each may be relevant on the first pass.

The plan should have *milestones* identified as key points in the project. Milestones are critical points within the project that should have due dates and deliverables associated with them. *Deliverables* are reports, analyses, education classes, or steps toward achieving the project's objectives. Detailed action items or tasks should be identified that will take the team to the next milestone. The plan is updated at each milestone. The project team should present the project status to the steering committee periodically and at milestones throughout the project.

Establish the Role of the Project Team.   The project team must immerse itself in the effort and the education. It will map out the details for what will happen, when, where, and how. The team should be cross functional so that all of the major departments that will be affected by the changes are represented. It should have the freedom to make recommendations to creatively reengineer the business to achieve the company's goals. This is not something that may be delegated to consultants—rather, the in-house team

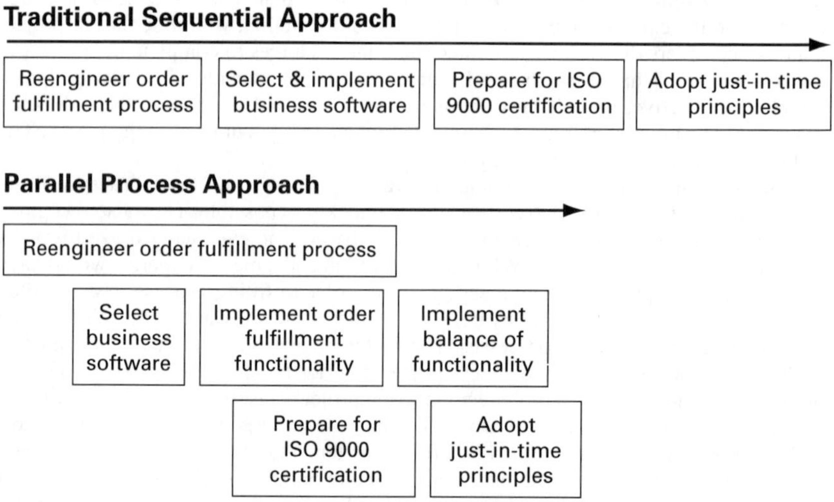

Traditional Sequential Approach

Reengineer order fulfillment process	Select & implement business software	Prepare for ISO 9000 certification	Adopt just-in-time principles

Parallel Process Approach

Reengineer order fulfillment process

Select business software	Implement order fulfillment functionality	Implement balance of functionality

Prepare for ISO 9000 certification	Adopt just-in-time principles

FIGURE 29.2   Two system design approaches.

must be responsible for the changes. Guidance and resources should be provided by the steering committee.

The team leader should represent the business, not the information systems. Many companies select a person who has demonstrated desirable qualities but is not a senior manager. If the project is merely an installation of software, this appointment is fine, but if major business improvements are expected, the more senior the team leader, the better. It is always best to select the most qualified, results-oriented person because the future of the business is riding on the project's success. The lack of project management or system skills is easily compensated for, but there is no replacement for a knowledge of the business and an ability to communicate effectively to all levels of the organization. The team leader should also be a member of the steering committee.

The team should be composed of representatives from all the key functional areas and/or business units. Certain skills must reside within the team, including analytical, communication, organizational, and problem-solving abilities. The core project team should be no more than six. Ad hoc or special-purpose teams may also be utilized. See Fig. 29.3 for a sample project organization chart.

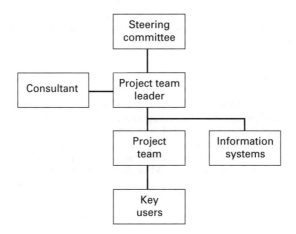

FIGURE 29.3   Project organization.

The team's level of participation on the project is a determining factor in developing the project plan. There is not a direct one-for-one correlation between the team's level of participation and the time required to complete the project. There tends to be an optimal point that varies by project, but 100 percent for the project leader and 40 percent for the balance of the team is reasonable. Any less than that and the team spends too much time getting reoriented to the project. Consultants can help to fill a gap in the type or amount of resources required, but they should not take over the project.

The consultant's role should be that of a catalytic agent, facilitator, coach, and guide. He or she should work behind the scenes in a low-profile manner in support of the project team and company's objectives. Active participation by the project team and its interaction with members of the company should be encouraged. The consultant's role is to jump-start the project, share his or her project and change management experience and software expertise, and apply concepts and techniques that will guide the team away from pitfalls. In the process, the team gains confidence, knowledge, and facility with the new system and processes. The company should not require outside help upon completion of the project.

Report Frequently on Project Status.   The steering committee must be kept informed of the status of the project. Project reporting is also critical to completing the project on time and within budget. When the project plan is developed, provision should also be made for the following types of project reporting:

- *Project status.* This report should state exactly how much work has been completed on each activity and how much remains to be done, as well as how much time and work remains until the planned cutover date.
- *Progress to plan.* This report should cover how much work was completed in the last week or period.
- *Expense to budget.* This figure may be broken out by type of resource, subproject, or phase. Special concern must be taken to track time and expenses for any consultants or vendors.
- *Outstanding implementation issues, a list of unresolved questions, problems or concerns, as expressed by the project team.*

Concept Education

Education of everyone touched by the changes means including almost everyone in the facility. The education must vary according to the needs of the different groups. Table 29.1 is a small piece of what the actual plan will look like. For example, each group will need to know different aspects of change management. The hourly workers need to understand what it is like to be the target of change, while the project team will need to master the role of being a change agent. While the education will be started at this point for the project team and executives, the education for everyone else should be timed to be delivered just prior to their need for it.

TABLE 29.1   Education Required by Position

	Executive	Project team	Management and professionals	Hourly
Understand strategy and reasons for change	*	*	*	*
Conceptual knowledge to support strategy	*	*	*	*
Conceptual knowledge to support particular processes		*	*	*
Skill to perform tasks and responsibilities				*
Project management		*		
Change management	*	*	*	*
Techniques and system skills		*	*	

PHASE 2: USING A CONFERENCE ROOM PILOT

Focus on Business Processes

Document what the processes are today and then what they will look like tomorrow, when the project is successfully completed. Many projects circumvent the definition of *as-is processes,* but it is difficult to map an implementation when you do not know where you are coming from and where changes will occur. Business software must be rigorously tested in a conference room pilot design prior to its introduction to the operating environment, which should never be used as a laboratory. The purpose of the pilot is not so much to make sure the system works but rather to test how it works. How should parameters and tables be set to accomplish business objectives? Where is there a gap between the software function and the way you want to run the business? This is not something that may be delegated to IS. It must be done by knowledgeable users who understand the business. Experience shows that with documented processes, the testing is often completed in dramatically less time simply because it offers a structured approach to a complex situation that most people have had no experience with.

As-Is Processes

Flowcharting, or business process flow modeling, should be used to document the as-is processes (see Fig. 29.4). This is often best done by a cross-functional team, as seldom will one person know how a whole process works. The purpose is to define *what* is being done by *whom*—not *how* it is done. A facilitator should work to capture the thoughts of personnel first and confirm them later. Then the process flow may be converted to a procedure format, or scripts, for the conference room pilot.

While many of the current processes will change, some will not. Unless you know what is done today, how can you determine a migration path or identify which jobs will change? Since this is familiar territory, some of the project team may feel more comfortable spending more time than is required at this step. Ask the question: Do we know *who* does *what* and *when?* You do not want to spend much time on *how* the work is completed.

Measurements should be collected for each process. How often is this process triggered? (How many transactions are there in a given time period?) What is the average

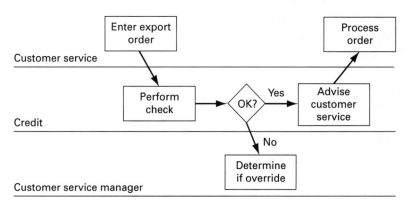

FIGURE 29.4   Process flow.

cycle time? What are the extremes? Are there peak periods or any special problems? These measurements do not need to be exact as they will be used only to establish relative priority.

The Conference Room Pilot

Sometimes called a *prototype* or *software test,* the *conference room pilot* is used to test the software in a simulated business environment.

Objectives
- Operate "business" using standard software.
- Identify and prioritize required changes in software and procedures.
- Continue the learning process.
- Identify, document, and resolve implementation issues.
- Identify required organizational and operational changes.
- Determine if additional hardware is required.

Identify
- Systems security setup
- System parameter requirements
- Master file setup
- Essential management reports
- Forms that require change
- Gains or losses in function
- Requirements for supporting documentation

Benefits
- Smooths the transition to the new system
- Simulates the operating environment
- Generates more reliable milestone dates
- Prepares project team for end-user training
- Minimizes the risk

Prerequisites
- Business concept education
- Software-specific training
- Business objectives
- Documented business processes

Critical Success Factors
- Management commitment
- Experienced consultant

- Good project management
- Education
- Dedicated project team
- Keep it simple

Conference Room Pilot Design Scenarios: Preparation

Before the conference room pilot can begin, the software must be installed. Software installation will often require a number of preparation activities. For example, the project team must receive software training to prepare for the conference room pilot. Other users will receive a combination of software-specific and new process or procedure training just prior to cutover. The timing is critical, as training received too early is not put to use and so is quickly forgotten.

The conference room pilot is often an intimidating portion of the project because it is a complex activity that most people are unfamiliar with and it has significant implications. Scripts must be developed to serve as a foundation for the testing process. A team member may then more easily follow the script and look for ways to improve or streamline the process. The *script* is a step-by-step test of the software, and it represents the current or potential way of doing business.

Script All Processes.   Script all processes, but if an as-is process is viewed as unsatisfactory, then a script should be created that represents the possible to-be process. The activities in creating a script are as follows:

1. Identify process objectives.
2. Determine if an as-is process meets the objectives.
3. If not, create a script for the proposed to-be process.
4. Convert processes to scripts.
5. Map process to software transactions and function.
6. Identify additional areas that need to be addressed (i.e., ISO 9000).

This is done in an iterative fashion until all relevant processes have a basic script. Figure 29.5 represents an example of a prepared script.

Each process may have several variations depending on the size, type of transaction, or the conditions that cause it to be initiated. Each variation is called a *thread,* which is

Process # 321 Thread # 7 Scenario # 4				
Description: Order Entry w/ credit problem, export				
Test	Description	Screen	Expected Results	Actual Results
1	Cust Serv enters export order.	OE35	Accepted	
2	Credit performs check	AR21	Over limit	
3	Credit advises CS	-	-	

FIGURE 29.5   Sample script on a test scenario form.

a possible path through a process. Most processes have more than one thread, and each must be documented so that they may be tested. For example, the order-fulfilling process would have many threads: one each for large, small, many more line items than usual, export, and rush orders. Combinations of these variations would also be documented as a separate thread because the software must be put through the paces in the laboratory of the conference room pilot as opposed to waiting until going live.

Build a Repository. A *repository* is a collection of all the reference documents found that relate to the processes and their use. The repository will be added to throughout the implementation. Included should be the following:

- Policies and procedures
- Interview notes
- Copies of screens and reports
- Process flowcharts
- Any metrics or other data
- Goals and objectives

The repository is invaluable when upgrading or modifying the software. It is often just a file cabinet or collection of notebooks organized by process.

Finalize Preparation for the Conference Room Pilot. The pilot preparations include reaching an agreement on a method for handling questions that arise, developing a schedule, and resolving any resource issues.

Open implementation issues are the difficult, unanswered questions that arise during any meeting, training class, or testing exercise. Often the particular moment in which an issue arises is not the best time to consider it, so the thought is captured for consideration later. A method to track and depoliticize the issue is required. One possible technique is the open implementation issue form shown in Fig. 29.6. The project manager should track each form. This can be an excellent measurement of the project's progress.

Ensure resource availability, including all team members, a well-equipped conference room, and a test database. The conference room pilot schedule has the following:

- A master plan that shows key accomplishments and milestones
- Assignments of responsibility for testing each process thread
- A detailed/rolling biweekly plan with assignments by person
- Weekly status meeting

The conference room should contain the repository, a large table, white board, flip charts, several computer terminals and a PC, a full set of the software documentation, and no phone. When the project team is meeting, they should be off limits to the rest of the company. The team should be able to plaster the walls with process definitions, the project plan, team rules, project objectives, and so on. Additionally the team must:

- Understand the objectives
- Have access to the repository
- Know of all assignments and all schedule and time requirements, and have the agreement of their direct supervisors
- Establish "team rules" such as: "Participants must be on time for meetings" and "Only one person may speak at a time."

- Agree to terminology   (*Customer order, allocation,* and *lead time* are all terms that are frequently confused.) Many companies use the *APICS Dictionary* for this purpose.

- Define and implement system security

Execute Conference Room Pilot Design

The conference room pilot is an iterative, ever-expanding cycle of using the scripts to test the new software. When a process does not perform satisfactorily (the process

<table>
<tr><td colspan="3" align="center">**Open Implementation Issue #** _____</td></tr>
<tr><td>DATE ISSUE RAISED: _____</td><td colspan="2">BY: _____</td></tr>
<tr><td>SUPERVISOR'S APPROVAL: _____</td><td colspan="2">DATE: _____</td></tr>
<tr><td colspan="3">TYPE OF ISSUE:</td></tr>
<tr><td>❑ POLICY</td><td>❑ MODIFICATION</td><td>❑ CONVERSION</td></tr>
<tr><td>❑ PROCEDURE</td><td>❑ ERROR IN SOFTWARE</td><td>❑ HARDWARE</td></tr>
<tr><td>❑ FORMS</td><td>❑ SECURITY ISSUE</td><td>❑ OTHER _____</td></tr>
<tr><td colspan="3">DESCRIPTION OF ISSUE: _____</td></tr>
</table>

DESCRIPTION OF ISSUE:

EXPECTED BENEFITS:

DATE REC'D: _____   ASSIGNED TO: _____   DATE: _____

ALTERNATIVES CONSIDERED:

WHO CAN RESOLVE

FINAL DISPOSITION

DATE CLOSED: _____

FIGURE 29.6   Open implementation issue form.

objectives cannot be achieved), alternatives must be identified and evaluated. When a single test is complete, another test or script may be added. Some tests can stand on their own such as cycle counting or adding a vendor, while others are part of a string of processes, as with order filling.

The connected tests may be performed individually at first and later by the team representing an actual event. This simulation drives unresolved questions to the surface so they may be addressed. The conference room pilot continues until all scripts have been included and questions resolved. The team leader must encourage creativity and be willing to challenge anything.

Many of the as-is processes will be altered in some significant manner. Remember that the software was not purchased so the business could continue operating the same way it always has. The future, or to-be, processes need to be identified and tested, alternatives evaluated, and then documented. Most software packages today make extensive use of parameters and tables. While the possible combinations are endless, there are usually several approaches to each key process or those that require improvement.

Weekly team meetings include a review of the week's work, test results, time it took to complete, any new open implementation issues, and status of all assignments. The team must then agree on the schedule and team assignments for the next 2 weeks. Changes must be noted as scripts are tested and changed so that during phase 3 the script will be up to date for the final test. The scripts will also be used to test future upgrades and changes. The conference room pilot may take as long as 8 to 12 weeks to complete, but it enables the implementation to move more quickly with less risk or disruption to the operation.

Identify Changes

During the conference room pilot a number of implementation issues will be identified. Some can be resolved immediately, while others will require that a change of some sort be made for the new system to function properly. These changes must be documented and a case made for why the change is required. Prior to making a significant modification, other alternatives should have been evaluated with a cost-benefit analysis identified. Some changes may not require as much research, but each change must be justified. Any modifications detract from the company's ability to upgrade to a new release of the software and so should be kept to a minimum.

The following should be prepared and presented to the steering committee during this step:

- *Recommended process changes.* Provide details for any alternatives that were considered.

- *Recommended organizational changes.* The team must identify any new, consolidated, or obsolete positions. For example, buyer-planner, master scheduler, or EDI coordinator are positions that might be added. In addition, positions where the responsibilities will significantly change, require additional skills, or require behavior changes should be noted. The amount of changes in the operation or the organization and the degree of difficulty must be assessed and costed.

- *Prioritized list of modifications.* The programming resources can then be applied accordingly, but every attempt must be made to minimize modifications so as to avoid future support and upgrading problems. For each modification the alternatives that were considered and a rough estimate of costs should be listed. All modifications should also be listed by the following:

1. Must have it to operate the business because it supports a mission critical process.
2. It would save significant time and resources.
3. Nice to have it, but can live without it.

- *Outline of data conversion.* Identify all current data that should be converted.
- *Interfaces.* Describe and estimate the cost to develop.
- *Cross references.* File existing reports to those in the new system.
- *Design of new or changed forms.* Include both computer-generated forms and those forms affected by process changes but that are manual.
- *Revised project plan.* Since more information is available than when the plan was originally created, the team should be able to project more accurate dates and resource requirements.

Review and Approve All Changes

The steering committee must review all of the recommended changes. They can approve recommended changes or request that alternatives be considered. If significant changes or modifications are being made, this step is repeated but in greater detail by providing a detailed design with tight resource and time estimates. The technical changes can be extremely expensive and time-consuming, so only the steering committee can authorize that expenditure.

PHASE 3: DEVELOPING THE CHANGES

Outlining the Changes

The changes were identified and evaluated during the conference room pilot and then approved by the steering committee. A detailed plan for managing the development effort must be made and the work started. The project team must monitor the effort and provide whatever assistance is required for testing. The changes include the following:

- Organization changes
- Procedural changes
- Modifications and interfaces
- Conversion

Some of the changes are the responsibility of the steering committee, but the project team must identify and justify them all.

Modifying Procedures and Tasks

The project team must develop or modify procedures, tasks, and forms. A procedure explains how an activity flows from one work group to another (who, what, and when). Procedures documentation should accomplish the following:

- Disseminate knowledge of the process
- Pool process knowledge and expertise
- Create positive interfaces between individuals and process elements

Testing the System with All Changes and Procedures

The final test uses the modified scripts from the conference room pilot to test the complete system with all modifications, interfaces, procedures, tasks, and forms. If the results of the test do not satisfactorily match the way the company wants to operate, then the gap needs to be identified.

Making Adjustments

Corrective actions must be identified and executed to eliminate the gap. The final test must be completed again and the cycle repeated until the results are satisfactory.

Planning for Rollout

The Management of Change. The need for changes in behaviors and attitudes must be addressed. Old habits are hard to break, but even more so if the reasons for change are not communicated properly that people are not motivated to change. Successful change agents recognize the difficulty of getting people to leave their present behavior. "The way we've always done things is safe, and we know how to be successful." To effect change, the future must be well defined and communicated. A degree of urgency must also be established. Jeanenne LaMarsh, in her new book *Changing The Way We Change,* describes an uncomfortable period between the present and future, called the *delta* (see Fig. 29.7).[3] The changes and much of the learning occur here. The project team must help people through the delta. The discomfort may be minimized by having fun. Creative and innovative special awards and recognition, such as an ice cream social or gift certificate for a video, may provide the energizing spark that is sometimes needed. Rewards should be immediate and tied to specific behavior or results if they are to be effective.

FIGURE 29.7   The change process.

Successful companies spend more effort on people than on tools. For instance, in the implementation of new software, the experienced project manager recognizes that the poor use of excellent software is a much more common cause of failure than is poor software. The changes must be carefully planned so that specific people targeted for change receive the right education and training just prior to the change. Their supervisor must be supportive as well. Behavior that helps to achieve the new goals should be rewarded and not the old behavior.

Performance Measurements. Frequent assessments will enable management to reinforce new behavior and accomplishments consistent with the new business objectives. Major changes are difficult enough to accomplish without being burdened by performance measurements that reward the old behaviors. If the goals are indeed valuable, then the actions required to achieve them should be recognized. Business and process performance should be the focal point, as opposed to departmental goals that subopti-mize the overall performance. Executive commitment and leadership play a significant role here, as there are many feathers that could be ruffled.

Gathering Support for the Change.   Mass support is essential, as eventually the new way of doing business must be embraced by the whole organization. Many excellent projects falter at this point, for a number of reasons:

1. Inadequate education and training are scheduled.

2. Job aids, procedures, or task reminders are not readily accessible after the training. This is one of the reasons that documentation plays such an important role in an ISO 9000 program. Business software implementations also require similar support. Have you ever wondered why the second shift does things differently than the first shift?

3. People realize management views the changes as the new program of the month and is not 100 percent behind them. This is often perceived because they are still being measured the same old way.

4. Lack of participation by the internal personnel creates a vacuum that is filled by third parties.

Supplying End-User Training

Training material must be developed for the end users. The training on the systems and techniques should be integrated with training on the new business processes, proce-dures, and tasks. Business concept education should have already been completed, but the lessons frequently referenced to reinforce the link. For instance, as inventory trans-actions on the new software are reviewed, places where mistakes could be made should be pointed out. Ideas and reasons for prevention of errors should be discussed.

The end-user training should come in short, digestible segments. The users need to return from the training with a job aid or "cheat sheet," to serve as an on-the-job reminder. Documented procedures, if they are accessible and easy to use, will also serve that purpose. Large manuals will sit on a shelf and gather dust, so find ways to make the procedures usable.

End-user training should be developed and facilitated by the project team for three reasons: *First,* the team must exhibit management's support and ownership of the changes. *Second,* the team is better able to apply the new concepts, techniques, and sys-tems to the specific business situations than an outsider can. And *third,* they have to understand the changes thoroughly so they can support them later on.

Reviewing the Implementation

At this point the project should almost be ready for cutover. Rather than discover a gap after going live, it makes sense to perform a complete review of the implementation. Cutting over to a new system represents a substantial risk to the operation. Mistakes and omissions can cause a serious disruption. Take the time to be sure you are ready. Some of the questions to be asked are the following:

• Has there been sufficient communication to the right people?

• Are all users adequately trained?

- Have all the resistance issues been addressed?
- Are all new forms available?
- Have all of the open implementation issues been resolved?
- Have all changes been completed and tested?

PHASE 4: MAKING THE CUTOVER TO THE NEW SYSTEM

Conversion of Data

Data should have been converted and prepared and tested during phase 3. The static data such as bills, routings, vendor and customer masters, and history can be converted early, as long as there is a plan to keep them synchronized. Variable data such as the inventory status, customer identification, and purchase and shop orders must be converted just prior to cutover, but the programs must be tested well ahead of time. A detailed plan should be developed for this conversion, with tight estimates of the time required for each program.

Cutover

The actual cutover to the new system and processes is usually done over a weekend and typically coincides with an accounting period close. The project team should closely monitor the use of the system for the first couple of weeks and be available to assist users in adapting to the changes. Executives must show complete support for the changes and celebrate even the minor successes.

For a long time, experts argued over the best approach to cutovers. Some preferred to operate both systems in parallel, but the duplicate efforts seldom were achievable. It was too easy to stay with the old system. Using a conference room pilot approach, as discussed in this chapter, is usually considered the most appropriate method today. A variation of this approach is to implement only the processes that were previously automated. The balance of the new system is then implemented by a second pass. This keeps the amount of change to a manageable level and reduces the risk of disruption to the operation, but it takes longer. Most multiplant organizations will produce a pilot system in one plant first and then roll it out to the other plants.

Comparison of Performance to Objectives

Shortly after the cutover, an assessment of the implementation should be made to verify that users have truly embraced the changes and that the system is being used properly. Are the project's objectives being achieved? Are there any gaps between what is desired and what is actually being done that need to be addressed? A plan to close the gaps must be developed and presented to the steering committee for approval. This plan may include retraining and process or system changes.

The ISO 9000 certification is a generic standard for quality and quality assurance that is used by manufacturing or service industries to document the quality system. It is not specific about techniques to be used. It is commonly used in contractual situations. If the company is pursuing an ISO 9000 certification, it would be appropriate to concentrate on it during a software system conversion, assuming the groundwork was laid during the implementation stage.

Adjustments and Corrective Actions

Implement the corrective actions, and then repeat the assessment and correction cycle every few months. The implementation of business software is an ongoing process of continuous improvement. Diligence and discipline are required to avoid slipping back to the old ways.

CRITICAL SUCCESS FACTORS

Many companies have discovered that it costs as much time and money to have a project fail as to successfully achieve the project's objectives. A focus on the following critical success factors will go a long way toward ensuring that the project's objectives will be achieved:

- *Executive commitment.* Set and communicate the vision and goals, while providing support.
- *Project plan.* Use a proven method.
- *Education.* Include business concepts, skills, and software.
- *Project team.* Include users and information systems.
- *Focus on entire business processes.* Do not focus on functions or modules.
- *Management of change.* Change behavior and attitudes of personnel.
- *Performance measurements.* Reward behavior and accomplishments consistent with the new business objectives.
- Mass support. Provide adequate training for the end users, and communicate the need for the support of the new system.

REFERENCES

1. Thomas F. Wallace: *MRP II: Making It Happen,* Oliver Wight Limited Publications, Inc., Essex Junction, Vt., 1990.
2. Michael Hammer and James Champy: *Reengineering the Corporation,* Harper Collins Publishers, Inc., New York, 1993.
3. Jeanenne LaMarsh: *Changing the Way We Change,* Reading, Mass., Addison-Wesley, 1995.

BIBLIOGRAPHY

Grauf, William M.: "Critical Success Factors of Manufacturing Improvement Projects," *APICS Performance Advantage,* November 1995.
Tincher, Michael G., and Sheldon, Donald H., Jr.: *The Road to Class A Manufacturing Resource Planning (MRP II),* Buker, Inc., Chicago, 1995.

CHAPTER 30
INTEGRATING BASIC MANUFACTURING SYSTEMS

Editor

Lloyd R. Andreas, CFPIM

Application Manager

Marcam Corporation, Atlanta, Georgia

Other chapters of this book have dealt with the fundamentals of different areas of production and inventory control—the underlying theories, operational practices, resource considerations, and so on. This chapter will discuss the major components of a basic computer-based manufacturing planning and control system from the perspective of implementation and integration. It will address the questions that always arise in initial systems implementations: "Where do we start?" and "What needs to be done?"

A distinction needs to be made among *development, implementation,* and *integration* of manufacturing planning and control systems. The *development* of a system involves the design, programming, testing, documentation, and other activities required to deliver a usable, working software package. The *implementation* of these systems, whether they are purchased from a software development company or built in house, involves the efforts to install and use the system to solve the problems that it was designed to address. The *integration* of a manufacturing system can be viewed from two perspectives: how the pieces of the system itself fit together and interact, and how the system interacts with other systems, both computerized and manual. This chapter will deal with issues of implementation and integration.

The chapter is organized to address first the general definition of a basic manufacturing planning and control system and second the definition of major data entities and their relationships. The information flows between modules will be stressed, highlighting the key data elements that need to be available and shared. Considerations for different manufacturing environments will be discussed at a high level where there is an impact on system scope and dependencies.

DEFINING THE PROJECT'S SCOPE

In most systems implementation projects, one of the first major challenges is defining the scope of the project—that is, understanding the business processes that the system is supposed to support and which problem(s) it is intended to address. Once this has been accomplished, the building blocks can be implemented in the proper sequence. Even when a packaged software product is purchased, it typically addresses many of a company's business processes. Implementation priorities need to be established that will help to ensure the following:

- Early successes in using the system effectively
- Systems acceptance by the users
- A quick return on the implementation investment

All those involved with or affected by the implementation of a manufacturing system will have different perspectives on what a manufacturing system is or should do. There will be disagreements on what the real requirements are and which requirements should be addressed first. Each operating area of the business will have differing priorities. Business decisions and trade-offs are required, and the scope of the system needs to be defined prior to the development or implementation of the system. Key integration points within the system and with other systems need to be defined, understood, and prioritized.

One view of a manufacturing planning and control system, as defined in the body of knowledge advanced by the American Production and Inventory Control Society, is illustrated in Fig. 30.1. All types of variations exist for this illustration, each with its own, often subtle, difference that highlights an area on which the originator is trying to focus. The profusion of acronyms and abbreviations like MRP, MRP II, ERP, COMMS, and MES also tends to distort the view of what is meant by a "manufacturing system,"

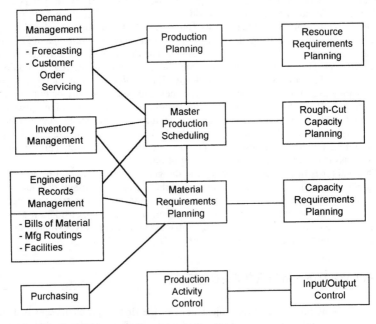

FIGURE 30.1   Manufacturing planning and control system.

or a "production and inventory control system." You will find similar terms representing the entire systems scope of a typical manufacturing enterprise. For example, where is the business process of "receiving production materials" located? Is it in inventory management? How about production activity control, or purchasing? Where do the cost accounting functions reside? For this level of discussion, it may not be that important to identify the elements of each of these major blocks. In reality, it may not even be feasible to construct a single diagram that illustrates all of the functional processes of a manufacturer and how they interrelate. However, some high-level picture needs to be constructed to define the scope of a systems implementation project. The objective of such a diagram should be to highlight the major areas for which systems requirements need to be defined. Business process modeling tools and methods can be applied in this arena to serve as a starting point for decomposition and further analysis.

The figure could be simplified to define a starting point for systems implementation. The major elements in this illustration might be summarized into six groups:

- *Business planning.* Although not clearly delineated in the illustration, this is what the executive management team uses to run the manufacturing company. Sales and operations planning, production planning, and resource planning are typical applications in this area.

- *Demand management.* The functions of forecasting future demands from both external and internal sources are supported by the modules in this block. In addition, this would include the booking and servicing of actual orders from customers, including those from other locations within the enterprise.

- *Manufacturing planning.* This application includes the traditional functions of master planning, material requirements planning, capacity planning, and other modules dealing with predicting the future need for materials, capacity, and other resources required to meet production goals.

- *Manufacturing execution.* These applications direct and support the daily activities of the production and inventory control personnel. A fundamental difference between a planning and an execution system is that an execution system authorizes the use of resources, that is, people, equipment, money, and so on. The execution system generates information that directs the production activities. It not only includes functions like manufacturing order release, schedule generation, dispatching, and shop reporting, it can also include the support of computerized physical control of production and inventory control.

- *Basic records management.* This element is rarely shown on diagrams of manufacturing planning and control systems, but it is the data foundation upon which all the other applications are built. References are frequently made to engineering data, such as bills of materials and routings, but they represent only a small, albeit important, piece of the mosaic. This subject will be covered in more depth in the next section of this chapter.

- *Supporting and reporting systems.* These tools and applications surround all of the other modules of the system to provide methods for users to access and extract information for a broad variety of reporting purposes and decision-making activities.

These groups are illustrated in Fig. 30.2.

The assumption in this book is that we are dealing with production and inventory control systems. Although there are integration dependencies with accounting systems, distribution functions, payroll and personnel, and many others, this chapter does not include implementation of these ancillary systems.

Systems & Application Architecture

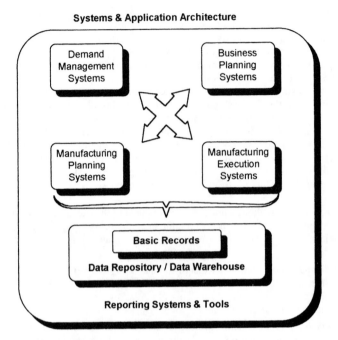

FIGURE 30.2 Basic elements of manufacturing systems.

THE ROLE OF TECHNOLOGY

There has to be an underlying architecture to support manufacturing systems. The architecture encompasses hardware, systems software, communications support, and operational support for the applications. All or portions of this architecture may already be defined by the systems currently in place or by the packaged-software developer. In many cases, the architecture of older application systems and of systems developed internally by the company tend to be more restrictive and inflexible. It becomes difficult to expand or change the systems to address new requirements and the changing business processes. Technology becomes important not because it is "the newest thing on the block" but because it supports more efficient development, integration, implementation, and use of application systems. Furthermore, it can provide the underlying architecture and tools to make it easier to adapt the system to changes that inevitably take place.

Investments in technology should be evaluated as any other financial decision. Whether it involves hardware, systems software, communications links, or development tools, the proposed solution must address the requirements in a way that provides an acceptable return on investment. As long as the solution continues to support the business requirements, it will continue to provide value. The recurring question then becomes one of whether or not a proposed change or replacement will provide a greater return and more value than retaining or enhancing the current solution. The financial analysis should include all aspects of investment and return, not just a single element. For example, when buying a manufacturing software package, the cost of the software may be a small part of the investment. Typically, there are annual maintenance or support fees required. Consulting services, education, and retraining may be needed to implement the system effectively. Additional systems design and development work may be required to interface to existing, "legacy" systems that will continue to be used in the company.

These evaluations should also include a subjective analysis of intangible benefits to be gained in a proposed change. Such things as the effect on employees' attitudes and morale, the impact on the company's competitive posture, and the potential overall increase in productivity should be considered. These are difficult areas to place a value on, but they can have a significant impact on the financial success of a systems project.

As with manufacturing systems, the terminology, abbreviations, and acronyms used in the hardware and software industry can be very confusing to many people. Even with the advent of personal and home computers, most users of information systems technology want only to accomplish tasks in a user-friendly manner. They do not want to have to understand the underlying technical details of hardware and programming. The bombardment of terms and marketing hype can be overbearing. Articles appear in a continuing stream in industry periodicals extolling the virtues of one approach or technology versus another—"Client-Server; 2-tier, 3-tier, or *n*-tier," "4th Generation Programming Languages Versus Object-Oriented Programming Systems," and the list continues. Even though the promises of new technology may often be oversold, they have to be evaluated because some of them will directly impact the end users of the manufacturing system. Others will impact the information systems staff. They will all affect the cost of implementation and operation to varying degrees.

The focus of this chapter is not on systems selection and development methods. A short description of key areas of consideration in these areas is warranted, however.

Hardware

Hardware can be viewed as tooling; you need it to get the job done, but it is designed for the operation to be performed. We don't make tooling and then look for something to manufacture. Hardware includes the host processors, file servers, communications controllers, workstations, data collection terminals, and programmable logic controllers similar to those found in automated machine tools on the shop floor. The hardware must fit the task, with respect to the following:

- *Capacity.* This includes both processing memory (RAM) and hard disk or other internal file or data storage media.

- *Performance.* The machine, when properly configured and utilizing the intended software, should provide transaction throughputs and interactive response times that meet business process goals. For example, a shortage check on a component for a manufacturing order should have a subsecond response time.

- *Reliability.* Tolerances for downtime need to reflect the impact of downtime on a company's operations. In certain process control environments, fault-tolerant systems may be desirable or necessary. Environmental factors must be considered.

- *Usability.* Ergonomic factors are extremely important in hardware that will be used directly by people. Safety features are of utmost importance. Although many of the useful features are attributes of the software being used, there are many hardware factors that can have a negative impact upon the user's productivity and can cause severe health problems such as the size of a monitor screen or the shape and configuration of a keyboard.

Systems Software

This is the software that supports communication between, and operation of, different hardware components, attached devices like workstations and printers, the communications network, and the database. Systems software often provides for systems security, backup and recovery, network management, and other administrative systems management tasks. Database management systems could be included in this category.

Development Tools

This includes compilers, fourth-generation languages, code generators, process and data modeling tools, and other "development environment" aids. Although the manufacturing system may be an off-the-shelf package, there may be a requirement to make modifications to it, extend the functionality, or modify the user interface. Many commercial software packages, for example, include report writers that allow the customer to create or modify reports without any programming.

As the push for "open systems" continues and supporting standards emerge, the tools used in the development and operation of the manufacturing system should conform to those standards. This will provide broader flexibility for expansion and wider solution availability. The emergence of object-oriented programming tools and techniques allows more rapid development of smaller, self-contained "objects" that contain data about things in the work environment, like parts, customers, and shop schedules, and what actions can be done with them. These objects are like standardized components. They can be reused and reconfigured to assemble a software solution specific to each environment. They may be customized without program modification.

Application Software

This is what the production and inventory control practitioner works with. Obviously, the most important consideration, when buying packaged software, is how well it addresses the company's requirements. There is often an attitude on the part of users that the software has to work "the way we've always done it." In many cases, the software may support more effective methods of completing tasks and accomplishing the business objectives. This is an area where business process reengineering projects can identify candidates for change prior to implementation of a new system. Application software should not make a job more difficult unless it provides a much greater benefit.

In most areas, application software should provide installation or run time options for functions that can be performed several ways. For example, inventory issues to manufacturing orders might be done at actual cost, average cost, or standard cost. Commercial software packages should support all these options.

Software Usability

The second consideration with application software is its usability. Will it be easy for the practitioner to learn how to use the system and to accomplish tasks using the software? Can the user be shielded from unnecessary actions, irrelevant or sensitive data, and a requirement to understand the technical operations of the system? Can the software be tailored to provide interfaces unique to individual users or groups of users? Tailoring may include the resequencing of data entry fields, the removal or addition of specific data fields on a display, and even the language that is used by each user.

Interfacing with Other Systems

A third consideration is the ability of the application to interface to other systems, to integrate other applications, or to change the function of the system, which are important to the long-term viability of the system and therefore the investment. This capability is determined not so much by the applications, such as the "inventory management" or "MRP" modules, but by the underlying architecture that ties the applications together and supports their operation, the development tools used, the systems software, and database management systems. The move to open systems is evident here, also.

An example of such a trend in the development of manufacturing software for industry is the *Open Applications Group,* founded by the Marcam Corporation and several other leading software vendors. Begun in 1995, this organization is composed of several committees whose charter is to develop protocols and interface standards between major components of manufacturing and financial systems. As these standards become available and are implemented by an increasing number of software developers, it will be much easier for a company to integrate application software packages from different suppliers.

Another systems problem not often considered is the availability of, and support for, each of the elements in the locations where they will be used. If the initial implementation is for one facility but it is intended for use in others, all possible locations have to be considered in the selection of system elements. It may be obvious that the hardware and systems software in each location have to be compatible to support the common application software, but there are many more subtle requirements that may be overlooked. For example, if the system will be used by plants in different countries, are translated versions of the software available? For support of translations such as Kanji (Japanese), Hanguel (Korean), Chinese, and Arabic, special hardware may be needed, such as special keyboards. The application software, development tools, and other software required to install and use the application or enhance it need to be *double byte enabled* to support such translations. Just because an international vendor offers a product on a global basis does not guarantee that localized versions are available.

By now, it should be apparent that a manufacturing planning and control system is composed of many elements. They must all be considered in deciding how best to implement a solution that addresses both short- and long-term requirements. Even though the stock clerk just wants to be able to input an inventory transaction easily, it is the underlying technology—a combination of hardware and software components—that determines how easily he or she can do that, now and in the future as the business process changes. Today, a user may enter a stock receipt by keying a part number, order number, and quantity. Next year, that user may just *wand* a bar code on a shipping container, and the EDI receipt acknowledgment will be sent to the supplier, while the inventory, accounts payable, purchasing, and other appropriate records are updated automatically. That's a gigantic leap in terms of systems function and application scope. It may have to be accomplished in several steps. It is *technology,* however, that will determine the relative difficulty, and cost, of making the transition.

IMPLEMENTATION SEQUENCE CONSIDERATIONS

When the requirements have been well defined and prioritized, the implementation sequence can be determined in a more logical fashion. Still, a broad view has to be taken, even though the initial effort will involve implementation of only a few components of the system as it is envisioned for the future. Certain dependencies already exist for manufacturing systems. For example, material requirements planning systems need to have bills of material and inventory data to operate, so some type of inventory system and bill of material database has to be implemented prior to MRP. Other dependencies that provide basic material availability data for MRP may be relatively straightforward but may not be satisfactory to support accounting.

The determination of which application area to address first should be guided by its potential benefit to the business, the probability of success, and the investment required. There is a tendency to "buy MRP and install accounts payable" when selecting and implementing commercial software packages. An analysis of the business areas in the company should point out which ones present the best opportunities. If material control is a major challenge, then perhaps the inventory management area should be attacked first. If shop orders are continually late, and work-in-process is out of control, then a shop floor control system might be the highest priority. In a make-to-order environment, the configuration and control of customer orders may present the biggest opportunity for improvement.

Generally, the relative importance of each application area will vary by industry and the type of manufacturing. In process industries, for example, sophisticated materials planning systems are usually not required. The focus is, instead, on planning the availability and efficient use of capacity. Food processors will receive raw materials but may not know exactly what can be manufactured until the materials are graded, sorted, or preprocessed in some fashion. The requirement to maintain inventory records that segregate lots of materials with different characteristics is fundamental to effective inventory management in this environment.

Figure 30.3 highlights the key production and inventory control areas and their relative importance based on the type of production; from a low-volume, build-to-order manufacturer of discrete products, such as aircraft, to a continuous-flow process environment, such as a refinery.

The scope of an implementation project has to be contained to ensure that benefits will begin to accrue in a reasonable time frame. The pressures will be enormous to "just add this small capability...while you're at it!"

GETTING STARTED: DEFINING THE BASIC RECORDS

To support any application, the basic records have to be in place: the data that define the company, its resources and products, and its external relationships. All the other data that are used in the organization are built through relationships between these basic elements and events or transactions. For example, think of an "item" as something that the company buys, manufactures, or sells. An item might be a purchased part, a subassembly, or a finished product. The basic record merely describes the item itself, not how much is in inventory or how many have been shipped to customers this month. Bills of material are defined by constructing relationships between items. It is in records that describe the relationships that we carry data about the relationship, as shown in the illustration in Fig. 30.4.

Item Records and Relationships

There are two types of basic records shown in Fig. 30.4: *item records* and a *location record*. The data that describe the relationships between them is shown in the relationship records. The records that show the parent-component relationship A between two item records define the bill of material. In the other example, there is a basic record

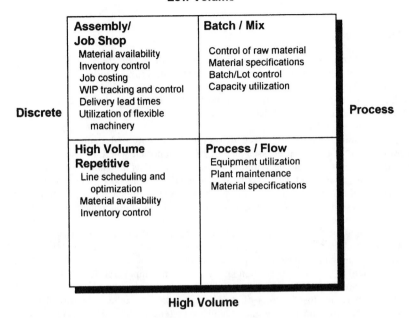

Low Volume

Assembly/ Job Shop	Batch / Mix
Material availability Inventory control Job costing WIP tracking and control Delivery lead times Utilization of flexible machinery	Control of raw material Material specifications Batch/Lot control Capacity utilization
High Volume Repetitive	Process / Flow
Line scheduling and optimization Material availability Inventory control	Equipment utilization Plant maintenance Material specifications

Discrete ... **Process**

High Volume

FIGURE 30.3 Focus areas by industry types: based on the volume-method matrix. (*Adapted from O. W. Thompson, "Practitioner, Know Thy Self,"* Computer Integrated and Flexible Systems Seminar Proceedings, *April 1985, pp. 240–247.*)

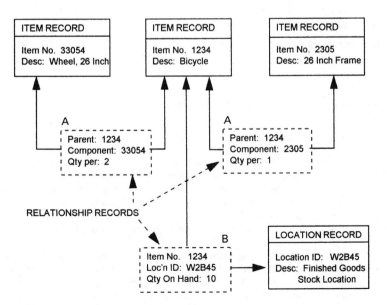

FIGURE 30.4 Basic records and relationships.

defining an inventory location. A relationship record B exists to record the stock level of a specific item at this location.

Relational Data Modeling

Relational data models are used to illustrate the difference between the fundamental data entities of a business and those data entities that describe relationships between two or more entities. Basic data entities can exist by themselves. Relationship entities, in contrast, have to have other entities to refer to. Relational data modeling is a very useful tool in understanding what data are used in the business and how the entities and the data elements are related.

The amount of data that is needed to describe an entity (the attributes) will vary according to the business processes that are to be supported. There is a lot of geometric data about a part that could be stored in an item record. This information may be useful, however, only if an interface to a computer-aided design (CAD) system is being implemented or if the data are required for direct download to automated machine tools by the scheduling system. The amount of data required by the system is related to the scope of the systems implementation.

By doing a good job up front of analysis and data modeling, future applications and interfaces can be recognized and planned. It is not necessary to go beyond the scope of the defined application in expanding and implementing the database. Preliminary modeling can help to ensure that the foundation is there to support future efforts.

So what are the "basic records" required by a manufacturing planning and control system? Where are the "origins of data" from which all other operational data are derived? When implementing a manufacturing system, what types of records, objects, or entities are needed? What data are typically used to define these?

If Fig. 30.2, the "Basic Elements of Manufacturing Systems" is used as a base, there are only five basic entities:

- The organizational units of the business
- The items that are planned and controlled
- The resources employed by the business
- The company's trading partners
- The ledgers used by the business

The next sections will explore each of these in more detail.

Defining the Organization

A business enterprise is composed of organizational units. These units are structured to support accounting, operational, and management purposes. This organization is usually reflected by the data that the enterprise uses such as company numbers and divisional identifications. These identifiers may find their way into areas of accounting and control. For example, the chart of accounts may be set up to follow organizational boundaries, with organizational identifiers embedded in the account numbers themselves.

To support a manufacturing system, the basic records for organizational data should define the lowest-level departments. To go lower than this would require identification of employees or other *resources*. The differences between an organizational unit such as a production department and a resource such as a work center can be confusing.

Generally, an *organizational unit* is a management-defined entity established for controlling the business. It is an aggregation point for the measurement of an activity. It usually implies "ownership" of company resources. The *resources,* on the other hand, can belong to different organizational units at different times. People can transfer from one department to another or inventory may be transferred between organizational units of the enterprise. Physical rearrangements of the production facility may result in new definitions of production departments that will have new configurations of equipment.

Once the basic unit is defined, for example, the department, other relationships can be constructed that describe the hierarchical structure of the enterprise. Different relationships may exist for different purposes, but they all spring from the definition of the smallest unit.

When implementing a manufacturing planning and control system, understanding the overall company structure is essential so that the proper unit identifications can be assigned for reporting and control. Data required to define a department should start with a departmental identifier and include a description. This may be all that is necessary. Grouping of departments into higher-level structures may not need any additional attributes. In effect, the organizational units of the business can be described in fairly simple tables.

Most commercial manufacturing software packages do not support an "organizational unit master file." Department and other structural identifiers are typically embedded in other records. Inquiries into the database can then selectively access data to generate the appropriate reports for a department, division, or any other defined unit. The challenge is to define these units prior to systems implementation so that operational reports and inquiries can be generated easily.

Item Definition Data

Items in this context are the things that a manufacturer buys, builds, converts, and sells. There are many types of items used in a production environment. Things such as raw materials, piece parts, fabricated parts, subassemblies, and final assemblies are all *items*. In the process industries, things like ingredients, fillers, compounds, and intermediates are also items. Items are physical things that can be inventoried and counted or measured.

In a general sense, an item could be considered a resource, like a machine tool or labor, that is needed to satisfy customer demand for a product. The class of items that are being described here, however, are differentiated in that they become, through the process of manufacturing, part of the physical product that the company eventually ships to customers. Other resources, which will be discussed in the next section, are used in the manufacturing process but do not become a physical part of the item being made.

Much of the PIC literature refers to the *item master file,* and this type of data entity can be found in most manufacturing databases. This is where the attributes that define an item can be found. When describing the attributes of an item, the first thing that usually comes to mind is an *item number,* or *part number.* The item number uniquely identifies the item. If the structure of the item, or its manufacturing process, changes in such a way as to alter its form, fit, or function, then another item number should be used. The other attributes of the item should always describe a unique item. For a particular part number, an attribute should have only one value at any time.

This is a good time to review the differences between basic data entities and relational entities that were discussed previously. The following lists a small sample of attributes usually associated with an item:

Item number

Item description

Engineering drawing number

Revision level

Unit of measure

Unit price

Unit cost

Item type (raw material, subassembly, etc.)

Replenishment source (manufactured, purchased)

Replenishment lead time

ABC classification code

Shrinkage factor

Standard lot size

If the manufacturing system is to be implemented for only one plant, with inventory being managed in a single warehouse, this type of data might be unique to each item number. In most situations, however, an item can be used and controlled at multiple locations within the company. A common assembly may be manufactured at two or more plants. Another part may be fabricated by one plant, sold by that location as a service part, and shipped to another plant where it is used as a component of a higher-level assembly. Items at one location may be sourced from multiple suppliers, including other plants within the enterprise.

Putting the "item" data shown above into a table such as Table 30.1 will help to show how this data may not be unique to the item number.

The item number in an integrated manufacturing system must represent the same item in every place it is used throughout the system. If the item is bought, built, stocked,

TABLE 30.1 Variation of Item Attributes

Attribute	Variation	
	Plant or warehouse	Revision
Item number		
Item description	X	
Engineering drawing number		X
Revision level	X	X
Unit of measure	X	
Unit price	X	X
Unit cost	X	X
Item type	X	X
Replenishment source	X	X
Replenishment lead time	X	X
ABC classification	X	X
Shrinkage factor	X	X
Standard lot size	X	X

or sold at multiple locations, much of the data about the item will probably be different at each location, as shown in the table. There are other qualifiers that could alter the data attributes of an item, such as a revision. A new revision of an item may not change the form, fit, or function, but it will usually have an effect on cost. Other attributes may change over time and need to be reflected showing an effective date.

Consider the lead time for items in Table 30.1. Even in an environment having one warehouse that is planned by MRP, an item may have more than one source, with significantly different lead times. Depending on how the MRP logic works, there may need to be a single planning lead time in the item number record, or the lead times may have to be reflected in a relationship record for each item and each replenishment source.

The critical factor in defining item data is how well the database can accommodate variations. If a person is developing a system from the ground up, the database should accommodate the definition of items for all locations and for all uses. In a commercial software package, the database design can be quite rigid, or it may have some flexibility. In any case, it should be capable of defining item data at a level that supports other applications. For example, a system with a single record for both item master level data and inventory balances will probably not support multiple warehouses.

The attributes required for each item will depend on the system's scope as to what specific item-related data are needed for other applications. This will be addressed further in the sections on building relationships. In general, the information should include item descriptive data and key elements related to the following:

Engineering

Production

Marketing and sales

Logistics and materials management

Accounting

"Invisible" Items

There may be a need to define items within the system that physically do not exist. In structuring bills of materials, an item number may be created for a *pseudoitem* that represents the parent in a planning bill of material. Such an item cannot physically be produced, but it has an item number and a record in the item file. An item number may exist for a nonstocked kit, that is, a group of parts that is used together or shipped with a product. In an assemble-to-order environment, an item may exist for the generic finished product, with the bill of material or other configuration mechanism specifying the features, options, or variants that may be part of a specific unit being ordered, built, or stocked. The configured item number only identifies the generic product. Additional data about the configuration will be needed to identify a specific physical unit.

Phantom items will also require an item number. In contrast to pseudoitems, phantoms physically exist. The phantom distinction is that it is usually built and used in the next level of manufacturing without being stocked and reissued. Planning items, kits, phantoms, and similar items need to be defined to support other applications in the system.

DEFINING MANUFACTURING RESOURCES

Two things are required to produce products: material and capacity. In this context, capacity is represented by resources that are used in manufacturing. The items that make up the product itself, or ship with the product—raw materials, parts, packaging materials, and so on—were dealt with separately.

These additional resources may be grouped into two broad categories: those that are usually inventoried and those that are not. Tooling is an example of a resource that is inventoried. A machining work center, on the other hand, is a resource that provides capacity but is not viewed as an "inventory item" (other than as a company asset that has to be maintained and accounted for). Resources that can be inventoried can sometimes be controlled by the same inventory management software that handles production materials inventories but treats resources as different types of items. The noninventoried resources are usually defined in separate files or as separate objects.

Consider the basic data requirements for several major resources: time, production facilities, people, location, and other support resources.

Time

Everything in a manufacturing system is eventually rooted to time! Even in the simplest MRP systems, everything starts with a date: a requirement date, a due date for a scheduled receipt, a shipment date promised to a customer. A major difference between production materials and capacity is that production materials are still available if not used, while capacity disappears with time. The machines or people may still be there, but there is no inventory of "old capacity" that can be used now.

The availability of resources, and therefore of capacity, is related to time. In manufacturing systems, time is typically defined by calendars. A single calendar may suffice in a small company to define which days are valid workdays for all business operations. More likely, the workdays will vary by facility or department. Within a calendar day, working hours and shifts will vary by resource. If manufacturing typically works a 6-day week but the receiving department works only 5 days, separate calendars may be required to ensure that production can be scheduled on Saturday, but materials needed for Saturday's production has to be received by Friday.

As the scope of the manufacturing system grows, more calendars may be required. Calendars identify days, but the availability of a resource may need to be defined in smaller increments that may vary by day. For example, a production calendar might exist for a work center that is operational 6 days per week. However, the work center works two shifts on weekdays and one shift on Saturdays. These variations in resource availability should be defined in the system, together with things like planned maintenance downtime.

Calendar data can be viewed as basic records support for manufacturing systems, whether single or multiple calendars are used. The definition of shifts and variable capacity will be considered as relationship records between calendars and specific resources.

Production Facilities

The smallest element of a production facility is usually an individual machine. In many of the commercial manufacturing software systems, and in earlier literature, groups of machines with similar capabilities, rates, tolerances, and so on can be grouped into *work centers*. The definition of production facilities has to be at a level that supports the scope of the manufacturing system. For example, the grouping of machines or people into work centers is usually adequate to support production activity reporting and capacity requirements planning. However, to really reap the benefits of *finite scheduling,* and other production optimization tools, data need to be defined for each individual resource to be scheduled. Even in this environment there remains a need to look at aggregate data. Overall work center capacity may still be needed for *capacity requirements planning* (CRP), but individual machine data must be available for finite scheduling. Efficiency, utilization, and queue statistics may be more useful at the work center level.

In a repetitive manufacturing environment, the *line* might be viewed as a single resource. Depending on the scope of the manufacturing system being implemented, this view may be adequate. To support reporting of production or yields at intermediate points in the line, however, the line may have to be broken down into a definition of workstations or reporting points.

People

Production personnel represent capacity. Whether or not individuals need to be defined in the manufacturing system depends on a number of factors. A labor-oriented work center that can be staffed with a varying number of employees depending on the schedule does not need to be broken down to define each individual and his or her work schedule. If an individual has a critical skill that is a frequent production bottleneck, however, it may be necessary to define the capacity at that level. A more common need for some minimal data about production people is to satisfy the accounting and control requirements of the system.

If the manufacturing system tracks actual costs of shop orders using employee pay rates and activities, that information will have to be available. If certain system activities can be initiated or performed only by specific employees, then employee IDs and passwords will have to be included. To facilitate labor distribution reports from production reports, a table of valid employee IDs will be needed.

Locations

Locations may be either physical or logical and organized into different hierarchies to support different business functions. A *physical location* might be an area identified by geographical coordinates, or it may be a carton on a pallet within a storage area on an aisle in a specific stockroom. A *logical location* usually represents a grouping of other locations so that data can be aggregated, a single point of control exercised, or common attributes can be shared. Using inventory locations as an example, it may be necessary to know specific locations where material is stored in the warehouse to support order picking. MRP will not usually need that level of location definition, but it will plan replenishment at the warehouse level. Purchasing needs to know only that a shipment should be delivered to a plant, but the plant warehousing system may need to know which locations are available to stock it when it is received.

In standard manufacturing software, location identifiers are often embedded in other records, like inventory balances. This can be restrictive as business processes change or if the system's scope needs to be extended. At a minimum, a table of factory locations should be available for editing.

Other Support Resources

Anything that needs to be planned, tracked, or managed within the scope of the manufacturing system needs to be defined in the database. This may include tooling, containers, special processing vessels, automated guided vehicles, and even utilities such as water or electricity. Although tooling inventory and control is a frequent requirement in

many environments, most of these resources are not accommodated in a basic manufacturing system, where the initial emphasis is placed more on production material and
work center capacities. Again, the scope of the implementation effort will determine
what resources need to be defined in the system and how they will be used.

Defining Trading Partners

Trading partners are those organizations with whom you do business. From a basic
manufacturing systems perspective, this includes customers and suppliers or vendors.
Trading partners can be internal or external organizational units, as discussed previously in the section on defining the organization. Most manufacturing systems software
supports a "customer master file" and a "vendor master file." Newer approaches may
have a "trading partner file." A supplier may often also be a customer. Another plant or
a distribution center within the enterprise may be a trading partner.

Basic trading partner records need to be defined for the lowest level at which the system will support business transactions. If the system scope includes shipping, for example, trading partner data has to be defined at the ship-to level. If the system includes
billing support and the trading partner is billed at a central location, that location also
has to be defined. For sales analysis purposes, a third level of trading partner relationship may be required. This is very similar to the definition of organizational units in that
a hierarchy of trading partner data can be defined through relationship records.

Constructing Ledgers

Integrated manufacturing systems usually provide fundamental support for the accounting functions. At a minimum, the inventory transactions should pick up an account identifier so that journals can be created, and ledgers updated properly. If shop activity
reporting is to be done directly through the manufacturing system, labor and other WIP
transactions should be created for cost accounting purposes and ledger posting. Account
numbers may be embedded in other basic data records for this purpose, but the chart of
accounts needs to be defined so that proper editing can take place.

Accounting systems often provide an excellent point for "decoupling" applications.
Even though the accounting functions are an integral part of a manufacturing enterprise,
the relationship between the production systems and the accounting systems can be
implemented primarily through transactions that flow between them. To accomplish
this, however, the manufacturing systems must include data elements and functional
capabilities that support the creation of accounting transactions that are accurate and
auditable. In an integrated system, this will reduce duplicate effort and the errors that
result from maintaining two sets of books.

BUILDING RELATIONSHIPS

Once the basic data entities have been defined, the relationships between those entities
can be constructed. In an integrated system, this is where the bulk of the enterprise data
will be found. Some of these relationships were discussed in the previous section, with
respect to the aggregation of basic records into groups or hierarchies. Those relationships tied together multiple records within the same set of basic entities. This section

will describe relationship entities that really broaden the enterprise's database to support manufacturing system functions.

Product and Process Definition

In the traditional fabrication and assembly manufacturing environment, the product and process data are generally separated into *bills of material* and *manufacturing routings*. Most of the manufacturing software available today maintains that separation, even though bills and routings have interrelationships that tie them together. For example, a component on the bill may specify the operation on the routing in which the component is used in the production process. Scrap statistics and operation yields from the routing can create additional component requirements over and above the "standard quantity per" in the bill of material.

Bills of Materials. The *product structure record* defines the relationship between two items, one the parent and the other a component. To avoid data redundancy and provide more flexibility, most commercial software uses this general approach of defining single-level bills of material within the database. In this way, a bill of material only needs to be defined once and can then be referenced wherever it is used. A multilevel view of an entire product structure can then be created starting at any point, as illustrated in Fig. 30.5.

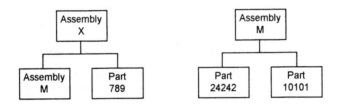

Connected to Form an Indented Bill of Material.....

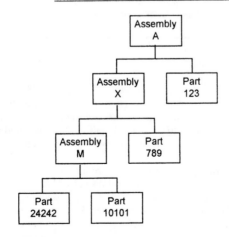

FIGURE 30.5   Single-level bills of materials.

TABLE 30.2   Commonly Used Attributes of Bills of Material

Bill of material attributes	Description
Parent item ID	Item number or identifier of the parent item.
Parent revision	Revision level of the parent item.
Component item ID	Item number or identifier of the component referred to in this relationship.
Reference designator	Sequence number, "find" number, "bubble" number, or other component reference when the component can be used multiple times on a bill.
Standard quantity per	The quantity of the component that is in a unit of the parent. This may also be defined in terms of the quantity per batch size of the parent, fixed quantities per order, etc.
Additional quantities	These specify the modifiers to the quantity per that are needed to actually manufacture the parent item. More of the component may be needed to account for yield loss, setup scrap, etc. This may also include updated averages from shop reporting in a yield-oriented environment.
Effectivities	This may include a "from date" and/or a "to date," a date based on projected inventory run out, a serial number, or other data reflecting when the component will be used.
Engineering-change number	The ECN associated with the implementation of this component in this bill.
Lead time adjustment	If this component is not needed at the beginning of production, an offset can be used to adjust requirement dates in the MRP and order release.
Option data	In a simple feature-option bill, data will be required such as codes, planning factors, etc., to facilitate construction and costing of specific bills for customer orders and manufacturing.

Other chapters in this handbook describe in detail the types of bills of material and how they can be structured. The emphasis here is on the data required to support the integration of the applications in a basic manufacturing system. The data attributes in the product structure relationship need to support all the functions included in the manufacturing system. Some of the more common types of data elements are shown in Table 30.2.

Different implementations of manufacturing software may or may not support all of these attributes or may associate them with other entities in the database. The data outlined in Table 30.2 provide a basis for analyzing the types of data required to define product structures for several manufacturing environments. In a company where yield loss is not a problem, some of this data will not be necessary. In a build-to-order business with complex product configuration rules, knowledge-based *configuration* software may be employed. Only common subassembly bills and configured bills will be included in the database.

Manufacturing Routings. Routings define the manufacturing steps used in building an item. The amount of routing data needed may range from very minimal to highly complex depending on the manufacturing system. Routings define relationships between items, manufacturing processes, and production resources. An item to be manufactured points to a routing that encompasses one or more operations. Each operation should specify the work center that performs the operation. It may also identify other resources required. Standard times for completing the operation are also included. Some statistics on actual times, such as smoothed averages for setup and run times, based on shop floor reporting, are often maintained in the routing records.

In many small-job shops, there are "standard operations" like milling or grinding that are used on many orders. The difference from order to order may be in, for example, the tolerances specified by the customer, the machine that needs to be used, or the estimated operation setup and run times. In these situations, since each item is built to order, there is no "item" to attach a routing to until an order is received and engineering work is done. The routings in this case are configured from the "standard operations," with changes being made to support the order specifications. This type of a routing can also be used for estimating and quoting delivery times and costs.

The level and amount of data in the routing needs to be adequate for all other functions within the manufacturing system, such as order scheduling, priority dispatching, cost accounting, and capacity planning. Table 30.3 highlights some of the key attributes of routing data.

Some of the software available to support process industries merges the bill of material and routing together to construct a model of the production process. This approach may more accurately reflect how an item is manufactured, even in the discrete manufacturing company. By focusing on the manufacturing process, it is easier to define all the inputs to and outputs from each operation. Manufacturing environments that deal with rework, remanufacturing, coproducts, and byproducts, for example, may find that a production model more closely resembles how they operate.

The example in Fig. 30.6 illustrates the basic concept of production models. The inputs to an operation or other defined process may be production items and other resources, and the outputs may consist of multiple things; the desired item to be produced, other usable items, waste that has to be controlled, or reusable resources. Even a traditional fabrication job shop can be modeled as shown. A metal-working shop may have NC machines programmed for the optimum cutting of sheets. The input to an operation may be a single metal sheet, with the output being the desired part together with other usable parts, and maybe some scrap. Figure 30.7 illustrates how a manufacturing bill of material and routing might be represented as a production model.

Defining the relationships between items, product structures, routings, work centers, and other resources, the database can become quite complex. The greater the extent and growth of the manufacturing system, the more data it requires. The future expansion of applications of the database need to be considered, even if they are not included in the initial implementation. In reviewing commercial manufacturing software offerings, the structure of the database should be analyzed carefully. Programming may be able to address many functional shortcomings, but only if the underlying data are organized in a way that it can be used or changed to accomplish the task.

TABLE 30.3 Key Attributes of Routing Data

Routing attributes	Description
Routing ID or item ID	An overall identification for the collection of operations that make up this routing. A "routing header" may exist that contains attributes that are not operation specific, such as a description, primary or alternate codes, and cumulative yields.
Operation sequence number	An identifier for each operation, typically numeric, that reflects the sequence in which the operations are usually performed.
Effectivity data	These data are used to include or exclude an operation based on dates or other criteria. In a feature-option environment, some operations may be common for all models and features, while others are used only for specific options.
Production facility ID	This specifies the department, line, or work center where the operation is performed, and it may also specify alternates.
Resources required	The specific resources that are required by the operation. This could include a specific machine, setup crew, labor skill, tool, or other defined resources.
Operation description	This should be a short description of the operation. Additional references could be made to drawings, procedure manuals, or multimedia aids such as film clips of setup procedures.
Setup times	These times can include the duration of setup for scheduling purposes, the standard setup labor and machine hours, and the average setup times.
Run times	These should include standards and averages for both machine and labor run times. There may need to be codes to denote how the rate is measured such as pieces per hour, hours per piece, hours per batch, or pieces per minute.
Move and wait times	Move time may be in the routing, or it could be in a matrix that defines all move times between any two work centers or other locations. Wait time is usually associated with the operation, as it reflects how long material will wait to be moved after it is completed at the operation.
Yields	Standard and average yields can be kept for each operation. Cumulative yields for a finished product can then be calculated from these values and requirements for components adjusted based on where they are introduced in the routing and how much upstream yield loss is expected. This is also important in costing.
Overlap factors	If operations are planned to overlap, as in a flow or repetitive environment, data elements are required to define when this operation can begin its setup or run time relative to the previous operation's setup or run. There may be several alternatives such as after so many pieces have been completed at the previous operation or after a fixed amount of time. There needs to be rules defined as to which portions of an operation, setup and/or run time, can be overlapped on the portions of the previous operation.

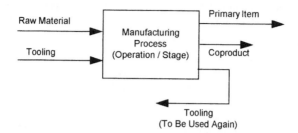

FIGURE 30.6   Production model example.

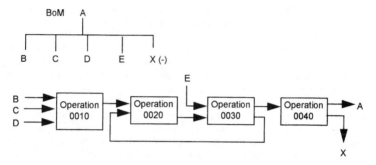

FIGURE 30.7   Bill of material and routing combined into a production model.

INVENTORY ASSETS

Inventory information is so fundamental to the operation of a manufacturing system that it could almost be considered as "basic records." In reality, inventory data define the relationship between an item and its physical existence at a particular location. The level of detail of the data required depends on the system functions to be supported. For example, material requirements planning may need to know only the total inventory of an item within a warehouse, but inventory management may need to know the individual bin locations when the shop order is released for efficient materials picking. In a contract-oriented environment, costs may have to be carried at the inventory lot level, although this is not required to support master scheduling.

Inventory needs to be defined at the lowest level required to satisfy all functions within the system scope. This should be viewed in conjunction with the definition of inventory locations. The lowest level of inventory that needs to be defined to the manufacturing system is a single unit of an item. This situation is usually found in a factory where each unit has a unique serial number and has to be tracked and accounted for by that identifier throughout the system. This is different than an item number. The item number merely identifies what the thing is. The serial number is associated with a specific physical unit.

Other item characteristics that will determine the level at which inventory should be defined can include the following:

- Revision level
- Configuration identifier
- Batch/lot identifier
- Potency
- Country of origin
- Condition (new, equivalent to new, reconditioned, etc.)

These are just a few of the *characteristics* that can be used to further identify an item in inventory. These and others are usually applicable to specific industries or types of manufacturing environments. The primary consideration is whether or not inventory items have to be identified by any of these characteristics to segregate and control inventory. Also, the characteristics may be used to control the logic in other functions of the system. Serial numbers are not necessary for finished goods if only recorded as order data when shipped to a customer. On the other hand, if lot tracking is required by a regulatory agency, inventory quantities will have to be identified by a batch-lot ID and perhaps segregated by stock locations. As a general rule, all inventory items must be identified for allocating, storing, moving, controlling, and using.

Low level identifiers can be organized into higher levels for system functions or reporting. To enhance system performance, the database may have to support both detail and summary inventory records. For example, the MRP function does not have to review every inventory location record, nor should it. Even though the item's availability data required by the MRP could be derived in this manner, it is usually maintained in some summary form that makes the MRP more efficient. An example of this kind of inventory hierarchy is illustrated in Fig. 30.8.

The types of inventory attributes maintained in inventory records are shown in Table 30.4. In the actual implementation of the manufacturing system, the level at which these attributes are defined in the database depends on the system functions being supported and on the level of summarization.

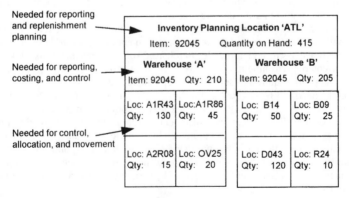

FIGURE 30.8   Summarizing inventory data.

TABLE 30.4 Types of Inventory Attributes

Inventory attributes	Description
Item number	The unique identifier of the item
Location	The physical or logical location of this inventory. This may range from a specific bin or stockroom location to a logical grouping of inventory into a summary location to address other needs.
Characteristics	These include any inventory *qualifiers* that further define this specific inventory—i.e., serial number, lot ID, etc.
Material review board status	Indication of material availability. This might include available for use, on QA hold, to be scrapped, etc.
Quantity on hand	The quantity of this item, with these characteristics, stored at this location.
Unit of measure	This could vary by location, with "cases" being carried in a bulk store area and individual units at a floor location. In some process industries, *catchweight* quantities may also be required.
Allocation quantities	This represents the quantities reserved (allocated) to specific demands. These might be maintained separately for customer orders, shop orders, etc.
Unit cost	This is the actual unit cost of this inventory.
FIFO date	The date the material was first placed into inventory. This is used to determine expiration dates when the material has to be retested, reassayed, or disposed of and to control usage in FIFO sequence.
Expiration date and/or days	These are used to determine when this inventory needs to be evaluated for further use or disposition.
Physical count data	These may include the date this location was last counted, the date for the next count, cutoff quantities, ID of the person who made the count, etc.

INVENTORY MANAGEMENT PARAMETERS

As discussed previously in the section on basic item data, there are many attributes that may pertain to an *item number* but vary based on how the item is planned and controlled at different locations. Planning factors, historical usage summaries, and replenishment parameters are some examples of this kind of data.

Items are needed to satisfy demands from customers, distribution centers, other plants within the enterprise, manufacturing, and others. This demand may be satisfied by either current or planned production or from existing inventory at some location. When inventory is stocked for expected demand, data must be accessible on how much inventory is on hand, how much is ordered, and when replenishment is needed and from where it can be retrieved. For MRP's planning purposes, these data are usually maintained for some aggregate level of inventory, like a warehouse, rather than for individual stocking locations. In a just-in-time environment, however, this type of data may also be associated with individual locations where replenishment is controlled using kanbans. Other data may be required to support usage analysis. As shown in Fig. 30.8, the definition of *location* for inventory management purposes may vary to address different purposes.

Some of these parameters, like lead times, will vary not just by the location of the item but by other factors such as the replenishment source. The database needs to accommodate this level of data definition. Some of the more common types of inventory management attributes are shown in Table 30.5.

TABLE 30.5   Inventory Control Attributes

Inventory control attributes	Description
Item number	The unique identifier of the item.
Location	The physical or logical location. This could be a specific line stock location in a JIT environment or a group of warehouses planned together by MRP.
Manufacturing lead times	These may include a single planning lead time, or they may be broken down into fixed and variable portions of lead time. These attributes could vary by production line or routing. Average lead times should also be maintained.
Purchase lead times	These can include shipment times, import-export times, dock-to-stock time, and other elements of the lead time for an outside supplier. Both planning and average actual times should be maintained.
Safety lead time	Safety lead time can be applied to cushion against variability in vendor lead time.
Unit costs	Costs may be specified at a summary level if not needed by lot. The summary level might be a warehouse or plant. This is generally where standard or average costs are maintained in a multisite environment.
Replenishment method	This identifies the approach used to plan and/or trigger replenishment, such as order point/order quantity, min/max, fixed quantity, periods of supply, and part period balancing.
Replenishment quantities	This includes order quantities, order-up-to levels, or other parameters to support the replenishment method being used for the item.
Order modifiers	When orders are planned, these parameters are used to adjust the order quantity to account for minimum run or order sizes, maximums, and multiple quantities.
Safety-stock quantity	This should be maintained at the "location" level where safety stock is carried. This might be a warehouse, plant, or centralized distribution center.
Usage summaries	Period and year-to-date data on the usage of the item (sales, issues, adjustments, etc.) are often maintained at a summary level. This can be in both units and currency. These data can be derived from inventory transaction history also.

In an integrated manufacturing system, there are literally hundreds of data elements that apply to the management and replenishment of inventoried items. Many of these attributes are control elements specific to the operation of the software or that support functional aspects unique to the implementation. The determination of what data are required and where they need to be maintained in the database should be based on the extent of the system.

Item Demands

Even the most basic inventory system must be able to inform users of how much inventory is actually available for a specific purpose. There may be a quantity of an item on hand, but some of it may already have been "promised" to customers or to manufacturing. To determine true inventory "availability," one needs to know what is on hand, what is needed (demands or requirements), and what is expected to be received. A simple inventory control application may have just enough data available to maintain the quantity on hand, the total quantity reserved for customers and manufacturing, and the total quantity expected to be received from manufacturing or on purchase orders. This system would be considered quite primitive in today's manufacturing environment. However, it helps to illustrate the additional information required by a full-function planning and control system, where time-phased records of demand and supply are needed to support master scheduling, MRP and the like. Again, the amount of data required and its detail will depend on the scope of the system being implemented.

Other chapters of this book have dealt with *independent* versus *dependent demand* and have explored planning and forecasting application areas in detail. The objective here is to define what specific data are required when integrating these applications, and where that data should be defined. For this section, demand will be split into four basic categories: forecasts, customer orders, dependent demands, and materials allocations.

Forecasts

Whether or not a formal forecasting procedure is within the scope of a manufacturing system, some estimate of demand is usually required to do an effective job of production planning, master scheduling, or materials requirements planning. Even in an engineer-to-order environment, the need to plan requirements for capacity, critical materials, or other resources calls for some level of forecasting of future demands. Some type of forecasting system may already be in use within the organization, or it may be included in the current implementation.

In this discussion, it is assumed that the forecast is based on past demand. Understanding what the forecast really represents is the key to the successful integration of a forecasting module and how it can be used for other applications. Figure 30.9 illustrates a *time line* of a customer order, showing key points of activity. If forecasting is really intended to forecast item *demand,* the historical data used by forecasting should reflect *how many the customer wants* and *when the customer wants them.* If the customer wants 100 units by a certain date but only 75 can be shipped, what is being measured as demand: 100 units or 75 units? The same challenge exists with dates. The customer may have requested delivery of the item on one date, the true date of demand, but then accepted a delivery date 2 weeks later. These data need to be captured when the customer order is being initially negotiated and entered into the system. If forecasts are generated based on adjustments to the customer's original demand date and quantity, error is introduced at the beginning.

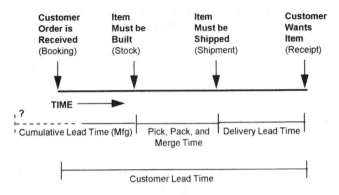

FIGURE 30.9   Demand forecast time points.

Historical "demand" data may actually represent *bookings* or *shipments*. When the customer order is received, it is considered a booking. Sales personnel are vitally interested in forecasting bookings, as are the financial executives. Bookings reflect additions to backlog. From a manufacturing perspective, bookings reflect future workload and are therefore of considerable concern. In a make-to-order environment, the backlog will translate to customer lead time. This is important information, but it will usually not support effective manufacturing planning.

For sales and operations planning, production planning, and master scheduling, the forecast should be based on the demand, the customer's original quantity ordered, and the date wanted. This information is reflected by the right margin of Fig. 30.9. When offset by delivery lead time, the date the item needs to be shipped from the producing location can be determined. Backing off still further, by the time needed to prepare the item for shipping, the forecast can determine when the item needs to be in stock or completed by manufacturing. Therefore, if the customer specifies a receiving date or a shipping date from the plant or distribution center, other key dates can be calculated by applying the appropriate lead times. Most planning systems are oriented toward either shipping dates or manufacturing completion dates. The demand forecasts used need to be expressed in the same manner.

The basic data required consists of an item number, location (if forecast at a location level), forecast period, and forecast quantity. Additional data may be maintained that track actual demand and calculate the "unconsumed" portion of the forecast. The forecasting system itself may be quite sophisticated, supporting different forecasting models and tools. Detailed forecasts may be developed for geographical areas, sales organizations, miscellaneous sources of demand, or other levels of detail or aggregation.

In the final analysis, what a forecasting system needs is to present to the manufacturing planning systems the best guess of what quantity of an item needs to be available to satisfy customer demands in each forecast period.

Customer Orders

The extent of a manufacturing system's implementation may include customer order management, or at least interfaces with an existing customer order application. This section does not address the functioning of such an application, but it does highlight the key data elements required for other manufacturing planning and control applications.

Customer order data serve as a basis for forecasting and are used for planning. They create reservations of inventory and drive production control in the make-to-order environment. Customer orders represent the origins of demand, and the information associated with them is used throughout an enterprise, from the manufacturing systems to the accounting applications.

The customer order attributes shown in Table 30.6 represent only a small part of the information included in an order. These attributes are generally required to support the manufacturing planning and control applications? Customer order data can have a variety of relationships. The order itself associates the trading partner (customer) with the organization unit of the enterprise that took the order. A critical relationship exists between the customer and the organization unit that will be shipping or manufacturing the item and who will maintain the data about the order status.

Booked customer orders should be used to reduce the forecast for planning purposes. Although there are several techniques that can be employed, the objective is to determine the projected level of demand for an item for each forecast period. As customer orders are booked, they should reduce the forecast for the period in which they are scheduled to be completed by manufacturing or shipped (depending on whether the

TABLE 30.6   Customer Order Data Required by Manufacturing

Customer order attributes	Description
Customer identifiers	This should include the trading partner's ordering location and ship-to location.
Order identifier	This provides a link to the customer order and can be used as a reference for "demand pegging."
Line number	This identifies the specific line on the order for this item.
Item number	This identifies the product being ordered.
Item characteristics	If customers can order an item with specific characteristics, those need to be identified. Examples like configuration ID, lot number, and new versus reconditioned were discussed in the section on inventory.
Quantity requested	The original quantity requested by the customer.
Requested date	The original delivery or ship date requested by the customer.
Quantity promised	The quantity that is currently booked.
Unit of measure	The customer's ordering unit of measure.
Date promised	This should include the scheduled ship date and may also contain the customer's promised "dock" date. These may differ from what the customer requested based on available-to-promise or other factors.
Supplying location	This identifies the organization unit of the enterprise that will build or ship the item.
Quantities shipped	This may be just a running total, or it may include period and to-date shipments.
Quantities backordered	If the trading partner accepts backorders for the item, this should reflect the quantity that cannot be shipped on the promise date.

forecast is aligned to stock dates or shipments). The unconsumed forecast quantity plus the actual customer order quantities in a period reflect the expected total demand for the period.

Dependent Demands

Forecasts and customer orders, as described above, represent *independent demands* on the manufacturing planning and control system. Whether the demand comes from outside the enterprise or from other locations within the enterprise, the assumption is that it cannot be calculated exactly by the system. *Dependent-demand item* requirements can be calculated from bills of materials or other network relationships. For example, material requirements planning uses the production demands for end items, as expressed in a master schedule, to generate the demand (requirements) for all lower-level subassemblies, parts, and raw materials needed.

From a manufacturing systems perspective, there are several types, or "stages," of dependent demand:

Gross Requirements.   This is the total quantity of an item that is required at a specific time. For MRP purposes, this quantity is usually expressed as a day, but it might also be expressed as a period.

Net Requirements.   This represents that portion of demand that cannot be satisfied by existing inventory or current scheduled receipts into inventory. It will have to be met by internal production or outside sources.

Planned Orders.   Net requirements may be *lot sized* to balance the ordering or setup costs with the costs of carrying inventory or to accommodate other factors such as container sizes. The parameters shown in Table 30.5 are used for this purpose. Planned orders become gross requirements (demands) for the components of the item if it is a manufactured product. If the item is procured from an outside source, the planned orders become requirements on the supplier.

Firm Planned Orders.   These are planned orders that are under the control of the planner, and they will not be rescheduled or changed automatically by MRP. The planner may want to "firm" a planned order's start or due date or its order quantity. Perhaps a change in the bill of material or routing needs to be specified. Within the "near-term" portion of the planning horizon, the firm planned order can be used to stabilize the schedule and reduce system "nervousness."

Dependent-demand records are typically generated by the manufacturing planning systems. The amount of data associated with these records depends on the function of the system. In its simplest application, MRP generates requirements records with an item number, due date, and quantity. If the requirements for multiple sites are being planned, the location needs to be included. To support *full pegging,* the source and quantity of each demand has to be kept separate through all levels of generation. When a planned order is created, the start date is added. If specific configuration data are required or if an alternate routing or process is to be used, pointers to these records must be included.

Material Allocations

Forecasts, actual customer orders, and manufacturing orders represent demand for inventory. The actual removal of inventory will take place when customer orders are *picked* or when material is issued to manufacturing. To help ensure that material is available when needed, inventory may be *allocated* to a customer order, manufacturing order, or production schedule. Usually these allocations are done at the latest possible moment so that inventory is not tied up unnecessarily. In some environments, inventory is allocated to a production location where it can be used to satisfy multiple-line schedules for multiple products or orders.

Material allocation records associate the inventory of an item at a particular location with the actual demand for the item dictated by a customer's order or a manufacturing order. Data in these records identify the quantity of the item that has been allocated and the location from which the material will be supplied and the order, schedule, or location to which it is allocated. When the inventory is issued on the order or schedule, the on-hand balance is reduced, and the allocation is reduced correspondingly.

Allocations may be made against inventory at a high level, such as the warehouse or stockroom, when any physical unit can satisfy the requirement. In some environments *discrete allocations* may be required. For example, the same chemical may have a different potency from lot to lot. The planning system may not be able to plan for the level of potency, so when the chemical is required in the production of some compound, a minimum potency may be ordered, or the required quantity may vary based on the potency. In a situation such as this, the characteristics of on-hand inventory may have to be reviewed and allocations done at the physical lot/location level.

ITEM SUPPLY

Demand and supply can be viewed as two perspectives of a single data entity in many manufacturing relationships. For example, in the previous discussion of dependent demands, a planned order generated by MRP becomes a demand for its components. It also represents a supply of the item itself. A purchase order for an item can be viewed as a demand on the supplier but also as a scheduled receipt (supply) by the ordering location.

Demand for an item may be satisfied by one or more supply sources. The source may be existing inventory, internal production, or an outside supplier. The "outside supplier" may be another location within the same company, whether or not it is incorporated into the same manufacturing system. The sources used to satisfy the demand for an item at a particular location need to be specified by parameters and rules within the manufacturing planning and control system. Some of these were discussed earlier.

In supply-chain management, the entire logistics network can be defined, from the customer end of the distribution network back through that network and all the manufacturing facilities to the suppliers. This macroview is illustrated in Fig. 30.10.

If the manufacturing system is to include *distribution requirements planning* (DRP) or even multisite MRP, then the network of materials flow from site to site has to be defined. Sourcing is usually specified for each item by planning site, as illustrated in Fig. 30.8. The planning site is a "location" that is considered as a single unit for DRP or MRP purposes, where demand, inventory, and supply are summarized. A distribution center, warehouse, or plant are examples of planning sites. An item might be assembled in one plant and used as a component in a final assembly at another plant. To support multisite planning, the system has to know that the item needs to be planned as a component at the final-assembly site before it can be planned in the item's producing location. The planned orders for the item in the final-assembly site will become gross requirements for the item at the producing site.

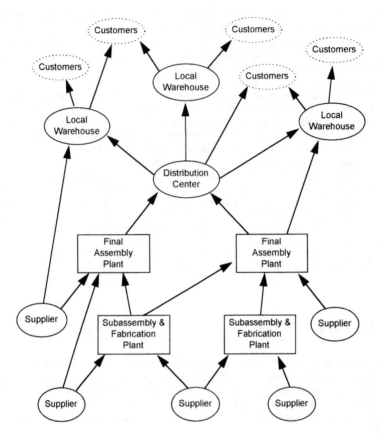

FIGURE 30.10 Materials flow through the logistics pipeline.

The sourcing of an item may be defined somewhat differently from an execution standpoint. Planning systems create a series of planned replenishments over the *planning horizon*. The actual triggering of materials movement may be based on the recommended start dates created by those systems or by other methods that more closely conform to a just-in-time procedure. Materials can be "pulled" to the location where they are required when actually needed. This may be done using manual requests, kanbans, or electronic signals for replenishment. A supplier may make frequent deliveries to keep a production line location stocked to a certain level. Order points may be used to trigger materials replenishment within the requirements established by MRP.

Figure 30.11 gives a microview from an execution systems perspective. Plant 1 in the figure is a planning entity for MRP. Items X, Y, and Z are planned by MRP, considering their entire inventory situation at plant 1. The output of MRP is sent to suppliers A, B, and C for their use in planning. At this point, planning can be separated from execution.

Item X is stocked at assembly line 1 only when production schedules require it, and then only in small quantities. Although the schedules on assembly line 1 might call for 200 units of item X, no more than 3 containers of item X, with 25 units per container, may be on the line at any time. When the stock of item X at assembly line 1 is down to 1

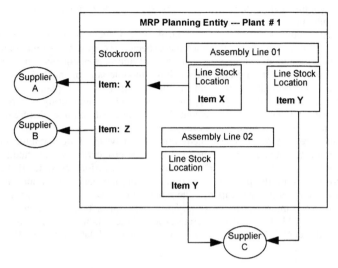

FIGURE 30.11   Material pulls versus planned replenishment.

container, a *pull signal* is sent to the stockroom to replenish the line with up to 2 more containers, as long as there are still unsatisfied requirements for the remaining schedules.

Item X may be stored at several locations within the stockroom. From a replenishment standpoint, however, the stockroom balance is considered as one location. The replenishment of item X in the stockroom is triggered by another order point. When the balance in the stockroom reaches that point, a pull signal is sent to supplier A to ship more of item X to plant 1's stockroom. Supplier A was made aware of this potential order earlier by the MRP output provided by plant 1. The pull signal is the supplier's authorization to ship the material.

Item Y is not stocked in the stockroom but at locations on assembly lines 01 and 02, where it is used as a common component in nearly every product made on those lines. MRP provides a forecast of demand for item Y on supplier C for all locations in plant 1. Supplier C is local and runs a truck over every production day to plant 1 where the line locations of item Y are restocked up to a specified level.

Item Z is stocked only in the stockroom and is issued directly to production orders as they are released to manufacturing. MRP plans orders for item Z and calculates a release date based on supplier B's quoted lead time. These planned orders are sent to supplier B each time MRP is run. Supplier B is authorized to ship item Z to plant 1 if the release date is within a 2-day horizon.

The example does not show all the possibilities for triggering replenishment, but it does help to illustrate how material replenishment can be planned at one level of aggregation and executed at a lower level using different mechanisms to trigger the physical movement of goods. Demand for the items manufactured in plant 1 may trigger the start of production on a line. Whether the "pull" is a signal to move material from another inventory location, from a supplier, or to start production, the separation of replenishment planning and execution can help a company move toward a JIT operation. Planning systems help ensure that the materials will be available at the supplying location when the pull is received.

Inventory locations were illustrated and discussed previously. The examples show how the definition of locations will vary based on what functions the system is meant to support. Replenishment parameters need to be specified at the appropriate level to facilitate both planning and execution.

The manufacturing planning and control system needs to have some minimum amount of information available about the expected receipts. If a shop floor control application is included in the system, it will provide data about open manufacturing orders and schedules. If a purchasing-receiving module is implemented, it should furnish data about expected receipts from suppliers or other plants. If planning systems are included, they will use the inventory, purchasing, and manufacturing data to generate planned replenishments. All of these contribute to the construction of different views of available inventory, in a time-phased sequence.

Scheduled receipt data describe the relationship between an item at a location and a supplier. For a manufactured item, the supplier is the production facility, and the scheduled receipt is typically a manufacturing order or production schedule. If the item is ordered from outside the planning function, the supplier may be another company or another location within the company. The scheduled receipt is usually represented by a purchase order or interplant order, or a *calloff* on a contract. As mentioned in the section on demands, MRP will also generate expected receipts in the form of planned and firm planned orders. Table 30.7 shows the key elements of data pertaining to scheduled receipts.

TABLE 30.7 Key Data Elements for Expected Receipts

Scheduled receipt attributes	Description
"Order" identifier	This should identify a unique entity such as a manufacturing order, purchase order or blanket release, or production schedule. This may be further qualified by line numbers on POs, etc.
Source	This should identify the supplier, be it another company, another unit of the enterprise, or internal production.
Item number	This identifies the item that is expected to be received.
Item characteristics	If items are ordered with specific characteristics, they need to be specified. Color, voltage, potency, new versus used, and revision level are some examples.
Item location	The inventory location that will receive this replenishment. This should be expressed at the lowest known level and extended to higher levels, or derived, for other functions.
Quantities	This should include the original requested quantity, the current promised quantity, quantity received to date in this period, and quantities returned and rejected.
Units of measure	The units in which the item will be received and counted. Multiple UMs may be specified and may be necessary in environments, e.g., catchweight.
Dates	These should include the date the order or schedule or pull was released, the original requested ship and/or delivery date, the promised delivery date, date of last receipt, and any other relevant dates.
References	This may include pointers to other data entities in the system. Examples might be the buyer or planner, the supplier contact, the catalog number, or drawing number.
Costs	Quoted or standard costs may be needed to support accounting functions.

In summary, demand can be satisfied by supplying items from inventory, production, or outside suppliers. The objective is to use the company's resources effectively and to meet demand better than the competition with respect to cost, quality, and delivery. Planning applications assist the company in projecting future needs for materials and other resources. Operational activities help to meet the objectives set by planning. A time-phased view of requirements and the materials and capacity available are major assets for a manufacturer. Inventory status, demand data, and information about expected receipts are integral parts of maintaining that view.

BUILDING A FIRM FOUNDATION

Data modeling can certainly help in determining from where business data come, how they are interrelated, and how they should be implemented in a database. But these tools and methods are not panaceas, and they still require a lot of work on the part of the business experts and analysts. Avoid the trap of getting locked into a never-ending analysis and modeling project. Also, the objective of *normalizing* the data to eliminate redundancy in the database can be pursued too far. This can cause excessive time being taken to complete the modeling effort and often results in system performance problems. In the end, all the data used by a business are related in some manner. Trying to discover and model all the relationships is outside the scope of most systems projects and will begin to produce diminishing returns.

Business process modeling and data modeling projects should precede major manufacturing systems implementation projects. Business simplification and reengineering can lead to reduced automation efforts. The extent of the modeling effort has to be well defined, as does the manufacturing system. Small projects are easier to manage, have shorter completion lead times, and have a higher chance of success. Whether it's a modeling project or a systems implementation, there should be some understanding of the relationships to data, processes, and systems outside the current project.

It may be relatively easy to have one group build a foundation for a house in one city, another group build a second floor bedroom in another city, a third group build a bathroom somewhere else, and so forth, but if everyone is working from a different set of plans and assumptions, there is little chance that the whole thing will ever come together as a house, much less a home!

MAINTAINING AN OPERATIONAL SYSTEM

Once the scope of the manufacturing system has been defined, equipment selection made, and appropriate software purchased or developed, the implementation begins. The installation of the hardware and manufacturing planning and control software is just the beginning. The database must be built or initialized and then maintained as events take place and business transactions are processed.

Building the Database

Certain elements of information are required by the system at the outset of operations. Obviously there is a need for the key attributes associated with basic records and many relationships. The question is where those data come from and how it gets into the database. If current systems are being replaced, much of the data may already exist in a database or files. Although it may not be a compatible system, much of the data can be moved or converted to the new system.

Existing data in the interfacing systems may be duplicated in the new system, although this data should have been identified during the modeling and analysis efforts. In some cases, the new system may be able to access and use the existing data, without having to replicate it in the new database. For example, there may be a customer file that is being used by an accounts receivable application. That file could be incorporated into the new database and perhaps expanded to include support for a customer order management module. The alternative is to maintain two or more sets of the same data, and that requires database synchronization programs to ensure that changes are made to all redundant data. Systems developed using object-oriented techniques or built on a comprehensive data model may help to dampen the negative impacts of these situations, but the older database may not necessarily be accessible by the newer system.

A third method of building the database is to use the old-fashioned data entry system, keying the data into the system. As part of the data modeling or database analysis process, forms can be designed to facilitate data entry. These might be paper forms or on-line templates. Commercially available manufacturing packages usually include both off-line and on-line maintenance support for the "master" files or major parts of the system. A method to expedite manual entry is the creative use of *mass maintenance capabilities.* For example, items can be coded in groups, as in the ABC classification system. Then a set of values can be developed for other attributes that are consistent for any items in the same group. A fairly common approach in client-server implementations is to select a subset of items by one or more attributes and then update other attributes of the selected items with a common set of values.

A *same-as-except capability* can help to support the creation of bills of material and routings by copying an existing set of records and then changing only those parameters that are different. Inventory data can be entered when cycle counting groups of items. Information from existing customer orders, manufacturing orders, and purchase or interplant orders may all have to be put into the system to support MRP or other planning or inventory functions. This process can be used as a training vehicle, by having the users actually create the orders on the system, release them, and then post the transactions to bring the orders up to their current status.

If order data or other basic records are not needed at system startup, then a phased approach to building the database may be acceptable. Items, bills, routings, and other records need be created only when they are first used. For example, work-in-process continues to be handled by the current methods; only new manufacturing orders are released and managed under the new system. There can be major drawbacks to this method, however. Dual systems have to be maintained and used, which can be quite confusing. In addition, inventory positions, cost data, or other data reported by the system may be incomplete and misleading until all relevant data are in the database.

Processing Transactions

The database, once established, will be maintained in two basic ways: directly updating records and transaction processing. The *direct update method* can be a combination of on-line interactive maintenance of records, direct updates that are triggered by other system or database events, or off-line maintenance programs that add, change, or delete records in a batch mode. *Transaction processing,* from a business perspective, is generally associated with the recording of some activity that causes records to be created or updated.

As an example, the basic records for items may be initially created through a conversion program from another system, using an off-line approach. As new items are created, they are put into the system interactively through a workstation. If an existing item's description is to be changed, it might also be updated directly through a workstation. Inventory data for the item could be entered initially in the same way, but after the inventory system becomes operational, things change. The inventory balance data from that point onward should be updated only by transactions—issues, sales, receipts, physical count adjustments, and so on. No one should be allowed to go into the database and directly change the inventory balance. Transactions provide control and audit trails.

When implementing and integrating manufacturing systems, the transactions used to support business processes need to be defined. If a component item is issued from the stockroom for a manufacturing order, there may be many updates that have to be made as a result of that transaction. First, the on-hand balance of the item at the location from which it was issued has to be reduced. If *allocations* were made, those have to be reduced also. The manufacturing order records should be updated to show the quantity issued. If interfacing with accounting systems, a whole new transaction needs to be created to reflect the movement of materials from an inventory account to a WIP account. The issue quantity may have to be added to an *issue-this-period* or *to-date-issues bucket* for use by other functions. The transaction itself may have to be written to another file for historical or auditing purposes. What started out as a reduction in stock may have ended up having a ripple effect across the manufacturing system and even into interfacing systems.

It is these types of transactions, this reporting of activity, together with the ongoing maintenance of the database, that keeps the system alive. If updates are not made correctly, if transactions are not entered accurately and on a timely basis, the database will become inaccurate. Inaccurate information will be presented, support invalid conclusions, and lead to bad business decisions.

Interfacing with Other Systems

Integrating new technology and new applications with existing systems is becoming easier over time, but it still poses major challenges. As mentioned previously, the use of open systems, and software development tools and methods, will facilitate the interaction and integration of different databases and functional applications. The typical problem at this time is how to get *legacy systems* to talk to new systems.

Legacy systems includes those old workhorses that were implemented previously but are still performing the task in an acceptable manner. The documentation, if there was any, may have disappeared. The original designers and development people are "gone." These systems are not necessarily the same as corporate systems that must be used throughout the enterprise, although the interface challenges are similar.

The scope of a new manufacturing system to be implemented may include replacing some or none of the functions of the older systems. Most likely, there will have to be communications between them. When feasible and logical, the new system should integrate with the legacy systems. This can help in gaining user acceptance and reducing data duplication and can result in less effort needed for maintenance and operation. *Integration* in this sense means sharing common database records and having the two systems interact in a program-to-program fashion.

If a legacy system cannot be integrated into the new manufacturing system, then interfaces may be required. Programs need to be written to pass data or transactions back and forth. Data may have to be reformatted to be acceptable to the receiving system. The interface may be either one way or bidirectional. Transactions and database updates should be supported by some type of synchronization mechanism to ensure that records are updated on both systems.

SUMMARY

The integration of the various pieces of a basic manufacturing planning and control system is like the formation of an orchestra. Do you want to perform great symphonies or arrangements suitable for a small ensemble? What kind of sound is desired? What is the prospective audience clamoring for? Do you want to augment the orchestra with extra instruments that may be needed only infrequently? How big is the concert hall?

The objectives have to be established early in the cycle. The scope has to be clearly defined and adhered to, but the outlying business processes and their interactions with the proposed system cannot be ignored. All of the pieces have to come together to produce the desired results; the instruments (hardware), the score (software), the musicians (developers and analysts), the conductor (project management), and the audience (users).

BIBLIOGRAPHY

Clement, Jerry, Andy Coldrick, and John Sari: *Manufacturing Data Structures: Building Foundations for Excellence with Bills of Materials and Process Information,* Oliver Wight Limited Publications, Inc., Essex Junction, Vt., 1992.

Fogarty, Donald W., John H. Blackstone, Jr., and Thomas R. Hoffman: *Production & Inventory Management,* 2d ed., South-Western Publishing Co., Cincinnati, Ohio, 1991.

Greene, James H. (editor in chief): *Production and Inventory Control Handbook,* 2d ed., McGraw-Hill Book Company, New York, 1987.

Rumbaugh, James, Michael Blaha, William Premerlani, Frederick Eddy, and William Lorensen: *Object-Oriented Modeling and Design,* Prentice-Hall, Englewood Cliffs, N.J., 1991.

CHAPTER 31
BAR CODE: AUTOMATING DATA COLLECTION

Editors

Kimberly Lombard
Public Relations Manager
Intermec Corporation, Everett, Washington

David Hunting
Freelance Technical Writer
Everett, Washington

Of all the modern production and inventory control technologies, bar code is perhaps the most common. It is found everywhere. It has been used in industries around the world for more than 25 years, and its uses in business continue to expand, evolve, and extend beyond the early implementations. While many people have grown familiar with bar code through everyday experience at the supermarket checkout counter or the public library, professionals have quickly come to value the technology for its significant contributions to increased productivity across a broad spectrum of industrial applications (Fig. 31.1).

Wherever we need to count, sort, pick, pack, trace, track, or locate a wide variety of items, bar code is there to expedite the transactions. By reducing the cost of data collection and increasing the amount of accurate, real-time information available for decision making, bar code directly contributes to increased profitability. In fact, automated data collection with bar code can be used to drive and control many industrial processes more profitably simply because it can handle large quantities of data faster and more reliably than people can.

But what, exactly, is bar code? How does it work? And how can we make sure

FIGURE 31.1 Application of bar coding. (*Illustrations courtesy of Intermec Corporation, Everett, Washington.*)

we use it most effectively? This chapter will take a closer look at the primary components of a bar-code data collection system, how the system is applied to the production and inventory control processes, and some of the key considerations for planning and implementing bar-code data collection technology at your site.

WHAT IS BAR CODE?

Simply put, *bar code* is an extremely reliable and cost-effective way to automate the data collection process. We collect data for many reasons in industry, from managing receiving and shipping, to work-in-process, and finished-goods inventories, from controlling work flow, quality, and mechanical processes, to cost accounting, labor tracking, scheduling, and resource planning.

A *bar-code symbol* consists of alternating parallel lines and spaces of varying widths that contain data. It is printed, either directly or on labels or tags, by a variety of economical printing technologies. And it is optically *scanned* and *electronically decoded*

FIGURE 31.2 Rapid scanning.

by a variety of fixed and/or portable *readers,* devices that have been adapted for a seemingly infinite number of industrial applications.

Some people like to think of bar code as a printed version of the Morse code with narrow bars representing dots and wide bars representing dashes. The code is read with a scanning device that moves across the symbol from one side to the other detecting the sequence of wide and narrow bars and translating the pattern into digital electronic form for processing by a computer (Fig. 31.2). In most cases the scanning activity happens so quickly that data capture can be considered a single-entry event even though the data captured may represent a string of alphanumeric characters equivalent to a "word" or "phrase."

In most industrial applications, the data included in bar code act to identify an item in much the same way as the letters and numbers on a license plate identify a vehicle on the road. Together with a database of information about the individual identifiers or "license plates," systems can be built to track each item, what it contains, where it is located, how it got there, who put it there, where it is headed, how much it cost, and so on. This has greatly reduced the clerical labor needed to manage business, and it has opened up new opportunities for achieving higher levels of productivity and quality improvement.

HOW DOES BAR CODE WORK?

Take the familiar example from the supermarket. When a box of breakfast cereal arrives at the checkout stand, its bar code is scanned by the checkout person. The scanning device recognizes the presence of bar code, and it reads and decodes the *Universal Product Code* (UPC) *number* from the series of lines and spaces printed on the side of the box. The checkout computer looks up the product code number and displays the product name and price information at the register, which adds the price to the tally and prints the customer receipt. In most cases, this transaction also decrements the store inventory, providing managers with the information they need to reorder and adding to the information base they use to measure the effect of their promotional activities and make strategic marketing decisions. All this takes place within a second or less, seemingly countless times each day.

To manually record, transcribe, calculate, and maintain this information without bar code and computer seems ludicrous in this day and age. Therein lies the power of automated data collection with bar code.

BAR-CODE USES IN A VARIETY OF APPLICATIONS ACROSS MANY INDUSTRIES

Perhaps the best way to understand the impact bar-code data collection has on production and inventory control is to look at some examples.

Shipping

A nationally recognized bedding manufacturer builds mattresses to order at 20 different plants around the United States. A bar-code label on each mattress is scanned when the mattress is completed in production and scanned again when it is loaded on a truck for delivery. The data travel instantly to a central order management computer. Previously this process was managed by handwritten production lists with keyboard data entry from each manufacturing site. Today production and shipping data are updated instantly and more accurately. The bar-code system is credited with having reduced shipping errors by a factor of 7 (Fig. 31.3).

FIGURE 31.3   Shipping room bar-code application.

Receiving

A major northeastern rail carrier receives new cars at an automaker's plant in Delaware and loads them on railcars for delivery to auto dealers across the United States. The new automobiles must be sorted and loaded in the proper order to assure that they are delivered to the right dealers. As a new car rolls off the assembly line, it receives a bar-code ID card. At the rail terminal, a driver inserts the card into a bar-code reader that tells him or her where to park for loading. Another bar-code reader is located at the loading ramp to each railcar to make sure that the automobiles are loaded in the proper sequence for delivery. The bar code system has reduced misshipments and has significantly cut the amount of time that the new cars spend in transit to the dealers.

Production Inventory

A national manufacturer of steel pipe and fittings for electrical conduit and fences makes different products at five different manufacturing sites across the United States. The pipe maker uses bar code to identify the finished goods, and a sophisticated satellite data communications system assures an accurate, up-to-date, nationwide finished-goods inventory. When a customer places an order for a product that is out of stock in Houston, the company knows what is available in New Jersey and Chicago. The company first started using bar code when several of its larger customers requested an industry standard, UI–approved bar-code label on the product.

Distribution

A major manufacturer of children's clothing in the fast-paced and highly competitive apparel industry added an extensive, real-time inventory management system based on wireless, portable bar-code readers and sophisticated distribution control software. In the first year since the system was installed, the incidence of stock-outs in the company's distribution center dropped from peaks of over 40 percent to less than 5 percent across the product line. Order cancellations resulting from stock-out conditions were reduced by 90 percent, recapturing significant revenues for the company. Today the company's employees can find out the status of any finished goods at any instant from the time the products leave the manufacturing sites to the time they are delivered to the customer (Fig. 31.4).

FIGURE 31.4 Apparel industry bar-code application.

Work-in-Process

A building products manufacturer makes aluminum, steel, and vinyl roof edge, window trim, rain gutters, siding, and accessories in a combination of cutting, forming, and painting processes that are distributed between two plants in separate midwest locations. Everything is made to order in a selection of 36 different colors, so it is important to know which orders are in which stages of production between the plants. To accommodate this constantly changing work-in-process inventory, all raw materials are labeled with bar code. Workers use portable bar-code readers in conjunction with electronic scales to track materials through different coating, cutting, and forming processes, generating new bar-code labels for product at each step in the process. In the first year of operation, the bar-code data collection system allowed the company to reduce its work-in-process inventory by over 50 percent while increasing production 20 percent to meet an increase in sales.

Raw Materials Inventory

In the textile industry, a furniture manufacturer stocks over 1500 upholstery fabrics from 50 different suppliers. They cut thousands of yards of fabric each week to produce thousands of pieces of fine furniture. Previously, fabric inventory was calculated based on the total amount of fabric purchased, the number of patterns cut, and an estimated yardage used for each pattern. Problems occurred when orders were taken based on the estimate and not enough fabric actually remained to fill the orders. Today the inventory is maintained more accurately by tracking the exact weight of each roll of fabric in the plant with bar-code readers linked to scales. They have dramatically reduced the number of man-hours tied up in completing physical inventories. In addition, they have reduced the number of unfulfillable orders by 90 percent.

Replenishment

A major Canadian metropolitan hospital relies on bar code to replenish supplies—everything from syringes and sterilized surgical procedure packages to soap and bedpans. Over 100 differently configured delivery carts in different departments on each floor of the hospital are labeled with bar codes for each item they carry. Using portable bar-code readers, nursing assistants scan the bar code and enter the number of items they want to reorder. The data are communicated to an automated central supply facility where orders are prepared and sent back to the departments. Previously the orders were entered on paper and by keyboard. Now the process is virtually paperless, data entry errors have been eliminated, and labor for the replenishment process has been reduced by nearly half thanks to the increased accuracy and timeliness of bar code.

Job Costing

A major U.S. aerospace company designs, builds, launches, and maintains communications satellites. The company uses bar code to track work-in-process on a wide variety of different projects and government contracts. In several of the assembly areas, workers use bar-code scanners at their workbenches to track the time they spend on each project, scanning their own bar-code identification badge, as well as a bar code printed on the documentation that travels with the project kits they assemble. The company estimates a savings of 1 hour per day per worker in data entry time alone. The system provides management with an accurate global view of work-in-process. Combined with a sophisticated materials-tracking bar-code system, the information is used to provide an accurate accounting of project costs.

Statistical Process Control

A progressive auto-parts manufacturer uses a sophisticated network combining data from bar code with input from electronic measurement devices to adjust machinery in process for greater quality control. As workers scan a part number, employee ID, and raw material lot number, the monitor at their workstation displays the specific machine setup parameters for the given part to be manufactured. Then as the worker samples the machine output using electronic measurement equipment (calipers and micrometer), the monitor displays graphs of the data to allow machine adjustments to be made to keep the finished product within specifications. In addition, the bar-code system updates accounting files, tracks labor, records scrap, and maintains the traceability of materials.

Lot Traceability

The research facility for a major international chemical manufacturer must keep track of each sample of the new organic chemicals it creates and tests. Each year, another seven to eight thousand new compounds are added to the archive, while as many as a dozen scientists a day check samples out of the archive for further testing. Some samples can represent thousands of dollars in lab work, and misplaced samples can be a nightmare for the scientists. Now samples are tracked using bar code in much the same fashion as books are checked out of a library. There are separate bar-code labels for each compound and separate bar-code identification symbols for each scientist.

Audit Trail

A major metropolitan police department uses bar code to track evidence from a crime scene, including everything from a few grams of drugs, to guns, money, and automobiles. By assigning a bar code to each new piece of evidence and scanning it each time it is transferred from precinct to storage to lab and to court, the police department is able to automatically generate an accurate audit trail representing the chain of custody. In the event that evidence tampering is alleged in court, the police can provide a detailed audit trail (Fig. 31.5).

These are just a few of the countless applications for automated data collection. As the technology continues to advance, the applications continue to unfold and multiply.

FIGURE 31.5   Audit trail with bar code.

AUTOMATED DATA COLLECTION

This chapter will focus on *nonretail* applications of bar code for *automated data collection* (ADC). There are several other ADC technologies sometimes associated with bar code including the following:

- *Magnetic stripe.* Magnetic recording of digital information used on most credit cards
- *Magnetic-ink character recognition.* A special set of alphanumeric characters originally printed with magnetic ink on most bank checks
- *Optical character recognition.* Optics and software combined to read standardized alphanumeric printing
- *Optical mark recognition.* Technology that recognizes marks made by hand on standardized forms such as academic tests and surveys
- *Radio-frequency identification.* Electronically programmable tags or labels that transmit data via radio frequency
- *Smart cards.* Cards with embedded microprocessor chips
- *Machine vision.* High-resolution video equipment used to recognize objects by size, shape, and color
- *Touchscreen.* Touch-sensitive computer display screens
- *Voice recognition.* Software capable of recognizing and converting a select vocabulary of oral commands into digital form for processing on computer

While these alternative technologies are appropriate in some unique industrial applications, and while some are occasionally used in combination with bar code, they will not be examined in detail here because they are not as widely used for production and inventory control applications as bar code alone.

Once data have been collected—automatically or otherwise—they can be manipulated, communicated, exchanged, and reported in a variety of ways. This is the function of production and inventory control software, which will be referred to only in passing here. And while bar code frequently is an enabling technology that makes things like advanced shipping notices and electronic data interchange between customers and vendors possible, those concepts rely primarily on long-range data communications, which is another topic for separate discussion. This chapter focuses exclusively on automating the data collection process with bar-code technology.

First the chapter will take a closer look at the benefits of automating the data collection process with bar code. Then it will examine the components of a bar-code data collection system in more detail: symbology, labels, printers, scanners, and network architecture. And finally the chapter discusses the process for planning and implementing a bar-code system.

THE BENEFITS OF ADC WITH BAR CODE

The benefits of automating data collection are clear and measurable. Quantifiable gains in productivity usually result in cost savings and sometimes can result in increased revenue as well. Companies frequently assess the financial return on their investment in bar-code technology by directly measuring the following:

- Reduction in the cost of carrying excess inventory, including reduced inventory obsolescence, and better facility utilization
- Reduction or elimination of defects, rework, and scrap through better quality control
- Improved customer service through reduced shipping errors and delays
- Improved cost analysis and planning resulting in more accurate bids and proposals
- Reduction of fixed labor costs through elimination of manual data entry and reductions in administrative costs such as correcting errors, expediting, scheduling, and overtime
- Reduction of indirect labor costs through improved accuracy allowing greater production control and reduced administrative, accounting, and payroll costs
- Increased customer satisfaction from faster response time, more accurate billing, higher-quality products, and so on

While individual return-on-investment calculations vary, bar-code systems commonly show a payback period of less than 18 months. Many show complete payback in less than a year from installation. Here's why.

Speed

Perhaps the most obvious benefit of bar-code data collection is speed. Consider the time required for a human operator preparing a shipping manifest to read and note a typical package label including a product name, serial number, count, and weight. Add the time required to enter the data at a keyboard. A detailed entry of even one order could take several minutes. With bar code the same data can be collected in seconds without clerical delay. Instantly, the shipping manifest can be automatically printed, the finished-goods inventory updated, an advanced shipping notice sent to the customer, and a notification for billing sent to accounting. Most bar-code system implementations realize considerable direct labor savings for this reason alone. It is simply much quicker and easier to scan a bar code than to write and/or keypunch data. Items on a moving conveyer belt can be scanned automatically while traveling at rates of 400 to 600 feet per minute without any human intervention.

In many cases, data collection has been a time-consuming, two-step process. First the data are written by hand on paper forms. Then the same data are entered into a computer in batches from the forms. With bar code, this batch process can be reduced to a single, instantaneous, on-line entry. There is virtually no delay between when the data are scanned and when they are made available. Real-time data collection provides the information to make just-in-time production methods possible.

Accuracy

In addition to speed, the accuracy with which data are collected using bar code is greatly enhanced. Studies have shown that manually keying data into a computer results in an error rate of approximately 1 substitution error (i.e., the transposition of a number or letter) for every 300 characters entered. Most of us know from direct experience how small data-recording errors can have a serious impact on business. Faulty information can result in critical miscalculations and significant logistical headaches.

In contrast, the substitution error rate for bar-code data entry is effectively zero because of built-in error checking and redundancy. In many cases, the use of bar-code data collection has not only saved time for front-line workers charged with gathering data as part of their production jobs, but the increased accuracy of bar code has reduced or eliminated the need for clerical personnel whose primary function was assuring the accuracy of data entry. In addition, labor savings have been realized in customer service time spent addressing shipping problems and in the cost of "making good" erroneous shipments.

Simplicity

With bar code, a single-entry event can result in the capture of a stream of data including many characters—a single scan gathers all the relevant information. In some cases this can be accomplished completely automatically without human intervention. When human operators are involved in the data collection process, very little skill or training is required.

Complex data entry routines are expedited and simplified with bar code. Many bar-code scanning or reading devices are programmable to prompt the worker through the data entry process. For instance, instead of keying in detailed production information about work-in-process on the shop floor, a worker might simply scan a bar code on the work order that he or she is about to work on, then scan a bar code indicating the machine or position where he or she is working, scan bar codes on the parts and supplies he or she will be using, and finally scan a bar code on his or her ID badge to indicate who is performing the work. The work-in-process inventory database is automatically updated with explicit production data time and date stamped for future reference.

Control

As a result of automating data collection with bar code, large quantities of data are made available in real-time, allowing us to closely manage production in process, rather than after the fact. Because more data can be gathered more quickly, accurately, and reliably with bar code and because computers allow us to process, analyze, and report that data more efficiently, we are now in a position to directly control industrial processes for measurably higher productivity. We can track, analyze, and act upon data where we might never have considered using it before simply because the data gathering process was too cumbersome.

For instance, a high-volume manufacturer uses bar-code labels to identify individual lots of incoming raw materials, then tracks the machines on which finished goods are produced from the raw materials. Machine tolerances are adjusted on-line according to data gathered in process. The manufacturer also uses bar code to identify the lots of finished goods for quality assurance. A complete audit trail of production allows higher-level statistical process control. The manufacturer has a record of which suppliers' raw materials perform best over time, which machines are frequently in need of repair, and which processes have the greatest impact on quality.

SELECTING AND APPLYING THE RIGHT TECHNOLOGY

Bar-code technology has evolved steadily over the past 25 years as it has been adapted to many different applications in many different work environments. Generally speaking, the technology involves encoding data with a specific *symbology,* then *printing* it on a select *media,* and finally *scanning and decoding* it with a variety of different types of *readers.* These individual components of the technology are most frequently tied together in a digital *data collection network.* Most systems are customized for the unique application and work environment.

Bar-Code Symbology

A *bar-code symbology* is the scheme or pattern whereby data are encoded as lines and spaces. Dozens of different bar-code symbologies have been developed over the years for different uses. But bar-code printers and readers must share the same symbology— that is, use the same language—in order to communicate. As a result, various data collection applications have standardized around specific symbologies.

While some bar-code readers can read multiple symbologies, most industrial applications rely on a single coding scheme and symbology standard. In fact, for many businesses the choice of a bar-code symbology has already been determined by agreement to use an industry standard so that the same bar-code label can be read by many different businesses in the industry. The UPC bar code used in the retail environment is one example of this. The UPC and printing specifications have been very tightly defined so that retailers can quickly and easily identify products from the different manufacturers.

Universal Product Code (UPC)

The *Universal Product Code* (UPC) is both a coding scheme and a symbology. To give you some idea of the considerations involved in bar-code symbology, here is a brief description of UPC bar code. UPC relies on a 10-digit coding scheme: the first 5 digits represent the manufacturer, and the last 5 digits represent a unique product identifier. Together, these 10 digits are preceded by a *number system digit* (representing a particular category important to participants in the system) and followed by a *check digit* (a way of checking for errors in reading the code). The UPC symbology is *fixed length:* It includes only the 12 characters described. It is *numeric:* Numbers only, no letters or other symbols are used. It is *continuous:* There are no gaps or spaces between the characters. It uses *four element widths:* The bars and spaces come in four different widths.

Code 39

Code 39 is the most common nonretail symbology. It has become a de facto standard in many industries. If a product is being shipped to the U.S. Department of Defense, it must be marked with Code 39 (Fig. 31.6). Unlike UPC, Code 39 does not represent a specific coding scheme but can be used to encode any type of data described with numbers and letters. That might be a part number, a serial number, a transaction code, a word or phrase, a quantity or weight, or any other type of data.

Code 39 is *variable length:* As many characters can be used as necessary. It is *alphanumeric:* It includes 44 different alphabetic, numeric, and graphic characters that can be combined to effectively represent the full 128 ASCII characters if necessary. It is *discrete:* Every character stands alone, and there are gaps between characters. It uses *two-element widths:* Each character is represented by a different combination of nine bars and spaces including three wide and six narrow elements. The typical Code 39 pattern for an individual character may be represented as a sequence of nine binary bits in computer memory.

The typical Code 39 symbol begins and ends with an asterisk, which is the symbol-

FIGURE 31.6 Department of Defense application.

ogy's stop-start code. And a Code 39 symbol usually includes a check character to allow the bar-code reader to check for errors in the scanning process. A check character is based on the mathematical relationship of the other characters in the symbol. It is used in conjunction with a preprogrammed algorithm in the bar-code reader to validate that the correct data have been decoded.

Bar Codes

Many other bar-code symbologies are in use for specific applications. For example, *Interleaved 2 of 5* is a continuous numeric symbology that has been used mainly in the distribution industry. *Codabar,* a self-checking, discrete symbology having 16 characters in its set, is frequently used in libraries, blood banks, and air parcel express applications. *Code 49* and *Code 16K* are "stacked" bar-code symbologies suited for labeling small objects (designed for use with a moving-beam scanner). These stacked symbologies are frequently referred to as *2D* (two-dimensional) *bar-code symbologies* since they must be scanned in two dimensions.

AIAG Bar Codes

Many industries have adopted bar-code application standards that specify a symbology for encoding data. In addition, these application standards may also specify characteristics such as symbol orientation, location, label format, minimum bar height, specific details to be included in the data, and human-readable content on the label. For instance, the *Automobile Industry Action Group* (AIAG) has generated several application stan-

dards for the automobile industry including vehicle identification numbers, parts identification labels, primary metals identification labels, and vehicle emission inspection
bar codes. Symbology standards include limits on dimensional tolerances, spots, voids,
edge roughness, reflectivity, and contrast. Automatic bar-code–verifying equipment is
designed to evaluate these various parameters to assure compliance.

BAR-CODE PRINTERS

Bar code can be printed directly on product packaging; however, in most production and
inventory control applications, bar-code labels are printed for individual items. Applied
on-site, bar-code labels may be *preprinted* or *printed on-demand* to identify materials
and products as they are produced and to include important new information as items
move through a production and distribution process. Most bar-code labels include
human-readable and/or graphic identification data as well. In some cases, label stock is
preprinted off-site with fixed data and graphics, then printed again with item-specific
bar codes on-site.

In addition to identifying items, bar-code labels are frequently used to identify shelf
or bin locations for storage and retrieval. Occasionally, bar-code labels are affixed to
schematic displays or are used to create menus for quickly identifying procedures and
speeding the data entry process. Sometimes menus of bar-code selections are created on
desktop computers and printed on standard office laser printers.

Media

Bar code is printed on a variety of *substrates* (i.e., labels, tags, or pages made of various materials), with a variety of inks or marking techniques, using a variety of mechanical and electronic printing technologies. While paper labels and tags are common,
materials that are tamper resistant, tear resistant, scuff resistant, water resistant, chemical resistant, and photoresistant have also come into popular use. And various adhesives
are available for different requirements.

Since the bar-code reading process depends on light reflected from the bar code, it is
most important to assure the proper reflective qualities of the substrate. It should be
noted that it is also possible for bar-code readers to use light waves falling outside the
visible-light spectrum (e.g., infrared), which in some cases allows bar-code symbols to
be concealed for security reasons. Obviously the right media should be selected for
durability and security as well as cost.

Off-Site Preprinting

Off-site preprinting is generally used to create medium to large quantities of identical or
sequenced bar-code symbols in a batch process. Many industrial applications can easily
be accomplished with preprinted bar-code tags or labels that simply identify large quantities of similar items in much the same way that license plates identify automobiles.
Preprinting can generate labels in large quantities at relatively low cost. Frequently used
printing techniques include letterpress, offset, flexography, rotogravure, and inking
wheel. In addition, there are a number of specialized printing techniques including
inkjet, laser, chemical etching, photocomposition, and hot stamping.

On-Site, On-Demand Printing

Many production and inventory control applications generate data that must be encoded on-site, requiring labels printed on-demand. Many different types of printers including desktop and portable models meet this need. On-demand printers have been designed with ruggedized components and dust-proof, and water-proof housings for a wide range of industrial working conditions.

The most common on-site printers use one of three different printing processes: dot matrix, thermal, and thermal transfer. Office laser printers are also occasionally used to economically print bar-code menus and/or run off a limited number of paper labels. However, most high-volume, on-site label printing applications dictate dedicated dot matrix, thermal, or thermal transfer printers both for reliability and economy of scale. These printers may be connected as peripheral equipment to a computer network either by wire or radio-frequency data communications.

Dot Matrix

The dot-matrix impact printer transfers ink from a ribbon onto the label when small "needles" force the ribbon against the label surface. A matrix of these needles is used to form a pattern of tiny dots, which in combination appear as solid lines or shapes on the printed label. The dot matrix is controlled electronically by software that describes the bar-code symbol, along with any human-readable characters or graphics to be printed. Dot-matrix printers, originally designed as computer output devices, can generate labels quickly and efficiently.

Thermal

Thermal printers generally use a paper label substrate that has been impregnated with a heat-sensitive, clear coating that changes to a dark color when exposed to a relatively high temperature. A thermal printer selectively heats localized areas of the label with a printhead that is controlled by logic built into the printer. Specialized thermal printers contain both rectangular heating bars used to print bar codes and a dot-matrix array of heating points used to print alphanumeric characters and graphics.

Thermal printing is a popular way to generate bar-code labels on demand because the image quality, speed, and flexibility make it cost effective. Because of the relative simplicity of this process, it has been possible to build portable, battery-powered label printers (Fig. 31.7). However, in some cases, the specially coated, heat-sensitive label substrate is inappropriate, especially if the label is going to be subjected to high temperatures and/or direct sunlight or ultraviolet light for a prolonged period of time.

Thermal Transfer

In thermal transfer printers, heat is used to transfer ink from a ribbon to a standard paper or polyester substrate. This eliminates the need for the special, heat-sensitive papers and specially prepared substrates required by thermal printing. It also means that the resulting image is more stable, unaffected by high temperatures and exposure to ultraviolet light (Fig. 31.8). Like thermal printers, thermal transfer printers use thermal print heads to heat the ink ribbon that transfers ink to the label. While thermal transfer printers have

FIGURE 31.7   Thermal printer.   **FIGURE 31.8**   Thermal transfer printer.

become a common standard for printing bar-code labels, many sites continue to find direct thermal and dot-matrix printers perfectly satisfactory.

BAR-CODE READERS

In its simplest form a bar-code reader can be considered as two separate elements: an input device and a decoder. The input device optically scans the bar-code symbol, and the decoder translates the resulting changes in light levels into raw data. After the bar-code symbol has been read, the data are commonly transmitted directly to a computer for processing, or they are stored in the reader's built-in memory for later transmission.

FIGURE 31.9   Interactive data processing.

However, over the years, bar-code readers have become considerably more versatile as technology has evolved to allow them to include more complex features. Some modern bar-code readers are essentially battery-powered, portable, handheld computers with keypads and displays, as well as bar-code input devices. They may communicate data via radio frequency with a host computer. This allows untethered, interactive data processing in real-time (Fig. 31.9).

For example, a worker scans a bar-code symbol, the data are transmitted and verified instantly by the host computer, and the screen on the bar-code reader displays a prompt to enter additional data by keypad. In some cases, data may even be processed by the handheld reader before it is transmitted. Similarly, the host computer screens may be processed for clear display on the handheld reader. First we will examine the fundamental *input* of the bar-code reader. Then we will discuss the *data interface functions.*

Input

Bar-code readers may be divided into two categories: fixed-beam scanners and moving-beam scanners. In *fixed-beam scanners,* the scanning motion across the bar-code symbol is accomplished by hand or by movement of the object symbol past the reader. In *moving-beam scanners,* the scanning motion across the bar code is accomplished by an electronic or mechanical scanning system built into the reader.

Fixed-Beam Scanners, Contact.   Handheld, fixed-beam, contact devices physically touch the symbol that is being scanned. The bar-code *wand* is the most common example (Fig. 31.10). Scanning is accomplished by dragging the wand across the bar-code symbol. Another example of a fixed-beam, contact scanner is the bar-code card reader. In slot or insertion style card readers, the sensing device stays in one place while the bar-code symbol slides past (Fig. 31.11).

Fixed-Beam Scanners, Noncontact.   Some fixed-beam readers work at close range without requiring contact. However, close-range, handheld, fixed-beam readers still require the operator to manually scan the light beam across the full length of the bar-code symbol. Fixed-mount, fixed-beam readers can take advantage of conveyors to provide the scanning motion moving the bar-code symbol past the reader (Fig. 31.12).

FIGURE 31.10   Contact reader.

FIGURE 31.11   Fixed-beam contact reader.

FIGURE 31.12   Fixed-beam reader.

However, as there is only one scanning opportunity in this scheme, the bar-code symbols must always pass by within range and the bar-code print quality must be consistently high.

All noncontact readers have limits to the range of distances over which a symbol can be successfully decoded, commonly described as the *depth of field*. Depth of field is a function of the printed bar-code symbol's dimension and "density" as well as the optical capabilities of the bar-code reader. When selecting bar-code technology, you should be aware of any limitations to the depth of field for your selected bar-code symbol-reader combination.

Charge-Coupled Device (CCD).   Another noncontact, fixed-beam reader relies on electronics to perform the scanning function. The *charge-coupled device* (CCD) *reader* contains no moving parts but does not require the operator or the bar-code symbol to move (Fig. 31.13). Instead, the CCD scanner focuses an image of the bar-code symbol on a linear array of light-sensitive photodiodes. The scanning motion is achieved by electronically sampling each of the individual photodiodes in sequence (Fig. 31.14). CCD scanners rely on flood illumination rather than a single beam of light. They have a relatively limited depth of field, but they are rugged and effective portable readers with no moving parts.

FIGURE 31.13   Charged-coupled device.

Moving-Beam Scanners.   Most contemporary industrial bar-code applications employ moving-beam scanners that use laser light. The light beam is commonly produced by a helium neon (HeNe) laser and sometimes by a laser diode. The laser light beam is mechanically or optically made to scan back and forth, up and down, or in many directions at high speeds, thus allowing multiple redundant scans of a single bar-code symbol. A typical scan rate in moving-beam laser scanners is about 40 scans per second. To the human eye, this gives the impression of a continuous scan line or multiple lines rather than a single point of light moving at high speed. Scan rates can be much higher, allowing laser scanners to effectively "blanket" a wide area to read bar codes oriented in a variety of different directions (Fig. 31.15). In addition, laser scanning sequence and direction can be managed to read two-dimensional bar-code symbologies.

FIGURE 31.14   Charged-couple device.

FIGURE 31.15   Moving-beam laser scanner.

Handheld Scanners.   Handheld, moving-beam, bar-code readers are popular because little operator training is required and because the high number of scanning attempts over a short period of time assures better readability for bar-code symbols with less-than-optimum print quality. In addition, handheld laser scanners have been adapted to provide greater depth of field and greater reliability in reading from curved surfaces (Fig. 31.16).

Fixed-Mount Scanners.   Fixed-mount, moving-beam readers are commonly used for untended scanning of bar-code symbols that pass by on a conveyor. They are frequently installed to aid in automatic sorting where the object symbol is brought to the scanner. The laser light beam is made to scan multiple times at high speed to assure a successful read. Decoders in these readers sometimes incorporate a "voting" algorithm whereby data from two or more scans are compared before decoding is completed (Fig. 31.17).

FIGURE 31.16   Handheld bar-code reader.

FIGURE 31.17   Fixed-mount, moving-beam reader.

Additionally, fixed-mount laser readers have been adapted to provide omnidirectional scanning in the form of a starburst, or multiangle, pattern to read bar-code symbols presented in different orientations.

DATA INTERFACE

After the bar code is read, the information can be stored, communicated, processed, and used to signal some activity.

Processing

Bar-code readers incorporate status lights and/or audible sounds to let the operator know that a bar-code symbol has been successfully read. Some wand readers and portable handheld readers provide this operator feedback through a separate decoder attached by cable to the scanning device. The decoder may also include a display device that shows the alphanumeric representation of the scanned bar-code symbol (Fig. 31.18). Once the bar-code symbol has been successfully read and decoded, its data can be processed immediately. The information may be used immediately to activate a sortation device on a conveyor line or call up a specific bin from an automated storage carousel.

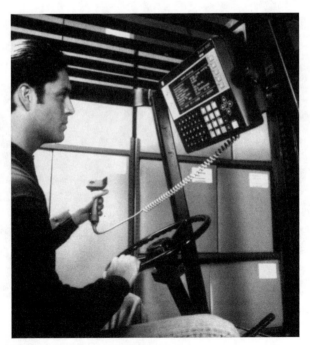

FIGURE 31.18 Decoder and display.

Some processing commonly occurs in the bar-code reader itself. An operator may scan in several different bar-code symbols to create a single transaction (e.g., part number plus serial number plus employee ID plus job code). The bar-code data may also be stored in memory to be communicated later in batch mode. Or it may be combined with other data and passed directly through to a host computer or network server.

Appended Data

Quite frequently additional data are appended to the data that have been read from the bar-code symbol. This appended data might include the date and time generated by a clock in the reader itself or the network server or host computer. Sometimes data identifying the bar-code reader itself or the reader's location are added electronically. Sometimes data from other sources are appended to a bar-code transaction, such as a weight from a digital scale, a measurement from some other digital device, or even an exact geographic location. In one application example from the mining industry, latitude and longitude data are derived from global positioning satellites and appended to each data entry.

Memory

Most bar-code readers provide a way of storing data in memory. Some readers are specifically designed to collect data and store them until an appropriate time when the information is uploaded in a batch usually via a hardwired docking station. This built-in memory can also serve as a fail-safe redundancy in on-line, real-time data collection networks.

Programmable Readers

Some readers may be programmed to prompt the operator for specific information and to reject bar-code readings that do not conform to specified criteria (Fig. 31.19). For instance, an operator may be prompted to scan the bar-code symbol containing a product serial number. Instead he scans the bar code on his ID badge by mistake. If the reader has been programmed to discriminate between different data types, it will reject the employee ID and prompt again for the product serial number.

Programmable bar-code readers have become increasingly sophisticated to the point where they can effectively serve as independent microcomputers. While some are programmable in proprietary programming languages specific to bar-code applications, others may be programmed in common PC software languages such as Basic, Visual Basic, C, and C++.

FIGURE 31.19   Programmable reader.

BAR-CODE DATA COMMUNICATIONS

Bar-code readers communicate data to a host computer or network server via hardwire connection (usually RS232 cable), modem, or radio frequency.

Wedge Readers

One common computing interface is the keyboard *wedge,* a hardwired device that allows the bar-code reader to be connected in series between the keyboard and the personal computer or the computer terminal (Fig. 31.20). The keyboard can still be used normally, but when a bar-code symbol is scanned, the alphanumeric data contained in the bar code are treated as though they originated from the keyboard.

Direct Connection

Bar-code readers may also be connected directly to host computers or network servers by dedicated connections. To conserve I/O ports on host computers, a *port concentrator* is used. A port concentrator prevents communications conflicts by regularly polling each bar-code reader in the system and reporting a single stream of data to the host.

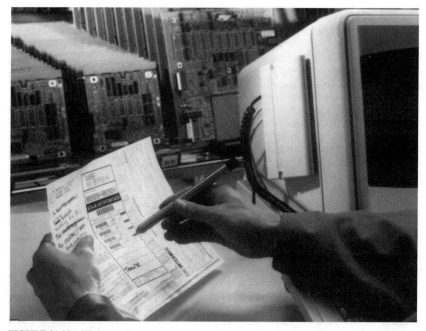

FIGURE 31.20   Wedge reader.

Local Area Network (LAN)

Many bar-code systems today are built upon *local area network* (LAN) *architecture* popularized by the proliferation of microcomputers. In this form, all bar-code devices (readers and printers) are connected on a multidrop network to a dedicated bar-code controller (server), which in turn may be connected to a network of other microcomputers with access to a corporate mainframe. In some cases, bar-code readers and printers may be linked to the network from remote locations by a modem.

Radio-Frequency Communication

Data communications via radio frequency rather than wire has recently become very popular in production and inventory control applications. Radio-frequency (RF) data communication offers significant benefits: real-time, two-way data communications providing increased portability, adaptability, and scalability with no need for costly and disruptive installation of cable runs. Two radio-frequency data communications technologies are commonly in use: *narrow band* and *spread spectrum.* Of the two, spread spectrum is the most popular.

Narrow-band technology relies on assigned frequencies for data transmission. Like commercial two-way radio communications equipment commonly used for dispatch and voice communications, narrow-band data communications requires licensing of an assigned frequency from the Federal Communications Commission. The operator is then required to transmit only within that narrow band so as not to interfere with others transmitting on adjacent narrow bands within the electromagnetic spectrum.

Spread-spectrum technology does not require licensing. Instead of avoiding interference with others by spacing different narrow-band transmissions at different frequencies, spread spectrum allows multiple broad-band transmissions to occur in the same portion of the radio spectrum. By spreading data communications over a wide range of frequencies with some redundancy, spread spectrum is able to achieve clear and reliable data communications at lower power with less risk of radio interference, or "jamming." In addition, spread spectrum provides greater data throughput (i.e., more data communicated faster). In the United States, 0.902- to 0.928-MHz bandwidth has traditionally been used for spread-spectrum RF traffic. In Europe, spread-spectrum transmissions in the 2.4-GHz bandwidth allow even faster data transmission rates.

Spread-spectrum technology was originally developed for military applications because of its antijamming capabilities. Although the range of operation or coverage area is somewhat less than narrow band, spread spectrum is considered to be the "industrial-strength" choice for RF data communications. Repeaters may be added to extend the coverage of spread-spectrum RF systems. A repeater will receive and retransmit radio frequency signals.

PLANNING AND IMPLEMENTING A BAR-CODE SYSTEM

Bar-code data collection systems have proven their value in all sorts of industrial applications. Nevertheless, not all automated data collection projects are instantly successful for their companies. A bar-code solution is made good only through the thoughtful planning, careful design, and well-executed implementation of the team that puts it in place.

Needs Analysis and Problem Definition

Key to the success of any automated data collection system is the early and continued involvement of a team leader who has a thorough understanding of the problems to be solved and a clear vision of the solution. This project champion must have the cooperation, assistance, and support of other professionals, from the front-line workers who will be instrumental in gathering the data to the managers who will allocate the resources to get the job done, as well as the outside vendors who will provide technical expertise.

Bar-code will change how some people do their jobs and make decisions. These people should be involved in planning the project from the very beginning. Diverse perspectives will bring critical input to important planning and design considerations. Be sure that the actual users of a proposed system take an active role at the beginning.

During the definition phase, it is especially important to evaluate operations objectively and systematically. Detail how information is currently collected, managed, and distributed. Diagram and model the existing flow of materials and information. Determine what information is acted upon immediately, what information must be archived for later action, and what information is reported for decision making. Identify all opportunities for automating data collection, and evaluate each by its direct impact on improving business processes and its long-term potential return on investment.

Set specific, quantifiable project goals. Most goals should have a measurable dollar value, usually in costs saved. Involve outside vendors and consultants early on. A vendor-partner can help at this early stage of project planning by showing examples of how other operations have solved similar problems and how they measure the results. A good vendor can also help to demonstrate quantifiable business benefits and cost justification methods. In addition, an outside perspective can identify important opportunities for cost savings that have been overlooked.

System Design, Funding, and Approval

Start with a general plan that will address the specific project goals identified in the problem definition stage. Give potential hardware and software vendors and consultants as much information as possible, and itemize any constraints such as timing, costs, information system platforms, and physical requirements. Specify how the data should be processed and organized. Recognize the time value of information. Traditional mainframe-based information systems may report what happened yesterday or last week. Real-time information systems allow managers to move from analysis of yesterday's problems—after they have taken their toll—to correction of today's problems—before they incur a significant cost.

Always consider two-way data communication—a conversation is more productive than a monologue. For instance, shipping data collection systems can tell managers which shipments contained errors, but two-way data communications with validation can warn dock workers not to put the package on the wrong truck. In warehouse picking functions, two-way communications allow computerized dispatching to direct operators through the most efficient work flow sequence to complete their tasks.

When presenting a bar-code project to management for approval and funding, remember that the technology itself is less important to managers than the ability of the system to help them reach their business objectives. Objectives should be linked directly to measurable improvements in the company's operations and profitability. Case studies from comparable installations at other sites can be effective illustrations.

Select vendors and consultants with care. Evaluate them specifically on their experience in the field of automated data collection. Seek references and examples of past work similar to the project you propose. Assess their ability to provide project management and ongoing support. Check their relationships with equipment suppliers. Once you have selected a vendor, work closely with them to determine how the system will be integrated with your company's strategic plans and goals. Be clear and explicit about what the vendor must do in order for your system to be considered a success. Plan for long-term reliability and the flexibility to meet future needs and expansion.

Implementation

Plan and schedule each stage of implementation thoughtfully. It is well worthwhile to set up a small pilot system first. Use the pilot system in tandem with existing procedures for a trial period. This provides time to resolve key aspects of the hardware and software interface, and it provides an opportunity for end users to become familiar with the system. Frequently a pilot project will reveal new ways to enhance productivity that can be built into the rollout of the full installation.

Communication with all parties affected by the new system is critical to assure a smooth installation. Training should begin before installation occurs. Allow time for hands-on trials with new equipment. Most workers will in fact be delighted with the speed and simplicity of scanning data rather than writing it down. Also be sure managers understand the system's reporting capabilities and characteristics, and consider how it will affect their decision making and strategic planning.

Test the system under worst-case scenarios early on so that you will be prepared for any problems that might occur. Then, after the system has been in operation for a reasonable period of time, review the operation against your original project goals, and make sure all adjustments have been made to capitalize on the system's capabilities. Also be sure that correct and adequate procedures are in place for system administration, maintenance, and review.

Adaptability and Scalability

The trend in automated data collection over the past few years has been toward the propagation of new and expanded portable data collection networks. Many sites have upgraded their hardwired and batch-oriented data collection capabilities with real-time, portable, radio-frequency bar-code readers. Modern bar-code systems have demonstrated their ability to evolve and expand as needs change. There has also been a trend for data collection manufacturers to move away from proprietary data collection networks toward more standard operating platforms. This will allow users to build on existing hardware and software capability while increasing the size and scope of their automated data collection systems to narrow the gap between data collection and data processing.

BIBLIOGRAPHY

Computer Identics: *Ten Steps to Bar Code Success,* 1994.
ID Systems Buyer's Guide, Helmer's Publishing, Peterborough, N.H., 1994.

Intermec Corporation: *Understanding Radio Frequency Data Collection,* Intermec Corp., Everett, Wash., 1992, 1993, 1994.

————: *Cost Justification/Automated Data Collection,* 1994.

Palmer, Roger C.: *The Bar Code Book,* Helmer's Publishing, Peterborough, N.H., 1991.

Sharp, Kevin R.: *Automatic Identification: Making It Pay,* Van Nostrand Reinhold, New York, 1990.

SECTION 7

MANAGING THE PIC FUNCTION

CHAPTER 32
MANAGING THE PIC ORGANIZATION*

Editors

C. Patrick Koelling, Ph.D.
Professor of Industrial Engineering
Virginia Polytechnic Institute and State University
Blacksburg, Virginia

Eileen Van Aken, Ph.D.
Professor of Industrial Engineering
Virginia Polytechnic Institute and State University
Blacksburg, Virginia

Production and inventory management can be defined as the management of the time, place, and physical facilities of production. This means having the right materials, workers, and facilities at the right time and in a manner that both maximizes the service to the consumer and minimizes the investment of the company.

This chapter presents a background of the *production and inventory control* (PIC) function along with its basic organizational concepts. The duties and responsibilities of the various functions are described and highlighted. The types of development and training programs that should be used are emphasized. In addition, one section discusses how to evaluate performance and reward personnel accordingly.

It is imperative that PIC personnel be able to relate to the various functions as well as to various levels of management. These interfaces are described in detail in this chapter.

The computer's impact is significant and is becoming more vital each day. Therefore, one section discusses the use of the computer in PIC systems. Finally, a hint is given as to the future challenges of the profession. It is a dynamic field; to progress, one must be alert to future opportunities.

*This chapter has been revised for the Third Edition. It is based on Chapter 26, *Management Concepts* of the *Production and Inventory Control Handbook,* Second Edition, Editor, Gary A. Landis; Assistant Editor, Julie A. Heard; Contributors, Ralph C. Edwards, Randell Eldridge, Robert J. Greene, and Mitchell Levy.

ORGANIZING THE FUNCTION

All organizations are supported by a structure consisting of the rules and regulations, policies and procedures, and operating methods employed by a business.

Defining Organizational Concepts

The basic concepts that define an organization are concerned with the manner in which it operates. Each individual organization must develop its own concepts. In essence, these concepts deal with planning and controlling the operation of the organization through the use of objectives, policies, and procedures.

Objectives.   Each organization and each manager within an organization must develop goals. Objectives deal with what is to be achieved by an organization, department, or individual. In most cases, objectives are specific and quantifiable. Examples include dollar or unit performance goals and efficiency goals. Such objectives provide a sense of direction and motivation and form the framework for establishing policies and procedures.

Policies and Procedures.   Once organizational objectives are established, a means of meeting those objectives must be developed. Policies and procedures focus attention on the how-to aspects of meeting objectives. Policies are generally guidelines for employees to follow. Policies can be either explicit or implicit, and they allow management to make decisions once rather than every time a situation arises. Most policies are concerned with decision-making responsibilities, employee behavior and requirements, and so on. Procedures, however, more often deal with the specific nature of how to accomplish an activity, such as paperwork routing, scheduling personnel training, and promotion. Policies tend to be broader and subject to interpretation, while procedures are generally more inflexible and detailed.

Rules.   Rules are generally derived from policies and are often very specific. Rules are established to clarify for the personnel specific behavioral offenses and the resulting penalties.

Budgets and Plans.   Budgeting and planning encompass many activities. Plans are specific operating guidelines for attaining the objectives and generally are established for the PIC activity in units of production and then translated to dollar terms for a budget.

Reporting Relationships

Reporting relationships within an organization depend on its structure to a great extent. Most often, line relationships exist, with each level reporting to the level above it. Authority and responsibility begin at the top of the organizational hierarchy and encompass ever-smaller areas further down the organization chart. In most organizations, the "staff" serves in an advisory capacity.

Types of Structures

Organizational structures vary greatly from one corporation to another. Many are simple and straightforward; others are extremely complicated. The basic types are functionalized structures, line structures, line-and-staff structures, committee structures, and project teams.

Functionalized Structure. Each individual function is a unit unto itself with its own specialized personnel and responsibilities. Generally, this type of structure has staff specialists with responsibility over line personnel. An example would be the quality-control department that is empowered to directly command production personnel in the activities related to quality. The primary advantage of such a structure is the true utilization of specialized skills. The basic weaknesses are that reporting requirements and authority lines become fuzzy and lower-level personnel suffer from having to report to many bosses.

Line Structure. Each functional area has a clear chain of command within the line structure. An example would be a corporation with marketing, manufacturing, and finance functions, each having a direct chain of command from top to bottom. Reporting relationships are generally simple and straightforward, as are responsibility and authority chains. Communication and decision making are generally quick processes. The primary disadvantage of this structure is the lack of specialized skills or knowledge that staff people often provide.

Line-and-Staff Structure. This structure attempts to blend the two methods described above to provide a clear, concise, and quick chain of command as well as the specialized skills of staff personnel.

Committee Structure. This structure attempts to use the skills and technical expertise of both line-and-staff personnel to solve problems and make decisions. The underlying theory is that two heads are better than one. Such committees may be standing or ad hoc and may be staffed permanently or temporarily. The committee process does allow input from many disciplines for decision making, and in some circles a decision by consensus is considered best. However, group decision making can often be a slow, painful process that does not necessarily produce the best decision. Rather, some feel that a group decision reflects the ideas of the most political, stubborn, or persistent member(s) of the group.

Project Teams. Like the committee structure, project teams solicit information, ideas, and involvement from many functional areas of an organization. Such teams are often formed for selecting and implementing a specific system. A project team is often superimposed on the existing line or functional structure. The project team structure has the same basic advantages and disadvantages as the committee structure. Project teams will be discussed later.

Each organization must develop its own "best" structure based on the type of industry it is and its personnel, goals, and reporting requirements. Information about structure can be gained from observing other organizations, but in the final analysis the custom-tailored structure is often superior.

Management Direction

Delegation is a talent required of all managers, and it must be included from the beginning during the design of the first tentative organizational chart. It is often said that accountability and decision making should be delegated to a person at the lowest possible level of management. This will affect his or her training and will allow him or her to achieve and receive added responsibility.

Exceptions Principle.   A manager controls the actions of subordinates to a considerable degree through policy formulation and the scope of the authority delegated to them. In this way, the superior sets limits within which the subordinates act without further consultation. When a problem arises that is not routine and is outside the scope of a subordinate's authority, it is understood that he or she should refer the matter to his or her superior. If his or her superior does not have sufficient authority to decide, the matter is referred upward in the hierarchy to a manager having sufficient authority. This process is called the *exceptions principle.* When it is followed correctly, the exceptions principle frees the manager of excessive detail and those decisions more efficiently made at lower levels. Similarly, subordinates are not obliged to make decisions best made at higher echelons.

Span of Control.   The number of subordinates reporting to a manager is the *span of control.* The concept associated with the span of a manager's control is that there is a limit to its size. When this limit is reached, it is wise to break up the group into subgroups. Decreasing the spans of control will increase the number of levels required and could hinder effective communication between top and bottom organizational levels. However, the number of levels can be decreased only by widening the spans of control. There is a limit to the degree to which the spans can be increased before the manager's ability to coordinate subordinates is impaired, even if the manager uses such techniques as assistants, staff organizations, and committees.

Maximum spans of control for various organizational levels have been suggested, although there is some question about their validity. A better conclusion is that the limits depend on the manager's abilities, the types of activities to be managed, and the capabilities of the subordinates. Certainly an energetic, capable manager can accommodate a larger span than someone possessing these qualities to a lesser degree. If the activities of subordinates are routine and change very little, a larger span is possible, particularly if the subordinates have been adequately trained. This fact explains why larger spans of control tend to be found in the lower echelons. Finally, larger spans are justified if the subordinates are able and willing to carry out their duties with little supervision.

Employee Characteristics.   Managerial direction involves getting employees to effectively accomplish the tasks dictated, but the effectiveness of departmental employees depends on both their ability and their willingness to contribute. The strength of these two employee characteristics depends on several factors. These factors may be grouped according to the degree of influence that the manager has over them. There are at least six factors over which the manager has little direct control:

1. The number and quality of outside job alternatives perceived by the employees. If economic conditions are adverse or employees' skills and experience are limited, the employees are likely to be very willing to contribute to the present organization.
2. The employees' attitudes, beliefs, and values that are formulated outside the work environment. These factors dramatically influence on-the-job behavior.
3. Group norms. The sanctions of informal groups exert enormous pressures on a member wishing to deviate from the norms of the group.
4. The emotional stability of subordinates.
5. The degree to which a manager can enlarge a subordinate's job to allow greater self-realization. Routine, uneventful jobs seldom evoke a strong loyalty and commitment on the part of an employee; yet the jobs must be done to achieve the economies of specialization.

6. The goals and expectations of employees as individuals and as a group. Yet the degree of compatibility between these goals and the realities of the work environment materially affect employee behavior and willingness to contribute.

Do not conclude that the manager has no control over these six factors. These factors act as constraints that must be recognized in dealings with subordinates. Furthermore, there are four categories of factors over which the PIC manager has considerable control:

1. The plans, job activities, authority relationships, and job interrelationships formulated in earlier phases of the management process

2. The payment and promotion systems of the department and the degree to which these reward systems are linked operationally to effective behavior

3. The training and development programs available to departmental employees

4. Interpersonal relationships with subordinates—more precisely, leadership style, communication methods, and the manner in which the manager takes disciplinary action.

Different aspects of some of these factors are discussed in greater detail since few answers apply to all situations. Although the progress in the state of the art has been extensive, there is considerable room for differences of opinion. A policy that works in one department, company, or geographical region may not work in another. Much depends on the precise nature of the situation.

Workforce Requirements. To operate any functional area, workers are required. After the initial staffing of the department, one of the primary management tasks is to continually review worker requirements and availability. The effective manager does not simply staff a department but also ensures that the right people in the right numbers are available at the right times and places to fulfill departmental responsibilities. A further responsibility of the manager is planning to ensure that personnel are trained and developed. By so doing, personnel can optimize the use of their talents and abilities and are less likely to suffer burnout. In addition, with a well-trained (and cross-trained) staff, personnel replacement problems are less likely to disrupt department operations.

Ratios. Personnel or manpower ratios, based on dollar or unit sales volume, have been developed as a result of extensive surveys of PIC departments. Such surveys can serve as a guideline to the manager concerned with how many of each type are required. Such ratios often do not take into consideration aspects of PIC such as types, numbers, and kinds of equipment, physical processes, or space required. Thus, reliance on ratios alone could cause the manager to make incorrect, and difficult to correct, staffing decisions.

Clerical Skills. As mentioned earlier, the PIC function was thought to be primarily clerical. Data collection and recording continues to be an important activity within the function. Without accurate data collection and recording procedures, decision making based on historical data would be impossible, financial accounting requirements would not be met, and product costing would be guesswork. The responsibility for such record keeping still falls within the PIC jurisdiction.

The purpose of record keeping is to provide accurate and timely information to decision makers and to offer input to the financial accounting system. Three basic types of records must be kept: availability records for materials, equipment, and tooling; basic information records, such as bills of materials, stock sheets, routing sheets, and work orders; and performance records (actual versus planned performance, order progress, etc.).

The simplest system possible to collect the necessary data should be used to provide the shortest, simplest reports possible to convey the necessary information for future planning, decision making, and performance evaluation.

Management Skills.   Throughout this chapter, management skills are discussed. These skills include the ability to effectively recruit, train, motivate, and discipline personnel. Effective management requires a thorough knowledge of the function and the ability to perform the administrative details inherent in any managerial job. Most importantly, good management entails skillfully leading a staff in the performance of the required duties to attain organizational goals and objectives.

Organizational Inefficiencies.   As in every organization, opportunities for inefficiency exist within PIC. Perhaps the most prevalent problem is functional-unit optimization. Each subsystem attempts to maximize the results of its activities but gives little consideration to the optimization need in other functional areas. The optimization of the entire system becomes less important than functional-unit optimization. As a result, each functional unit may appear to be prospering while the entire organization is faltering. Conflict in such situations can be resolved only when top-level management clearly identifies overall company goals and brings functional-unit goals into conformance in such a way that each unit's performance and the overall company performance are optimized.

As organizations become increasingly complex, so do information and communication flows between functional units. Faulty information from one unit to another is often cited as a cause of poor decision making, poor planning, and poor coordination. In structuring information and the communication flows, the shortest and simplest path is often best. PIC professionals are often inundated with information, with much of it arriving in reports cluttered with needless detail and too late to be of much use for current problem correction and future planning. Again, the best solution is the simplest, fastest information format possible needed to convey data.

PIC Subsystems.   Several systems within the production control area support the primary system. Each functions somewhat independently of the primary system and the other subsystems. Each such subsystem is responsible for providing data to the primary system and to other subsystems. The two primary subsystems involved are materials handling and storage and indirect materials control. The materials-handling and storage subsystem is responsible for moving materials from internal and external sources to and from the storeroom and various work centers. It is responsible for record keeping regarding the storage and movement of such materials. The indirect materials control subsystem is responsible for purchasing, storing, controlling, handling, and issuing all indirect materials. These materials are essentially for the manufacture of products but are not accounted for as raw materials. Examples are nails, screws, maintenance supplies, and perishable tools.

In addition to these two subsystems, many consider warehousing and/or shipping and purchasing to be PIC subsystems. However, they appear to have developed into systems that are related to, but are independent of, PIC.

Recruiting.   One of the major responsibilities of managers is staffing their departments. Included in staffing is recruiting both from within the company and from external sources. Generally, it is an accepted practice that promotions from within the organization, whenever possible, are most desirable. This attitude is based on the premise that promotions from within stimulate higher productivity, creativity, motivation, and commitment. In addition to their willingness to promote from within, most organizations have programs to actively train and educate employees to prepare for such promotions.

Despite the best efforts of a manager, sometimes promotion or recruiting from within is simply not possible. At that point, other likely sources include professional and trade societies, employment agencies, personnel consultants, and personal contacts. When a suitable candidate is located, care must be taken to promote a positive attitude on the part of current employees who will report to the new person.

Equal Employment Opportunity Commission. Each department should provide a policy statement that prohibits discrimination because of age, sex, race, or national origin. Hiring and promotional considerations should be based on job performance, applicable experience, and demonstrated competence. Proper documentation should be maintained whenever hiring, promotions, or demotions are affected. Each manager or supervisor should maintain an employee file for each individual under her or his jurisdiction. All pertinent information should be placed in this file. In this manner, objectivity can be maintained.

Duties and Responsibilities

Many types of organizational structures are used in the materials management field. These vary from company to company and from plant to plant. In one company, the materials group may perform strictly clerical functions whereas in another company a similar group may perform significant staff work and have substantial line responsibility and accountability.

Organizational structures also vary greatly depending on the size of the company. When job descriptions are reviewed, functions rather than titles should be stressed. No matter how small the company, all functions must be performed to some degree. The supervisor and clerk in a 25-employee shop may spend only a few minutes each week reviewing inventory while a large firm has a staff of several people perform the same basic task. As a company expands, the functions of the materials management group do not change; they simply receive more emphasis.

Many large corporations, even those that are very decentralized, have a corporate materials management group. The size and organization of these groups vary. As a result, their relationship with the plant-level materials management department varies widely from close daily control and supervision to providing primarily educational services. The most common corporate responsibility is purchase-contracts administration, typically the negotiation of contracts with major suppliers that service several corporate divisions or plants. In companies with several plants producing similar products, a central group might exist to develop long-range production plans and master production schedules. In that case, the plant materials group would focus on development and execution of short-range plans.

In spite of industry-to-industry variations and the many possible types of corporate structures, certain functions are generally accepted as the responsibility of materials management.

- Production control and inventory management, including master scheduling and physical stock control
- Distribution, including shipping, receiving, and traffic and frequently customer order entry and field warehousing
- Purchasing, including purchase-contract administration

Job Descriptions.   Job titles and short descriptions of positions and functions generally found at the plant level in a manufacturing company are essential. Their purpose is
to aid in communication among materials, management personnel, students, and others
interested in the field. Fortunately, standardization of terminology for job titles and
descriptions is underway. The title *master scheduler,* for example, is now used to
describe people who share the same general range of duties and responsibilities in different industries.

The sample organizational charts shown in Figs. 32.1 and 32.2 illustrate job relationships and job progression. As mentioned earlier, job functions rather than job titles
should be used in these charts and in a comparison of these jobs and those in a specific
company.

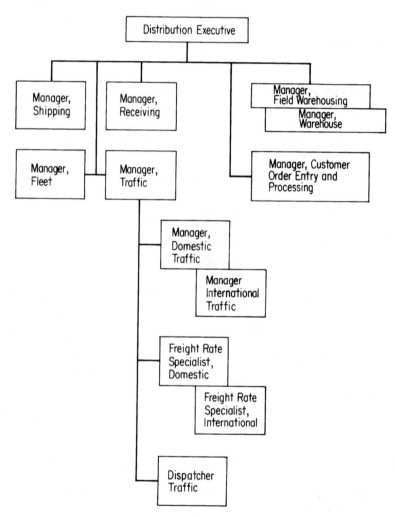

FIGURE 32.1   Distribution function organization chart.

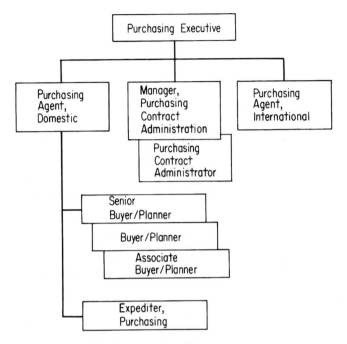

FIGURE 32.2 Purchasing organization chart.

Managerial, supervisory, and exempt positions are emphasized in these charts. Lower-level jobs such as those of stock clerks and materials handlers tend to vary greatly among companies of different size and industry.

The sample job description shown in Fig. 32.3 represents the type of writeup that should be prepared for all the positions in a company as part of a formal wage and salary administration program. Information such as salary grade would be added by the company.

Materials Management Executive This is the top materials management position. This person is generally responsible for most of or all the following: production planning and control, inventory planning and control, distribution, and purchasing. This person reports to higher-level manufacturing or operations management.

FIGURE 32.3 Sample job description.

Managerial Influence and Flexibility

The sample job descriptions make it clear that materials management personnel have considerable contact with other functional areas and, for many positions, considerable latitude in how they organize their own jobs and staffs. The following are examples of contact and influence with other areas:

1. Engineering
    a. Structuring of the product and its bills of materials to simplify production scheduling
    b. Establishing schedules for new products and engineering changes
2. Data processing
    a. Participation in the design and implementation of a variety of business systems
3. Cost accounting
    a. Stockroom and work-in-process inventories represent significant investments for most manufacturing companies
    b. Changes in production schedules can have a major impact on the distribution of fixed costs
4. Sales
    a. In many companies the materials management group has full responsibility for on-time delivery of finished products, from the time of entering the customer's order to shipment of the products

Other groups can also have a major impact on the operation of a materials management group. For example, marketing provides the sales forecast that is the prime input to the master scheduling group. Cost accounting may prescribe requirements for auditing of various processes and records, for example, cycle counting of inventory. The quality-control group is important, too. Unexpected problems with product quality can undo months of careful planning. In addition, purchasing and traffic personnel typically support the entire company, not just manufacturing departments.

Materials management groups include, in general, a broader mix of hourly, exempt, and supervisory positions than other functions in manufacturing companies. This mixture allows for greater flexibility in job definition for individual employees. A data entry clerk, for example, can be prepared for eventual promotion by being taught to review input documents for reasonableness.

Employee Development and Training

As the PIC profession continues to grow, the employee development and training needs become greater. The process really entails four aspects: (1) A program should be created to offer guidance to the employee through career development. (2) A program for both management and personnel development should be generated. (3) Specific education, from both a generic and a company standpoint, should be provided. (4) Training specific to today's environment should be offered. This relates to systems software and the specific computer hardware.

Motivation.   Employees are willing to contribute to their departments only if they perceive that by doing so they gain more than they lose. This implies the need for a certain degree of congruency between individual and organizational goals. Understanding the goals of individual employees introduces the topic of motivation. The study of motivation begins with seeking out and cataloging the motivators of employees, to relate them to the reward system of the organization.

Perhaps the best of these cataloging schemes is called the *needs hierarchy*. Humans are said to be *wanting* animals that always seek to satisfy their needs. These needs exist in a hierarchy. As lower-level needs are satisfied, humans turn their attention and energies to higher-level needs, which become increasingly more difficult to satisfy. As humans attempt to satisfy their needs, they are motivated. It is interesting that a satisfied need is no longer a motivator.

Physiological and safety needs comprise the first and basic level of needs as humans seek protection from danger and threats. Being in a somewhat dependent relationship, an employee responds favorably to managerial behavior that is consistent and fair and that does not cause an undue amount of fear of discharge. The all-important payment system relates to this basic level of needs.

The next level of the hierarchy consists of *social needs*. Humans are social animals who seek a sense of belonging and acceptance. The prevalence of informal groups in the industrial setting gives adequate testimony to the human social requirement. Managerial action thwarting an employee's social needs may lead to behavior detrimental to the organization. To the extent that an employee is a social being, the manager should be aware of the employee's feelings and need to belong.

The highest rung of the needs hierarchy encompasses *egoistic and self-actualizing needs*. People seek autonomy, self-respect, status, and the experience of continual self-development. The manager is no longer the motivator and controller. Instead, the manager's role is to provide the framework and climate within which the employee's existing motivation and drives can be harnessed to serve organizational purposes.

Basing reward systems solely on one of these three simplified views of human needs would be naive. Humans are too complex to be described adequately as striving solely for one level of needs. People are highly variable; they are capable of acquiring new motives and needs. The PIC manager must, therefore, be capable of detecting the differing and changing needs of each subordinate. The manager has at hand a repertoire of behavior patterns, to facilitate adjustment to the needs of employees. The manager's behavior in motivating subordinates manifests itself along three dimensions: leadership, communication, and disciplinary practices.

Types of Education and Training.   Every PIC department should have a formally documented educational program. This program should be time phased to focus the individual's education on specific functional responsibilities.

Education and training should be thought of as programs having different objectives. Education should teach concepts and theories, while training should provide hands-on practical instruction. Both are necessary for PIC personnel. Various types of education and training should be utilized. The best approach to use depends on the objectives of the program.

Independent Study.   This is one of the least costly methods of educating and training, and it allows the individual to use time as it becomes available. This method should always be used in conjunction with other techniques.

APICS Certification Workshops.   This approach is specifically oriented to the certification test. The curriculum thoroughly reviews the terminology and state of the art for specific manufacturing operations. This method is particularly important for new members of the department or old members who need a refresher course.

Consultants.   Working with a professional automatically offers exposure to knowledge otherwise unavailable. In addition, this type of individual can offer formal educational programs on a specific subject tailored to the company's needs.

Seminars and Workshops.   These are available throughout the country and cover every subject. Private consultants, educators, American Production and Inventory Control (APICS) chapters, and the APICS all offer programs of this nature. This type of education is suitable for new employees, seasoned professionals, and anyone wanting more knowledge.

Tutorial Sessions.   This approach uses videotapes, audiovisual presentations, and coordinators. As video equipment becomes more accessible, this type of technique will certainly be used more.

Software and Hardware Vendors.   Almost all major software and hardware manufacturers publish literature on manufacturing control systems, and many offer training as part of the systems support. Once again, this method is good for every level of information required. But the reader or listener should be able to discriminate between fact and salesmanship.

Who Should Educate and Train.   Education and training can be accomplished by various types of individuals. Many companies hire training managers for their personnel departments. If properly informed, these individuals can be effective. Many new system implementations place a full-time project director in charge. This individual is usually qualified to satisfy any educational needs.

One untapped resource that most companies consider last is their own employees, managers or otherwise. As more of the staff become certified by APICS as a CPIM or CFPIM, their knowledge should be applied to training others. These individuals usually become good instructors.

External and Internal Training.   A balance of both external and internal education is most beneficial. External training helps the trainee assess what others are doing as well as apply these lessons specifically. External education gives the individual exposure to other companies' successes and failures. It also provides generic education and the understanding of basic principles and techniques. It shows how to use specific approaches to solving problems. Therefore, a blend of both the external and internal approaches is needed. Thus the employee learns to assess situations objectively.

Teams as a Management Strategy

Employee involvement strategies in particular teams are an increasingly common strategy in helping organizations improve their performance and competitive position. A significant portion of Fortune 1000 organizations surveyed reported that a large part of their workforce uses many employee involvement practices, including teams.[1] Teams are becoming the essential building blocks of the organization whether for the purpose of organizing employees in different ways for delivering products and services to customers or for identifying and implementing ways of improving work.

Forms of Teams.   There are many forms of teams used in organizations: continuous improvement teams, quality circle teams, process improvement teams, cross-functional teams, self-directed work teams, task forces, product design teams, to name just a few examples. These types of teams always bring a group of people together to work for a common goal or purpose.

One of the simplest ways to classify teams is to identify three essential types:

- *Standing team.* A permanent team whose members generally do not work full time on team efforts but have regular job responsibilities in addition to the team's work
- *Ad hoc team.* A temporary team whose members do not work full time on the team and who disband once the team has accomplished its mission
- *Natural team.* A permanent team whose members are a dedicated resource and perform the core work of the organization

An example of a standing team is a management team for a manufacturing plant consisting of managers and leaders in the plant who make decisions about strategic direction, resource allocation, product development, and so on. An example of an ad hoc team is a cross-functional process improvement team consisting of representatives from operations, engineering, human resources, production control, accounting, and so on to improve a business process that spans the organization. Once the team has identified and implemented improvements, the team is disbanded. An example of a natural team would be a work team (e.g., in production) that works to deliver products to customers. Note that the work team may be traditionally managed (i.e., it may have a supervisor who has primary decision-making responsibility) or self-managed (i.e., it may have increased decision-making responsibility).

Characteristics of Effective Teams. One of the key questions about forming teams is what will lead to an effective team? Given the resources (time, money, education, and training, etc.) that are required to assemble and manage a team, understanding what leads to team effectiveness is of interest to many.[2] The elements that lead to team effectiveness are the following:

Commitment. A person's intention and desire to contribute to the team

Capability. Knowledge, skills, ability, and diversity of team members

Resources. Information, time, money, authority, and organizational support

Purpose. A clear sense of why the team exists, a direction

Scope. Boundaries, limits, and constraints for the team

Processes. Internal (e.g., communication, meeting management, or decision processes) and external (interacting with external stakeholders)

This list can be used when putting a team together as a checklist of important team member attributes. Or the list can be used as a tool to help a struggling team identify ways to improve.

Team Charters. The next question that can be asked is: If these characteristics lead to effective teams, how can we increase the chances that a team will be effective. A *team charter* is a critical tool in helping a team to be more effective. A charter documents important information about what a team will do and how it will function. The elements of a charter are described in Table 32.1. The *team's sponsor* (someone in management who provides direction, guidance, resources, and approval to a team) must be involved in developing the charter. The sponsor should draft a charter, focusing on the elements relating to *what the team will do* (purpose, scope, deliverables). The team should review and complete the charter, focusing on elements relating to *how the team will function* (team processes, team roles, etc.).

A team charter can be related significantly to higher levels of team performance.[3] A sponsor should work with a team at the start to develop a charter so that the team will have laid the foundation for successful work.

Team Resources

There are many resources available for teams that can be helpful in problem solving, decision making, and identifying ways to improve a product or process. Two resources for teams in general (i.e., any type of team brought together to improve a product or process) are *Continuous Improvement Teams and Tools*[4] and *The Team Handbook.*[5] Both are in the form of a workbook intended for all team members to use, and both cover how to apply many problem-solving and quality-improvement tools in a team setting. A third resource for a team is *Skill-Building for Self-Directed Work Team Members.*[6] This is specifically intended for self-directed teams such as a group of 8 to 15 employees organized around a whole product or process. The team will have the responsibility and

TABLE 32.1   Elements of a Team Charter

Mission (provides direction to the team)	What is the team's essential mission (e.g., redesign an inventory process, improve a scheduling process, etc.)? What specific goals or objectives must be accomplished as part of this mission?
Sponsor (provides accountability and guidance to the team)	Who is the individual or group that initiated the team? To whom is the team accountable for its results?
Boundaries (defines the scope of work for the team)	What is the target system, or unit to be improved, on which the team will focus (e.g., a department or a work process)?
Deliverables or products (defines what products the team is expected to produce)	What plans, reports, or documents, does the sponsor expect the team to create?
Time line (defines time constraints for the team)	Within what time frame must the team accomplish its mission and objectives?
Measures of effectiveness (defines success for the team)	What key measures of effectiveness will be used to tell if the team has been successful (e.g., percent of on-time deliveries, cycle-time reduction, or quality improvement in the target system)? Who will assess the success of the team and when? What goals or expectations do sponsors have for improving results in the target system?
Team-to-team interactions (defines interactions and communication with other teams)	With what other teams or groups must the team interact and coordinate (e.g., other improvement teams, a steering committee, leadership teams, or other stakeholder groups)? In what ways will the team coordinate and communicate with these teams?
Resources to the team (defines the resources the team has available)	What resources does the team have (e.g., budget or education and training opportunities)? What resources can the team call upon if necessary for help (e.g., in technical content areas, group facilitation)?
Membership of the team (defines who is on the team)	Who specifically is a member of the team? Who are temporary members? What skills are needed on the team? What viewpoints are needed on the team?
Intrateam processes (defines how the team will operate)	How often and where will the team meet? How will the team make decisions? What principles will be used in decision making? What process will the team use for problem solving or identifying improvement areas? What problem-solving or quality tools will the team use?
Team roles (clarifies roles within the team)	What formal roles will the team use to distribute workload (e.g., team leader, recorder, or facilitator)? What are the responsibilities of each role?

Queue Priority.   This describes the order in which individuals are served. The most common queue discipline is the first-come, first-served (FCFS) rule. However, there are many other possible rules including *service in random order* (SIRO) and *shortest processing time* (SPT).

Service Rate.   The time spent serving an individual includes only the time spent with the individual. If this time follows an exponential distribution, then the service rate is a Poisson distribution. As with arrival rates, queueing formulas can model several different probability distributions for service rates.

Exit.   There are different exits that an individual can make from the system. After leaving the system, the individual might be eligible to reenter the queue or might enter a different population that does not enter the service system for some time. For example, the probabilities of a machine needing service before and after an overhaul should be quite different.

Shop-Load Queueing Example.   A work center has been exhibiting excessive lead times. While the average input to the work center (7.75 jobs per day) has been less than the average output (8 jobs per day), the work center's lead times and backlogs seem excessive. Even though the average input is less than the average output, the variability of each causes large backlogs and long lead times. To better understand how the backlog could increase under these conditions, a queueing model is selected to model the system.

The input to the work center has the frequency distribution shown in the Poisson distribution. The mean input rate is 7.75 jobs per day. A chi-square goodness-of-fit statistical test reveals that the distribution is consistent with the Poisson. The output rate (Fig. 34.5b) is also a random variable described by a Poisson distribution with a mean of 8 jobs per day.

The shop scheduling system uses a first-come, first-served queue discipline. The number of jobs that can wait in the work center is large; therefore, the queue length is assumed to be infinite, and the population of possible jobs is also infinitely large. These characteristics describe a single-server, single-phase queueing system with a Poisson arrival rate, a Poisson service rate, an FCFS queue discipline, an infinite queue length, and infinite population size. This model is often noted using Kendall's notation $M/M/1$, where the first M denotes a Poisson arrival rate, the second M denotes a Poisson service rate, and the 1 denotes the number of servers. The M notation refers to a Markovian (Poisson) process.

Queueing Formulas.   The mathematical formulas of an $M/M/1$ model are given in the following example. The derivation of these formulas is beyond the scope of this handbook; however, one does not need to know how these formulas were developed to apply queueing models properly, but one does have to understand the assumptions underlying the formulas. After confirming that the assumptions are valid, the system is analyzed using the following formulas:

System utilization ρ

$$\rho = \frac{L}{M} = \frac{7.75}{8.00} = 97 \text{ percent utilized} \tag{34.1}$$

Because the average input to the system is slightly less than the average output, the system is utilized 97 (idle 3) percent of the time.

Mean number in queue $\overline{n}_q$

$$\overline{n}_q = \frac{L^2}{M(M-L)} = \frac{7.75^2}{8(8-7.75)} = 30.03 \text{ jobs} \tag{34.2}$$

action that can reinforce established limits. Discipline should always be administered in a private discussion between the employee and the superior. It should take place virtually immediately after the action requiring discipline and should be applied both consistently and impersonally. To be effective, disciplinary action should involve only breaches of known, established standards and limits.

Lack of discrimination in applying discipline is critical to the future relationship between superior and subordinate, as is an impersonal attitude on the part of the superior. Only when discipline is administered fairly will the superior continue to be regarded as a source of help, encouragement, and motivation.

Audits.   Personnel audits for each employee are beneficial in matching employees with jobs. Such an audit should cover a wide range of information about employees, including education, goals, outside interests, and abilities. Matching employees with jobs is difficult, but by relating job descriptions to personnel audits the task becomes easier. Promotion from within an organization is a valuable motivational tool accomplished most successfully through such matching.

Measuring Departmental Efficiency.   A necessary step in improving systems and processes is evaluation based on past performance. Within the PIC area, such evaluation is a difficult process owing to the interaction with other disciplines. Performance and actions of those other disciplines can affect the ability of PIC to perform effectively and efficiently.

Care must be taken to evaluate both the department and the individual employees based on only those areas of responsibility over which they exercise adequate control. A major problem occurs when different functions do not share common objectives. For example, if purchasing is evaluated based on the purchase price of raw materials and PIC is evaluated based on inventory levels, a conflict is sure to arise, and one group is bound to have a negative evaluation. Such conflicts are, to some extent, unavoidable. However, every effort should be made to reduce the impact of such conflicts on departmental (and individual) performance evaluations. Each measure should be studied individually to determine the various factors that affect it. The objective of performance measurement—process system control and improvement—is admirable; the specific techniques used, however, are the source of many problems and conflicts.

Appraisals.   In performance evaluation activities, appraisals serve the same purpose as feedback systems in a closed-loop control system. The established reason for appraisals is to evaluate the employee's past performance and establish future criteria. Almost as an afterthought, the results of the appraisal are usually related verbally to the employee. Too often, employee appraisal meetings do not happen in that way. At times, such appraisals become nothing more than a general superior-subordinate conversation; at other times, they are a one-sided discussion of the past and future. Research has shown that employees resent their inability to affect the future course of their work. Alternate processes, such as management by objectives, have been developed in the past several years. Because they involve the employee directly in planning and evaluating performance, these methods serve as a motivational tool rather than simply as the annual appraisal that must be endured.

Promotion Systems.   Promotion systems exist in most organizations. Components of promotion programs are personnel audits, job descriptions, and performance appraisals. These elements tend to be very subjective and, as such, are apt to be criticized. Research has indicated that direct measures of performance, such as budgetary responsibility and specific performance standards and goals, are effective in rating employees. Promotion policies can greatly affect employee motivation. The employee who sees management being hired from outside the organization will not be as performance or goal oriented as the employee who sees the link between job performance and career possibilities. Company policies and procedures related to promotion systems should be clearly stated, to encourage employees to set personal career goals and strive to attain them through superior performance.

REMUNERATION

For an organization to attract and retain the quality workforce necessary to meet its business objectives, reward systems must be offered. To be effective, such reward systems must be equitable, competitive, legal and defensible, understandable and appealing, and efficient to administer. The manner in which such systems are designed and administered has a major impact on the ability to motivate employees to be productive and to contribute to the organization's success.

Every manager must ensure that the organization's reward systems are appropriate and adequate for the unit or function. The PIC function requires people with specific skills, although it is unlikely the organization will develop reward systems specifically for PIC. The responsible manager must ensure that these systems do not cause difficulties with recruiting, turnover, and employee motivation.

Reward systems include nonfinancial rewards such as recognition, challenging work, and a good environment as well as financial rewards. Frequently the absence of such nonfinancial incentives forces the employer to make up the difference with dollars. PIC management is responsible for ensuring that their employees receive adequate nonfinancial and financial rewards and that the balance between the two is appropriate.

Financial rewards consist of the following:

- Direct pay, salary, and short-term incentives
- Long-term incentives such as capital-accumulation programs, retirement plans, stock-based programs, and profit sharing
- Employee benefits such as group health and life insurance and paid time off
- Employee services and perquisites such as education reimbursement, membership in professional organizations, and company-provided services

PIC management generally has control over and input to the determination of direct pay levels for employees, while benefits and other rewards are generally the same throughout the organizations.

Direct pay for an employee is a function of both the nature and the relative value of the job performed. Typically job descriptions are used to classify employees and identify them with a specific job title based on the value of their work. Frequently job descriptions become a major input for organizational analysis and job or work team design efforts. The relative value of the job performed is measured by four universal factors:

1. Skill
    a. Knowledge (education and experience)
    b. Analytical
    c. Manual
    d. Interpersonal

2. Effort
    a. Mental
    b. Physical
3. Responsibility
    a. For assets and information
    b. For work of others
    c. For safety of others
    d. For internal and external contacts
    e. Latitude exercised and potential impact
4. Working conditions
    a. Adverse conditions
    b. Hazards

Employers must be able to defend the method of assigning relative job values both to employees and to government regulatory agencies. Employees are concerned about internal equity, which involves the relationship of one job to other jobs in the job-worth hierarchy; inequity is known to cause dissatisfaction and unwanted turnover.

The market rate for a job, in addition to being equitably valued within an organization, must compare with prevailing competitive rates in the relevant labor markets. Each organization must decide in which labor market it competes, who its competitors for personnel are, and what the competitive posture will be relative to prevailing pay levels.

The process of setting pay levels is complex because of differences in the rates for specific disciplines or jobs. New jobs constantly emerge as a result of technological change—for example, that of a robotics engineer. These new positions make the assessment of an organization's competitive ability even more difficult.

The Materials Management Association (MMA) has developed an annual materials management compensation survey for determining prevailing market rates for key jobs in the field. Included are job definitions for new or changing disciplines such as master scheduling, capacity planning, and manufacturing data administration as well as for more traditional jobs in the stockroom, shipping, receiving, and traffic. By using the survey, current pay levels for materials management jobs can be compared with other jobs in the organization and with similar jobs in other organizations. Analysis of the materials management survey produces two pay relationship patterns which are similar to those widely found in other disciplines (see Tables 32.2 and 32.3).

Once an organization has determined the relative internal values of jobs, these jobs are usually grouped into job grades, each containing jobs of equal or similar value. The market values of the jobs are then used to establish pay ranges for each grade. A pay structure is the result, as shown in Fig. 32.4.

TABLE 32.2 Managerial Pay Relationships at Corporate Level

Materials management executive	Percentage of average pay for materials management executive
PIC, distribution, and purchasing executives	70–80
Manager of production planning, traffic, inventory planning, field warehousing, master scheduling, and fleet; purchasing agent; purchasing contract advisor	55–65

TABLE 32.3   Pay Relationships: Nonmanagerial Jobs within a Job Family*

Job title	Pay difference
Supervisor, quality control (QC) Senior QC specialist QC specialist Associate QC specialist	Average difference between adjacent levels = 15 percent

*A *job family* is a group of jobs involving work of the same nature but performed at different skill and responsibility levels.

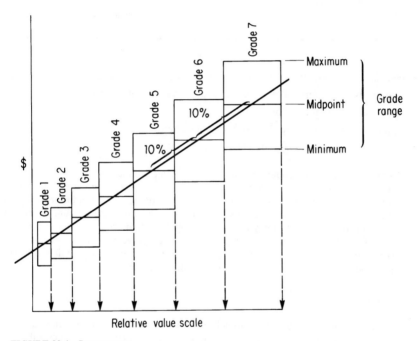

FIGURE 32.4   Pay structure.

Pay ranges allow for the difference in rates between people on the same job. These rate differences are usually attributable to differences in one or more of the following: seniority, command of job-related skills, and performance. The profile shown by Table 32.4 describes a pay range and what each type of employee should be paid.

To administer pay rates within established pay ranges on the basis of performance, an organization must design and effectively administer a performance appraisal plan based on job-related results. A sound appraisal system has the following characteristics:

• Performance standards are defined in advance.
• Performance standards are communicated in advance.

TABLE 32.4   Pay Range Profile

Pay level	Ranking	Type of employee who should be paid at this level
Maximum	4th Quarter	Employees whose performance is consistently outstanding and is sustained over extended period
Midpoint	3rd Quarter	Employees whose performance consistently exceeds standards
	2nd Quarter	Employees whose performance meets standards or who have acceptable performance but are still learning the remainder of the job
Minimum	1st Quarter	Employees whose performance occasionally meets standards or very new (minimally qualified) employees who are clearly in a learning capacity in the job

- Performance standards are based on job-related results and are as objective as possible.
- Appraisals are performed by someone who knows the employee's work.
- Appraisals are performed by a trained person.
- Appraisals are written and reviewed with the employee.
- An appeals mechanism is available to employees.

Organizations are confronted by different economic conditions over time. Business cycles, technological change, competitive conditions, and government intervention may all affect the funds available for employee rewards. Pressure to maintain profit levels may precipitate cost-cutting programs, which typically affect the amount of money available for increasing direct pay levels. It is important that each manager ensure that an adequate share of the available funds goes to the employees in his or her organizational unit. Pay levels should be kept competitive so that the organization does not find itself without the key employees needed for the organization's success.

Interfaces

To effectively fulfill assigned responsibilities, the PIC professional must interact with other company personnel from other disciplines. The key ingredients to successful interaction are communication and recognition of company-wide goals and objectives. Too often, one's own discipline appears to be the only important functional area of a business, and organizational goals are subjugated to area goals.

Human Relations.   In the past decade, increased emphasis has been placed on the human relations aspects of the organization. Employee needs are given greater consideration. The result appears to be increased employee commitment and motivation. Effective leadership, good communication skills, and encouraging employee participation and motivation are all key elements in creating a positive atmosphere in the workplace. Employees need to feel that they are getting as much as they are giving. The company that maintains good human relations with its employees will have committed and loyal employees.

To be effective in their jobs, PIC personnel must be able to relate to peers, superiors, and subordinates. Special training and an understanding of human relations are imperative. PIC personnel act as the focal point or coordinating function for most of the operations with which they deal. They more than any others must be able to get other people to respond through persuasion. All people in staff positions must rely on behavioral techniques to accomplish tasks.

Top Management.   Top management in many organizations is drawn from disciplines other than PIC. Frequently, top management comes from accounting, marketing, or the legal department. As a consequence, many top managers have relatively little understanding of the actual systems and processes in manufacturing and PIC. Despite their lack of understanding, they are ultimately responsible to stockholders for performance in both manufacturing and materials management.

The interaction between PIC and upper-level manufacturing and materials managers is generally easier because these positions are filled from the areas they represent. The practicing PIC professional deals with many details in day-to-day activities, and the top management for this activity is responsible for the overall company objectives, as well as the smooth performance of the area of responsibility. Thus, interaction with upper-level management is likely to be broad and general in nature rather than involving specific operating techniques.

An open-door policy on the part of upper-level management has become common. Such a policy encourages employees to channel information or grievances through the appropriate levels until they are satisfied with the outcome. Employees do not feel as cut off from the company when they are aware that such a channel is open to them. Top management's primary responsibility is the overall operation of the organization. A key to ensuring the success of an organization is to keep all the players working as a team. Disputes between functional areas resulting from differing goals can be settled and eliminated only by top-management involvement.

Subordinates.   The manager's relationship with his or her subordinates is critical. The responsibilities of management include providing leadership and motivation for employees and good communication.

Employee motivation is a subject that has been discussed and debated widely. Current theory suggests that participation is a key element to motivation. When employees are involved in establishing organizational objectives, they take a more active interest and are committed to a much greater degree. Some participation techniques that stimulate motivation include management by objectives, quality circles, and financial rewards for process or system improvements.

Leadership styles abound, from democratic to authoritative and everywhere on the continuum between. Research indicates that the more democratic form of leadership encourages worker commitment, innovation, and self-fulfillment. This form of leadership is better accepted by employees and creates a more positive atmosphere. Communication skills are essential in every aspect of life but perhaps nowhere more so than in creating positive superior-subordinate relationships. The ability to concisely convey instructions, relate necessary information, and encourage, motivate, and discipline employees can be a manager's most effective tool and can have a most positive effect on overall objective attainment.

Relationships with Other Departments.   PIC is frequently involved in disputes and/or conflicts with other departments. In part, such conflicts are the result of conflicting goals. Each department should concentrate on overall organizational objectives rather than simply ignoring all but its own objectives. Communication and education are additional tools for strengthening organizational unity. Too frequently, the functions involved simply do not understand the objectives of others. Often when people from two departments do try to communicate, they cannot understand each other. As technology has made specialists of us all, separate languages have evolved that tend to be very specific. Learning about the other subjects involved in an organization is a difficult and often frustrating task, but one well worth the trouble because of the many positive results to be achieved.

Integration of New Techniques.   The technological state of the art in PIC changes almost daily. Computer-aided design/computer-aided manufacturing (CAD/CAM) group technology, computer-integrated manufacturing (CIM), and kanban and materials requirements planning (MRP) represent advances in the body of knowledge. Detailed explanations of these techniques are inappropriate here; however, each of these technological advances requires interdisciplinary cooperation and education. Once again, education and communication in the various techniques are the keys to maximizing the benefits.

IMPACT OF THE COMPUTER

Technological developments in computer hardware and software have had an enormous impact on PIC. As computers have become smaller and processing times shorter, computers are seen more frequently in the manufacturing facility, both in the offices of PIC professionals and on the shop floor.

Systems Responsibilities

Through an extended process of trial and error, it has been decided that responsibility for system implementation must rest with the user. In the early evolution of computerized systems the entire responsibility for systems design, development, and installation rested with the data processing department. Installation of a workable accounting system was a relatively easy task. Formal, written procedures existed based on the manual record-keeping system in use. In contrast to the ease of installing accounting software, PIC systems were difficult to design or purchase and nearly impossible to install. Historically, PIC worked primarily from informal systems that did not even perform well manually. Written documentation and procedures were scarce. The changing day-to-day activities and priorities made formal manual systems impractical.

Most inventory managers were not sure what they wanted or needed in a system. They were even less aware of the systems available to them. Each individual made decisions to keep supplies available and production running based on experience and knowledge. Thought processes used to make such decisions were, at best, vague and difficult to explain.

During this period, relatively few software packages were available to adapt to PIC use. Therefore, data processing was faced with the task of developing totally new systems for individuals who had little understanding of what they wanted. As a consequence, PIC systems were developed that did not provide appropriate information for decision making, were difficult to use, and did not provide timely information. Thus, such systems soon deteriorated into informal systems that were less effective than the manual systems they replaced. During this evolution, it was determined that the only truly successful systems were those developed and installed by users of the system.

Successful system design and implementation depends on a person being held responsible for making it work. To ensure success, the end user must be involved and responsible. The user must be involved at all stages, including software selection, task force creation, management, implementation, and test data preparation. To assist in a system installation, a task force should be established with members from all involved departments. The head of the task force should be the end user in the highest position within the company. At least one member of the task force should have full-time responsibility to work on the installation.

Importance of Change

The installation of computers and computer systems has been one of the most significant changes in PIC management. Historically, the PIC function had been bogged down in routine paperwork, constantly fighting emergencies in order to keep the day-to-day activities going. The computer necessitated the development of formal, written procedures for inventory management. This procedure formalization process has been instrumental in speeding the emergence of the PIC body of knowledge.

Including the computer system in formal procedures leaves the inventory manager free to manage business more effectively. The result has been inventory reductions, improved customer service, and more efficient plant operations. The computerization of the factory results in increased recognition of PIC as a profession. During recessions many companies are caught with excessive raw materials and finished-goods inventories. This results in layoffs, capital shortages, and inventory obsolescence. Membership in APICS increased by leaps and bounds as companies realized that properly trained and educated personnel were essential to prevent a resurgence of excess inventory after the recession ended.

Upgrading Skills

Changes brought about by the widespread use of computer systems necessitate numerous changes in the educational requirements of the PIC professional. Decisions must be made after careful analysis of the data and information provided by the computer. Such analysis requires a thorough understanding of the techniques and formulas used to manage inventory. Computer systems include sets of decision rules designed to make routine recommendations. With a thorough understanding, the PIC professional will know which decisions require intervention and which decisions should be left to the computer.

Inventory affects every department of a company. Marketing must supply forecasts to plan materials requirements, production must provide feedback on quantities produced, purchasing must provide order status, and sales must provide data on actual customer orders. To be effective, the PIC manager must have at least a working knowledge of all company functions and be able to analyze how they affect the decision-making process.

The PIC manager is affected now, as never before, by activities outside the company. Rapid changes in technology create a ripple effect throughout all industry. The PIC professional faces constant changes in customer demand for new products, government relations, economic conditions, and manufacturing methods. Remaining aware of such changes and staying technically abreast of those that affect one's industry are crucial.

Given the rapidly advancing state of the art and body of knowledge, constant reeducation becomes a prerequisite for success. New management techniques are being described in the APICS publication *Production and Inventory Management Journal,* in the *APICS News,* in other trade magazines, and in newsletters and publications by consultants. Most hardware and software vendors gladly supply material related to their products. Some of their literature is generic in design and offers an excellent, inexpensive way to stay abreast of the latest technology.

To be useful, education must be applied, and the ability to analyze data to determine the best course of action is of the highest priority. Also, the ability to communicate actions and justification of decisions is required.

Flexibility

The only constant in today's business environment is change. The computer provides the flexibility to deal with change in a timely manner, making good management decisions with confidence possible. Previously, all data were manipulated manually and could not be handled rapidly enough for decision making. Consequently, decisions were often made with partial, sometimes inaccurate information. Companies can no longer afford to make decisions based on partial information provided by manual systems.

Companies dealing with retail customers must react quickly to changes in demand. Many retail stores now have point-of-sale terminals tied to a central database for providing daily sale quantities of individual items. Customer demands are recognized immediately and have an immediate effect on orders sent to the manufacturer. The manufacturer must be able to react to new demands by ordering raw materials, scheduling, producing, and shipping to retail outlets. Conversely, a manufacturer must react to cancel raw materials orders and reschedule production capacity to produce salable products if necessary.

The emerging trend in building new or modernizing older factories is toward the development of a *flexible manufacturing system* (FMS). In an FMS, production equipment can be converted from producing one type of item or product line to another with little modification or loss of time. In addition, more operations are performed with a single machine, thus reducing queue and move times. Another feature built into some systems is computerized quality control. Flexible manufacturing systems contribute to lower in-process inventory, faster reaction to change, decreased manufacturing time, and production of higher-quality products.

Using the Computer as a Tool

Computers manipulate large quantities of data in relatively short periods to provide information for decision making. Software systems should be evaluated based on this fact, and users must be trained and educated to ensure that the full advantage of such a tool capability is recognized.

FUTURE CHALLENGES

Technology is constantly changing, requiring upgrading the PIC function. To most PIC professionals, the challenge is to keep abreast of new technology and determine which is right for the particular manufacturing environment.

Systems Challenges

Personal computers.   Personal computers (PCs) offer significant opportunities for the PIC professional to profit from the capabilities of the computer with little or no involvement of data processing personnel. Many have experienced the frustration of waiting for computer programming services, an especially difficult task for professionals responsible for making things happen. Little time and training is required to learn how to program and operate a PC that can provide usable information. Several advantages of current PC systems are the shortened development time, increased user acceptance, minimal delay in making changes, and less reliance on other departments. All of these are large pluses for the PIC professional.

Caution should be exercised, however. The ease with which PCs are used can give users a false sense of security. For example, blind reliance on data generated from a spreadsheet built by a casual computer user can lead to disaster. Because of the power of computers and their ease of use, extra care must be exercised. Commercial, off-the-shelf software is very powerful and a wonderful development. However, any programs or small systems created quickly and easily should be scrutinized for errors.

The world of computing continues to change rapidly. Network communications and electronic mail, including electronic data interchange (EDI), is having an enormous effect on the PIC function. So it is important for the PIC professional to stay abreast of the latest developments in this fast-changing arena.

Properly regulated and used, PCs can play an ever-increasing role in inventory management. It is essential that system developments occur in a way that the necessary continuity of the PIC functions is maintained. Also, it is critical that the computers use, address, and support overall business goals.

Input-Output Devices Challenges. Computers are able to manipulate data at a faster pace than input can be received or output generated. The rapid development and deployment of I/O devices significantly enhances computer applications. Devices such as point-of-sale terminals, magnetic-tape readers, bar-code readers, laser scanners, and printers allow most input to be processed immediately, on-line, without manual intervention. In addition, the PIC professional may also be involved with EDI with either suppliers or customers. This extremely rapid and accurate method of data transmission of order information is having a large impact on the PIC function. The PIC professional will receive timely information for making management decisions so that decisions will be made and actions taken at a more rapid pace than at present.

Computer-Integrated Manufacturing. With cheaper and more powerful computers, integration of all company activities can now be achieved. Manufacturing resource planning (MRP II) was a significant advance toward this aim. CIM goes beyond that and includes new technologies such as CAD, CAM, computer-aided engineering (CAE), and computer-aided process planning (CAPP).

Installation of a CIM system will lead to new opportunities and responsibilities for the PIC professional. One challenge will be to ensure that sufficient interfaces are established to provide the PIC professional with appropriate information to manage inventories. Therefore, one must stay abreast of the latest technologies and maintain a working knowledge of current capabilities.

Robots. The rapid deployment of robots is an inevitable development for the factory of the future. The use of robots will provide more reliable production quality and more dependable production rates.

In addition to the innovations mentioned above, various techniques and software packages have been available for many years but have not been implemented successfully. For example, in most companies, computer-controlled storage is not tied into the centralized database, to obtain maximum use of the available capabilities. The challenge to PIC is to fully utilize the available technology. All systems must be integrated and used to manage and further the overall goals of the company. Failure to properly implement such systems results in the deterioration of the competitive posture in the world markets, resulting in slow economic growth of companies and the nation.

Management Involvement

With the advent of the computer and the subsequent system opportunities, management must become more involved. Some managers have attempted to avoid this confrontation but have realized the advantages of these tools. Managers at higher levels will operate in teams without friction. They will be more supportive of the production plan and the master production schedule. They will be evaluated on the basis of their contribution in making and executing these plans.

Three significant developments should be expected in the future: (1) The trend toward simpler systems that users can understand should continue. (2) Better production plans need to be developed and executed. (3) Human resources need to improve. Problems must be solved by the priority of their importance.

It is obvious that PIC professionals have come of age. If they are to retain their leadership role, they must continue to be aware of new opportunities for improving inventory management techniques and be able to offer more efficient and effective methods of manufacturing.

REFERENCES

1. E. E. Lawler, III, S. A. Mohrman, and G. E. Ledford: *Employee Involvement in Total Quality Management: Practices and Results in Fortune 1000 Companies,* Jossey-Bass, San Francisco, 1992.

2. Cornelius and Associates: "Team Facilitation and Team Management Skills," *Workshop Notebook,* Columbia, S.C., 1994.

3. E. M. Van Aken and D. S. Sink: "Key Learnings in Chartering Design Teams," *Proceedings of the 1996 Annual Quality Congress,* American Society for Quality Control, Milwaukee, Wis., 1996.

4. R. F. Lynch and T. J. Werner: *Continuous Improvement Teams and Tools: A Guide for Action,* QualTeam, Atlanta, Ga., 1992.

5. P. Scholtes: *The Team Handbook,* Joiner Associates, Madison, Wis., 1988.

6. A. Harper and B. Harper: *Skill-Building for Self-Directed Work Team Members,* MW Corporation, Mohegan Lake, N.Y., 1992.

7. R. M. Kanter: *The Change Masters: Innovation and Entrepreneurship in the American Corporation,* Simon and Schuster, New York, 1984.

8. P. Hersey and K. Blanchard: *Management of Organizational Behavior,* 4th ed., Prentice-Hall, Englewood Cliffs, N.J., 1982.

CHAPTER 33
PARTNERING FOR PRODUCTION

Editor

Patricia E. Moody, CMC
President, Patricia E. Moody Inc.
Marblehead, Massachusetts

Companies interested in acquiring new ideas, faster and more robust product introductions, and collective clout have discovered the power created by *partnering*. With partnerships, these players—some competitors, some neighbors, some adversaries even—have created an entirely new organization. But partnering offers considerable challenges to a traditional organization that is skilled in leveraging and other techniques intended to create "false partners."

What are the elements of true partnering, and how can an organization begin to develop and strengthen them? There are many models of companies doing it the wrong way. There are extreme examples of squeezing, leveraging, and otherwise pressuring supplier "partners" for price cuts and other concessions. These tactics are intended for short-term advantage, at best. Moreover, because of the severe and destructive impact they have on smaller organizations, they cause some suppliers to seek relationships with better partners, or World Class Customers.

SEVEN DRIVERS OF BREAKTHROUGH PARTNERING

The entire process of developing new, long-term relationships with suppliers starts with a few basic supports that cement the relationship. The Seven Drivers of Breakthrough Partnering are quality, timeliness, communications, flexibility, an attitude of continuous improvement, the habit of collaboration, and trust. Each of these elements must be securely in place for a strong partnership to develop. Examine each one, and how to best develop them.

1. Quality

When the pioneers of just-in-time thinking formulated this approach to production and supply management, they based the success of its application on acceptance of total quality, or zero defects, production. Now, over 15 years after JIT's common acceptance, superior quality is the minimum ticket to most marketplaces. Just as quality reinforces good work practices, the goal of superior quality unites partners seeking mutual advantage.

Motorola Corporation understands the value of driving an entire organization by its vision of total quality, Six Sigma (or 3.4 defects per million). *Motorola University,* in addition to offering standard, required training for every Motorola employee, has become a quality methods training ground for its customers, suppliers, and even competitors.

Stick to the Basics. Customers and suppliers, and other alliance members, have, however, been known to get carried away with the superficial tools associated with "The Quality Crusade." Quality cannot be inspected or audited into an out-of-control process. Many suppliers, for example, are inundated with a variety of quality audits, each superficially different but drawn typically from the same database. NCR, Motorola, and Xerox have recently collaborated on simplifying their supplier audit standards and have adopted Motorola's survey instrument, *Quality System Review* (QSR), as the single audit standard to be used for periodic review of this billion-dollar business. The result has been a reversal of the pre-QSR, 1-man-month-per-year expenditure of supplier time. Moreover, this document is written so that its *Maturity Index* allows practitioners to learn where they are in the maturity-of-quality practices, moving on a continuum from relatively inexperienced to worldclass.

Good measures of supplier performance typically include statistics on the number of defects received by the customer and also the number of items received late on site. Some organizations also track shipping quality (on-time, damages, etc.), invoicing, and other record-keeping quality. The importance of basic quality information is that it must be understood and developed by the personnel in the organization who also have the ability to make improvements. For that reason, the data should also be represented in an easy-to-read format—pie charts and bar graphs, for example—that show visual trends as well as irregular patterns.

Partnering quality basics, therefore, require that procurement personnel, as well as production and engineering professionals, be comfortable with daily quality measures of product and process "goodness."

2. Timeliness

The other basic JIT performance requirement is timeliness—that is, timeliness in delivering a product on time to meet the original customer request, or "need" date. Zero days early and zero days late is as basic a measure of process "goodness" as is quality. In fact, Honda of America supplier's quality awards include an award to producers that consistently meet their very demanding, sometimes hourly, delivery requirements.

But perfect, consistent, on-time delivery of shipments requires more than expedited premium transport logistics; it requires complete control of the entire product delivery cycle—from order entry down through production, and out to shipping. Suppliers that want to minimize disruptions and all causes of lateness need to monitor and troubleshoot late-delivery problems as seriously as they would product or process quality defects.

3. Communications

The third partnership element, communications, is, next to trust (to which it contributes greatly) the biggest challenge would-be partners face in initiating and maintaining strong partnerships. For the purpose of partnering, the term *communications* has a very specific meaning. It is the careful and thorough sharing of information vital for all partners to perform well in the partnership. Most customers frequently and usually consistently communicate their requirements through a variety of communications tools—production schedules, contracts, daily expedite notices, and various audit and qualification instruments.

Partnering communications, however, cannot be confined to information or requests coming from only one side of the partnership. Boeing's 777 project is a good model for customer-supplier communications and cooperation. For the design of this aircraft, Boeing took an approach very different from its previous rollouts. Because the objective of the design team was to produce a service-ready airplane that incorporated very innovative interior and service-ready features, Boeing chose to include key customers in the design from the start. Philip Condit and several other executives worked for 3 weeks on a statement of their partnership. The resulting handwritten, one-page document summarizes the intent of their partnership: to produce the best aircraft design in the industry. But this single page reflects more than that objective—in fact, it reflects the process of developing this agreement, working out the details of specifically what and how much information each partner would share, and what the lines of communications would include.

Once the partners have stated their intent and worked out parameters of sharing information, regular and open communications become key to maintaining the agreement. Innovative companies like Williams Technologies in South Carolina, a remanufacturer to GM, Honda, and other major automotive suppliers, has pioneered a variety of partnership communications techniques. Along with monthly customer-supplier reviews, Williams undergoes regular supplier audits and conducts its own customer audit that they regularly use to elicit useful information from their bigger customers.

When designing a partnership communications program, remember that effective communication is brief, consistent, and designed to give both parties the information they need to do their jobs well. Most suppliers need technical product information, as well as market positioning concepts, as early in the idea stage as customers can allow. Most customers need assurance of quality, delivery, and cost performance. Beyond these basics, companies must be selective about information that employees can absorb—sticking to the basic works best.

The next four partnering drivers—flexibility, an attitude of continuous improvement, the habit of collaboration, and trust—take the organization from JIT competency to strong, long-term partnerships.

4. Flexibility

Partnering can be a challenge to rule-bound, hierarchy-driven organizations. Flexibility, however, is key to the success of two manufacturing drivers: *lean* (sometimes also called *agile*) *manufacturing* and *partnering*. *Flexibility* typically is a code word for a supplier's willingness to change production schedules overnight or to adjust product mix to fit new forecasts. Now, however, *flexibility* is a broader, more strategic term that encompasses a partner's willingness and ability to flex to meet new market opportunities. Flexibility becomes the main characteristic of fluid, changeable organization structures populated by multifunctional teams.

5. Attitude of Continuous Improvement

Organizations that practice true partnering are usually committed to continuous improvement. Companies like Honda, Motorola, Nypro, and many others demonstrate this with their education initiatives. Motorola University, for example, is open to customers, suppliers, and even competitors. These companies demonstrate their belief that workforce development "raises the bar" for all industries, and they spend substantial amounts of their net profits, sometimes over 5 percent, to fulfill that commitment.

Continuous improvement can be driven by other corporate initiatives, like reward systems that favor suggestions or promotion policies that rotate professionals through engineering, production, and purchasing positions. Teams tend to nurture continuous improvement if they work on real problem-solving activities; at one East Coast temperature-controls company, all employees serve on at least three teams per year. The culture has developed an openness to new ideas and a willingness to try new production approaches that started with member participation in an improvement team.

6. Habit of Collaboration

The habit of collaboration appears at many levels. Internally, if employees are encouraged and rewarded for working on teams with professionals from other disciplines, and if the results are generally good, they will continue to seek new partnerships internally and externally. Some world-class companies foster the habit of collaboration by sponsoring industry consortia and otherwise finding ways to share resources and information. Varian, for example, has decided that rather than attempting to identify and source world-class suppliers, they will offer quality training and other much-needed assists to help suppliers develop to the level of performance that they need.

7. Trust

Trust, the last and most important element of partnering, rests on the successful development of the previous six strengths. Although trust is the "fuzziest" term, it is easy to identify actions that destroy trust. Suppliers complain of partners that talk value but buy on price. Customers complain of suppliers that promise high performance, then forget their commitments. The list of trust destroyers is endless.

Any operation serious about extending its power beyond the factory walls can learn to partner, and trust lies at the heart of all partnering activities. If your intent is to build a network of strategically linked partners, you should avoid adversarial activities like purchase price variance awards and bid-and-quote selection.

Think carefully about specific actions that build trust. Start with day-to-day operating issues at the "basic JIT" end of operations because when companies perfect JIT scheduling and low inventory levels, they must trust suppliers to keep their operations running. Companies such as Honda and Motorola that excel in partnering work hard to build trust around specific issues through supplier councils, resource grants to small suppliers, supplier awards, and benchmarking projects.

TOOLS THAT BUILD PARTNERSHIPS

Most partnerships start with excellent and frequent communications. Among customers and smaller suppliers, however, the additional basic element that builds partnering capabilities is manufacturing excellence practices. World-class manufacturing methods like visual systems, self-directed work teams, and a variety of total quality tools are well understood and used by larger customers, but small- and medium-sized companies have fewer resources and less time to develop training in these areas. Companies like

Motorola and Honda, Varian and Xerox, that share their training resources—videos, courses, books, and instructors—are at an advantage at building and keeping partnerships.

Other simple tools that build trust and strong communications in the partnership include the following:

1. The World-Class Customer Survey[1]
2. The Motorola QSR
3. Benchmarking surveys and visit
4. Supplier advisory councils and awards
5. In-plants and other innovative organization structures
6. The world-class customer concept

The World-Class Customer Survey

Partnership communications need not be one-sided. Both partners have information requirements that can best be met when they state clearly and specifically what they need to perform well. Surveys administered by neutral third parties meet this need.

Honda surveyed its 300 suppliers using the World Class Customer Survey to discover what the company needed to do better to help suppliers perform well. This two-page survey is structured to determine where an organization may be offering inconsistent information or where one area in a company may be giving insufficient or incorrect information on topics like product specifications, schedules, critical-path items, and new-product introduction and obsolescence plans. Honda learned two critical lessons from the survey:

1. Suppliers complained that contact personnel rotate too frequency. Although job rotation has been a good internal training method, suppliers find it confusing.

2. *Kintori amay* ("same face"): Suppliers need to receive the same, consistent message from different areas of the organization. *Kintori amay* refers to a Japanese spaghetti-like candy; wherever one cuts a cross section, the same face of an ancient Samurai warrior, Kinton, appears!

In-plants

Colocation of suppliers on the customer site, or *in-plants,* are a creative way to break communications barriers and to bring supplier expertise into the heart of the product development and production process. EMC Corporation in Massachusetts, Bose Corporation, Honeywell, and others have initiated arrangements that open planning systems and other key areas to supplier representatives. Most of these arrangements are intended to deemphasize the selling phase of the partnership and cut down paperwork and expediting between the partners. In fact, at EMC the supplier representative has access to most information used by internal employees. At Bose, in-plants cut purchase orders on their own companies. Although they are not paid by Bose, they have a desk and phone at the company and carry a Bose badge.

Relationships among manufacturing companies, customers and suppliers both, used to be organized in hierarchical tiers—big fish fed on and leveraged little fish. Leverage and pressure tactics were the tools that big organizations regularly applied to smaller ones; smaller ones retaliated in kind, by setting prices high enough to compensate or by maintaining a large stable of "captive" customers. Breakthrough Partnering, however, advances the short- and long-term objectives of all partners. By building on the Seven Drivers of Breakthrough Partnering—quality, timeliness, communications, flexibility, and attitude of continuous improvement, the habit of collaboration, and trust—and by becoming a World Class Customer, companies can develop a collective enterprise advantage that gives them larger markets, access to innovation, stability, and flexibility.

BIBLIOGRAPHY

1. *World Class Customer Survey,* Copyright Patricia E. Moody, Inc., Marblehead, Mass.
2. P. E. Moody, *Breakthrough Partnering,* Wiley, New York, 1994.
3. D. Nelson, P. E. Moody, and R. Mayo, *Powered by Honda,* Wiley, New York, 1997.

SECTION 8

QUANTITATIVE METHODS FOR PIC

CHAPTER 34
QUANTITATIVE METHODS

Editor
Stephen A. De Lurgio, Ph.D., CFPIM
Professor of Operations Management
University of Missouri, Kansas City, Missouri

The term *quantitative methods* (QM) has several meanings, including the synonyms *operations research* (OR) and *management science* (MS). Simply defined, QM is the application of the scientific method to solutions of managerial problems. Historically, OR/MS became a recognized discipline during World War II. It has since grown to include many techniques that can be effective in planning, executing, and controlling operations. In the past, there have been some technical and behavioral problems in using QM. Fortunately, more help is now available to both managers and analysts because (1) the effectiveness of computers and software has improved greatly, including built-in spreadsheet capabilities, (2) knowledge has improved on how to apply QM successfully,[1-7] and (3) comprehensive and accessible QM textbooks exist.

This chapter illustrates QM that solve *production and inventory control* (PIC) problems and discusses the assumptions, limitations, benefits, and disadvantages of QM. Its objective is to provide enough information so you will (1) recognize when QM is applicable, (2) be able to solve important PIC problems, and (3) know where to find additional information about QM. Because this chapter cannot present all the methods of QM, several references are included for further study.[8-15]

CHARACTERISTICS OF QUANTITATIVE METHODS

In general, the purpose of QM is to assist managers in solving problems by using models; thus, the fundamental objective of QM is to provide information for better decisions. Information is derived through the collection of data, the formulation of hypotheses, and the construction, validation, and implementation of models. Modeling is an essential part of QM because both the modeling process and the model assist problem solvers in analyzing, predicting, and controlling real-world systems.

Because models are abstractions of the essence of real systems, the process of modeling requires both art and science. Too often, those responsible for modeling and decision making ignore the interaction of analyst science and managerial art.

While many forms of models exist, such as physical, schematic, graphical, mathematical, analog, and digital, this chapter only discusses the mathematical and logical models implemented by digital computers. Some people mistakenly believe that the only purpose of QM is to provide optimal solutions; although this is certainly an important purpose, much modeling activity in QM is directed to providing insightful information for better decisions.[7] The reduction of uncertainty through what-if simulations and experiments is one of the most important purposes of modeling. In practice, the best measure of a model's validity is its ability to improve the decisions of management.

Solution Methods

Two types of solution methods exist for solving quantitative problems: deductive and inductive. *Deductive methods,* such as *economic order quantity* (EOQ) *formulas,* derive solutions directly from mathematical techniques, such as the maxima-minima theorem of calculus. In contrast, *inductive methods* employ iterative procedures to search for good solutions to problems. Because simple and complex problems are solvable using inductive methods, they are applied more frequently. The procedures of decision theory, mathematical programming, simulation, part-period balancing, computer spreadsheet models, and MRP what-if analyses are inductive procedures.

Sometimes problems are forced to fit a familiar, easy, or optimal solution procedure. This is not the best procedure. We should remember that a good solution to a realistic model is sought, not an optimal solution to an unrealistic model. Therefore, the solution procedure should be selected after problem formulation and modeling, not before.

Types of Models

In general, two types of models exist: deterministic and probabilistic. In a *deterministic model,* the values of all factors are known with certainty. In contrast, a *probabilistic model* includes variables that are randomly distributed and therefore are described by appropriate probability distributions. Obviously, probabilistic models are more general than deterministic models.

Deterministic Models. If a system has mathematical relationships that are known with certainty (synonym: *deterministic*), then powerful mathematical methods can be used to achieve optimal solutions. For example, in scheduling production with known demands, capacities, and materials, a deterministic model can be used. Deterministic solution methods include linear programming and the continuous mathematical optimization methods of calculus, as used in the derivation of EOQ formulas.

If the deterministic assumption is valid, then deterministic techniques provide insightful information about the behavior of the system. However, when the deterministic assumption is invalid, then the model may be meaningless or misleading. One should always critically evaluate the assumptions of a quantitative model. However, the assumptions of a model may not have to be perfectly accurate because solutions are often insensitive to violations of those assumptions, a condition called *robustness.* For example, the EOQ model has been found to be valid in a variety of situations that violate its assumptions.

Most often, systems are not perfectly deterministic. If a system is dominated by deterministic events, certainty may be assumed or what-if experiments can be used to explore the effects of uncertainties—a procedure called *sensitivity analysis.* However, if sensitivity analysis shows that the uncertain events greatly affect system behavior, then a probabilistic model should be used.

Probabilistic Models. Systems that possess one or more random variables may have to be modeled using frequency or probability distributions. In general, probabilistic systems are more difficult to model than are deterministic systems. However, most systems exist in uncertain environments. For example, if considerable uncertainty exists in demand, it may be necessary to use probability distributions to describe demand. Consider the following probabilistic model: A manufacturer sells a product under two different retail brand names, A and B. The brand A forecast yields two possible order quantities and probabilities, a 40 percent chance of 100 and a 60 percent chance of 140, while the brand B forecast yields a 50 percent chance of 200 and 50 percent chance of 300. Knowing these, what is the mean (expected) demand for the products?

Let $P_{A,1}$ = probability that brand A demand equals quantity 1 $(Q_{A,1})$

$P_{A,2}$ = probability that brand A demand equals quantity 2 $(Q_{A,2})$

$P_{B,1}$ = probability that brand B demand equals quantity 1 $(Q_{B,1})$

$P_{B,2}$ = probability that brand B demand equals quantity 2 $(Q_{B,2})$

Assuming that the demands for each brand are independent of each other, the laws of probability and statistics yield the following forecast:

$$\text{Expected sales A} = P_{A,1}(Q_{A,1}) + P_{A,2}(Q_{A,2})$$
$$= 0.40(100) + 0.60(140) = 124$$

$$\text{Expected sales B} = P_{B,1}(Q_{B,1}) + P_{B,2}(Q_{B,2})$$
$$= 0.50(200) + 0.50(300) = 250$$

$$\text{Expected sales (A + B)} = \text{expected sales A} + \text{expected sales B}$$
$$= 124 + 250 = 374 \text{ units}$$

In this simple example, only two random variables exist; however, when the number of random variables increases to more than a few, it may be necessary to use simulation. Simulation is one of the most powerful analytical tools of management, and is discussed in Chapter 36.

Essentials of Quantitative Methods

The QM approach to managerial problem solving has three essential characteristics: a systemwide perspective, the use of an interdisciplinary team, and the use of the scientific method

Systemwide Perspective. A problem must be identified, modeled, and solved in the context of the specific environment in which it exists. In solving systems problems, one must study the system, its environment, its parts, and their interrelationships, interactions, and purposes.

Interdisciplinary Teams. Many complex managerial problems require a variety of perspectives, skills, and knowledge. A proper mix of managers and analysts will achieve more effective results than will specialized groups. It is always important to have an interdisciplinary perspective when solving complex problems.

Scientific Method.   The essential characteristic of the scientific method is the systematic and objective repetition of observation, measurement, experimentation, and hypothesis testing. Through these activities, one can define valid models of essential system behavior. Figure 34.1 illustrates the scientific method and the steps of QM, of which the most important step is the problem formulation—from which all other activities follow. While the scientific method is shown sequentially, the steps are executed somewhat simultaneously and repetitively.

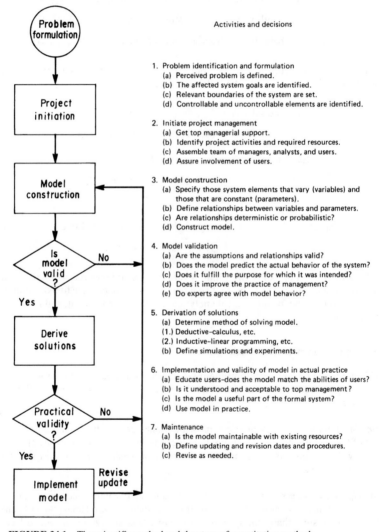

FIGURE 34.1   The scientific method and the steps of quantitative methods.

Use of Quantitative Methods

Surveys have shown that over a span of 30 years, the percentage of firms using QM in production has increased to well over 90 percent. These surveys have shown that the quantitative methods used most in PIC are inventory models, exponential smoothing, regression analysis, linear and mathematical programming, program evaluation review techniques and the critical-path method (PERT/CPM), simulation, heuristics, and (with considerably less frequency) queueing theory, dynamic programming, decision theory, game theory, and Markov analysis. However, the discipline of QM continues to evolve and new methodologies such as artificial intelligence, expert systems, and artificial neural networks are finding more and more applications in PIC.

This chapter presents the QM of PIC in an accessible manner. Accessibility is a primary objective here because research has shown that when managers lack knowledge of QM, then there are few QM applications, even when proposals are received from subordinates. Because the benefits of QM are great, the firm suffers when they are applied improperly or not applied at all.

PROBABILISTIC METHODS

Because simulation models are the most flexible and comprehensive of all QM, they have been one of the most widely used techniques in PIC. The continuing increase in the availability of low-cost simulation software and hardware has resulted in even more applications.

Simulation

Simulation is the process of seeking optimal solutions to complex problems through dynamic experimentation with system models, usually using computers. The term *dynamic* has particular importance, denoting that models are experimented with as time or other system elements are varied. Dynamic behavior can be included manually through computer spreadsheet programs or through what-if analysis in manufacturing resource planning (MRP II) and distribution resource planning (DRP II); however, the most powerful method of experimenting is a technique called *Monte Carlo sampling,* which is fully developed in another chapter.

Decision Analysis

Production and inventory managers most often make decisions under uncertain conditions. This section introduces QM for making decisions in ill-structured, nonroutine situations under risk and uncertainty.

Risk describes a situation in which alternative events and their probabilities are known; for example, risk was illustrated previously when the sales of products of A and B were calculated using probability estimates. In contrast, uncertainty describes a situation in which events can be identified, but probabilities cannot be estimated. Uncertainty is the most difficult situation under which to make good decisions. The purpose of decision analysis is to optimize the outcomes of decisions while facing uncertainty or risk.[16-20]

A manufacturer-distributor is currently medium in size and complexity; however, this complexity will increase or decrease as the sales volumes and the number of products, production facilities, and distribution centers increases or decreases. The manu-

TABLE 34.1 PIC Systems, Events, Probabilities, Decisions, and Outcomes

			Decision	
			System 1, d_1	System 2, d_2
Event			Outcomes	
company complexity,	Event probability			
j	x_j	$P(x_j)$	$O(d_1, x_j)$	$O(d_2, x_j)$
1	Low, x_1	0.3	12	-2
2	Medium, x_2	0.5	18	18
3	High, x_3	0.2	15	24
Expected ROI			15.6	13.2

facturer-distributor is deciding which of two production information control (PIC) systems to purchase. System 1 is currently more desirable, but it is not as easily expanded as system 2. Forecasting, product management, and manufacturing have provided three scenarios concerning the company's complexity levels and their probabilities. Table 34.1 shows low, medium, and high company complexity with the returns on investments in percentages of each PIC system. Based on this information, the company must decide which system to purchase.

Elements of Decision Problems.   There are five common elements to most decision problems. Each is considered in this solution.

Goals.   Assume that the goal of this firm is to maximize the expected (mean) return on investment (ROI). The laws of probability denote that the expected values EV of a decision alternative d_i are

$$EV(d_i) = \sum_{i=1}^{n} \sum_{j=1}^{m} [P(x_j)O(d_i, x_j)]$$

where n = number of alternative decisions
   m = number of different events
 $P(x_j)$ = probability of event x_j occurring
$O(d_i, x_j)$ = outcome value of decision d_i when events x_j occurs

For example, the expected value (EV) of a gamble with a 60 percent chance of winning $10 and a 40 percent chance of losing $10 is $2:

$$EV(\text{gamble}) = 0.60(\$10) + 0.40(-\$10) = \$2$$

Courses of Action (Alternative Decisions).   In this case, the decision maker has two alternative actions: purchase system 1, d_1, or purchase system 2, d_2.

Random Events.   Depending on sales, one of three possible company complexities will occur: x_1 = low, x_2 = medium, *or* x_3 = high.

Probabilities of Events $P(x_j)$.   The probabilities in Table 34.1 were forecast using historical and subjective data.

Outcomes of Decision-Event Combinations $Q(d_i, x_j)$.   The returns on investments associated with decision-event combinations are shown in the table. Assume that these were determined using a spreadsheet model and the best input of those most knowledgeable about such investments.

Optimal Decisions Using Expected Values.   A frequent criterion used to select optimal solution is the maximization of the expected value. The following describes the expected returns on investments of each decision.

Decision 1, System 1

$$\text{Expected ROI}(d_1) = P(x_1)O(d_1,x_1) + P(x_2)O(d_1, x_2) + P(x_3)O(d_1, x_3)$$

$$= 0.3(12) \qquad + 0.5(18) \qquad + 0.2(15) = 15.6 \text{ percent}$$

Decision 2, System 2

$$\text{Expected ROI}(d_2) = P(x_1)O(d_2, x_1) + P(x_2)O(d_2, x_2) + P(x_3)O(d_2, x_3)$$

$$= 0.3(-2) \qquad + 0.5(18) \qquad + 0.2(24) = 13.2 \text{ percent}$$

The best decision is to purchase system 1 because it yields the highest expected return on investment. "Highest expected" denotes that over the long run, with repetitions, this decision will yield the highest *average* return on investment. The assumption of repetitions (called *repeated trials*) is an important one, meaning that this or similar decisions are made frequently. In repeating similar decisions, one achieves the highest profit by selecting that decision having the highest *average* profit. The highest average profit yields the highest total long-run profit. In contrast, if such a decision were made only once in a lifetime, then maximizing the expected value might not be the best criterion.

Limitations of Expected Values.   In general, the expected value is the most rational decision criterion when probability estimates exist. However, there are several situations in which expected values are not effective.

Infrequent Decisions.   When a decision is made very infrequently and therefore the repeated-trials assumption is not valid, the expected-value criterion may be invalid. A decision maker may see an opportunity in one action that may never be available again. Seizing or avoiding an opportunity despite its lower expected value may take precedence over the highest expected-value criterion.

Whole Distribution.   Because it does not describe the whole distribution of possible outcomes, the expected value ignores important information concerning extreme values. Therefore, when a decision yields extremely undesirable outcomes (such as bankruptcy, loss of job, or death), one might not choose the decision with the highest expected value. In such situations, those decision alternatives with unacceptable outcomes should be ignored.

In contrast, one might face a situation in which a decision with a low expected value has an outcome that is very desirable. Given a choice between the following alternatives, different executives may react differently: Decision 1, d_1, yields a 50 percent chance of $10 million and a 50 percent chance of $-$15 million; decision 2, d_2, yields 70 percent chance of $2 million and a 30 percent chance of $-$1 million. The expected values of each are as follows:

$$\text{Expected value}(d_1) = 0.50(10,000,000) + 0.50(-15,000,000) = -\$2,500,000$$

$$\text{Expected value}(d_2) = 0.70(2,000,000) + 0.30(-1,000,000) = \$1,100,000$$

Decision 2 has the highest expected value. However, some individuals, for example, entrepreneurs, might have a preference for decision 1 after considering the whole distribution of outcomes. Thus, they choose decision 1. A more formal approach to making decisions using such personal preferences is available through the use of *utility functions*.

Utility Functions. One desires outcomes from decisions because of their utility (their inherent personal value). Utility is simply a way of representing the intrinsic value of money. While normally the utility that one receives from money is greater for higher sums than for lower sums, the utility may not be in proportion to the monetary sums. For example, an individual may view a potential loss of $1 million as quite different than just double the loss of $500,000, particularly if the larger loss will result in bankruptcy or job loss.

While a full discussion of the construction of utility functions is beyond our scope, utilities are not difficult to arrive at through an interview process. Assume that three executives have been interviewed concerning the utility of the monetary values of column 1, Table 34.2. Utility scales are commonly chosen to run from 0 to 1. In this case, a 1.0 utility is associated with a $20 million gain, while a 0.0 utility is associated with a $20 million loss.

TABLE 34.2 Utility Values for Three Executives

Values of sum equal to, dollars	Individual 1 (risk avoider), utility	Individual 2 (risk neutral), utility	Individual 3 (risk seeker), utility
−20,000,000	0	0	0
−15,000,000	0.250	0.125	0.100
−1,000,000	0.500	0.475	0.300
2,000,000	0.560	0.550	0.400
10,000,000	0.775	0.750	0.725
20,000,000	1.000	1.000	1.000

Expected Utility. To calculate the expected utility of the previous decisions, d_1 and d_2, simply substitute the utility values of Table 34.2 for monetary sums in the expected-value formulas. Let $U_i(\$X)$ represent the utility that individual i receives from the monetary sum of $\$X$.

Individual 1, the risk avoider, chooses decision 2 because its expected utility is highest:

Expected utility $d_1 = 0.50U_1(10,000,000) + 0.50U_1(-15,000,000)$

$= 0.50(0.775) + 0.50(0.250) = 0.512$

Expected utility $d_2 = 0.70U_1(2,000,000) + 0.30U_1(-1,000,000)$

$= 0.70(0.560) + 0.30(0.500) = 0.542$

Individual 2, the risk neutral, will by definition always choose that decision which is best using expected monetary values; therefore, the risk-neutral executive chooses decision 2:

Expected utility $d_1 = 0.50(0.750) + 0.50(0.125) = 0.4375$

Expected utility $d_2 = 0.70(0.550) + 0.30(0.475) = 0.5275$

Individual 3, the risk seeker, chooses decision 1 because of the relatively high utility of $10 million as opposed to the relatively low utility of the $2 million gain of decision 2:

Expected utility $d_1 = 0.50(0.725) + 0.50(0.100) = 0.4125$

Expected utility $d_2 = 0.70(0.400) + 0.30(0.300) = 0.370$

Utility functions can be important decision aids, yet there are some problems in their use: (1) A derived utility function is only valid for the given decision maker; (2) the shape of the utility function for an individual may change over time, therefore making periodic revisions necessary; and (3) it is very difficult to determine reliable utility functions for groups of individuals.

Offsetting these disadvantages are several advantages: (1) Utility functions do express the intrinsic value associated with alternatives, (2) utility functions can be useful in measuring the value of trade-offs between monetary and nonmonetary alternatives, (3) multiattribute utility functions provide a method for evaluating several different measures of goals and outcomes (loss of occupation, bankruptcy, pollution, etc.). Finally, while the construction of utility functions is not a common practice in PIC, an understanding of the utility functions is important. Utility functions explain the behavior of different decision makers and stakeholders in firms. Thus, they can aid the professional PIC manager who needs to assess the consequences of alternative actions.

Decision Criteria under Uncertainty. While uncertainties (unknown event probabilities) make decision making more difficult than when facing conditions of risk in which probabilities are known, decision criteria do exist to assist the executive.

The *equally likely* criterion assumes that when probabilities are unknown, each outcome has an equal probability of occurring. One chooses the decision having the highest expected value under the assumption that all events have an equal probability. Using this criterion, reconsider the problem concerning the production information control (PIC) system in Table 34.1. Assuming that each of the three events has a 1/3 probability of occurring:

d_1 yields $\frac{1}{3}(12) + \frac{1}{3}(18) + \frac{1}{3}(15) = 15$ percent

d_2 yields $\frac{1}{3}(-2) + \frac{1}{3}(18) + +\frac{1}{3}(24) = 13.33$ percent

Therefore, d_1 is the best decision.

The *maximin* (maximum of the minimums) *criterion* directs one to choose that decision which has the maximum of the minimum outcomes. This is d_1, with a 12 percent ROI. The maximin criterion is a conservative approach that has general appeal.

The *maximum likelihood criterion* states that one should choose that decision which is best with the most likely event. As shown in Table 34.1, the most frequently occurring event is "medium complexity"; d_1 and d_2 both yield 18 percent returns when the most likely event occurs. Therefore, this criterion leaves one indifferent between d_1 and d_2.

The *maximax* (maximum of the maximums) *criterion* identifies the best decision as that which yields the outcome with the maximum value, regardless of the probability of the outcome. In this case, d_2 yields the maximum of the maximum ROIs, 24 percent.

However, d_2 also yields the lowest ROI, -2 percent. This criterion is often illogical because it ignores the probabilities of negative events. Yet, if the probabilities are unknown and the decision maker is a "gambler" or entrepreneur, this rule may be relevant.

These criteria are useful decision guides under uncertainty. However, when event probabilities are known, then the equally likely, maximum likelihood, and maximax criteria become less relevant. But even when the probabilities are known, the maximin criteria is often relevant because many decision makers are risk avoiders. As discussed later, their criteria are also very important in game theory, where intelligent competitors react to each other's decisions.

Decision Trees for Sequential Decisions. Frequently, one faces sequential decisions that are influenced by random events. In such situations, decision trees such as shown in Fig. 34.2 are valuable. Reconsider the selection of the best PIC system described in Table 34.1. In selecting decision 1, management was concerned about the low return on investment (15 percent) if the company's size and complexity became high. As shown in the figure, management has determined that a second decision can be made to expand system 1 if the company's complexity is high. This system expansion has an 80 percent probability of being successful with a 26 percent ROI and a 20 percent probability of being unsuccessful, in which case the ROI of system 1, with high company complexity, is only 12 percent.

To learn the main elements of a decision tree, refer to Fig. 34.2. Decision nodes are shown as squares and represent points at which decisions must be made. Random-event nodes are shown as circles. After constructing a decision tree, an optimal solution is

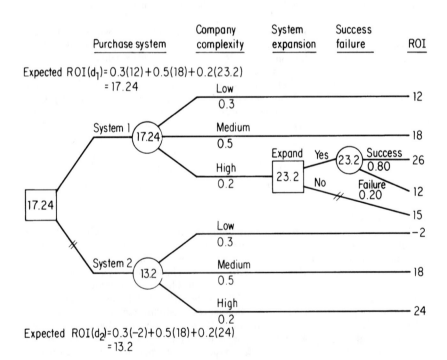

FIGURE 34.2   Decision tree for PIC system acquisition and expansion.

found by working backward from each decision node and trimming or slashing (//) those decisions with lower expected values. The values shown in the squares and circles are the expected values of decisions or events. The sequence of decisions that remains after trimming is optimum. As shown, the optimal decision is to purchase system 1 and to expand it later if the organization's complexity increases.

Decision analysis and decision trees are particularly powerful tools for complex, ill-structured situations. Decisions such as the acquisition and development of a computer-based information system, facility planning, and location analysis are candidates for decision analysis.

There are several other decision-analysis tools available to the PIC professional. These are described in other references and fortunately, there are a number of decision analysis software packages available. Applications of decision analysis have not been reported in the literature as much as one would infer from its relative ease of application, low computational costs, and potential benefits. In many cases, these applications are not reported because of the sensitive nature of the important decisions that were modeled. As improvements in information and decision support systems continue, the number of reported applications should increase.

Queueing Models

Typical *queues* (waiting lines) include calls at telephone switchboards, trucks waiting at docks, jobs waiting in job shops, orders arriving at distribution centers, machinists waiting at tool cribs, customers waiting at service counters, and interactive users of computers. Many of these systems could be designed and managed more effectively by using queueing models.[21-23]

Queueing theory was originated by the Danish mathematician and engineer A. K. Erlang in 1909 as he designed and configured telephone switching equipment. The basic purpose of queueing theory is to design a service facility so as to maximize the profit or ROI from serving or having individuals (such as parts, products, paperwork, or people) wait. Providing service usually requires a fixed cost (such as adding more machines or docks) and a variable cost (such as the hourly wages of workers), while the cost of waiting includes having individuals idle (as a result, for instance, of late orders, poor customer service, or poor efficiency).

Only the simplest queueing model, the single-server single-phase system, is presented here. This is typified by a single-server retail counter, a single-person tool crib, or a single machine. Note that the concepts illustrated here are very useful in analyzing a wide variety of systems using queueing and other methods including simulation. Simple queueing systems have simple equations for modeling system behavior. In contrast, complex queueing systems may not be validly modeled using mathematical formulas; consequently, Monte Carlo simulation as developed in Chapter 36 is used for such systems.

Queueing System Structure. A *single-server, single-phase queueing system* is shown in Fig. 34.3*a*. As shown, the number of servers, or channels, refers to the number of servers at each *phase* of the system. Figure 34.3*b* illustrates a *single-server, multiphase queueing system*. As shown, two servers exist in the system, but they provide only a single path (or channel) for service; therefore, this is referred to as a *single-server, or single-channel, queueing system*. In contrast, a multiserver single-phase system has several servers to provide only one service (Fig. 34.3*c*). An example of this is a multiserver retail counter where patrons either take a number or wait in a single line. Figure 34.3*d* is a multiserver, multiphase queueing model. Consider Fig. 34.4 which summarizes some common assumptions concerning queueing models. Please refer to this when studying the following.

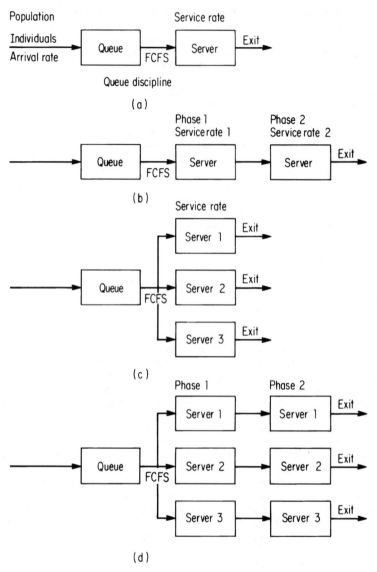

FIGURE 34.3   Basic queueing system.

Population Size.   A system serving a very small population behaves differently from one serving a large population. For example, the probability of one machine needing repair from a large population of machines is easily described by using simple probability statements; however, if the population consists of only eight machines, two of which are in the shop for repair, the probability distribution of breakdowns becomes more complex. Thus, when the population is relatively small (such as 50), then special

A simple single-server (channel), single-phase queueing model

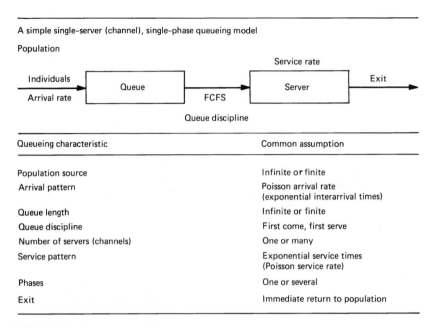

FIGURE 34.4 Characteristics of typical queueing systems.

queueing tables must be used to describe the system. However, frequently, it is possible to assume that the system serves a very large (i.e., infinite) population.

Arrival Rate. Probability distributions are used to describe the arrival patterns of individuals entering a queueing system. Many theoretical and empirical distributions can be used to describe arrivals. These include constant, Poisson, random, Erlang, hyperexponential, and general distributions. One of the most common is the Poisson distribution (see Fig. 34.5*a* and 34.5*b* for examples).

Poisson and Exponential Distributions. The *Poisson distribution* describes the rate of occurrences of a random event. The concept of rate is important. It measures occurrences per unit of space or time, such as the number of phone calls arriving at a switchboard per hour or the number of orders received per week. If the rate of an event is the result of a relatively large number of minor, independent chance influences, and the probability of the event in any one unit of time or space is very low, and the number of possible points of occurrence is very large, then the event follows a Poisson distribution. For example, the probability of a phone call arriving at a switchboard during the next second is very low, but the number of seconds per hour is quite large; therefore, the arrival rate may follow a Poisson distribution. The other characteristics of the Poisson distribution are that it describes discrete events that are independent of each other and possesses a constant mean.

If the rate of an event follows a Poisson distribution, then the time between occurrences follows an exponential distribution. The *exponential distribution* has a mean equal to the inverse of the mean of the Poisson distribution. Therefore, the rate of arrivals is described by the Poisson distribution, and the time between arrivals is described by the exponential distribution.

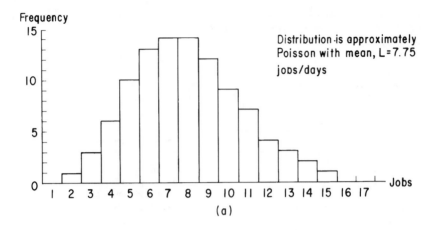

FIGURE 34.5 Poisson distributions: (*a*) daily input rates to the shop for 100 days; (*b*) daily output rates of the shop for 100 days.

Statistical *goodness-of-fit methods* can be used to identify the theoretical distribution of the actual arrival rate of a system. If the pattern of arrivals does not follow a known theoretical distribution like the Poisson or exponential, it can be modeled as a general empirical distribution; or, when queueing formulas fail, Monte Carlo simulation methods can be used.

Queue Length. If a service facility (for example, a conveyor) has a limited number of spaces in its queue, then it will behave differently than if there were no limit. Models exist for both infinite and finite queue lengths. How the system behaves with a full queue may not be easily modeled. If individuals balk (that is, do not enter) when the queue is full, then this may be modeled easily, but if individuals behave differently, then the model may be too complex for queueing analysis.

Queue Priority.   This describes the order in which individuals are served. The most common queue discipline is the first-come, first-served (FCFS) rule. However, there are many other possible rules including *service in random order* (SIRO) and *shortest processing time* (SPT).

Service Rate.   The time spent serving an individual includes only the time spent with the individual. If this time follows an exponential distribution, then the service rate is a Poisson distribution. As with arrival rates, queueing formulas can model several different probability distributions for service rates.

Exit.   There are different exits that an individual can make from the system. After leaving the system, the individual might be eligible to reenter the queue or might enter a different population that does not enter the service system for some time. For example, the probabilities of a machine needing service before and after an overhaul should be quite different.

Shop-Load Queueing Example.   A work center has been exhibiting excessive lead times. While the average input to the work center (7.75 jobs per day) has been less than the average output (8 jobs per day), the work center's lead times and backlogs seem excessive. Even though the average input is less than the average output, the variability of each causes large backlogs and long lead times. To better understand how the backlog could increase under these conditions, a queueing model is selected to model the system.

The input to the work center has the frequency distribution shown in the Poisson distribution. The mean input rate is 7.75 jobs per day. A chi-square goodness-of-fit statistical test reveals that the distribution is consistent with the Poisson. The output rate (Fig. 34.5*b*) is also a random variable described by a Poisson distribution with a mean of 8 jobs per day.

The shop scheduling system uses a first-come, first-served queue discipline. The number of jobs that can wait in the work center is large; therefore, the queue length is assumed to be infinite, and the population of possible jobs is also infinitely large. These characteristics describe a single-server, single-phase queueing system with a Poisson arrival rate, a Poisson service rate, an FCFS queue discipline, an infinite queue length, and infinite population size. This model is often noted using Kendall's notation *M/M/*1, where the first *M* denotes a Poisson arrival rate, the second *M* denotes a Poisson service rate, and the 1 denotes the number of servers. The *M* notation refers to a Markovian (Poisson) process.

Queueing Formulas.   The mathematical formulas of an *M/M/*1 model are given in the following example. The derivation of these formulas is beyond the scope of this handbook; however, one does not need to know how these formulas were developed to apply queueing models properly, but one does have to understand the assumptions underlying the formulas. After confirming that the assumptions are valid, the system is analyzed using the following formulas:

System utilization ρ

$$\rho = \frac{L}{M} = \frac{7.75}{8.00} = 97 \text{ percent utilized} \tag{34.1}$$

Because the average input to the system is slightly less than the average output, the system is utilized 97 (idle 3) percent of the time.

Mean number in queue $\bar{n}_q$

$$\bar{n}_q = \frac{L^2}{M(M-L)} = \frac{7.75^2}{8(8-7.75)} = 30.03 \text{ jobs} \tag{34.2}$$

Even though the work center's average input is less than its average output, there is an average backlog of 30.03 jobs waiting in the system. Also, the backlog frequently exceeds 30.03 jobs. It may seem illogical that the system is sometimes idle and at other times has long backlogs, but this is nonetheless true.

Mean Number in System $\bar{n}_s$

$$\bar{n}_s = \frac{L}{M - L} = \frac{7.75}{(8 - 7.75)} = 31 \text{ jobs} \tag{34.3}$$

The average number of jobs in the system is 31. As shown above in Eq. (34.1), the system is 97 percent utilized. Consequently, on the average, there is 0.97 of a job at the server plus 30.03 jobs in the queue, and therefore 31 jobs in the system.

Mean Time in Queue $\bar{t}_q$

$$\bar{t}_q = \frac{L}{M(M - L)} = \frac{7.75}{8(8 - 7.75)} = 3.875 \text{ days} \tag{34.4}$$

The average job waits 3.875 days before being worked on.

Mean Time in System $\bar{t}_s$

$$\bar{t}_s = \frac{1}{M - L} = \frac{1}{8 - 7.75} = 4.0 \text{ days} \tag{34.5}$$

The average job takes 4.0 days to be completed, 3 days 7 hours (or 3.875 days) waiting, and 1 hour being processed.

Probability of 40 Jobs in the Shop P_n

$$P_n = \left(1 - \frac{L}{M}\right)\left(\frac{L}{M}\right)^n$$

$$P_{40} = \left(1 - \frac{7.75}{8}\right)\left(\frac{7.75}{8}\right)^{40} = 0.0087 \tag{34.6}$$

While the probability that there will be exactly 40 jobs in the shop is quite low (0.00877), the probability that there may be 40 or more jobs in the shop is quite high. Figure 34.6 illustrates the cumulative probabilities of different backlogs. For example, there is approximately a 27 percent probability of more than a 40-job load in the shop; that is, the shop will have more than 40 jobs waiting 27 percent of the time.

While the results of this analysis may be counterintuitive, they are accurate when the assumptions of the model are valid. The interaction of the random arrival and service rates results in large backlogs in some periods and idle times in others. This situation is the curse of many systems that cannot or do not control their input and output rates. However, management can design systems to preclude these random influences. For example, if the arrival rate and the service rate were constant, then a work center could operate with a 100 percent utilization and no backlogs.

Limitations of Simple Analytical Models.   While queueing models are very useful, there are limitations to their applicability. First, queueing formulas describe the behavior of the service system after reaching a steady state. If the actual system never reaches a steady state or if one is interested in describing the dynamics of reaching a steady state, than queueing models are less applicable. Second, formulas for complex queueing applications may not exist, and simulation procedures may therefore be needed.

Queueing models have been successfully used in a variety of applications, most recently in the design of computer and communications systems. Thus, queueing models are important tools in the management of complex information systems. They will

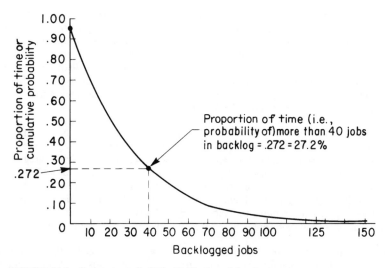

FIGURE 34.6   Cumulative probability distribution of shop load.

become more important in PIC as managers become more knowledgeable of the advantages and limitations of QM and as production systems become more automated.

DETERMINISTIC METHODS: LINEAR PROGRAMMING

Linear programming (LP) *methods* are a subset of *mathematical programming* (MP) *methods.*[24–27] MP and LP provide optimal solutions and insights when allocating scarce resources in many deterministic environments. They are applicable in determining where, when, and how limited resources should be allocated so as to achieve the highest level of effectiveness (maximum profit, minimum cost, shortest time, smallest square footage, and so on). The term *programming* may be misleading because LP applications are implemented using software that facilitates problem formulation and model construction but do not require programming expertise.

Some people have the misconception that LP is a tool only for the process industries. This is not so. LP methods are general and are effective in managing a variety of manufacturing operations.[28–33] While the dimensions of a complex manufacturing system may be too large for the cost-effective use of LP, there are many other complex problems that are solvable by LP. In fact, the forte of LP models is their ability to find optimal solutions to extremely large problems within very little computer time.[34–36] Thus, the continuing interest in JIT and repetitive manufacturing has renewed interest in LP.

Typical Applications of LP

LP has been used in almost every conceivable environment.[26–27] In several surveys, LP has emerged as one of the most frequently applied QM in production and inventory control. The LP capabilities of popular spreadsheets have made these methods much more accessible for applications in production, distribution, and logistics. LP can be very useful in determining the lowest-cost shipment routes from existing *distribution centers* (DCs) to retail outlets or from factories to DCs. In addition, LP is useful in determining the best location for DCs given the existing or future locations of factories or retail outlets. Also, LP has been used to plan the production, inventory, and distribution of parts for shipment among plants and distribution centers. These applications do not eliminate MRP/JIT or *distribution resource planning* (DRP) *systems,* but they enhance them through improved aggregate and detailed planning.

Aggregate Production Planning.   LP has been used in scheduling the lowest-cost or highest-profit production rates for product groups over finite planning horizons. The OR/MS literature is abundant in the areas of "production smoothing" or aggregate production planning and scheduling. The benefits of LP have increased through the widespread use of shorter time fences, "frozen" master schedules, rough-cut capacity-planning procedures, planning bills, and the analysis of bottleneck work centers. These approaches remove the uncertainty and instability of production plans and master schedules and therefore enhance the effectiveness of LP in manufacturing.

Product-Mix, Blending, and Cutting-Stock Problems.   Associated with master scheduling and production planning is *product-mix planning,* which is the determination of the optimal mix of products, given constraints on labor, materials, and sales. LP has been used to solve product-mix problems in a variety of manufacturing and process industries.

Blending problems in the process industries are ideally suited for solution by MP procedures. The lowest-cost (highest-profit) blend of ingredients must meet technological, chemical, nutritional, or palatability requirements. The blending of human or animal foods, of petroleum products, and of menus are a few examples.

The *cutting-stock problem* is one in which a mill desires to minimize the waste in cutting and trimming stock for a variety of products (which have different widths, lengths, and thicknesses, for instance), subject to the available stock of materials, technical specifications, and demands for the final product.

Hierarchical Applications.   While LP can be used to solve extremely large problems in operations, many situations have exceedingly large dimensions.[29-32] A medium to large MRP II system is a good example. For such systems, LP procedures have been embodied in a larger system of models arranged in a hierarchical or sequential manner. The hierarchical approach recognizes the top-down and bottom-up relationships and feedback loops that exist in most systems. When a system is very complex, it may be impossible to model the effects of decisions at all levels simultaneously, but it is possible to solve problems systematically and sequentially—much as is done iteratively and heuristically in an MRP II system. In the hierarchical approach, an LP model can be used for medium- to long-term planning, and a simulation or MRP model can be used for immediate- to short-term planning.

Other Applications.   Other applications of LP are too many to mention; however, references 24 through 36 provide many examples.

Important Assumptions of LP

The term *linear* means that LP relationships are assumed to be linear. For example, in maximizing the profits from manufacturing, linearity denotes that if twice as many products are produced, the costs will double. In contrast, the costs might be more or less than double in a nonlinear relationship. The linearity assumption does not significantly reduce LP's applicability because linearity is often valid and it is possible to include some nonlinearities in LP models by using approximations of nonlinear functions. When these approaches fail, *nonlinear programming* (NLP) can be used. Several popular spreadsheets include NLP capabilities.

Another assumption of LP is that the environment being modeled is relatively certain (that is, deterministic). Costs, demands, priorities, and capacities are assumed to be known with certainty. When a few uncertainties exist, what-if procedures (called *sensitivity analyses*) can be used to explore the effects of uncertainty. However, when there are a number of probabilistic processes, then the simulation methods are applicable. These important assumptions of LP are considered in the example below.

Production-Planning Example of LP

A firm desires to maximize its profit by selling all the gas-powered G and wind-powered W turbines it can produce. However, it is constrained by capacity in two departments: fabrication and assembly. When sold, each G yields a profit contribution of $70, and each W, $50. The profit contribution is the difference between the selling price and the cost per unit. Each G requires 5 fabrication hours and 20 assembly hours; each W, 1 fabrication hour and 30 assembly hours. There are 200 and 2400 hours of capacity available in the fabrication and assembly departments, respectively. Using this information, an LP model is formulated and solved for the maximum profit.

Step 1. Objective Function Formulation.   The most important step in a problem formulation is the identification of the related system objective, such as maximizing profits, or ROI, or minimizing costs. This objective function measures the optimality of different decisions. In this situation, the objective has been clearly defined: Maximize the profit Z, from producing G's and W's. Mathematically, this is as follows. Maximize:

$$\text{Profit } (Z) = \$70 \text{ for each } G + \$50 \text{ for each } W$$

$$= \$70G + \$50W$$

Step 2. Constraint Formulation.   Identify constraints that limit the upper or lower values of the variables (such as G's and W's). In general, constraints are technical, regulatory, economic, or policy limits on the number of units of a variable that can exist in the solution. The constraints in the example are as follows:

Lathe (i.e., Fabrication) Constraint.   5 hours for each G plus 1 hour for each W must be less than or equal to the 200 hours available in the lathe department:

$$5G + 1W \leq 200 \tag{34.7}$$

Assembly Constraint.   20 hours for G plus 30 hours for each W must be less than or equal to the 2400 hours available in the assembly department:

$$20G + 30W \leq 2400 \tag{34.8}$$

Nonnegativity Constraint.   In addition to the above constraints, it is mathematically necessary to eliminate negative values of G and W as solutions. That is, all variables in LP are restricted to be nonnegative:

$$G \text{ and } W \geq 0 \tag{34.9}$$

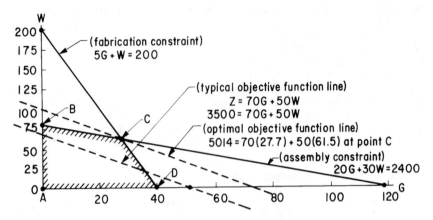

FIGURE 34.7   Feasible region and optimal solution at point *C*.

Definitions.   The constants on the right side of the inequality sign are called *right-hand sides* (RHSs). The variables *G* and *W* are called *decision variables,* and the coefficients or multipliers (that is, 70 and 50, and 5, 1, 20, and 30) are referred to as *objective-function coefficients* and *constraint coefficients,* respectively. Now that this problem has been formulated, which is normally the most difficult step, consider the graphical solution shown in Fig. 34.7.

Step 3. Solution.   The vertical axis represents the number of *W*'s produced, and the horizontal axis the number of *G*'s produced. Also plotted are an *objective-function line,* the fabrication constraint, and the assembly constraint. The less-than portion of the constraints lies below and to the left of each line. The shaded area (*ABCD*) of the figure outlines the region, called the *feasible region,* of all possible combinations of *G*'s and *W*'s that meet the requirements of all constraints, that is, combinations that do not exceed the capacities of the fabrication and assembly departments.

As points move up and to the right of the origin, where *G* = 0 and *W* = 0, the values of *G* and *W* increase, and therefore the profit increases (that is, 70*G*+50*W* increases). To calculate the profit at any point, just find the values of *W* and *G* at that point, and substitute them into the objective-function equation. The plotted objective function is one of many possible profit lines. It was chosen to conveniently display the slope of the objective function. In this case, a profit of $3500 yields two convenient points on the *W* and *G* axis. Given *Z* = 70*G*+50*W* = $3500: When *G* = 0, then *W* = 70, and when *W* = 0, then *G* = 50.

When written in standard algebraic form, with the vertical variable on the left-hand side of the equal sign, the objective-function equation is the following:

$$Z = 70G + 50W$$

$$50W = Z - 70G$$

$$W = \frac{Z}{50} - \frac{70}{50}G$$

where $-70/50$ is the slope (that is, the change in W resulting from a 1-unit change in G) and $Z/50$ is any conveniently chosen value of the objective function, such as the \$3500 in the figure.

The slope of the objective function is important in determining the optimal combination of G's and W's. A graphical solution is obtained by moving the objective-function line as far away from the origin as possible while still touching the feasible region and thereby not exceeding any of the constraints. This is done by taking a ruler and moving the objective-function lines parallel to the original line and as far from the origin as possible in the feasible region. In this case, point C is the farthest point; therefore, given the current objective-function slope and constraints, C yields the highest profit. As shown on the graph, at the optimal point C:

$$G = 27.7 \tag{34.10}$$

$$W = 61.5 \tag{34.11}$$

$$\text{Maximum profit} = \$70(27.7) + \$50(61.5) = \$5014 \tag{34.12}$$

$$\text{Lathe utilization} = 5(27.7) + 1(61.5) = 200 \text{ hours} \tag{34.13}$$

$$\text{Assembly utilization} = 20(27.7) + 30(61.5) = 2400 \text{ hours} \tag{34.14}$$

This is the highest-profit combination of all feasible G's and W's. In this solution, both departments' constraints were fully utilized, but in the general problem, some departments will be fully utilized while others will be underutilized. In addition to the information given above, LP solutions provide planning information called *postoptimality analysis*.

Postoptimality Analysis.   One of the benefits of LP is the what-if planning information it provides. How these data are derived will not be obvious from our discussion, but they are a standard output of commercially available mathematical programming software, including spreadsheets. The postoptimality analysis for this problem is as follows.

Marginal Values.   As shown in Eq. (34.13), the lathe department is fully utilized (that is, its load is 200 hours). Logically, additional profit could be achieved by increasing its capacity. Postoptimality analysis provides a variable called a *marginal value* (also known as the *dual price, shadow price, reduced cost,* or *imputed value*) for every constraint in the model. In this case, the marginal value of the fabrication department denotes that a 1-hour increase in capacity (from 200 to 201 hours) will increase profits by \$8.46. In addition, the marginal value for the assembly department is \$1.38, thus, profits can be increased by \$1.38 for each added assembly hour. These incremental profits are generated by producing additional G's and W's. Clearly, if additional resources were available, it would be most profitable to allocate them to the fabrication department (\$8.46/hour versus \$1.38/hour).

In addition to answering questions concerning increases in capacity, the marginal values are useful in simulating reductions in capacity. That is, the values also denote that if the available capacity of the fabrication or assembly departments were reduced by 1 hour, then the profit would go down by \$8.46 and \$1.38, respectively.

Ranges.   Marginal values are only valid over a finite range of increases or decreases. In this case, postoptimality analysis yields the following: the fabrication capacity could increase to 600 hours or decrease to 80 hours, and the profit would increase or decrease, respectively, by \$8.46 for each hour of capacity change.

Postoptimality analysis also yields other planning information. The current solution ($G = 27.7$ and $W = 61.5$) is the optimum with respect to the slope of the objective function ($-70/50$). The slope will change if the profit coefficients of G and W change. If the coefficients of G and W change, will the optimal solution change as a result of changes in the coefficients? In this case, if the profit for G remains in the range of \$34 to \$105, then the current solution is still optimum. These ranges can be determined graphically on the figure by rotating the objective-function line at G until it touches point D, then B. These two slopes set the ranges quoted above.

Simplex Method.   It is impossible to solve realistic problems graphically because three dimensions are insufficient to represent multidimensional problems. Each decision variable (such as G and W) adds a dimension to the graph. Fortunately, the simplex procedure quickly solves LP problems with large numbers of decision variables from 30,000 to 100,000 and up to 16,000 constraints. The method is very efficient because the optimal solution to constrained resource problems is always at a corner point of the feasible region when the objective function and the constraints are linear; this is called the *simplex theorem*. The simplex method only has to evaluate a fraction of the corner points of the feasible region to determine the optimal solution. Note that point C in Fig. 34.7 was a corner point representing the intersection of two linear equations in two unknowns. In general, at corner points there are n linear equations of n unknowns, an easily solved system of equations.

The simplex method does algebraically what was done graphically in Fig. 34.7. It efficiently moves the objective function from corner point to corner point until it finds that corner point at which the profits of all adjacent corner points are lower. For example, the profit at point C is higher than at the adjacent corner points of B and D.

Linearity is a necessary assumption of LP and the simplex method because it yields a feasible region that is a convex polygon. A simplex in mathematics is a multidimensional convex polygon. Figure 34.8 illustrates convex and concave polygons. Because of its shape, a convex polygon ensures that a corner point is optimal when all of its adjacent corner points have lower profits (maximization) or higher costs (minimization). The simplex procedure locates the optimal solution to large problems by evaluating only a few corner points; often the number of points evaluated equals the number of constraints.

Whereas a convex polygon has all internal angles less than or equal to $180°$, a concave polygon has one or more internal angles greater than $180°$. These large internal angles give the concave polygon the "caved-in" shape that makes it difficult to find an optimal solution.

Each of the figures illustrates two objective-function lines. Given these two polygons and objectives lines, the optimal solutions are at points C and E, respectively.

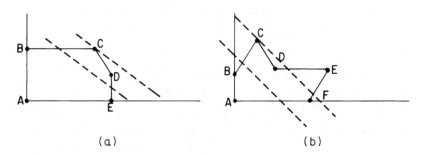

FIGURE 34.8   (*a*) Convex and (*b*) concave polygons.

When the simplex method is used, it evaluates one corner point on either side of C and finds that the profit decreases at B and D; therefore, C is the optimal solution and the search stops. In contrast, if nonlinearities exist, a concave polygon might describe the feasible region. Because the simplex procedure does not have a graph as an aid when it is used, it may mistakenly converge on C as the optimal solution because the profits are lower at B and D; however, point E is the optimum. Mathematically, the simplex method cannot look ahead more than one corner point; therefore, concavity might hide optimal points that are more than one corner away. Point C of the concave polygon is called a *local optimum,* while point E is the *global optimum.*

Production Planning Using Dynamic LP. Consider a more complex LP application. A firm desires to schedule production to maximize the profits from selling two product lines, wagons W and bicycles B. The firm must minimize regular production, overtime production, and inventory-holding costs while meeting known demands. Using a bill of capacity, the firm has estimates of the fabrication F and assembly A times for each product. Also, the planning horizon consists of two periods. While this problem has been contrived to have two periods, two products, and two work centers, the general case of many products, periods, and work centers is a simple extension that is easily solved using LP. However, an extremely large problem with more than 20,000 constraints, for example, might be too costly to implement. To formulate this LP model, consider the price, cost, demand, and capacity requirements provided in Table 34.3.

To solve this problem, express the profit function as the total revenue minus the total cost. Table 34.4 provides definitions of the variables used in this problem in order to facilitate its formulation and solution. From this information, formulate this problem as a linear programming problem.

Model Formulation. Now that the decision variables and coefficients of the problem are defined, the LP formulation is given below.

Objective function. Maximize the profit:

$$
\begin{aligned}
Z = \;& 20(DW_1) & + 25(DB_1) & + 20(DW_2) & + 25(DB_2) & - 3(WFR_1) & - 4.5(WFO_1) \\
& - 4(BFR_1) & - 6(BFO_1) & - 6(WAR_1) & - 9(WAO_1) & - 8(BAR_1) & - 12(BAO_1) \\
& - 1(EIW_1) & - 1(EIB_1) & - 3(WFR_2) & - 4.5(WFO_2) & - 4(BFR_2) & - 6(BFO_2) \\
& - 6(WAR_2) & - 9(WAO_2) & - 8(BAR_2) & - 12(BAO_2) & - 1(EIW_2) & - 1(EIB_2)
\end{aligned}
$$

subject to period 1 fabrication constraints. Production in period 1 = demand 1 + ending inventory 1 − ending inventory 0. That is, produce enough at least to meet the demand of period 1. This also assumes that the ending inventory of period 0 is 0:

$$
WFR_1 + WFO_1 = DW_1 + EIW_1 - EIW_0
$$

$$
BFR_1 + BFO_1 = DB_1 + EIB_1 - EIB_0
$$

Period 1 assembly constraints. Assembly quantities are forced to equal fabrication quantities:

$$
WAR_1 + WAO_1 = WFR_1 + WFO_1
$$

$$
BAR_1 + BAO_1 = BFR_1 + BFO_1
$$

TABLE 34.3 Prices, Costs, Demands, and Capacities

	Wagons	Bicycles
Price ($/unit)	20	25
Cost of fabrication ($/unit):		
Regular time	3	4
Overtime	4.5	6
Cost of assembly ($/unit):		
Regular time	6	8
Overtime	9	12
Cost of holding ($/unit/period)	1	1
Bill of capacity (hours/unit):		
Fabrication	2	2.67
Assembly	1	1.33
Demand (units/period):		
Period 1	25	15
Period 2	15	25

Departmental capacity, hours/period	Fabrication	Assembly
Period 1:		
Regular time	80	40
Overtime	20	10
Period 2:		
Regular time	80	40
Overtime	20	10

TABLE 34.4 Definition of Variables

Period 1 terms
WFR_1 = wagons fabricated on regular time in period 1
WFO_1 = wagons fabricated on overtime in period 1
WAR_1 = wagons assembled on regular time in period 1
WAO_1 = wagons assembled on overtime in period 1
EIW_1 = ending inventory of wagons in period 1
BFR_1 = bicycles fabricated on regular time in period 1
BFO_1 = bicycles fabricated on overtime in period 1
BAR_1 = bicycles assembled on regular time in period 1
BAO_1 = bicycles assembled on overtime in period 1
EIB_1 = ending inventory for bicycles in period 1
DB_1 = demand for bicycles in period 1
DW_1 = demand for wagons in period 1

Period 2 terms are identical in definition to those of period 1.

Period 1 capacity constraints. Input to work centers must be less than or equal to capacity:

$$2WFR_1 + 2.67BFR_1 \leq 80$$
$$2WFO_1 + 2.67BFO_1 \leq 20$$
$$1WAR_1 + 1.33BAR_1 \leq 40$$
$$1WAO_1 + 1.33BAO_1 \leq 10$$

Period 2 fabrication constraints. Production 2 = demand 2 + ending inventory 2 − ending inventory 1. That is, produce enough at least to meet the demand of period 2:

$$WFR_2 + WFO_2 = DW_2 + EIW_2 - EIW_1$$
$$BFR_2 + BFO_2 = DB_2 + EIB_2 - EIB_1$$

Period 2 assembly constraints. Assembly quantities are forced to equal fabrication quantities:

$$WAR_2 + WAO_2 = WFR_2 + WFO_2$$
$$BAR_2 + BAO_2 = DFR_2 + BFO_2$$

Period 2 capacity constraints. Input to work centers must be less than or equal to capacity:

$$2WFR_2 + 2.67BFR_2 \leq 80$$
$$2WFO_2 + 2.67BFO_2 \leq 20$$
$$1WAR_2 + 1.33BAR_2 \leq 40$$
$$1WAO_2 + 1.33BAO_2 \leq 10$$

Period 1 and 2 demand constraints. Demand is shown as a variable to facilitate planning and what-if analysis. These values are for the next two periods: future planning can use different values:

$$DW_1 = 25$$
$$DB_1 = 15$$
$$DW_2 = 15$$
$$DB_2 = 25$$

Ending inventory of period 0. This constraint is not necessary unless the right-hand side is greater than zero. It is shown for generality here:

$$EIW_0 = EIB_0 = 0$$

Nonnegativity constraint. No variable can be negative.

Model Assumptions.   Prices, costs, demands, and capacities are known constants.

- Holding costs are $1 per unit per period of ending inventory.
- Shortages or back orders are not allowed.
- Linear relationships adequately define the system.

While these assumptions are operable here, each of these can be relaxed in other applications.

The optimal solution is illustrated in Table 34.5. Like all LP solutions, it has fractional values for the decision variables. This is a consequence of the continuous, linear assumption. In this application, one can round the results to achieve a good integer solution. However, integer solutions will always be less than or equal to that of the continuous, linear solution. Postoptimality analyses of constraints and variables are not presented here; however, these are available as output of LP computer software packages.

Now that this problem has been solved and validated, it is very easy to update the demands by using a rolling planning horizon. That is, to plan production for months 2 and 3, only the forecasted demands and beginning inventory need be changed. Thus, the plan is easily rolled over each month.

TABLE 34.5   Optimal Solution to Dynamic LP Problem
Profit Z = $900.01

Period 1	Period 2
Wagons	
Fabrication:	
WFR_1 = 25	WFR_2 = 15
WFO_1 = 0	WFO_2 = 0
Assembly:	
WAR_1 = 20.0	WAR_2 = 6.67
WAO_1 = 5.0	WFO_2 = 8.33
Inventory:	
EIW_1 = 0	EIW_2 = 0
Bicycles	
Fabrication:	
BFR_1 = 11.24	BFR_2 = 18.75
BFO_1 = 3.76	BFO_2 = 6.25
Assembly:	
BAR_1 = 15.0	BAR_2 = 25
BAO_1 = 0	BAO_2 = 0
Inventory:	
EIB = 0	EIB_2 = 0
Demands	
DW_1 = 25	DW_2 = 15
DB_1 = 15	DB_2 = 25

Summary of LP

The purpose of LP is to maximize or minimize some linear objective function subject to linear constraints. It assumes that certain, linear, and continuous relationships exist. *Certain* means that the constants and relationships are known with certainty (deterministic). *Linear* denotes, for example, that doubling the inputs yields a doubling of output. However, if slight nonlinearities exist, there are methods of approximating nonlinear functions by using piecewise separable methods. *Continuous* denotes that variables can equal fractional values. When the values of variables are large, then rounding may be a valid approach to integer solutions; otherwise, integer programming may be necessary.

The simplex algorithm finds solutions to very large problems in a short time on a computer and guarantees that an optimal solution has been achieved. LP software packages are capable of routinely solving and maintaining LP models with tens of thousands of variables and constraints. The capabilities of spreadsheet software may be considerably less than those of dedicated LP software. The simplex theorem states that the optimal solution occurs at a corner point of a convex polygon; at a corner point there are n linear equations in n unknowns, a deterministic and easily solved system of equations.

Postoptimality information is provided by commercial software. This information is important in exploring what-if analysis under conditions of uncertainty. The marginal values measure the increase or decreases in the objective function as the right-hand-side coefficients are changed.

Finally, LP has been widely applied in PIC and will become even more widely used in future PIC applications, especially with the increasing availability of spreadsheet optimization software.

NETWORK MODELS

The *transportation method* (TM) and *assignment method* (AM) are special cases of LP referred to as *network models*. While they solve problems similar to those discussed in the preceding section, they are simpler models and are computationally more efficient, making possible the solution of exceedingly large problems with hundreds of thousands of relationships.[37-39] In addition to efficiency, these methods always guarantee an optimal integer solution. Briefly review the transportation and assignment in Fig. 34.9 before discussing other network methods.

From	To			Supply
	Quebec	Los Angeles	New York	
Kansas City	$10 +5.0	$9.0 ⑩	$8.0 ⑫	22
Toronto	$1.5 ⑫	$12.0 +6.5	$4.5 ⑩	22
Demand	12	10	22	44 = 44

FIGURE 34.9   Optimal shipment schedule by transportation method.

Transportation Method

The TM optimally allocates scarce resources from many sources to many destinations given a linear objective function (such as to maximize profits, minimize travel distance). Its applicability should be obvious after an example.

Distribution Example. International Tire, Inc., operates two distribution centers (Kansas City and Toronto) from which it ships unit loads of tires to three warehouses. Transportation costs are a significant determinant of profitability, and the distribution centers have limited supplies of tires. Orders from the three warehouses (in Quebec, Los Angeles, and New York) are received weekly at central distribution office. During a typical week, Quebec orders 12 unit loads, Los Angeles 10, and New York 22. What is the minimum shipment cost, given the supply of 22 units at both Kansas City and Toronto?

The general transportation problem is described in Fig. 34.9. The unit shipping costs are given in the coefficient cells (smaller squares), the supply at each source in the right-hand column, and the demand in the bottom row. The circled values are the optimal shipment quantities, while the values with + signs are the marginal values (explained shortly). The solution procedure, although not illustrated here, is very straightforward. Study the solution of how the supply and demand for each location is met: The 12 units demanded in Quebec are shipped from Toronto, the 22 units demanded in New York are met from Kansas City and Toronto, and the 10 units demanded in Los Angeles are shipped from Kansas City. The minimum shipment cost totals $249.00. Table 34.6 illustrates this solution using a different format.

TABLE 34.6   Costs and Allocations of the Optimal Solution

Units	From	To	Unit cost	Total cost
10	Kansas City	Los Angeles	$9.00	$90.00
12	Kansas City	New York	8.00	96.00
12	Toronto	Quebec	1.50	18.00
10	Toronto	New York	4.50	45.00
44				$249.00

There are a number of different algorithms for solving transportation problems. These include the simplex method of the previous section, the stepping-stone procedure, which is frequently used with the *northwest-corner method* and *Vogel's approximation method* (VAM). Other, more efficient algorithms include the *SHARE out-of-kilter code* and the *transshipment code.* The transshipment code is efficient for solving very large problems. Fortunately, the basics of all solution methods are easily learned by users with little mathematical background.

Postoptimality Information. Postoptimality information is a byproduct of the transportation method, just as it is for the simplex method. Alternative solution costs are given by the noncircled numbers in the allocation cells of Fig. 34.9. These *marginal values* are the increased costs of shipping from nonoptimal locations instead of from optimal locations. For example, shipping 1 unit from Toronto to Los Angeles will increase the total cost by $6.50. Each unit shipped from Kansas City to Quebec will increase the cost of the schedule by $5. Because a shipment from Kansas City to Los Angeles is an optimal shipment route, its marginal value (while not shown) is zero.

By using marginal values, we can consider alternative shipping schedules. Table 34.7 is an alternative schedule that forces shipments from Toronto to Los Angeles. As shown, it cost $6.50 each more (or $255.50) to ship by this schedule than by the optimal schedule, even though the number of units shipped is 44 in each plan.

TABLE 34.7 Nonoptimal Alternative Solution

Units	From	To	Unit cost	Total cost
9	Kansas City	Los Angeles	$9.00	$81.00
13	Kansas City	New York	8.00	104.00
1	Toronto	Los Angeles	12.00	12.00
12	Toronto	Quebec	1.50	18.00
9	Toronto	New York	4.50	40.50
44				$255.50

While not obvious from this presentation, the transportation method is a special case of linear programming. If one were to formulate and solve this problem using the simplex method, it would be seen that the assumption and form of the TM are the same as those of the general LP model except that the left-hand-side constraint coefficient are all 1s or 0s.

There are many applications in which TM can provide effective solutions. Its structure and solution are easily understood, and when the TM is applicable, it provides important information. In addition, the TM has the advantage of providing integer solutions to extremely large problems by using fast algorithms. For example, one can easily combine the previous production planning example with the distribution example to form a single, integrated production-distribution optimization model.

Assignment Method

The assignment method optimally allocates scarce resources when *n* supply sources are to be assigned to *m* demands and only one resource assignment is made from supply to demand (such as assigning 12 jobs to 12 machines). The efficiencies, times, costs, or profits from each assignment are known, and the objective is to find the optimal assignment of all jobs, such as the lowest cost or highest profit.

Figure 34.10 illustrates a simple minimum-cost assignment problem with the optimal solution and costs shown circled. While not illustrated here, the manual and computer solution methods are very straightforward. If one were to formulate and solve this problem using the simplex method, one would see that the assumptions and form of the AM are the same as those of the general LP model except that the left-hand-side constraint coefficients and the right-hand-side constants are all 1s or 0s. However, solutions via simplex are not efficient for large problems as simpler approaches; nonetheless, they are no less optimum.

The importance of the AM and the TM is their ability to find optimal solutions to very large allocation problems. If a problem possesses the structures illustrated, then significant improvement in costs and profits are possible through the use of the AM or

Jobs	Machine			
	A	B	C	D
1	20	15	(12)	35
2	(10)	5	7	22
3	45	(24)	30	47
4	12	75	44	(22)

FIGURE 34.10   Optimal assignment of jobs (1 through 4) to machines (A through D).

TM. In addition, the simplicity and efficiency of these approaches make them effective algorithms of more complex planning and allocation systems.

Other Network Algorithms

In addition to TM and AM, several other network methods exist. These include the *shortest-path problem,* the *longest-path problem,* the *maximal-flow problem,* and the *critical-path method.* There have been several computation improvements in network models in recent years. These techniques represent methods that can be very useful in routing vehicles, scheduling and tracking thousands of jobs in a job shop environment, and other specialized problems.

Project Planning and Scheduling Using PERT/CPM

Large projects can be managed with specialized network algorithms and software.[40–44] In recent years there has been a rapid growth of project management systems with the popularity of microcomputers and powerful microsoftware. (See Chapter 13 for further discussion of project management.)

ADVANCED MATHEMATICAL PROGRAMMING

Goal Programming (GP)

Decision makers often face problems that have multiple goals that must be considered in achieving good solutions.[45–47] The standard LP approach optimizes only a single-objective function and may therefore not be useful in finding good solutions if there are conflicting goals. Fortunately, *goal programming* (GP) methods exist to solve such problems. GP is a special case of LP which is no more difficult to solve than an LP problem and has many applications in PIC.

Integer Programming

LP methods solve continuous, linearly constrained problems very efficiently, and the fractional values of a continuous solution frequently cause no problems.[24,25,27,36,48] For example, if in a production planning problem, the optimal number of units to be produced on regular time is 1000.5, then little loss of optimality exists in rounding the solution to 1000 or 1001. But if in a facility planning problem the optimal solution is to build 3.4 distribution centers with 13.3 loading docks supplied by 2.8 factories, then there can be considerable difference in the optimality of rounded solutions. In such situations, *integer programming* (IP) methods are necessary.

A simple example of an integer programming problem is the previous production planning of gas and wind turbines. The optimal integer solution arrived at through enumeration is shown in Table 34.8, where the continuous LP values are given in parentheses.

The optimal integer solution ($4990) is always lower than the optimal LP continuous solution ($5014) as shown by this example; consequently, the continuous solution always provides a benchmark in judging alternative integer solutions. In addition, the search for integer solutions can provide insights to alternative solutions. For instance, during the enumeration process of this example, it was noted that $40 additional profit could be generated by adding 5 hours of capacity to the fabrication department. This alternative solution is shown in Table 34.9.

This solution illustrates the ability to undertake what-if analysis by using LP and IP methods. Such explorations can be insightful even if the model does not perfectly fit the environment.

There are several types of IP problems: integer problems in which all variables are integers [*pure integer programming* (PIP)]; *mixed integer programming* (MIP) *problems,* in which both continuous and integer values are in the solution; and *zero-one integer programming* ($0 - 1$P), which can be mixed or pure integer. A number of IP methods work very well with these problems if the model does not possess more than a thousand integer variables; these methods include the cutting plane, branch and bound, and implicit enumeration methods of IP. By far the most popular solution method is the branch-and-bound method. The cutting-plane method has not been found to be of value

TABLE 34.8   Integer Solution to Production Planning Using LP

	Integer	Continuous LP
$G = 27$		(27.7)
$W = 62$		(61.5)
Maximum profit = $70(27) + $50(62) = $4990.00		($5014)
Lathe utilization = 5(27) + 1(62) = 197 hours		(200)
Assembly utilization = 20(27) + 30(62) = 2400 hours		(2400)

TABLE 34.9   Integer Solution with Increased Capacity

	Integer
$G = 29, W = 60$	
Maximum profit = $70(29) + $50(60)	= $5030.00
Lathe utilization = 5(29) + 1(60)	= 205 hours
Assembly utilization = 20(29) + 30(60)	= 2380 hours

in practice, and the implicit-enumeration method works best with integer variables that have only values of 0 or 1.

Nonlinear Programming

Nonlinear functions frequently occur in business and economics.[24,25,27,36] Costs, revenues, and production may be nonlinear because of the law of diminishing returns, geometric growth, the time value of money, and so on. Often these can be modeled using linear approximations of the nonlinear function; that is, a nonlinear curve can be separated into a number of linear line segments and solved as an LP problem; this is called *separable programming*. When this is not possible, *nonlinear programming* (NLP) methods may often, but not always, solve the problem.

Because there is an infinite variety of nonlinear forms of equations, the NLP problem may be considerably more difficult to solve than the LP problem. There is not one nonlinear method but many different methods; consequently, NLP methods solve only one subclass of nonlinear problems. Also, the formation and solution of nonlinear problems may be quite difficult, very often requiring skills not available to many manufacturers. These limitations reduce the importance of NLP in solving the general problems facing PIC managers.

Dynamic Programming

Dynamic programming (DP) is a general approach to determining the optimal solution to sequences of decisions made over time or space.[49–51] There is no standard mathematical formulation or procedure for solving dynamic programming problems; different solution techniques (such as linear programming or differential calculus) are used to find optimal solutions. The familiar Wagner-Whitin algorithm is a good example of a forward DP method, and the solution procedure used in the decision tree shown in Fig. 34.2 is an example of a backward DP algorithm. While DP can be very complex, there are many situations in which DP can be easily and effectively applied.

OTHER QUANTITATIVE METHODS

There are many quantitative methods. Those not discussed in this chapter include statistical and probability methods, forecasting methods, inventory models, and project-planning methods, all of which are discussed in other chapters. In addition, neural networks, game theory, and Markov processes are only briefly described below because they are not widely applied as yet in production and inventory management. Also worthy of mention are heuristic procedures, which are embodied in most PIC systems and techniques such as the part-period balancing method.

Game Theory

Game theory is used to model the relationship between two or more competing entities, such as individuals, corporations, or governments. These competing entities anticipate and react to each other's decisions. While it is not widely used at the operational (tactical) level, game theory is an important tool at the strategic level.

Markov Processes

These are useful in describing how the state of a system changes over time.[52-53] A *Markov process* is a probabilistic method for which the future state depends only on the immediately preceding state. Markov processes have been used in marketing to model brand switching, and in PIC to study equipment adjustment, maintenance, and quality control. Like queueing analysis, Markov models can become very complex and difficult to solve in the general case—but if the specific situation fits a Markovian process, then considerable benefit can be achieved from Markov analysis.

Heuristic Procedures, Artificial Intelligence, or Expert Systems

These methods use empirically derived rules to achieve good solutions to complex problems.[54-56] They are used whenever an optimal procedure is too costly, impossible to use, or unavailable. There have been many applications of heuristics in PIC, including the part-period balancing and least-total-cost methods of inventory control. The future growth of *expert systems* (ES) and *artificial intelligence* (AI) will yield more sophisticated and useful heuristic procedures. A study of AI/ES will assist those desiring more knowledge of heuristic.

Artificial Neural Networks

The artificial intelligence movement of the 1970s and 1980s has resulted in the development of computer models that mimic the essential processing capabilities of the human brain.[56-58] The discipline that attempts to model the decision-making and pattern-recognition capabilities of the brain is called *neural-network computing* (NNC) or *artificial neural networks* (ANN). These approaches simulate massive parallel processes of the neurons of the human brain, of which there are about 100 billion. These artificial neurons receive information from external sources that are then transformed into external outputs using a weighting scheme that is learned through an iterative process of reweighting and relearning. The inputs can be data (e.g., past demands) where the output can be a production plan or forecast similar to those developed earlier in this chapter.

For example, consider a firm wanting to develop an ANN for forecasting demand. The learning process begins by setting initial weights on a function such as past demands, prices, product promotions, temperatures, and precipitation. These initial weights are set using heuristics or even through a random process. Using mathematical processes beyond our scope, these weights are applied to the inputs. The results yield an estimated output that is then compared to the actual demand. The objective of the learning process in forecasting is to minimize the difference between the actual demand and the estimated output. Thus, we see that these weights are coefficients or relative strengths given to each of the input variables at the various layers of the ANN. The values of these weights will be varied to improve the prediction and control of the output variable.

The output of an ANN is a solution to a problem. For example, in the production-planning example, the ANN might provide estimates of the regular, overtime, and inventory as done with the LP model. A disadvantage of ANN is that it requires considerable time to learn. Another disadvantage is that if a human cannot do a task well, then an ANN will most likely not do the task well either. Nonetheless, the applications of ANN will grow as the software to support them becomes more available.

BIBLIOGRAPHY

Periodicals Featuring QM in PIC

AIIE Transactions
Computers and Industrial Engineering
Computers and Operations Research
Decision Sciences
Harvard Business Review
Industrial Engineering
Interfaces
International Journal of Operations and Production Management
International Journal of Production Research
Journal of Operations Management
Journal of the Operational Research Society
Management Science
Operations Management Review
Operations Research
Production and Inventory Management
Project Management Journal
Project Management Quarterly
Simulation
Sloan Management Review

Abstract Services Reviewing PICS Applications of QM

APICS Bibliography, American Production and Inventory Society, Falls Church, Virginia

Applied Science and Technology Index, H. W. Wilson, New York

Business Periodicals Index, H. W. Wilson, New York

Dissertation Abstracts, University Microfilm, Ann Arbor, Michigan

Engineer Index, Engineering Information, Inc., New York

Government Reports Index, National Technical Information Service, Springfield, Virginia

Information Services in Mechanical Engineering, Data Courier, Louisville, Kentucky

International Abstracts in Operations Research, Operations Research Society of American, Baltimore, Maryland

Operations Research/Management Science (OR/MS) Abstracts, Executive Sciences Institute, Whippany, New Jersey

Quality Control/Applied Statistics (QC/AS) Abstracts, Executive Science Institute, Whippany, New Jersey

Science Citation Index, Institute for Scientific Information, Philadelphia, Pennsylvania

Online Literature Search Services

The most efficient way to research the OR/MS literature is to use online literature retrieval services that provide access to the abstract services above. These can be done at your local library or through computer services such as Compuserve or America Online. Electronic services include ABI/Inform, ERIC, Management Contents, Compendex, INFOTRACS, DIALOG, and SciSearch, to name a few. In some cases it is recommended that a professional librarian do the online literature search.

REFERENCES

General QM Implementation and Survey References

These references discuss the role of QM in business and the proper methods of implementing QM.

1. J. S. Hammond: "The Role of the Manager and Management Scientist in Successful Implementation," *Sloan Management Review* (15), winter 1974, pp. 1–24.

2. S. Eilon: "The Role of Management Science," *Journal of the Operational Research Society* (31:1), 1980.

3. H. M. Wagner: "The ABC's of OR," *Operations Research,* Vol. 19, Oct. 1971.

4. A. A. Assad, E. A. Wasil, and G. L. Lilien: *Excellence in Management Science Practice,* Prentice-Hall, Englewood Cliffs, N.J., 1992.

5. R. G. Batson: "The Modern Role of MS/OR Professionals in the Interdisciplinary Teams," *Interfaces,* May–June 1987.

6. R. L. Schultz and D. P. Slevin (eds.): *Implementing Operations Research/Management Science,* American Elsevier, New York, 1975.

7. A. M. Geoffrion: "The Purpose of Mathematical Programming Is Insight, Not Numbers," *Interfaces* (7:1), 1976, pp. 81–92.

Comprehensive Introductory Quantitative Methods Textbooks

These references introduce QM in a manner accessible to managers and analysts possessing basic algebra skills. They are comprehensive in their coverage of all techniques discussed in this chapter. These are suggested "first" references for a study of specific quantitative methods. References of specific techniques, 16 to 58, will vary in their mathematical sophistication.

8. D. R. Anderson, D. J. Sweeney, and T. A. Williams: *An Introduction to Management Science: Quantitative Approaches to Decision Making,* 7th ed., West Publishing, St. Paul, Minn., 1993.

9. Saul I. Gass and Carl M. Harris: *Encyclopedia of Operations Research and Management Science,* Kluwer Academic Publishers, New York, 1996.

10. F. S. Hillier and G. J. Lieberman: *Introduction to Operation Research,* 5th ed., Holden-Day, San Francisco, 1990.

11. N. K. Kwak and S. A. De Lurgio: *Quantitative Models for Business Decisions,* Duxbury Publishing, North Scituate, Mass., 1980.

12. R. E. Markland: *Topics in Management Science,* 2d ed., Wiley, New York, 1985.

13. H. A. Taha: *Operations Research: An Introduction,* 5th ed., Macmillan, New York, 1992.

14. Efraim Turban and Jack R. Meredith: *Fundamentals of Management Science,* 6th ed., Irwin Publishing, Burr Ridge, Ill., 1994.

15. H. M. Wagner: *Principles of Management Science,* 2d ed., Prentice-Hall, Englewood Cliffs, N.J., 1982.

Decision Analysis

16. J. F. Magee: "Decision Trees for Decision Making," *Harvard Business Review,* July–August 1964.

17. R. O. Swalm: "Utility Theory–Insights Into Risk Taking," *Harvard Business Review,* November–December 1966, pp. 123–136.

18. R. Keeney and H. Raiffa: *Decision with Multiple Objectives: Preferences and Value Trade-offs,* Wiley, New York, 1976.

19. J. Ulvila and R. V. Brown: "Decision Analysis Comes of Age," *Harvard Business Review,* September–October 1982, pp. 130–141.

20. D. E. Bell et al.: *Decision Making,* Cambridge University Press, New York, 1988.

Queueing Theory

21. M. F. Aburdene: *Computer Simulation of Dynamic Systems,* William C. Brown, Dubuque, Ia., 1988.

22. O. J. Boxma and R. Syski (eds.): *Queueing Theory and Its Applications,* North-Holland, Amsterdam, 1988.

23. R. Hall: *Queueing Methods for Service and Manufacturing,* Prentice-Hall, Englewood Cliffs, N.J., 1991.

Mathematical Programming

24. R. B. Darst (ed.): *Introduction to Linear Programming: Applications and Extensions,* Dekker, New York, 1990.

25. J. E. Calvert et al.: *Linear Programming,* Harcourt Brace Jovanovich, New York, 1989.

26. H. M. Salkin and J. Saha: *Studies in Linear Programming,* Elsevier, New York, 1975.

27. N. K. Kwak: *Mathematical Programming with Business Applications,* McGraw-Hill, New York, 1973.

28. S. Eilon: "Five Approaches to Aggregate Production Planning," *AIIE Transactions* (7), 1975, pp. 118–131.

29. G. Bitran, E. Haas, and A. Hax: "Hierarchical Production Planning: A Two Stage System," *Operations Research* (30:2), March–April, 1982.

30. A. M. Geoffrion: "A Guide to Computer-Assisted Methods for Distribution Systems Planning," *Sloan Management Review,* winter 1975.

31. A. M. Geoffrion: "Better Distribution Planning with Computer Models," *Harvard Business Review,* July–August 1976.

32. A. C. Hax and H. C. Meal: "Hierarchical Integration of Production Planning and Scheduling." In M. A. Geisler (ed.), *Studies in the Management Sciences,* Vol. I, Logistics, North Holland-Elsevier, Amsterdam, 1975.

33. K. D. Lawrence and S. H. Zanakis: *Production Planning and Scheduling, Mathematical Programming Applications,* Industrial Engineering and Management Press, Norcross, Ga., 1984.

34. R. E. Markland and R. J. Newett: "Production-Distribution Planning in a Large Scale Commodity Processing Network," *Decision Sciences,* October 1976.

35. J. N. Hooker: "Karmarkar's Linear Programming Algorithm," *Interfaces,* July–August 1986, pp. 75–90, and January–February 1987, p. 128.

36. L. Schrage: *LINDO User's Manual* (release 5.0), Scientific Press, San Francisco, 1991.

Network Models and PERT/CPM

37. M. S. Bazaraa and J. J. Jarvis: *Linear Programming and Network Flows,* 2d ed., Wiley, New York, 1990.

38. D. Klingman and J. M. Mulvey (eds.): *Network Models and Associated Applications,* Elsevier, New York, 1981.

39. F. Glover and D. Klingman: "Network Applications in Industry and Government," *AIIE Transactions,* December 1977.

40. L. J. Goodman and R. N. Love: *Project Planning and Management: An Integrated Approach,* Pergamon Press, New York, 1980.

41. A. B. Badiru: *Project Management in Manufacturing and High Technology Operations,* Wiley, New York, 1988.

42. H. Kerzner: *Project Management: Effective Scheduling,* Van Nostrand Reinhold, New York, 1991.

43. J. Knudson: *How to Be a Successful Project Manager,* American Management Association, Saranac Lake, N.Y., 1989.

44. J. R. Meredith and S. J. Mantel, Jr.: *Project Management: A Managerial Approach,* 2d ed., Wiley, New York, 1989.

Advanced Mathematical Programming

45. M. J. Schniederjans: *Linear Goal Programming,* Petrocelli Books, New York, 1984.

46. R. E. Steuer: *Multiple Criteria Optimization: Theory, Computation, and Applications,* Wiley, New York, 1986.

47. J. P. Ignizio: *Linear Programming in Single & Multiple Objective Systems,* Prentice-Hall, Englewood Cliffs, N.J., 1982.

48. S. Walukiewicz: *Integer Programming,* Kluwer Academic, New York, 1991.

49. H. M. Wagner and T. M. Whitin: "Dynamic Version of the Economic Lot Size Model," *Management Science* (5), 1958, pp. 89–96.

50. R. Bellman and S. E. Dreyfus: *Applied Dynamic Programming,* Princeton University Press, Princeton, N.J., 1962.

51. A. D. Esogbue: *Dynamic Programming for Optimal Resource Systems Analysis,* Prentice-Hall, Englewood Cliffs, N.J., 1989.

52. W. J. Anderson: *Continuous Time Markov Chains,* Springer-Verlag, New York, 1991.

53. D. T. Gillespie: *Markov Processes,* Academic Press, New York, 1991.

54. T. S. Saaty: *Decision for Leaders: The Analytic Hierarchy Process,* University of Pittsburgh, Pittsburgh, Pa., 1990.

55. S. H. Zanakis and J. R. Evans: "Heuristic Optimization: Why, When and How to Use It," *Interfaces,* October 1981.

56. E. Turban: *Decision Support Systems and Expert Systems,* 3rd ed., Macmillan, New York, 1993.

57. R. Dixon and F. Bevin: *Neural Networks Tutor,* Advanced Technology Transfer Group, Whitby, Ontario, Canada, 1996.

58. B. Widrow, D. E. Rumelhart, and Michael A. Lehr: "Neural Networks: Applications in Industry, Business and Science", *Communications of the ACM* (37:3), 1994, pp. 93–105.

CHAPTER 35
STATISTICS*

Editor

Stephen D. Roberts, Ph.D.

Professor and Head
Department of Industrial Engineering
North Carolina State University
Raleigh, North Carolina

Statistics deals with the collection, display, and characterization of data and with the use of data to draw conclusions and make decisions. The word *data,* the plural of the Latin word *datum,* means facts. Statistics is concerned with facts about events and entities and the processes that generate or affect them. The relevant characteristics of the events of interest are represented by variables, which are either qualitative or quantitative. A *quantitative variable* may take on numerical values, while a *qualitative variable* takes on categorical values. For example, part size, stated as small, medium, or large, is a qualitative variable, while part weight, measured in pounds, is a quantitative variable. If a quantitative variable assumes only certain values such as integers, it is referred to as a *discrete variable.* If the variable can assume any value in a given range, then it is referred to as a *continuous variable.*

The value of a variable is not known until it is actually measured or determined in some way. The process of determining the value of a variable may be conceived of as an experiment whose outcome is uncertain or subject to chance and so is referred to as a *random variable.* A variable that can assume a single value is no longer random and is actually a constant. Here, the concern is mainly with the use and analysis of data in the form of numerical random variables.

The term *population* denotes the set of entities about which conclusions are being drawn, and the term *example* indicates the part of the population for which data were actually collected. For instance, one may take a sample of 20 units and measure the weight in pounds to draw a conclusion regarding the weight of the population of units in a particular production run.

A population can be finite or infinite. Very large populations, even though finite, may be considered infinite for practical purposes. Most statistical techniques assume that data were collected from a *random sample,* which is a sample selected such that all members of the population are equally likely to be included.

---

*Parts of this chapter were included in the first edition in Chapter 28, "Statistical Theory," edited by Dr. Warren H. Thomas, Chairman, Department of Industrial Engineering, State University of New York at Buffalo, Buffalo, New York.

It is randomness in the sample that allows inferences to be made from statistics to population parameters. The sample must be not only random but also representative. This means that one must be careful that the sample taken is in fact characteristic of the population. Hence, the sample must be large enough to adequately reveal the population characteristics. Sometimes special schemes such as stratification, proportionality, and so forth are used to ensure proper representation. These schemes form the foundation of sampling theory and statistical inference.

From a set of sample observations one can calculate *statistics,* which are numerical values that characterize the sample. In a similar manner, a population is characterized by a set of descriptive measures known as *parameters.* The techniques used to draw conclusions about the parameters of a population based on the values of sample statistics are referred to collectively as *statistical inference.* The underlying theory that allows one to draw these conclusions is known as *probability theory.*

DESCRIPTIVE STATISTICS

There are many methods of obtaining information, from personal observations to elaborate automated systems. Important internal sources of data for production control include such reports as the production records, sales forecasts, routings, materials supply schedules, budgets, and scrap reports. This information can be collected by hand (manually), by electronic data processing equipment, and by many other methods. Most management information systems provide means of collecting and storing of data. Therefore, familiarization with these modes of collection can greatly aid in obtaining information.

Frequently, external data sources must be consulted. This is especially true in forecasting. In this case one might consult such publications as *Survey of Current Business* or other external sources.

Display of Data

After data are collected, it is helpful to display them in some insightful fashion. This display can often reveal useful properties about data and imply important characteristics, presenting data that can be understood with a minimum of explanation. In general, there are two methods of display: tabular and graphical.

Tabular Displays.   These displays of numerical values emphasize some relevant fact. The three displays of primary interest are the historical table, the research table, and the frequency table.

Historical Table.   The *historical,* or *reference, table* is a means of collecting concise reference material. It generally takes the form shown in Table 35.1. This specific table illustrates the number of employees for each department for 3 separate years. The basic parts indicated in the table should be used as a guide in the preparation of such tables. It is important that emphasis be placed where most desired. People have a tendency to read from left to right and from top to bottom, so the data in the upper left-hand corner should be most prominent. In general, the arrangement should be easily understood and yet provide sufficient information to effectively communicate valuable ideas. Footnotes should provide additional explanation, and the information source should be acknowledged.

Research Table.   The *research table,* sometimes called the *analytical* or *cross-reference table,* serves as an aid for more specific analysis of data. An example of this kind

TABLE 35.1 Average Number of Employees per Department

	Year		
Department	1	2	3
Stock	3	4	5
Plating	7	7	8
Screw machine	8	9	10
Milling	10	12	12
Drilling	5	5	6
Miscellaneous parts	15	15	17
Stores	5	5	6
Assembly	20	22	23
Warehousing	6	7	7

TABLE 35.2 Effects of Machine Speed, Feed, and Material on Scrap Rates

	Material A		Material B		Material C	
	Feed, in/rev		Feed, in/rev		Feed, in/rev	
Speedy, ft/min	0.005	0.010	0.005	0.010	0.005	0.010
200	0.05	0.06	0.04	0.08	0.08	0.02
250	0.04	0.07	0.05	0.07	0.06	0.03
300	0.02	0.06	0.07	0.07	0.05	0.03
350	0.01	0.05	0.09	0.08	0.06	0.04

of table is shown in Table 35.2. This table presents the effects of machine speeds, feeds, and material types on scrap rates and the interrelationships among the variables. Since the table contains three variables—speed, feed, and materials—it is sometimes called a *three-way table.*

Frequency Table. Of primary importance in descriptive statistics is the *frequency table.* This is described best with an illustration. Suppose one is interested in customer orders outstanding which are late. Table 35.3 presents the data as they are collected. There are 40 tardy orders. Obviously the data, as collected, are difficult to understand

TABLE 35.3 Tardiness of Orders (Days)

10	11	20	1	0
9	12	16	6	17
16	15	9	31	19
12	12	11	15	2
8	4	6	14	8
7	13	3	2	7
5	17	10	11	18
13	14	12	5	22

in present form, so one would like to present them in a more usable and effective manner. In their original form the data are often referred to as *raw data.*

For this case, the data may be ordered according to the degree of tardiness, as presented in Table 35.4. This is sometimes called a *frequency array,* since the number of times, or frequency, of a particular number of days tardy is presented as well as the days tardy. However, reduction to a frequency array usually does not greatly improve the compactness of the presentation. Consequently, it is often convenient to group the data into classes, or groups, of specified intervals. For this case it could be accomplished by using a class size of 5. These grouped data are then tabulated in Table 35.5. Such a tabulation is called a *frequency distribution.* A *class* refers to the designation of information within a given interval, while the interval itself is called a *class interval.* For this case there are five classes, each with an interval of 5. The boundaries of the classes, 0, 4, 5, 9, and so on are referred to as the *class limits.*

Note, however, that while this presentation does give a clear and concise picture of tardiness, it was achieved through some loss of information. This is illustrated by the fact that one cannot decipher from the table which orders are more than 19 days late. To obtain this information, one must refer to the raw data.

TABLE 35.4   Frequency Array of Tardiness

Days tardy	Frequency	Days tardy	Frequency
0	1	11	3
1	1	12	4
2	2	13	2
3	1	14	2
4	1	15	2
5	2	16	2
6	2	17	2
7	2	18	1
8	2	19	1
9	2	20	1
10	2	22	1
		31	1

TABLE 35.5   Frequency Distribution of Tardiness

Days tardy	Number of orders
0–4	6
5–9	10
10–14	13
15–19	8
Over 20	3
	40

Consequently, the reduction of the data to a more concise form depends directly on the number of classes chosen. This is not easy to determine and requires much insight. If there are too many classes, the resulting frequency distribution becomes bulky, and the concentrations of the data are difficult to ascertain. If there are too few classes, much of the information is concealed within the class intervals, and the frequency distribution becomes so compact that an important pattern may be completely grouped within a class. A good rule of thumb states that the number of classes should range between 5 and 15. Obviously in some special situations 15 may be too few or 5 too many, but without any other insight the rule has proved very useful.

Selection of the class interval and class limits is also difficult. The class limits should not be overlapping but should be exclusive. If, for example, the class limits were 0 to 5 for the first class and 5 to 10 for the second, an order having a tardiness of 5 could be placed in either the first or second class. If the class interval and limits are established before the data are collected, this consequence should be considered so that accurate data are obtained. To make the table easy to understand and construct, the class intervals should be equal. This was done in constructing Table 35.5, and the reasons should be clear.

For discrete data it is not difficult to define class limits because the data can assume only certain values. Consequently, the limits were 0 to 4, 5 to 9, 10 to 14, and so forth, since this guaranteed that all data would be contained in mutually exclusive classes. However, this is difficult to do if the data are continuous. Suppose, for example, that the tardiness were measured in half-days. A tardiness of 4.5 would not lie within the limits of any class boundary. Thus the class limits would have to be revised. To avoid this ambiguity, one usually represents the class limits to one decimal point more than that of the data. For example, the class limits could be revised to the following: 0.00 to 4.54, 4.55 to 9.54, 9.55 to 14.54. Since the data are measured to only one decimal place, the new class limits will be nonoverlapping, and the class intervals remain equal. Note that this may always be done since any time data are collected they are made discrete to some extent; thus class limits may be constructed, so that all information will fall within a class.

It is important that there be no separation between classes. Often this is difficult to avoid without using too few classes. Therefore, it is sometimes convenient to utilize *open-ended classes*. This is, in fact, what the fifth class is in the table. An open-ended class has only one class limit. It is useful when part of the data appears far away from the major concentration of the information. In the tardiness example, the use of an open-ended class avoided the use of an empty class (25 to 29). Notice that open-ended classes can occur at the beginning of a frequency distribution as well as at the end. The disadvantage of such classes is that they cover an extremely large range and do not provide any magnitude information such as how many days over 20 are the orders late.

In addition to the class intervals, limits, size, and so forth, the *midpoints* of the classes are important. The midpoint is merely the sum of the class limits divided by 2, or just the average of the class limits. The midpoint of the classes should be of such a magnitude that its value can actually be obtained. For continuous data this presents no problems. However, for discrete data the values of the data are restricted to a certain set of values. The midpoint is important since data within a class are often represented by their value, and the data should tend to cluster about this point. Thus the use of the classes in the table appears satisfactory.

An important type of frequency table is called the *percentage table*. This table represents the proportion, or percentage, of data that may be found in a certain class. Thus it is merely the frequency table transformed to percentage data. An illustration of this for the tardiness example is given in Table 35.6. This table indicates, for example, that 25 percent of the orders are 5 to 9 days late. If these 40 orders were a random sample of

TABLE 35.6   Percentage Table

Days tardy	Percentage
0–4	15.0
5–9	25.0
10–14	32.5
15–19	20.0
Over 20	7.5
	100.0

some larger population, we might use the percentage table to reflect the tardiness character of the population itself.

Sometimes it is even useful to collect cumulative data. For example, suppose we wanted the number of orders less than or equal to 9 days late. Table 35.7 supplies this type of information. This is sometimes called a *less-than table*. Note that this may also be presented in percentage form, as indicated by the previous table. One may construct an equivalent *more-than, cumulative table*. The less-than table *begins* with zero, while the more-than table *ends* with zero. Often the *cumulative frequency table* (of the less-than type) is referred to as the *cumulative distribution,* and it represents an important concept in descriptive statistics.

Graphical Display.   As with the tabular display, the *graphical display* is used to emphasize some particular aspect of the data but through a visual or pictorial medium. Graphical presentations may be used to highlight certain significant facts and are often used in conjunction with tabular results. Management appreciates graphical displays that present, at a glance, simple and clearly significant points. Often graphical displays are used for presentation of information to a group of people where a large display can provide a persuasive exhibit. There are many types of graphical displays, but among the most important are bar charts, line charts, pie charts, pictograms, histograms, and frequency polygons.

Bar Charts.   The *bar chart* is one of the most popular of the graphical displays. It is simple to construct and easy to understand. The basic characteristic of the bar chart is that it is strictly one-dimensional. In other words, only the lengths of the bars vary. An example of a bar chart is given in Fig. 35.1. This presents the distribution of people during the year for the plant departments. Notice that the bars are separated for ease of identification, and normally the bars are placed in increasing or decreasing order unless they

TABLE 35.7   Cumulative Frequency Table

Days tardy	Cumulative number of orders	Cumulative percentage
0–4	6	15.0
5–9	16	40.0
10–14	29	72.5
15–19	37	92.5
Over 20	40	100.0

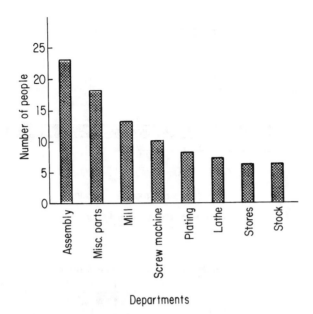

FIGURE 35.1   Distribution of people during the year for plant departments.

are fixed by something such as time. The height of the bar represents the number of people. More specifically, this bar chart is called a *simple vertical-bar chart,* or *column chart.* This chart may be turned on its side, and then is called a *simple horizontal-bar chart.* The preference for vertical or horizontal is simply a question of which makes the most effective presentation and which is simplest to construct.

In addition to the simple bar charts, there exist other types of bar charts. Among the most widely used are the *component-part bar chart,* the grouped bar chart, and the two-directional bar chart. These charts are illustrated in a horizontal fashion in Figs. 35.2, 35.3, and 35.4.

The *component-part bar chart* is recognized because the bars themselves are composed of components. This type of chart permits a visual comparison of the contribution

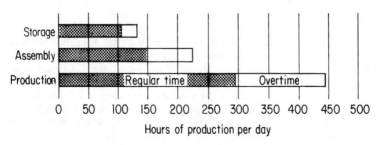

FIGURE 35.2   Component chart—breakdown of production hours.

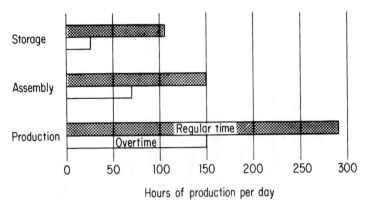

Hours of production per day

FIGURE 35.3 Grouped bar chart—breakdown of production hours

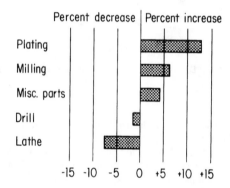

FIGURE 35.4 Two-directional chart: percentage change in department performance for 2 years.

of regular time and overtime to the total production hours per day for each departmental group. However, all overtime components have different origins on the scale, and so it is difficult to compare the overtime among the departmental groups.

This disadvantage is overcome by the *grouped bar chart*. In this chart, both overtime and regular time may be compared with each other and also with those of the other departmental groups. But this chart has a disadvantage which the component-part chart does not possess. Comparisons are difficult between the total production hours for each departmental group when a total includes the sum of overtime and regular time.

When relative gains and losses are desired, the *two-directional chart* emphasizes the characteristics. The percentage change in departmental performance for 2 years is presented. The departments are ranked from the most positive to the most negative, so analysis is simplified. Note that component-type bars may be used as well as grouped bars. These types of charts are extremely useful to indicate improvements or losses on the same chart around a common base of zero. In the example, one is able to pinpoint which department's performance is deteriorating or improving.

In constructing bar charts, it is important that direct labeling be used, as illustrated, so that they are easily read. For the component-part or grouped charts, the bars should be shaded, crosshatched, or colored so that each bar is distinct. Also the bars should be spaced, for ease in identification. Grouped bars of the grouped bar chart are, however, often side by side. The central theme in construction should be clarity and ease of presentation and identification.

Line Chart. Line charts are particularly useful whenever the variable is a function of or depends on time. Sales forecasts are examples of this type of need. Normally time is plotted on the horizontal axis while the quantity of interest is plotted on the vertical. Line charts may be *simple* or of the *component-part type* similar to bar charts. Figure 35.5 illustrates the simple line chart for the personnel requirements of three major departmental groups—assembly, production, and storage. The vertical axis could be of the same form as in Fig. 35.2, except the line segments connect components of the data, thus forming a component-part line chart. The series of connecting lines is called a *curve* and represents the variable of interest as the time varies. The major advantage of such a chart is the ability to visualize the character of the data as they change with respect to time.

Pie Charts. Pie charts or *circle charts* are used to portray components of a total. The pie chart is particularly eye-catching, but application is limited to component-type characteristics. An example is presented in Fig. 35.6. In constructing the pie chart, a protractor is useful to obtain the desired proportions. Also it is desirable to arrange the sectors according to their magnitude. Colors can produce a more striking appearance. Pie-chart suitability lies in its eye-catching appeal, and so it is useful for public presentation. However, it lacks the accuracy of other charts.

Pictograms. Like the pie chart, the *pictogram* is used because of eye appeal and is particularly useful for a wide range of audiences. The pictogram is simply a bar chart constructed from symbols that serve the same purpose as the bars in the bar chart. A typical pictogram is shown in Fig. 35.7, denoting the number of employees for each shift. Note that in constructing such a chart, the symbol has a numerical relationship with the data, and thus each symbol represents a certain segment of the data. Sometimes the size

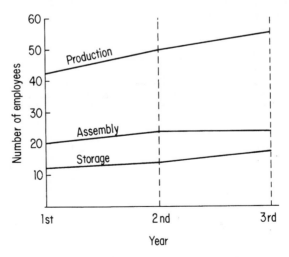

FIGURE 35.5 Personnel requirements for departmental groups.

1st Shift	♀♀♀♀♀♀♀
2nd Shift	♀♀⟩
3rd Shift	♀

FIGURE 35.6 Pie chart for proportion of inventory.

FIGURE 35.7 Pictogram of number of employees per shift.

of the symbol represents the data, and often fractional symbols are used. The pictogram should illustrate the data clearly and should not distract from the importance of the result. In constructing such a chart, avoid the pitfall of displaying too much information, thus confusing the viewer.

Histograms.   The *histogram* is a means of graphically illustrating a frequency distribution. In many ways it is similar to a vertical bar chart; however, it is two-dimensional in that both the width and height of the bars are variables. Consider the frequency distribution of Table 35.8, which depicts the distribution of daily demand for stock over a period of 160 days. Figure 35.8 illustrates the histogram constructed from this frequency distribution and using the class limits and frequency. The frequency for each class is represented by the height of the bar, while the width of the bar for each class is governed by the class limits. The bars are usually not separated, so the numbers on the horizontal axis practically form a continuous span.

TABLE 35.8 Frequency Distribution of Bar-Stock Demand

Number of bars demanded	Frequency of demand
30–34	1
35–39	4
40–44	13
45–49	26
50–54	50
55–59	39
60–64	20
65–69	5
70–74	2
	160

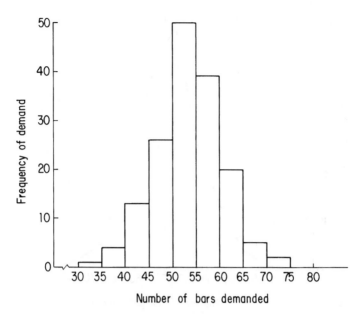

FIGURE 35.8   Distribution of bar-stock demand.

Note that a histogram cannot be constructed for distributions that have open-ended classes. One should also avoid using a histogram for distributions when classes are not equal. The histogram may be altered if classes are unequal but closed by making the frequency within each interval proportional to the area of the bar for the class. For example, if one class interval is twice as wide as the rest, then the height of the bar for this particular class should be reduced by one-half. In general, however, one cannot use the histogram for cases involving open-ended classes, and care must be used if the class intervals are unequal.

Frequency Polygons.   The frequency polygon is an alternative method for graphically illustrating the frequency distribution and performs a function similar to that of the histogram. The frequency polygon for the data in Table 35.8 is shown in Fig. 35.9. The frequency polygon is formed by letting the midpoints of the classes assume the frequency of the class. Then these points are connected by a set of line segments, thus forming a type of curve. Note that the extra classes with zero frequency are artificially augmented at both ends of the distribution so that the curve will meet the horizontal axis on both ends, thus enclosing the frequency within the polygon.

As with the histogram, the frequency polygon cannot be constructed if one of the classes is open-ended. If the class intervals are unequal, the same adjustment must be made for the frequency polygon as has to be done for the histogram.

The choice of whether a frequency distribution is to be represented by a frequency polygon or histogram is a matter of personal preference. The only advantage of a frequency polygon lies in comparing two or more distributions plotted on the same chart, but the histogram seems to be preferable when a discrete set of data is presented.

Cumulative Frequency Representation.   Like the frequency table, the frequency polygon or the histogram may be represented in cumulative form. For example, if the

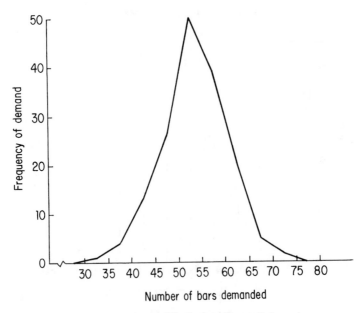

FIGURE 35.9   Frequency polygon of distribution of bar-stock demand.

less-than distribution were to be graphed for Table 35.8, its cumulative frequency representation in polygon form would look like Fig. 35.10. Note that the vertical axis may be represented by frequency or by percentage.

Sometimes these types of curves are called *ogives*. Note that the ogive differs from the frequency polygon in that the cumulative frequency is plotted at the upper class limit

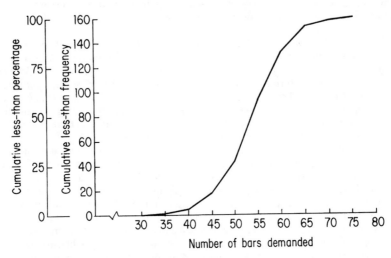

FIGURE 35.10   Cumulative bar-stock demand.

(or between the upper limit of the class and the lower limit of the next class), so that the less-than notion agrees with the graphed display.

Naturally a cumulative histogram could be constructed in the same manner. Cumulative representations tend to be S shaped, rising from zero at the lower left to the maximum at the upper right. These curves allow interpolation and are very similar to their continuous counterpart, the distribution functions. These are widely used in simulation studies, particularly those of the Monte Carlo variety.

MEASURES OF LOCATION

The frequency distribution is useful to characterize the pattern of variation of variables. The frequency table provides a tabular form of the distribution, while the frequency polygon presents a graphical display. However, working directly with the frequency distribution is quite cumbersome, and one may wish to investigate the data by summarizing some of the more important properties. This discussion is directed particularly to developing measures of the location, or position, of the distribution. Specifically, one wishes to know about what point the distribution seems to be concentrated. Methods of measuring such a point are referred to as *measures of location.* Sometimes they are called *measures of position, measures of central tendency,* and *measures of central values.* In general, the measures of location tend to summarize the distribution in the sense that they characterize by a single value the location, or position, of the frequency distribution.

Mean

This first measure of location is called the *average,* or *mean,* or, more accurately, the *arithmetic mean.* Consider n observations whose values are $x_1, x_2, x_3, ..., x_n$. The mean is defined as follows:

$$\text{Mean} = \frac{x_1 + x_2 + \cdots + x_n}{n} = \frac{\sum_{i=1}^{n} x_i}{n}$$

where $\sum_{i=1}^{n} x_i = x_1 + x_2 + \cdots + x_n$

To illustrate this computational method, suppose in a particular shop there are five screw machines whose production capabilities are as follows (in parts per hour): 255, 215, 157, 230, and 188. By the above formula, the mean production capability of the screw machines is:

$$\frac{255 + 215 + 157 + 230 + 188}{5} = \frac{1045}{5} = 209$$

If the mean is calculated from the entire population, it is denoted by the Greek letter μ (mu) and thus represents a population parameter. However, if the calculation is made for a sample, the mean is denoted by $\bar{x}$ (x bar) and is thus a statistic. For a particular population, μ is a constant; however, $\bar{x}$ for the same population is a variable since the sample mean will depend on the values of the sample chosen. Hence for different samples from the same population, there will probably be a different mean.

Mean of the Frequency Distribution

The mean may be computed from the frequency distribution as well as the raw data or data array. Consider the frequency distribution of Table 35.8 for the demand of bar stock. Obviously, one cannot work with the individual demands in this case since they have been grouped into classes. Consequently, one must make an assumption regarding the distribution. It is assumed, usually validly, that all frequencies located within each class may be represented by the midpoint. Hence, this emphasizes the necessity for selecting the classes and their midpoints with care. For most distributions found in production and inventory control, the errors introduced by this assumption tend to cancel themselves eventually. However, the formula for calculating the mean must be modified:

$$\text{Mean from a frequency distribution} = \frac{\sum_{i=1}^{k} x_i f_i}{\sum_{i=1}^{k} f_i} = \frac{\sum_{i=1}^{k} x_i f_i}{N}$$

where $\sum_{i=1}^{k} f_i = N$ and f_i is the number of observations in class i.

An illustration of this calculation for the mean bar-stock demand of Table 35.8 is given in Table 35.9. Since these are results from a sample (and this is always the case unless it is indicated otherwise), one may assert that $\bar{x} = 8490/160 = 53.0625$, upon application of the previous formula. The table includes the general method for accomplishing the calculation. Of major importance are the columns containing x_i, f_i, and $x_i f_i$, since they form the basis of the calculation. The first four columns are taken from Table 35.8, while the last column is simply the product of the midpoints and frequencies.

Weighted Mean

Suppose one wishes the average space utilization in all three storage areas—rough stock, in-process stock, and finish stock. The arithmetic average of the utilization in each of the three areas is inappropriate since more than likely each store occupies a dif-

TABLE 35.9   Calculation of Mean of Bar-Stock Demand

Class	Bar demand	Midpoint x_i	Frequency f_i	$x_i f_i$
1	30–34	32	1	32
2	35–39	37	4	148
3	40–44	42	13	546
4	45–49	47	26	1222
5	50–54	52	50	2600
6	55–59	57	39	2223
7	60–64	62	20	1240
8	65–69	67	5	335
9	70–74	72	2	144
			$\sum_{i=1}^{g} f_i = 160$	$\sum_{i=1}^{g} x_i f_i = 8490$

ferent area. Suppose the utilization in rough stock is 21 percent, 33 percent in in-process stock, and 47 percent in finish stock; and the area of rough stock is 700 square feet, in-process stock is 400 square feet, and finish stock occupies 1050 square feet. Therefore, the overall space-utilization mean for all stores is:

$$\frac{(0.21)(700) + (0.33)(400) + (0.47)(1050)}{700 + 400 + 1050} = 0.359, \text{ or } 35.9 \text{ percent}$$

Thus by weighting each utilization with the proper area, a more representative mean is calculated. In this way the size of the area is incorporated along with its utilization.

In general, suppose we have a set of n values $x_1, x_2,...,x_n$, whose importance is reflected by the weights $w_1, w_2,...,w_n$. Thus the *weighted mean* may be defined as:

$$\text{Weighted mean} = \frac{\sum\limits_{i=1}^{n} w_i x_i}{\sum\limits_{i=1}^{n} w_i}$$

Another application of the weighted mean utilizes the combination of several means. For example, suppose one knows the mean number of personnel in each of n departments. Let $\bar{x}_1, \bar{x}_2,..., \bar{x}_n$ be the mean number of people in each of the n departments. Suppose the sizes of the departments are given by $m_1, m_2,..., m_n$. Then the overall (sample) mean number of people in the n departments is:

$$\bar{x} = \frac{\sum\limits_{i=1}^{n} m_i \bar{x}_i}{\sum\limits_{i=1}^{n} m_i}$$

Hence one may use the above formula to calculate overall means, which are in essence a form of the weighted means. Consequently, overall means may be formulated from the means of several sets of data.

Properties of the Mean

The following are among the most important characteristics of the mean:

1. The mean is a concept of general familiarity and is easily understood.
2. The mean always exists and so always may be calculated.
3. For a given set of values, only one mean can be calculated. Thus the mean is unique.
4. The mean is influenced by every value in the sample. If the data are classified by a frequency distribution, then all midpoints and class frequencies affect the mean.
5. The unit of measure of the mean is identical to the unit of measure describing the data; that is, if the data are in units of demand, then the mean is described in units of demand.
6. The algebraic sum of the differences between the mean and the data is zero. Expressed mathematically, this is:

$$\sum\limits_{i=1}^{n} (x_i - \bar{x}) = 0$$

7. The sum of the squares of the differences between the mean and the data is a minimum. In other words, the sum of the squares of the differences between the data and any point other than the mean will produce a larger value. This property may be demonstrated by merely calculating the sum of the squared difference first about the mean and then about any other value. The interested reader may verify this for Table 35.9, utilizing the mean and any other values. This characteristic has a special significance in computing a measure of the variation called the *standard deviation,* which is discussed later.

Median and Other Quartiles

In a series of ordered data (either increasing or decreasing), the *median* is the middle value, or the value that divides the total frequency in half. If the number n in the ordered series is an odd number, then the median is merely the $(n + 1)/2$ value, counting from either end. For example, consider the following ordered series composed of five numbers:

$$15 \quad 17 \quad 23 \quad 24 \quad 26$$

Since the number of values in the series is odd, the median is $(5 + 1)/2$, or the third number from either end. Thus the median of the above series is 23. If the n values of the ordered series are odd, then the median is the mean of the middle values. To illustrate, consider the following ordered series composed of six numbers:

$$12 \quad 17 \quad 18 \quad 22 \quad 26 \quad 28$$

Since 18 and 22 are the middle two values, the median is $(18 + 22)/2 = 20$. Hence the median is a positional measure since the values of the numbers in the series do not, in general, have a critical effect on the median. For example, one may change 12, 17, 26, and 28, and the value of the median will be unaffected *as long as the order in the series is maintained.*

Quartiles, Deciles, and Percentiles

If the total frequency is divided into 4 equal proportions, the 3 values at the division are called *quartiles.* If the frequency is divided into 10 equal proportions, the 9 dividers are referred to as *deciles.* Likewise, if the frequency is divided into 100 equal parts, the 99 dividers are called *percentiles.* Note that the number of dividers is always 1 less than the number of parts because both ends of the frequency are not counted.

The quartiles in general are determined in a manner similar to the median. Again, interpolation is required when data come from the frequency distribution.

Properties of the Median

The following are among the most important characteristics of the median:

1. The median is simple to calculate and always exists for any set of data.
2. For any set of data, it is a unique value.
3. It is relatively unaffected by extremes in the data and is influenced by the position rather than by the actual value of each data entry.

4. It can be calculated from a frequency distribution with open classes or unequal intervals (as long as the median does not fall in an open interval).

5. The sum of the absolute value of the differences between a set of values and the median is a minimum. The interested reader may verify this for a series of values.

Mode

The *mode,* which is a measure of location, is the value most frequently found in a set of data. Consequently, it is often referred to as the most "probable" value in the set of data since it occurs the most often. Many times, in every day usage, the mode is the most "typical" value. For example, the typical grade received by a student is a C.

To demonstrate how to locate the mode in a data array, consider the following list of numbers:

$$9 \quad 11 \quad 10 \quad 8 \quad 12 \quad 10 \quad 9 \quad 13 \quad 9 \quad 7$$

The most frequently repeated number in this set is 9, and it is repeated three times. Thus 9 is the mode for this set of data.

Mode of the Frequency Distribution. The mode may be determined from a frequency distribution by first noting which class has the highest frequency of occurrence. This class is commonly called the *modal class.* If two adjacent classes have the highest (equal) frequency, then the mode is merely the boundary between the two classes.

Properties of the Mode. The following are among the most important characteristics of the mode:

1. It is extremely easy to calculate and enjoys a meaningful interpretation as a typical value.

2. It is unaffected by extremes in the data and may be computed from distributions involving open classes or classes having unequal intervals.

3. It may not be unique in that the maximum frequency may be attained by more than one value. Also if all values have equal frequency, it does not exist at all.

Comparison of the Mean, Median, and Mode

For distribution whose general shape is perfectly symmetric, the mean, median, and mode are identical (Fig. 35.11). If the shape of the distribution is not symmetric and the mass of the data tends to be concentrated toward the high numbers, tailing off slowly with lower numbers, then the mean will have the lowest number, followed by the median and then the mode. If the concentration of the data appears skewed toward lower values, then the mode will be the smallest number, followed by the median and then the mean.

For distributions that are moderately skewed, there exists an approximate relationship among the mean, median, and mode. These are roughly related as follows:

$$\text{Mode} = \text{mean} - 3(\text{mean} - \text{median})$$

In general, the mean, median, and mode each measure the location of the frequency distribution. The mean represents the average, or center of gravity, while the median indi-

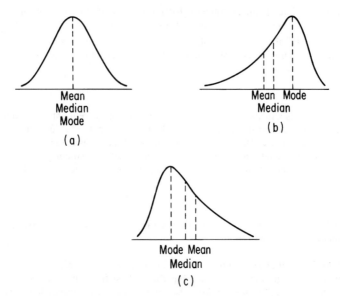

FIGURE 35.11   Examples of symmetric and skewed frequency distributions.

cates a central, or middle, value and the mode indicates the most typical value. The question as to which should be used depends on the application and interpretation required of the results.

MEASURES OF VARIATION

It is a characteristic of frequency distributions and variables to contain *variation,* or *variability.* Sometimes this variation is referred to as *dispersion.* Variables such as the mean, median, and mode measure the position or *central tendency*; however, these measures do not adequately describe the degree of scatter often encountered.

Variation, or dispersion, in a frequency distribution is very important in decision making, especially in production and inventory control. Consider the demand of bar stock given in Table 35.8. Because of the variation in this demand, one cannot merely stock the average demand required (where average may be mean, median, mode, etc.) because the demand may be very high in certain periods and an "average" value of stock on hand will not suffice. This was illustrated by the frequency distribution in the table. Thus the degree of variation determines the amount of safety stock carried for the bar stock. Consequently, the variation in the frequency distribution can be very important, and to describe this characteristic, one must determine measures that reflect this variation, or dispersion.

Range

The simplest and most easily obtained measure of variation is the *range*. It is calculated as the difference between the highest and lowest values in a group of data. For example, consider the following data:

$$15 \quad 5 \quad 17 \quad 18 \quad 9 \quad 13 \quad 15$$

The range for this example is merely $18 - 5 = 13$. Although easiest to calculate, the range is normally not a satisfactory method to measure variation. It reflects only the extremes in the data and does not account for the dispersion throughout the remaining data. Its main advantage is that it is simple to calculate and may be most useful when a rough, quick measure of the variation is required.

Interquartile and Interdecile Range

Sometimes it is common to eliminate extreme values in computing ranges. If the upper and lower quarters of the data are removed, the resulting range is called the *interquartile range*. This measure reflects the range in which 50 percent of the data is contained. If one lets Q_1, be the first quartile and Q_3 the third, the interquartile range is simply the difference between Q_3 and Q_1, or $Q_3 - Q_1$.

If one calculates the first decile D_1 and the ninth decile D_9, then the *interdecile range* is merely $D_9 - D_1$. This range includes 80 percent of the values and so describes more of the data than the interquartile range.

Interquartile and interdecile ranges are better than simple ranges because they are *location based*. This refers to the fact that their bases stem from the median and are thus related, to some extent, to a representation of the position, or location, of the data. Hence, in general, they reflect more of the dispersion of the data and are less subject to extremes. Also interquartile and interdecile ranges are quickly obtained from frequency distributions even if there are open classes.

Average Deviation

To overcome the disadvantage of the range measure of variation, one might consider the deviation of individual values from some positional value such as the mean or median. This would allow all items in the data to influence the measure of variation. A method for accomplishing this scheme is to calculate the average of the absolute values of the deviations about the mean. This measure of variation is commonly referred to as the *average deviation*. For lists of data, it may be expressed as:

$$\text{Average deviation} = \frac{\sum_{i=1}^{r} |x_i - \bar{x}|}{n}$$

where $\bar{x}$ is the mean of the data under consideration.

Therefore, for data which tend to be concentrated about the mean, the average deviation is low. As the dispersion in the data becomes more pronounced, the average deviation *increases* to reflect this increased variability.

For data grouped into a frequency distribution, the deviations are calculated from the class midpoints. Thus, for calculating the average deviation from a frequency distribution:

$$\text{Average deviation} = \frac{\sum_{i=1}^{k} (|x_i - \bar{x}|f_i)}{N}$$

where x_i = midpoint of the ith class
    f_i = class frequency
    k = number of classes
    N = total frequency

For the bar-stock example of Table 35.8, the computation of the average deviation is given in Table 35.10. The average deviation is shown to be:

$$\text{Average deviation of bar-stock demand} = \frac{879.7500}{160} = 5.498$$

It might be preferable to sum the absolute deviations about the median rather than the mean since it is a minimum (see property 5 of the median); however, it has been common practice to use the mean. Although the average deviation does represent an improvement as a measure of variation over the range, it is used very infrequently. The main reason is that more mathematically complex analysis cannot be performed because of the use of absolute values.

Variance and Standard Deviation

Another commonly used measure of dispersion is the variance s^2, which is defined as the mean squared deviation from the mean value:

$$s^2 = \frac{\sum\limits_{i=1}^{n} (x_i - \bar{x})^2}{n - 1}$$

Notice that the denominator is $n-1$ rather than n. This is due to some theoretical considerations that are not discussed here.

The units of s^2 are the square of the units of x. For instance, if x is measured in pounds, s^2 is given in square pounds. In many cases it is more meaningful to consider the square root of the variance, which has the same units as the original variable. This quantity, referred to as the *standard deviation,* is calculated as follows:

TABLE 35.10   Calculation of Average Deviation of Bar Stock

Class	Midpoint x_i	f_i	$|x_i - \bar{x}|$*	$f_i|x_i - \bar{x}|$
1	32	1	21.0625	21.0625
2	37	4	16.0625	64.2500
3	42	13	11.0625	143.8125
4	47	26	6.0625	157.6250
5	52	50	1.0625	53.1250
6	57	39	3.9375	153.5625
7	62	20	8.9375	178.7500
8	67	5	13.9375	69.6875
9	72	2	18.9375	37.8750
		160		879.7500

*$\bar{x}$ = 53.0625.

$$s = \sqrt{\frac{\sum\limits_{i=1}^{n} (x_i - \bar{x})^2}{n - 1}}$$

Frequently this formula is awkward to use and is especially subject to rounding errors. An alternative formula, which gives identical results, is:

$$\text{Standard deviation} = \sqrt{\frac{\sum\limits_{i=1}^{n} x^2 - \left(\sum\limits_{i=1}^{n} x\right)^2 / n}{n - 1}}$$

Table 35.11 illustrates the calculation of the standard deviation of an array of six x values. For this table:

$$s = \sqrt{\frac{46}{5}} = \sqrt{9.2} = 3.033$$

Some General Aspects of the Standard Deviation.   The following are among the most important aspects of the standard deviation as a measure of variation:

1. For many of the distributions found in production and inventory control, about 68 percent of all values in a particular distribution do not deviate from the mean by more than 1 standard deviation; about 95 percent of the values do not deviate from the mean by more than 2 standard deviations; and about 99 percent of the values do not deviate from the mean by more than 3 standard deviations. In general, at the very worst, $1 - 1/k$ of the values will not deviate from the mean by more than k standard deviations.

2. The standard deviation provides a measure of variability such that statistical tests regarding properties of the data can be analyzed. For example, one may wish to know if the production rates on two screw machines are statistically different.

3. The standard deviation provides a basis for inference regarding a population parameter. For example, one may calculate an interval in which he or she is almost sure the average bar-stock demand will lie.

TABLE 35.11   Calculation of the Standard Deviation

	Array		
x_i	$(x_i - \bar{x})$*	$(x - \bar{x})^2$	x_i^2
6	−5	25	36
10	−1	1	100
11	0	0	121
11	0	0	121
13	2	4	169
15	4	16	225
66		46	772

*$\bar{x} = {}^{66}\!/_{6} = 11$.

4. Use of the standard deviation and variance establishes the groundwork for more sophisticated statistical analysis of data such as regression analysis, correlation analysis, analysis of variance, and so on.

Relative Measures of Variation.   The previously discussed measures of variation deal with an absolute measure of variation in the sense that the magnitudes of the units are not considered. For example, suppose one is interested in the variation in departmental sizes. Suppose from historical records department A has a standard deviation of 2.3 men, while that of department B has more variation than department A. However, the mean number of men in department A is 10, while that of B is 20. Since the magnitude of the means is not similar, this suggests the use of some relative measure of variation.

Perhaps the most popular of the relative measures is one which simply expresses the standard deviation as a percentage of the mean. The measure called the *coefficient of variation* may be expressed as follows:

$$\text{Coefficient of variation} = \left(\frac{\text{standard deviation}}{\text{mean}} \right) 100$$

The advantage of such a measure is that variation is expressed as a percentage. Hence not only can variation involving different magnitudes be compared but also the variation in data involving different units of measure such as time and distance may be compared.

Another measure of relative variation is called the *coefficient of quartile deviation.* This is especially useful for relative measures of variation involving open-end distributions. It is defined simply as the interquartile range as a percentage of the sum of Q_1 and Q_3, as follows:

$$\text{Coefficient of quartile deviation} = \left(\frac{Q_3 - Q_1}{Q_3 + Q_1} \right) 100$$

This again reduces the variation to a percentage, making comparisons possible. The coefficient of quartile deviation is simply calculated through the use of quartiles, as discussed earlier.

MEASURES OF THE SHAPE OF THE FREQUENCY DISTRIBUTION

Although measures of variation and location indicate two of the most important characteristics of the frequency distribution, they do not indicate completely its shape. Although applications of measures of shape are found infrequently, they are important as a further description of the frequency distribution.

Skewness and Symmetry

The *skewness* in a distribution refers to the position of the concentration of the mass of the data with respect to the total distribution. In general, whenever the mean, median, and mode are not identical, skewness is present in the distribution. A distribution is said to be *symmetric* if the shape of the distribution above the mean is a *reflection* of the distribution below the mean. Whenever symmetry is present, the mean, median, and mode of the distribution are identical. Figure 35.11*a* illustrates a symmetric distribution.

A distribution such as that in Fig. 35.11*b* is said to be *skewed to the left* when there is a prominent "tail" to the left. In general, for this type of skewness the mean will be exceeded by the median, which in turn will be exceeded by the mode. Figure 35.11*c* illustrates a distribution skewed to the right and the typical positions for the mean, median, and mode.

Kurtosis, or Peakedness

Kurtosis refers to the peakedness of the distribution. A distribution possessing relatively flat tails but very peaked is called *leptokurtic*. This type of shape is illustrated in Fig. 35.12*a*. Figure 35.12*b* indicates a *platykurtic distribution,* distinguished by very thin tails and a long broad hump.

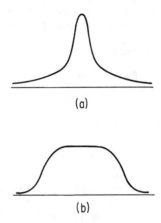

(a)

(b)

FIGURE 35.12   Leptokurtic and platykurtic distributions.

ELEMENTS OF PROBABILITY THEORY

The purpose of this section is to provide an elementary foundation in probability theory sufficient to make meaningful the subsequent consideration of statistical methods. The treatment of probability is brief and is clearly oriented toward the particular use that will be made of it in this chapter.

Probability Distributions

Although there are several definitions for the term *probability,* the "frequency" definition is the most common. It embodies the notion that as the number of times an experiment is rerun (trials) increases toward infinity, the probability of an occurrence of a certain value for the random variable equals the fraction of trials in which that value would occur.

It is convenient to discuss separately the probability distributions of discrete and continuous random variables. However, the basic concepts are similar.

Discrete Random Variables. Let x_i denote a particular value that can be assumed by a discrete random variable. For example, roll two dice and define a random variable equal to the sum of the two faces. This variable takes on values:

$$x_i = 2, 3, 4, \ldots, 12$$

Next let $p(x_i)$ represent the probability that the random variable takes on value x_i. This is known as the *probability distribution function of x_i*.

Given unbiased dice in which all face values are equally probable, the probability distribution function for the random variable equal to the sum of two faces is as shown in Table 35.12. This random variable is now completely defined. All values that it might take on are specified, as are the probabilities that each of these might occur.

It is often convenient to describe the probability distribution functions graphically with a line on the x axis corresponding to the probability of occurrence of each value of x. Table 35.12 thus gives rise to Fig. 35.13.

Two properties must be satisfied by every discrete random variable:

1. The range of the probability function must be 0 to 1:

$$0 \leq p(x_i) \leq 1$$

2. The sum of all probabilities is equal to 1:

$$\sum_{\text{all } x_i} p(x_i) = 1$$

The first property specifies that the probability of occurrence of any value x_i must be nonnegative and cannot exceed 1. The second property specifies that the sum of the probabilities over all values of x_i must equal 1. These are useful checks in attempting to enumerate all possible values of x_i and $p(x_i)$. Note that the random variable defined in Table 35.12 satisfies both these requirements.

It is often of interest to have available the probability that a random variable takes on values less than or equal to a specified value. For this we define the *cumulative distribution function*. Let $F(b)$ equal the probability that the random variable takes on values less than or equal to b. Hence:

$$F(b) = \sum_{x_i \leq b} p(x_i)$$

The cumulative distribution function for the random variable defined in Table 35.12 is listed in Table 35.13. Note that $F(b)$ is necessarily a nondecreasing function. A graphical interpretation is frequently useful and is shown for the example in Fig. 35.14. This is a *step function* since only discrete x_i values may occur. The probability that the ran-

TABLE 35.12   Probability Distribution Function: Sum of Two Dice

x_i	2	3	4	5	6	7	8	9	10	11	12
$p(x_i)$	$\frac{1}{36}$	$\frac{2}{36}$	$\frac{3}{36}$	$\frac{4}{36}$	$\frac{5}{36}$	$\frac{6}{36}$	$\frac{5}{36}$	$\frac{4}{36}$	$\frac{3}{36}$	$\frac{2}{36}$	$\frac{1}{36}$

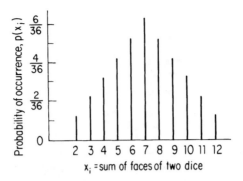

FIGURE 35.13 Probability distribution function of a discrete random variable.

TABLE 35.13 Cumulative Distribution Function

x	2	3	4	5	6	7	8	9	10	11	12
$F(x)$	$\frac{1}{36}$	$\frac{3}{36}$	$\frac{6}{36}$	$\frac{10}{36}$	$\frac{15}{36}$	$\frac{21}{36}$	$\frac{26}{36}$	$\frac{30}{36}$	$\frac{33}{36}$	$\frac{35}{36}$	$\frac{36}{36}$

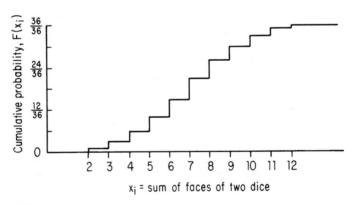

FIGURE 35.14 Cumulative distribution function of a discrete random variable.

dom variable takes on values less than or equal to 3.4, for example, is equal to $p(2)$ + $p(3)$. Hence $F(b)$ is the same for all values of b from 3 to, but not including, 4.

Continuous Random Variables.   A continuous random variable is one that may take on any value within a range of possible values. Therefore, it conceptually may take any one of an infinite number of possible values in the range. It is meaningless to consider the probability of a particular value occurring. We therefore deal with the probability that the random variable takes on a value within some specified interval.

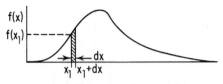

x = a continuous random variable

FIGURE 35.15 Probability density function of a continuous random variable.

The probability that the random variable (RV) takes on values in the interval $(x, x + dx)$ for a very small value dx (see Fig. 35.15) is:

$$\Pr\{x_i < \text{RV} < x_i + dx\} = f(x_i)\, dx$$

where $f(x)$ is the probability density function. And $f(x)$ is most conveniently interpreted when it is plotted as in the figure. The area of the slice of height $f(x_i)$ and width dx corresponds to the probability of the random variable taking on values in that particular interval.

The probability that the random variable takes on a value between any two values a and b can be obtained by measuring the area under $f(x)$ from a to b, as represented by the shaded portion in Fig. 35.16. This area can be found mathematically by integrating $f(x)$ from a to b:

$$\Pr\{a < x < b\} = \int_b^a f(x)\, dx$$

For $f(x)$ to be a probability density function, it must satisfy the conditions:

$$f(x) \leq 0 \qquad \text{for all } x$$

and

$$\int_{-\infty}^{\infty} f(x)\, dx = 1$$

As with discrete random variables, it is frequently of interest to find the probability that the variable takes on a value less than or equal to a specific value, say, b. This can be found by:

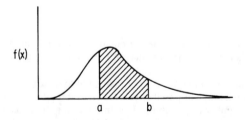

x = a continuous random variable

FIGURE 35.16 Probability that $a < x < b$.

$$\Pr\{x < b\} = \int_{-\infty}^{b} f(x)\, dx$$

This is defined as the *cumulative distribution function F(b)*.

Note that this is analogous to the discrete case discussed previously with the summation replaced by the integration operation. The probability that x falls between a and b can now be rewritten in terms of the difference in two values of the cumulative distribution function as:

$$\Pr\{a < x < b\} = \Pr\{x < b\} - \Pr\{x < a\}$$

$$= \int_{-\infty}^{b} f(x)\, dx - \int_{-\infty}^{a} f(x)\, dx = F(b) - F(a)$$

The cumulative distribution function can be evaluated for all possible values of x and plotted as shown in Fig. 35.17. This figure illustrates two basic properties. First, $f(x)$ must start at zero on the left-hand end and second, it must reach 1 on the right-hand side.

Consider as a specific example the uniform distribution in which the probability density function is constant in the interval 0 to a. The density function is shown in Fig. 35.18a. Note that:

$$f(x) = \begin{cases} 1/a & \text{for } 0 \le x \le a \\ 0 & \text{elsewhere} \end{cases}$$

which follows from the requirement that the area under the curve equal 1. It can be found by solving:

$$\int_{0}^{a} K\, dx = 1$$

for the constant K.

The cumulative distribution function is found by:

$$F(x) = \int_{0}^{x} \frac{1}{a}\, dx = \frac{x}{a}$$

which is plotted in Fig. 35.18b.

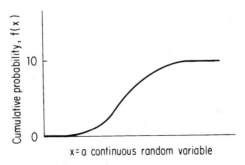

FIGURE 35.17 Cumulative distribution function of a continuous random function.

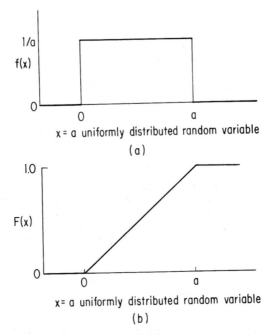

x = a uniformly distributed random variable

(a)

x = a uniformly distributed random variable

(b)

FIGURE 35.18 A uniformly distributed random variable.

Note that the slope of $F(x)$ at any point x corresponds to the height of $f(x)$ at that point. In this case the slope $F(x)$ is constant everywhere on the interval $(0, a)$ corresponding to the uniform density function in the interval.

POPULATION PARAMETERS

The mean and variance of a sample have been defined. In a similar manner, one may define the mean (or expected value) and variance of a particular population described in terms of a probability distribution (or density, in the continuous case) function.

By denoting the mean by μ and the variance by σ^2, the following equations are obtained for a discrete distribution:

$$\mu = \sum_{i=1}^{n} x_i\, p(x_i)$$

$$\sigma^2 = \sum_{i=1}^{n} (x_i - \mu)^2 p(x_i)$$

For the continuous case:

$$\mu = \int_x xf(x)\, dx$$

$$\sigma^2 = \int_x (x - \mu)^2 f(x)\, dx$$

The standard deviation of a population is equal to the square root of the variance and is denoted by σ. Notice that μ and σ^2 are constant for a given population while $\bar{x}$ and s^2 depend on the specific values included in the sample and may vary among different samples taken from the same population.

Normal Distribution

The most common distribution encountered in statistical work is the *normal distribution*. A normally distributed random variable x is a continuous random variable whose probability density function $f(x)$ is given by:

$$f(x) = \frac{1}{\sqrt{2\pi}\sigma} \, e^{-(x-\mu)^2/(2\sigma^2)}$$

where μ is the mean and σ the standard deviation. For convenience we occasionally use here the shorthand notation $N(\mu, \sigma^2)$ to represent a normally distributed random variable with mean μ and variance σ^2.

When it is graphed, the *density function* appears as shown in Fig. 35.19a. Note that the distribution is symmetrically centered about the mean μ. Knowledge of μ and σ is sufficient to completely define the distribution. It is therefore referred to as a *two-parameter distribution.*

The cumulative distribution function:

$$F(x) = \int_{-\infty}^{x} f(x) \, dx$$

appears, when plotted, as depicted in Fig. 35.19b. One frequently needs to evaluate the area under the density function to determine relevant probabilities. For example, given μ and σ, what is the probability that the random variable x exceeds b? Mathematically it is given by:

$$\Pr(x > b) = \int_{b}^{\infty} f(x) \, dx$$

which is equivalent to finding the shaded area of Fig. 35.20.

The normal density function is unfortunately a function that cannot be easily evaluated. In practice, the scheme is to use a table of the cumulative area. However, we would need a separate table for all combinations of μ and σ—clearly an impossibility. Instead, we use a table of the *standardized normal distribution* and use a simple transformation to relate it to the particular problem at hand. Let z represent the standardized normal variate:

$$z = \frac{x - \mu}{\sigma}$$

This is the appropriate transformation relating the distribution of x to the z distribution.

The standardized normal variate has a mean of 0 and a variance of 1 $[N, (0, 1)]$. The density function is:

$$f(z) = \frac{1}{\sqrt{2\pi}} \, e^{-z^2/2}$$

In the example below, let z_α represent the value of z for which:

$$\Pr\{z > z_\alpha\} = \int_{z_\alpha}^{\infty} \frac{1}{\sqrt{2\pi}} \, e^{-z^2/2} \, dz = \alpha$$

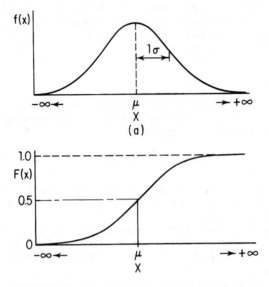

FIGURE 35.19   Normally distributed random variable.

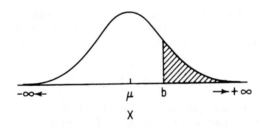

FIGURE 35.20   Probability that $x > b$.

Graphically this is equivalent to the shaded area in Fig. 35.21. For example, Table A.2 in the Appendix shows that:

$$\Pr\{z > 1\} = 0.1587$$

and

$$\Pr\{z > 1.645\} = 0.05$$

The probability is 0.1587 that z will take on a value greater than 1 and 0.05 that it will take on a value greater than 1.645.

Our interest is, however, not in z but in x, which is $N(\mu, \sigma^2)$. Given b a particular value in the distribution of μ, and recalling that $z = (x - \mu)/\sigma$, we find:

$$\Pr\{x > b\} = \Pr\left\{z > \frac{b - \mu}{\sigma}\right\} = \Pr\{z > z_\alpha\} = \alpha$$

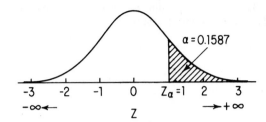

FIGURE 35.21 Standardized normal distribution.

This is represented graphically in Fig. 35.22. For example, given x, which is $N(10, 4)$, the probability that x will take on a value greater than 12 can be found as follows. Let:

$$z_\alpha = \frac{b - \mu}{\sigma} = \frac{12 - 10}{\sqrt{4}} = 1$$

Then

$$\Pr\{x > 12\} = \Pr\{z > 1\} = 0.1587$$

Instead of seeking the probability that x take on a value greater than b, the problem might be to find b such that the probability that $x > b$ is equal to a given α. For example, given x as $N(10, 4)$, what is b for which:

$$\Pr\{x > b\} = 0.05$$

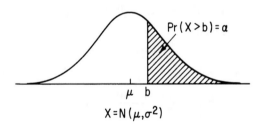

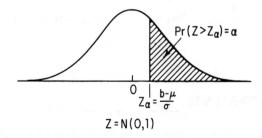

FIGURE 35.22 Area under normal curve of interest.

We solve this by finding z_α corresponding to $\alpha = 0.05$. From the tables we found above $z_\alpha = 1.645$ satisfies this requirement; that is:

$$\Pr\{z > 1.645\} = 0.05$$

Set

$$z_\alpha = \frac{b - \mu}{\sigma}$$

and solve for b:

$$1.645 = \frac{b - 10}{2}$$

from which we obtain:

$$b = 13.29$$

Hence:

$$\Pr\{x > 13.29\} = 0.05$$

By utilizing the fact that the area under the entire curve from $-\infty$ to $+\infty$ equals 1, one can find:

$$\Pr\{x < b\} = 1 - \Pr\{x > b\}$$

or

$$\Pr\{z < z_\alpha\} = 1 - \Pr\{z > z_\alpha\}$$

Again using the above example:

$$\Pr\{x < 12\} = 1 - \Pr\{x > 12\} = 1 - 0.1587 = 0.8413$$

Since the function is symmetric, tables contain entries only for the right-hand half (i.e., $x > 0$). Because of this symmetry and since the standardized normal has a zero mean:

$$\Pr\{z < -z_\alpha\} = \Pr\{z > +z_\alpha\}$$

Consider the task of finding:

$$\Pr\{x > 8\}$$

given that x is $N(10, 4)$. First find:

$$z_\alpha = \frac{8 - 10}{2} = -1$$

$$\Pr\{z_\alpha > -1\} = \Pr\{z_\alpha < +1\} = 1 - \Pr\{z_\alpha > +1\} = 1 - 0.1587 = 0.8413$$

The above can be combined to yield answers to questions of the form:

$$\Pr\{a < x < b\}$$

STATISTICAL INFERENCE

Statistical inference consists of drawing conclusions about a population based on the results of a sample. Even though the actual probability distribution of the population may not be known, the *central limit theorem* allows one to use the normal distribution or one of its derivatives to develop statistical techniques for drawing conclusions. The central limit theorem states that the means of samples of size n, drawn from any population of mean μ and finite variance σ^2, have a distribution that tends to the normal distribution as n is increased. The mean of the distribution is μ, and its variance is σ^2/n.

In addition to the normal distribution, discussed to some extent in the previous section, two other distributions are often used in statistical inference: the t distribution and the χ^2 (chi-square) distribution. Both are, in effect, a family of distributions, indexed according to a quantity known as *degrees of freedom,* which is related to the number of observations in the sample used for inference.

HYPOTHESIS TESTING

The purpose of hypothesis testing is to examine the reasonableness of a statement regarding a population parameter in the light of sampling results. Although the details of hypothesis testing are beyond the scope of this book, the procedure involves specifying two complementary hypotheses: a null hypothesis, denoted by H_0, and an alternative hypothesis, denoted by H_1. The null hypothesis is assumed to be true, and the results of sampling are examined to see whether they refute this assumption. If such is the case, then H_0 is rejected and H_1 is accepted as true. Most often, the null hypothesis H_0 is the one for which erroneous rejection has more serious consequences.

The fact that a hypothesis is accepted may be the result of one of two reasons. First, the hypothesis may be, in fact, true. Second, there may be such a large degree of variability inherent in the data that any actual difference between the hypothesized parameters and the actual population parameters may be masked. Additional data from a larger sample may enable one to remove some of the masking due to chance variation, thus possibly leading to rejection of the hypothesis where at first acceptance was the only possible conclusion. It is not possible to completely remove the effect of this inherent chance variation without examining the entire population. However, then the problem would no longer be one of statistical inference, for complete information would be available.

Typical Applications

Quite frequently one wishes to compare two populations to ascertain whether they are different. For example, one may want to find out whether there is a difference in the mean production rate for two machines.

The test of a proportion is useful when one wishes to draw conclusions about a proportion such as the fraction of tardy orders or the proportion of defective units in a production batch.

The theory of hypothesis testing and its applications may be found in many statistical books.

ESTIMATION

Estimation consists of determining the likely values of the population parameter(s) based on sample results. An *estimator* is a function of sample values that provides an estimate of a population parameter. There are two basic types of estimates: point estimates and interval estimates.

Point Estimation

A *point estimate* is a single value used to estimate the population parameter of interest. In each case a random sample is taken from the population of concern. A statistic is then calculated that provides an estimate of a corresponding population parameter. Several estimators of interest are presented here. These have been shown to provide quality estimates, a discussion of which, however, is beyond the scope of this chapter.

1. To estimate the population mean μ, use the sample mean $\bar{x}$ computed by:

$$\bar{x} = \frac{\sum\limits_{i=1}^{n} x_i}{n}$$

2. To estimate the variance of a population σ^2, use:

$$s^2 = \frac{\sum\limits_{i=1}^{n} (x_i - \bar{x})^2}{n-1}$$

3. In estimating the population proportion ρ of a binomial population, use:

$$\rho = \frac{k}{n}$$

where ρ = estimate of π, true proportion of population
k = number of occurrences
n = sample size

Interval Estimates

Estimation by point estimates does not permit the inclusion of information about the degree of variability associated with the variable used in the estimates. For example, a sample may yield a point estimate that the true production rate for a process is 50 units per minute. It may be important, however, to know whether the true value is between 49 and 51 or 40 and 60. To provide this type of information, interval estimates are employed.

An *interval estimate,* sometimes called a *confidence interval,* is the specification of two values obtained from a single sample between which a parameter of interest is estimated to lie with a prescribed degree of confidence. Procedures are described in the references for establishing confidence limits for several parameters. Although the details may differ, every interval estimation follows the same general approach:

1. A sample is drawn from the population of interest.

2. A sample statistic is calculated from the sample.

3. Upper and lower limits are established for the appropriate population parameter.

REGRESSION AND CORRELATION

Often it is of interest to examine the effects that some variables exert (or appear to exert) on others. The techniques of regression and correlation are useful in this examination.

In *regression* we wish to establish a relationship whereby the value of one variable can be predicted, given knowledge of other variables. Let x represent an *independent variable* that can be set to either a desired value, such as months for forecasts, or values that can be observed but not controlled (such as business indexes or competitive prices). This is used to predict a *dependent,* or response, *variable y* as product demand.

In simple linear regression, one seeks to determine the coefficients a and b of the linear function:

$$y = a + bx$$

where a is the y-axis intercept and b is the slope. Given a value of the independent variable x, a prediction can be made about the value of the dependent variable. For example, one may wish to predict sales on the basis of knowledge of some general index of business activity.

Simple linear regression analysis makes the prediction with a single independent variable. Correlation analysis also is used to examine relationships. Instead of deriving a prediction equation, correlation analysis provides a measure of the degree to which variables are associated.

Development of Regression Equations

Given a set of n data pairs in which values for the independent variable x and the dependent variable y are simultaneously measured for each of n observations, establish a linear relationship. Consider as an example the data of Table 35.14 in which for each of 8 years a particular industry's domestic sales are recorded along with the consumer disposable income. With an estimate of disposable income, it should be possible to predict domestic sales for the industry. Disposable income, in this case, is the independent variable x, and domestic sales is the dependent variable y.

The first step in the analysis is to construct a *scatter diagram* of the sample data to provide a visual portrayal. The procedure is to plot for each value of x a point corresponding to the value of y (Fig. 35.23). Hence, there will be n data points, each representing an (x, y) pair of observations.

Clearly an apparent linear relationship exists. The scatter diagram is particularly useful in the detection of nonlinear relationships. The techniques for linear regression may be accepted to fit a best-fitting straight line even though the relationship might actually be nonlinear. Hence, visual examination of the relationships displayed by the data is desirable.

Given the n data points, we want to determine a straight line of the form $y = a + bx$ through these points. One method is to simply establish visually a line of reasonable fit.

TABLE 35.14　Domestic Sales Versus Disposable Income

Disposable income x, billions of dollars	Domestic sales y, billions of dollars
181.6	0.435
206.1	0.621
226.1	0.819
236.7	0.879
250.4	0.933
254.8	0.970
274.0	1.070
284.0	1.180

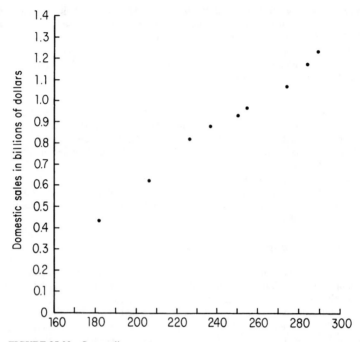

FIGURE 35.23   Scatter diagram.

For some purposes such a scheme might be satisfactory. However, usually it is not. As dispersion of the points from the line increases, visual fitting becomes more difficult. Hence there is need for a quantitative method.

Underlying the method of linear regression is the existence of a true (although unknown) relationship between the x_1 and y_i described by the model

$$y_i = \alpha + \beta x_i + \epsilon_i$$

where α is the true value of the y intercept and β is the true slope of the straight (or regression) line describing the relationship.

If all data points lie on a straight line, one has the equation of a straight line $y_i = \alpha + \beta x_i$. Inasmuch as not all observations lie on such a line, an additional term must also be present. This term is defined as the error ϵ_i that identifies the error associated with the ith observation and enters the model in an additive manner:

$$y_i = \alpha + \beta x_i + \epsilon_i$$

Since the true regression coefficients α and β are not known, we wish to obtain estimates of them based on the information contained in the sample of n data points generated by the true model. Let a be an *estimate* of the true intercept and b be an *estimate* of the true slope such that the line:

$$y_i = a + bx_i$$

determined from the data produces an estimate of the true linear relationship:

$$y_i = \alpha + \beta x_i$$

The objective of the regression analysis is to find a and b such that some function of the error is minimized. The minimization of the sum of errors is unsatisfactory inasmuch as positive and negative errors cancel in the sum. Moreover, minimizing the sum of the absolute deviations, while theoretically satisfactory, is characterized by significant computational difficulties. However, if the errors are squared, the problem of cancellation in the sum is overcome, yielding a tractable computational problem. Hence the *method of least squares* determines the coefficients a and b of the best-fitting straight line such that the sum of the squares of the deviations of the observations from the line is a minimum.

Minimizing the sum-of-error squares results in the following equations for a and b:

$$b = \frac{\sum\limits_{i=1}^{n} x_i y_i - \left(\sum\limits_{i=1}^{n} x_i \sum\limits_{i=1}^{n} y_i \right) \Big/ n}{\sum\limits_{i=1}^{n} x_i^2 - \left(\sum\limits_{i=1}^{n} x_i \right)^2 \Big/ n}$$

and

$$a = \frac{\sum\limits_{i=1}^{n} y_i}{n} - b \frac{\sum\limits_{i=1}^{n} x_i}{n} = \bar{y} - b\bar{x}$$

Table 35.15 shows the calculations of the various sums and sums of squares and products required to compute a and b for the sample data. This table yields:

$$n = 8 \qquad \Sigma xy = 1709.2985$$
$$\Sigma x = 1913.7 \qquad \Sigma x = 465{,}959.09$$
$$\Sigma y = 6.907 \qquad \Sigma y^2 = 6.366957$$

from which:

$$\bar{x} = 239.21 \quad \text{and} \quad \bar{y} = 0.8634$$

TABLE 35.15 Details of Calculations

x	y	x^2	xy	y^2
181.6	0.435	32,978.56	78.9960	0.189225
206.1	0.621	42,477.21	127.9881	0.385641
226.1	0.819	51,121.21	185.1759	0.670761
236.7	0.879	56,026.89	208.0593	0.772641
250.4	0.933	62,700.16	233.6232	0.870489
254.8	0.970	64,923.04	247.1560	0.940900
274.0	1.070	75,076.00	293.1800	1.114900
284.0	1.180	80,656.00	335.1200	1.392400
1,913.7	6.907	465,959.07	1,709.2985	6.366957

The slope is found to be:

$$b = \frac{1709.2985 - (1913.7 \times 6.907)/8}{465,959.09 - (1913.7)^2/8} = 0.00698$$

and the intercept:

$$a = \frac{6.907}{8} - (0.00698)(1913.7) = -0.8056$$

The estimate of the regression line is:

$$y = -0.8056 + 0.00698x$$

where y is the domestic sales and x is disposable income, both in billions of dollars. This line is plotted in Fig. 35.24.

For larger data sets, it becomes quite cumbersome to perform the various calculations manually. Extensive computer software is available to assist in these types of analysis.

Correlation

In correlation the interest lies in determining the *degree of relationship* between the two variables rather than predicting one from the other. Correlation differs theoretically from regression in the manner in which the observations are measured. In regression, the independent variable x is assumed measured without error, whereas the dependent

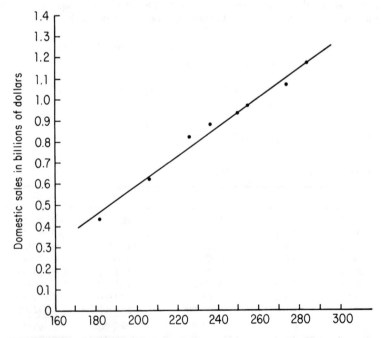

FIGURE 35.24   Sales forecast by regression.

variable y is measured with error. In correlation both variables x and y are assumed to be measured with error, there being no differentiation between independent and dependent variables.

Clearly a least-squares straight line can be fitted to any set of data whether or not the data really follow a linear relationship. We therefore desire some measure that reflects the degree of joint behavior of two factors. This measure is the unitless *coefficient of correlation r*, computed by:

$$r = \frac{\displaystyle\sum_{i=1}^{n}\sum_{j=1}^{n} x_i y_i - \left(\sum_{i=1}^{n} x_i \sum_{j=1}^{n} y_j\right)\bigg/ n}{\sqrt{\left[\displaystyle\sum_{i=1}^{n} x_i^2 - \frac{\left(\displaystyle\sum_{i=1}^{n} x_i\right)^2}{n}\right]\left[\displaystyle\sum_{j=1}^{n} y_j^2 - \frac{\left(\displaystyle\sum_{j=1}^{n} y_j\right)^2}{n}\right]}}$$

The coefficient of correlation lies between -1 and 1.

Interpretation of Correlation Coefficient. The magnitude or absolute value of r, denoted by $|r|$, reflects the quality of the relationship. A high value indicates a good relationship; a low one, a poor relationship. The sign of r specifies the direction. A plus means that y increases with increasing x, while a minus sign shows that y decreases with increasing x.

Now $|r| = 1$ would indicate a perfect fit, whereas $|r| = 0$ would result if there were no relationship whatsoever. Figure 35.25 provides graphical interpretation of the coefficient of correlation.

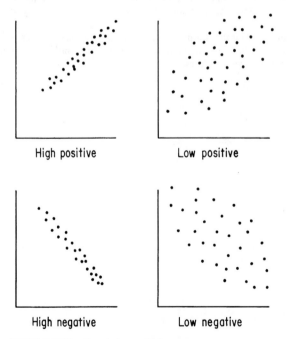

FIGURE 35.25 Correlation coefficient.

Another useful measure is the *coefficient of determination,* defined as r^2. Obviously, r^2 is always positive and falls in the range between 0 and 1. It may be interpreted as the percentage of variation in y that is explained by x. Thus, a high value of r^2 indicates that x is related to y and actually explains its variation. For a test of hypotheses related to regression and correlation coefficients, refer to a statistics book.

It is possible to perform regression and correlation analysis on data with more than one independent variable. The calculations, however, become quite voluminous. Therefore, it is recommended to utilize statistical software.

SUMMARY

This chapter presents you with the statistical tools used for managing production and inventory control. Some will use this material as an introduction to statistics, while others will use it as a review of the subject.

The statistical tools the chapter presents will help you display and explain information. The part about dispersion of data as described by means, medians, modes, variance, and standard deviations will add to your understanding of a process.

Statistical concepts are the foundation for modern forecasting, economic lot size theory, quality control, scheduling, product reliability, cost estimating, and simulation. So it is important to know the fundamentals of statistics to take full advantage of current manufacturing procedures.

It would be nearly impossible to take advantage of the statistical tools without the computer to compute and manipulate the data. There are numerous computer software packages available to perform the procedures discussed—there seems to be a new one coming out daily, and as in selecting any software, it is important to find the best product to serve your needs. This is where you will have to depend on your knowledge of statistics.

Your computer program library should include *spreadsheet* capabilities. Spreadsheets will give you the opportunity to organize and manipulate information to determine what effect changes would have.

CHAPTER 36
SIMULATION

Editor
Hank Grant, Ph.D.
Director, School of Industrial Engineering
University of Oklahoma, Norman, Oklahoma

Contributors
Michael Pidd, Ph.D.
Lancaster University

Jerry Banks, Ph.D.
Georgia Institute of Technology

David Kelton, Ph.D.
University of Minnesota

Ken Musselman, Ph.D.
Pritsker Corporation

Gordon Clark, Ph.D.
Ohio State University

Digital simulation uses a mathematical model to represent a real or hypothetical physical system. A computer simulation model of a physical system provides a laboratory in which alternative designs can be explored and analyzed. The model, executed on the computer, is a software replica of the manufacturing system and is controlled so that the system's behavior can be studied and analyzed. Decisions can be made concerning production alternatives. For example, adding a new lathe can be considered without disrupting the actual physical system.

Simulation depends on describing a system in terms acceptable to the computer language used. To do this, it is necessary to have a *system-state description,* which is typically characterized by a set of state variables included in the computer program that make up the simulation model. The various combinations of values that these variables can take on characterize the unique states of the system. Sufficient variables must be defined to represent all of the pertinent details of the system. As the values of the variables are changed, the system effectively moves from state to state. The process of building a simulation model consists of defining the state variables of the system and the operating procedures that cause the state variables to change over time. Simulation is the process of moving the system from state to state according to the rules that characterize the operational procedures of the system. Simulation is an extremely important tool for engineers in industry. There are numerous examples of major savings in the analysis and prediction of system performance prior to the actual construction and modification of facilities.

This chapter presents several subjects detailing various aspects of simulation. The first subject provides an introduction to simulation and how it works. The subject will discuss the most important simulation software tools and their availability. Later sections will address the analysis of simulation output, the management of simulation projects, and the application of simulation in industry.

AN INTRODUCTION TO COMPUTER SIMULATION*

Provided here is an introduction to the fundamentals of computer simulation. The difference between the various approaches in common use is discussed, and the importance of a carefully considered approach to modeling is highlighted. Its main stress is on discrete-event methods, and within that topic is described conceptual modeling, statistical aspects, and the types of computer software that are available.

WHYS AND WHEREFORES OF COMPUTER-BASED MODELING

Computer simulation methods have been in use since the 1950s, and they are based on the idea that an experimental or gaming approach can be a useful support to decision making. The idea is to try out a policy before it is implemented. Clearly, there are several ways in which this could be done:

- The policy could be tried in the real world, but in a controlled way so that its effects can be understood and analyzed. There are obvious problems with this approach, especially in systems that are dangerous or expensive to operate in which experimenting with the real system could turn out to be experimenting with disaster. Nevertheless, this type of direct experimentation does have its place, especially when training people.

- A second option would be to develop a mathematical model of the system being studied, and this is the specialty of operations research. This approach works well for some types of application (for example, in simple queuing systems) but not so well in others. The basic problem is that the mathematical knowledge needed to represent a complex dynamic system may be impossible to solve or virtually impossible to formulate without excessive approximations.

- Hence, the third option is to simulate the system of interest in a computer-based model and then carry out experiments on that model to see what might be the best policy to adopt in practice.

*Courtesy of *1994 Winter Simulation Conference Proceedings*. Michael Pidd, Ph.D., The Management School, Lancaster University, United Kingdom. J. D. Tew, S. Manivannan, D. A. Sadowski, and A. F. Seila (eds.), pp. 7–14.

In addition, a simulation approach is sometimes used to understand how an existing system operates or how a proposed system might operate. What are believed to be the rules governing the behavior of the system are captured in a computer-based model, and the behavior of this model is used to infer how the system being modeled might itself operate.

The Essence of Computer-Based Modeling

A computer-based model is at the heart of any computer simulation, and the question that has to be faced is, how can the important details of the system to be simulated be captured within such a model? A later section of this chapter will discuss the main features of simulation models, but before considering these features, it is a good idea to give some brief consideration to the process of modeling.

At the core of this process is one or more human beings who are concerned that their model is appropriate for the purpose for which it is intended. To do this, it is useful to consider the main features. The *tangible system* that they are attempting to model is separate from them, and to use the ideas of Zeigler (1976, 1984), provides a source of data from which a model will be constructed. Different people may well hold different notions about the operation of this tangible system, and these can be described in *conceptual models* that are themselves the result of reflection about the tangible system. The *simulation model,* which eventually becomes a computer program, stems from the conceptual model and is expected to be much simpler than the tangible system. Were it not simpler, then it would be as difficult to use for experimentation as the tangible system itself.

Hence, computer-based modeling is a process of simplification and abstraction in which the modeler attempts to isolate those factors believed to be crucial in the operation of the system being modeled. This process of abstraction depends on data and information about the tangible system and also on the intended purpose of the simulation.

Modeling Complicated Dynamic Systems

Given enough time, money, expertise, and computer power, almost any system can be simulated on a computer, but this may not be sensible. Hence the next question to face is, to what type of systems are modern computer-simulated methods best suited? The following features tend to characterize the systems best suited to computer simulation:

- They are *dynamic,* that is, they display distinctive behavior that is known to vary through time. This variation might be due to factors that are not well understood and may therefore be amenable to statistical analysis—for example, the apparently random failures of equipment. Or they might be due to well-understood relationships that can be captured in equations—for example, the flight of a missile through a nonturbulent atmosphere.

- They are *interactive,* that is, the system is made up of a number of components that interact with one another, and this interaction produces the distinctive behavior of the system. For example, the observed behavior of aircraft under air traffic control will be due to the performance characteristics of the individual aircraft, the intervention of the air traffic controllers, the weather, and any routing problems due to political action on the ground. This mix of factors will be varying all the time and their interaction will produce the observed behavior of the air traffic.

- They are *complicated,* that is, there are many objects that interact in the system of interest, and their individual dynamics need careful consideration and analysis.

Continuous, Discrete, and Mixed Approaches

It is normal to classify approaches to computer simulation into three groups, and this will be done here, but it should be noted that these distinctions are ones made by the modeler and are not ones that occur in the real world being simulated.

Discrete-Event Simulation:

- *Individual entities.* The behavior of the model is composed of the behavior of individual objects of interest that are usually called *entities.* The simulation program tracks the behavior of each of these entities through simulated time and will be minutely concerned with their individual logics. The entities could be truly individual objects (e.g., machines, people, vehicles) or could be a group of such objects (e.g., a crowd, a machine shop, a convoy of vehicles).

- *Discrete events.* Each entity's behavior is modeled as a sequence of events, where an event is a point of time at which the entity changes state. For example, a customer in a shop may arrive (an event), may wait for a while, his or her service may begin (an event), his or her service will end (an event), and so on. The task of the modeler is thus to capture the distinctive logic of each of these events (e.g., what conditions must hold if a *begin-service event* is to occur?). The flow of simulation time in a discrete-event simulation is not smooth, as it moves from the event time to event time and these intervals may be irregular.

- *Stochastic behavior.* The intervals between events is not always predictable—for example, the time taken to serve a number of customers in a shop will be observed to vary. There may sometimes be obvious and entirely predictable reasons for this (the server may speed up as the queue of waiting customers increases), or there may be no obvious reason to explain things. In the latter case, the varying intervals between events has to be modeled stochastically by using sampling methods based on probability theory.

Continuous Simulation.   A quite different approach to simulation is taken in *continuous simulation,* which is an approach that is popular among engineers and economists. The main building blocks of this approach are as follows.

- *Aggregated variables.* Instead of a concern with individual entities, the main concern is with the aggregated behavior of populations—for example, the changing sales of a product through time.

- *Smooth changes in continuous time.* Rather than focusing on individual events, the stress is on the gradual changes that happen as time progresses. Thus, just as the graph of a variable might be smooth, the aim is to model the smooth changes of the variable by developing the suitable continuous equations.

- *Differential or difference equations.* The model consists mainly of a set of equations that define how behavior varies through time; thus these tend to be differential equations or, in simpler cases such as system dynamics (Forrester, 1961, and Wolstenholme, 1990), difference equations.

Nature does not present itself labeled neatly as discrete or continuous; both elements occur in reality. Modeling, however, as mentioned above, involves approximation, and the modeler must decide which of these approaches is most useful in achieving the desired aim of the simulation.

Mixed Discrete-Continuous Simulation. In some cases, both approaches are needed, and the result is a *mixed discrete-continuous simulation.* An example of this might be a factory in which there is a cooking process controlled by known physics that is modeled by continuous equations. Also in the factory is a packing line from which discrete pallets of products emerge. To model the factory will require a mixed approach.

The Role of Software. Computer software plays an essential role in the development and use of computer simulations and is available to support the following aspects:

- *Statistical analysis of input data.* In a discrete simulation it will probably be necessary to model certain aspects by taking samples from probability distributions within the model. Thus the modeler needs to consider which distributions are appropriate for the system being considered. This requires the modeler to collect data (e.g., the times between failure) and to try to fit an appropriate distribution. There are a number of products available to support this task. Examples include UniFitII (Vincent and Law, 1993) and SIMSTAT 2.0 (Blaisdale and Haddock, 1993).

- *Rapid modeling.* The last 10 years have seen the development of *visual interactive modeling systems* (VIMS) such as Witness (AT&T, Istel, latest version), XCELL + (Conway et al., 1990) and ProModel (Harrell and Leavy, 1993) and Stella/I Think (Richmond and Peterson, 1988). These allow the modeler to develop the logic of a model on-screen using a graphic-user interface and also control the running of the model.

- *Simulation model programming.* It is sometimes necessary to write a "proper" computer program, and this can be done using a purpose-designed simulation language such as SIMSCRIPT II.5 (CACI, 1987), a general-purpose language such as C, or even a spreadsheet or database program.

- *Statistical output analysis.* It is not always easy to interpret the results of a simulation, especially one that includes a large number of stochastic elements, and the resulting output may need careful statistical analysis. There are tools to support this task; some are specifically for simulation modeling (e.g., SIMSTAT, Blaisdale and Haddock, 1993), and others are more generally available packages such as SPSS and SAS.

MODELING IN DISCRETE SIMULATION

The rest of this section will concentrate on discrete-event simulation.

Events and Their Logic

A computer program that represents a discrete simulation model will have a number of components:

- *The event logic.* A precise definition of the conditions that govern the state changes of the entities to be included in the model

- *An executive or control program.* A program that ensures that the entities' events occur at the right time and in the correct sequence and thus that their aggregate behavior is a model of the system being simulated

- *Other components.* Examples are sampling routines, integration algorithms, graphics, and other features needed for a particular model

If the modeler is using a VIMS or a simulation programming language, then he or she need be concerned only with the event logic; everything else will be provided by the system vendor. If a bespoke program is being written in a general-purpose language, then all of the features will have to be provided.

Capturing System Logic

Parsimony Principle.   Perhaps the best way of modeling complicated event logic is to bear in mind the *principle of parsimony,* which is to keep things as simple as possible for as long as possible. This requires an evolutionary approach to modeling, starting with a deliberately oversimplified model that is gradually elaborated on until it is agreed to be valid for the intended purpose. The initially oversimplified model should represent the skeletal logic of the system and should not be elaborated until the modeler is happy with the validity of the skeleton.

Using Diagrams.   One way of ensuring a parsimonious approach to modeling is to try to capture the essential system logic within some type of network diagram. In some cases, such diagrams can be drawn on-screen or described textually to a computer program that will itself generate the computer-based model. In this chapter, only a simple type of diagram—the *activity cycle diagram* (ACD)—will be presented, though other forms (for example, Petri nets and GPSS flowcharts) have been used in discrete simulation.

An ACD is an attempt to show how the processes of different entity classes interact, at least in a skeletal form. An ACD has just two symbols as shown in Fig. 36.1 and described below:

- An *active state* is one in which time duration can be directly determined at the event that marks its start. This might be because the time duration is deterministic (the bus will definitely leave in 5 minutes) or because its duration can be sampled from some probability distribution handling random and unpredictable behavior.
- A *dead state* is one in which duration cannot be so determined but can be inferred only by knowing how long the active states may last. In most cases, a dead state is one in which an entity is waiting for something to happen, and thus some writers refer to the dead states as *queues.*

These two symbols, active and dead states, are used to represent the logic of a system as in the following simple example: Consider a theater booking office staffed by one or more clerks who have two tasks: answering the phone and attending to personal callers at the theater. As this is a skeletal model, suppose that the theater has a call queuing system with infinite capacity, that there is no limit on the number of waiting per-

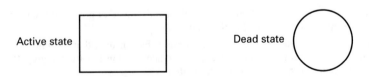

FIGURE 36.1   Activity cycle diagram symbols.

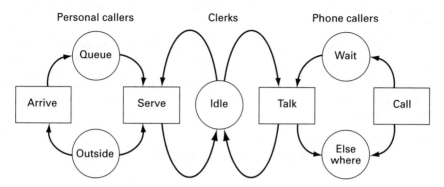

FIGURE 36.2   Harassed booking clerks' ACD.

sonal customers, and that all waiting callers are infinitely patient. Hence the diagram of Fig. 36.2 can be drawn.

The skeletal logic of the system can be clearly understood from the activity cycle diagram. For example, a personal service can begin only if two conditions hold: There must be an idle clerk and a waiting personal inquirer. Similarly, it shows that any clerk may engage in two tasks: attending to personal inquirers or answering the phone. It also shows some of the ambiguities. For example, what should a clerk do if faced, at the same time, with waiting inquirers and a ringing phone?

This type of conceptual representation must eventually become part of a computer program that might involve some programming or could involve a description of the logic being fed as data to a simulator, which may be a VIMS. (See the section "Software Support for Discrete Simulation.")

HANDLING RANDOM AND UNPREDICTABLE BEHAVIOR

As was made clear earlier, one aspect of systems that are well suited to discrete-event simulation is that they may have behavior which can be modeled only statistically—for example, the time interval between intervals may be observed to vary, and the variation may be modeled by fitting a probability distribution to that variation. To cope with this variation, discrete simulation models employ sampling procedures.

Basics of Random Sampling

The idea of random sampling is to ensure that a set of samples is produced that is representative of the distribution from which they were taken and within which set no pattern is evident. This is usually achieved by a two-stage sampling process that uses pseudorandom numbers. A truly random number stream is a sequence of numbers produced by a device that is believed to be random—for example, a roulette wheel, which some people find curiously interesting. Truly random number streams are not used in discrete simulations because most such devices are slow (millions of random numbers may be needed), and also they cannot be repeated—an important consideration, as will become clear shortly.

A pseudorandom number stream is a sequence of numbers that behaves exactly as a stream of random numbers would be expected to behave but that is produced by a well-understood mathematical process. Thus, when the sequence is examined, it is found that there is no pattern in the sequence and all values covered by the range of the random numbers occur equally often. In statistical terms, the sequence must be independent and uniformly distributed with a dense coverage of the range of values. The two-stage process is as follows:

- Generate 1 or more pseudorandom numbers.
- Convert these into the samples needed by some suitable algorithm.

Top-Hat Sampling.   To illustrate the basic idea, consider *top-hat sampling,* which is a common approach to taking samples from histograms. Figure 36.3 shows the probability of a clerk's selling a certain number of tickets during the service of a customer. Figure 36.4 is the cumulative histogram.

The vertical axis represents the cumulative probability of ticket sales. It runs over the (0, 1) interval and can be replaced by a range of pseudorandom numbers that also runs over (0, 1). Thus, if the pseudorandom sequence includes a set of numbers (0.38, 0.75, 0.53), then reading from the graph, these correspond to a set of ticket sales (2, 4, 3). The simple two-stage process for top-hat sampling involves the following:

- Generate a pseudorandom number.
- Look up the corresponding value from the graph or a look-up table.

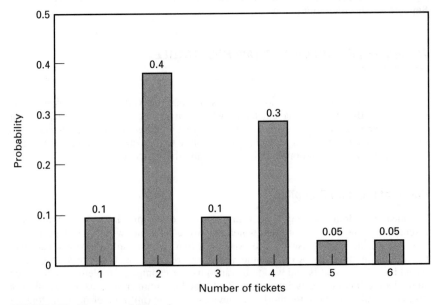

FIGURE 36.3   Histogram of ticket sales.

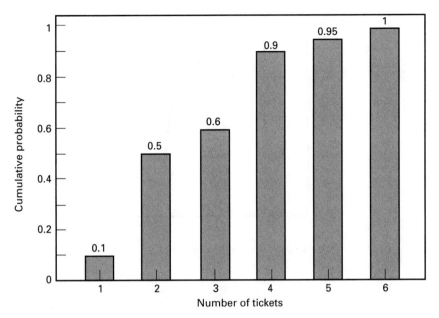

FIGURE 36.4 Cumulative histogram of ticket sales.

As well as a top-hat sampling, there are many algorithms in use for different types of probability distribution. Law and Kelton (1991) have more details.

The Effects of Statistical Variation

Due to its sampling procedures, a discrete simulation may display complicated behavior, which needs careful analysis. For example, there may be separate samples taken for the personal inquirer's arrival time, the phone call arrival time, the personal service duration, and the length of conversation duration even in a simple model such as the harassed booking clerk.

Typical two-stage sampling procedures use the pseudorandom numbers for two purposes. The first is to ensure that the sequence of samples is pattern free; the second is to select the set of values that are contained in the sequence. These two sources of sampling variation, which will be combined as different samples are combined, mean that any discrete simulation which has stochastic elements needs to be regarded as a sampling experiment. In such an experiment, it must be recognized that there is a risk of coming to the wrong conclusion. For example, consider Figs. 36.5 and 36.6 which show the (imagined) results from two sets of separate simulations in which policy A is being compared with policy B—the idea being to decide which one generates the highest profit.

The variation due to the pattern-free sequence is very desirable (this is random behavior); that due to a badly selected set is undesirable and is due to the set being of finite (and possibly rather small) size. This set effect means that the distributions of the samples may not properly represent the distributions from which they came.

In both cases the mean value of the experiments with policy B exceeds those with policy A, but it would be possible to be much more confident that this is a true inference

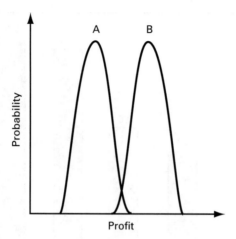

FIGURE 36.5   First set of experiments.

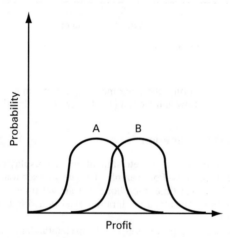

FIGURE 36.6   Second set of experiments.

if the experiments turned out like the first set shown in Fig. 36.5. The difference between the two sets of experiments is that the output variances are much lower in Fig. 36.5 than in Fig. 36.6 and thus the risk of a wrong inference is lower. The output variance is a function of the sampling variation that must be controlled.

Some Cautionary Advice

In any experimental comparison, whether using real systems or a simulation, it is important to ensure that the comparison is a fair one. That is, the comparisons should be made with the system (real or simulated) operating under similar and typical conditions for all policy options.

Run-in Periods. Suppose that someone wished to simulate the effect of adding an extra runway to a civil airport, and in particular he or she wished to discover what extra traffic, if any, this would permit. Part of the experimental control would be to ensure that simulations of the existing runway configuration and the extra runways were conducted in such a way that both options were compared under the same starting conditions. There is probably never a time when a large civil airport has no activity, and thus starting the simulations with no activity would not be representative of real conditions. Indeed, there is a risk that this may bias the comparison one way or the other.

Two ways of coping with this are to use "typical starting conditions" or to use a run-in period. Of the two, the latter is preferable, but why? The risks with using "typical starting conditions" are twofold. First, we may know what these are for the existing system configuration, but we do not know what they are for the novel alternative. Indeed, if we knew this, then there would be no need for the simulation. The second reason is that use of "typical starting conditions" may bias the results. For example, in the airport example, we might reasonably believe that an extra runway will allow extra flights, and we may thus ensure that the starting conditions for this policy have more activity than those for the current system configuration. If we are interested in assessing whether the extra runway will permit extra traffic, then there is a great danger of a self-fulfilling prophecy.

Hence, it is better to employ a run-in period. The idea of this is that if a simulation starts with no activity, then it should be allowed to run for some time until it is believed to have settled down into some form of steady state. During this run-in period, the output from the simulation is ignored, and only output generated after that point will be used in the analysis. Of course, there are simulations in which no form of steady state is possible (e.g., a missile chasing a jinking target), in which case the transient effects are the main focus of interest. In such cases, run-in periods should not be used.

Variance Reduction. As was pointed out, the accuracy of simulation results is related to the observed variation in the sampling processes of the model. Thus it is important to control these if at all possible. There are many techniques available to help in this (for a thorough discussion, see Law and Kelton, 1992, and Kleijnen and van Groenendal, 1992). The simplest approach when comparing different policies is to use *common random numbers,* a technique which works by synchronizing sampling processes across policy comparisons.

To use common random numbers, the analyst must ensure that each sampling process has its own controllable pseudorandom number stream. Hence, in the harassed booking clerk example introduced earlier, this means that four streams will be needed for each simulation run (one each for personal arrivals, phone calls, personal service, and phone conversations) if there is just one clerk, and $2 + 2n$ if there are n clerks.

The technique works by controlling the set of random numbers that are used to generate the required samples. If each policy option is compared using the same random numbers, then the same samples will, as far as is possible, be used for each policy comparison. If each policy option is being replicated m times, then the modeler will need to ensure that each of these m replications uses common random numbers and thus will need access to $m(2 + 2n)$ streams in the above example. This need for control of the random number streams is the main reason why pseudorandom numbers are preferred over truly random streams.

SOFTWARE SUPPORT FOR DISCRETE SIMULATION

A thorough review is given in Pidd (1992), but a summary here will help to place things in context.

Coding in a General-Purpose Language

Early simulations were written in whatever primitive programming languages were available on the simple computers of the day. This approach, like the rest, persists to this day, and it seems likely that a reasonable proportion of simulations are written in languages such as C (Crookes, 1989), C++ (Joines et al., 1992, and Pidd, 1993), Pascal (Pidd, 1989) and even in Fortran and Basic (Pidd, 1988). Using such an approach means that very flexible and bespoke software can be created, but the cost is that such program development is very slow and requires considerable skills and highly specific knowledge in detailed computer programming.

Using a Library

Rather than starting each program from scratch, it has also long been possible to construct some parts (occasionally, most parts) of a discrete simulation application out of program building blocks taken from a "library." This allows quicker program development but still requires detailed programming skills—and faith in the library that is being used.

Simulation Programming Languages

Many simulations are written in special-purpose simulation languages such as SIM-SCRIPT II.5 (CACI, 1987) because these ease the task of program development by providing language constructs that are designed for discrete simulation. Thus, these languages usually provide the even-scheduling mechanisms that underpin discrete simulations and also have a syntax that eases the expression of the logical interaction of the simulation entities. However, as with the other two approaches, such software still requires detailed programming skills if it is to be used effectively.

Flow Diagram Systems

A different approach to easing model implementation is taken in flow diagram systems such as HOCUS (Szymankiewicz et al., 1988). In these systems, the user develops a flow diagram such as an activity cycle diagram and then uses a defined command set to describe the features of the flow diagram to the flow diagram system. This description is, in essence, data for a generic simulation model which is suited to a particular domain (e.g., queuing systems). As originally developed, these flow diagram systems did not permit the user to develop or generate a simulation program in any meaningful sense.

The main advantage of this approach is that it supports rapid program development. The main snag is that, without considerable effort, it is very difficult to model complex systems. It is interesting to note that so-called block-structured languages such as GPSS are, at root, flow diagram systems.

Interactive Program Generators

These, for example CAPS/ECSL (Clementson, 1992) and SIGMA (Schruben, 1991), attempt to combine the benefits of rapid development from flow diagram systems and the flexibility of direct programming. They represent the start of attempts to provide layered software development tools for discrete simulation. Their initial use resembles that of a flow diagram, but, instead of treating the diagram description just as program data, they are used to generate a working program in some target languages by linked-together, edited prewritten fragments of program code. This code may then be edited so as to allow the modeling of complex systems. Because the user can develop the simulation model at different levels, these interactive program generators represent the start of layered program development systems.

Visual Interactive Modeling Systems

These are flow diagram systems brought up to date, in the sense that they make good use of recent developments in general computing. There are many examples available on the current market such as Witness (AT&T Istel, latest version), Pro-Model (Harrell and Leavy, 1993), and SIMFACTORY (CACI, latest version). To use them, the modeler must conceptualize the system of interest as a network around which elements flow, changing their state at the nodes of the network. Icons are placed on-screen and linked together so as to represent the network logic. In some systems, there is considerable capacity for expressing the event logic at nodes by the use of specially designed macro-type languages. However, it is not normal for these VIMSs to generate proper program code that the user may modify, though some (for example, Witness) have a simplified coding language, and they are thus best suited to relatively straightforward network-type applications.

Choosing Software by Type of Application

Some tools are better suited to certain applications than to others. To use an analogy of house painting, if the walls and windows of a house need to be painted, then, the best way to paint the walls is probably to use a large roller or paint-spray. But if these are used on the windows, the results tend to obscure the view!

The discrete simulation equivalents of the paint-sprayers are the VIMSs, which provide a rapid way of developing models with attractive graphics. For relatively straightforward applications, many of which are found in factories and back-office processing, these tools are hard to beat. However, there are times when very detailed systems need to be modeled, and this will require the use of tools that make it easier to express complex system logic, which usually involves programming. Thus, for a smaller proportion of discrete simulations (probably less than 20 percent), there is no escape from the skilled process of developing a computer program.

Required Features of Software. The next issue to face is the detailed demands that will be placed on the software. Examples of these issues are the following:

- Is graphical display important?
- Does the software need to interface with corporate systems (e.g., databases)?
- Do you need strong statistical support for input and output analysis?

- Is security important?
- Are debugging tools required?
- What hardware/software platform will it be run on (e.g., UNIX or DOS/Windows)?

The software vendors need to be asked to specify a system to meet your requirements.

Vendor Support and Prices.   Finally, no user can ignore two very practical issues. How much will the software cost?—and remember that software prices are soft, so negotiation is often possible. Also ask what support you can reasonably expect from the vendor given the vendor's size and given your physical location.

*SIMULATION SOFTWARE**

Specifically designed computer simulation languages provide many features for managing the updating of the state variables and advancing time. They also provide features for recording system performance statistics and for generating random numbers to introduce system randomness.

The lowest level of computer language typically used is Fortian or Basic. This requires that the entire simulation model be coded, which is labor intensive. High-level languages, such as SLAM, SIMSCRIPT, and GPSS, facilitate simulation because they provide subroutines for time advancement, entity maintenance, and statistic collections. Higher-level simulation languages are designed for special purposes; MAP/1, SPEED, and MAST are three designed for the simulation of manufacturing systems.

Some simulation languages can produce animations. This permits the simulation to be illustrated graphically on a computer terminal so that the analyst can see the system in action and observe its interactions and behavior, a visual function beyond the scope of standard reporting technique. For example, TESS (a software program) provides animation, as well as model-building and output analysis capabilities, for the SLAM simulation language. The following paragraphs review many state-of-the-art simulation languages.

The next two sections describe general-purpose and manufacturing-oriented simulation software, respectively. The third section describes simulation environments. Then, an animator for simulation is discussed. Finally, some simulation support software is described.

General-Purpose Software

Applications of simulation exist in many arenas such as manufacturing, materials handling, health services, military decision support, natural resources, public services, transportation, and communications, to mention a few. These simulation applications are usually accomplished with the use of specially developed simulation software. This tutorial describes the software in two categories. The first of these is software for general purposes. This type of software can solve almost any discrete simulation problem. In this section, five products, GPSS/H, GPSS/World, SIMAN V, SIMSCRIPT II.5, and SLAMSYSTEM, will be discussed to provide a feel for this type of software.

---

*Courtesy of *1994 Winter Simulation Conference.* Jerry Banks, Ph.D., School of Industrial Engineering and Systems Engineering, Georgia Institute of Technology, Atlanta, Georgia. J. D. Tew, S. Manivannan, D. A. Sadowski, and A. F. Seila (eds.), pp. 26–33.

GPSS/H. GPSS/H is a product of Wolverine Software Corporation, Annandale, Virginia (Smith and Crain, 1993). It is a flexible, yet powerful tool for simulation. It provides improvements over GPSS V that had been released by IBM many years earlier. These enhancements include built-in file and screen I/O, use of an arithmetic expression as a block operand, interactive debugger, faster execution, expanded control statement availability, and ampervariables that allow the arithmetic combinations of values used in the simulation. The latest release of GPSS/H is Version 2.0. It added a floating-point clock, built-in math functions, and built-in random-variate generators. Options available include Student GPSS/H, Personal GPSS/H within the 640K memory limit, and GPSS/H 386 providing unlimited model size.

GPSS World. GPSS World, from Minuteman Software, is a complete redesign of GPSS/PC (Cox, 1991). It is designed as a high-power environment for simulation professionals. It includes both discrete and continuous simulation. Its features include interactivity, visualizability, and configuration flexibility. It utilizes 32-bit computing, virtual memory, preemptive multitasking, symmetric multiprocessing, and distributed simulation. Highlights include drag-and-drop model building, 512 megabytes of virtual memory for models, point-and-shoot debugging, and embedded programming language, built-in probability distributions, multiple data types, and many other improvements to GPSS/PC.

The GPSS World family is a set of three software products including:

1. GPSS World as the center of the family. This self-contained modeling environment includes local Simulation Server capabilities.

2. Simulation Server provides simulation services on a remote networked computer. It does not include a model-building user network.

3. Simulation Studio provides hierarchical modeling and user-drawn simulation capabilities.

There is an enhanced-memory version of GPSS/PC that is also available. It allows access of up to 32 Mb of memory.

SIMSCRIPT II.5 SIMSCRIPT II.5, from CACI Products Company, is a language that allows models to be constructed that are either process oriented or event oriented (Russell, 1993). The microcomputer and workstation version include the SIMGRAPH-ICS animation and graphics package. SIMSCRIPT can be used to produce both dynamic and static presentation-quality graphics such as histograms, pie charts, bar charts, levels of meters and dials, and time plots of variables. Animation of the simulation output is also constructed using SIMGRAPHICS. SIMGRAPHICS can be used also to produce interactive graphical front ends or forms for entering model input data. An input form may include such graphical elements as menu bars with pull-down menus, text or data boxes, and buttons that are clicked on with a mouse to select an alternative. The graphical model front end allows for a certain set of modifications to the model to be made without programming, facilitating model use by those that are not programmers.

SIMAN V. SIMAN V, from Systems Modeling Corporation, is a general-purpose program for modeling discrete and/or continuous systems (Glavach and Sturrock, 1993, and Banks, Burnette, Jones, and Kozloski, 1995). The program distinguishes between the system model and the experiment frame. The system model defines components of the environment such as machines, queues, and transporters and their interrelationships. The experiment frame describes the conditions under which the simulation is conducted including machine capacities and speeds, and type of statistics to be collected. What-if questions can usually be asked through changing the experiment frame rather than by changing the model definition. Some important aspects of SIMAN V are as follows:

1. Special features that are useful in modeling manufacturing systems include the ability to describe environments as work centers (stations) and the ability to define a sequence for moving entities through the system.

2. Constructs enable the modeling of materials-handling systems including accumulating and nonaccumulating conveyors, transporters, and guided vehicles.

3. An interactive run controller permits breakpoints, watches, and other execution control procedures.

4. The ARENA environment includes menu-driven point-and-click procedures for constructing the SIMAN V model and experiment, animation of the model using Cinema, the Input Processor that assists in fitting distributions to data, and the Output Processor that can be used to obtain confidence intervals, histograms, correlograms, and so on. (More aspects of the ARENA environment are discussed later.)

5. Portability of the model to all types of computers.

SLAMSYSTEM. SLAMSYSTEM, from Pritsker Corporation, is an integrated simulation system for PCs based on the Microsoft Windows (O'Reilly, 1993). All features are accessible through pull-down menus and dialog boxes and are selected from the SLAMSYSTEM Executive Window. A SLAMSYSTEM project consists of one or more scenarios, each of which represents an alternative system configuration. A project maintainer examines the components of the current scenario to determine if any of them have been modified, indicates whether tasks such as model translation should be performed, and allows the user to accomplish these tasks before the next function is requested. SLAMSYSTEM allows multiple tasks to be performed in parallel while the simulation is operating in the background. Some of the features of SLAMSYSTEM are as follows:

1. Models may be built using a graphical network builder and a forms-oriented control builder, or text editor. Using the first method, a network symbol is selected with the mouse; then a form is completed specifying the parameters for that symbol. The clipboard allows many other operations such as grouping one or more symbols and placing them elsewhere on the network.

2. Output analysis includes a "report browser" that allows alternative text outputs to be compared side by side. Output may be viewed in the form of bar charts, histograms, pie charts, and plots. Output from multiple scenarios can be displayed at the same time in bar chart form. Using the Windows environment, multiple output windows can be opened simultaneously.

3. Animations are created under Windows using the Facility Builder to design the static background and the Script Builder to specify which animation actions should occur when a particular simulation event occurs. Animations can be performed either concurrently or in a postprocessing mode. Two screens can be updated simultaneously, and up to 225 screens can be swapped into memory during an animation.

4. SLAMSYSTEM was designed to be used in an integrated manner. For example, historic data may be read to drive the simulation. CAD drawings may be loaded. Output charts and plots created by SLAMSYSTEM may be exported via the clipboard to other applications.

The newest release of SLAMSYSTEM is Version 4.0. Some of its unique features include the following:

1. *Multiple networks in a single scenario.* Networks can be constructed in sections and combined at run time. The sections can be reused in future models.
2. *New output graphics.* These graphics support 3-D, *X-Y,* grids and the display of point plot data.
3. *Direct interface to SimStat (product of MC² Analysis Systems).* These files may be loaded for advanced statistical analysis.
4. *OS/2 metafiles for graphics.* The OS/2 metafile format can be read for animation backgrounds or icons.

Manufacturing-Oriented Software

The software discussed in this section is limited to those associated with manufacturing and further to only six within that category including SIMFACTORY II.5, ProModel for Windows, AutoMod, Taylor II, WITNESS, and AIM. References for these software packages include the following: Goble (1991) for SIMFACTORY II.5; Harrell and Leavy (1993) for ProModel; Norman and Farnsworth (1993) for AutoMod; Thompson (1993) for WITNESS; and Hillen and Warner (1993) for Taylor II. For AIM, the references are Lilegdon (1993) and Lilegdon, Martin, and Pritsker (1994).

SIMFACTORY II.5.   SIMFACTORY II.5 is a factory simulator written in SIM-SCRIPT II.5 for engineers who are not full-time simulation analysts. It operates on the PC under Windows 3.*x* and OS/2 2.0, or on many workstations. A system amenable to SIMFACTORY II.5 can be modeled rapidly. A model is best constructed in stages by first defining the layout consisting of processing stations, buffers, receiving areas, and transportation paths, defining the products, then the resources, next the transporters, and finally the interruptions. The animation automatically follows from the definition of the model. These model elements are pulled from a pallet rather than a menu bar. The resulting model may be changed with a text editor. Flexible flow modeling is supported. For example, OR logic may be used (as in Request Part A or Part B).

The layout is created by positioning icons, selected from a library, on the screen. As each icon is positioned, characteristics describing it are entered. The products are defined by process plans that define the operations performed on each part and the duration of that operation.

Resources are added to the model in two steps. First, the resource is defined, and its quantity is set. Second, the stations requiring specified resources are identified. While resources are moving, simulation time can elapse. Resource requirements are flexible—namely, one unit of resource A and two units of resource B can be requested.

Transporters may be batch movers such as forklifts, or they may be conveyors. Characteristics of a transporter are specified (pickup speed, delivery speed, load time, unload time, and capacity of a forklift, as an example). The transporter path is identified on the screen. Transporters can avoid each other by collision detection, and they can carry resources.

Any interruptions, planned or unplanned, can be applied to any model element or group of elements (e.g., conveyors, queues, resources, and transporters). Interruptions can require any combination of resources.

Reports are available concerning equipment utilization, throughput, product makespan, and buffer utilization. Multiple business graphics (pie charts, histograms, and plots) can be compared at the same time. Data can be compared across multiple runs. Text reports can be customized, and specific statistics can be collected on the elements of interest. A summary report of all replications provides means, standard deviations, and confidence intervals on the model output.

ProModel for Windows.   ProModel for Windows, from PROMODEL Corporation, has programming features within the environment, and the capability to add C or Pascal type subroutines to a program. Some of the features of ProModel for Windows are as follows:

1. Models are created using a point-and-click approach. Intuitive interfaces, interactive dialog, and on-line help are provided. An auto-build feature guides the user through the model-building process. An on-line trainer is available.

2. The software operates in the Windows and OS/2 environments, as a 32-bit application, taking advantage of memory management techniques, synchronized windowing, and data exchange. Windows fonts, printer drivers, cooperative multitasking, and the Dynamic Link Library are available.

3. Virtually unlimited model size is offered.

4. The simulator offers a 2-D graphics editor with scaling, rotating, and so on. Icons can be defined using either vector-based or pixel graphics. These icons are saved as bitmaps at run time for fast animation during the simulation.

5. CAD drawings as clipart can be imported as well as process information and schedules. Customized output reports and spreadsheet files can be produced. If the data are in another Windows application, cutting and pasting can be accomplished.

6. The static and dynamic elements of the animation are developed while defining the model. That is, the simulation model and animation are integrated.

7. Business output graphics are automatically provided and may be printed in color.

8. Only standard hardware is required (IBM or compatible with VGA graphics). No special graphics cards, monitors, or math coprocessor chip are needed.

9. Preprogrammed constructs are provided. This allows for fast modeling of multiunit and multicapacity locations, shared and mobile resources, downtime, shifts, and so on.

10. Automatic statistics are available.

11. Submodels allow the creation of a library of templates of work steps, activities, or subprocesses that can be reused. This allows for model construction to be accomplished by a team with later merger of submodels into one model.

12. A free run time, multiple scenario, capability is provided.

A model is constructed by defining a route for a part or parts, defining the capacities of each of the locations along the route, defining additional resources such as operators or fixtures, defining the transporters, scheduling the part arrivals, and specifying the simulation parameters. The software then prompts the user to define the layout and the dynamic elements in the simulation.

AutoMod.   AutoMod, from AutoSimulations, Incorporated, has general programming features including the specification of processes, resources, loads, queues, and variables. Processes are specified in terms of traffic limits, input and output connections, and itineraries. Resources are specified in terms of their capacity, processing time, MTBF, and MTTR. Loads are defined by their shape and size, their attributes, generation rates, generation limits, and start times, as well as their priority.

The simulator is very powerful in its description of materials-handling systems. AGVs, conveyors, bridge cranes, AS/RSs, and power and free devices can be defined. The range of definition is extensive. For example, an AGV can be defined in terms of the following: multiple vehicle types, multiple capacity vehicles, path options (unidirectional or bidirectional), variable speed paths, control points, flexible control and scheduling rules, arbitrary blocking geometries, automatic shortest-distance routing, and vehicle procedures.

Numerous control statements are available. For example, process control statements include if-then-else, while-do, do-until, wait-until, and wait-for. Load control, resource control, and other statements are also available. C functions may be defined by the user. Attributes and variables may be specified.

The animation capabilities include true 3-D graphics, rotation, and tilting, to mention a few. A CAD-like drawing utility is used to construct the model. Business graphics can be generated.

The latest release, Version 7.0, contains a simulator within AutoMod. Features of the simulator include its spreadsheet interface. This eliminates the need for programming in building models. The spreadsheet interface also allows the definition of models outside of AutoMod. Another option as a separate utility is AutoStat. It provides simulation warmup capability, scenario management, confidence interval generation, and design of experiments capability.

Taylor II.   Taylor II is a Dutch product developed by F&H Logistics and Automation B.V. Working with Taylor II starts with building a model. All model building is menu driven. A model in Taylor II consists of four fundamental entities: elements, jobs, routing, and product. The element types are in-out, machine, buffer, conveyor, transport, path, aid, warehouse, and reservoir. One or more operations can take place at an element. The three basic operations are processing, transport, and storage.

Defining a layout is the first step when building a model. Layouts consist of element types. By selecting the elements in sequence, the product path or routing is defined. Routing descriptions may be provided from external files. The next step is detailing the model. In this step the parameters are provided. In addition to a number of default values, Taylor II uses a macro language called TLI for Taylor Language Interface. TLI is a programming language that permits modifications of model behavior in combination with simulation-specific predefined and user-definable variables. TLI can also be used interactively during a simulation run to make queries and updates. An interface to C, Basic, and Pascal is also available. Local and global attributes are available.

During simulation, zoom, pan, rotate, and pause are possible. Modifications can be made on the fly. The time representation is fully user definable (hours, days, seconds, and so on can be mixed). Output analysis possibilities include predefined graphics, user-defined graphics, predefined tabular reports, and user-defined reports. Examples of predefined graphics are queue histograms and utilization pies. User outputs include bar graphs, stacked bars, and other business graphics. Predefined tables include job, element, and cost reports.

Animation capabilities include both 2-D and 3-D. The 3-D animation can be shaded. Standard indicators can be shown for elements. Icon libraries for both 2-D and 3-D animation are provided. Each of these libraries contain more than 50 icons.

Additional features include 500 pages of on-line, context-sensitive help with index and page-search capability. Educational support materials are available.

WITNESS.   WITNESS, from AT&T Istel, contains many elements for discrete-part manufacturing. For example, machines can be single, batch, production, assembly, multistation, or multicycle. Conveyors can be accumulating or nonaccumulating. Options exist for labor, vehicles, tracks, and shifts. WITNESS also contains elements for continuous processing including processors, tanks, and pipes.

Variables and attributes may be specified. Parts arrivals may be scheduled using a file. Distributions and functions can be used for specifying operation times and for other purposes. Machine downtime can be scheduled on the basis of operations, busy time, or available time. Labor is a resource that can be preempted, use a priority system, and be scheduled based on current model conditions.

Track and vehicle logic allow requests for certain types of jobs, vehicle acceleration and deceleration, park when idle, and change destinations dynamically. Many types of routing logic are possible in addition to the standard push and pull. For example, if-then-else conditions may be specified.

Simulation actions, performed at the beginning and end of simulation events, may employ programming constructs such as for-next, while-end, and go to-label. The user can look at an element at any time and determine the status of a part.

Reporting capabilities include dynamic on-screen information about machines and elements. Reports may be exported to spreadsheet software.

Tools within the language include access to the model database through C language, arithmetic and logical operators, save current status of model, built-in status functions, and many others. In addition, all of the above-mentioned features can be enhanced through the use of C language.

Debugging or brainstorming can be accomplished by stopping the model, changing desired parameters, and continuing with the model from the same point in simulation time.

An animation is constructed along with the model definition. This animation and statistical feedback can be turned on or off during any run. Many changes to the model may be made at any time.

Built-in experimentation capabilities are available from the menu bar. The results of the experiments are output to a CSV file by default, or other file types by user choice. The CSV file is in a format that allows the internal statistics package to create confidence intervals.

The latest release of the software is Version 6. Its capabilities include the following:

1. Storage of up to 15,000 variables or attributes
2. Up to 1000 distinct random number streams
3. Bitmap import-export with icon sizes increased to 256×256 pixels
4. "Module" element for hierarchical modeling—one icon represents the detail existing in another portion of the model
5. "Selector bar" for filling fields with rules, distributions, built-in functions, and so on, for defining elements on-the-fly

AIM.   AIM (Analyzer for Improving Manufacturing), from Pritsker Corporation, is one of three applications of FACTOR. Other packages are Factor Production Manager and Leitstand. Factor Production Manager performs detailed planning-scheduling or operations, order promising, order release, and supply-chain management. All of these applications use the same database.

AIM models are OS/2 based and built graphically with icons that represent machines, operators, conveyors, and so on, placed directly on the screen. The animations are created in a virtual window. The current release of AIM is Version 5.3. During a simulation, the model can be stopped to check its status or to add other components; then the simulation can be continued. Performance data are dynamically updated and displayed while the simulation is running. A dynamic Gantt chart is provided for tracking machine and operator status. Inventory levels and materials-handling utilization can also be graphed dynamically. Outputs include bar charts, pie charts, and plots of inventory levels. Alternately, information can be transferred to other software for development of presentation graphics. Features of AIM include the following:

1. *Manufacturing representation.* Manufacturing-specific modeling components can represent a variety of discrete manufacturing processes. Standard rules provide choices that are interpreted with processes. Custom rules may be written to extend the logic.

2. *Integration with scheduling applications.* Models written with AIM can be used with other FACTOR applications providing support for capacity, logistics, production scheduling, supply-chain analysis, and schedule management.

3. *Manufacturing data.* AIM is built around a relational database that stores the manufacturing operation and simulation output. Part descriptions, process plans, order-release schedules, machine locations and schedules, shift schedules, and so on can be transferred from other data sources to the AIM database.

4. *Animation support.* AIM models are built graphically and are animated automatically during model construction.

5. *Interactive model building and simulation.* Components are located on a scaled facility background. Intelligent defaults are provided for all components. Components are customized by completing forms. During execution, the modeler can change the status of a component and observe the simulated impact on the manufacturing system.

6. *Comparison of alternatives.* The AIM project framework organizes all aspects of a manufacturing simulation project. Alternative models of the manufacturing process are stored. Comparison reports show model performance data to identify differences between alternatives.

7. *AIM Gantt charts.* The latest release of AIM supports the creation of Gantt charts for the improved verification and validation of models. Model performance can be reviewed in the Gantt chart to follow a single load or the decisions of a resource.

8. *Cost modeling methodology.* AIM includes a detailed cost modeling capability. AIM models represent alternative costing philosophies such as standard cost and ABC.

Simulation Environments

A simulation environment contains many utilities to conduct a simulation study. These capabilities include input data analysis, model entry support, scenario management, animation, and output data analysis. ARENA, a product of Systems Modelling Corporation, is intended to provide the power of SIMAN to those for whom learning the language is burdensome and enhance the use of tools used by SIMAN modelers (Collins and Watson, 1993). Assume that a person, other than a simulation analyst, wants to use SIMAN. Currently, he or she must understand the block used in the model and the elements used in the experiment frame to proceed. Under ARENA, the user could extract a module, place it in its appropriate location, and parameterize it without learning the SIMAN language. For SIMAN language modelers, ARENA is intended to increase their functionality, eliminating the need for writing similar code in different models.

SIMAN is the engine for ARENA, and Cinema is the animation system that is used. Other products included in ARENA are an input processor and an output processor. A shop floor analysis capability is also being developed and will be supported by ARENA. This latter product will be oriented toward scheduling and real-time shop floor applications of simulation.

The term *modules* is used to represent the building blocks available for creating models. The fundamental feature of ARENA is that a simulation analyst can construct a module definition for use by others. These module definitions may be combined to create other modules. SIMAN Base Modules form the lowest possible level of modules.

These correspond to basic SIMAN modeling constructs (blocks and elements). All other modules, called *Derived Modules,* are built from Base Modules or other Derived Modules. This increases the speed at which models can be built and aids in understanding by those not familiar with SIMAN blocks and elements. Templates provide modelers with a domain-specific Module Definition set. For example, a Manufacturing Template could be sold by Systems Modelling or by third parties.

A much-revised Cinema is contained within ARENA. This animation capability is integrated with ARENA modules. For example, when adding a module to represent a manufacturing process, a modeler might get both the modeling logic to represent the process, as well as the Cinema components representing work-in-process, and the status of the resource (busy, idle, in repair, etc.)

Animators

Most simulation animators are integrated with the software. However, this is not always the case, and the introduction of general-purpose animation packages allows the use of custom-made environments.

Proof animation is a product of Wolverine Software Corporation (Earle and Henriksen, 1993). Any software that can write ASCII data to a file can drive Proof Animation. Thus, Basic, C, Fortran, GPSS/H, SIMAN V, and SIMSCRIPT II.5, among others, can serve as drivers. Animation is accomplished by using a static background, the layout file, and a trace file that contains dynamic events. Some of the features of the software are as follows:

1. Graphics are vector based, similar to CAD programs.
2. Zoom in and zoom out are supported. Maximum resolution is guaranteed at any scale as the drawing is recalculated.
3. Drawing takes place on a coordinate grid using mouse-driven primitives.
4. Moving objects are defined internally by their geometry.
5. Statistics can be displayed dynamically.
6. Animation occurs in a postprocessing mode.
7. Motion is smooth on VGA PCs.
8. There is a steady ratio of animated (simulation) time to viewing (wall clock) time. This ratio may be varied while the animation is running.
9. The top view can be changed to isometric and changed back to top view instantly.
10. An option allows the construction of a demo disk.
11. CAD layouts can be imported and exported through an optional utility.

As an example of the integration of Proof with other simulation software, consider the interface with MOGUL from High Performance Software, Inc. The user can graphically build a model using Proof, complete the model using MOGUL, execute the model using GPSS/H, and view an animation using Proof.

Simulation Support Software

Two products, among many that are available, are discussed in this section. The first is UNIFIT II from Averill M. Law and Associates, for input data modeling (Vincent and Lay, 1993). The second is SIMSTAT from MC^2 Analysis Systems for input and output data analysis (Blaisdell and Haddock, 1993).

UNIFIT II is used to model input data distributions. The product can be used in conjunction with the major simulation software in producing the necessary code to enter distributions. The software actually augments the built-in distribution capability of most of the software described previously. For example, GPSS/H has 4 built-in distributions, but UNIFIT increases that number to 21. The software can be operated in three different modes. *Guided selection mode* automatically determines the best fitting distribution. *Manual selection mode* is designed for experienced simulationists allowing them to select the appropriate statistical tools and the order of application in determining an appropriate distribution. Finally, the *no-data model selection mode* assists in choosing a source of randomness when no corresponding data exist.

SIMSTAT 2.0 is an interactive graphical software tool that performs statistical analysis on simulation input and output data. It is designed to work seamlessly with many simulation packages. The software uses pull-down menus and is integrated into the Windows environment. Data are maintained in a spreadsheet format for editing, examination, and analysis. SIMSTAT takes advantage of the Windows clipboard. Some of the many graphical capabilities of SIMSTAT include the fitting of input distributions to data, the determination of initialization bias, and autocorrelation plots.

Summary

Described was software for simulation organized in four categories. The first of these was general-purpose software. The second was manufacturing-oriented software. Next, a simulation environment was discussed. Then, an animator was described. Finally, some simulation support software was discussed.

*OUTPUT ANALYSIS**

The analysis of simulation output is often a difficult and time-consuming process. Many assumptions must be verified in order to draw accurate conclusions from the information generated in simulation runs. This process can be simplified greatly if some basic procedures are followed. The following presents the concepts of simulation output analysis and provides methods for their application.

Building a good simulation model can be a lot of work. You have to figure out how to model the system, express the model in whatever software you are using, collect data on the corresponding real system (if any) to set the simulation model's input parameters, verify that the simulation model, as expressed in the software, is working properly, and validate the simulation's output against the corresponding output from the real system (if any). After all that, you should feel pretty good.

But not *too* good. If you stop there, you have wasted a lot of effort since it is now the simulation model's turn to go to work. And that does not mean just running it (once) on the computer and looking at the results (which you doubtless did anyway just to get it to run). What you really have now is far more than just "a" simulation model—you have a great vehicle to test out a lot of different ideas without a lot more work on your part (although your computer will now get very busy). You can now learn a lot about your model and the system it is simulating in terms of performance and possible improvement.

To do all this effectively, though, you have to think carefully about how you are going to exercise your model. And, perhaps unfortunately, the most common kinds of

---

*Courtesy of *1994 Winter Simulation Conference Proceedings.* W. David Kelton, Ph.D., Department of Operations and Management Science, Carlson School of Management and Supercomputer Institute, University of Minnesota. J. D. Tew, S. Manivannan, D. A. Sadowski, and A. F. Seila (eds.), pp. 62–68.

simulation models can fool you (although not intentionally) if you are not circumspect about how you interpret their output.

The purpose here is to call attention to these issues and indicate in general terms how one can deal with them. There will not be great depth or a lot of technical details, but we will instead make reference along the way to any of several texts on simulation that do, to introduce matters on this subject in the last few Winter Simulation Conferences (WSC), to more advanced and specialized WSC reviews.

Then, issue will be taken on randomness in simulation, planning the runs, and looking at the role of time in simulation. Analysis of a single variant will be described, as well as alternative variants, variance reduction, sensitivity estimation, metamodels, and simulation optimization.

DIDO Versus RIRO

Some simulations take as input only fixed, nonrandom values, typically representing parameters that describe the model and the particular variant being evaluated. If the system you are simulating is really like this, then you can get by with such a *deterministic* simulation model. The nicest thing about this is, since there is no randomness in the input, there is no randomness in the output either—if you repeat the simulation, you will get the same thing over again. Thus, the answers are exact, at least up to roundoff. Figure 36.7, DIDO (deterministic in, deterministic out) simulation, illustrates the idea in a manufacturing example, where the inputs are the machine cycle times, the interarrival times between successively arriving batches of parts, and the sizes of these batches; the outputs are the hourly production and the machine utilization. The big dots for the inputs represent their (deterministic) values, and the big dots for the outputs represent the (deterministic) output performance measures obtained by transforming the input via the simulation's logic into the output. To abuse the computer science anti-maxim of GIGO (garbage in, garbage out), you might still have to make a lot of different runs, but for the purpose of evaluating a lot of different input parameter combinations rather than deal with uncertainty in the output.

But many (maybe most) systems involve some kind of uncertain, random input, so realistic simulation models ought to provide for such variable input as well; these are called *stochastic simulation models*. In fact, ignoring randomness in the input can cause

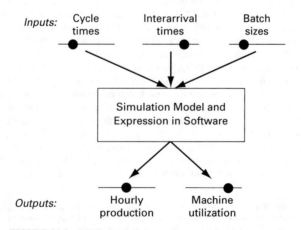

FIGURE 36.7   DIDO simulation.

dangerous errors in the simulation output. For instance, even in simple queuing models, which form the basic building blocks for a lot of simulations, the averages (expected values) of output performance measures like queue length and waiting time depend directly on the *variance* (as well as other things) of the service time distributions. So ignoring randomness actually gets the wrong answer, rather than just complicating life. Besides, you might be interested in the output's randomness itself—like variability in hourly production. Of course, if you put random things into the simulation logic, it is going to give you random things out—RIRO (random in, random out). Figure 36.8, RIRO simulation, illustrates the idea in the same manufacturing example, except now the inputs are probability distributions for the three quantities, regarded as random variables. The simulation proceeds by "drawing" realizations from the input probability distributions (indicated by the multiplicity of big dots from the input distributions) and transforms them into *an* observation on each of the (unknown) output distributions (indicated by the *single* big dot from each of the output distributions).

The whole point of this can be pretty much summed up by the fact that there is only a single big dot from the output distributions. The purpose of such a simulation is to learn (infer) something about these unknown output distributions, such as their expected values, variances, or probabilities on one side of some fixed tolerances. But all you get from one run of a stochastic simulation is a single observation on each of the output distributions, from which you obviously cannot tell much about the governing output distribution (especially if, by unluck of the draw, you got an unusual value of the output under its distribution).

So you have to think of a simulation run's output on some performance measure as a single observation on the output distribution; something very different could just as well have happened, just as something very different could just as well have happened on some other day in the actual manufacturing facility. Thus, you have to take care to perform the right kinds of simulation runs (design the simulation experiments) and do the right kinds of statistical analyses on the output data generated from the simulation. The rest of this tutorial will indicate some of the issues involved in these statistical questions as they apply to output data from a stochastic simulation.

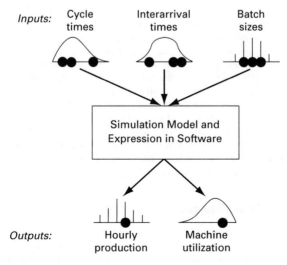

FIGURE 36.8 RIRO simulation.

Experimental Design or Simulation

Regardless of the type of simulation you have, you need to think ahead of time about exactly what scenarios you will be asking your model to evaluate. Sometimes this is easy, having been specified by executive fiat or being just plain obvious. But most of the time it is not so clear, and you will find yourself wondering what values the input parameters should take, and in what combinations with each other. You might also want to know what the effect is of changing some input parameter and perhaps whether the effect of such a change might depend on (interact with) where the other parameters are set.

In these situations, formal experimental design procedures can be of great help; you just need to think differently about them in the context of a simulation model. Traditionally, the "experiment" is some kind of physical situation; an agricultural experiment might be aimed at evaluating the effect of factors like different seed hybrids, fertilizers, and watering schedules on the yield of tomatoes, so an experiment with different factor-level combinations would be run and analyzed. The only things different about a simulation experiment are that you have a computer program rather than a tomato plant, the responses are the output measures like hourly production and machine utilization rather than yield of tomatoes, and the input factors are parameters like mean cycle times, variance of interarrival times, and maximum batch sizes, rather than seed hybrid, fertilizer, and watering. So you can design the simulation experiment in the same way and analyze it similarly as well in terms of measuring effects of factors and interactions among them.

Big simulations usually involve a lot of input factors, and you will have to do some paring down of their number before you can do a workable analysis. For this purpose there are several factor-screening designs to help separate which factors matter (and should thus be retained as factors) and which ones do not (which should be frozen at some reasonable values and eliminated as factors). For more on experimental design in the simulation context, see Chapter 12 of Banks and Carson (1984), Cook (1992), Hood and Welch (1992), Chapter 12 of Law and Kelton (1991), and Ramberg et al. (1991).

Does Time Go By?

An issue that has as great an impact on what you do with your model as the deterministic-stochastic issue is whether time plays a role in the system and your model of it. Some simulations do not involve the passage of time and are called *static*; examples include Monte Carlo evaluation of integrals and prediction with a cross-sectional regression model. The design-and-analysis approach is conceptually simple here (although may still be computationally tedious): just repeat, or *replicate,* the model as many times as necessary to get the precision you need. Methods from classical statistical analysis can usually be used directly. For instance, in estimating an integral via a static Monte Carlo simulation, just get many independent estimates and then take the average, standard deviation, and maybe form a confidence interval in the elementary way.

But most simulations of industrial interest involve the passage of time as an important element; these are *dynamic simulations,* and the design-and-analysis approach can be a lot harder. From here on assume that a dynamic simulation is what you have.

Evaluating a Single Configuration

As a first step, one might want to evaluate the output from just a single configuration of the model. This section discusses issues involved with this, which will then be components of more ambitious goals like comparing alternative configurations or optimizing.

What to Watch. In a stochastic simulation a person would really like to know all about the output distributions in the previous figure, RIRO simulation, but that is asking way too much in terms of the number and maybe length of the replications. So you usually have to settle for various summary measures of the output distributions. Traditionally, people have focused on estimating the expected value (mean) of the output distribution, and this can be of great interest. For instance, knowing something about the *average* hourly production is obviously important.

But things other than the means might be interesting as well, like the *standard deviation* of hourly production, or the *probability* that the machine utilization for the period of the simulation will be above .80. In another example you might observe the *maximum* length of the queue of parts in a buffer somewhere to plan the floor space; in this connection it might be more reasonable to seek a value (called a *quantile*) below which the maximum queue length will fall with a probability of .95.

So think beforehand about what you would like to get out of your simulation; it is easier to ignore things you have than go back and get things you forgot.

Multivariate Output. You will probably want to get several different things out of your simulation. The stylized simulation (shown in the previous figure) indicates two outputs, but dozens or scores would be more like it. Since these are all coming out of the same simulation runs, they are likely to be related in some way. For instance, high hourly production is probably associated with high utilization of the machine. So what you really have is a *vector* of output measures, and so multivariate statistical analyses can sometimes help with estimating all the output parameters simultaneously, as well as with understanding how they might be related to each other. For details in the simulation context and further references, see Charnes (1991), Section 9.7 of Law and Kelton (1991), and Seila (1991, 1992).

How Long? A fundamental issue in your planning is whether you want performance measures over the long run (technically infinite, sometimes called *steady state*) or for a specific (finite, sometimes called *terminating*) fixed time period. The answer to this question is not a simulation issue but rather one concerning the goals of the study. The answer also has obvious impact on how long you run your simulations; it also, perhaps less obviously, affects the kind of statistical analyses you can do on your output.

If a terminating simulation is appropriate for your goals, things are easy (at least in concept). Just run your model for whatever time period is called for, and get your output measures. That is one (replication, that is). Then repeat (replicate) until you are happy with your results (described in more detail in the next section). A complete run of the simulation constitutes a sample of size 1 (so it is not worth much), but standard statistical methods can be applied to the results across independent replications. On the other hand, if you really want steady-state measures, the statistical analysis problems become a lot harder (and, of course, the simulation runs become a lot longer). There are some things you can do, though, which are described below.

How to Express Things? Traditionally, simulation experts have expressed statistical analyses in the form of confidence intervals (or confidence regions in the case of multivariate output). Compared to hypothesis tests, many people feel that confidence intervals are more informative and useful. Increasingly, though, clever graphical displays are being used, which may not even involve formal inferential statistical analysis. For instance, histograms or dot plots of the output can indicate clear patterns that might not otherwise emerge from numerical measures. For more on graphical tools for describing simulation output, see Grier (1992).

Of course, animation has become very popular and, in some important ways, effective. But it is essential not to let yourself get swept along in the obvious visual appeal of animation to the exclusion of a proper statistical evaluation. For the 15 simulated minutes that you had the patience to watch the animation, how do you know that the model was not in some weird state that is not representative of conditions as a whole?

Difficulties and Cautions. Alas, there are some pretty bad things you can do to yourself if you are not pretty careful about how your statistical analysis goes. Maybe the biggest mistake is to take as the basic data points for statistical analysis the individual observations coming out of a simulation over time. For instance, you dare not use the sequence of times in queue of successive parts in their raw form in standard statistical calculations (like "sample" variances). The problem is that they are not independent— if one part has a big delay in queue, the next one probably will too—which renders most of classical statistical theory invalid, sometimes with disastrous consequences. For instance, the sample variance of the individual part delays in queue will be biased low, perhaps severely, causing you to underestimate the variance and place more confidence in your results' precision than you ought to.

On the bright side, though, people have worked out some fairly simple and practical methods for dealing with simulation-generated data that usually work out pretty well. If you have a terminating simulation, for instance, you just make multiple replications and treat the summary statistics from each replication (averages, proportions, extremes, etc.) as the basic "data" points, which *can* be plugged into standard statistical formulas since the replications *are* independent of each other. With steady-state simulations, though, things are not quite as easy. Here are some ideas that people have come up with and tested out.

Replication. Even though you want (simulated) time to go to infinity, you cannot do that. So just make runs as long as the results give you a picture of being "in" steady state. You then have independent replications, just as in the terminating case, that you can plug into classical statistics. The problem with this is that the initial conditions you use to start the simulation (like everything's empty) are probably pretty atypical of steady state, which biases the run's output, at least for a while. You can make some plots and try to see where things stabilize, deleting the output data prior to that point, or maybe try to find better initial conditions that are more representative of steady state.

Batch Means. Since you want to get as close as you can to steady state, just make one enormously long run. But then you really have only one replication, so you cannot do statistical analysis. To manufacture more observations out of this, split the run up into "batches" of observations, and treat the means of these batches as being independent unbiased observations of what is going on in steady state. While the initial-condition bias is less severe than with the replication method, the batch means are not really independent; the key is to have big batches, and people have developed ways to help you decide how big the batches need to be for your output data.

Time-Series Models. The correlated, nonstationary simulation output series can be thought of as a time series, just like economic data such as stock prices or housing starts over time. Then a time-series model (like AR or ARMA) is fit to the data, and the fitted model is used for inference.

Standardized time series. A process version of the central limit theorem is applied to "standardize" the output series, and methods for statistical analysis have been worked out based on this.

Regeneration cycles. Some simulations return now and then to a state from which they "start over" probabilistically. For instance, if a queue empties out at some point, it looks just like it did at the beginning (assuming it started empty). This creates independent *cycles* that are manipulated for statistical analysis.

Spectral analysis. Estimates of the correlation structure of the process are used to form a variance estimate for statistical analysis.

One gets the idea that this is a hard problem and that there is no completely satisfactory solution. There is a very large selection of literature available on this subject, and the above list is a pretty thin tour of these methods, but they are all explained in detail elsewhere; see Alexopoulos (1993); Chapter 11 of Banks and Carson (1984); Chapter 3 of Bratley, Fox, and Schrage (1987); Charnes (1993); Chapters 2, 3, and 5 of Fishman (1978); Goldsman (1992); Chapter 7 of Khoshnevis (1994); Kleijnen (1987); Chapter 9 of Law and Kelton (1991); Lewis and Orav (1989); Chapter 6 of Ripley (1987); Seila (1991, 1992); and Chapter 6 of Thesen and Travis (1992). In the last-named volume, you will find a tutorial by Alexopoulos covering these subjects in depth as well.

Comparing Alternatives

Most of the time you will be considering several different configurations of a simulation model, perhaps distinguished from each other by input-parameter values or by logical and structural differences. On the basis of some output performance measure, you might like to estimate the difference between various pairings of the configurations, perhaps expressed as a confidence interval for the difference or maybe a test of the null hypothesis that there is no difference. Most of the methods described can be adapted for these kinds of goals. For instance, in a terminating simulation, you can use paired-sample confidence intervals for the difference, discussed in any elementary statistics book. The same difficulties and cautions apply, though, if you are interested in steady state.

Simulation is an ideal setting in which to apply any of several selection and ranking methods. For instance, you can invoke statistical methods (basically telling you how much data you need to collect) that allow you to declare one of your alternatives as being the best on some criterion, and be highly confident that you are right about your choice. What makes simulation an attractive setting for this is that these methods often require two-stage or sequential sampling (deciding on the sample size on the fly), which is easier to do in simulation than in growing tomatoes. For more depth on these subjects, see Chapter 12 of Banks and Carson (1984); Goldsman, Nelson, and Schmeiser (1991); Chapter 10 of Law and Kelton (1991); Chapter 7 of Thesen and Travis (1992); or the tutorial by Nelson and Goldsman in the last-named volume.

Variance Reduction

Some of the difficulties and dangers in dealing with simulation data have been presented, but on the positive side are some important opportunities not available when experimenting with tomatoes. Ease of sequential sampling, as mentioned, was one example. But a more important example is that the variance of the output can be reduced without any extra work. Such *variance-reduction techniques* often proceed by exploiting the ability to control the random-number generator driving the simulation, and reuse random numbers to induce helpful correlations that reduce the noise in the output.

For instance, when comparing alternative configurations, you could use the same random numbers, properly synchronized, to drive them all. This would result in the same jobs' arriving to the alternative manufacturing facilities at the same times, and with the same processing requirements. Whatever differences in performance you observe are due to system differences rather than to "environmental" differences in the arriving jobs (since there weren't any). While intuitively appealing, there is actually firm statistical foundation for this, and the variance of the difference is usually reduced. This strategy, known as *common random numbers,* is often used unconsciously by just starting the runs for all alternatives with the same random number streams and seeds.

There are many other sophisticated variance-reduction ideas; for details see Chapter 2 of Bratley, Fox, and Schrage (1987); Chapter 3 of Fishman (1978); Chapter 11 of Law and Kelton (1991); Kleijnen (1987); Lewis and Orav (1989); Chapter 7 of Morgan (1984); Nelson (1992); and Chapter 5 of Ripley (1987).

What If You Want Sensitivities?

Related to the question of comparing alternatives is the more microlevel question of measuring the effect on the output due to a change in one or several of the inputs. For example, how much would hourly production increase if the mean cycle time on the machine were reduced by a small amount? Viewing the output as a (complicated) function of the input, this is a question about a partial derivative of the output with respect to one of the inputs.

A direct way to answer this is to make two sets of runs—one at the original value and another at the changed value of the input parameter—and then look at the difference. There are other ways of doing this, though, that are more clever (and maybe more complicated), yet are also more economical from the point of view of the amount of simulating you have to do. Details on these methods can be found in Chapter 12 of Law and Kelton (1991); Glasserman and Glynn (1992); Ho (1992); L'Ecuyer (1991); and Strickland (1993).

Metamodels

Thinking of the simulation logic and action as being a transformation of inputs into outputs, the notion arises that a simulation is just a function, albeit a pretty complicated one, that you cannot write down as some little formula. But it might be possible to *approximate* what the simulation does with some little formula, which could be particularly useful if a large number of input-factor combinations are of interest and it takes a long time to run the simulation.

So people sometimes fit a regression model to the simulation model, with the dependent variable's being the input parameters to the simulation. All the usual techniques for building regression models came into play, like selecting important subsets of the independent variables, modeling nonlinearities, and considering interactions. Since this is a (regression) model of a (simulation) model, it's sometimes called a *metamodel.*

For more on metamodeling, see Barton (1992); Hood and Welch (1993); Kleijnen (1987); and Chapter 12 of Law and Kelton (1991).

Finding Optimal Configurations

The ultimate, maybe, in using a simulation model is to find input-factor settings that optimize some performance measure. This could involve several of the above issues, including gradient estimation, metamodeling, and comparing alternatives. Now optimization of nonlinear functions is a hard enough problem in itself, but in a stochastic simulation you have uncertainty in terms of measuring the response, as well as the statistical difficulties described. So this is truly a tall order.

People have made important advances in this, though. One idea is to estimate the partial derivatives at a point (the gradient), then move in the direction of steepest descent (if you are minimizing) or steepest ascent (if you are maximizing). You could also fit a regression metamodel as in the preceding section and then use simple calculus to optimize it in lieu of the simulation itself. There are, to be sure, many more techniques (like adaptation of stochastic-programming methods) that have been developed or are under investigation; for more details see Azadivar (1992); Chapter 12 of Law and Kelton (1991); or the tutorial by Fu in the latter volume.

Conclusions

While all the details, methods, and cautions of doing a good job at output analysis may seem bewildering, you really owe it to yourself to try to get as much honest, precise information out of your hard-built simulation model as you can. While there are dangers and difficulties at times, there are also reliable and robust methods available. Moreover, some simulation software products now have output analysis capabilities built in to facilitate things.

*SIMULATION PROJECTS**

Simulation projects are often challenging and complex to plan and manage. There are typically several groups involved in the studies from various parts of a company, and their goals often differ. Also, simulation models are very much a function of the analysis goals of the individuals involved and must be constructed accordingly. The following discussion provides insights into the process.

When system performance improvements result from carrying out a simulation project's recommendations, the feeling on the project team can be euphoric. Their sense of pride is self-evident. Unfortunately, not all project teams experience this, for not all projects are successful. Some never finish. Others finish, but not with enough credence to persuade the customer to take any action. And still others fail to finish in time to make a difference.

While success cannot be guaranteed, conducting a simulation project according to certain guidelines can improve the team's chance of success. The guidelines presented here are straightforward, even commonplace, actions that have repeatedly proven their value. Technical fundamentals are not emphasized. This is not to minimize their importance, for technical knowledge and competence are necessary conditions for success. Rather, the purpose is to emphasize the role practical management plays in every successful project.

Project Steps and Guidelines

A simulation project is a process of interpretive, developmental, and analytical steps—see Pritsker, Sigal, and Hammesfahr (1989); Banks and Carson (1984); and Law and Kelton (1991). These steps, which are intrinsic to all simulation projects, generally

---

*Courtesy of *1994 Winter Simulation Conference Proceedings.* Kenneth J. Musselman, Ph.D., Pritsker Corporation, West Lafayette, Indiana. J. D. Tew, S. Manivannan, D. A. Sadowski, and A. F. Seila (eds), pp. 88–95.

include problem formulation, model conceptualization, data collection, model building, verification, validation, analysis, documentation, and implementation.

A functional definition is given below for each step in the simulation process (Pritsker 1986, and Pritsker Corporation 1993). Following each definition, guidelines are presented. These guidelines affect the success of the project at this point in the process. Keep in mind, however, that a particular guideline may need to be initiated well ahead of where it is placed here and could be engaged repeatedly.

Problem Formulation

Define the problem to be studied, including a written statement of the problem-solving objective.

Work on the Right Problem.   Nothing is less productive than finding the right solution to the wrong problem. While this is usually not one's intention, it happens more frequently than it should. Often, this is due to misunderstood or poorly stated objectives. For this reason, establishing sound objectives is critically important. Obscure objectives make it difficult to succeed. Construct objectives that are precise, reasonable, understandable, and action oriented to convey a proper sense of direction and to distinguish between primary and subordinate issues. Then continue to focus on these objectives throughout the project.

Maxim: Fuzzy objectives lead to unclear successes.

Listen to the Customer.   Good listening habits are essential for success. Learn to listen more and talk less. Give the customer a chance to change your way of thinking. Remember, the goal is to solve the customer's problem, not yours. Work on suspending judgment until you better understand the system and the situation. Know who the customer is, what is being asked, and why. Concentrate on what is, as well as what is not, being said. Draw out the facts, and encourage further clarification. Do not let vague answers or unfamiliar terminology curb your need to know.

Be as aware of your question selection as you are of your customer's answers. Learn to probe with pro-active questions. "What if we release it later? Earlier? Suppose we do it more often? Less often? How about eliminating it altogether?" Try compressing, adding, subtracting, multiplying, substituting, combining, and reserving your way through the system.

Also be more circumspect. Part of finding a solution involves understanding its implications. Continually sensitize yourself to the customer's needs, values, beliefs, and attitudes. Be on the alert for clues into how the customer views the problem and the project. Then couch your comments, reports, documents, and presentations accordingly.

Maxim: Don't look for a solution without first listening to the problem.

Communicate.   Poor communication is the single biggest reason projects fail. There is simply no substitute for good communication. Start by reaching an understanding with the customer about the project. Settle on objectives, scope, assumptions, how the system functions, key questions to be addressed, model input, and model output. At this point, you want everyone to understand clearly the project team's collective knowledge and intent.

Next, orient the customer by establishing a project plan. Gain the customer's support by explaining how the project will proceed and what to expect. Emphasize the benefits associated with doing the project as planned, and prepare the customer for potential problems. In short, give the customer a "road map" of the project. By knowing what is coming and why, the customer is in a better position to lend support. Without this knowledge, the customer may unintentionally work against you.

Finally, keep the customer informed. People like knowing where they are. Have plenty of "sign posts" along the way. Easily identifiable deliverables are excellent for this.

Maxim: Keep people informed, for the journey is more valuable than the solution.

Predict the Solution. In the beginning of a project, people often miss an excellent opportunity to properly set the stage. They are too eager to get started. As a result, they fail to do a simple, yet effective, exercise.

At project initiation, ask the customer to conduct a quick, even crude, analysis of the problem. This does several things for you. First, it gets the thought process started. The customer begins to concentrate on the problem more than the model. This can provide early insight into the problem. Caution is advisable, however. Preconceived ideas can restrict thinking. Do not let this happen. Keep creativity alive. You want this exercise to strengthen the thought process, not stop it.

Second, this starting solution provides a base for comparison. If the project's results turn out differently, you arouse interest. This leads to exploration into why these differences exist and, eventually, to an even deeper understanding of system behavior.

Finally, predicting the solution establishes where the customer's thinking was at the beginning of the project. Eventually, you want to show how the project advanced understanding. Without this beginning reference point, you have no way of doing this. Accordingly, the project's true value could be discounted.

Maxim: Only by knowing where you started you can judge how far you have come.

Model Conceptualization

Abstract the system into a model described by the elements of the system, their characteristics, and their interactions, all according to the problem formulation.

Direct the Model. The best guide for formulating a simulation model is a well-defined set of objectives. These objectives establish the criteria against which all modeling decisions can and should be judged. With these objectives as a basis, use a backward pass to reach the model specification stage. This is accomplished as follows. As shown in Fig. 36.9, "Model Formulation Procedure," first generate a list of specific questions that support the project's objectives. These questions provide the direction needed to identify the most important areas in the system. Next, determine what output measures are necessary to answer these questions. Then, by limiting the discussion to just these measures, begin to define and determine the scope of the model. This process helps ensure that the model is consistent with the project's objectives.

Formulating the model backward as suggested above results in a leaner model. This provides several benefits: easier model verification, quicker initial results, and improved ability to adjust the model as necessary.

Maxim: Advance the model by formulating it backward.

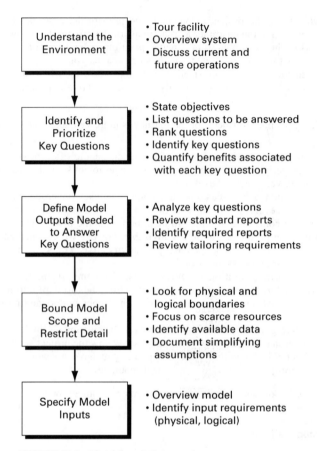

FIGURE 36.9   Model formulation procedure.

Manage Expectations.   Successful projects require continuous management of the customer's expectations. It is important to have these expectations agree with the project's objectives. Otherwise, you can find yourself obligated to perform tasks only to satisfy an expectation, not an objective.

Start by setting the correct expectations up front. Be enthusiastic, but be careful not to oversell. Make sure the customer understands what issues the model will and will not address. It is far better to discuss restrictions from the beginning than to state them for the first time when you present results. Then continually manage the customer's expectations. Quickly throttle any unrealistic hopes or ideas. Do not let the customer assume you are delivering capability you cannot or do not intend to deliver. Work together to understand each other's viewpoint and come to a mutually acceptable resolution. If you cannot reach agreement immediately, look for a way to work around the issue. You want to keep the project moving forward. If the issue is technical, consider using the model to explore options or to bound the problem to see if the issue really matters.

Maxim: It is easier to correct an expectation now than to change a belief later.

Data Collection

Identify, specify, and gather data to support the model.

Question the Data. Challenge all data you get for the model. Do a quick audit. Consider the source, what was collected, and how it was collected. Do the data make sense? Is it representative of the process? Is it at an appropriate level of detail? Is it within the scope of the project? Is it going to bias the results?

Strive to get all the data you need, but be open to compromising the model to better suit the data you *can* get. Then test the sensitivity of the model's outputs to the full range of input possibilities. If sensitivity exists, you now have a good reason to get the data you need.

Maxim: Do not take data for granted.

Make Assumptions. Data collection will inevitably be on the critical path. Do not be held captive by the information you lack. Be willing to make assumptions to keep the project moving forward. Take an educated guess at what you do not know. Then use the model to judge the sensitivity of this information. You may find it is of little consequence.

Making an assumption does not mean you must hold to it. Learn to revise your thinking and your assumptions throughout the project. Making unconfirmed assumptions is a problem only if you treat them as if they were fact. Finally, review your assumptions regularly, and be sure to validate them before presenting results.

Maxim: Be willing to make assumptions.

Model Building

Fit the conceptualized model to constructs available in a simulation language or system.

Focus on the Problem. Many simulation projects inappropriately concentrate on model building more than problem solving. Getting the model up and running becomes the overriding objective, so understanding the problem and deriving possible solutions become subordinate.

Consider, instead, spending more time modeling and experimenting and less time building. Use the process of modeling to gain more insight into the problem and possible solutions. New ideas will come with the knowledge gained in modeling the process. You want to give the model a chance to contribute to the process of originating new ideas. Remember, building the model is not the main task at hand; implementing the right solution is.

Maxim: Focus on the problem more than the model.

Start Simple. Use the model to reduce the problem to your ability to solve it. If you build a complex model, you undermine your ability to understand the outputs produced by it and, ultimately, your ability to arrive at a solution. Therefore, initially avoid making the model too complex. Try, instead, to capture just the essence of the system. Then use your judgment skills to fill in the details.

Starting with a simple model also enables you to learn about the system in stages. By incrementally building the model both down and out, you will better understand why things happen as they do and what the impact of each new state is.

A simple model also helps you maintain modeling freedom. If you build a detailed model that now must be redone or significantly modified, you can find yourself arguing against change only because of the effort involved. It is best to maintain modeling freedom as long as possible.

Maxim: Add complexity; do not start with it.

Curb Complexity.   Complexity can easily creep into a model. With perfect information available, a model's control logic for example, can become so sophisticated it allows the model to out-perform the actual system. This level of control in the model can conceal fundamental system design flaws. Seek to expose these flaws, not hide them. Moreover, do not lose sight of what is reasonable to implement. Consider, for example, the situation in which you are choosing the next best job to run on a machine. By including both waiting and incoming jobs in your search, system performance will likely improve. Yet how intelligent should the model be? Can you implement the logic? Be ever mindful of what is practical. It can save precious modeling time and effort.

Maxim: Do not let the model become so sophisticated that it compensates for a bad design, or so complex that it goes beyond your ability to implement.

Verification and Validation

Establish that the model executes as intended and the desired accuracy or correspondence exists between the model and the real system.

Control Changes.   Change requests are inevitable. Therefore, expect them, plan for them, and, most of all, control them.

Begin by being smart from the start. Do not accept a small change just because the project is going well now. Stay true to the project's objectives and scope. Argue against a change that is not in line with the objectives or within scope. The true implications of a change usually become evident much later in the project, namely, during verification, validation, acceptance testing, and implementation. Large costs and delays can easily result from even a minor change.

Agree to a change only if you must. When you do, be aware that you open yourself to more changes, with possibly even bigger consequences. Therefore, proceed with caution. Remember also that changes can delay deliverables that others are expecting. Consequently, be sure to communicate to all affected parties the implications of each change, especially the added time and costs.

Consider delaying changes by moving them to a later phase of the project. Get baseline results out first. Then look to incorporate the changes you deferred. This allows you to show progress under the original schedule and still satisfy the request.

Include the customer in change-request meetings. This gets the customer to think occasionally about the project's objectives and scope. It will also help the customer begin to appreciate, in advance, the reasonableness of these requests and their impact on the project.

Get all change requests in writing. A record of these requests and their judgments fosters good customer relations. If you have no record of what you agreed to or, more importantly, what you did not agree to, you are more likely to consent to the change.

Be especially mindful of changes in project personnel. If possible, argue against them. However, if you have no choice, immediately hold a project meeting. Review the team's accomplishments, what tasks remain, and who needs to be involved. Take the time necessary to properly transition all technical and administrative information. Make sure each team member knows what this means to him or her personally. Poorly executed transitions can quickly cause an otherwise secure project to fail. Do not miss this opportunity to get the project back on track. At the end of the project, it is too late to take time to do it right.

Maxim: Verbal agreements are not worth the paper they are printed on.

Be Mindful of the Customer's Perceptions.   Through experience you develop a way of doing things that works well for you. You know what is important to establish early and what can be left for later. The customer, on the other hand, may have a different viewpoint. That which is unimportant to you may be very important to the customer. A small programming error, for example, if left unattended, can greatly undermine the customer's confidence in the simulation model and the project. Therefore, quickly correct any mistakes the customer perceives as a problem.

Maxim: Customer perceptions require attention.

Analysis

Analyze the simulation outputs to draw inferences and make recommendations for problem resolution.

Sell Success.   Selling the value of a project continues throughout its life…and beyond. It starts with the proposal and continues past implementation. Seize every opportunity to explain the value of what you are doing. Aggressively pursue these opportunities. Success will not come to you; you need to go after it.

Learn to accentuate the positive. You will have enough support in exposing the negative. Moreover, sell success, not underachievement. Compare your progress to where you were, not to where you are going. You will always be short of your objective until the end. Continue to remind everyone where the project started and how far it has come. At every opportunity, make known what you *have* accomplished.

Maxim: Report successes early and often.

Question the Output.   Challenge the model's outputs. Can you explain them? Do they make intuitive sense? Can you defend them without getting into technical details?

Believe in yourself as much as the outputs. If the outputs are counter-intuitive, check your work. Something is wrong! Examine your assumptions. Reverify and revalidate the model. There must be a rational explanation.

In the end, compare the model's outputs with the crude estimate you asked the customer to perform at the beginning of the project. Are they different? If so, why? If not, examine why you did a simulation study so you can avoid doing "confirmation" projects in the future.

Maxim: If it doesn't make sense, check it out.

Understand the Model's Limits.   At best, a model is less than reality. By its very nature, it is an abstraction of the system. This means a solution for the model is not necessarily a solution for the system. A degree of interpretation must accompany each analysis. Be careful not to stray beyond reasonable limits. Revisit the model's assumptions and inputs to help define what is reasonable.

Models do not replace individual thought. The customer, in the end, must rule on the worth of a particular solution. The model cannot do this. Its purpose is to support the thought process, not supplant it.

Maxim: People decide; models don't.

Know When to Stop.   You can always do more. For example, you can expand the model by extending it upstream and downstream, adding detail, improving the data, and reformatting the output. You can expand the analysis by testing the sensitivity of the results to boundary conditions, conducting a more rigorous statistical evaluation, examining other alternatives, and training the customer. The list is never-ending.

Prepare the customer for this eventuality. During the project, work with the customer to define a suitable stopping point. This is a judgment call, but one with which the customer must feel comfortable. You can help by instructing the customer on how to continue the process. This could involve teaching the customer how to change input, modify the model, interpret output, stay within scope, and decipher errors. The customer will deem the project far more successful if progress can continue following your departure.

Maxim: Ultimate truth is not affordable.

Present a Choice.   The customer asks for a solution, but wants a choice. Therefore, present a range of possibilities to the customer. This gives the customer a sense of freedom and involvement and a better understanding of why the best is best. Besides, with a choice, it is harder to find fault. It is much easier to dispute one solution than a set of solutions.

Maxim: People do not resist their own discoveries.

Documentation

Supply supportive or evidential information for a specific purpose.

Report Progress.   Progress reports provide an important, written history of a project. They give a chronology of work done and decisions made. This can prove to be invaluable as you endeavor to keep the project on course.

Reporting should occur at least monthly. In this way, people who are not directly involved in the project's day-to-day activities can stay involved. By knowing the project's status and plans, they still have an opportunity to further the project and your chance of success.

Regular reporting also surfaces misunderstandings early in the process, when problems can often be easily solved. You cannot afford to have them fester. Give them immediate visibility. Handling them without delay minimizes their impact.

Keeping a project log is also important. The log provides a comprehensive record of accomplishments, noteworthy problems, change requests, key decisions, ideas for follow-up work, and anything else of major or even minor importance. This can be indispensable when developing a historical record of the project.

Maxim: Document, Document, Document!

Maintain Momentum.   A simulation project is a journey. Along the way, it is important to give the customer a reading of where you are. By showing progress and having the customer acknowledge this progress, enthusiasm for the project is kept high. One means of doing this is by having frequent deliverables. These need not be major pieces of work. The best deliverables are easy to accomplish, hold value for the project, and are clearly identifiable. Examples include a model specification, prototype demonstrations, model delivery, animations, training, analyses, model documentation, progress reports, presentations, and a final report. Timing these deliverables judiciously over the project gives the customer a reliable measure of progress.

Maxim: It is better to work with many intermediate milestones than with one absolute deadline.

Implementation

Fulfill the decisions resulting from the simulation.

Foster Teamwork. A simulation project is more than building a model or managing a process; it is working with people if the project is to succeed, for success is in the minds of people.

Working well together means taking full advantage of the team's collective talents. Learn to work as a unified body, with all members' being aware of their role and importance to the general outcome of the project. By having the team search, discover, and grow together, you enrich the project and increase your chance of success.

Maxim: Focus on possibilities, not personalities.

Involve Key Decision Makers. Know who the key decision makers are and work to involve them in the project. Periodically meet with them to incorporate their ideas and allay their concerns. Be sure to involve the process owners from the beginning, even if they are not the key decision makers. In the middle of the project, you do not want either camp coming in with a different set of expectations. This can be both costly and demoralizing.

Watch for signs of the project's not being a priority, such as data gathering delays, end-user difficulties, upper-management unavailability, decision postponements, deadline slippages, and apathetic or even hostile attitudes. When these signs appear, call on the key decision makers to reset the priorities.

Maxim: Pull in key decision makers to prevent being pushed out.

Advocate Improvement. If done right, a simulation project results in system improvements. These improvements are the result of change, such as a new operating policy, a different cell configuration, or a new job allocation scheme. Whatever the change, expect resistance and take action to overcome it. Enlist management support; educate those affected as to the value of the change; sell the project team on the importance of being pro-active and enthusiastic about the change; and educate the customer as to the benefits associated with implementing the change. By involving everyone in the change process, you help mitigate any resistance.

Success in making a change is heavily dependent on the customer's confidence to take action. Giving the customer a sense of control over the project helps to instill this confidence. Learn, therefore, to guide the simulation process without usurping the customer's control. With loss of control, the customer becomes either angered or uninterested. In either case, the project falls into disfavor, and any action to implement the necessary changes is unlikely.

Maxim: Be a change agent; have a bias for action.

Conclusion. Simulation projects demand strong technical and managerial skills. The guidelines presented here highlight the managerial skills needed in each step of the simulation process. They cover directing the process, controlling model development and analysis, and improving customer relations. By following these guidelines, the technical aspects of the project can continue with fewer distractions and disruptions. The result is improved project performance and increased likelihood of the project's recommendations being implemented.

*MANUFACTURING APPLICATIONS**

Computer simulation has two important applications in industry: design and control. In design, the typical application is for analyzing a production system. Simulating a design is appealing because the components of the model are well detailed and have a one-to-one correspondence to the physical system. Because there are very few theoretical considerations, the model can represent many of the subtle system nuances; and with such a detailed model, the analyst can gain the confidence of the people using the simulator. Performance measurements, such as the number of parts passing through the system per day, can give an insight into the system's dynamic operation.

When simulation is used as a control aid, it is used to generate and analyze possible production schedules. Since simulation models are used based on very accurate predictions of system behavior, it is logical to use these powerful predictive techniques to develop precise schedules. Highly complex operating rules can be implemented in a model and then downloaded to the shop floor in the form of production schedules with operation start and end times. The following provides insights into the application of simulation in industrial settings.

Manufacturing is one of the earliest simulation application areas (Naylor et al., 1966), and the attendance at the manufacturing application conferences indicates that manufacturing remains as one of the most popular application areas. Simulation is used to improve the performance of manufacturing systems because of the following:

- Many manufacturing systems are too complex to be analyzed and improved by simply thinking and talking about possible approaches.

- Simulation can predict system performance resulting from interactions among system components.

System components can be people, machines, tools, materials-handling devices, and materials, as depicted in Fig. 36.10. The result of interactions among these components

---

*Courtesy of Gordon M. Clark, Ph.D., Department of Industrial and Systems Engineering, The Ohio State University. From *1994 Winter Simulation Conference Proceedings,* J. D. Tew, S. Manivannan, D. A. Sadowski, and A. F. Seila (eds.), pp. 15–21.

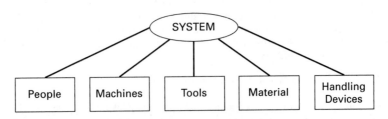

FIGURE 36.10 System components.

may be very difficult to predict without the use of a model, and a simulation model is frequently the easiest model to use. This section introduces simulation applications for manufacturing systems by illustrating:

- Diverse uses of simulation
- Use of random and deterministic variables in simulation models
- A structured process for applying simulation

Three example applications are used to illustrate the above points. The first example is a single-machine-failure model. It illustrates the value of using a model even when studying the performance of a single machine. The second example is a study to determine effective operating policies for a manufacturing cell. This example illustrates the steps and process that one ought to follow in a simulation study. The third example is the use of simulation in an on-line mode to schedule a manufacturing system. The simulation model is a completely deterministic model in this application.

Single-Machine-Failure Model

Results from the single-machine-failure model illustrate the need for a model in analyzing a machine purchasing decision, and the model shows requirements for using a simulation. Law and Kelton (1991) present similar results. A company is considering the purchase of a machine from a vendor that advertises that the machine has the following performance characteristics:

- Constant time to process a job in 1 minute
- A mean time to failure of 540 minutes, that is, 9 hours, of actual operating time
- A mean time to repair a failure of 60 minutes, that is, 1 hour

Operating time does not include idle time. The company wants to predict the effect of the machine characteristics on throughput rate, work-in-process (WIP), and throughput time. *Throughput time* is the total time at the machine including both queuing time, processing time, and waiting for a repair to be completed.

The above characteristics permit one to calculate an upper limit on the capacity or the throughput rate of the machine. The first step is to obtain a mean service time for a part on the machine. Service time will include the processing time and any time a job has to wait for the machine to be repaired. Define a *cycle* as starting when the machine is repaired, operates until failure, undergoes repair, and then starts another cycle. The cycle length is 10 hours, and the machine is being repaired for 1 hour, or 10 percent of the cycle length. Thus, the effective mean time to service a job is 1/0.9 minutes. An equivalent viewpoint is that a job will require 1 minute of processing plus any time to remedy a failure. On the average, one out of every 540 jobs will experience a failure, and have to wait for repair. Since the mean repair time is 60 minutes, the mean service time for a part is $1 + 60/540 = 1/0.9$ minutes. The mean service time of 1/0.9 minutes implies a mean service rate of $1/(1/0.9) = 0.9$ jobs per minute. Define the following quantities, having units of jobs per minute, that apply over an extended time period:

$$\lambda = \text{the average arrival rate of jobs to the machine}$$

$$\theta = \text{the average throughput rate}$$

In this case, $\theta = \text{minimum } (\lambda, 0.9)$. The above example illustrates that we can calculate the mean throughput rate without a simulation model.

The prediction of the average WIP and throughput time will be shown by a simulation. The variability in job interarrival times and job service times is important in predicting queuing and queuing times. However, the distribution of times to failure and of machine repair times are unknown. Assume that the probability distribution of job interarrival times is negative exponential with mean 1.25 minutes. Then, $\lambda = 1/1.25 = 0.8$ jobs per minute. Thus, $\theta = 0.8$ jobs per minute. For the simulation of job service times, consider the three cases shown in Table 36.1.

Results for the three cases will show the effect of variability in service times. We simulated 100 independent shifts of 8 hours' production for each case. A machine under repair at the end of a shift will be operable at the start of the following shift. Also, each shift starts with the machine and its associate queue being empty and idle. Table 36.2 gives 90 percent confidence intervals for mean throughput time, WIP, and number in the queue. Observations on Table 36.2 are the following:

- Service time variability has an important effect on WIP and throughput time.
- The timing of machine failures and/or stoppages must be explicitly represented as opposed to allocating an average downtime to the processing time of each job. Law and Kelton (1991) make this observation.
- A deterministic representation of time to failure and time to repair gives larger throughput time and WIP estimates than allocating average downtime to each job.
- The STOFAIL and DETFAIL confidence intervals overlap; thus, one should run more than 100 replications for these two cases.

This single-machine-failure model illustrates an important property of simulation models. A simulation is an atomistic model in that the simulation describes the performance of individual system components and their interactions. Given this description, the simulation model can trace the changes in system state over time. This means that the sim-

TABLE 36.1   Job Service Times

Case	Description
STOFAIL	Operating time to failure has a negative exponential distribution with mean 540 minutes.
	Repair times have a lognormal distribution with mean 60 minutes and standard deviation 20 minutes.
DETFAIL	Operating times to failure are a constant 540 minutes.
	Repair times are a constant 60 minutes.
NOFAIL	Service times are a constant $1/0.9 = 1.111$ minutes.

TABLE 36.2   Confidence Intervals

Case	Throughput time	WIP	Number in queue
STOFAIL	17.6 ± 4.0	14.4 ± 3.0	13.5 ± 3.0
DETFAIL	12.3 ± 1.6	10.2 ± 1.3	9.3 ± 1.3
NOFAIL	5.02 ± 0.32	4.06 ± 0.29	3.18 ± 0.28

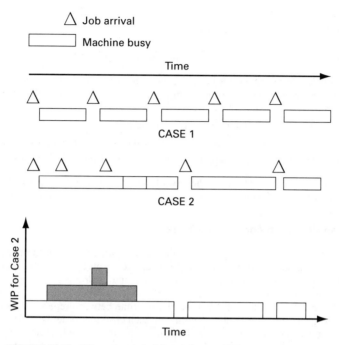

FIGURE 36.11 Effect of statistical fluctuations on WIP.

ulation user must specify a description of the system components and their performance characteristics to implement a simulation. In the preceding example, the user specified the distribution of job interarrival and service times for each case. To represent the variation in machine failure times, the user must specify or select a particular distribution.

Why is variability so important in estimating WIP and throughput time? Any utilization close to 1 will result in excessive WIP if there is any variation in service times or times between arrival of lots to the respective machines. Figure 36.11 illustrates the effect of fluctuations in job interarrival times and job operation times on WIP for a single machine. The top sequence, called case 1, of job arrivals and service times for each arrival follows a perfect uniformly spaced pattern that has no variation. That is, the times between each arrival are all equal, and the service times are also all equal. The proportion of time the machine is busy represents the machine utilization, which is close to 1. Because of this lack of variation, case 1 gives no queuing and no instances of WIP greater than 1. The lower sequence, called case 2, of service and interarrival times has precisely the same mean and gives the same overall machine utilization, which is the proportion of time the machine is busy. However, this statistical fluctuation increases the WIP, which becomes as large as 3. The shaded area in plot at the bottom of Fig. 36.11 shows the jobs waiting in the machine queue.

Potential sources of variations in job service times are the following:

- Tooling failures.
- Machine cycle length changes due to different types of jobs, that is, a machine performs operations on nonidentical parts. For example, a machine processes an XYZ123 job and then an ABC123.

- Machine failures and adjustments.
- Variations in human-paced task times.

Variations in interarrival times could result from the following:

- Any variation in the times between release to production due to the company planning system or customer order times, for example, job release times that vary with the hour of the day or the day of the week
- Variations in the times materials arrive from vendors
- Variations in the initiation of production caused by tools not being available
- Variations in the times jobs depart from upstream workstations in the job's route

See Law and Kelton (1991) for another list of potential sources of statistical variations in manufacturing simulations.

Gear Manufacturing Throughput Time

Clark and Cash (1991) used simulation in a study to identify preferred operating policies for a rough steel cell used in the manufacture of precision gears. Figure 36.12 depicts the three cells used to produce gears. The manufacturer produces gears to order, rather than making gears for stock. Customer orders may specify a gear that the manufacturer has produced in the past, but the elapsed time between repeat orders is so long that making gears for stock is not economical. Each customer order specifies a quantity of gears that varies over a wide range. The flow allowance is the lead time quoted to the customer specifying the promised delivery date. Currently, the type of gear determines the flow allowance, but no allowance is made for the number of gears in the customer order. The manufacturer currently releases work to production as soon as raw materials are available to produce the customer order; thus, the number of gears in a job has a considerable range of variation. The manufacturer uses manual procedures for tracking and scheduling work in the plant. This process includes the following steps:

- Specify study objectives.
- Specify performance measures.
- Determine alternatives to investigate.
- Describe systems to be simulated.
- Create simulation model.
- Prepare input data.
- Formulate experimental design.
- Conduct simulation experiments.
- Analyze results.
- Make recommendations.

FIGURE 36.12   Gear production flow.

Study Objectives. The manager of manufacturing engineering and the director of engineering requested a study to determine policies for scheduling work in the rough steel cell. These scheduling policies consist of policies for controlling the release of work to the cell and sequencing work in the cell. The objectives for these policies are the following:

- Reduce throughput time through the cell.
- Reduce WIP.
- Reduce quoted lead time.
- Reduce tardiness.
- Reduce cost.

The tardiness objective requires establishing flow allowances and due dates specifically for the rough steel cell. This study emphasized simplified procedures for scheduling because of the following:

- The objective of reducing cost
- The lack of a computerized procedure for tracking work in the plant

Performance Measures. The primary performance measures are the following:

- Average WIP
- Average system time
- Average number of tardy jobs per year
- Average time a tardy job is late
- Quoted lead times for each type of job

Alternatives Investigated. The alternatives investigated included fixed-capacity buffers, a modified due-date procedure, an upper limit on job size, and a sequencing rule. The following describe the alternatives.

Fixed-Capacity Buffers. The use of fixed-capacity buffers at each workstation is a simplified means for reducing WIP. A station is blocked, becoming inactive when it completes work on a job and the next station in a job's route has a full buffer. Reducing WIP also simplifies the scheduling problem for work in the cell. If the buffers do not significantly reduce capacity, by the occurrence of blocking, the reduced WIP will reduce throughput time. The use of buffers forces incoming orders to wait in a backlog when the first workstation in the processing plan has a full buffer. Thus, the use of buffers introduces a control on the timing of production release. A similar alternative is to define an upper limit on the number of jobs in the entire cell. This alternative is known as the *CONWIP* alternative (Spearman et al., 1990).

Modified Due-Date Procedure. A modified due-date procedure was defined that incorporated the number of gears in an order to determine the flow allowance. The modified flow allowance has two components: one for the aggregate setup time and one for the aggregate run time per gear. The run time component is proportional to the order quantity. For most customer orders, the modified procedure has a shorter flow allowance than the current flow allowances.

Job Size. An upper limit on job size, the number of gears in a job, will reduce the large variation in the number of gears in a job. Large jobs tend to create floating bottlenecks. A customer order for more gears than the job size limit will result in multiple jobs to fill an order.

Sequencing Rules.   Investigated were two sequencing rules for work at a workstation. They were *first-in, first-out* (FIFO) and *earliest due date* (EDD).

System Description

Figure 36.13 depicts the system studied. The rough steel cell has the following workstations: lathes hobs, shapers, and generators. Each workstation may have a buffer and
multiple machines. The buffer sizes and number of machines in each workstation are
inputs. The service time for a job at a machine has a setup time and a run time component. The setup times and single-part run times are lognormal random variables. The
total service time for a job is the sum of the setup time and lot size independent run
times, where lot size is the number of gears in the job. The system represents a number
of different gear types, and each gear type has its own processing plan. A processing
plan gives the route through the cell for each gear type and the standard setup and run
times. The arrival times of customer orders are exogenous, deterministic inputs.

Experimental Conditions

The director of engineering and the manager of manufacturing engineering selected 50
gear types for analysis—that is, number of gears = 50. The gears selected were representative of future business. They supplied the process plans for each gear type. The manager
of information systems supplied historical job release times over the previous 4 years.
These data became the basis for the exogenous customer order times. The study used three
different customer order patterns, known as *release schedules,* that is, RS1, RS2, and RS3.
Each release schedule specified the time materials were available for production for each
customer order over a 1-year period. The intent was to represent more than a single scenario to increase the robustness of the study's conclusions. These release schedules presented the lathe workstation with average utilization levels of 65, 85, and 95 percent for
RS1, RS2, and RS3, respectively. These averages apply over a 1-year period.

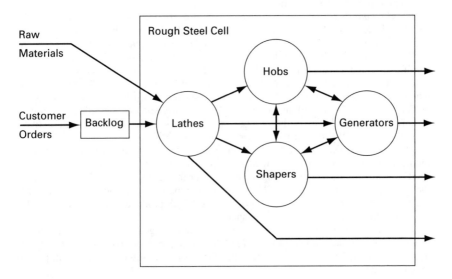

FIGURE 36.13   System studied.

Study Requirements

The five previous steps—that is, specify study objectives, performance measures, alternatives to investigate, systems to simulate, and experimental conditions—place requirements on the study. They dictate the detail in the simulation model and the data to be collected. All those concerned should review the results of these steps prior to making simulation runs and recommendations.

Simulation Model

The simulation model was programmed in WITNESS, which permitted animation of the simulations. The animated display was effective in showing company management the nature of the simulation. Two additional programs, written in C++, simplified the use of WITNESS considerably. These programs prepared inputs for WITNESS and analyzed the WITNESS output data. The extensive inputs required to represent the large number of different gear processing plans, that is, 50, and their flow allowances motivated the input program.

Prepare Input Data

An analysis of shop labor records, supplied by the manager of information systems, provided historical actual times to implement the process plans for the 50 gears. The study assumed that the coefficient of variation for setup and run times at a machine group was the same for all 50 gears. That is, the ratio between the standard deviation and the mean of a setup (run) time was a constant for a machine group. The estimation of these coefficients of variation used historical data.

Experimental Design

The primary objective of the first set of simulation experiments was to determine the effectiveness of buffers in limiting WIP without significantly reducing capacity. This set of experiments imposed no limit on job size. These experiments had four factors, that is, buffer configuration, flow allowance procedure, release schedule, and sequencing rule. Table 36.3 shows the levels of each factor. Each possible combination of the levels for each factor was simulated in the first set of experiments for a total of 72 simulation runs.

Stochastic simulations of this type present two experimental problems (Law and Kelton, 1991): that is, the initial condition effect and run length so that confidence intervals are sufficiently narrow. The release schedules applied over a 1-year period. Each simulation run consisted of 11 consecutive years by repeating the appropriate release schedule 11 times. Thus, the final simulation state at the end of December became the initial condition for the next January. The C++ postprocessor program deleted the first year to reduce the initial-condition effect. The analysis assumed that statistics for each subsequent year were independent and identically distributed, which is the batch means procedure. The postprocessor program employed these assumptions in calculating 90 percent confidence intervals, which were sufficiently narrow.

Based on results from the first set of experiments, the analysis identified a preferred buffer configuration, sequencing rule, and flow allowance procedure. Further simulation experiments investigated the upper limit on job size.

TABLE 36.3 Four-Factor Experiment

Factor	Levels
Buffer, configuration	Buffer size of 1 at each station
	Buffer size of 2 at each station
	Buffer size of 3 at each station
	CONWIP with WIP limited to x
	CONWIP with WIP limited by y
	No WIP control (unlimited buffer size)
Flow allowance	Current procedure
	Modified
Release schedule	RS1
	RS2
	RS3
Sequencing rule	FIFO
	EDD

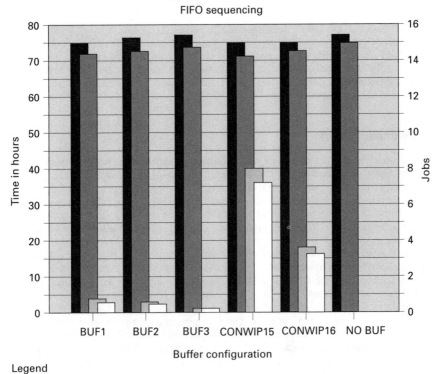

FIGURE 36.14 Throughput time and WIP.

Simulation Results

Figures 36.14 and 36.15 illustrate the results from the simulation experiments. In both figures, the use of buffers at each station dominates the CONWIP results. The system and WIP performance measures applied to the shop after leaving the backlog. Throughput time and WIP are less with a buffer size of 1 at each station. However, the total of backlog time and throughput time are slightly larger than the results with no buffers. Figure 36.15 clearly shows the superiority of the modified due-date procedure. Also, for the modified procedure, the tardiness results with no buffers. The manufacturer prefers a buffer size of 1 since:

- WIP is less, reducing costs, improving quality, and simplifying scheduling.
- Tardiness is lower.

Major Points Illustrated

The gear-manufacturing throughput time example illustrates the overall steps required to apply simulation to influence management decisions. An important milestone is to review the first five steps with all those concerned before collecting data and program-

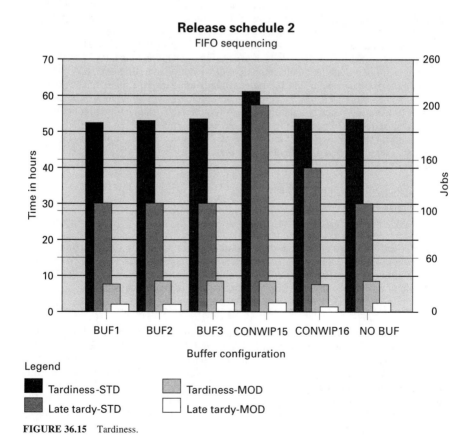

FIGURE 36.15   Tardiness.

ming the model. Then, affected individuals will feel they are a part of the study. Also, the simulation experimental results can address the study objectives and provide the proper outputs. The effort in programming the simulation is usually a small part of the overall study effort. Data collection can occupy a major part of the study effort.

SIMULATION-BASED SCHEDULER

FACTOR (Pritsker Corporation, 1989) is an example of a simulation-based scheduling system. A scheduler will use FACTOR in an on-line mode. That is, FACTOR will take inputs from an existing database and generate schedules after a short time delay such as a half-hour. The database will specify the status of all jobs and resources such as machines in the system and will process plans for these jobs, including standard setup and run times. For many applications, the principal output for the simulation is a schedule giving the times that jobs are processed by resources. Shop personnel can use this schedule to ensure that other resources such as tools are available when the schedule requires them. The schedule also identifies which jobs will probably be late.

The simulation can do what-if comparisons. As an example, the simulation may compare sequencing rules such as earliest due date and shortest processing time. The motivations for using simulation is that it automates the scheduling task and the simulation is capable of generating realistic schedules. The schedules are realistic in the sense that the simulation represents the finite capacity of resources in a detailed manner.

FACTOR has a completely deterministic simulation. That is, FACTOR does not sample from probability distributions in generating a schedule. Since the scheduler must generate a single schedule, a deterministic representation simplifies this task. Also, by accessing a database specifying the process plans and standard times for all jobs, the nature of each simulated task is known in more detail than simulating in a planning mode. For example, when simulating to identify preferred designs for a production line, the precise sequence of each job type may not be known.

Cheselka (1992) describes the use of FACTOR to schedule Timken's Gambrinus Thermal Treatment Facility. Scheduling that facility was challenging because the scheduler had to balance three conflicting objectives:

- Complete orders by their due date.
- Maximize furnace utilization.
- Minimize energy costs.

These objectives can conflict because maximizing utilization and minimizing energy costs would sequence jobs to avoid changes in furnace temperature and speed of materials-handling devices transporting jobs through the furnace. FACTOR uses a scheduling logic that first identifies the highest-priority jobs using critical slack:

Critical slack = firm plan date − current time − estimated processing time

If the critical slack for a job is less than 30 hours, then the job is considered critical. The system assigns a higher priority to critical jobs, and they are scheduled first. Within the same priority level, FACTOR will maximize furnace utilization by searching for a job that matches the current furnace setup after completing a job. The setup includes furnace temperature and speed of the materials-handling device. The timeliness of schedules depends on the ability to quickly obtain inputs from an existing database. At Timken, the data inputs to FACTOR include data from the following databases:

- The VAPP database supplies job due dates and current job work center locations.
- The RODS database supplies detailed order information such as product size and special processing data.
- The Heat Chemistry database supplies a heat chemistry analysis for each job.

CONCLUSIONS

The three examples summarized illustrate important applications of simulation in manufacturing. Simulation is a powerful approach to modeling manufacturing systems in that many complex and diverse systems can be represented. Simulation can predict system performance measures that are difficult to assess without a model. However, simulation requires data that characterize the behavior of system components. Also, individuals contemplating the use of simulation should use a structured process such as the one described in the section "Gear Manufacturing Throughput Time."

REFERENCES

Alexopoulos, C.: "Advanced Simulation Output Analysis for a Single System." In G. W. Evans, M. Mollaghasemi, E. C. Russell, and W. E. Biles (eds.): *Proceedings of the 1993 Winter Simulation Conference,* WSC Board of Directors, Washington, 1993, pp. 89–96.

AT&T Istel: *Witness System Manual,* AT&T Istel, Redditch Wores, UK (latest version).

Azadivar, F.: "A Tutorial on Simulation Optimization," In J. J. Swain, D. Goldsman, R. C. Crain, and J. R. Wilson (eds.): *Proceedings of the 1992 Winter Simulation Conference,* WSC Board of Directors, Washington, 1992, pp. 198–204.

Banks, Jerry, and John S. Carson, II: *Discrete-Event System Simulation.* Prentice-Hall, Englewood Cliffs, N.J., 1984.

Banks, J., B. Burnette, J. D. Rose, and H. Kozloski: *SIMAN V and CINEMA V,* Wiley, New York, 1995.

Barton, R. R.: "Metamodels for Simulation Input-Output Relations." In J. J. Swain, D. Goldsman, R. C. Crain, and J. R. Wilson (eds.): *Proceedings of the 1992 Winter Simulation Conference,* WSC Board of Directors, Washington, 1992, pp. 289–299.

Blaisdale, W. E., and J. Haddock: "Simulation Analysis Using SIMSTAT 2.0." In *Proceedings of the 1993 Winter Simulation Conference,* Los Angeles, Calif., 1993.

Blaisdell, W. E., and J. Haddock: "Simulation Analysis Using SIMSTAT 2.0." In G. W. Evans, M. Mollaghasemi, E. C. Russell, and W. E. Biles (eds.): *Proceedings of the 1993 Winter Simulation Conference,* Association for Computing Machinery, New York, 1993, pp. 213–217.

Bratley, P., B. L. Box, and L. E. Schrage: *A Guide to Simulation,* 2d ed. Springer-Verlag, New York, 1987.

CACI: *SIMFACTORY Introduction and User's Manual,* La Jolla, Calif. (latest version).

Charnes, J. M.: "Multivariate Simulation Output Analysis." In B. L. Nelson, W. D. Kelton, and G. M. Clark (eds.): *Proceedings of the 1991 Winter Simulation Conference,* WSC Board of Directors, Washington, 1991, pp. 187–193.

Charnes, J. M.: Statistical analysis of output processes. In G. W. Evans, M. Mollaghasemi, E. C. Russell, and W. E. Biles (eds.): *Proceedings of the 1993 Winter Simulation Conference,* WSC Board of Directors, Washington, 1993, pp. 41–49.

Cheselka, Michael C.: "The Timken Company's Gambrinus Thermal Treatment Facility Scheduling System." In J. J. Swain, D. Goldsman, R. C. Crain, and J. R. Wilson (eds.): *Proceedings of the 1992 Winter Simulation Conference,* Institute of Electrical and Electronics Engineers, San Francisco, Calif., 1992, pp. 833–841.

Clark, Gordon M., and Charles R. Cash: *Reduction of Gear Manufacturing Throughput Time: Rough Steel Cell Operating Policies,* Department of Industrial and Systems Engineering, The Ohio State University, Columbus, 1993.

Clementson, A. T.: *The ECSL Plus System Manual,* available from A. T. Clementson, The Chestnuts, Princess Road, Windermere, Cumbria, UK, 1991.

Collins, N., and C. M. Watson: "Introduction to ARENA." In G. W. Evans, M. Mollaghasemi, E. C. Russell, and W. E. Biles (eds.): *Proceedings of the 1993 Winter Simulation Conference,* Association for Computing Machinery, New York, 1993, pp. 205–212.

Conway, R., W. L. Maxwell, W. L. McClain, and S. L. Worona: *User's Guide to XCell Factory Modeling System,* Release 4.0 (3rd ed.), Scientific Press, San Francisco, 1990.

Cook, L. S.: "Factor Screening of Multiple Responses." In J. J. Swain, D. Goldsman, R. C. Crain, and J. R. Wilson (eds.): *Proceedings of the 1992 Winter Simulation Conference,* WSC Board of Directors, Washington, 1992, pp. 174–180.

Cox, S. W.: "GPSS World: A Brief Preview." In B. L. Nelson and G. M. Clark (eds.): *Proceedings of the 1992 Winter Simulation Conference,* Association for Computing Machinery, New York, 1991, pp. 59–61.

————: "Simulation Studio." In J. J. Swain, D. Goldsman, R. C. Crain, and J. R. Wilson (eds.): *Proceedings of the 1992 Winter Simulation Conference,* Association for Computing Machinery, New York, 1992, pp. 347–351.

Crookes, J. G.: "Simulation." In M. Pidd (eds.): *Computer Modeling for Discrete Simulation,* Wiley, Chichester, 1989.

Earle, N. J., and J. O. Henriksen: PROOF Animation: Better animation for your simulation. In G. W. Evans, M. Mollaghasemi, E. C. Russell, and W. E. Biles (eds.): *Proceedings of the 1992 Winter Simulation Conference,* Association for Computing Machinery, New York, 1993, pp. 172–178.

Fishman, G. S.: *Principles of Discrete Event Simulation,* Wiley, New York, 1978.

Forrester, J. S.: *Industrial Dynamics,* MIT Press, Cambridge, Mass., 1961.

Glasserman, P., and P. W. Glynn: "Gradient Estimation for Regenerative Processes." In J. J. Swain, D. Goldsman, R. C. Crain, and J. R. Wilson (eds.): *Proceedings of the 1992 Winter Simulation Conference,* WSC Board of Directors, Washington, 1992, pp. 280–288.

Glavach, M. A., and D. T. Sturrock: "Introduction to SIMAN/Cinema." In G. W. Evans, M. Mollaghasemi, E. C. Russell, and W. E. Biles (eds.): *Proceedings of the 1993 Winter Simulation Conference,* Association for Computing Machinery, New York, 1993, pp. 190–192.

Goble, J.: "Introduction to SIMFACTORY II.5." In B. L. Nelson, W. D. Kelton, and G. M. Clark (eds.): *Proceedings of the 1991 Winter Simulation Conference,* Association for Computing Machinery, New York, 1991, pp. 77–80.

Goldsman, D., B. L. Nelson, and B. Schmeiser: "Methods for Selecting the Best System." In B. L. Nelson, W. D. Kelton, and G. M. Clark (eds.): *Proceedings of the 1991 Winter Simulation Conference,* WSC Board of Directors, Washington, 1991, pp. 177–186.

Goldsman, D.: "Simulation Output Analysis." In J. J. Swain, D. Goldsman, R. C. Crain, and J. R. Wilson (eds.): *Proceedings of the 1992 Winter Simulation Conference,* WSC Board of Directors, Washington, 1992, pp. 97–103.

Grier, D. A.: "Graphical Techniques for Output Analysis." In J. J. Swain, D. Goldsman, R. C. Crain, and J. R. Wilson (eds.): *Proceedings of the 1992 Winter Simulation Conference,* WSC Board of Directors, Washington, 1992, pp. 314–319.

Harrell, C. R., and J. J. Leavy: "ProModel Tutorial." In *Proceedings of the 1993 Winter Simulation Conference,* Los Angeles, Calif., 1993.

Harrell, C. R., and J. J. Leavy: "ProModel Tutorial." In G. W. Evans, M. Mollaghasemi, E. C. Russell, and W. E. Biles (eds.): *Proceedings of the 1993 Winter Simulation Conference,* Association for Computing Machinery, New York, 1993, pp. 184–189.

Hillen, D. W., and D. Werner: "Taylor II Manufacturing Software." In G. W. Evans, M. Mollaghasemi, E. C. Russell, and W. E. Biles (eds.): *Proceedings of the 1993 Winter Simulation Conference,* Association for Computing Machinery, New York, 1993, pp. 276–280.

Ho, Y. C.: "Perturbation Analysis: Concepts and Algorithms." In J. J. Swain, D. Goldsman, R. C. Crain, and J. R. Wilson (eds.): *Proceedings of the 1992 Winter Simulation Conference,* WSC Board of Directors, Washington, 1992, pp. 231–240.

Hood, S. J., and P. D. Welch: "Experimental Design Issues in Simulation with Examples from Semiconductor Manufacturing." In J. J. Swain, D. Goldsman, R. C. Crain, and J. R. Wilson (eds.): *Proceedings of the 1992 Winter Simulation Conference,* WSC Board of Directors, Washington, 1992, pp. 255–263.

Hood, S. J., and P. D. Welch: "Response Surface Methodology and Its Application in Simulation." In G. W. Evans, M. Mollaghasemi, E. C. Russell, and W. E. Biles (eds.): *Proceedings of the 1993 Winter Simulation Conference,* WSC Board of Directors, 1992, pp. 115–122.

Joines, J. A., K. A. Powell, and S. D. Roberts: "Object-Oriented Modelling and Simulation in C." In *Proceedings of the 1992 Winter Simulation Conference,* Arlington, Va., 1992.

Khoshnevis, B.: *Discrete Systems Simulation,* McGraw-Hill, New York, 1994.

Kleijnen, J. P. C.: *Statistical Tools for Simulation Practitioners,* Marcel Dekker, New York, 1987.

Kleijnen, J. P. C., and W. van Groenendal: *Simulation: A Statistical Perspective,* Wiley, Chichester, 1992.

Kiviat, P. J., R. Villaneuva, and H. Markowitz: *The SIMSCRIPT II Programming Language,* Prentice-Hall, Englewood Cliffs, N.J., 1969.

Law, A. M., and W. D. Kelton: *Simulation Modeling and Analysis,* 2d ed., McGraw-Hill, New York, 1991.

Law, Averill M., and W. David Kelton: *Simulation Modelling and Analysis,* 2d ed., McGraw-Hill, New York, 1991.

L'Ecuyer, P.: "An Overview of Derivative Estimation." In B. L. Nelson, W. D. Kelton, and G. M. Clark (eds.): *Proceedings of the 1992 Winter Simulation Conference,* WSC Board of Directors, Washington, 1991, pp. 28–36.

Lewis, P. A. W., and E. J. Orav: *Simulation Methodology for Statisticians, Operations Analysis, and Engineers,* Vol. 1, Wadsworth, Belmont, Calif., 1989.

Lilegdon, W. R., Martin, D. L., and A. A. B. Pritsker: "FACTOR/AIM: A Manufacturing Simulation System." *Simulation* (62), 1994, pp. 367–372.

Miner, Robin J., and Laurie J. Rolston: *MAP/1 User's Manual,* Pritsker & Associates, West Lafayette, Ind., 1983.

Morgan, B. J. T.: *Elements of Simulation,* Chapman and Hall, London, 1984.

Musselman, Kenneth J.: "Conducting a Successful Simulation Project." In J. J. Swain, D. Goldsman, R. C. Crain, and J. R. Wilson (eds.): *Proceedings of the 1992 Winter Simulation Conference,* Washington, 1992, pp. 115–121.

————: "Guidelines for Simulation Project Success." In G. W. Evans, M. Mollaghasemi, E. G. Russell, and W. E. Biles (eds.): *Proceedings of the 1993 Winter Simulation Conference,* Los Angeles, 1993, pp. 58–64.

Naylor, T. H., J. L. Balintfy, D. S. Burdick, and K. Chu: *Computer Simulation Techniques,* Wiley, New York, 1966.

Nelson, B. L.: "Designing Efficient Simulation Experiments." In J. J. Swain, D. Goldsman, R. C. Crain, and J. R. Wilson (eds.): *Proceedings of the 1992 Winter Simulation Conference,* WSC Board of Directors, Washington, 1992, pp. 126–132.

Norman, V. B., and K. D. Farnsworth: "AutoMod." In G. W. Evans, M. Mollaghasemi, E. C. Russell, and W. E. Biles (eds.): *Proceedings of the 1993 Winter Simulation Conference,* Association for Computing Machinery, New York, 1993, pp. 249–254.

O'Reilly, J. J.: "Introduction to SLAM II and SLAMSYSTEM." In G. W. Evans, M. Mollaghasemi, E. C. Russell, and W. E. Biles (eds.): *Proceedings of the 1993 Winter Simulation Conference,* Association for Computing Machinery, New York, 1993, pp. 179–183.

Payne, James A.: *Introduction to Scheduling,* McGraw-Hill, New York, 1982.

Pidd, M.: *Computer Simulation in Management Science,* 2d ed., Wiley, Chichester, 1988.

————: "Simulation in Pascal." *Computer Modelling for Discrete Simulation,* edited by M. Pidd, Wiley, Chichester, 1989.

————: *Computer Simulation in Management Science,* 3rd ed., Wiley, Chichester, 1992.

————: "Object-Orientation and Three Phase Simulation." In *Proceedings of the 1992 Winter Simulation Conference,* Arlington, Va., 1992.

Pritsker, A. B.: *Introduction to Simulation and SLAM II,* 2d ed., Pritsker & Associates, West Lafayette, Ind., and Wiley, New York, 1984.

————: *Introduction to Simulation and SLAM II,* 3rd ed., Wiley, New York, 1986.

Pritsker, A. B., C. Elliott Sigal, and R. D. Jack Hammesfahr: *SLAM II Network Models for Decision Support,* Prentice-Hall, Englewood Cliffs, N.J., 1989.

Pritsker Corporation: *FACTOR Version 4.0 Implementation Guide,* Pritsker Corporation, Indianapolis, Ind., 1989.

————: *Simulation: A Decision Support Tool,* Pritsker Corporation, West Lafayette, Ind., 1993.

Ramberg, J. S., S. M. Sanchez, P. J. Sanchez, and L. J. Hollick: "Designing Simulation Experiments: Taguchi Methods and Response Surface Metamodels." In B. L. Nelson, W. D. Kelton, and G. M. Clark (eds.): *Proceedings of the 1991 Winter Simulation Conference,* WSC Board of Directors, 1991, pp. 167–176.

Richmond, B. M., and S. Peterson: *A User's Guide to STELLA,* High Performance Systems, Lyme, N.H., 1988.

Ripley, B. D.: *Stochastic Simulation,* Wiley, New York, 1987.

Russell, E. C.: "SIMSCRIPT II.5 and SIMGRAPHICS Tutorial." In G. W. Evans, M. Mollaghasemi, E. C. Russell, and W. E. Biles (eds.): *Proceedings of the 1993 Winter Simulation Conference,* Association for Computing Machinery, New York, 1993, pp. 223–227.

Schriber, T.: *Simulation Using GPSS,* Wiley, New York, 1974.

Schruben, L.: SIGNAL: *A Graphical Simulation System,* The Scientific Press, San Francisco, 1991.

Seila, A. F.: "Output Analysis for Simulation." In B. L. Nelson, W. D. Kelton, and G. M. Clark (eds.): *Proceedings of the 1991 Winter Simulation Conference,* WSC Board of Directors, Washington, 1991, pp. 28–36.

————: "Advanced Output Analysis for Simulation." In J. J. Swain, D. Goldsman, R. C. Crain, and J. R. Wilson (eds.): *Proceedings of the 1992 Winter Simulation Conference,* WSC Board of Directors, Washington, 1992, pp. 190–197.

Smith, D. S., and R. C. Crain: "Industrial Strength Simulation Using GPSS/H." In G. W. Evans, M. Mollaghasemi, E. C. Russell, and W. E. Biles (eds.): *Proceedings of the 1993 Winter Simulation Conference,* Association for Computing Machinery, New York, 1993, pp. 223–227.

Spearman, M. L., D. L. Woodruff, and W. J. Hopp: "CONWIP: A Pull Alternative to Kanbans," *International Journal of Production Research* (22), 1990, pp. 879–894.

Standridge, Charles R., et al.: *TESS User's Manual,* Pritsker & Associates, West Lafayette, Ind., 1984.

Strickland, S. G.: "Gradient/Sensitive Estimation in Discrete-Event Simulation." In G. W. Evans, M. Mollaghasemi, E. C. Russell, and W. E. Biles (eds.): *Proceedings of the 1993 Winter Simulation Conference,* WSC Board of Directors, Washington, 1993, pp. 97–105.

Szymankiewicz, J., J. McDonald, and K. Turner: *Solving Business Problems by Simulation,* McGraw-Hill, Maidenhead, 1988.

Thompson, W. B.: "A Tutorial for Modelling with the WITNESS Visual Interactive Simulator." In G. W. Evans, M. M. Mollaghasemi, E. C. Russell, and W. E. Biles (eds.): *Proceedings of the 1993 Winter Simulation Conference,* Association for Computing Machinery, New York, 1993, pp. 159–164.

Thesen, A., and L. E. Travis: *Simulation for Decision Making.* West Publishing Company, St. Paul, Minn., 1992.

Vincent, S. G., and A. M. Law: "UniFitII: Total Support for Simulation Input Modelling." In *Proceedings of the 1993 Winter Simulation Conference,* Los Angeles, Calif., 1993.

Vincent, S. G., and A. M. Law: "Unifit II: Total Support for Simulation Input Modelling." In G. W. Evans, M. Mollaghasemi, E. C. Russell, and W. E. Biles (eds.): *Proceedings of the 1993 Winter Simulation Conference,* Association for Computing Machinery, New York, 1993, pp. 199–204.

Wolstenholme, E. S.: *System Enquiry: A System Dynamics Approach,* Wiley, Chichester, 1990.

Zeigler, B. P.: *Theory of Modelling and Simulation,* Wiley Interscience, New York, 1976.

————: *Multifaceted Modelling and Discrete Event Simulation,* Academic Press, New York, 1984.

————: *The GASP IV Simulation Language,* Wiley, New York, 1974.

————: *Modeling and Analysis Using Q-GERT Networks,* Halstead Press, New York, and Pritsker & Associates, West Lafayette, Ind., 1977.

SECTION 9

CERTIFICATION

Chapter 37. APICS Certification Programs

CHAPTER 37
APICS CERTIFICATION PROGRAMS

Editor
Thomas R. Hoffman, Ph.D., CFPIM
Carlson School of Management
University of Minnesota, Minneapolis, Minnesota

APICS offers two comprehensive educational programs to help resource management professionals meet the changing needs of business. Both programs allow people to work at their own pace and within their own schedule. While the programs both culminate in certification, their true purpose is to provide the opportunity for professional growth and self-assessment.

The *Certified in Production and Inventory Management* (CPIM) *program* develops "vertical," in-depth capabilities throughout every aspect of production and inventory management. The *Certified in Integrated Resource Management* (CIRM) *program* expands management capabilities by providing a "horizontal," generalist business education by improving the understanding of the interrelationships of all the different business functions.

DESCRIPTION OF THE PROGRAMS

Because the two programs are completely separate, a person does not need to be certified in one before starting the other. The choice will depend on the nature of each individual's experience, the knowledge he or she has already acquired, and his or her goals for the future. The CPIM program prepares a person for specialized, functional management in production and inventory management; CIRM prepares one for a management role that involves interaction with other functional areas.

The CPIM Program

Introduced in 1973, the Certified in Production and Inventory Management program is recognized internationally for its value to corporations and employees. The program is designed to develop specialized knowledge in the very latest production and inventory management techniques and trends, including production planning, materials and capacity requirements planning, just-in-time, and systems and technologies.

The CIRM Program

The Certified in Integrated Resource Management program is designed to transform professionals from functional specialists into organization leaders. The program develops an understanding of multiple business functions and how they affect each other. Furthermore, people from varied disciplines learn to work together to establish and achieve common goals. The result: highly valued leaders who have a comprehensive view of the entire enterprise and are comfortable within the kind of team-based, cross-functional approach being adopted by a growing number of progressive, competitive organizations worldwide.

After successful completion of an entire CPIM or CIRM program, a person will be awarded certification by APICS. Upon achieving certification, a person is entitled to use the initials CPIM or CIRM after his or her name. He or she also receives a certificate to signify the achievement. Even more meaningful, though, is the reward of increased capability and knowledge that leads to professional growth throughout one's career.

PREPARING FOR CERTIFICATION

APICS certification programs are divided into several study units, or modules, each concentrating on a specific subject area. At their own pace, individuals can expand their knowledge of each area by referring to books, study guides, and other materials available through APICS, as well as participating in chapter-sponsored courses and workshops. The broader their exposure to professional education sources, the more effective their professional performance will be. They can use as many or as few resources as needed to build knowledge to certification levels. Obviously, more preparation will be needed for those subject areas that are less familiar. The focus—and the value—of CPIM and CIRM is not on passing a particular examination but on expanding expertise and growing professionally.

Competence in each module topic is tested through the APICS examinations. The tests are administered by the *Educational Testing Service* (ETS) at more than 200 test sites around the world. CPIM and CIRM examinations are administered throughout the year. CPIM certification is awarded after successful completion of six examinations. CIRM certification is awarded after successful completion of a different set of five examinations.

The amount of time required to become certified depends upon a person's knowledge and experience. There is no ceiling on the amount of time taken between study modules. Many participants in the CPIM program do, however, take between 1 and 2 years to become certified.

The Cost of Certification

The total cost of certification varies for each participant. There is a base cost for each CPIM and CIRM module examination, and study materials and workshops are priced separately. Many employers, recognizing the value of a more knowledgeable and capable workforce, *do* pay for APICS certification. Some firms may pay for workshops, others may already have invested in APICS reference materials for the corporate library, and others may pay for certification examinations.

In 1994, approximately 60,000 CPIM examinations were given. Approximately 1000 colleges and universities may recommend college credits for the successful completion of CPIM exams.

Demographics of Candidates

The work experience and education levels of persons who took recent exams are shown in Tables 37.1 and 37.2. For CPIM test takers, 45 to 50 percent have 10 or more years of experience while for CIRM, Tables 37.3 and 37.4, the figures are 60 to 80 percent. Approximately 65 percent of the CPIM test takers and over 80 percent of the CIRM test takers are college graduates.

TABLE 37.1 Number of Years of Work Experience in Industry for CPIM Candidates

figures in percent of candidates taking examination

Responses	Inventory management	JIT	Master planning	PAC	M&CRP	Systems and technology
None	2.4	2.8	3.2	1.3	3.1	1.1
0 to 1.99 years	10.5	9.6	9.5	7.5	11.5	6.7
2 to 5.99 years	25.6	24.2	23.3	23.9	25.2	23.9
6 to 9.99 years	17.2	17.9	18.7	20.2	17.6	18.6
10 or more years	44.2	45.5	45.3	47.0	42.6	49.8

TABLE 37.2 Highest Level of Education Reached for CPIM Candidates

figures in percent of candidates taking examination

Responses	Inventory management	JIT	Master planning	PAC	M&CRP	Systems and technology
Some high school	0.6	0.7	0.4	1.0	0.8	0.5
High school graduate	8.1	9.0	7.9	10.0	8.4	6.3
Some postsecondary education	24.8	24.9	25.2	23.5	25.8	24.4
College graduate	41.5	41.6	40.8	38.8	39.9	39.4
Some graduate work	9.1	8.8	9.5	8.8	9.5	10.8
Master's degree	13.7	12.8	13.8	15.3	13.2	15.0
Graduate work beyond MS	1.7	1.6	1.7	2.2	1.7	3.2
Doctorate	0.5	0.5	0.8	0.4	0.7	0.4

TABLE 37.3 Number of Years of Work Experience in Industry for CIRM Candidates

figures in percent of candidates taking examination

Responses	Logistics	Customers and products	Support functions	Manufacturing processes	Integrated enterprise management
None	0.0	0.9	0.5	0.8	0.0
0 to 1.99 years	1.8	2.2	1.6	1.3	0.4
2 to 5.99 years	16.3	15.4	13.2	15.5	9.0
6 to 9.99 years	20.9	17.6	16.2	18.5	11.6
10 or more years	61.0	63.8	68.6	63.9	79.0

TABLE 37.4 Highest Level of Education Reached for CIRM Candidates

figures in percent of candidates taking examination

Responses	Logistics	Customers and products	Support functions	Manufacturing processes	Integrated enterprise management
High school graduate	3.1	3.8	0.9	1.9	0.0
Some postsecondary education	15.5	13.1	13.5	13.3	12.2
College graduate	37.6	41.1	39.9	38.5	25.8
Some graduate work	14.1	11.9	15.5	17.2	16.7
Master's degree	26.1	25.8	23.7	22.4	35.8
Graduate work beyond MS	2.7	3.4	5.8	5.4	7.6
Doctorate	1.0	0.9	0.7	1.3	1.9

CPIM CURRICULUM

The CPIM curriculum is divided into six complementary modules. Certification is awarded upon successful completion of six examinations, one in each field. Certification in production and inventory management confirms the understanding of the design, operation, and control of systems for the manufacture and distribution of products and services.

Inventory Management Module

Objectives and Policies

Objectives and performance measures of inventory management

Functions of inventory

Factors affecting inventory

Categories of inventory

Inventory Systems

Independent-demand systems

Dependent-demand systems

Environmental factors

Subsystem factors

Information system considerations

Techniques

Aggregate methods

Multi-item methods

Item-level management

Inventory accounting

Physical control

Strategies and choices

Distribution Inventory Planning and Control

Management considerations

Techniques

Transportation and physical distribution

Just-in-time distribution

Distribution network structure

Just-in-Time Module

Concepts

Objectives

Principles

Scope

Human Resources

Development and involvement
Flexibility
Compensation
Changing responsibilities within the organization
Relationships
Motivation
Education

Total Quality Control

Basic concepts
Problem selection
Determining root cause
Eliminating root cause

Techniques

Pull signals
Production considerations
Materials logistics
Planning and scheduling
Transaction paperwork reduction

Integration and Application

Finance
Engineering
External customer relationships or partnerships
External supplier relationships or partnerships

Implementation Considerations Unique to JIT

Justification and commitment
Determining what to do
Managing change
Performance indicators
Implementation phases

Master Planning Module

Forecasting

Concepts
Management considerations
Data sources and requirements
Techniques
Forecast accuracy

Order Servicing

Concepts and management considerations
Data sources and requirements
Available to promise
Customer communications
Monitoring the customer service policy

Production Planning

Concepts
Management considerations
Data sources and requirements
Developing, validating, and maintaining the production plan

Master Scheduling

Concepts
Management considerations
Data sources and requirements
Developing the master production schedule and rough-cut capacity plan
Developing the final schedule
Managing the master production schedule

Materials and Capacity Requirements Planning Module

Concepts

MRP
CRP
Factors affecting both CRP and MRP

Data Sources and Requirements

Bill of materials
Routing
Work center data
Inventory data
Item master data
Order file data
Master production data

Materials Requirements Planning

Characteristics
Mechanics
Using MRP
Performance measurements

Capacity Requirements Planning

Characteristics
Mechanics
Using CRP

Production Activity Control (PAC) Module

Scope

Objectives of PAC
Production environment
PAC relationships

Capacity Control

Determining capacity
Input-output control
Production leveling
Line balancing and flow balancing

Priority Control

Scheduling techniques
Production authorization and release

Lead Time Management

Elements of lead time
Factors affecting lead time
Lead time control

Supplier Interfaces

Relationships
Scheduling and control

Reporting and Measurement

Data sources and requirements
Production reporting
Measurements

Systems and Technologies Module

Strategic Drivers That Affect Production and Inventory Management

Competitive advantage and market planning
Product volume and variety issues

Choices Affecting Production and Inventory Management

Facilities

Factory layout and manufacturing technology choices

Strategies for changing capacity

Supply chain structure

Quality choices

Information technology

Organization choices and people issues

Configuring and Integrating Production and Inventory Management Functions

Business and priority planning processes

Capacity-planning processes

Product-planning and design processes

Supply-chain management

Cost accounting processes

Inventory-planning and control processes

Managing the Implementation of Systems and Technologies

Project evaluation and justification

Change management

Project management

Project planning and control

Measuring Organization Performance

Fundamental measurement concepts

Aggregate productivity measurement

Product cost measurement

Quality measurement

Delivery speed measurement

Delivery reliability measurement

Flexibility measurement

CPIM EDUCATION SUPPORT

The educational benefits of preparing for CPIM examinations are as important as the achievement of certification. To facilitate thorough study, APICS has developed a wide variety of materials and options:

APICS Handbook

A study guide outlining the curriculum of each module and suggested reference resources for further study

The *APICS Dictionary*

Reprints of articles on module study areas

Reprints of *Harvard Business Review* articles on some topical areas

Reference books on specific module topics

Workshops

Materials for in-house CPIM educational programs, including student guides and instructor guides for each module

Sample tests for CPIM modules

Chapter educational programs and networks

THE CIRM PROGRAM

Industry recognizes the need for workers with both a greater depth of skill *and* a greater breadth of knowledge. Only by emerging from their silos of functional expertise and acquiring a broader-based understanding of business can managers keep up with today's ever-changing technology and customer needs. They must provide the cross-functional abilities demanded by streamlined organizations in order to succeed in an era of integrated manufacturing structures. Certified in Integrated Resource Management is an educational and self-assessment process developed by APICS to help managers expand their capabilities and enhance their flexibility and performance. The process explores 13 different business functions at work in a manufacturing enterprise and how they interact with each other. It provides managers with the knowledge and skills required to assume a greater diversity of responsibilities, to make better-informed decisions, and to implement those decisions expertly—on their own and as part of a team. Ultimately, the CIRM process results in professionals who can positively influence and efficiently manage the many ongoing changes.

Profile of Candidates for CIRM

CIRM is oriented toward practicing project managers and team leaders and aspiring managers, operations staff, and consultants—virtually every professional who currently is in or is being developed for a decision-making position. This includes employees involved in the enterprise who would benefit from an understanding of other business functions such as management information systems, human resources, finance, marketing, engineering, and production.

CIRM Curriculum

The CIRM process is divided into five curriculum modules; each concludes with an examination. The first four components cover the scope of various functions and their interdependencies within an enterprise, while the fifth module unites the enterprise and addresses the strategy it employs.

The Customers and Products Module.   This module relates to the design, marketing, and service of a product, beginning with the recognition of a need and assurance that customers receive full value from the product throughout its life cycle. This module contains four major topics: marketing and sales, field service, product design and development, and their relationships.

The Logistics Module. This module represents the market-driven activities necessary to plan and procure materials, control manufacturing, and distribute products to customers throughout the supply chain. This module addresses production and inventory control, procurement, distribution, and the relationships among these areas.

The Manufacturing Processes Module. This module examines the methods companies use in process design, production, and facilities management. Manufacturing processes provide the execution components to the other activities of an integrated manufacturing system. The manufacturing processes module draws on four different but very interrelated subsystems: industrial facilities management, process design and development, manufacturing, and their relationships.

The Support Functions Module. This module covers the broader activities an organization undertakes to assist its own internal departments. While these activities usually do not directly create a product or bring revenues into the organization, they support those functions that do. This module covers total quality management, human resources, finance and accounting, and information systems.

The Integrated-Enterprise Management Module. This module provides a holistic view of the business enterprise. The module builds on the knowledge acquired from the first four CIRM modules and on the interactions among all the disciplines in the business environment. It also includes the interplay of personal and interpersonal skills required for effective team interaction. The module emphasizes implementing strategic business decisions, plans, and measurement systems that are consistent with the enterprise's mission and vision and stresses the integration of the collective knowledge and skills needed for an effective and profitable organization. High levels of customer service through an environment of continuous improvement are paramount.

Content Organization

The body of knowledge for each functional area is organized into five major topics:

Objectives. The conceptual nature of the area

Strategic issues. Ways in which the objectives are pursued

Functional responsibilities. Tactics for dealing with the strategic issues

Directions. Leading-edge issues and activities

Performance measures. How the function is evaluated

The Integrated Enterprise Management examination differs from the rest of the CPIM and CIRM exams in that two-thirds of it is in the form of case analysis and open-ended response instead of the traditional multiple-choice format questions.

CIRM Education Support

The most important end product of the CIRM process is the learning that occurs while participants are preparing for the CIRM examinations. APICS facilitates this education by developing study materials and making them available to companies and candidates:

The APICS Handbook

A study guide outlining coverage of each module and suggesting reference resources for further study

The *APICS Dictionary*

Reprints of articles on module study areas

Reprints of *Harvard Business Review* articles on topical areas

Reference books on specific module topics

Workshops

Materials for in-house CIRM educational programs, including student guides and instructor guides for each module

Chapter educational programs and networks

The APICS offers CIRM examinations that are administered by the ETS several times per year at numerous locations throughout the world.

Further Information

Although the preceding describes the APICS certification programs as of the present, the programs continue to evolve as the body of knowledge changes. For current information, write to or phone the APICS at 500 Annandale Road, Falls Church, Virginia 22046-4274 or call 800-444-2742.

APPENDIX

TABLE A.1 Greek Alphabet

A α	alpha		N ν	nu
B ß	beta		Ξ ξ	xi
Γ γ	gamma		O o	omicron
Δ δ	delta		Π π	pi
E ε	epsilon		P ρ	rho
Z ζ	zeta		Σ σ	sigma
H η	eta		T τ	tau
Θ θ	theta		Υ υ	upsilon
I ι	iota		Φ φ	phi
K κ	kappa		X χ	chi
Λ λ	lambda		Ψ ψ	psi
M μ	mu		Ω ω	omega

TABLE A.2 Normal Distribution

This table gives the area α under the standard normal curve from z_α to $+\infty$.

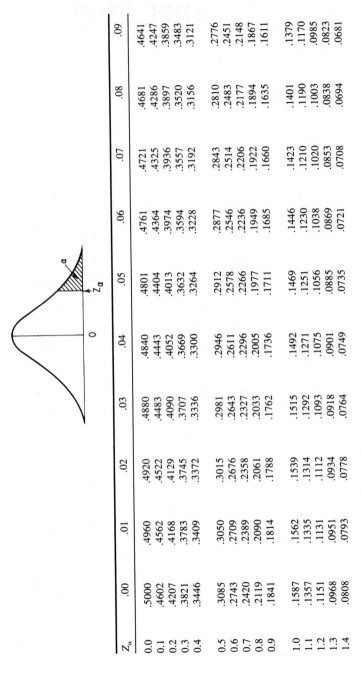

Z_α	.00	.01	.02	.03	.04	.05	.06	.07	.08	.09
0.0	.5000	.4960	.4920	.4880	.4840	.4801	.4761	.4721	.4681	.4641
0.1	.4602	.4562	.4522	.4483	.4443	.4404	.4364	.4325	.4286	.4247
0.2	.4207	.4168	.4129	.4090	.4052	.4013	.3974	.3936	.3897	.3859
0.3	.3821	.3783	.3745	.3707	.3669	.3632	.3594	.3557	.3520	.3483
0.4	.3446	.3409	.3372	.3336	.3300	.3264	.3228	.3192	.3156	.3121
0.5	.3085	.3050	.3015	.2981	.2946	.2912	.2877	.2843	.2810	.2776
0.6	.2743	.2709	.2676	.2643	.2611	.2578	.2546	.2514	.2483	.2451
0.7	.2420	.2389	.2358	.2327	.2296	.2266	.2236	.2206	.2177	.2148
0.8	.2119	.2090	.2061	.2033	.2005	.1977	.1949	.1922	.1894	.1867
0.9	.1841	.1814	.1788	.1762	.1736	.1711	.1685	.1660	.1635	.1611
1.0	.1587	.1562	.1539	.1515	.1492	.1469	.1446	.1423	.1401	.1379
1.1	.1357	.1335	.1314	.1292	.1271	.1251	.1230	.1210	.1190	.1170
1.2	.1151	.1131	.1112	.1093	.1075	.1056	.1038	.1020	.1003	.0985
1.3	.0968	.0951	.0934	.0918	.0901	.0885	.0869	.0853	.0838	.0823
1.4	.0808	.0793	.0778	.0764	.0749	.0735	.0721	.0708	.0694	.0681

Z_a	.0	.1	.2	.3	.4	.5	.6	.7	.8	.9
1.5	.0668	.0655	.0643	.0630	.0618	.0606	.0594	.0582	.0571	.0559
1.6	.0548	.0537	.0526	.0516	.0505	.0495	.0485	.0475	.0465	.0455
1.7	.0446	.0436	.0427	.0418	.0409	.0401	.0392	.0384	.0375	.0367
1.8	.0359	.0351	.0344	.0336	.0329	.0322	.0314	.0307	.0301	.0294
1.9	.0287	.0281	.0274	.0268	.0262	.0256	.0250	.0244	.0239	.0233
2.0	.0228	.0222	.0217	.0212	.0207	.0202	.0197	.0192	.0188	.0183
2.1	.0179	.0174	.0170	.0166	.0162	.0158	.0154	.0150	.0146	.0143
2.2	.0139	.0136	.0132	.0129	.0125	.0122	.0119	.0116	.0113	.0110
2.3	.0107	.0104	.0102	.00990	.00964	.00939	.00914	.00889	.00866	.00842
2.4	.00820	.00798	.00776	.00755	.00734	.00714	.00695	.00676	.00657	.00639
2.5	.00621	.00604	.00587	.00570	.00554	.00539	.00523	.00508	.00494	.00480
2.6	.00466	.00453	.00440	.00427	.00415	.00402	.00391	.00379	.00368	.00357
2.7	.00347	.00336	.00326	.00317	.00307	.00298	.00289	.00280	.00272	.00264
2.8	.00256	.00248	.00240	.00233	.00226	.00219	.00212	.00205	.00199	.00193
2.9	.00187	.00181	.00175	.00169	.00164	.00159	.00154	.00149	.00144	.00139
3	.00135	$.0^3968$	$.0^3687$	$.0^3483$	$.0^4337$	$.0^3233$	$.0^3159$	$.0^3108$	$.0^3723$	$.0^4481$
4	$.0^4317$	$.0^4207$	$.0^4133$	$.0^5854$	$.0^5541$	$.0^5340$	$.0^5211$	$.0^6130$	$.0^6793$	$.0^6479$
5	$.0^6287$	$.0^6170$	$.0^7996$	$.0^7579$	$.0^7333$	$.0^7190$	$.0^7107$	$.0^8599$	$.0^8332$	$.0^8182$
6	$.0^9987$	$.0^9530$	$.0^9282$	$.0^9149$	$.0^{10}777$	$.0^{10}402$	$.0^{10}206$	$.0^{10}104$	$.0^{11}523$	$.0^{11}260$

SOURCE: Reproduced by consent of publisher from Frederick E. Croxton, *Elementary Statistics with Applications in Medicine*, Prentice-Hall, Englewood Cliffs, N.J., 1953, p. 323.

A.3

TABLE A.3 *t Distribution*

This table gives specified values of t for d degrees of freedom and a one-tail area of α.

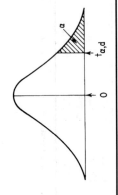

Value of α

d	.40	.30	.20	.10	.05	.025	.01	.005	.001	.0005
1	.325	.727	1.376	3.078	6.314	12.71	31.82	63.66	318.3	636.6
2	.289	.617	1.061	1.886	2.920	4.303	6.965	9.925	22.33	31.60
3	.277	.584	.978	1.638	2.353	3.182	4.541	5.841	10.22	12.94
4	.271	.569	.941	1.533	2.132	2.776	3.747	4.604	7.173	8.610
5	.267	.559	.920	1.476	2.015	2.571	3.365	4.032	5.893	6.859
6	.265	.553	.906	1.440	1.943	2.447	3.143	3.707	5.208	5.959
7	.263	.549	.896	1.415	1.895	2.365	2.998	3.499	4.785	5.405
8	.262	.546	.889	1.397	1.860	2.306	2.896	3.355	4.501	5.041
9	.261	.543	.883	1.383	1.833	2.262	2.821	3.250	4.297	4.781
10	.260	.542	.879	1.372	1.812	2.228	2.764	3.169	4.144	4.587
11	.260	.540	.876	1.363	1.796	2.201	2.718	3.106	4.025	4.437
12	.259	.539	.873	1.356	1.782	2.179	2.681	3.055	3.930	4.318
13	.259	.538	.870	1.350	1.771	2.160	2.650	3.012	3.852	4.221
14	.258	.537	.868	1.345	1.761	2.145	2.624	2.977	3.787	4.140

15	.258	.536	.866	1.341	1.753	2.131	2.602	2.947	3.733	4.073
16	.258	.535	.865	1.337	1.746	2.120	2.583	2.921	3.686	4.015
17	.257	.534	.863	1.333	1.740	2.110	2.567	2.898	3.646	3.965
18	.257	.534	.862	1.330	1.734	2.101	2.552	2.878	3.611	3.922
19	.257	.533	.861	1.328	1.729	2.093	2.539	2.861	3.579	3.883
20	.257	.533	.860	1.325	1.725	2.086	2.528	2.845	3.552	3.850
21	.257	.532	.859	1.323	1.721	2.080	2.518	2.831	3.527	3.819
22	.256	.532	.858	1.321	1.717	2.074	2.508	2.819	3.505	3.792
23	.256	.532	.858	1.319	1.714	2.069	2.500	2.807	3.485	3.767
24	.256	.531	.857	1.318	1.711	2.064	2.492	2.797	3.467	3.745
25	.256	.531	.856	1.316	1.708	2.060	2.485	2.787	3.450	3.725
26	.256	.531	.856	1.315	1.706	2.056	2.479	2.779	3.435	3.707
27	.256	.531	.855	1.314	1.703	2.052	2.473	2.771	3.421	3.690
28	.256	.530	.855	1.313	1.701	2.048	2.467	2.763	3.408	3.674
29	.256	.530	.854	1.311	1.699	2.045	2.462	2.756	3.396	3.659
30	.256	.530	.854	1.310	1.697	2.042	2.457	2.750	3.385	3.646
40	.255	.529	.851	1.303	1.684	2.021	2.423	2.704	3.307	3.551
50	.255	.528	.849	1.298	1.676	2.009	2.403	2.678	3.262	3.495
60	.254	.527	.848	1.296	1.671	2.000	2.390	2.660	3.232	3.460
80	.254	.527	.846	1.292	1.664	1.990	2.374	2.639	3.195	3.415
100	.254	.526	.845	1.290	1.660	1.984	2.365	2.626	3.174	3.389
200	.254	.525	.843	1.286	1.653	1.972	2.345	2.601	3.131	3.339
500	.253	.525	.842	1.283	1.648	1.965	2.334	2.586	3.106	3.310
∞	.253	.524	.842	1.282	1.645	1.960	2.326	2.576	3.090	3.291

SOURCE: Reproduced by consent of publisher from A. Hald, *Statistical Tables and Formulas*, Wiley, New York, 1952, p. 39.

A.5

TABLE A.4 Chi-Square Distribution

This table gives specified value of χ_α^2 for d degrees of freedom and a tail area of α.

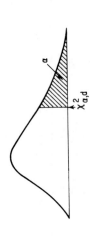

α

$\chi_{\alpha,d}^2$

					Value of α					
d	.995	.99	.98	.975	.95	.90	.80	.75	.70	.50
1	$.0^5393$	$.0^4157$	$.0^3628$	$.0^4982$	$.0^3393$	.0158	.0642	.102	.148	.455
2	.0100	.0201	.0404	.0506	.103	.211	.446	.575	.713	1.386
3	.0717	.115	.185	.216	.352	.584	1.005	1.213	1.424	2.366
4	.207	.297	.429	.484	.711	1.064	1.649	1.923	2.195	3.357
5	.412	.554	.752	.831	1.145	1.610	2.343	2.675	3.000	4.351
6	.676	.872	1.134	1.237	1.635	2.204	3.070	3.455	3.828	5.348
7	.989	1.239	1.564	1.690	2.167	2.833	3.822	4.255	4.671	6.346
8	1.344	1.646	2.032	2.180	2.733	3.490	4.594	5.071	5.527	7.344
9	1.735	2.088	2.532	2.700	3.325	4.168	5.380	5.899	6.393	8.343
10	2.156	2.558	3.059	3.247	3.940	4.865	6.179	6.737	7.267	9.342
11	2.603	3.053	3.609	3.816	4.575	5.578	6.989	7.584	8.148	10.341
12	3.074	3.571	4.178	4.404	5.226	6.304	7.807	8.438	9.034	11.340
13	3.565	4.107	4.765	5.009	5.892	7.042	8.634	9.299	9.926	12.340
14	4.075	4.660	5.368	5.629	6.571	7.790	9.467	10.165	10.821	13.339
15	4.601	5.229	5.985	6.262	7.261	8.547	10.307	11.036	11.721	14.339
16	5.142	5.812	6.614	6.908	7.962	9.312	11.152	11.912	12.624	15.338
17	5.697	6.408	7.255	7.564	8.672	10.085	12.002	12.792	13.531	16.338
18	6.265	7.015	7.906	8.231	9.390	10.865	12.857	13.675	14.440	17.338
19	6.844	7.633	8.567	8.907	10.117	11.651	13.716	14.562	15.352	18.338
20	7.434	8.260	9.237	9.591	10.851	12.443	14.578	15.452	16.266	19.337
21	8.034	8.897	9.915	10.283	11.591	13.240	15.445	16.344	17.182	20.337
22	8.643	9.542	10.600	10.982	12.338	14.041	16.314	17.240	18.101	21.337
23	9.260	10.196	11.293	11.688	13.091	14.848	17.187	18.137	19.021	22.337
24	9.886	10.856	11.992	12.401	13.848	15.659	18.062	19.037	19.943	23.337
25	10.520	11.524	12.697	13.120	14.611	16.473	18.940	19.939	20.867	24.337

Table continued from previous page (d = 26–30)

d	.001	.005	.01	.02	.025	.05	.10	.20	.25	.30
26	25.336	21.792	20.843	19.820	17.292	15.379	13.844	13.409	12.198	11.160
27	26.336	22.719	21.749	20.703	18.114	16.151	14.573	14.125	12.879	11.808
28	27.336	23.647	22.657	21.588	18.939	16.928	15.308	14.847	13.565	12.461
29	28.336	24.577	23.567	22.475	19.768	17.708	16.047	15.574	14.256	13.121
30	29.336	25.508	24.478	23.364	20.599	18.493	16.791	16.306	14.953	13.787

Value of α

d	.30	.25	.20	.10	.05	.025	.02	.01	.005	.001
1	1.074	1.323	1.642	2.706	3.841	5.024	5.412	6.635	7.879	10.827
2	2.408	2.773	3.219	4.605	5.991	7.378	7.824	9.210	10.597	13.815
3	3.665	4.108	4.642	6.251	7.815	9.348	9.837	11.345	12.838	16.268
4	4.878	5.385	5.989	7.779	9.488	11.143	11.668	13.277	14.860	18.465
5	6.064	6.626	7.289	9.236	11.070	12.832	13.388	15.086	16.750	20.517
6	7.231	7.841	8.558	10.645	12.592	14.449	15.033	16.812	18.548	22.457
7	8.383	9.037	9.803	12.017	14.067	16.013	16.622	18.475	20.278	24.322
8	9.524	10.219	11.030	13.362	15.507	17.535	18.168	20.090	21.955	26.125
9	10.656	11.389	12.242	14.684	16.919	19.023	19.679	21.666	23.589	27.877
10	11.781	12.549	13.442	15.987	18.307	20.483	21.161	23.209	25.188	29.588
11	12.899	13.701	14.631	17.275	19.975	21.920	22.618	24.725	26.757	31.264
12	14.011	14.845	15.812	18.549	21.026	23.337	24.054	26.217	28.300	32.909
13	15.119	15.984	16.985	19.812	22.362	24.736	25.472	27.688	29.819	34.528
14	16.222	17.117	18.151	21.064	23.685	26.119	26.873	29.141	31.319	36.123
15	17.322	18.245	19.311	22.307	24.996	27.488	28.259	30.578	32.801	37.697
16	18.418	19.369	20.465	23.542	26.296	28.845	29.633	32.000	34.267	39.252
17	19.511	20.489	21.615	24.769	27.587	30.191	30.995	33.409	35.718	40.790
18	20.601	21.605	22.760	25.989	28.869	31.526	32.346	34.805	37.156	42.312
19	21.689	22.718	23.900	27.204	30.144	32.852	33.687	36.191	38.582	43.820
20	22.775	23.828	25.038	28.412	31.410	34.170	35.020	37.566	39.997	45.315
21	23.858	24.935	26.171	29.615	32.671	35.479	36.343	38.932	41.401	46.797
22	24.939	26.039	27.301	30.813	33.924	36.781	37.659	40.289	42.796	48.268
23	26.018	27.141	28.429	32.007	35.172	38.076	38.968	41.638	44.181	49.728
24	27.096	28.241	29.553	33.196	36.415	39.364	40.270	42.980	45.558	51.179
25	28.172	29.339	30.675	34.382	37.652	40.646	41.566	44.314	46.928	52.620
26	29.246	30.434	31.795	35.563	38.885	41.923	42.856	45.642	48.290	54.052
27	30.319	31.528	32.912	36.741	40.113	43.194	44.140	46.963	49.645	55.476
28	31.391	32.620	34.027	37.916	41.337	44.461	45.419	48.278	50.993	56.893
29	32.461	33.711	35.139	39.087	42.557	45.722	46.693	49.588	52.336	58.302
30	33.530	34.800	36.250	40.256	43.773	46.979	47.962	50.892	53.672	59.703

Reproduced by consent of publisher from Frederick E. Croxton, *Elementary Statistics with Applications in Medicine*, Prentice-Hall, Englewood Cliffs, N.J., 1953, pp. 328–329.

TABLE A.5 Table of Random Digits

2380	4072	3008	1403	1341	5417	0429	2183
1100	0011	0163	0876	3790	4854	5012	6793
3056	4643	0353	0324	8766	9682	9196	5561
3596	3171	6664	1438	8653	8974	5965	5347
7054	0858	1663	2252	8541	0973	8965	2839
0932	5976	7465	1000	8810	3864	3891	7094
2586	2239	156	0779	3270	2610	6227	7875
3300	1457	9042	1136	5435	2379	5360	2489
7794	6527	9013	5338	0907	7399	6226	0850
7761	6076	6604	4934	0167	6590	8035	8335
9340	7971	3762	0827	1103	9175	5124	2922
3617	3321	7369	4324	9618	8791	6179	6110
6654	2553	5427	9580	8636	5595	5847	4881
2305	0902	4666	9875	7255	4653	2628	6974
0891	7370	6201	0871	9413	8637	7107	4457
9978	5992	6144	2937	2324	7506	4124	3677
2205	4959	9903	4788	9595	4481	0526	5784
0642	2127	6986	2767	3726	7450	1164	6878
2687	4597	3392	8976	3333	9208	5249	4190
8033	2356	1841	9836	2445	6147	4872	1725
0236	5882	3172	6088	7979	3084	6690	3820
9055	9955	8230	9779	4607	9625	6288	6388
3216	1799	1854	4927	2873	2897	1521	8034
5440	0327	3002	5066	3378	4667	7600	5022
6444	3467	2802	5606	8420	0065	4607	5035
9523	1816	5194	4815	2139	9497	7735	8564
6365	1116	9403	6377	3633	4400	3697	3864
7140	8066	4131	2196	5990	6177	3149	0751
6259	0797	8446	3501	4987	8410	5582	0765
8551	4419	9560	7380	9443	8433	5610	8901
1088	6418	8721	4560	8866	2152	3119	8163
2864	3715	6513	5614	5227	589	6487	7956
2124	1140	7718	6047	6817	6473	7486	4725
5729	1844	9502	415	6974	8109	5881	3885
9655	2965	0890	8657	3933	5677	8664	4906
5471	8666	2756	8542	6441	1771	2653	7186
5998	1310	3875	1453	3846	9997	5363	2828
2228	7915	7436	3379	3349	9686	7969	9936
9139	5404	0172	2394	2820	5370	6836	8621
4480	9288	5408	8852	4436	6947	1760	3907

INDEX

ABOUT THE EDITOR

James H. Greene, Professor Emeritus of Industrial Engineering at Purdue University, is a leading consultant in operations management and the author of many widely used books in the field. He has worked as a consultant for the European Productivity Agency, and as a Fulbright Lecturer at Finland's Institute of Technology. In the United States, Dr. Greene's clients have included the Ford Motor Company, Caterpillar, RCA, and the Century Geophysical Corporation. He is a Fellow of the American Production and Inventory Control Society (APICS), and has served on the Society's advisory council, accreditation committee, and inventory control committee.